CRITICAL SURVEY OF

Long Fiction

Fourth Edition

CRITICAL SURVEY OF

Long Fiction

Fourth Edition

Volume 10
Topical Essays
Resources
Indexes

Editor
Carl Rollyson
Baruch College, City University of New York

SALEM PRESS
Pasadena, California   Hackensack, New Jersey

Editor in Chief: Dawn P. Dawson

Editorial Director: Christina J. Moose   *Research Supervisor:* Jeffry Jensen
Development Editor: Tracy Irons-Georges   *Research Assistant:* Keli Trousdale
Project Editor: Judy Selhorst   *Production Editor:* Joyce I. Buchea
Manuscript Editor: Desiree Dreeuws   *Design and Graphics:* James Hutson
Acquisitions Editor: Mark Rehn   *Layout:* William Zimmerman
Editorial Assistant: Brett S. Weisberg   *Photo Editor:* Cynthia Breslin Beres

Cover photo: (Hulton Archive/Getty Images)

Some of the essays in this work, which have been updated, originally appeared in the following Salem Press publications: *Critical Survey of Long Fiction, English Language Series* (1983), *Critical Survey of Long Fiction, Foreign Language Series* (1984), *Critical Survey of Long Fiction, Supplement* (1987), *Critical Survey of Long Fiction, English Language Series, Revised Edition* (1991; preceding volumes edited by Frank N. Magill), *Critical Survey of Long Fiction, Second Revised Edition* (2000; edited by Carl Rollyson).

∞ The paper used in these volumes conforms to the American National Standard for Permanence of Paper for Printed Library Materials, Z39.48-1992 (R1997).

Library of Congress Cataloging-in-Publication Data

Critical survey of long fiction / editor, Carl Rollyson. — 4th ed.
     p.   cm.
Includes bibliographical references and index.
    ISBN 978-1-58765-535-7 (set : alk. paper) — ISBN 978-1-58765-536-4 (vol. 1 : alk. paper) —
ISBN 978-1-58765-537-1 (vol. 2 : alk. paper) — ISBN 978-1-58765-538-8 (vol. 3 : alk. paper) —
ISBN 978-1-58765-539-5 (vol. 4 : alk. paper) — ISBN 978-1-58765-540-1 (vol. 5 : alk. paper) —
ISBN 978-1-58765-541-8 (vol. 6 : alk. paper) — ISBN 978-1-58765-542-5 (vol. 7 : alk. paper) —
ISBN 978-1-58765-543-2 (vol. 8 : alk. paper) — ISBN 978-1-58765-544-9 (vol. 9 : alk. paper) —
ISBN 978-1-58765-545-6 (vol. 10 : alk. paper)
1. Fiction—History and criticism. 2. Fiction—Bio-bibliography—Dictionaries. 3. Authors—Biography—
Dictionaries. I. Rollyson, Carl E. (Carl Edmund)
   PN3451.C75 2010
   809.3—dc22

2009044410

First Printing

PRINTED IN CANADA

CONTENTS

COMPLETE LIST OF CONTENTS

Volume 1

Volume 2

VOLUME 3

VOLUME 4

VOLUME 5

VOLUME 6

VOLUME 7

Contents . . . .

VOLUME 8

VOLUME 9

VOLUME 10

PRONUNCIATION KEY

Foreign and unusual or ambiguous English-language names of profiled authors may be unfamiliar to some users of the *Critical Survey of Long Fiction*. To help readers pronounce such names correctly, phonetic spellings using the character symbols listed below appear in parentheses immediately after the first mention of the author's name in the narrative text. Stressed syllables are indicated in capital letters, and syllables are separated by hyphens.

VOWEL SOUNDS

Symbol	Spelled (Pronounced)
a	answer (AN-suhr), laugh (laf), sample (SAM-puhl), that (that)
ah	father (FAH-thur), hospital (HAHS-pih-tuhl)
aw	awful (AW-fuhl), caught (kawt)
ay	blaze (blayz), fade (fayd), waiter (WAYT-ur), weigh (way)
eh	bed (behd), head (hehd), said (sehd)
ee	believe (bee-LEEV), cedar (SEE-dur), leader (LEED-ur), liter (LEE-tur)
ew	boot (bewt), lose (lewz)
i	buy (bi), height (hit), lie (li), surprise (sur-PRIZ)
ih	bitter (BIH-tur), pill (pihl)
o	cotton (KO-tuhn), hot (hot)
oh	below (bee-LOH), coat (koht), note (noht), wholesome (HOHL-suhm)
oo	good (good), look (look)
ow	couch (kowch), how (how)
oy	boy (boy), coin (koyn)
uh	about (uh-BOWT), butter (BUH-tuhr), enough (ee-NUHF), other (UH-thur)

CONSONANT SOUNDS

Symbol	Spelled (Pronounced)
ch	beach (beech), chimp (chihmp)
g	beg (behg), disguise (dihs-GIZ), get (geht)
j	digit (DIH-juht), edge (ehj), jet (jeht)
k	cat (kat), kitten (KIH-tuhn), hex (hehks)
s	cellar (SEHL-ur), save (sayv), scent (sehnt)
sh	champagne (sham-PAYN), issue (IH-shew), shop (shop)
ur	birth (burth), disturb (dihs-TURB), earth (urth), letter (LEH-tur)
y	useful (YEWS-fuhl), young (yuhng)
z	business (BIHZ-nehs), zest (zehst)
zh	vision (VIH-zhuhn)

CRITICAL SURVEY OF

Long Fiction

Fourth Edition

GERMAN LONG FICTION TO THE MID-NINETEENTH CENTURY

German narrative literature had its beginnings in the medieval epics of such poets as Wolfram von Eschenbach and Hartmann von Aue. Although the novels of the Middle Ages were composed in highly stylized verse, conforming to specific metric patterns, they nevertheless exhibit many elements that are characteristic of later prose fiction. Among the significant features shared by these early romances and the productions of modern novelists are divisions of the presentation into chapters, projection of the plot against a broad world background, detailed development of a variety of characters, careful painting of substantial landscapes, and the artistic interweaving of multiple strands of action. The tremendous literary force of major works that were written during the twelfth and thirteenth centuries derives from the effective combination of fullness of life with rhythmic form of exposition. One of the most significant creations of the period was Wolfram's *Parzival* (c. 1200-1210; English translation, 1894), which is, in many respects, a forerunner of the bildungsroman.

Substance for these sophisticated lyric tales came from the common European cultural heritage. Arthurian legend had an especially strong impact on writers of the time, as did Germanic sagas and material pertaining to the world of Charlemagne. Typically, the resulting products were heroic stories of love and adventure that taught carefully calculated lessons about particular chivalrous ideals. In their essence, these components of the courtly ethic are spiritualized and ascetic; at their center is the concept of moderation, which leads to a harmonious life through the exercise of discipline, decency, and decorum. Other advocated virtues include courage, humor, loyalty, constancy, and gentleness. Illustrations of these ideas are offered within the context of portrayals of the problems of the times. The primary focus is knighthood and its attendant phenomena. Courtly love is a key theme, as are the tensions that arise out of certain existential polarities, especially this world and the hereafter, the material and the spiritual aspects of life, and beauty and sin. Heavily pronounced qualities of this medieval fiction are orientation toward the ideal, distance from reality, aristocratic exclusiveness, clarity, and artful simplicity.

During the late Middle Ages, the rise of the middle class and the shifting of the religious-political balance of power in favor of the state had a marked impact upon the evolving literature. As the burghers began to demonstrate increased interest in education, they traveled more and became professionally involved in the arts. One important outgrowth of this situation was the decline of verse and the rise of prose as the new medium of narration.

At the beginning of the fifteenth century, three factors strongly contributed to the expanded use of prose in German fiction. The propagation of expository documents—especially the writings of prominent mystics, including Meister Eckhart (c. 1260-c. 1328), Heinrich Seuse (c. 1300-1366), and Johannes Tauler (c. 1300-1361)—served as a stimulus for the refinement of prose style. On another level, the decay of courtly culture fostered the appearance of prose versions of the heroic epics. Perhaps most important of all, German-language writers began to translate stories and novels that had been written in other European languages. These translations from foreign literatures, particularly from the French, Latin, and Italian masters, offered needed models to writers who were interested in genres that were more suited to the real-world bent of the era. Among the most significant accomplishments of this kind were Elisabeth von Nassau-Saarbrücken's renderings of examples of the French *chanson de geste* into German prose and the translation into German of novellas from Giovanni Boccaccio's *Decameron: O, Prencipe Galetto* (1349-1351; *The Decameron*, 1620) by Heinrich Arigo, Niklas von Wyle, and Heinrich Steinhöwe. Many of the *Volksbücher* (folk-books) that appeared as the Middle Ages waned had their origins in these and other translation efforts.

Narrative prose created during the fourteenth and fifteenth centuries shows little originality in substance or approach. Its tone was dictated to some extent by the melancholy mood of an era subject to famine, pestilence, and disease. An inclination toward concern for things real and useful is manifest in the emergence of social, political, historical, and travel fiction. Didactic stories became increasingly widespread, favoring the employment of allegory and satire.

Aside from the verse epics of the Middle Ages, major achievements in long fiction written prior to the eighteenth century are primarily isolated occurrences that participate in no true continuum of development in point of technical approach or artistic orientation. Nevertheless, individual works and authors did exert significant influence on the later evolution of the novel and the novella in German literature.

Despite the Reformation-inspired Humanistic direction of intellectual life in the sixteenth century, few authors made noteworthy contributions to the prose narrative in German. There were two closely related reasons for that situation. First, the main written language of the Renaissance was Latin; second, much of the energy of creative minds was devoted to religious and technical writings that documented the theological and political controversies of the day. As a result, most of the novels and stories that circulated in German-speaking areas were merely works of popular entertainment with little or no lasting artistic value. The basic tone of these productions was more pedagogical than poetic, and didactic tales were commonly satiric, with religious and political overtones. In addition to novels, various kinds of novellas and *Volksbücher* were widely read.

There are two notable exceptions to the otherwise undistinguished progress of German long fiction during the Renaissance. The first is the early middle-class family story *Fortunatus* (1509). Written by an unknown author, it is unique for its time and certainly the best instructional narrative of the beginning part of the century. The basic account, which describes the life of the title character, whose pursuit of riches rather than wisdom leads to the eventual downfall of his family, is enhanced by fairy-tale elements (a wishing hat and an inexhaustible purse) that contribute to the work's success as literary art. More important within the history of German letters are the books of Georg Wickram (c. 1505-c. 1561), Germany's earliest successful prose novelist. Wickram moved from tortuously involved novels based on common European themes to clearly organized instructive presentations

that combined traditional narrative features with personal experience. Among the characteristic stylistic devices that he introduced into his prose were long monologues and conversations, songs that revealed things that the singer could not say directly, and letters that conveyed information about relationships among characters. With his *Der jungen Knaben Spiegel* (1555; mirror of boyhood), based on the then-popular biblical motif of the prodigal son, he became the true founder of the German middle-class novel.

Wickram's creations had little immediate influence on other writers, and after his death, there was a break of many years before significant novels were produced again in German. Much of the popular narrative literature of the last half of the sixteenth century consisted of translations and various free interpretations of material that originally had appeared in other languages.

The first calculated attempts to set up meaningful artistic criteria for German fiction were made by Martin Opitz (1597-1639) in the seventeenth century. Opitz worked as a literary organizer, seeking to bring order to belles lettres through the establishment of a well-defined poetics and the generation of paradigms for the various genres. Major authors of the baroque period regarded Opitz as their spiritual father; following his lead, they did away with many of the remains of medieval influences, overcame the dominance of the Latin tradition, and formed the basis for an artistic prose style.

Narratives created under the sway of Opitz's reforms were certainly not uniform in quality and lasting value. What did emerge, however, was a new general orientation toward literary art. It specifically reflected broad cultural developments in other areas. German baroque literature is a part of the art of the Counter-Reformation and documents a definite clash between antiquity and Christianity, with no attempt to find a synthesis of the two. The pessimistic approach to life that was a direct product of the Thirty Years' War (1618-1648) colors many of the novels of the time, with fear of death and hunger for life appearing as characteristic attitudes. Typical productions are heavy with Christian content that focuses on the dualism between extravagant lifestyles and asceticism by balancing Christian stoicism against passion and enjoyment of existence. Important themes are the transitoriness of everything earthly, a special awareness of death, absolutism in church and state, and the rejection of individualism and subjectivism.

The prevailing style of German baroque fiction is best described as massive and ornate. Overemphasis on form is especially visible in works that incline toward accumulation and expansion of substance. A strong tendency to gather, pile up, and vary forms and devices of antiquity is paralleled by a love for affectation, ornamentation, the farfetched, and the allegorical. Opitz's demand for mastery of technique and aesthetic principles was greeted by a fashion of fastidiousness.

During the seventeenth century, epic literature was largely a product of the Protestant regions of northern and eastern Germany. Although occasional novellas appeared, the predominant form was the novel, of which there were three main types: pastoral love stories, historical narratives that were based upon materials from a broad range of sources, and earthy, humorous, picaresque tales, all of which became popular to varying degrees.

Pastoral creations are found in all baroque genres, including poetry and drama. They arose out of a longing for naturalness, for a golden age of peaceful existence, and out of a love for masquerade. Anacreontic forms were introduced into German literature by Opitz. Apart from him, only a few authors composed successful bucolic prose. Opitz set the pattern for this kind of writing with his slender volume *Die Schäfferey von der Nimphen Hercinie* (1630; the pastoral life of the nymph Hercinie). Among its paradigmatic characteristics are the setting in an idyllic landscape; employment of verse inserts; use of the narrative as a vehicle for intellectual discussion; exposition about elements of nature such as mountains, rocks, and water; and the emphasis placed on family history. The Anacreontic novel's predilection for the treatment of problems related to love is perhaps best illustrated in Philipp von Zesen's *Die adriatische Rosemund* (1645; Adriatic Rosemund), the most important pastoral work of the period. Its love conflict is centered on the special German situation of the insurmountable obstacle that is erected by a difference in religious confessions.

Baroque novelists achieved their greatest breadth and diversity in political and social accounts framed in historical settings. These works are notable for their sheer bulk (multiple volumes involving thousands of pages in many instances), proliferation of primary characters, labyrinthine webs of many plots and subplots, vast scope, and richness of detail. Events and situations of immediate local Germanic interest are often clothed in the trappings of Romanic or Asian history. More frequently than not, heterogeneous masses of material make the presentation ungainly, while accumulations of figures and relationships inhibit the story's progress and contribute to weak epic development. Anton Ulrich von Braunschweig provided significant models for the complicated baroque history in his *Die durchläuchtige Syrerin Aramena* (1669-1673; the illuminated Syrian woman Aramena) and the more famous *Die römische Octavia* (1677-1707; Octavia of Rome). One of the more powerful literary monuments of the seventeenth century is Heinrich Anshelm von Ziegler und Kliphausen's *Die asiatische Banise: Oder, Das blutige, doch muthige Pegu* (1689; Banise of Asia, or the bloody but courageous Pegu), an exotic novel that is peculiar for its extremes of terrifying events coupled with indifference of feeling.

The most important accomplishments in German baroque fiction were made in the picaresque novels of Hans Jakob Christoffel von Grimmelshausen. Indeed, the only seventeenth century prose epic with substantial artistic significance beyond its own time is Grimmelshausen's slice of life from the time of the Thirty Years' War, *Der abenteuerliche Simplicissimus* (1669; *The Adventurous Simplicissimus*, 1912). Factors that contribute to its unprecedented narrative success include the humanness of the central character; the fascinating flow of the story; the inexhaustible wisdom that is integrated into the partially autobiographical account of the hero's life; the vividness and plasticity of individual scenes; the stark portrayal of raw reality in a difficult, tumultuous, confused era; and, above all, the pulsating vitality of the whole. *The Adventurous Simplicissimus* is especially noteworthy within the framework of German literary history as the first authentic example of the novel of personal development.

Unlike other writers of his day, Grimmelshausen had profound impact on his contemporaries and immediate successors. There were many imitations of *The Adventurous Simplicissimus*, although none was very successful from an artistic point of view. The only other seventeenth century picaresque novel of any real literary magnitude is Christian Reuter's *Schelmuffskys wahrhafftige curiöse und sehr gefährliche Reisebeschreibung zu Wasser und Lande* (1696, 1697; *Shelmuffsky*, 1962), a mendacious travel novel that presents sharp criticism of the society and times in a guise of comical exaggeration, pointed distortion of material reality, and clever social caricature.

During the early part of the eighteenth century, development of the novel and the novella as artistic literary genres languished. At the same time, substantial amounts of mediocre and low-quality entertainment prose were published. Three kinds of light fiction became popular with middle-class readers: The courtly novel had shallow ties to some forms of baroque literature; so-called gallant narratives satisfied the never-ending public craving for stories about love; and tales of travel and adventure provided escape into exotic realms.

An especially representative example of the courtly novel is Johann Michael Freiherr von Loën's *Der redliche Mann am Hofe: Oder, Die Begebenheiten des Grafen von Rivera* (1740; the honest man at the court). A didactic account of intrigue, its central theme is the realization of the ideal of integrity through personal action. Impressive for its combination of utopian scope with interpretation of reality, the work features a typically involved pattern of episodic situations, tested human relationships, life stories, and social challenges.

Gallant fiction was commonly composed in the manner of the courtly historical novel, but it lacked the elements of heroic adventure and involvement in national political processes. It was smoothly written, characterized by the clever arrangement of many captivating episodes, and presented love as an amusingly frivolous play of confusions and mistakes. The writers who created this kind of fiction were quite prolific but produced nothing of lasting importance. Among them were figures such as August Bohse, who published more than twenty volumes, Christian Friedrich Hunold, whose four novels each appeared in several editions, and Leonhard Rost, the author of at least nine books.

A rather interesting phenomenon was the rapid proliferation of adventure novels patterned after Daniel Defoe's *Robinson Crusoe* (1719). Within a few years after the first German translation of Defoe's masterpiece was circulated in 1721, between thirty and forty imitations had appeared in print. Especially attractive to the German reader were the ideas of complete isolation and individual activity outside the constraints of society. The German imitations were generally much weaker than Defoe's original; they usually combined elements of traditional adventure stories with the English author's ideas, but they lacked the component of moral education that characterizes *Robinson Crusoe*. Many of the books were simply tales of travel that capitalized on Defoe's many possibilities for exciting episodes while ignoring the profound psychological development of the central character that had been so important for the Englishman. Of all the German novels of this type, only Johann Gottfried Schnabel's *Wunderliche Fata einiger See-Fahrer, absonderlich Alberti Julii . . .* (1731-1743, 4 volumes; also known as *Die Insel Felsenberg*) is worthy of note as a minor artistic achievement.

Toward the middle of the century, taste and cultural attitudes changed, leading to far-reaching effects on the artistic evolution of German long prose forms. These modifications were a specific product of the Enlightenment. Classicistic in orientation, the new spiritual-intellectual trend emphasized the ideas of tolerance, cosmopolitanism, and philosophical and general education, thereby fostering the reuniting of religious, social, and political elements of life that had become separated during the seventeenth century. The movement had its theoretical basis in the English empiricism of John Locke and David Hume, as mediated on the Continent by Voltaire.

An important contributor to German Enlightenment thought was the philosopher Gottfried Wilhelm Leibniz, who sought to devise a complementary union of theological-teleological and physical-mechanical views of the world. Leibniz took the position that body and soul exist in a preestablished harmony with each other, and he argued that the artist imitates God in the creative process. As a reflection of nature, art must be formed according to rules. Production thus becomes subordinate to theory. Christian von Wolff popularized and systematized Leibniz's philosophy, emphasizing its practical application and underscoring the ideals of healthy human understanding and virtue as sources of mortal happiness. In turn, Johann Christoph Gottsched spread Wolff's teachings and established their relationship to literature, advocating German adherence to French classicistic, Roman, and classical Greek styles as the realization of reason and nature. Gottsched's demands were later opposed by Gotthold Ephraim Lessing, who insisted that truly German literature was more closely related to English models.

While coming to grips with Enlightenment ideas, German novelists pursued definite goals in their narrative presentations. One of the most pronounced of these goals was a concerted effort to free people from their traditional ties to the world beyond, in order to bring about a universal independent development of human intellect. Especially visible manifestations of this thrust were attacks against the supernatural aspects of Christian theology by people educated in physical science and the promotion of Deism as a more acceptable natural religion. Absolute rationalistic dogmatism that demanded the achievement of social progress through the advancement of reason was tempered only by a parallel insistence upon humanistic behavior, which promoted an attitude of religious tolerance.

Prose literature that was produced under the influence of these ideas is characteristically optimistic in tone and meticulously precise in style. It was intended to be both useful and entertaining. Leibniz's doctrine of the best of all possible worlds finds reflection in works that affirm the complex realities of mortal experience while expressing both doubts about the validity of revelation and a coincident firm belief that everything can be explained. Humans stand in the foreground as entities in the process of perfecting themselves through the exercise of will and reason. They learn to control their drives by basing their conduct upon purposeful rational action that leads in the direction of beauty and social harmony. The most important key to Enlightenment storytellers' approach to the problem of humans in their world is the perception that ethical and aesthetic values are the same.

At the beginning of the Enlightenment period, a literary art that was dominated by feeling had special meaning for the rise of prose fiction as a major mode of expression, not only during the middle years of the century but also during the Sturm und Drang era. Political and social repression of the middle class found a relief valve in writings that were filled with the rapture of self-satisfied sensitivity and enthusiasm, often connected with patriotism and a more subjectively than objectively encountered hatred of tyranny. In contrast to the strongly rationalistic bent of the mature Enlightenment, many of these works were molded by Pietistic tendencies toward a renewal of mysticism. They document the intensification of emotional life that is based on inner experience of salvation and rebirth. Significant substance is provided by a new sense of communality that has as a side effect the participation in spiritual events that takes place within other individuals. A general tie between the literature of sentimentality and mainstream Enlightenment philosophy exists in the emphasis placed upon piousness of the heart that serves as a basis for practical humanistic discipleship in Christ.

Primary stimuli for German propagation of sentimental fiction came from England. During the 1740's and 1750's, Samuel Richardson's narratives about family and virtue, especially *Pamela: Or, Virtue Rewarded* (1740-1741) and *Sir Charles Grandison* (1753-1754), established patterns that became extremely popular in Germany. Richardson's influence was particularly strong in connection with development of the epistolary novel. The works of Henry Fielding became important as models for a deliberate separation of author and narrator with regard to the focus of presentation. Following Fielding's lead, German novelists began to introduce fictive storytellers who became focal figures in creations that revealed the nature of their inner worlds. Even more significant for their impact upon German writers were Laurence Sterne's *Tristram Shandy* (1759-1767) and *A Sentimental Journey Through France and Italy* (1768). Sterne stressed the experiences of thinking and feeling, amplifying the concept of the fictional narrator by styling his novels as conversations between storyteller and reader. Employment of the motif of the journey as a frame for the depiction of humanity's internal life became a definitive characteristic of German emulation of his techniques. One other Englishman whose writing profoundly affected German prose throughout the last one-third of the eighteenth century was Oliver Goldsmith. Through its powerful revelation of the central figure's strength of spirit, his famous book, *The Vicar of Wakefield* (1766), reinforced existing tendencies toward intense portrayal of inward experience.

Critical Survey of Long Fiction

The English preoccupation with artistic analysis of human sensitivities is mirrored in the German creation of three types of the sentimental novel. In the first variety, fictional life stories, often told in the first person, mingle the objective narration of events and circumstances with subjective reflections, explanations, and interpretations. Emotionally charged travel narratives constitute a second type, in which the focus is on the hero's heartfelt responses to external impressions; to some extent, these writings are socially critical, but they also frequently feature displays of empathy for meaningless objects and phenomena. Heavily autobiographical accounts form a third kind of sentimental novel that is related to the other two in its intensity of often religiously based self-examination.

Among the more noteworthy examples of the German "life and opinions" novel are Christian Fürchtegott Gellert's *Leben der schwedischen Gräfin von G . . .* (1747-1748; *The Life of the Swedish Countess of G . . .*, 1752), Sophie von La Roche's *Geschichte des Fräuleins von Sternheim* (1771; *The History of Lady Sophia Sternheim*, 1776), Friedrich Nicolai's *Das Leben und die Meinungen des Herrn Magister Sebaldus Nothanker* (1773-1776; *The Life and Opinions of Master Sebaldus Nothanker*, 1798), and Johann Karl Wezel's *Lebensgeschichte Tobias Knauts, des Weisen, sonst der Stammler genannt* (1773-1776; the life story of Tobias Knaut the wise, otherwise known as Stammler). Gellert and La Roche were conscious followers of Richardson, while Nicolai and Wezel leaned more toward Sterne. *The Life of the Swedish Countess of G . . .* was the first substantial novel of this type. With its first-person narrative, frequently epistolary form, alternating compression of narrated time and detailed expansion of specific happenings, stress on aesthetic beauty and the perfection of sensually perceived experience, and changing situations, perspective, and mode of expression, it provides a compendium of literary trends of the times. *The History of Lady Sophia Sternheim*, a well-arranged account presented in letters, is the earliest significant German novel by a woman. It is remarkable for its individualization of characters and its representation of the finding of self through social action. The two novels by Nicolai and Wezel, consciously patterned on Sterne's *Tristram Shandy*, illuminate specific ethical and moral conflicts

in the individual's interactions with society. *The Life and Opinions of Master Sebaldus Nothanker* is a work of special moment in its expression of contemporary middle-class taste and its capturing of the atmosphere of Berlin.

Sentimental travel novels are closely related to the fictional biographies in their epistolary style and their focus on bourgeois social conditions. They especially reflect the increased fascination with Sterne that began with the first German translation of *A Sentimental Journey Through France and Italy* in 1768. Like the life stories, they often represent notable firsts in the history of German narrative prose, although they lack, for the most part, true artistic power. Included in this group are Johann Timotheus Hermes's five-volume creation, *Sophiens Reise von Memel nach Sachsen* (1770-1772; Sophie's journey from Memel to Saxony), the first major German novel to focus in depth on the middle-class situation, and Moritz August von Thümmel's *Reise in die mittäglichen Provinzen von Frankreich im Jahre 1785 bis 1786* (1791-1805; *Journal of Sentimental Travels in the Southern Provinces of France, Shortly Before the Revolution*, 1821), a narrative of extreme epistolary breadth.

The single most significant representation of the autobiographical novel of sentiment pinpoints the link between the literature of sentimentality and the major productions of the Sturm und Drang (storm and stress) movement. Titled *Heinrich Stillings Jugend* (1777; Henry Stilling's youth), it was written by Johann Heinrich Jung, who was known to his contemporaries as Stilling. Although it was created in Strasbourg under the influence of Johann Wolfgang von Goethe at the height of Sturm und Drang activity, its intense inwardness and peculiar realism tie it closely to the sentimental novel.

Parallel to sentimental fiction, but informed more by the rationalistic secularization tendencies of the Enlightenment than by the emotion-dominated spiritual demands of Pietism, other authors composed narrative works that at last firmly established the novel and the novella as intellectually valid genres of serious literary expression. These writings exhibit careful structuring, the conscious interdependence of form and central idea, powerful tone of language, and an infinite wealth of personal experience, reflection, and ideas. Like the sentimentalists, their creators were influenced by Richardson, Fielding, and other English novelists, but they were not simply imitators of British trends. Rather, they were concerned with relating German long prose to the totality of European literature. Written for a broad readership that was largely unprepared for them, their productions were poorly received and not understood in their time. Lessing accurately identified the factors that separated these new documents from everything that had gone before when he characterized a representative example as a novel for the thinking person with classical taste. Despite their initial lack of popularity, these creations formed the true beginnings of a new German fiction through their exploration of specifically modern problems, including disillusionment, contradiction between appearance and reality, illusion versus truth, and the freedom of the individual from traditional or psychological blindness. Within the mainstream of artistic prose, themes and approaches were introduced and new literary avenues were opened that anticipated key developments of the decades to come. Particular examples are the focus on the life and fate of the artist within society, experiments with open-ended form and the elimination of continuous plot, the illumination of fundamental existential questions, the examination of the human condition from psychological perspectives, and the employment of devices such as debate, reflection, and essay in the formulation of the philosophical novel.

The outstanding master of Enlightenment narrative was Christoph Martin Wieland, whose compositions became paradigms for the works of the most influential figures of the literary movements that stirred the late decades of the eighteenth century. His first major novel, *Der Sieg der Natur über die Schwärmerey: Oder, Die Abentheuer des Don Sylvio von Rosalva, worrin alles Wundebare natürlich zugeht* (1764; *Reason Triumphant over Fancy, Exemplified in the Singular Adventures of Don Sylvio de Rosalva: A History in Which Every Marvelous Event Occurs Naturally*, 1773; commonly known as *The Adventures of Don Sylvio of Rosalva*), a picaresque romance with obvious ties to Miguel de Cervantes' *Don Quixote de la Mancha* (1605, 1615), was unique in German literature of the time. It had a profound impact on Goethe and on the German Romantics as a model for their many treatments of youthful, Ro-

mantic heroes who wander through the world following ideal concepts. *Geschichte des Agathon* (1766-1767; *The History of Agathon*, 1773), in many respects Wieland's finest work, established significant patterns for psychological and philosophical fiction; it was also the first German historical novel to accurately capture the aura of classical antiquity. The carefully conceived satire *Die Geschichte der Abderiten* (1774; *The Republic of Fools*, 1861), remarkable for its perfection of style and cosmopolitan grace, was the first comprehensive novel of social criticism in eighteenth century Germany. Wieland's last masterpiece, *Aristipp* (1801), exemplifies the preoccupation of the era with themes such as superstition, spiritualism, secret organizations, and problems of faith and deception. It carries the epistolary form in a new direction in which the exchange of ideas and opinions between letter writers unveils a broad social landscape rather than illuminating a single traditional main character.

One other major consequence of Wieland's concerted endeavor to raise the literary level of German prose fiction was the emergence of the novella as a viable artistic form. Earlier eighteenth century specimens of the medium-length narrative, including the folk novellas of Christian Friedrich Daniel Schubart, were pedestrian in style and unsettled in approach. Wieland's cultivation of the genre inspired further experimentation—first by Goethe, later by the Romantics—and was the first critical step toward the ultimate perfection of the form during the nineteenth century.

Beginning shortly before 1770, a rather strong reaction against the spirit of the Enlightenment ignited the relatively brief literary upheaval that was subsequently called Sturm und Drang. The spiritual father of the movement was Johann Gottfried Herder, whose programmatic demand for the subordination of the critic to the creative artist's genius became the basis for writings that defied the restraints of rationalism. Herder and his followers insisted that Enlightenment thought and the resulting literature treated the irrational dimensions of human life improperly and unnaturally. Sturm und Drang writers therefore placed concepts such as heart, feeling, suspicion, and instinct in opposition to reason in generating works that glorify the goal of natural social order for natural humans. In some respects, these creations served to satisfy a longing for action that, under despotism, was otherwise impossible, by concerning themselves with the solution of the primarily moral tasks of politics. There was also a strong tendency to deify a nature that had been robbed of its spiritual essence by the rationalists.

Typical Sturm und Drang productions are dominated by clearly identifiable attitudes. Among the most definitive of these attitudes are cultural pessimism complemented by natural optimism and idealism (that is, a clear perception that natural humans are higher than cultural humans) and strong sympathy for specific human types, including innocent children, naïve women, rural people, artisans, petit bourgeois, primitive people, the ancient Greeks, the old Germanic tribes, and original, earthy power figures. The Sturm und Drang view of life is focused in Faustian duality, a peculiar conflict between a sense of the value of all elements of temporal reality and the opposing feeling for the inner endlessness of nature and life in the face of which all worldly things lose their meaning. Application of these approaches to existence results in a variety of specific characteristic manifestations. Especially visible is an intensification of sensual experience and personal consciousness of individual phenomena. Emphasis on individuality corresponds to a picture of life as a restless changing of forms. A new relationship to history and tradition is created, in which the Bible becomes a parable for the fate of humanity as a whole, and humanity's position within the natural order is defined by a philosophy of dynamic pantheism that identifies the divine aspect not as an incalculable person but rather as the highest cause of all things.

Like sentimental literature, creations of German Sturm und Drang were influenced by intellectual and artistic developments in other parts of Europe. Jean-Jacques Rousseau's *Discours sur les sciences et les arts* (1751; *The Discourse Which Carried the Praemium at the Academy of Dijon*, 1750; also known as *A Discourse on the Arts and Sciences*, 1913), with its famous advocation of a return to nature, was especially significant for the philosophical approach of Sturm und Drang novelists. Because of their focus on intimate experiences of feeling, novels such as Sterne's *A Sentimental Journey Through France and Italy* were almost as important as models for the representatives of the genius cult as they

were for the sentimentalists. There was, however, one distinctive difference in the results. In productions of the Sturm und Drang movement, intense inner sensitivity is frequently pathological; the deep psychological penetration of characters opens to view a spiritual malaise that becomes symbolic for the inward decay of modern cultural humans.

Despite the energy with which they wrote, representatives of Sturm und Drang produced relatively few prose narratives of consequence. By far the most outstanding work was Goethe's *Die Leiden des jungen Werthers* (1774; *The Sorrows of Young Werther*, 1779), which upon publication became an immediate international sensation and for many years remained the most famous novel in the German language. *The Sorrows of Young Werther* is at once a compendium of Sturm und Drang tendencies and a superb illustration of the eighteenth century German novel in general. Both the idea of sensitivity as a dangerous force and the concept of nature as a model for aesthetic and ethical education receive detailed elaboration in an epistolary presentation that responds perfectly to the demand that the novel portray the inner history of an individual who is subjected to a series of changing conditions. Theme, substance, language, narrative technique, figures, situations, milieu—in short, everything that contributes to the story's progress—is oriented toward the revelation of internal processes that are carefully integrated with external events. The result is a clearly crafted work of art that combines for the first time in German fiction a weighty, deeply personal mirroring of the author's own inner world with a vital, direct representation of contemporary life.

The patterns set by *The Sorrows of Young Werther* were unique in their artistic achievement, making the prose writings of other Sturm und Drang authors appear pale and shallow by comparison. Friedrich Heinrich Jacobi's confessional illumination of his own experience and suffering in *Eduard Allwills Papiere* (1775-1776; also known as *Allwills Briefsammlung*, 1792) combines a portrayal of Jacobi's innermost concerns with sharp social criticism in pointing out the tragic dangers that exist within a society that submits to the domination of feeling. In *Anton Reiser: Ein psychologischer Roman* (1785-1790; *Anton Reiser: A Psychological Novel*, 1926), Karl Philipp Moritz continued the trend established by Goethe with the description of the hypochondria of a youth who must grow up in totally negative circumstances. Only Wilhelm Heinse's *Ardinghello: Oder, Die glückseligen Inseln* (1787; *Ardinghello: Or, The Artist's Rambles in Sicily*, 1839) attained a measure of freshness and vitality through its utopian interpretation of Rousseau. A cycle of novels by the dramatist Friedrich Maximilian Klinger began to appear in 1791; although primarily philosophical in direction, they are nevertheless tied to the Sturm und Drang movement through their employment of Faustian motifs.

Beginning with Sturm und Drang and continuing well into the nineteenth century, the general tone of major developments in German belles lettres was set by Goethe's epoch-making writings and by specific artistic responses to them. When Goethe consciously renounced his Sturm und Drang tendencies in the early 1780's, he single-handedly inaugurated the classical era of German literature, which overlapped the final stages of the Enlightenment and the beginnings of German Romanticism. Although only a few key authors can be regarded as authentically representative of classicism, their works made contributions to German fiction that have affected its evolution ever since.

The primary defining characteristic of German classicism is cultural idealism. Goethe and similarly inclined authors sought to create a literature of high artistic value that was devoted to well-defined ideals of Greek and Roman antiquity. Key concepts were balance, order, and the application of aesthetic principles to moral and ethical goals; the ultimate aim was harmonious agreement of spirit and intellect in service to all humanity. Two different approaches to the process of cultural purification reflect the respective influences of Enlightenment and Sturm und Drang thought: Goethe's natural and Friedrich Schiller's rational idealism.

Classical idealism had its philosophical bases in the writings of Immanuel Kant, especially his *Kritik der reinen Vernunft* (1781; *The Critique of Pure Reason*, 1838) and *Kritik der praktischen Vernunft* (1788; *The Critique of Practical Reason*, 1873). In *The Critique of Practical Reason*, he examined the process of action, the morality of which is a function of pure, unconditional will. Arguing that nothing is unequivocally good except goodwill, he arrived at his famous categorical impera-

tive. It advocates that activity be based upon the principle that humanity in self and others be employed always as purpose, never as means. Kant associated the aesthetic element of human experience with moral idealism in his *Kritik der Urteilskraft* (1790; *The Critique of Judgment*, 1892). There he stated that the objects of aesthetics are the beautiful and the sublime and that a central property of beautiful art is humanity as a general feeling of participation. According to Kant, the eternal models for this humanistic art are found in the culture of classical Greece.

In coming to grips with the aesthetic and ethical aspects of their own creations, Schiller and others also employed key defining concepts or refinements thereof that were provided by other thinkers, notably Leibniz; Anthony Ashley Cooper, third earl of Shaftesbury; Johann Joachim Winckelmann; and Wilhelm von Humboldt. From Leibniz and Shaftesbury came the principle of harmony that is central to the worldview of classicism. Goethe and Schiller focused on the ideal of a concord in which the physical and moral condition of the individual come into play with each other as a substantial characteristic of the beautiful soul. They perceived harmony as a natural condition that had been broken down by culture and was in need of restoration, a goal that could be realized only through aesthetic education. Specifically applying the idea of harmony to works of art, Winckelmann derived from Greek masterpieces the programmatic notions of noble simplicity and quiet grandeur. In turn, Humboldt related the problem of harmonious education to Kant's humanistic aesthetics by insisting that the ultimate aim of the former is human self-perfection, or the purification of the individual through humanity.

The political and social climate of the final quarter of the eighteenth century also had a significant impact upon both the substance and the tone of German classical prose. The French Revolution of 1789, which affected all of Europe, left a deep mark on German intellectuals and fostered the application of philosophical idealism to practical existence. As a result, novelists and storytellers began to treat such themes as cosmopolitanism, the union of nations, individual self-determination, and freedom from subjection to traditional institutions.

During the classical period, the German novel rose from the status of solid artistic legitimacy that had been achieved by Enlightenment authors to one of new creative mastery. Out of the spirit of idealism, gifted writers sought to present in their long fiction a kind of integrated summary of human existence. The bildungsroman became the symbolic expression of the times. It was based upon a biological mode of observation within which the concept of organism became fundamental to the realization of classical goals of education. A number of definite manifestations are especially characteristic of the progress of the genre toward its modern identity. Increased concern for poetic language and style augmented the aesthetic power of narrative prose. The humanistic application of philosophical idealism to temporal reality established the broad spectrum of humanity's condition as focus and material for a new kind of didactic literature. Special attention given to the inner lives of characters paved the way for intense psychological exploration of human problems through the use of refined techniques. Expansion of perspective beyond the limitations of customary travel and adventure stories permitted the novel to become a vehicle for the presentation of an entire worldview, while the finely detailed creation of characters as concrete, rounded individuals made possible revelations concerning the true nature of humanity. In this regard, classical authors became particularly concerned with the identification and modeling of the qualities that mark the great soul. At the same time, notably in more humorous works, a concerted effort was made to offer a sharp portrayal of that which is typical in life.

As had been the case with the Sturm und Drang novel, Goethe fashioned the pinnacle masterworks of German classical long fiction. The central prose narratives of the period are *Wilhelm Meisters Lehrjahre* (1795-1796; *Wilhelm Meister's Apprenticeship*, 1824), *Die Wahlverwandtschaften* (1809; *Elective Affinities*, 1849), and *Wilhelm Meisters Wanderjahre: Oder, Die Entsagenden* (1821, revised 1829; *Wilhelm Meister's Travels*, 1827). Virtually all the literary developments of the eighteenth century lead up to *Wilhelm Meister's Apprenticeship*, which—with its originality, multiple layers of plot, uniformity of presentation, immediacy, careful organization, lucid elaboration, perfection of form, and powerful representation of the atmosphere of the times—had a profound effect on the German novel from that time forward. The theme of education, on which the

entire work is built, is treated from a variety of perspectives that allow the author to mix traditional motifs with his own inventions, leave decisions open, and move from ironic expression to symbolic meaning. *Wilhelm Meister's Apprenticeship* is of great import as the direct prototype of the nineteenth century bildungsroman and the primary stimulus for the rise of the open-ended novel, in which resolution of plot is no longer the essence of the artistic presentation. In *Elective Affinities*, Goethe produced the first work in a new trend away from the illumination of the individual's inner world and toward the literary analysis of a topical problem. *Elective Affinities* exhibits the richest development of German classical prose style and is the literary high point of classical humanism. Finally, *Wilhelm Meister's Travels* glorifies the ethic of usefulness in what is regarded by many critics as the first truly significant German social novel.

Three other authors made interesting contributions to the evolution of the novel during the classical period. Although he wrote only a few prose works, Schiller demonstrated in them uncommon facility with the psychological penetration of characters and situations, intense revelation of vital human experience, and the effective handling of background and mood. Johann Paul Friedrich Richter, an extremely popular novelist who wrote under the pen name Jean Paul, emulated Goethe in cultivating the bildungsroman as a portrait of contemporary social conditions. His perception of world history as an endless novel enabled him to capture in his writings a forceful sense of the fragmentary nature of existence. At the same time, a special feeling for the humorous aspects of life lent his creations a unique flavor. The writer whose work best exemplifies the ideal of harmony between modern culture and Greek antiquity is the poet Friedrich Hölderlin (1770-1843). His novel *Hyperion oder der Eremit in Griechenland* (1797, 1799; *Hyperion: Or, The Hermit in Greece*, 1965), an extremely original work, is peculiar for its lyric, open style, its powerful symbolism, its uncommon tone and language, and its carefully perfected integration of form and content.

Meaningful events in German long fiction were certainly not limited to the novel during this period. Various writers consciously cultivated the novella, which won its particular definitive form as a direct result of the classicists' experimentation and theorizing. The most important models for the German novella were provided by Boccaccio and Cervantes, although Goethe also translated examples from French and other literatures. From the efforts of Goethe and his contemporaries, there emerged a formal conception of the novella as a narrative focused on a single incident or theme presented in limited space such that no deviation from the exposition of the central problem is permitted. In spite of explicit structural restrictions, the story was to bring forth the environment in all of its color and mood, while portraying characters as multidimensional individuals. Aside from the limited plot, the most important particular of the German novella is the programmed involvement of symbols and motifs that highlight the singularity of the work's focal situation.

Although Wieland, Schubart, and others had had some success in producing novellas before Goethe, it was once again he who perfected the form and provided the patterns for later emulation. His *Unterhaltungen deutscher Ausgewanderten* (1795; *Conversations of German Emigrants*, 1854), a series of stories framed within the milieu of the French Revolution, is the first cycle of its type in German literature. A separate work, simply titled *Novelle* (1826; *Novel*, 1837), was intended as a paradigm of the genre and is especially attractive for its lyric elements. Additional writers of the classical period who created medium-length narratives worthy of note were Schiller and Jean Paul.

Near the end of the eighteenth century, the articulators of German idealism separated themselves into two distinct groups. Goethe, Schiller, and certain other authors continued to pursue the artistic goals of classicism, while a new generation rejected them in favor of the tendencies that are now most commonly associated with Romanticism.

Within the framework of German literary history, the Romantic movement represents a sharp surge away from traditional ideas about the substance, purposes, and techniques of belles lettres. In many respects, it is the direct opposite of classicism. Specific characteristics of the Romantic approach to literature include a focus on Nordic, Germanic, and southern Romanic culture of the Middle Ages; synthesis of irrational and rational components of life; a picturesque lack of rules; emphasis on a particular feeling for nature that glorifies the beauty of the wild and the mystery of ancient ruins; and infatuation with the unknown and with the notion of giving infinite meaning to things that are finite and common. Of special import is a process of reflection that illuminates the tensions between conscious and unconscious dimensions of experience and places dreams, longings, the abysses of the soul, and the power of the demoniac in vivid perspective as vital existential forces. The typical Romantic author perceived life as an unending process of becoming and stressed accordingly the categories of the elemental and the universal.

Like the classicists, the German Romantics derived their worldview from interpretations of Kant's philosophical idealism. Using Kant's doctrines as his starting point, Johann Gottlieb Fichte promulgated the theory of subjective idealism, according to which the individual is center, creator, and master of the external world. Friedrich Wilhelm Joseph von Schelling amplified Fichte's system and transformed his primarily natural philosophy into a strongly religious one. Several aspects of his teachings had tremendous importance for the literary creations of the Romantics. Schelling believed, for example, that nature and spirit form a unity such that nature is visible spirit and spirit is invisible nature. In that context, nature becomes a progressive revelation of spirit because everything in physical existence has a soul. Based upon his religious renderings of Fichte's philosophy, Schelling came to the conclusions that art is the highest form of everything earthly and that history is the prophetic explanation of absolute reality. As a consequence of Schelling's ideas, the Romantics came to regard knowledge and belief, philosophy and religion as inseparable. Religion became the very soil from which their myth-centered art grew.

Schelling's approach was most productively interpreted by Friedrich Schleiermacher, whose essays fostered a reconciliation between idealism and Christianity. Schleiermacher contributed to the body of Romantic thought a perception of religion as the connection between humans and that which is infinite and eternal, a feeling for that which is beyond the reach of the senses, a means of endless observation of the universe. Among the most significant reflections of this new *Weltanschauung*, or worldview, in Romantic letters are a visible return to mysticism and a focus on death as a central human experience that leads either to destruction or to salvation in Christian, especially Catholic, dogma.

Romantic authors cultivated long fiction as a dominant form of what they called "progressive universal poetry," a literature of total synthesis. Within it, they sought to combine all elements of education and cultural development. In direct contradiction to classical demands for consistency, clarity, and Enlightenment theories such as Lessing's separation of visual and literary arts, they advocated the union of writing, painting, and music and the dissolution of boundaries between art and science. Novels and shorter prose works were informed by the principle that all life should be poetized. Accomplishment of this goal required that the narrative unite all the separate genres. Romantic theoreticians insisted that the perfect novel would combine poetry with philosophy and rhetoric; it would contain dramatic monologues and dialogues, both natural and artistic lyric poetry, various prose forms, including novellas, anecdotes, and short tales, as component cells of the epic whole. The inclusion of criticism, episodes, letters, and reflections would assist in making the work a kind of personal bible, a compendium of the entire spiritual and intellectual life of the genial individual. By definition, Romantic universal poetry was to be infinite and free; its first postulate was that the caprice of the writer is not to be considered subject to any law.

What emerged from the pursuit of these goals was a prose fiction that is rich in fantasy and unfettered creativity. The demand for diversity and imagination fostered the renewal of old forms, particularly fairy tales, *Volksbücher*, and sagas. Because improvisation, experimentation, and lack of strict conception are more characteristic than concern for consistency and perfected structure, many Romantic narratives are unfinished fragments that reflect in a peculiar way the intense relationship between the artists' lives and personalities and their literary utterances. Especially visible are manifestations of these authors' ability to lift themselves above everything else, including their own work. The result is Romantic irony that shatters the illusion that has been created and intensified through the careful selection of word, word form, sentence structure, and rhythm in the telling of the story. Other typically Romantic devices are the use of the archaic chronicle style to invoke a feeling of past time and distant milieu and the tearing down of the logical context of situations as a prelude to entry into the fantastic dimension.

As to the nature of its intellectual and artistic activity, German Romanticism can be separated into two relatively well-defined phases. Early Romanticism was more critically and theoretically oriented. Its representatives leaned toward the formation of closed intellectual communities that concerned themselves not only with the creation of new works but also with various philological endeavors, including translation of William Shakespeare and the collection of folk literature. Notable theorists and writers in this group were Friedrich von Schlegel and his brother August Wilhelm von Schlegel, Ludwig Tieck, and Novalis (Friedrich von Hardenberg). Mature Romanticism was less speculative, although it was often strongly irrationalistic. Excepting a small group in Heidelberg, the later Romantics for the most part worked separately. They were also less antagonistic toward contemporary life and more likely to remain within the framework of reality. Among the more remarkable of the later Romantics were Clemens Brentano, Joseph von Eichendorff, and E. T. A. Hoffmann.

The most important prose genre of the initial period was the novel. With its masterful integration of diverse literary forms and its exemplary portrayal of an artistic quest, Goethe's *Wilhelm Meister's Apprenticeship* was a key model for the Romantic bildungsroman. Heinse's *Ardinghello: Or, The Artist's Rambles in Sicily* and Jean Paul's impulsive, sometimes formless works also exerted considerable influence. All early Romantic novels remained fragmentary torsos characterized by sentimentalism and heavy authorial subjectivism. Intense longing, glorification of the Middle Ages, special sensitivity to nature, and the employment of the narrative as a backdrop for the revelation of the writer's inner world are prominent features of this fiction.

A basic pattern for a work of literature that satisfies both the historical and the philosophical yearnings of a seeker for humanity's lost golden age was set by Novalis (1772-1801) in his famous *Heinrich von Ofterdingen* (1802; *Henry of Ofterdingen*, 1842). Enflamed by *Wilhelm Meister's Apprenticeship*, Novalis sought to surpass Goethe in content, power, variety, and thoughtfulness of presentation while spending his whole life on a single novel that would become the ultimate description of humanity's transition from the finite to the infinite. *Henry of Ofterdingen* is especially typical of the early Romantic novel in its happy mixture of reality and fairy tale, its deliberate poetizing of the world, its insertions of lyrics and shorter stories into the narrative structure, and its use of the narration as both elaboration and example of fundamental principles of literary art. Friedrich von Schlegel, in connection with the writing of his less successful *Lucinde* (1799; *Lucinda*, 1913-1915), had insisted that the Romantic novel be at once a theory of the novel and an illustration of the theory. In *Henry of Ofterdingen*, Novalis achieved early Romanticism's most impressive approximation of that ideal.

Although mature Romanticism produced a substantial number of novels, there were few outstanding accomplishments among them. Many of these works adhered to the synthesis principle of Schlegel's literary theory, as, for example, in Achim von Arnim's *Armut, Reichtum, Schuld und Busse der Gräfin Dolores* (1810; poverty, wealth, guilt, and repentance of the countess Dolores), a social novel that interweaves novellas, poems, and dramatic episodes; and Eichendorff's *Ahnung und Gegenwart* (1815; suspicion and presence), a creation that integrates problems of the times with a typical Romantic quest in vague episodes, moonlit forest scenes, and confused situations. Others experimented with radically new forms and substance. Particularly intriguing in this respect are Hoffmann's *Die Elixiere des Teufels: Nachgelassene Papiere des Bruders Medardus, eines Kapuziners* (1815-1816; *The Devil's Elixirs: From the Posthumous Papers of Brother Medardus, a Capuchin Friar*, 1824) and *Lebensansichten des Katers Murr, nebst fragmentarischer Biographie des Kapellmeisters Johannes Kreisler in zufälligen Makulaturblättern* (1819-1821; *The Life and Opinions of Kater Murr, with the Fragmentary Biography of Kapellmeister Johannes Kreisler on Random Sheets of Scrap Paper*, 1969; also known as *The Educated Cat*). The former is notable for its mixture of horror, crime, and guilt motifs with a profound examination of the psychological basis for events. Its themes of obsession and demoniac possession occupied later writers well into the twentieth century. *The Life and Opinions of Kater Murr* opened new avenues of approach to the problem of narrative presentation of ma-

terial. In it, Hoffmann totally shattered conventional notions of orderly form. The account offers two stories simultaneously, in a peculiar jumble of fragments that are interspersed with each other without benefit of transitions and clear definition of beginning or end of either tale.

At least as important as the Romantic novel for the history of German long fiction are the unique achievements of this period in narratives of medium length. The dominant type of Romantic novella is the fairy tale, of which there are two kinds. Natural fairy tales were created after models provided by folk literature. Substance and atmosphere were commonly taken from legends and sagas of the Middle Ages, and the orientation of the stories is often didactical. The best examples of natural fairy tales are found among Tieck's early novellas. An especially famous one is *Der blonde Eckbert* (1797; *Fair Eckbert*, 1913-1915, 1969). Mature Romanticism favored the artistic fairy tale, although this form also had its beginnings during the early period, in the writings of Novalis. He patterned his work after *Das Märchen* (1795; *The Tale*, 1823), the enigmatic concluding story in Goethe's *Conversations of German Emigrants*. The artistic fairy tale is characterized by a fantastic setting in a highly symbolic world, carefully crafted personalities, bizarre situations, and substantial philosophical content. Particularly representative of this sort of production are works such as Hoffmann's "Der goldene Topf" ("The Golden Flower Pot") and Brentano's animal stories.

In addition to fairy tales, the Romantics wrote social and historical novellas that parallel their novels in approach and themes. Pertinent examples include Eichendorff's *Aus dem Leben eines Taugenichts* (1826; *Memoirs of a Good-for-Nothing*, 1866), a charming quest narrative, and Hoffmann's "Das Fräulein von Scudéri" ("Mademoiselle Scudéri"), a story of murder and suspense set in the Paris of Louis XIV. Within their fairy tales and other novellas, the Romantics left a lasting legacy of conquest of new literary material, psychological penetration of portrayed reality, and original treatment of historical figures and basic human problems.

Although German Romantics did foster an identifiably conservative political posture with their patriotic allegiance to country and national tradition, they were relatively uninvolved in practical politics. In 1830, however, the July Revolution in France awakened hope for an end to the reactionary era, and certain representatives of the younger generation began to demand active literary contact with political and social life. Mediated by Ludwig Börne's *Briefe aus Paris* (1832-1834; letters from Paris), the social, political, and philosophical ideas of French liberalism found fertile ground in Germany, notably in the southwest. The result was the birth of a new German political literature, created initially by the loosely connected Young Germans and later by other concerned writers.

Narrowly speaking, the main figures of the Young German movement were Börne, Heinrich Heine, Ludolf Wienbarg, Theodor Mundt, Heinrich Laube, and Karl Gutzkow. In 1835, in response to their open attacks on traditional institutions and values and their revolutionary political stance, the writings of these authors were officially banned in Germany, on the grounds that they were blasphemous and immoral.

The political and social doctrines of the Young Germans, which informed their literary creations, were products of interpretations of Georg Wilhelm Friedrich Hegel's philosophy. Hegel viewed world history as the development of the concept of freedom. He insisted that in a reasonable state, laws and ordinances are nothing but the realization of freedom in its basic destiny. As the father of critical idealism, Hegel had a deep influence on political thought throughout Europe. Karl Marx and others followed his lead in the search for a rational system of government. In Germany, adaptation of Hegel's teachings ultimately led to the definition of specific political goals that rapidly became the focus for activist literature. Among these aims were the rise of the middle class to political power, territorial unity of the German states, constitutional freedom, and the removal of prior social, religious, and national political restrictions.

In addition to Hegel, other thinkers contributed to the Young German political philosophy. Henri de Saint-Simon amplified Rousseau's and Voltaire's ideas, basing an individual and social ethic upon reason and nature. Fundamental tenets of his Christian socialism were the emancipation of the individual, women, and the flesh; rejection of the exploitation of humans by humans; and the overcoming of social conflict through brotherly love. In response to this stimulus, Ludwig Feuerbach

expanded Hegel's philosophy, replacing God with nature and faith with knowledge and reason. Attacking Christian institutional dogma from a psychological point of view, he dismissed God and traditional religion as the products of wishful thinking. The Young Germans' decidedly negative view of contemporary social conditions was further influenced by David Friedrich Strauss's rejection of Christian theology as myth and allegory and by Lord Byron's *Weltschmerz*.

Influenced by Hegelian philosophy, the Young Germans put forth a theoretical program in which political freedom constituted the primary prerequisite for a German national literature. Its direction was democratic, liberalistic, and consistently materialistic. Moreover, it renounced Romantic escape to an imaginary past world of ideal heroism and love. The new trend was toward a poesy that is tied to practical questions of life—not the life of the individual but that of a new national society unified in its struggle to attain clearly defined political goals. Young German theoreticians, especially Wienbarg, proclaimed the task of literary art to be a representation of beauty in real life and individual situations. Wienbarg argued that proper depiction of reality requires political, social, and scientific knowledge. Despite the repeated employment of political and social criticism as their point of departure, however, the resulting creations were not realistic in nature. Rather, the Young Germans produced a rationalistic, often utopian literature of critical reflection. There was no longer any true concern for the inner, spiritual life of humans; more significant were revolutionary acts and ideas. Works of epic narrative began to examine tensions arising out of various polarities, including national feeling and cosmopolitanism, Christianity and rationalistic criticism, individualism and socialism, tradition and progress, middle-class morality and the emancipation of the flesh. Emphasis was on the improvement of life through reform and revolution, with special attention to things new and modern in anticipation of the future.

Young German writers considered prose to be the most appropriate medium for timely presentation of reality. Accordingly, they cultivated a variety of forms, ranging from diary-type sketches to weighty novels. The novella was a very popular genre during this era, because it was particularly well suited to the clear exposition of pertinent individual problems and themes. Most of the longer works were either social treatments of contemporary issues or novels of personal development used as a frame for panoramic illumination of the times. Although the Young Germans were quite prolific, they produced very little prose of lasting value. Only Heine's fragmentary historical novels represent a measure of enduring artistic accomplishment.

In spite of the general mediocrity of Young German prose, there did emerge one interesting new approach to the novel that had some significance for the further development of long fiction later in the century. Gutzkow, whose *Wally, die Zweiflerin* (1835; *Wally the Skeptic*, 1974) was the immediate cause of the political ban that was placed upon Young German literature, created two massive, relatively unsuccessful political-social narratives: *Die Ritter vom Geiste* (1850-1851; knights of the spirit) and *Der Zauberer von Rom* (1858-1861; the magician of Rome), each of which consists of nine volumes. In these works, the author experimented with presentation based on a principle of simultaneous rather than sequential organization of substance. That is, the primary concern was not the progressive unfolding of a traditional plot but rather the broad rendering of a many-sided, almost static mural of the age. Unfortunately, Gutzkow seldom achieved the desired effect of simultaneity. The remarkable breadth of his portrait of German life did not have the power to counteract the weakness of plot and make the novels appealing to the reader.

Lowell A. Bangerter

BIBLIOGRAPHY

Beutin, Wolfgang, et al. *A History of German Literature: From the Beginnings to the Present Day*. 4th ed. Translated by Clare Krojzl. New York: Routledge, 1993. Comprehensive, oft-used work provides a basic historical and critical overview of German literature. Includes bibliographical references and an index.

Craig, Gordon Alexander. *The Politics of the Unpolitical: German Writers and the Problem of Power, 1770-1871*. New York: Oxford University Press, 1995. Examines the attitudes of German authors toward the issue of national unification in the period leading up to the first Germany. Includes bibliographical references and an index.

Diethe, Carol. *Towards Emancipation: German Women Writers of the Nineteenth Century*. New York: Berghahn Books, 1998. Presents a rare systematic analysis of the literary contributions of German women, beginning with the late Romantics and moving through the 1848 revolutionary period to the late nineteenth century. Explores the wide-ranging and varied attitudes of these writers concerning women's emancipation.

Hardin, James, ed. *German Baroque Writers, 1580-1660*. Detroit, Mich.: Gale Research, 1996.

_____. *German Baroque Writers, 1661-1730*. Detroit, Mich.: Gale Research, 1996. These reference works provide brief biographies of German writers of the baroque period. Supplemented with lists of sources for further study.

Hill, David, ed. *Literature of the Sturm und Drang*. Rochester, N.Y.: Camden House, 2003. Collection of critical essays addresses the important themes and major works of German authors during the period of the Sturm und Drang.

Kontje, Todd Curtis. *Women, the Novel, and the German Nation, 1771-1871: Domestic Fiction in the Fatherland*. New York: Cambridge University Press, 1998. Examines the lives and works of fourteen women writers in regard to their roles in molding attitudes on class and gender prior to German unification as a nation. Includes bibliographical references and an index.

Mahoney, Dennis. *The Literature of German Romanticism*. Rochester, N.Y.: Camden House, 2004. Discusses long fiction from the beginnings of German Romanticism in the eighteenth century to the reception of this literature in the twentieth century.

Sagarra, Eda. *A Companion to German Literature: From 1500 to the Present*. Malden, Mass.: Blackwell, 1997. Readable overview surveys nine eras of German literature—from the Reformation and Renaissance to the late twentieth century—providing cultural and historical context for both well-known and neglected authors, including many women. Includes maps and an index.

Vivian, Kim, ed. *A Concise History of German Literature to 1900*. Columbia, S.C.: Camden House, 1992. Collection of essays by various scholars includes contributions covering German literature in different periods as well as essays on such topics as the Enlightenment and Romanticism. Includes illustrations, bibliographical references, and an index.

Watanabe-O'Kelly, Helen, ed. *The Cambridge History of German Literature*. New York: Cambridge University Press, 1997. Thorough overview from the Carolingian period to the unification of Germany in 1990 provides historical, political, and cultural context for both the student of German literature and the general reader. Quotations are translated into English.

Wellbery, David E., and Judith Ryan, eds. *A New History of German Literature*. Cambridge, Mass.: Belknap Press, 2004. Invaluable reference work contains more than two hundred scholarly essays. Covers various aspects of German literature, ranging from the ancient sagas to the twentieth century.

German Long Fiction from the Mid-Nineteenth Century to World War I

According to the historian Arnold Toynbee, historical periods and entire civilizations may be likened to lights that shine brightly for a time and then grow dim. German literature in the nineteenth century was such a light. The literary luminescence of German classicism and Romanticism and the dynamic, internationally oriented activism of the Young Germans were followed by decades of darkness, a period in which German writers seem to have lost international attention and recognition. Even a well-read person will draw a blank when asked to name German writers between Heine, who died in 1856, and Gerhart Hauptmann, whose first play was performed in 1889, or Thomas Mann, whose early novellas appeared in the 1890's. From the 1840's to the late 1880's, German literature was out of step with the rest of European literature. Where is the German Honoré de Balzac or Stendhal? The German Charles Dickens or William Makepeace Thackeray? The German Fyodor Dostoevski or Leo Tolstoy? The German Nathaniel Hawthorne or Herman Melville? Yet any history of German literature lists Annette von Droste-Hülshoff, Eduard Mörike, Franz Grillparzer, Adalbert Stifter, Friedrich Hebbel, Jeremias Gotthelf, Gottfried Keller, Theodor Storm, and other major writers of prose, poetry, and plays who were active around the middle of the century.

One reason that most of these writers were only rarely or belatedly translated and thus reached only a limited audience is that they persisted in exemplifying the attitudes and techniques of German idealism and Romanticism, a heritage that kept them out of the mainstream of European realism. When histories of German literature discuss the German variety of realism—which extended roughly from the 1840's to the 1880's—they often modify the word *Realismus* with an adjective such as *poetisch*, *psychologisch*, or *bürgerlich*.

The concept of poetic realism seems like a contradiction in terms and is peculiar to German literature. The term, coined by the philosopher Friedrich Schelling as early as 1802 and later popularized by Otto Ludwig in his studies of Shakespeare, refers both to a style and to a period. Poetic realism may be regarded as the most characteristic expression of the German *Bürgertum* around the middle of the nineteenth century. It reflected the relatively stable political and social structure of the middle class, a structure that was soon challenged by Heine, Karl Marx, Friedrich Nietzsche, and others. In contrast to the age of Romanticism, when the *Bürger* had been decried as a philistine, *bürgerlich* was now an entirely respectable appellation. The poetic realists strove for an aesthetically transformed depiction of reality; avoiding pathos and passion, their style was craftsmanlike, muted, and sober, reflecting a tension between the objective and the subjective.

Victor Lange has pointed out that "German fiction has . . . been provincial in setting and parochial in its belief," and it should be borne in mind that the German writers of this period lacked the coherence and unity of experience that the writers of other European nations possessed. The abortive revolutions of 1848 fostered a Biedermeier-like mood of resignation among these writers; as the Austrian playwright Johann Nestroy put it, "The noblest nation is resignation." The political structure encouraged provincialism and regionalism, and disillusionment with political and social activism caused these writers to retreat into an idyllic, simplistic world and concern themselves with their writings with morality, humaneness, conciliation, and adaptation. The great advances that were made in the 1850's in the natural sciences, technology, and industrialism, as well as the growing pains attendant upon the transformation of a largely agrarian country into a highly organized industrial society, found little reflection in this literature. Only at a later time were class differences and the contrast (sometimes conflict) between rural and urban life given adequate literary expression. Instead, German fiction focused on the *Innerlichkeit*, the inner development and psychology of its characters. Two great bildungsromans, novels of development in the manner of Johann Wolfgang von Goethe's Wilhelm Meister novels, were produced during that period: Keller's *Der grüne Heinrich* (1854-1855, 1879-1880; *Green Henry*, 1960) and Stifter's *Der Nachsommer* (1857; *Indian Summer*, 1985).

Above all, the writers of poetic realism seemed afraid to write about the burgeoning big cities, with their multifarious economic and social problems, and preferred instead to depict country life in the regions they knew best. The anthropological religion of this-worldliness that was preached by Ludwig Feuerbach influenced writers such as Hebbel and Keller. Arthur Schopenhauer's pessimistic philosophy of suffering and resignation, as expressed in his magnum opus, *Die Welt als Wille und Vorstellung* (1819; *The World as Will and Idea*, 1883-1886), became widely known only around the time of the philosopher's death in 1860 and influenced Wilhelm Raabe and Ferdinand von Saar, among others. Such philosophies supplied a modicum of support in an age characterized by rapid industrial, scientific, and technological development—changes that threatened to bring about a loss of religious faith and an unraveling of the social fabric, as well as skepticism and despair at the prospect of increasing dehumanization. The coming decades were to be marked by the polar forces of reaction and rebellion, with entrenched privilege fighting a rearguard action against the forces of change. The last novel of the Swiss writer Keller, *Martin Salander* (1886; English translation, 1964), portrays the struggle of a principled individual against new political and social conditions. As Georg Lukács has pointed out, Keller's basic orientation was toward the idyllic, and thus his world crumbled as he tried to give an unvarnished portrait of the coming age.

THE *GRÜNDERZEIT*

The Franco-Prussian War of 1870-1871 was followed by several decades of general peace, prosperity, and pride in the (Second) Reich fashioned by Otto von Bismarck, who served as chancellor from 1871 to 1890. The early period after the unification of Germany is known as the *Gründerzeit* or the *Gründerjahre*, the time of the founders, builders, and speculators. Factories, cities, and whole industrial empires were expanded, banks were set up, and the export and import trade flourished. The boom led to the creation of a myth of national greatness and vigor that was hardly affected by financial fluc-

tuations, crashes such as the one of 1873, and other growing pains of the *Gründerzeit*. A line from Emanuel Geibel's 1861 poem "Deutschlands Beruf" (Germany's calling), published in 1871 in the series *Heroldsrufe*, "Und es mag am deutschen Wesen einmal noch die Welt genesen" (someday the German spirit may yet cure the world's ills), became a sort of Pan-German slogan; Wilhelm II quoted it in his Münster speech of 1907.

As great numbers of people moved from the country to the city, an industrial proletariat came into being, and this strengthened the workers' movement. What has been called "the dilemma of the industrialized agrarian state" did not have a salutary effect on literature and culture. As the spirit of 1870-1871 focused attention on Germany's political and geopolitical aims—its quest for a place in culture, its pursuit of material advancement, and its enjoyment of luxurious living—intellectual life was bound to decline. Nietzsche believed that the victory over France was having deleterious effects on Germany: "Deutschland, Deutschland über alles," he said in reference to a line from Hoffmann von Fallersleben's poem, which ultimately served as Germany's national anthem from 1922 to 1945; "I fear that was the end of German philosophy." Political unification and material advancement were placed above the kind of freedom of spirit for which the Young Germans had fought some decades earlier. Philosophers such as Nietzsche, Jacob Burckhardt, and Wilhelm Scherer warned of what would happen to the German spirit and culture if the feverish speculative boom, the expansionism, the unbridled realpolitik, and the self-indulgent philistinism of the *Gründerjahre* were not kept in check. There was increasing tension between those writers who maintained a conservative, nationalistic bent and those who adopted a more progressive, socially conscious, cosmopolitan stance.

Many writers of the 1870's and 1880's were aware of the seamy side of the "economic miracle" and the "social question." Their sensitivity to the decline of the bourgeoisie and the plight of the proletariat made them skeptical of traditional values and solutions. This uncertainty and insecurity could only work to the detriment of creativity. It has become axiomatic to say that political power and success tend to go hand in hand with cultural decline. Literary historian Richard M. Meyer discerns such a decline in the 1870's, and the contemporary critic

Henry Hatfield believes that "around 1880 German literature was at the lowest point it had reached in over a century."

REALISM

Before the major writers after the middle or late 1880's can be discussed, it is necessary to take a brief look backward at the fictional forms of German realism. Paul Heyse not only wrote more than one hundred *Novellen*, issued in two dozen volumes between 1850 and 1914, but also became one of the chief theoreticians of the genre. According to his *Falkentheorie* (derived from the story of the falcon in Giovanni Boccaccio's *Decameron: O, Prencipe Galetto*, 1349-1351; *The Decameron*, 1620), a *Novelle* must have a clearly delineated basic motif and a characteristic that sets it apart from all other stories. In 1871, Heyse wrote that a *Novelle* should present "a significant human fate, a spiritual, intellectual, or ethical conflict, revealing through an uncommon occurrence a new side of human nature." (The "uncommon occurrence" seems to be the same *unerhörte Begebenheit* that Goethe specified as the hallmark of the genre.) Despite the fact that the prolific Heyse was once widely read and, in 1910, became the first German to receive the Nobel Prize in Literature, he is all but forgotten today, possibly as a result of what George Wallis Field called the "sentimental fragrance of old lace and lavender which lingers in most of [his] narratives."

Theodor Storm, another prolific practitioner of the genre, gave his own definition of the *Novelle* in an 1881 letter to Keller. Storm wrote,

> Today's *Novelle* is a sister of the drama and the most defined form of prose. Like the drama, it deals with the profoundest problems of human life and demands for its perfection a central conflict around which the entire story organizes itself. Consequently it requires the most compact form and the elimination of everything nonessential.

Storm, whose reputation has grown over the years, produced a great variety of *Novellen* and in his last decade favored the forms of the *Chroniknovelle* and the *Problemnovelle*, such as *Ein Bekenntnis* (1888; a confession), which deals with euthanasia. ("How does a person get into the position of killing the person he loves most?" wrote Storm to Keller. "And when it has happened, what becomes of him?") In Storm's last work, *Der Schimmelreiter* (1888; *The Rider on the White Horse*, 1915), the protagonist is presented in conflict with nature. Storm also made masterful use of the *Erinnerungsnovelle*, presenting a character's memories in the form of a *Rahmenerzählung*, the framework technique that anticipates the flashbacks of the cinema.

Another outstanding writer of *Novellen*, some of them long enough to rate as novels, was the Swiss Conrad Ferdinand Meyer. This prim patrician and emotionally unstable man wrote passionately and dramatically about the Italian Renaissance and the religious strife of the sixteenth and seventeenth centuries. Meyer's choice of characters, periods, and themes reflects not only his need for strong, vital figures but also the interest of his contemporaries in the late Middle Ages, the Renaissance, the Reformation, and the Counter-Reformation (though he did not share their fascination with the evolutionary process of history). Famous historical figures such as Thomas à Becket, Dante, Cosimo de' Medici, Lucrezia Borgia, Gustavus Adolphus, Louis XIV, and Michel Eyquem de Montaigne appear in Meyer's work, yet he was not so much concerned with historical personages and events as with the ethical problems of their (and his) age. Meyer was a master of the artistic reactivation of history, though he sometimes reactivated it in rather ambivalent fashion and as though from behind a mask of objectivity and detachment. His response to the spiritual cataclysms of a declining age was the presentation and therapeutic working out of what he regarded as timeless psychological, ethical, and philosophical problems. His eleven *Novellen* are thus primarily *Problemnovellen*, accounts of contending polar forces inherent in events or figures. These chronicles of spiritual and intellectual conflicts typically take the form of *Rahmenerzählungen* with copious use of dialogue and poetically stylized language.

Meyer stood at the end of a line of development. As Field put it, "In his turning away from contemporary life to history and distanced violence, there is also an element of fin de siècle aestheticism, reflecting the decay of the *Bürgertum* in which the *Novelle* had developed and flourished." E. K. Bennett adds Heyse to the representatives of the forces disintegrating from within and without—in the case of Meyer, his morbidity and neurotic susceptibility to the spiritual malaise of his age, and in the case of Heyse, his facile individualism and cosmopolitanism—that undermined the *Bürgertum* and its characteristic literary form. While Bennett pays due tribute to the sheer strength of will that enabled Meyer to transmute his chronic depression into the art of a virtuosic storyteller, he sees in his work "weakness masquerading as strength, uncertainty and insecurity disguised by the bold gesture" and points out that in Meyer's work "form and subject matter are nearly always in conflict."

Several minor masters, most of whom did not outlast their age, endeavored to inform, inspire, and entertain their contemporaries with massive, frequently multivolume historical novels that have rightly been deprecated as *Professorenromane*, the kind of tedious novels an academician might produce. Gustav Freytag, whose novel *Soll und Haben* (1855; *Debit and Credit*, 1855) painted a positive picture of the German middle class and its business morality, published a cycle of novels between 1872 and 1880 titled *Die Ahnen* (the ancestors; first two volumes translated as *Ingo: The First Novel of a Series Entitled "Our Forefathers,"* 1873, and *Ingraban: The Second Novel of a Series Entitled "Our Forefathers,"* 1873), an equally ambitious and ponderous panorama of German life from the fourth century to the author's own time. In 1870, Freytag followed the Prussian armies in their advance across eastern France and averred that he had encountered the type of ancient German hero he had glorified in these novels. The quintessential "professorial novel" is Felix Dahn's *Ein Kampf um Rom* (1876; *A Struggle for Rome*, 1878), about the decline and fall of the Ostrogothic empire in Italy. Dahn's *Kleine Romane aus der Völkerwanderung* (little novels from the great migration) appeared in thirteen volumes between 1883 and 1901, and his work led Bismarck, the "Iron Chancellor" himself, to call his novels appropriate reading for persons concerning themselves with serious things.

Not all such historical fiction is uncritically patriotic or chauvinistic, to be sure. In some instances, these novels represent efforts to come to terms with the present by providing parables of contemporary political events. Thus, Georg Ebers wrote about Egypt (*Eine ägyptische Königstochter*, 1864; *The Daughter of an Egyptian King*, 1871), Robert Hamerling about classical Greece (*Aspasia*, 1876; English translation, 1882), and Ernst Eckstein about ancient Rome (*Nero*, 1889; English translation, 1889). Others were undisguised *Zeitromane* with contemporary settings and criticism of many aspects of the present, such as the unsound development of the economy and untrammeled speculation. Heyse also wrote novels of this type. In *Über allen Gipfeln* (1895), he tried to rise to the challenge of Nietzsche by telling the story of a Nietzschean, the Prussian official Erik von Friesen. In *Sturmflut* (1876; *The Breaking of the Storm*, 1877), by Friedrich Spielhagen, a tidal wave in the Baltic that takes the life of a speculator is related to the economic tidal wave, with one catastrophe shedding light on the other.

WILHELM RAABE AND THEODOR FONTANE

The two outstanding German storytellers of the latter part of the nineteenth century were Wilhelm Raabe and Theodor Fontane, writers whose reputations grew during the last several decades of the twentieth century. Since at least some of their work falls in the fin de siècle period, a more extended discussion of their contribution is in order here.

Raabe was a curiously isolated figure who had no real successors, although some of his narrative techniques foreshadow those of Thomas Mann. In his quirky ambivalence, wry humor, whimsy, and latter-day Romantic irony, this subtle and sophisticated storyteller harks back to Sterne and Jean Paul, but these qualities also bespeak an affinity with Dickens and Thackeray. Raabe grasped the moral dilemmas of his world and portrayed that world honestly and truthfully. His social range was rather narrow, his intellectual penetration not very profound, and he had little passion or reformers' zeal. Yet his admitted philistinism had a gleam of true wisdom that has been called "simply an acknowledgment of the inscrutable fitness of things," and his pessimism is somehow uplifting and cheering as often as it is despairing and depressing. Lange sees Raabe as the continuator of a fertile tradition, that of the German baroque imagination, and concludes that "his work represents the impressive climax of the literature of German bourgeois idealism." Barker Fairley calls Raabe's work "the most richly conceived body of fiction in the German language."

"Look up to the stars! Watch life in the streets!" This admonition reflects what may be termed Raabe's idealistic realism as he foreshadows the coming German (and indeed European) crisis of morals. His best-known novels portray the eventual triumph of inner strength and integrity over the forces of decay and dissolution. The individual must stand inviolate amid all onslaughts: "We want to remain what we must be." There is more tension than action in Raabe's novels; his subjective style and multiple narrative perspectives may have been intended to facilitate communication with a wider readership, but in effect, his subtleties were lost on many readers, and his modest, pseudonaïve disclaimers were accepted at face value.

Raabe's basic theme is humanity in an age of social change. After 1870, he remained loyal to the Reich, but he was troubled by the political developments and the social upheavals he witnessed, and his late novels reflect his disillusionment with Bismarck's nationalistic policies. *Pfisters Mühle* (1884) deals with the clash of the old and the new as a rural landscape is rapidly transformed into an industrial one. The novel takes the form of a reminiscence of a young Berlin schoolmaster who is spending his honeymoon in his father's mill, soon to make way for a factory. It turns out that the water of the millstream is polluted by the effluvia of a beet-sugar factory. Even though the father wins a lawsuit against the factory, it is a Pyrrhic victory, for he dies knowing that the old way of life is doomed. The conflict between the old and the new worlds is personified by Dr. Asche, who in his youth enjoyed the mill but as an industrial scientist and founder of a dye business aligns himself with the forces of "progress." Yet the fact that he remains essentially humane shows that the march of time need not drown out the harmonies of tradition. *Im alten Eisen* (1887) is less optimistic; the wheel of history rolls over the human community. *Das Odfeld* (1889; *The Odin Field*, 2001), set during the Seven Years' War, is about some uprooted civilians who are guided back to their homesteads to rebuild their lives. *Die Akten des Vogelsangs* (1896) tells the story of three children who experience the breakup of an old-fashioned neighborhood in a town that is being modernized. In an ironic concession to popular taste,

Raabe called his novel *Stopfkuchen: Eine See-und Mordgeschichte* (1891; *Tubby Schaumann: A Tale of Murder and the High Seas*, 1983) a "murder and sea story"; he also described it as his best and most subjective book. The title is the nickname of a nibbler named Heinrich Schaumann, a warm and humane Biedermeier type, who tells the story of his life to Eduard, a prosperous settler in Africa who is on his way home after a visit to his native Germany. In its attack on tendencies to idealize the past and its deflation of the materialistic person of action, this wry commentary on a quarter-century of change may be regarded as anti-*Faust*.

Pointing out that Raabe "presents metaphysical problems in a precisely described social and historical milieu," Eda Sagarra formulates some basic, penetrating questions that Raabe posed in his most mature novels: Should life be lived in conformity with changing patterns of society at the cost of spiritual and intellectual values, or should it be lived in self-imposed seclusion? Can one be involved in the process of historical change without sacrificing one's humanity?

Theodor Fontane, a Prussian of French Huguenot ancestry, had already been a pharmacist and journalist and was almost sixty years old when he published his first novel, *Vor dem Sturm* (1878; *Before the Storm: A Novel of the Winter 1812-13*, 1985), set in Brandenburg just before Napoleon's defeat in Russia and the Wars of Liberation. In two decades, he followed this novel with fifteen more works of fiction that finally placed the German novel in the European mainstream. Roy Pascal has called him "the first German writer since Goethe to stand in easy contact with the public issues of the European world." Betraying the influence of Jane Austen, George Eliot, Thackeray, and the Russian Realists, Fontane actually belongs more to European realism than to the literary tradition of his own country. Though he never enjoyed the kind of worldwide recognition that has been accorded to such writers as Leo Tolstoy and Gustave Flaubert, Fontane did prepare the ground for Thomas Mann and other literary giants of the twentieth century.

Fontane expressed himself repeatedly about the mission of the novel and his own contributions to the genre. He compared German fiction with the works of Ivan Turgenev, to the detriment of the former: "It lacks veracity, objectivity, reality. People constantly do and say things that, given the way they are, they could never do and say." "The task of the modern novel," he wrote elsewhere,

> seems to me to be the description of a life, a society, a group of people, as the undistorted reflection of the life we lead. . . . The novel should be a picture of the times to which we belong, or at least the reflection of the times adjacent to ours, about which our parents have told us.

In reading a novel, Fontane pointed out, one should feel a congruence between the invented life and real life, the only difference being that which arises from "that intensity, clarity, transparency, roundedness, and, consequently, that intensity of feeling which is the transfiguring task of art." This patriotic but remarkably unchauvinistic Prussian chose to write mainly about the declining Prussian nobility, the Junker class, because of its historical importance in the evolution of modern Germany and because of its embodiment of the essence of the contemporary situation.

A relentless critic of the new Reich and its rigid, antiquated, decadent social order, Fontane satirized the self-satisfaction, smugness, and pretentiousness of the titled and moneyed, particularly the nouveau-riche bourgeoisie. He was less concerned with the proletariat, though lower-class characters do appear in his writings. His social novels highlight three basic problems: liaisons between an upper-class male and a lower-class female, misalliances, and adultery. Fontane was aware that his time was witnessing the end of the *Bürgertum*, its established values and social code. The moral code was becoming relativistic rather than absolute, and Fontane, a worldly-wise old man who tended to shrink from scenes of intense passion and action and who was an eminently conciliatory spirit, was content to leave some questions unanswered and certain conflicts unresolved. While he came to believe that the reevaluation of all values for which Nietzsche called needed to take place, he also believed that for the sake of preserving inner integrity a moral law was needed to keep order in life, especially where the human passions were concerned. Fontane's style is controversial, allusive in its skillful employment of symbols and leitmotifs, and full of anecdotes and epigrams that illuminate the personality, problems, and behavior of a character. Not infrequently, comic and tragic elements intermingle.

Fontane is particularly noted for his series of Berlin novels, beginning with *L'Adultera* (1882; *The Woman Taken in Adultery*, 1979). The theme of *Irrungen, Wirrungen* (1888; *Trials and Tribulations*, 1917; also known as *A Suitable Match*, 1968) can be stated in this question: Can an individual find happiness in the face of a rigid order and an unsympathetic environment that in its social and moral pressures harks back to the past? An illicit liaison must here be dissolved in accordance with the code of honor of the Prussian aristocracy, on the one hand, and that of the petite bourgeoisie, on the other. With his distaste for "noise in feelings," the author comes down on the side of traditional order. In *Stine* (1890; English translation, 1969), however, a count wants to break through the barriers of convention, but a poor seamstress knows her place and rejects him, whereupon he kills himself. *Frau Jenny Treibel* (1893; *Jenny Treibel*, 1976) contains a subtle critique of the anti-intellectualism of the bourgeoisie. The protagonist, who has moved up from poverty, claims to be an idealist, but when her son wishes to marry an impecunious girl, she reveals her materialistic attitude.

Fontane's best-known novel, widely regarded as the German *Madame Bovary*, is *Effi Briest* (1895; English translation, 1914, 1962). The adultery committed by the protagonist out of boredom is discovered years later by her stodgy, older husband, Baron von Instetten, and avenged by him not so much out of passion as out of pedantic "correctness." A divorcée and social outcast, Effi dies an early, lonely death. While Fontane seems to condemn the hollowness of society's code of honor, his message is "Marriage is order." It is interesting to note, though, that he lets similar instances of marital infidelity in *The Woman Taken in Adultery* and *Effi Briest* be treated differently by society. In *Die Poggenpuhls* (1896; *The Poggenpuhl Family*, 1979), problems of mésalliance in an impoverished aristocratic family are solved by the legacy of a wealthy relative. Fontane designated his last work, *Der Stechlin* (1898; *The Stechlin*, 1996), as a political novel, but the ambiguity of the title, which is the name of a lake, a forest, a village, and a castle in addition to that of its principal character, lifts it to a symbolic-mythical plane. The author's original plan was to show the aristocracy as it ought to be, but he wound up painting an unvarnished portrait of fin de siècle Prussian society. This novel points back to Fontane's first, in which the author had concerned himself with the task of the Prussian aristocracy and questioned the nature and limits of patriotism. As he contrasts the worlds of the old and the young Stechlin, Fontane bids an optimistic farewell to an irretrievably lost age. The words spoken by a pastor at Dubslav von Stechlin's funeral also apply to the author: "Nothing human was alien to him, because he thought of himself as a human being and was at all times conscious of his own human weaknesses."

Fontane was a Janus-like figure, both the apogee of nineteenth century bourgeois realism and the anticipator of trends and techniques to come. He was in no way an extremist, an innovator, an activist, a utopian thinker, or a propagandist. Yet it is characteristic of him that he became the beloved mentor of a new literary generation, the naturalists, in particular Gerhart Hauptmann, whom he championed without recoiling at the sordidness and disorder in their work. With his vaunted wit and irony, however, Fontane supplied a critical perspective when he played on one of the buzzwords of the day: "Modern? Sprechen Sie das Wort einmal anders aus!" The meaning of the adjective *modern*, stressed on the second syllable, is obvious; the verb *modern*, stressed on the first syllable, means "to decay." Fontane's pun may be reproduced in English by predicting that today's new mold will have mold on it tomorrow.

THE THEORY OF NATURALISM

"Our world is no longer classical," wrote Arno Holz; "our world is no longer romantic; our world is modern." Terms such as *modern* and *die Moderne* (coined by Eugen Wolff) became battle cries as a new generation of writers strove to modify Germany's feudal and parochial structure sufficiently to admit cultural currents from elsewhere in Europe and to allow a heightened realism finally to take hold in German literature. Marxism became increasingly influential in the 1870's and 1880's, and the doctrines of Charles Darwin as presented by his chief German disciple Ernst Haeckel promoted a more materialistic *Weltanschauung*. Nietzsche's rejection of conventional morality and his call for a "new man" appealed to a younger generation of activists, who de-

scribed themselves as "Das jüngste Deutschland" in programmatical reference to "Das junge Deutschland" earlier in the century. What has been termed *Hochrealismus* but is generally known as *Naturalismus* depended heavily on foreign prototypes. Émile Zola's twenty-volume cycle of novels, *Les Rougon-Macquart* (1871-1893; *The Rougon-Macquarts*, 1896-1900), viewed human nature as determined by the all-important factors of heredity and environment. Zola's kind of experimental novel, as described in *Le Roman expérimental* (1880; *The Experimental Novel*, 1893), combined objectivity with personal expression, and from him German writers, who tended, according to Felix Bertaux, to alternate "between microscopic treatments of fact and vast empty structures of thought," derived a broadly humanistic view of life. Other influential Frenchmen were Maurice Barrès, who enunciated an ego psychology in his trilogy *Le Culte du moi* (1887-1891); Paul Bourget, whose *Cosmopolis* (1893; English translation, 1893) highlights the figure of the dilettante; and Edmond de Goncourt and Jules de Goncourt with their family novel *René Mauperin* (1864; English translation, 1888). Turgenev, Tolstoy, and Dostoevski became important models, but the greatest number of mentors and models were supplied by the Scandinavian countries: the critic Georg Brandes, the dramatists August Strindberg and Henrik Ibsen, and the novelists Jens Peter Jacobsen, Hermann Bang, Alexander Kielland, Knut Hamsun, Ola Hansson, Peter Nansen, Henrik Pontoppidan, Björnstjerne Björnson, Holger Drachmann, Jonas Lie, Arne Garborg, Hans Jaeger, and Christian Krogh. The example of these authors enabled the naturalists to reject the works of predecessors such as Heyse as epigonal, false, and effete; to turn away from the princes, knights, and other heroes evoked by Freytag and Dahn; and to shine a spotlight on the lowly, the economically and socially disadvantaged, and the seamy side of life. The modern successor of the traditional hero was the passive hero or the irresolute "half-hero" in the manner of Jacobsen's Niels Lyhne.

The theoretical foundation for naturalism was laid by the Hart brothers, Heinrich and Julius. Their six brochures titled *Kritische Waffengänge* appeared between 1882 and 1884 and made Berlin one of the centers of the movement, spawning a number of journals and associations, such as the Der Verein "Durch" (1886), the Freie Bühne Verein (1889), and the Friedrichshagener Kreis (founded 1890). The leading figures of the Berlin circle were, in addition to the Harts, Arno Holz, Johannes Schlaf, Hermann Conradi,Gerhart Hauptmann, and Karl Henckell. Munich was the second center, and the chief focus there was Michael Georg Conrad's journal *Die Gesellschaft*. Carl Bleibtreu regarded the Sturm und Drang firebrands of the 1770's as the spiritual ancestors of the young writers; once again, "original genius" was to be given its due.

Holz, who believed that "an art can be revolutionized only by revolutionizing its means," originated the idea of a *konsequenter Naturalismus* (consistent naturalism). To Zola's dictum "Une oeuvre d'art est un coin de la nature, vu à travers un tempérament" (a work of art is a corner of nature seen through a temperament), he opposed his own definition (in *Die Kunst: Ihr Wesen und ihre Gesetze*, 1891-1892): "Die Kunst hat die Tendenz, wieder die Natur zu sein. Sie wird sie nach Massgabe ihrer jeweiligen Reproduktionsbedingungen und deren Handhabung." This can be expressed in a simple formula: Art equals Nature minus X, with X representing the unavoidable limitations of the artist's medium and the way it is used or applied. Nature means strict limitation to factual, empirical reality and the exclusion of imaginative or inventive additions by the artist. Holz wished to completely eliminate the omniscient narrator in order to achieve the illusion of perfect objectivity and complete realism; by grasping and conveying everything a character sees and hears, a "phonographic method" was to overcome "paper language." Holz and his collaborator Schlaf called for the employment of *Sekundenstil*, a kind of staccato style making for unretouched snapshots of life that actually anticipated cinematic techniques, a microscopic precision in registering every nuance of setting and atmosphere as well as every inflection of speech. Conrad came to describe the *konsequenter Naturalismus* as an "asphalt plant of a big-city street without fragrance or seeds—an astonishing wonder of technology."

"No more verses, no more novels," wrote Holz, "only the open, living scene exists for us now." It was neither prose nor poetry but the theater that offered the naturalists the most effective pulpit for their preachings, the best

forum for their muckraking, and the best proving ground for their techniques. It should be emphasized that their fiction was no match for the power, brilliance, and international stature achieved by a dramatist such as Hauptmann. While few of the narrative works written under the banner of naturalism are still read today, this fiction and its writers nevertheless bespeak a lively and varied literary scene.

THE FICTION OF NATURALISM

The naturalists favored the novel over the *Novelle* or other forms of short prose, but a few outstanding examples of the latter genre deserve pride of place. In Hauptmann's symbolistic masterpiece *Bahnwärter Thiel* (1888; *Flagman Thiel*, 1933), a railroad gatekeeper is haunted by his deceased first wife even while he is under the erotic spell of his current one, who mistreats his little son and through carelessness causes the boy to be killed by a train, whereupon the Woyzeck-like Thiel goes mad and murders her. Equally tragic is the prose sketch *Papa Hamlet* by Holz and Schlaf, published in 1889; that year Hauptmann dedicated his first play, *Vor Sonnenaufgang* (pr., pb. 1889; *Before Dawn*, 1909), to the fictitious Scandinavian Bjarne P. Holmsen, the pseudonym used by Holz and Schlaf. This prose study tells the story of Niels Thienwiebel, a broken-down, brutish, egotistical actor who chokes his infant son. The grandiloquent quotations from Shakespeare, with their highflown idealism, provide an ironic counterpoint to the sordid goings-on in the dim-witted actor's reality. The deterministic helplessness of the characters is expressed in their very language, which is choppy, stuttering, and fragmented. "Holz often worked on a sentence for a whole day," wrote Schlaf, "because he found it impossible to go on until it sparkled with color, resonance, and even fragrance."

The early naturalists cultivated the *Grosstadtromane*, novels set in big cities, particularly the capital, Berlin. The most noteworthy among the somewhat melodramatic, Dickensian Berlin novels of Max Kretzer are *Meister Timpe* (1888), about the losing fight of an urban craftsman against encroaching mechanization, and *Das Gesicht Christi* (1897), in which the Savior becomes a symbol for the destitute of Berlin. In his story "Die letzte Pflicht" (the last duty), the Scottish-born John Henry

Mackay paints an altogether bleak cityscape as he follows a small-town schoolteacher across Berlin in search of a friend; this "story without a plot" is bound to end tragically and conveys the message that "the sad thing is not death but life." Mackay's novel *Die Anarchisten* (1891; *The Anarchists*, 1891) marks his turning to a sort of anarchistic individualism. The short-lived Hermann Conradi wrote two novels, including *Adam Mensch* (1889), in which he gave such a radical analysis of his time that he was condemned by the courts and his writings were labeled as immoral. Conrad Alberti (pseudonym of Konrad Sittenfeld), "the swashbuckler of naturalism," published *Plebs* (1887), a collection of stories set among Berlin workers. Peter Hille, the legendary Berlin vagabond poet, wrote *Die Sozialisten* (1886), a novel with such thinly veiled characters as Beber and Triebknecht. Carl Bleibtreu's "pathological novel" *Grössenwahn* (1887) has a Bohemian setting. Its hero retreats from the world to find salvation in Darwin. In *Der Büttnerbauer* (1895; *Farmer Büttner*, 1915), a novel praised by Tolstoy, Wilhelm von Polenz described the destructive force of capitalism in a rustic setting. *Frau Sorge* (1887; *Dame Care*, 1891), by Hermann Sudermann, about an East Prussian peasant who incurs debts but finally manages to free himself from the ghosts of his youth and win the love of people who guide him to a better life, was once widely read and admired, but Lange judges the author harshly when he says that "he merely turned the impartial conscientiousness of Zola and Tolstoy into German sentimentality." In the first decade of the twentieth century, Schlaf published two trilogies in which he attempted to present a typology of people in search of a new lifestyle, a new society, and a new human.

There was no "Munich novel" as such, but M. G. Conrad, the chief German apostle of Zola, attempted a ten-volume German pendant to *The Rougon-Macquarts*, though only three novels appeared, beginning with *Was die Isar rauscht* (1888), set in Schwabing, the artists' district of Munich. The once-popular *Jörn Uhl* (1901; English translation, 1905), by Gustav Frenssen, is also about a farmer who struggles to preserve an encumbered farm. This novel is an example of *Heimatkunst*, both a throwback to the regionalism of poetic realism and a forerunner of the nefarious *Blut und Bodenliteratur*

(blood and soil literature) favored by the Nazis. Other works of this type, imbued with an almost mystic belief in the purity and inviolability of the ancestral soil and those living on it, are the stories *Leute eigner Art* (1904; people of a special kind), by Timm Kröger, and *Der Wehrwolf* (1910; *Harm Wulf*, 1931), by Hermann Löns, a gory chronicle of German peasants during the Thirty Years' War who fight for their homesteads like werewolves.

The autobiographical *Roman aus der Décadence* (1898), by Kurt Martens, is set among troubled Leipzig intellectuals and indicates that by then many naturalists had turned from Marx to Nietzsche, from socialism to individualism and anarchism in the spirit of Max Stirner or Peter Kropotkin. The controversial novel *Werther, der Jude* (1893), by Ludwig Jacobowsky, the Berlin editor of *Die Gesellschaft*, presents an autobiographical portrait of a young Jew who experiences the tragic duality of being inadequately rooted in the Jewish tradition and incompletely integrated into German culture and society, which means discrimination, despair, and death.

A more positive note is struck by Julius Stinde, who wrote a series of novels about the cozily materialistic middle-class Buchholz family; by Heinrich Seidel, who produced a group of novels about the lovable eccentric Leberecht Hühnchen; and by Ludwig Thoma, whose *Lausbubengeschichten* (1905-1907) are delightful and durable Bavarian bad-boy stories. The physicist Kurd Lasswitz anticipated space travel in his novel *Auf zwei Planeten* (1897); giving the Martians a higher form of culture than the earthlings enables the author to criticize contemporary conditions. A new kind of *Professorenroman* was attempted by the noted natural scientist Wilhelm Bölsche: In *Die Mittagsgöttin* (1891), the example of an aristocrat done in by spiritism leads a young man to recapture his belief in a better future based on science and socialism. Carl Hauptmann, Gerhart's brother, is remembered for his roman à clef *Einhart der Lächler* (1907), set among artists. In novels such as *Leonore Griebel* (1900) and *Der begrabene Gott* (1905), by the Silesian Hermann Stehr, a brooding awareness of suffering and a mystic religiosity are in evidence. Otto Julius Bierbaum is mainly remembered for two works: *Stilpe* (1897), "a novel from a frog's perspective," is a roman à clef with a Berlin bohemian setting in which a megalomaniacal writer sinks in the social scale and commits suicide. *Prinz Kuckuck* (1907-1908), subtitled *Leben, Taten, Meinungen und Höllenfahrt eines Wollüstlings* (life, deeds, opinions, and descent to hell of a voluptuary), betrays the influence of Joris-Karl Huysmans and Oscar Wilde. This great panorama of the Wilhelmian Age has been extravagantly praised by Klaus Günther Just as "the first great German novel of contemporary life before *The Magic Mountain.*"

Cäsar Flaischlen's autobiographical novel *Jost Seyfried* (1905) chronicles, in the form of letters and diary entries, the development of a young writer of the *jüngstdeutsche* persuasion; this "new man" slips back into comfortable middle-class mediocrity. *Modernus* (1904), by Heinrich Lilienfein, is also autobiographical, a novel of development suffused with the spirit of Richard Wagner, Schopenhauer, and Nietzsche, the three sections of which are headed "How I Lost God," "How I Lost the World," "How I Lost Myself." Its hero, however, moves from irresponsible aestheticism and decadent living to a meaningful life. A portrait of fin de siècle aristocracy is given in the trilogy *Deutscher Adel um 1900* (1897-1901), by Georg von Ompteda. The Satanist of German literature was Polish-born Stanisław Przybyszewski, who was indebted to Nietzsche and Huysmans. His interest in Satanism, occultism, demonology, and nihilism is reflected in such works as *Homo sapiens* (1895-1898; English translation, 1915), *Satans Kinder* (1897), and *Androgyne* (1906). Jethro Bithell believes that Przybyszewski's importance "lies in his preaching of sex as the ineluctable purpose of life and as the creative organ of art and literature."

Gerhart Hauptmann's novel *Der Narr in Christo Emanuel Quint* (1910; *The Fool in Christ: Emanuel Quint*, 1911) is indebted to Dostoevski's figure of the Grand Inquisitor. It is a Tolstoyan tale about a Silesian carpenter who tries to emulate Christ; the world is not ready for this, and the man is banished. *Atlantis* (1912; English translation, 1912) foreshadows the wreck of the *Titanic* in a symbolic presentation of a prewar culture that seems destined to founder.

The outstanding women writers of the time were Clara Viebig and Ricarda Huch. Although Viebig lived mostly in Berlin, her socially conscious and compassionate fiction is set mainly in her native Rhineland or the Polish borderland. "Das Miseräbelchen" is a touching story about a deformed child, "a cacophony in Creation, a mockery of jubilant Nature." *Die Rheinlandstöchter* (1897) pleads for the emancipation of women, and "Halbtier!" is a story about a "new woman" who rebels against her traditional role. *Das Weiberdorf* (1900) is set in a village populated by sex-starved women whose husbands work in distant mines. A trilogy of (somewhat belatedly) naturalistic Berlin novels appeared between 1910 and 1915. Similar subjects are dealt with in the fiction of Helene Böhlau, Gabriele Reuter, Helene Voigt-Diederichs, and Lulu von Strauss und Torney.

Lou Andreas-Salomé, who occupied an important place in the lives of Nietzsche, Rainer Maria Rilke, and Sigmund Freud, published empathic stories such as "Menschenkinder" and novels such as *Ruth* (1895) and *Im Zwischenland* (1902). Ricarda Huch's *Erinnerungen von Ludolf Ursleu dem Jüngeren* (1893; *Recollections of Ludolf Ursleu the Younger*, 1913-1915, 1969) anticipates Mann's *Buddenbrooks* in its account, from the silence of a cloister, of the decline of a patrician Hamburg merchant family because of a passionate love. In *Aus der Triumphgasse* (1902), an old Trieste mansion serves as the squalid domicile of paupers and other outcasts of society.

COUNTERCURRENTS TO NATURALISM

Various countercurrents to naturalism made themselves felt at an early stage of the movement; as early as 1891, the Austrian critic Hermann Bahr wrote a monograph about its *Überwindung* (transcending). Apart from the fact that "consistent naturalism" and other doctrinaire forms were bound to be limited and short-lived, there was a general tendency to abandon the empirical and "scientific" for the irrational, the intuitive, the psychic, the aesthetic, the mystic, and the mythological—to shift from the problems of the time to the problems of the individual. Remembering Goethe's insight that "Art is called art precisely because it is not Nature," the antinaturalists pointed out that the methods of the laboratory and the photographer's studio were not those of the writer. A "return to living things" and a quest for a "literature of nerves" replaced what Bahr described as the "street clothes of truth" and the "insolent despotism of dead things." A desire to give words their due and a striving for inspired language, however, soon produced a new psychological crisis, the awareness of the insufficiency of words.

The prose writers were slower to free themselves from the traditions of realism and naturalism than were the poets and dramatists. While the novel often retained the *Sekundenstil*, fiction, in general, became more subtle and more lyric, concentrating on a second reality of dreams and visions and showing multifarious interconnections between the rational and the irrational. "Without the binding force of nineteenth century Realism and social consciousness," writes H. M. Waidson, "the novel became open to fragmentation through visionary perception and at the same time exposed to that revaluation of all values which so frequently led to nihilistic amorality." The French Symbolists, Oscar Wilde, Walt Whitman, and the Belgians Émile Verhaeren and Maurice Maeterlinck, as well as Huysmans (particularly his antinaturalist novel *Là-bas*, 1891; *Down There*, 1924; better known as *Là-Bas*, 1972), all became important influences on what was generally a European countermovement. This period of intellectual ferment and multiplicity has been classified under many rubrics: Symbolism, neo-Romanticism, neoidealism, neoclassicism, regionalism, aestheticism, art for art's sake, and even incipient expressionism (which Waidson defines as an "ecstatic radicalism which strove to combine visionary awareness with practical social purpose"). The terms "impressionism" and "expressionism" were derived from art, as was Jugendstil (Art Nouveau), which refers not to a youthful style but to the trendsetting periodical *Jugend*, founded in 1896 and aimed at aesthetic refinement in art and literature. This periodical resisted the notion of fin de siècle weariness, decadence, or cultural pessimism of Nietzschean or Schopenhauerian provenance: "We are not living among the last gasps of a dying epoch; we are in the morning of a perfectly healthy age. It is a pleasure to live!"

In novels such as *Beate und Mareile* (1903; *The Curse of the Tarniffs*, 1928), Eduard, Graf von Keyserling—the scion of a noble Baltic family and in some ways a continuator of Fontane—describes a thin upper crust trying to live in style above a less refined but more vital lower social stratum, the only contact between these two levels being an occasional and fleeting amorous relationship. Karl May, an enduring phenomenon as a best-selling author, between 1892 and 1910 published thirty-three volumes of what he modestly called his *Reiseerzählungen* (travel tales), exemplifying Wilhelmian Germany's longing for colorful adventures in faraway places. On a higher literary level are the exotic adventure stories and novels of Maximilian Dauthendey, such as *Lingam* (1909) and *Raubmenschen* (1911), as well as the grotesque narratives of Paul Scheerbart, the antierotic *Tarub, Bagdads berühmte Köchin* (1896), and the "snob novel" *Rakkóx der Billionär* (1900).

The fiction of Frank Wedekind, who challenged society on the basis of Freud's thesis that "civilization is based on the permanent subjugation of the human instincts," often is a pendant to his dramas. *Feuerwerk* (1906), a collection of stories, presents such fireworks of eroticism as "Der Brand von Egliswyl," in which a voluptuary, rendered impotent by a girl's rejection of him, sets the entire village on fire to prove his machismo. Wedekind's novel, *Mine-Haha: Oder, Über die körperliche Erziehung der jungen Mädchen* (1903), is a utopian glorification of physical fitness. The early novels of Waldemar Bonsels, *Mare, die Jugend eines Mädchens* (1907) and *Blut* (1909), fasten on the conflict between passion and conscience. In *Freund Hein: Eine Lebensgeschichte* (1902), Emil Strauss took up a subject repeatedly treated in fiction: the anguish of a student who sees suicide as the only way out of a rigid, uncaring school and social system. Friedrich Huch's first novel, *Peter Michel* (1901), deals with a village boy who vainly tries to break out of a confining environment. Similar themes are found in the early novels of the Swabian Hermann Hesse. *Peter Camenzind* (1904; English translation, 1961) depicts a flight to and from people as a country boy, disappointed at what he finds in the city, returns to a simpler life. The protagonist of *Unterm Rad* (1906; *Prodigy*, 1957; also known as *Beneath the Wheel*, 1968) is an ambitious and sensitive student who perishes "under the wheel" of an authoritarian, dehumanizing system.

In 1900, Heinrich Mann published his novel *Im Schlaraffenland* (*In the Land of Cockaigne*, 1925), a scathing indictment of corruption among Berlin's nouveaux riches, which foreshadows the author's later social satires. The trilogy *Die Göttinnen* (1902; *The God-*

dess, 1918; also known as *Diana*, 1929) deals with the gifted and ambitious Duchess d'Assy, and *Die Jagd nach Liebe* (1903) presents a caricatured panorama of Munich high society. In *Professor Unrat* (1905; *Small Town Tyrant*, 1944), an autocratic schoolmaster falls under the spell of an entertainer at a dubious tavern and then takes revenge for his social ostracism by ensnaring his fellow citizens and ruining their morals and reputations. (Twenty-five years later, this novel formed the basis of the celebrated film *Der blaue Engel*, 1930; *The Blue Angel*.) *Zwischen den Rassen* (1907) highlights the contrast between the Nordic and the Latin, and in *Die kleine Stadt* (1909), submerged passions erupt when a troupe of actors appears in a small Italian town.

The great theme of Thomas Mann, Heinrich's more celebrated brother, is the tenuous position of the artist in society, his unassuaged longing for both full acceptance and the "joys of the commonplace," and his status as an anguished outsider. *Buddenbrooks: Verfall einer Familie* (1901; English translation, 1924), as impressive a first novel as has ever been written, is not really a modern novel but a masterful restatement of, and farewell to, the narrative tradition of the nineteenth century. Replete with both naturalistic and impressionistic elements and techniques, it chronicles the decline of a Hanseatic merchant family (clearly in Mann's native Lübeck). Sensitive young Hanno, of the fourth generation, knows that with his artistic sensibilities he represents the end and willingly, almost incidentally, succumbs to a disease. Mann's second full-length novel, *Königliche Hoheit* (1909; *Royal Highness*, 1916), is a modern fairy tale, complete with a happy ending. An impecunious petty prince leaves his ivory tower and achieves an "austere happiness" through his marriage to the daughter of a German American millionaire. The story "Der kleine Herr Friedemann" ("Little Herr Friedemann") represents the artist as cripple; the emphasis on the physical causation of his "chosenness" suggests Zola. In the novella *Tristan* (1903; English translation, 1925), a rather seedy writer living in a sanatorium for the sake of discipline acts as Tristan to a patient's Isolde, and the price of her spiritual-artistic-erotic awakening is her "parodistic" death estranged from her commonplace family. The most mature and enduring among Mann's early *Novellen* is *Tonio Kröger* (1903; English translation, 1914). An escapee from his father's bourgeois world and rejected by the attractively mindless and charming people of this world, the protagonist finds the artistic life unsatisfying and is crushed when a confidant suggests that he may be "a commoner gone astray"; in the end, Tonio realizes that his outsider status may be the very source of his creativity and that his true mission may be ironic mediation between life and art.

STORYTELLERS FROM SWITZERLAND, AUSTRIA, AND CZECHOSLOVAKIA

The foremost Swiss prose writer after Conrad Ferdinand Meyer was Carl Spitteler, the recipient of the Nobel Prize in Literature in 1919. A Symbolistic critic of the materialism and utilitarianism of his age, he expressed many psychological insights in his fiction. The story *Conrad der Leutnant* (1898) deals with a young man and his overbearing family. The title of *Imago* (1906), the story of a sexual obsession sublimated in devotion to art and a love attachment emerging from repression, supplied Freud and his circle with the name of both a significant psychoanalytic concept and a journal. *Die Mädchenfeinde* (1907; *The Little Misogynists*, 1923) is a sensitive and colorful tale about boys and girls on the verge of adolescence. The three novels of Robert Walser, who lived in psychiatric clinics for the last twenty-seven years of his life, are partly autobiographical. The subtly ironic Walser foreshadows Franz Kafka (who appreciated him) in that familiar details of everyday life are used as the stepping-stones to fantasy. In *Jakob von Gunten* (1909; English translation, 1969), the author exposes the moral ambivalence of his age through the diary entries and musings of a boy at a boarding school, a sort of urban "magic mountain," who manages to take an imaginary trip that removes him from European culture. In *Konrad Pilater* (1910), by Jakob Schaffner, a young man is torn between political radicalism and love. Jakob Christoph Heer and Ernst Zahn dealt with aspects of Swiss cantonal life in their novels *Der König der Bernina* (1900) and *Albin Indergang* (1901), and the priest Heinrich Federer wrote *Lachweiler Geschichten* (1911), Swiss village tales in the tradition of Jeremias Gotthelf and Keller.

The Vienna of the end of the nineteenth century has attracted considerable attention in recent years. In the last decades of the old, moribund Habsburg Empire there was a greater consciousness of decline and dissolution in Austria than in Germany, and this sense of life found expression in impressionistic and Symbolistic terms. Naturalism never took hold in Austria, where industrialization was a much slower process, for writers there did not share the political activism of their German colleagues. Most of the *Jung Wien*, or Young Vienna, writers (Hermann Bahr, Arthur Schnitzler, Hugo von Hofmannsthal, Felix Salten, Richard Beer-Hofmann, Peter Altenberg, Stefan Zweig, and Leopold, Freiherr von Andrian-Werburg) were of an upper-middle-class background and thus tended to be conservators rather than reformers.

The great theme of the older generation of writers was the impact of modernization and early capitalism on the landed gentry and the upwardly mobile bourgeoisie. The melancholy Ferdinand von Saar strove to depict society in the manner of Turgenev; his stance of scientific detachment and sympathy for those defeated by change links him to the naturalists. Saar is particularly remembered for his cycle *Novellen aus Œsterreich* (1877-1897; a literary picturebook of Francisco-Josephinian Austria) and the novel *Schloss Kosternitz* (1892). The dramatist Ludwig Anzengruber wrote the powerful novel *Der Sternsteinhof* (1885). The fiction of Peter Rosegger, including the novel *Jakob der Letzte* (1888), is rooted in his native Styria.

The senior member of Young Vienna, the dramatist and critic Bahr, has been called a "virtuoso of receptivity." His considerable amount of fiction includes his first novel, *Die gute Schule* (1890), subtitled *Seelenstände* (psychic states), which tells the story of a young painter whose overcoming of a creative crisis in Paris makes him conclude that love is "the good school of true wisdom," and *Theater* (1897), a roman à clef set in Viennese theatrical circles. The most striking among the few works of Berlin-born Leopold, Freiherr von Andrian-Werburg, is the *Novelle Der Garten der Erkenntnis* (1895), about a narcissistic young nobleman's education, travels, interpersonal relationships, and early death. In Richard Beer-Hofmann's short novel *Der Tod Georgs* (1900), the decadent Paul experiences the death of his "wife"—ostensibly an extension of himself—in a dream and then suffers the death of his gifted friend Georg. Paul's reveries and stream-of-consciousness reflections

on his aesthetic existence lead him to an affirmation of life and of his Jewish heritage.

In his stories and novels, Arthur Schnitzler, a great diagnostician of earthly evanescence, decadence, cultural decay, and moral relativism, "combined the naturalist's devotion to fact with the Impressionist's interest in nuance." Schnitzler's first *Novelle*, *Sterben* (1895; dying), already stamps him as a master of the psychological story. A young man doomed by tuberculosis watches in consternation as his lady's joie de vivre breaks their death pact; his death is prefigured in the fading of their love. The epistolary story "Die kleine Komödie" features the role-playing of an egocentric playboy and a former actress who aim for "atmosphere." *Leutnant Gustl* (1901; *None but the Brave*, 1925) takes the form of an inner monologue and brings out the emptiness of conventional morality, specifically the military code of honor. Schnitzler's roman à clef, *Der Weg ins Freie* (1908; *The Road to the Open*, 1923), is a *Diskussionsroman* in which the author presents a typology of Viennese society (including Jews trying to come to terms with anti-Semitism and Zionism) seeking freedom and fulfillment. Robert Musil's *Die Verwirrungen des Zöglings Törless* (1906; *Young Torless*, 1955) is a haunting story of adolescent sexual perversion and brutality in a boarding school. A curiosity of literary history is the pornographic novel *Josefine Mutzenbacher* (1906), purportedly the autobiography of a Viennese prostitute; it appeared anonymously but has been attributed to Felix Salten.

In the works of the German storytellers from Czechoslovakia, most of whom were Jews, a definite undercurrent of mystical ecstasy may be discerned. Prague, that alchemistic melting pot, was a city of raconteurs and Magical Realists. After the older generation, which produced a wealth of rural legends and ghetto stories, there was increasing concern with the city. The life span of Moravian-born Marie von Ebner-Eschenbach (Countess Dubsky) coincided with that of Emperor Franz Josef. In her numerous novels and stories, she artistically captured the mellow, slightly decadent atmosphere of her country. In her several volumes of *Dorf- und Schlossgeschichten* (1883; tales of village and castle life), she is critical of her own class, but her realism is always tempered with gentleness. The novel *Das Gemeindekind* (1887) tells the story of a boy of unfortunate parentage who overcomes prejudice and discrimination through strength of character. Auguste Hauschner was influenced by naturalistic trends and interested herself in the social problems of women (*Frauen unter sich*, 1901). *Die Familie Lowositz* (1909) presents a kaleidoscopic view of Prague in the 1870's.

Bohemian-born Fritz Mauthner, a major philosopher of language, followed his *Berlin W* trilogy (1886-1890) with depictions of the Bohemian milieu such as *Die böhmische Handschrift* (1897). Moravian-born Jakob Julius David, who was hard-hit by poverty and infirmity and who lived in Vienna from 1891 on, wrote melancholy stories and novels that are marked by a pronounced social consciousness, including *Das Höfe-Recht* (1890); *Das Blut* (1891), about problems of Jews living in rural areas; *Die am Wege sterben* (1900), about the misery of students in Vienna; and *Der Übergang* (1902), about the decline of a Viennese family. David's collection *Die Hanna* (1904) contains stories of Moravian village life. Philip Langmann, who also lived in Vienna from 1900 on, published several volumes of naturalistic stories, including *Arbeiterleben* (1893) and *Realistische Erzählungen* (1895).

Hugo von Salus, who practiced medicine in Prague, also published collections of stories (*Novellen des Lyrikers*, 1904). Gustav Meyrink is remembered for his later novel *Der Golem* (1915; *The Golem*, 1928), but his interest in the grotesque, occultism, and spiritism is also reflected in such early tales as *Orchideen* (1904) and *Das Wachsfigurenkabinett* (1907). Prague-born Oskar Wiener is known not only as an anthologist but also for his novel *Im Prager Dunstkreis* (1919). Grete Meisel-Hess is the author of novels (*Fanny Roth*, 1902) and stories (*Suchende Seelen*, 1903) that reflect her interest in social reform, feminism, occultism, and sexual and moral problems. Robert Saudek published the novel *Dämon Berlin* in 1907.

After three early prose works—the autobiographical story *Ewald Tragy* (written in the 1890's but not published until 1929; translated into English in 1958), the Tolstoyan *Vom lieben Gott und Anderes* (1900; republished as *Geschichten vom lieben Gott*, 1904; *Stories of God*, 1931, 1963), and the popular *Die Weise von Liebe und Tod des Cornets Christoph Rilke* (1906; *The Tale of the Love and Death of Cornet Christoph Rilke*, 1932)—

the Prague-born poet Rainer Maria Rilke published *Die Aufzeichnungen des Malte Laurids Brigge* (1910; *The Notebooks of Malte Laurids Brigge*, 1930; also known as *The Journal of My Other Self*). In the form of the notebook of a Danish aristocrat who tries to live in Paris as a poet, this is an impressionistic depiction of disintegration and decay, with childhood recollections dredged up as a counterpoint to the distressing urban reality.

Finally, this was the milieu that produced one of the greatest writers of the twentieth century, Franz Kafka, whose impact began to be felt in the 1920's with the posthumous publication of his uncompleted novels *Der Prozess* (1925; *The Trial*, 1937) and *Das Schloss* (1926; *The Castle*, 1930). Appearing only a few years after the fin de siècle fiction already discussed, Kafka's masterpieces nevertheless belonged to another world: the world after World War I. In fact, only *The Castle* was written after the war (*The Trial* was begun in 1914 and was abandoned, unfinished, in 1915), yet Kafka's novels, like his stories, which began appearing in book form in 1913, seemed peculiarly suited to the "age of anxiety" ushered in by World War I. Indeed, many readers see in the nightmarish logic and bureaucratic evil of *The Trial* and *The Castle* a prescient vision of the Holocaust and all the other totalitarian horrors of the twentieth century.

Harry Zohn

BIBLIOGRAPHY

Adams, Jeffrey, and Eric Williams, eds. *Mimetic Desire: Essays on Narcissism in German Literature from Romanticism to Post Modernism*. Columbia, S.C.: Camden House, 1995. Collection of scholarly essays focuses on the theme of narcissism in the works of several German writers, including Thomas Mann, Gottfried Benn, Max Frisch, Christa Wolf, and Thomas Bernhard.

Berman, Russell A. *The Rise of the Modern German Novel: Crisis and Charisma*. Cambridge, Mass.: Harvard University Press, 1986. Explains the rise of the German novel by looking at the social processes and political tensions in modern society.

Beutin, Wolfgang, et al. *A History of German Literature: From the Beginnings to the Present Day*. 4th ed. Translated by Clare Krojzl. New York: Routledge, 1993. Comprehensive, oft-referenced work provides a basic historical and critical overview of German literature. Includes bibliographical references and an index.

Diethe, Carol. *Towards Emancipation: German Women Writers of the Nineteenth Century*. New York: Berghahn Books, 1998. Presents a rare systematic analysis of the contributions of German women writers, beginning with the late Romantics and moving through the 1848 revolutionary period to the late nineteenth century. Explores the wide-ranging and varied attitudes of these writers concerning women's emancipation.

Hardin, James, and Siegfried Mews, eds. *Nineteenth-Century German Writers, 1841-1900*. Detroit, Mich.: Gale Research, 1993. Second of two volumes in the Dictionary of Literary Biography series that provide biographical sketches of the periods' writers. Includes bibliographical references and indexes.

Hill, David, ed. *Literature of the Sturm und Drang*. Rochester, N.Y.: Camden House, 2003. Collection of critical essays addresses the important themes and major works of German authors during the period of the Sturm und Drang.

Koelb, Clayton, and Eric Downing, eds. *German Literature of the Nineteenth Century, 1832-1899*. Rochester, N.Y.: Camden House, 2005. Collection of critical essays examines German literature after the passing of Romanticism. Discusses realism, naturalism, symbolism, and impressionism in novels, poetry, drama, and opera. Includes a critical bibliography.

Kontje, Todd Curtis, ed. *A Companion to German Realism, 1848-1900*. Rochester, N.Y.: Camden House, 2002. Collection of essays addresses major themes and writers of German realism as well as lesser-known women and gay writers.

Mahoney, Dennis. *The Literature of German Romanti-cism*. Rochester, N.Y.: Camden House, 2004. Discusses long fiction from the beginnings of German Romanticism in the eighteenth century to the reception of this literature in the twentieth century.

Sagarra, Eda. *A Companion to German Literature: From 1500 to the Present*. Malden, Mass.: Blackwell, 1997. Readable overview surveys nine eras of German literature—from the Reformation and Renaissance to the late twentieth century—providing cultural and historical context for both well-known and neglected authors, including many women.

Vivian, Kim, ed. *A Concise History of German Literature to 1900*. Columbia, S.C.: Camden House, 1992. Collection of essays by various scholars includes contributions covering German literature in different periods as well as essays on such topics as the Enlightenment and Romanticism.

Watanabe-O'Kelly, Helen, ed. *The Cambridge History of German Literature*. New York: Cambridge University Press, 1997. Thorough overview from the Carolingian period to the unification of Germany in 1990 provides historical, political, and cultural context for both the student of German literature and the general reader. Quotations are translated into English.

Weedon, Chris. *Gender, Feminism, and Fiction in Germany, 1840-1914*. New York: Peter Lang, 2006. Examines German literary explorations of women and education, politics, the world of work, and the family. Includes a bibliography.

Wellbery, David E., and Judith Ryan, eds. *A New History of German Literature*. Cambridge, Mass.: Belknap Press, 2004. Invaluable reference work contains more than two hundred scholarly essays. Covers various aspects of German literature ranging from the ancient sagas to the twentieth century.

German Long Fiction Since World War I

The Austrian novelist Stefan Zweig, in his autobiography *Die Welt von Gestern* (1941; *The World of Yesterday*, 1943), reminisces about Europe at the beginning of the twentieth century and the then-prevalent hopes for the future. Social and political security were the foundation for all further developments as the new age dawned: Diplomats provided peace, science was steadily eliminating disease and pain, morality became more liberal and more tolerant, the economy provided a comfortable life for millions and work for most, and prosperity was evident in the attractive modern cities as well as in the individual lives of Europeans. Comfort was no longer a dream but rather a reality for most. Mass production had enriched the daily lives of all citizens, and technology promised the widespread availability of indoor plumbing, telephones, radios, and hundreds of labor-saving devices, not to mention such luxuries as the cinema, the automobile, and the airplane. For Zweig and for millions of his fellow Europeans, this was the onset of the true Golden Age. Yet, despite continued astonishing developments in technology, science, and industry, paradise soon slipped from their grasp.

THE POST-WORLD WAR I NOVEL

World War I represented a watershed, marring Zweig's wonderful dream with a horrible reality. By 1920, the social and political security so necessary for equilibrium and progress had disappeared. For some, the new era was to prove exhilarating, a time for new beginnings, but for many others, the chaos resulting from the war caused severe trauma and would lead to a later and greater catastrophe in the ensuing search for stability.

The loss of tradition and continuity was felt in all areas of life and thus in the world of literature, which mirrored these social tremors. Some writers accepted the challenge of revaluing cultural traditions in quest of a new future, while others bemoaned the irretrievable loss of "the good old days." This dichotomy, conspicuous in their works, is responsible for a remarkable variety and vitality of expressions—the hallmark of German fiction since 1920.

With the resounding defeat of the Central Powers in 1918, long-standing problems emerged to confront the German-speaking nations. Within fifty years, Germany had developed from a predominantly agrarian society to a modern, industrialized nation. Traditional middle-class values of an earlier age were no longer sufficient in an era of metropolitan anonymity, of mass conformity and blind obedience to emperor and state. The change was so drastic and so sudden that Hermann Hesse was to write in his *Der Steppenwolf* (1927; *Steppenwolf*, 1929) of one individual's reaction: "Now there are times when a whole generation is caught . . . between two ages, two modes of life, with the consequence that it loses all power to understand itself and has no standard, no security, no simple acquiescence." The many strikes, revolutions, mutinies, putsches, and related forms of chaos during the 1920's were merely reactions to external events that had become unfathomable. In the German-speaking countries, the shame of defeat was compounded by the humiliating terms of the Treaty of Versailles. Germany and Austria saw long-standing monarchical rule replaced by republican forms of government. All colonies were surrendered, territories were ceded or occupied, and the army was limited to 100,000 soldiers. In addition to the loss of a generation of men, the Central Powers had to accept sole responsibility for the war and then make reparation payments to reimburse the victors.

Within a period of five years, Germany and its allies had gone from world powers to shrunken remnants of once-great nations. The shock, humiliation, and confusion could not have been greater. Since all were treading a foreboding terra incognita, it became the task of the writers to understand and clarify their situation, to create new values by which all could live.

Aside from the many problems of modernity, dealing with the immediate past was a necessity. War novels abounded, the most popular being Ernst Jünger's *In Stahlgewittern: Aus dem Tagebuch eines Strosstruppführers von Ernst Jünger* (1920; *The Storm of Steel: From the Diary of a German Storm-Trooper Officer*, 1929), Ludwig Renn's *Krieg* (1928; *War*, 1929), Walter Flex's *Wanderer zwischen beiden Welten* (1917; the wanderer between two worlds), Arnold Zweig's *Der*

Streit um den Sergeanten Grischa (1927; *The Case of Sergeant Grischa*, 1928), and Ernst Glaeser's *Jahrgang 1902* (1928; *Class of 1902*, 1929). Yet only Erich Maria Remarque, in his controversial *Im Westen nichts Neues* (1928, serial; 1929, book; *All Quiet on the Western Front*, 1929), was able to capture the boredom and horror, the naïve enthusiasm and ultimate despair of World War I. Translations immediately communicated the experience to other participants around the globe, and a motion picture with the same title proved equally popular on an international scale. Even for Remarque, a journalist by trade, the gestation of the book took some time—it appeared in 1929, fully ten years after the conclusion of the war. In Austria, Joseph Roth required even more time to contemplate the loss of his beloved Habsburg monarchy. His novel *Radetzkymarsch* (1932; *The Radetzky March*, 1933) and its sequel *Die Kapuzinergruft* (1938; *The Emperor's Tomb*, 1984) trace the ascent and demise of Emperor Franz Joseph through parallel developments in three generations of one Austrian family. For Roth, the death of Franz Joseph is synonymous with the irreplaceable loss of traditional Habsburg Austria and the simultaneous advent of modern existential uncertainty.

This ambivalence, encouraged in the philosophical and scientific writings of Søren Kierkegaard and Friedrich Nietzsche, of Sigmund Freud and Albert Einstein, was to result in a generation of "outsiders." Four novelists of the time represented the concerns of many in their recognition of such isolation. The first, Hermann Hesse, had become famous and wealthy in the ten years preceding the war through popular romantic novels such as *Peter Camenzind* (1904; English translation, 1961) and *Unterm Rad* (1906; *The Prodigy*, 1957; also known as *Beneath the Wheel*, 1968). Yet with the outbreak of war, such tales appeared trivial in the light of world events, and, as suspicion of Hesse's patriotism increased, his popularity rapidly dwindled, causing him to have a nervous breakdown. Following these personal crises (and psychological treatment), Hesse began to examine more thoroughly his life and those of his contemporaries. *Demian* (1919; English translation, 1923), published under a pseudonym, was an instant success, becoming the bible of an entire generation.

For the next ten years, Hesse was to chronicle in ever-

changing format the trials and tribulations of the disaffected individual. *Siddhartha* (1922; English translation, 1951), *Steppenwolf*, and *Narziss und Goldmund* (1930; *Death and the Lover*, 1932; also known as *Narcissus and Goldmund*, 1968) were all products of the turbulent 1920's, each a literary solution to the existential despair of its titular heroes. Employing exotic settings or, as in *Demian* and *Steppenwolf*, elements of the fantastic and the occult, Hesse introduced a novelistic alienation effect by which the reader could gain intellectual distance from the fictitious events, all the better to arrive at an objective solution to these pressing problems. It was Hesse's unfortunate fate that youthful readers often ignored this objectivity, transforming him into a cult figure for narcissistic escapists. On a primitive level, Hesse's heroes encourage such identification, for they popularize the outsider in the twentieth century: Split personalities of intellect and sensuality, they grope and suffer near suicide for a meaning to their lives, to the "self." In his mature works, however, Hesse renounced this popular preoccupation, promoting a "selfless" solution; in *Die Morgenlandfahrt* (1932; *The Journey to the East*, 1956) and *Das Glasperlenspiel: Versuch einer Lebensbeschreibung des Magister Ludi Josef Knecht samt Knechts hinterlassenen Schriften* (1943; *Magister Ludi*, 1949; also known as *The Glass Bead Game*, 1969), the protagonists devote their lives unselfishly to higher causes.

Nobel laureate Thomas Mann, a friend of Hesse, was also preoccupied with the philosophical problems posed by an existence that often seemed alien and hostile to the individual. Mann's first novel, the two-volume *Buddenbrooks: Verfall einer Familie* (1901; *Buddenbrooks*, 1924), achieved popular success despite its length. Influenced by the ideas of German philosophers Arthur Schopenhauer and Nietzsche, Mann traced the decline of a commercial family over three generations. The story asked whether the artistic temperament might be at odds with the "will to live" that these philosophers argued lay at the core of existence. As younger, sensitive, and aesthetically oriented members of the Buddenbrooks family take control of the business, the firm slides into failure.

Decadence, the opposition between art and life, and the interplay of philosophical ideas continued to dominate Mann's work. The novella *Der Tod in Venedig* (1912; *Death in Venice*, 1925) dealt with the passion of an aging writer for a pretty young boy. Mann's massive novel *Der Zauberberg* (1924; *The Magic Mountain*, 1927) presents the story of the ordinary, middle-class citizen Hans Castorp, who is transported to the rarified atmosphere of a tuberculosis sanatorium in the mountains. Away from everyday concerns, Castorp engages in a seven-year philosophical examination of life. He socializes with characters who represent extremes of emotion and reason, and Castorp learns the value of moderation. The ending of the novel is ambiguous, though, because Castorp leaves the mountaintop and is drafted into the German army during World War I. In the last scene, he faces apparently fatal enemy gunfire.

Later biographers of Mann tended to interpret the novelist's concerns with decadence and conflict as products of his psychological turbulence, rather than as purely philosophical matters. Ronald Hayman, in *Thomas Mann: A Biography* (1995), draws a portrait of a man tormented by fits of depression and frustrated bisexuality, who had difficulty forming close relations with family members. Donald Prater's massive biography, *Thomas Mann: A Life* (1995), describes Mann as a closeted homosexual whose inability to demonstrate feelings for others led to a passion for abstract ideas. Anthony Heilbut, in *Thomas Mann: Eros and Literature* (1996), maintains that an idealized love for a series of young men ran through all of Mann's writing. Hermann Kurzke, in *Thomas Mann: Life as a Work of Art* (2002), also stresses Mann's sexuality but focuses on Mann's efforts to create and preserve his reputation as an artist.

The Austrian novelist Robert Musil, in his massive, unfinished magnum opus *Der Mann ohne Eigenschaften* (1930, 1933, 1943; *The Man Without Qualities*, 1953, 1954, 1960), created a new kind of novel reflecting the worldview of modern science and philosophy. Trained as an engineer with a broad scientific background, Musil rejected the reductive positivism of the Vienna Circle yet drew on his scientific and philosophical studies to view his characters in a manner unprecedented in fiction: both analytically, from a great distance, and in sympathy with the most intricate movements of thought and feeling. In *The Man Without Qualities*, the collapse of the Austro-Hungarian Empire represents the larger crisis in European culture and, on an even larger scale, the existential dilemma of modern man.

Finally, Alfred Döblin's *Berlin Alexanderplatz* (1929; *Alexanderplatz, Berlin*, 1931; better known as *Berlin Alexanderplatz*), a monumental novel, asserts that even the lower-class working person can find himself (or herself) an outsider in his own environment. Döblin's hero, a truck driver, is released from prison into the labyrinthine jungle of modern Berlin. He believes that he can control his own destiny but soon is forced to join a gang of thieves. His personal failure and helplessness culminate in the murder of his beloved, a blow that drives the hero insane. Döblin emphasized the chaos of modern life through the hapless reactions of his hero-victim; stylistically, he employed stream-of-consciousness techniques and other impressionistic qualities to depict the unrelenting bombardment of external stimuli on a vulnerable individual.

The works of these four novelists, of course, do not represent the entire range of attitudes and responses characteristic of the post-World War I era. One writer who deserves mention in this context is the Austrian novelist Hermann Broch. Like his compatriot Musil, Broch came to the novel from an extraliterary background; a successful executive in the textile industry, he also had training in philosophy and mathematics. Like Musil, Broch used the novel as an instrument of philosophical inquiry; his great novel *Die Schlafwandler* (1931-1932; *The Sleepwalkers*, 1932) rivals Musil's *The Man Without Qualities* as an exploration of the malaise of modern European culture. Broch's second masterpiece, *Der Tod des Vergil* (1945; *The Death of Virgil*, 1945), was completed during his exile in the United States, to which he emigrated after being briefly imprisoned by the Nazis in 1938.

THE WORLD WAR II NOVEL

Indeed, in one sense, the existential crisis of German culture in the post-World War I era was resolved not by philosophical treatises or literary masterpieces but by political fiat. With the ascension of the Nazi Party to power in 1933, all facets of culture were to be monitored and manipulated by the state. Membership in the respected Prussian Academy of Arts was soon to require an oath of loyalty to the government; similar organizations experienced a similar fate. Another omen of the proscriptive measures to come could be seen in the spring of 1933, when university professors, students, and Nazi Party members publicly burned books written by "undesirables." The works of Freud were consigned to the flames for their purported immorality. Remarque's famous novel was branded as "pacifistic," while the social satires written by Heinrich Mann, Thomas Mann's older brother, were found to be derogatory. Authors of nonconforming racial background, religious preference, or political taint were blacklisted and banned from publishing on German soil. The list of prominent writers (along with scientists, politicians, and other civilian leaders) grew to include literally thousands of prominent Germans. Some were allowed to stay in the country, though they were forbidden to write except along party lines; most were forced into exile, under the threat of imprisonment or death. Thus, from Sweden to Russia, from Mexico to California, "the real German culture" (as one exile phrased it) struggled to survive.

As a result of the Nazi cultural monopoly, three distinct types of German literature emerged during the twelve years from 1933 to 1945. First, there was the "officially approved" literature by those writers who had remained in the Third Reich or whose works had been appropriated by the Nazis, such as Hans Grimm's massive *Volk ohne Raum*, published in 1926. This *Blut und Bodenliteratur* (blood and soil literature), extolling the virtues of the Germanic race and its cultural roots, was not a product of National Socialist ideology. As in most things cultural, the Nazis adopted earlier works and traditions that had existed long before Adolf Hitler came to power. *Heimatkunst* (or regional art), neo-Romanticism, and expressionism provided powerful, already extant sources from which to draw—novels such as *Der Hitlerjunge Quex* (1932; quest of the Hitler Youth), by Karl Aloys Schenzinger, *Die S.A. erobert Berlin* (1933; the S.A. conquers Berlin), by Wilfrid Bade, and *Die grosse Fahrt* (1934; the great journey), by Hans Friedrich Blunck. Parallel to Hitler's penchant for historical figures, a spate of historical novels appeared after 1933. Although purporting to depict ages and situations past, these works attempted to extol current Nazi values. As J. M. Ritchie postulates in his *German Literature Under National Socialism* (1983), Blunck's *Die grosse Fahrt* is typical in many ways: "Essentially the view presented is undemocratic, nationalistic and irrational. There is no

analysis of society: instead the novel directs the reader away from reality towards a mystical, Utopian solution to Germany's problems."

These writers were awarded all the literary prizes at the state's disposal, were granted access to publishing houses and the precious supplies of paper, and were reviewed enthusiastically by critics and scholars sympathetic to the Nazi cause. This group remains problematic for the student of literature today: The backlash after the war branded them all as "brown," or as Nazi hacks who merely churned out propaganda for Hitler. Not until late in the twentieth century did scholars begin to evaluate the literature of these writers with a dispassionate eye.

Of those writers not employed by the Nazis, two basic groups must be considered. One body consists of authors who remained in Germany, unable to publish, but who nevertheless insisted on the right to be considered members of an "inner emigration." The second, more distinct body is composed of those countless individuals who were forced to flee their homeland. Their individual tales of hardship, of terror and suffering, of despair and accommodation constitute an entire chapter of literary history. Of the thousands of anecdotes created by their exile, the most uplifting recounts Franz Werfel's escape from the Gestapo: While fleeing through France, Werfel was forced to hide in Lourdes, the site of a shrine of miracles. He prayed for a miraculous escape and vowed to dedicate his next novel to the legendary vision of Lourdes. Upon his safe arrival in New York, he wrote the inspiring best seller of hope and faith, *Das Lied von Bernadette* (1941; *The Song of Bernadette*, 1942).

Simply to live and write on foreign soil became an arduous task for the exiled writers. Some continued to write in German for small exile presses and for even smaller audiences. A few were fortunate in finding competent translators; Vicki Baum, for example, was the beneficiary of such a luxury through her publisher, Doubleday, and consequently her fiction was widely sold through the Book-of-the-Month Club. Another struggling novelist, Stefan Heym, did not trust his literary fate to luck, learning English so well that he continued to write all of his novels in this second language after the war. These writers all wished that the madness in Germany would soon end, that they could return to Germany as productive and respected writers. Yet as the years dragged on without hope, as Germany attacked Poland and war began, their despair grew. Stefan Zweig emigrated first to England, then to Brazil; though wealthy and cosmopolitan, he could not bear the isolation and committed suicide. Others, such as Thomas Mann, reconciled themselves to their fates and survived as best they could, vowing never to return to a Germany they no longer recognized.

As one would expect, the utopian novel flourished during the war years. From around the globe, writers constructed visions of a new and better society; among the more significant were Hesse's *The Glass Bead Game*, Werfel's *Stern der Ungeborenen: Ein Reiseroman* (1946; *Star of the Unborn*, 1946), and Jünger's *Heliopolis: Rueckblick auf eine Stadt* (1949). However, the realities of the first years following the war—the incredible destruction of population and property, starvation and deprivation considerably worse than in the waning years of Nazi domination, and the mandatory occupation by the victorious Allied powers—effectively stifled this genre and its implied hope for the future. Although the Allies introduced policies of denazification and publicly judged individual Germans in Nuremberg for their complicity in war crimes, their decision to rebuild Europe through such instruments as the Marshall Plan created the basis for a new Germany. The postwar years thus brought fundamental changes to the political and cultural structures of the German-speaking countries. The defeated Germany was divided into two separate nations: The Federal Republic of Germany was allied with the North Atlantic Treaty Organization and Western Europe, while the German Democratic Republic became a member of the Warsaw Pact under Soviet influence. While Austria ultimately became a neutral republic, Switzerland experienced a unique development as the only German-speaking country not directly involved in World War II. These experiences and those of the war itself provided German writers with abundant material for their novels. With the demise of the Nazi dictatorship, additional literary impulses stimulated cultural life: The works of exiled writers and those previously burned and banned were reintroduced into the occupied lands, along with hundreds of works of world literature previously forbidden by the Nazis as "decadent."

WEST GERMAN FICTION

West German fiction after 1945 was strongly marked by the Nazi years. Gradually, many of the exiled authors returned to Europe, though generally with diminished productivity. Of the major writers of the post-World War I era, Musil was no longer living; Hesse wrote no fiction between 1943 and his death in 1962; Mann lived in Switzerland until his death in 1955, publishing one of his greatest works in the immediate postwar years, the novel *Doktor Faustus* (1947; *Doctor Faustus*, 1948); Döblin returned to Germany and died there in 1957, leaving little impact on the new society; and Broch, who had long since emigrated to the United States, died there in 1951. This generation of writers had fought the early battles with modern ambivalence, but the changing times would encourage others to continue the struggle. Soldiers who had survived the war, the prison camps, and denazification surveyed a devastated homeland and broken families. Some, like Heinrich Böll, would commit their experiences, feelings, and observations to paper. Civilians were to comment on their own memories, as in the case of Walter Kempowski. More censorious authors instigated critical investigations of the German people during the Nazi era; here, Günter Grass, Siegfried Lenz, and Uwe Johnson come to mind. Indeed, no writer in the postwar years could escape the reality of the Nazi era and especially the genocidal "final solution" that led to the Holocaust.

The Holocaust proved an enormous stumbling block for all sides—for the victims and survivors of the death camps as well as for the perpetrators and their descendants. In purely literary terms, the obstacles appeared almost insurmountable: How could one explain or describe the depth and breadth of this abomination? What literary forms existed to portray this singular horror? What narrative perspective would allow a truthful and accurate presentation of the common fate of thirteen million individuals? How could one convey the inhumanity of this atrocity persuasively, so that it can never happen again? These were but a few of the perplexing literary considerations to have confronted the writer in Germany after 1945.

Scholars often write of an imaginary "zero point" immediately after the war, a starting point where the culture had to be rebuilt from ground zero. This implies that all literary trends from the pre-Nazi years were effectively extinguished by Hitler's rise to power, that there was no continuity between the literature of the Third Reich and that of the new Germany to follow. The emerging literature is frequently designated *Trüimmerliteratur* (literature from the ruins), conveying not only the immediate surroundings but also the psychological state of the authors themselves. In the words of Heinrich Böll, this development was the result not of normal organic growth but of the catastrophe of war. To write optimistic literature would be cruel in the face of so much destruction, and there was no time for the luxury of reflection, comparison, and thoughtful objectivity. The result was sober and realistic description, neither heroic nor romantic, often couched in autobiographical reports which signaled a new realism.

A younger generation with different experiences and viewpoints dominated West German literature after 1945. Like all novices, the new writers struggled to master their craft, to attract publishers and an audience. To provide mutual support in their efforts to produce a new literature, these authors banded together at the invitation of Hans Wemer Richter to establish a working forum for critical discussions of their art; in commemoration of their first annual meeting, they became known as Gruppe 47, which functioned successfully for fifteen years to promote a new German literature of high standards and of world renown—though the group has often been discussed as much for its political engagement as for the fine literature it produced.

The group's activism may be clearly seen in the fiction of Heinrich Böll, Nobel Prize winner and a major German writer. Böll's early prose depicted World War II in a dispassionate manner, focusing on the senseless destruction and waste of human lives. In later works, such as *Billiard um halbzehn* (1959; *Billiards at Half-Past Nine*, 1961) and *Ansichten eines Clowns* (1963; *The Clown*, 1965), he portrayed civilian corruption and hypocrisy during the Nazi period and during the postwar "economic miracle." Böll's social criticism was often exaggerated to the point of grotesque satire, and the figure of the clown was the perfect medium for such criticism; the clown is an artist who lives and performs in society, magnifying its features through pantomime and monologue while maintaining his independence and distance from social convention. Still, the conclusion of Böll's novel was more realistic than many cared to admit, for the clown's independence and social criticism only cause him personal grief; though irritated by his presence, society is able to maintain the status quo by dint of its sheer size and political influence. Despite the fact that Böll experienced a similar reception in his own artistic career, he continued to criticize the prosperous, consumer-oriented Federal Republic of Germany. His novels of the 1970's, including *Gruppenbild mit Dame* (1971; *Group Portrait with Lady*, 1973), *Die verlorene Ehre der Katharina Blum* (1974; *The Lost Honor of Katharina Blum*, 1975), and *Fürsorgliche Belagerung* (1979; *The Safety Net*, 1982), were thinly veiled exposés of actual living persons and contemporary institutions in the West Germany of the time.

The other major figure in West German fiction, Günter Grass, burst upon the literary scene with his overnight best seller *Die Blechtrommel* (1959; *The Tin Drum*, 1961). His grotesque and irreverent "dwarf" offered, literally, a different perspective on the events from 1933 to 1945 and on into the early postwar years. The dwarf may make noise on his drum, shatter glass with his voice, or merely outrage people with his behavior and audacious narration, but the reader cannot ignore him or the controversy that Grass's book caused. Although none of his subsequent novels gained quite the international attention (or national notoriety) accorded *The Tin Drum*, Grass himself became a lightning rod for German political engagement. He participated in election campaigns on behalf of the liberal German Socialist Party, and his "Heilbronn Declaration" of 1983—challenging the constitutionality of nuclear missiles being stationed in West Germany—indicated a return to political activism after the torpid decade of the 1970's. Grass embodied the artist's political responsibility to society, a position that caused many West Germans discomfort, especially since Grass was an outspoken liberal.

The social criticism present in the fiction of Böll and Grass became a fixture in much of the literature that appeared in the late 1960's and early 1970's during the student protests. Political demonstrations were mounted against foreign targets, especially during the Vietnam War, and national issues such as the West German laws excluding suspected communists from governmental service came under heavy attack. Other groups, disadvantaged or previously ignored, received special attention during this period of heightened awareness and personal involvement. Both workers' literature and women's literature thrived. Max von der Grün's *Stellenweise Glatteis* (1973) marked a conscious (and successful) attempt to develop a style and narrative stance appropriate to the milieu and problems of contemporary workers. In addition, the growing body of literature by and about women explored a new dimension. Ingeborg Bachmann's *Malina* (1971) and Karin Struck's *Die Mutter* (1975) attracted public attention and stimulated controversy among the general public, not to mention among their fellow writers—compare Grass's *Der Butt* (1977; *The Flounder*, 1978).

While these writers' provocative contributions reexamined social conventions around 1970, subsequent trends toward apathy and isolation diminished the effect of their criticism. The alternative culture provided an antidote to realistic and documentary literature of the 1960's, replacing political and social involvement with an increasing concern for the individual. Here more personalized literature was evident: Biographies, reminiscences, and diaries were popular genres for portraying intimacy. It must be emphasized, however, that such intimacy and spontaneity were often artificial; in the "diaries" of Max Frisch, for example, the various entries were carefully crafted literary constructions obviously intended for public consumption.

This "new sensibility" attempted to capture the alienation and isolation in modern life, as exemplified in the works of Botho Strauss. His *Marlenes Schwester* (1975), *Die Widmung* (1977; *Devotion*, 1979), and *Paare, Passanten* (1981; *Couples, Passersby*, 1996) explored the sterility in society and the impossibility of human communication. Basing his fiction on physical and astronomical observations—that the planets are moving inexorably away from one another into the void—Strauss sought to recognize similar physical phenomena among people. His work is thus characterized by lonely individuals who speak primarily in monologues, underscoring the impossibility of communication and therefore of human contact. This trend was also clearly evident, to a lesser degree, in the works of the popular novelist Martin Walser. His early works—*Ehen in Phillippsburg* (1957; *The Gadarene Club*, 1960; also known as *Marriage in Phillippsburg*), for example—were critical of the conformist striving to succeed in the materialistic world of the economic miracle. Later works, such as the novels *Seelenarbeit* (1979; *The Inner Man*, 1984) and *Das Schwanenhaus* (1980; *The Swan Villa*, 1982), and the classic novella *Ein fliehendes Pferd* (1978; *Runaway Horse*, 1980), explored the problems of middle age. Walser devised an initial Kafkaesque shock to jolt the "hero" from his established routine, then traces the latter's soul-searching through monologue, indirect discourse, and interior monologue. The realistic, informal language and the unerring accuracy of his portraits provided psychic identification and understanding between his troubled protagonists and the reader. These writers were only a few of the many and varied talents on the West German literary scene.

The writers of West Germany made use of a variety of novelistic forms and techniques. While some experimental literature tended to the extreme of *Unkunst*, or nonart, such as the do-it-yourself novel, which required the reader to construct the plot, most novelists struggled earnestly to communicate their individual yet typical concerns. As noted earlier, modern ambiguity or isolation may be transmitted effectively through monologue— that is, a subjective utterance in place of pronouncements by the traditional omniscient narrator. Indeed, the inadequacy of any narrator has resulted in novels that "tell themselves." Techniques borrowed from film and radio sometimes eliminated chronological narration, utilizing techniques such as the flashback, dream sequences, and fades. The most resilient, versatile, and thus popular form for presenting simultaneity and complexity in fiction was that of the montage, an arrangement of elements from several different sources joined so that each distinct element contributed to a new composition or totality. Wolfgang Hildesheimer, for example, allowed his first-person narrators to pile fantasy upon fantasy in an attempt to construct a new reality that they can comprehend and thus master. In *Tynset* (1965) and *Masante* (1973), the main character is an insomniac whose imagination creates a pseudoreality in which he can barely survive.

Günter Grass utilized variations of the montage to

create a synthesis of *Vergegenkunft*, of past-present-future, emphasizing their interrelation and importance as a continuous process; from *Örtlich betäubt* (1969; *Local Anaesthetic*, 1969), *Aus dem Tagebuch einer Schnecke* (1972; *From the Diary of a Snail*, 1973), *The Flounder* to *Kopfgeburten: Oder, Die Deutschen sterben aus* (1980; *Headbirths: Or, The Germans Are Dying Out*, 1982), and *Im Krebsgang* (2002; *Crabwalk,* 2003), Grass interspersed historical details from the past and actions from the present with conjecture relating to future developments in order to illuminate the historical process and educate the reader as to the consequences of his or her individual actions.

Christoph Meckel combined documentary materials, personal recollections, and poetic fiction in a composite *Suchbild: Über meinen Vater* (1980; *Image for Investigation About My Father*, 1987), at once a portrait of his father and an allegory of two generations of Germans. In *Der Mensch erscheint im Holozän* (1979; *Man in the Holocene*, 1980), Max Frisch inserted encyclopedic excerpts into his text as a sobering counterpoint to his main character's improbable assumptions, offering an austere critique of the modern tendency to confuse information with knowledge. Another Swiss author, Gerold Späth, allowed more than two hundred individual characters to narrate their life stories in *Commedia* (1980), each distinct autobiography contributing to a larger story, the mosaic of an entire community.

As a result of its size and potential audience, its marketing capabilities and critical coverage, West Germany enjoyed a preeminent role in the German-speaking publishing world in the years before reunification. The other German-speaking countries—East Germany, Austria, and Switzerland—were all somewhat dependent upon West Germany for inspiration and stimulation. Though their authors may have a core of faithful readers at home, to be published in West Germany was the ultimate sign of critical and financial success.

EAST GERMAN FICTION

In an article in the volume *Deutsche Gegenwartsliteratur* (1981), Frank Trommler observed that East German literature existed under tenuous circumstances: It was only one of many national literatures among its Soviet bloc neighbors and ranked as only a variant

within the literature of German-speaking nations. The result was an inferiority complex and an identity crisis on a national scale, creating a situation in which East German literature was dependent on that of West Germany for critical resonance, contrast, and thus confirmation of its "otherness." Ironically, West German scholars were the first to recognize East German literature as a cohesive body, and they wrote literary histories in the mid-1970's on its evolution.

The literature of East Germany (after 1949, the German Democratic Republic) was initially created by returning emigrants. Socialists and members of the Communist Party exiled from West Germany moved to the Soviet-occupied zone in the hope of contributing to the establishment of a new society. Their participation in a proletarian-revolutionary movement was encouraged by the government in the form of conferences, subsidies, and various awards, and through the Literature Institute at the University of Leipzig. The Soviet zone thus attracted many returning exiles, among them Arnold Zweig, Bertolt Brecht, and Johannes R. Becher, whose prestige and productivity lent respectability to the socialist sector.

One of the most prominent authors was Anna Seghers. Her most popular novel, *Das siebte Kreuz* (1942; partial translation as *The Seventh Cross*, 1942), and an earlier novella, *Aufstand der Fischer von St. Barbara* (1928; *The Revolt of the Fishermen*, 1929), had gained critical recognition. *Transit* (1944; English translation, 1944) chronicled the exploits of refugees and their attempts to escape the Nazis in Marseilles during the first years of the war. Two complementary novels, *Die Toten bleiben jung* (1949; *The Dead Stay Young*, 1950) and *Die Entscheidung* (1959), offered a broad portrait of developments in Germany from 1918 to 1945 and from roughly 1945 to 1951, respectively, as seen through the lives of representative characters. For the author, a member of the Communist Party since 1929, these descriptions supported the working class and its struggle for sustained influence in German life. She consciously contrasts capitalist and socialist societies and, while admitting the tensions and difficulties present in the life of the workers, ultimately sides with the latter.

The anti-Fascistic tone of the exiles' works was short-lived. The Third Party Congress in 1950 suggested that literature's function was to depict the accomplishments of socialist renewal—the first of continuing reminders that literature was to be subservient to the needs of the party. In response to the congress, the "positive hero" became the programmatic effort to provide a didactic model of enthusiasm for achievement, especially in an industrial setting such as those found in the so-called factory novels. Not surprisingly, few of these early works could claim even moderate success.

By 1956, several prominent authors discussed the unfortunate absence of confrontation with the recent (that is, Nazi) past, encouraging the younger generation to fictionalize their personal experiences. Dieter Noll's *Die Abenteuer des Werner Holt* (1960) was a bildungsroman that contrasted the young protagonist's ideals with the reality of the war years. Through an inordinate number of adventures, Noll endeavored to trace the development of a "typical" individual who coincidentally served as the representative of an entire collective society. Christa Wolf, arguably East Germany's finest writer, ventured a thoughtful innovation within this general theme. Most novels that deal with the Third Reich constantly rephrase the question, How could the Holocaust have happened? In her *Kindheitsmuster* (1976; *A Model Childhood*, 1980; also known as *Patterns of Childhood*, 1984), Wolf offered a pedagogical twist, insisting that such a historical past is overcome only through a thorough analysis and present awareness; her new, incisive question was, How have we become the people that we now are?

Another example of the state's initiatives in the field of literature was the conference in Bitterfeld in 1959, which signaled the official trend toward workers' literature. The Bitterfeld Way further encouraged writers to collect concrete experiences in the factories and fields. Erwin Strittmatter revived the cliché of the 1950's positive hero and transformed it into an admirable tragic figure. In *Ole Bienkopp* (1963; English translation, 1966), the titular hero dedicates himself to the development of a collective farm and must struggle against the entrenched bureaucracy and various Communist Party opportunists. Scholar Marc Silberman labeled Bienkopp an "anticipatory hero," to account for his individual initiative within a collective society: Though Beinkopp disagrees with established socialist policies and the capricious func-

tionaries behind them, his overriding dedication to others (in the form of the collective) leads him to take actions which are later adopted by the party as new policy. Bienkopp's striving is not against the old policies but merely anticipating the new.

With the construction of the Berlin Wall in 1961, it became necessary to justify East Germany's enforced isolation, if not convince its citizens that they were actually in the better half of Germany. Wolf first tackled this dilemma in her novel *Der geteilte Himmel: Erzählung* (1963; *Divided Heaven: A Novel of Germany Today*, 1965), articulating the problems inherent in the mass migrations from East to West Germany before the wall was built. Günter de Bruyn accentuated the importance of individual commitment as a positive step in reaffirming one's allegiance to the socialist ideal; his *Buridans Esel* (1968; *Buridan's Ass*, 1973) was a vivid depiction of an indecisive character whose lack of commitment is paralyzing.

By the 1970's, the new directive was to refocus the novel toward the recognition of the numerous problems within East German society, but from the perspective of their resolution. In this type of fiction, the new heroes were to be the planners and managers—in other words, those individuals in decision-making positions who were actively participating in the advancement of the socialist state. The managers, however, would not inherit this world without a struggle; the student unrest, protest, and celebration of individuality that rocked the West during the late 1960's and early 1970's did not spare East Germany. One cause célèbre was the appearance of Ulrich Plenzdorf's *Die neuen Leiden des jungen W.* (1973; *The New Sufferings of Young W.*, 1979). A conscious juxtaposition of Johann Wolfgang von Goethe's classic *Die Leiden des jungen Werthers* (1774; *The Sorrows of Young Werther*, 1779) and J. D. Salinger's *The Catcher in the Rye* (1951), this novel employed pop jargon of the younger generation to undermine the socialist work ethic, extolling instead the virtues of individuality and creativity. The sympathetic young protagonist drops out of the ranks of the loyal workers and attempts to find himself, only to be electrocuted while inventing a better paint sprayer. The work's immediate success and popularity (especially in the West, where it served in some quarters as confirmation of the evils of communism) were more the result of its daring theme than its artistic merit.

Despite the sporadic declaration of "official" guidelines for literature, periods of relative liberalization encouraged East German writers to attempt more original themes, though always at the risk of fines, house arrest, censorship, and even deportation. A case in point is that of Stefan Heym. Disaffected by American politics during his exile in the United States, Heym returned to the fledgling East German state only to find even greater repression. The shock resulting from the Berlin Revolt in 1953 removed any illusions Heym may have fostered concerning the humanistic ideals of the Communist rulers. His subsequent novels dealt with suppression in historical situations, culminating in his *Fünf Tage im Juni* (1974; *Five Days in June*, 1977), the first literary work in East Germany to deal with the 1953 revolt; as a consequence, Heym was at times forbidden to publish in East Germany (as happened between 1963 and 1973), and several of his works could be published only in the West. Nevertheless, writers less bold (or more ingenious) than Heym managed to package their criticism in seemingly harmless forms; fantastic novels (including science fiction), children's literature, and fairy tales all offered an outlet for social commentary. Manfred Bieler and Günter Kuner, who both settled in the West, employed these genres to call into question commonly accepted practices and casual assumptions.

One direct result of the political repression, especially after the appearance of the Berlin Wall, was the isolation of East German literature from many of the trends, influences, and experiments in the West, with resulting stagnation. Also, because of the programmatic nature of their literature, few East German authors gained international recognition. Those few who were critical of East German society or the socialist bureaucracy were well received in the West; the basis for this recognition was primarily political, however, and often had little to do with the literary merits of the individual works.

GERMAN FICTION AFTER REUNIFICATION

The collapse of socialism in East Germany and the reunification of West and East Germany into a single country in 1990 enabled works to be published in the East that would have been banned previously. Uwe Saeger's partly autobiographical novel *Die Nacht danach und der Morgen* (1991) looked at the issue of the border guards who had been charged with keeping easterners from fleeing to the West. Karl Mickel published *Lachmans Freunde* (1991), a novel set in the 1950's and actually written between 1968 and 1983, which considered the problems of socialist society that had led to East Germany's end. Erich Köhler treated the same subject in a novel that blended elements of realism and fantasy, *Sture und das deutsche Herz* (1990), a history of Germany from the Middle Ages to reunification, told from the point of view of a troll.

Despite the new freedom, the specter of East German communism continued to haunt German literature. In 1992, East German state documents revealed that the renowned East German writer Christa Wolf, along with other intellectual leaders, had collaborated with the communist secret service. After these revelations, Wolf wrote the novel *Medea: Stimmen* (1996; *Medea: A Modern Retelling*, 1998). She portrayed the ancient Greek mythical character Medea, who betrayed her own father and murdered her own children, as a victim caught up in political oppression and complex interpersonal relations. Many critics read the apology for Medea as an apology for Wolf's own past.

The foremost writer of the former West Germany also continued to be active after reunification. *Unkenrufe* (1992; *The Call of the Toad*, 1992), by the literary giant Günter Grass, considered the question of Germany's past and future relations with its neighbors. In this novel, an aging German art historian forms a romantic relation with a Polish woman in the Polish city of Gdańsk, which was formerly German Danzig. The two work out their cultural differences, but their plans to establish a cemetery of reconciliation, in which Poles and Germans will rest together, are complicated when German business enterprises become involved; the German free market land-grabbing in Poland becomes reminiscent of the Nazi invasion. Novelist Frank Werner saw a different sort of similarity between the German past and the German present in his novel *Haus mit Gästen* (1992), which drew parallels between the end of Nazi Germany and the end of the communist regime of East Germany. In 1999, Grass was awarded the Nobel Prize in Literature. He became the center of a new controversy in 2006, when he revealed in the autobiographical *Beim Häuten der Zwiebel* (*Peeling the Onion,* 2007) that as a young man at the end of World War II he had served with the Waffen-SS, a combat unit remembered for its members' strict adherence to Nazi ideology. Because of his long career as a social critic—a critic of Germany's Nazi past—Grass was branded a hypocrite by some, while others attempted to find a way to balance his lifetime of work against his youthful mistakes.

AUSTRIAN FICTION

The nearly seven-century-old Habsburg monarchy of Austria dissolved in 1918 with national and global consequences. Gone were the giant empire, the cultural influence and prestige, the political alliances, and the practical administration of everyday affairs. While still grieving over their loss, the Austrians were annexed by Nazi Germany and engulfed by the Third Reich. Only after the war, when occupation forces withdrew and exiles returned to aid in the cultural reconstruction, could one envision a restoration of timeless Austrian values. Certain qualities such as stability and equilibrium, an aversion to extremes, an appreciation for timeless and lasting values, a sense of tradition, and an allegiance to a specific geographical region and national culture have always appealed to the Austrian mentality. These traits had survived for centuries, had provided stability and a sense of security under the Habsburgs, and could be trusted once again to provide a solid foundation in uncertain times.

Older writers such as Heimito von Doderer and the revival or rediscovery of Austrian masters such as Musil and Broch influenced the younger novelists in the 1950's and early 1960's, so that critics were convinced of a timeless continuity. Indeed, older and younger authors alike propagated these values during the twenty years following the war. Their efforts for the rejuvenation of literature in Austria centered on the journal *Plan* after its inception in 1945. Young authors were encouraged to publish in this journal and could gain needed recognition and a receptive audience. The Austrian ministry for education began to award subsidies to young authors in 1950, and since that time, Vienna and other provinces have introduced similar incentives. The Austrian Society for Literature, founded in 1960, has also provided international contacts and exposure for native writers, encouraging a broader perspective and higher standards for budding authors.

Critics and writers both agreed that postwar Austrian literature represented a continuation of prewar values and traditions. Novels such as George Saiko's *Auf dem Floss* (1948, revised 1954; on the raft) only tended to confirm these suspicions. In this superbly crafted work, Saiko's subjects move in the present but with attitudes out of the distant past. Society may be adrift, but like his contemporaries, Saiko disdained current issues in favor of a distinctly Austrian melancholy romanticism. With the liberal waves that swept across other industrialized nations, Austria's isolation and innocence too were challenged. New critics appeared, young authors who questioned Austrian society and its influence on the individual, represented by the Wiener Gruppe (1952-1964) and the Forum Stadtpark in Graz. The Viennese pioneered the use of dialect in their works as a conscious commentary on modern language and thus on modern institutions. Provincial novels resurrected the unspoiled, timeless qualities in nature, far from the industrialized metropolis. In its critical phase, however, the novel of the province may also reduce the nation to its lowest common denominator, the village, where all the vices of contemporary life can be exposed.

One of the major representatives of the provincial novel was Franz Innerhofer's *Schöne Tage* (1974; *Beautiful Days,* 1976). Written in a touchingly native, primitive style, the novel chronicles an adolescent's experiences on an isolated farm. The cruelty, brutality, and despair of everyday life eventually drive the youth to the big city, there to overcome the debilitating aspects of his development. Innerhofer's first novel, apparently autobiographical, was successful primarily because his unpolished prose complemented the rustic personality of his protagonist. In subsequent volumes of this trilogy, *Schattseite* (1975) and *Die grossen Wörter* (1977), he affected a more elevated form of language to indicate his hero's intellectual maturation—with painfully mediocre results.

The 1960's brought forth a new generation of novelists who, like Innerhofer after them, were to pose embarrassing and often painful questions. One of Austria's more celebrated writers, in drama as well as in prose, was Thomas Bernhard. From the titles of two representative works, the novel *Frost* (1963; English translation, 2006) and the memoir *Die Kalte: Eine Isolation* (1981; *In the Cold*, 1985), one can infer his concern with alienation in modern life. In his presentation of the weak, the sick, and the insane, Bernhard stressed the senselessness of striving; his bucolic settings thus became monstrous traps from which the individual could not escape. *In Verstörung* (1967; *Gargoyles*, 1970), the reader is assaulted by the personal recollections of a young student as he accompanies his father, a country doctor, on his various rounds; here the descriptions of mental and physical illness, of brutality and pain, create an image of an insane world. Further proof, if required, abounds in *Das Kalkwerk* (1970; *The Lime Works*, 1973), the testimony of a mine owner, Konrad, relating his failures in business, in his studies, and in his torturous marriage to his crippled wife, whom he has killed.

Like Bernhard, Peter Handke gained international recognition for his dramatic works and his fiction alike. Handke's initial successes occurred in the theater, where he made dramatic history of a sort by insulting his audiences in the mid-1960's. After 1970, however, he devoted his considerable talents mainly to fiction. Early novels such as *Die Angst des Tormanns beim Elfmeter* (1970; *The Goalie's Anxiety at the Penalty Kick*, 1972), *Der kurze Brief zum langen Abschied* (1972; *Short Letter, Long Farewell*, 1974), and *Die Stunde der wahren Empfindung* (1975; *A Moment of True Feeling*, 1977) project an increasing subjectivity, a sensitivity to external impressions as well as to the innermost feelings of people. While Handke was long considered an avant-gardist interested in structural linguistic problems (and as such became a cult figure among deconstructionist critics), his developing preoccupation with the "New Sensibility" became most obvious in *Wunschloses Unglück* (1972; *A Sorrow Beyond Dreams*, 1975), the reconstruction of his own mother's life and suicide. Despite objections by feminists such as Karin Struck, Handke's sensitive yet objective portrayal of his mother's life—the boredom, the disappointment of unfulfilled expectations, the suffering and despair—is an insightful literary portrait colored by sociological observation and the personal scars the son obviously still bears. Handke's novels of the late 1970's reveal a shift in

emphasis, with a positive, almost visionary conception of the writer's role unusual in postwar literature; in this regard, Handke has spoken of the influence of the nineteenth century Austrian novelist Adalbert Stifter.

Perhaps Austria's best-kept secret is the prose of Elias Canetti. This master craftsman wrote and published for more than fifty years, yet until he was awarded the Nobel Prize in Literature in 1981, he attracted little attention. The bulk of his writings were essayistic, aphoristic reflections on his travels and on his experiences during and after the war; here one would include *Masse und Macht* (1960; *Crowds and Power*, 1962), *Die Stimmen von Marrakesch: Aufzeichnungen nach einer Reise* (1967; *The Voices of Marrakesh: A Record of a Visit*, 1978), *Die gerettete Zunge: Geschichte einer Jugend* (1977; *The Tongue Set Free: Remembrance of a European Childhood*, 1979), *Die Fackel im Ohr* (1980; *The Torch in My Ear*, 1982), and *Nachträge aus Hampstead* (1994; notes from Hampstead). Canetti's novel *Die Blendung* (1935; *Auto-da-Fé*, 1946; also known as *The Tower of Babel*) deserves special mention. The main character, Peter Kien, is a scholar unable to cope with the uncertainty of reality. His fear of life becomes paranoia, and he withdraws ever deeper into his library and scholarship. Love is also threatening to Kien, so it is only poetic justice that his wife turns into a vile creature. In his denial of life, Kien destroys himself, both literally and figuratively. Despite Canetti's often humorous and satiric treatment, this is a disturbing novel because of the insights it provides into the modern aversion to life, to change, and to love. An article by Claudio Magris in *Modern Austrian Literature* (1983) reflects that Canetti's depiction of a frightening attraction for death has, in effect, transformed the author into a powerful advocate of life. This, too, is the Austrian legacy.

Other contemporary Austrian writers of note include Christoph Ransmayr and Elfriede Jelinek. Ransmayr's first novel, *Die Schrecken des Eises und der Finsternis* (1984; *The Terrors of Ice and Darkness,* 1991), which combines history, travelogue, and fiction in an account of the Austro-Hungarian polar expedition of 1872-1874, was a critical and popular success. His other works include *Die letzte Welt* (1988; *The Last World,* 1990), *Morbus Kitahara* (1995; *The Dog King,* 1997), and *Der fliegende Berg* (2006; the flying mount). Jelinek, the

2004 winner of the Nobel Prize in Literature, is a feminist novelist and playwright whose works, according to the Nobel Committee, "reveal the absurdity of society's clichés and their subjugating power." Her novels include *Die Liebhaberinnen* (1975; *Women as Lovers,* 1994), *Die Klavierspielerin* (1983; *The Piano Teacher*, 1988), *Lust* (1989; English translation, 1992), and *Gier: Ein Unterhaltungsroman* (2000; *Greed*, 2006).

SWISS FICTION

Although Switzerland is politically neutral, the country and its people are not disinterested in world affairs. They are clearly aligned with the democratic West and have always maintained close cultural ties with the other German-speaking countries in Europe. For this reason, the onset of German fascism was a blow to Switzerland, and in the area of cultural exchange, many Swiss authors could no longer be published in the larger German market. Direct contact among individual writers was often halted, while many German authors attempted to enter Switzerland so that they could continue writing for a native-language audience during their exile.

Because of its long tradition of neutrality, Switzerland was able to survive the war years intact, indeed as a bulwark of German-language culture. Untarnished by National Socialism's excesses, the Swiss could continue the tradition of European humanism so abruptly interrupted in Germany and Austria. Because of their cosmopolitan outlook, Swiss authors provided an enlightened, objective perspective on the events that corrupted German culture.

Although 1945 was not a crucial year in Swiss history, as in the war-ravaged Germany and Austria—there was no "zero point" from which to recover in Switzerland—the Swiss were not untouched. The country had been on military alert since the beginning of the war, and in an unwritten code of solidarity, rigorous self-examination had been postponed for the duration. Now came the time for introspection: Governmental policies concerning refugees from Nazi Germany, private and official collaboration with Hitler's regime, and military plans for the nation's defense all came under consideration. The economic resurgence following the war (with the accompanying problems of imported foreign workers) made the Swiss even more protective in preserving

their miniature paradise. Criticism, though ever-present, was seldom welcome, and the Swiss reluctantly endured the milder forms, such as the intrusion of satire and ironic criticism as a literary corrective. In fact, it seems that Swiss authors have perfected these forms, for with the exception of the bildungsromans of Jakob Schaffner, the most noteworthy Swiss novel between 1920 and 1945 was Meinrad Inglin's *Schweizerspiegel* (1938). It was left to the younger generation to resume a critical appraisal of the relationship between the individual and Swiss society.

The image, or rather the myth, of Switzerland as the "land of Heidi"—of rustic clockmakers, alpine pastures, beauty and serenity, independence and democracy—was propagated for centuries in literature, from the itinerant Hans Jakob Christoffel von Grimmelshausen to the natives Gottfried Keller, Jeremias Gotthelf, and Conrad Meyer. Switzerland, however, was not to be spared the crass realities of modern existence. Typical problems of twentieth century life also invaded paradise. Material success and greed have often spoiled the landscape and the tranquillity of small-town life. Problems of identity and self-worth have plagued the Swiss as well. In addition, distinctly Swiss dilemmas have arisen: A suffocating demand for conformity and order has alienated a sizable portion of the youth who must live in this "golden cage." Hypocrisy and bureaucracy only compound the problem.

The more critical Swiss authors have been engaged for some time in examining their national myth and offering correctives. It is difficult to convey the concern that Swiss authors harbor for their country. Critics often chide (or revile) them as traitors, yet their devotion to their native land is sincere and should not be underestimated. They view with distrust any attempts, either accidental or willful, to ignore or conceal national problems. Typical is the accusatory tone displayed in Walter Matthias Diggelmann's *Die Hinterlassenschaft* (1965), in which criticism focuses on Swiss treatment of refugees during World War II; Diggelmann's exposé of selfish, unchristian behavior is a broad indictment of the Swiss as a people. Such attempts at criticism often fall upon deaf ears, provoking harsher and more exaggerated criticism. One example was the scandalous novel by Fritz Zom, *Mars* (1979; English translation, 1980), in which the author, dying of cancer, accused society of causing such destructive illnesses; repression, anger, and frustration are all carcinogenic agents of a society as stifling as that of the Swiss. If Zom overstated his case, many other Swiss novelists provide a more balanced perspective.

As early as 1949, a young architect and writer explained why he was obligated to concern himself with social developments at home and abroad.

> When people who speak the same language as I, who like the same music as I, when they are not immune from becoming inhuman, where can I gain the assurance from now on, that I am immune from similar actions?

This young writer's name was Max Frisch. It was this same Max Frisch who, by the middle of the century, had raised Swiss prose to world prominence; together with the dramatist Friedrich Dürrenmatt, Frisch had brought a previously moribund, provincial literature to world attention. In fact, purists would insist that there is no Swiss fiction beyond Frisch. His *Tagebuch, 1946-1949* (1950; *Sketchbook, 1946-1949*, 1977) reports and reflects on the issues and events immediately following World War II, but with the second volume, *Tagebuch, 1966-1971* (1972; *Sketchbook, 1966-1971*, 1974), Frisch began to focus his attention on more personal issues. Two of his early novels, *Stiller* (1954; *I'm Not Stiller*, 1958) and *Mein Name sei Gantenbein* (1964; *A Wilderness of Mirrors*, 1965), explore the questions of personal identity and freedom in regimented Switzerland. After 1975, however, Frisch dealt with the problems of aging, love and human relationships, knowledge and its absence during senility, self-worth and ultimate accountability for the sins of omission and commission during an entire lifetime. In *Montauk* (1975; English translation, 1976), Frisch unflinchingly investigates the personal failings of his (autobiographical?) main character. *Man in the Holocene* portrays the poignant results of senility and self-imposed isolation on the aged. His *Blaubart* (1982; *Bluebeard*, 1983) relies on the background of a courtroom investigation to initiate an unrelenting search for accountability in the public as well as in the private sphere. Ultimately, according to Frisch, each life must be examined in minute detail to discover the extent of one's failings in relation to those of other human beings.

Among the younger Swiss authors, Adolf Muschg also mirrors these crises in Swiss life and, like Frisch, is able to elevate them from the merely provincial to the general, as attested in such prose works as *Im Sommer des Hasen* (1965), *Fremdkörper* (1968), *Albissers Grund* (1974), and *Gegenzauber* (1967). Like Fritz Zom, Muschg was interested in the relationship between illness and society. His own experiences with group therapy encouraged him to delve deeper into the mystery of humans as social animals. Muschg dismissed the argument that literature should serve as a form of therapy, either for the writer or for the reader, positing instead that critical self-evaluation is preferable. Muschg prized in his fiction that moment when the protagonist can differentiate between the person he thought he was or had hoped to be and the person that he is in reality. This frightening moment of recognition, of ultimate isolation and truth, can lead to the process of honest evaluation of the person as a complete human being. Only in this way can isolation be overcome and spontaneity and life be restored.

To avoid wallowing in self-pity or self-delusion, Muschg expanded the apparently egotistical literature of the New Sensibility, directing it outward into political activism. An interview with Muschg in *Studies in 20th Century Literature* (1984) records these observations:

> Individuals who take their own needs seriously cannot be misused to serve the needs of politicians. It is an immunization process. . . . People who are aware of their real needs tend to be more courageous, more rebellious, even in the public sector. They are less corruptible than the flag wavers of every persuasion, including the left.

Here he defends individuality as a counterbalance to mass (social and political) pressures.

Gerold Späth created an enviable collection of works in little more than ten years—novels and short stories that exhibit an amazing versatility and virtuosity. His first novel, the picaresque *Unschlecht* (1970; *A Prelude to the Long Happy Life of Maximilian Goodman*, 1975), was received with critical acclaim. Here and in *Balzapf: Oder, Als ich auftauchte* (1977), Späth investigated the significance of custom and tradition, the importance of wealth and lineage that provide prestige and freedom within Swiss society. His protagonists are rogues who survive and thrive without the external trappings of a prosperous life, all the while gently mocking those who feverishly pursue "the good life." *Die heile Hölle* (1974) depicts a representative family—father, mother, daughter, son—that has acquired material and social success at the expense of happiness; their desperate attempts to find meaning in their lives climax with the son's suicide, which serves as an end to both his pointless existence and the continuation of this familial folly, since he dies childless. Späth's most ambitious project was the novel *Commedia* (1980). Its two distinct parts correspond to the isolated individuals of a modern community, individuals who have become divorced from the accoutrements and traditions that bring meaning to their environment and thus to their lives.

The leading figure of the German "pop literature" that developed in the mid 1990's is the Swiss novelist and journalist Christian Kracht. His first two novels, *Faserland* (1995) and *1979* (2001), deal with contemporary decadence and materialism, showing the emptiness of those who pursue lives defined by consumerism. In *Ich werde hier sein im Sonnenschein und im Schatten* (2008; I'll be there in sunshine and in shadow), he presents a dystopic view of a communist, colonialist Switzerland fighting a perpetual war.

THE CHALLENGE OF MODERN GERMAN FICTION

For all the notable achievements in poetry and drama, the modern period has been a high point for German fiction. One superficial illustration of this is the fact that six of the seven German-language writers who won the Nobel Prize in Literature from the 1920's through the first decade of the twenty-first century were novelists: Thomas Mann in 1929, Hermann Hesse in 1946, Heinrich Böll in 1972, Elias Canetti in 1981, Günter Grass in 1999, and Elfriede Jelinek in 2004. Thanks to an abundance of competent translators and a voracious reading public, readers around the globe are now able to enjoy the works of many German novelists, thus bringing great change to the personal circumstances of the individual writers. With the mass production of books (and the innovation of the paperback book in Germany after 1950), writing and publishing have become big business. Since

the eighteenth century, the writer has been accepted as a moral force, as the nation's conscience, and as prophet or guru for an entire generation. Now the writer has become a public figure as well, a creation of the culture industry that organizes publicity, prizes, receptions, autograph parties, and, ultimately, a reading public on the writer's behalf. For a writer to ignore or to refuse the benefits of this highly organized machine has proved increasingly difficult. Authors have always been dependent on readers. Today, however, the stakes have grown to astronomical proportions: Aside from the material advantages to be gained from a best seller, critical success has become crucial to the continued existence of the *freischaffender Schriftsteller*, or professional writer.

While books have become more readily available and affordable, their authors would admit that they have not become easier to write. The highly publicized "death of the novel" had a significant effect on German literature, for traditional (that is, nineteenth century) means of narration proved inadequate to express or describe the events of the twentieth century. Writers such as Michael Ende, Johannes Mario Simmel, and Heinz Konsalik will always find a large reading public for their conventional novels told by a third-person narrator in chronological sequence. Indeed, the complaint of the average reader continues to be: Why don't the famous authors write something I can understand? Those writers most highly prized by critics are not often readily understandable. Here the reader must exercise a good bit of effort (and goodwill) to decipher the new medium or the new message. A changing world seemingly requires changing forms of expression to capture adequately the significance of the new, and the twentieth century certainly provided a rapid succession of changes, overwhelming events, and bewildering circumstances.

The changing circumstances of German society have caused some German writers and the German reading public to question whether German literature is too ponderous and takes itself too seriously. In 1994, the editor of the S. Fischer publishing house, Uwe Wittstock, publicly posed the question, "Is German literature boring?" Wittstock answered that it was, and he claimed that German writers should follow English and American examples and try to be more entertaining. Other writers and literary critics, however, disagreed with Wittstock's verdict and defended the continued relevance of German literature.

One characteristic of German prose has been the attempt to reflect the upheavals in contemporary society while realizing the inherent complexity of modern life. Writers often produce extremely large novels, thereby hoping to encompass the variety and depth of reality. To reflect the impossibility of comprehension, the absence of order, and the lack of individual control, one can note the virtual disappearance of the omniscient narrator. These considerations represent an evolution in literature and expose the writer's insistent questions: What can and do I know? What can I write? What forms are appropriate? How can I master a language that has become suspect as a result of its abuse in the hands of politicians, advertising-slogan writers, and other mass manipulators?

The ambiguity frequently encountered and so often criticized in the modern novel must also be considered from nonphilosophical perspectives. While critics are often confused by an author's seemingly ambivalent stance—and attribute this indecision or hesitancy to the chaos or the complexity in modern life—the rhetorical effects of such ambiguity must not be overlooked. By refusing to fashion a satisfactory conclusion or happy ending, the novelist encourages the reader to evaluate the circumstances for him- or herself, to become involved in the world of the novel (and thus in its "reality"), prompting the reader to participate actively in the decisions of life. This controversial stance consciously creates provocative situations and events, yet without providing morals or related answers. Readers are aware that writers are not without opinions, that they do, in fact, have beliefs, ideals, and causes. Yet through their literary works readers are challenged to reach their own conclusions in regard to political, social, and cultural issues.

Todd C. Hanlin; Carl L. Bankston III
Updated by Cynthia A. Bily

BIBLIOGRAPHY

Adams, Jeffrey, and Eric Williams, eds. *Mimetic Desire: Essays on Narcissism in German Literature from Romanticism to Post Modernism*. Columbia, S.C.: Camden House, 1995. Collection of scholarly essays focuses on the theme of narcissism in the works of several German writers, including Thomas Mann, Gottfried Benn, Max Frisch, Christa Wolf, and Thomas Bernhard.

Beutin, Wolfgang, et al. *A History of German Literature: From the Beginnings to the Present Day*. 4th ed. Translated by Clare Krojzl. New York: Routledge, 1993. Comprehensive work provides a basic historical and critical overview. Includes bibliographical references and an index.

Durrani, Osman. *Fictions of Germany: Images of the German Nation in the Modern Novel*. Edinburgh, Scotland: Edinburgh University Press, 1994. Examines portrayals of the German nation in works by Alfred Döblin, Hermann Hesse, Thomas Mann, and Günter Grass. Maintains that novels are historical documents and that the literary value of the works of these authors is enhanced by connections between the novels and actual social events.

Gay, Peter. *Weimar Culture: The Outsider as Insider*. 1968. New ed. New York: W. W. Norton, 2001. One of the preeminent American historians of modern Europe offers a short overview of major cultural figures and institutions in Germany in the troubled but artistically productive period after World War I.

Ritchie, James M. *German Literature Under National Socialism*. London: C. Helm, 1983. Unique in its efforts to take National Socialist literature seriously, this work looks both at writers who remained in Germany during the Nazi years and at those who wrote in exile.

Sagarra, Eda. *A Companion to German Literature: From 1500 to the Present*. Malden, Mass.: Blackwell, 1997. Readable overview surveys nine eras of German literature—from the Reformation and Renaissance to the late twentieth century—providing cultural and historical context for both well-known and neglected authors, including many women. Includes maps and an index.

Stoehr, Ingo Roland. *German Literature of the Twentieth Century: From Aestheticism to Postmodernism*. Rochester, N.Y.: Camden House, 2001. Presents analyses of the important movements in German fiction, from aestheticism through expressionism, Dadaism, and modernism, and examines the influences of Nazism and unification.

Taberner, Stuart. *German Literature of the 1990's and Beyond: Normalization and the Berlin Republic.* Rochester, N.Y.: Camden House, 2005. Focuses on the connections between realism and "pop" literature and those between Germany's past and its present.

_____, ed. *Contemporary German Fiction: Writing in the Berlin Republic.* New York: Cambridge University Press, 2007. Collection of critical essays addresses the important trends, writers, and works in German fiction since unification. Includes discussions of Turkish German writers and the writings of German Jews.

Watanabe-O'Kelly, Helen, ed. *The Cambridge History of German Literature.* New York: Cambridge University Press, 1997. Thorough overview from the Carolingian period to the unification of Germany in 1990 provides historical, political, and cultural context for both the student of German literature and the general reader. Quotations are translated into English. Includes bibliographical references and an index.

Wellbery, David E., and Judith Ryan, eds. *A New History of German Literature.* Cambridge, Mass.: Belknap Press, 2004. Invaluable reference work contains more than two hundred scholarly essays. Covers various aspects of German literature ranging from the ancient sagas to the twentieth century.

IRISH LONG FICTION

Irish literature falls into two distinct categories. Written in the Irish language, the first category includes bardic poems and Celtic sagas. The second category, Irish literature written in English, includes what is often called Anglo-Irish literature because it was created by Protestants of English extraction. This phenomenon can be explained by England's historical colonization of Ireland and the acceptance of Irish writers within the British literary tradition.

THE EIGHTEENTH CENTURY

Although Irish writers are recognized for their contributions to poetry and drama, Irish writers beginning in the eighteenth century contributed also to the rise of the English novel. Irish writers also played a large role in the evolution of the English novel throughout the nineteenth and twentieth centuries. Very little eighteenth century Irish fiction deals with Irish subject matter. On the contrary, Irish fiction deals with humor, the sense of the grotesque and fantasy, the significance of anecdote, and the importance of the storyteller, all of which categorize the constructs of the Irish novel.

Irish long fiction took root in the eighteenth century with the writings of Jonathan Swift (1667-1745). His exuberant use of humor and fantasy, as well as his expansive imagination, demonstrates the deep influence of Ireland on his psyche and firmly distinguishes him as an Irish writer. Recognized as the foremost prose satirist in the English language, Swift spent much of his life trying to escape Ireland, which was considered then as a place of exile from England. However, politics dictated that he spend the bulk of his life as dean of St. Patrick's Anglican cathedral in Dublin.

Although Swift penned verse early in his life, his true genius did not surface until he turned to prose satire. His *A Tale of a Tub*, published anonymously in 1704, is a satire against religion and education. The book isolated Swift as a genius of satiric wit. His greatest novel, *Gulliver's Travels* (1726), assured his permanent place in literary history. The ironic tension Swift creates prompts questions about the author's views on humankind. In each of the novel's four books, Lemuel Gulliver sets sail on a voyage and ends up in a strange land. In book 1, Gulliver finds himself a giant prisoner of the six-inch-high Lilliputians, whom he saves from invasion from the neighboring Blefuscu. He escapes when he is charged with treason.

In book 2, the hero travels to Brobdingnag, where he finds himself as tiny as a toy in a world of giants. Although loved and pampered as a pet, in fear for his life he manages to escape in the talons of a large bird. In book 3, Gulliver visits the floating island of Laputa, where the islanders are so obsessed with scientific activity, particularly those in the Academy of Lagado (a parody of England's Royal Society), that they are blind to commonplace hazards. Book 4 finds Gulliver in the utopian land of the admirable, enlightened, rational horses, the Houyhnhnms, and the degraded, filthy humans, the Yahoos. Although first accepted as a curiosity by the gentle creatures, Gulliver is soon ousted as despicable because of his human physical characteristics. Although, at the end of his fourth voyage, he returns to England, he finds himself no longer able to tolerate human company and lives out his days in the company of horses.

Swift's ironic novel has no clear-cut explanation. Swift utilizes the various places his hero visits to satirize the folly of humankind. Of the human beings he encounters, the Lilliputians and the Brobdingnagians are impractical and mean-spirited, and the intellectuals in book 3 lack any wisdom, if they are not outright mad. The humanlike Yahoos are contemptible and powerless to express any reason whatsoever, but the Houyhnhnms, the horses, are reasonable and kind.

Swift was certainly not the only esteemed eighteenth century Irish writer. In *Tristram Shandy* (1759-1767), humorist Laurence Sterne (1713-1768) made a critical contribution to English literature, which secured him the reputation of a major novelist. The book is generally considered the progenitor of the psychological novel and the twentieth century stream-of-consciousness novel popularized by James Joyce and Virginia Woolf.

In the novel, the narrator, Tristram, sets out to do the seemingly impossible: to tell the story of his own life. Beginning at the narrator's moment of conception,

Sterne parodies the emerging novelistic form by exploring the relativity of time in human experience. Throughout, the author disorders experiences and mocks the development of narrative by providing no consistent plot or conclusion and by inserting outrageous and lengthy digressions. Ultimately, Tristram realizes the telling of his life's story takes longer than the living of it.

Sterne also penned *A Sentimental Journey Through France and Italy* (1768) in an attempt to teach humans to love their fellow creatures. The novel, which parodies the era's wide range of travel books, had a major impact on the campaign toward sentimentalism prevalent in the second half of the eighteenth century. This movement associated acute sensibility and a sympathetic, tender heart with true virtue. In the novel, the narrator, Parson Yorick, who is frequently moved to tears, sets out to travel through France and Italy in search of "sentimental commerce," or genuine human contact.

Frances Sheridan (1724-1766), mother of the famous Irish dramatist Richard Brinsley Sheridan and much influenced by Samuel Richardson, author of *Pamela: Or, Virtue Rewarded* (1740-1741) and *Clarissa: Or, The History of a Young Lady* (1747-1748), wrote the popular sentimental *Memoirs of Miss Sidney Bidulph* (1761), which considers the effect of extreme suffering on ideal virtue by focusing on the social role assigned to women in eighteenth century society. She also wrote the highly acclaimed and didactic Eastern-themed novel, *The History of Nurjahad, by the Editor of Sidney Bidulph* (1767), much in keeping with Samuel Johnson's *Rasselas, Prince of Abyssinia: A Tale by S. Johnson* (1759).

Although Oliver Goldsmith (1728 or 1730-1774) achieved eminence as an essayist (*The Citizen of the World*, 1762), a poet (*The Deserted Village*, 1770), and a dramatist (*She Stoops to Conquer: Or, The Mistakes of a Night*, pr., pb. 1773), he is also well recognized as a novelist for his pastoral novel *The Vicar of Wakefield* (1766). Early in his life, his first calling as a physician was soon submerged by his writing talent, which gained him much literary renown. He was one of the founding members of the famous Literary Club, which included Samuel Johnson, Sir Joshua Reynolds, David Garrick, Edmund Burke, and James Boswell.

The melodramatic *The Vicar of Wakefield* presents a picture of idealized rural village life and the unforgetta-

ble vicar, Dr. Charles Primrose. The family's troubles begin when the vicar loses his income and is forced to move the family near the estate of Squire Thornhill, who abducts his daughter Olivia. Next, the vicar's son George is imprisoned after his attempt to avenge his sister. The vicar's troubles continue when his other daughter, Sophia, is also abducted. After the family's house burns down, the vicar is imprisoned for debt. Despite such hardship, the vicar remains unfailingly charitable throughout. Goldsmith, who had the ability to crystallize the human personality, provides a comic look at the human predicament.

Maria Edgeworth (1768-1849) authentically captures eighteenth and nineteenth century rural Irish life in her popular novels and children's stories. Deeply involved with issues of nationality and cultural identity, Edgeworth is known for presenting the first believable children in the English novel form in the collection *The Parent's Assistant: Or, Stories for Children* (1796, 1800). Her actual involvement in running her father's estate in Ireland provided her with the knowledge necessary to authentically characterize rural Irish society in her first novel, *Castle Rackrent* (1800), said to be the first fully developed regional novel and the first true historical novel in English. Edgeworth focused attention on the much-maligned practice of absentee English landowning in *The Absentee* (1812), said to influence Sir Walter Scott (1771-1832) to finish his novel *Waverley: Or, 'Tis Sixty Years Since* (1814). *Patronage* (1814) and *Ormond* (1817) explore the relationship between culture and politics and heightened Edgeworth's literary reputation. During the Irish famine in 1846, Edgeworth became a spokesperson for Irish relief.

William Chaigneau (1709-1781) contributed one of the earliest Irish novels, *The History of Jack Connor* (1752). A picaresque novel in the tradition of Miguel de Cervantes's *Don Quixote de la Mancha* (1605, 1615) and later Henry Fielding's *The History of Tom Jones, a Foundling* (1749; commonly known as *Tom Jones*), *The History of Jack Connor* concerns the cultural identity of a young Irish man forced to become an English soldier.

THE NINETEENTH CENTURY

The nineteenth century saw progress from sentimentalism to sensationalism with the development of the

Irish gothic tradition, which made use of gothic architecture, convoluted plot, emotional intensity, and supernatural agency. The Irish gothic was popularized by Charles Robert Maturin (1780-1824), author of *Melmoth the Wanderer* (1820), which was set inside seventeenth century madhouses, and by Joseph Sheridan Le Fanu (1814-1873), author of *The House by the Churchyard* (1863), a tale of a ghostly hand that taps on windows.

Undoubtedly, however, the most popular Irish gothic writer is Bram Stoker (1847-1912), the author of the horror tale *Dracula* (1897), the subject of many films. Told principally through multiple diary entries, the tale features the unforgettable undead vampire Count Dracula, who travels to England and victimizes young Lucy Westerna. Dr. Van Helsing and the young solicitor Jonathan Harker attempt to overpower Dracula and keep him from Mina, Harker's fiancé. After his return to Transylvania, Dracula crumbles to dust after he is beheaded and stabbed through the heart by his captors. Stoker is also the author of the lesser-known *The Snake's Pass* (1890), *The Mystery of the Sea* (1902), *The Jewel of Seven Stars* (1903), and *The Lady of the Shroud* (1909).

Oscar Wilde (1854-1900), another renowned Irish writer better known as a dramatist (*Lady Windermere's Fan*, pr. 1892, and *The Importance of Being Earnest: A Trivial Comedy for Serious People*, pr. 1895) contributed to the Irish gothic tradition by creating one of the most popular nineteenth century novels. *The Picture of Dorian Gray* (serial 1890, expanded 1891) blends supernatural elements with French decadence. The novel caused a great deal of scandal: Wilde declared in the preface that there was no such thing as a moral or immoral book.

In the novel, the beautiful youth Dorian Gray has his portrait painted before he turns to a life of vice and corruption. However, the painting has supernatural powers and grows more and more degenerate and corrupted, reflecting the actual appearance of Gray, who maintains his youthful appearance. At the end, Gray kills the artist and stabs the painting; he is discovered as the very image of depravity, a knife through his heart, while the painting depicts an innocent youth. Wilde, a leader of the aesthetic movement in England and a well-known and flamboyant social wit, was greatly influenced by Walter Pater (1839-1894), who advocated art for art's sake.

Although not as popular, George Moore (1852-1933)

nevertheless deserves consideration for his innovations in fiction. In his first novels, *A Modern Lover* (1883), set in artistic bohemian society, and *A Mummer's Wife* (1884), he introduced French naturalism into English literature, coming later to utilize the realistic techniques of Gustave Flaubert and Honoré de Balzac. Moore counted among his friends Irish poet and dramatist William Butler Yeats and played a role in the development of the Abbey Theatre. Moore is best known for *Hail and Farewell: A Trilogy* (1911-1914), a comic, autobiographical satire in monologue form that features Yeats and Irish dramatist Lady Augusta Gregory and records the history of the Irish Literary Revival.

THE TWENTIETH CENTURY

While the twentieth century Irish Literary Revival encouraged the publication of poetry, drama, and folklore, Ireland continued producing long-fiction writers. James Joyce (1882-1941), arguably one of Ireland's best novelists, is highly celebrated for his experimental use of language. In 1904, in the company of a young girl named Nora Barnacle, Joyce left his native Dublin for the European continent to begin his writing career in earnest. His early stories, and all his later works, feature the city of Dublin—socially frozen and inanimate—and deal almost exclusively with Irish subject matter. Concerned with both the Symbolist and realist literary movements, Joyce integrated both styles, utilizing every word he composed to provide meaning. His autobiographical novel, *A Portrait of the Artist as a Young Man* (serial 1914-1915, book 1916), sketches the development of young Stephen Dedalus, who ultimately leaves Dublin for Paris to dedicate his life to art.

Joyce's best-known novel, *Ulysses* (1922), parallels Homer's *Odyssey* (c. 800 B.C.E.). The action in *Ulysses* takes place in Dublin on a single day, June 16, 1904, which has popularly come to be known as Bloomsday. The novel features Dedalus, the hero of Joyce's earlier novel; Leopold Bloom, an advertising salesman; and his wife, Molly Bloom—all modern representations of the mythic Telemachus, Ulysses, and Penelope. Through interior monologue, or the stream-of-consciousness technique, their myriad thoughts, impressions, and feelings—rational and irrational—are revealed as they make their way through the day in Dublin.

Finnegans Wake (1939), written in a unique and extremely difficult but comic style, features the archetypal family, about whom everyone dreams, metaphorically falling and rising. The novel characterizes a Dublin tavern-keeper, Humphrey Chimpden Earwicker; his wife, Mrs. Anna Livia Plurabelle; and their children, Shem, Shaun, and Isabel in a dream sequence throughout the course of one night. In pervasive dreamlike fashion, Joyce utilizes puns throughout and merges various languages, mythic images, and literary and historical characters to show, albeit obscurely, how history predominates over human experience and relationships.

Although, like Goldsmith and Wilde, Samuel Beckett (1906-1989) was more popularly known as a dramatist, he also was widely recognized as a novelist. Strongly influenced by Joyce (whom he met in Paris), Beckett's popular novel *Murphy* (1938) concerns an Irishman in London who becomes a nurse in a mental institution. While hiding in France during World War II, Beckett wrote *Watt* (1953), a highly abstract novel that deals with a servant who continues to work for a master whom he never meets until he is dismissed. Between 1946 and 1949, Beckett wrote *Molloy* (1951; English translation, 1955), *Malone meurt* (1951; *Malone Dies*, 1956), and *L'Innommable* (1953; *The Unnamable*, 1958). Beckett, winner of the Nobel Prize in Literature in 1969, attempts to analyze people's social relationships with one another. His work is thick with literary, historical, and philosophical allusions and draws heavily on thirteenth century Italian poet Dante Alighieri, seventeenth century French philosopher René Descartes, and seventeenth century Dutch philosopher Arnold Geulincx, whose philosophy attempts to integrate both the physical and the spiritual sides of men and women. Beckett puzzled continuously over the human condition.

Like the work of Joyce, Edna O'Brien's (born 1930) work was banned by the Catholic Church in Ireland. Her strict Catholic convent education provided the impetus to write her popular first novel, *The Country Girls* (1960), which concerns solitary women seeking identity and a sense of belonging. This first volume of *The Country Girls Trilogy and Epilogue* (1986) features two Irish girls who leave their strict rural convent school for a more exciting, less curtailed life in Dublin. Their lives are subsequently recorded in *The Lonely Girl* (1962; also known as *Girl with Green Eyes*, 1964) and *Girls in Their Married Bliss* (1964). Disillusioned, both girls leave Dublin for London, finding neither a meaningful connection with men nor happiness in marriage.

O'Brien's novels express despair over women's repression and place in contemporary society. Lonely and empty, her female characters, although at times happy, continuously seek fulfillment in doomed erotic relationships. Her portrayals of her characters' sexuality was deemed too frank for the 1960's, and the Country Girls trilogy was banned in Ireland for a time. O'Brien's twentieth book of fiction, *The Light of Evening* (2006), uses stream of consciousness to look back on the life and relationships of an elderly widow. The novel returns to O'Brien's themes of an oppressive church and a search for female autonomy.

Although Irish writers are highly recognized for their enormous contributions to poetry and drama, the legacy of Irish long fiction is splendid and rich as well. In addition to Joyce, Beckett, and O'Brien, Forrest Reid (1875-1947), Brinsley MacNamara (1890-1963), Peadar O'Donnell (1893-1986), Joyce Cary (1888-1957), Elizabeth Bowen (1899-1973), Francis MacManus (1909-1960), Flann O'Brien (1911-1966), Mary Lavin (1912-1996), and John McGahern (1934-2006) carried on the Irish long fiction tradition in the twentieth century.

IRISH LITERATURE INTO THE
TWENTY-FIRST CENTURY

Prizewinning novelists Roddy Doyle (born 1958) and Patrick McCabe (born 1955) are two of Ireland's finest contemporary novelists, following in the footprints of earlier Irish literary giants. Doyle's humorous *The Barrytown Trilogy* (1992; includes *The Commitments*, 1987; *The Snapper*, 1990; and *The Van*, 1991) centers on the irrepressible working-class Rabbitte family in Dublin.

Doyle's first novel, *The Commitments*, traces the everyday life of the Rabbitte family and their uproarious encounters with a group of working-class Irish teenagers who form a soul band, the Commitments. *The Snapper* deals hilariously with pregnancy. When nineteen-year-old Sharon Rabbitte becomes pregnant, she refuses to name the father of her "snapper." Her father, Jimmy, Sr., at first feels embarrassed and blames his daughter but eventually takes an active part in Sharon's pregnancy, coming to wonder at the marvels of life and loving. *The Van* examines male friendship. When Jimmy, Sr., loses his job, what he misses most are his evenings out at the pub with his friends. Although he joins the library and cares for his baby granddaughter, it is not until he and his best pal, Bimbo, buy a beat-up fish-and-chips van that he gains back his enthusiasm for life. All sections of the trilogy were made into successful films.

One of Doyle's strengths is his ability to give voice to a range of characters. In his Booker Prize-winning comic novel, *Paddy Clarke, Ha-Ha-Ha* (1993), Doyle captures the wonder and carefree days of youth through the speech patterns of childhood. Ten-year-old Padraic Clarke, or Paddy, runs wild through the streets of Barrytown with his gang of bullying friends, setting fires, playing "cowboys and Indians," and generally having a good time. *The Woman Who Walked into Doors* (1996) and its sequel, *Paula Spencer* (2006), concern a battered wife who uses her wits and a sharp tongue to deal with substance abuse and economic hardship.

McCabe has been compared to Joyce and Beckett, yet he could easily be classified within the Irish gothic tradition. McCabe's *The Butcher Boy* (1992), acclaimed as a masterpiece of literary ventriloquism, was shortlisted for the 1992 Booker Prize. This finely crafted novel tells the story of a young adolescent's descent into madness and murder. Although Francie Brady, a schoolboy in a small town in 1960's Ireland, has a drunken father and careless mother, his buddy Joe Purcell keeps him on track. When the boys con Philip Nugent out of his comic book collection, Philip's mother calls Francie's family "pigs." Francie the "pig boy" internalizes this insult and comes to hate the socially aspiring Mrs. Nugent. After his own mother enters a mental hospital, Francie runs away to Dublin. He discovers upon his return that she has committed suicide. Feeling extreme guilt, he breaks into Mrs. Nugent's house and is then sent to reform school: His best friend, Joe, befriends Francie's nemesis Philip Nugent, and Francie is lost. He continues his descent into darkness.

McCabe's *Breakfast on Pluto* (1998), part of the author's preferred humorous-macabre genre, is another tale of a youngster unable to come to terms with the conflicts of life. The emotionally overwrought Patrick "Pussy" Braden writes his outrageous memoirs for his psychiatrist, Dr. Terence. A product of the Tyreelin parish priest and his housekeeper, Patrick is abandoned and placed in a foster home with an alcoholic, Hairy Braden. The youngster finds deliverance in dreams of stardom and female fashion, winding up with a new name, Pussy, and a new life as a cross-dressing hooker in London. The protagonist soon finds himself overwhelmed, however, when he starts working for Irish Republican Army terrorists. McCabe is also known for his novels *Music on Clinton Street* (1986), *Carn* (1989), *The Dead School* (1995), *Call Me Breeze* (2004), *Winterwood* (2007), and *The Holy City* (2009).

Other important Irish writers of the early twenty-first century include Anne Enright (born 1962), whose novel *The Gathering* (2007) won the Booker Prize, Sebastian Barry (born 1955), Joseph O'Connor (born 1963), and Antonia Logue (born 1972). Novelist Eoin Colfer (born 1965) reached a massive worldwide audience with his Artemis Fowl fantasy series, intended for young adults but enjoyed by adults for their humor and wit. The series, about a ruthless teenage criminal mastermind, began in 2001 with *Artemis Fowl*.

M. Casey Diana
Updated by Cynthia A. Bily

BIBLIOGRAPHY

Cahalan, James M. *Modern Irish Literature and Culture: A Chronology*. New York: G. K. Hall, 1993. Examines events in Irish literature and culture after 1600, connecting historical and political developments with Irish fiction, poetry, and drama.

Coughlan, Patricia, and Tina O'Toole, eds. *Irish Literature: Feminist Perspectives*. Dublin: Carysfort Press, 2009. Questions traditional narratives of Irish studies and argues for a renegotiated study of the relations of feminism with nationalism. A good contribution to contemporary debates about Irish culture, gender, and identity.

Hogan, Robert Goode, and Zack R. Bowen. *Dictionary of Irish Literature*. Rev ed. Westport, Conn.: Greenwood Press, 1996. Through critical interpretation, the authors focus primarily on Anglo-Irish writers, especially major and later Irish writers. Discusses principal themes of Irish literature and the history of Irish writing in English.

Jeffares, A. Norman, and Peter Van de Kamp. *Irish Literature: The Nineteenth Century*. Dublin: Irish Academic Press, 2006-2007. Focuses on literature of the mid-nineteenth century, and on the Great Famine and the rise of cultural nationalism.

Kelleher, Margaret, and Philip O'Leary, eds. *The Cambridge History of Irish Literature*. 2 vols. New York: Cambridge University Press, 2006. First comprehensive history of Irish literature in the Irish, English, medieval Latin, and Norman languages. Includes a chronology, maps, and suggestions for further reading.

Leerssen, Joep. *Mere Irish and Fíor Ghael: Studies in the Idea of Irish Nationality, Its Development, and Literary Expression Prior to the Nineteenth Century*. South Bend, Ind.: Notre Dame University Press, 1997. Examines the idea of Irish national identity, Irish historical background, and how Ireland and fictional Irish characters are represented in English literature.

Powell, Kersi Tarien. *Irish Fiction: An Introduction*. New York: Continuum, 2004. Handbook designed to introduce readers to Irish fiction, explore themes common among most Irish writers, and examine key novels that have shaped the genre.

Shaffer, Brian W., ed. *A Companion to the British and Irish Novel, 1945-2000*. Malden, Mass.: Blackwell, 2005. Collection of critical essays on the major issues, themes, writers, and works of the second half of the twentieth century.

Welch, Robert, ed. *The Oxford Companion to Irish Literature*. 1996. Reprint. New York: Clarendon Press, 2001. More than two thousand entries cover the major works and writers, literary genres, folklore, and mythology, along with articles on Protestantism, Catholicism, Northern Ireland, the Irish Republican Army, and the political and cultural background necessary to understand Irish literature.

ITALIAN LONG FICTION

Giovanni Papini (1881-1956) argued that Italians are less suited temperamentally to writing novels than to writing poetry, essays, and biographies. Certainly, the art of storytelling has long been esteemed in Italy; Baldassare Castiglione, in *Il cortegiano* (1528; *The Book of the Courtier*, 1561), listed it as one of the attributes of the perfect gentleman. It was simply the length of the fictional narrative that Italians were slow to elaborate. This lack of experimental spirit probably had more to do with historical factors—such as illiteracy, lack of a unified country, and the persistent *questione della lingua* controversy—than with temperament.

Besides drawing upon the *novellino* (storybook) tradition of Giovanni Boccaccio, Franco Sacchetti, Matteo Bandello, and many other early Italian writers, would-be Italian novelists of the nineteenth century looked to the narrative-in-verse genre of the eighteenth and nineteenth centuries, such as Johann Wolfgang von Goethe's *Hermann und Dorothea* (1797; *Herman and Dorothea*, 1801), and to the novels and verse of Sir Walter Scott. In Scott, especially, Italians saw the possibility of using adventurous tales of a more substantial length to publicize their cause of political unification.

Giovanni Berchet (1783-1851), whose famous *Lettera semiseria di Grisostomo al suo figliuolo* (1816; semiserious letter from Grisostomo to his son) was conceived in support of Madame de Staël's recommendation that Italians imitate the new Romantic tendencies of the German writers, himself contributed a major work to the narrative-in-verse genre with his anti-British *I profughi di Parga* (1823; the refugees of Parga). Tommaso Grossi (1790-1853), who wrote Romantic novellas in octaves, bridged the gap between the verse novel and the prose novel in 1834 when he published *Marco Visconti* (1834; *Marco Visconti: A Romance of the Fourteenth Century*, 1907), set in Lombardy in the fourteenth century.

The year 1827 was a milestone in the development of the novel in Italy. In that year the following novels were published: *Il castello di Trezzo* (the castle of Trezzo), by Giambattista Bazzoni (1803-1850); *Sibilla Odaleta* by the "Italian Sir Walter Scott," Carlo Varese (1793-1866); *La battaglia di Benevento* (*Manfred: Or, The Battle of Benevento*, 1875), by Francesco Domenico Guerrazzi (1804-1873); and *I promessi sposi* (1827, revised 1840-1842; *The Betrothed*, 1828, revised 1951), by Alessandro Manzoni (1785-1873). The historical novel became so fashionable in subsequent years that Manzoni himself felt compelled, out of his respect for the incontrovertible facts of history, to decry its further cultivation as a genre in his nonfiction work *Del romanzo storico* (1845; on the historical novel).

Like most of the other Italian novelists of this period, Manzoni was Milanese; his grandfather was the humanitarian criminologist Cesare Beccaria (1738-1794), whose treatise *Dei delitti e delle pene* (1764; *On Crimes and Punishments*, 1767) is credited with eliminating from European criminal law the use of torture. Manzoni's mother, Giulia Beccaria, separated from his father, and, in 1805, the future novelist went to live with her in Paris, where his friendship with Claude Fauriel brought him under the influence of the Romantic movement. Manzoni's wife's conversion from Calvinism to Roman Catholicism was soon followed by his own, and it was still under the influence of his conversion that he began work on his masterpiece, *The Betrothed*. The impulse to write a historical novel came mainly from his reading of Scott, but his idea for the plot came from a proclamation that he happened to read regarding forced or prevented marriages, issued in 1627 by the Spanish governor of Lombardy.

Although Manzoni finished writing the novel in 1823, its publication was not complete until 1827. Displeased with his style, Manzoni began a thorough revision and visited Florence "to wash his rags" in the Arno River and thereby increase his sensitivity to the Tuscan literary standard, which would thirty years later become the language of a united Italy. The revised edition, greatly improved in style and in lexical choice but hardly changed at all in content, was published in parts between 1840 and 1842. Writing within a tradition that emphasized the pompous and academic rhetoric of the medieval and Renaissance masters, Manzoni—with a superb ear for dialogue—achieved a remarkable reconciliation between the spoken and the written language as the vehicle for his narrative. Joining the *questione della lingua* controversy that has plagued Italy since the time of Dante Alighieri, Manzoni argued to the end of his life that Italian writers should conform to the contemporary usage of cultured Florentines.

The Betrothed takes place in Lombardy between 1628 and 1631; the protagonists, the humble silk-weavers Renzo and Lucia, are already betrothed when the story opens. Lucia has attracted the attention of the unscrupulous Don Rodrigo, who is determined to have her. His henchmen prevent the village priest from performing the marriage, and for their own safety, the two are separated (Renzo is sent to Milan, Lucia to Monza). Throughout the rest of the novel, the reader lives, suffers, and hopes with the ill-starred couple at the mercy of the whims of the rich and powerful and menaced by war, famine, and plague. Manzoni depicts his large cast of characters with a gentle humor that stems from his own delight in the variations of the human personality. As a fictional creation, Renzo is thoroughly convincing; Lucia, however, is more a Romantic period piece than a typical peasant girl.

Although *The Betrothed* was widely read and translated, it failed to win an important place in the gallery of Western literary achievements. Manzoni failed to assimilate fully his historical material; many of his pages are unadulterated history, some encumbered by lengthy quotations from documents and others footnoted with references to actual historical texts.

Manzoni's ever-present Catholicism is perhaps another factor that accounts for his novel's lack of worldwide popularity. The glow of his religious belief, which allows the unfortunate couple to persevere against all odds and serves to counterbalance the dark, cruel world that they must inhabit, does not communicate itself well to many modern readers. Alberto Moravia observed that Manzoni had to choose the seventeenth century as the setting for his novel precisely because that was the last time that Catholic belief was strong, even in Italy. Renzo and Lucia survive because they are sheltered by a magical and encompassing Providence. Providence is what moves the hardened brigand L'Innominato ("The Unnamed") to pity when he hears the supplications of Lucia; Providence is responsible for striking Don Rodrigo

dead with plague; and Providence is what makes an eventual reunion of the lovers possible.

Manzoni's son-in-law, Massimo D'Azeglio (1798-1866), a member of an aristocratic Piedmontese family who became an important figure in the Risorgimento, wrote historical novels to inspire Italians with pride in their past. *Ettore Fieramosca* (1833; English translation, 1854) takes its title from a famous challenge made by thirteen Italian knights at Barletta to a like number of French knights, as recorded by Francesco Guicciardini (1483-1540) in his *Storia d'Italia* (1561-1564; *The Historie of Guicciardin*, 1579; better known as *The History of Italy*, 1753-1756), to which plot D'Azeglio added the story of a despondent protagonist who commits suicide. Another of D'Azeglio's novels, *Niccolò dei Lapi* (1841; English translation, 1860), follows the siege of Florence in 1530 and the fortunes of a republican family; this same siege was used in the title of a novel by Guerrazzi, *L'assedio di Firenze* (1836; the siege of Florence).

The novel from the era between Manzoni and Giovanni Verga (1840-1922) that is most esteemed today is *Le confessioni di un ottuagenario* (1867; partially translated as *The Castle of Fratta*, 1954), by the Paduan journalist and poet Ippolito Nievo (1831-1861). Nievo's narrator, Carlo Altoviti, is an octogenarian who, though Venetian, wishes to die an Italian. The old man tells his story from before the time of the French Revolution; his youthful love affair with Pisana at the Castle of Fratta is the portion of this very long and sometimes digressive novel that was excerpted and translated into English. Nievo, a colonel in Giuseppe Garibaldi's Thousand fighting against the Bourbons, died the untimely victim of a shipwreck in the Tyrrhenian Sea at the age of thirty.

NATURALISM

The Sicilian Luigi Capuana (1839-1915) did much to incorporate the precepts of French naturalism into Italian literature. Capuana saw the novel as a purely scientific study and as a means to social progress. With great versatility, he wrote short stories, children's books, criticism, and plays in Sicilian dialect; he was a birdwatcher, teacher, folklorist, and twice mayor of his native town of Mineo in Sicily. Capuana's novel, *Giacinta*

(1879), one of the first realistic novels written in Italian, is marred by an incongruous emphasis on the occult. In *Il profumo* (1890; perfume), Capuana explored an abnormal erotic situation. His most lasting work is *Il marchese di Roccaverdina* (1901; the marquis of Roccaverdina), a detective novel of sorts about a Sicilian landowner and his murdered agent. Capuana's characterization of Agrippina Solmi, the landowner's humble peasant mistress, elicited high critical praise, notably from Benedetto Croce. Capuana's influence on Italian fiction, however, stems not from his novels (he never got beyond a dependence on gimmicky, weird effects) but rather from his short stories and from his influence on his friend, Verga.

Verga, who is accorded the honor of following Manzoni in the hierarchy of Italian novelists, left Sicily and, following the example of Manzoni, went to Florence in 1865 to perfect his Italian. In Florence, he acquired instant fame for *Storia di una capinera* (1871; *Sparrow: The Story of a Songbird*, 1994), about a young nun in love. There followed four more similarly sentimental novels before he found his true métier, depicting the world of the Sicilian peasant, in the short story "Nedda" (1874; English translation, 1893). The characters that began to interest Verga in this new, more mature period of his career were poor people, farm workers, or fishermen, and he describes them sparely, without authorial introduction or commentary. Readers of Verga, like readers of William Faulkner, are offered a fictional world that they must interpret for themselves.

While it is true that for Verga the author's lot is to record and not to judge, Verga's fiction nevertheless pulsates with the compassion that he dared not put into words. His attitude toward the precarious existence of his beleaguered peasants, so completely at the mercy of natural forces that remain indifferent to the concerns of humans, is reminiscent of the poetic stance of Giacomo Leopardi (1798-1837). Whereas the ultimate reality had been for Manzoni a boundless Catholic faith, it was for Verga a fatal inevitability, contingent upon circumstances and conditioned somewhat by economic security.

In the six years after helping to found *Verismo*, or Verism (the Italian literary movement that partakes of both realism and naturalism), Verga wrote short stories and one minor novel but was concerned mainly with the preparation of his greatest work, *I malavoglia* (1881; *The House by the Medlar Tree*, partial translation 1890, 1953; complete translation 1964). The good-hearted but frugal grandfather, Master 'Ntoni, watches his brood of grandchildren grow up to disappoint his fondest dreams of prosperity for the family. Nature is at its harshest in a storm at sea that destroys a boatload of lupine purchased on credit and in a cholera epidemic that takes its toll on members of his family. To pay for the lost cargo of lupine, the family must give up their beloved house by the medlar tree. When the grandfather hears that his oldest grandson and namesake has been brought to trial for smuggling, he has a stroke and dies. A younger grandson, Alessi, Verga's symbol of faith in traditional hard work, is able to buy back the house by the medlar tree, and the novel ends with the suggestion that, despite the reversals of fortune, once again the Malavoglia may be as "numerous as the stones on the old Trezza road."

Even before the publication of this novel, Verga had conceived the idea—probably inspired by Honoré de Balzac and Émile Zola—of composing a cycle of five novels entitled La marea (the tide) or I vinti (the doomed), which would study successive stages in the human struggle for material security. *The House by the Medlar Tree* was to be the first of the cycle, depicting the struggle for minimal needs alone, but only one of the four projected novels was finished—*Mastro-don Gesualdo* (1889; English translation, 1893, 1923), the epic of a self-made man who lusts insatiably after greater and greater wealth and who, as a result of his greed, must die alone.

Although it was Capuana who influenced Verga to write in the manner of Zola and Gustave Flaubert, Verga had always been a pessimist and did not require a model on which to base his gloom. Although he is seen as the *verista* par excellence of Italian fiction, he was not dogmatic about his literary ideas. His greatest achievement was to "invent" a language that, while not employing the Sicilian dialect that his peasant characters would naturally speak, echoed their dialect in its phrasing, cadences, simplicity, and repetitions. This echoing of the Sicilian dialect in standard Italian is perceived even in portions of Verga's fiction that are not written in direct discourse. His style is laconic and inherently tragic in its intensity, yet in its selectivity it is also poetic.

One of Verga's closest friends, Federico De Roberto (1861-1927), was born in Naples but grew up in Sicily and considered himself Sicilian. Torn between Verga's regionalism and the emphasis on the psychological analysis of author Paul Bourget (1852-1935), he abandoned the peasant world of his early fiction for a more complex middle- and upper-class cast of characters. De Roberto's masterpiece *I vicerè* (1894; *The Viceroys*, 1962) is a historical and psychological study of three generations of the aristocratic Uzeda family, as well as a bitterly ironic indictment of politicians. According to Sergio Pacifici, there is enough packed into this sweeping novel to satisfy all tastes: a Manzonian taste for miniature biographies that probe psychology, Verga's emphasis on economic causes of people's fate, the psychological approach of Bourget and Capuana, the scientific approach of Zola, the regional approach of *Verismo*, and the stylistic clarity of Flaubert.

Despite its poverty and backward social conditions, Naples during the second half of the nineteenth century was a center of literary creativity, producing significant works of criticism (by Croce and Francesco De Sanctis), philosophy (by Croce and Bertrando Spaventa), poetry (by Salvatore Di Giacomo), and theater (by Roberto Bracco). It was in Naples that Greek-born Matilde Serao (1856-1927), of mixed Italian and Greek parentage, chose to make her home, depicting it realistically in her fiction. Fiction for Serao was not so much an art form as a mission, and the effect of Zola's naturalism is evident from her first works. The heroes of her fiction are lowly slum dwellers, and she is at her best describing the hopes and broken dreams of children and the emotions of women who are betrayed in love. Her best work is *Il paese di Cuccagna* (1890; *The Land of Cockayne*, 1901), a study of the lottery and the evil effects that it wreaks on all classes of society. The precision of her Neopolitan settings and her keen powers of empathy for the poor is marred by excessive sentimentality, a lack of unity, and occasional grammatical carelessness.

Despite the inevitable recognition of Verga's genius, for a quarter century following the publication of *Daniele Cortis* (1885; English translation, 1887), it was the Vicenzan Antonio Fogazzaro (1842-1911) who was viewed as the heir presumptive of Manzoni in the line of Italian novelists. Fogazzaro remains a good example of

how desperately the Italian bourgeoisie tried to believe during a time in the post-Risorgimento period when belief was seriously questioned. Since Fogazzaro deals exclusively with the social class to which he so comfortably belonged and seemed impervious to the socioeconomic problems of his recently unified country and the misery in which the majority of his compatriots lived, his books have less relevance to the majority of readers today than they did to a minority during the time they were written.

Content to perpetuate the traditional prose style of Manzoni, Fogazzaro employs a lofty vocabulary that could now be considered decadent. He was, nevertheless, the first major novelist to incorporate dialect into his literary Italian; this earned for him the censure of many critics. In the manner of Scott's introduction of "braid Scots" into portions of his novels dealing with Scottish life, Fogazzaro availed himself of Lombard, Venetian, Tuscan (with its guttural *gorgia*, or burr), Roman, and Sicilian words and accents to render character more faithfully. His forte was characterization rather than plot, and he was noted for the skill with which he captured the natural beauty of the Italian lake region.

Fogazzaro's masterpiece, *Piccolo mondo antico* (1896; *The Patriot*, 1907), depicts the idealized little world of the late Risorgimento and is a love story, as are many of Fogazzaro's plots. Through his protagonists, Franco and Luisa Maironi, the author explores two opposing views of life: the religious view of Franco and the skepticism of Luisa. When their child Obretta is drowned, the disconsolate mother dabbles in spiritualism; Fogazzaro, like Capuana, was interested in the occult, although not enough to classify him as a decadent author. The novel ends happily as Luisa conceives another child, Piero. Fogazzaro's next two novels concern Piero's development through his worldly stage (*Piccolo mondo Moderno*, 1900; *The Man of the World*, 1907) into his spiritual stage (*Il santo*, 1905; *The Saint*, 1906). After Piero becomes a lay brother in the latter novel, he assumes the name Benedetto and ultimately takes on the pope himself, lecturing the sympathetic but virtually powerless pontiff on the four "evil spirits" that infect the Church—falsehood, greed, immobility, and clericalism.

Leila (1910; English translation, 1910), the last novel

of the Piero Maironi tetralogy and Fogazzaro's swan song, addresses the question of what can be done now that all the proposed solutions have been rejected. Like Luisa, Leila represents the skeptical nature of Italian immoralism. She eventually marries Massimo Alberti, a favorite disciple of Benedetto "the Saint" who, after his own disillusionment with the Church, takes refuge in the pure altruism of his medical practice. While sadly accepting the official decision of the Church, Fogazzaro can only recommend the diverting solace of humanitarianism.

Fogazzaro was caught in the middle: His ideas about church reform brought charges of Protestantism from the papal contingent, and his novel *The Saint*, soon followed by *Leila*, was placed on the Index, the Catholic Church's list of banned books; his sympathy with the less radical aspect of socialism, however, was not Marxist enough to please the Marxists. Besides a greater openness within the Church itself, Fogazzaro advocated a stricter application of Christian morality to everyday life. If Italians of subsequent generations were indifferent to the issue of church reform, the issue later regained some of its former immediacy, and the novels of Fogazzaro managed to retain a reading public through the generations. Films and television dramatizations were made from some of his novels, and the future novelist Mario Soldati (1906-1999) wrote the screenplay for a 1941 film version of Fogazzaro's *Piccolo mondo antico*.

Another contender for second place in the literary hierarchy after Manzoni, one whose reputation declined even more sharply than Fogazzaro's, is Edmondo De Amicis (1846-1908), born in Oneglia in Liguria on the Italian Riviera. Indeed, in his treatise *L'idioma gentile* (1905; pure language), which reaffirms the superiority of the Florentine dialect, he stands out as a staunch Manzonian, at least in linguistic matters. Educated for the army, De Amicis fought in the Battle of Custozza (1866), which established Italy as a kingdom. His first book of sketches, the short-story collection *La Vita militare* (1868; *Military Life in Italy*, 1882), was based on his military experience. He was a great traveler and a prolific writer of travel books, about foreign countries (Morocco, Spain, Holland), foreign cities (London and Paris), and even remote regions within Italy (Basilicata).

De Amicis's best short-fiction work, immensely suc-

cessful but hopelessly sentimental by today's standards, is *Cuore* (1886; *The Heart of a Boy*, 1895), a series of sketches describing the life of a twelve-year-old boy attending the Turin public school system. The book was used in Italian schools until the advent of Fascism and was long a favorite for teaching Italian in the United States. Despite the disrepute into which his sentimentalism fell (a contemporary dubbed him Edmondo the Languorous), one cannot but admire De Amicis's conviction that there is something wondrous and lovable in every child. Nor was De Amicis indifferent to the social ills of his day; in 1891, he became a socialist. His long novel *Sull'oceano* (1889; *On Blue Water*, 1897), no more than a mere string of anecdotes, is devoted to the ordeal of illiterate emigrants as they make their interminable ocean crossing from Italy to a new life in the New World. In a subsequent novel, *Il romanzo d'un maestro* (1890; *The Romance of a Schoolmaster*, 1892), which deals with the idealism of a young schoolteacher pitted against uninspired politicians and supervisors, De Amicis showed the same lack of constructive ability, and in his final years, which were saddened by the suicide of his son, he turned his attention to linguistic matters.

Another novelist noted for his strong moral sense and his compassion for his fellow humans is the Milanese Emilio De Marchi (1851-1901), who has also been compared to Manzoni but who lacks much of the latter's stylistic elegance and religious feeling. Nevertheless, Sergio Pacifici suggests that a reevaluation of De Marchi's contribution to Italian literature is in order, noting with optimism that in 1994 a film was made of his detective novel about a murdered priest, *Il cappello del prete* (1888; the priest's hat).

Avoiding all mention of contemporary events, De Marchi was committed to depicting the sad reality of the monotonous bourgeois life led by some Italians, and for this reason, he has been compared to the French naturalists. His most accomplished novel is *Demetrio Pianelli* (1890), about a simple office clerk who is transformed, through a series of reversals, from an unheroic, retiring type of individual into a caring individual who learns to give without thought of reward (for example, he arranges the marriage of his widowed sister-in-law, Beatrice, to a wealthy relative, even though he himself is enamored of Beatrice).

THE EARLY TWENTIETH CENTURY

The leading novelist of the first decades of the twentieth century was the Sardinian Grazia Deledda (1871-1936), who became the second woman and the second Italian to win the Nobel Prize in Literature (1926). By the time of her marriage in 1900 and her subsequent removal from Sardinia to Rome, she had already published several collections of essays. Inasmuch as the best of her twenty-five novels are set in Sardinia and depict the primitive conditions of the island, Deledda is classified as a regionalist writer.

Deledda's characters struggle against their primitive background, as in *Elias Portolu* (1903; English translation, 1992), in which the hero, returning from imprisonment for a crime he did not commit, falls in love with his brother's fiancé and, in desperation, is forced to become a priest. *Le colpe altrui* (1914; the faults of others), a novel of tragic perplexities in which good and evil seem to be enmeshed and whose conclusion recognizes the inevitability of evil, is a plea for mutual forgiveness. *La madre* (1920; *The Mother*, 1923, 1974; also known as *The Woman and the Priest*, 1922) is the bitter tale of a mother who strives to make her son—a priest—forget the woman he loves. At the moment of crisis, when the priest seems about to be exposed by his mistress before his congregation, the mother dies, and her son knows instantly that the "shock of that same grief, that same terror which he had been enabled to overcome," was responsible for her death. The entire plot unfolds within the space of two days, and the story is told chiefly in the mother's emotional reactions to the situation.

After 1920, Deledda abandoned the Sardinian background, and her last novels show the influence of Fyodor Dostoevski. Despite her prolonged use of the Sardinian setting, she is more complex than the average regionalist realist writer; her concerns are, rather, the struggle between good and evil and the temptation of sensual love. In the words of the Swedish Academy, she was honored "for her idealistically inspired writings which with plastic clarity picture the life on her native island and with depth and sympathy deal with human problems in general."

Deledda enjoyed something of an international revival when she and her works were subjects of a wave of critical articles and books and several of her works were translated into English: for example, *Canne al vento* (1913; *Reeds in the Wind*, 1999), *La chiesa della solitudine* (1936; *The Church of Solitude*, 2002), and *Cosima* (1937; English translation, 1988). A full-length critical biography in English, *Grazia Deledda: A Legendary Life*, by Martha King, was published in 2005.

One of the most widely discussed writers of all of Italian literature, Gabriele D'Annunzio (1863-1938), versatile, prolific, and charismatic, is generally dealt with in Italian literary histories more as a poet and as a dramatist than as a novelist, though his fiction was undeniably popular. In fact, D'Annunzio turned from poetry to fiction because he believed that the novel was the genre of the future.

D'Annunzio was a sensualist in the tradition of the Marquis de Sade, Charles Baudelaire, Joris-Karl Huysmans, and Oscar Wilde, and the Romantic novels that he wrote represent a break both with *Verismo* and with the historical novel. The scientific and sociological preoccupations of the *veristi* are replaced in D'Annunzio by a realism of the senses. Pathological psychology, such a noticeable feature of Capuana's short stories, is present in D'Annunzio as well. For example, Tullio, in *L'innocente* (1892; *The Intruder*, 1898), fantasizes about making love to a woman while she is ill—but his novels are weak on plot and characterization. D'Annunzio himself is his own main character, and all of his novels involve a strikingly joyless search for pleasure; his strength lies in his sensitivity to the musical potential of combinations of words.

Il piacere (1889; *The Child of Pleasure*, 1898) is the story of Andrea Spinelli, who is saturated with art, "demanding only experience and more experience of the sharpest kind to feed it," and who moves in a world of duels, fox hunts, and intrigue. D'Annunzio's next attempt at the novel, *The Intruder*, is a psychological study of a Nietzschean Superman, Tullio Hermil, who conspires with his wife to murder her son born of an extramarital indiscretion. Finding this novel "the least D'Annunzian" of D'Annunzio's novels, Luchino Visconti more than eighty years later made a film of *The Intruder* (1975). To accommodate contemporary realism, Visconti felt it necessary to make only one change in his script: Whereas D'Annunzio allowed Tullio to survive the murder "at a level of experience beyond conventional standards of good and evil," Visconti has Tullio commit suicide.

Less pretentious, more unified, and possibly D'Annunzio's best novel is *Il trionfo della morte* (1894; *The Triumph of Death*, 1896), in which Giorgio Aurispa loves a woman so intensely that he feels he must destroy her. This novel particularly benefits from its vivid sense of the primitive quality of life in D'Annunzio's native Abruzzi region. *Il fuoco* (1900; *The Flame of Life*, 1900), which baldly details the liaison between a young poet and an older actress, was based on the author's own affair with Eleanora Duse. The descriptions of Venice in this novel are noted by the *Encyclopedia Britannica* (1956) as "perhaps the most ardent glorification of a city existing in any language." A master of embellishment, D'Annunzio is remembered in the annals of Italian fiction primarily for the decorative effect of what he wrote rather than for its content.

Although D'Annunzio fancied himself the mentor and soothsayer of Benito Mussolini, and indeed he contributed to Fascism the famous war cry *Eja, Eja, allala* and was responsible for the militia uniform with the tasseled cap, the thrill of literary creation was always more important to D'Annunzio than groveling for power. In the late twentieth century, there was a minor reassessment of D'Annunzio as a writer, and he was noted for his influence on Stefan George, Hugo von Hofmannsthal, Heinrich Mann, and Henry de Montherlant; one scholar, Jackson I. Cope, argued that D'Annunzio influenced the young James Joyce (see *Joyce's Cities: Archaeologies of the Soul*, 1981).

A novelist who wrote in the same vein as D'Annunzio is Alfredo Oriani (1852-1909), a Decadent vulgarian later lionized by the Fascists. Born in Faenza, this tireless writer of novels, plays, and political commentary began as a *verista* and was greatly influenced by French journalism and parliamentary oratory. When he abjured the excesses of the Decadents, it was to embrace the excesses of colonial messianism. Many of his ideals are found in what is considered his best novel, *La disfatta* (1896; the defeat), the drama of a scholar and the woman whom he loves and eventually marries. As he sees his son and his friends die and fails to win recognition for his scholarly pursuits, he comes to the disconsolate realization that his life is empty and that his defeat consists in his failure to move onward with life. Oriani's characterizations are effective, and the many ideas that crowd his novels are at least vitally represented, but he stands out more as an intuitive thinker of Hegelian stripe than as a novelist.

As D'Annunzio's novels were being hailed in their French translations as proof of a Latin Renaissance, one writer who found D'Annunzian conventions congenial and faithfully echoed them in her early stories of unhappy heroines is the feminist writer Sibilla Aleramo (1876-1960). Born Rina Faccio in Alessandria of bourgeois parents, she was often drawn to men—and women—of artistic temperament, and the life she lived is in itself suitable for a novel. Her first novel, *Il passaggio* (1919; the passage) was based on her year-long relationship with Lina Poletti (1885-1971), one of the first women in modern Italy to live openly as a lesbian. When a young poet forty years her junior came to interview the sixty-year-old Aleramo about her liaison with the poet Dino Campana (1885-1932), the subject of the young poet's university thesis, he himself became involved in a decade-long liaison with the older woman.

Although D'Annunzio dubbed Aleramo his "attentive sister" and she herself was dubbed a female D'Annunzio, her D'Annunzian stance was significantly tempered by her encounter with the sociology of Guglielmo Ferrero (1871-1942). In 1906, she wrote *Una donna* (1906; *A Woman*, 1908), a lightly fictionalized memoir hailed immediately as an international classic and taken as a proclamation that women are human beings entitled to fulfill their ideals. Although she was one of the few courageous intellectuals who dared to sign Benedetto Croce's anti-Fascist manifesto, she eventually supported Mussolini and said she envied D'Annunzio for having been spared the horror of witnessing the outcome of Fascism. Still later, however, she became a militant communist and read from her poetry at proletarian rallies.

Although originally an admirer of D'Annunzio and, like D'Annunzio, sympathetic with Fascism, the Sicilian Luigi Pirandello (1867-1936) managed to break free of D'Annunzian influence. In 1929, before the Italian Academy, Pirandello boldly took his revenge for a full thirty years of fame that D'Annunzio had usurped from him by broadly categorizing human types as either superficial "spinners of words" or more productive "spinners of things." It was the theater in which Pirandello excelled and for which he won the Nobel Prize in 1934, but he was also a master of the novella. He began his literary career as a poet and, at the urging of the ever-influential Capuana, applied himself to long fiction in 1893, the year he returned from his philological studies in Germany.

Pirandello wrote several novels, the third of which, *Il fu Mattia Pascal* (1904; *The Late Mattia Pascal*, 1923), a significant influence on the *teatro grottesco* of Luigi Chiarelli (1880-1947), is his most acclaimed novel. Tired of his marriage and his job as a librarian, Pascal uses a false newspaper report of his suicide as an excuse to flee and assume a new identity. Assuming this new identity, however, is impossible, because he lacks proper identification, and when he decides to return home, he finds that because his wife has remarried, he has lost his old identity as well. Pirandello's powerful sense of irony, evident here as well as in his drama, derives from Ludovico Ariosto and Niccolò Machiavelli and was tempered by Verga's vision of humanity (although Pirandello abhorred being called a *verista*) as a world of vanquished souls bound together in a religion of compassion. This novel stands thematically at a point midway between Pirandello's early emphasis on humans as a type within society and his later emphasis on the inner nature of humans, and structurally between the novels emphasizing plot and setting and those that abandon external reality to explore the characters' inner reality.

In an age of D'Annunzian rhetoric that followed a period of brutally candid *Verismo*, the uncomplicated storytelling of the conservative Romagnol Alfredo Panzini (1863-1939) must have been welcomed by more than a few readers. Although he had a fine sense of balance, tempering his criticism with humor, Panzini was a thoroughly bourgeois writer, unmoved by the wretchedness of the masses, and while he could represent pathos, he could not depict tragedy. *Io cerco moglie* (1920; *Wanted—A Wife*, 1921), his only novel translated into English, purports to analyze different kinds of women but reveals the author's conviction that there are only two: those a man falls in love with and those a man marries. His best novel, *La madonna di mamà* (1916; the madonna-mother), traditional in every sense, elaborates the theme of a young man's move from the country to the

city and turns into a war novel with crepuscular overtones.

Marino Moretti (1885-1979), one of the original three poets to whose work the gifted critic, novelist, and playwright Giuseppe Borgese (1882-1952) first applied the term *crepuscolari* (twilight poets) in 1910, was also a novelist and, like Panzini, from Romagna. Moretti's fiction is meditative, Catholic in the tradition of Manzoni, and particularly effective when dealing with the melancholy nature of the humble characters for whom Moretti cherished a special love. His peasants are from his native Romagna, a region with a long history of violence and sensuality capable of producing within a single generation the likes of Mussolini and Giovanni Pascoli. The gallery of Moretti's characters, who suffer but do not despair, is remarkably large, and he is particularly effective in his portrayal of women characters, as in *Il sole del sabato* (1916; the sun of the Sabbath).

Sometimes classified together as Tuscan storytellers par excellence are Enrico Pea (1881-1953), Bruno Cicognani (1879-1971), and Aldo Palazzeschi (1885-1974). As a result of having had little formal education and an early period spent living in Egypt, Pea was freer than most of his contemporaries from hampering literary conventions. He wrote from personal rather than intellectual or literary experience, and his books (for example, *Moscardino*, 1922) create a fablelike atmosphere that depends little on structure or chronology.

More intellectual is Cicognani, a Florentine lawyer who used his daily practice for human observation and, like Pea, worked outside the literary mainstream. His first novel, *La crittogama* (1908; the cryptogram), was written under the influence of D'Annunzio, while *La velia* (1923; the shrike) is an Italian version of Gustave Flaubert's *Madame Bovary* (1857; English translation, 1886). Although his portraits of immoral women place him with the French naturalists and his cultivation of Florence as his setting links him with *Verismo*, the psychological dimension he gives to his characters aspires to universality.

Palazzeschi, born Aldo Giurlani and an only child of bourgeois parents, first turned to poetry and participated in both the Futurist and the crepuscular movements. His first novel, dispensing with plot, dramatic action, and dialogue, was the epistolary *Riflessi* (1908), about a love affair between a Roman prince, Valentino Core, and a young Briton, John More. In order that the relationship remain pure and perfect (and therefore socially acceptable), any depiction of bodily contact is scrupulously avoided; the prince writes Johnny daily letters until one day the prince mysteriously vanishes, apparently a suicide. The decadence of its setting and language is reminiscent of D'Annunzio; this influence persists in the futuristic *Il codice di Perelà: Romanzo futurista* (1911, revised as *Perelà: Uomo di fumo*, 1954; *Perelà: The Man of Smoke*, 1936, and *Man of Smoke*, 1992) and *La piramide* (1926; the pyramid).

There is, however, the flavor of Manzoni in Palazzeschi's *Sorelle Materassi* (1934; *The Sisters Materassi*, 1953), a tableau of Tuscan life during the 1930's depicting the relationship of two lonely women with their orphaned adolescent nephew, Remo, who brings warmth into their empty house but takes advantage of them financially. As a narrator, Palazzeschi is sympathetic but aloof, and his gentle laughter is the only judgment that he makes on the all-too-human folly of his characters. The contrast between the misguided dreams of the young and the materially adequate but spiritually deficient ambience that they must inhabit reappears as the theme of his less successful later novels, *I fratelli Cuccoli* (1948; the Cuccoli brothers) and *Roma* (1953; English translation, 1965).

Another Tuscan writer, Federigo Tozzi (1883-1920), whose abrasive genius contrasts with the traditional emphasis on *il bello stile* (beautiful style), underwent a reevaluation during the postwar period and became ranked by Alberto Moravia in fourth place among Italian novelists, after Manzoni, Italo Svevo, and Verga. The product of an unhappy childhood, Tozzi wrote tragic and autobiographical fiction, tempered only by a trace of Dostoevskian compassion. Like his mentor Verga, he was interested in the effect of property on people's lives; material wealth for Tozzi was an obstacle to be overcome. In *Il podere* (1921; the farm), remarkable for its suffusion of tragedy rather than for its plot, Remigio returns home to take over the management of a farm from his dying father, a return that for Tozzi betokens a retrogression and a setting forth on the road toward death.

The novel *Tre croci* (1920; *Three Crosses*, 1921) takes its title from the graves of the three brothers whose lack of moral fortitude leads to their successive catastrophes. The brothers inherit a bookstore from their father. Business is bad, so they borrow money, eventually become involved in fraud, and nevertheless continue to waste money that they do not have on gormandizing. The portraits of the three, with their idiosyncrasies, fears, temper tantrums, and gluttony, are studies of unusual depth. The author's own untimely death deprived him of seeing either of these novels in print, but overdue recognition is granted him as a forerunner of Franz Kafka and existentialism.

Farther removed from the mainstream than even Tozzi is Svevo (1861-1928), literally Italo the Swabian, the pen name of Aron Hector Schmitz. Born in Trieste of Jewish parents, his father was of German-Italian parentage and his mother a native Triestine. Svevo's father sent him to Germany to perfect his German, which was vital to the boy's future in what was then the Austro-Hungarian port city of Trieste. He was an Italian citizen only for the last decade of his life.

Although he always yearned to be a writer, Svevo's literary success was hampered first by economic necessity and then, after the appearance of *Una vita* (1892; *A Life*, 1963) and *Senilità* (1898; *As a Man Grows Older*, 1932; also known as *Emilio's Carnival*, 2001), by public indifference. For the next quarter of a century, Svevo did not publish, although he did continue to write. His friendship with James Joyce led eventually to the publication of his third novel, *La coscienza di Zeno* (1923; *Confessions of Zeno*, 1930; also known as *Zeno's Conscience*, 2001), which became popular in France and only later in Italy.

Svevo's antiacademic writing style—dry, too close to the Triestine dialect, and perhaps influenced by the author's greater fluency in German—alienated many critics, although those readers nourished on Verga and Tozzi admired him. His helpless characters are intelligent anomalies, portrayed in the first two novels with the objectivity of the French naturalists. *A Life* is about the insincerity of Alfonso Nitti's love affair with his employer's daughter and his humdrum white-collar life, and it ends with an official communication announcing Nitti's suicide. *As a Man Grows Older*, an improvement in subtlety and psychological penetration, is about Emilio Brentani, who falls in love with a prostitute and achieves senility at the age of thirty-five when his dying sister tells him the truth about his lover. After Svevo discovered Sigmund Freud, around 1912, he used the idea of psychoanalysis in the writing of *Confessions of Zeno*. The morbid Zeno Cosini seeks his salvation through psychoanalysis, recounting his life supposedly to find the origin of his smoking habit, as well as his innumerable other psychosomatic diseases, and thereby exposing his contradictory ideas and desires.

As a pro-Italian Austro-Hungarian subject, a Jew, a businessman who liked literature, and a pacifist during World War I, Svevo lived as an outsider prone to the pleasures of introspection. His novels project an absurdist world where people are prevented by their spinelessness and other foibles from assuming the responsibility for their own weakness and are unable to share happiness or sorrow with others. To probe this sorry state, Svevo analyzes human consciousness (the Italian *coscienza* of his title suggests both "consciousness" and "conscience"), and because his work provides such a detailed look at the contradictions between reality and personality (Zeno habitually says the opposite of what he thinks and does the opposite of what he wants to do), Svevo has a modern flavor for the contemporary reader.

The founding of the journal *La voce* (1908), which provided a much-needed forum for serious writing by many gifted writers, foreshadowed both the Hermetic (obscurantist) tradition in poetry and the journal *La ronda* (1919-1923), which championed a reactionary return to classic tradition, emphasizing clear style, well-constructed syntax, and literary vocabulary. The versatile Riccardo Bacchelli (1891-1985) was the only one of the *rondisti* to make his imprint on the novel, and this he did with his two-thousand-page historical epic, *Il mulino del Po* (1938-1940; *The Mill on the Po*, 1950). It follows successive generations of the Scacerni family, from the time of Napoleon to the end of World War I. Political events are not important to Bacchelli per se, but rather as they affect the lives of his characters. In his many, diverse attempts at the novel and other forms of narrative, in which he was only cautiously experimental, he followed the formalism of Manzoni and, like Fogazzaro, dignified his own robust sensuality under a veil of Catholic unction.

In 1926, the gifted Massimo Bontempelli (1878-

1960) and Curzio Malaparte (1898-1957) attacked the aesthetic formalism of the *rondisti* as well as the popular realism (which scored its final triumph in Deledda's Nobel Prize of 1926) by founding the review *"900,"* *Cahiers d'Italie et d'Europe*, also known as *Il novecento* (the twentieth century). Although short-lived, the review attempted, by publishing its material in French, to expose Italians to the influences of French and Continental literature. Bontempelli was a critic, playwright, aphorist, novelist, and short-story writer as well as an editor. His literary creed was "to clothe in a smile the most sorrowful things and with wonderment the most common things" in order to evoke the surreal inherent in the real. Four of his novels have been translated into English: *La scacchiera davanti allo specchio* (1922; *The Chess Set in the Mirror*, 2007); *Il figlio di due madri* (1929; *The Boy with Two Mothers,* 2000); *Vita e morte di Adria e dei suoi figli* (1930; *The Life and Death of Adria and Her Children*, 2000); and *L'amante fidele* (1953; *The Faithful Lover*, 2007).

The younger Malaparte, pen name of Kurt Erich Suckert, was the son of a German father and an Italian mother and was born in Prato. Controversial and contradictory, he wrote his best book, *Kaputt* (1944; English translation, 1946), while confined to Finland after he had angered the Nazi command. *Kaputt* is an apocalyptic vision of Europe crumbling under the violence of war. Later in 1944, his experiences as Italian liaison officer with the Allies in Naples offered the material for his most controversial novel, *La pelle* (1949; *The Skin*, 1952), whose Surrealism was mistaken for documentary realism. Both novels were international best sellers. The comparison with D'Annunzio is inescapable, but as Luigi Barzini points out, while D'Annunzio was both admired and loathed by his outstanding contemporaries, Malaparte managed to strike only the obscurest of his contemporaries as irritating or charming.

The founding of the Florentine review *Solaria* in 1926 represented an attempt to reconcile the stylistics-oriented *rondisti* with the current dedicated to modern European trends responsible for Bontempelli's *Il novecento*. *Solaria* was pledged to introducing Italians to such modern figures as Kafka, Marcel Proust, T. S. Eliot, and Joyce and to refurbishing the images of such underrated Italian authors as Svevo and Tozzi, to whom they dedicated special commemorative issues. The *solariani* did not oppose regionalism: It was their successful blend of regional and universal concerns that gave rise to the work of Cesare Pavese, Elio Vittorini, Ignazio Silone, Carlo Levi, Vasco Pratolini, Vitaliano Brancati, Corrado Alvaro, and Giorgio Bassani. *Solaria*, however, had a formidable enemy in Fascism; the *solariani* were called "Jew-lovers" for their devotion to the likes of Kafka and Svevo, and by 1937, they were forced to close their doors.

Vittorini (1908-1966), from a middle-class Sicilian family of Syracuse, left home in 1928 with his wife, Rosa Maria, the sister of poet Salvatore Quasimodo, to settle in Gorizia in northeastern Italy. His contribution to Italian intellectual life figures more in terms of his work as literary critic and organizer than in his narrative output, and he became a sort of Italian Jean-Paul Sartre, dispensing theories about the necessity of updating literature.

Vittorini's first short story appeared in *Solaria* in 1929, and soon he began working for the periodical as a proofreader and office assistant. In 1933, he published his first translation, of D. H. Lawrence's *St. Mawr: Together with the Princess* of 1925. In February of 1933, *Solaria* began serializing Vittorini's own novel *Il garofano rosso* (1948; *The Red Carnation*, 1952). Because the novel explored the fascination that Fascism held for young people, especially emphasizing the sexual-sadistic element, the censors stopped its publication after the third installment, and Vittorini, in the wake of interest in American literature stimulated by the awarding of the Nobel Prize in Literature to Sinclair Lewis in 1930, continued his work on translations of Edgar Allan Poe, Faulkner, William Saroyan, and Erskine Caldwell.

Vittorini's masterpiece, *Conversazione in Sicilia* (1941; *In Sicily*, 1948; also known as *Conversation in Sicily*), was confiscated by the censors but reprinted in 1942. It was immediately praised for its lyric beauty, its innovative style, and its emotional impact; later, Italo Calvino (1923-1985) would call it the basis for modern Italian literature. The story of thirty-year-old Silvestro as he travels from the north back to Sicily to see his mother and the conversations he has with various people are converted by Vittorini into a rare allegory on the need to rekindle hope in freedom and justice. The book cir-

culated in French and German translations in Nazi-governed countries and was a great inspiration in those dark days of oppression.

In 1943, Vittorini joined the Resistance movement, was jailed, and used the experience for *Uomini e no* (1945; *Men and Not Men*, 1985), the story of a Resistance group and a work that was immediately hailed as a wartime classic and the cornerstone of the neorealistic movement (although Vittorini himself denied the neo-realism of the book). A few years later, Vittorini wrote *Le donne di Messina* (1949, 1964; *Women of Messina*, 1973), whose first edition was a wordy novel seven hundred pages long. It involves a group of displaced people (many of whom are from the Sicilian city of Messina, which has risen phoenixlike from its ashes many times in its history) who resettle an abandoned village. It is the story of a society that is reborn, but Vittorini was always dissatisfied with the novel.

Vittorini believed that Italians had more in common with Americans than they had with Italian life of Manzoni's era, and he demanded that authors be more responsive to contemporary sensibility than the Italian literary idols of the past, such as D'Annunzio and Croce. He accused authors who persisted in writing from the omniscient point of view of catering to the "mystic enjoyment" of a reactionary reading public, and he rejected his own novel *Women of Messina* because it smacked of the nineteenth century. This explains his disapproval of Verga and why, as an editor, he rejected Giuseppe Tomasi di Lampedusa's *Il gattopardo* (1958; *The Leopard*, 1960) as typifying an obsolete literature that barred the way for works of more responsible and revolutionary conception. Long novels he felt were passé, and literature as a system of representing relations with the modern world must not fail to incorporate the newest technological changes. He fiercely defended science in the hope that humans could someday come to win control over the machines that are understood so little.

Vittorini founded and directed the *I gettoni* (literally "gambling chips") series for Einaudi, which published first works by such budding authors as Mario Tobino, Carlo Cassola, Giovanni Arpino, and Calvino. Vittorini also founded and served as editor of the controversial and short-lived periodical *Il politecnico*, which he intended to serve as a vehicle for former Fascists to shrive themselves of their wartime complicity. He also established the avant-garde periodical *Il menabò*, and just before he died in 1966, he was trying to organize "Gulliver," an international periodical.

NEOREALISM

"Neorealism" is the blanket term applied to the socially aware postwar movement in literature, the fine arts, and cinema. It was probably most successful in the great films in the decade following the war when directors such as Roberto Rossellini, Vittorio De Sica, and Luchino Visconti were producing some of the most original films in the Western world. Factors contributing to this heightened sensibility were the anti-Fascist struggle, the postwar social and political struggle within Italy, and the spread of Marxism arising from the rediscovery of the works of Antonio Gramsci. In their concern for the condition of the common people, many writers (including some northern Italians such as Pavese and Levi), freed of the bonds of Fascist censorship, came to refocus on the plight of the Italian South in the tradition of Verga, Capuana, Serao, and Di Giacomo. The poor South (called the *mezzogiorno*) is a special enigma to the Italian nation. Because southern Italians are admittedly a frugal and hardworking people at the mercy of an inhospitable terrain and the feudal legacy of the latifundium, or landed estate, it would seem reasonable that with proper guidance they could be made into an asset instead of a liability for the country.

At this time, a great number of Italian writers arose to place the urgent problems of the South squarely in view of the Italian reading public. The three southern writers chosen by Sergio Pacifici as typical of three different tendencies within the category of the "southern novel" are Corrado Alvaro (1895 or 1896-1956), Vitaliano Brancati (1907-1954), and Lampedusa (1896-1957).

The Calabrian Alvaro grew up under the style-conscious influence of *La ronda*, which gave to his style a complexity and richness that does not quite qualify as neorealism. His fiction is reminiscent of Verga in its emphasis on a cruel destiny, in his distance from his characters, and in his sense of irony; his masterpiece *Gente in Aspromonte* (1930; *Revolt in Aspromonte*, 1962), which elaborates the difficult life led by a family of Calabrian shepherds and their struggle to survive the reversals that

ultimately obliterate their modest dreams, resembles *The House by the Medlar Tree*. By the beginning of World War II, Alvaro had produced twelve volumes of fiction, ten of nonfiction, three of poetry, two plays, and translations from English, Russian, and Greek. After the war, he wrote a trilogy of Rinaldo Diacono novels—of which *L'età breve* (1946; the brief age) was the only one published in its finished form—that focus on Italian bourgeois society under Fascism and after the war through the eyes of a young, urbanized, transplanted southerner who longs for his native land, which he has idealized beyond recognition.

Unlike Alvaro, who created a world full of dramatic tension, the Sicilian Brancati employed a more comic approach to portray southern Italian morals and manners. Writing in reaction to D'Annunzio's glorification of sexual freedom, Brancati satirized in *Don Giovanni in Sicilia* (1941; Don Juan in Sicily) *gallismo*, the aggressive eroticism of southern males who are reared in a matriarchal society only ostensibly ruled by men, where honor consists of saving face and morality consists of conformity. Originally a Fascist, Brancati was disabused of his early loyalties when he migrated to the mainland and made the salutary acquaintance of Giuseppe Borgese and Croce. Because neither Alvaro nor Brancati proposed any radical solutions to the plight of the *mezzogiorno*, neither received more than a passing recognition from the Marxist-oriented criticism of modern Italy.

A literary anomaly—it is the only novel that is frankly decadent to appear in the postwar period—but undeniably one of the most extraordinary and most written-about books of modern Italian literature is Lampedusa's *The Leopard*. Despite his international education and his love of literatures other than Italian (he especially liked William Shakespeare, Leo Tolstoy, Marcel Proust, and Thomas Mann), Lampedusa felt so thoroughly Sicilian that it was about Sicily that he felt compelled to write.

The odyssey of Lampedusa's manuscript is remarkable; in 1957, the year of his death, he submitted the manuscript to Mondadori of Milan and to Einaudi of Turin, two of the most prestigious publishing houses in Italy, headed respectively by Vittorio Sereni and Elio Vittorini. The book was rejected by both, and after Lampedusa's death, his widow gave Elena Croce (the daughter of Benedetto Croce) a handwritten copy of the manuscript. She passed it on to Giorgio Bassani, a senior consulting editor at Feltrinelli of Milan; this time the novel was accepted.

Lampedusa's "leopard," named for the proud beast emblazoned on the family coat of arms, is Don Fabrizio, Prince of Salina, modeled on the author's own great grandfather, an enlightened despot who ruled over vast estates on the eve of Garibaldi's landing in Sicily. Too intelligent to resist the inevitable future but reluctant to join the present, he views the fall of the Bourbon monarchy with "historic nausea," as well as a strange equanimity, for in Lampedusa's frankly pessimistic representation of Don Fabrizio's world, despite the appearance of change, nothing really changes.

The novel *Fontomara* (1930, 1933, revised 1958; English translation, 1934, revised 1960), is a forerunner of this trend to enlighten readers about the poor conditions in the South. Its author, Ignazio Silone (1900-1978), the pen name of Secondo Tranquilli, here undertook to communicate to the free world from his exile in Switzerland the totalitarian repression of Fascism, which served only to compound the misery of the southern Italian *cafoni* (peasants). Nothing is going to change, according to Silone, unless the *cafoni* can unite their forces to create change. *Fontamara*, however, is not quite a realistic novel, for its peasants are idealized and its Fascists are caricatured. *Pane e vino* (1937, revised as *Vino e Pane*, 1955; first pb. as *Brot und Wein*, 1936; *Bread and Wine*, 1936, revised 1962) and *Il seme sotto la neve* (1942; first pb. as *Der Samen unterm Schnee*, 1941; *The Seed Beneath the Snow*, 1942) are set in the same barren land of the Abruzzi and chronicle the life of Pietro Spina, a revolutionary disguised as a priest who rediscovers a renewed way of life tending the soil of his homeland but who eventually dies for another man's crime. Silone invests in his character Spina his own transformation from communist to primitive Christian socialist. Strangely enough, Silone is more widely known in the United States than in Italy.

Like Silone, Carlo Levi (1902-1975) was an intellectual in exile when he wrote about the condition of southern Italian peasants. More for his anti-Fascist sentiments than for being a Jew, Levi, a painter and physician, was sent to a small town twenty miles from the nearest rail-road station in remote and impoverished Basilicata in the instep of the Italian boot. Here, for the first time, Levi did not feel the sting of racial prejudice, for "his" peasants, as he came to call them, did not know what a Jew was. The title of his masterpiece, *Cristo si è fermato a Eboli* (1945; *Christ Stopped at Eboli: The Story of a Year*, 1947), refers to the peasants' belief that they were by-passed by Christianity and even by civilization: "Christ never came this far, nor did time, nor the individual soul, nor hope, nor the relation of cause to effect, nor reason nor history."

The book, which depicts a people so worn down by the gratuitous insults of life and nature that Mussolini's Fascism is hardly a matter of importance to them, ends when the author is freed by a political amnesty in 1936. It was written eight years later while Levi was living in Florence as a hunted member of the Resistance; it was published after the war and immediately became an international best seller. The spirit of Levi's moving diary-novel set the tone for much of the truth-seeking neorealism that was to follow, and it also marks the beginning of a new vogue for the subgenre of books that combine travel and observation, such as Carlo Bernari's *Il gigante Cina* (1957; gigantic China), Alberto Moravia's *La rivoluzione culturale in Cina* (1967; *The Red Book and the Great Wall*, 1968), and Levi's own book on the Soviet Union, *Il futuro ha un cuore antico: Viaggio nell'Unione Sovietica* (1956; the future has an ancient heart).

Francesco Jovine (1902-1950) conjured up his own brand of poetic realism describing the peasants of his native Molise region. His best novel, *Le terre del Sacramento* (1950; the estate in Abruzzi), is the epic of a depressed people who succeed in occupying uncultivated land. At the center of this peasant insurrection against the privileges of the ruling class is Luca Marano, who was called one of the most felicitous creations of contemporary Italian fiction.

The northerner Giovanni Arpino (1927-1987), who normally depicts the Piedmontese countryside in his fiction, employed a southern setting to expose the absurdity of the practice of the southern vendetta in *Un delitto d'onore* (1961; *A Crime of Honor*, 1963). In a small town south of Naples, a leading citizen murders his wife when a doctor certifies that she was not a virgin at the time of their marriage. The narrative is permeated with black irony but is also remarkable for the author's understanding of the traditions involved.

Leonardo Sciascia (1921-1989), whom Luigi Barzini considers "perhaps one of the best of all" contemporary Italian writers, evokes the Sicilian mentality. The author of a number of scholarly works on Sicilian history, Sciascia is primarily concerned in his fiction with exposing the crimes of the Italian Mafia and the strict primitive adherence of Sicilians to *omertà* (the code of silence). Sciascia's novels are generally classified as mysteries in the United States. As Herbert Mitgang observes of *A ciascuno il suo* (1966; *A Man's Blessing*, 1968; also known as *To Each His Own*), Sciascia's murder stories exemplify the gemlike difference between a simple mystery and a work of fiction that does not depend upon a tidy solution for its vitality.

Sardinia, which is considered part of the Italian South, is portrayed by Giuseppe Dessí (1909-1977), a follower of *Solaria* and a reader of Proust and Mann with a lyric gift for blending autobiographical detail with regional realism, especially evident in *Michele Boschino* (1942). *Paese d'ombre* (1972; the forests of Norbio), perhaps a little too dependent on the Sardinian ambience for an American audience, is the life story of Angelo Uras and his anger at the wanton destruction of the magnificent forests of Norbio, sacrificed to fuel the insatiable furnaces of technology.

The teeming metropolis of Naples is the preferred subject matter of Neopolitan novelists Carlo Bernari (1909-1992), one of the forerunners of neorealism with his *Tre operai* (1934; three factory workers), which deals with the urban proletariat of his native city; Michele Prisco (1920-2003); and Domenico Rea (1921-1994). Prisco and Rea both write short stories as well as novels; Prisco is fond of describing the aristocracy and the petite bourgeoisie, whereas Rea is more interested in the tragicomic condition of the common people.

Depicting the southernmost province of Calabria are Fortunato Seminara (1903-1984), who probes the psychological motives for the archaic social structures of the area, and Saverio Strati (born 1924), who creates a world of day laborers, coal miners, and masons who dream of emigration to more civilized and charitable lands to escape the squalor of their lives and who sometimes return empty-handed to Calabria after an odyssey abroad. Prisco, Rea, Seminara, and Strati are not well-known in the United States, which is lamentable—and ironic, because a majority of Italian Americans have their roots in precisely the areas of Italy that these authors describe.

A northern writer who wrote his first novel while a political exile in Calabria is the Piedmontese Cesare Pavese (1908-1950), whose short novels constitute, according to Italo Calvino, the "most dense, dramatic, and homogeneous narrative cycle" of modern Italian literature. Although his fiction was a major influence upon neorealism, his novels cannot be said to be realistic, for he is not as much interested in the outside world as he is in how his characters come to terms with their world.

Pavese, who was asthmatic, was judged unfit for military service and for the same reason could not participate in the guerrilla warfare of the Resistance movement. A reading of his diary through the war years reveals only a few offhand references to the war and a lack of involvement for which he would later be criticized. Pavese was a major interpreter of American and English letters for Italians, translating works by Lewis, Gertrude Stein, Herman Melville, William Faulkner, Charles Dickens, and Daniel Defoe, among others; he admired F. Scott Fitzgerald and Ernest Hemingway so much that he claimed he did not dare to translate them. He worked as an editor for Einaudi, the publishing house that he had helped to found in Turin.

A sensitive man who believed that life was not worth living unless for the sake of others, Pavese nevertheless found it difficult to relate to other people. Despite his belief that the advance of civilization rested on men overcoming their misogyny, he was obsessed by his love for individual women and ended his life by his own hand, recognizing that he was sexually hopeless. He came to the novel from poetry, which he freed from formal metrical requirements, emphasizing rhythm and synthesis and preoccupied with the problem of solitude.

Like Elio Vittorini, Pavese wished to infuse new vitality into what he perceived as a tired tradition by the introduction of American literature and by making technical innovations, which for Pavese involved mixing local dialect with literary Italian, and experimentation with ungrammatical, unliterary language. (He was fascinated by the American slang in the novels he translated.)

Using the "return of the wanderer to his homeland" theme elaborated into such a powerful allegory by Vittorini, Pavese wrote *La luna e I falò* (1950; *The Moon and the Bonfire*, 1952), emphasizing memory as a key to understanding past experiences, which can in turn be prodded by immersing again in the past (hence, Pavese's realism). His character, Anguilla ("eel" in Italian, referring to the eel's characteristic return to its birthplace), returns to his mountain village after an absence of twenty years in America (which he characterizes as an illusory heaven, a land where, like the moon of Pavese's title, there is nothing, no real women and no wine), re-creates his idyllic past and then suffers the anguish of seeing these memories disintegrate in the present. Although he finds that nothing has really changed, he does become reconciled to what he perceives as his own destiny, his own identification with the people of his homeland and with the natural forces (the mountains) that shaped them all.

Pavese's women characters are more convincing than his men; this is particularly evident in *Tra donne sole* (1949; *Among Women Only*, 1953), set in the world of haute couture. The Rosetta of this novel, like Rosalba in *Il diavolo sulle colline* (1949; *The Devil in the Hills*, 1954), finds suicide the only escape—a solution to which Pavese himself resorted on August 27, 1950.

The Resistance novel treats an area of such overwhelming and specialized interest to Italian readers that some critics have attempted to call it a subgenre of the novel. The Resistance novel, however, does not admit of a facile definition, especially considering that for many who use the term, it is generously applied even to those novels of wartime or postwar activity by or about those who were not even sympathetic to the Resistance movement.

British and American critics understandably exclude from the category such novels as *Tiro al piccione* (1953; *The Day of the Lion*, 1954), by Giose Rimanelli (born 1926), or *Il cielo è rosso* (1947; *The Sky Is Red*, 1948), by Giuseppe Berto (1914-1978). The former, a sympathetic presentation of the losing side and based on the author's own experiences, depicts a rebellious adolescent's escape from the boredom of his southern Italian village to join the bedraggled Fascist army and his subsequent emergence from the ruins able to accept the future. The latter, written about four adolescents who come together after their families have been killed and form a nucleus of life amid the ruins of 1943 to 1944, was conceived while the author was in a prison camp in Hereford, Texas; its style was even affected by some of the American authors that Berto read while in prison (for example, John Steinbeck, Melville, Faulkner, Hemingway).

The first of what are unequivocally called Resistance novels by British and American standards is Vittorini's *Men and Not Men*, which employs the 1944-1945 struggle of a group of Milanese partisans to suggest that World War II was a conflict between men and "nonmen." Vittorini portrays his Nazis and Fascists as either stupid, unfeeling automatons or sadists, and his anti-Fascists as simple people who react with human sensitivity. Vittorini's protagonist is identified only by his code name N2; the other characters are not well drawn, and the dialogue, which reveals the influence but not the skill of Hemingway, is repetitive and banal.

Two years later, Italo Calvino published *Il sentiero dei nidi di ragno* (1947, 1957, 1965; *The Path to the Nest of Spiders*, 1956). It deals with a partisan movement originating in the mountains around Genoa and has as its hero an unloved orphan boy named Pin who finds in the partisans with whom he associates a camaraderie new to him. Although the partisans offer Pin at least the hope of redemption, Calvino is careful not to idealize his characters, who remain ordinary, even shocking in their crudity.

Renata Viganò (1900-1976), born in Bologna and a prolific writer of short stories, enshrined the touching heroism of her communist peasant woman protagonist in *L'Agnese va a morire* (1954; Agnese goes to her death). In a narrative unencumbered by speculation and rhetoric, Agnese, whose aged husband has been carried off to a German work camp, where he perishes, performs faithfully the instructions of the partisans with whom she works until she is killed in an encounter with an enraged German soldier.

The Resistance novels of Pavese, Carlo Cassola (1917-1987), and Mario Tobino (1910-1991) are more complicated and reflect more on the failures of the movement than do Vittorini, Calvino, or Viganò. In Pavese's *La casa in collina* (1949; *The House on the Hill*, 1956), his introspective and alienated protagonist

Corrado cynically observes that all humans, unless they throw bombs or otherwise risk their lives in combat, are Fascists. *Fausto e Anna* (1952; *Fausto and Anna*, 1960), by Roman author Cassola, active in the Resistance fighting in Tuscany and later a schoolteacher, spans a period of eight years and of all the Resistance novels portrays most successfully the tension of those years. The joyful disbanding of the partisans of Cassola's novel betokens a return to a normality that does not promise to be better than before. Fausto, previously devoted both to Anna and to the Communist Party, loses both of them by the end of the novel.

Like Pavese's Corrado, the Tuscan Tobino is unstinting in his accusation in his *Il clandestino* (1962; *The Underground*, 1966, 1967) that the vast majority of Italians were Fascists and that it was precisely these people who were responsible for the war. In this novel, Tobino gives a collective character to the Resistance movement and deprives his story of a single protagonist. Despite an overpopulated cast of characters, what emerges from the novel is a remarkably complete picture of the Resistance period. Like Cassola, however, Tobino is not sanguine about a renewal or a restructuring of Italian society.

L'ombra delle colline (1964; shadow on the hills), by Giovanni Arpino (1927-1987), presents a protagonist who returns to the Langhe Hills in Piedmont years after he has worked with the Resistance there as a youth. In this novel, there is the wistfulness about the lost ideals of the Resistance, the sad acceptance of the status quo, and the conflict between myth and history that had tortured Pavese.

Resistance novels continued to be written, most notably by Beppe Fenoglio (1922-1963), who seems to have intended to produce a panoramic cycle of the Italian civil war from September, 1943, through April, 1945. Fenoglio, who was born in Alba and spent his entire life in the Langhe region of the Piedmont, was an Anglophile who made extensive use of English words and phrases in his novels and translated a variety of English works, including Kenneth Grahame's *The Wind in the Willows* (1908). His lightly fictionalized autobiographical hero appears first as an officer cadet in Rome in *Primavera di bellezza* (1959; spring of beauty) and continues through *Il partigiano Johnny* (1968; *Johnny the Partisan*, 1995); finally, the former partisan's readjustment to civilian life

is examined in *La paga del sabato* (1969; Saturday's wages). Fenoglio's World War II novel, *La trappola amorosa* (1988), was translated into English as *A Private Affair* in 2007.

Of the northern Italian writers who partook of the vogue of neorealism, perhaps the Florentine Vasco Pratolini (1913-1991) is the most typical; certainly he is one of the most prolific. His realism, as opposed to the *Verismo* of Verga, does not emphasize folklore and local color per se but rather uses the setting as a backdrop for a drama of ordinary human emotion. Neither does Pratolini strive to be scientifically objective or shrink from intervening to plead the case of one of his characters, if necessary. Pratolini's masterpiece is *Cronache di poveri amanti* (1947; *A Tale of Poor Lovers*, 1949), which Frank Rosengarten considers a Resistance novel because it depicts so graphically a microcosm of the Italian world (in the mid-1920's) on the eve of political tyranny.

The postwar works of the Vicenzan Guido Piovene (1907-1974) are sometimes classed as neorealistic despite their overtones of D'Annunzian decadence. Pier Paolo Pasolini (1922-1975), born in Bologna, came to the novel from poetry and abandoned the novel for film; he also made his mark on literary history as a critic. Because literary language is a reflection of the ruling classes so distasteful to Pasolini's Marxism, he rejected it; with the scholarship of a philologist, he followed the example of Carlo Emilio Gadda (1893-1973) and employed the crude dialect of the Roman undesirables for much of his first two novels, *Ragazzi di vita* (1955; *The Ragazzi*, 1968) and *Una vita violenta* (1959; *A Violent Life*, 1978).

Giorgio Bassani (1916-2000) was a chronicler of Ferrara who created vulnerable characters such as Jews and gays and examines them in times of stress. *Il giardino dei Finzi-Contini* (1962; *The Garden of the Finzi-Continis*, 1965), made even more popular by Vittoria De Sica's 1970 film, is a pathetic story of a wealthy Jewish family whose members live impervious to the growing turmoil outside their garden walls, which will lead to their own persecution. The novella *Gli occhiali d'oro* (1958; *The Gold-Rimmed Spectacles*, 1960; revised as *The Gold-Rimmed Eyeglasses*, 1975) is the no less pathetic story of a gay doctor eventually forced to commit suicide; the story is narrated by a sympathetic young

Jew who is growing more and more aware of the anti-Semitism that he himself must inevitably face.

Writing during these years with the spirit of an *avant gardista* was Dino Buzzati (1906-1972), who was born in Belluno. Best known for his short fiction, Buzzati was a journalist and an editor by profession and a gifted painter as well as a writer. In 1940, he published an allegorical novel reminiscent of Franz Kafka, *Il deserto dei Tartari* (*The Tartar Steppe*, 1952). His more conventional *Un amore* (1963; *A Love Affair*, 1964) is about a dignified middle-aged man in love with a shameless prostitute. Although Buzzati filled his fiction with historical characters, this was not, in the words of Sergio Pacifici, to encourage realism, but "simply to heighten the irony of a world teetering on the brink of madness."

Another author of this period who does not conform to neorealism is Gadda, a civil engineer born in Milan of an Italian father and a German mother; he is the author of the Italian equivalent of James Joyce's *Ulysses* (1922). Written in a mixture of standard Italian and Roman dialect with liberal admixtures of Milanese, Venetian, and Neapolitan dialects, *Quer pasticciaccio brutto de via Merulana* (1957; *That Awful Mess on Via Merulana*, 1965), seems to be a detective story, but it soon becomes clear that Gadda is more interested in the welter of possibly sapphic, or lesbian, relationships that could have provided the motive than he is in solving the crime itself.

In a separate category are several authors whose works are substantially more popular in the United States than in Italy. Giovanni Guareschi (1908-1968), born near Parma and a prisoner of the Germans from 1943 to 1945, was a sort of James Thurber who illustrated his own works. By confining himself to whimsy, Guareschi managed to publish books under Fascism even before he emerged in his true light as a political satirist with his Don Camillo sketches (*Mondo piccolo: Don Camillo*, 1948; *The Little World of Don Camillo*, 1950), which satirize extremists of both the Left and the Right.

Another contemporary author less esteemed in Italy than abroad is Carlo Coccioli (1920-2003), a participant in the Resistance. Influenced by modern French authors, he typified, according to Thomas F. Staley, the postexistential novelist who tried to integrate existential thought with unorthodox Christian idealism. His *Il cielo e la terra* (1950; *Heaven and Earth*, 1952) is a controversial novel about a priest who gathers strength as he struggles with the many conflicts of life. Beginning in 1955, Coccioli, following an Italian tradition that extends from Marco Polo to Giovanni Papini and Gabriele D'Annunzio, chose to write in French rather than in Italian.

Alberto Moravia (1907-1990), the son of a Jewish agnostic from Venice and a Catholic mother, is without question the dominant figure of postwar fiction. His first novel, *Gli indifferenti* (1929; *The Indifferent Ones*, 1932; also known as *The Time of Indifference*, 1953), was published at his own expense and was an instant success. It was rightly interpreted as an indictment of the bourgeoisie and an exposé of the corrupt social situation that allowed Fascism to develop. This novel, which remains one of his most important works, contains most of the themes seen in his later works and would be his last explicitly ideological novel until *Il conformista* (1951; *The Conformist*, 1951). The novel was made into a film by Bernardo Bertolucci in 1969.

While it is often claimed that Moravia is a founder of neorealism (because of his reportorial scrutiny applied to the hypocrisies of the middle classes), such a claim conflicts with his undeniably strong existentialism. If *La ciociara* (1957; *Two Women*, 1958) can be called neorealistic because of setting, characterization, subject, and a certain idealism represented by its protagonist, his next novel *La noia* (1960; *The Empty Canvas*, 1961), must be recognized for its return to a philosophical, almost Sartrean emphasis.

Seeking to avoid Mussolini's censors, Moravia turned to indirect modes of expression, cloaking his stories in satire and Surrealism; nevertheless, *La mascherata* (1941; *The Fancy Dress Party*, 1952) was personally censored by Mussolini, and by 1943, Moravia was forced to flee his home in Rome with his wife, novelist Elsa Morante (1912-1985). The couple spent nine months hiding with peasants and living in a pigsty; the experience strengthened Moravia's tendencies toward Marxism and inspired *Two Women* (made into a film by Vittorio De Sica in 1960, starring Sophia Loren), about a mother and daughter's struggle to survive wartime violence.

When Moravia's characters seek reality, they usually embark on their search through sexuality, which, according to Moravia, replaced love in the modern world;

because an estranged man can find a moment's solace with a prostitute, some of Moravia's most sympathetic characters are prostitutes. (As a result of his treatment of sexual matters, the Catholic Church, in 1952, placed all of his books on its Index of prohibited works.) This is not to say that this search for sexual satisfaction has even a chance of being successful; the sexual act itself is perceived by Moravia as ugly and unnatural, and the typical Moravian character who is searching for happiness through sex meets with nothing more than failure.

Moravia is not a structural innovator, nor is he fancy with words, nor does he waste time. Wishing to expose for his readers hidden realities, which he attempts to isolate for them, Moravia's aims as a storyteller are openly didactic. Unlike most Italian novelists of the middle class, who prefer to write about the working class, Moravia is fascinated by the mores of his own class. His clinical method of analyzing character may have been inherited from Italo Svevo, and his works are saturated with passages and situations absorbed from his prodigious reading of the classics of other generations and literatures.

By the late 1950's, most everything that could be said about the wretchedness of the lower classes in Italy had been said, and a literary backlash inevitably occurred. While some awaited the appearance of a second D'Annunzio, there came to the attention of the public the ironic Calvino, with his love of fantasy from earlier centuries. Calvino, born in Cuba of Italian parents and already famous for his somewhat fablelike *The Path to the Nest of Spiders*, turned to the Renaissance and to his favorite poet, Ludovico Ariosto (1474-1533), for inspiration; like Ariosto, the author of *Orlando furioso* (1516, 1521, 1532; English translation, 1591), Calvino uses his fanciful narration to convey an implicit moral. His trilogy comprising *Il visconte dimezzato* (1952; *The Cloven Viscount*, 1962), *Il barone rampante* (1957; *The Baron in the Trees*, 1959), and *Il cavaliere inesistente* (1959; *The Non-existent Knight*, 1962) was also issued in a single volume as *I nostri antenati* (1960; *Our Ancestors*, 1980).

Also a folklorist, Calvino produced a monumental anthology of Italian fairy tales (*Fiabe italiane: Raccolte della tradizione popolare durante gli ultimi cento anni e transcritte in lingua dai vari dialetti*, 1956; partially

translated as *Italian Fables*, 1959, and completed as *Italian Folktales*, 1980) and turned to science fiction in *Le cosmicomiche* (1965; *Cosmicomics*, 1968), a collection of stories depicting a world peopled by ciphers and essences. His *Se una notte d'inverno un viaggiatore* (1979; *If on a Winter's Night a Traveler*, 1981) became one of the best-known postmodern works of metafiction and helped make Calvino the most-translated Italian writer at the time of his death.

Like Calvino, the Sicilian Ercole Patti (1904-1976) worked in a surrealistic medium. His last novel, *Gli ospiti di quel castello* (1974; the guests of that castle), tells the story of a twenty-three-year-old man who suddenly finds himself forty years older. Also breaking away from realism in a quest for hallucinatory memories of the past is Elsa Morante (1918-1985). Her masterpiece, *L'isola di Arturo* (1957; *Arturo's Island*, 1959), is the haunting recollection of a lonely adolescence rudely punctuated by a boy's awareness of his infatuation with his young stepmother and of the fact that his father is gay. Morante's language is musical, rich, and allusive, and her imagery is poetic. Her long-awaited *La Storia* (1974; *History: A Novel*, 1977) is an allegory with appeal to both Christian and Marxist readers. Set in Rome during World War II, the novel portrays death and violence as dominating human experience.

In addition to Morante, there is Natalia Ginzburg (1916-1991), the daughter of a Jewish biology professor and a Gentile mother. Married to Russian expatriate Leone Ginzburg, who was murdered by the Nazis after his arrest for editing an anti-Fascist newspaper, Ginzburg writes prose of unsentimental reminiscence, observation, and invention, often autobiographical and exhibiting a Hemingwayesque precision. Several of her works have been translated into English. Her *Lessico famigliare* (1963; *Family Sayings*, 1967; also known as *The Things We Used to Say*) is a recollection of her childhood and early adulthood and a portrait of Italy between the wars. *La città e la casa* (1984; *The City and the House*, 1987) is an epistolary novel depicting the rich variety of characters living in Rome.

The periodical *Il menabò*, founded by Vittorini and Calvino in 1959, especially encouraged writers who sought to analyze the phenomenon of Italian industrialization. Depicting the effect of technology upon humanity is the primary interest of such novelists as the Roman Ottiero Ottieri (1924-2002), Paolo Volponi (1924-1994), from Urbino, and Luciano Bianciardi (1922-1971), from Grosseto. Bianciardi, who coauthored the social inquiry *I minatori della maremma* (1956; the miners of Maremma), also wrote *La vita agra* (1962; *La Vita Agra = It's a Hard Life*, 1965), about the anxiety that develops in an idealistic intellectual who comes to the city with a revolutionary mission and is defeated by the daily grind of making a living.

Lucio Mastronardi (1930-1979), born near Milan, wrote in the experimentalist tradition of Gadda and Pasolini, drawing heavily on the Milanese and Neapolitan dialects. He was interested in the southern Italian who goes north for economic reasons and meets with undisguised prejudice from the northerners, especially in *Il meridionale di Vigevano* (1964; the southerner of Vigevano).

Also interested in the plight of the southern Italian who finds him- or herself at the mercy of the northern cities is Giovanni Testori (1923-1993), who applies his vigorous religious belief to social problems. His five-volume cycle *I segreti di Milano* (the secrets of Milan) contains his novel *Il fabbricone* (1961; *The House in Milan*, 1962), a proletarian version of William Shakespeare's *Romeo and Juliet* (1595-1596), and the stories of *Il ponte della Ghisolfa* (1958; the bridge on the River Ghisolfa), which inspired Luchino Visconti's film *Rocco e suoi fratelli* (1960; *Rocco and His Brothers*, 1960). The film portrays the disintegration of a southern family upon contact with the industrial North. Testori's experimental fiction moves between French, English, and the Lombardy dialect spoken in northern Italy.

The zeal fostered by neorealism for examining situations with reportorial accuracy persisted into the 1960's—for example, in the social criticism of Sicilian social reformer Danilo Dolci (1924-1997) and the controversial theater criticism of enfant terrible Alberto Arbasino (born 1930), who is also the author of the best-selling novel *Super-Eliogabalo* (1969; super-Heliogabalus), which explores self-destructive power. Mario Soldati (1906-1999), a journalist and fiction writer best known for directing films, had his first success in long fiction with *Le lettere da Capri* (1954; *The Capri Letters*, 1956), a study of a poorly matched American couple in Allied-occupied Rome. A sort of Henry James in reverse, Soldati was fascinated by Americans; in 1935, he wrote *America primo amore* (America, first love), a novelist's sort of travel book destined to be influential in forming the Italian conception of the United States during those years. In *La confessione* (1955; *The Confession*, 1958), Soldati explores a young man's odyssey from the proscriptions of his Jesuit upbringing to homosexuality, and in *La busta arancione* (1966; *The Orange Envelope*, 1969), he depicts the friction of a destructive mother-son relationship.

In 1960, the most aggressive adherent of neorealism was Pasolini, who pronounced the demise of neorealism in verse that parodied Marc Antony's funeral oration for Caesar: "Friends, Romans, countrymen, lend me your ears./ I have come to bury Italian realism, not to praise it." Recalling the glorious genesis of neorealism in the light of the Resistance, Pasolini blames Lampedusa, the neo-experimentalists, and his own erstwhile friend Carlo Cassola for dealing the deathblows. The term "neo-experimentalist"—which, in the words of Olga Ragusa, refers here to the expressionistic rather than the mimetic subversive use of language in the creation of poetry—was sanctified to use by Pasolini himself and was the term adopted by the avant-garde writers who riotously convened in Palermo in 1963 and subsequently called themselves the Gruppo 63.

These writers argued that literature is essentially antirational, and they heartily rejected literary works that imitated or mirrored reality. Thus, while they accepted Gadda, Svevo, and Pirandello, they rejected Moravia, Pasolini, Bassani, Cassola, and most of the other Italian authors. Nevertheless, many of the writers belonging to the Gruppo 63 had different responses to and personal ways of experiencing the criticism they were transferring to Italy's recent narrative past. Most of the discussions took place in the monthly journal *Quindici*, which appeared in Rome in 1967. Very soon the Gruppo 63 was declared finished, and the focus became the political activity surrounding the 1968 movement. *Quindici* itself was short-lived, and the critic and writer Umberto Eco (born 1932), a member of the Gruppo 63, defined the question of whether literature should be devoted to direct political action. He proposed the criticism of culture as the only direction to take. The lively debate created a variety of literary productions that followed different routes: Some authors continued with neorealism, while others preferred a more experimental technique. Individual creativity offered various solutions, generating a profusion of interesting novels that are difficult to situate in precise categories.

Among those who pursued neorealistic models was Cassola, who was able to combine that vein with an existential motif that distinguishes his works from neorealism. After his most important novel, *La ragazza di Bube* (1960; *Bebo's Girl*, 1962), he wrote *L'antagonista* (1976; the antagonist), *La disavventura* (1977; the misfortune), and *Un uomo solo* (1978; a lonely man). Despite the criticism of him by the Gruppo 63, his novels achieved a distinct public success.

Writers often mixed the realistic flavor and the description of everyday life with an emphasis on universal human values and feelings. This was the case, for example, with Giorgio Saviane (1916-2000), who devoted most of his books to an attentive analysis of peasant culture in the Veneto region and to the values that surrounded it, particularly its religion and sense of sin. These reverberate in many of his books: *Il papa* (1963; *The Finger in the Candle Flame*, 1964), the famous *Eutanasìa di un amore* (1976; euthanasia of a love affair), and *Getsèmani* (1980; Gethsemane). More part of subaltern culture is Gavino Ledda (born 1938), whose widely read *Padre Padrone* (1975; my father, my master) recounts the narrative autobiography of a shepherd in Sardinia and who grew up under the care of a traditionally authoritarian father, the last surviving example of the disappearing patriarchal culture of the island.

THE LATE TWENTIETH AND EARLY TWENTY-FIRST CENTURIES

Writers such as the Neapolitan Michele Prisco, on the other hand, although starting in the area of neorealistic regionalism and later analyzing the static cultural situation, arrive at a novel centered on psychological analysis and introspection of characters. These themes are revealed by Prisco in *Una spirale di nebbia* (1966; *A Spiral of Mist*, 1969), which examines the decay of a bourgeois marriage; *I cieli della sera* (1970; evening skies); *Gli ermellini neri* (1975; black ermines); and *Le parole del silenzio* (1981; the words of silence).

Another novelist who cannot be neglected is Primo Levi (1919-1987), who became immediately famous with the publication after World War II of his nonfiction work *Se questo è un uomo* (1947; *If This Is a Man*, 1959; revised as *Survival in Auschwitz: The Nazi Assault on Humanity*, 1961). Levi's autobiographical first novel, *La tregua* (1963; *The Reawakening*, 1965), narrates the adventures and the return home of a group of young men after they are liberated from a Nazi concentration camp. *Se non ora, quando?* (1982; *If Not Now, When?*, 1985) is also based on the postwar chronicles of Jewish partisans fighting for the rediscovery of their dignity. Jewish characters are also at the center of his last book, a nonfiction work called *I sommersi e I salvati* (1986; *The Drowned and the Saved*, 1988).

Among the women writers who in the 1970's and 1980's made everyday life and everyday people the centers of their narratives was Lalla Romano (1906-2001), who won the Strega Prize with *Le parole tra noi leggere* (1969; light words between us). Written like a journal, this novel analyzes with psychological detail the relationship between mother and son. It began a series of narratives, which from *L'ospite* (1973; the guest) to *Ho sognato l'ospedale* (1995; I dreamt about the hospital) became increasingly dramatic. Her semiautobiographical *La penombra che abbiamo attraversato* (1964) was published in English translation as *The Penumbra* in 1999.

Quite different is the writing of Piero Chiara (1913-1986), who instead of simply describing the quiet bourgeois life of the Lago Maggiore, especially that of Luino, reverses narrative traditions with his highly sarcastic tone, sometimes reaching the grotesque. This is evident in *Il piatto piange* (1962; the kitty is short), *Il balordo* (1967; the fool), *La stanza del Vescovo* (1976; the bishop's room), *Il cappotto di astrakhan* (1978; the Astrakhan coat), and *Una spina nel cuore* (1979; a thorn in the heart).

Although the description of ordinary life dominated Italian novels of the 1970's, the ideological novel was not completely abandoned; some writers who pursued it found international fame. Oriana Fallaci (1929-2006), in her more successful stories, chooses a mixture of journalistic narrative and polemical prose to engage either in the issue of abortion, in *Lettera a un bambino mai nato*

(1975; *Letter to a Child Never Born*, 1976), or in the biography of young Greek dissident Alexandros Panagulis, in *Un Uomo* (1979; *A Man*, 1980). *Niente e così sia* (1969; *Nothing, and So Be It*, 1972) engages in the political events connected with the Vietnam War, while *Insciallah* (1990; *Inshallah*, 1992) translates into fiction stories about oppression in Beirut. *Un cappello pieno di ciliege* (2008) is a historical novel about Fallaci's ancestors.

Another genre, the detective novel, grew in popularity in the 1960's and 1970's in a very peculiar way. The detective novel assumed characteristic national forms and themes in the *giallo all'italiana*. It is important to study this genre's evolution in this period to understand its future implications in the novels of Umberto Eco. Following the tradition of Sciascia, Giorgio Scerbanenco (1911-1969) puts a fragile and sentimental detective in charge of investigating the mediocre criminality of Milan (*I milanesi ammazzano di sabato*, 1969; the Milanese kill on Saturday). What is at stake in Scerbanenco's novels is not the aristocratic murder of Arthur Conan Doyle's stories but the violence and the frustration of crime among the lower classes.

Carlo Fruttero (born 1926) and Franco Lucentini (1920-2002) exploited literary consumerism by creating novels that would easily attract readers. In their cowritten novels, such as *La donna della domenica* (1972; *The Sunday Woman*, 1973), *A che punto è la notte* (1979; at what stage is the night?), and *Enigma in luogo di mare* (1991; *An Enigma by the Sea*, 1994), murder is central, but the detective novel plot is enriched by a number of characters with peculiarities and problems. The team's last novel together (both also wrote separately) was *I nottambuli* (2002).

This genre reached one of its most interesting peaks with Eco's best seller *Il nome della rosa* (1980; *The Name of the Rose*, 1983), which sold about five million copies around the world. Eco explained the formidable success of the book by attributing it to the formula he used, that of the detective novel imbued with historical facts and erudite citations, creating a postmodern mixture that attracted readers of every nationality. William of Baskerville, the astute detective and semiotician of *The Name of the Rose*, in the end fails to solve the murders he was hired to investigate, while the murderer kills

himself and burns the building—the library—at the center of the diabolic plot.

Eco demonstrated with his four following novels that *The Name of the Rose* had not been a fluke. With *Il pendolo di Foucault* (1988; *Foucault's Pendulum*, 1989), Eco returns to the detective novel, but this time he sets the action in the Italian cultural sphere of the 1980's and surrounds the murders with the aura of conspiracy inherent in the actions of secret orders such as those of the Templars and the Rosicrucians. In *L'isola del giorno prima* (1994; *The Island of the Day Before*, 1995), Eco abandons the detective genre in favor of historical fiction, following Manzoni's legacy but portraying the state of mind, memories, and hallucinations of a young man shipwrecked just off an island in the seventeenth century. Roberto, longing to reach the island that stretches in front of him but unable to swim, dreams and creates possible worlds in which his fantasies and fears are played out, including his desperate love for the beautiful Signora. In *La misteriosa fiamma della regina Loana* (2004; *The Mysterious Flame of Queen Loana: An Illustrated Novel*, 2005), the main character is an antiquarian book dealer who loses his memory.

No writer of Eco's generation equaled his international success, but the productions of different kinds of novels in the late twentieth century enriched the Italian literary sphere. Gesualdo Bufalino's *Diceria dell'untore* (1981; *The Plague-Sower*, 1988) achieved much popular and critical success. Bufalino (1920-1996) was unknown at the time his book was published and was already past sixty years old, but the way in which his book narrates the events surrounding war victims who are enmeshed in the degradation of a sanatorium in Sicily is fresh. Bufalino's admirable style, sometimes elaborate, sometimes crystal clear, always has the effect of a personal and precious testimony of human debasement. Although still admirable, his later books, *Museo d'ombre* (1982; museum of shadows), *Argo il cieco: Owero, I sogni della memoria* (1984; *Blind Argus: Or, The Fables of Memory*, 1988), and *Tommaso e il fotografo cieco* (1996; *Thomas and the Blind Photographer*, 2000), did not enjoy the same level of success.

Alberto Bevilacqua (born 1934) is another writer and film director who became extremely popular in Italy in the second half of the twentieth century. Although his writing style was often under attack, he first was noted in the 1960's with the novels *La Califfa* (1965; *Califfa*, 1969) and the Campiello Prize-winning *Questa specie d'amore* (1966; this type of love). Enriched by flashbacks, memories, anticipations, and dreamlike events, Bevilacqua's novels sometimes appear verbose and excessive. When he writes about his hometown, Parma, however, he achieves his most sincere results, as in *La festa parmigiana* (1980; celebration in Parma), *Curioso delle donne* (1983; curious about women), or *Donna delle meraviglie* (1984; the woman of wonders).

Two novelists very different from Bevilacqua are Giuseppe Pontiggia (1934-2003) and Ferdinando Camon (born 1935). Pontiggia relates a journalistic account of the events of contemporary times in a clean and readable style, but not without interpreting and situating the stories in a dreamlike zone, as in *Il giocatore invisibile* (1978; *The Invisible Player*, 1988), *Il raggio d'ombra* (1983; ray of shadow) and *La grande sera* (1989; *Born Twice*, 2003), winner of the prestigious Strega Prize. Camon, on the other hand, began by writing about the people of his own area, the Veneto region, and linguistically reproduced the musicality of their way of speaking. His fictional memoirs form a trilogy: *Il quinto stato*, (1970; *The Fifth Estate*, 1987), *La vita eterna* (1972; *Life Everlasting,* 1987), *Un altare per la madre* (1978; *Memorial*, 1983). He later moved to the realistic novel, turning his analysis to introspective and psychological aspects of relationships, as in *La malattia chiamata uomo* (1981; *The Sickness Called Man*, 1992), *La donna dei fili* (1986; the woman of threads), and *Il canto delle balere* (1989; the whales' song).

Women also became more prominent as writers in the last decades of the twentieth century. Many, following the legacy of Sibilla Aleramo, chose to focus on the rights of women through the heroines of their novels. Dacia Maraini (born 1936), inspired by history and historical figures to critique the condition of women, made her debut in the 1960's with the novels *La vacanza* (1962; *The Holiday*, 1966), *L'età del malessere* (1963; *The Age of Malaise*, 1963), and *A memoria* (1967; by heart). She is best known, however, for her novels *Storia di Piera* (1980; story of Piera) and, especially, *La lunga vita di Marianna Ucrìa* (1990; *The Silent Duchess*, 1993), which won the Campiello Prize. She won the

1999 Strega Prize for *Buio* (1999; *Darkness*, 2002), a collection of short stories.

Another feminist writer is Gina Lagorio (1922-2005). After *La spiaggia del lupo* (1977; the wolf beach), in which she followed the itinerary of a young woman toward emancipation, she published *Tosca dei gatti* (1983; Tosca of the cats). In this novel, Lagorio portrays the loneliness of a common middle-aged widow, whose heroism consists of her being able to evoke the best qualities in the people who surround her; she is similar to Michele, the main character of Lagorio's next novel, *Golfo del paradiso* (1987; the gulf of paradise). Like Maraini, Lagorio turns to history in search of exemplary heroines. In *Tra le mura stellate* (1991; within starred walls), for example, she remembers Countess Lara, also a writer; in *Il bastardo* (1996; the bastard), Lagorio relates the love affairs and the vicissitudes of Don Emanuel of Savoy.

Isabella Bossi Fedrigotti (born 1948) found in her family's home a wealth of historical documents referring to the Italian Risorgimento and used them as sources for her novels. *Amore mio uccidi Garibaldi* (1980; my love, kill Garibaldi) and *Casa di guerra* (1983; house of war) are directly inspired by her interest in historiography. She achieved national fame with *Di buona famiglia* (1991; of a good family), winner of the Campiello Prize, in which two sisters from high society spend their time imagining opposite lives. Fedrigotti has published eleven books, including *Il primo figlio* (2008). Other popular women novelists include Francesca Duranti (born 1935), also a winner of the Campiello Prize, for *Effetti personali* (1988; *Personal Effects*, 1993); Paola Capriolo (born 1962), whose novels include *Vissi d'amore* (1992; *Floria Tosca*, 1997), *La spettatrice* (1995; *The Woman Watching*, 1998), and *L'amico invisibile* (2006); and Susanna Tamaro (born 1957), whose *Va' dove ti porta il cuore* (1994; *Follow Your Heart*, 1994) was an international best seller and the single best-selling Italian book of the twentieth century. A sequel, *Ascolta la mia voce* (listen to my voice), was published in 2006.

Countless Italian novelists critique—and have critiqued—society, often through developing in their stories a nostalgia for a lost age. Carlo Sgorlon (born 1930) shows that in a computer age, human beings have an even greater need to narrate and listen to stories. In *Il trono di legno* (1973; *The Wooden Throne*, 1988), he explores the value of writing, and his writing vocation, through the stories of an old carpenter. In *Gli dei torneranno* (1977; the gods will come back) his focus is on the courageous people (to which he belongs) of the Friuli region in northern Italy, who react to natural disasters with a peculiar strength. In later novels, including *La conchiglia di Anataj* (1983; Anataj's seashell), *L'armata dei fiumi perduti* (1985; *Army of the Lost Rivers*, 1998), and *Il caldèras* (1988; the coppersmith), he writes about the victims of history who have been cheated and beguiled by society. In *Il regno dell'uomo* (1994; the kingdom of man) and *La malga di Sîr* (1997; the "malga" of Sîr), Sgorlon focuses once again on the everyday lives of the common people of Friuli.

The same belief in the capacity of literature to restore lost values is shared by Raffaele Crovi (1934-2007). Crovi passes from the political interests manifested in his first novel, *Il franco tiratore* (1968; the sniper), to the denunciation of technology in *Il mondo nudo* (1975; the naked world), and finally arrives at descriptions of his own personal experiences and the formulation of his creed in his next two novels, *La convivenza* (1985; living together) and *Le parole del padre* (1991; the words of the father).

Giorgio Montefoschi (born 1946) prefers to transfigure reality in a dreamlike atmosphere. In *La terza donna* (1984; the third woman) and *La felicità coniugale* (1982; happiness in marriage), he takes on the fundamentally abstract concepts of love, time, and existence; he also examines interpersonal relations, especially between husband and wife. Other works include *La sposa* (2003; the bride), winner of the Mondello Prize, and *Le due ragazze con gli occhi verdi* (2009; the two girls with green eyes).

In *Da Verga a Eco* (1989), a study of contemporary Italian novels, Angela Ferraro identifies writers whose fiction implicitly denies the possibility of narration. That is, they wish to deconstruct the novel, choosing to reveal secret narrative mechanisms by showing the contradictions and the inconsistencies of stories. Among these writers is Luigi Malerba (1927-2008), who in *Salto mortale* (1968; *What Is This Buzzing, Do You Hear It Too?*, 1969) chooses the detective novel format but subverts it by manifesting different points of view and multiple narrators: The detective, the murderer, and the sus-

pects are all named Giuseppe. Similarly, in *Il pianeta azzurro* (1986; blue planet), three different narrators recount the same story, but they continuously contradict themselves.

Antonio Tabucchi (born 1943) belongs to this same group of writers of metafiction. His *Notturno indiano* (1984; *Indian Nocturne*, 1988) presents a narrator occupied in his search for a lost (or nonexistent) friend. Two discourses are revealed in which the roles are inverted, and the friend searches for the narrator. This disrupts all literary conventions, resulting in the disenchantment of the reader. The same technique is used in Tabucchi's next novel, *Il filo dell'orizzonte* (1986; *The Edge of the Horizon*, 1990), in which linear narration becomes circular; the detective strongly resembles the murdered victim discovered in the beginning of the book. Tabucchi won the Compiella Prize for *Sostiene Pereira: Una testimonianza* (1994; *Pereira Declares: A Testimony*, 1995), a thriller about a newspaperman working under Fascism. His other works available in English translation include *Si sta facendo sempre più tardi: Romanzo in forma di lettere* (2001; *It's Getting Later All the Time*, 2006) and *Requiem: Uma alucinação* (in Portuguese, 1991; in Italian as *Requiem: Un'allucinazione*, 1992; *Requiem: A Hallucination*, 1994).

Italian novels of the late twentieth and early twenty-first centuries reflect on the nature of the text. They also are intent on the implicit deconstruction of the subject. The challenge to narrative structure and the fragmentation of the individual subject do not seem to impair the ongoing proliferation of themes in these novels. On the contrary, modern Italian authors reveal creative ways of approaching the loss of tradition and an optimistic view of the subject's possibilities.

Jack Shreve; Cristina Farronato
Updated by Cynthia A. Bily

BIBLIOGRAPHY

Arico, Santo L., ed. *Contemporary Women Writers in Italy: A Modern Renaissance*. Amherst: University of Massachusetts Press, 1990. Collection of essays dedicated to exploring the works of Italian women writers, including Elsa Morante, Natalia Ginzburg, Lalla Romano, Gina Lagorio, Dacia Maraini, and Oriana Fallaci.

Bondanella, Peter, and Andrea Ciccarelli, eds. *The Cambridge Companion to the Italian Novel*. New York: Cambridge University Press, 2003. Describes the development of the Italian novel from the seventeenth through the twentieth century. Explores major themes common among novelists and discusses works by several important writers.

Brand, Peter, and Lino Pertile, eds. *The Cambridge History of Italian Literature*. New York: Cambridge University Press, 1996. This first substantial history of Italian literary culture written in English provides a comprehensive survey of the literature. Excellent overview of Italian literature.

Caesar, Ann Hallamore, and Michael Caesar. *Modern Italian Literature*. Cambridge, Mass.: Polity Press, 2007. Chronological survey of Italian literary culture, beginning with the eighteenth century, to the creation of modern Italy between 1816 and 1900, to the twentieth and twenty-first centuries.

Cervigni, Dino S., ed. *Italy 1991: The Modern and the Postmodern*. Chapel Hill: University of North Carolina Press, 1991. Contains an analysis of Italian contemporary literature, with particular references to what characterizes the modern and postmodern in the works of the Italian writers of the late twentieth century.

Gordon, Robert S. C. *An Introduction to Twentieth-Century Italian Literature: A Difficult Modernity*. London: Duckworth, 2005. Discusses many of the important writers and works of Italian literature and examines the central motifs and movements of the modern Italian novel.

Marotti, Maria Ornella, ed. *Italian Women Writers from the Renaissance to the Present: Revising the Canon*. University Park: Pennsylvania State University Press, 1996. Collection of essays, written by eminent scholars of Italian, which centers on the twin themes of canon formation and canon revision in Italian women's literature from the Renaissance through the late twentieth century.

Marrone, Gaetana, Paolo Puppa, and Luca Somigli, eds. *Encyclopedia of Italian Literary Studies*. Boca Raton, Fla.: CRC Press, 2007. A two-volume reference work with more than six hundred entries covering the major writers, works, themes, movements, and genres.

Japanese Long Fiction

The earliest text in Japan that shows essential characteristics of long fiction is the *Kojiki* (712 C.E.; *Records of Ancient Matters*, 1882, 1968). Presented to the Japanese imperial court shortly after the establishment of the first permanent capital in 710 C.E., in what is now called the city of Nara, *Records of Ancient Matters* was compiled from narratives that traditional storytellers handed down through generations. The text combines history and myth. The graphemes, or written characters, used to record the text are Chinese. Because there was no independent Japanese writing system at the time, the Chinese characters used to transcribe *Records of Ancient Matters* were employed sometimes to project the semantic sense of their Chinese meaning and sometimes to convey the phonetic value of Japanese proper nouns, elements of song, and passages of incantation.

EARLY YEARS

Japanese long fiction in its formative aspects and for much of its tradition of nearly thirteen centuries may be treated basically as a recitative form, derived from the human impulse to tell a story, sing a song, do a dance, or paint a picture. As such, it may be readily related to the development of narrative prose elsewhere. In Japan, as in China, India, and Persia, however, the narrative, or recitative, mode became interpenetrated with both lyric and dramatic modes of projection. Thus, fiction and poetry, story and song, drama and recitation were frequently mixed. This was already true of the earliest texts, *Records of Ancient Matters* as well as the *Nihon shoki*, or *Nihongi* (720 C.E.; *Chronicles of Japan*, 1896), which was also presented to the court early in the Nara period; and the early eleventh century court romance *Genji monogatari* (c. 1004; *The Tale of Genji*, 1925-1933), by Murasaki Shikibu (c. 978-c. 1030), all of which combined narrative and lyric modes of representation. Poetic elements were harnessed to augment the narrative, as in long Chinese fiction and as discussed by Anthony C. Yu, the translator of *Xiyou ji* (pb. 1952; also known as *Hsi-yu chi*; *The Journey to the West*, 1977-1983), by Wu Chengen, in that book's volume 1 introduction.

Typically, the lyric element in traditional Japanese long fiction served to project a character or person's state of mind or emotion, and the narrative element provided description, something like a pattern inscribed on a vase or embroidered on a cloth background. A sense of drama and immediacy came from dialogue, which is found in the earliest examples of Japanese narrative prose.

Narration and dialogue in *Records of Ancient Matters* and in the Bible, for instance, afford a useful comparison. Both texts are third-person narratives. In the preface to *Records of Ancient Matters*, however, the storyteller is identified as O no Yasumaro (I, Yasumaro), whereas in the Bible, the reportorial voice remains anonymous. Although such a view is admittedly speculative, these two widely separated traditions from eastern and western Asia may conceivably be linked by oral traditions that span the entire Eurasian landmass, which from prehistoric times was inhabited by various nomadic peoples. Indeed, such oral traditions may even have been transmitted into the New World with the migrations of people across what is now the Bering Strait and down the land corridors of North America.

Accordingly, concepts such as specificity and universality may be employed in analyzing Japanese long fiction: The first of these concepts makes Japanese long fiction uniquely Japanese; the second guarantees general intelligibility and translatability. For example, the personal names of the procreative deities that appear in *Records of Ancient Matters*, Izanagi and Izanami, the male and female figures of the land-creating myth in the text, require familiarity with the Japanese cultural code in order to take on meaning, but their function allows readers everywhere to understand their role in a theogonic story of creation.

Although *Records of Ancient Matters* may be discussed in terms of its mythological, historical, or religious significance, both it and the companion work, *Chronicles of Japan*, deserve close attention as the earliest recorded texts that allow readers to investigate the roots of Japanese long fiction. In terms of physical size, they make up generous one-volume editions in modern movable-type format, whether in the original Chinese script, modern Japanese, or English. The question of fictionality, however, needs some qualification. A reader who expects fully rounded characters and a sense of individual growth will surely be disappointed. Other fictional elements, nevertheless, can readily be identified. These may be classified as structural, on one hand, or semantic, on the other. For example, putative conversations, which are embedded in a narrative framework, may be treated as a fictional element of a structural nature. The following passage provides an example:

> "This bird's cry is ominous. It must be shot to death."
>
> As soon as she thus advised him, Ame-no-waka-hiko took the bow of hagi wood and the deer-slaying arrows and shot the pheasant to death.

The narrative voice and the storyteller's, or reciter's, frame may be defined as structural rather than semantic; they provide shape and form rather than referential meaning to the narrative.

By contrast, many episodic units in *Records of Ancient Matters* involve adventures, interpersonal relationships, human activities as well as their consequences, the passage of time, descriptions of settings, and the attribution of feeling to characters. Such units may be analyzed as fictional elements of a semantic nature; the sequence in book 1, chapters 17 to 37, known as the Izumo sequence, which tells how a new land was subdued and pacified, represents a case in point.

THE TALE OF GENJI

Thus, both myth and folklore may be seen as sources of long fiction in Japan. Later, in *The Tale of Genji*, by Murasaki Shikibu, which describes the career of Prince Genji and two generations of his progeny as well as the society in which they lived, examples abound. To mention only one example, in the last ten chapters of *The Tale of Genji*, water spirits derived from Japanese mythology appear to be personified as female characters. Indeed, this most widely admired part of the text acclaimed as the supreme masterpiece of Japanese literature may be read as an extended allegory of female water spirits who invite the love of human men and who pass away like water flowing swiftly in its course from mountain springs to the salty sea, leaving behind sad memories.

The lyric, or poetic, element in Japanese long fiction is exemplified by its function in *The Tale of Genji*. Distributed throughout the narrative are nearly eight hundred examples of thirty-one-syllable poems known as *waka* or *tanka*. Sometimes these poems furnish the germ for a situation or mood that is then developed in the text; at other times, a verse recapitulates emotions that a character experiences, summarizing a situation and serving as a distillation of human feeling. More of these short poems appear in *The Tale of Genji* than in the shortest of the imperial anthologies of such verses, which were compiled between the tenth and fifteenth centuries under court auspices.

It is no wonder, then, that by the twelfth century in Japan, poets and critics expressed great admiration for *The Tale of Genji*, not so much because of the story and plot as because of the role of the poetry in the tissue of the text. The poet and critic Fujiwara Shunzei (1114-1204), for example, taught that familiarity with the tale was essential to every poet's education. To him, the individual episodes together with the verses with which they were integrated conveyed the essence of various aspects of love, of the human response to the beauty of nature, and of the poignancy of human situations such as suffering, old age, and death. All these features may be subsumed under the classical Japanese exclamatory word *aware*, which in a nominative sense became *mono no aware*, a term used in the vocabulary of criticism and aesthetics to suggest great sensitivity and a range of powerful human feeling, especially with regard to objects and "things."

Besides its sensitivity, *The Tale of Genji* came to exemplify another classical Japanese aesthetic quality, *miyabi* (courtly elegance), which exerts a soothing and civilizing influence. In large measure because *The Tale of Genji* survived through centuries of social upheaval and civil war, literary and artistic culture became irrevocably embedded in the fabric of Japanese culture. To Shunzei and successive generations of critics, *The Tale of Genji* remained a handbook for poets.

In yet another way, *The Tale of Genji* manifests a characteristic of traditional Japanese long fiction. This relates to connections between what may be termed "icon" and "logos"—picture and word. Unlike in England, where as late as the eighteenth century there existed a great tradition of literature with virtually nothing "that could be called a native tradition of painting," as Ronald Paulson observes in *Book and Painting* (1982), Japan, as *The Tale of Genji* reveals, saw word and picture develop hand in hand.

Within the text itself, word descriptions could be projected by means of visual terms: When a young boy, as if especially dressed for the occasion, walked out among flowers early on a misty summer day, his trousers wet with dew, and picked a morning glory, the narrative relates, "He made a picture that called out to be painted." Already by the time *The Tale of Genji* was written, there existed a pictorial tradition that accompanied such fictional narratives. Chapter 17 of the tale, "A Picture Contest," describes in fictional terms how word and picture were connected. In fact, *The Tale of Genji* may be seen as a confluence of literary and iconographic systems, in which iconocentric and logocentric aspects of the human imagination are combined and integrated in a fresh and appealing way. The tradition of combining picture and word continued virtually through modern times. Successive editions of *The Tale of Genji* are marvelously illustrated, and other novels and romances are similarly illuminated. Even now, in long fiction published serially in newspapers, illustrations retain a prominent place.

By way of contrast, early English novels had little connection with illustrations. As Paulson points out, in the European tradition, word came first and image followed, whereas in Japan, picture and story emerged together; icon might even take primacy over logos. In the twelfth century, an edition of *The Tale of Genji* already existed in the form of *e-maki* (illustrated scrolls) that combined literary text and painted scenes in a harmonious way. Later, a system of complex iconographic conventions developed, as Miyeko Murase describes in *Iconography of "The Tale of Genji"* (1983). The illustrator's pictorial imagination was often regarded as deserving credit equal to that of the author, especially in a kind of short Japanese chapbook that foreshadowed modern comic books.

Long or short, any fictional configuration that employs language as its principal medium needs two basic elements. The first of these is structural, involving narrative techniques and devices. The second is semantic and involves the extended units or episodes that relate to human feeling. In *The Tale of Genji*, much of the sense of universality and psychological realism that amazes many modern readers may be traced to episodes that depict basic human relationships in terms of dyads and triads.

As the basis for all simple and complex relationships between two people, various sorts of dyads may be analyzed. One common kind is a competitive dyad. This is best characterized by Genji and his long-standing companion Tō no Chūjō. Similar in age as well as social station and growing up together, the two men are fond of each other and resemble each other in many ways, sometimes being virtually indistinguishable. As the people around them make incessant comparisons between them, rivalry develops, leading in time to animosity. Eventually, in chapter 33, a degree of reconciliation takes place, as if to suggest restoration of a pristine harmony. Other dyads, too numerous to mention in a brief survey, figure in the tale. The dyadic unit may be traced throughout the course of Japanese long fiction, exemplifying the type of semantic configuration that guarantees translatability.

A further example may be drawn from *Nansō Satomi hakkenden* (1814-1842; Satomi and the eight dogs), by Kyokutei Bakin (1767-1848). In this long, historical romance of several thousand pages, one male dyadic relationship is especially reminiscent of that between Genji and Tō no Chūjō. Shino and Gakuzō, two of the eight heroes (all of whom have emblematic and symbolic canine connections), grow up together and develop a lifelong friendship, reflecting a universal literary phenomenon known variously as doubling, twinning, and splitting, as R. Rogers describes in *A Psychoanalytical Study of the Double in Literature* (1970). Similarly, the two women Yōko and Komako in the highly acclaimed novel *Yukiguni* (1935-1937, 1947; *Snow Country*, 1956), by Yasunari Kawabata (1899-1972), form a female dyadic relationship.

In *The Tale of Genji*, certain dyads involving women are characterized by rancor or jealousy. Two characters, the Rokujō lady and Lady Aoi, one loved by Prince Genji and the other married to him, came to be celebrated in drama and painting as well as in prose fiction as archetypes of destructive female jealousy. Other women in

The Tale of Genji, such as Murasaki and the Akashi lady, to mention the most exemplary case, barely avoid falling into such a destructive and futile relationship.

Another kind of dyad in *The Tale of Genji* touches on incest. Bonds between men and women that would normally be considered taboo are treated in various ways in *The Tale of Genji*. The boldest exploration of the incest theme involves Prince Genji and his stepmother, Fujitsubo. Prince Genji's later marriage to one of his nieces, the Third Princess, would be regarded in the West as incestuous, as would that of Genji's son, Yūgiri, to his cousin, Kumoinokari. Modern Japanese writers of fiction, whether short or long, from time to time continue to construct situations that remind Western readers of the ancient Greek story of Oedipus and Jocasta. The presence of incest in the literature of virtually all societies suggests a universal recognition of its existence and of the emotional strain to which such relationships give rise.

Another extended semantic confrontation skillfully treated in Japanese long fiction and particularly in *The Tale of Genji* involves triads. Surely the relationship most often depicted in world literature, such triangles may be broken down into three component dyads, each of which overlays the other two. In a relationship of this sort, people experience a mixture of joyous and painful emotions. Negative feelings and tragic consequences may come from the need, as in Ukifune's case toward the end of *The Tale of Genji*, to decide to which of two rival lovers a woman ought to grant her affections. Unable to make the decision, Ukifune first attempts suicide and then becomes a nun.

Turning one's back on the world of love gives rise to an independent theme, that of renunciation. Especially during the Middle Ages, under the influence of Buddhism, the idea of renouncing the world and taking religious orders was often treated in long Japanese fiction.

Within the Japanese tradition, *The Tale of Genji* stands out as a compendium of themes that give life to the extended episodes and sequences serving to make up narrative structures. One that reflects universal appeal is a man's search for a perfect woman or, conversely, a woman's quest for a dependable and loving mate. In Prince Genji's case, such a search stems from the early loss of his own mother and his admiration for Fujitsubo, his father's later consort and in effect his own stepmother. This admiration leads to a secretive love affair and to the birth of a son believed by the world to be the Emperor's but who in reality is Genji's.

Love in *The Tale of Genji* and elsewhere in Japanese long fiction involves the idea of substitution. Genji's father, the Emperor, finds Fujitsubo as a substitute for his lost love, Genji's departed mother. Genji, in turn, takes Murasaki as a replacement for the unattainable Fujitsubo, and so on. Tamakazura, a woman who appears in chapter 22, emerges as a substitute for the Lady of the Evening Faces, whose life was snuffed out in chapter 5 under mysterious circumstances.

In the last part of the tale, one of the main characters is Kaoru, Genji's putative son, who is in fact the offspring of a clandestine affair between Genji's young wife of his later years, the Third Princess, and the son of Tō no Chūjō, Genji's best friend. For Kaoru, two women, Nakanokimi and then Ukifune, become substitutes for Oigimi, who prefers death to the uncertainty of a love commitment. Behind such complex interconnections lies a relatively simple repertory of basic patterns and situations. In Kawabata's modern novel *Snow Country*, for example, the hero, Shimomura, and two women, Yōko and Komako, form such a triangle.

Long fiction would be tedious if narrative situations were always limited to people interacting in twos and threes. As in the orchestration of musical instruments in symphonic productions, long fiction often involves scenes of mass action, festive occasions, or public mourning when many people come together. Japanese long fiction is no different in this regard from that of other traditions. By virtue of the irony and contradictions that life involves, effective portrayal of human feeling and emotion may result from juxtaposing a collective atmosphere of gaiety, auspiciousness, or victory to a private mood of sadness, distress, or death. In Western literature, for example, Ulysses' victory at Troy is counterpointed by Achilles' defeat and death.

Often, *The Tale of Genji* involves a similar kind of irony. In chapter 9, the Kamo festival, a gala religious and social event something like the Mardi Gras, with a grand procession of people vying to display their finery, represents a case in point. Against this backdrop of collective joy, the tragic rivalry between the Rokujō lady and Lady Aoi reaches its climax, resulting in Aoi's death by the ghostly possession of the Rokujō lady's living spirit as Aoi is giving birth to Genji's son, Yōgiri. That such techniques are exploited in the tale stands as a tribute to the author's artistic mastery and as a testimony that Japanese long fiction from early times attained a high degree of subtlety and sophistication.

By the eleventh century, a broad repertory of literary ideas and themes was available. A literary language, albeit with a relatively narrow vocabulary, and a writing system that combined a phonetic syllabary of Japanese invention with the semantic resources of Chinese characters allowed compositions to be recorded, disseminated, and preserved. These and other developments enriched literary culture, remaining part of the tradition to the present day, as J. Thomas Rimer points out in *Modern Japanese Fiction and Its Traditions* (1978).

THE HEIKE MONOGATARI

About one hundred and fifty years after the appearance of *The Tale of Genji*, Japanese society entered a period of turmoil that ushered in cataclysmic social and political change. One of the works of long fiction that grew out of the collective experience of the age was the epic chronicle known as the *Heike monogatari* (*The Heike Monogatari*, 1918-1921; also known as *The Tale of the Heiki*, 1975, 1988). As an account of the rise and fall of the Taira family in the late twelfth century, *The Heike Monogatari* took form gradually in the following century. Originally intended for recitation to the musical accompaniment of the Japanese lute, it stands out in form and impact over the centuries since as the nearest equivalent in Japan to a great epic. Written in a heightened style and dotted with about one hundred short lyric verses, the text, like *The Tale of Genji*, has much of the tone of narrative poetry. Although *The Heike Monogatari* is now admired chiefly for its literary qualities, it was formerly read for its historical content; the same was true with *Records of Ancient Matters*. This point suggests that in the tradition of Japanese long fiction, certain texts exemplify the idea of telling a tale that combines elements of both make-believe and truth.

Above all, the unifying force in *The Heike Monogatari* is the passage of time; various transitional seg-

ments and expressions suggest the temporal flow of events. In turn, this theme is related to the philosophical concerns of Buddhism. In the epic, both lyric descriptions and the development of character are subordinated to karma, or the concept of fate, the vanity and transitoriness of life, and the value of abandoning ordinary pursuits in favor of monasticism. A profound moralistic bent also runs through *The Heike Monogatari*, which can be traced to the Chinese influence of Confucianism. Confucian moralism appears in the form of an emphasis on intense personal loyalty; an unstinting spirit of service that links master and retainer, husband and wife, parent and child in *The Heike Monogatari* is also a product of Confucian values. The interplay of the Buddhist and Confucian worldviews imparts a sense of poignancy and a tone of tragedy to *The Heike Monogatari*, lending it an elegiac quality. Modern Japanese critics have observed that, in a text that superficially focuses on armed conflict, the reader finds surprisingly few descriptions of actual bloodshed.

Narrative techniques and conventions that came to maturity in *The Tale of Genji* are found in *The Heike Monogatari*. This partly explains why it has endured as a sourcebook for long Japanese fiction. Approximately two hundred episodes make up the epic's twelve numbered books and the culminating book known as the *Kanj-no maki*. Each book is divided into twenty or more episodes, suggesting units suitable for oral reading or recitation to the accompaniment of the Japanese lute.

Matsumura Gekkei (1752-1811; also known as Goshun), a prominent haiku poet and painter, chose the image of a spotted fawn with a humped back, a furry tail like that of a rabbit, and a face as meek as that of a mouse to illustrate a famous and representative passage of *The Heike Monogatari*. The episode tells of an emotionally charged moment in the life of a former empress who lost her child in the conflict between the two rival clans that figure in the book. The former empress is forced to take refuge in a lonely mountain temple amid the fallen leaves of the surrounding oak trees. Hearing a rustling sound, as if someone were approaching her retreat, she asks her companion to see who is coming and to signal her if she should hide. Discovering that the sound was only that of a deer passing by, the lady, her eyes filled with tears, recites a poem: "What visitor dares/ Tread this rocky mountain path/ To see my lady?/ It was only a young stag/ That rustled the fallen oak leaves,/ Only a deer is stirring,/ As it passes on its way."

More than episodes involving heroic action in battle or tragic and untimely death, the description of the frightened empress's forlorn existence as a nun in a remote temple among moss-covered rocks, frost-laden bushes, and withered chrysanthemums characterizes the mood of the text and the tone of the best Japanese long fiction.

The Heike Monogatari was composed in a noble style that mixes Chinese characters with Japanese phonetic symbols, in contrast to *Records of Ancient Matters*, which was written completely in Chinese characters. Stylistically, the language of *The Heike Monogatari* represents a literary forerunner of the modern mixed-colloquial style of Japanese narrative prose.

Recognition that beauty is related to frailty and perishability lends an aesthetic coherence to the tale, making the text more than merely a series of episodes describing the fall of the Taira clan. Read and reread, *The Heike Monogatari* still functions as part of the living culture of Japan. In early modern times, popular authors such as Bakin drew on it for inspiration. Several later novelists have reworked it, the most notable being Eiji Yoshikawa (1892-1962), author of *Shin Heike monogatari* (c. 1940; *The Heike Story*, 1956). Films and television shows based on the original tale continue to appear, and every year thousands of young people still visit places made famous by the story.

THE THIRTEENTH THROUGH THE SEVENTEENTH CENTURIES

About two hundred works of narrative prose fiction produced in Japan between the thirteenth and the seventeenth centuries are extant into the twenty-first century. Besides those that have survived, some two hundred other titles remain in name only, being mentioned in anthologies, catalogs, and the like, largely from the Middle Ages. Most of these titles, however, are short fiction, retold versions or elaborations of parts of *The Tale of Genji* and *The Heike Monogatari*. In time, the best of these became *yfkyoku*, or librettos, for Japanese theatrical performances known as Nō drama, or *mai-no-hon* (literally, dance books), as texts for singing and chanting a form of

medieval ballad were called. James T. Araki, in *The Ballad Drama of Medieval Japan* (1964), discusses this aspect of Japanese literature, which combines the art of narration or recitation with that of performance.

Similarly, a tradition of historical and literary texts analogous to *The Heike Monogatari* developed. Accounts of events organized in chronological fashion and composed of narrative units with partly fictional material were compiled by monks and scribes. One such title is the *Taiheiki* (1318-1367; English translation, 1959, 1961). Now valued primarily as a historical sourcebook, it is also praised for its narrative technique and rhetorical excellence.

In addition to such chronicles, there were also literary tales, consisting mostly of short fiction typically preserved in illustrated manuscripts. A third kind of compilation also deserves attention. From the ninth century on, there appeared collections of anecdotal tales and narratives called *setsuwa* (explained stories), the earliest of which were written in Chinese. Around the beginning of the twelfth century, one such work was recorded in a mixed style of Chinese characters and Japanese syllabary foreshadowing that of *The Heike Monogatari*. This work was the *Konjaku monogatari* (pb. 1972; partial translation, *Tales of Times Now Past*, 1979). W. Michael Kelsey's *Konjaku monogatari-shū* (1982) discusses this massive collection of thirty sections and 1,039 titled items, which in total length exceeds *The Tale of Genji*.

Quite different from elegant court literature, the *Konjaku monogatari* and its successors reflect a primitive oral impulse. In later Japanese long fiction, whenever a suggestion of salaciousness, a strain of ribald humor, or a flight of farfetched fantasy occurs, the influence of anecdotal tales and narratives is usually at work. Modern authors such as Ryūnosuke Akutagawa (1892-1927), best known for his short stories about fantastic, grotesque, and macabre topics, turned to such sources for inspiration, as Beongcheon Yu points out in *Akutagawa: An Introduction* (1972).

JAPANESE LONG FICTION AFTER THE SEVENTEENTH CENTURY

With the reestablishment of an era of peace in the early seventeenth century following a period of civil war, conditions became conducive to literary production. The total number of titles of narrative prose preserved from the seventeenth to the mid-nineteenth centuries amounts to more than ten times as many as those dating from the eighth through the sixteenth centuries. In the twentieth century, Japanese literary historians developed a complex generic terminology for narrative prose. As authorship of long fiction gradually proliferated, the distinction between practical, historical, philosophical, dramatic, and poetic compositions, on one hand, and works of narrative prose, on the other hand, became somewhat more clear-cut.

Moreover, new titles of long fiction—as distinct from newly printed editions of old titles previously available only in manuscript—increased in number. Three essential conditions were met: First, authors had the leisure to write; second, readers had time to read, and third, a system of dissemination evolved with the spread of woodblock printing and illustration. By the end of the early modern, or Edo, period (1600-1868), Japanese long fiction was read and admired not only in urban centers such as Edo (modern-day Tokyo), Kyoto, and Osaka but also in the remote countryside, as Bakin pointed out, wherever small boats could pass or people would walk the mountain pathways between distant villages.

By the late eighteenth century, new titles of long and short fiction alike were appearing every year in woodblock printed editions. Typically, these editions were sold in soft paper covers in sets of as many as five or more thin volumes. Only the longer items deserve to be classified in the category of fiction discussed here. Besides the connections with court romances, literary tales, chronicles, and anecdotal narratives (including permutations and pastiches), one new influence deserves to be pinpointed. Literary and colloquial fiction from China had a fresh impact on Japanese long fiction.

Such an influence can be traced to the publication of a collection of short tales, *Otogi bōko* (1666; the storyteller's servant). The compiler, Asai Ryōi (1612-1691), acknowledged indebtedness to a collection of Chinese tales, *Jian deng xin hua* (late fourteenth and early fifteenth centuries; new tales for lamplight). Thereafter, Chinese fiction had a growing impact on literary and intellectual life in Japan, extending to virtually every author of long fiction. The influence of Chinese fiction in early modern Japan foreshadowed the impact of

Western literature on Japanese long fiction after the late nineteenth century. Without the attention that Japanese authors of the Edo period paid to Chinese literature, especially literary and colloquial fiction, Japanese authors and readers could hardly have been as receptive to new literary currents from the West.

Publication of *Kōshoku ichidai otoko* (1683; *The Life of an Amorous Man*, 1964), by Ihara Saikaku (1642-1693) marked a significant event in the history of Japanese long fiction. First, the idea of engaging dialogue and lively conversation amid a realistic urban setting imparted a fresh impulse to long fiction in Japan. For decades afterward, other authors emulated Saikaku, as Howard Hibbett observes in *The Floating World in Japanese Fiction* (1959) and as Blake Morgan Young discusses in *Ueda Akinari* (1982). While seeming to break with traditions and conventions of the past, Saikaku actually extended them in new and original directions.

The very title of *The Life of an Amorous Man* evokes the world of *The Tale of Genji* and other texts of the courtly tradition. More obvious, the fifty-four episodes in *The Life of an Amorous Man* match the number of chapters of *The Tale of Genji*. Finally, just as Prince Genji gathered around him a large number of female companions, Saikaku's hero, Yonosuke, during the fifty-four years of his life, "enjoys" 3,742 women.

Instead of the world of the aristocrat or the warrior, however, *The Life of an Amorous Man* deals with the newly prosperous townspeople. By writing of their life in a realistic vein, Saikaku broke with the traditions of earlier narrative prose. Nevertheless, epoch-making though *The Life of an Amorous Man* was, the influence of the past should not be overlooked. Besides allusions to *The Tale of Genji*, examples of indebtedness to the rhetoric and conventions of traditional poetry abound. Not so much a direct response to the aristocratic *waka*, the text is derived from the more popular and plebeian *haiku*. Although a number of Saikaku's titles have been translated into English, there is no successful and complete version of either of Saikaku's most widely acclaimed works of long fiction. The second of these, *Kōshoku ichidai onna* (1696), was translated by Ivan Morris as *The Life of an Amorous Woman* (1963). As Bakin appreciatively commented in 1811, "Writing about daily things that people see with their own eyes and moreover to do this in an amusing manner began with Saikaku."

In its day, *The Life of an Amorous Man* struck readers as a shocking and salacious book, especially emerging as it did from the milieu of the townsperson. Its plebeian origins in a class-structured society prevented its consideration on a par with titles in the aristocratic tradition, such as *The Tale of Genji*. Until almost the middle of the twentieth century, even in modern, movable-type editions, certain passages of Saikaku's works were regarded as inappropriate for study in schools and universities, mainly because free love between men and women in the context of a neo-Confucian code of morality was held to be a threat to the social fabric. Wine, women, and wealth were regarded as the three temptations that men must resist.

The hero of *The Life of an Amorous Man*, Yonosuke (whose name suggests an allegorical meaning, man-of-the-world or worldly man), far from eschewing contact with women, has an insatiable craving for female companionship and for sexual intercourse. Exactly as young Prince Genji in his seventh year is described as having been taken to visit the women's quarters in the imperial palace and presumably initiated to sexual experience, young Yonosuke in his seventh year is also introduced to coitus, his partner being an older and experienced maidservant. The choice of such an improbably young age may stem from the traditional Confucian injunction that by the age of seven, boys and girls should begin to lead segregated lives.

Until the modern era and the transformation of Japanese literature under influence from the West, long fiction continued to be integrated with lyric modes of expression, and Saikaku's case was no exception. His training and apprenticeship as an author were in *haikai* (amusing) poetry, a popular, plebeian, and comparatively light form of *renga* (linked verse), which was a communal variety of chain poetry that developed in aristocratic circles and gradually spread during the Middle Ages to all classes of society. It was from such circles that *haiku* emerged.

No wonder, then, that each of the fifty-four short chapters, or sections, of *The Life of an Amorous Man* begins with a rhetorical flourish reminiscent of the all-important opening verse of a chain poem. In terms of structure, each segment of the text in a cryptic and anecdotal manner describes scenes from stages of the hero's life. Depiction of the manners and customs of people that Yonosuke meets enriches the texture. Human foibles and contradictions are exaggerated in a dry and humorous manner. Each part ends in a witticism, paralleling the conventions that govern linked verse. Thus, Saikaku's text, like earlier representative examples of Japanese long prose, amounts to a composite form with rhetorical elements common to both prose and poetry. Not until the late nineteenth century was this pattern broken.

The weakness of Saikaku's style, as well as that of his successors and imitators, lies in excessive abbreviation of an underlying expository narrative; the result is something like rice without enough gluten to hold the grains together. Initiated readers can exercise their imaginations and complete the tale as they please, but outsiders often experience frustration at trying to discern the basic outline. Thus, Saikaku's prose has a relatively low level of translatability. To the present day, certain kinds of Japanese long fiction still have the same weakness, creating difficulties for translator and reader alike.

Japanese long fiction of the traditional epoch culminated in Bakin's *Nansō Satomi hakkenden*. An illustrated historical romance in nine sections and 181 chapters, *Nansō Satomi hakkenden* describes the fortunes of a warrior family. Falling in defeat during the fifteenth century, the Satomi family's fortunes are revived with the aid of eight "dog" warriors and a host of other loyal retainers and dedicated citizens. Such a restoration may be seen as a paradigm both for the Meiji Restoration of 1868 and for Japan's dramatic revival following World War II. Literary themes both reflect and feed social ideals. Art both follows and shapes nature.

Nansō Satomi hakkenden, which was the longest literary work hitherto written in Japan, reflected Bakin's personal outlook and particularly his deeply moral sensibility, tempered by compassion and a belief in human dignity. Loyalty, filial piety, and the restoration of hard-pressed or destitute samurai families like his own were Bakin's main themes. In *Nansō Satomi hakkenden*, as well as his other full-length historical romances, special attention to Chinese and Buddhist philosophy was tempered by belief in the efficacy of the Japanese gods and a concern for language and style. Bakin's work represents a culmination of a Japanese literary response to nearly fifteen centuries of Chinese cultural influence, dating from the introduction of the Chinese writing system in about the fifth century.

As a pivotal work in the tradition of Japanese long fiction, *Nansō Satomi hakkenden* illustrates Japanese transformation of Chinese literary conventions into a rich and distinctive body of long fiction (to say nothing of the other literary forms, such as poetry and drama). With this precedent, Japanese long fiction of the modern era could accommodate powerful outside influences from the West without losing a sense of its own identity.

Structurally, *Nansō Satomi hakkenden* may be divided into three parts. Chapters 1 through 14 describe the establishment of the Satomi clan in what is today the Chiba area near modern Tokyo; chapters 15 to 131 tell how the eight dog warriors assemble under the Satomi banner; and finally, chapters 131 to 181 relate the struggle of the Satomi clan against the combined forces of other powerful clans and opponents, who contest their right to live in peace and enjoy prosperity.

After the Satomi victory, the eight dog warriors accompany a clan embassy to the traditional capital of Kyoto to pay respects to the Emperor as well as the Shogun and to ask that Fusehime (the daughter of the Satomi patriarch and a kind of sacrificial victim who offered herself to the cause of familial restoration) be recognized as a goddess. A shrine is built in her honor because of the many miracles she performed. At the end, each of the eight warriors is married to one of the patriarch's eight daughters. The Satomi clan then flourishes in peace for generation after generation until the virtue of the founding patriarch of the clan is seemingly exhausted. Like that of the Taira clan in *The Heike Monogatari*, the Satomi glory becomes but an evanescent dream.

"When people control their desires, govern their passions, store up good and not work evil," Bakin wrote in his didactic voice as narrator near the end of *Nansō Satomi hakkenden*, "and when they show discretion in their acts, while alive they need feel no shame on earth, and after death their descendants will continue to flourish." Owing to the great virtue of the first two generations of Satomi lords, Bakin records with a flourish at the end, "The citizens of the domain remembered them and responded to their profound influence." Bakin con-

cludes with three verses, one in Chinese and two in Japanese, the last of these reflecting a conventional gesture of self-depreciation: "Like a floating weed/ Passing countless dreary hours,/ I've tried hard to write,/ But my brush may seldom touch/ Elusive words that have no roots."

Even today, when compared with their Western counterparts, most Japanese novels lack an architectonic sense of plot, tending to be episodic and notoriously lacking in overall shape and structure. This characteristic partially stems from the legacy of medieval linked verse. The early conventions of narrative recitation and the rhetorical techniques of court poetry have also played their part. Structural coherence in Japanese long fiction derives more from associations of idea and image than from well-wrought unity in a classical Western sense.

Nevertheless, *Nansō Satomi hakkenden* stands as an exception. Indeed, Bakin's long historical romances, known as *yomihon* (reading books), belong in a class of their own, distinguished by the author's close attention to plot construction and conscious technique, for both of which he was much indebted to Chinese influences. In *Nansō Satomi hakkenden*, the action includes an escape from the flaming ruins of a besieged castle (which bears comparison to a parable about a burning house found in the *Lotus Sutra*, the most widely read Buddhist holy book in East Asia). A death curse of a usurper's malicious concubine evokes ideas and imagery found in an early Chinese classic that warns against women sharing in the highest affairs of state. These are but two of the motifs from which the overall structure is generated.

Eight lost jewels from a charmed rosary—the same number as the *Lotus Sutra* has parts—foretell how eight heroes will break the sinister curse and help institute a benevolent rule. The name of the Satomi daughter, Fusehime, is written with Chinese characters suggesting "Princess of Man and Dog," the morpheme "Fuse-" (from a verb meaning to submit, to lie in wait, or to be hidden) employing a character with the "man radical" and "dog." Fusehime's fate is linked to that of a wolflike dog, Yatsufusa (Eight Patches). This canine beast, in turn, is a reincarnation of the malicious concubine of the usurper already mentioned.

Retiring into the mountains with the dog, the girl seems to become pregnant (a phenomenon inspired by Chinese accounts of a woman's miraculous conception through a beast). Fusehime thereby becomes the god-mother of eight warriors who mysteriously possess eight jewels from her rosary. She serves as their protective deity as well as that of the Satomi house.

Farfetched as such a plot might sound, within the overall form and structure of a historical romance of an allegorical nature, fantastic elements help to sustain reader interest over several thousand pages of text and add to the suggestive power of the narrative. On the one hand, a literal meaning unfolds. Scenes and situations describe an imaginative likeness of what happened in history. On the other hand, a complex allegory is revealed. Good and evil are imagined as persons who serve as emblems as well as human characters in their own right. History and make-believe are combined in an aesthetic structure that bears special comparison with texts of long Chinese fiction such as Shih Naian's (c. 1290-1365) novel *Shuihu zhuan* (possibly fourteenth century; translated by Pearl S. Buck as *All Men Are Brothers*, 1933; also as *Water Margin*) and *The Journey to the West*.

Restoration of a family that has unjustly fallen on hard times is the basic theme of *Nansō Satomi hakkenden*. Morality is described as the foundation for such a restoration. Fate in a Buddhist sense is a force ensuring that morality prevails. Good and evil are interwoven "like tangled strands of thread." Religious and ethical beliefs that people's behavior may influence fate are expressed in literary terms. Good is seen to benefit one's progeny more than oneself. Evil deeds meet punishment in one's own lifetime. Good and evil may both activate supernatural forces. Bakin accordingly expounds Confucian and Buddhist ideas that fate is linked to morality and embodies this concept in the imaginative structure of his lengthy romance.

Even in modern times, long Japanese fiction—especially in its popular manifestations—shows a strong didactic bent. Fictionalized history remains a common form of reading matter. *Nansō Satomi hakkenden* exemplifies the interpenetration of history and fiction in Japan and marks the high point of the didactic function of literature. A modern version appeared serially in one of the mass circulation daily newspapers, *Asahi shimbun*, and a critical exposition of Bakin's text by Takada Mamoru, *Hakkenden-no sekai* (1980; the world of Satomi and

the eight dogs), sold an impressive number of copies in a paperback edition.

About twenty years after the Meiji Restoration, Japanese authors of long fiction began to respond to Western literary influences. The period of modern literature began. Like that of other nations, Japanese literature, in response to various new modes of communication and cross-cultural discourse, has increasingly converged with the currents of its world counterpart. By the time the twentieth century began, the chief impetus in Japanese long fiction involved a concerted effort to break with older traditions. This force has had both a positive and a negative side. In a positive sense, Japanese writers embraced Western literary movements and theories, trying to model their works on particular European or American examples.

Although the result of turning to Europe and America was imitative in many cases, the impulse to reach out and adapt Western literature to native needs was basically constructive. Western literature brought fresh vitality to traditions and conventions that reached back a millennium and a half. On the negative side, writers turned away from their own heritage, rejecting many native myths, archetypes, and conventions.

Tradition, however, dies hard in Japan. The conservative impulse remains strong. Albeit undergoing transformation, classical modes of long fiction and various conventions that developed alongside them have survived. Old texts regularly appear in new editions or in fresh garb, as the serial version of *Nansō Satomi hakkenden* suggests. Indeed, long fiction together with its short counterpart has emerged as the principal literary genre. Enriched by new examples introduced from the outside world and having overshadowed lyric and dramatic forms, Japanese long fiction remains indebted to an indigenous lineage of narrative prose that goes back to *Records of Ancient Matters*, *The Tale of Genji*, and many other predecessors.

THE TWENTIETH CENTURY

By the beginning of the twentieth century, the modern counterpart of older forms of Japanese long fiction proved to be a medium capable of dealing with the main theme of twentieth century Japanese literature—awareness of the self. Japanese writers espoused the ideology of individualism. A characteristically Japanese form of long fiction, the *shishosetsu* (literally, I novel), emerged. Concurrently, Japanese authors capitalized on newfound personal freedom to deal with topics that indicated heightened social and political awareness. One of the most famous I novels is *An'ya kuro* (1921-1937; *A Dark Night's Passing*, 1976), by Naoya Shiga (1883-1971); it was described by Edwin McClellan, the book's translator, as "an intensely private and self-centered novel," in which the "identification of the author with his hero is complete."

A widely acclaimed early twentieth century novel that deals with social problems is *Hakai* (1906; *The Broken Commandment*, 1974), by Shimazaki Tōson (1872-1943). According to Natsume Sōseki (1867-1916), a critic and widely translated author of long fiction, *The Broken Commandment* is "the first [genuine] novel of the Meiji era."

Although the I novel deserves to be seen as a manifestation of a newfound sense of individual identity, reflecting the process of Westernization, it also has connections with earlier Japanese literary genres. In addition to forms discussed previously, the *nikki* (diary) and the *zuihitsu* (miscellaneous essay) involved the concept of a private self, as distinct from that of a group, or corporate, self. Certain situations in *A Dark Night's Passing* call to mind parallels with *The Tale of Genji*. Likewise, the idea of socially engaged literature predates *The Broken Commandment*. Bakin's tales and romances, as well as the works to which they are indebted, presaged Tōson's morally committed novel. Thus, older Confucian views of literature, which stressed a didactic function, found a new direction in modern literary movements that emphasized an ideological reference.

Besides such dichotomies as old and new, native and Western, self and other, which permeate twentieth century Japanese literature, other dualities also deserve mention. For example, a split between the *jun-bungaku* (pure literature) and *taishn bungaku* (literally, mass literature or, by extension, popular literature) unavoidably implies class differences of high and low. Similar distinctions such as *gabun* (elegant writings) and *zokubun* (common writings) existed in earlier times. *The Tale of Genji* exemplifies the former. Compilations of anecdotal tales and narratives such as *Konjaku monogatari* led to

the latter. Now, the literature of court salons and of plebeian groups has been replaced by modern overtones of social or educational class. Pure literature is thought to belong to an elite level of society and mass literature to the ordinary people. Certain critics dismiss mass literature as being beneath contempt.

To be sure, most critical attention in modern Japan has been on a succession of elite writers who have dominated the literary scene. Popular writers, whose work has a strong emotional appeal and continues to capture the Japanese imagination, have been ignored if not scorned by literary scholars. One such author is Kaizan Nakazato (1885-1944), whose *Daibosatsu tōge* (1913-1941; *Daibosatsu Toge: Great Bodisattva Pass*, 1929) is a saga about a nihilistic master of Japanese swordsmanship. This novel combines elements of the Japanese narrative tradition with the humanism of Western literature. Another example is Eiji Yoshikawa's *Miyamoto Musashi* (1936; *Musashi*, 1981). A historical romance of travel and adventure about a late sixteenth and early seventeenth century warrior, the novel has been widely read in North America. Many business people believe that the book reveals important cultural and organizational traits that have helped Japan achieve its dramatic success as a leading economic power in the contemporary world.

Another popular author, Hisashi Inoue (born 1934), is a leading exponent of the Japanese tradition of satire and parody. Debunking orthodoxy and exploiting the seamy and ribald side of human life goes back to the very beginnings of Japanese long fiction; even in *The Tale of Genji*, comic scenes appear. The Akashi Lay Monk, father of the Akashi Lady, for example, is presented as a garrulous, tiresome, and eccentric person who "seemed ridiculous as he bustled around seeing to Genji's needs." Inoue's proud Gallic priest, a French teacher at S. University in Tokyo, in the best-selling novel *Mokkimpotto-shi-no ato-shimatsu* (1974; *The Fortunes of Father Mokinpott*, 1976), represents a modern counterpart. Father Mokinpott, incidentally, has been called perhaps "the first living, breathing, fully realized non-Japanese character in Japanese literature." While Inoue has devoted much of his career to writing for the theater, he continues to publish novels, including *Kirikirijin* (1982), which won the Seiun Award for Japanese science fiction.

One twentieth century author who was adept at creating both "pure" and "popular" literature was Yukio Mishima (1925-1970). His bucolic novel *Shiosai* (1954; *The Sound of Waves*, 1956) belongs to the latter category and *Kinkakuji* (1956; *The Temple of the Golden Pavilion*, 1959) belongs in the former. His tetralogy, *Hōjō no umi* (1969-1971; *The Sea of Fertility: A Cycle of Four Novels*, 1972-1974), represents an attempt to create a hybrid form of long fiction in a dazzling richness of style that might appeal to both classes of readers in Japan.

Other general points that relate to Japanese long fiction of the twentieth century include the centralization of literary activity in the capital city of Tokyo. This, too, had its earlier counterpart in literary history; the names of Japanese literary periods, such as Nara, Heian, Kamakura, Muromachi, and Edo, come from centers of political power. In this sense the modern age may be called the Tokyo period. One of the first authors to write about Tokyo and describe its people in long fiction was Nagai Kafu (1879-1959). A native of the city, he was heir to the older traditions of Edo, the former name of Tokyo. Most modern Japanese authors live and work in Tokyo or nearby cities and towns and depend upon the communications and distribution system that is centered in Tokyo.

Newspapers and serials published in Tokyo serve as a primary medium of disseminating novels. Formerly, woodblock editions of long fiction were published in serial form; for example, Bakin took twenty-eight years to finish *Nansō Satomi hakkenden*. At first, installments appeared every two or three years; later, they were issued annually. Even in the early twenty-first century, the book version of a novel often follows serialized publication in the daily, weekly, or monthly press. More than in English-speaking countries, authors are public personalities, giving them added reason for living and working in the Tokyo area. Izumi Kyōka (1873-1939), whose reputation enjoyed a revival in Japan, was one of many early twentieth century authors of long fiction whose works first appeared serially.

Another characteristic of modern Japanese long fiction involves style. Today, the colloquial language is the main medium of expression; a larger gap formerly existed between the style of literary texts and ordinary discourse. This change took place gradually and needs to be seen in the context of the entire tradition. Two stages, however, may be singled out. First, late in the nineteenth century, people searched for a suitable idiom for translating Western literature into Japanese. Futabatei Shimei (1864-1909) dominates as the author of long fiction who brought literary composition into line with everyday speech.

The second stage dates from after World War II. Between 1948 and 1952, a number of reforms in language and education took place. Meanwhile, the use of Chinese (the earliest literary language in Japan and the writing system of *Records of Ancient Matters*) declined. Study and translation of literature flourished. Virtually all the famous European and American works of long fiction became available as models for would-be writers and as a reference for readers and critics. Nowhere is there a more world-oriented literary culture than in Japan. So complex has the Japanese literary code become that any given work of long fiction may at least hypothetically involve allusions to Homer's *Odyssey* (c. 800 B.C.E.), Shikibu's *The Tale of Genji*, and Hermann Hesse's (1877-1962) *Siddhartha* (1922; English translation, 1951) in the same text. Critics of Mishima's *The Sound of Waves* have compared it to Longus's *Daphnis and Chloë*, a second century Greek pastoral romance.

Modern world literature took root in Japan primarily after the Russo-Japanese War (1904-1905). A new era in Japanese long fiction brought fame and popularity to young writers. When Japan forced Russia to sue for peace, authors, including several who remained active into the 1940's and 1950's, felt a surge of inspiration and confidence. Innovations by young writers still in their thirties hastened the break with tradition. Novelists such as Shimazaki Tōson, whose goal was to depict life as it is, without glossing over the seamier side, established the naturalistic novel.

Meanwhile, authors such as Natsume Sōseki opposed the naturalists' excesses of lurid sensationalism and thinly disguised autobiographical exhibitionism. Sōseki, especially, still holds a firm place in the Japanese reader's affections; his crisp conversational style continues to influence young writers. In *Kusamakura* (1906; *The Three-Cornered World*, 1965), he taught that the leisurely moments one devotes to art and letters offer relief from the unavoidable suffering of existence. This belief contrasted with the unrelieved gloom and despair of naturalists such as Tōson. In spite of a period of study in England, Sōseki's philosophy and theory of literature show an affinity for those of an earlier poet, diarist, and critic, Matsuo Bashō (1644-1694). However, in *Kokoro* (1914; English translation, 1941), written toward the end of his life, Sōseki, whose thought combined art for art's sake and pronounced Buddhist tenets, granted humans only three equally dreary choices: death, madness, or religion. Actually, the intellectual differences between Japanese naturalists and antinaturalists often seem small or even nonexistent.

Toward the end of the Meiji period (1868-1912) and into the Taishō era (1912-1926), writers who shared criticism of the naturalists' excesses published a periodical called *Shirakaba* (1910-1923; white birch) with serialized works of long fiction as well as other forms of literature and criticism. Humanitarian in outlook and aristocratic in temperament, the group's members included Naoya Shiga and Takeo Arishima (1878-1923). Curiously enough, the outspoken and emotional tone of Arishima's best-remembered novel, *Aru onna* (1919; *A Certain Woman*, 1978), stands at variance with his prevailing image as a quiescent, scholarly humanist of strong ethical bent.

Although the boundary between naturalist and antinaturalist now seems vague, such distinctions at least show how modern writers in Japan have tended to band together into small, independent groups and how critics, at least in Japan, continue to follow such categories. One of the leading modern writers of long fiction was Jun'ichirō Tanizaki (1886-1965). Tanizaki explored human life with daring, sensitivity, and psychological acumen; his long fiction appeals readily to Western readers, and his work has achieved worldwide recognition. His most ambitious novel, *Sasameyuki* (1943-1948, 1949; *The Makioka Sisters*, 1957), published in three volumes in Japanese, deals with such matters as the conflict between traditional ways of life and superficial Westernization. Other titles include *Kagi* (1956; *The Key*, 1960) and *Fūten rōjin nikki* (1961-1962, 1962; *Diary of a Mad Old Man*, 1965), which date from the productive last years of his life.

Taishō literature usually takes in several years of Meiji and the early part of the Shōwa era (1926 to the present). Although Japanese commentators have criticized Taishō authors for failing to transcend traditional, feudal, or nationalistic concepts, during the 1910's and 1920's a number of novels with delicately wrought detail were produced. Some writers—despite or because of their acute perception of life—shirked social responsibility and feigned moral decadence. Western readers may readily discover untranslated literary works that are at once original and part of the twentieth century Zeitgeist. Reevaluation of the contribution Taishō authors have made to the creation of a distinctly modern sensibility is comparatively recent.

Among writers whose careers began in the 1920's, Yasunari Kawabata was one of those who advanced such European causes as Futurism, expressionism, and Dadaism. Kawabata, however, developed an intuitive, subjective, sensual, and faintly decadent tone that owed as much to classical Japanese texts as to modern European "isms." Among his works of long fiction, three titles in particular stand out. In addition to *Snow Country*, the novels *Sembazuru* (1949-1951, 1952; *Thousand Cranes*, 1958) and *Yama no oto* (1949-1954, 1954; *The Sound of the Mountain*, 1970) best convey the atmosphere of Kawabata's long fiction. Kawabata was the first Japanese writer to win the Nobel Prize in Literature.

For a time in the 1920's, it seemed that leftist literature might overshadow the efforts of avant-garde writers and modernists such as Tanizaki and Kawabata. Despite the support of many established writers, however, the proletarian movement was suppressed. Some prominent leftist authors failed to survive World War II; others lived through government repression and the hardships of war, resuming literary activity after Japan's defeat in 1945.

Writers who were not on the left and who were active during the 1930's include Ibuse Masuji (1898-1993), one of the most underrated of modern Japanese novelists. His fictitious journal of the atomic bombing of Hiroshima in August, 1945, brought him well-deserved fame. A make-believe diary of a Hiroshima resident at the time of the bombing, *Kuroi ame* (1966; *Black Rain*, 1969) strikes the reader as an extraordinary interpretation of the event. *Black Rain* relates how Japanese society carried on in the wake of the atomic holocaust. The author's deep belief in the futility of war and a tone of gentle irony toward the militaristic and bureaucratic mentality permeate the book. A feature film based on the novel was made in 1989.

AFTER WORLD WAR II

Best typifying the immediate postwar period, the autobiographical novels of Osamu Dazai (1909-1948) describe a time of excruciating self-examination and extreme nihilism in Japan. In some respects, they anticipated Beat literature. *Shayó* (1947; *The Setting Sun*, 1956), about the privation and despair that an aristocratic family endures, gave birth to a new expression in the Japanese language, "setting sun people," which referred to anyone who fell from a position of comfort and prosperity to one of abject misery, much like the Heike clan at the end of the twelfth century. *Ningen shikkaku* (1948; *No Longer Human*, 1958) particularizes the gloomy postwar years in Japan.

Many other writers emerged after World War II. Paradoxically, in the same way as victory over Russia in 1905 stimulated literary activity, defeat by the Allies in 1945 led to a renaissance in literature and art as well as to economic revival. The most notable postwar author of long fiction was Yukio Mishima. Mishima may be best remembered for focusing on individuals who groped—often without success—for new directions in a fragmented, dislocated society. His characters suffer from the aftereffects of the most disastrous war in the nation's history. In microcosm, they represent a country still struggling to transform itself from an isolated and ingrown local society in East Asia to an economic and political power on the world stage. Mishima's characters' wild, bizarre, and perverse behavior contrasts with the collective ideals, restraints, and discipline that held the desperate nation to its course. In 1970, he committed seppuku, or ceremonial suicide, in the manner of the Edo-period samurai; Mishima's highly theatrical suicide was followed by Kawabata's self-asphyxiation in 1971.

While Mishima was making his reputation as a fiery young author, Fumiko Enchi (1905-1986), twenty years his senior, was exploring the experience of betrayal and sensuality with keen insight and haunting beauty. Her novel *Onnamen* (1958; *Masks*, 1983) unfolds against a background that involves the medieval Japanese theatri-cal form, No, which is still widely patronized in Japan. She published a well-received and highly praised new translation into modern Japanese of *The Tale of Genji*. Shūsaku Endō (1923-1996), one of the few Christian writers in Japan, has been compared by Western critics to Graham Greene; among Endō's many novels translated into English are *Umi to dokuyaku* (1957; *The Sea and Poison*, 1972), *Chinmoku* (1966; *Silence*, 1969), *Kuchibue o fuku toki* (1974; *When I Whistle*, 1979), and *Fukai kawa* (1993; *Deep River*, 1994).

An author representative of the immediate postwar years is Yasushi Inoue (1907-1991). Several of his historical novels have been translated into English: *Tempyō no iraka* (1954; *The Roof Tile of Tempyo*, 1975), which is set in eighth century Japan; *Tonko* (1959; *Tun-huang: A Novel*, 1978); *Furin kazan* (1953; *The Samurai Banner of Furin Kazan*, 2006); and *Aoki ōkami* (1959; *The Blue Wolf: A Novel of the Life of Chinggis Khan*, 2008). The setting for the latter is a Central Asian oasis community along the ancient Silk Road, over which desert caravans ensured connections between East and the West until navigational techniques allowed for the more dependable use of sea routes.

In the 1960's, new writers continued to appear, and postwar authors such as Kōbō Abe (1924-1993) extended their literary reputation. Abe's long fiction has been widely translated and read outside Japan. He combines a scrupulous attention to the individual's emotional state, characteristic of the best traditional Japanese long fiction, with a deft appreciation of the present human situation, in which, as Arthur Kimball wrote in *Crisis in Identity* (1973), "the outlines of one's identity may become an unreadable confusion."

Kenzaburō Ōe (born 1935), in *Kojinteki na taiken* (1964; *A Personal Matter*, 1968), probed modern youth's confrontation with sex and society. His feisty and diminutive hero, Bird, despite appearances, demonstrates that right will prevail over might, light will prevail over darkness, and order will prevail over chaos. The hero's abrupt about-face at the end has led critics to complain that the conclusion is unconvincing. Ōe was the second Japanese writer to win the Nobel Prize in Literature. His 1994 citation praised his creation of "an imagined world, where life and myth condense to form a disconcerting picture of the human predicament today." Among his works are *Man'en gan'nen no futtoboru* (1967; *The Silent Cry*, 1974), the semiautobiographical *Atarashii hito yo mezameyo* (1983; *Rouse Up, O Young Men of the New Age*, 2002), and *Chūgaeri* (1999, 2 volumes; *Somersault*, 2003).

During the 1970's, other fresh authors contributed to the vibrant state of Japanese long fiction. For example, a controversial, best-selling fantasy of sex, drugs, and violence by Ryū Murakami (born 1952), *Kagirinaku tōmeini chikai burū* (1976; *Almost Transparent Blue*, 1977), won the coveted Akutagawa Prize. By means of rich imagery and often crude language, a repellent world in an advanced state of disintegration, decay, and corruption is projected, as the author explores the tensions created by the U.S. military stationed in Japan.

THE LATE TWENTIETH CENTURY AND BEYOND

After the early 1980's, a number of shifts occurred in the attempts by younger authors in Japan to reveal in their novels a broader representation of the complexities of contemporary Japanese life. Older distinctions between "high" and "popular" fiction have been steadily breaking down. Some critics see parallels between the situation in contemporary Japan and the United States, where postmodern concerns often preempt attention from older forms of modernism.

In some ways, this trend began as early as the 1960's in Japan, when the work of two important writers attracted and sustained widespread attention. The first of these is Morio Kita (pseudonym of Sokichi Saito, b. 1927), whose lengthy novel *Nireke no hitobito* (1964; *The House of Nire*, 1984-1985) helped characterize, often with trenchant humor, the life of his family, spanning the often tumultuous years between the two world wars. Saito's father was a noted poet and psychiatrist, and the son's disguised portrait of his father is as vivid as it is compelling. Saito was one of the first to introduce elements of humor into this kind of family chronicle, although the work harbors shadows. The success of this novel helped launch the author's subsequent career as a humorist.

The second of these writers, Saiichi Maruya (pseudonym of Nemura Saiichi, b. 1925), also introduces humor into his delineation of the contemporary social scene, notably in his novel *Tatta hitori no hanran* (1972; *Singular Rebellion*, 1986). While dealing with such volatile issues as the antiwar demonstrations current at the time, the tonality of the book (particularly because of the delightful old lady who, straight from prison, enters the narrator's family to become the book's main character) is surprisingly successful in creating a relaxed, even droll atmosphere.

In this context, the tonality of Saiichi's writing is considerably different from that of, say, Ōe. Ōe may well represent the last of the significant writers in Japan to maintain this stance. Younger novelists, on the whole, tend to either withdraw into themselves to compose highly introspective fiction or turn to writing in a more hedonistic, often fanciful way, which they often define as postmodern or cutting edge. As the twenty-first century began, a spectrum of important writers were working, ranging from the modernist or postmodernist writers to those who still made at least some use of the long heritage of Japanese culture and tradition. In this sense, these writers may be said to mirror the variegated, sometimes contradictory nature of contemporary Japanese culture itself.

The cutting-edge writers in particular have taken an interest in international popular culture. The characters in their novels often live abroad, and many have foreign friends. Video, film, animation, and computer games also figure in their aesthetic. Perhaps the most widely read of these authors is Ryū Murakami, who wrote a number of best sellers, in particular *Koin rokkā beibīzu* (1980; *Coin Locker Babies*, 1995), which deals with the surprising, often grotesque adventures of two boys in the Tokyo labyrinths, abandoned and originally brought up in an orphanage. Another writer somewhat in the same vein is Eimi Yamada (born 1959), who often sets her stories abroad and who deals with controversial issues including sexuality and race. Her novel *Torasshu* (1991; *Trash*, 1994), set in New York, is both ironic and harrowing as it explores the complex relationship between the heroine, her African American boyfriend, and his son, Jesse. Yamada, who is known as Amy Yamada for her works in translation, has won nearly every important literary prize in Japan, including the Bungei Prize for *Beddotaimu Aizu* (1985; *Bedtime Eyes*, 2006).

Another writer, Banana Yoshimoto (pseudonym of Mahoko Yoshimoto, b. 1964), became well known outside Japan after the publication of the first of her twelve novels, *Kitchin* (1988; *Kitchen*, 1993), in which she first displayed the kind of heroine—at the same time both vulnerable and optimistic—that made her works so popular around the world. *Kitchin* won several prizes, sold thousands of copies, and was made into a television movie. *Hādoboirudo* (1999; *Hardboiled and Hard Luck*, 2005), a novel told as three connected stories, demonstrates the ease with which the author moved between traditional Japanese and Western approaches to storytelling.

Among those writers who make use of some of the kinds of larger concerns found in earlier modern Japanese literature is Yūko Tsushima (born 1947), the daughter of the novelist Dazai. Among her many compelling novels, *Yama o hashiru onna* (1980; *Woman Running in the Mountains*, 1991), which chronicles the travails of an unwed mother, is breathtaking for both its powerful human insights and its lack of sentimentality. Even more popular is the postmodernist Haruki Murakami (born 1949), who developed a large readership around the world. His many novels often possess the kind of laid-back characters that may seem somewhat familiar to those who know the works of the American crime novelist Raymond Carver, some of whose works Murakami translated into Japanese. In one of his later novels, however, *Nejimaki-dori kuronikuru* (1994-1995, 3 volumes; *The Wind-Up Bird Chronicle*, 1997), Murakami does touch for the first time upon Japan's role in Asia during World War II. Here, too, some of his writing shows the creation of a kind of science-fiction universe. His successful *Sekai no owari to hāoboirudo wandārando* (1985; *Hard-Boiled Wonderland and the End of the World*, 1991) creates parallel worlds that reveal an eerie dimension to commonsense understandings of contemporary urban society. *Umibe no Kafuka* (2002; *Kafka on the Shore*, 2005) is a fantasy novel combining Shintoism, popular culture, Magical Realism, and humor. His novel *Afutādāku* (2004; *After Dark*, 2007), a tale of alienation, has been translated into many languages, including Chinese, Czech, Dutch, French, Norwegian, Polish, Romanian, Russian, and Serbian.

Finally, two other late twentieth century writers reveal still closer ties to the great traditions of Japanese literature. The first of them, Yoshikichi Furui (born 1937),

a student of German literature, translated works by such significant modern writers as Hermann Broch and Robert Musil into Japanese. Furui's compelling novella, *Yōko* (1971; *Child of Darkness*, 1997), about the discovery by the narrator of a mysterious woman sitting in a ravine, reveals Furui's ability to question the very structures of human identity. These and other works support the claim that Furui is one of the most powerful writers of the entire postwar period, although much of his writing since the 1970's has been in the short-story form.

Kenji Nakagami (1946-1992) is another writer with close ties to the great traditions of Japanese literature. An acknowledged master of postwar prose, Nakagami died at a relatively young age, ending the career of one of the most powerful postwar voices. Born in a poor area of Japan known as Shingû, a port at the edge of the mountainous peninsula south of Osaka, Nakagami used the legends and history of his region, plus his own early experiences as a day laborer, to write about the basic instabilities of human nature. The most important themes in his works are the shifting, usually unarticulated relationships between humans and nature and the cruelties of racism in Japanese society. Nakagami won the Akutagawa Prize for *Misaki* (1976; *The Cape,* 1999).

The ultimate origins of fiction in Japan, as elsewhere, can be found in the human need to form interpersonal relationships and to share common experience by the use of language. Japanese long fiction reflects the continuing vitality of a prosperous nation of more than one hundred million people. For celebrated writers, the rewards are enormous, in terms of both wealth and public acclaim. Nevertheless, the current educational system places little emphasis on creative writing, which as an occupation is generally discouraged, making it all the more of a marvel that so much energy and attention is devoted to writing.

Even with the notoriety of Japanese poetry and drama, long fiction is most likely that country's greatest contribution to world literature. Japanese fiction of all eras commands the attention of students of literature worldwide, not because of its supposedly exotic qualities but because of its technical artistry and its attention to everyday life and common people.

Leon Zolbrod; J. Thomas Rimer
Updated by Cynthia A. Bily

BIBLIOGRAPHY

Bowring, Richard. *Murasaki Shikibu: "The Tale of Genji."* New York: Cambridge University Press, 2004. Lucid and thoughtful guide to Japan's greatest classic novel, *The Tale of Genji*. Examines the cultural context in which the novel was written, the novel's language and style, and its impact on the literature that followed.

Gessel, Van C. *Three Modern Novelists: Sōseki, Tanizaki, Kawabata*. New York: Kodansha International, 1993. Three brief but balanced biographical accounts of the lives and works of three modern masters of Japanese fiction.

Kato, Shuichi. *A History of Japanese Literature: The First Thousand Years*. New York: Kodansha International, 2002. Sweeping historical survey that begins with the seventh century, examines the major works of Japanese literature since that time, and also examines Chinese and Western influences on the literature.

Kawana, Sari. *Murder Most Modern: Detective Fiction and Japanese Culture*. Minneapolis: University of Minnesota Press, 2008. First full-length study of Japanese detective fiction written between the two world wars.

Keene, Donald. *Dawn to the West: Japanese Literature of the Modern Era—Fiction*. Vol. 3 in *A History of Japanese Literature*. New York: Columbia University Press, 1998. Massive study of the fiction produced since the Japanese enlightenment of the nineteenth century. Individual chapters feature major writers, discuss important advances in technique, and highlight key issues dealt with by many writers. Other volumes examine earlier centuries. Keene is a renowned scholar of Japanese literature and culture.

Lewell, John. *Modern Japanese Novelists: A Biographical Dictionary*. New York: Kodansha International, 1993. Excellent reference work, with plot summaries, useful critical opinion, and bibliographies of works available in English translation.

Richie, Donald. *Japanese Literature Reviewed*. New York: ICG Muse, 2003. This introduction to Japanese literature includes reviews of works by more than one hundred writers. Coverage from *Tale of Genji* and literature of the Edo period to the end of the twentieth century.

Rimer, J. Thomas. *A Reader's Guide to Japanese Literature*. 2d rev. ed. New York: Kodansha International, 1999. Guide to all periods of Japanese literature, with extended discussions of more than fifty works, mostly long fiction. Includes bibliographies of translations and secondary works.

Rubin, Jay, ed. *Modern Japanese Writers*. New York: Charles Scribner's Sons, 2001. Twenty-four critical essays, covering the eighteen Japanese writers most frequently translated into English.

Latin American Long Fiction

Inherent in the ideology underlying the conquest and colonization of Latin America were certain factors that severely curtailed the development of the novel there. Notable among those factors was the Roman Catholic Church's view that the novel form was harmful to morals, coupled with the vision of Latin America as a mission field, from which such negative influences could and should be excluded. Thus, in 1531, it was forbidden for books such as *Amadís de Gaula* (1508; *Amadis of Gaul*, partial translation, 1567, 1803; better known as *Amadís*) to be imported.

While it is true that from 1580 on, all sorts of fiction did enter the region—and it even appears that a sizable portion of the first edition of Miguel de Cervantes' *Don Quixote de la Mancha* (1605, 1615) came to the New World—the law is indicative of an attitude that, in the Spanish-speaking regions, successfully prevented until 1816 the production of anything that might properly be called a novel.

In Brazil, in contrast, the attempt to exclude the form was not so successful. It was, in fact, a churchman who produced Brazil's first novel. Four years after the publication of John Bunyan's *The Pilgrim's Progress* (1678, 1684), the Jesuit Alexandre de Gusmão (1628-1724) published *História do predestinado peregrino e seu irmão Precito* (1682). Also in the allegorical mode is the *Compêndio narrativo do peregrino da América* (1728), by Nuno Marques Pereira (1652-1728), and Teresa Margarida da Silva e Orta's *Aventuras de Diófanes* (1752). These attempts to turn the form to the service of morality left no progeny, and when the Brazilian novel returned, it was in the fullness of the Romantic movement.

The outstanding Brazilian novelist of the Romantic period was José de Alencar (1829-1877), whose early work consists of a series of sentimental novels of adventure, dealing particularly with the idealized "Indian," modeled on Chateaubriand's "noble savage," who predominated throughout Latin American literature in this era. Alencar's more mature works, including *Lucíola* (1862), *Iracema* (1865; *Iracema, the Honey-Lips: A Legend of Brazil*, 1886), and *Senhora* (1875; *Senhora: Profile of a Woman*, 1994), are more concerned with the portrayal of urban society, as is the notable *Memórias de um sargento de milícias* (1854; *Memoirs of a Militia Sergeant*, 1959), by Manuel Antônio de Almeida (1831-1861), which concentrates on Rio de Janeiro. At the same time, Bernardo Guimarães (1825-1884) was dealing with nationalistic themes.

The nineteenth century

The first novel of Spanish America, as well, appeared within the politically liberal orientation of nascent Romanticism. With the accession of the Bourbons to the Spanish throne in 1700, considerable French influence began entering the colonies, and the Enlightenment left its mark on their literature.

José Joaquín Fernández de Lizardi (1776-1827), known as the Mexican Thinker, was fundamentally a pamphleteer and essayist who traveled with a portable printing press, turning out material in support of the war of independence. His first novel, *El periquillo sarniento* (1816; *The Itching Parrot*, 1942), was a statement of reason at the same time that it led to a current of Romantic novels in the region. Although the picaresque genre in Spain had been an instrument of the Church, useful in the preaching of morality, Lizardi's picaresque novel is brutally anticlerical even while its entertaining narrative is marred by lengthy sermons. This tendency toward essay in the novel perhaps had its roots in the missionary traditions of the colonies and has continued to the present day, particularly in the fiction of Mexican writer Carlos Fuentes. In the Mexican novel, there is also a tendency to employ circular structures, which are already visible in Lizardi's work. Each episode presents the reader with a turn of the Wheel of Fortune, as the protagonist becomes successful only to end in desperate straits again.

The vast majority of Latin America's nineteenth century novels appeared in the second half of that century, although one notable work spans nearly a half century in itself: *Cecilia Valdés* (first part 1839, completed 1882; *Cecilia Valdés: A Novel of Cuban Customs*, 1962), by the Cuban author Cirilo Villaverde (1812-1894). Like nearly all fiction following the attainment of independence by most of Latin America (although not yet by

Cuba), *Cecilia Valdés* is Romantic in character; following the example set by Lizardi, Villaverde's is a political Romanticism, relatively unconcerned with nature.

The Latin American short story has its roots in the celebrated narrative "El matadero," by Esteban Echeverría (1805-1851). Another hard-to-categorize work from the same era, *Vida de Juan Facundo Quiroga* (1845; *Facundo: Life in the Argentine Republic in the Days of the Tyrants: Or, Civilization and Barbarism,* 1868), by Domingo Faustino Sarmiento (1811-1888), exercised considerable influence on the novel for decades to come. A combination of biography, novel, and essay, it establishes with its subtitle, *Civilización y barbarie,* the theme of the struggle between the relatively sophisticated, often Europeanized, cities of Latin America and the developing, "barbaric" outlying areas, be they the Argentine pampas or the Venezuelan llanos. In general terms, the novel of the nineteenth century tends to contrast the refinement of Europe with the crudeness of the New World. The sons of Brazilian planters, for example, received the finest education that Europe could offer, often returning to bewail their homeland's lack of culture.

The most prominent of a number of novels written in opposition to the Argentine dictator Juan Manuel de Rosas was *Amalia* (first part 1851, second part 1855; *Amalia: A Romance of the Argentine,* 1919), by José Mármol (1817-1871), who learned his craft from Sir Walter Scott and Alexandre Dumas, *père.* In his struggle against injustice, Mármol's Daniel Bello is the prototype of the Romantic hero, while the heroine, Amalia, is representative of European refinement surrounded by New World vulgarity. In this era, many novels were serialized in newspapers, among them *Amalia,* which exhibits the episodic character of this type of composition.

Probably the most widely read Latin American novel of the nineteenth century was *María* (1867; *María: A South American Romance,* 1890), by Jorge Isaacs (1837-1895). At this stage, the Romantics were generally more concerned with nature, and the heroine of Isaacs's novel appears to be almost a projection of the landscape of Colombia's Cauca Valley. The tale is typical of the novels of its day, involving an encounter of soul mates who are separated and then reunited at the conclusion, only to learn that fate has made their marriage impossible. In this

case, the couple are brother and sister by adoption, and her death prevents their marriage. A variation on the theme appears in *Cumandá* (1879), by the Ecuadoran Juan León Mera (1832-1894): After the lovers have overcome many obstacles, the proposed marriage is prevented by the revelation that the couple are brother and sister, separated in infancy. In *Cumandá,* Mera lays the foundations for the modern novel of protest against the inhuman treatment of Indians, concerning whom he has solid documentary knowledge.

In 1889, the same type of novel, overlaid with European sentimentalism and full of fateful coincidences and melodramatic surprises, including the usual impossible marriage of siblings, appeared in Peru under the title *Aves sin nido (Birds Without a Nest: A Story of Indian Life and Priestly Oppression in Peru,* 1904). The author, Clorinda Matto de Turner (1854-1909), wrote a preface within the tradition of the moralistic essay, declaring that her purpose in writing was to exhibit the unjust treatment of the Peruvian Indian and argue for the marriage of priests. It is a prime example of the nineteenth century Romantic novel, far more concerned with theme than with technique. Nevertheless, it exercised a powerful influence in Latin America.

Cuban-born Gertrudis Gómez de Avellaneda (1814-1873) published *Sab* (English translation, 1993) in 1841, with a black slave as protagonist, anticipating by nearly a century the handful of novels that would attempt to set black people's situation in relief. Also significant is her *Guatimozín* (1846; *Cuauhtemoc, the Last Aztec Emperor: An Historical Novel,* 1898), a well-researched historical novel dealing with the conquest of Mexico, one of the two most important historical novels of the century—the other being *Durante la reconquista* (1897), by Alberto Blest Gana (1831-1920).

French literary influences gradually gained momentum throughout Latin America in the nineteenth century, and critics are often hard-pressed to identify the influences on a given writer or work. While Romantic tendencies underlie nearly all the novelistic production of the region until 1880 or so, writers were beginning to feel the influence first of Honoré de Balzac and Émile Zola and then of the Parnassian and Symbolist movements, and to experiment with them. In Brazil, *Inocência* (1872; *Innocencia: A Story of the Prairie Regions of Brazil,*

1889), by Alfredo de Escragnolle Tarmay (1843-1899), represents something of a transition from the dominance of Romanticism to realism in that country. The well-known *Martín Rivas* (1862; English translation, 1916), by Blest Gana, is illustrative of his desire to become the Balzac of Chile, although at its base it is still a Romantic work rather than a realistic one. It has, in fact, been termed the best example of Romantic realism in Latin America, and it exhibits the typical polarity that is so evident in the novels of this period: city against country, reality against appearances, good characters against evil ones.

The Mexican writer Ignacio Manuel Altamirano (1834-1893) attempted to raise the quality of the Latin American novel by urging his fellow authors to read widely to gain a more universal literary vision, something that Lizardi and others had already been doing. Although an Indian himself, and desirous of making the novel more realistic, Altamirano tended to produce romantically stereotyped characters, Indian or otherwise, and failed to plead the Indian's case strongly. His *Clemencia* (1869; mercy) and *La Navidad en las Montañas* (1871; *Christmas in the Mountains*, 1961) are worthy novels, but his considerable ability to tell a good adventure story is best displayed in *El Zarco: Episodios de la vida Mexicana en 1861-1863* (1901; *El Zarco, the Bandit*, 1957), in which he attempts to break with Romanticism yet employs as an omen an owl in the tree where his title character is to be hanged. There are two couples, one positive and the other negative, the one illustrating what is good for Mexico and the other illustrating what threatens to destroy it.

About 1880, the call of writers such as Altamirano bore fruit, for there was at that time a considerable increase in both the quantity and the quality of Latin American fiction, corresponding, perhaps coincidentally, to the emergence of naturalistic tendencies. These were mixed with what remained of Romanticism and realism, the best of which led to the regionalist novel as the writer became increasingly preoccupied with accurately describing the circumstances on the land. *Costumbrismo*, as the term indicates, involves the more or less superficial portrayal of types and customs in a given region. The term *criollismo* is related, but the *criollista* writer is more deeply involved in the subject of study. In the last two

decades of the century, these tendencies became mixed with the emerging *Modernismo*, whose most powerful impetus was provided by the publication in 1888 of *Azul*, a collection of short stories and poems by Rubén Darío (1867-1916).

Modernismo in the Spanish-speaking countries (in contrast to the modernism of Brazil) was a truly indigenous movement, the roots of which, however, were in French Parnassianism and Symbolism. *Modernismo* is a movement characterized by refined sensibilities, even hyperaestheticism, and in contrast to *criollismo*'s desire to come to grips with Latin American reality, its aim in general was to rise above it in a manner of escape. It left its mark on prose fiction in a greater concern on the part of the writer for sound artistic accomplishment and in an increase in the use of imagery in prose style, issuing ultimately in some novels that must be read almost as poetry because of the intensity of their language.

In the Spanish-speaking countries, the leading exponent of naturalism is probably Eugenio Cambacérès (1843-1890), whose *Pot-pourri* (1881; *Pot-Pourri: Whistlings of an Idler*, 2003) and *Música sentimental* (1884), while clearly influenced by Zola, still exhibit realistic tendencies. In Mexico, the most prominent of those deeply influenced by naturalism was Federico Gamboa (1864-1939), a careful artist whose most important works are *Suprema ley* (1896) and *Santa* (1903). The latter was more successful than any Mexican book up to its time and strongly influenced the later prominent Mexican novelist Mariano Azuela (1873-1952). Gamboa's principles are drawn from French naturalism, but his work serves as a bridge between the Romantic realism of the nineteenth century and the regionalism of the twentieth century. Another Mexican novelist, Emilio Rabasa (1856-1930), was the first to address the social issues leading to the Mexican Revolution of 1910, and as such anticipates the novel of that revolution. The Cuban Carlos Loveira (1882-1928) produced a late example of the naturalist novel, *Juan Criollo* (1927), whose protagonist, reared in a family of higher social class, is nevertheless condemned to a life of misery by his lower-class birth.

In Brazil, the most prominent writers in the realist-naturalist camp were Aluísio Azevedo (1857-1913), whose best works are *Casa de Pensão* (1884) and *O cortiço* (1890; *A Brazilian Tenement*, 1926; also as *The*

Slum, 1999), and Adolfo Caminha (1867-1897), whose *Bom crioulo* (1895; *Bom-Crioula: The Black Man and the Cabin Boy*, 1982), concerning homosexuality in the Brazilian navy, produced a national scandal. Among the Brazilian writers whose novels defy classification are Euclydes da Cunha (1886-1909), whose *Os sertões* (1902; *Rebellion in the Backlands*, 1944), regarded as one of the masterpieces of Brazilian literature, deals with war in the backlands and is similar to Domingo Faustino Sarmiento's *Facundo* in its mixture of genres, and Raul Pompéia (1863-1895), whose *O Ateneu* (1888) employs a boys' boarding school as a microcosm of society.

Equally difficult to classify is the person generally considered to be Brazil's greatest writer, Joaquim Maria Machado de Assis (1839-1908), whose principal model was Laurence Sterne. Machado de Assis ignored naturalism to explore the psychological dimensions of alienation. Although he is considered a pioneer of psychological realism, his major concern is not with character development but with novelistic technique, so that his work both fits into the emerging aestheticism of the Spanish-speaking countries and anticipates the later Latin American novel's preoccupation with language as such, in the handling of which he is an acknowledged master. His first work of excellence is *Memórias póstumas de Brás Cubas* (1881; *The Posthumous Memoirs of Brás Cubas*, 1951; better known as *Epitaph of a Small Winner*, 1952), but it was only with *Quincas Borba* (1891; *Philosopher or Dog?*, 1954; also as *The Heritage of Quincas Borba*, 1954) and *Dom Casmurro* (1899; English translation, 1953) that his greatness was generally recognized.

A significant novel later retrieved from critical oblivion was important in the development of technical excellence in the late nineteenth century: *Mitío el empleado* (1887), by the Cuban Ramón Meza (1861-1911), is characterized by what has been described as a picaresque *costumbrismo* similar to that of Emilio Rabasa. It exhibits a Wheel of Fortune structure somewhat similar to that of *The Itching Parrot*, as the hero experiences a rise, a fall, and finally what is presumably a permanent rise in Mexico. The work's picaresque qualities, rooted in the Cuban *choteo*—the Trickster-like practice of mocking everything—anticipates a persistent humorist theme in the modern Spanish American novel.

Known as one of the foremost *Modernista* poets, the Colombian José Asunción Silva (1865-1896) produced *De sobremesa* (1896; *After-Dinner Conversation: The Diary of a Decadent,* 2005), a lesser-known novel important for the understanding of the direction the genre was taking around the end of the nineteenth century. Rooted in the aesthetic decadentism that was one of the primary characteristics of urban Latin American culture at that time, it presents a protagonist whose values are emphatically those of the *Modernistas*, just as the earlier Colombian writer Jorge Isaacs's Efraín (in Isaacs's novel *María*) is the quintessential Spanish American Romantic hero. The *Modernista* concern for aesthetic values as opposed to those of pragmatism is delineated in a long essay by the Uruguayan José Enrique Rodó (1871-1917). This work, *Ariel* (1900; English translation, 1922), is perfectly placed for psychological impact at the opening of the new century. In it, Rodó insists that the developing culture of Latin America, while taking advantage of the admirable advances of technology in North America, reject its materialistic values in favor of those of the spirit. *Ariel* profoundly influenced an entire generation of Latin American intellectuals.

THE EARLY TWENTIETH CENTURY

In the novel at this time, there is an increasing commitment to technical quality, along with an attempt at a more skillful analysis of the regions in which the authors lived. Regionalist tendencies were accentuated in the first decades of the twentieth century by the relative isolation of national capitals from one another, and added to the geographical isolation was the almost worshipful attention paid by authors in each region to what was taking place in Europe, so that a writer in Lima, Peru, and one in Santiago, Chile, might each be far more aware of the literary scene in Paris than in the other's city. Therefore, the regionalist tendency became strong within a general *criollista* current.

One of the most skillful of the regionalist writers was Tomás Carrasquilla (1858-1940), whose novels, including *Frutos de mi tierra* (1896), *Grandeza* (1910), *La marquesa de Yolombó* (1928), and *Hace tiempos* (1935), are set in the city and countryside of Colombia's Antioquia, a region of difficult access before the advent of air travel. Correspondingly, the circumstances of

Carrasquilla's characters are static, as is generally the case in the early regionalist novels of Latin America. Characterization for Carrasquilla is largely by way of regionalist speech.

In Chile, Alberto Blest Gana had a successor in Luis Orrego Luco (1866-1949), whose *Casa grande* (1908) was the first novel to analyze in depth the life of the Chilean upper classes. Orrego Luco's concern, that of the psychological penetration of a social sphere that interests him, using a calm, controlled, polished language, is typical of Chilean fiction, from its inception to the present day, and is especially evident in the work of José Donoso (1924-1996). Orrego Luco is something of a transitional figure, standing between nineteenth century realism and twentieth century *criollismo*. Another transitional figure is Manuel Gálvez (1882-1962), who straddled the gap between Romanticism and *Modernismo*, producing books of unbridled subjectivism, a quality associated with both schools. As typically Argentine as Orrego Luco was Chilean, Gálvez sought to analyze his nation's reality in terms of his own ongoing spiritual crisis, to produce an opus illustrative of his and Argentina's anxiety and hope for the future. His *La maestra normal* (1914) is a prime example of the *costumbrista* novel, but in its agonized introspection it anticipates the novels of Eduardo Mallea (1903-1983) as well as the call for social reform and women's rights.

Among the Brazilian regionalists, the most prominent was Lima Barreto (1881-1922), who, like Machado de Assis, was black. Unlike Machado de Assis, however, Barreto reacted violently against the racism that he felt even in his relatively easygoing country, becoming a militant anarchist. His bitter parodies of the Brazilian mainstream caused the critics of his day to ignore him.

Out of the wave-interference pattern of sometimes contradictory literary movements, there emerged some novels of clearly definable *Modernista* character, while others whose *Modernista* aesthetic is discernible, such as *El embrujo de Sevilla* (1922; *Castanets*, 1929) and *El gaucho florido* (1932), by the Uruguayan Carlos Reyles (1868-1938), betray the melodramatic character of the old Romanticism. Among the better *Modernista* novelists was the Chilean Augusto d'Halmar (1882-1950).

In 1902, Manuel Díaz Rodríguez (1868-1927) published *Sangre patricia* (English translation, 1946), in

which he struggled to force psychological penetration beyond the limits of *Modernismo*'s usual superficiality. In it, however, even the protagonist's suicide becomes a positive aesthetic event. Another tour de force is *La gloria de don Ramiro* (1908; *The Glory of Don Ramiro*, 1924), by Enrique Larreta (1865-1961), which employs a historical setting in Toledo as the basis for a transformation of that reality into a sensorial experience—a process betraying *Modernismo*'s roots in Symbolism, in which the object perceived is gradually metamorphosed into a representation of the observer's psychic state. Some critics have mistakenly placed Rafael Arévalo Martínez (1884-1975) and his works, such as the short-story collection *El hombre que parecía un caballo* (1916), in the naturalist camp because his characters are often compared to animals. In fact, this process in his stories is also an example of Symbolist transformation.

The advent of modern communications eventually began unifying Latin America to the extent that authors came to have freer access to one another. There are some modern authors who have commented that, as their centuries-long insularity finally gave way, they became aware of their common goals, and several have even spoken of "the novel that we are all writing." Carlos Fuentes, in his *Terra nostra* (1975; English translation, 1976), attempts to pick up the quests of the heroes of several novels written by his peers and complete them, even bringing a number of those heroes together at the conclusion of his novel. This attitude stands in contrast to that of many nationalistic leaders of the individual countries, who at times insist that there is no real Latin America— that each individual nation is an entity in itself and impossible to classify with others.

As the authors of Latin America came to an increasing awareness of their common experience and concerns, regionalist tendencies gradually became less important, and the focus came to be upon America as a problem. While European literary currents continued to exercise a strong influence, a complex series of events moved the Latin American novel into the channels it was to follow. Rodó's plea for a continuing stress on Latin American cultural identity was very much in the minds of these writers, as they wrote in the *costumbrista* and *criollista* modes. This Latin American identity was reinforced in 1910 by the centennial of the outbreak of the wars for independence from Spain. Intellectuals became preoccupied with what Latin America had become in those hundred years, and their stress on America as a viable, powerful entity in itself, rather than a stepchild of Europe, became known as *mundonovismo*.

Because little had changed with independence save the replacement of Spanish-born political leaders by governors of Spanish descent born in the New World, in many cases government had deteriorated into dictatorship. One of the worst of these governments in terms of its emphasis on progress at the expense of the cynical exploitation of the poor was that of Porfirio Díaz, who was president of Mexico from 1876 to 1880 and 1884 to 1911. In another instance of timing with considerable symbolic value, in the centennial year of 1910, a true revolution (as opposed to the typical Latin American replacement of one dictator by another) broke out in Mexico. Latin Americans, already profoundly concerned with the direction to be taken by their region, watched closely as, in the midst of the Mexican Revolution, World War I broke out, and then, before either war was concluded, the Russian Revolution began. Sociopolitical upheaval was a way of life, and Latin America already had a well-established tradition of writers influencing the course of such events.

This confluence of currents produced, among other effects, a subgenre of the regionalist novel, that of the Mexican Revolution, the first example of which appeared in the course of the fighting. *Los de abajo* (1916; *The Underdogs*, 1929) is most notable for the ability of its author, Mariano Azuela (1873-1952), to transform living experience into fiction as it occurred. The work has the typically Mexican circular structure, the protagonist dying at the same location at which he begins his successful career in the revolution. While this has been termed an epic structure, it may also be viewed as another turn of the Wheel of Fortune, indicative not only of the nature of one revolutionary's fortunes but also of the lot of the nation as a whole as its revolution was to lead to new forms of death-dealing oppression. *The Underdogs* was largely ignored until 1925, when journalists rediscovered it and brought it to the public's attention.

Martín Luis Guzmán (1887-1976) also published a work linked to journalism, *El águila y la serpiente*

(1928; *The Eagle and the Serpent*, 1930), which is a novel of the sort that a war correspondent might be expected to write; it nevertheless contains some of the best prose of its day. The next year he produced *La sombra del caudillo* (1929), in which he, like Azuela, views the Mexican people as being swept inexorably along by the revolution. For him, its story is one of *caudillos*, the petty regional dictators whose story was to emerge in its most powerful form in a work by Juan Rulfo (1918-1986), *Pedro Páramo* (1955; English translation, 1959).

Gregorio López y Fuentes (1897-1966), in his *El indio* (1935; English translation, 1961), bridges the gap between the novel of the Mexican Revolution and the Indianist novel, examining the role played by Indians in the conflict and questioning their treatment since that time. In doing so, he moves away from the traditional narrative technique of Mexico's novel involving the common people, treating them as masses rather than as individuals. Many other authors turned to a portrayal of the Indian plight during the 1920's and 1930's. If America was a problem, then at its roots was the situation of its peoples, who had been raped, slaughtered, enslaved, and generally exploited throughout the centuries since the conquest.

John S. Brushwood pointed out that three stages should be recognized in the development of Indian-oriented fiction in Latin America. The first has its roots in some of the earliest writings of the region, in works such as *Arauco domado* (1596; *Arauco Tamed*, 1948), by Pedro de Oña (1570-c. 1643). In this epic poem, the indigenous are glorified and made to conform to European ideals of language, behavior, and even physical appearance. Later, under the influence of French writers such as Chateaubriand, these conceptions were reinforced in the "noble savage" mode, as in Avellaneda's *Guatimozín* or Mera's *Cumandá*. The second stage involves a concern for Indians, describing and protesting against social injustice and dealing with them in terms of what has been called social realism, as in *El indio*. Finally, there are novels such as *Los ríos profundos* (1958; *Deep Rivers*, 1978), by José María Arguedas (1911-1969), and *Oficio de tinieblas* (1966; *The Book of Lamentations*, 1996), by Rosario Castellanos (1915-1974), in which the author actually writes from the Indians' viewpoint, revealing their vital experience from within. These works belong to a period of more universal concerns in the novel in general.

In the regionalist mode of the second stage, one of the important novels is that of the poet César Vallejo (1892-1938), *El tungsteno* (1931; *Tungsten*, 1988), dealing with the concerns of Indians working in the mines of Latin America. In other Indianist novels, the stress is on the unjust distribution of land, not merely for the purpose of pointing out the problem of economic exploitation but because of the Indians' need for a sense of belonging. In this connection, it should be stressed that to the extent that Marxist concepts entered Latin American thinking in this area, they tended to be received in terms not so much of their economic import as of their cultural import, which is in part the result of the fact that these writers derived their Marxist ideals from the Ukrainian Nikolay Berdyaev (1874-1948) rather than the more economically oriented theoreticians.

Thus, while the Indians in these second-stage novels are generally portrayed as masses, they are never simple adjuncts to an economic theory, but rather a people in quest of ethnic wholeness. An early example by Alcides Arguedas (1879-1946), *Raza de bronce* (1919), deals with the impossible position in which Indians find themselves, even while the author fails to call for any radical change. Jorge Icaza (1906-1978), in his *Huasipungo* (1934; *The Villagers*, 1964), chose to employ scenes of unspeakable atrocity to shock the reader into indignation, while the Mexican Mauricio Magdaleno (1906-1986) makes use of astronomical metaphors to depict the Indians' situation in *El resplandor* (1937; *Sunburst*, 1944), reflecting the preconquest belief of the people in a destiny set in the heavens. The last significant novel in this stage, by the Peruvian Ciro Alegría (1909-1967), was *El mundo es ancho y ajeno* (1941; *Broad and Alien Is the World*, 1941), in which the Indians are dispossessed by the greed of white people. The novel is most notable for its creation of a powerful individual, the chief Rosendo Maqui, a sign of hope; in his human qualities he towers over his oppressors in their venality.

One of the issues that greatly intrigued the regionalists was the response of Americans to a nature that was often perceived as overwhelming. During the 1920's, this concern resulted in a series of landmark novels, each dealing with the issue in a different manner. The novelist

of the Colombian jungle, José Eustacio Rivera (1889-1928), wrote of how "men disintegrate like worms and nature closes implacably over them." His *La vorágine* (1924; *The Vortex*, 1935) treats the jungle as an irresistible destructive force, reducing human beings to pitiful shells and then swallowing them. Domingo Faustino Sarmiento's civilization-versus-barbarism theme was transferred to the plains of Venezuela by Rómulo Gallegos (1884-1969), who later was to become president of that country. His *Doña Bárbara* (1929; English translation, 1931), complete with allegorical names, portrays the victory of city-based enlightenment over superstition and the raw lust for power found in the outlying regions.

In Sarmiento's Argentina, however, what appeared in *Facundo* as an ambivalent Romantic attitude toward the gaucho is transformed into a *Modernista* presentation of him as, paradoxically, the Romantic ideal of humans in harmony with nature in both suffering and triumph: *Don Segundo Sombra* (1926; English translation, 1935), by Ricardo Güiraldes (1886-1927), is a sort of bildungsroman for Argentine youth, in which the hero is drawn from his "effeminate" civilized surroundings into the "masculine" gaucho world, eventually to return as a landowner. The cycle of major novels dealing with humans and nature is completed, as humans have been viewed as dominated by nature, dominant over it, and in harmony with it. Each of the novels deals with the problems of a specific region, even while creating an experience to which all Latin Americans can relate. That the three can be seen almost as a loose sort of unwitting trilogy on humans and nature is indicative of the growing tendency of Latin American writers to write on the same topics in ways that indicate shared experiences and concerns.

THE 1920'S AND 1930'S

There has been a critical tendency to treat the situation of prose fiction in the 1920's and 1930's as if the only significant works were of the regionalist variety, whether they deal with the Mexican Revolution, social issues of some other sort, or more general Latin American themes. For this reason, many have viewed later Latin American novels as if they had been created ex nihilo or pieced together from foreign sources. The fact is that there had been a more or less steady and consistent development of the vanguardist novel, parallel to those works preoccupied with sociopolitical issues. The most important link between the two lay in the profound rejection of existing social values in virtually all the novels of this period. From that point on, there was a divergence, as some writers, as in the nineteenth century, became more concerned with their message than with the language in which it was couched, while others were primarily concerned with their novels as works of art.

In the first few years of the twentieth century, the Chilean poet Vicente Huidobro (1893-1948) produced his "Creationist Manifesto," in which he rejected the demand that the artist reproduce external reality to make mimetic art, asserting instead the right to invent new realities, in an art involving genetic processes. Huidobro's view is that the poet is "a little god," so that each literary work is a new creation in the world. In the full flush of social commitment, his cries were ignored by a considerable percentage of writers, but many more followed his lead and those of other influential writers, among whom Marcel Proust, James Joyce, and the Peninsular author Benjamín Jarnés are the most frequently mentioned. In the 1920's, these theories were displayed most prominently in a series of often short-lived literary magazines.

At this time, vanguardist writers experimented with such techniques as antichronological development and interior monologue. In the fiction of this period, characterization is radically interiorized, and there are often variations in the narrative point of view. There is an increasing concern with visual effects and the use of startling imagery, along with an interest in playing with typography. Underlying it all, there is the conviction that the author is under no obligation to reproduce visible reality. *El café de nadie* (1926), by Arqueles Vela (1899-1977), is heavy with radical innovations, including the concept of a fictional space within which the plot develops, and some early experiments with Surrealism.

Even when a novel of this time bears a regional cast, the increasing interest in a psychological penetration of the characters often places the universal orientation of an author in bold relief. The best examples in this period are two works of the Chilean Eduardo Barrios (1884-1963): *El niño que enloqueció de amor* (1915; *The Little Boy Driven Mad by Love*, 1967), in which a young boy falls in love with his mother's friend, and *El hermano asno* (1922; *Brother Asno*, 1969), a study of the emotional torment of a saintly monk. In the same decade, *La educación sentimental* (1929), by Jaime Torres Bodet (1902-1974), focuses on interior experience to such a degree that there is virtually no action.

In the Argentine tradition of novels dealing with anguished characters obsessed with questions concerning the meaning of an alienated existence is *Los siete locos* (1929; *Seven Madmen*, 1984), by Roberto Arlt (1900-1942), in which the revolutionary impulse has motives solely of personal gain. The Nietzschean will to power figures largely, as does Joycean interior monologue. In Chile, what Fernando Alegría terms the "deathblow to *criollismo*" was produced in two stages. In 1934, María Luisa Bombal (1910-1980) published *La última niebla* (*The Final Mist*, 1982; previously published as *The House of Mist*, 1947), which deals in a cool and elegant style with both the universal human condition and specifically feminine psychology. It was not until 1951, however, that Manuel Rojas (1896-1972) completed the process with *Hijo de ladrón* (*Born Guilty*, 1955), a completely secular novel—something virtually unknown before this time in Latin America—that examines the life of a modern people in the cosmopolitan vein.

MODERNISM

In Brazil, the regionalist tendency was first challenged by that country's version of modernism, which represents a combination of vanguardist currents. Modernism suddenly appeared on the scene in 1922 and had the effect of making poetry dominant until 1930, when a series of neorealistic novels of a social orientation began appearing, among them *Vidas sêcas* (1938; *Barren Lives*, 1965), by Graciliano Ramos (1892-1953), a novel of psychological realism in the tradition of Joaquim Maria Machado de Assis focusing on character development rather than plot.

Still another major contribution to the complex set of influences on the Latin American novel was made by Jorge Luis Borges (1899-1986), who never wrote a novel himself but whose short stories serve as the primary impetus of what Seymour Menton calls *cosmopolitismo*. Borges's major scholarly interests lie in medieval Northern Europe and England, and Nordic mythology therefore plays a role in his stories. He is known for his play with mythic and philosophical concepts, and his stories are rife with paranormal events, which differ from those of writers interested in the African and indigenous traditions mainly in having their roots in European mythologies and philosophies.

In the work of Borges, who wrote in Buenos Aires, prose fiction tends to move away from rural, regional concerns and into more urbane, universal settings, with the result that in the last several decades of the twentieth century there was a curious split in the best Latin American novels: Some, such as *Rayuela* (1963; *Hopscotch*, 1966), by Julio Cortázar (1914-1984), were set in the great cities of Europe and America, and others, most notably *Cien años de soledad* (1967; *One Hundred Years of Solitude*, 1970), by Gabriel García Márquez (born 1928), were set in remote rural areas but nevertheless universal for it.

In Borges, the author's demand for the right to invent his or her own reality comes to full fruition. His *Ficciones, 1935-1944* (1944; English translation, 1962) and *El aleph* (1949, 1952; translated in *The Aleph, and Other Stories, 1933-1969*, 1970) appeared at exactly the right moment, as the Latin American novel was ready to move into a new phase and take its place as one of the world's most creative and active. Even before Borges's landmark works, however, Juan Filloy (1894-2000) had produced a radical piece of fiction entitled *Op Oloop* (1934, 1967, 1997; English translation, 2009) in the Joycean tradition, particularly in its innovative language. In 1941, Macedonio Fernández (1874-1952) published *Una novela que comienza*, insisting in the text that if he can locate a certain woman he has seen and incorporate her into the work, the novel can get under way. In this period, throughout Latin America, the general inclination to express dissatisfaction with social values was giving way to a cultural internationalism on one hand and political liberalism on the other. *Adán Buenosayres* (1948), by Leopoldo Marechal (1898-1970), presents a character attempting to re-create Buenos Aires through language in order to make it conform to such ideals.

The Surrealists took a deep interest in inner landscapes. As painters, they portrayed visions supposedly arisen from the unconscious mind, while the poets, following André Breton's model of "the chance occurrence, upon a dissecting table, of a sewing machine and an umbrella," wanted to be the first to join two words together. Such a preoccupation with the unconscious and the seemingly irrational involves a flight from normal, supposedly logical, visions of reality that merge with several other concerns of the Latin American novelists of this era, among them an interest in penetrating beneath the surface of the Indians' world into their often radically different vision of the cosmos. The word "primitive" began to lose its negative connotations as archaeologists and anthropologists revealed that the pre-Columbian civilizations had been vastly superior in many aspects to that of the Europeans who conquered them. Latin American writers began to realize that the myths, folktales, and rituals of even the modern descendants of the Mayas and Incas could not be dismissed as inferior, childish attempts to be civilized in the European sense.

Contributing to this change in attitude was the decreasing influence of the Catholic Church, which had condemned such myths and rituals as pagan and satanic. Furthermore, Europe was experiencing yet another resurgence of interest in its own ancient mythologies, which were proving to be fascinatingly similar to those that anthropologists were collecting around the world. One result, in a world in which it appeared that the values of Western civilization were leading only to war and chaos, was a sense that the concepts that had aided in structuring the ancient societies of a region should be examined in search of their possible values for the same region in the twentieth century. Writers such as Joyce appeared to be searching for significance in their characters' acts by relating them to the archetypal deeds of the heroes of the past. Joyce, whose influence has been considerable in the Latin American novel, early on used Odysseus as a model and later seemed to allude to the Irish hero Finn MacCool and the expectation of his return to life in *Finnegans Wake* (1939).

Much of Latin America had placed its hope in European values. Sarmiento, having reluctantly rejected the gauchos (who were mainly mestizos) as a viable social force, called for European immigration as the salvation of Argentina. Civilization must prevail over the barbarity of the plains, and Rómulo Gallegos echoed the cry from Venezuela eight decades later. By 1929, with

Roberto Arlt's *Seven Madmen*, it was becoming evident that Sarmiento's theories were not working in a most significant area of concern, that of the human spirit.

Other voices had been heard, although they had been overwhelmed for a considerable length of time. Eugenio María de Hostos (1839-1903), active in education in the Caribbean, declared in the essay "El cholo" that the hope of America lay in the fusion of the three major racial groups: Caucasian, African, and Indian. Later, in *La raza cósmica* (1925; *The Cosmic Race*, 1979), José Vasconcelos (1882-1959), a Mexican writer, expressed the theory that Latin America had the unique opportunity to reunite those racial groups, drawing on the strengths of each to build a great new society.

To do so, the intelligentsia would have to examine and come to a comprehension of the roots of the thinking of those groups, as expressed in Latin America. One early attempt was made by the Cuban Alejo Carpentier (1904-1980), in *¡Ecué-Yamba-O! Historia Afro-Cubana* (1933), an attempt to penetrate the experience of the Afro-Cuban religious cults. Later, the author was to repudiate the work, having realized that he had been far from any true understanding of the premodern thought of the people involved. The 1967 Nobel Prize winner from Guatemala, Miguel Ángel Asturias (1899-1974), was the first to make a serious attempt to deal adequately with Indian mythology, with his *Leyendas de Guatemala* (1930), in which he recovers as much as possible of the thought of the Mayas as it survived in their descendants. Asturias serves as something of a transitional figure, for his social commitment is abundantly clear in his attacks on Latin American dictatorship and the United Fruit Company in works such as *El Señor Presidente* (1946; *The President*, 1963) and *Hombres de maíz* (1949; *Men of Maize*, 1975), while at the same time he laid the foundation for what was to become known as Magical Realism in Latin American prose fiction. In *Men of Maize*, he revealed the continued effect of the *Popol Vuh* (c. 1550), or book of the community, on the life of the Central American Indian.

MAGICAL REALISM

The term "magical realism" is nebulous, and many authors and critics prefer *lo real maravilloso*, which is based loosely on the Surrealist concept of *le merveilleux*.

Magical Realism is fundamentally a reflection of the twentieth century's departure from what has been perceived as bourgeois categories. Psychology and sociology have shown that rational categories are not necessarily dominant in determining the course of the life of a person or society, and even physics has departed from the Newtonian model, with its more or less mechanistic bias. While the nineteenth century realist wanted to show life as it was actually lived, the Magical Realist believes that true reality is that which underlies the ordinary events of daily life. In this sense, the term "realism" is accurate, for writers in this vein believe that, once found, reality will always prove to have a paranormal, magical cast. Typically, in this type of fiction, supernatural occurrences are narrated in a matter-of-fact manner, as if they formed a part of normal daily life.

Demetrio Aguilera Malta (1909-1981) had been experimenting with such alternative realities in the early 1930's, along with writers such as Carpentier and Asturias. Aguilera Malta's *Don Goyo* (1933; English translation, 1942, 1980) reveals an early animistic tendency to personify nature that was to contrast sharply with the views of French writer Alain Robbe-Grillet, whose *Pour un nouveau roman* (1963; *For a New Novel: Essays on Fiction*, 1965) contains a fierce repudiation of the pathetic fallacy of the Romantics. Aguilera Malta commented that if the works that he and others were writing in this vein during the 1930's had been received more enthusiastically, they would have continued writing them, but the social realist tendency nearly swamped the other. Only in 1970 did Aguilera Malta return with one of the best examples of the novel of Magical Realism, *Siete lunas y siete serpientes* (*Seven Serpents and Seven Moons*, 1979), with its eerie, brooding evocation of the Ecuadoran jungle. People are transformed into animals or appear to be manifestations of otherworldly beings, and even the narrator is unsure of whether to believe what he has recounted. By the time he provides the reader with a rational explanation, the reader is not persuaded the explanation is valid.

In the context of the same great pre-Columbian culture, the Peruvian José María Arguedas, while not an Indian himself, lamented the inadequacy of the Spanish language to express the realities experienced by the descendants of the Incas, for his native language was the

Quechua of the Indian household servants among whom he spent his first few years. His powerful *Yawar fiesta* (English translation, 1985) was published in 1941.

In the same period, however, there was another current in Latin American fiction, based in the Río de la Plata (often referred to as River Plate) region, which has experienced little influence from indigenous groups. The Argentine Eduardo Mallea was extremely influential in the years between 1934 and 1940, and in 1941 his *Todo verdor perecerá* (*All Green Shall Perish*, 1966) was published. It is a vaguely existentialist work of human alienation, angst, and the impossibility of meaningful communication between people, yet it lacks the existentialist's concept of self-affirmation through struggle. The works of the Uruguayan Juan Carlos Onetti (1909-1994) are in much the same vein. His *Tierra de nadie* (*No Man's Land,* 1994) also appeared in 1941, and his later works, such as *El astillero* (1961; *The Shipyard*, 1968), present the same dismal atmosphere of hopelessness.

The Argentine Ernesto Sábato (born 1911) deals with psychological and sociological issues. In *El túnel* (1948; *The Outsider*, 1950; also known as *The Tunnel*) he, too, presents the case of people together physically but spiritually isolated from one another. Later, in *Sobre héroes y tumbas* (1961; *On Heroes and Tombs*, 1981), he makes use of the Borgesian labyrinth as his hero descends to the network of sewers underlying Buenos Aires. His *Abaddón, el exterminador* (1974; *The Angel of Darkness*, 1991) focuses on the Argentine apocalyptic motif, seen earlier in Arlt's short story "La luna roja" and in Mallea's work.

A number of novels that might be considered transitional appeared between the older regionalist and vanguard tendencies and the explosive New Novel. In them, there is what Fernando Alegría calls a thirst for universality, along with a further development of the long-standing movement from mimetic to genetic forms. If the Impressionist artist had demanded the right to portray his or her subjective reactions to the perceived, and Huidobro had insisted that the poet is a creator rather than an imitator, Borges would absorb such theory and delight in creating a mixture of philosophy, fantasy, and play elements. The novelists accepted Borges's spirit of inventiveness, using language to draw the reader into a new sort of participatory experience.

Among the important transitional novels is *Al filo del agua* (1947; *The Edge of the Storm*, 1963), by Agustín Yáñez (1904-1980), a work regional in its setting but more concerned with the interpersonal and intrapersonal conflicts of the characters and with the use of whatever narrative techniques the author believes are most effective in presenting them. Another experimenter is Asturias, whose *The President* uses vanguard techniques to re-create the atmosphere of dread that characterizes Latin American dictatorship. In 1949, Carpentier published *El reino de este mundo* (*The Kingdom of This World*, 1957), introducing his preoccupation with the cyclical nature of tyranny and revolution and employing a highly cerebral style. In *Los pasos perdidos* (1953; *The Lost Steps*, 1956), Carpentier experimented with time and captured the ongoing American fascination with the marvelous qualities of the land. In this novel, the protagonist is able to travel backward in time by departing from a modern city into the ever more primitive wilderness. Ten years later, Carpentier's masterful *El siglo de las luces* (1962; *Explosion in a Cathedral*, 1963) brought the historical novel firmly into the stream of the new fiction.

The Mexican novel, with its rich tradition leading from *The Itching Parrot* through the works of its revolution and those of Yáñez, began to come to full maturity in Juan Rulfo's *Pedro Páramo*. Like much of Mexican fiction, it is preoccupied with death, and the reader eventually learns that all the characters, including the narrator, are dead. In a sense, this, too, is a transitional work, in that its setting is regional and it deals with the *caudillo* system and the revolution. However, in the novel the act of making art is the controlling factor, and the predominant impression gained by the reader is one of the magical atmosphere into which the protagonist descends as he visits the town of his birth, an atmosphere made up of classical mythology, pre-Columbian ideologies, and even voodoo.

In his first novel, *La región más transparente* (1958; *Where the Air Is Clear*, 1960), Carlos Fuentes (born 1928) deals with the betrayal of the Mexican Revolution in a generally realistic manner, while frankly admitting the influence of Joyce, John Dos Passos, and several other foreign writers on his technique. Fuentes attempts to incorporate an element of *lo real maravilloso* in the form of a character known as Ixca Cienfuegos, a sort of incarnation of Mexico's indigenous heritage, who, as a quasi-mythic being, is not very well integrated with the other characters. In his later novels, Fuentes moved more fully into the mythic mode, with the exception of *Las buenas conciencias* (1959; *The Good Conscience*, 1961) and *La muerte de Artemio Cruz* (1962; *The Death of Artemio Cruz*, 1964); in them and his short stories, he was refining the themes and techniques he was to use in his massive *Terra Nostra*.

Terra Nostra attempts to mythologize the history of the West for the past two thousand years. In its extremely free handling of time, multiple reincarnations, appearances of supernatural beings such as Satan, and other features, it represents a manifestation of Magical Realism carried to the limit. While *Terra Nostra* is Fuentes's most important novel, his best technical achievement remains *The Death of Artemio Cruz*, a masterpiece of novelistic construction in which another character guilty of betraying the Mexican Revolution is viewed at the time of his death. Narration is variously in the first, second, and third persons, and in the present, future, and past tenses, respectively. Fuentes continued to experiment with narrative voice. His *Todas las familias felices* (2006; *Happy Families*, 2008) is a novel comprising short first-person accounts in different voices, interspersed with a chorus in the form of poetry.

THE NEW LATIN AMERICAN NOVEL

Fuentes's works are central to the related but separate phenomena known as the new Latin American novel and the Latin American boom. The former refers to what most critics would call the coming of age of the Latin American novel, a gradual process that was accelerated in the 1950's. At that time, Latin American prose fiction was worthy of moving into the realm of world literature and exercising a good deal of influence of its own.

The Latin American boom, somewhat difficult to define at best, is fundamentally a phenomenon of the 1960's and early 1970's and involves a more general recognition of the quality of the novels of a limited group of authors, some of whom believe that the boom was essentially a phenomenon of public relations and economics. That is, many believed the boom was a time in which a few authors—including Fuentes, García Márquez,

Cortázar, Rulfo, Carpentier, Guillermo Cabrera Infante, Donoso, and Mario Vargas Llosa—became celebrities and were at last able to make a living from their writing. The Chilean Donoso wrote about the boom in his *Historia personal del "boom"* (1972; *The Boom in Spanish American Literature: A Personal History*, 1977), while Fuentes produced an excellent analysis of the larger movement, *La nueva novela hispanoamericana*, in 1969.

Donoso's novelistic production represents an advance in the novelist's art in Chile at the same time that it continues that country's tradition of examining a segment of society by the use of carefully controlled language. His *Este domingo* (1965; *This Sunday*, 1967) dissects the wealthy class of Santiago, while the shorter *El lugar sin límites* (1966; *Hell Has No Limits*, 1972) deals with the lower classes. His best novel, *El obsceno pájaro de la noche* (1970; *The Obscene Bird of Night*, 1973), employs more radical techniques.

The work of Julio Cortázar (1914-1984) presents a major example of the movement of the Latin American novel into the universal sphere. The novel that first attracted the world's attention to him was *Rayuela* (1963; *Hopscotch*, 1966). Moving from the sterile atmosphere of most of the Argentine novels of his generation, he presents a far more authentic existentialist hero in Horacio Oliveira (although author and character would deny the latter's adherence to the existentialist philosophy), who converses with others in Buenos Aires and Paris and almost reaches them. The essential point is that Oliveira is a person in motion, creating a persona, however defective, as he moves. There is humor in the work, the title of which presents the reader with a child's-play version of Borges's characteristic labyrinth. The chapters are not presented in any prescribed order; Cortázar only suggests a hopscotch order in which the reader might approach them. One of his important contributions to the New Novel is his insistence that the reader participate in the creative act with him.

Five years after *Hopscotch*, speculating on the possibility of constructing a novel on the basis of "found" materials, including chapter 62 of the earlier novel, Cortázar produced *62: Modelo para armar* (1968; *62: A Model Kit*, 1972). Among Cortázar's other novels is *Libro de Manuel* (1973; *A Manual for Manuel*, 1978), a handbook for a child growing up in a world of radical change.

The Cuban exile Cabrera Infante (1929-2005) produced two novels based on humor—especially puns and other forms of wordplay—and, as in *Hopscotch*, the frenetic search for creativity in chaotic language. *Tres tristes tigres* (1967, 1990; *Three Trapped Tigers*, 1971) challenges its reader to discover a meaningful structure, which emerges only on the level of a nebulous mythology created by language as it disintegrates. After a series of books of essays and short stories, Cabrera Infante published *La Habana para un infante difunto* (1979; *Infante's Inferno*, 1984), a bildungsroman dealing with the sexual initiation of a young would-be Don Juan in pre-Castro Havana.

Another explosive experiment with language and mythology in Cuba was *Paradiso* (1966; English translation, 1974), the only novel of the premier poet of that country, José Lezama Lima (1910-1976), a work that in a sense constitutes his poetics. A dense atmosphere is created as the author overlays his characters' words and deeds with metaphor, in one expression of what the critics have termed the "Cuban neobaroque." Lezama Lima, too, appears to be attempting to lend significance to his characters' acts by comparing them to the archetypal deeds of heroes.

Another major writer of the Cuban baroque tendency is Severo Sarduy (1937-1993), who wrote a number of novels characterized by an explosive language and humor, among them *De donde son los cantantes* (1967; *From Cuba with a Song*, 1972) and *Cobra* (1972; English translation, 1975). Reinaldo Arenas (1943-1990), forced to leave Cuba in 1980, combines features of Magical Realism with a baroque style in *El mundo alucinante* (1969; *Hallucinations: Being an Account of the Life and Adventures of Friar Servando Teresa de Mier*, 1971) but generally withdrew from both in his more important *El palacio de las blanquísimas mofetas* (1975; as *Le Palais des très blanches mouffettes*, 1980; *The Palace of the White Skunks*, 1990).

Carpentier, who had done much to provoke the baroque movement in Cuba by his use of a self-consciously erudite style, published *El recurso del método* (1974; *Reasons of State*, 1976), which is one of a number of Latin American novels appearing in various countries in

the space of a few years to deal with the subject of dictatorship. One of the persistent themes of the Latin American novel for more than a century is the "shadow" of the dictator, the man depersonalized and viewed more as a malevolent force, as in *Amalia* or, a century later, in *The President*. In some of the new novels of dictatorship there is a tendency analogous to the presentation of Indians from their own perspective: The reader is now inside the dictator's palace and, in some cases, inside his mind.

Alejo Carpentier creates a powerful effect by the use of interior monologue to characterize his *Primer Magistrado*. In *Hijo de hombre* (1960; *Son of Man*, 1965), by the Paraguayan Augusto Roa Bastos (1917-2005), the emphasis is still on the action of the people against tyranny as exemplified by the individual dictator, while Aguilera Malta moved into a radically mythic vision with *Seven Serpents and Seven Moons* in 1970, only to descend to an often ludicrous level through an excess of Magical Realism in *El secuestro del general* (1973; *Babelandia*, 1985). The novel in this vein receiving the most attention is *El otoño del patriarca* (1975; *The Autumn of the Patriarch*, 1975), by Gabriel García Márquez, a novel presenting the personal view of the perennial dictator in decline. Exaggerating the already incredible events typical of such a dictator's rule, García Márquez attempts to re-create the stifling atmosphere of tyranny, an atmosphere that is communicated to the text itself.

García Márquez, who was awarded the Nobel Prize in Literature in 1982, previously dealt with the towns of the Caribbean coast of Colombia, in that often seemingly regional focus of the New Novel that nevertheless takes on universal appeal in the nature of the experience created in the text. His *La hojarasca* (1955; *Leaf Storm, and Other Stories*, 1972) and *El coronel no tiene quien le escriba* (1961; *No One Writes to the Colonel, and Other Stories*, 1968) had already established his reputation when he published *One Hundred Years of Solitude* in 1967, the Latin American novel that has had the greatest impact worldwide. The novel is the history of a fictional town called Macondo and of the Buendía family. Reversing normal values so that the commonplace appears marvelous and vice versa, and exercising the storyteller's right to exaggerate and embellish, García Márquez created another prime example of Magical Realism, one in which the atmosphere is the private property of author and reader, bearing little relationship to reality outside the text.

García Márquez turned from Magical Realism in *El general en su laberinto* (1989; *The General in His Labyrinth*, 1990), a historical novel about the last days of Simón Bolívar, but returned to it in *Del amor y otros demonios* (1994; *Of Love and Other Demons*, 1994) and *Memoria de mis putas tristes* (2004; *Memories of My Melancholy Whores*, 2005). Subsequently, it became difficult to establish trends and tendencies in other Latin American fiction, which has featured a wide variety of subjects and treatments. The Argentine Manuel Puig's tongue-in-cheek satires on pop culture can be seen in his *La traición de Rita Hayworth* (1968; *Betrayed by Rita Hayworth*, 1971) and *Pubis angelical*, 1979 (English translation, 1986), and the dense, brooding works of José María Arguedas can be seen most notably in his *Deep Rivers*.

One of the foremost novelists of the newer generation is the Peruvian Mario Vargas Llosa (born 1936), much of whose work focuses on the military establishment, prostitution, or a combination of the two. He established his literary credentials with *La ciudad y los perros* (1962; *The Time of the Hero*, 1966), whereas *La casa verde* (1965; *The Green House*, 1968) and *Conversación en la catedral* (1969; *Conversation in the Cathedral*, 1975) continued in the vein of almost bitter analyses of Peruvian society. With *Pantaleón y las visitadoras* (1973; *Captain Pantoja and the Special Service*, 1978), however, he was drawn into a humorous treatment of the military and prostitution themes; this approach continued in *La tía Julia y el escribidor* (1977; *Aunt Julia and the Scriptwriter*, 1982), a masterful example of the New Novelist's concern with revealing in his or her work the process involved in that work's composition. Vargas Llosa's *La guerra del fin del mundo* (1981; *The War of the End of the World*, 1984) is a long, difficult, and powerful novel based on the same historical incident that inspired Euclydes da Cunha's *Rebellion in the Backlands*. Twenty years later, Vargas Llosa wrote the political thriller *La fiesta del chivo* (2000; *The Feast of the Goat*, 2001), based on the dictator of the Dominican Republic, Rafael Trujillo, who ruled from 1930 to 1961.

Around 1960, Brazilian writers began to reject the emphasis on the social message of the novel and instead began to focus on the craft of the writer. The most prominent novelists of this generation were João Guimarães Rosa (1908-1968) and Clarice Lispector (1925-1977). Guimarães Rosa's interest in universalizing local experience leads to a focus on the mythic and folkloric traditions of the Brazilian outback, expressed in a Joycean language rich in neologisms and regional speech. His work culminates in *Grande sertão: Veredas* (1956; *The Devil to Pay in the Backlands*, 1963). Lispector's mentor was Lúcio Cardoso (1912-1962), whose *Crônica da casa assassinada* (1959) is considered one of the best of modern Brazilian novels. Lispector herself departs from Guimarães Rosa in emphasizing thematic development over technique, in works such as *A maçã no escuro* (1961; *The Apple in the Dark*, 1967). One of Brazil's most popular novelists is Jorge Amado (1912-2001), whose works contain some of the finest treatments of female experience in Latin American literature.

THE LATE TWENTIETH CENTURY AND BEYOND

The decade of the 1980's was the era of the post-Latin America boom, and it signaled a new era in which women, gays and lesbians, and Afro-Hispanics were finally accepted into the literary canon. While a boom-era novel typically portrays the earnest search of the protagonist for the meaning of life, the postboom novel is more likely to describe a journey of this kind with parodic humor; pastiche is its favored trope. It is true that the boom writers continued to publish during the 1980's—García Márquez wrote *Crónica de una muerte anunciada* (1981; *Chronicle of a Death Foretold*, 1982), Fuentes wrote *Gringo viejo* (1985; *The Old Gringo*, 1985), and Vargas Llosa wrote *Quién mató a Palomino Molero?* (1987; *Who Killed Palomino Molero?*, 1987)—but this era was especially characterized by a group of new writers.

Luna caliente (1983; *Sultry Moon*, 1998), by the Argentine Mempo Giardinelli (born 1947), tells the story of a young man named Ramiro Bermúdez, who recently returned to Buenos Aires from Paris. He has a distinguished career before him but his life swiftly disintegrates once he becomes fascinated with Araceli, the thirteen-year-old daughter of a doctor friend, whom he rapes and kills (or so he thinks). The novel parodies the genre of the *novela negra* (hard-boiled crime novel) to produce a gripping plot, combined with a Cortazarian sense of the uncanny that unexpectedly explodes that world from within. Giardinelli's other novels include *El décimo infierno* (1999; *The Tenth Circle*, 2001).

Ardiente paciencia (1985; *Burning Patience*, 1987; also as *The Postman*, 1993), by the Chilean-Croatian writer Antonio Skármeta (born 1940), centers on the love affair and eventual marriage of Mario Jiménez and Beatriz González. To win Beatriz's heart, Mario seeks the help of the famous Chilean poet Pablo Neruda, for whom he works as the postman. In a playful parody, literature is depicted in the novel as a cultural reservoir that plays a direct formative role in the everyday lives of ordinary people. The novel *Gazapo* (1985), by the Mexican Gustavo Sainz (born 1940), tells the story of a group of adolescent boys living in Mexico City, who share with each other their tales of sexual and criminal exploits. The novel suggests that the telling of the stories is more important than the events they allegedly relate, giving the novel a playful feel.

Female authors captured the reading public's attention after the boom. Even though women of this time had written earnest political novels—*Conversación al sur* (1981; *Mothers and Shadows*, 1986), by Marta Traba (1930-1983), was the prototype—it was the mixing of politics with Magical Realism, as in *La casa de los espíritus* (1982; *The House of the Spirits*, 1985), by Isabel Allende (born 1942), which captured the readers' imagination in Latin America and Europe. *The House of the Spirits* traces the political struggle in twentieth century Chile between the Left (symbolized by Pedro García and his son and grandson) and the Right (personified by Esteban Trueba). Whereas the Left is presented in terms of continuity through family lineage, the Right is shown finally to be issueless; Esteban Trueba's male progeny either become Marxists or dropouts, and his female progeny fall in love with revolutionaries. Allende's novel is ultimately a positive and playful affirmation of the value of solidarity in the face of political oppression and other evils.

Como agua para chocolate: Novela de entregas mensuales con recetas, amores, y remedios caseros (1989; *Like Water for Chocolate: A Novel in Monthly Installments with Recipes, Romances, and Home Rem-*edies, 1992), by the Mexican Laura Esquivel (born 1950), is redolent of the television soap opera (a great favorite in Mexico). The novel is also, in essence, a feminist reinterpretation of the Mexican Revolution, offering a "kitchen-eye view" of those turbulent years at odds with the masculinist rhetoric of the history books. This novel is one of the best to emerge in the postboom era, and its humor and metaphoric flair are successfully carried over into the 1985 film version of the novel, which was a box-office hit in the United States as well as Mexico. Esquivel continues to explore the power of desire in *Tan veloz como el deseo* (2001; *Swift as Desire*, 2002) and in the historical novel *Malinche* (2006).

The most significant Latin American writer who also was gay, and whose novels set the scene for the acceptance of writing by gays and lesbians in the following decade, is the Argentine Manuel Puig (1932-1989). His major works were published in the 1970's, including his masterpiece *El beso de la mujer araña* (1976; *Kiss of the Spider Woman*, 1979). The novel *La nave de los locos* (1984; *The Ship of Fools*, 1989), by the Uruguayan-Spanish writer Cristina Peri Rossi (born 1941), is a postmodern, gay-themed text that rewrites the alphabet of Christian culture. The novel describes the misadventures of a character, whose name is simply a letter of the alphabet, *equis* (or "x"), in a variety of urban settings. Making up the tale are sordid sexual encounters, far-fetched dream sequences, and Equis' philosophizing about life and the universe with his companions, Vercingetorix and Graciela. Rossi's work typically explores the sexuality of male protagonists, as in *La última noche de Dostoievski* (1992; *Dostoyevsky's Last Night*, 1994) and *El amor es una droga dura* (1999; love is a hard drug).

Otra vez el mar (1982; *Farewell to the Sea*, 1986), by the gay Cuban writer Reinaldo Arenas, is written from the perspective of a young Cuban couple spending a holiday on the beach. The novel has a plot of sorts (a woman moves with her son into the cabin next door, and the latter, mysteriously, is found dead later that day), but more striking is the story's Joycean rejection of the limitations of Euclidean space and time and its playful use of language.

Afro-Hispanic literature also took a place in the new literary canon of the 1980's. The major work of this period is *Changó: El gran putas* (1983), by the Colombian

Manuel Zapata Olivella (1920-2004). The novel has five parts, each of which traces successive historical eras in which Africans struggled against oppression in the New World.

A new wave of novelists continues to experiment with form and style into the twenty-first century, but these writers frequently are telling stories of political struggle and cultural identity, much like their literary elders. Feminist Chilean writer Diamela Eltit (born 1949) examines women's oppression and sexuality. Puerto Rican poet and novelist Giannina Braschi (born 1953), working at the boundaries of Spanish and English, published what is thought to be the first novel in "Spanglish," *Yo-Yo Boing!* (1998). Roberto Bolaño (1953-2003), who wrote several important volumes of poetry in a short career, achieved international fame with the parodic *Los detectives salvajes* (1998; *The Savage Detectives*, 2007). His last novel, *2666* (2004; English translation, 2008), is more than one thousand pages in length and examines the degradation of society through historical moments in the twentieth century. The novel brings the Latin American political story into the twenty-first century, dealing with, among other topics, the unsolved murders of hundreds of women and girls in and around Ciudad Juárez, Mexico, beginning in 1993. Colombian writer Fernando Vallejo (born 1942) examines the Medillín drug cartel in his novel *La virgen de los sicarios* (1994; *Our Lady of the Assassins*, 2001).

William L. Siemens; Stephen M. Hart
Updated by Cynthia A. Bily

BIBLIOGRAPHY

Boland, Roy C., and Sally Harvey, eds. *Magical Realism and Beyond: The Contemporary Spanish and Latin American Novel*. Madrid: Vox/AHS, 1991. Articles in this edited collection explore Magical Realism in the works of Latin American and Spanish novelists of the twentieth century.

Comprone, Raphael. *Four Major Latin American Writers: Pablo Neruda, Mario Vargas Llosa, Carlos Fuentes, and Gabriel García Márquez*. Lewiston, N.Y.: Edwin Mellen Press, 2008. Drawing on one major work by each of the four named novelists, Comprone creates a coherent history and theory of Magical Realism in Latin American literature.

Febles, Jorge, ed. *Into the Mainstream: Essays on Spanish American and Latino Literature and Culture*. 2006. New ed. Middlesex, England: Cambridge Scholars, 2008. Edited collection of critical articles examining the acceptance of Latin American literature as part of the mainstream literary canon and Latin American culture in general.

González, Aníbal. *A Companion to Spanish American "Modernismo."* Rochester, N.Y.: Tamesis, 2007. An introduction to *Modernismo*, the literary movement that thrived from about 1880 to 1920. Examines the movement's contribution to the various Latin American literary genres, its social and historical context, and its relevance to the work of contemporary authors.

Hart, Stephen M. *A Companion to Latin American Literature*. Rochester, N.Y.: Tamesis, 2007. Solid reference work that introduces the major movements of Latin American literature and its writers and their works. Surveys the fifteenth century to the twentieth century and twenty-first century writings of gays and lesbians, Afro-Hispanics, Afro-Brazilians, and New Novelists.

King, John, ed. *Modern Latin American Fiction: A Survey*. London: Faber & Faber, 1987. Excellent collection of first-rate, readable essays on all the major novelists of the Latin American boom, including Gabriel García Márquez, Carlos Fuentes, Mario Vargas Llosa, and Julio Cortázar.

Martin, Gerald. *Journeys Through the Labyrinth: Latin American Fiction in the Twentieth Century*. New York: Verso, 1989. Elegantly written overview of the development of the Latin American novel in the twentieth century. Recommended resource for all readers of the Latin American novel.

Shaw, Donald L. *The Post-Boom in Spanish American Fiction*. Saratoga Springs: State University of New York Press, 1998. Authoritative survey of the main figures of the post-Latin American boom novel written by an acknowledged expert. Includes chapters on the transition between "booms" and on the work of Isabel Allende.

Sommer, Doris. *Foundational Fictions: The National Romances of Latin America*. Berkeley: University of California Press, 1991. Excellent study of the Latin

American novel of the nineteenth century. Chapters examine the novels *Amalia*, *Sab*, and *Iracema, the Honey-Lips*, studying the interplay between the path toward nationhood and the journey of love in those novels.

Swanson, Philip. *The New Novel in Latin America: Politics and Popular Culture After the Boom*. New York: Manchester University Press, 1995. Authoritative overview of the work of the postboom novelists. Contains separate chapters on Manuel Puig and Isabel Allende, among others.

Williams, Raymond L. *The Columbia Guide to the Latin American Novel Since 1945*. New York: Columbia University Press, 2007. Comprehensive account of the postwar Latin American novel. Includes an introduction to the novel, chronological and regional surveys, encyclopedic entries on select titles, and an annotated bibliography.

THE MIDDLE EASTERN NOVEL

The novel did not begin to take root in the Middle East until after World War I and did not develop into a serious genre until after World War II. Although Arabic, Kurdish, Persian, and Turkish literatures have a long and rich assortment of oral narrative forms, it seems that none of them has become a major narrative type in the way of the European novel. Lacking a native tradition of their own, Middle Eastern novelists thus turned to Western models for inspiration and guidance.

Prior to the outbreak of World War I, there was some contact between the West and the Middle East. Napoleon invaded Egypt in 1798; following the French withdrawal, the country's ruler, Muhammad Ali, began to send missions to Italy and France to study military tactics and new weaponry. In 1882, the British occupied Egypt. However, nonmilitary contact with the West, including the sharing of literature, did not occur to any significant degree until after the region came under French and British domination following the collapse of the Ottoman Empire in 1923.

Many Western editors argue that the literatures of the Middle East are always about politics. This is indeed often the case. However, this should not be surprising. The Middle East has been a volatile region politically. The widely publicized Arab-Israeli conflict is only one of several conflicts in the Middle East. In addition, regional secularism and freedom of expression have faced ongoing challenges from orthodox Islam and undemocratic systems of government. Under these circumstances, it is difficult to imagine literature not entering political life.

THE EGYPTIAN NOVEL

Egypt has long been the region's undisputed cultural capital. In 1927, Muhammad al-Muwaylihī's novel *Fatra min al-zaman* (1907; a period of time), better known as *Hadīth ʿēsā ibn Hishām* (the story of ʿēsa ibn Hishām), was adopted as a school text. Two years later, Muhammad Husayn Haykal's novel *Zaynab*, completed in 1911 and published in 1913, went into its second printing. These two literary events generated so much interest in the novel that in 1930 a competition in novel writing was

announced. The winner was Ibrāhīm al-Māzinī's 1931 novel *Ibrāhīm al-kātib* (*Ibrahim the Writer*, 1976).

Muwaylihī's novel proved quite popular, largely because of the way it juxtaposed two very different ways of life—one Egyptian, the other European. Many Egyptians found it fascinating to read about the inventions and technological marvels displayed at the Great Paris Exhibition of 1899. The novel led to a new literary theme—the European visit—and it became the focus of many novels published during the 1940's and 1950's. This period included serious and prolonged debate about the advantages and disadvantages of contact with Europeans.

Even those novels without a European theme display the influence of the West. In Haykal's novel, for example, Zaynab is prevented by tradition from marrying the man she loves. In Māzinī's novel, Shushu's marriage cannot take place until after her older sister is married. Exposure to European ways turns both protagonists against tradition, which they see as confining and outdated. Forces of change—government bureaucracy, the justice system, and secularism—also lead to conflict in *Yawmiyāt naʾib fi al-aryaf* (1937; *Maze of Justice*, 1947), by Tawfiq al-Hakim (1898-1987).

These novelists played an important role in the development of the novel in the Middle East. However, the writer who contributed the most to the genre and who has been the most influential is Naguib Mahfouz (1911-2006). Born in Cairo and educated at King Fuad I (now Cairo) University, Mahfouz worked as a civil servant for a number of years; he did all his writing at night. His first novel, *ʿAbath al-Aqdār* (*Khufu's Wisdom*, 2003), appeared in 1939, but it was his later novels that won him international recognition and the 1988 Nobel Prize in Literature. These novels include *Zuqāq al-Midaqq* (1947; *Midaq Alley*, 1966, revised 1975), *Bayn al-qasrayn* (1956; *Palace Walk*, 1990), *Qasr al-shawq* (1957; *Palace of Desire*, 1991), and *Al-Sukkariya* (1957; *Sugar Street*, 1992). These last three titles are known collectively as *Al-Thulāthiya*, or *The Trilogy*.

The Trilogy, some fifteen hundred pages long, is in the great novelistic traditions of Leo Tolstoy, John

Galsworthy, Anthony Trollope, and Victor Hugo. In tracing the life, beliefs, tragedies, and difficulties of al-Sayyid Ahmad Abd al-Jawad and his family in the years leading up to World War II, this massive work serves as a vast historical study of a society in transition. The first volume centers on the father, Ahmad, who follows tradition and rules the family with an iron fist. No one dares to oppose him. In volume two, his son, now attending college and sick of tradition, begins to challenge his father. In volume three, the father, now weak and old, has relinquished most of his authority to his son. It is a changed world: Boys and girls attend school together, people talk about communism and the impossibility of belief in God, the young rebel against tradition and openly embrace European ways, fathers are the subject of ridicule and hate, and the old constantly complain about change but are powerless to stop it.

Although Mahfouz never joined any political party, he said that politics were "the very axes" of his thinking. He once credited George Bernard Shaw and Karl Marx for his development into a socialist and a believer in science. He strongly supported the 1952 revolution that brought Gamal Abdel Nasser to power in Egypt, hoping that Nasser would create a "true socialism and true democracy." When that did not happen, and Nasser grew increasingly autocratic, Mahfouz responded with a series of critical novels: *Ḥikāyāt Ḥāratinā* (1975; *The Fountain and the Tomb*, 1988), *Al-Liṣṣ wa-al-kilāb* (1961; *The Thief and the Dogs*, 1984), *Al-Shaḥḥādh* (1965; *The Beggar*, 1986), and *Al-Karnak* (1974; *Karnak*, 1979; *Karnak Café*, 2007).

Of these novels, *The Beggar* is the bleakest. It is the story of Omar, a former poet, revolutionary, and socialist who is now a wealthy, middle-age lawyer. He is married and has two daughters, but he has lost all interest in living. He has become alienated from everyone around him, but what appalls him the most is the government's intolerance of any form of dissent and the terrible economic mess it has created in the name of socialism. All this proves too much for Omar. He tries one diversion after another—travel, drink, sex—but to no avail. As the novel comes to a close, he goes mad.

Mahfouz also criticized his country's Muslim fundamentalists after they assassinated President Anwar Sadat in 1981 for making peace with Israel. Mahfouz re-

sponded with the novella *Yawm Qutila al-Za'īm* (1985; *The Day the Leader Was Killed*, 1989), which underlines his belief that society, to overcome violence, intolerance, and poverty, must grow out of its need for religion. When Muslim fundamentalists assassinated author Farag Foda in 1992, Mahfouz accused the group of "intellectual terrorism." In 1994, Mahfouz himself became the target: A young militant Muslim stabbed the author in the neck while he was waiting for a ride; Mahfouz was hospitalized for two weeks.

Mahfouz was well versed in Western philosophy and literature and was greatly influenced by such important authors as William Shakespeare, James Joyce, Franz Kafka, Thomas Mann, Eugene O'Neill, Henrik Ibsen, and Shaw. Some Arab nationalists accused Mahfouz of going too far in embracing Western ideas and traditions.

THE QUESTION OF PALESTINE

Many Arab and Israeli novelists came into prominence after the creation of Israel as a nation in 1948. Arab novelists have focused mostly on the plight of the Palestinians and the ongoing Arab-Israeli conflict. Ghassān Kanafānī (1936-1972), who was assassinated in Beirut, Lebanon, at the age of thirty-six, gained a wide readership after the publication of *Rijāl fil al-shams* (1963; *Men in the Sun, and Other Palestinian Stories*, 1978) and *Mā tabaqqā lakum* (1966; *All That's Left to You*, 1990). Both focus on the horrendous difficulties that Palestinians face as they try to find a home. In the first book, three young men brave the scorching heat of the Jordanian desert trying to make it to the Kuwaiti border on foot, where a truck driver agrees to smuggle them into the country for an exorbitant fee. After a long delay, the driver manages to make the crossing with his hidden human cargo undetected. By the time he crosses the border, however, the men have all suffocated to death inside the water tank. The driver throws the bodies into a garbage dump. Out of this tragic event, Kanafānī creates a tale that carries with it, from beginning to end, the pain of national dispossession and its consequences for ordinary people.

As another novel of dispossession, *All That's Left to You* is the moving story of Hamid and Maryam, a brother and sister who are separated from each other and their mother. Hamid, on his way to Jordan in search of his mother, must cross the desert at night so that he will not be detected by the border guards. His sister, impregnated by Zakariyya, who is already married and the father of five children, has no choice but to marry the man, a Palestinian paid by Israel to spy on his fellow Palestinians. The end is bloody: Maryam stabs her husband to death in self-defense, and Hamid kills an Israeli border guard. Both end up in prison for life. Kanafānī published nineteen books in his short career, including the novella *ʿĀʾid ilá Ḥayfā* (1970; *Returning to Haifa*, 2000).

Like Kanafānī, Syrian writer Ḥalīm Barakāt (born 1933) deals exclusively with the question of Palestine. *Sittat Ayyām* (1961; *Six Days*, 1990) is an eerie anticipation of the Arab-Israeli Six-Day War of 1967, while *ʿAwdat al-ṭāʾir ilá al-baḥr* (1969; *Days of Dust*, 1974) is a response to the same conflict. In *Days of Dust*, Ramzi Safadi is a Western-educated professor at the American University in Beirut. As a displaced Palestinian, he cannot call Lebanon home. His dream is to one day return to Palestine; he and his students are led to believe by the national media that this might actually happen. However, the war turns out to be a crushing defeat for the Arabs. With their illusions shattered, Ramzi and his students find themselves in a state of shock and disbelief. For Ramzi, this is a turning point. Enraged by American and British support for Israel, he turns against everything Western. Apart from its vividness of character and description, the novel is popular because it succeeds in demolishing the myths of Arab invincibility and the West's neutrality in the Arab-Israeli conflict. It forces Arab readers to ask themselves whether they, too, are implicated in this national defeat and whether they need to rethink their attitude toward the West. In *Taʾir al-hawm* (1988; *The Crane,* 2008), Barakāt again creates a displaced protagonist, this time a college student who settles in Washington, D.C., but remains nostalgic for the small Syrian village where he grew up.

OTHER ARAB NOVELISTS

The appearance of Ṭayyib Ṣāliḥ's *Mawsim al-hijra ilá al-shamāl* (1967; *Season of Migration to the North,* 1969) was a major literary event in the Middle East. Ṣāliḥ (1929-2009), who was educated in London and worked for the British Broadcasting Corporation's Arabic Service before joining the United Nations Educational,

Scientific and Cultural Organization, created the first truly postcolonial Middle Eastern novel.

Told by two British-educated narrators, one unnamed and the other a father of three named Mustafa, the novel moves back and forth between a small village in the Sudan and a London slowly emerging from the devastation caused by World War I. Just like the author, Mustafa has been sent on a scholarship to London. As a student, he frequents the bars and clubs of the Chelsea and Hampstead districts, attends gatherings of the Bloomsbury Group, and develops a strong affinity for Shaw and other Fabian socialists. He marries an Englishwoman and acquires the nickname the Black Englishman. He earns a Ph.D. in economics from the world famous London School of Economics. As he becomes increasingly critical of capitalism and colonialism, however, Mustafa begins to refer to himself as "a lie" and sets out to erase it. He turns his back on everything English and European and returns to his native village, where he marries a local woman and begins farming. He seems to blend in easily.

Mustafa is attempting in this novel what postcolonial critics call the process of resistance and reconstruction: confronting the past in order to purge it of colonial influence and domination. However, this is an impossible task. On one hand, the English language has taken him further and further away from his roots. On the other hand, he declares war on hybridity at a time when the world is becoming increasingly hybridized. His suicide, as the other narrator makes clear, is meant to underline the futility of his undertaking. The novel seems to conclude that although hybridity might be painful, it should, as Chinua Achebe and Edward Said have said, be appropriated rather than discarded. In 2001, the Arab Literary Academy named *Seasons of Migration to the North* "the most important Arabic novel of the 20th century."

What is most surprising about Ṣāliḥ is this: While the region's other novelists seemed unable or unwilling to disengage from the troubling political upheavals sweeping the region, Ṣāliḥ offered a novel oblivious to all the troubles, focusing instead on such postcolonial themes as identity, sexuality, spirituality, materialism, modernity, change, and the problem of belonging and not belonging to East and West. What is more, unlike his earlier work *ʿUrs az-Zen* (1966; *The Wedding of Zein, and Other Stories,* 1968), *Seasons of Migration to the North* appropriated the techniques and forms of the European novel to create a stunning narrative of displacement that is rich in imagery and tone and multiple and fragmentary in scope.

Abdelrahman Munif (1933-2004), another gifted contemporary Arab novelist, favors themes that deal with Arab nationalism and the impact of the discovery of oil on Middle Eastern societies. Because of his involvement in Arab nationalism, an ideology highly critical of the role of the United States in the Middle East, Munif was stripped of his Saudi Arabian citizenship in 1963, after which he moved to Damascus, Syria. Munif's 1975 novel, *Sharq al-Mutawassiṭ* (the Mediterranean), is a bitter denunciation of the Arab governments that fought Israel in 1976. Despite their crushing defeat, these governments continued to talk about victory and the near annihilation of Israel, and they severely punished anyone who dared to speak against government policy. To underline the significance of the issue, the novel starts out with a quotation from the United Nation's Universal Declaration of Human Rights.

In later works, Munif focused on the way that the discovery of oil changed age-old traditions and led to an increase in the region's domination by the West. His novel *Sibāq al-masāfāt al-ṭawīlah: Rihlah ila al-Sharq* (1979; the long competition) is generally understood to be an allegorical study of Iran in the early 1950's. The United States, represented by the protagonist, cannot allow a popularly elected government to pursue independent oil policies. The Central Intelligence Agency overthrows the government and installs a puppet prime minister.

Al-Tīh (1984; *Cities of Salt*, 1987), the first volume in Munif's City of Salt quintet, dwells on a similar theme in a country resembling modern Saudi Arabia, perhaps one reason why the novel has been banned there. Americans arrive with equipment to look for oil. They bring with them prefabricated houses and air conditioning, and they start building roads and recreational facilities, all of which seem to be quite at odds with a nomadic way of life in this desert nation. Some of the Saudi citizens try to resist, but they are unsuccessful. The powerful clan leaders, with American support and supervision, transform the region into a modern police state. Such rivalries and disagreements about the United States and the forces of

modernization are also the subject of the other volumes in the quintet: *Al-Ukhdūd* (1985; *The Trench*, 1991), *Taqāsīm al-layl wa-al-nahār* (1989; *Variations on Night and Day*, 1993), *Al-Munbatt* (1989; the uprooted), and *Bādiyat al-ẓulumāt* (1989; the desert of darkness). However, the industrial world is not the only threat faced by the nomadic peoples of Munif's fiction. In *Al-Nihāt* (1978; *Endings*, 1988), the conflict is with nature, in the form of a sandstorm.

ISRAELI NOVELISTS

Since its creation in 1948, Israel has produced many highly gifted novelists who explore in a variety of forms and techniques what it means to be Jewish in a land where identity and nationality are challenged. One of the most distinguished novelists is the Ukrainian-born Holocaust survivor Aharon Appelfeld (born 1932), a speaker of many languages who also writes in Hebrew. His early shorter works, *'Ashan* (1962; smoke), *Ba-gai ha-poreh* (1963; in the fertile valley), and others, are in the collection *In the Wilderness: Stories* (1965); the stories feature a series of dream sequences involving his experience with the Holocaust. The novels feel allegorical; they are dark and philosophical, poetic, and sometimes obscure. The novel *Badenheim, 'ir nofesh* (1975; *Badenheim 1939*, 1980) portrays a Europe in which to be labeled a Jew is tantamount to a death sentence. The protagonists were all born in Badenheim, but the Austrian authorities refuse to accept them as citizens and have no qualms about sending them to a concentration camp in Germany. The Jews live a life of isolation, uncertainty, fear, and denial. This is also the case with the protagonist of *Bartfus ben ha-almavet* (1988; *The Immortal Bartfuss*, 1988), who, in Appelfeld's words, "has swallowed the Holocaust whole." To survive, he must remain silent and distance himself from those around him.

In *To the Land of the Cattails* (1986; also known as *To the Land of the Reeds*), Appelfeld takes readers once again to a Europe dominated by Adolf Hitler. It is the summer of 1939. A woman insists on going back to the land of her childhood, "the land of the cattails," not far from Appelfeld's own birthplace. She is accompanied by her son, Tony. The mother is caught by the Nazis and is shipped by train to an unknown destination. In desperation, Tony turns to alcohol and begins to negotiate an identity for himself based on his Jewish and Gentile heritage. In the end, suffering gives him no choice but to reject everything that is not Jewish. *Mesilat barzel* (1991; *The Iron Tracks,* 1998) deals with the aftermath of the Holocaust, as a survivor obsessively rides trains throughout Europe searching for his former concentration camp guard.

Another distinguished Israeli novelist, A. B. Yehoshua (born 1936), also has written a number of short stories, plays, and screenplays. In his novels, Yehoshua tends to focus on issues that became central to the Israeli experience after the Six-Day War: the relationship between Jews and Arabs, the fight over territory, Israeli national borders, the large-scale displacement of Palestinians, and the conflict between Orthodox and secular Jews. His novel *Bi-tehilat kayits 1970* (1972; *Early in the Summer of 1970,* 1977) takes readers to a postwar Israel. A father is still mourning a son killed in the Six-Day War. Midway through the story, however, the father learns that the reported death was a case of mistaken identity; the corpse discovered was not that of his son. Although he receives proof that his son is still alive, the father cannot stop grieving. The story is constructed in a circular pattern: The final chapter repeats the first with only a slight variation.

Yehoshua uses a similar technique in his first novel, *Ha-meahev* (1977; *The Lover,* 1978), a series of monologues by different persons that intentionally leaves things murky. Readers do not know the exact identity of the "lover" of the title or, for that matter, why he has been adopted by the couple Asya and Adam. Also, readers do not know what bearing these personal events have on the national situation, such as the ongoing war with the Arabs. Reader also do not know what to make of the Arab Naim, who plays an important part in the novel.

Things are less obscure in *Molkho* (1987; *Five Seasons,* 1989), *Mar Mani* (1990; *Mr. Mani,* 1992), and *Gerushim me'uharim* (1982; *A Late Divorce,* 1984). *A Late Divorce* concerns an American Jew who travels to Israel to divorce his Israeli-born wife. The story is meant to parallel the national debate on the relationship between Israel and the Diaspora of the Jews. After the divorce, in a clearly symbolic act meant to stress the inextricable linkage between the personal and the national, the man starts wearing his former wife's clothes.

Yehoshua has won several prizes, including the 1995 Israel Prize for Literature. He also has published several novels in English translation, including *Ha-Kalah ha-meshahreret* (2001; *The Liberated Bride,* 2003) and *Esh yedidutit* (2007; *Friendly Fire,* 2008).

No contemporary Israeli novelist matches Amos Oz's innovative writing about the Jewish experience in the Holy Land. Born in Jerusalem in 1939 and educated at Hebrew University, Oz became Israel's best-known novelist. After working as a visiting professor at a number of prestigious schools in the United States and Europe, he became a professor of Hebrew literature at Ben Gurion University in 1987. In addition to novels and novellas, Oz has written short stories, literary criticism, and political essays.

Oz's first novel, *Makom aher* (1966; *Elsewhere, Perhaps,* 1973), juxtaposes two realities that seem to be at odds with each other. On the surface, the kibbutz life seems orderly, rational, peaceful, and fulfilling. Beneath the surface lurks a different reality, eleven times alluded to in the novel as the "other place." The place, however, remains mysterious throughout the novel; it is at once the source of yearning and revulsion, pain and gaiety. The upright father, Reuben, and his beautiful daughter, Noga, have come to the kibbutz to build a society that will presumably know no discrimination, injustice, or economic disparity. However, Noga finds herself drawn to Siegfried, the sinister visitor from Germany; much to Reuben's surprise and revulsion, Noga needs little persuading to give up her life on the kibbutz for a new one in Germany.

Oz's highly popular novel *Mikha'el sheli* (1968; *My Michael,* 1972) also is set in a world in which the personal is a much stronger force in shaping people's lives than are national considerations. Told in the form of a memoir, the story is built around the mind of the leading female figure and narrator, Hannah, who remembers in vivid detail how she and Michael met, became engaged, and married in 1950. Within this personal narrative, readers also know that the national scene in Israel is peaceful, prosperous, and optimistic. This world of conformity and stability is juxtaposed with the private world of Hannah's fantasies, which involves Arab twins, rape, terror, surrender, domination, and suicide. While Israel happily celebrates its first decade of independence, Hannah's mind begins to disintegrate, creating a sharp contrast between two seemingly irreconcilable realities.

Oz's writing is easily accessible, and his stories take place in recognizable Israeli settings. However, an element of mystery often surrounds his characters' private lives. *La-da'at ishah* (1989; *To Know a Woman*, 1991) and *Matsav ha-shelishi* (1991; *Fima*, 1993) present characters that seem to be on one level quite ordinary but on another level mysterious and perplexing.

Another Israeli novelist, David Grossman (born 1954), had a considerable boost in stature after he received an award from the Book Publishers' Association of Israel in 1985. Like Oz, Grossman welds the political with the personal in a writing style that mixes stream-of-consciousness technique and journalistic reporting. A good example is Grossman's first novel, *Hiuch ha-gedi* (1983; *Smile of the Lamb*, 1990), a vivid representation of life in the West Bank under Israeli occupation. The story is told by both Israeli and Arab protagonists, the governors and the governed, and is a conflicting account of personal and political considerations. Although the novel seems to cast doubt on certainties, it nevertheless can be interpreted as making a case against the Israeli occupation of the West Bank and in favor of Arab self-determination, a position Grossman restates unequivocally in his book of documentary nonfiction *Ha-zeman ha-tzahov* (1987; *The Yellow Wind*, 1988).

Grossman's novel, *Ayien erech: Ahavah* (1986; *See Under: Love*, 1989), also uses multiple voices and modes. The first section, "Momik," reconstructs the Holocaust through the mind of a nine-year-old boy who relies more on his imagination than on his surviving relatives' accounts to understand exactly what happened at the concentration camps. The next three sections challenge chronology and traditional narrative techniques even further by making the boy rely entirely on fantasy to understand Bruno Schulz's death and Anshel Wasserman's experience in Auschwitz. *Sefer hadikduk haprimi* (1991; *The Book of Intimate Grammar*, 1994) does away with the adult narrator by making the child the fictionalized memoir's only voice. Several of Grossman's works of fiction are available in English translation.

Again, for many Israeli writers, the political is inseparable from art. Israeli novelists have taken seriously their role as intellectuals with power and influence. Oz has long been an advocate of a two-state solution for the Israeli-Palestinian conflict, Grossman is a well-known peace activist, and Yehoshua is active in the Israeli peace movement. In 2006, in the middle of an armed conflict between Israel and Lebanon, Grossman, Oz, and Yehoshua held a joint press conference calling for a cease-fire and a negotiated solution.

THE RISE OF WOMEN NOVELISTS

The late 1950's saw the emergence of many women novelists in the Middle East, most famous among them Nawāl al-Sa'dāwī (born 1931), Ḥanān al-Shaykh (born 1945), and Ghādah al-Sammān (born 1942). These writers embraced the novel form to address a critical issue in the religiously, socially, and culturally conservative Middle East: women's oppression.

Sa'dāwī, trained as a gynecologist, achieved fame through her many novels, short stories, plays, and critical essays that passionately crusaded for women's rights. Her first novel, *Mudhakkirāt Tabībah* (1958; *Memoirs of a Woman Doctor*, 1988), which has been translated into many languages, is the story of a girl who becomes a doctor, and who remains nameless throughout the novel. As a child, the narrator becomes aware of the limitations imposed on her by a male-dominated culture. Unlike her brother, she cannot play in the street, cannot wear what she likes, cannot have short hair, and cannot go anywhere without her parents' permission. Out of frustration, she first turns against herself: "The first real tears I shed in my life weren't because I'd done badly at school or broken something but because I was a girl." She then begins questioning God's fairness as she starts to menstruate.

Later, as a physician trying to dissect a male body, she is astounded by its unattractiveness; in a fit of anger and revenge against men for oppressing and harming women, she violently and repeatedly stabs the body. Her most shocking realization about what it means to be a woman in a patriarchal society comes when she is forced to give up her human rights in order to get married. Predictably, the marriage soon ends in a divorce. The doctor's fight is against an entire society and tradition. In agreeing to perform an abortion on a woman who had been raped, the doctor seems to speak for the author:

"How could I punish her alone when I knew that her society as a whole had participated in the act?"

Sa'dāwī's 1987 novel, *Suqūt al-Imām* (*The Fall of the Imam*, 1988), undermines the patriarchal order by taking on the very system upon which it is based. The imam, a religious and political figure of enormous authority, represents patriarchy. In the novel, to protect his authority, he must hide the fact that his own daughter is illegitimate. The novel then becomes a test of will between a father who is the ultimate symbol of power and tradition and his young daughter, who is determined to challenge that power. In the end the father is assassinated by an enraged public, and the daughter is hailed as a female Christ.

Sa'dāwī's writing demonstrates how difficult it is for a woman to write under patriarchy. Like Sa'dāwī, Lebanese novelist Shaykh is both admired and vilified in the Middle East because of her feminism. Shaykh's first novel, *Ḥikāyat Zahrah* (1980; *The Story of Zahra*, 1986), although hailed as a hallmark of Arab feminism, was banned in several Middle Eastern countries because of its vivid discussion of female sexuality. In the novel, Zahra quickly learns that to be a girl is to be condemned to lifelong servitude. Her brother, Ahmad, gets the best of everything and has the freedom to talk, play, and bring home friends. As she grows up, Zahra realizes that to be a woman is even worse; she is repeatedly raped by a cousin and later by a family friend. She has two abortions before reaching adulthood. In her helplessness, Zahra turns against herself and inflicts severe scars on her own face in the hope that men will no longer find her attractive. Her ordeal continues even in marriage, as she has to deal with an extremely abusive husband.

Shaykh's *Misk al-ghazāl* (1988; *Women of Sand and Myrhh*, 1989) is equally daring in its attack on patriarchy; it, too, was banned in most Middle Eastern countries. It is the story of four women living in an unnamed desert kingdom closely resembling modern Saudi Arabia. Their lives consist of series of less-than-fulfilling events and activities that center on the home, in which the women wear makeup and tight jeans, take pleasure in one another's bodies, and talk openly about their sexual problems. Two of them start a passionate lesbian romance. Another woman, a young widow by the name of Tamar, struggles to start a sewing business of her own.

Because her father is dead, she is required to get her brother's permission to start the business. After he refuses, Tamar goes on a hunger strike, forcing the brother to give his consent. She then goes to an office to get permission from the government and is told that women are not allowed to enter the building. In the end, and against all odds, she gets the state's permission to open her business. Shaykh's novel is not just a dry narrative of social criticism. In sharp contrast to Sa'dāwī's novels, *Women of Sand and Myrrh* is a highly readable book, full of tension and nastiness, but also joy, beauty, and laughter. Similar elements are also seen in Shaykh's *Barīd Bayrūt* (1992; *Beirut Blues*, 1995), an epistolary novel about an architect living amid war in Beirut, and in *Innahā Landan yā 'azīzī* (2001; *Only in London*, 2001), about four strangers from the Middle East who meet on a plane heading for London.

The status of women in the Middle East is also an important theme in the works of Syrian-born Lebanese resident Sammān. For her, women's oppression cannot end until both men and women are liberated from dogma and repressive traditions. Sammān studied English literature at the American University in Beirut and, after a short career in teaching, became a full-time writer in 1966, publishing four collections of short stories before writing her first novel in 1975. The novel, *Bayrūt 75* (*Beirut '75*, 1995), whose events coincide with the 1975 Lebanese civil war, begins with a taxi ride from Damascus, Syria, to Beirut, Lebanon, a city where the characters hope their dreams will come true. Farah wants to become a successful businessman, while Yasimina, a young woman who is fed up with her society's insistence that women belong in the home, hopes to find romance and a more fulfilling career than teaching at a convent. The taxi is black, the driver is unable to speak, and the three women passengers are all dressed in black—details clearly designed to foreshadow the novel's bleak outcome.

In Beirut, success eludes Farah. For a while, Yasimina seems to be doing well. She spends her time in the company of a rich boyfriend sunbathing nude on his yacht. After years of seeing her body as "a burden, a corpse," she begins to discover it "as a world of pleasure." The pleasure, however, is short-lived. The daily bombing by Israeli planes of Palestinian targets in and around Beirut puts a stop to the normal flow of life. Yasimina's boyfriend breaks up with her. In desperation, she turns to her brother, a longtime Beirut resident, who takes her money and, after accusing her of tarnishing the family honor through her sexual transgressions, stabs her to death. Sammān clearly intends the novel to be an exposé of horrific forms of social and political oppression, the responsibility for which must lie with both men and women. As she herself has said, "We should demand rights for women and men together—that is, demand rights for the repressed human race of which women form such a large part."

Sammān returns to this theme in her next novel, *Kawābis Bayrūt* (1976; *Beirut Nightmares*, 1997), which is in the form of a series of nightmares involving a nameless female narrator's many struggles in a patriarchal society amid civil war. A stray bullet from a sniper goes through the narrator's apartment window, grazing her ear. She puts the bullet next to her pen, then comments, "this particular bullet . . . seemed to me at first sight as long as my pen. Then it grew and became a pillar of fire, while my pen trembled and shrank." Another bullet scores a direct hit at her university diploma. Later, a missile pierces her apartment, destroying her entire library. Through these images, Sammān is trying to determine if violence can be justified in the name of revolution. The narrator herself has been trying to start some sort of a peaceful revolution against society: "My library was not merely books. It was a dialogue. Every book was a man with whom I had argued." She soon realizes that a peaceful revolution will have little chance of success in a war-torn country. At the end of the book, the narrator, despite serious misgivings ("I need it, but I still detest it"), begins to carry a pistol along with her pen.

Other women writers of this region have broken new ground in the novel. Israeli Batya Gur (1947-2005) wrote a series of internationally respected and highly literary mystery novels featuring police detective Michael Ohayon. The novels include *Retsah be-Shabat ba-boker* (1988; *The Saturday Morning Murder: A Psychoanalytic Case*, 1992) and *Retsah be-Derekh Bet Lehem* (2001; *Bethlehem Road Murder*, 2004). Hudā Barakāt (born 1952) of Lebanon is the author of *Ḥajar al-Ḍaḥik* (1990; *The Stone of Laughter*, 1994), the first book by an Arab author to feature a gay protagonist.

TURKEY

In its early days, the Turkish novel, especially those of Ahmet Mithat (1844-1912), Halit Ziya Uǎakligil (1866-1945), and Peyami Safa (1899-1961), extolled the virtues of Turkish society while at the same time stressing the importance of Western knowledge for material success. Safa's *Fatih-Harbiye* (1931) is a naturalistic portrayal of life in Fatih, an old Istanbul district where age-old traditions give men and women contrasting gender roles, and in Harbiye, a sprawling suburb of European-style homes and businesses where women work outside the home and do not have to cover their faces. Other early novelists, most notably Refik Halit Karay (1888-1965) and Reǎat Nuri Güntekin (1889-1956), found inspiration in the country's heartland, the Anatolia region, where the peasantry's seemingly harmonious relationship with nature proved alluring to them. This gradually developed into what came to be known as the peasant novel, and Yashar Kemal (born 1923), who emerged as Turkey's most famous novelist during the 1950's, was its undisputed perfecter.

Kemal's many novels have been translated into some thirty languages, and he has been a frequent candidate for the Nobel Prize in Literature. The recipient of numerous awards, including the 1997 German Book Trade Peace Prize, Kemal was born in Turkey's southeast to the only Kurdish family in the poverty-stricken village of Hemite. Although Kemal moved to Istanbul in the early 1950's, the region of his birth and its poor peasantry continued to dominate his novels. Like William Faulkner, who was a strong influence on Kemal, the Turkish writer returned time and time again to his birthplace, weaving out of its people, their songs and legends, their lyrical ways with language, their many struggles, and their age-old traditions stories of epic proportions.

Kemal's 1955 novel, *İnce Memed* (*Memed, My Hawk*, 1961), is the story of Memed, a fatherless peasant boy who must work long hours in the field to support himself and his mother. Unusually mature for his age, Memed puts up with an abusive, tyrannical landowner and scorching summer heat; the only bright spot in his life is his sweetheart, Hatche. However, the landlord, Abdi Agha, tries to force Hatche to marry his nephew, Veli. Hatche and Memed elope. In a shootout with the Agha and his men, Memed kills Veli, wounds the landlord, and escapes to the mountains. Hatche is eventually captured, charged with Veli's death, and thrown into prison. The story, however, is the stuff of legend: Memed returns, rescues his sweetheart, gives chase to the Agha, and divides his fields among the peasantry. As can be seen from this brief sketch, the novel is action-packed, cinematic, and quite lyrical in its rendering of the peasant imagination.

These are also the qualities that characterize other Kemal novels that have been translated into English, especially *Ölmez otu* (1968; *The Undying Grass*, 1977) and *Yılanı öldürseler* (1976; *To Crush the Serpent*, 1991). Though the latter is much shorter than *Memed, My Hawk*, its scope and style are easily recognizable. Esme is forced to marry Halil, whom she does not love, and the couple soon have a son, named Hasan. Esme's lover murders Halil, but most everyone in the village blames Esme for it. Killing a woman in revenge is out of the question. According to popular belief, however, failure to avenge the murder would result in the community being terrorized by Halil's spirit, which would return in the form of a poisonous snake. The burden is now on the young Hasan to avenge his father's death, but he decides to leave for the city rather than stay and become trapped in and possibly destroyed by violence. This plot twist reflects Kemal's outspoken criticism of feudalism.

The novels of Orhan Pamuk (born 1952), highly acclaimed for their technical innovation and mesmerizing prose, have been translated into more than one dozen languages. Appropriating the techniques of such European writers as James Joyce, Marcel Proust, and Thomas Mann, Pamuk has created stories that explore Turkey's Ottoman past, its troubled present, and its uncertain future.

Pamuk's international fame came with his third novel, *Beyaz kale* (1985; *The White Castle*, 1990). Set in the 1690's, the time when the Ottoman Empire began a decline, it tells the story of a Venetian aristocrat and a Turkish inventor known only as Hoja. Hoja sees the West as the source of all scientific knowledge. He invents a war machine with which he helps the sultan's army lay siege to a white castle in southern Poland. Hoja settles in Europe, while the Venetian retires to Anatolian exile. The identities of the two men remain unclear: Even though one is from the East and the other is from the West, they are interchangeable.

The novel questions the notions of cultural and racial purity. The Venetian character is created out of all the fictions that the narrator has read and appropriated. There is also nothing real about the Ottoman character, for he, too, is created out of myths and stories that the Turkish state requires schoolchildren to learn as facts. The novel's theme is clearly postmodern: Where do the Turkish people living on the margins of Europe belong? East or West? Such questions are complicated even further, given that modern Turkey was founded on secular and Western, rather than religious and Eastern, principles. After the Ottoman defeat in World War I, modern Turkey was created in the West's image. Religion was banned as something backward and outdated, the Latin alphabet was introduced, the Turkish language was purged of its Arabic and Persian words, and the dervish sects were outlawed. As a result, most Turks today cannot read their own classical texts. Another complication comes from the fact that Turkey became a member of the North Atlantic Treaty Organization in 1954, yet its attempts to join the European Union have been repeatedly rebuffed.

Pamuk challenged himself to explore this enduring identity crisis, revisit the past rejected by the postwar government, and study the lines of filiation between East and West. *Yeni hayat* (1994; *The New Life*, 1997) is the story of a student who is greatly influenced by a mysterious book he has been reading. His country is big and sparsely populated; some of it is modernized and Westernized, but most of it remains tribal and traditional. The more the student tries to find out where he belongs, the more troubling and confusing the notion of identity becomes for him. Pamuk's view, expressed in this novel, is that all Turks, being in the "provinces of world culture," suffer from "this feeling of being off the track" and "forgotten." His next novel, *Kar* (2002; *Snow*, 2004), is set in the border city of Kar and examines the conflict between Western and Islamic cultures in Turkey. In 2006, Pamuk won the Nobel Prize in Literature, in recognition of his "quest for the melancholic soul of his native city" and his discovery of "new symbols for the clash and interlacing of cultures."

IRAQ

The novel had a promising start in Iraq, a country with a long, rich literary tradition. Mahmud Ahmad al-Sayyid (1904-1937) and Dhū al-Nūn Ayyūb (1908-1996) began writing in the late 1930's, and Ayyūb's 1939 *Al-Duktūr Ibrāhīm* (Dr. Ibrahim), which deals with the moral bankruptcy of a Western-educated physician, became a best seller in Iraq. The establishment of Saddam Hussein's dictatorship in 1968 dealt a heavy blow to the novel as the state incorporated all forms of artistic and literary production into its massive propaganda machine in support of the leader. The policy forced many to quit writing altogether, but some chose to collaborate with the state. Typical of such work is the massive *Al-Ayyam al-tawila* (1978-1981; *The Long Days*, 1979-1982), a novel by 'Abd al-Amīr Mu'allah that transforms Hussein into a heroic figure of mythic proportions. Under Hussein, the novel was mandatory reading for soldiers, students, and government employees, and it was made into a six-hour film. Hussein himself published four novels—tawdry romances—during his rule; it is assumed that they were ghostwritten. The years of sanctions and oppression under Hussein, and the subsequent war with the United States and allies begun in 2003, has made it nearly impossible for a new era of artistic expression to emerge.

Sabah A. Salih
Updated by Cynthia A. Bily

BIBLIOGRAPHY

Allen, Roger. *The Arabic Novel: An Historical and Critical Introduction*. 2d ed. Syracuse, N.Y.: Syracuse University Press, 1995. Organized chronologically, this readable study examines the development of the Arabic novel into a serious literary genre after World War II. Provides detailed analyses of many novelists and their works.

Chertok, Haim. *We Are All Close: Conversations with Israeli Writers*. New York: Fordham University Press, 1989. Thorough and detailed discussion of themes, techniques, and ideological positions that have become the hallmark of such Israeli writers as David Grossman, Amos Oz, Abraham Yehoshua, and Aharon Appelfeld.

Fuchs, Esther. *Israeli Mythogynies: Women in Contemporary Hebrew Fiction*. Albany: State University of New York Press, 1987. Thought-provoking study that surveys Israeli literature from a feminist perspective. Examines the representation of gender and related issues in the works of male and female writers of Hebrew fiction.

Mehrez, Samia. *Egyptian Writers Between History and Fiction: Essays on Naguib Mahfouz, Sonallah Ibrahim, and Gamal al-Ghitani*. Rev. ed. Cairo: American University in Cairo Press, 2005. Thorough literary-historical study of three influential Egyptian novelists. Mehrez attempts "to bridge the gap between the literary and the historical, the personal and the collective, the aesthetic and the ideological."

Meyer, Stefan G. *The Experimental Arabic Novel: Postcolonial Literary Modernism in the Levant*. Albany: State University of New York Press, 2001. Discusses modernism, experimentation, "Arabization," and questions facing Arab writers as they employ a postcolonial perspective in their modernist works.

Mikhail, Mona. *Seen and Heard: A Century of Arab Women in Literature and Culture*. Northampton, Mass.: Olive Branch Press, 2004. Study examining the ways women have been represented in Arabic texts and the ways they have represented themselves. Chapters include "Masculine Ideology or Feminine Mystique: A Study of Writings on Arab Women," "I Light Ten Candles: Women and Vow-making," and "'A New Vision of the Veil,' by Iqbal Barraka."

Orfalea, Gregory. "The Arab American Novel." *MELUS* 31, no. 4 (Winter, 2006): 115-133. Scholarly but accessible look at the Arab American novel, part of a special issue on Arab American literature. A journal of the Society for the Study of the Multi-Ethnic Literature of the United States (MELUS).

Ramras-Rauch, Gila. *The Arab in Israeli Literature*. Bloomington: Indiana University Press, 1989. A useful and accessible discussion of how the Arab-Israeli encounter has been portrayed in the novels of David Grossman, Abraham Yehoshua, Amos Oz, Aharon Appelfeld, and others.

Shaaban, Bouthaina. *Voices Revealed: Arab Women Novelists, 1898-2000*. Boulder, Colo.: Lynne Rienner, 2009. Demonstrates the innovations women have brought to the Arabic novel, and traces the parallels between the reception of the novels of female authors and their changing position in Arab countries. Argues that "Arab women were pioneers in the creation of the Arab novel—though until now they have been little known."

Silberschlag, Eisig. *From Renaissance to Renaissance: Hebrew Literature in the Land of Israel.* New York: KTAV, 1977. A solid and thorough discussion of the origins, developments, themes, and circumstances of early Israeli literature, with a long chapter on the novel.

Suleiman, Yasir, and Ibrahim Muhawi, eds. *Literature and Nation in the Middle East.* New York: Columbia University Press, 2006. Analyzes the representation of the idea of "nation" in the literature of Egypt, Iraq, Israel, Lebanon, Palestine, and the Sudan.

Russian Long Fiction

The eighteenth century is generally considered the beginning of modern Russian literature for several reasons. The most important is that a clear break occurred with the age of faith, as Serge Zenkovsky calls it in the introduction to his anthology, *Medieval Russia's Epics, Chronicles, and Tales* (1974). The acceptance of Christianity in 988-989 C.E. by Vladimir the Great (who ruled Kievan Rus from 980 to 1015) from culturally superior Byzantium established the authority of the Orthodox Church and enabled it to determine the nature of literature, such as it was, for several centuries. Written by clergy and monks in Old Church Slavonic, a language elaborated for the Slavs in the ninth century by Saints Cyril and Methodius, the literature ("writings" would perhaps be a better term) consisted of the Bible, liturgical texts, Church books, sermons, saints' lives, chronicles and annals, military tales, and some translated literature. The latter included popular works of a secular nature, such as the historical heroic romances *Aleksandriya* (c. twelfth century; the story of Alexander the Great) and *Troyanskoe deyanie* (c. eleventh century; Trojan deeds), which, however, often contained religious motifs. Didactic stories offering instruction in the form of a fable or homily, such as "Varlaam i Yosafat" (c. thirteenth century; Barlaam and Yosaphat), a Christian version of the story of Buddha, were also common. It is important to note that the great classical Greek and Roman heritage was not transmitted to Rus: The Byzantines regarded the Russians as culturally inferior, unworthy of this heritage, while the Orthodox Church considered such writings pagan literature.

The destruction of Kievan Rus by the Mongols from 1238 to 1240 was followed by more than 150 years of Tatar domination (the Tatar Yoke, as it is called), which ended with the rise of Muscovy as the new center of power. Religious literature continued to dominate throughout the fifteenth and sixteenth centuries, although secular themes, realistic details, and the vernacular gradually became more widespread. This is particularly evident in the gradual changes in the canonical form of the saint's life, which by the seventeenth century was supplanted by secular biography, autobiography, and first-person confession. A good example of this is "Povest o Yulianii Lazarevskoy" (c. 1620; the life of Juliania Lazarevsky), which, although written in the traditional form of a saint's life, is, in fact, a secular biography in conception.

There was also a gradual shift from Church Slavonic, a language that virtually none but clergy spoke, toward the vernacular, a shift that was closely linked to the rise of secular literature. Consequently, an account of a Tver merchant's journey to India, "Khozhdeniye za tri morya Afanasiya Nikitina 1466-1472 gg" (c. 1475; "The Travels of Athanasius Nikitin"), describing its exotic animals, lush landscapes, and strange customs, is written in a language almost entirely free of Church Slavonicisms. The vernacular was also dispersed by numerous stories satirizing corruption, irreligious practices among the clergy and monks, and a host of other common abuses, as seventeenth century literature moved to a closer portrayal of everyday life.

Modern Russian literature

The passage from the age of faith into modern Russian literature is strikingly illustrated by the story "Povest o Frole Skobeyeve" (late seventeenth century; "Frol Skobeev, the Rogue," 1963). The story introduced a new type for Russian literature, the rogue, the social outsider who managed through his scheming to rise in station. Sharply satiric in its portrayal of the relationships between the rich and the poor, the story also contains erotic scenes and realistic details of Moscow life. Written in the vernacular, it is devoid of any religious features and is an excellent example of native Russian literature of the Petrine period (1682-1725).

In addition to the secularization of literature, there are other reasons for considering the eighteenth century as the beginning of modern Russian literature. The efforts of Peter the Great (1682-1725) to westernize Russia increased contacts with Western Europe and freed Russia from its relative isolation. This led to a large influx of foreign literature, which served as a model for Russian authors and stimulated their own literary efforts; it also prepared the ground for the acceptance of French classicism—which was, however, modified by native Russian traditions.

French classicism exerted its greatest influence on Russian poetry, which was the dominant genre of the eighteenth century. Prose, which was not regarded as on an equal footing with serious art such as poetry or drama, had to struggle for recognition and legitimacy, and rose to prominence only in the last quarter of the century, after the demise of classicism in the early 1770's. In keeping with the distinction made by classicism between high and low genres, Russian prose fiction of the eighteenth century tended primarily toward the low genres—the picaresque, the satire, the adventure story, and the romance—rather than the high genres—the tragedy or the *Staatsroman*, the novel concerned with how the ideal state should be governed. The latter was influenced by the Enlightenment belief in reason and centered on the discussion of the correct way a monarch was to rule his or her subjects; it was considered, therefore, to have a serious purpose. The former, the lower genres, were considered mere amusement and diversion. These popular forms were, however, much more widely read, and as a result, they furthered the penetration of the vernacular into literature.

The eighteenth century also saw the first conscious efforts made to fix the standard of the Russian literary language, which to that time consisted of an incongruous mixture of Church Slavonic, the vernacular, chancellery terms, and foreign borrowings. Under the influence of classicism, Mikhail Lomonosov (1711-1765), a prominent poet and scholar, established the doctrine of three styles—high, middle, and low—which were distinguished by the relative abundance of Church Slavonicisms. The high style, with its predominance of archaisms and Church Slavonicisms, was deemed appropriate for heroic poems, odes, and prose orations on important matters; the middle style, for epistles in verse, satires, eclogues, theatrical productions, and elegies; and the low style, for comedies, songs, humorous epigrams, and prose letters to friends. As one can see, prose fiction was not an art form recognized by Lomonosov, although he accepted the satiric novel as a tool for edification. In the ongoing debate concerning the novel, the principle of usefulness was, in fact, often invoked by its defenders, who pointed out that the novel conformed to Horace's doctrine of *dulce et utile* and therefore deserved to be recognized. The expectation that literature should serve as a force for social change, a notion upheld throughout the nineteenth century as well, was fostered by the Russian satiric tradition and the hostile reaction of the nativists to the flood of popular French literature entering Russia.

Translations of European novels, primarily French but later German and English, played a crucial role in the development of Russian prose fiction of the eighteenth century. They provided models for Russian authors and were themselves very popular. Handmade copies of novels circulated extensively among the aristocracy—which, by and large, spoke French, as did nearly every educated Russian of the eighteenth century. The French novels generally provided entertaining reading, especially the popular adventure novel, which described travels to strange countries, exotic landscapes, fantastic encounters, and amorous adventures. Consisting of loosely connected episodes, the popular novels emphasized melodramatic action rather than character development. They first appeared in large numbers in the early 1760's; only one novel was published in Russian between 1725 and 1741, and that was a translation of Paul de Tallemant's *Voyage à l'isle d'amour* (1663; Russian translation, 1730).

The influence of French literature is evident in the works of Russia's first novelist, Fyodor Emin (c. 1735-1770). He wrote six original novels between 1763 and 1769, intertwining melodramatic plots characteristic of the adventure novel with verbose digressions on politics, society, geography, and love. He made extensive use of clichés in his portrayal of character and wrote in a pathetic-emotional style, but he was also among the first to voice sympathy with the plight of the peasants. His first novel, *Nepostoyannaya fortuna ili pokhozhdenie Miramonda* (1763; fortune inconstant, or the voyage of Miramond), is a typical adventure novel in which the hero travels through Europe and offers a commentary on geography, political systems, the relationship between rich and poor, and so on. Similar topics appear in his *Priklyucheniya Femistokla* (1763; the adventures of Themistocles), which is set in the Athenian age and consists of conversations between a father and son about politics and society—in particular, the way an enlightened monarch should govern. In this regard, Emin was influenced by François Fénelon's popular novel *Les Aventures de Télémaque* (1699; *The Adventures of Telemach*, 1720; Russian translation, 1766), the translation of which went through eight editions in Russia by 1800, and by his wish to flatter Catherine the Great (r. 1762-1796), who fancied herself an enlightened monarch. Emin's most noted work is his four-volume novel *Pisma Ernesta i Dovravry* (1766; the letters of Ernest and Dovravra), the first Russian epistolary novel. Influenced by *Julie: Ou, La Nouvelle Héloïse* (1761; *Eloise: Or, A Series of Original Letters*, 1761; better known as *The New Héloïse*), by Jean-Jacques Rousseau (1712-1778)—but without its social conflict—it is the story of the unhappy love of the socially equal but poor nobleman Ernest for the wealthy Dovravra. Its weaknesses are its style, too clumsy and awkward for depicting the fine sentiments of the two lovers; its overly melodramatic and emotional tone; and its numerous digressions. It was through these digressions, however, that Emin expressed his criticism of the aristocracy, corruption, and political inequality, and his sympathy for the plight of the peasants. The novel also foreshadowed the rise of a later literary movement, sentimentalism, by some twenty years.

PICARESQUE LITERATURE

Along with the adventure novel, another popular genre of the eighteenth century was the picaresque. Although the picaro had appeared in earlier works of Russian literature, the popularity of the genre was primarily the result of the translations of the works of Alain-René Lesage (1668-1747). The Russian translation of Lesage's *Histoire de Gil Blas de Santillane* (1715-1735; *The History of Gil Blas of Santillane*, 1716, 1735; better known as *Gil Blas*, 1749, 1962), for example, went through eight editions from 1754 to 1800, while Lesage's *Le Diable boiteux* (1707; *The Devil upon Two Sticks*, 1708, 1726) went through five editions from 1763 to 1800, quite an achievement when one considers that in eighteenth century Russia, only twenty works of belletristic prose went through more than four editions. The popularity of the picaresque novels prompted Russian authors to try their hand at the genre.

Although itself not a picaresque novel, *Peresmeshnik: Ili, Slavyanskie skazki* (1766; the mocker, or Slavic

tales), by Mikhail Dmitrievich Chulkov (c. 1743-1792), combined elements of the picaresque with those of the fairy tale and knightly romance. Influenced by Giovanni Boccaccio's *Decameron: O, Prencipe Galetto* (1349-1351; *The Decameron*, 1620) and *The Arabian Nights' Entertainments* (fifteenth century; Russian translation, 1763), Chulkov's novel consists of separate stories told by three narrators, and, in comparison to other works of fiction of its time, it stands out for its native Russian character. His second work, *Prigozhaia povarikha: Ili, Pokhozhdenie razvratnoy zhenschiny* (1770; *The Comely Cook: Or, The Adventures of a Depraved Woman*, 1962), was the first Russian work to present a picara: It is the story of a young widow's trials and amorous adventures told in the form of a confession and limited to her naïve perspective. There is, however, very little that is genuinely Russian—the characters' names are foreign, the places and events are typical of the genre rather than specifically Russian, and virtually no Russian customs or traits are mentioned.

The most frequently published work influenced by the picaresque (as well as by the Russian satiric tradition) was "O Vanke Kaine, slavnom vore i moshennike kratkaya povest" (1775; a short tale about the famous thief and swindler Vanka Kain). The story of a real Moscow thief and police informer, it went through three versions and sixteen editions, thus surpassing all other single works of belletristic prose published in the eighteenth century. Strongly influenced by the Russian folktale, it describes real Russian types and the actual setting of Moscow; it contains few foreign words and many folk sayings and expressions, and even includes thieves' jargon, with translations provided in the footnotes by the unknown author, who maintains the first-person narration and the satiric intent characteristic of the genre. In 1779, it was reworked by Matvey Komarov (eight of the sixteen editions are of his version), who included witnesses' statements, police reports, and folk songs about Kain. He also added a moralistic, sentimental tone and stressed the value of education in turning evil into good, points uncharacteristic of the picaresque.

Works containing picaros or tricksters continued to appear throughout the century and maintained their popularity until the early 1830's, but by the 1780's a gradual shift in literary taste had occurred. Once again, translations of European works—Rousseau's *Émile* (1762; Russian translation, 1779), Johann Wolfgang von Goethe's *Die Leiden des jungen Werthers* (1774; Russian translation, 1781), Oliver Goldsmith's *The Vicar of Wakefield* (1766; Russian translation, 1787), Samuel Richardson's *Pamela: Or, Virtue Rewarded* (1740-1741; Russian translation, 1787), and the idylls of Thomas Gray, Edward Young, and Goethe—played a crucial role in shaping the movement called sentimentalism. Sentimentalism (also referred to as pre-Romanticism) asserted the primacy of the individual and the emotions (instead of reason) as the source of moral virtue and developed the cult of friendship and sensibility. It emphasized the virtues of the countryside as opposed to the corrupt city and the honest simplicity of the peasant as opposed to the worldly veneer of the aristocrat.

The transition to sentimentalism can be seen in the works of the minor writer Nikolay Emin (died 1814), son of Fyodor Emin. His *Roza* (1786; Rosa) and *Igra sudby* (1789; the play of fate) combine the classicist conflict of duty versus feelings with the melodramatic plot of the adventure novel and attempt, unsuccessfully, to incorporate the new sensibility in describing fine emotions. The influence of foreign works can also be seen in the absence of real Russian characters. The same is true of another minor writer, Pavel Lvov (1770-1825), in his novel *Rossiyskaya Pamela: Ili, Istoriya dobrodetelnoy poselyanki* (1789; the Russian Pamela, or the history of a virtuous peasant girl). Influenced by the idyll and the adventure novel as well as by Richardson's *Pamela*, it, too, contained very few Russian elements.

SENTIMENTALISM

Critics of the time were quick to point out that few of the numerous stories written in the sentimental vein described Russian reality and characters. Striving for grace and pleasantness (*priyatnost*) in literature, sentimentalist writers offered idyllic images of Russia and its society that occasionally ended in absurdity, especially in the portrayal of peasants, who were often shown speaking in the high style and occasionally even singing songs from French operas. The influence of the French rococo, with its emphasis on playfulness and lightness, was also evident in the predilection for short fiction of various types, designated by a number of sometimes overlap-

ping terms: *skazka, rasskaz, romanets, novost* (from the French *nouvelle*), or *povest* (which could refer to a short story but more often designated a long tale, a novella, or a short novel). The absence of clearly defined generic features merely reflected the nascent stage of Russian prose fiction.

One of the leading writers of the sentimental *povest* was Nikolai Mikhailovich Karamzin (1766-1826). Among his most important contributions was the development of a smooth, readable literary style, achieved by forgoing the heavy syntax of Lomonosov's German model and approximating the lightness and elegance of French. This Karamzin accomplished by shortening the syntactic period, avoiding Slavonicisms, and establishing a middle style of educated speech. Although criticized by Admiral Aleksandr Semyonovich Shishkov (1754-1841) and the conservatives (*Arkhaisty*) for his rejection of native Slavonic words and his introduction of Gallicisms, Karamzin's reform shaped the language in which the poetry of Russia's golden age was written and established an elegance that was imitated but unsurpassed in the eighteenth century. His most famous tale was "Bednaya Liza" (1792; "Poor Liza," 1803), with its theme of seduced innocence. Contemporaries praised his artistic rendition of the two lovers, the weak nobleman Erast and the poor country girl Liza, and their emotional and psychological portrayal. The story's great success was also a result of the absence of exaggeration, the careful use of detail, and the native Russian elements, such as the character types and the setting (Moscow and its environs). The story's immense popularity led to numerous literary imitations and even to pilgrimages to the pond near Simonov Monastery, where, in the story, Liza drowned herself. Karamzin also wrote one of the first Russian gothic tales, "Ostrov Borngolm" (1793; "The Island of Bornholm," 1821). A gloomy, Romantic atmosphere is evoked by features typical of the genre—a subterranean dungeon, vaults, a gothic castle, nocturnal settings, storms, fogs, and the suggestion of a terrible sin (incest) that has doomed the hero.

In addition to his stories, Karamzin left a fragment of a novel (thirteen chapters were published), *Rytsar nashego vremeni* (1803-1804; a knight of our time), in which he focused not on plot or incident but on the psychological portrait of his hero, the young boy Leon. Influenced by Rousseau's *Les Confessions de J.-J. Rousseau* (1782, 1789; *The Confessions of J.-J. Rousseau,* 1783, 1790; Russian translation, 1797), which also deals with childhood, and by Laurence Sterne's *Tristram Shandy* (1759-1767; partial Russian translation, 1791-1792), with its whimsical play with narration, the fragment remains an interesting if incomplete document. Another of Karamzin's contributions to long fiction was his popular travelogue *Pis'ma russkogo puteshestvennika* (1797; *Letters of a Russian Traveler, 1789-1790,* 1957). The epistolary form enabled him to combine personal expression and commentary with factual description of his journey through Europe. The later entries, however, resembled essays, as Karamzin shifted his attention from his surroundings to general philosophical topics. The success of Karamzin's work was a result of his moderate use of facts and statistics, the absence of pronounced sermonizing, and his elegant literary style.

THE TRAVELOGUE

The travelogue was the most popular genre at the end of the eighteenth century and the start of the nineteenth century. One of the first Russian authors in this genre was Denis Fonvizin (1745-1792), with his "Pisma iz vtorogo i tretego puteshestvij po Evrope" (written 1777-1778, 1784-1785, and published in his complete works of 1959; letters from the second and third journeys abroad). Addressed to his sister and his friend, Count Peter Panin, these letters were written in colloquial Russian and were not necessarily intended as a finished literary work. The patriotic Fonvizin wished, however, to point out that social and economic conditions were not better in France than in Russia. By exposing sham, corruption, hypocrisy, and immorality in European countries, Fonvizin wished to show that human vices and frailties were universal and that Russian imitation of European culture was, therefore, pointless.

Because of its political significance, the best-known Russian work in this genre is *Puteshestvie iz Peterburga v Moskvu* (1790; *A Journey from St. Petersburg to Moscow,* 1958), by Aleksandr Radishchev (1749-1802). Without undertaking an actual journey, Radishchev utilized the form of the travelogue to launch an attack against Catherine II and the Russian nobility, arguing for a constitutional monarchy and the abolition of serfdom.

In spite of the illusion of a real journey, there is little description of the countryside or local customs. Instead, Radishchev discusses law, the individual's rights in relation to the state, new concepts of morality, and a variety of other subjects. Often relying on allegory to convey his didactic message, Radishchev wrote in a ponderous, uneven style incorporating Church Slavonic syntax, Latinisms, archaisms, and grammatical forms of his own creation in order to approximate the elevated high style established by Lomonosov. While the work has its faults, Radishchev was admired (and is today) for his courageous protest, for which he was sentenced to death for sedition, a sentence commuted by Catherine II to ten years' exile in Siberia.

Censorship was a problem facing literature throughout the eighteenth century (and it continues to be a problem in modern times). During Catherine II's reign, the struggle between the autocracy and literature was graphically played out in the satiric journals. Publishing her own rather harmless satiric journal, *Vsyakaya vsyachina* (1769; all kinds of things), Catherine encouraged others to follow suit, and several leading literary figures did so, only to have the censors close the journals for their hostile attitudes toward the government: Nikolai Ivanovich Novikov (1744-1818) published *Truten* (1769-1770; the drone); Chulkov published *I to i se* (1769; this and that); and Emin published *Adskaya pochta* (1769-1774; hell's post). In addition to the political significance of the satiric journals, which were sharply critical of the autocracy, the nobility, and serfdom, they sustained native Russian traditions by presenting Russian reality and characters, folk sayings, and customs, serving as a counterbalance to the influx of European literature. They were closely watched and were frequently shut down by the censors, particularly following the Pugachov Rebellion (1772-1774), after which not a single satiric journal appeared until the end of the 1780's.

Censorship was again vigorously enforced by Catherine as news and reports of the French Revolution (1789) became known in Russia; her fear of radical ideas and political unrest led to Radishchev's arrest in 1790. It also led to Novikov's arrest in 1792 and the burning of twenty thousand books published by him, as well as the burning of Karamzin's translation of William Shakespeare's *Julius Caesar* (pr. c. 1599-1600) as seditious.

As a means of increasing government control over literature, Catherine closed down all private publishing houses
in 1796, the last year of her reign. Matters did not improve under Paul I (r. 1796-1801), who well understood
the potential political danger inherent in literature. This
point was also grasped by many of the leading political
and social thinkers of the nineteenth century, who wished
to make literature a tool for edification and social criticism, an issue that remained hotly debated throughout
the nineteenth century.

THE NINETEENTH CENTURY

The first three decades of the nineteenth century are
appropriately referred to as Russia's golden age of poetry, an age that was dominated by Russia's greatest
poet, Alexander Pushkin (1799-1837). Unable to rival
the achievements of poetry, prose fiction continued to
struggle for acceptance as a serious art form. Many of the
issues facing prose fiction in the eighteenth century remained unresolved by the relatively minor authors who
wrote in the popular prose genres of the previous century. Minor contributions to the travelogue, which continued to enjoy popular success, were made by Vasily
Zhukovsky (1783-1852), with *Puteshestvie po Sakson-
skoy Shveytsarii* (1821; journey to Saxon Switzerland);
Konstantin Batyushkov (1787-1855), with "Puteshestvie
v Zamok Sirey" (1814; journey to the Chateau Sirey),
an essay describing his visit to Voltaire's château at
the conclusion of the Napoleonic War; and Aleksandr
Aleksandrovich Bestuzhev (1797-1837), with *Poezdka
v Revel* (1821; journey to Revel).

Translations of picaresque novels also enjoyed continued success, as evidenced by the four editions of *Gil
Blas* and the two editions of *The Devil upon Two Sticks*
that appeared between 1800 and 1821. The influence of
Lesage is seen in *Rossiiskii Zhilblaz: Ili, Pokhozhdeniia
kniazia Gavrily Simonovich Chistiakova* (1814; complete version, 1938; the Russian Gil Blas, or the adventures of Prince Gavrilo Simonovich Chistakov), by Vasilii
Trofimovich Narezhny (1780-1825), the last three parts
of which were forbidden by the censor. The novel was
immensely popular for its Russian character and
spawned numerous imitations. One of the most famous
of these was *Ivan Vyzhigin: Ili, Russkiy Zhil Blas* (1825;
Ivan Vyzhigin, or the Russian Gil Blas), by Faddei

Bulgarin (1789-1859), excerpts of which appeared in
the journal *Severny arxiv* (the northern archive). In the final version, it was called *Ivan Vyzhigin, nravstvenno-
satiricheskiy roman* (1829; *Ivan Vejeeghen: Or, Life in
Russia*, 1831); the novel went through three editions by
1830 and was translated into French, German, Polish,
English, Swedish, and Spanish. Its popularity resulted
from Bulgarin's successful adaptation of the picaresque
novel to Russian conditions. Modifying the traditional
worldview of the picaro, Bulgarin focused on descriptions of the Russian countryside, villages, and customs,
and on the life of the middle class. In this respect,
Bulgarin shrewdly assessed the literary tastes of the
newly established average reader, who was primarily interested in entertaining books about Russian life.

The major task of forming a readership, shaping public opinion, and introducing Russian authors and European literary and philosophical movements to the public
was carried out by the journals and newspapers. As in
the eighteenth century, their significance extended to
the political arena as well. Often advocating a particular
literary tendency, they were carefully scrutinized by
the censors, and many were suppressed—*Moskovskiy
Telegraf* (1825-1834), *Literaturnaya gazeta* (1830-1831),
Evropeets (1832), and the monthly *Teleskop* (1830-
1836), to name but a few. Survival depended less on the
literary qualities of the publications than on coming to
terms with the authorities and successfully catering to
the public, a point not lost on publishers and editors
scrambling to increase circulation.

Fueled by the defeat of the French in the Napoleonic
War (1814), new demands were being placed on prose
fiction—namely, that it represent Russian reality. The
current genres were considered inadequate: The travelogue, while interesting, focused on foreign countries and
had no specific form; the picaresque form, in spite of
adapting to Russian conditions, lacked the dignity appropriate for high art; and the sentimental novel of manners, although presenting scenes from everyday life, was
unable to express the new sense of national pride.

THE HISTORICAL NOVEL

In the 1820's, the Russian sense of national pride
found expression in the historical novel, which combined everyday reality (*byt*) with the heroic fate of the

nation. Elements of the historical novel could already be found in Bestuzhev's early works, *Zamok Neygauzen* (1824; the castle of Neuhausen) and *Revelskiy turnir* (1825; the tournament at Revel), which were influenced by Sir Walter Scott's Waverley novels. It was not until 1829, however, that the historical novel proper made its presence felt with the appearance of the popular *Iurii Miloslavskii: Ili, Russkie v 1612 godu* (1829; Yuriy Miloslavskiy, or the Russians in the year 1612), by Mikhail Nikolaevich Zagoskin (1789-1852), which he followed with *Roslavlev: Ili, Russkie v 1812 godu* (1831; Roslavlev, or the Russians in the year 1812). So successful was the historical novel that it soon outpaced all other genres of prose fiction of the time; numerous authors, among them the popular Ivan Lazhechnikov (1792-1869) and even the great writers Pushkin and Nikolai Gogol (1809-1852), turned to this Romantic genre. Its success was, however, short-lived, and by the mid-1830's it had lost its appeal to a public demanding that fiction reflect contemporary life.

The late development of the historical novel is indicative of the delayed influence of Romanticism on Russian literature. Reacting against classicism, with its distinct genres, rules, and emphasis on clarity, Romanticism sought to fuse disparate elements into new forms by combining reality with fantasy and the rational with the irrational. It introduced the folk and folklore as subjects worthy of attention; it championed the individual's sincerity and passion over society's hypocrisy and constraints. In Russia, the influence of Romanticism was spread through the works of Scott, Lord Byron, the English and German balladeers, and the German Romantics, particularly Goethe, Friedrich Schiller, Ludwig Tieck, and E. T. A. Hoffmann. The full development of Russian Romantic long fiction was slowed by peculiarly Russian conditions. First, the novel was still in its early stages of development, and therefore there were no models of successful novels; second, the readership demanded a Russian national literature representing Russian reality; and third, by the time the Romantic influence affected Russian prose, Western European literature was already turning to realism. Nevertheless, a limited impact of Romanticism can be seen among both major and minor writers and both short and long fiction in nineteenth century Russia.

In addition to the historical novel, the influence of Romanticism on prose is evident in the current theme of the alienated hero in conflict with his surroundings, a conflict already expressed in Russian poetry of the 1820's, particularly in Pushkin's southern poems and in the poetry of Mikhail Lermontov (1814-1841). Several popular writers of the Russian novel of the 1830's incorporated this theme into their works. Nikolai Polevoy (1796-1846), in his *Mechty i Zhizn* (1834; dreams and life), presented the theme as a conflict between the alienated artist-genius and his society, a popular interpretation. Bestuzhev treated it in his *Frigat Nadezhda'* (1833; the frigate *Hope*) as a conflict between the hero's code (being true to himself) and society's code, but in his *Mulla-Nur* (1836), it received a new twist: The mountain tribesman Mulla-Nur overcomes his alienation and returns to society. Similar themes and variations thereof were widespread in the literature of the 1830's as prose fiction supplanted poetry as the dominant form.

In spite of the steady rise of prose fiction, several major problems remained. The language of prose fiction still had to be elaborated, for neither the rhetorical bookish style nor the measured precision of poetry was appropriate for depicting everyday reality. Writers also faced the problem of defining the form of the novel, their readership, and themselves as writers of Russian literature. In the 1830's, the novel was still an eclectic genre characterized by narrative digressions, fragmentation, lyric pathos, and episodic plots. There were as yet no brilliant successes that could have served as models for the large form. A transitional step appeared in the guise of the story cycle, a form that provided the justification for unifying separate stories into a larger whole. Fairly common in the 1830's, this form also appeared among the major precursors of Russian realism—Pushkin, Gogol, and Lermontov.

THE STORY CYCLE

Pushkin's first attempt at prose fiction resulted in a fragment of a planned historical novel, *Arap Petra velikogo* (1828-1841; *Peter the Great's Negro*, 1896). Although he made several attempts at long fiction, he had only limited success, leaving several prose fragments and only one completed novella, *Kapitanskaya dochka* (1836; *The Captain's Daughter*, 1846), a historical romance about the Pugachov Rebellion, influenced by Scott. Pushkin's most famous work, the long narrative poem *Evgeny Onegin* (1825-1832, 1833; *Eugene Onegin*, 1881), subtitled *A Novel in Verse*, is of interest because of its subsequent influence on long fiction. The work is remarkable for its fine portraiture, its factual description of Moscow and Saint Petersburg, and its details of everyday life (it has been called an encyclopedia of Russian life), all of which produced an accurate description of the period and milieu and served to individuate the characters. In prose, Pushkin was more successful with short forms; in 1831 he published *Povesti Belkina* (*Russian Romance*, 1875; better known as *The Tales of Belkin*, 1947), a collection of five stories parodying current genres and styles.

Pushkin's lack of success with long fiction and his turning to the story cycle, a form then in vogue, are indicative of the ongoing efforts to master the large form. Although he reformed and shaped the language of poetry, he did not choose to take up this issue in regard to prose. His prose language, influenced by the constraint, precision, and simplicity of his poetry, gave the impression of artificiality and was not well suited to bridging the gap between the normal spoken language and the bookish style. This step in the development of prose language was successfully carried out by his younger contemporary, Nikolai Gogol.

Gogol's importance for Russian prose rests on several notable achievements. He was able to develop a middle prose style that raised the spoken idiom to an acceptable literary standard, which he achieved by blending Russian and Ukrainian, a language (to many Russians a dialect) in which the stylistic distinction between the literary language and the spoken language was not as pronounced as in Russian. This fusion arose quite naturally out of his cycle of stories about the Ukraine: *Vechera na khutore bliz Dikanki* (1831, 1832; *Evenings on a Farm near Dikanka*, 1926) and *Mirgorod* (1835; English translation, 1928). The latter collection included Gogol's historical romance *Taras Bulba* (expanded 1842; English translation, 1886), an exaggerated heroic account of the Polish-Cossack conflict. The stories were well received by the reading public, which perceived Ukraine, with its bountiful landscape, colorful peasants, and former Cossacks, as exotic and foreign yet still within the Russian sphere. In spite of presenting an abundance of realistic details of everyday life, Gogol did not fall into ethnographic realism. Contemporaries were misled by the details and considered him a realist, often overlooking the comic devices and the presence of the mysterious and supernatural—the latter influenced by the German Romantics Tieck and Hoffmann.

Stories about Ukraine, often referred to as Little Russia (Malorossiya), had appeared earlier, in the works of the minor Romantic writers Aleksey Perovsky (the pseudonym of Antoni Pogorelsky, 1787-1836) and Evgeny Grebenka (1812-1848), and for a time rivaled the exotic Caucasus as a literary subject. Gogol's treatment of the subject spurred interest in folklore and in the folk (*narod*), as well as demands for their portrayal in works about Russian life. Not surprisingly, Russia turned to Gogol after Pushkin's death in 1837, expecting him to create the national literature, and was not disappointed by his two fine novels *Myortvye dushi* (1842, 1855; *Dead Souls*, 1887) and *Taras Bulba*, the latter an expanded version of a short story published in 1835. Influenced by Henry Fielding, Sterne, Lesage, and Narezhny, Gogol's novel is full of stylistic devices—non sequiturs, hyperboles, illogicalities, obfuscation, and lyric digressions. Contemporaries, however, attracted by the wealth of accurate details from Russian life, the Russian types, and the passages concerning Russia's destiny, proclaimed Gogol a realist. Only a fragment remains of part 2 of the novel, the bulk of which Gogol burned in 1852 under the influence of the mystical religious orientation that dominated the last decade of his life. Gogol's influence on Russian literature has been immense; many of his characters have served as prototypes, and many of his stylistic devices have been imitated by later writers. He developed the theme of the abused little man (usually a government clerk) and of Saint Petersburg (the artificial city created by the will of Peter the Great), themes introduced by Pushkin in his poem *Medniy vsadnik* (1837; *The Bronze Horseman*, 1899). Gogol's Petersburg tales brought forth a host of stories about poor clerks and prompted Fyodor Dostoevski (1821-1881) to offer his own interpretation of those two themes. Gogol's influence extends into the twentieth century, when he was rediscovered and reinterpreted by the Symbolists, and is still vital today.

Gogol's contemporary Mikhail Lermontov was, like Pushkin, a poet who later turned to prose, and his prose work was of great importance to the development of the Russian novel. Lermontov's first two attempts at prose produced the fragment *Vadim* (written 1832-1834 but not serialized until 1873; published in book form, 1935-1937; English translation, 1984) and the unsuccessful novel *Knyaginya Ligovskaya* (written 1836-1837; published in book form 1935-1937; *Princess Ligovskaya*, 1965). His third attempt was the remarkably successful novel *Geroy nashego vremeni* (1839, serial; 1840, book; *A Hero of Our Time*, 1854). Influenced by Benjamin Constant's *Adolphe* (1816; Russian translation, 1831) and the Byronic tradition of the alienated hero who despises society for its hypocrisy and corruption, the novel is set in the Caucasus—an exotic region popular in the literature of the time, as evidenced by Bestuzhev's popular tale *Ammalat bek* (1832; English translation, 1843). Using the travelogue and diary forms, Lermontov's book consists of five stories set within a frame narrative. Although he avoided many of the shortcomings typical of the novel in the 1830's, he was unable to show character developing over time and had to rely on the form of the story cycle to illustrate different aspects of his hero's character. The static portrayal of the hero does not, however, detract from the novel's significant achievements—Lermontov's ability to create atmosphere and his excellent psychological study of the hero, the ironic, analytical Pechorin.

REALISM

The psychological study of the individual was a significant step in the development of realism, as was the focus on details of everyday life. The latter point was the hallmark of the natural school (*naturalnaya shkola*) that appeared in the 1840's. Paying careful attention to details, they presented the unpleasant, harsh side of reality commonly found among the poor and the peasants. This aspect was dealt with by the minor writer Dmitri Grigorovich (1822-1899) in his two novels, *Derevnya* (1846; the village) and *Anton Goremyka* (1847), in which he attempts to describe peasant and village life from the peasant's point of view. The striving for verisimilitude and accurate detail was also apparent in the physiological sketch (*fisiologichesky ocherk*) popular-

ized by the writers of the natural school. Influenced by the French *feuilleton*, the sketches describe social types and milieus, city quarters, and nature in minute detail.

The demand for verisimilitude was not, however, the only expectation placed upon literature in the 1840's. The influential literary critic Vissarion Belinsky (1811-1848) also insisted that literature should be inspired by socially significant ideas, and similar views were to be heard throughout the nineteenth century. First attracted to the German Idealists Friedrich Schelling (1775-1854), Johann Gottlieb Fichte (1762-1814), and Georg Wilhelm Friedrich Hegel (1770-1831), Belinsky later adopted a materialistic position that judged literature not in aesthetic terms but in terms of its utilitarian social function. Oriented toward Europe, Belinsky and the Westernizers were sharply attacked by the Slavophiles, who stressed the superiority of native Russian traditions, institutions, and laws and championed the Russian soul. For both parties, the question concerned Russia's relationship to Europe, an issue frequently found in the novels of Russia's great realists, Ivan Turgenev (1818-1883), Dostoevski, and Leo Tolstoy (1828-1910).

The late 1840's witnessed the development of a remarkable range of novelistic talents. While the novel *Dvoynaya zhizn* (1848; *A Double Life*, 1978), by Karolina Pavlova (1807-1893), reflects the passing of the Romantic era by contrasting a young society woman's stifling daytime experiences with the rich dream world that opens up to her at night, other works display the pronounced shift toward realism urged by Belinsky. For example, Dostoevski's first novel, *Bednye lyudi* (1846; *Poor Folk*, 1887), was enthusiastically reviewed by Belinsky himself and was soon followed by *Dvoynik* (1846; *The Double*, 1917) and "Gospodin Prokharchin" (1846; "Mr. Prokharchin," 1918). Polemicizing with but not parodying Gogol in these three works, Dostoevski gave his own interpretation to the themes of the little man and St. Petersburg. The stories also reflected the influence of the natural school, as evidenced by his focus on ugliness, poverty, and the dull, dirty milieu of the city. The Petersburg theme surfaced in a very different guise, as a dreamer's city, in his "Khozyayka" (1847; "The Landlady," 1917) and "Belye nochi" (1848; "White Nights," 1918), the latter published in the year in which Dostoevski was arrested for being a member of the Petrashevsky Circle, a group that discussed socialist ideas and criticized existing conditions in Russia. His four years of penal service in Siberia and subsequent military service interrupted his literary activity; he did not return to St. Petersburg until 1859.

From 1850 to 1880, Russian literature was dominated by three writers—Turgenev, Dostoevski, and Tolstoy—whose works defined the form of the novel as well as the broad literary movement called realism. Their focus on details of everyday life, on the surroundings, on the social milieu, on individuals and their psychology, and their narrative technique of staging scenes rather than commenting through narrative intrusion, became the hallmarks by which realism was defined.

Although the 1850's were dominated by Turgenev, several writers made significant contributions to the novel in this period, among them Tolstoy, who published his first major work, a nonautobiographical trilogy about a young boy growing up: *Detstvo* (1852; *Childhood*, 1862), *Otrochestvo* (1854; *Boyhood*, 1886), and *Yunost'* (1857; *Youth*, 1886). Influenced by Sterne, Charles Dickens, Rousseau, and Rodolphe Töpfler, Tolstoy utilized a child's own peculiar angle of perception to present familiar objects and experiences in a new and unusual manner—an example of the device, frequent in Tolstoy's works, which the Russian Formalist critic Viktor Shklovsky calls *ostranenie* ("making strange," or "defamiliarization"). A similar subject was treated by Sergey Aksakov (1791-1859) in his trilogy of family generations and a young boy's development: *Semeynaya khronika* (1856; *Chronicles of a Russian Family*, 1924), *Vospominaniya* (1856; *A Russian Schoolboy*, 1917), and the best-known volume, *Detskiye gody Bagrova-vnuka* (1858; *Years of Childhood*, 1916). The last of these, an example of an *Entwicklungsroman*, is a captivating study of a child's psychology as he begins to understand the conflicts and tension among members of his own family; it is also remarkable as a realistic narrative of ordinary life.

Another author known for a realistic narrative of ordinary life was Ivan Goncharov (1812-1891), whose first novel, *Obyknovennaya istoriya* (1847; *A Common Story*, 1890), was hailed by Belinsky as an example of realistic fiction second only to Dostoevski's *Poor Folk*. His novel *Oblomov* (1859; English translation, 1915) is

best known for its phlegmatic eponymous hero, whose philosophy of resignation and inactivity aroused the ire of many activists—including the radical socialist critic Nikolay Dobrolyubov (1836-1861), who wrote an article, "Chto takoye Oblomovshchina?" (1859-1860; "What Is Oblomovism?" 1903), in which he denounced the gentry for being an obstacle to progress.

These relatively minor achievements of the 1850's were overshadowed by Turgenev's success, which was readily acknowledged by critics and the public. Turgenev began his literary career writing poetry, but by the late 1840's, he had turned to writing the stories that he later incorporated into his collection *Zapiski okhotnika* (1852; *Russian Life in the Interior*, 1855; better known as *A Sportsman's Sketches*, 1932), which made him an overnight success. The volume was noted for its lyric mood and atmosphere evoked by the detailed nature descriptions and for its sympathetic portrayal of the serfs. In addition to this volume, Turgenev wrote many stories, several plays, and six novels. In the novels, plot is secondary to character, which is skillfully revealed through polished dialogue and social milieu. Turgenev's novels are generally structured around a romance between a morally superior woman and a weak, irresolute man, a theme made famous by Pushkin in *Eugene Onegin*, and at the same time, around a current political issue. Although he was a civil-minded liberal Westernizer, Turgenev avoided becoming tendentious in his depiction of the ideological struggle between the generations (between the fathers and the sons). He supported the cause of the young radicals but failed to portray a positive Russian political activist. Stung by the radicals' criticism of his portrayal of Bazarov, the nihilistic hero of *Ottsy i deti* (1862; *Fathers and Sons*, 1867), Turgenev decided to remain abroad and settled in France for most of the remainder of his life. In his last two novels, *Dym* (1867; *Smoke*, 1868) and *Nov* (1877; *Virgin Soil*, 1877), he gave vent to his bitterness toward Russia, but although it was clear that he had lost touch with Russian life, he remained a popular writer. Pushkin's influence is evident in Turgenev's poetic prose, masterfully shaped for expressing nuance, atmosphere, and character. Turgenev was the first Russian author to achieve fame in Western Europe, particularly in France, where he died in 1883.

While Turgenev was a member of the nobility and a Westernizer, Dostoevski was a *raznochinets* (educated plebeian). His experience in prison, which he chronicled in his novel *Zapiski iz myortvogo doma* (1861-1862; *Buried Alive: Or, Ten Years of Penal Servitude in Siberia*, 1881; also known as *The House of the Dead*, 1915), produced a profound change in his personal and political views. Arrested for his socialist and Western views, Dostoevski returned from exile having rejected them along with Rousseauism, utopianism, rationalism, and Schillerian Romanticism and having embraced Christ, a belief in Russia and its elect status, and the human need for freedom. He was the first in world literature to find a literary medium for the metaphysical novel, which he combined with the crime story, a combination found in varying degrees in all five of his major novels but particularly evident in his famous *Prestupleniye i nakazaniye* (1866; *Crime and Punishment*, 1886).

Plumbing the depths of his characters' souls, Dostoevski presents the dialectic struggle of good and evil. His characters are shown testing the strength of their rational position against their emotions. Salvation for the proud, the guilty (murders are committed in four of the major novels), and the "supermen" (those who assume that they are beyond good and evil) can be achieved, according to Dostoevski, only through suffering and humility, which will lead to faith in Christ, an issue masterfully illustrated in his *Bratya Karamazovy* (1879-1880; *The Brothers Karamazov*, 1912). Dostoevski also assigned to God a crucial role in Russia's salvation and messianic mission. In perhaps his best novel, *Besy* (1871-1872; *The Possessed*, 1913; also known as *The Devils*), he attacked the atheistic ideological offspring of the liberals of the 1840's (the novel included a vicious satire of Turgenev). *The Possessed* is an excellent example of polyphony, in which each character's voice is given equal weight in the frequent metaphysical arguments. Aspiring to a "higher realism," Dostoevski sought to penetrate to the essence of his characters, avoiding narrative intrusion, and this remains one of his major achievements.

The literary activity of Leo Tolstoy, one of the greatest figures in world literature, falls into two distinct periods, divided by his spiritual crisis in 1879, after which Tolstoy the moral philosopher took precedence over Tolstoy the artist. In his early long fiction, written in the 1850's—the childhood trilogy, the Sevastopol stories, *Kazaki* (1863; *The Cossacks*, 1872), and *Semeynoye schast'ye* (1859; *Family Happiness*, 1888)—he introduced many of the themes he developed further in his two great novels, *Voyna i mir* (1865-1869; *War and Peace*, 1886) and *Anna Karenina* (1875-1877; English translation, 1886): the morality of killing, the enigmatic question of death and the meaning of life, and the question of how one should live, to mention but a few. In his pursuit of truth, he debunked many popular myths concerning war, patriotism, and romantic heroism, particularly in *War and Peace*. In form, *War and Peace* resembles a classic epic, charting the collective experience of the Russian nation during the Napoleonic era; at the same time, it is a modern novel in which the individual searches for meaning and his or her relation to the collective, to society. While Tolstoy's heroes often serve as subjective centers, their individual perceptions revealed through the devices of estrangement (*ostranenie*) and interior monologue, the objectivity of outside reality is not challenged. Tolstoy's interest in the development of character and society over time (and in the question of causation) led him to focus on the individual's changing relationship to family and society. Through this self-reflection within a social setting, an influence of sentimentalism, his characters learn the obligations of responsibility and responsiveness.

This theme also appears in Tolstoy's *Anna Karenina*, a novel about upper-class society of the 1870's. Structured around two contrasting love relationships, the novel focuses on the moral and personal dilemma of transgressing society's ethical code for the sake of love. Through the introduction of stream of consciousness, Tolstoy gives an excellent rendition of the heroine's psychological and emotional turmoil, adding a consummate truth to an already memorable portrait of an individual human being.

Carefully differentiating even minor characters by specific details or traits, even in his large works, Tolstoy was not content with remaining only an observer; he felt the need to guide the reader to the truth by means of direct appeals, narrative intrusions, and digressions. Tolstoy's tendency to instruct, a characteristic feature of his fiction, and his personal search for faith and the meaning of life led to a spiritual crisis that culminated in his work *Ispoved'* (1884; *A Confession*, 1885). Thereafter, his long fiction took on an increasingly moralizing tone, attacking the state, the church, and society as he turned literature into a vehicle for his views. He still produced several great works, such as the novellas *Smert' Ivana Il'icha* (1886; *The Death of Ivan Ilyich*, 1887) and *Khadzi-Murat* (1911; *Hadji Murad*, 1911), but in the last two decades of his life his fame rested not on his fiction but on his moral teachings.

The thirty years from 1850 to 1880 were also a period of activity among socialist critics whose articles and novels were of literary and political significance. Among them was the influential critic Aleksandr Herzen (1812-1870), the author of the *povest Kto vinovat?* (1847; *Who Is to Blame?*, 1978) and publisher of the enormously influential weekly *Kolokol* (1857-1867), which was frequently smuggled into Russia, where it had a wide readership. He advocated a positivist, national socialism and was close to the Slavophiles. Much more radical were N. G. Chernyshevsky (1828-1889), who wrote the famous and tendentious radical novel *Chto delat?* (1863; *What Is to Be Done?*, 1886) and who was arrested in 1862 and later exiled to Siberia, and Dobrolyubov, who was the most influential critic after Belinsky. They both advocated a scientific rationalism as a means to achieve progress, and they professed great faith in the Russian peasant, whose emancipation from serfdom (granted in 1861) they ardently championed. Dobrolyubov also served as the literary critic of the successful journal *Sovremennik* (1836-1866) and had a great impact on succeeding generations.

In addition to the great realists, numerous writers of varying caliber also appeared, among them Aleksey Pisemsky (1820-1881). His novels were known for their unadorned, unidealized view of humankind and for their portrayal of Russian characters not of noble birth, whose dialect Pisemsky expertly rendered. Another notable writer of this period was Mikhail Saltykov-Shchedrin (1826-1889), acclaimed for his many satiric novels, some excessively topical and written in Aesopian language. His crowning achievement, which established his place among the realists, was *Gospoda Golovlyovy* (1872-1876; *The Golovlyov Family*, 1955), a gloomy depiction of the materialistic provincial gentry. Other

civic or plebeian writers include Nikolay Pomyalovskiy (1835-1863), Gleb Uspenskiy (1843-1902), and Ivan Kushchevsky (1847-1876). Populist novels celebrating the virtues of the peasants also appeared, generally written by minor authors, such as Nikolay Zlatovratsky (1845-1911) and Pavel Zasodimsky (1843-1912).

A writer of considerable talent was Nikolai Leskov (1831-1895), known for his excellent rendition of speech, which he often expressed through *skaz*, a narrative form in which the narrator's presence is marked by his or her individualized language and tone. Leskov, who excelled in short fiction, was contemptuously treated by the critics for his portrayal of the radicals and for his works on ecclesiastical life, which he sympathetically described in his popular novel *Soboriane* (1872; *The Cathedral Folk*, 1924).

THE 1880'S AND 1890'S

The early 1880's are generally taken as a watershed in the history of the Russian novel. Two of the great realists had passed from the scene, Dostoevski in 1881 and Turgenev in 1883, and Tolstoy, after his crisis, produced no major novels. There was also a change in the political climate following the assassination of Alexander II (r. 1855-1881), an event that ended the period of political reforms and introduced the repressive measures of Alexander III (r. 1881-1894). In the prose fiction of the 1880's and 1890's, there was a movement away from long fiction, from the globalism (the philosophical questions of existence and the thorough representation of everyday life) of the nineteenth century novel, toward shorter forms with a narrower field of vision.

Several minor but popular writers of this period continued, however, to make use of the novel. One such writer was Aleksandr Ertel (1855-1908), known for his popular novel *Gardeniny, ikh dvornya, priverzhentsy i vragi* (1888; the Gardenins, their retainers, their friends, and their enemies), the second edition of which was prefaced by Tolstoy himself. The novel presents a vast panorama of contemporary life on a provincial gentry estate in southern Russia. Another popular author of the time was Vladimir Korolenko (1853-1921), known for his romantic though rather shallow *povesti* with nature descriptions reminiscent of Turgenev, whose works enjoyed a revival at that time. Also popular was N. Garin (the pseudonym of Nikolay Georgievich Mikhaylovskiy, 1852-1906), whose trilogy about a young boy's education was immensely successful.

In addition to the short form of prose, poetry flourished once again, dominated by the Symbolists, who heralded in Russia's silver age of poetry. The Russian Symbolists, influenced by their French counterparts, spoke of a higher reality existing beneath the surface of everyday life. Defending the aesthetic value of literature, one of the leading Symbolist critics, Dmitry Sergeyevich Merezhkovsky (1865-1941), who also wrote a trilogy of novels in the 1890's, blamed the social tendentiousness of the civic critics for the decline of Russian literature. This new critical position, which denied the basic tenets of the nineteenth century, is indicative of the social crisis experienced by the intelligentsia and the writers. It forced a reevaluation of their relationship to literature and society, as well as a reconsideration of the role of literature itself. These issues, raised at the close of the nineteenth century, became even more pertinent in the twentieth century.

THE EARLY TWENTIETH CENTURY

Russian literature of the twentieth century began like the literature of the nineteenth century, with the dominance of poetry and under the influence of Western European writers, among them Henrik Ibsen (1828-1906), August Strindberg (1849-1912), the French Symbolist poets, and the German philosopher Friedrich Nietzsche (1844-1900). There was, however, a distinct break with the commonality of issues and viewpoints characteristic of the nineteenth century. Instead of consensus, division prevailed among schools of poetry, whose positions were provocatively stated in literary manifestos, an entirely new phenomenon in Russian literature.

The Symbolists, the leading school of poetry in the first decade of the twentieth century, also produced several interesting novels. They believed that the visible world is symbolic of a higher reality behind it and that the poet, as a superior being (a Romantic conception of the artist), is able to articulate this truth, which can only be alluded to, through art. Their writing is, therefore, intentionally vague and ambiguous. They question the identity of objects and only hint at the essence hidden beneath the surface. These traits are clearly evident in

Melkiy bes (1907; *The Little Demon*, 1916; also known as *The Petty Demon*, 1962), written by Fyodor Sologub (the pseudonym of Fyodor Terternikov, 1863-1927), a work strongly influenced by Gogol, whom the Symbolists reinterpreted. Similar qualities inform the works of another Symbolist novelist, Valery Bryosov (1873-1924), whose best-known novel was *Ognenny angel* (1908; *The Fiery Angel*, 1930). Both were surpassed by Andrey Bely (the pseudonym of Boris Bugayev, 1880-1934), a Symbolist poet and a disciple of Rudolph Steiner's Anthroposophy. Although best known for his poetry, Bely wrote several novels, the most remarkable of which was *Petersburg* (serial 1913-1914, book 1916, revised 1922; *St. Petersburg*, 1959; better known as *Petersburg*), considered by the renowned novelist and critic Vladimir Nabokov (1899-1977) to be one of the best novels of the twentieth century. Revised several times, it offers a philosophical and metaphysical interpretation of Russian history in terms of two opposing forces—Western rationalism and a destructive Asiatic-Tatar element of irrationalism. Complex in style and structure, and full of literary allusions, it continues the great tradition of the Petersburg theme, portraying the city's malevolent atmosphere and artificial existence.

There were few identifiable schools of prose fiction prior to the Russian Revolution (1917); one small group of writers, however, did appear. Centered on the journal *Znanie*, from which it took its name, this group was led by the internationally renowned Maxim Gorky (the pen name of Aleksey Maksimovich Peshkov, 1868-1936). The group consisted of Aleksandr Kuprin (1870-1938), known for his realistic novels of military life and his compassionate novel about prostitutes, *Yama* (1909-1915; *Yama: The Pit*, 1929); the minor writer Mikhail Artsybashev (1878-1927), whose popularity rested on his sensational novel *Sanin* (1907; *Sanine*, 1917), with its violence, erotic scenes, and empty metaphysical discussions; Leonid Andreyev (1871-1919), an extremely popular writer of stories focusing on the pathos of the soul; and Ivan Bunin (1870-1953). Bunin was a direct descendant of the nineteenth century realist tradition, as is evident from his short novel *Derevnya* (1910; *The Village*, 1923) and its companion piece *Sukhodol* (1912; *Dry Valley*, 1935). After the Russian Revolution, he emigrated to Paris, where he continued to write on Russian subjects. In 1933, he was awarded the Nobel Prize in Literature, the first Russian to receive the award.

The most significant member of the *Znanie* group, which soon dissolved, was Gorky, who in the Soviet Union became the center of a personality cult, although he himself was critical of the revolution and suspicious of the masses. Having developed from an early Nietzschean Romanticism, Gorky turned from the principle that literature should beautify life to the depiction of current political issues. His novel *Mat* (1906; *Mother*, 1906), based on the events of a May Day demonstration in Sormovo in 1902, gave the first comprehensive portrait of the Russian revolutionary movement. Influenced by Tolstoy, whom he knew personally, Gorky wrote an autobiographical trilogy depicting the hard life of the lower classes in the provinces, of which the first volume, *Detstvo* (1913; *My Childhood*, 1915), is the best. Living in Italy for many years because of poor health, Gorky did not return to Russia for good until the early 1930's. Up to the time of his death, a suspicious affair, he worked on his four-volume "novel-chronicle" *Zhizn Klima Samgina* (1927-1936; *The Life of Klim Samgin*, 1930-1938). It has something of the scope of Tolstoy's *War and Peace*, offering a vast panorama of historical events and social change seen through the eyes of a developing intellectual. Often rhetorical, uneven, and heavy-handed in his fiction, Gorky the publicist outweighed Gorky the artist. While serving as a bridge between the two centuries, he continued the nineteenth century tradition of the Russian writer acting as a public figure. He had an immense influence on the progress of literature and the arts in the Soviet Union and has been called the father of Soviet literature.

THE BOLSHEVIK REVOLUTION

The most decisive event in twentieth century Russian history was the revolution that brought the Bolsheviks to power. It had a profound impact on all spheres of life, including literature. Control over literature was only gradually asserted, however, and as a result, the 1920's were years of relative artistic freedom. Although a radical break with the past political system had occurred, that was not so with regard to culture; the nineteenth century literary tradition continued to exist alongside modernist experiments. Intellectuals, writers of the intelligentsia,

often derogatorily referred to as "fellow travelers," had not yet been displaced by the proletarian writers who swarmed to the metropolis to establish the new literature, to reflect the new morality.

The issue facing the writers of the 1920's was how the novel should depict the new reality. World War I, the revolution, and the bitter Russian Civil War (1918-1921) had shattered the belief in the wholeness of the world, in the collective experience so frequently reflected in the nineteenth century novel. In the West, this experience led to the sense of alienation, epitomized by the lost generation. While the same was true for some Russians, in particular for the intellectuals and those who emigrated, the strong sense of an ending was countered by a firm belief that a new and better time was at hand. The sense of fragmentation did indeed lead to a reassessment of the individual's relationship to society, to the new collective, but the 1920's were still a period of optimism. These issues surfaced in various forms in the prose fiction of nearly every literary school or movement of the time, which made the 1920's a variegated and productive literary period.

The intellectual exuberance of the early 1920's is particularly evident in the works of the Formalist critic Viktor Shklovsky (1893-1984). The Formalists—whose influence on modern criticism, both direct and via French structuralism, has been enormous—emphasized the internal dynamics of literary works, the devices by which they are "made." (Thus, in a characteristic passage, Shklovsky boasts, "I know how Don Quixote is made.") Shklovsky's *Sentimental' noye puteshestviye: Vospominaniya, 1917-1922* (1923; *A Sentimental Journey: Memoirs, 1917-1922*, 1970), *Zoo: Ili, Pis'ma ne o lyubvi* (1923; *Zoo: Or, Letters Not About Love*, 1971), and *Tret'ya fabrika* (1926; *Third Factory*, 1977) combine a sophisticated awareness of literary forms with a strikingly original tone; part novel, part memoir, part literary criticism, these works are marked by the spirit of artistic freedom for which Shklovsky and others were to be attacked in the late 1920's.

Shklovsky's language, fresh and colloquial yet able to accommodate technical literary terms, reflects in part the influence of Aleksey Remizov (1877-1957). Remizov, who emigrated from Soviet Russia to Berlin in 1921, settling in 1923 in Paris, where he remained for the rest of his life, sought to invigorate the Russian literary language with a return to its native resources. In his novels, which resist translation, Remizov forged a style at once racy and ornate, drawing heavily on colloquial speech, proverbs, and folktales, mixing many different levels of diction and different genres within a single work.

One loosely organized group of nonproletarian writers active in the 1920's was the Serapion Brotherhood. Vaguely influenced by E. T. A. Hoffmann but also by Shklovsky and the Formalists, they combined reality and social criticism with fantasy and action plots. Not unsympathetic to the revolution, they resisted pressure to write works praising the new society and focused instead on the individual consciousness in an alienated world. An excellent illustration of this theme appears in *Zavist'* (1927; *Envy*, 1936), a novel that made Yury Olesha (1899-1960) an overnight success. The historical background of the 1920's is present in the novel but on a reduced scale, and reality becomes subject to the laws of fantasy. Olesha creates this fantasy through his method of "magic photography," whereby he transforms reality into images of an alternative world for his superfluous, imaginative little man, estranged from the materialistic, pedestrian new world he envies.

The theme of alienation is also expressed by Konstantin Fedin (1892-1977) in his novel *Goroda i gody* (1924; *Cities and Years*, 1962). Using the technique of montage to convey the fragmentation of reality, Fedin traces the demise of a superfluous man, an intellectual, not able to fully accept the revolution and the new regime. His second novel of the 1920's, *Bratya* (1928; brothers), also portrays a sensitive intellectual out of step with the times.

One of the most interesting novels to appear in the 1920's was *My* (corrupt text published 1927, reissued 1952; *We*, 1924), written in 1920-1921 by Yevgeny Zamyatin (1884-1937), a member of the Serapion Brotherhood. The novel was first published in English and was not published in the Soviet Union for several decades because it is an antiutopian novel. Combining two genres, the diary and the utopian novel, it denies the possibility of utopian happiness and, by implication, the possibility of a future communist paradise. Zamyatin's novel appeared before the rise to power of Joseph Stalin

(1879-1953) and is not, therefore, merely a satire on totalitarianism; it is also a novel about communication and language. The conflict between the individual and the state is expressed through the hero's discovery of many languages—the languages of love, poetry, and the past—that create a threatening polyphony that the authorities suppress in the name of collective happiness. After the publication of *We*, Zamyatin served as head of the Leningrad section of the Union of Writers until 1929, when the Stalinist crackdown on literature began. He was fortunate to be allowed to emigrate in 1931.

Utopias and the future were topics widely discussed in the 1920's. Another novel that raises similar questions is *Chevengur* (1972, written 1928-1930; English translation, 1978), an idiosyncratic novel with an unusual history of publication. Written by the unorthodox Andrey Platonov (1899-1951), the novel is constructed as a pilgrimage through the steppe, as a search for utopian solutions. Full of literary allusions to Dostoevski, Novalis (1772-1801), and Miguel de Cervantes' *Don Quixote de la Mancha* (1605, 1615), it ironically focuses on the inherent contradiction of the revolution as a dynamic, ongoing force and utopia as a static state of collective happiness.

A critical appraisal of the revolution also appears in *Goly god* (1922; *The Naked Year*, 1928), written by an influential writer of the 1920's, Boris Pilnyak, also a member of the Serapion Brotherhood. Influenced by Andrey Bely's prose style, the novel is composed of episodes and fragments that intentionally disrupt and obscure the chronology and logical sequence of events to convey the disruptive force of the revolution itself. The revolution is represented as an elemental deed of blind biological forces and organized, machinelike movement. Pilnyak wrote several other novels, and his style and manner were widely imitated during the 1920's.

In contrast to the critical attitude of many intellectuals, the proletarian writers widely acclaimed the revolution, glorifying its heroes and achievements. Forming their own groups, such as Proletcult, Pereval, and the Smithy, they were quite conservative as writers and continued the literary traditions of the nineteenth century. Their novels are simple and straightforward rather than experimental and convey a social message that usually takes precedence over artistic and technical considerations. Their heroes are portrayed as individual representatives of the collective, for which they make personal sacrifices in combat or on the industrial front. The relationship of the individual to the collective created problems that became the center of considerable debate in the 1920's and that remained an unresolved issue in Soviet literature.

Among the works glorifying the revolution and the revolutionary hero was the novel *Chapayev* (1923; English translation, 1935), by Dmitri Furmanov (1891-1926). Basing the novel on events from Vasily Chapayev's life, Furmanov subordinated this charismatic figure (an actual leader of Red partisans) to the historical context and produced a kind of documentary, not a photographic realism, but a "literature of fact" (*literatura fakta*), a literary phenomenon of the 1920's. Not as well known, Furmanov's second novel, *Myatezh* (1925; the uprising), was also about the partisan movement in the southeastern steppe.

In the enthusiasm for glorifying the revolution, many early works of the proletarian writers portrayed the revolution as a historical movement and overemphasized the role of the collective. A case in point is the popular epic *Zhelezny potok* (1924; *The Iron Flood*, 1935), by Aleksandr Serafimovich (the pen name of Aleksandr Popov, 1863-1949). The novel describes the transformation of an anarchic mass into an organized fighting force that overcomes the Whites. Although ideologically sound, the novel was criticized for its abstractness, its undistinguished characters, and the absence of an individuated revolutionary hero.

The novel that successfully struck a balance between portraying the hero as an individual yet representative of the collective, as resolute and disciplined but with human weaknesses, was the popularly acclaimed *Razgrom* (1927; *The Nineteen*, 1929), by Aleksandr Fadeyev (1901-1956). Fadeyev adequately presented the Marxist notion of historical processes (the revolution) finding expression through concrete individuals. The novel was later praised as a paragon of Socialist Realism, and Fadeyev was proclaimed the "Red Leo Tolstoy." Tolstoy's influence on Fadeyev and the proletarian writers in general was pronounced: Attempting to establish the legitimacy of the new literature, the proletarian writers turned to the classic author of Russian realism, Tolstoy,

with whose concept and portrayal of reality they could identify.

Tolstoy's influence is particularly apparent in *Tikhii Don* (1928-1940; partial translation *And Quiet Flows the Don*, 1934; also known as *The Don Flows Home to the Sea*, 1940; complete translation *The Silent Don*, 1942; also known as *And Quiet Flows the Don*, 1967), an extremely popular novel in four volumes that has often been compared to *War and Peace*. Written by Mikhail Sholokhov (1905-1984), the novel focused on the turbulent and brutal events among the Don Cossacks from World War I to the end of the civil war. Controversy arose concerning both authorship (charges of plagiarism were made, revived in the 1970's by Aleksandr Solzhenitsyn) and the portrayal of the reflective hero, who questions the legitimacy of the revolution and thus suggests the possibility of a third way, the existence of which is denied by communism. Avoiding simplistic oppositions and taking a critical attitude toward the communists, Sholokhov achieved a complexity and verisimilitude that was immediately acknowledged by readers and critics alike.

Few works written by the proletarian writers went so far as to suggest the possibility of a third way between communism and capitalism. Even when presenting the shortcomings of the revolution or the defeat of the communist forces, such setbacks were presented as temporary, as heroic sacrifices necessary to achieve the goals of the revolution. Such a position is taken by Yury Libedinsky (1898-1959) in his novel *Nedelya* (1922; *A Week*, 1923), in which a small detachment of communists is sacrificed for the general good. Libedinsky also wrote two novels on a subject current in the 1920's—the reappearance of bourgeois influences during the period of the New Economic Policy (NEP), a particularly disturbing phenomenon for orthodox communists and one sharply attacked in the novel *Shokolad* (1922; *Chocolate*, 1932), by Aleksandr Tarasov-Rodionov (1885-1938).

Anecdotes, stories, and novels satirizing the return of philistinism, the ineptness of the bureaucracy, and the mundane concerns of everyday life during the NEP were a welcome relief from the steady stream of novels about the revolution. Particularly popular were the satiric novels of Ilya Ilf (1897-1937) and Evgeni Petrov

(1903-1942), such as their *Dvenadtsat stuliev* (1928; *The Twelve Chairs*, 1961) and *Zolotoy telyonok* (1931; *The Little Golden Calf*, 1932). Another author of interest was Ilya Ehrenburg (1891-1967), who had been allowed to travel to the West and later wrote several works critical of Western culture and the capitalist economic system. Some of the first Russian science fiction also appeared during the NEP. One writer of Wellsian fantasies was Aleksey Tolstoy (1883-1945), who is better known for his unfinished historical novel *Pyotr Pervy* (1929-1945; *Peter the First*, 1959). Although of aristocratic background, he was a willing apologist for the Stalin regime.

The conditions under which literature developed during the NEP did not continue for long. In 1928, the First Five-Year Plan was adopted, and the Communist Party decided that literature was to be harnessed to the needs of the state. By 1932, all autonomous literary organizations were disbanded by a party directive, and all writers were exhorted to follow the precepts of Socialist Realism. Socialist Realism remained an intentionally vague term, to be defined as the authorities wished; novelists were to avoid psychological realism focusing on the individual and objective realism revealing negative aspects of Soviet life, concentrating instead on the positive, inspiring aspects of Soviet life. In 1934, the First Congress of Soviet Writers was held, and the Union of Writers was launched; membership was virtually obligatory. During the 1930's, many writers were forced to publicly admit their errors and "heresies"; arrests were frequent, and many writers and poets perished in the charged atmosphere of the infamous Stalinist purges from 1936 to 1938. Those who survived were forced to be silent or accept a role as an instrument of education and propaganda within the Soviet apparatus.

The novels of the 1930's primarily focused on the subject of industrialization, a topic that had already replaced revolutionary romanticism in the 1920's. The model for the writers of the 1930's was *Tsement* (1925; *Cement*, 1929), by Fyodor Gladkov (1883-1958), which downplayed the hero's family tragedy and emphasized his constructive role in rebuilding a local factory. Virtually all the major writers responded with novels on the theme of industrialization: Sholokhov wrote about collectivization, as did Fyodor Panferov (1896-1960);

Pilnyak wrote about the construction of a great dam and hydroelectric station; Valentin Katayev (1897-1986) wrote about the construction of a huge metallurgical plant in the Ural Mountains in *Vremya vperyod!* (1932; *Time Forward!*, 1933); Ehrenburg also contributed to the subject, as did many others.

The 1930's also saw the appearance of autobiographical educational novels such as *Kak zakalialas' stal'* (1932-1934; *The Making of a Hero*, 1937; also known as *How the Steel Was Tempered*, 1952), by Nikolai Alekseevich Ostrovsky (1904-1936), and *Pedagogicheskaya poema* (1935; *The Road to Life*, 1954), by Anton Makarenko (1888-1939). Such novels depicted the development of exemplary communists in the face of great obstacles and the process of disciplining the dynamic forces of the revolution. They were clearly intended to inspire the reader with appreciation for the sacrifices made and to provide the proper ideological orientation.

The literature of the 1940's was concerned with the patriotic efforts of the Red Army, the party, and the *narod* (the folk) in the defense of the motherland, a theme that remained a staple of popular Soviet literature. Again, writers responded to social demand and produced novels of varying quality. Among the more interesting are Gladkov's *Klyatva* (1944; the vow), Fadeyev's *Molodaya gvardiya* (1946; *The Young Guard*, 1958), and *V okopakh Stalingrada* (1946; *Front-Line Stalingrad*, 1962), by Viktor Nekrasov (1911-1987). In spite of the emphasis on the role of the collective in the war effort, several works "rediscovered" the individual. One such novel was *Sputniki* (1946; *The Train*, 1948), by Vera Panova (1905-1973). In her presentation of the members of a medical team during World War II, she focused on their personal lives and portrayed the collective as a group of individuals with a common goal: a new conception of the collective. The 1940's were also saturated with memoirs relating to the war experience.

THE POST-STALIN NOVEL

A significant change in Soviet literature occurred after the death of Stalin in 1953. Commonly referred to as the "thaw," after the title of Ehrenburg's novel *Ottepel* (1954, 1956; *The Thaw*, 1955; also known as *A Change of Season*, 1962), it led to the revival of the novel genre and reasserted the individual's role within the collective.

Mild criticism of the system, evident in *Vremena goda* (1953; *The Span of the Year*, 1956), by Panova, and *Russkii les* (1953; *The Russian Forest*, 1966), by Leonid Maksimovich Leonov (1899-1988), was not, however, a departure from the tradition of the Russian novel (as one can see from the novels of the nineteenth century), but it was an attempt to break away from the dogmatic treatment of political and social issues. Such works were indicative of the paradoxical relationship between literature and politics. The demand by authorities that literature reflect the goals and needs of the state allowed a realistic (convincing) portrayal of characters in conflict, but it introduced contradictions and ambiguities that obscured the simplistic Communist Party point of view. At such moments of crisis, as in 1954, the party periodically stepped in to reassert its control over literature.

It is not surprising, therefore, that the famous poetic novel of Boris Pasternak (1890-1960), *Doktor Zhivago* (1957; *Doctor Zhivago*, 1958), which was announced in the journal *Znamya* as forthcoming, was rejected when submitted in 1956 and had to be published abroad. Concerned with symbolic truth, Pasternak gave a metonymic representation of the revolution and the civil war, as witnessed by the passive but receptive poet Yuri Zhivago. The novel provides a remarkable portrait of an individual in the nineteenth century tradition and opens a critical dialogue with the past.

This dialogue was continued by the publication of the rediscovered works of Mikhail Bulgakov (1891-1940), written some thirty years earlier. Among his novels satirizing Soviet life and deflating Soviet institutions was his masterpiece *Master i Margarita* (written 1940; censored version 1966-1967; uncensored version 1973; *The Master and Margarita*, 1967). A modern treatment of the Faust theme with a fantastic, dreamlike atmosphere, it is a metaphysical inquiry into the evil of Stalin and the cult of personality; it is also a novel about the creative process, about the writing of a novel about Christ and Pilate. The appearance of the novel created a sensation in Russia, and in the context of Soviet literature, it was indeed a magnificent achievement.

Another author whose works were rediscovered was Platonov. His *Chevengur* (mentioned earlier) and his novel *Kotlovan* (1968; *The Foundation Pit*, 1973, 1975) were not originally published in the Soviet Union, though

samizdat (underground) copies of both circulated widely. Full of symbolic images and folklore and written in a peculiar style, *The Foundation Pit* is a dark, ironic satire of early Soviet industrialization and education.

A work that focused on a relatively unexplored side of the Soviet past was *Odin den' Ivana Denisovicha* (1962; *One Day in the Life of Ivan Denisovich*, 1963), by Aleksandr Solzhenitsyn (1918-2008). Its appearance was made possible by a change in the political climate following a speech by Nikita Khrushchev at the Twentieth Congress of the Communist Party in 1956, in which he acknowledged Stalin's "mistakes" (that is, his crimes). The next year, Vladimir Dmitrievich Dudintsev (1918-1998) published his novel *Ne khlebom yedinym* (1957; *Not by Bread Alone*, 1957), in which he defended the individual's rights against the vulgar careerists wielding power. Dudintsev was sharply attacked by the Communist Party, which quickly moved to curb the liberal tendencies appearing after Khrushchev's speech. Three years later, however, controls were eased again, and with Khrushchev's personal intervention, Solzhenitsyn's novel was published.

One Day in the Life of Ivan Denisovich is a stunning indictment of the labor camps of the Stalin era. Describing life in reduced situations, a characteristic of nearly all of his fiction, Solzhenitsyn illustrates the struggle of the *zeks* (prisoners) to survive with dignity. He portrays the harshness of the prison but points out that, paradoxically, freedom is possible only within the camp. Introducing a wide range of characters in his novels *V kruge pervom* (1968; *The First Circle*, 1968) and *Rakovy korpus* (1968; *Cancer Ward*, 1968), Solzhenitsyn skillfully renders their speech and creates a polyphony of views that constitute a complete picture of Soviet society. Solzhenitsyn's position as a moral conscience and a voice for those not able to speak out is well in evidence in his monumental *Arkhipelag GULag, 1918-1956: Opyt khudozhestvennogo issledovaniya* (1973-1975; *The Gulag Archipelago, 1918-1956: An Experiment in Literary Investigation*, 1974-1978), which exposed the magnitude of the evil of Stalin's camps. It is a historical document shaped by an artist into a powerful and profound epic.

Of the many works written about the camps and the purges, most are a mixture of history, biography, confession, and memoir, emphasizing the factual nature of the content, its truth value. Many courageous people did leave accounts: Varlam Shalamov (1907-1981), who wrote of his experiences in Kolyma; Evgenia Ginzburg (c. 1906-1977), who wrote of her arrest in the purges; and Anatoly Marchenko (1938-1986), who was arrested several times for his defiance of the state, are but a few.

Three major waves of emigration from Russia occurred in the twentieth century: after the revolution, after World War II, and during the 1960's and 1970's. A number of Russian novelists found themselves cut off from their homeland and confronted with a new reality, a new freedom that affected their creativity in various ways. Among the more prominent Russian writers outside the Soviet Union were Bunin, Merezhkovsky, Remizov, Zamyatin, the minor novelists Boris Zaitsev (1881-1972) and Ivan Shmelyov (1873-1950), both of whom wrote about the émigré experience, and Mark Aldanov—the pen name of Mark Landau (1886-1957), a prolific and serious writer of novels on Russian history. One of the most accomplished writers to have emigrated was Vladimir Nabokov, who, before turning to English, wrote eight novels in Russian, only two of which are not about émigrés. An exquisite craftsman influenced by Gogol and Bely as well as by Marcel Proust (1871-1922), Franz Kafka (1883-1924), and the German expressionists, Nabokov enjoyed great success with his English-language novels such as *Lolita* (1955) and *Ada or Ardor: A Family Chronicle* (1969). Several other émigré writers of note are Andrei Sinyavsky (1925-1997), who often wrote under the pen name Abram Tertz, the author of surreal novels and tales in the tradition of Gogol, as well as of brilliant, idiosyncratic critical studies; Vassily Aksyonov (born 1932), a prolific and original novelist; Vladimir Voinovich (born 1932), best known for his satiric Chonkin trilogy; and Vladimir Maximov (1932-1995), whose novels exhibit a pronounced hostility both to communism and to Western liberalism—views similar to those of Solzhenitsyn, who was himself forced into exile and only allowed to return to Russia in the mid-1990's. Two other émigrés who created distinctive works of fiction are Sergei Dovlatov (1941-1990) and Sasha Sokolov (born 1945), whose novel *Shkola dlia durakov* (1976; *A School for Fools*, 1977) offers a unique vision of the lyric freedom found in mental illness.

Many of the émigré writers had published in the Soviet Union before arriving in the West. Aksyonov and Voinovich both represented the young generation, critical of the stale abstractions, political slogans, and dullness of Soviet life. Others had to rely on samizdat to circulate their work; among these was Venedikt Erofeev (1938-1990), whose novel *Moskva-Petushki* (1973; *Moscow to the End of the Line*, 1980), about alcoholism as an escape from the banality of Soviet life, had no chance of being officially published. While not officially sanctioned, the literature of protest was tolerated to a certain degree, the limits of which fluctuated with the political climate. When necessary, the authorities simply reasserted their control.

A significant trend in Soviet literature appeared in the late 1950's. Writers of the same generation as the writers of protest turned to village and rural themes. Surprisingly, the nineteenth century did not produce a single significant work about peasant life, while in the twentieth century, the Marxists have found little more in the peasant than an obstacle to progress, to socialism. The village writers were the first to show a reverence for peasants, describe their traditions, present their uneven struggle with the bureaucracy, and portray them as individual human beings. Many of the novels on peasant life espouse such conservative and traditional Russian values as love of nature and pride in one's work. They are critical of collectivization, often seeing it as the reason for the poor state of Russian agriculture, and of the treatment that the peasants have received at the hands of government officials. These themes can be found throughout the works of some of the leading village writers: Fyodor Abramov (1920-1983), Vasily Belov (born 1932), Valentin Rasputin (born 1937), and the popular and talented Vasily Shukshin (1929-1974).

THE LATE TWENTIETH CENTURY AND BEYOND

Also widespread in the 1960's and the 1970's were novels dealing with urban themes. They focused on problems in the workplace, the harried life of women in Soviet urban society, careerism, and the mundane concerns of everyday life. Novels returning to the subject of the revolution and World War II also continued to appear, focusing primarily on the individual's private experience. The major writers on such themes include

Yury Trifonov (1925-1981), I. Grekova (the pseudonym of Elena Ventzel, born 1907), Yury Kazakov (1927-1982), Andrei Bitov (born 1937), Vasily Bykov (1924-2003), and Viktoria Tokareva (born 1937).

The elevation of Mikhail Gorbachev to the post of general secretary of the Communist Party in 1985 opened a new era for Russia's writers. Eager to reform the stagnant economy, Gorbachev encouraged a new openness (glasnost) in Soviet society. During the last few years of the Soviet Union, from the mid-1980's to 1991, many works that had hitherto been prohibited from publication were allowed to appear in print for the first time. The year 1988, for example, saw the first Soviet publication of Pasternak's *Doctor Zhivago*, Zamyatin's *We*, several works by Nabokov, and the controversial novel by Vasily Grossman (1905-1964), *Zhizn i sudba* (finished in 1960, published in the West in 1980; *Life and Fate*, 1985). Many of the newly published works, including Grossman's novel and the novel *Deti Arbata* (wr. 1966, pb. 1987; *Children of the Arbat*, 1988), by Anatoly Rybakov (1911-1998), countered official views of Soviet society and politics, and they generated considerable debate among the reading public. Yet while much attention was focused on works previously unavailable for general consumption, other developments in literature also triggered excited discussion. New writers appeared in print, along with some older writers whose work had not been readily accessible. Among the most celebrated of the "new" writers are Lyudmila Petrushevskaya (born 1938), Vladimir Makanin (born 1937), Yevgeny Popov (born 1946), Vyacheslav Pyetsukh (born 1946), and Viktor Erofeev (born 1947), all of whom depict the seamier side of Soviet life. Their writing ranges from the farcical to the grotesque. Although they often prefer shorter genres, they also have produced longer works of haunting intensity, such as Petrushevskaya's *Vremya noch* (1992; *The Time: Night*, 1994), which challenges the myth of the "nurturing mother" in Russia.

Women, including the familiar Lyudmila Petrushevskaya, achieved a new literary prominence at the end of the twentieth century and the beginning of the twenty-first century. Tatyana Tolstaya (born 1951) is best known for her short fiction, but her dystopian novel *Kys* (2001; *The Slynx*, 2003) has been widely read internationally.

Lyudmila Ulitskaya (born 1943) has been both a critical and a popular success, beginning with her first novella, *Sonechka* (1992; *Sonechka, and Other Stories*, 1998). Her later works include *Kazus Kukotskogo* (2000; Kukotsky's case), which won the Russian Booker Prize, and her American debut, *Veselye pokhorony* (1998; *The Funeral Party*, 1999). Aleksandra Marinina (born 1957; pen name of Marina Anatol'evna Alekseeva) is a best-selling writer of detective novels, a genre that has become increasingly popular in Russia.

The swirling currents of change came to a head in 1991, when the failed coup attempt by a group of hardline Communists led to the final dissolution of the Soviet Union. This breakdown of traditional state authority had major consequences in the literary sphere as well. Writers and publishers could no longer count on hefty state subsidies to support their work; publishing houses had to adapt to the pressures of a free market economy. For a year or two, Russian intellectuals fretted about a crisis in literature. In their rush to make a profit, publishers began to turn out an enormous quantity of pulp fiction, from detective stories to erotic thrillers. Demand for "serious" literature diminished considerably. Without official constraints on what could appear in print, literature was deprived of its traditional role as the prophetic voice or moral conscience of the nation. Within a few years, however, the sense of crisis died down, and Russian literature saw a new flowering of individual talents. The creation of the Russian Booker Prize in 1992 helped provide a focus for the literati, and signs of renewed growth soon became evident. In addition to the original publication of long-suppressed or buried works, such as the memoir-novel *Vremenà* (1994; *How It All Began*, 1998), written by the Bolshevik Nikolay Ivanovich Bukharin in prison in 1937-1938 before his execution at Stalin's behest, fresh writers appeared in print. Many of the authors who came to prominence in the 1990's were distinguished by their innovative approach to fiction writing, and several seemed to reflect a particularly Russian brand of European postmodernism. Among the most interesting of these writers are Vladimir Georgievich Sorokin (born 1955) and Victor Pelevin (born 1962). Their work, including Pelevin's *Zhizn' nasekomykh* (1994; *The Life of Insects*, 1996), raise existential questions through extraordinary forms of pastiche and parody. With the arrival of this new generation of writers, the prospects for the future development of Russian literature once again looked bright.

George Mihaychuk
Updated by Julian W. Connolly

BIBLIOGRAPHY

Barker, Adele Marie, and Jehanne M. Gheith, eds. *A History of Women's Writing in Russia*. New York: Cambridge University Press, 2002. Collection of essays presents topics in chronological order, beginning with the images of women in medieval Russian literature and continuing through the years of perestroika.

Brown, Deming. *The Last Years of Soviet Russian Literature*. New York: Cambridge University Press, 1993. Examines currents in Russian literature that surfaced in the Soviet Union between 1975 and 1991. Designed to follow the author's earlier book, *Soviet Russian Literature Since Stalin* (1978).

Cornwell, Neil. *The Routledge Companion to Russian Literature*. New York: Routledge, 2001. Extremely useful reference work contains introductory essays to major topics in Russian literature, biographical essays, and articles on numerous individual works.

Emerson, Caryl. *The Cambridge Introduction to Russian Literature*. New York: Cambridge University Press, 2008. Excellent chronological literary history provides analysis of the major works, writers, and themes. Includes a glossary, pronunciation guide, and bibliography of primary and secondary sources.

Freeborn, Richard. *The Rise of the Russian Novel*. New York: Cambridge University Press, 1973. Stimulating study examines some of the most famous works of nineteenth century Russian literature, including *Eugene Onegin, Dead Souls, A Hero of Our Time, Crime and Punishment*, and *War and Peace*.

Jones, Malcom V., and Robin Feuer Miller, eds. *The Cambridge Companion to the Classic Russian Novel*. New York: Cambridge University Press, 1998. Fourteen essays by prominent scholars cover a wide range of subjects reflected in the Russian novel, from politics and religion to psychology and gender.

Kelly, Catriona. *A History of Russian Women's Writing, 1820-1992*. New York: Oxford University Press, 1994. Comprehensive study of the evolution of women's writing in Russia combines sociohistorical analysis with close readings of individual works.

_____. *Russian Literature: A Very Short Introduction*. New York: Cambridge University Press, 2001. Explores the role of literature in Russian culture, using one of Russia's most influential writers, Alexander Pushkin, to illustrate the major ideas.

Ledkovsky, Marina, Charlotte Rosenthal, and Mary Zirin, eds. *Dictionary of Russian Women Writers*. Westport, Conn.: Greenwood Press, 1994. Contains a wealth of information on a broad range of literary figures.

Moser, Charles A., ed. *The Cambridge History of Russian Literature*. New York: Cambridge University Press, 1989. Collection of essays by noted scholars traces the evolution of Russian literature from the medieval period to 1980.

Shneidman, N. N. *Russian Literature, 1995-2002: On the Threshold of the New Millennium*. Toronto, Ont.: University of Toronto Press, 2004. Analyzes Russian literature after the breakup of the Soviet Union, considering how the economy and the market have shaped literary production.

Scandinavian Long Fiction

The earliest prose in Scandinavia consists of medieval law collections, chronicles, legends of saints, and other didactic literature; fictional prose came later, with the emergence of the Icelandic sagas. The so-called kings' sagas and family sagas are set in the period from 850 to 1200; the contemporary sagas are set in the authors' own time, from 1180 to 1350; and a special group, the *fornaldar* sagas, remove the action to a distant past before the discovery of Iceland.

Before 1800

Apart from a number of the kings' sagas, most of the sagas are anonymous. No original manuscripts exist; the sagas are preserved only in a number of widely varying copies. They are based partly on oral, partly on written tradition, and the sources—often anecdotal or legendary—are used with great freedom. Their composition was guided primarily by artistic considerations rather than by principles of historical accuracy.

The sagas reached their zenith in the thirteenth century. In the following century, they were superseded by translations of an ecclesiastic character (for example, sagas about the Virgin Mary and about saints) and of European romances. The earliest written are the kings' sagas, which to a larger extent than the others can be conjectured to contain historical facts. Even in the kings' sagas, however, these facts are subordinate to purely artistic principles of composition, as in the oldest, from about 1180, *Olafs saga helga* (Saint Olaf's saga). In approximately 1230-1235, Snorri Sturluson (1178 or 1179-1241) wrote his version of the saga, which he later included in his major work, *Heimskringla* (English translation, 1844), a history of Norway until 1177. Sturluson proceeds as a modern, critical historian, but, despite his striving for historical truth, he does not neglect the artistic rendition, the colorful, significant detail, and the pithy dialogue. Many episodes from Old Norse history, regardless of their authenticity, achieved their classic form in Sturluson's vivid prose.

The family sagas, the climax of the genre, are somewhat younger. They resemble historical novels, often following several generations. The scene is primarily local, but voyages are frequent. In these passages, the narration shifts from the factual and realistic to the fantastic in intricate stories of the Icelanders' deeds in exotic lands and their success with foreign kings and chiefs as a result of their physical courage and skaldic art. About 1220, the family saga reached full maturity with *Egils saga* (*Egil's Saga*, 1893). Especially fine is its portrait of the tenth century skald, Viking, and farmer Egil Skallagrímsson (c. 910-990), a historical figure and a prolific and innovative poet. His life in Iceland, as well as on exciting trips abroad, is followed from the time when, at three years of age, he composes his first poetry to the day when, as a blind and helpless old man, he tricks his heirs by burying his life's fortune in a secret place.

While Egil still reveals elements of barbaric savagery in his character—as when, for instance, he bites through the throat of an adversary—and while he worships the old gods, an atmosphere of European chivalry permeates *Laxdæla saga* (English translation, 1899). In this somewhat later saga from about 1250, the main protagonists, Bolli and Kjartan, have been baptized in Norway, and the woman whom they both love, Gudrun, the source of their rivalry and ruin, lives out the remainder of her life as the first nun in Iceland. Pagan fatalism persists, however, in another saga written around the same time, *Gísla saga* (*The Story of Gísli the Outlaw*, 1866), a story of unprovoked criminality and death. Even here, however, fatalism is tempered by the psychological nuances of the hero's relationships with those closest to him. Gísli vacillates between hope and fear when faced with his destiny via two phantasms, the good and evil women of a dream, who in turn offer him consoling and ghastly omens. The saga moves inexorably toward Gísli's destruction, a reflection of the author's own disillusionment.

The masterpiece of the family sagas, *Njál's Saga* (English translation, 1861), from the end of the thirteenth century, is pure tragedy. Its center is the friendship between Gunnar and Njál, a friendship that survives the vicious designs of their wives. Despite Gunnar's placidity and Njál's wisdom, however, destiny takes its course. Njál's good advice leads to catastrophe; finally, with bitter acceptance, he relinquishes his hopeless fight against fate and allows himself to die in the fire that destroys his home. The author excels in characterization, penetrating and multifaceted to a degree unique in saga literature. Even though the story ends weakly in the reconciliation of the survivors, *Njál's Saga* stands out as one of the great prose tragedies of world literature.

Among the contemporary sagas are a number of accounts of the Icelandic bishops, but more important are the secular sagas—which, teeming with people and events, constitute a unique source for knowledge of life in Iceland. The main work is *Íslandingasögur* (saga of the Icelanders) from the 1270's, written by Sturla Þórðarsson (1214-1284), a nephew of Snorri Sturluson. This saga makes up one-third of the somewhat later *Sturlunga saga* (saga of the Sturlungs), compiled by Þórðr Narfason (died 1308), which describes the history of Iceland during the twelfth and thirteenth centuries. Þórðarsson's masterful narration clearly anticipates the twentieth century documentary novel. He took an active role in political life and often steps forth as a direct eyewitness of or participant in the dramatic events he describes: violence, arson, family feuds, and revenge.

Elements of the fairy tale and folk legend dominate the *fornaldar* sagas. Their characters are stereotyped, and the authors concentrate on describing dramatic Viking raids, trolls, giants, and fabulous animals, far from any realism. They often paraphrase Germanic heroic poetry, such as the *Volsunga saga* (c. 1270; English translation, 1870) and Old Norse lays, occasionally preserving a few stanzas. There has been a tendency to regard these sagas as a degeneration of the more realistic family sagas, but both types probably existed simultaneously; the family sagas might even have taken some of their more imaginative traits from the *fornaldar* sagas. Undoubtedly somewhat later—from the fourteenth century—is the purely romantic *Frithiofs saga* (1825) and the fairytale saga *Örvar-Odds saga* (*Arrow-Odd: A Medieval Novel*, 1970), with its magic tools and unimpeded shift of scenery from Iceland to Palestine. The *fornaldar* sagas, with their dramatic plots and easy prose, gained immense popularity; thus, they became a favorite source for later Scandinavian writers.

In artistic quality, however, they cannot compare with the family sagas and kings' sagas. Here one finds

components that elevate these Icelandic novels to the level of world literature. The narration's objectivity—perhaps sometimes more formal than real—renders characters' feelings and thoughts through their physical reactions and particularly through their own speech. Powerfully understated dialogue is unusually frequent and contributes to the drama of the sagas' moods. The protagonists are complex and passionate personalities, often compelled by warring impulses: falseness and loyalty, love and hate. Always apparent, however, is the admiration for courage in catastrophe. The saga authors fully recognize that sudden death strikes even the most innocent—fate disregards moral justice—and their works affirm spiritual grandeur in the face of abysmal tragedy.

Icelandic literature's predominance declined during the fifteenth century as new Continental trends gained a footing in the Nordic countries. The historiography of the early Middle Ages found its climax with the *Gesta Danorum* (twelfth century) of Saxo Grammaticus (fl. mid-twelfth century-early thirteenth century), a history of Denmark from the first legends of the country's foundation to contemporary events. The leading genre of this period was the anonymous folk ballad, especially in Denmark and Sweden. A more pronouncedly epic genre, the chivalric verse novel, emerged in the early fourteenth century—again following Central European models. In Sweden, the didactic religious writing that dominated the era produced only one figure of lasting importance, the Holy Birgitta (1301-1373), whose *Revelationes* (published in 1492) is a distinguished example of the period's mysticism.

In all the Nordic countries, the Reformation brought a rupture with the European cultural tradition. In this period, Scandinavian literature was dominated by hymns, Bible translations, anti-Catholic satires, and prayer books, and strong theological orthodoxy suppressed free artistic expression. Not until the end of the sixteenth century were the ideas of Humanism and the Renaissance accepted; they dominated the first half of the seventeenth century, demanding the creation of a national literature based on the classic traditions of genre, style, and meter. Poetry was enthroned in Sweden with Lars Wivallius (1605-1669) and Georg Stjernhielm (1598-1672), and in Denmark with Anders Arrebo (1587-1637); the predominant genres were the didactic epic and occasional poetry.

This development betokened the secular consolidation that followed the ecclesiastical one in Denmark and Sweden. At this time, Iceland was under Denmark's trade monopoly and was falling into economic dependency and cultural isolation. Norway was completely under Danish control, while Finland was under Swedish control; Sweden thus evolved to become a European superpower in bellicose rivalry with Denmark. This led to a strengthening of both monarchies, which—in Denmark in 1660 and in Sweden after 1680—established them as autocratic. Under absolutism—and under the impact of the Thirty Years' War—baroque literature, with its mixture of stately commendation, ornamentation, and strong consciousness of death, flourished. The greatest prose work of the period is *Jammersminde* (1869; *Memoirs of Leonora Christina*, 1872), the autobiography of the Danish princess Leonora Christina (1621-1698). She describes her imprisonment in Copenhagen Castle from 1663 to 1685 with rare sensitivity to situations and people and with natural dialogue, which was, for that time, unique.

Early in the eighteenth century, French classicism reached Scandinavia and merged with the ideas of the Enlightenment. Central in this development was the Dano-Norwegian Ludvig Holberg (1684-1754), whose thirty-three plays are both bitingly comical and realistic. Holberg was also the master of this period's prose, with his *Moralske Tanker* (1744; moral thoughts); *Epistler I-IV* (1748-1750; *Epistles I-IV*, 1955) and *Epistler V* (1754; *Epistles V*, 1955); and the novel *Nicolai Klimii iter subterraneum* (1741; *Journey to the World Underground*, 1742). In Latin, Holberg tells of Klim's journey through the interior of the earth. First he visits the ideal Potu ("utop[ia]" backward), based on absolutism and Deism; then Martinia, a caricature of France, its citizens pleasure-seeking monkeys; and finally Quama, an underdeveloped country that slavishly proclaims Klim emperor. Pride in one's cultural superiority goes before a fall, however, and Klim has to escape, returning to the surface of the earth. The novel is both a satiric travelogue in the style of Jonathan Swift and a moralizing bildungsroman recommending moderation and tolerance.

In Sweden, these ideas were promoted in a periodical of Olaf von Dalin (1708-1763), *Them Swänska Argus* (1732-1734), modeled after the English *Spectator*. This periodical, together with von Dalin's political fable *Sagan om hästen* (1740; the tale about the horse), became the foundation for modern Swedish prose. To von Dalin's model was added further precision and lucidity with Emanuel Swedenborg's (1688-1772) mystical and philosophical writings, while the travelogues of Carl von Linné (better known as Linnaeus, 1707-1778), contributed stylistic elegance.

Throughout the eighteenth century, to counterbalance the Enlightenment, a lyric and sentimental undercurrent—often connected with Pietistic religiosity—led to pre-Romanticism. In Denmark, a major exemplar was the lyric poet Johannes Ewald (1743-1781), whose autobiography, *Levnet og meninger* (1804-1808; life and opinions), broke sharply with the more academic prose style. *Levnet og meninger* resembles eighteenth century English author Laurence Sterne's novels; the action is only a pretext for digressions in which—through dialogue, lyric sketches, and penetrating self-analysis—Ewald describes the ecstasy he finds in wine and love. This strategy is continued by the travelogue *Labyrinten* (1792-1793; the labyrinth), by Jens Baggesen (1764-1826). With Sterne and French philosopher Jean-Jacques Rousseau as models, Baggesen places the capricious self of the poet in the center, and from that vantage he describes the surrounding world: a journey through Germany, Switzerland, and France, transformed by the artist's impulsive temperament.

In Sweden, the eighteenth century was dominated by King Gustav III and his brilliant, French-oriented court. The greatest writer of the period was the bohemian lyric poet Carl Michael Bellman (1740-1795); indeed, poetry, drama, and opera were the predominant artistic modes. The prose of this period was mainly nonfictional and retains only historical interest. Two travelogues, however, are noteworthy: *Min son på galejan* (1781; my son on the galley), by Jacob Wallenberg (1746-1778), is a humorous account of a voyage to East India in an agile but nevertheless precisely descriptive style; by contrast, *Resa till Italien* (1786; travel to Italy), written and illustrated by C. A. Ehrensvärd (1745-1800), forgoes description for laconic, aphoristic reflections on the author's encounter with nature and art.

The few Danish and Swedish plagiarisms of foreign novels are negligible. Periodical literature, on the other hand, includes several fictional discursive accounts of contemporary life. These efforts culminated in Sweden with two picaresque novels by Fredrik Cederborgh (1784-1835), *Uno von Trasenberg* (1809-1811) and *Ottar Trallings leftnads-målning* (1811-1818). Like Voltaire's Candide, the title characters are inexperienced young men confronted with the folly of the world and finally taught by experience. Cederborgh's rather kindhearted satire partly ridicules the haughtiness of the nobility and the greediness of the petite bourgeoisie and partly attacks the defects of the judicial and prison system. Thus, Cederborgh provides a connection among the Enlightenment, Romanticism, and the bourgeois realism characteristic of the mid-nineteenth century.

ROMANTICISM AND POETIC REALISM

During the first decades of the nineteenth century, Danish and Swedish literature alike was dominated by a pantheistic, universal Romanticism. In Sweden's Erik Johan Stagnelius (1793-1823), this trend manifested itself in Platonic nature and love poems, while Denmark's Adam Oehlenschläger (1779-1850) based his works, often dramas, on Nordic mythology or history. Oehlenschläger led Romanticism into its second phase, national Romanticism. Following Sir Walter Scott, Bernhard Severin Ingemann (1789-1862) wrote historical novels based on Denmark's Middle Ages, among which *Valdemar Seier* (1826; *Waldemar, Surnamed Seir: Or, The Victorious*, 1841) stands out with its perfect composition and exciting plot. All of Ingemann's works—so typical of Danish national Romanticism—combine nationalism with religion: The spirit of the people, and thus the power of the country, blossoms only when church and state ally. Ingemann's contemporary novel *Landsbybørnene* (1852; the village children) is an optimistic *Entwicklungsroman* (novel of development) that intersperses elements of Hans Christian Andersen's life with the story of the poet-protagonist. Despite its realistic milieu, the novel idealistically champions simple ethics over personal and social egotism.

Johannes Carsten Hauch (1790-1872), also familiar with Scott, was less concerned with historical accuracy than was Ingemann. After two novels set in previous centuries, he wrote *En polsk familie* (1839; a Polish family), a love story set against the Polish rebellion of 1830-1831. Structurally, the novel recalls German writer Johann Wolfgang von Goethe's Wilhelm Meister tales in its alternation among epic, lyric, and dramatic strategies. The fragmentary novel *En dansk students eventyr* (1843, wr. 1824; the adventures of a Danish student), by Poul Martin Møller (1794-1838), is more single-mindedly directed toward character delineation; its straightforward attack on sentimentality introduced critical realism to Denmark. The trend's finest representative is Steen Steenson Blicher (1782-1848), but better known are the novels of Hans Christian Andersen (1805-1875). All view life as a fairy tale that might just as easily end catastrophically as happily. *Improvisatoren* (1835; *The Improvisatore*, 1845) describes a poor young poet's road to success—recalling Andersen's own stay in Italy and forecasting his own career. *O.T.* (1836; English translation, 1845) is likewise optimistic, although darkened by the main character's having been born in a prison and the consequent speculations about fate. The protagonist of *Kun en spillemand* (1837; *Only a Fiddler*, 1845) also grows up in a poverty that overrules his artistic talent. This work is episodic, like the philosophical novel *At være eller ikke være* (1857; *To Be, or Not to Be?*, 1857), an indictment of nineteenth century materialism. Indeed, Andersen's novels live in single episodes and a host of acutely realized secondary characters. Andersen's novels indicate how descriptions of contemporary society gradually gained recognition, especially after the social analyses of Honoré de Balzac and Charles Dickens replaced Scott's historical novels as models in all Nordic countries.

The Danish novel, however, retained its ties to the *Entwicklungsroman*. While Andersen's characters pursue artistic and social recognition, those of Mär Aron Goldschmidt (1819-1887) strive for ethical triumph, searching for an ideal that is not reached because of an old guilt. This concept of nemesis is not fully developed in Goldschmidt's first work, *En jøde* (1845; *The Jew of Denmark*, 1852), about a disappointed idealist who, like a Byronic hero, participates in European freedom struggles but ends up as a Copenhagen usurer. Less negative is *Hjemløs* (serialized 1853-1857; *Homeless: Or, A Poet's Inner Life*, 1861), in which the hero realizes on his deathbed that life is not something to be demanded but a debt to be paid. Another bildungsroman, by Hans Egede Schack (1820-1859), *Phantasterne* (1857; the phantasts), follows three young men to show that a good life must subordinate fantasy to reality. With its brilliant psychology and its attack on sentimentality in the period's idealistic literature, Schack's work prefigures naturalism.

In Sweden, naturalism had been anticipated in 1839 with a novel by Carl Jonas Love Almqvist (1793-1866), *Det går an* (*Sara Videbeck*, 1919), which both questions the institution of marriage and defends a woman's right to choose her own profession. Besides August Strindberg, Almqvist is the most complex figure in Swedish literature. From 1832 to 1851, he published *Törnrosens bok* (the book of the briar rose), a diverse mix of novels and tales, plays and essays, and lyric and epic poems, held together by a frame story, "Jagtslottet" (the hunting seat). His *Drottningens juvelsmycke* (1834; the queen's jewel) is also unique—cryptic and inaccessible. The external action takes place at the Rococo court of Gustav III, where the androgynous Tintomara appears; she embodies both Almqvist's dream of a new human being and elements of his own personality.

The realistic trend seen in *Sara Videbeck* continued with Fredrika Bremer (1801-1865), who in 1828 had made her debut with the first part of *Teckningar utur hvardagslifvet* (*The Novels of Fredrika Bremer*, 1844-1849, 11 volumes)—the collective title she gave her novels through the 1830's—the epistolary novel *Axel och Anna* (1836; *Axel and Anna*, 1844), which depicts a confined and restrained woman. During these years, Bremer created the Swedish family novel, a genre that, in only slightly idealized detail, describes life in the well-to-do bourgeois homes and manor houses. A stay in the United States from 1849 to 1851 prompted her to work out her thoughts on women's oppression, culminating in *Hertha* (1856), which passionately discusses social equality between the sexes.

Overall, Swedish literature in the mid-nineteenth century was characterized by an insipid academic idealism, especially prevalent in a number of forgotten poets; not until Viktor Rydberg (1828-1895) was there a significant writer. Rydberg's historical adventure novel *Fribytaren på Östersjön* (1857; the freebooter in the Bal-

tic Sea) also propagandizes against the tyrannical nobility and the religious intolerance of the seventeenth century. Its detailed description of a witch-hunt evidences Rydberg's cultural and historical concerns, but his style and characterization are still immature. Nor is his best-known novel, *Den siste Athenaren* (1859; *The Last Athenian*, 1869), artistically polished, marred as it is by the complicated intrigues common to popular novels. As an argument for spiritual freedom, however, it is significant, its picture of fanaticism in third century Greece exposing that of Rydberg's own time. The novel *Singoalla* (1857; *Singoalla, a Medieval Legend*, 1903), about the love of a young knight for a Gypsy girl, set in the legendary Middle Ages, includes mystical and Platonic elements that make it a beautiful and stately culmination of Swedish Romanticism.

In Norway, early nineteenth century literature was shaped by the decisive events of 1814, when Denmark was forced to cede the country to Sweden. Not until the work of Henrik Wergeland (1808-1845) did Norwegian literature become original. Wergeland is regarded as his country's greatest lyric poet. His bold imagination highlighted the breakthrough of Romanticism, which did not actually take place until the 1840's, when the young nation revived its national history, harking back to the epoch before its union with Denmark in 1397. The center of gravity was the lyric poem, and the novel was almost neglected. The first modern Norwegian novel, *Amtmandens døttre* (1855; the governor's daughters), was written by Wergeland's sister, Camilla Collett (1813-1895). With this artistically rather insignificant book, she not only paved the way for realistic problem fiction but also introduced the subject of the social position of women, which was carried further by Henrik Ibsen and Jonas Lie and ended in the tendentious works of Alexander Lange Kielland and Arne Garborg of the 1880's.

NATURALISM

The ideas of naturalism had been heralded in Scandinavia since the 1830's, but their sudden and definite breakthrough in the early 1870's should be credited to the Danish critic Georg Brandes (1842-1927). His dictum "That a literature exists in our time is shown by the fact that it sets up problems for debate" focused anew on social, sexual, and religious problems.

In Denmark, the major names in this new literary generation were Jens Peter Jacobsen (1847-1885) and Holger Drachmann (1846-1908). Jacobsen was by nature a dreamer, and his essential motif is the ongoing struggle between dream and reality. His artistic maturity was established with his story *Mogens* (1872; included in *Mogens, og andre Novellen*, 1882; *Mogens, and Other Stories*, 1921), the first naturalistic Scandinavian novella, containing precise impressions from nature and a perception of humans as physiological as well as spiritual beings. Jacobsen's *Fru Marie Grubbe* (1876; *Marie Grubbe*, 1917) signals a renewal of the historical novel. Realism was the goal; the means to that goal was an exhaustive study of sources in archives and libraries; and the result was a magnificently executed period piece. Marie's story—her fall through the social strata into the depths—from castle to hut to the primitive and strong man who can dominate her—is unrelievedly naturalistic. *Niels Lyhne* (1880; English translation, 1896), on the other hand, is more contemporary. It portrays the development of a man ill suited for life, escaping into dreams because he expects too much from reality; it is also a problem novel about a freethinker whose heart cannot keep pace with his brain and who longs for "a god to accuse and to worship." Jacobsen had learned much about psychological portrayal from French writers such as Stendhal and Gustave Flaubert, but he was no French naturalist. In his acute understanding of human beings and his melancholy tone, he more closely resembles the Russian novelist Ivan Turgenev, whose books were very popular at that time in all the Nordic countries. Thus, Drachmann, in his novel *En Overkomplet* (1876; a supernumerary), employs Turgenev's favorite motif of a strong woman versus a weak man. Drachmann was primarily a lyric poet; nevertheless, he wrote one of the most remarkable novels of the nineteenth century, *Forskrevet* (1890; signed away). Its characterization of men as unpredictable beings whose existence is paradoxically determined by dark fate is so mature and intense that it far surpasses the realistic works of the period.

Outside the Brandes camp stood the two greatest figures of the 1880's, Herman Bang (1857-1912) and Henrik Pontoppidan (1857-1943). Bang, a critical realist, emphasized that realism ought to be founded in aesthetics, not partisanism. His first novel, *Haabløse Slægter* (1880; generations without hope), is a naturalistic novel of inheritance and degeneration, a theme basic to Bang and derived from the French naturalists Balzac and Émile Zola. During his peak as a writer, from 1885 to 1890 (thereafter he devoted his efforts to stage direction), Bang wrote *Tine* (1889), which, against a historical backdrop—the Dano-Prussian war of 1864—plays the tragic love story of a servant girl. Tenderness, desire, and destruction are likewise stages of development in *Ludvígsbakke* (1896; *Ida Brandt*, 1928). Here, Bang portrays the relationship between husband and wife as a torture leading to life's destruction. His last novel, *De uden fædreland* (1906; *Denied a Country*, 1927), though marred by a mannered style and a hysterical tone, best shows Bang's style: The main action occurs in one afternoon, exposition having been given in a prologue. As in Bang's other impressionistic works, the novel is a drama: Everything happens before the eye of the reader; everything is situation, action, and direct speech.

The pessimism of the late decades of the nineteenth century, which determined Bang's view of life, found even more powerful expression in the works of Pontoppidan, who was a cowinner of the Nobel Prize in Literature in 1917. He was a confirmed realist, an opponent of complacency, but he also sharply criticized naturalism. Scorn and biting irony lift his writing to an irrational sphere of passion and fantasy. His trilogy *Det forjættede land: Et tidsbillede*, 1892 (*The Promised Land*, 1896) is at once a satire on the times, a penetrating study of the soul of a religious dreamer, and a tragedy of an idealist. Like the main protagonist, Emanuel, the title character of Pontoppidan's next cycle, *Lykke-Per* (1898-1904; lucky Per), also searches for happiness, but whereas Emanuel pursues altruistic goals and perishes as a result, Per is interested only in his own happiness and finally finds it by losing everything except himself under the influence of medieval mysticism. In the novel *Isbjørnen* (1887; *The Polar Bear: A Portrait*, 2003), the conflict is between a vicar and his clergymen, or between open-mindedness and provinciality. At the beginning of the twentieth century, in *De dødes rige* (1912-1916; the realm of the dead), Pontoppidan condemns his own epoch by showing how the characters, in their conflict with moral and political conditions, demean themselves or are even destroyed. The basic theme of the cycle is the emptiness of human existence owing to the absence of love; this religious experience of the nothingness of life, combined with the moral experience of its valuelessness, makes it unique in Nordic literature.

In Sweden, the new intellectual and literary movement of naturalism was not established until around 1880, with the ground-breaking novel *Röda rummet* (1879; *The Red Room*, 1913), by August Strindberg (1849-1912). What makes the work a breakthrough is the sharp criticism of economic and political conditions in Sweden, of the early rise of capitalism. Yet in spite of the indignation, the mood is not bitter. Strindberg's style sparkles with subtle observations and impressionistic technique—an example is the famous panorama of Stockholm in the early pages of the book. After a number of strictly naturalistic dramas, Strindberg returned to fiction with a novel about people and nature in the archipelago, *Hemsöborna* (1887; *The Natives of Hemsö*, 1959). A foreman from the mainland, Carlsson, comes to reorder a neglected farm—and to win financial security by marrying the owner's widow—but throws away his chances because of his desire for a younger woman. Carlsson, although he belongs to the lower class, represents a superior type of human being. Strindberg was, therefore, ready when Brandes, in 1888, called his attention to the writings of Friedrich Nietzsche, whose homage to strong personalities is clearly reflected in Strindberg's novel *I havsbandet* (1890; *By the Open Sea*, 1913). The novel has an explicit antidemocratic prejudice. Its Nietzschean superman is Borg, an inspector of fisheries and Strindberg's alter ego, an absolute individualist of superior intelligence, battling a world of mediocrities.

Strindberg became a model for a group of writers called Young Sweden, which emerged during the 1880's, wanting to mirror reality in all its everyday banality and tragedy. In the spirit of Brandes they took passionate positions on current problems and thus brought the social realism of the 1840's to a sharper and more insistent naturalism. The driving force behind Young Sweden, the prolific Gustaf af Geijerstam (1852-1909), illustrates the period's pessimism, suggested by the title of his first volume of novellas, *Gråkallt* (1882; gray cold).

In Norway in the 1880's, naturalism took a much more bellicose character than it did elsewhere, and doctrinaire writing became a force in society. Kristian Elster (1841-1881), strongly influenced by Turgenev, wrote *Farlige folk* (1881; dangerous people), contrasting modern ideas of progress with their reception in a small Norwegian provincial town. To Amalie Skram (1846-1905), Brandes's program gave the courage to break up an unhappy marriage in 1877 and to choose a career as a writer. She became the most consistent representative of naturalism in Scandinavia. The lives of many of her heroines were based on personal experience; in the cycle of novels *Hellemyrsfolket* (1887-1898; the people from Hellemyr), she penetratingly portrays a woman's unsatisfied desire for love in a deterministic, desolate world. Compared with the work of several of her contemporaries, Skram's work is more widely available in English, thanks in part to renewed interest by feminist scholars at the end of the twentieth century. These novels include *Constance Ring* (1885; English translation, 1988), *Lucie* (1888; English translation, 2001), *Forrådt* (1892; *Betrayed*, 1986), and *Professor Hieronimus* (1895; English translation, 1899; also known as *Under Observation*, 1992).

While Elster and Skram openly expressed their hopeless views of life, Alexander Kielland (1849-1906) concealed his behind the elegance of his style. His novels *Garman og Worse* (1880; *Garman and Worse*, 1885) and *Skiper Worse* (1882; English translation, 1885) portray with warmth and humor the members of an old trading firm in a plot interspersed with critical comments on social injustice, stifled conventions, and religious hypocrisy. More direct in attacking social dishonesty are *Gift* (1883; poison) and *Fortuna* (1884), translated together as *Professor Lovdahl* (1904), while Kielland's last novel, *Jacob* (1891), satirizing the vulgar careerist in a democracy, marks him as the most acerbic ironist of his generation. Despite this emphasis on day-to-day problems and the topicality of his themes, Kielland's best novels are masterpieces of vivid psychology, completely transgressing the ideology of naturalism.

More typically transitional is Arne Garborg (1851-1924), whose entire body of work is informed by a dread of life and by religious longing. As a Christian journalist for a conservative newspaper, he at first opposed Brandes, but after an intensive study of the Danish critic—and of Charles Darwin—he changed his mind. In 1878, Garborg published the novel *Ein fritenkjar* (a free-thinker), which clearly shows this shift in opinion, describing a radical theologian's disappointment in orthodox Christianity, which is for him a caricature of true faith. The novel, however, like Garborg's later ones, suffers from excessive theorizing and tendentiousness. In 1891 came a clear renunciation of Garborg's belief in naturalism as an ideology that can solve all social and individual problems: In *Trætte mænd* (*Weary Men*, 1999), he repudiated the materialism and dogmatic atheism of the time. In diary form, he portrays the spiritual despair and self-criticism, and finally the conversion to Christianity, of the main protagonist—a development that clearly anticipates the changing ideological climate of the 1890's.

Completely outside the dogmatic naturalistic school was Jonas Lie (1883-1908), whose visionary fantasies were expressed in essentially realistic writing. His first novel, *Den fremsynte* (1870; *The Visionary*, 1984), embodies the mysticism of northern Norway, a world in which the borders between the real and the unreal are strangely blurred by powerful nature. *Livsslaven* (1883; *One of Life's Slaves*, 1895), which treats the problem of poverty and social disparities, shows that Lie had developed into a writer of modern realistic novels, whose partisanship, however, never interfered with his art. In the same year, Lie's *Familien paa Gilje* (1883; *The Family at Gilje*, 1894), was published—a major Norwegian work. Protesting a marriage of convenience, Inger-Johanna breaks her engagement, thus sacrificing an advantageous match, but does not get the man she really loves. In *Kommandørens Døttre* (1886; *The Commodore's Daughters*, 1892), the title of which refers to Camilla Collett's earlier novel, the question of the emancipation of women, already touched upon in *The Family at Gilje*, is treated in a similarly undogmatic way. In the 1890's, Lie abandoned contemporary topics, publishing two volumes of tales titled *Trold* (1891-1892; partial translation *Trolls* in *Weird Tales from Northern Seas*, 1893). The concept of a demoniac lower stratum in the soul dominated Lie's next works, giving a symbolic character to many of them. He creates a delicate impressionistic style from allusions and characteristic details that appeal to the imagination of the reader.

A national Finnish literature did not arise until the nineteenth century. The cultural language was primarily Swedish, the scholarly language Latin. The publication of the medieval epic *Kalevala* in 1835 (English translation, 1888), by Elias Løhnrot (1802-1884), laid the foundation for an independent Finnish literature and a national revival. Johan Ludvig Runeberg (1804-1877) and Zacharias Topelius (1818-1898) also attempted to promote Finnish nationalism through literature. Topelius found the material for his long series of novellas, *Faltskärns berättelser* (1853-1867; *The Surgeon's Stories*, 1883-1887), in historical events in Sweden and Finland during the seventeenth and eighteenth centuries. Influenced by Sir Walter Scott and Edward Bulwer-Lytton, he added excitement and adventure to his skillful narratives.

Both Runeberg and Topelius wrote in Swedish. A Finnish literary language was not created until Aleksis Kivi (1834-1872). Thereafter, Finnish and Finno-Swedish literature diverged. Kivi's novel *Seitsemän veljestä* (1870; *Seven Brothers*, 1929) tells how seven brothers leave their ancestral farm to settle in the wilderness, mature through hardship into social-minded citizens, and return to civilization. It is a novel that fluctuates between Romanticism and realism, baroque humor and seriousness; at the same time, it offers a symbolic history of Finnish culture.

After Kivi's death, literary activity stagnated for almost a decade, until 1880. At that time, Finnish literature became strongly influenced first by French and Scandinavian naturalism and later by Leo Tolstoy's doctrines of altruism, self-denial, and social responsibility. Common people, everyday life, and the socially oppressed were increasingly treated by young writers, who in 1885 formed a group called Nuori Suomi (Young Finland), led by Minna Canth (1844-1897) and Juhani Aho (1861-1921). *Papin tytär* (1885; the daughter of a clergyman), Aho's first attempt at a tendentious depiction of the middle class, stresses the experience of Elli, a passive being, doomed to tragic resignation in unsympathetic surroundings—a typical motif in Nordic literature of the 1880's, found, for example, in the novels of Lie and Bang. The tone became sharper in Aho's depiction of student life in *Helsinkiin* (1889; to Helsinki), but around 1900 he moved from Zola-influenced realism toward a more impressionistic lyricism. This shift is clearly reflected in his masterpiece, *Papin rouva* (1893; the wife of a clergyman), a sequel to his novel of 1885. Here, description and epic elements are secondary; instead, the emphasis is on the psychological analysis of the minister's wife and of her brief passion, doomed from the outset, for a blasé, cosmopolitan houseguest.

Iceland's contact with European cultural life was not very extensive until the eighteenth century, and it is impossible to speak of a Romantic movement there before 1830. The country finally achieved political and financial autonomy in 1874. Because Iceland did not have its own university until 1911, Icelanders had to study in Copenhagen. There, around 1880, Icelandic realism and naturalism developed, under the influence of Georg Brandes. These currents, however, were not as influential in Iceland as they were in other Nordic countries, primarily as a result of the lack of urban centers and an industrial proletariat. The 1870's and 1880's were years of great hardship in Iceland; one-fourth of the nation's people emigrated to North America during this period.

Radical views were proclaimed in the periodical *Verðandi* (1882). Promoting a new realistic prose were Gestur Pálsson (1852-1891) and Einar Hjörleifsson Kvaran (1859-1938). Their pessimistic short stories analyze injustice and hypocrisy in contemporary society. Kvaran's attacks on conservatism give way in his later writings to psychological portrayal of the oppressed, not the oppressors, but they are devoid of any propagandistic tendency. This development, influenced by William James's theories of the subconscious, is also manifest in Kvaran's novels. *Ofurefli* (1908; overwhelming odds) and *Gull* (1911; gold) offer the first realistic depictions of the Reykjavík bourgeoisie, the main theme being the victory of liberal theology against orthodoxy. Yet in *Sálin vaknar* (1916; the soul awakens), a murder story, Kvaran supports immortality and spiritualism; the novel's optimistic tone also permeates Kvaran's later writings.

To World War I

Nordic literature in the 1890's generally departed from past traditions—in Sweden, Finland, and Iceland perhaps less than in Norway and Denmark. Even in these countries, however, neo-Romanticism and Symbolism clashed with naturalism and realism. The ethical demand for truth was succeeded by the aesthetic demand for beauty, and rationalism was met by a new metaphysics and a mystically colored religiosity. Nature and history became favored subjects, and lyric poetry, which had been totally neglected, was revived.

In Sweden, this change was evident in the novel *Hans Alienus* (1892), by Verner von Heidenstam (1859-1940), which treats antiquity both historically and imaginatively. A strong bond to the homeland, based on an ideal conception of heroic death, raises Heidenstam's historical novellas *Karolinerna* (1897-1898; *A King and His Campaigners*, 1902; better known as *The Charles Men*, 1920) to the level of tragic national epic. *Folkungaträdet* (1905-1907; *The Tree of the Folkungs*, 1925), a two-volume novel, is Heidenstam's greatest historical work. Composed as a unit, it was based on extensive studies of Swedish society and language. Heidenstam was awarded the Nobel Prize in Literature in 1916.

Swedish history and folklore form the basis for the works of Selma Lagerlöf (1858-1940). Her best-known novel—a true masterpiece—the two-volume *Gösta Berlings saga* (1891; *The Story of Gösta Berling*, 1898; also known as *Gösta Berling's Saga*, 1918) is a modern lyric and dramatic epic. In place of the coherent plot characteristic of the naturalistic novel, Lagerlöf favored episodic narratives; here, diverse episodes are joined by unity of place: an old estate and its surroundings in the author's home province of Värmland, the domain of adventurers, drunks, and artists who live unreflectively for the passion of the moment. Though Lagerlöf renders their dealings in a lyric style influenced by Thomas Carlyle, she morally condemns them. In 1896, she visited a colony of Swedish farmers in Jerusalem who had experienced a religious awakening in the province of Dalecarlia. Leaving farms and families, they had emigrated to practice works of mercy and to await the second coming. Lagerlöf describes them in *Jerusalem I: I Dalarne* (1901; *Jerusalem*, 1915) and *Jerusalem II: I det heliga landet* (1902; *The Holy City: Jerusalem II*, 1918); the first volume of this two-volume novel is the most significant, with its brilliant psychological portrayal of an old farming family and the world of their thoughts.

Lagerlöf was in total agreement with the national movements of her time when, in 1906 and 1907, she published her next major work, *Nils Holgerssons under-*

bara resa genom Sverige (*The Wonderful Adventures of Nils*, 1907, and *The Further Adventures of Nils*, 1911), written as a geography reader for elementary schools. Nils, an ill-mannered farm boy, is changed into a Tom Thumb and carried off by a wild goose, in a situation reminiscent of Rudyard Kipling's *The Jungle Book* (1894). Not content with this main plot, Lagerlöf incorporates numerous fairy tales, legends, and short stories, all designed to spur Nils's progress toward honesty and duty. In 1909 she won the Nobel Prize for Literature "in appreciation of the lofty idealism, vivid imagination and spiritual perception that characterize her writings." Not until 1925 did Lagerlöf again publish a major work, the first volume of the Löwensköld trilogy, *Löwensköldska ringen* (*The General's Ring*, 1928), followed by *Charlotte Löwensköld* (1925; English translation, 1928) and *Anna Svärd* (1928; English translation, 1928); a translation of the three volumes of the trilogy appeared in English as *The Ring of the Löwenskölds: A Trilogy* (1928). The trilogy suggests Lagerlöf's frequent inability to differentiate between the original and the banal; nevertheless, she possesses a great talent for epic construction, for vivid characterization, for rich fantasy, and for other neo-Romantic features, which can also be found among the works of many writers of the next generation.

Most of these writers, however, turned toward realism, especially in a newly vigorous precision in the treatment of social classes. Having lost faith in evolution's implied optimism, they maintained their belief in its determinism. The influence of the 1890's persisted in the disillusioned skepticism—expressed earlier in European literature in the works of Oscar Wilde, Anatole France, and Herman Bang, among others, and finding a significant representative in Hjalmar Söderberg (1869-1941). The protagonist of his novel *Martin Bircks ungdom* (1901; *Martin Birck's Youth*, 1930), unstable and melancholy, is typical of the period. Plot is subordinated to feeling and thought; especially distinctive are the shattering of Martin's illusions about his vocation and love and his role as an ironic observer of existence.

Among the writers of the first decade, Hjalmar Bergman (1883-1931) had the most expansive imagination. About 1900, he, too, progressed from neo-Romanticism to realism, never, however, abandoning a symbolic treatment of his subjects. Thus, in the trilogy *Komedier i Bergslagen* (1914-1916; comedies in Bergslagen), the mixture of fairy-tale world and colorful and realistic description elevates the episodic portrayal of human suffering and spiritual ailments, reminiscent of Dostoevski, to an inspired expression of Bergman's pessimism. The violent, brutal quarrels between father and son, the tormenting jealousy and unhappy love, all unmask life's demoniac forces.

Bergman's succeeding novels, *Markurells i Wadköping* (1919; *God's Orchid*, 1924) and *Farmor och vår Herre* (1921; *Thy Rod and Thy Staff*, 1937), describe, with elements of comic relief, a tragic narrative—the theft of illusions. By contrast, epic plot gives way to the psychology of the subconscious life of a businesswoman—an approach influenced more by Dostoevski than by Sigmund Freud—in Bergman's last great prose work, *Chefen fru Ingeborg* (1924; *The Head of the Firm*, 1936). Bergman's work is an attempt to compensate for the blind game of fate with humor and satire—learned from Balzac and Dickens—and to overcome disharmony and destruction through art.

The reorientation in the Norwegian literature of the 1890's is perceptible in the works of many older authors, such as Jonas Lie and Arne Garborg. The fruitless debates and analyses had grown wearisome, and disappointment over the inconclusiveness of radical ideas led to a skeptical attitude toward democracy, as in the works of Hans Ernst Kinck (1865-1926) and Knut Hamsun (1859-1952).

Most outstanding among the nationalistic neo-Romantics was Kinck. Half poet, half cultural philosopher, well-read in history and psychology, Kinck describes periods of transition in which two cultures combat each other or an individual combats society. Thus, in *Herman Ek* (1923), Kinck portrays the clash between the old peasant culture and the modern urban culture. The trilogy *Sneskavlen brast* (1918-1919; the avalanche broke) gathers all of Kinck's essential themes: inhibited eroticism, rejected tenderness, and the relationship of the farmer to the estate holder. Kinck's figures are always shown in the context of their cultural milieu; yet he always emphasizes the subconscious mind's interaction with nature. External events are for him only unfocused and counterfeit images of the private psyche.

Hamsun also searched for the primitive and the natural. His novel *Sult* (1890; *Hunger*, 1899) introduced a new epoch in Norwegian literature. It portrays the hopeless struggle of a poverty-stricken writer. Tormenting hunger is scientifically analyzed as it slowly destroys his nervous system and self-control, strictly omitting all social and political perspectives. In Hamsun's next book, *Mysterier* (1892; *Mysteries*, 1927), the main character, Johan Nagel, who suddenly appears one day in a small Norwegian town, is, like the poet in *Hunger*, a stranger in life. Hamsun, however, makes no attempt to explain his behavior, wanting to demonstrate the mysterious depths of the human soul. The Nagel type appears again in the lyric, first-person narrative *Pan* (1894; English translation, 1920); Lieutenant Glahn is also a maverick, a hunter and a man of nature, rejecting modern civilization.

In the twentieth century, Hamsun moved from subjective to more objective narration, unfolding fully in *Børn av tiden* (1913; *Children of the Age*, 1924) and its sequel *Segelfoss by* (1915; *Segelfoss Town*, 1925). Hamsun, whose interest had been limited to his protagonists, here created a wide-ranging realistic picture of the social range of northern Norway, especially the clash between the old, patriarchal feudal system and material progress. The epic novel *Markens grøde* (1917; *Growth of the Soil*, 1920), instrumental in Hamsun's winning the 1920 Nobel Prize in Literature, tells the story of the settler Isak, who stubbornly makes the wilderness arable and establishes his own farm. As Isak's estate grows, other settlers move into the woods and establish a new self-supporting community. Such optimism yielded to social bitterness and criticism in Hamsun's novels *Konerne ved vandposten* (1920; *The Women at the Pump*, 1928) and *Ringen sluttet* (1936; *The Ring Is Closed*, 1937); in the latter, once again, a maverick figure shuns, with aristocratic contempt, bourgeois society.

The Finnish neo-Romantics were deeply influenced by Hamsun's cult of nature and Lagerlöf's imaginative narrative art, and they found their motifs not only in Finnish history and folklore but also in distant countries, antiquity, mythology, and the Bible. Most were lyric poets, such as Eino Leino (1878-1926) and Otto Manninen (1872-1950); Leino also wrote several rather superficial novels on contemporary life in Helsinki. The only prolific prose writer of the neo-Romantic period was Johan-

nes Linnankoski (the pseudonym of Vihtori Peltonen, 1869-1913). His novel *Laulu tulipunaisesta kukasta* (1905; *The Song of the Blood-Red Flower*, 1920) is uneven but was tremendously successful; it sets the Don Juan motif in contemporary Finland among lumberjacks and timber floaters. With *Pakolaiset* (1908; the refugees), Linnankoski created a masterpiece. Descriptions of nature are subordinated to dramatic suspense in the story of a young wife's faithlessness to her older husband and his hard-won inner development when he discovers her deception.

The Finnish Civil War of 1918 brought about a skeptical and apocalyptic mood; melancholy and hedonism became popular. In *Onni Kokko* (1920), by Jarl Hemmer (1893-1944), the civil war forms an ominous backdrop to the complex ethical question of suffering in a presumably just world order. Christianity colors Hemmer's major work, the Dostoevski-like novel *En man och hans samvete* (1931; *A Fool of Faith*, 1936). With existential commitment, Hemmer analyzes suffering and death, the quest for consolation in religion, and, finally, the belief in sacrificial death as a possible means of salvation.

As in Finland, the foremost writers of the 1890's in Iceland were lyric poets. Home rule in 1904, however, encouraged nationalism and the revival of traditions that precluded introversion and ennui. The novels of Guðmundur Kamban (1888-1945) deal mainly with Iceland's history from the Middle Ages into the twentieth century. The monumental *Skálholt* (1930-1935; parts 1 and 2 translated as *The Virgin of Skalholt*, 1935) analyzes the psychology of love set against a panorama of everyday seventeenth century life, based on extensive historical study. In *30. Generation* (1933; thirtieth generation), Kamban returned to a portrayal of contemporary Reykjavík, while his last novel, *Jeg ser et stort, skønt land* (1936; *I See a Wondrous Land*, 1938), retells the discovery of Greenland and Vineland (America).

Writers of the new literary generation in Denmark were not, as in Sweden and Iceland, rediscoverers of the national past, but rediscoverers of the soul. The primary Danish Symbolists were all lyric poets, with the exception of Johannes Jørgensen (1866-1956), whose five short novels from 1888 to 1894 describe uprooted students from the provinces being confronted with the modern metropolis. After his conversion to Catholicism in 1896, Jørgensen achieved a place as an international Catholic author with his extensive, knowledgeable biographies, *Den hellige Frans af Assisi* (1907; *Saint Francis of Assisi*, 1912) and *Den hillige Katerina af Siena* (1915; *Saint Catherine of Siena*, 1938).

The lyric introverted literature of the 1890's was followed in Denmark by a new realistic and rationalistic wave, different from the naturalism of the 1870's and 1880's in its decided materialism and occasional socialism. Two directions can be distinguished in the literature of this period: regionalism and social agitation. Regional literature was dominated by two vastly different writers, Johannes V. Jensen (1873-1950) and Jakob Knudsen (1858-1917).

The first major work of Knudsen, the novel *Den gamle Præst* (1899; the old pastor), concerns the clash between social convention and the individual's conscience. Knudsen's partially autobiographical two-volume novel *Gjæring-Afklaring* (1902; fermentation-clarification) portrays with both satire and empathy the spiritual situation of Knudsen's own generation. Until this point, peasants had been merely secondary figures in Knudsen's works. In his artistically most significant novel, *Sind* (1903; temper), nature and the rural population are primary. In *Fremskridt* (1907; progress), Knudsen confronts the old peasant community's social, political, and spiritual development with modern reform politics.

One of the most influential figures in modern Danish literature was Jensen, who won the Nobel Prize in Literature in 1944. Influenced by Jørgensen and Hamsun, Jensen's early novels *Danskere* (1896; Danes) and *Einar Elkær* (1898), in the decadent mood of the 1890's, have as protagonists introverted, self-centered students from the provinces. Fresher is Jensen's first masterpiece, the collection of stories *Himmerlandsfolk* (1898; Himmerland people), immortalizing his home region, its traditions and its people. In its regional setting, the novel *Kongens fald* (1900-1901; *The Fall of the King*, 1933) is linked to *Himmerlandsfolk*. It focuses on the figure of the sixteenth century king Christian II. The king's character is secondary, but his skepticism, which leads to the dissolution of all plans and energy into reflection and dream, symbolizes the paralysis Jensen perceived as a major flaw in the Danish character. Scenes of harsh naturalism alternate with passages of exquisite lyricism. *The Fall of the King* is a historical novel—the most significant in Danish literature—but Jensen broke decisively with the historical naturalism of Flaubert and J. P. Jacobsen. The apparently accidental juxtaposition of tableaux and situations creates a myth of loneliness, transitoriness, and death.

A journey to the United States in 1902 and 1903 resulted in two novels, *Madame d'Ora* (1904) and *Hjulet* (1905; the wheel), both of which reveal Jensen's confrontation with the modern United States. Their brilliant descriptions of New York and Chicago coexist, however, with shopworn attempts at suspense. At the same time, they turn against all speculations concerning immortality. Jensen's finest narrative art—aside from *The Fall of the King*—is in the smaller prose pieces of *Myter* (myths), which appeared in eleven volumes between 1907 and 1944. The "myths" elevate visionary existentialism over conventional plot. Several are studies for the great series of novels *Den lange rejse* (1908-1922; *The Long Journey*, 1922-1924, 1933, 1945). This history of the world begins before the Ice Age in the tropical Danish forests and encompasses the epochs of the tribal migrations and Viking raids to the discovery of America. It tells of the progenitors of the "Gothic race," of their longing for distant places, and finally of their departure from their northern homeland toward the lost land before the Ice Age. Influenced by Darwin's evolutionary theories, Jensen attempts to explain universal human symbols and conceptions, purely on the basis of practical experience.

Martin Andersen Nexø (1869-1954) was the first significant writer of the Danish workers' movement, the first to make the proletariat central. In his novel *Pelle Erobreren* (1906-1910; *Pelle the Conqueror*, 1913-1916), Nexø traces the growth of the Danish workers' movement in the last decades of the nineteenth century. The novel contains many agitatory passages, and the later parts of the novel are frequently utopian and naïve without the artistic merit of earlier parts. *Pelle the Conqueror* is nevertheless carried along by the epic power of the narrative and by Nexø's social commitment. His second major work, *Ditte Menneskebarn* (1917-1921; in three volumes as *Ditte: Girl Alive!*, 1920; *Ditte: Daugh-*

ter of Man, 1921; *Ditte: Towards the Stars*, 1922), is based on the same human and social concerns as *Pelle the Conqueror*. Like Pelle, Ditte begins at the very bottom, ambitious and hungry for life, but her fate is different. Whereas Pelle becomes involved in politics in order to build a new social order, Ditte fights alone against poverty and finally succumbs. Nexø was the only Danish Marxist writer of his generation, but he obviously differed from the socialist authors of the 1930's; he still adhered to an idealistic belief in human goodness that, cutting across all social and economic relationships, asserts itself despite everything.

BETWEEN THE WORLD WARS

The democratization of Sweden after World War I clearly shows in its literature. Around 1910, several writers emerged from the working class to portray the lowest social strata, a dominant feature of twentieth century Swedish literature, yet their realistic material and naturalistic techniques posed new aesthetic problems. For many, Zola was the master; above all, the proletarian writers were strongly influenced by Maxim Gorky, Upton Sinclair, and the Scandinavian pioneer of proletarian writing, Nexø.

The satiric novels of Jan Fridegård (1897-1968) describe the conflicts of the poor with society—as in his major work, the autobiographical "Lars Hård" cycle (1935-1951). Ivar Lo-Johansson (1901-1990) was the first of the proletarian novelists of the 1930's to depict poor farmhands collectively, in *Godnatt, jord* (1933; good night, earth). In a number of social novels, Lo-Johansson continued his treatment of working-class problems; *Analfabeten* (1951; the illiterate) is the first of an eight-volume autobiographical series, concluding with *Proletärförfattaren* (1960; the proletarian writer).

The first novel of Vilhelm Moberg (1898-1973), *Raskens* (1927), introduced the character type of the exploited farmhand in an unsentimental story of a peasant soldier, his large family, and their fight against misery and poverty. Moberg's major work is his partly documentary prose epic about the nineteenth century emigration of Swedish farmers to the United States, the multivolume *Romanen om utvandrarna* (1949-1959), which includes *Utvandrarna* (1949; *The Emigrants*, 1951), *Invandrarna* (1952; *Unto a Good Land*, 1954),

Nybyggarna (1956), and *Sista brevet till Sveriga* (1959; *The Last Letter Home*, 1961, is an abridged version of the last two volumes). It is at once a social chronicle, a myth about the search for happiness, and a satire of Swedish bureaucracy and social hierarchy.

The postwar mentality, familiar from world literature, shattered all illusions; any belief in moral order seemed ludicrous. The nihilism of the lost generation was eventually evident in all countries, in the works of Ernest Hemingway, André Malraux, and Erich Maria Remarque—in Denmark in the work of Tom Kristensen and in Iceland in that of Halldór Laxness.

In Swedish prose, next to Pär Lagerkvist, Eyvind Johnson (1900-1976) probably most accurately expresses this postwar attitude. Whereas Lagerkvist's angst is primarily metaphysical, Johnson's is more pragmatic. The expressionism of his early works gives way to more humanistic democratism, as in the trilogy *Krilon* (1941-1943), which attacks fascism and Sweden's neutrality during World War II. After the war, Johnson wrote two historical novels that depict his essential theme—the hopeless battle of the right and good for a better world. *Strändernas svall* (1946; *Return to Ithaca: The Odyssey Retold as a Modern Novel*, 1952) reworks Homer's *Odyssey* (c. 725 B.C.E.; English translation, 1614) from a modern point of view, fragmenting the firmness of the classical figures. *Drömmar om rosor och eld* (1949; *Dreams of Roses and Fire*, 1984) expresses Johnson's pessimism, treated in *Molnen över Metapontion* (1957; clouds over Metapontion) on three time levels: ancient Syracuse, World War II, and the 1950's, suggesting that freedom and love are always threatened and that history is unpredictable and senseless. His most successful treatment of this theme is *Hans nådes tid* (1960; *The Days of His Grace*, 1968), set in Charlemagne's France, describing how several young rebels become either tools of imperial power or sink into paralysis. The narrative experiments are continued in *Livsdagen lång* (1964; life's long day), which combines several stories from different epochs, held together by the narrator. In *Några steg mot tystnaden* (1973; a few steps toward silence), the action again shifts between different periods to illustrate the futile effort of Western humanism to retain integrity when threatened by injustice and violence. Johnson was awarded the Nobel Prize in Literature in 1974, "for a narrative art, farseeing in lands and ages, in the service of freedom."

The central figure of the 1920's was another Nobel laureate, Lagerkvist (1891-1974), who received the prize in 1951. His early pessimism is overcome in *Det eviga leendet* (1920; *The Eternal Smile*, 1934), the setting of which is the realm of the dead, where the dead philosophize about the meaning of life and alternately decide to seek out God, to demand an explanation. The political crises of the 1930's are clearly reflected in Lagerkvist's works. The first part of the novella *Bödeln* (1933; *The Hangman*, 1936) is set in a medieval village inn, the second part in a dance hall in the Fascist present. The medieval hangman, Lagerkvist suggests, was watched with anxious fascination; his counterpart in the Fascist era is celebrated. In 1944, in the novel *Dvärgen* (*The Dwarf*, 1945), Lagerkvist again investigated the psychology of evil, this time through the diary of a dwarf at the court of an Italian Renaissance prince. A kind of Antichrist, the dwarf comprehends only inhumanity, gruesomeness, and the struggle for power. This work brought Lagerkvist to the reading public, leading up to his international breakthrough with the novel *Barabbas* (1950; English translation, 1951), about the liberated robber who, though incapable of love or sacrifice, is filled with a vague metaphysical yearning for something beyond himself.

With *Barabbas*, Lagerkvist began to express a new longing for a distant God. In *Sibyllan* (1956; *The Sibyl*, 1958), which brings together a seeress from Delphi and the wandering Jew Ahasuerus, the theme is the human encounter with God. Only at the end of *Ahasverus död* (1960; *The Death of Ahasuerus*, 1962) does the restless wanderer find quiet in a monastery, where he experiences Christ not as the Son of God but as an unhappy fellow man. This novel and the following two, *Pilgrim på havet* (1962; *Pilgrim at Sea*, 1964) and *Det heliga landet* (1964; *The Holy Land*, 1966), all set in the European Middle Ages, describe restless pilgrims who find peace through love. Lagerkvist's last book, *Mariamne* (1967; *Herod and Mariamne*, 1968), carries the same message, expressed, as in his other mature works, through the greatest possible stylistic simplicity and lucidity.

Two significant—and very different—interwar novels were written by lyric poets. Karin Boye (1900-1941) wrote the utopian *Kallocain* (1940; English translation,

1966) based on her travels in Germany and the Soviet Union; this work is stylistically indebted to Aldous Huxley's *Brave New World* (1932) and to Franz Kafka's novels. It depicts a totalitarian state that has eliminated all personal freedom, without, however, completely denying the survival of humanity. This humanism found an outstanding representative in Harry Martinson (1904-1978), particularly in his poem cycle *Passad* (1945; trade winds). In his novel *Vägen till Klockrike* (1948; *The Road*, 1955), Martinson shapes the theme of humanism's clash with science in the portrayal of a vagabond who renounces society to find spiritual poise in meditation and nature.

Knut Hamsun's development after 1900 into a social critic accorded with the increasing preoccupation of Norway's younger generation with social issues. The working class grew at a pace unknown in the other Nordic countries, and the population shift from country to city and factories led inevitably to political radicalization, expressed most clearly in works by Johan Falkberget (1879-1967) and Kristofer Uppdal (1878-1961). In Falkberget's trilogy *Christianus Sextus* (1927-1935), set in the 1720's, the miner appears for the first time in Norwegian literature. In the tetralogy *Nattens brød* (1940-1959; bread of night), Falkberget unforgettably pictures the upheaval in the life of the late seventeenth century peasants who gave up their property to work in the foundries. Falkberget's work is not only realistic but also has a Romantic vein, as his religiously colored optimism remains victorious over the described misery. It fell to Uppdal to depict the workers as a class and to found the modern Norwegian social novel. His uneven ten-volume novel cycle, *Dansen gjenom skuggeheimen* (1911-1924; the dance through the shadow land), is based on the clash between the feudal structures of the villages and those of modern industry.

Two Norwegian writers, the world-renowned Sigrid Undset (1882-1949) and the lesser-known Olav Duun (1876-1939), stand above most of the Nordic writers of the epic in the twentieth century. In his main work, the six-volume family saga *Juvikfolke* (1918-1923; *The People of Juvik*, 1930-1935), Duun chronicles a peasant family over a one-hundred-year period to the end of World War I. He explores the relationship between individual and environment in a collective portrait of the spiritual life of the Norwegian people as they develop from feudalism to a society of high ethical standards. Duun's last book, *Menneskene og maktene* (1938; *Flood-tide of Fate*, 1960), which embodies all of his essential ideas and motifs, envisions apocalypse in the story of the inhabitants of a small island and their dread of being swallowed up by the sea. In modern point-of-view technique, each scene is told from more than one character's perspective.

The work of Undset was more traditional. Her historical novels of the Middle Ages—including two trilogies, *Kristin Lavransdatter* (1920-1922; English translation, 1923-1927) and *Olav Audunssøn i Hestviken* and *Olav Audunssøn og hans børn* (1925-1927; *The Master of Hestviken*, 1928-1930, 1934)—constitute a significant contribution to world literature and were recognized in Undset's Nobel Prize in Literature citation in 1928. *Kristin Lavransdatter*, set in the fourteenth century, begins with the struggle of the title figure for the man she loves. After her husband's death, Kristin's life becomes a humble pilgrimage toward final peace in service to God and her fellow humans. Undset's conversion to Catholicism in 1925 shaped *The Master of Hestviken*, a thirteenth century tragedy of love and marriage that glorifies religion. As in *Kristin Lavransdatter*, the major motif is the struggle between willfulness and obedience to God. Undset returned to the twentieth century in the two-volume novel *Gymnadenia* (1929; *The Wild Orchid*, 1931) and *Den brændende busk* (1930; *The Burning Bush*, 1932), portraying a young man's harrowing progress from humanism to Catholicism. Contemporary settings also characterize Undset's two novels of marriage, *Ida Elisabeth* (1932; *Ida Elizabeth*, 1933) and *Den trofaste husfru* (1933; *The Faithful Wife*, 1937), strongly attacking modern materialism.

Although Norway was neutral in World War I, many younger authors felt the unsettling events of the period. Several embraced socialism on one hand and Sigmund Freud's theories on the other. Outside all political groups stands Cora Sandel (the pseudonym of Sara Fabricius, 1880-1974), whose works analyze women's inhibitions and feelings of inferiority. Her trilogy comprising *Alberte og Jacob* (1926; *Alberta and Jacob*, 1962), *Alberte og friheten* (1931; *Alberta and Freedom*, 1963), and *Bare Alberte* (1939; *Alberta Alone*, 1965) follows a woman's hard-won independence in a narrow petit bourgeois milieu, finally leading to her personal and artistic liberation.

Sigurd Hoel (1890-1960) was, in contrast to Sandel, a cool and ironic commentator. His first significant work, and the first attempt by a Norwegian to write a collective novel, was *En dag i oktober* (1931; *One Day in October*, 1932)—modeled on Elmer Rice's play *Street Scene* (pr., pb. 1929)—concerning an Oslo apartment house and its inhabitants. Hoel's most penetrating psychological work of the interwar period, *Fjorten dager før frostnettene* (1935; fourteen days before the frosty nights), focuses on a man who deserts his beloved because he is incapable of love. In 1943, during the German Occupation, Hoel fled to Sweden. There he began *Møte ved milipælen* (1947; *Meeting at the Milestone*, 1951), which asks the crucial questions, Why did so many Norwegians become traitors to their country? and To what degree is everyone responsible? The novel contains superb descriptions of the Occupation years, but it is more absorbing in its sophisticated structure, constantly shifting between time planes, a technique that one finds even in Hoel's prewar novels. In his last novel, *Trollringen* (1958; *The Troll Circle*, 1991), possibly Hoel's greatest artistic achievement, fantasy can again unfold freely, unburdened by the satiric comments on the period that pervade so many of his works.

Around 1930, Tarjei Vesaas, Aksel Sandemose, and Johan Borgen made their appearance. Their work was influenced by the period's growing political tension, but the excesses of totalitarianism also challenged these writers to a psychological investigation of human nature. This group was much influenced by translations from other modern literatures, particularly from American literature.

Vesaas (1897-1970) was the Norwegian novelist who broke most consistently with realism. In the novel *Kimen* (1940; *The Seed*, 1964), the forces of destruction haunt a peaceful island community, symbolized in a merciless hunt for a mentally disturbed man who has killed a girl. Vesaas's next novel, *Huset i mørkret* (1945; *The House in the Dark*, 1976), likewise portrays the present in its depiction of the occupation of Norway, yet the plot is elevated to an allegory concerning the essence of evil. In *Bleikeplassen* (1946; *The Bleaching Yard*,

1981), realism and symbolism are blended in a suggestive world, and the process of spiritual purification and salvation through death is analyzed. *Fuglane* (1957; *The Birds*, 1968) follows the same development: When Mattis discovers the love between his sister and another man, he knows he is standing in their way; his death upon the water is viewed as a sacrifice for his sister and her love. Vesaas's last novel, suggestively titled *Båten om kvelden* (1968; *The Boat in the Evening*, 1971), gathers sixteen semiautobiographical sketches into a symbolic pattern that suggests the miraculous and enigmatically ominous elements in nature and human existence.

Sandemose (1899-1965), on the other hand, was fascinated by the struggle between the individual and the masses. Though he insisted that environment inevitably overcomes free will, he remained critical of dogmatic materialism. In Sandemose's novel *En sjømann går i land* (1931; a sailor goes to shore), Espen Arnakke escapes off Newfoundland from the ship on which he has fought to be accepted by his comrades; he murders a friend in a crime of passion. In the sequel, the episodic *En flyktning krysser sitt spor* (1933; *A Fugitive Crosses His Tracks*, 1936), set seventeen years later, Espen comes to understand that the murder was rooted in his childhood. The atmosphere of death dominates *Vi pynter oss med horn* (1936; *Horns for Our Adornment*, 1938), a novel in which Sandemose depicts the relationships among the crew members of a schooner bound for Newfoundland. *Det svundne er en drøm* (1946; the vanished is a dream) offers the journal entries of a Norwegian American's visit to his homeland, from 1938 to 1940, in order to reexperience the past. Another novel dealing with traumas rooted in the past is Sandemose's last significant work, *Varulven* (1958; *The Werewolf*, 1966), a sequel to which, *Felicias bryllup* (Felicia's wedding), appeared in 1961. The werewolf symbolizes the repression that precludes happiness; typically, Sandemose weds love to murder and lust to death in his attempt to track down the elusive, self-destructive, irrational mind.

Borgen (1902-1979) was the most innovative stylist of the period. The question of identity is central to his work: Is it merely created by societal expectation and the private need for concealment? His major work, the trilogy *Lillelord* (1955-1957; English translation, 1982), describes a shattered, middle-class Oslo boy just before

World War I who grows into a lonely man, masking his destructive amorality with good upbringing. *Den røde tåken* (1967; *The Red Mist*, 1973) shapes Borgen's most characteristic themes into a single inner monologue. Through the entire volume, the reader follows one person's consciousness, behind whose search for harmony is concealed a lost self, who has committed a crime. In *Eksempler* (1974; examples), about a dissolving marriage, Borgen is skeptical about the possibilities for personal integrity, as a result of the inability of language to serve as a medium of communication.

World War I's impact was stronger in Danish literature than in that of the other Nordic countries. A new generation of lyricists emerged spontaneously, affirming life amid the threat of war. The two most prominent were Emil Bønnelycke (1893-1953) and Tom Kristensen (1893-1974). One year after his poetic debut, Kristensen published a novel, *Livets arabesk* (1921; arabesque of life), conveying a desperate view of life as absurd, rendered in a colorful, expressionistic style. Kristensen's major novel, *Hærværk* (1930; *Havoc*, 1968), can be read as an autobiography, a roman à clef, or a case study of psychological decline. The main motif is the paralyzing fear of the major character, Ole Jastrau, that he cannot realize himself. In his decline, Jastrau ironically experiences not only joy in his self-destruction but also a sense of infinity. Formally, *Havoc* is indebted to James Joyce's *Ulysses* (1922), and Jastrau's search for identity is reminiscent of the characters in Aldous Huxley's *Point Counter Point* (1928). As an unsentimental examination of the postwar character, however, *Havoc* stands forth as one of the most significant and independent expressions of the "lost generation" in world literature.

Next to Kristensen, Jacob Paludan (1896-1975) is most typical of his generation. Both writers occupied themselves with postwar crises, but whereas Kristensen felt the chaos within himself, Paludan critically observed and condemned it from a conservative standpoint. The interwar period's dehumanizing technological concentration is dramatized in the social novel *Fugle omkring fyret* (1925; *Birds Around the Fire*, 1928). The victim's revenge comes when the sea destroys the new harbor, which had been built as a financial speculation. This pessimism is somewhat alleviated in Paludan's major work and the most significant *Entwicklungsroman* in modern Danish literature, *Jørgen Stein* (1932-1933; English translation, 1966). Paludan demonstrates the changes that occur because of the outbreak of World War I—in the countryside, the provinces, and in Copenhagen—especially for the young generation. The main themes are cultural decline and the futile attempt to bring oneself into harmony with a fast-changing world, another significant expression in Danish literature of the mood of the lost generation.

Nis Petersen (1897-1943) most convincingly expresses the period's nihilism. In 1931, his major work *Sandalmagernes gade* (*The Street of the Sandalmakers*, 1933) broadly portrayed the uprootedness and uncertainty of Marcus Aurelius's Rome. Superficially a historical novel, the work actually suggests modern Copenhagen, and its author shows how it, like Rome, stands in a negative relationship to the Gospels' message of love. The thoroughly realized setting and society are rendered through the use of ironic anachronisms and a modern, subjective style.

Another significant prose work of the period is the collective novel *Fiskerne* (1928; *The Fishermen*, 1951), by Hans Kirk (1898-1962). In the naturalistic tradition of Pontoppidan and Nexø, it tells of a group of families who leave a barren coastal area for a milder environment. Though clearly separate from the inhabitants of the new region, their cohesiveness and their strong faith conquer the community's strong resistance from within. The basic viewpoint of the novel is sociological and Marxist, but this bias is somewhat offset by credible characterization.

Kirk influenced a number of collective novels by the Faroese writer William Heinesen (1900-1991). The first, *Blæsende gry* (1934; *Windswept Dawn,* 2009), offers a cross section of a small island's struggle between old and new and the exploitation of the poor by the wealthy merchants and ship owners. *Noatun* (1938; *Niels Peter*, 1940) adds to these themes the individual's battle with harsh Faroese nature. In this novel, as well as in his masterpiece, *De fortabte spillemænd* (1950; *The Lost Musicians*, 1971), Heinesen's imagination is freed and combined—in the latter, with a grotesquely humorous portrayal of eccentric musicians and poets threatened by the material world. Comedy and tragedy are also inge-

niously mixed in *Det gode Håb* (1964; the good hope), an epistolary novel set in the seventeenth century, while Heinesen's childhood provided the material for *Tårnet ved verdens ende* (1976; *The Tower at the Edge of the World*, 1981); in about seventy brief chapters made up of a young boy's dreams and fantasies, the novel provides a vehicle for the aging author's magnificent farewell to life, its lyric, occasionally humorous, language masking a deep sadness and resignation.

Hans Christian Branner (1903-1966) was skeptical of his time's ideological and social systems. As an early influence of psychoanalysis on Branner diminished, that of existential philosophy—its concepts of angst, responsibility, and loneliness—increased. *Drømmen om en kvinde* (1941; dream about a woman) deals with human isolation, in particular with the two situations in life in which men and women stand completely alone, birth and death. Branner uses a complex inner monologue which gives way in *Rytteren* (1949; *The Riding Master*, 1951; also known as *The Mistress*, 1953) to brief dialogues in a story about four people whose lives are dominated from beyond the grave by the riding master of the title. World War II darkened almost everything Branner wrote after 1939, but not until 1955 did he use the war itself as material. In the novel *Ingen kender natten* (1955; *No Man Knows the Night*, 1958), he portrays members of the Resistance as well as collaborators, though his main concern is with the personal dispossession of a man dominated by nihilism and Freudianism.

Martin Alfred Hansen (1909-1955), who began as a realistic social critic, became by the late 1940's a major advocate of religious and antinaturalistic trends. The picaresque novel *Jonatans rejse* (1941; English translation, 1961) builds on the old fable of the blacksmith who lures the devil into a bottle and thus is able to acquire all the world's riches. In Jonatan and his analytical comrade, Askelad, the modern and the more harmonious medieval worldviews clash. Similarly, Hansen's next book, *Lykkelige Kristoffer* (1945; *Lucky Kristoffer*, 1974), combines picaresque form and historical material, with Miguel de Cervantes' *Don Quixote de la Mancha* (1605, 1615) as the model. The novel depicts the collapse of the Middle Ages itself and calls into question its universal figures, the knight and the priest. Hansen's last fictional work, the novel *Løgneren* (1950; *The Liar*, 1954), tells of a sexton and teacher, Johannes Vig, the liar of the title, who sketches his life in his diary for a confidant, Nathanael, whose name is meant to evoke that of the biblical prophet who was "without deceit." Johannes is a dilettante of faith who finally confronts and conquers evil; in the terms of Søren Kierkegaard, whose philosophy inspired the novel, Johannes advances from the ethical to the religious stage.

Prose literature in interwar Finland was dominated by several authors writing in Finnish, who, during the years of the 1918 civil war between the Right and the Left, rejected neo-Romanticism and addressed themselves to social themes—in contrast to the Finno-Swedish lyric poets' sophisticated modernism. Realistic prose flourished, sharply contrasting with earlier idealizations of Finnish folk life but offering no clear political program.

Thus, Joel Lehtonen (1881-1934) expected no substantial political change to result from the social criticism of his novels and short stories. In his major work, *Putkinotko* (1919-1920), naturalistic characterization and dialogue are framed with impressionistic, colorful descriptions, alleviating the poverty and misery of the family described. More negative is Lehtonen's last novel, *Henkien taistelu* (1933; the struggle of the spirits), a series of loosely connected scenes from everyday life, framed by a philosophical discussion between God and Satan about good and evil in human beings.

The interwar author most connected with his native soil was Frans Eemil Sillanpää (1888-1964). The merger of the self and nature in his first novel, *Elämä ja aurinko* (1916; life and the sun), inspired by Hamsun, proved to be a successful novelty in Finnish literature. *Nuorena nukkunut* (1931; *The Maid Silja*, 1933; also known as *Fallen Asleep While Young*, 1939), which brought Sillanpää international recognition, tells the story of the destruction of an old peasant family, interwoven with sensitive descriptions of the Finnish summer. The poverty and illness of the protagonists recedes before their inner strength as they face death—showing the spirit's victory over matter. The atmosphere of Sillanpää's first novel was resumed in his novels of the 1930's, *Miehen tie* (1932; the way of man) and *Ihmiset syviyössä* (1934; *People in the Summer Night*, 1966). The first is a love story, accompanied by seasonal changes; the second offers a cross section of human destinies during a few days

and nights. Sillanpää received the Nobel Prize in Literature in 1939, in recognition of "his deep understanding of his country's peasantry and the exquisite art with which he has portrayed their way of life and their relationship with Nature."

With the novel *Alastalon salissa* (1933; in the living room of Alastalo), Volter Kilpi (1874-1939) created the most interesting Finnish prose experiment of the period. On the surface, the novel is a didactic story in the manner of Kivi's *Seven Brothers*. The external action takes place in only six hours, but Kilpi adds a mystical dimension; the characters function not only in the present but also in the past and in the future. *Kirkolle* (1937; on the road to the church)—concerning the gathering of some churchgoers, their journey in a boat, and their arrival—takes place in only three hours. Again, thoughts and feelings are primary, and the narrative moves between past and present.

As the most original talent in Finnish prose, Kilpi has found a limited audience. More traditional is Mika Waltari (1908-1979). His best work was written in the 1930's: the trilogy comprising *Mies ja haave* (1933; a man and a dream), *Sielu ja liekki* (1934; the soul and the flame), and *Palava nuoruus* (1935; burning youth), published in one volume as *Isästä poikaan* (1942; from father to son), about a family that settles in Helsinki, and *Vieras mies tuli taloon* (1937; *A Stranger Came to the Farm*, 1952), a novel with a rural setting. In the postwar years up to 1964, Waltari wrote six historical novels that made him the best-known Finnish author of all time. These works were translated into most major languages, and the first, *Sinuhe, egyptiläinen* (1945; *The Egyptian*, 1949), was filmed in Hollywood. Behind the historical facade, Waltari here analyzes the disillusionment after Finland's defeat by Russia in 1944.

Icelandic literature after 1920 moved toward greater realism and receptiveness to foreign influences. An intense cult of the self, the present, and sexuality emerged, together with a greater political consciousness. Gunnar Gunnarsson, Kristmann Guðmundsson, and Halldór Laxness brought prose to a high level of perfection during the late 1920's. Gunnarsson (1889-1975), though he wrote in Danish during his residence in Denmark from 1897 to 1939, deals exclusively with Icelandic topics in his more than forty volumes. His first success, the tetralogy *Af Borgslægtens Historie* (1912-1914; partial translation *Guest the One-Eyed*, 1920), re-creates Iceland in a family saga whose protagonist is a legendary saint. Of the philosophical middle-class problem novels that Gunnarsson began during World War I, the most important is the contemporary story *Salige er de Enfoldige* (1920; *Seven Days' Darkness*, 1930), about the struggle between a humanitarian doctor and his cynical opponent, ending with the doctor's defeat and internment in an insane asylum.

Gunnarsson eventually found faith in humankind through recognition of the past. With *Jón Arason* (1930), the story of the last Catholic bishop in Iceland, Gunnarsson resumed work on a monumental cycle of twelve novels on Iceland's history, begun in 1918 with a description of the early saga period in *Edbrødre* (*The Sworn Brothers*, 1920). The masterpiece of the series is *Svartfugl* (1929; *The Black Cliffs*, 1967), a story of eighteenth century crime and punishment. As a whole, the series tells of the founding of a nation, its unification, then its decline and disintegration caused by egotism and aggression.

Guðmundsson (1902-1983) became the most frequently translated Icelandic novelist—into more than thirty languages. His best works, such as *Den første vår* (1933; the first spring), describe youthful love, sometimes resulting in disillusionment, sometimes ending on an optimistic note. *Brudekjolen* (1927; *The Bridal Gown*, 1931) and *Livets morgen* (1929; *Morning of Life*, 1936) are well-constructed family chronicles. Guðmundsson also wrote historical works. *Gyðjan og uxinn* (1937; *Winged Citadel*, 1940), for example, is a romance set in Mycenaean Crete yet clearly alluding to World War II politics.

After writing his first work, a romantic story influenced by Hamsun, entitled *Barn náttúrunnar* (1919; child of nature), Halldór Laxness (1902-1998) visited Denmark and Sweden and stayed in Germany and Austria between 1921 and 1922; in 1923, he converted to Catholicism. The autobiographical *Vefarinn mikli frá Kasmír* (1927; *The Great Weaver from Kashmir*, 2008) comes to terms with the conflicts of the postwar times from a Catholic viewpoint, making Laxness the Icelandic representative of the lost generation. During a stay in the United States from 1927 to 1929, Laxness turned to the socialistic views that would shape his work in the following decade. The first result was the two-volume novel comprising *Þu vínviður hreini* (1931; O thou pure vine) and *Fuglinn í fjörunni* (1932; the bird on the beach), published together in English as *Salka Valka: A Novel of Iceland* (1936). In a small fishing village, the first trade union is established, a strike breaks out, and the domination of the local capitalist merchant is threatened. *Sjálfstætt fólk* (1934-1935; *Independent People*, 1946) is the story of the impoverished farmer Bjartur at the threshold of modernity, a physical giant betrayed by his traditions and stubborn individualism. The protagonist of the four-volume *Heimsljós* (1937-1940; *World Light*, 1969), on the other hand, is a poet whose genius is cramped by his surroundings; the novel is an analysis of the artist's eternal problem, rendered as social criticism.

After World War II, Laxness's distinct individualism led him far from his socialist views. In *Brekkukotsannáll* (1957; *The Fish Can Sing*, 1966), the narrator recalls the life of his grandparents in Reykjavík, who honored simple, traditional values but also allowed themselves to be deceived by them. Similarly, the farmer in *Paradísarheimt* (1960; *Paradise Reclaimed*, 1962) leaves his homestead and family to travel to Utah, the promised land of the Mormons; realizing his mistake, he returns, only to find the ruins of his old farm. This revolt against ideology continues in Laxness's humorous fable *Kristnihald undir Jökli* (1968; *Christianity at Glacier*, 1972). Laxness never stagnated; he had the courage to give up accepted viewpoints, just as he continuously chose new artistic directions—he was also an excellent lyric poet and a productive dramatist.

POSTWAR DEVELOPMENTS

The turbulent years after the outbreak of World War II began with Finland's Winter War against Russia (1939-1940) and continued with German aid to Finland (1941-1944), the occupation of Denmark and Norway by German troops (1940-1945), the occupation of the Faeroe Islands and Iceland by the British (1940-1945), and Sweden's armed neutrality. Approaching the 1960's, Nordic literature became increasingly political. The modern welfare state and growing materialism were sharply attacked, as was the ivory-tower attitude, defended by some writers as the means of artistic survival. In addition, the 1960's led to a radical questioning of women's role in society. Consequently, a fierce debate arose about the artist's position and responsibility, as well as speculations on the relationship of language to reality.

The first of the Swedish prose writers of the 1940's, Lars Ahlin (1915-1997) belonged to the generation of young people who suffered from the economic crisis of the 1930's; the resulting sense of disenfranchisement stayed with him. Ahlin's first book, *Tåbb med manifester* (1943; Tåbb with the manifesto), lays down his program: The young proletarian Tåbb is a "zero being" and seeks a worldview corresponding to his life. He finds communism existentially inadequate, but he is attracted to the Lutheran view that the human being is essentially a sinner, to be judged according to his or her deeds.

Next to Ahlin, Stig Dagerman (1923-1954) is the most significant prose writer of the postwar years in Sweden. For him, too, point zero was the necessary point of departure, but, unlike Ahlin's characters, Dagerman's never find a solution to contemporary anxiety. In his first novel, *Ormen* (1945; *The Snake,* 1995), Dagerman symbolically writes of the terror that spreads among the soldiers in a barracks as they realize that an escaped snake is loose among them. The novel *De dömdas ö* (1946; *Island of the Doomed,* 1991) also deals with the stresses of the time in its picture of seven people who, shipwrecked on an uninhabited island, face an agonizing death.

The writing of the 1940's had been informed by a common, pessimistic worldview; this was not true in the 1950's. Certain common traits, however, can be noted—particularly an inclination toward aestheticism and optimism. Lars Gyllensten (1921-2006) is an exception. His first two prose works, *Moderna myter* (1949; modern myths) and *Det blå skeppet* (1950; the blue ship), stand in a dialectical relationship to each other. The first is aphoristic and ironic. The second, a complex story of a youth growing up on a ship, employs rituals and myths in a romantic manner. Both modes—the intellectual/analytical and the romantic/naïve—are combined in Gyllensten's masterpiece, *Barnabok* (1952; children's book). This psychologically intense and verbally precise work follows the progressive ruination of a marriage and of a human being. Both *Sokrates död* (1960; the death of Socrates), questioning the value of the philosopher's death,

and *Kains memoarer* (1963; *The Testament of Cain,* 1967), defending Cain in a number of aphorisms, suggest that truth is relative. A similar tack is taken in *Grottan i öknen* (1973; the cave in the desert), based on the Orpheus and Eurydice myth, and in *I skuggan av Don Juan* (1975; in the shadow of Don Juan).

Two authors of the 1950's, Sara Lidman (1923-2004) and Per Wästberg (born 1933), treat the problems of the developing countries, a theme which several other authors were to treat during the next decade. Lidman's novels *Tjärdalen* (1953; the tar valley) and *Hjortronlandet* (1955; the land of cloud-berries) introduce modern Swedish neoprovincialism. Here one finds her recurrent outcast figure and the topics of guilt and responsibility, a moralistic approach that becomes even more pronounced in her two-volume novel *Regnspiran* (1958; *The Rain Bird,* 1962) and *Bära mistel* (1960; to carry mistletoe). In the 1960's, Lidman's stay in Africa resulted in the novels *Jag och min son* (1961; I and my son) and *Med fem diamanter* (1964; with five diamonds), sharply attacking apartheid and neutrality. In 1968, she returned to a Swedish setting with *Gruva* (mine), a mixture of fiction and social reportage which strongly advocates a strike among the miners of northern Sweden.

Per Wästberg's early writings are deft but somewhat disinterested portrayals of a dreamy childhood world. In *Arvtagaren* (1958; the heir), Wästberg's hero leaves the Swedish idyll to learn about postwar Europe. In the trilogy comprising *Vattenslottet* (1968; the water castle), *Luftburen* (1969; *The Air Cage,* 1972), and *Jordmånen* (1972; *Love's Gravity,* 1977), the author returns to a Stockholm setting to synthesize his earlier explorations of freedom and to exemplify the shift from provincialism to internationalism.

Swedish fiction of the 1960's was strongly influenced by the New Novel, especially the work of Alain Robbe-Grillet. His disciple, Torsten Ekbom (born 1938), like Robbe-Grillet's Danish contemporary Svend Åge Madsen, insisted that an author should interest himself (or herself) not in what his characters perceive but in how they perceive. Thus, *Signalspelet* (1965; the signal game) is a work composed from a popular boys' book, cut into pieces and reassembled, picturing the haphazardness of existence.

One implication of Ekbom's theories is the preoccupation with the relationship of the author to objective reality. This question culminated in the extensive use of a documentary and journalistic style. In *Ekspeditionen* (1962; *The Expedition*, 1962), Per Olof Sundman (1922-1992) used Sir Henry Morton Stanley's jungle expedition to investigate relationships among a group of people isolated by their surroundings. *Ingenjör Andrées luftfärd* (1967; *The Flight of the Eagle*, 1970) is an account of an actual balloon trip, in 1897, from Spitzbergen to the North Pole, which failed as a result of poor planning. The reader learns nothing of the physical and psychological burdens of the characters, and their fate is presented without melodrama. On the contrary, Sundman created a double documentary by publishing his preliminary research for the novel as *Ingen fruktan, intet hopp: Ett collage om Salomon August Andrée, hans medresenärer och hans polarexpedition* (1968: no fear, no hope: a collage on S. A. Andrée, his fellow travelers, and his polar expedition).

The question of subjectivity versus objectivity is also the topic of a novel by Per Olov Enquist (born 1934), *Färdvägen* (1963; the direction of travel), a picaresque journey through life's alternatives. Enquist gained international recognition with *Legionänerna* (1968; *The Legionnaires*, 1973). The point of departure of this documentary novel was the Swedish government's turning over to the Russians, in 1946, Baltic prisoners of war who had served in the German army—an action undertaken by the government against a storm of public protest. Enquist weaves his own personality into the presentation, and with constant revision and discussion, it becomes an example of how one's understanding of a political situation can be altered when one works one's way into it more deeply.

An alternative to the objectivity inspired by the New Novel is offered by Sven Delblanc (1931-1992) and Per Christian Jersild (born 1935), who tell fantastic stories, partly burlesque, partly serious. Delblanc's *Åsnabrygga* (1969; the donkey's bridge) is an extreme example of the Swedish semidocumentary novel. Whereas Sundman sets forth historical material about Andrée's balloon trip and Enquist and Lidman attempt to present actual circumstances objectively, Delblanc's book—his own diary—shows how subjectively he relates to traditional

objectivity, implicating himself to such a degree that he crosses the line between fiction and autobiography, thus again questioning the role of the artist—a theme also discussed in his novel *Kastrater: En romantisk berättelse* (1975; *The Castrati: A Romantic Tale*, 1979).

In the work of Jersild, there is a sharper satiric interest in society than one finds in the novels of Delblanc or Sundman. Jersild's major novel, *Grisjakten* (1968; the pig hunt), deals with the perfect civil servant, who loyally and unthinkingly follows orders. Jersild again warns against such manipulation in *Djurdoktorn* (1973; *The Animal Doctor*, 1975), a satiric novel envisioning a repressive system which absorbs its few revolts with appeals to solidarity and tolerance. The human compassion underlying this work also permeates *Babels hus* (1978; the house of Babel), a penetrating satiric analysis of Swedish health policy.

Lars Gustafsson (born 1936) stands outside all the literary trends in contemporary Sweden. His works—which range across many genres, including fiction and nonfiction, poetry and prose—explore questions of human identity and the relations between the self and objects with acuity and nearly mystical imagination. His novel *Poeten Brumbergs sista dagar och död* (1959; the last days and death of the poet Brumberg) is a mosaic from the literary legacy of the title character, including quotations from his Renaissance novel and recollections from his friends. In the allegorical novel *Bröderna* (1960; the brothers), Gustafsson discusses how environment shapes personality and perception. Whereas Gustafsson's earlier works were marked by defeatism and bewilderment, his novel cycle "Sprickorna i muren" (the cracks in the wall) is more extroverted, more pragmatic, and more hopeful. It begins with *Herr Gustafsson själv* (1971; Mr. Gustafsson himself), a presentation of the narrator and his confrontation with political reality, and concludes with *En biodlares död* (1978; *The Death of a Beekeeper*, 1981), the tragic but heartwarming story of a man dying of cancer.

Swedish writers of the 1970's were increasingly skeptical about the value of fiction; they attempted to establish new connections with reality, often forsaking fiction to encourage solidarity and a growing political awareness of oppression outside and inside Sweden. A work by Jan Myrdal (born 1927), *Rapport från kinesisk* by (1963; *Report from a Chinese Village*, 1965), typical of this trend, is a detailed description of everyday life in China after the revolution; the results of the Cultural Revolution are analyzed in *Kina: Revolutionen går vidare* (1970; *China: The Revolution Continued*, 1970).

The form of the pseudodocumentary, employing the diary of a fictitious hero, was taken up by Per Gunnar Evander (born 1933). Many of his novels are reconstructions of actual events. *Sista dagen i Valle Hedmans liv* (1971; the last day in Valle Hedman's life) deals with the accidental death of the title character through evidence and police reports actually fabricated by the author, while *Judas Iskariots knutna händer* (1978; the fists of Judas Ischariot) matter-of-factly describes the last days of Jesus through the eyes of Judas.

The more experimental trend is represented by Lars Norén (born 1944), inspired by French Surrealism. In 1970, he published the first part of a trilogy, *Biskötarna* (the beekeepers), followed in 1972 by *I den underjordiska himlen* (in the underworld heaven), an autobiographical, semidocumentary work dealing with human evil and cruelty, replete with symbolic structures interrupted by realistic dialogue.

After the first coming to terms with war and occupation, Norwegian literature suddenly shifted to lyric poetry after 1945. There were few dramas; prose, with the exception of Paal Brekke's novels, did not break with psychological realism until the 1960's, when it joined the currents of European modernism. Thematically, ethics dominated Norwegian postwar prose, which rejected the arbitrary divisions of the courageous and cowardly, the active and passive for the hard-won conviction that all are equally responsible for crime and war. Sigurd Hoel attempts in his novel *Meeting at the Milestone* to explain the Nazi motivation of the Norwegian traitors during the German Occupation. Younger authors also attacked this problem, such as Sigurd Evensmo (1912-1978) in his *Oppbrudd etter midnatt* (1946; departure after midnight), the somewhat glossy tale of a Fascist farmer whose patriotic feelings bring him into conflict with the Germans. This novel is surpassed by Evensmo's best book, *Englandsfarere* (1945; *Boat for England*, 1947), which deals with the capture and execution of a group of Resistance fighters.

A strong ethical commitment characterizes the prose of poet and playwright Jens Bjørneboe (1920-1976). His first novel, *Før hanen galer* (1952; before the cock crows), depicts the medical experiments in the German concentration camps. Bjørneboe, however, does not seek the specific causes of Nazism but investigates evil as a schism between feeling and intellect. Human cruelty is likewise analyzed in his trilogy comprising *Frihetens øyeblikk* (1966; *Moment of Freedom*, 1975), *Kruttårnet* (1969; the gunpowder tower), and *Stillheten* (1973; the silence), one of the most significant works of postwar Norwegian prose, a running chronicle of violence and torture.

In 1951, in his wordy Joycean novel *Aldrende Orfeus* (aging Orpheus), Paal Brekke (1923-1993) analyzed the generation gap before and after the war, strongly attacking conventional mores. *Og hekken vokste kjempehøy* (1953; and the hedge grew enormous) is clearer. Here the theme of human isolation is interwoven with an exciting murder plot, revealing that all the characters in the book could be guilty of the crime.

A more traditional approach is taken by Terje Stigen (born 1922), whose lyric novels are strongly influenced by Hamsun. Like Hamsun's *Hunger*, Stigen's *Nøkkel til ukjent rom* (1953; key to the unknown room) tells of a hypersensitive man who fluctuates between an ironic view of his misfortune and anarchy. In his succeeding novels, Stigen employed a more epic treatment of extroverted men of action. With *Det flyktige hjerte* (1967; the fickle heart), perhaps Stigen's best work, he turned to the period around 1800. The main character is a student of theology who becomes a pastor north of the Arctic Circle. His travel experiences are linked to the idea of love as erotic perversion, as he exploits love for his own artistic development and falsifies the life of feeling.

Stigen's realism contrasts sharply with the symbolic prose of Finn Carling (1925-2004), especially in Carling's novels, such as *Arenaen* (1951; the arena) and *Piken og fuglen* (1952; the girl and the bird). All treat the same theme despairingly: The artist betrays life by removing himself from it. The documentary technique is used in *Resten er taushet* (1973; the rest is silence), about death and humanity's relationship to it. *Fiendene* (1974; the enemies) contains prose sketches and poems about violence, fear, and isolation, posted against a glimmer of hope. Carling's *Dagbok til en død* (1993; *Diary for a*

Dead Husband, 1998), the story of a woman who gradually emerges from her husband's shadow after forty years of marriage, was adapted for the stage in 2004.

Foremost among contemporary Norwegian prose authors stands Finn Alnæs (1932-1991). Including the entire cosmos in his thinking, he showed human insignificance in a demoralized and nihilistic world. His novel *Gemini* (1968) is a polemical argument against the times, treating the ethical and aesthetic position of the artist in a modern welfare society from the vantage of a conservative worldview. This individualism also permeates *Musica* (1978), the first part of a cycle in eight volumes titled *Ildfesten* (the fire feast), a family chronicle of disintegration and adherence to tradition.

Many of the most interesting writers of contemporary Norwegian literature contributed to *Profil* (established in 1943), originally a philological journal, which became an organ of Marxist theory in the early 1970's. Tor Obrestad (born 1938), the oldest of the *Profil* rebels, was for a long time regarded as this group's central force. Marxism is conspicuous in his most important work, the novel *Sauda! Streik!* (1972; Sauda! strike!), a semidocumentary based on an illegal strike at an ironworks.

The most controversial revolutionary Norwegian author—and the most celebrated author in Norway—is Dag Solstad (born 1943). The title character in his *Arild Asnes 1970* (1971) seeks to escape from his limited milieu and finally finds an answer in Marxist-Leninist ideology. Solstad's *25. september-plassen* (1974; the twenty-fifth of September square) chronicles the working class of postwar Norway. Less convincing are the first two parts of a projected trilogy: *Svik: Førkrigsår* (1977; betrayal: prewar years) and *Krig: 1940* (1978; war: 1940), social, realistic works marked by superficial characterization. Solstad's two novels that have been translated into English, *Genanse og verdighet* (1994; *Shyness and Dignity*, 2006) and *Ellevte roman, bok atten* (2001; *Novel 11, Book 18*, 2008), deal with aging men trying to make sense of modern society.

Several others of the *Profil* group turned from the individualistic to the social but refused to enter the political arena. Einar Økland (born 1940) combines prose, poetry, and drama in *Gull-alder* (1972; golden age), in which he makes startling associative leaps to reflect on his childhood and his role as a writer. In *Anne* (1968), by

Paal-Helge Haugen (born 1945), the documentary approach is sustained for the first time in Norwegian literature. The story of a girl who dies of tuberculosis at an early age is commented on with excerpts from medical books, a reader, and the Bible, interspersed with lyric fragments. Haugen's anti-ideological viewpoint is shared by Kjartan Fløgstad (born 1944), whose novel, *Rasmus* (1974), levels strong attacks at fashionable trends. The picaresque *Dalen Portland* (1977; *Dollar Road*, 1989) mirrors contemporary Norwegian society, portrayed in both comic and tragic, fantastic and realistic ways, a technique characteristic of the general antidogmatic trend in contemporary Norwegian literature.

Among the contemporary Norwegian novelists not associated with the *Profil* group, one of the most significant is the prolific Tor Edvin Dahl (born 1943), who is known for short stories, detective novels (under the pseudonym David Torjussen), cultural criticism, studies of true crime, and a variety of other works in addition to mainstream novels. Reared in a family that was active in Norway's Pentecostal Church, Dahl explores issues of sin and guilt, responsibility, and spiritual striving. His first novel, *Den andre* (1972; the other), indicts materialistic modern society for the amorality that permits a student to remorselessly murder a friend. The trilogy comprising *Den første sommeren* (1980; the first summer), *Renate* (1981), and *Abrahams barn* (1982; Abraham's children) reveals the pervasiveness of evil, both individual and social, with little explicit hope for redemption.

Most prose writers in Danish literature after World War II followed the traditions of the 1930's, whereas the poets were more innovative. Many of them contributed to the journal *Heretica* (1948-1953)—"heretical" in relation to the dominant rationalism and materialism. The common ground was a recognition of the "cultural crisis," analyzed by Ole Sarvig (1921-1981), his generation's leading poet and the major representative of a modern metaphysical trend. His first novel, *Stenrosen* (1955; the rose of stone), is set in postwar Berlin, a city that was destroyed because it was a manifestation of demoniac modernism. In the dreamy *Havet under mit vindue* (1960; *The Sea Below My Window*, 2003), a woman awakens with amnesia on a mysterious island. In *Limbo* (1963), lyricism predominates at the expense of more traditional structure in its description of a woman's waiting and her dead husband's continued life in her soul. Sarvig's most significant novel is *De rejsende* (1978; the travelers). On one level, it tells the story of a middle-aged Danish American and his attempt to settle accounts with his childhood myths; on a more philosophical level, it deals with finding oneself in today's world.

Typical of several prose writers of the 1950's is the atmosphere of myth and fairy tale; also characteristic is a renewed interest in the work of Isak Dinesen (pseudonym of Karen Blixen, 1885-1962), particularly noticeable in the novels of Willy-August Linnemann (1914-1985). Along with fantasy, Danish prose of the 1950's evinces experimentation in the short stories of Villy Sørensen (1929-2001) and Peter Seeberg (1925-1999), the latter also a noted novelist. His first novel, *Bipersonerne* (1956; secondary characters), breaks consistently with realism. It portrays the shadowy existence of foreign laborers in a German film studio during World War II. In *Fugls føde* (1957; *The Imposter,* 1990), Seeberg deals with deliberate escapism. Tom, a writer, is a dreamer whose plans miscarry; at the same time, he is sharply aware of human follies and ruthlessly exploits them. *Hyrder* (1970; shepherds) is an apparently realistic story that suggests that people must be one another's shepherds in order to survive catastrophe. Such confidence is less apparent in Seeberg's last novel, *Ved havet* (1978; at the sea), but in his entire authorship it places him among the great humanists of recent Nordic literature.

Less exclusive is Leif Panduro (1923-1977), whose work primarily revolves around a person divided by his or her ties to the past. In this theme, Panduro, like many other Danish writers, was influenced by Villy Sørensen's treatment of humankind's psychological and social inadequacies. *Rend mig i traditionerne* (1958; *Kick Me in the Traditions,* 1961) is based on Panduro's favorite subject: the trials of puberty, when one capitulates to the seemingly ordered and normal adult world. Both the action-filled *Daniels anden verden* (1970; the other world of Daniel) and Panduro's last novel, *Høfeber* (1975; hay fever), are variations on the normal/abnormal theme as well as fascinating psychological analyses of love and responsibility.

The political climate of the years immediately after the war had favored a quest for the cosmic or metaphysical. In the mid-1950's, however, a gradual shift to a lyric rendering of social reality was perceptible. This lyric blossoming was largely attributable to Klaus Rifbjerg (born 1931), who, in addition to poetry, writes film scripts, plays, and numerous short stories and novels. Like Panduro's *Kick Me in the Traditions*, Rifbjerg's first novel, *Den kroniske uskyld* (1958; chronic innocence), portrays the mystery of unprotected and vulnerable puberty. The problems of insecure youth are also explored in the novels *Arkivet* (1967; archives) and *Lonni og Karl* (1968; Lonni and Karl). In a series of novels, Rifbjerg also treats the psychology of the adult world. *Operaelskeren* (1966; *The Opera Lover,* 1970) portrays the love of a mathematician for an opera singer, which eventually ends in catastrophe as the cool rationalist discovers that his well-ordered world is undercut by irrational powers. The full consequences of such a situation are experienced by the principal character of *Anna(jeg)Anna* (1969; *Anna(I)Anna,* 1982), a diplomat's neurotic wife who escapes from her luxurious life to travel with a young criminal hippie across Europe. In the complex *R.R.* (1972), Rifbjerg again criticizes the crippling effects of rationalism to which the main character, a Faust-like figure, has sold his soul. The broad chronicle *De beskedne* (1976; the modest ones), on the other hand, which tells of Danish everyday life during the 1950's and 1960's, is more accessible. Along with the subsequent novels *Tango* (1978), *Joker* (1979), *Krigen* (1992; *War,* 1995), and *Rod* (2008), *De beskedne* confirms Rifbjerg's position as an exceptionally sensitive writer.

Around 1960, Danish prose modernism became the focus of topical debate. Authors now turned from the experiences of the war, and the novel form was transformed under the influence of the New Novel, subordinating traditional plot and sharply distinguishing a novel's narrator from its characters. Clearly influenced by the New Novel is a work by Svend Åge Madsen (born 1939), *Besøget* (1963; the visit), that contrasts different narrative perspectives. In *Otte gange orphan* (1965; eight times orphan), seven independent stories are told in the first person in a monotonous and image-free language, suggesting that literature does not describe but rather creates reality according to the author's notions of it. In *Dage med Diam* (1972; days with Diam), readers must combine characters and events to create not the story they want to read but the reality they want to experience. A renewal in Madsen's writing is evident in the pseudodocumentary novel *Tugt og utugt i mellemtiden* (1976; decency and indecency in the meanwhile), a political and social analysis of Denmark in the 1970's. *Den ugudelige farce* (2002; the ungodly farce) shows from multiple viewpoints what happens to a jazz musician when he loses his unconscious mind after a head injury.

Myth predominates in the writings of playwright and novelist Ulla Ryum (born 1937); her attempt to create an ambiguous and associative dream language is reminiscent of the work of the American writer Djuna Barnes. Ryum's main interest revolves around those tragic figures who find meaning only in death. Such a person is the protagonist of *Natsangersken* (1963; the night singer), a psychological and symbolic portrait of a woman abandoned by life and love.

The neorealistic trend that emerged in the mid-1960's had a forerunner in Thorkild Hansen (1927-1989), who achieved great success with *Det lykkelige Arabien* (1962; *Arabia Felix*, 1964), based on two archaeological expeditions to Kuwait and the Nubian desert and focusing on scientists torn from their cultural milieu. *Jens Munk* (1965; *The Way to Hudson Bay*, 1970) deals with a sailor's bold but unsuccessful attempt to find the Northwest Passage to India and China. The theme of Hansen's "Slave Trilogy"—comprising *Slavernes kyst* (1967; *Coast of Slaves,* 2002), *Slavernes skibe* (1968; *Ships of Slaves*, 2003), and *Slavernes øer* (1970; *Islands of Slaves*, 2004)—is the slave trade practiced by the Danes between the Gold Coast of Africa and the West Indies. Hansen, however, oversteps the bounds of objective reporting through his subjective style, the use of inner monologue and literary leitmotifs, turning the trilogy into a masterful literary achievement.

The most popular of the neorealists is Anders Bodelsen (born 1937). His novels of 1968, *Hændeligt uheld* (*Hit and Run, Run, Run*, 1970) and *Tænk på et tal* (*Think of a Number*, 1969), cleverly combine the realistic novel with the thriller. *Frysepunktet* (1969; *Freezing Point*, 1971) approaches science fiction. In Bodelsen's writing—as in most of the realistic Danish authors—the close of the 1960's brought increased interest in the social mechanisms of the modern welfare state. *Bevisets*

stilling (1973; *Consider the Verdict*, 1976), based on a much-debated contemporary criminal case, describes a taxi driver falsely accused of murder, concluding in a violent accusation of judicial inhumanity. Things as they are, however, predominate in *De gode tider* (1977; the good times) and its sequel *År for år* (1979; year by year), which deal with the economic boom of the 1960's and the growing political awareness of the period.

Christian Kampmann (1939-1988) was also critical of middle-class mores, but his analyses have a wider psychological perspective. Thus, in *Nærved og næsten* (1969; near and nearly), social problems give way to existential ones in the picture of six married couples' attitudes toward love, isolation, and death. Kampmann's most significant achievement is his cycle, begun in 1973 with *Visse hensyn* (certain considerations), about the Copenhagen bourgeoisie after World War II, which reflects the Cold War of the 1950's, the prosperity that followed, and finally the economic crisis of the 1970's.

The dogmatic demand of the 1960's for social and political commitment in Denmark is also evident in reportorial writing, especially feminist novels. Documentary literature is represented in a number of studies of the work environment done by collectives, students, and the workers themselves; it has also influenced fictional writing, as in the novels of Jette Drewsen (born 1943) and Jytte Borberg (1917-2007). A more traditional neorealism, however, is demonstrated by Ole Hyltoft (born 1935) and Henrik Stangerup (1937-1998).

In the work of Ebbe Kløvedal Reich (1940-2005), Thorkild Hansen's historical documentary is combined with undogmatic political awareness. In 1977, Reich published his story of the Cimbrian march against Rome (c. 100 B.C.E.), *Fæ og frænde* (cattle and kinsman). Clearly referring to the European Economic Community, Reich has Rome represent everything evil: economic, political, and cultural imperialism.

Often the demand for a new society is expressed as a romantic, revolutionary dream. This dream is realized in *Smukke tabere* (1970), by Vagn Lundbye (born 1933); the title is a direct translation of Leonard Cohen's *Beautiful Losers* (1970). The narrator's diary records the feelings of a religious relationship with a partisan group on its way to blow up a nuclear reactor. In the novels *Tilbage til Anholt* (1978; back to Anholt) and *Hvalfisken*

(1980; the whale), Lundbye calls for a return to "the original condition—a life-style between light and darkness, cold and warmth, closeness and cosmos."

During World War II, almost all literary activity ceased in Finland. Finnish literature of the 1950's was self-critical, nationalism gave way to disillusionment, and, on the whole, authors shunned any participation in the debates on current political and social issues.

Paavo Haavikko (1931-2008), Finland's great modernistic poet, also wrote a number of plays and novels. Whereas Haavikko's plays are nearly absurdist, his prose treats social and political events pessimistically as the meaningless actions of insignificant individuals. Hence, the protagonist of *Yksityisiä asioita* (1960; private matters) experiences the political events of 1918 only as an occasion for profitable business deals. Likewise pessimistic is the novel *Tohtori Finckelman* (1952; Doctor Finckelman), by Jorma Korpela (1910-1964), which represents one of the earliest postwar breaks with traditional Finnish prose style.

The remaining prose of the 1950's is primarily distinguished by its factual style. War is generally seen as a personal, relativistic experience. Even when the narration is realistic, as in the popular war novel by Väinö Linna (1920-1992), *Tuntematon sotilas* (1954; *The Unknown Soldier*, 1957), such relativity is present. Linna's description of the destiny of a single platoon's actions at the front is free of nationalistic mythmaking and permeated with a redeeming sense of humor. Realism and humor are also foremost elements in the trilogy *Täällä pohjantähden alla* (1959-1962; here under the polar star), which tells of the civil war of 1918 from the perspective of the vanquished, confirming Linna's position as a great epic narrator in the tradition of Kivi and Sillanpää.

Whereas Linna represents a more traditional trend within modern Finnish prose, Veijo Meri (born 1928), more experimental, follows in the steps of Korpela. Meri's basic themes are also the war; he often contrasts war's irrationality with the soldiers' discipline in a way that exposes the absurdity of the military events themselves. This is demonstrated in *Manillaköysi* (1957; *The Manila Rope*, 1967). The hero, Joose, smuggles home a piece of rope on his leave, thus risking his life without understanding his motives. A deserter is the main character in *Sujut* (1961; quits), about the Russian military breakthrough in 1944, but Meri's soldiers lack the inner stability that makes Linna's soldiers act correctly.

Meri pursues objective reporting. The most typical representative of such a purely factual approach, however, is Antti Hyry (born 1931), whose work forms a Finnish parallel to the French *nouveau roman*. Thus, *Maailman laita* (1967; the edge of the world) simply describes a fishing trip in which a boat drifts away but is recovered the next day. Hyry's religious view of life is expressed in the novel *Kevättä ja syksyä* (1958; spring and fall) through the character Niilo, who experiences childhood as a paradise, a spontaneous realization of God and the world, which is lost in the materialistic world of adults.

Standing outside all literary groups is Paavo Rintala (1929-1999), whose novels blend all the trends of the 1950's in their treatment of religious and ethical issues. Rintala shares with Hyry the northern Finnish milieu and the view that urban life is spiritually alienating. In his trilogy *Mummoni ja Mannerheim* (1960-1962; Grandmother and Mannerheim), Hyry attempts to dismiss the myths about Finland's national heroes during the civil war and World War II. Even more controversial is *Sissiluutnatti* (1963; *The Long Distance Patrol*, 1967), an unvarnished picture of the horrors of war. During the 1960's, Rintala assembled a documentary on the siege of Leningrad, followed by other accounts of major twentieth century crises, including the first Nordic novel to deal exclusively with the Vietnam War, *Vietnamin kurjet* (1971; the cranes from Vietnam). This documentary trend, of which Rintala is the most talented Finnish representative, continues in *Nahkapeitturien linjalla* (1976; the tanner's line), which reevaluates the events at the Finnish-Russian front during World War II.

The wave of report and debate literature reached its crest around 1970, most convincingly represented by an accusatory report on the textile industry by Marja-Leena Mikkola (born 1939), *Raskas puuvilla* (1971; heavy cotton). Less radical than Mikkola, who is also one of the few Finnish contributors to Nordic feminist literature, is Samuli Paronen (1917-1974), whose novels depict social needs rendered in traditional prose. The foremost representative of this style is Hannu Salama (born 1936), whose novel *Juhannustanssit* (1964; the midsummer night dance) aroused strong public debate with its alleged blasphemy. Less controversial and characterized by a more objective approach is the first volume of a planned series about contemporary Finland, *Kosti Herhiläisen perunkirjoitus* (1976; Kosti Herhiläisen's inventory). With pessimism Salama portrays a man who searches his past for something with which to face a present that is threatened by decay and catastrophe.

In the 1970's, the provincial narrative returned in a rediscovery of long-forgotten cultural traditions. The novels of Eeva Kilpi (born 1928), such as *Häätanhu* (1973; summer dance), reflecting a Rousseau-inspired dream, depict the village as a place of security and redemption, whereas the city, with its impersonal efficiency, is strongly attacked—as, for example, in a novel by Eina Säisä (1935-1988), *Kukkivat roudan maat* (1971; the lands of flowering frost).

The major representative of modern Finnish and Swedish prose is Tito Colliander (1904-1989). The strong influence of Dostoevski is especially noticeable in *Förbarma dig* (1939; have mercy), a study of the psychology of suffering, guilt, and atonement. A longing for salvation recurs in *Bliv till* (1945; come into being) and likewise in a work by Göran Stenius (1909-2000), *Klockorna i Rom* (1955; *The Bells of Rome*, 1961), which relates the author's conversion to Catholicism. It is acknowledged as the best religious novel in Finland after World War II.

Political commitment, on the other hand, characterizes the novels of Christer Kihlman (born 1930), among them *Se upp salige!* (1960; pay heed, O blest!), which satirizes a small town and its self-centered Finno-Swedish bourgeoisie, and *Den blå modern* (1963; the blue mother), which follows two brothers through childhood, revealing what is hidden beneath their superficial respectability. A true masterpiece is *Dyre prins* (1975; *Sweet Prince*, 1983), both a humorous satire on the Finnish nouveau riche after the war and a penetrating Dostoevskian psychological study. The same intensity and commitment to his subjects characterizes Anders Cleve (1937-1985); however, in his novels such as *Vit eld* (1962; white fire), he employs a much more diffuse and occasionally fragmentary language to express the chaos from which the narrator tries to escape.

The two most significant Finno-Swedish prose writers of the 1970's were the married couple Märta and Henrik Tikkanen. Märta Tikkanen (born 1935) speaks for the oppressed, focusing on the situation of modern woman, as in *Män kan inte våltas* (1975; men cannot be raped). Henrik Tikkanen (1924-1984) achieved his literary breakthrough in 1975 when he published the first part of his confessions, *Brändövägen 8 Brändö. Tel. 35* (*A Winter's Day*, 1980), followed by *Bävervägen 11 Hertonäs* (1976) and *Mariegatan 26 Kronohagen* (1977)—the titles refer to three important addresses in his life. Rather than exposing the corruption of Tikkanen's environment and within his own family in particular, the three volumes primarily attack hypocrisy and taboos in the Finno-Swedish upper class in general.

After World War II, Icelandic writers became less insular. Numerous translations were published, especially of English and American writers, including Aldous Huxley, D. H. Lawrence, Ernest Hemingway, John Steinbeck, and Sinclair Lewis. Halldór Laxness's development was typical of the postwar period. After writing a dramatic account of Iceland's materialistic decadence, he turned to historical novels and increasingly occupied himself with questions of literary form. In spite of the political optimism of 1944, when the final dissolution of the union with Denmark was proclaimed, a pessimistic, almost nihilistic note was sounded among the younger writers—inspired by the Swedish modernistic poetry of the 1940's.

A return to preindustrial Icelandic tradition and history as a remedy for existential anguish is evident in poetry as well as in prose, dominated into the 1960's by an epic, realistic narration. Thus, the setting of the novel *A bökkum Bolafljots* (1940; on the banks of the Bola River), by Guðmundur Daníelsson (1910-1990), is his native southern lowlands, but the time is the past. Ólafur Jóhann Sigurðsson (1918-1988) is a more sophisticated stylist, employing a richly nuanced, lyric language. His most convincing novel, *Fjallið og draumurinn* (1944; the mountain and the dream), is set in the provinces and contains overtones of social criticism. After many years of near silence, Sigurðsson published the novel *Hreiðrið* (1972; the bird's nest), a bitter critique of modern welfare society.

Sigurðsson's distaste for the contemporary scene is also characteristic of the work of Indriði Þorsteinsson

(1926-2000), whose books focus on those who have moved to the city from the country, the only source of permanent value, and who no longer belong anywhere. This motif recurs in the novels *Land og synir* (1963; land and sons) and *Norðan við strið* (1971; north of the war), dealing with the Allied occupation of Iceland during World War II and its negative consequences for the old peasant society.

The most significant stylistic renewal of Icelandic prose occurred in the work of Thor Vilhjálmsson (born 1925), who was influenced by Kafka and—following a stay in postwar Paris—by existentialism. In Vilhjálmsson's first novel, *Fljótt, fljótt sagð i fuglinn* (1968; fast, fast said the bird), which deals with death and erotic love, the dimensions of personality, time, and space are absent. In *Fuglaskottís* (1975; bird dance), the action unfolds during a twenty-four-hour stay in Rome and depicts two Icelanders' search for two missing girls, which at the same time is a search for their own identity in an absurd world. A similar search is the main theme of *Mánasigð* (1976; crescent moon), executed with such artistic sophistication that Vilhjálmsson stands out as his generation's most distinguished prose writer.

In the late 1960's, there was a considerable upsurge of leftist literature, turning in particular against foreign political and economic influences. Thus, for example, *Astir samlyndra hjóna* (1967; the love of a harmoniously married couple), by Guðbergur Bergsson (born 1932), depicts the threatening conformity of modern Iceland and attacks the United States and its relation to Icelanders. Reality merges with absurdity and takes on mythic dimensions in the two-volume novel *Það sefur í djúpinu* (1973; it sleeps in the depths) and its sequel *Það rís úr djúpinu* (1976; it rises from the depths). In surpassing reality to disclose the extreme, grotesque, and negative in everyday life, Bergsson became the leading experimenter in Icelandic prose. The diversity of his work is an excellent example of the universal perspective that characterizes the principal writers of the five Nordic countries.

THE MODERN WELFARE STATE

The 1980's brought a reevaluation of Scandinavia's political and literary position. The radical politicizing of large segments of the population, increasing interdependence on the global market, financial burden of government services, and ever-growing immigrant populations all served to fragment what had been a homogeneous society. In Sweden, government support of literature aimed to preserve a diversity of national literatures while taking a negligible role in the quality of literature. Political novels remained popular, including those by Per Wästberg, who wrote extensively about Swedish colonialism in Africa. Stockholm was the setting for *Vindens låga* (1993; the flame of the wind), in which he explored dark love relationships. Documentary novelist Per Olov Enquist turned to psychological themes in *Nedstortad ängel* (1985; *Downfall: A Love Story*, 1986), an intense tale of altruistic love, and *Kapten Nemos bibliotek* (1991; *Captain Nemo's Library*, 1992), which explores how the power of imagination can shape reality. Per Gunnar Evander examined the psychological theory that life achieves meaning only through relationships in such novels as *Mörkrets leende* (1987; smile of darkness).

Sven Delblanc's family saga explored the recent past in *Samuels bok* (1981; Samuel's book), *Samuels döttrar* (1982; Samuel's daughter), *Kanaans land* (1984; the land of Canaan), and *Maria ensam* (1985; Maria alone). Delblanc's recurring theme of the overbearing father is personalized in his terrifying autobiographical novels *Livets ax* (1991; gleanings from life) and *Agnar* (1992; chaff). Kerstin Ekman (born 1933) brought a balancing feminist perspective to the historical novel in *Rövarna i Skuleskogen* (1988; *The Forest of Hours*, 1998). In the acclaimed *Händelser vid vatten* (1993; *Blackwater*, 1995), Ekman combined aspects of the detective story with a rich portrayal of northern Sweden. Göran Tunström (born 1937) placed his novels in the province of Värmland, including *Juloratoriet* (1983; *The Christmas Oratorio*, 1995), which resembles a musical composition, and *Tjuven* (1986; the thief), which explores betrayal and the human cost of artistic endeavor.

The biting social satire of Per Christian Jersild used science and technology to manipulate individuals in *En levande själ* (1980; *A Living Soul*, 1988) and speculated on the nature of being human in *Efter floden* (1982; *After the Flood*, 1986). He returned to bureaucratic satire with *En lysande marknad* (1992; a wide-open market). The writings of Stig Claesson (born 1928) concern people whom the welfare state has forgotten in *Min vän Charlie*

(1973; my friend, Charlie) and *Utsikt från ett staffli* (1983; view from an easel). The most important of the social satirists is Lars Gustafsson, whose reputation was well established by the 1980's. His masterpiece of international intrigue *Bernard Foys tredje rockad* (1986; *Bernard Foy's third castling*, 1988) demonstrates that nothing is as it seems. Gustafsson examined personal isolation in the workers' novel *En kakelsättares eftermiddag* (1991; *A Tiler's Afternoon*, 1993) and a Texan bankruptcy judge in *Historien med hunden* (1993; *The Tale of a Dog: From the Diaries and Letters of a Texan Bankruptcy Judge*, 1998).

Bunny Ragnerstam (born 1944) wrote about the Swedish labor movement in *Uppkomlingen* (1980; the upstart) and *Ett prima liv* (1983; a first-rate life), known collectively as *En svensk tagedi* (a Swedish tragedy). Reidar Jönsson (born 1944) achieved international recognition when his autobiographical novel *Mitt liv som hund* (1983; *My Life as a Dog*, 1989) was made into an award-winning film in 1987.

Literary feminism gained prominence through the novels of such writers as Inger Alfvén (born 1940), who wrote about female discontent. In *Ur kackerlackors levnad* (1984; from the lives of cockroaches) and *Lyckans galosch* (1986; lucky dog) she examines relationships involving more than two people, and in *Judiths teater* (1989; Judith's theater) she explores the relationship between a mother and a daughter who love the same man. The poet Sun Axelsson (born 1935) interprets her own life from a feminist perspective in the trilogy *Drommen om ett liv* (1978; *A Dreamed Life*, 1983), *Honungsvargar* (1984; honey wolves), and *Nattens årstid* (1989; night's season). The work of Heidi von Born (born 1936) concerns material deprivation in *Månens vita blod* (1988; white blood of the moon) and the devastating effect of childhood neglect in *Tiden år en tjuv* (1989; time is a thief).

One of the most internationally famous Swedish writers of the twenty-first century is detective writer Henning Mankell (born 1948), author of several books featuring Inspector Kurt Wallander of the Ystad police department. Wallender is a middle-aged man who struggles with depression, his ability to connect to others, and the line between right and wrong. From 1991 to 1999, Mankell published a new volume in the series each year,

and all, from *Mördare utan ansikte* (1991; *Faceless Killers*, 1996) through *Pyramiden* (1999; *The Pyramid, and Four Other Kurt Wallander Mysteries*, 2008), sold well throughout Europe and North America. In addition, Mankell has published more than a dozen other works of fiction, including *Djup* (2004; *Depths*, 2006), about a naval depth sounder who meets a mysterious woman on an isolated island.

As the Cold War drew to a close and the economic problems facing the modern welfare state developed, Norwegian literature increasingly reflected an ironic postmodernism that examined the contradictory paradoxes of existence. Two writers emerged during the 1980's as prototypic Norwegian postmodernists: Kjartan Fløgstad (born 1944) and Jan Kjærstad (born 1953), both of whom wrote in Nynorsk (new Norwegian). Fløgstad began the new decade with *Fyr og flamme* (1980; fire and flame), an amalgam of different styles that both tells a story and comments upon its themes. In *U3* (1983), Fløgstad fabricates devices as part of the narrative in order to interpret information that otherwise would not be available to his characters. Using the "retrospectroscope," the protagonist, Alf Hellot, interprets how the downing of the American U2 spy plane affects Norwegian defense policy. Fløgstad's controversial *Det 7. klima: Salim Mahmood i Media Thule* (1986; the seventh climate) is a social commentary on the effect of thousands of immigrants on Norwegian culture and intellectual life. *Det 7. klima* was written in a perplexing style that purposefully obscured its meaning and caused such extensive reader frustration that Fløgstad published a debate about the novel titled *Tyrannosaurus text* (1988).

Kjærstad achieved prominence as editor of the literary journal *Vinduet* (the window). He conducts a search for love among the remnants of a Norwegian society grounded on writing in *Det store eventyret* (1987; the great adventure). Taken with *Det 7. klima*, Fløgstad and Kjærstad defend a traditional Norwegian culture being replaced by the transitory images of the popular media.

Modern feminism is advocated in the novels of Cecilie Løveid (born 1951) and Karin Moe (born 1945), both of whom utilize language in an expressionistic manner. Løveid combines poetry and prose to examine nurturing in *Sug* (1979; *Sea Swell*, 1986), while Moe mirthfully plays on the fact that the title can mean either "mother-daughter" or "murder again," depending upon how the word is divided in *Mordatter* (1985). Popular poet-novelist Eva Jensen (born 1955) speculates that life can best be interpreted through language in *Teori nok for eit kort liv: Roman-roman* (1987; theory enough for a short life: novel-novel).

Although generally considered to be of minimal quality, postmodernist thinking in Danish literature challenged social humanism during the 1980's, examining the relationship between the individual's life and society. Martha Christensen (1926-1995) can be singled out as the most popular of these writers, particularly for *Dansen med Regitze* (1987; dancing with Regitze), with its message of petty-bourgeois humanness. Dagny Joensen (born 1944) emerged as the preeminent feminist writer by depicting the destructive nature of marriage for three women, *Gerandislangnur* (1981; everyday fates).

Just as Danish literature seemed to be sinking into a quagmire of mediocrity, Peter Høeg (born 1957) published his first novel, *Forestilling om det tyvende århundrede* (1988; *The History of Danish Dreams*, 1995), a saga covering 450 years of history interpreted through the eyes of everyday people. Høeg's second novel, *Frøken Smillas fornemmelse for sne* (1992; *Smilla's Sense of Snow*, 1993), tells a tale of international intrigue. The book's protagonist is a remarkable half-Dane, half-Greenland Inuit glaciologist whose innate knowledge of snow allows her to recognize that a child's death was not accidental, but murder. The novel has been translated into more than a dozen languages, and it established Høeg as the first internationally renowned Danish writer after Isak Dinesen. A motion picture adaptation of the novel was released in 1997. Høeg's *Da måske egnede* (1993; *Borderliners*, 1994) is the harrowing tale of three orphaned youths at the center of a social experiment that shows the real consequences of a so-called enlightened social policy. *Kvinden og aben* (1996; *The Woman and the Ape*, 1996), an experiment in evolutionary theory, continues Høeg's investigation of Danish social issues in a manner that appeals to an international audience. His thriller *Den stille pige* (2006; *The Quiet Girl,* 2007) draws on elements of science, Magical Realism, and the music of Bach. Høeg has single-handedly raised standards for Danish and Scandi-

navian literature with his artistic freshness, love of language, depth of learning, characterization, and intensity of storytelling.

In the twenty-first century, Morten Ramsland (born 1971) has emerged as one of the most popular of the Danish novelists. His first novel, *Akaciedrømme* (1998), is rather experimental in its prose style, and like many first novels it was praised when it appeared more for its promise than for its success. Ramsland's family saga *Hundehoved* (2005; *Doghead,* 2008), his second novel, won four important awards in Denmark and became a best seller in Europe; it has been translated into more than a dozen languages. This work comprises a series of vignettes about three generations of the dysfunctional Eriksson family, from a war profiteer grandfather to a young boy with comically large ears. Ramsland's deft handling of both coarse comedy and pathos has led his American publishers to dub him a "Danish John Irving."

Sven H. Rossel; Gerald S. Argetsinger
Updated by Cynthia A. Bily

BIBLIOGRAPHY

Bredsdorff, Elias, Brita Mortensen, and Ronald Popperwell. *An Introduction to Scandinavian Literature from the Earliest Time to Our Day*. Cambridge, Mass.: Harvard University Press, 1951. Excellent single-volume history begins with Old Norse and extends through the early postwar period.

Horn, Frederik Winkel, Rasmus Björn Anderson, and Thorvald Solberg. *History of the Literature of the Scandinavian North from the Most Ancient Times to the Present*. Reprint. Honolulu, Hawaii: University Press of the Pacific, 2002. Valuable study of Scandinavian literature. One of few books on the topic available in English. Includes a bibliography.

Naess, Harold S., ed. *A History of Norwegian Literature*. Lincoln: University of Nebraska Press, 1993. Second volume of a Scandinavian literature series begins with Viking literature, extends through the 1980's, and includes chapters on women's and children's literature.

Neijmann, Daisy L., ed. *A History of Icelandic Literature*. Lincoln: University of Nebraska Press, in cooperation with the American-Scandinavian Foundation, 2006. Fills a gap in the study of contemporary Icelandic literature and, especially, scholarship on that literature in English.

Nestingen, Andrew K. *Crime and Fantasy in Scandinavia: Fiction, Film, and Social Change*. Seattle: University of Washington Press, 2008. Examines both Scandinavian popular culture and genre fiction. Part of the New Directions in Scandinavian Studies series.

Rossel, Sven H. *A History of Scandinavian Literature, 1870-1980*. Minneapolis: University of Minnesota Press, 1982. Excellent work that provides thorough coverage of modern Scandinavian literature.

_____, ed. *A History of Danish Literature*. Lincoln: University of Nebraska Press, 1992. First volume of a Scandinavian literature series provides analysis of Danish writings in greater depth than is available in single-volume histories. Leading scholars examine topics extending from Runic literature through the early 1990's. Separate chapters discuss Faroese and women's and children's literature.

Schoolfield, George C. *A History of Finland's Literature*. Lincoln: University of Nebraska Press, 1998. Fourth volume of a Scandinavian literature series begins with Finnish literature of the sixteenth century and extends through the mid-1990's.

Warme, Lars G., ed. *A History of Swedish Literature*. Lincoln: University of Nebraska Press, 1996. Third volume of a Scandinavian literature series covers Swedish literature from the Middle Ages through the early 1990's.

Zuck, Virpi, Niels Ingwersen, and Harald S. Naess, eds. *Dictionary of Scandinavian Literature*. Santa Barbara, Calif.: Greenwood Press, 1990. One of the most comprehensive reference works on Scandinavian literature available in English, covering almost four hundred authors as well as themes, movements, and genres. Includes a thorough bibliography.

SOUTH ASIAN LONG FICTION

The Indian subcontinent, or what geographers call South Asia, includes India, Pakistan, Bangladesh, Sri Lanka, Nepal, and Bhutan. Though world leaders can change borders and create new political entities, they cannot persuade men and women of letters to observe such artificial boundaries. Thus, even though she is not an Indian in the narrow sense of the word but "technically Pakistani," a writer such as Bapsi Sidhwa is included in *Mirrorwork: Fifty Years of Indian Writing, 1947-1997* (1997). As coeditor Salman Rushdie explains, "This anthology has no need of Partitions"; indeed, he recognizes Sidhwa's *Ice-Candy-Man* (1988), published in the United States as *Cracking India* (1991), as a valuable re-creation of "the horror of the division of the subcontinent."

Even if political divisions are disregarded, however, there are other issues confronting any student of South Asian long fiction. One is how to deal with the many worthwhile novels and short stories written in the vernacular. Since there are fourteen major languages in the state of India alone, it is obvious that if these works are to receive the general recognition they deserve, they must be translated into English. Though there are objections to the use of a colonial language for such purposes, they are outweighed by practical considerations and even broad social benefits. In their introduction to *The Penguin New Writing in India* (1995), editors Aditya Behl and David Nicholls express their belief that such translations will enable people long separated by language to come to a better understanding of other cultures, thus enabling them to interact more successfully in what has always been a multicultural and multilingual society.

The fact that so many South Asians are choosing English as the language in which they express themselves has also dismayed some critics. However, these writers evidently feel more comfortable in English than in the vernacular, and they are well aware that works written in English will be more likely to reach readers throughout the world. They may also point out literary precedents early in the nineteenth century.

ENGLISH IN INDIA

Two years before Thomas Babington Macaulay introduced his famous "Minute" on English education in India (1835), Raja Rammohan Ray, one of several Indian writers who were using the English language successfully even before compulsory English education was officially introduced to India, died in Bristol. It was Macaulay who insisted that all funds appropriated for education in India be set aside for English education alone. In insisting on English education in India, Macaulay was recognizing that Indians could use English advantageously. In fact, he praised the linguistic competence of the people he knew, describing the town natives as "quite competent to discuss political or scientific questions with fluency and precision in the English language." Macaulay also recognized that the use of English opened up a vast information source and audience to the Indians. Thus, an empire was built not only for the British but also for modern Indian writers, providing them with both a form and an audience.

Before Macaulay, Christian missionaries had been teaching English in schools and colleges around the country. Indians, for their part, were eager to obtain a Western education and link people in their nation with the changing world. By the early part of the nineteenth century, Indian literary activity in English had already begun. Henry Louis Vivian Derozio (1807-1831), Kasiprasad Ghose (1809-1873), Michael Madhusudhan Dutt (1824-1873), and Bankim Chandra Chatterjee (1838-1894) were some of the early Indians to use English for their creative and social purposes. By the latter half of the nineteenth century, educated Indians were using English for all purposes, from mundane government work to poetry.

Today, English has become a naturalized member of the citizenry of Indian languages. Along with Hindi, it is used throughout India, unlike other Indian languages. Jawaharlal Nehru, in dealing with the question of a national language for India, noted that English, like Sanskrit and Persian before it, was the language of invaders but had become totally assimilated into Indian life.

The introduction of English to India brought with it an introduction to English literature. The reading public in India soon discovered the novel form and took it over. While India has a long, tradition of fiction in the form of the oral tale, the short morality story, and the *Pañcatantra* (between 100 B.C.E. and 500 C.E.; *The Morall Philosophie of Doni*, 1570; the Indian equivalent of *Aesop's Fables*), it was to the current British forms that nineteenth century Indian writers turned. Nick Wilkinson, writing about the modern Indian novel, notes that the novel was imported from England and patterned after the popular works of Sir Walter Scott and Charles Dickens. The genre as it has developed in India is a product of the two cultures.

Two major habits that were thus inculcated in Indian authors were the forcing of Indian subject matter into European forms and the imitation of the trendiest of these European forms. In addition, the audience was seen as a European audience hungry for an Asian element in their lives. The exoticism of Indian myth and culture was soon to be exploited even further. As they met with critical acclaim abroad, Indian writers seemed to be writing for the Western critics, who were amazed at and patronizing of their achievements, expressing wonder at the ability of Indian writers to write in English, a second language, and at their ability to use the European form of the novel. At the same time, Indian writers themselves manifested an ambiguity toward their Indian roots. This ambiguity was primarily manifested in the overwhelming choice of English as the medium for their creativity. Questions of nationalism or alienation became inextricably linked with both the development of Indian literature and its criticism. Even the "father of the Indian novel," Rabindranath Tagore (1861-1941), felt compelled to translate his work into English and then even to compose in English. This turn to English drew from William Butler Yeats the following disclaimer. In a letter to William Rothenstein in 1935, Yeats lamented

Damn Tagore, we got three good books and because he thought it more important to see and know English than to be a great poet he brought off sentimental rubbish. No Indian knows English. Nobody can write music and style in a language which is not their own.

This dictum became a significant issue both in the formulation of Indian literature and in its criticism. To this day, critics wrangle over whether English or one of the many Indian vernaculars is an appropriate medium for the development of a literature in India's multilingual, multicultural setting. This is not to imply, however, that any literary development in Indian fiction can be attributed entirely to the influence of English.

THE INDIAN TRADITION

Ancient Indian manuscripts written on *bhurjapatra*, or palm leaves, are for the most part lost, extant only in Chinese and Tibetan translations that testify to their previous existence. Excluding well-known works—such as the epic poetry of the Rāmāyana (c. 350 B.C.E.), Mahābhārata (c. fifth century B.C.E.), and Bhagavad Gita (c. fifth century B.C.E.) and the Sanskrit drama of Kalidasa and the critical work on drama *Nātya-śāstra* (c. 100 C.E.)—a whole body of short works of fiction exists. Their origins can be dated to the Jātakas (birth stories), the Buddhist tales that describe the cultural encounter between the indigenous Dravidians and the Aryans. In the popular Sanskrit literature, drama reigned supreme.

The tales from the epics were dramatized on festival days. This was so until the Muslim invasion of the twelfth century C.E., and under the Moguls, Persian literature was dominant. An Indian critical tradition, however, remained significant in the shaping of the literary tradition. Drawing upon the critical theory in the *Nātya-śāstra* of the concepts of *rasa* (meaning) and *dhwani* (undertones or poetic language), Indian literature has always been preoccupied with poetic expression to the detriment of the development of prose and prose fiction. Tracing the growth of Indian literature from the Middle Ages to the Renaissance, Nehru noted in his *Discovery of India* (1946) that popular literatures in Hindi, Gujarati, Marathi, Urdu, Tamil, and Telugu were developing an oral tradition. With the use of the printing press, some of these orally transmitted epics and collections were documented. Nehru notes, however, that these works were in the form of memorizable songs and collections of poems. Hence, it was not until the early Christian missionaries brought English and English education to India that a canon of fiction developed.

THE INDIAN NOVEL

By the 1920's, English education in India was all-pervasive, and by the end of the nineteenth century, English literature held sway over the Indian imagination. Nevertheless, the Indians trained under Rammohan Ray's system of English education in India were not simply to remain Baboos and clerks in British government offices. Their newly acquired language found expression in creativity in a newly learned form. The ancient traditions of the oral epic tales came together with Scott's serialized, romantic *Waverley: Or, 'Tis Sixty Years Since* (1814) to found the annals of a new *Rama Katha* (epic of Rama). The traditional story of the adventures of the Hindu deity Rama, told night after night by the village elder at the local temple, was transformed, in the nineteenth century Indian literary tradition, into nationalist Indian novels written sometimes in English and sometimes in the vernacular, largely about the oppression of the poor by the middle class and the British. These novels sometimes described situations related to tyrannical customs, sati, arranged marriages, and child marriages; sometimes, however, as in the work of Tagore, they merely evoked sentimentality for Indian mysticism.

Because Bengal was the first geographic region to come in contact with the British, the first Indian novel was written in Bengali—a distinction customarily granted to Bhudeva Chandra Mukherjee's *Anguriya Binimoy* (1857). Chatterjee's *Raj Mohan's Wife* was serialized in 1864 in the fashion of Scott's novels. Lal Behari Day's *Govinda Samantha* (1874) is a documentary of peasant life in Bengal. The zamindar professed interest in the lives of the peasants; Day described his novel as a "plain and unvarnished tale of a plain peasant living in the plain country of Bengal . . . told in a plain manner." The story of the peasant Govinda and his exploits with a money-lender, *Govinda Samantha* is the first in a long tradition, culminating in Munshi Prem Chand's social-realist *Godān* (1936; *Gift of a Cow*, 1968), to describe the oppression of peasants by feudal lords. Govinda and his relative Kalamanik attempt to pay off a debt to the zamindar, who responds by levying a new tax against them and falsely charging them with having borrowed money, in order to keep them indebted to him. When they refuse to pay him, their homes are burned. In the midst of this story of oppression, Day describes the fam-

ine of 1873, thus depicting the poverty and the uncertainty that characterize Indian agriculture to this day.

In fin de siècle Indian fiction, a need to explore the Indian in relation to the Westerner, including an attempt to educate the West about Indian customs and mores, shaped the themes. Sochee Chunder Dutt's *The Young Zemindar* (1885) presents the cross-cultural encounter, the weighing of Eastern and Western traditions, and the question of whether East and West can in fact meet as a major theme in the development of any Anglo-Indian or Indo-Anglian literary tradition. Indian traditions are outlined, and the effect of the British on these traditions is analyzed. In the novel, a sannyasi leads the main character, Monohur, to places of religious importance and describes the customs of those places. Legends connected with the major subcontinental rivers—the Ganges, the Indus, and the Brahmaputra—are retold, as are the stories of the Mahābhārata and the Rāmāyana. Even the Muslim festival of the martyrdom of Mohammed, Moharrum, is pictured. All of this is an effort to show that the British government was attempting to interfere with Indian customs.

The vernacular novel continued to be developed under the shadow of Scott, but the themes tended to be nationalist, emphasizing the importance of traditional Indianness or describing the oppression of the people by feudal lords and the British government. In Hindi, Kishorilal Goswami's *Labangalata* (1891) and Devki Nandan Khatri's *Chandrakāntā* (1892) established themes that lasted into the 1920's and were picked up by the Progressive Writers' Union; such themes were definitely nationalist and, if the term may be used, socialist. Hari Narayan Apte's first novel in Marathi, *Maisorcha Wagh* (1890), is a translation of Meadows Taylor's *Tippoo Sultan* (1840) and refers to him as the Lion of Mysore. *Maisorcha Wagh* brought the celebration of Tippoo Sultan, the great nationalist Indian guerrilla fighter, to the people of his region. In Malayalam, Raman Pillai wrote *Martanda Varma* (1891). At the same time, the retelling and documenting of Indian sacred tales continued: Dwijendranath Neogi published *Sacred Tales of India* (1916), *True Tales of Indian Life* (1917), and *Anecdotes of Indian Life* (1920).

In all of this diverse activity in the writing of fiction, Rabindranath Tagore stands out. For his translations of lyrics composed in Bengali, entitled *Gitānjali* (1910; *Gitanjali (Song Offerings)*, 1912), Tagore was awarded the Nobel Prize in Literature in 1913. With the encouragement of his English publisher, Tagore translated several collections of his own poetry and fiction. His best-known work of fiction is *Gora* (1910), the English translation of which was published in 1924. Tagore's next novel, *Ghare bāire* (1916; *Home and the World*, 1919), reflects the changing politics of Bengali society. Both novels again have nationalist themes. Gora, meaning "white," is a foundling reared as an orthodox Hindu who learns that his mother was Irish. This brings to the forefront questions of caste and religion, leading to an eventual preference for Indianness. Nationalism returns even more aggressively in *Home and the World*. The concept of *Swadeshi*, or Indian, which was to become a key element of the Gandhian movement, is a central concept in this novel about revolutionary Bengal in 1905. Even the conservative Indian wife is drawn by the call of the outside world. Sandip, another character in the novel, would like to move toward Western modernization. Hence the novel portrays the traditional clash between the Western and the Indian.

What constituted the modern, the new, the Western? Was it sociological or technological advancement into the modern era? Was it a recognition of one's roots as reflected through the prism of Westernization? Was it a breaking from the acquiescence that kept Indians under oppressive rulers, whether Muslim or British? These are the questions that were forced to the forefront during the first four decades of the twentieth century, and, whether in English or in one of the vernaculars, these were the questions that were articulated in Indian fiction. With the documentation of a social milieu and with the changing feelings of the moment, the literature of the Indian people seemed to turn toward the novel of social realism.

THE DEVELOPMENT OF THE INDO-ENGLISH NOVEL

The tradition of the Indo-English novel took deep root during the early twentieth century. K. S. Venkatramani (1892-1952), whose long poem *On the Sand Dunes* (1923) was highly derivative of Tagore's *Gitanjali (Song Offerings)*, was more original as a novelist. His *Murugan, the Tiller* (1927) and *Kandan, the Patriot* (1932) were harbingers of the realism that was to mark Indian literature during what in Indian history is called the Gandhian era (1920-1947). World War I had replaced fin de siècle Romanticism and Georgian effusions with a new idiom and new role models that the Indian writers were soon to imitate. The war also brought to India an awareness of socioeconomic problems and of the British exploitation of India's human and economic resources, a feeling that was to be enhanced later in World War II and embodied in Mahatma Gandhi's call for noncooperation with the Stafford proposal of cooperation with the Allies and postponement of the Quit India movement. The impact of Marxism and an accompanying attraction to socialism are also apparent in the Indian novel of this period.

Venkatramani's two novels are notable chiefly as works marking the general turn away from poetry toward the novel. With the appearance of Mulk Raj Anand (1905-2004), Indian writing gained its first major fiction writer; his first novel, *Untouchable* (1935), established social realism as a rich vein for the Indian novel. British-educated and a member of the intellectual Bloomsbury group in the early 1920's, Anand began his writing career with a Joycean stream-of-consciousness "tract" about an untouchable. It was not until his conversion to Gandhism that he was able to move past his interest in stylistic imitation to a primary interest in subject matter. *Untouchable* became the first of a trilogy of novels. Various options to the tyrannical caste system are discussed as the plot develops around the incidents of maltreatment of the main character, Bakha, and his sister. As E. M. Forster pointed out in his foreword to the book, it is another story of the difference between tradition and modernity, the Mahatma and the machine, in Indian fiction. The same theme runs through the other two novels of the trilogy, *Coolie* (1936) and *Two Leaves and a Bud* (1937): The poor remain poor, exploited, and Indian.

In "Why I Write?" (in *Indo English Literature*, 1977), Anand describes his first attempt at "Tagorean singsong rubbish." Anand got the same reaction from his Bloomsbury friends when he read them his confessional narrative-turned-novel about Bakha, the untouchable.

I had borrowed the technique of word coinage from James Joyce's *Ulysses* [1922] and made the narrative rather literary, and that the novel was a prose form not an epic poem like [John] Milton's *Paradise Lost*. Only one thing they liked about my fictional narrative: that it faced the poverty, the dirt and squalor of the "lower depths" even more than Gorky had done. And I was confirmed in my hunch that, unlike Virginia Woolf, the novelist must confront the total reality, including its sordidness, if one was to survive in the world of tragic contrasts between the "exalted and noble" vision of the blind bard Milton and the eyes dimmed with tears of the many mute Miltons.

Realism had become Anand's hallmark, and he steadfastly espoused it. In *The Sword and the Sickle* (1942) he portrayed the horrors resulting from the independence movement and the subsequent partition. In a succession of works—*The Village* (1939), *Across the Black Waters* (1940), *The Barber's Trade Union, and Other Stories* (1944), *The Big Heart* (1945), *Seven Summers* (1951), *The Old Woman and the Cow* (1963), *The Road* (1962), and *Morning Face* (1968)—he remained steadfast in his depiction of the wronged poor.

In espousing realism, Anand had in fact taken up the cause of the 1920's British intellectuals; to that extent he was imitative. He made no apologies for this formative influence on his writing and was singularly forthright in his admissions. In "The Story of My Experiment with a White Lie" (in *Critical Essays on Indian Writing in English*, 1972), he acknowledged all the intellectual influences on him.

I had become conscious, after the suppression of the general strike of the South Wales miners by [Winston] Churchill, of the kind of defiance which, under democratic conditions, the better off untouchables of Europe could indulge in. . . . I am not sure whether the *Confessions* of [Jean-Jacques] Rousseau, which I had just then read, or some of the books of the Russian writers like [Nikolai] Gogol, [Leo] Tolstoy and [Maxim] Gorky . . . were not then forcing me to acknowledge what most Indian writers of the modern period, like Bankim Chandra Chatterjee, Ratanath Sarshar and Rabindranath Tagore, had not accepted in their novels that even the so-called lowest dregs of humanity, living in utmost poverty, squalor and degradation, could become the heroes of fiction.

Pursuing the cause of realism and Indianization, Anand moved beyond word coinage by incorporating in his fiction English as spoken in the Indian streets, generously sprinkled with Indian words.

"INDIANIZING" ENGLISH

At the same time, mindful of the nationalism at home and of the general call to abandon English from their daily lives, most Indian writers, whose only medium of expression in some cases may have been English, responded with efforts to "Indianize" the English language. In 1938, Raja Rao's preface to *Kanthapura* expressed the problem of conveying through English the speech and thought patterns of a people whose language was not English. In *Kanthapura*, an oral tale of the coming of Gandhism told by an old crone to her village, Rao (1908-2006) attempted to capture the rhythms of Indian speech in English. Told in the lyric, lilting voice of the village crone, *Kanthapura* gave the English language a new meter and a new rhythm, so skillfully developed that it seems to have been a unique achievement both for the writer and for other writers. Rao's other novels, including *The Serpent and the Rope* (1960), *The Cat and Shakespeare: A Tale of India* (1965), and *The Chessmaster and His Moves* (1988), resort to conventional English, varied only for dialogue.

All About H. Hatterr (1948), by G. V. Desani (1909-2000), a deliberate attempt to capture Indian English, is perhaps more ambitious and less successful than *Kanthapura*; it is almost impossible for most readers to comprehend. In part, the language is meant to fit the character of H. Hatterr, who is of mixed blood and mixed cultural background. Yet, as Anthony Burgess notes in his introduction to the 1970 Bodley Head edition, "it is the language that makes the book a sort of creative chaos that grumbles at the restraining banks." Burgess compares Desani's language with that of Joyce; indeed, in the language and the rambling stream-of-consciousness technique of the novel, the influence of Joyce is evident and ultimately fails to transcend stylistic imitation. It is no puzzle that the book went underground and became a "coterie pleasure," as Burgess observes. The language itself is an obstacle for readers both in India and abroad.

While other Indian writers in English were focusing on imitations or language experimentation, R. K.

Narayan (1906-2001) was creating a style of his own. Various labels have been used to describe him—the Indian Jane Austen or the Indian Anton Chekhov—but Narayan is in a class all his own, combining the skills of those two literary giants and at the same time creating his own fictional world. In a career of more than fifty years, he won for his imaginary South Indian town of Malgudi a permanent place on the literary map, along with William Faulkner's Yoknapatawpha County. From *Swami and Friends* (1935) to *The World of Nagaraj* (1990), readers around the world have lived with the characters from Malgudi, felt with them, and seen the history of India evolve from the coming of Gandhism (*Waiting for the Mahatma*, 1955) to the coming of "American ways" (*The Sweet-Vendor*, 1967; also known as *The Vendor of Sweets*). Narayan's best-known work, *The Guide* (1958), was made into both a film and an unsuccessful Broadway production—both versions disliked by Narayan himself. Narayan focuses in a Malrauxian manner on the disparity between humanity's hope and humanity's fate, yet he does not spend time musing on large philosophical questions. There is in his work no Indian religiosity, nor is there any attempt to describe exotic India for the Westerners; there is simply the presentation of situations and moments of character revelation and awareness.

Narayan's language is straightforward, traditional English. English, for him, was a tool for the person who can use it. Contrary to other Indian writers, Narayan believed that English is a very adaptable language. In his descriptions of South Indian life, Narayan makes a deliberate effort to incorporate the Indianized English heard in the Indian streets and households. It is because of the Indian English that his descriptions and vignettes come through with an effectiveness that would make any effort to convey such an essence through language variations superfluous, for they are simply descriptions of life, of universal moments.

Thus, Narayan's portrayal realistically captures a distinct variety of English as spoken by a sizable body of Indians. His style includes all the features formed in English through a process of hybridization—collocations of English words with Indian words (for example, "marriage pandal" or "lathi charge") or compounding of words ("high caste" or "low caste") or expressions of Indian English speech ("your good self"). Another exam-

ple comes from *The Dark Room* (1938): "If the cook can't cook properly, do the work yourself. What have you to do better than that?" The last phrase is a nativized idiom. So is this construction: "Ramani would keep calling the servant Ranga in order to tell him what he was and where he ought to be for not polishing the boots properly." In using Indian English straightforwardly, Narayan is the Indian writer writing in English who has most successfully avoided the self-consciousness implicit in the situation of being an Indian writer writing in English. In his career he successfully resisted attempts to shape his writing according to current literary trends.

Some Indian critics bemoan the fact that Narayan was guided primarily by his desire to be an entertaining storyteller. Such criticism reveals some of the prejudices that have been inherent in the Indian critical response to a literature written in English: The literature cannot be any good if it does not imitate what is produced abroad; it cannot be any good if it is written in English by someone who has not been abroad (implicit in this attitude is the judgment that Indians cannot use English effectively without Western guidance); writers cannot produce great literature if they are not concerned with the "profound" issues, which can range from Indianizing English to expressing Indian philosophical problems to dealing with the current nationalistic issues; and writers are suspect if they have received acclaim abroad. In such a response to Narayan, one can see recapitulated the conflicts that have beset Indian literature in English since its birth. Against these odds, those writers who have had the courage to pursue their own course have endured, while those who have shaped their writing to suit either Western or Indian ideals have failed.

DUAL PERSPECTIVES

The same prejudices that motivated the attacks on Narayan and other writers of his generation are evident in the critical response to later writers. Typical is the case of Kamala Markandaya (1924-2004), who wrote with a solid command of the English language. Could this be a sign of alienation? Markandaya's situation was particularly disconcerting to the critics. Married to an Englishman, she wrote about India from abroad, with a perspective identified as Western. Her fiction often depicts the difference between the Eastern and Western views of life, as in *Nectar in a Sieve* (1954), *Some Inner Fury* (1955), *A Handful of Rice* (1966), *The Coffer Dams* (1969), *Two Virgins* (1973), and *Pleasure City* (1982; published in the United States as *Shalimar*, 1983), which incorporate descriptions of India through Western eyes while they remain essentially accurate portrayals of urban and rural poverty. The plight of Rukhmani, the peasant woman in *Nectar in a Sieve*, reflects the poignant and passive acceptance of poverty in India. It also juxtaposes the traditional and the modern as the peasants are displaced by a leather factory and neglected by their modernized sons in the city. When Rukhmani and her husband move to the city in search of their son, they find themselves singularly unequipped to deal with it and are able to find employment only as stone breakers. While they are living on handouts at a temple, Rukhmani's husband dies, leaving Rukhmani to return to the village. The only voice of reason in the novel is that of the English doctor Kenny. *A Handful of Rice* again reflects poverty in the city; here, however, the emphasis is on the rich taking advantage of the poor. Both the conflict between the city and the country and the issue of exploitation are explored in *Shalimar*. However, while the author recognizes that there will be a certain loss of innocence when a luxury resort, Shalimar, is built in a coastal area up to now inhabited only by simple fishermen, she also knows that there is nothing admirable about being hungry. As a realist, Markandaya does not wax sentimental about poverty, just as she refuses to romanticize the colonial past, as represented in this novel by the beautiful, decaying house called Avalon.

Ironically, Markandaya's very honesty has brought her works under attack. Her sympathy for the poor and her poignant descriptions of their often desperate lives have been perceived by nationalists as evidence of Markandaya's alienation from her native land. If she had any feeling for India, they argue, she would have shown it at its best rather than at its worst. In contrast to the critical view of her as an alienated writer, as the Commonwealth writer overseas, Markandaya saw herself as having "the blessing and the bane of duality." The strength of Markandaya's ties to India is demonstrated by her use of language. In her early works, she generally kept to standard English. However, she later modified this view, believing that Indian writers can use their own dialect

forms or localisms with the same brio that American counterparts use Americanisms.

A writer who uses her double perspective as an arch, Ruth Prawer Jhabvala (born 1927), though born in Germany of Jewish parents, reared in England, and living in the United States since 1975, has been acclaimed by some critics as truly Indian. In a career that began while she was living in India, Jhabvala has explored and described upper-middle-class Indian life—particularly as she saw it in New Delhi. Her *Esmond in India* (1958) is almost an allegory of contemporary Indian civilization. Gulab, the Indian girl married to the Englishman Esmond, is an embodiment of traditional India. Shakuntala, the young college girl with whom Esmond later develops a relationship, is the personification of the new India—modernized, sprightly, and yearning for achievement—embarrassed by her slower and more traditional counterpart. Despite his knowledge of Indian culture, civilization, and languages, Esmond remains the foreigner, unable to understand the simultaneous existence of the modern and the traditional, attracted only to exoticism and unable to fit in. Jhabvala seems to concede that such is the position of the foreigner in the mixed, pell-mell Indian society.

Jhabvala's later novels are both broader in scope and more complex in structure than her earlier ones, but their themes are the same: the conflict between East and West, old ways and new, alienation, and the search for meaning. Jhabvala won a Booker Prize for *Heat and Dust* (1975), a brilliant juxtaposition of two stories about young British women in India. Letters written by the narrator's stepgrandmother, who deserted her husband for an Indian prince in 1923, mark the way for her descendent a half century later, as she, too, succumbs to India. Jhabvala's Westerners like to believe that either the East or Eastern practices can assuage their pain. If they do not travel to India, they look for a guru to follow, like the Jewish refugee who takes charge of a group of German Jewish immigrants in Jhabvala's *In Search of Love and Beauty* (1983). The wealthy innocents in *Three Continents* (1987) turn over their lives and their fortunes to an Indian known as the Rawul. In both novels, the gurus are revealed as self-serving and dangerous people, who deprive their followers of their wills and of whatever good sense they may at one time have had.

Three Continents is set in New York, London, and Delhi. *Poet and Dancer* (1993) takes place in Manhattan, but it has two important Indian characters. *Shards of Memory* (1995) moves from place to place as easily as *Three Continents*, chronicling the adventures and misadventures of a mixed Indian-American-British family over the course of four generations. Again, an Indian guru is important to the plot, though he never appears and leaves no record of his teachings. The "shards" of the title are the random recollections of family members, all of whom are affected in one way or another by this unprincipled, charismatic figure. *My Nine Lives: Chapters of a Possible Past* (2004), which Jhabvala labeled "autobiographical fiction," is a series of nine first-person accounts by women describing events that "might have" happened to the author, or things she "might have" wished for.

From the beginning of her literary career, when she wrote what were termed novelistic comedies of manners, Jhabvala has satirized fools, and she often seems as unsympathetic to the Westerners duped by these gurus as she is sympathetic to some of her Indian characters—like the wise, compassionate patriarch in *Shards of Memory*. It is not Indians but India itself that Jhabvala finds so perilous. Her tales of gurus and disciples remind Westerners drawn to India that they will have a difficult choice to make. If they do not renounce their Western identity and become totally Indian, they must live with a sense of alienation. In "Introduction: Myself in India," which prefaces her volume *Out of India: Selected Stories* (1986), Jhabvala comments that Europeans and many modern Indians sometimes find India, "the idea, the sensation of it," so overwhelming, so "intolerable," that they either leave or retreat into themselves, and even those who leave will eventually have to return. Jhabvala has concluded that the primary subject of her fiction is, as she states it, "myself in India." Certainly India, or the "idea" of India, is somehow present in everything she writes.

STYLE AND SUBJECT

Because of the critical emphasis on theme and subject matter, the question among the new generation of Indian novelists of the 1960's and the 1970's was not, Should we use English? or How can we Indianize English? but rather, How best can we use the English language to reflect our society and culture? Manohar Malgonkar (born 1913) and Nayantara Sahgal (born 1927), for example, both experimented in form and structure, but they did not do so at the expense of their subject matter. Many of Malgonkar's novels, including *Distant Drum* (1960), *Combat of Shadows* (1962), *The Princes* (1963), and *A Bend in the Ganges* (1964), deal with the transition from British colonialism to Indian nationalism. Life in the Indian army, the tea estates, the princely states, and the role of wars in India's recent history are the subjects of Malgonkar's fiction.

Sahgal's novels, beginning with *A Time to Be Happy* (1958), reflect the changing political history of India that began with the independence movement. The conflict between modernity and tradition is one of the major themes in Sahgal's novels. In his *This Time of Morning* (1965) and *Storm over Chandigarh* (1969), symbols control structure. The dawning of the Indian nation is seen in the functioning of politicians' lives and ethics; it is still morning for a new nation, yet innocence has no place in the political world. Both of these novels show that a changing order is taking over postindependence India. India is strike-ridden; the nonviolent movement of Gandhi's day has given way to stone-throwing, factory-burning mobs. In *Storm over Chandigarh*, the city of Chandigarh, designed and built by Le Corbusier and commissioned by Nehru to be built with starkly simple lines, is a symbol of Westernization and represents the imposition of the strange, Westernized ways of an alien political order on Indian lives. For men such as Harpal Singh, one of the older politicians in the novel, the starkly simple lines become symbolic of a terrifying, angular coldness in the new order. "It's a revolution in architecture and what's more a revolution in people's thinking . . . but revolutions are sudden and have peculiar results." The gray starkness of the architecture, one of the women in the novel reflects, is opposed to the Indian warmth and effusiveness embodied in the traditional Indian woman.

One of the most highly acclaimed Indian novels in English is *Midnight's Children* (1981), by Salman Rushdie (born 1947). In expressing an alienation from contemporary political India, the novel concentrates heavily on stylistic innovation. *Midnight's Children*, perhaps more clearly than any other postwar Indian novel, highlights the failure of criticism—a criticism that continuously calls for stylistic imitation and pushes Indian writers in the direction of imitating modern British writers. The clue to the theme of *Midnight's Children* lies in the individual's connection to history and in the individual's power to make history. With the gift of extrasensory perception, Saleem Sinai, the narrator, attempts to reconstruct and remake Indian history. The metaphorical manifestation of his attempts finds him cutting up newspaper headlines and rearranging them to make scandal notes that incite trouble. Rushdie's novel reflects the communal feelings of a Muslim family as it experiences the history of India. The communal fighting and killing that pervaded the independence movement and later the "Widow's Rule" is described as graphically in Rushdie's novel as it is in Richard Attenborough's film *Gandhi* (1982). *Midnight's Children* actually reflects regret at the departure of the British. The narrator assesses the end of the second five-year plan in 1961: "The number of landless and unemployed masses actually increased, so that it was greater than had ever been under the British Raj . . . illiteracy survived unscathed; the population continued to mushroom." "Maybe I am wrong. Maybe we are not ready yet," Gandhi had said after the first general strike after which Adam Aziz, the narrator's grandfather, had felt so optimistic about India. Perhaps the lack of readiness, particularly to give up on individual needs and their accommodation, continues to be the root of India's problems; this is the theme of *Midnight's Children*. The novel won the Booker Prize in 1981, and in 1993 it won the Booker of Bookers Prize, as the best of the Booker Prize winners in the award's twenty-five-year history; in 2008, it won the Best of the Booker award as the best Booker winner in forty years.

Rushdie's fourth novel, *The Satanic Verses* (1988), became one of the most notorious and honored books of the end of the twentieth century when the supreme leader of Iran, the Ayatollah Khomeini, issued a religious decree, or fatwa, that Rushdie be killed. Muslims in several countries considered the novel to be blasphemous and considered fulfilling the fatwa to be a religious imperative. For a decade, Rushdie lived in hiding, but he continued to write fiction as well as essays and letters condemning censorship.

Fiction in the vernacular

The development of fiction in the vernacular most clearly demonstrates the imitative tendency among Indian writers. There has been a continual imitation of European trends from the social realism of the 1930's in Munshi Prem Chand's writing to the self-consciously modernist idiom, not only in English but also in its translated forms in the vernacular and the self-consciously experimental forms of fiction such as that published in *Matrubhumi* (Malayalam), *Dharmayug* (Hindi), and similar literary magazines.

Like Anand, Prem Chand (1880-1936), the best-known and one of the most respected Hindi writers, began with the romanticized socialist themes of the previous generation of European writers. His *Gift of a Cow* is a prose epic of the peasants' battle with the moneylender and the zamindar. Other themes of social concern in his work are early marriage and widowhood in *Nirmalā* (1928), the dowry system and prostitution in *Sevā-Sadan* (1918), and the rise of capitalism in *Rangabhümi* (1925). The same themes of social reform mushroomed in the other vernaculars with few variations: in Bengali in *Palli Samaj* (1916), by Sarat Chandra Chatterjee (1876-1938); in Malayalam in *Rantitangazhi* (1949; *Two Measures of Rice*, 1967), by Thakazhi Pillai (1912-1999; and in works by Rajendra Singh Bedi, Pannalal Patel, and Jaswant Singh "Kaneval." In this period, from the 1930's to independence in 1947, Bengal remained the most prolific source of fiction. Novels written in Bengali include Bibhutibhusan Bannerjee's *Pather Panchali* (1929; English translation, 1968), filmed by Satyajit Ray as part of his Apu Trilogy, and Manik Bandopadhyaya's well-known *Putul nacher itikath* (1936; dance of the dolls); several anthologies of short stories in Bengali have also appeared. Social realism was quickly developing into a nationalist consciousness, and Indian literature began to reflect the move toward independence.

Gandhi and Gandhism

Ironically, the best and perhaps the only Indian nationalist fiction appeared in English. Rao celebrated Gandhi in *Kanthapura*, while Narayan dealt with him in the lighthearted, humorous *Waiting for the Mahatma*. Anand's trilogy *The Sword and the Sickle* depicts the turbulence of the Quit India movement, and Khushwant

Singh's *Train to Pakistan* (1955) documents the immense violence of the partition of India and Pakistan. A well-known Marathi writer, Prabhakar Machwe, however, notes that Gandhi seems to have failed to provide inspiration for those writing in the vernacular. In his *Four Decades of Indian Literature: A Critical Evaluation* (1976), Machwe recalls,

> Gandhi's non-violent and non-cooperation movement found still less place in fiction published in the Indian languages. In the celebrations of Gandhi's centenary in 1969, it was difficult to locate even one literary classic which was a reflection of contemporary events, or which documented the impacts of the movements.

This fact, however, is not at all surprising. Astute politician that he was, Gandhi recognized the usefulness of English in uniting the country; the great nationalist debates and arguments, even the one for Hindustani as a national language, were made in English. The irony of this situation was heightened when a noted Bengali writer and nationalist critic, Buddhadeva Bose, claimed in the 1963 edition of *The Concise Encyclopedia of English and American Poetry* (edited by Stephen Spender and Donald Hall) that "Indo-Anglican literature" (by which he means literature written in English by Indians) is "a blind alley lined with curio shops."

VERNACULAR FICTION AFTER INDEPENDENCE

It was after independence and the call to abandon the "imperialist" yoke of English that fiction in the vernaculars began to struggle to make some advancements. In its nationalist impulse, however, it quickly turned to European models. P. Lal, in his review "Contemporary Hindi Fiction" (in *The Concept of an Indian Literature*, 1968), notes the influences of Jean-Paul Sartre, Søren Kierkegaard, and particularly Sigmund Freud. Freudian themes, symbols, and impulses permeate Hindi fiction, particularly of the magazines—Lal recalls the celebration of the sesquicentennial of Kierkegaard's birth by a popular Hindi literary magazine. The impulse toward European modernism rather than toward an experimental idiom that turned to folk and indigenous roots has been demonstrated in the plastic arts. While experimental artists pursue what is new in the West, the more individualistic artists, such as Narayan, work in their own distinctive style.

A similar precedent has not been established in the vernacular fiction.

Among the vernacular novels since independence, there are, however, some landmark achievements. *Chemmeen* (1956; English translation, 1962), by Sivasankara Pillai (1912-1999), deals with the superstitions and lives of the tribal fisherfolk who live along the Malabar coast. Karuthamma, the heroine, believes that the dishonesty of her parents will make the sea go dry. In her own dishonesty in taking a lover, she darkens Arundhati, the star that guides fishermen, thus killing her husband, Palanni, in a storm at sea as he attempts to bait a shark. The novel has something of the fablelike quality of Ernest Hemingway's *The Old Man and the Sea* (1952). Pillai's masterpiece is the massive *Kayar* (1978; *Coir*, 1997), a tale of four generations of a family from feudalism in the 1880's through the India industrial revolution in the 1960's.

Amrita Pritam's *A Line in Water* (1975) is reminiscent of Kate Chopin's *The Awakening* (1899) in that it deals with a woman's feelings, often not communicable to a male sensibility. Pritam (1919-2005) creates characters, like Chopin's, who are caught in the whirlwind of tradition and change, and such concepts as "widowhood without even a wedding," while revolutionary in Indian fiction, underscore the permanent and universal in her work. *Jalavatan* (1969) contains two short novellas, *Jalavatan* (the exile) and *Kala Gulab* (the black rose). The latter is autobiographical, with descriptions of symbolic dreams leaning toward the Freudian tendency in Hindi modernism. *Pinjar* (1963; in *The Skeleton, and Other Writings*, 1964), an existential novel about violence against women, was made into an award-winning film in 2003 and sparked a renewed interest in—and new editions—of Pritam's work.

In Punjabi, the work of Kartar Singh Duggal (born 1917), as well as *I Take This Woman* (1967), by Rajendra Singh Bedi (born 1915), also reflects the changing social scene in India. Bedi's novel was translated into English by Khushwant Singh (born 1915), himself an Indian novelist in English. Other Indian writers who belong to the generation of novelists of independence and deserve mention include Ka Naa Subramanyam (1912-1988), who wrote in Tamil; Khwaja Ahmad Abbas (1914-1987), author of *Inquilab* (1945; revolution), who wrote in both Urdu and English; Chaman Nahal (born 1927), who wrote *Azadi* (1975; independence) in English; and K. M. Munshi (1887-1971), who is considered the founder of Gujarati fiction.

U. R. Anantha Murthy (born 1932), the Kannada writer and scholar, is best known as a theorist who has questioned the turning to Western models: "Why do we import even our radicalism via [Allen] Ginsberg, [John] Osborne or [Jean-Paul] Sartre?" In several speeches and essays, he has urged a "search for identity." He, too, has recognized that while Indian writers cannot return to their roots per se, they must take into consideration the race, moment, and milieu of their own writing—the interaction of the current idiom of the contemporary scene in India with its ancient roots. Buddhadeva Bose (1908-1974), also a theorist of Indian literature, attempted this cultural merger by creating the dramatic novel in Bengali, wherein an Indian consciousness is cast in a dramatic monologue. His novels include *Lal Megh* (1934), *Kalo Haoa* (1942), and *Tithidor* (1949).

Among translations into English recommended by the Authors' Guild of India are Jainendra Kumar's *The Resignation* (1946; originally in Hindi as *Tyaga patra*, 1937); Kalinidi Charan Panigrahi's *A House Undivided* (1973; originally in Oriya as *Matiro manisha*, 1930), Neela Padmanaban's *The Generations* (1972; originally in Tamil as *Talaimnraikal*, 1968), M. T. Vasudevan Nair's *The Legacy* (1975; originally in Malayalam as *Kalam*, 1969), S. H. Vatsyayan's *To Each His Stranger* (1967; originally in Hindi as *Apane apane ajanabi*, 1961), and Lokenath Bhattacharya's *Virgin Fish from Babughat* (1975; originally in Bengali as *Babughatera kumari macha*, 1972). This list demonstrates that literary activity in vernacular remained healthy as the century progressed. However, few critics can overcome the barriers presented by at least fourteen languages, many in different linguistic families and alphabets. Therefore they remain dependent upon translators and interpreters for an understanding of works written in languages beyond the two, or at most three, with which they are familiar.

TRENDS AT THE END OF THE
TWENTIETH CENTURY

At the end of the twentieth century, the fiction of the Indian subcontinent had not yet found a voice and a method of its own. Critics and authors alike seemed uncertain as to how they might rekindle the techniques and values of India's ancient tradition, how to come to terms with its mixture of cultures and languages without allowing one of them to become dominant, and how to move away from Eurocentric models and criticism while still aiming at high standards and at the communication of universal values. One fact was obvious: The only literary works that could reach an audience throughout the entire subcontinent were those either written in English or translated into English. It was also evident that the English language alone could make possible the worldwide recognition and the impressive sales figures for which South Asian writers hoped. By the end of the century, practical considerations had effectively stifled the nationalists' protests, and to all intents and purposes English had become the literary language of the Indian subcontinent.

As long as India was striving for independence, it was difficult for Indian writers to view the colonial past or the British with any objectivity. One of the first to do so was Kamala Markandaya, who in *The Golden Honeycomb* (1977) demonstrated how entrenched traditions and the colonial system prevented decent people—such as the maharajah, his son, and the British resident—from fully understanding each other, much less the people for whose welfare they were responsible. Gita Mehta's novel *Raj* (1989) reveals the frustration of a capable maharajah's daughter, prevented from assuming a position of leadership simply because of her gender. In *Olivia and Jai* (1990) and its sequel *The Veil of Illusion* (1995), both of which are set in the middle of the nineteenth century, the pseudonymous Rebecca Ryman emphasizes how difficult it was to ignore the ethnic distinctions on which the colonial system depended.

In the final decades of the century, writers also reexamined the tumultuous period immediately after independence, when India was torn apart by religious and ethnic differences. Like Rushdie's *Midnight's Children*, most of the novels about this terrible era focused less on actual events than on the way the atmosphere of fear and distrust affected individuals. In *Cracking India*, Sidhwa incorporated horrifying details about the riots in and around Lahore into a comic account of daily life in a prosperous Parsee family, seen through the eyes of the young protagonist. Like *Cracking India*, *Funny Boy* (1994), by the Sri Lankan writer Shyam Selvadurai (born 1965), is a story about coming of age, made doubly difficult by the enmity between neighbors and former friends. The protagonist of *Funny Boy* has to come to terms with being gay and with being a member of the Tamil minority in a largely Sinhalese community; he learns firsthand how cruel human beings can be. Selvadurai's *Cinnamon Gardens* (1998), set in a suburb in colonial Ceylon, shows characters struggling against conventional ideas about women's roles, sexual identity, and social and cultural identity. The novel's attention to the small details of dress, style, and manners have led some critics to compare the author with Jane Austen.

A Fine Balance (1995), by Rohinton Mistry (born 1952), is a massive, sweeping novel about life for the desperately poor during the State of Emergency called in India between June 25, 1975, and March 21, 1977. It follows four characters from different castes as they struggle to find economic stability. *A Fine Balance* sold widely outside India and was selected in the United States for Oprah's Book Club in 2001, guaranteeing further sales. Mistry's next novel was the award-winning *Family Matters* (2001). A decade after *A Fine Balance*, another best-selling Indian novel drew international attention: *Q and A* (2005), by diplomat Vikas Swarup (born 1963), about a waiter from the slums of Mumbai who wins a record-breaking amount of money on a television quiz show. After a 2008 film based on the novel won eight Academy Awards, including Best Picture, the book was reissued under the film's title, *Slumdog Millionaire*. In its two incarnations, the book has been translated into more than forty languages. Swarup's next novel, *Six Suspects* (2008), is a murder mystery set in New Delhi.

WOMEN WRITERS, WOMEN'S LIVES

Intolerance and injustice based on ethnic and religious differences were not the only targets of post-independence South Asian fiction. There had been hints of a demand for women's rights in Indian literature as early as the 1930's. For example, in his atypical novel *The Dark Room*, R. K. Narayan told the story of a devoted Hindu wife driven into rebellion by her husband's infidelity but helpless to make good her escape. In the second half of the twentieth century, the drive for Indian independence, the worldwide feminist movement, and the proliferation of women writers combined to make women's issues one of the dominant subjects in South Asian fiction. It is significant that the protagonists of five of the novels written by Nayantara Sahgal between 1966 and 1985 were women and that in three instances these women left their husbands.

Like Rushdie's *Midnight's Children*, *Clear Light of Day* (1980), by Anita Desai (born 1937), is set in 1947. Desai's focus, however, is not on India's success in gaining independence from Great Britain but on the need for India's women to be freed from a stifling, patriarchal society, a theme the author repeats in *Fasting, Feasting* (1999) and other works. In novels such as *That Long Silence* (1988) and *The Binding Vine* (1993), Shashi Deshpande (born 1938) asks questions to which there are no easy answers, including whether an arranged marriage is safer than one based on love; if there is no prior emotional involvement, one is less likely to be hurt. Deshpande is enough of a realist to understand how difficult it is for Indian women to become assertive when for centuries they have been taught that submissiveness is a virtue; she also shows how hard it is for modern daughters to feel close to their traditional mothers, who so often feel inadequate and are possessed by despair. Deshpande decries the obsession with female purity, which can cause women who have been raped to commit suicide rather than live in shame.

The women in *Listening Now* (1998), by Anjana Appachana, may seem contented, but the purpose of the novel is to show how angry they are at being denied both passion and a sense of self-worth. Appachana shares the conviction of feminists throughout the world that the political upheavals and social changes of the twentieth century did not suddenly cause women to become dissatisfied with their lot but instead brought forth women writers who could voice their feelings and protest against centuries of systematic oppression.

THE DIASPORA

Twentieth and twenty-first century South Asian fiction also reflects the effects of the diaspora from the Indian subcontinent, usually motivated by the hope of a better life but often resulting in a profound sense of alienation. In an early novel, *Wife* (1975), Bharati Mukherjee (born 1940) shows the tragic results when a young Indian woman is married to a stranger and transported to the United States, where she is supposed to act the part of an obedient Indian wife, ignoring the fascinating world around her. It is hardly surprising that she retreats into a fantasy world and eventually explodes into madness. Mukherjee's novel *Desirable Daughters* (2002) and its sequel, *The Tree Bride* (2004), are narrated by Tara Chatterjee, a woman in San Francisco who faces the consequences of her family's actions in pre-independence Bengal.

The complexity of the American immigrant experience is also explored in *The Mistress of Spices* (1997) and *Sister of My Heart* (1999), by Chitra Banerjee Divakaruni (born 1956). In the first of these novels, a shopkeeper in Oakland, California, uses her magical powers for the benefit of confused new immigrants; in the second, it is only the sisterly love two cousins feel for each other that enables them to survive. The protagonist of Divakaruni's *Queen of Dreams* (2004) is a single mother in Berkeley whose mother can interpret dreams. She discovers after the terrorist attacks of September 11, 2001, that her stature as a citizen of the United States is not as solid as she had imagined.

In some novels, the immigration experience leads to a rejection of the past. The recently widowed title character in Bharati Mukherjee's novel *Jasmine* (1989) plans a *sati*, or ritual self-immolation, as soon as she gets to the United States; instead, she kills a rapist, settles down in Iowa with a man, then leaves him for another and heads toward California. Jasmine seems to have become an American. The Pakistani Parsee student in Sidhwa's *An American Brat* (1993) may be appalled by the violence and immorality she sees in the United States, but she decides to remain there rather than returning to Pakistan, with its repressive policies toward women.

Sometimes writers explore the differences between East and West by having a South Asian return home. This device is utilized by Indira Ganesan (born 1960) in *The Journey* (1990), Arundhati Roy (born 1961) in *The God of Small Things* (1997), and Vikram Chandra (born 1961) in *Red Earth and Pouring Rain* (1995), a brilliant novel in which a returning student's lapse from custom

prompts the intervention of the gods and enables the author to recapitulate Indian history. The theme of East versus West also underlies novels in which the major characters are Europeans or Americans in India, perhaps seeking spiritual fulfillment, as in Jhabvala's *Three Continents* and Desai's *Journey to Ithaca* (1995), or perhaps, like the displaced Jew in Desai's poignant *Baumgartner's Bombay* (1988), wishing for nothing more than a safe place to live.

A NEW COSMOPOLITANISM

South Asian writers, too, are involved in the diaspora from their subcontinent. For years, promising students have attended universities in Great Britain or the United States, but more and more writers have either made their homes outside of the subcontinent or divided their time among various countries. Bharati Mukherjee, Chitra Banerjee Divakaruni, Anjana Appachana, Ruth Prawer Jhabvala, and Bapsi Sidhwa moved to the United States, while Kamala Markandaya and Salman Rushdie relocated to Great Britain. Gita Mehta moves among the United States, England, and India; Anita Desai moves between the United States and the United Kingdom; and Vikram Seth (born 1952), author of the monumental work *A Suitable Boy* (1993) and *An Equal Music* (1999), is equally at home in Mumbai and Washington, D.C. Although they may have born in South Asia and use material from their heritage, many of these writers are generally considered—and consider themselves—American writers or British writers (a condition that is not, of course, limited to writers from this region). In 1999, Divakaruni was named one of the "most promising under-forty American writers of the new millennium." Shauna Singh Baldwin (born 1962) is sometimes described as a Sikh Canadian living in Milwaukee.

Admittedly, the diaspora may sometimes lead to a diminished use of South Asian subject matter, as with Jhabvala. The first four novels by Meira Chand, who was born in London of an Indian father and Swiss mother, were set in Japan, where she lives; not until *House of the Sun* (1989) did Chand write a story about Indians in India. On the other hand, though Kiran Desai's home is in New York City, her hilarious *Hullaballoo in the Guava Orchard* (1998) is as convincing a story of Indian village life as one finds in the fiction of

R. K. Narayan, who spent his life in Madras. If it is true that only by observing other cultures can one arrive at a real understanding of one's own, the diaspora may do far more good than harm. Indeed, the new cosmopolitanism may well account for the technical complexity, thematic density, and amazing variety that have become the salient characteristics of South Asian long fiction.

In the twenty-first century, women writers of the South Asian diaspora have assumed a prominent place, attracting a large readership. Bharti Kirchner (born 1940), also an award-winning author of cookbooks, has received popular acclaim for *Sharmila's Book* (1999) and *Pastries: A Novel of Desserts and Discoveries* (2003). Mystery writer Sujata Massey (born 1964) has written a series of five novels featuring the detective Rei Shimura. Shauna Singh Baldwin won the Commonwealth Prize in the Canada/Caribbean division for her first novel, *What the Body Remembers* (1999), about two women in a polygamous marriage in preindependence India. Jhumpa Lahiri (born 1967) won the Pulitzer Prize in fiction with her first collection of short stories about Indian immigrants, *Interpreter of Maladies* (1999). Her first novel, *The Namesake* (2003), was made into a feature film (released in 2006). Monica Ali (born 1967) is author of the best-selling *Brick Lane* (2003), about a woman in an arranged marriage living in London's Bangladeshi community. The novel, which was made into a feature film (released in 2007), raised controversy among some Bangladeshis, who viewed the novel's portrayal of their community as too negative.

Feroza Jussawalla; Rosemary M. Canfield Reisman
Updated by Cynthia A. Bily

BIBLIOGRAPHY

Arya, Sushma, and Shalini Sikka, eds. *New Concerns: Voices in Indian Writing*. New Delhi: Macmillan India, 2006. Collection of critical papers explores the opportunities and challenges presented to Indian authors who write in English. Includes discussion of both resident and expatriate writers.

Behl, Aditya, and David Nicholls, eds. *The Penguin New Writing in India*. New York: Penguin Books, 1995. Anthology of poetry and prose originally written in thirteen different languages, including English, fea-

tures new and relatively unknown Indian writers. Published originally in 1992 as a special issue of the *Chicago Review*.

Brians, Paul. *Modern South Asian Literature in English*. Westport, Conn.: Greenwood Press, 2003. Presents analyses of fifteen important novels by writers including Tagore, Rao, Desai, Sidhwa, and Mistry.

Clark, T. W., ed. *The Novel in India: Its Birth and Development*. Berkeley: University of California Press, 1970. Traces the evolution of prose fiction in the six major languages of India and Pakistan, devoting a chapter to each.

Dodiya, Jaydipsinh, and K. V. Surendran, eds. *Indian Women Writers: Critical Perspectives*. New Delhi: Sarup & Sons, 1999. Collection of twenty-four critical essays includes examinations of the works of writers such as Anita Desai, Kamala Markandaya, Arundhati Roy, and Shobhaa Dé.

Hogan, Patrick Colm, and Lalita Pandit, eds. *Literary India: Comparative Studies in Aesthetics, Colonialism, and Culture*. Albany: State University of New York Press, 1995. Essays by various scholars compare works from very different literary traditions, considering such topics as caste and race, home and exile, political and social change, and language. Interview with Anita Desai is also included. Indexed.

Mukherjee, Meenakshi. *Realism and Reality: The Novel and Society in India*. New York: Oxford University Press, 1985. Eminent scholar demonstrates how the conflict of value systems in colonial society was reflected in the form and content of novels written before the twentieth century. Includes a bibliography and an index.

Nelson, Emmanuel Sampath. *Writers of the Indian Diaspora: A Bio-bibliographical Critical Sourcebook*. Westport, Conn.: Greenwood Press, 1993. Reference work covers the lives and works of fifty-eight writers as well as their critical receptions. Includes an extensive primary and secondary bibliography.

Rushdie, Salman, and Elizabeth West, eds. *Mirrorwork: Fifty Years of Indian Writing, 1947-1997*. New York: Henry Holt, 1997. Includes fiction and nonfiction, translations and works written in English. Rushdie's introduction is excellent.

Sanga, Jaina C. *South Asian Novelists in English: An*

A-to-Z Guide. Westport, Conn: Greenwood Press, 2003. Comprehensive reference work provides biographical information and critical analysis. Includes a bibliography.

Silva, Neluka. *The Gendered Nation: Contemporary Writings from South Asia*. Thousand Oaks, Calif.: Sage, 2004. Examines writing in the contexts of nation-building and the anticolonial struggle in India, Sri Lanka, Pakistan, and Bangladesh.

Tharu, Susie, and K. Lalita, eds. *Women Writing in India: 600 B.C. to the Present*. 2 vols. New York: Feminist Press, 1991-1993. Volume 1 is titled *600 B.C. to the Early Twentieth Century*; volume 2, *The Twentieth Century*. Introductory essays provide a feminist context for the works in this monumental anthology, which does not include works by authors from Pakistan, Bangladesh, and Sri Lanka. Contains a guide to pronunciation, a bibliography, and an index.

SPANISH LONG FICTION

The prose form that eventually came to be called the novel has always been the least precisely defined of literary genres. For that reason, it is difficult to assign a beginning to the history of the novel in Spanish literature. Most of the prose of the Middle Ages and much of that written during the eighteenth century does not fit very well into the category of long fiction of which the nineteenth century realistic novel is the synthesis. Poetry could be defined—at least until the advent of the experimental poetry of the twentieth century—as a literary form in which the language is ordered through rhyme and meter, and drama is identified by the fact that it is intended for live presentation on a stage. The characteristics that make a work of prose "novelistic," however, have eluded most attempts at precise identification.

The history of the novel in Spain is the history of a form that is constantly new, or "novel." The shape of that history is determined to some extent by a concern for the purpose of the novel, which is really a concern for the effect of the novel on the reader. Throughout the development of long fiction in Spain, as in many other Western cultures, reading for pleasure was considered an idle and potentially dangerous pursuit and reading for edification an admirable pastime. The novel was subjected to a process of more or less subtle censorship by the official institutions of society, which tended to make it justify itself as something other than pure entertainment, as something useful. This social phenomenon is most obvious in the case of the masterpiece of Spanish fiction, Miguel de Cervantes' *Don Quixote de la Mancha* (1605, 1615), but it is manifest even in the earliest extant imaginative prose writing in Spain, the exemplum literature of the thirteenth century.

EARLY DIDACTIC FICTION

The first examples of exemplum prose fiction—probably translations or adaptations of Arabic works—include *Calila e Dimna* (c. 1251; Calila and Dimna) and the *Libro de los engaños e los asayamientos de las mujeres* (c. 1253; *Book of Women's Wiles and Deceits*, 1882). The propagation of these early didactic works was facilitated by the increase in the manufacturing of paper in Spain during the thirteenth century and the invention of eyeglasses toward the end of it. This exemplum literature belongs to the tradition of short fiction because of its form—collections of brief prose pieces, each serving as an example of appropriate or inappropriate social conduct—but it presages some of the characteristics of the longer prose forms that eventually evolved into the novelistic form of the seventeenth century and after. As the titles of some of these collections indicate—the anonymous *Libro del consejo e de los consejeros* (early 1200's; book of advice and advisers) and the *Libro de los exemplos del Conde Lucanor y de Patronio* (1328-1335; *Count Lucanor: Or, The Fifty Pleasant Stories of Patronio*, 1868) of Juan Manuel (1282-1348)—the exempla are linked together by a fictional device involving the relationship of central characters: usually an older, wiser counselor who tells the stories to a naïve, inexperienced person for whom the counselor is in some way responsible. Although the "short stories" that form the text may be unrelated to one another, they are unified by the presence and concerns of the teacher and the student.

The collections of exemplary literature were important antecedents of the novel in that the history of long fiction is replete with examples of a great diversity of experience portrayed in a single work, synthesized into a unified narrative through some point of reference, such as one character, locale, or theme. The obviously didactic intent, which often seems to be only a necessary justification for the "idle pleasure" of reading ingenious, sometimes satiric stories, is another characteristic that the novel inherited from medieval prose literature. The tendency toward a more imaginative fictional representation was evident throughout the fourteenth and early fifteenth centuries, culminating in *El Arcipreste de Talavera*, commonly known as *El corbacho* (1498, written 1438; first three parts as *Little Sermons on Sin*, 1959), of Alfonso Martínez de Toledo (1398-c. 1482), who held the position of archpriest of Talavera, and in the work of Diego de San Pedro, a late fifteenth century writer about whom almost nothing is known. His sentimental novels of courtly love, which include the *Tratado de amores de*

Arnalte y Lucinda (c. 1481; *Arnalte and Lucenda: A Certayne Treatye Most Wyttely Devysed Orygynally Written in the Spaynysshe*, 1543) and the *Cárcel de amor* (1492; *The Castell of Love*, c. 1549), were precursors of the pastoral and chivalric fiction of the sixteenth century.

CHIVALRIC AND PASTORAL ROMANCES

The advent of a long fictional form that resembled in some ways the modern novel occurred only after the invention of movable type in the late fifteenth century. Although there are two significant examples of adventure fiction in the early 1300's—the *Libro del caballero Zifar* (book of the knight Zifar) and the *Gran conquista de Ultramar* (the great overseas conquest)—the sixteenth century was the first period of extensive dissemination of long prose works. Some of this fiction was from the late fifteenth century, but the large, diverse audience that was the prerequisite for the development of the modern novel did not exist until the advent of printing made books accessible to less than wealthy readers.

The most popular works of fiction were, unquestionably, the romances of chivalry. The primary source of the Spanish version of the Arthurian legend was *Amadís de Gaula* (*Amadis of Gaul*, partial translation, 1567, 1803), originally in Portuguese and widely circulated in manuscript during the fourteenth century, then revised about 1492 by Garci Rodriguez de Montalvo (c. 1480-c. 1550), who published it in 1508. It was so popular that it had been reprinted thirty times by 1587. In the sixteenth century, there appeared a total of twelve books about Amadis and his descendants, including Montalvo's *Las sergas de Esplandián* (c. 1510; *The Sergas of Esplandián*, 1664), *Amadís de Grecia* (sixteenth century; *Amadis of Greece*, 1694), *Lisuarte de Grecia* (1514; *Lisuarte of Greece*, 1652) by Feliciano de Silva (c. 1492-1558), *Palmerín de Oliva* (1511; *Palmerín d'Oliva*, 1588), and *Primaleón* (1512; *Primaleon of Greece*, 1595-1596). The great popularity of the romances of chivalry is evident in the records of the number published and the frequent attempts by the government to ban their publication. The histories of the perfect knights and the rigid codes of honor and courtly love were evidently out of touch with the actual experiences of the readers but surely embodied some important aspiration or truth for the sixteenth century. The romances of chiv-

alry presented an ideal world of absolutes that surely seemed to be more manageable than the vagaries of actual everyday experience.

The pastoral romances, which achieved a popularity almost equal to that of the romances of chivalry, presented an equally ideal world, one based on the Neoplatonic concept of cosmic love as the controlling force of the universe. The reflection of this universal love in the chaste relationship of perfect lovers and the vicissitudes of those who love unwisely dominated novels such as *Los siete libros de la Diana* (c. 1559; *The Seven Books of Diana*, 1596), by Jorge de Montemayor (1520-1561), and *Primera parte de Diana enamorada* (1564; *First Part of Enamored Diana*, 1598), by Gaspar Gil Polo (c. 1519-1585). The pastoral novels were not only representations of shepherds stricken by love but also somewhat polemical as they expounded various humanistic theories about the nature and effects of true love. Miguel de Cervantes (1547-1616) contributed to the genre with *La Galatea* (1585; *Galatea: A Pastoral Romance*, 1833) and continued until his death to promise that he would produce a second part of this successful story. The first two novels of the most important and prolific dramatist of the time, Lope de Vega (1562-1635), were in the pastoral mode: *La Arcadia* (1598) and *Los pastores de Belén* (1612; the shepherds of Bethlehem).

Chivalric and pastoral fiction represented an evasion of reality, in that their portrayal of experience was based on an idealized concept of the world. Their appeal was in part a result of the fact that, even though they were not what could be called realistic, they did deal in some way with the real concerns of the reading public—honor, love, and suffering—and in part because those concerns were portrayed in the exotic contexts of heroic exploits and peaceful, bucolic settings. Even more exotic was the subject matter of the Byzantine novel, which often took the form of a Moorish novel and experienced a period of popularity in the sixteenth century. The most successful was the anonymous *Historia de Abindarráez y Xarifa*, more commonly known as the *Historia del Abencerraje y la hermosa Jarifa* (three versions, in 1561, 1562, and 1565; history of the Abencerraje and the beautiful Jarifa) or simply the *Abencerraje*, which narrates a story of love and chivalry in the context of Christian-Moorish conflicts along the Andalusian frontier during the retaking of Spain from the Moors. Another significant example of this genre was the widely read historical novel by Ginés Pérez de Hita (c. 1544-c. 1619), *Las guerras civiles de Granada* (1619, written 1595-1597; *The Civil Wars of Granada*, 1803).

LA CELESTINA AND THE PICARESQUE

Throughout the sixteenth century, the development of long fiction took two directions. Paralleling the novelistic prose that portrayed the world in the idealistic terms of the chivalric, pastoral, and Byzantine modes was a type of fiction more firmly based on the truth of sixteenth century experience. The earliest example is one of the masterpieces of Spanish literature, first published anonymously in 1499 as the *Comedia de Calisto y Melibea* (comedy of Calisto and Melibea). It reappeared several years later in a series of expanded versions titled *Tragicomedia de Calisto y Melibea* (1502; *Celestina*, 1631), in which there was textual evidence that the author of at least the major part of the work was Fernando de Rojas (c. 1465-1541). The printers of the novel changed the title to *La Celestina* because of the popularity of the main character, an earthy old woman who uses her skills of witchcraft to further her professional reputation as a go-between. It is a story of the passionate love of Calisto and Melibea, doomed to failure by the circumstances of their birth. Some critics have called *La Celestina* the first novel in Spanish, because it portrayed characters from all social classes in a more realistic manner than did the romances, which tended to idealize and perfect the world that they created.

La Celestina became a very popular work, and the name of the old witch, Celestina, entered the lexicon of Spanish as the generic term for a go-between or pimp. Throughout the sixteenth century, there were imitations of *La Celestina* and examples of prose fiction influenced by Rojas's work that presented a fairly realistic portrayal of certain baser aspects of sixteenth century life. A surprisingly frank and erotic account of the life of a prostitute appeared in the *Retrato de la lozana andaluza* (1528; *Portrait of Lozana, the Lusty Andalusian Woman*, 1987), by Francisco Delicado (c. 1480-c. 1534), a priest who published in the following year a treatise on a supposed cure for syphilis, a disease from which he himself suffered.

The sixteenth century work of fiction that had perhaps the greatest impact on the development of the European novel was *La vida de Lazarillo de Tormes y de sus fortunas y adversidades*, published anonymously in 1554 and translated into English as *The Pleasant Historie of Lazarillo de Tormes* (1576; commonly known as *Lazarillo de Tormes*). His work was the first example of what later was called the picaresque novel, the fictional biography (or often, as in this case, autobiography) of a parasitic delinquent. Lazaro, the picaro who narrates his own story, rises above his miserable surroundings by serving a series of masters, using all of his cunning and wit to survive in a cruel society. As he changes from a child to an adult, he accumulates the experience of sustained contact with a deceptive world and becomes as cynical and dishonest as the people who have exploited and mistreated him. *Lazarillo de Tormes* is extraordinary for its brutal satire and comic narrative, particularly in the context of the prevailing literary vogue of heroic chivalric adventures, courtly conduct, and pastoral love.

Lazarillo de Tormes continued the tradition of social realism established by *La Celestina*, and part of that realistic portrayal of society was its consideration of the nature of honor—whether it is something intrinsic or something acquired through conduct. In the later manifestations of the picaresque genre, the theme of honor became more important and often was related to the more specific question of *limpieza de sangre* (purity of blood), a concern central to the plot of *La Celestina*. Particularly after the expulsion or forced conversion of the Jews in 1492 and the Muslims in 1502, purity of blood became a significant question. To be a *converso* (convert, or New Christian) was to be a second-class citizen, barred from positions of public prominence and respect and often harassed and mistreated. Because of the implication that, if honor was inherited and dependent on the purity of Christian blood, a *converso* was not honorable, the theme of intrinsic or acquired honor represented an actual, socially conditioned anxiety of the time.

The concern over discovery of questionable ancestry and the pursuit of recognition of one's honor pervades the satiric exposure of society's hypocrisy that emerges from the texts of the picaresque novel. *La vida y hechos del pícaro Guzmán de Alfarache* (part 1, 1599, part 2,

1604; *The Rogue: Or, The Life of Guzman de Alfarache*, 1622; also known as *The Life and Adventures of Guzman d'Alfarache: Or, The Spanish Rogue*; best known as *Guzmán de Alfarache*), by Mateo Alemán (1547-c. 1614), is the fictional autobiography of a reformed delinquent who, because he has established himself as a respectable citizen, can moralize about Original Sin and redemption as he narrates his devilish escapades. Significant examples of the picaresque novel with innovative variations appeared well into the seventeenth century. The *Libro de entretenimiento de la pícara Justina* (1605; *The Life of Justina, the Country Jilt*, 1707) of Francisco López de Úbeda (died 1620) uses the picaresque form as a thinly veiled satire of the Spanish court. *La hija de Celestina* (1612; *The Hypocrites*, 1657), by Alonso Jerónimo de Salas Barbadillo (1581-1635), was primarily an exploitation of the genre, an entertainment without the moralizing overtones.

In 1618, Vicente Espinel (1550-1624) published a pseudo-picaresque novel, the *Relaciones de la vida del escudero Marcos de Obregón* (*The History of the Life of the Squire Marcos de Obregón*, 1816), which tells the episodic adventures not of a delinquent, but of a respectable man. In the *Segunda parte de la vida de Lazarillo de Tormes, sacada de las crónicas antiguas de Toledo* (1620; *The Pursuit of the Historie of Lazarillo de Tormes*, 1622), Juan de Luna (c. 1590-c. 1650) used the picaresque genre as an attack on the clergy and the Inquisition. The most enduring of the genre, after *The Pursuit of the Historie of Lazarillo de Tormes*, was the *Historia de la vida del Buscón llamado don Pablos* (1626; *The Life and Adventures of Buscón, the Witty Spaniard*, 1657), written by one of the most extraordinary poets of the seventeenth century, Francisco Gómez de Quevedo y Villegas (1580-1645). The history of Don Pablos, a disadvantaged young man who longs to be a gentleman, is an example of the picaresque returning to the witty, humorous narrative of grotesque brutality that characterized *Lazarillo de Tormes*. There is an implicit didacticism in the constant punishment that Don Pablos suffers for trying to move from his lower social class to the more respectable station of the nobility. The tradition of the picaresque novel is, in fact, a continuation of the tradition of the early didactic prose, the exemplum literature of the thirteenth century, another manifestation of the tendency

to justify literature as something other than pure entertainment or art.

The motifs of satire and social criticism of the picaresque novel were also evident in other forms of fiction during the sixteenth and seventeenth centuries. *El crotalón* was a satiric dialogue in the style of Lucian (second century C.E.), written and circulated in 1553 (though not published until 1871), which bore the pseudonym Christóphoro Gnósopho and has been attributed to the Erasmian writer Cristóbal de Villalón (c. 1500-1558). Quevedo published a series of *Sueños* (1607-1622; *The Visions of Dom Francisco de Quevedo Villega*, 1667), witty, conceit-filled satires of social types in the form of extravagant hallucinations, and Baltasar Gracián (1601-1658) created a monumental allegorical narrative of prudence, optimism, and pessimistic disenchantment with the world in *El criticón* (1651-1657; *The Critick*, 1681). *El diablo cojuelo* (1641; the lame devil, published in English as *Le Diable Boiteux: Or, The Devil upon Two Sticks*, 1741) of Luis Vélez de Guevara (1579-1644) was an extensive panorama of Spanish society, as were the less successful but more satiric works of the prolific novelist Francisco Santos (c. 1617-c. 1697), which include *Día y noche de Madrid* (1663; day and night in Madrid) and *El arca de Noé y campana de Belilla* (1697; Noah's ark and Belilla's bell). In 1632, Lope de Vega Carpio produced *La Dorotea* (the story of Dorotea), an autobiographical novel in dialogue influenced by the realistic portrayal of characters in *La Celestina* that deals with the illusions and disillusionment of love and the emptiness of a life restricted to the pursuit of sensual pleasures.

Miguel de Cervantes

The life of Cervantes fell in the two centuries of the Spanish Golden Age, the sixteenth and seventeenth. The publication of his monumental *Don Quixote de la Mancha* was a culmination of the previous trends of prose fiction in Spanish and a point of departure for the novelistic works not only of the remaining years of the Golden Age but also of the prose literature of the eighteenth century. Examples of all the significant forms of fiction that had developed by 1600 are found in Cervantes' writing. His *Galatea* is a pastoral romance. The picaresque as well as reflections of the early didactic tales appear in the collection of his short novels, the *Novelas ejemplares* (1613; *Exemplary Novels*, 1846), while *Los trabajos de Persiles y Sigismunda* (1617; *The Travels of Persiles and Sigismunda: A Northern History*, 1619) is a Byzantine novel. The chivalric tradition is the foundation of *Don Quixote de la Mancha*, but this vast panorama of Spanish life and literary tradition contains interpolated, self-contained stories that represent all of these styles of literature. *Don Quixote de la Mancha*, in fact, is a work of fictional literature that deals directly with fictional literature and its relationship to real, historical experience. It is a culmination of the tendency to regard literature as serving some motive other than pleasurable entertainment, yet it is as much a satire of that tendency as a restatement of the conviction that literature does—and perhaps should—influence its audience in an edifying manner.

The emphasis on literature and its audience is clear in the basic presuppositions of the history of Don Quixote—that his insanity is the result of reading too many chivalric romances and that his assuming the role of a knight errant is the result of his interpreting the romances as history rather than fiction. The episodes with moralizing commentary of Don Quixote and his squire Sancho Panza are reminiscent of the early exemplum literature but are rendered ironic by the insanity of the counselor and the shifting of roles of the knight and the squire as teacher and student. This vast and complex novel seems to be concentrated on a theme of the fickleness of human perception, but it is in fact an exploration of the nature of reality and the various illusions to which humans succumb in the course of their ambitious quest for respectability, honor, or mere survival.

The history of Don Quixote is, above all, the narrative of a continual process of experiencing the world as it really is, a slow disintegration of idealistic visions, both optimistic and pessimistic, of the world. *Don Quixote de la Mancha* is unquestionably what it has been called by numerous critics, the first modern novel. The astounding diversity of motifs and perspectives present in the narrative signify a radical departure from all the previous forms of prose fiction. While the pastoral, the chivalric, the picaresque, the Byzantine, and the sentimental novel begin with presuppositions or postulates about the nature of reality and are developed, for the most part, according to those a priori convictions, Cervantes' novel is an exploratory text that develops independent of any fixed notion about the nature of reality or the strictures of a particular literary genre.

Although *Don Quixote de la Mancha* has often been described as a satire of the romances of chivalry, it is more accurate to interpret the novel as a satire of the tendency to regard an idealistic concept of reality as a valid model for human conduct. Don Quixote believes that the codes and rituals of chivalry are viable in his historical reality. The humorous satire of the text derives from the futility of transferring that fictional vision to his real experience. In his prologues and his novel, Cervantes creates characters who proclaim that *Don Quixote de la Mancha* was written with the intent of destroying the influence of the romances of chivalry. Throughout the seventeenth and eighteenth centuries, that claim of authorial intent was repeated in hundreds of critiques, imitations, and adaptations of Cervantes' novel. It is more likely that the popularity of the literature of chivalry and the fact that there were many nobles who actually performed chivalric rituals as a form of entertaining, idle pastime provided Cervantes with a theme that would be at once ridiculous and credible, and provide an incomparable opportunity to develop the dichotomy of appearance and reality that forms the unifying concept of his novel. As he proclaimed the efficacious intent of his work, Cervantes was also exploiting the commonplace notion of the potentially pernicious effect of idle reading and participating in the tendency to justify literary art by its usefulness.

Because of the widespread success of *Don Quixote de la Mancha*, there were many imitations. One of the most interesting and significant cases occurred before Cervantes had completed the second part, which was published in 1615. In 1614, someone published the *Segundo tomo del ingenioso hidalgo Don Quixote de la Mancha* (*A Continuation of the Comical History of the Most Ingenious Knight, Don Quixote de la Mancha*, 1705) under the pseudonym Alonso Fernández de Avellaneda. Most critics have judged this spurious second part, commonly referred to as the "false Quixote," to be inferior to Cervantes' work and to be a ridiculous, unimaginative attempt at Cervantine satire. Understandably, Cervantes was furious and even included a critique of the false Quixote in his own second part.

THE EIGHTEENTH CENTURY

Although *Don Quixote de la Mancha* had considerable influence in the seventeenth century, the most significant manifestations of the impact of Cervantes' work on Spanish literature appeared during the Enlightenment, along with evidence of the influence of Quevedo and Gracián. That these three writers were emulated during the eighteenth century is understandable, for it was the supreme age of social criticism and the last great attempt in European culture to renovate society according to rational principles. It was a time of supreme optimism, in which intellectuals were convinced that, through judgment, insight, and good taste, a perfect world could be established. Thus, Quevedo and Gracián, as social satirists, were appealing enough to be imitated by Diego de Torres Villarroel (1693-1770) in his satiric fantasy of life in Madrid, the *Visiones y visitas de Torres con Don Francisco de Quevedo por la corte* (1727-1728; visions and visits of Torres with Don Francisco de Quevedo in the court). Cervantes was also attractive as the writer who, according to the generally accepted critical judgment of the century, had single-handedly driven out a contemporary social evil, the romances of chivalry.

Many writers prefaced their works with comments about Cervantes' accomplishment and the promise that they would do the same—eradicate some flaw of society through a judicious satire. The most notable examples were Francisco de Isla (1703-1781) and José Cadalso (1741-1782). Isla's voluminous *Historia del famoso predicador Fray Gerundio de Campazas, Alias Zotes* (part 1, 1758, part 2, 1770; *The History of the Famous Preacher Friar Gerund de Campazas, Alias Zotes*, 1772) is a satiric attack on the extravagant preachers of the day, whose sermons were so filled with ingenious conceits and convoluted language that no one understood much of what they said. Cadalso's major work was the *Cartas marruecas* (1789; Moroccan letters), a collection of letters exchanged among a young Moor living in a Christian household in Spain, his Moorish mentor in Morocco, and the Christian host. The epistolary work has no significant evidence of Cervantine influence, but Cadalso's preface compares his attempt to improve society through social criticism to Cervantes' intent.

There is a paucity of significant eighteenth century Spanish novels, for the Spanish Enlightenment was primarily an age of the essay, didactic poetry, and exemplary drama. The most interesting form of prose literature was a hybrid form, a type of essayistic prose work that made use of novelistic devices such as the portrayal of imaginary characters who represented more or less obviously real people or fictional characters from the Spanish literary tradition. It was an age of polemics, and much of the "essayistic fiction" was pointedly didactic and argumentative, often witty and ingenious in its direct attacks on certain individuals. Most of the major writers of the second half of the century engaged in the literary exchanges, though most did so through poetry or short prose pieces. The two most significant examples of works that can be termed novelistic in the context of the literary values of the period are *Los literatos en cuaresma* (1773; writers during Lent), by the poet and fabulist Tomás de Iriarte (1750-1791), and *Los gramáticos: Historia chinesca* (c. 1783; the grammarians: a Chinese history), a fierce attack on Iriarte and his entire family, by Juan Pablo Forner (1756-1797).

Of the more traditional novelists, the notable examples were Pedro de Montengón y Paret (1745-1824), who wrote sentimental historical novels, and José Mor de Fuentes (1762-1848), whose epistolary novel *El cariño perfecto: O, Los amores de Alfonso y Serafina* (c. 1795; perfect affection, or the love of Alfonso and Serafina) continued the Renaissance literary tradition of praise of country life and scorn of the court.

ROMANTICISM AND *COSTUMBRISMO*

During the early years of the nineteenth century, few novels were published in Spain; in part, this was a consequence of a particularly strong expression of the recurring idea that prose fiction is immoral and detrimental to its readers. Indeed, the government attempted, with some success, to suppress the publication of novels. In spite of an official ban on translated fiction, a Valencia publishing house began in 1816 to publish a collection of novels that introduced foreign novelists to the evergrowing Spanish reading public.

The Romantic influences prevalent during the 1820's and 1830's resulted in a spate of historical novels, some written by the outstanding literary figures of the Spanish Romantic movement. The dramatist Francisco Martínez de la Rosa (1787-1862) published his historical novel

Doña Isabel de Solís, Reyna de Granada in parts from 1837 to 1846. One of the finest Romantic poets, José de Espronceda (1808-1842), developed the typical Romantic themes of spiritual vacuity and despair over the failure of love in *Sancho Saldaña* (1834). Mariano José de Larra (1809-1837), the satiric essayist whose suicide and funeral rallied the Romantic writers to a proclamation of unity against a disapproving Establishment, published *El doncel de don Enrique el doliente* (1834; the squire of Sir Henry the Sufferer). The best of the historical novels appeared several years after a strong ideological reaction to Romanticism had set in. *El Señor de Bembibre* (1844; *The Mystery of Bierzo Valley: A Tale of the Knights Templars*, 1938), by Enrique Gil y Carrasco (1815-1846), is unusual because of its strong evocation of a regional Leonese setting and its development of the conflict between traditional values and the Romantic despair that results from a loss of faith in the moral, religious, and intellectual beliefs that formed those values. There were also hundreds of historical novels published by lesser-known writers such as Wenceslao Ayguals de Izco (1801-1873), Francisco Navarro Villoslada (1818-1895), and Manuel Fernández y González (1821-1888), who, in spite of their popularity, never gained the attention of literary scholarship.

Particularly popular during the Romantic period and the remainder of the nineteenth century were the *novelas por entregas*, or *folletines*, serialized novels that appeared either in magazines or in separate installments that were sold a chapter at a time. The most striking feature of early nineteenth century historical fiction and the serial novels was the apparent indifference to a careful, convincing portrayal of physical reality; this is the feature that also distinguished this fiction from the literary tradition of works such as *La Celestina*, *Lazarillo de Tormes*, and *Don Quixote de la Mancha*, as well as from post-1850 fiction. More in the tradition of fiction based on preconceived notions about the nature of reality and experience—the tradition of the pastoral and the chivalric romance—the nineteenth century historical novel did not contribute significantly to the development of the novel as an artistic form until the advent of the most notable novelist of the century, Benito Pérez Galdós (1843-1920).

A major influence on the novel at midcentury was the importation of the French novels of Eugène Sue (1804-1857), six of which were translated and published in 1844 alone. Sue's novels inspired in Spanish writers an interest in a different type of historical novel, one that dealt with recent events and propagated social and political ideas. Significant examples were Ayguals's *María: O, La hija de un jornalero* (1845-1846; Mary, or the daughter of a day laborer) and *Misterios de las sectas secretas: O, El francmasón proscrito* (1847-1852; mysteries of secret sects, or the proscribed Freemason) by José M. Riera y Comas (1827-1858).

The more careful observation of recent historical reality evident in these novels had a parallel in another type of fiction that pervaded the middle years of the century—the *costumbrista* literature. The popular *costumbrista* sketches portrayed specific "authentic" aspects of everyday life in Spain in precise detail and often with a nostalgic attitude toward the quaint, typical customs that were disappearing with the advance of the modern world. The *costumbrista* tradition influenced two important novelists who began publishing in the mid-nineteenth century, Fernán Caballero (pseudonym of Cecilia Böhl von Faber, 1796-1877) and Pedro Antonio de Alarcón (1833-1891). Fernán Caballero is an unusual case in the history of Spanish fiction. Usually credited with preparing the way for the important realistic novelists of the second half of the century, she wrote her novels in German or French and had them translated for publication by her agent. She was best known for *La gaviota* (1849; *The Sea-Gull: Or, The Lost Beauty*, 1867), which is typical of all of her novels, moralizing and somewhat sentimental, superficially descriptive in the tradition of the *costumbrista* sketches.

Alarcón was an aggressive proponent of the conservative Catholic point of view. Except for his delightful, whimsical *El sombrero de tres picos* (1874; *The Three-Cornered Hat*, 1886), which inspired the ballet by the Spanish composer Manuel de Falla (1876-1946) and is reminiscent of the exemplum literature of the Middle Ages and the *Exemplary Novels* of Cervantes, his novels are rather severely ideological. *El final de Norma* (1855, wr. 1850; *Brunhilde: Or, The Last Act of Norma*, 1891), *El escándalo* (1875; *The Scandal*, 1945), and *El niño de la bola* (1880; *The Child of the Ball*, 1892; also known as *The Infant with the Globe*, 1959) are attacks on irreligion, immorality, and the liberal ideas that were prevalent during Alarcón's career. *La pródiga* (1882; *True to Her Oath: A Tale of Love and Misfortune*, 1899) is a more interesting novel; it narrates the story of a woman's illicit sexual behavior and suicide, stimulated by an idealized Romantic attitude toward love.

REALISM

The triumph of the nineteenth century "liberal" movement in Spain, the September Revolution of 1868, which dethroned the Bourbon monarchy and led to the establishment of the short-lived republic in 1873, was a turning point in the history of the novel. The aspirations, problems, and anxieties of Spanish society were, rather suddenly, appropriate material for narrative fiction, and the decade of the 1870's was fertile ground for the thesis novel, a type of fiction in which the theme seems to unduly determine the structure, characterization, and plot development. It was also the decade of intense interest in the idealism of the German philosopher Karl Christian Friedrich Krause (1781-1832). The intellectual movement appropriately called Krausism, which emphasized a harmony of the spiritual and the rational and stressed principles of liberal education, led to the establishment in 1876 of the Institución Libre de la Enseñanza (Free Institute of Teaching) by Francisco Giner de los Ríos (1839-1915), a disciple of the Spanish intellectual leader Julian Sanz del Río (1814-1869), who was in turn a student and disciple of Krause. Krausism had a considerable, if temporally limited, effect on the novelists of the period, such as Juan Valera (1824-1905) and Pérez Galdós, whose novel *El amigo Manso* (1882; *Our Friend Manso*, 1987) is a disenchanted portrayal of a Krausist professor. During the 1870's, Pérez Galdós established himself as a significant novelist with the thesis novels that would bring him extensive recognition as an enemy of religious and social intolerance—*Doña Perfecta* (1876; English translation, 1880), *Gloria* (1876-1877; English translation, 1879), and *La familia de León Roch* (1878; *The Family of León Roch*, 1888).

In contrast to Pérez Galdós's liberalism, which was moderate but impressive for its contrast to prevailing social attitudes, the regional novels of José María de Pereda (1833-1906), published during the 1870's, are characterized by a reinforcement of traditional values

and institutions, as in *Los hombres de pro* (1872; the supporters), *El buey suelto* (1877; the freed ox), and *Don Gonzalo González de la Gonzalera* (1878). Pereda went on to write the most widely read novelistic accounts of provincial life in Spain, characterized by a *costumbrista* nostalgia and idealism about rural society—*El sabor de la tierruca* (1881; the smell of the land), *Sotileza* (1884; English translation, 1959), and *Peñas arriba* (1895; atop the mountain). Pereda's fiction had an enormous appeal for its own kind of exoticism, the life of the simple country people, but his lack of detached, objective narrative rendered his fiction less significant to the development of the dominant trend of nineteenth century fiction—realism—in spite of the astounding wealth of descriptive details in his novels.

A more significant novelist was Juan Valera (1824-1905), who began his career with *Pepita Jiménez* (1874; *Pepita Ximenez*, 1886), an elegant, refined, and subtle work that in less judicious hands would have been a blatant thesis novel. His later works, which include *Las ilusiones del doctor Faustino* (1875; *The Illusions of Doctor Faustino*, 2008), *Doña Luz* (1879; English translation, 2002), *Juanita la larga* (1896; English translation, 2006), and *Genio y figura* (1897; spirit and form), presented idealized studies of the difficulties of love and the emotional frustrations resulting from the conflict between worldliness and spirituality.

The other novelist of the time who, with Valera, Alarcón, and Pérez Galdós—for *Pepita Ximenez, The Three-Cornered Hat*, and *Doña Perfecta*—gained considerable recognition in Europe and the United States was Armando Palacio Valdés (1853-1938). The less familiar novels of Palacio Valdés were more significant to the development of nineteenth century fiction than the immensely popular *Marta y María* (1883; *The Marquis of Peñalta*, 1886), *José* (1885; English translation, 1901), and *La hermana San Sulpicio* (1889; *Sister Saint Sulpice*, 1890). *La espuma* (1891; *The Froth*, 1891) and *La fé* (1892; *Faith*, 1892) are innovative novels of social and religious protest with fantastic elements that imply political symbolism.

The most significant novelists of the century were, unquestionably, Emilia Pardo Bazán (1851-1921), Clarín (pseudonym of Leopoldo Alas, 1852-1901), and Benito Pérez Galdós. Pérez Galdós was the literary giant of the century, for the quantity and sustained quality of his fiction, while Clarín's reputation and importance as a major novelist rested on a single, monumental work, *La regenta* (1884; English translation, 1984). Although Emilia Pardo Bazán produced many novels that were widely read and continues to gain the somewhat qualified respect of literary scholarship, she was most influential for her activities as a literary critic and her rather outrageous public image. A robust woman who smoked cigars in public and alienated many with her feminist ideas and outspoken manner, Pardo Bazán was the first writer in Spain to publish commentaries on French naturalism—*La cuestión palpitante* (1883; the burning question)—and was instrumental in creating widespread interest in the nineteenth century Russian novelists. While she praised the literary talent of Émile Zola (1840-1902), she condemned the impersonal, scientific observation characteristic of his naturalistic fiction. She proposed instead a balance of naturalistic and idealistic fictional motifs, a sort of hybrid ideological approach that was the perspective, if not the theory, of the realists.

Pardo Bazán's pronouncements were considered rather scandalous, and her novels were equally offensive to the conservative establishment. *La tribuna* (1883; *The Tribune of the People,* 1999) portrays the struggles of a young woman caught in the unpleasantries of urban working-class life. *Los pazos de Ulloa* (1886; *The Son of the Bondwoman,* 1908; also known as *The House of Ulloa,* 1992) and *La madre naturaleza* (1887; mother nature), her best-known novels, are somewhat idealized portraits of lusty, earthy conflicts between the idle aristocracy and the greedy, rural working class. The themes of sometimes illicit sexual behavior and class conflicts dominate *Insolación* (1889; *Midsummer Madness,* 1907) and *Morriña* (1889; *Morriña: Homesickness,* 1891), but in the later novels, such as *La quimera* (1905; the chimera) and *La sirena negra* (1908; the black siren), Pardo Bazán's perspective shifted to one of more conservative and religious ideology.

The career of Clarín was also established primarily through his activities as a literary critic, but his personality was more serene and his public image more that of an intellectual, humanistic spokesman for the liberal consciousness. Except for his elegant and moving narrative *Su único hijo* (1890; *His Only Son,* 1970), Clarín's only

novel was *La regenta,* a vast panorama of life in a provincial capital developed around the interior conflict of Ana Ozores, a young woman married to a much older man and tempted by her sexual attraction to her priest and the local playboy. Clarín's judicious and subtly satiric portrait of the manners and mores of Spanish society is rivaled in excellence and perceptivity only by the *novelas contemporáneas* of Pérez Galdós.

BENITO PÉREZ GALDÓS

Since the death of Pérez Galdós in 1920, the general reading public of Spain has been more familiar with his historical novels, the *Episodios nacionales* (1873-1912; national episodes), than with his realistic novels of contemporary urban society, the *novelas españolas contemporáneas* (contemporary Spanish novels), although these have always received more serious attention from scholars. The forty-six *episodios* form a fictionalized history of Spain's recent past, from the Battle of Trafalgar in 1805 to the Restoration of the Bourbon monarchy in 1874. While these are historical novels, they are somewhat unusual in that all the principal characters are fictional personages whose lives are intertwined with historical figures and events to a greater or lesser degree, depending on the particular novel. Throughout the *episodios,* which Pérez Galdós published at the amazing rate of from one to five per year from 1873 to 1879 and again from 1898 to 1912, the recent past is revealed as primarily a struggle between two opposing ideologies, the traditional Carlist point of view and the progressive, liberal ideas that led to the revolution of 1868 and the establishment of the First Republic in 1873. In contrast to the development of the historical novel in Spain and elsewhere, Pérez Galdós's *episodios* are very much a part of the realistic fictional mode that dominated the second half of the nineteenth century. While they are somewhat more ideologically directed than the *novelas españolas contemporáneas,* they lack the nostalgic idealization of the past evident in most historical fiction before Pérez Galdós.

After the thesis novels of the 1870's, which usually are referred to as Pérez Galdós's *novelas de la primera época* (novels of the first period), the novelistic development of Pérez Galdós changed dramatically. With *La desheredada* (1881; *The Disinherited Lady,* 1957),

Pérez Galdós began what eventually became an all-encompassing portrait of urban middle-class life in Madrid. The twenty-eighth novel, *Casandra* (1905), is usually considered the end of the series, because Pérez Galdós's last two novels—*El caballero encantado* (1909; the enchanted knight) and *La razón de la sinrazón* (1915; the reason of nonreason)—are markedly different and so peculiar that they are often disregarded as unfortunate postscripts to a remarkable career.

Pérez Galdós was known for his liberal tendencies, as indicated by the title of the first biography published in English, H. Chonon Berkowitz's *Benito Pérez Galdós: Spanish Liberal Crusader* (1948). The label of liberal, however, must be understood in the context of the last decades of the nineteenth century. Pérez Galdós's novels are not primarily political, and they certainly are not radical in their treatment of middle-class society. They are, rather, fairly objective representations of the established institutions of urban Spain and the amazing variety of human experience that one might expect in such a diversified society. The censure of morally aberrant behavior that is evident in the work of many novelists of the century is replaced by a sympathetic understanding in novels such as *Tormento* (1884; *Torment*, 1952), *Ángel Guerra* (1890-1891), and *Tristana* (1892; English translation, 1961), which was the source of a 1970 film version by the Spanish director Luis Buñuel, who also made a film version of Pérez Galdós's *Nazarín* (1895; the Nazarene) in 1958. In novel after novel, Pérez Galdós exposed with masterfully subtle irony the hypocrisies and foibles of the middle class.

Whether he was portraying the unfortunate plight of a mediocre bureaucrat fired from his job with only months to go before acquiring a retirement pension in *Miau* (1888; English translation, 1963) or the excruciating task of a pretentious housewife trying to solve the riddle of bourgeois society—how to get away with spending ten times what one earns—in *La de Bringas* (1884; *The Spendthrifts*, 1951), Pérez Galdós maintained a congenial and benevolent narrative voice. Through his consummate ability to give the impression that his narrative is more objective than it in fact is, Pérez Galdós creates characters who reveal themselves as they really are. The variety and complexity of their aspirations, of their admirable spirit or deplorable lack of it, of

their naïveté or cynical wisdom are evident in all of Pérez Galdós's contemporary novels, but more so in his two longest works, *Fortunata y Jacinta* (1886-1887; *Fortunata and Jacinta: Two Stories of Married Women*, 1973) and the Torquemada cycle (published in English translation as *Torquemada* in 1986)—*Torquemada en la hoguera* (1889; *Torquemada in the Flames*, 1956), *Torquemada en la cruz* (1893; *Torquemada's Cross*, 1973), *Torquemada en el purgatorio* (1894; Torquemada in purgatory), and *Torquemada y San Pedro* (1895; Torquemada and Saint Peter). The epic history of Fortunata, an earthy, uneducated young woman from the slums of Madrid, and Jacinta, a respectable, middle-class woman, both in love with the same errant playboy, is one of the most extraordinary novels of the European realist tradition. The story of Francisco Torquemada, a moneylender of questionable social origin who establishes himself as a prominent member of the new upper middle class through his financial dexterity and his marriage to an impoverished aristocrat, is in some ways the most important fictional work of Pérez Galdós. At no other point did he explore so thoroughly the essence of the nineteenth century social phenomenon of the dependence of respectability on the acquisition of material wealth. It is significant that Pérez Galdós dominated the development of the realistic novel in the last decades of the nineteenth century, for he created a vast body of fiction that exemplifies all that the realistic tradition in fiction has, in retrospect, been judged to represent—an artistic creation through which the varied truths of nineteenth century urban existence are revealed.

Generation of '98

At the beginning of the twentieth century, several nineteenth century novelists, such as Pérez Galdós, Pardo Bazán, and Palacio Valdés, were still active, and there were others whose principal work retained the tone and the concerns of the late nineteenth century. Vicente Blasco Ibáñez (1867-1928), after the enormous success of naturalistic novels such as *La barraca* (1898; *The Cabin*, 1917) and *Cañas y barro* (1902; *Reeds and Mud*, 1928), turned to the anti-German wartime novels that became popular in Spain and abroad—*Los cuatro jinetes del Apocalipsis* (1916; *The Four Horsemen of the Apocalypse*, 1918) and *Mare Nostrum* (1918; English translation, 1919). The ultraconservative Catholic novelist Ricardo León (1877-1943) continued the tradition of the thesis novel with *Casta de hidalgos* (1908; *A Son of the Hidalgos*, 1921) and *El amore de los amores* (1917; *The Wisdom of Sorrow*, 1951), and Concha Espina de la Serna (1877-1955) published *La esfinge maragata* (1914; *Mariflor*, 1924) and *El metal de los muertos* (1920; the metal of the dead), novels characterized by an unusual combination of subjective sentimentality and social protest in response to the deplorable conditions of the life of the working classes.

While these and other novelists cultivated a wide reading public, the prose fiction that is recognized as of extraordinary importance was produced by another group of writers, many of whom formed a sort of informal literary alliance that came to be called the Generation of '98. These novelists, poets, dramatists, and essayists held two things in common—their attempts at innovation in their literary work and a concern for the regeneration of Spain after the humiliating defeat suffered in the Spanish-American War in 1898. The second of these concerns—the quest for a rebirth through a spiritual awakening and an affirmation of authentic, individual values—was the subject of much essayistic and journalistic writing, and it passed into the fiction of the period, usually as a subtle ideological base rather than as an overt expression. A concurrent movement in Spanish American literature that cultivated a conscious aestheticism through radical innovations in prose and poetry, *Modernismo*, was related to the artistic concerns of the writers of the Generation of '98 and had considerable influence on their search for innovative expressive forms.

Certain novelists of the period, such as Miguel de Unamuno y Jugo (1864-1936), Pío Baroja (1872-1956), Azorín (pseudonym of José Martínez Ruiz, 1873-1967), and Ramón Pérez de Ayala (1880-1962), were clearly participants in the ideological and artistic Generation of '98, according to the three following prerequisites aptly defined by the British Hispanist Donald L. Shaw:

> participation in a personal quest for renewed ideals and beliefs; interpretation of the problem of Spain in related terms, i.e., as a problem of mentality, rather than as political or economic and social; and acceptance of the role of creative writing primarily as an instrument for the examination of these problems.

The other major novelist of the time, Ramón María del Valle-Inclán (1866-1936), seemed disinterested in the "Spanish problem," although the satiric observation of Spanish society in many of his works indicates that his interest was greater than suggested by the lack of direct, soul-searching statements that characterize the novels, plays, poems, and essays of other writers of the Generation of '98. Valle-Inclán's interest was primarily aesthetic, however, and his first important novels, the four exotic *Sonatas*—*Sonata de primavera* (1904; spring sonata), *Sonata de estío* (1903; summer sonata), *Sonata de otoño* (1902; autumn sonata), and *Sonata de invierno* (1905; winter sonata), which were published together in English as *The Pleasant Memoirs of the Marquis de Bradomín: Four Sonatas* (1924)—show a marked influence of *Modernismo* in their apparent indifference to questions of morality and their emphasis on the development of pure aesthetic artifice. Valle-Inclán's later novels, notably *Tirano Banderas: Novela de tierra caliente* (1926; *The Tyrant: A Novel of Warm Lands*, 1929) and *El ruedo ibérico* (1927-1958; the Iberian arena)—*La corte de los milagros* (1927; the court of miracles), *Viva mi dueño* (1928; long live my master), and *Baza de espadas* (serialized 1932, published 1958; spade trick)—present a bitter censure of all levels of Spanish society, both rural and urban, through an aesthetic distortion achieved by a systematic deformation of the characters and the milieu. This type of fictional narrative, which Valle-Inclán called earlier in his career the *esperpento* (distorted mirage), anticipated the *tremendismo* of the post-Spanish Civil War novel initiated by Camilo José Cela (1916-2002).

Azorín, who adopted his pseudonym from the name of the protagonist of his early novel *La voluntad* (1902; the will), was obsessed for a short period with the problem of the struggle between thought and action, a major preoccupation of the Generation of '98. *La voluntad* develops the alternatives of acceptance of nihilism or resignation to the Nietzschean doctrine of eternal recurrence. The anguish of *La voluntad* became a quiet resignation mixed with nostalgia for the past in *Antonio Azorín* (1903) and *Las confesiones de un pequeño filósofo* (1904; confessions of a little philosopher). In later novels, such as *Don Juan* (1922; English translation, 1923) and *Doña Ines* (1925), the emphasis remained on a frustrated resignation in the face of time and its destructive power. The last novels of Azorín, written after 1927, were experimental departures from the traditions of realism, but they are generally regarded by critics as being more ambitious than successful.

The most astounding novelist of the early twentieth century, for the sheer volume of his work if not for its artistic accomplishment, was Pío Baroja, whose more than fifty novels form a fictional document of modern Spanish society equaled only by the novels of Pérez Galdós. Baroja is indeed a curious case. From 1901, the year of his first significant novel, *La casa de Aizgorri* (the house of Aizgorri), to his last novels in the 1950's, his novelistic technique and the ideological bases of his work remained essentially unchanged. The style is simple, direct, and unadorned by the aesthetic mannerisms that characterize at least some of the work of almost every major twentieth century novelist. The ideological vision is clear throughout his work, and on it is founded his early trilogy *La lucha por la vida* (1904; *The Struggle for Life*, 1922-1924)—*La busca* (1904; *The Quest*, 1922), *Mala hierba* (1904; *Weeds*, 1923), and *Aurora roja* (1904; *Red Dawn*, 1924). Life is a struggle for survival, and only the fittest survive through the only remedy that exists for the inevitable *abulia*, or lack of will—individual action, action without aim, finality, or social implications of any kind. Any hint of meaning in life, any emotion—love, for example—is simply a *mentira vital* (vital lie) that enables the individual to bear the truth of the lack of meaning in the world. The intellect destroys illusions, as Sacha realizes in *El mundo es ansí* (1912; the world is thus), and action is the only alternative to the paralysis of the will that leads to the disillusionment and suicide of Andrés Hurtado in *El árbol de la ciencia* (1911; *The Tree of Knowledge*, 1928).

Baroja wrote what at first seems to be a variety of fiction—adventure novels, historical novels, biographical and autobiographical fiction—but his approach scarcely changed as he moved from one to the other. Some are dominated by narrated action, and some are made up almost entirely of conversations in which his characters reveal their own manifestations of the conflict of the intellect and the emotions. Baroja's strongest trait is his ability to evoke a sense of the physical atmosphere through a careful choice of details. It is perhaps not sur-

prising that Baroja had many admirers, including Cela, who asserted that the entire twentieth century Spanish novel stems from Baroja, and Ernest Hemingway (1899-1961), who declined the invitation to serve as a pallbearer at Baroja's funeral, claiming to be unworthy of the honor.

The truly monumental figure of the Generation of '98 was Miguel de Unamuno y Jugo, essayist, poet, dramatist, philosopher, philologist, and novelist. Partly because of the enormous prestige that he had acquired by the first years of the twentieth century, he was unofficially designated as the father of the Generation of '98. After his first attempt at fiction, *Paz en la guerra* (1897; *Peace in War*, 1983), his novels represented an extraordinary break with the realist tradition of the nineteenth century and embodied the spiritual and ontological anguish that characterized much of the work of the early twentieth century Spanish writers, as well as the existentialist writings of French authors such as Jean-Paul Sartre (1905-1980) and Albert Camus (1913-1960). The scene in *Niebla* (1914; *Mist*, 1929) in which the despairing hero Augusto Pérez confronts the author Unamuno and asserts his independence from him is frequently cited as an important precursor of the techniques of the Italian playwright Luigi Pirandello (1867-1936). This scene is equaled in its fantastic and ridiculous but serious implications only by the novel's prologue, written by another character in the novel, Víctor Goti, who calls Unamuno a liar, and by the epilogue, written by Augusto Pérez's dog.

This "game of fiction," as Unamuno's narrative tricks have been called, has serious existentialist implications that Unamuno continued to explore in *Abel Sánchez: Una historia de pasión* (1917; *Abel Sánchez*, 1947), a fascinating version of the Cain and Abel story. It is a complex history of ontological envy, developed through a simple, straightforward narrative interspersed with fragments of Joaquín's (Cain's) confessional journal and a suggestion that the entire story is a novelistic text written by Abel's son. Unamuno further questioned existence and its relationship to fictional characters in the strange, autobiographical *Cómo se hace una novela* (1927; *How to Make a Novel*, 1976) and *La novela de don Sandalio, jugador de ajedrez* (1930; the novel of Don Sandalio, chess player). Unamuno's last novel, which is in a sense a fictionalization of *Del sentimiento trágico de la vida en los hombres y en los pueblos* (1913; *The Tragic Sense of Life in Men and Peoples*, 1921), his famous treatise on the conflict of faith and reason, was *San Manuel Bueno, mártir* (1931; *Saint Manuel Bueno, Martyr*, 1956). Again Unamuno plays with fiction in a Cervantine fashion, as the novel, which is the confessional memoir of a young woman who suspects that her priest does not believe in eternal life, turns out to be a manuscript found by a fictionalized Unamuno who claims to have only edited it for publication. Unamuno's fiction was a radical departure from the realist tradition, for at almost no point did it attempt to objectively portray contemporary historical reality. It did, however, transform the novel into what it would be throughout much of the twentieth century, a means of investigating and reflecting on the question of human existence.

Ramón Pérez de Ayala, like Unamuno, began his career with a novel in the realist tradition, *Troteras y danzaderas* (1913; trotting and dancing around), and then began to experiment with more innovative narrative devices. His *Prometeo, Luz de domingo, La caída de los Limones: Tres novelas poemáticas de la vida española* (1916; *Prometheus, Sunday Sunlight, The Fall of the House of Limón: Three Poematic Novels of Spanish Life*, 1920) are not poetic in the usual sense, but grotesque, brutal distortions of the literary legends of Prometheus and Odysseus (*Prometheus*), of the daughters of the Spanish epic hero El Cid (*Sunday Sunlight*), and of the Spanish conquistadores (*The Fall of the House of Limón*). *La pata de la raposa* (1912; *The Fox's Paw*, 1924), *Belarmino y Apolonio* (1921; *Belarmino and Apolonio*, 1931, 1990) and, to a lesser extent, the 1923 novel published in two parts, *Luna de miel, luna de hiel* and *Los trabajos de Urbano y Simona* (published together in English translation as *Honeymoon, Bittermoon*, 1972), create complex situations of varied perspectives on single realities. The two final novels of Pérez de Ayala, published in 1926, *Tigre Juan* and *El curandero de su honra* (combined in English translation as *Tiger Juan*, 1933), are generally considered to be his finest accomplishments. As a restatement in Freudian terms of the story of Don Juan and the theme of honor and sexual fidelity so pervasive during the Golden Age, these novels are further manifestations of Pérez de Ayala's penchant for creating fiction from the legends and classics of early Spanish literature.

Three other novelists, contemporaries of the writers of the Generation of '98 but lacking achievements as substantial as those of Unamuno, Baroja, and Azorín, were Gabriel Miró (1879-1949), Ramón Gómez de la Serna (1888-1963), and Benjamín Jarnés (1888-1949). Miró's reputation among literary scholars has grown over the years, but his refined aestheticism and his refusal to turn his novels into topical studies of the "Spanish problem" limited the popular appeal of his work in the early part of the twentieth century. Much of his prose work consisted of collections of short pieces, and his novelistic production was limited to four penetrating psychological novels about the complexities of human behavior, *Las cerezas del cementerio* (1910; the cherries of the cemetery), *El abuelo del rey* (1915; the king's grandfather), *Nuestro Padre San Daniel* (1921; *Our Father San Daniel*, 1930), and *El obispo leproso* (1926; *The Leper Bishop,* 2008), in which Miró evoked the experience of provincial life in Spain in an elegant narrative style.

Gómez de la Serna, quite in contrast to Miró, created for himself a significant reputation as the creator of the *greguería*, a form of epigrammatic statement made up of witty, surprising, and often trivial metaphors. Some of his novels, such as *El doctor inverosímil* (1914; the unbelievable doctor), seem to be little more than collections of *greguerías*, and only his novel about the relationship of the game of fiction to human existence, *El novelista* (1923; the novelist), is of particular interest. Eight of his novellas were published in English translation under the title *Eight Novellas* in 2005. Jarnés was a much more substantial novelist, with an ideological perspective that recalls Unamuno and an elegant, elaborately cultivated style similar to Miró's. There is much introspective concern in his texts for the creative act of narrative observation and for the meaning of existence. Jarnés's unconventional narrative techniques in novels such as *Locura y muerte de nadie* (1929; madness and death of a nobody) and *Teoría del zumbel* (1930; theory of the top-string) made his work too esoteric for a general audience. His later work—*Lo rojo y lo azul: Homenaje a Stendhal* (1932; the red and the blue: homage to Stendhal) and *Venus dinámica* (1943; dynamic

Venus)—is more conventional, with a more traditional approach to plot and characterization.

THE CIVIL WAR AND THE FRANCO ERA

The Spanish Civil War (1936-1939), a bloody conflict between the conservative Nationalists and the liberal Republican forces that led to the establishment of the dictatorship of Francisco Franco (1892-1975), had an extraordinary effect on the history of the twentieth century Spanish novel. Many of the outstanding literary figures went into exile and produced their most important novels in countries other than Spain. Also, the war experience became the material with which the novel dealt, in much the same way that the social malaise resulting from the disaster of 1898 had become the subject matter for novels in the early part of the century.

The two novelists who established themselves most successfully as representatives of postwar fiction are Camilo José Cela (1916-2002) and Juan Goytisolo (born 1931). Cela's *La familia de Pascual Duarte* (1942; *The Family of Pascual Duarte*, 1946, 1964) initiated the literary vogue of *tremendismo*, a pessimistic cultivation of the shocking, grotesque aspects of human experience. A later novel, *La colmena* (1951; *The Hive*, 1953), portrays the wretchedness of life in postwar Madrid through multiple narrative perspectives. Goytisolo's early novels, *Juego de manos* (1954; *The Young Assassins*, 1959) and *Fiestas* (1958; English translation, 1960), attacked the repression and psychological deprivation of Franco's Spain in a conventional narrative style typical of social realism. His principal contribution to the innovative postwar novel is his trilogy of exile—*Señas de identidad* (1966; *Marks of Identity*, 1969), *Reinvindicación del conde Don Julián* (1970; *Count Julian*, 1974), and *Juan sin tierra* (1975; *John the Landless*, 1975). The first of the trilogy is a fictionalized autobiographical account of the exile's return to Barcelona that makes use of diverse narrative techniques and multiple points of view but remains a rather conventional novel for its time. The second and third novels of the trilogy, however, are bitter, grotesque experimental narratives that attempt to convey an overwhelming repulsion and an obsession with the destruction of every traditional value of society. Over the course of his career, Goytisolo has published more than two dozen works of fiction. His later novels

include *La saga de los Marx* (1993; *The Marx Family Saga*, 1999) and *Carajicomedia: De Fray Bugeo Montesino y otros pája de vario plumaje y pluma* (2000; *A Cock-Eyed Comedy: Starring Friar Bugeo Montesino and Other Faeries of Motley Feather and Fortune*, 2002).

Other postwar novelists experimented with narrative techniques, conveying an equally pessimistic view of Spanish society in a less shocking way than Goytisolo. *El Jarama* (1956; *The One Day of the Week*, 1962), by Rafael Sánchez Ferlosio (born 1927), and *Tiempo de silencio* (1962; *Time of Silence*, 1964), by Luis Martín-Santos (1924-1964), are portraits of Spanish society that are made up of fragmented, anecdotal mosaics, examples of a kind of social realist subject matter transformed through experimental narrative devices.

Luis Goytisolo (born 1935), the brother of Juan Goytisolo, first attracted critical attention with *Las afueras* (1958; the suburbs), a novel that portrays postwar Catalonia in terms of the contradictory forces at work in the economic and class structures of society. Gonzálo Torrente Ballester (1910-1999), a professor of history and literature and well-known drama critic, produced an impressive series of successful novels beginning with *El señor llega* (1957; the master comes), many of which are unusual narratives about the process of novelistic invention. For his most ambitious and successful work, *La saga/fuga de J. B.* (1972; the legend/flight of J. B.), Torrente Ballester won the coveted Crítica Prize, only one of many literary awards that he received during his career.

José María Gironella (1917-2003) and Miguel Delibes (born 1920), two novelists who remained in Spain during and after the wartime experience, represent two very different trends in fiction. Gironella's epic war trilogy—*Los cipreses creen en Dios* (1953; *The Cypresses Believe in God*, 1955), *Un millón de muertos* (1961; *One Million Dead*, 1963), and *Ha estallado la paz* (1966; *Peace After War*, 1969)—is among the most widely read accounts of the Spanish Civil War. Delibes is a less popular novelist, but he is respected for his elegant style, his sympathetic portrayal of the simple, natural life of the country, and the gradual evolution of his work. *El camino* (1950; *The Path*, 1961) is a charming story of rural society. *Mi idolatrado hijo Sisí* (1953;

my beloved son Sisí) is a cynical but delicate satire of middle-class aspirations. *Cinco horas con Mario* (1966; *Five Hours with Mario*, 1988) is an experiment in interior monologue, and *Parábola del náufrago* (1969; *The Hedge*, 1983), a technically innovative allegorical fantasy. *El hereje* (1998; *The Heretic*, 2006) is a dense historical novel that is built out of dialogue rather than narrative.

Some of the best postwar fiction was produced by a group of novelists who were adults at the time of the war and remained in exile after 1939. Ramón José Sender (1902-1982), the only one of these to achieve wide recognition, produced a vast amount of fiction beginning with the appearance of his first successful novel, *Imán* (1930; *Earmarked for Hell*, 1934; also known as *Pro Patria*, 1935). Sender's work is characterized by an Unamunian preoccupation with the meaning of human existence. In novels such as *Crónica del alba* (1942-1966, 3 volumes; *Before Noon*, volume 1, 1957) and *La esfera* (1947, 1969; *The Sphere*, 1949), published first in 1939 as *Proverbio de la muerte* (proverb of death) and subsequently published in an expanded version with the new title, he achieved a distinctive fusion of realistic and fantastic techniques.

Antonio Barea (1897-1957), Francisco Ayala (born 1906), and Max Aub (1903-1972), the other exiled novelists of considerable significance, did not match the volume of work that Sender produced, nor did they enjoy his success. Barea's *La forja de un rebelde* (1941-1944; *The Forging of a Rebel*, 1941-1946) is a fictionalized autobiographical memoir of the prewar and war years in Spain. Ayala, a prolific novelist as well as a short-story writer, created a brutal, cruel portrait of life in a fictional Spanish American republic in *Muertes de perro* (1958; *Death as a Way of Life*, 1964) and its sequel, *El fondo del vaso* (1962; the bottom of the glass). Ayala's *El jardín de las delicias* (1971; the garden of delights), the source of the 1970 film by the Spanish director Carlos Saura (born 1932), is a dazzling display of novelistic art, a mosaic of references to the painting by Hieronymus Bosch (1450-1516) that forms the narrative of the psychic suffering of a twentieth century industrialist left paralyzed after an automobile accident.

The most esoteric of these novelists was the avant-garde writer Max Aub. His cycle of novels about the war experience, *El laberinto mágico* (1943-1968; the magic labyrinth), is a complex tapestry of fragmented characterizations and conversations that together form an interpretation and analysis of the psychological manifestations of wartime experience. Aub's most unusual work is *Jusep Torres Campalans* (1958; English translation, 1962), a painstakingly detailed biography of a fictitious artist and friend of Picasso. As if following the tradition of Unamuno, Aub evoked through this "biography" questions of the relationship between art and life.

During the late 1940's and the 1950's, a new generation of novelists began to emerge who were dedicated to a neorealist fictional mode as a means of exploring the nature of the human condition, particularly as it is manifested in a repressive society. Ignacio Aldecoa (1925-1969), author of *El fulgor y la sangre* (1954; lightning and blood), was an active stimulus to this revival of the novel through his journalistic criticism and his association with other writers such as Sánchez Ferlosio, Jesús Fernández Santos (1926-1988), Juan Goytisolo, José Luis Castillo Puche (1919-2004), and Carmen Martín Gaite (1925-2000).

A striking feature of the period after the Spanish Civil War was the unusual number of women who established themselves as successful novelists. In 1944, Carmen Laforet (1921-2004) won the prestigious Nadal Prize for her neorealist novel of tedium and repression, *Nada* (English translation, 1958). The prominence achieved by Laforet, Martín Gaite, Dolores Medio (1911-1996), and Ana María Matute (born 1926), whose *Primera memoria* (1960; *School of the Sun*, 1963) also was awarded the Nadal Prize, is a significant phenomenon, given the disadvantaged position of women during the Franco era. Of these writers, Martín Gaite has received the most lasting and serious attention from critics for works such as *El balneario* (1954; the spa), *Ritmo lento* (1963; slow rhythm), and *El cuarto de atrás* (1978; *The Back Room*, 1983), *La reina de las nieves* (1994; *The Farewell Angel*, 1999), and *Lo raro es vivir* (1996; *Living's the Strange Thing*, 2004).

While this group of women novelists enjoyed considerable success, the Spanish novel of the 1970's and 1980's was dominated by men, particularly Juan Goytisolo, Juan Marsé (born 1933), and Juan Benet (1927-1993)—the novelist who, according to some critics, established the new direction in fiction evident in Goytisolo's *Count Julian* and in Delibes's *The Hedge*. Benet's trilogy consisting of *Volverás a Región* (1967; *Return to Región*, 1985), *Una meditación* (1970; *A Meditation*, 1982), and *Una tumba* (1971; a tomb) is the complete antithesis of the realist tradition of Pérez Galdós and the neorealist tradition of the postwar novel. The narrative style is so difficult that the work seems almost unintelligible at first, though the identity of the characters and the details of the plot begin to emerge toward the end of the first novel through various techniques that reveal the text as an exaggerated evocation of memory. Marsé's first success was *Últimas tardes con Teresa* (1966; last afternoons with Teresa), a kind of "suburban" novel characterized by a blend of psychological and objective realism. The irony of Marsé's tone, however, limits the novel's tendency toward social realism. Marsé also attracted considerable critical attention for *Si te dicen que caí* (1973; *The Fallen*, 1976), a narrative of ambiguous accounts of the war years woven into the details of social existence in postwar Spain, and for *El embrujo de Shanghai* (1993; *Shanghai Nights,* 2006) and *Rabos de lagartija* (2000; *Lizard Tails,* 2003). He won the Cervantes Prize in 2008.

As the dictatorship ended with the death of Francisco Franco in 1975, the Spanish novel gradually ceased to be a discourse concentrated on a response to the circumstances of life under the existing totalitarian regime. It became, rather, primarily a consideration of the various forces at work in society as the post-Franco struggle for power began to take shape.

THE NOVEL AFTER FRANCO

The Spanish novel from 1950 to the end of the Franco regime in 1975 was dominated by two significantly different trends that have characterized the novel throughout its history. The neorealist mode is a continuation of the attempt of prose fiction to create an aesthetic experience that parallels the varied experiences of historical, "real" human existence. The other trend, represented by the diverse textual experimentation of the more innovative novelists such as Juan Goytisolo and Benet, represents the attempt to portray the authentic nature of human experience more effectively through a nontraditional narrative.

These two tendencies in prose fiction continued to be apparent in the novel after 1975, but there is evidence of a preference for a less complex narrative style. One of the manifestations of this trend is the emergence of a significant number of novelists working in the genre of detective or crime fiction. The first novel of Eduardo Mendoza (born 1943), *La verdad sobre el caso Savolta* (1975; *The Truth About the Savolta Case*, 1992), is an example of the genre, as are many of the novels of Lourdes Ortiz (born 1943), Benet's *El aire de un crimen* (1980; scent of a crime), and *Visión del ahogado* (1977; a drowned man's vision), by Juan José Millás (born 1946). Manuel Vázquez Montalbán (1939-2003) cultivated the genre with a series of novels about his fictional hero Pepe Carvalho, a bodyguard for U.S. president John F. Kennedy turned detective. Among his many novels of this type, all characterized by a perverse sense of humor unusual in the Spanish fiction of the period, are *Yo maté a Kennedy* (1972; I killed Kennedy), *Los mares del sur* (1979; *Southern Seas*, 1986), and *El delantero centro fue asesinado al atardecer* (1988; *Offside*, 1996).

Many of the novelists who established themselves before and during the Franco era continued to publish in the period after 1975. Cela's *Mazurka para dos muertos* (1983; polka for two dead people) and Delibes's *Los santos inocentes* (1981; the innocent saints) are evidence of the continued vitality of the older writers. Cela won the Nobel Prize in Literature in 1989, "for a rich and intensive prose, which with restrained compassion forms a challenging vision of man's vulnerability." The principal novelists of the 1960's and 1970's, such as Juan and Luis Goytisolo, Benet, Marsé, and Martín Gaite, continued to enjoy considerable success and enhanced their reputations as significant figures in the history of the Spanish novel.

In the last decade of the twentieth century and the beginning of the twenty-first, decisive changes were occurring in the novel, not so much in terms of narrative form as in ideology. After the end of the Franco era, the principal discourse of the novel gradually ceased to be a dialogue with the social forms that thrived under the totalitarian regime. It became instead a response to the emerging ideological factions of the new democratic society. The younger novelists, such as Lourdes Ortiz, Rosa Montero (born 1951), Antonio Muñoz Molina (born 1956), Esther Tusquets (born 1936), and Terenci Moix (1943-2003), produced numerous novels that explore the influences of popular culture and the various conflicting ideologies (sexist, fascist, communist, capitalist) that shaped Spanish society in the late twentieth century. Muñoz Molina, who resides in the United States, set *Beltenebros* (1989; *Prince of Shadows*, 1993) in post-Civil War Madrid. After he moved to New York, several of his works were published in English translation, including *Beatus ille* (1986; *A Manuscript of Ashes*, 2008), set near the end of Franco's dictatorship; *El invierno en Lisboa* (1987; *Winter in Lisbon*, 1999), about a jazz pianist; *Sefarad* (2001; *Sepharad*, 2003), whose narrator is a man in Madrid nostalgic for the village in which he grew up; and *En ausencia de Blanca* (1999; *In Her Absence*, 2006), about a Spanish civil servant.

Tusquets is a leading feminist voice in Spanish fiction, and her work is marked by powerful images of female and lesbian sexuality. *El mismo mar de todos los veranos* (1978; *The Same Sea as Every Summer*, 1990), the first novel in a trilogy, was one of the first Spanish lesbian novels. The protagonist in *Para no volver* (1985; *Never to Return*, 1999) is a straight middle-aged woman undergoing psychoanalysis. In *Con la miel en los labios* (1997; with honey on the lips), Tusquets depicts the struggles of student activists and lesbians during the last years of Franco's rule. Catalan writer Moix, a self-educated anarchist, published eleven novels, most of them criticizing oppression under Franco, especially as experienced by gay men. His works have sold millions of copies in Spain, but he has remained virtually unknown outside the country. His best-known works include *No digas que fue un sueño* (1986; say not that it was a dream) and *El amargo don de la belleza* (1996; the bitter gift of beauty).

From its beginning, Spanish prose fiction has portrayed the circumstances of human existence in terms of the surrounding reality and the predominant ideological perspectives of the period in which it was created. The novelistic narrative of the late twentieth century period was characterized by considerations of issues that were suppressed either by official governmental actions or by societal taboos during the earlier years of the century. The novel of this era posed questions about concepts of gender, homosexuality, psychoanalysis, and the dominant power structures of society, questions that often were presented in terms of the conflict between the prevailing ideologies of Francoist Spain and those gaining prominence in the Spain of the new democracy. Prose fiction continues to be marked by the opposing tendencies that have characterized the genre from its beginning, the struggle between realist representation and various experimental, innovative modes of portraying the world. In its diversity of form and its singularity of purpose—the representation of human experience—the complex genre of linguistic and literary art that is the novel in Spain is heir to the tradition of Cervantes.

Gilbert Smith
Updated by Cynthia A. Bily

BIBLIOGRAPHY

Charnon-Deutsch, Lou. *Gender and Representation: Women in Spanish Realist Fiction*. Philadelphia: J. Benjamins, 1990. Significant study addresses the sexual polarization of nineteenth century Spanish society and the patriarchal values and ideologies of gender inscribed in the fictional discourses of the major novelists, including José María de Pereda, Juan Valera, Clarín, and Benito Pérez Galdós.

Close, Anthony. *The Romantic Approach to Don Quixote*. New York: Cambridge University Press, 1978. Critical overview that had considerable repercussions in Hispanic studies. Presents a general discussion of the Romantic interpretation of *Don Quixote de la Mancha*, from the time of the Romantic movement through the realist period, the Generation of '98, and twentieth century criticism.

Dunn, Peter N. *Spanish Picaresque Fiction: A New Literary History*. Ithaca, N.Y.: Cornell University Press, 1993. Significant work by a prominent Hispanist presents a study of the reading public and the cultural implications of the picaresque form of fiction.

Gies, David Thatcher. *The Cambridge History of Spanish Literature*. New York: Cambridge University Press, 2004. Comprehensive history of Spanish literature covers the years from the early Middle Ages to the early twenty-first century. Includes a chronology of Spanish history, literature, and art.

Gold, Hazel. *The Reframing of Realism: Galdós and the Discourses of the Nineteenth Century Novel*.

Durham, N.C.: Duke University Press, 1993. Effective study examines the novels of Pérez Galdós from the perspective of narrative frame theory. Discusses his work in the context of the nineteenth century novel.

Johnson, Carroll B. *Don Quixote: The Quest for Modern Fiction*. Boston: Twayne, 1990. Provides a general introduction to the historical context of Cervantes' novel and the characteristics of the book-reading public of the seventeenth century.

Landeira, Ricardo. *The Modern Spanish Novel, 1898-1936*. Boston: Twayne, 1985. Introductory study covers the period from the Generation of '98 to the beginning of the Spanish Civil War in 1936, including discussion of the works of Vicente Blasco Ibáñez, Miguel de Unamuno y Jugo, Pío Baroja, Ramón María del Valle-Inclán, and Ramón Pérez de Ayala.

Moss, Joyce. *Spanish and Portuguese Literatures and Their Times: The Iberian Peninsula*. Detroit, Mich.: Gale Group, 2002. Analyzes fifty works in about ten pages each, tracing the connections between the works and the political and social contexts in which they were written.

Sánchez Conejero, Cristina, ed. *Spanishness in the Spanish Novel and Cinema of the Twentieth-Twenty-first Century*. Newcastle, England: Cambridge Scholars, 2007. Collection of essays focuses on authors—including Manuel Rico, Juan Goytisolo, and lesser-known writers—whose works explore the meanings of Spanish and Iberian identity.

Schumm, Sandra J. *Reflection in Sequence: Novels by Spanish Women, 1944-1988*. London: Associated University Press, 1999. Examines seven novels whose protagonists struggle for self-realization in a restrictive Spanish society.

Solé-Leris, Amadeu. *The Spanish Pastoral Novel*. Boston: Twayne, 1980. Provides a general introduction to the pastoral novel and the literary tradition of which it is a product, with considerations of the novels of Montemayor, Gil Polo, and Cervantes.

Thomas, Gareth. *The Novel of the Spanish Civil War, 1936-1975*. New York: Cambridge University Press, 1990. Discusses the portrayal of the Spanish Civil War and the conditions of exile in the novels of José María Gironella, Max Aub, Francisco Ayala, Antonio Barea, Castillo Puche, and Ana María Matute. Presents interesting considerations of the propagandistic Republican novel and the process of myth creation in Nationalist fiction.

Turner, Harriet, and Adelaida López de Martinez, eds. *The Cambridge Companion to the Spanish Novel: From 1600 to the Present*. New York: Cambridge University Press, 2003. Collection of essays by a variety of scholars covers the development of the Spanish novel from Cervantes to the modern novelists. Includes a chronology and a bibliography.

NORTH AMERICAN LONG FICTION

African American Long Fiction

Slave narratives

Nineteenth century American fiction influenced the form and content of many of the slave narratives of the time, while nineteenth and twentieth century African American fiction owes a great debt, in form and content, to the slave narrative. Thus, the development of African American fiction can be traced to nineteenth century American fiction only by way of the slave narrative.

Just as Africans arriving in the Americas staked their claims to humanity on the basis of the cultural models available to them—European Enlightenment and Christian values—so too did the first "authors" of the slave narrative model their testimonies on the Christian confessionals of Jonathan Edwards and the sentimental fiction of Harriet Beecher Stowe. Despite these debts to Puritanism and sentimentality, the best and most influential narratives transcended their origins to create an entirely new prose genre. Thus, an achievement such as Frederick Douglass's *Narrative of the Life of Frederick Douglass, an American Slave, Written by Himself* (1845) is instructive, if rare.

Because the slave narrative was, by definition, a collaborative effort between white and free black abolitionists, political or social supporters, and the slave, a great number of reputed slave narratives were outright frauds concocted by abolitionists to fan the flames of the antislavery movement or, occasionally, by proslavery forces determined to demonstrate the slaves' satisfaction with their lives. Yet even in those slave narratives that have been generally authenticated by meticulous historical research, the voice of the slave is often muffled under letters of support, prefaces, introductions, reproductions of bills of sale, and appendixes, all deployed to assure the reader of the truthfulness of the tale. Indeed, insofar as many of the slave narratives are careful to depict the slave's freedom as having been the result of the aid of sympathetic white people, the narrative moral reinforces its collage format: The story of a slave's flight to freedom is inconceivable without the support and aid of northern and, occasionally, southern whites.

Narrative of the Life of Frederick Douglass, an American Slave, Written by Himself is distinguished, however, by both its literary élan and political independence. This well-known narrative boldly rises above its encumbering supplementary materials to depict one man, one slave, fighting his way to freedom. Of course, both luck and friendly white hands play a role in Douglass's flight to freedom, just as they do in every other slave narrative. However, the thrust of Douglass's narrative is that he, and he alone, took his life into his hands and forged for himself a new destiny. This theme also was evident in Olaudah Equiano's *The Interesting Narrative of the Life of Olaudah Equiano: Or, Gustavus Vassa, the African, Written by Himself* (1789).

Such independence and bravado were not always available for enslaved African American women, as demonstrated in Harriet Jacobs's narrative, written under the pseudonym Linda Brent. *Incidents in the Life of a Slave Girl* (1861) has many parallels with Harriet E. Wilson's novel, *Our Nig: Or, Sketches from the Life of a Free Black, in a Two-Story White House, North. Showing That Slavery's Shadows Falls Even There* (1859). Wilson's protagonist, Alfrado, submits to a marriage with a fugitive slave who abandons her while she is pregnant, forcing her to work for an abusive white female employer. For Jacobs, affirming her gender means that she will be forced to submit to her sexual identity as an African American woman to escape sexual exploitation by her white master. The central psychological crisis for Jacob occurs when she decides to take a white man as a lover in order to block the predatory sexual advances of her master. For Jacobs, the submission to sexuality as a form of power over her circumstances is humiliating, but it is a humiliation redeemed, if only in part, by her choice to decide with whom she will have illicit sexual relations. Having learned that literacy is not enough to affirm and defend her humanity (her freedom), she must affirm her racial and sexual difference—her status as a black woman—by a decision that ironically ensures her identity as both a woman and a human.

The narratives escape the limitations of their origins and their utility as propaganda for the antislavery cause precisely because they emphasize specific individuality rather than a vague "humanity." That they differ in terms of gender stereotypes—physical prowess for the men, sexual wiliness for the woman—only underscores the narrow band of options available for those attempting to escape slavery. More important, Douglass and Equiano can demonstrate their humanity with a number of virile activities, while Jacobs has only one way to demonstrate her humanity: sexuality. This imbalance in the range of choices, along with the stereotypical, sentimental, and fiction-derived narrative of flight, disguise, conceal-ment, near discovery, and final freedom, orients the tra-jectory of the African American novel along lines that consistently wed identity to gender, which then orient the positions authors take on issues such as class, caste, and skin-color distinctions; individualism and integra-tion; and cultural nationalism.

Before these themes are considered, however, it is necessary to examine a subgenre of the slave narrative known as the narrative of revolt. *The Confessions of Nat Turner* (1832) is a peculiar document of some twenty pages, a reputed record of Nat Turner's descriptions of the revolt he launched against white Virginian men, women, and children in 1831. Augmented with the usual preface attesting the truthfulness of what follows, *The Confessions of Nat Turner* resembles in form the stereo-typical slave narrative. However, the witnesses in ques-tion are proslavery white men, and the content of the narrative is indeed a "confession" of the conception, planning, and execution of the revolt. This slave narra-tive is thus not an attempt to affirm the humanity of the "author." Instead there is only the justification of righ-teous violence, the inspired zealot wreaking judgment upon the sinners—that is, the slave owners. Thus, just as white abolitionists created the format of the slave narra-tive to depict the horrors of slavery, so too was *The Con-fessions of Nat Turner* created to justify not only the con-tinuation of slavery but also the ruthless suppression of the few privileges permitted selected slaves.

The Confessions of Nat Turner may well have bene-fitted the proslavery cause, but it also inspired other slave revolts, as well as the first protest novel in the Afri-can American literary tradition, *Blake: Or, The Huts of America* (serial 1859), by Martin Delany, himself an Af-rican American. *Blake* did not appear as a book until 1970, but it first ran serially in a black abolitionist news-

paper. *Blake* is a call to arms, an explicit justification for open slave revolt and the establishment of a black sover-eignty. It is, in some respects, the novelistic version of *Walker's Appeal, in Four Articles* (1830), by David Walker, judged to be so inflammatory that a large num-ber of people called for its suppression; it also allegedly cost the author his life a short time after its publication. Like *Walker's Appeal, in Four Articles*, *Blake* rejects the possibility of slaves integrating into American society. Instead, Delany imagines a black-ruled Cuba as the only viable option for the enslaved Africans. Both *The Con-fessions of Nat Turner* and *Blake* imagine violence as the only solution to slavery and link this violence to mas-culinity.

POST-RECONSTRUCTION

Francis E. W. Harper's *Iola Leroy: Or, Shadows Up-lifted* (1892), Charles Waddell Chesnutt's *The Marrow of Tradition* (1901), and Paul Laurence Dunbar's *The Sport of the Gods* (1902) represent three different reactions in the African American novel to the post-Reconstruction United States, although Harper's ideal-ized treatment of injustice, suffering, and redemption stands in marked contrast to the bitterness evident in the works by Chesnutt and Dunbar.

Harper's *Iola Leroy* is the story of a woman who is, unknown to herself and others, a mulatto (of mixed race). Iola Leroy believes she is white until the unex-pected death of her father spurs her uncle, who has long resented his brother's interracial marriage, to sell Iola and her mother separately into slavery. Aside from the search for her mother and abolitionist arguments that function as subplots, the novel focuses on Iola's court-ship by two men, one a white abolitionist doctor, the other a mulatto like herself. Though tempted by the doc-tor's offer to "pass" into white society, Iola steadfastly rejects the opportunity. Instead, she weds herself to the cause of abolition by agreeing to marry the mulatto. The novel's happy ending suggests that Harper preferred to invoke the nineteenth century sentimental novel of man-ners rather than the "tragic mulatta," a figure who had al-ready appeared in William Wells Brown's *Clotel: Or, The President's Daughter: A Narrative of Slave Life in the United States* (1853; revised as *Miralda: Or, The Beautiful Quadroon*, 1860-1861; *Clotelle: A Tale of the*

Southern States, 1864; and *Clotelle: Or, The Colored Heroine*, 1867).

On the other hand, Chesnutt's *The Marrow of Tradition* and Dunbar's *The Sport of the Gods* are much darker assessments of African American life during the so-called decades of disappointment. Based loosely on the Wilmington, North Carolina, riot of 1898, Chesnutt's novel follows the lives of several white and black characters whose unacknowledged but intertwined lives culminate in a literal "revelation" amid a murderous riot. Ostensibly a depiction of the end of Reconstruction—the riot is fomented by white people who want to "take back" their town—*The Marrow of Tradition* is also a morality tale concerning the futility of hate and violence, themes that Chesnutt links to the obsession with racial purity. For Chesnutt, miscegenation is the only viable solution to the race problem.

If Chesnutt offers some hope to his audience, Dunbar's vision of the destiny of the newly freed slaves is relentlessly desolate. *The Sport of the Gods* concerns the dissolution of a postslavery African American family forced to flee to New York City after the father is jailed on trumped-up burglary charges. Every family member ends up losing his or her moral integrity in the urban landscape; even when the parents are reunited near the end of the novel, it is clear that their lives will be cheap imitations of their shattered dreams. Dunbar's dismal vision of the urban landscape, a vision anticipated by *Our Nig*, looks forward to those novelists of the Harlem Renaissance whose portraits of city life effectively undermine any romantic notions of what it might mean to have come "up from slavery."

THE HARLEM RENAISSANCE

The concern with skin color, particularly with miscegenation, became particularly urgent during the Harlem Renaissance (1919-1929), as the possibility of an "authentic" African American culture began, however tentatively, to take shape. Insofar as the fledgling culture had to partake of the culture of its former oppressors, the tensions and arguments over who and what was, in fact, "Negro" took on a certain urgency. However, not every African American writer treated this issue with morbid seriousness. Wallace Thurman's *Infants of the Spring* (1932) is an excoriating roman à clef about the

central figures of the Harlem Renaissance. Its vicious attacks on the petty prejudices of the leading personages of the day echo themes developed in his first and most popular novel, *The Blacker the Berry* (1929), which concerns skin-color prejudice within African American culture.

Less known but in many respects a better work, George Schuyler's *Black No More: Being an Account of the Strange and Wonderful Workings of Science in the Land of the Free, A.D. 1933-1940* (1931) is a hilarious send-up of the obsession with "race advancement" among members of newly formed organizations such as the National Association for the Advancement of Colored People (NAACP) and the obsession with racial purity among members of the Ku Klux Klan. Thurman's and Schuyler's satires on race, class, and gender mock the absurdities of politicians and artists identified with the Harlem Renaissance.

James Weldon Johnson's *The Autobiography of an Ex-Coloured Man* (1912), for example, represents a logical extension of the reconciliation themes evident in the novels of Harper and Chesnutt. If, in their works, the mulatto or mulatta appears to embody the race's best chance for advancement, then passing—mulattoes and mulattas "disappearing" into white society—would obviously be the next logical step. Johnson's novel idealizes the passing motif even as it rehearses its tragedy: the mulatto as a wanderer between separate cultures, never at home in either.

At the opposite end of the spectrum is Nella Larsen. Her two novels, *Quicksand* (1928) and *Passing* (1929), contain depictions of the tragic mulatta. In *Quicksand*, Helga Crane, a mulatta never at ease among African Americans or Caucasians, marries and has children. In *Passing*, Clare Kendry is a mulatta passing for Caucasian while her friend, Irene Redfield, is both disgusted and envious of her freedom. Kendry's sudden death offers her escape from the humiliation of being unveiled as a "nigger" by her white, racist husband.

Larsen's analyses of middle-class mulattas represents an extension of Jean Toomer's *Cane* (1923), a collage of poetry and fiction centered on multiple themes in early twentieth century African American life: the juxtaposition of urban and rural lifestyles, tensions between the North and the South, and "purebred" or "mixed-blood" characteristics. As with Harper, Chesnutt, and others, Toomer links the resolution of these oppositions to the mulatto. Like Larsen, however, Toomer is not optimistic about this figure, who is shunned and scorned by both African Americans and whites.

Between Johnson's idealism and Larsen's cynicism lie authors such as Claude McKay and Zora Neale Hurston on one hand and Jessie Redmon Fauset on the other. McKay's novel *Home to Harlem* (1928) was a commercial success, which some critics, including W. E. B. Du Bois, attributed to its exotic treatment of Harlem nightlife. Richard Wright made similar criticisms of Hurston's novel *Their Eyes Were Watching God* (1937), arguing that Hurston created laughable caricatures of African Americans.

Like the novels of Larsen, Fauset's three best novels, *There Is Confusion* (1924), *Plum Bun: A Novel Without a Moral* (1928), and *The Chinaberry Tree: A Novel of American Life* (1931), concern the plight of middle- and upper-class African American women struggling with racial passing, material possessions, marital prospects, and self-worth. Unlike Larsen, and in some respects more like Johnson, Fauset delineates the pitfalls of racial confusion without the melodrama of tragedy. At the same time, Fauset's protagonists are clearly more sensitive to, and more psychologically damaged by, the perplexing anxieties of the color caste system in African American culture.

POST-RENAISSANCE REALISM

If the problem of the color caste system dominated African American fiction as a concern before and during the Great Depression, perhaps it was because of the effects of post-Reconstruction migrations of African Americans from the South to the North. Although writers such as Dunbar attempted to unmask the urban dreamscape, the struggle by so many writers to confront color prejudice among African Americans is linked to the social problems associated with mass migrations: poverty, joblessness, overcrowding, and, in the case of African Americans, class distinctions tied to the presence or absence of "white" blood. Underlying the tendency to privilege or castigate on the basis of miscegenation was a belief that becoming white was either a way to escape the stigma attached to African blood or a way

to delude oneself that white America would accept African Americans if they acted less "African."

Richard Wright's groundbreaking first novel, *Native Son* (1940), changed the terms of the debate, dramatizing the conflict between race and class. Wright's portraits of communists—the naïve Mary, the careless Jan, and the rough-hewn Max—were augmented by his negative portraits of both liberal Caucasians, such as the Daltons, and African American women, such as Bigger's mother, sister, and girlfriend. Wright's realist novel was widely criticized, and in this respect Dunbar's equally desolate, if less brutal novel, *The Sport of the Gods*, can be seen as its most immediate ancestor. A similar combination of gritty realism and broad criticism can be seen in two other writers of the period: Chester Himes and Ann Petry.

Himes's postwar work is an effective combination of the hard-boiled detective fiction of Raymond Chandler and the protest fiction of Wright. His best novel, *If He Hollers Let Him Go* (1945), is a masterful hybrid of these two genres. On one hand, as Wright does in *Native Son*, Himes compresses his story into a short time frame (four days) that allows him to explore the effects of unrelenting racism on the consciousness of his narrator-protagonist, Bob Jones. At the same time, Himes pays tribute to the detective story as Jones struggles to figure out why a Caucasian coworker has fabricated a rape charge against him. His later novels, such as *Retour en Afrique* (1964; *Cotton Comes to Harlem*, 1965), owe more to the detective genre than to the protest novel, perhaps because Himes wrote them after his expatriation to France.

Petry's fame rests primarily on the basis of her novel *The Street* (1946), the first novel by an African American woman to sell more than one million copies. While some critics have compared the novel to Wright's *Native Son* because of its intense focus on urban decay and squalor, a case could also be made for linking it to Dunbar's *The Sport of the Gods* and Hurston's pioneering *Their Eyes Were Watching God*. Just as Hurston's novel concerns Janie's triumph over the patriarchal traditions of white male racism and black male chauvinism, so, too, does Petry's novel focus on Lutie Johnson's attempts to eke out a meager living away from the brutality of her father. Like those of the mother in Dunbar's novel,

Lutie's dreams to provide for herself and her son are driven by a naïveté that drags her even further down the social ladder. If Hurston's Janie seems like an idealized role model for all women to emulate, Petry's Lutie is a grim reminder of what so many black women actually go through in their daily lives.

Compared to the grim urban realism of Wright, Himes, and Petry, the fiction of Ralph Ellison offers a way out of the morass of frustration, rebellion, defeat, and despair. *Invisible Man* (1952), Ellison's only novel published during his lifetime, has been heralded as one of the greatest American novels ever written, and it is precisely the role of "Americanism" in the work that has made it a lightning rod for political debates since its appearance.

Told in a flashback by an unnamed narrator, *Invisible Man* chronicles the misadventures of a naïve high school graduate in the grand tradition of the episodic, picaresque novel. Boiled down to its essential themes, the novel traces the gradual awakening of a potential leader who believes that the key to the salvation of his community is organized group action, the most notorious of which turns out to be the Brotherhood, a political organization loosely based on the Communist Party of America. In the epilogue, however, the narrator realizes that individualism is the answer to his, and his community's, problems, that all groups are, to one degree or another, straitjackets of intolerance.

Ellison's novel was thus read as a direct rebuke to *Native Son*, though Wright himself saw more affinities than differences between the two works. Nevertheless, Ellison was heralded as the successor to Wright, whose commitment to the communist cause, if not the Communist Party, isolated him and his later work in the context of, and fallout from, McCarthyism. Moreover, a chorus of new voices began to declaim their relevancy and militancy, a phenomenon that had the effect of elevating Wright while demoting Ellison.

The writer who not only functions as a transitional figure between the 1950's and 1960's but also inherited all the contradictions and conflicts between the two decades, represented by the trajectories of Wright's and Ellison's careers, is James Baldwin. Baldwin authored six novels, but his fame rests almost entirely on his provocative essays, especially "Everybody's Protest Novel,"

which signaled his aesthetic break from his mentor, Wright. Just as Baldwin slays his literary father in the essay, so too does his first novel, *Go Tell It on the Mountain* (1953), a depiction of the Oedipal struggle between a religious father and an unconventional young son, seem to be directed at his real-life stepfather, David Baldwin.

Baldwin's next two novels, *Giovanni's Room* (1956) and *Another Country* (1962), explore homosexuality and black pride as avenues toward individualism. More ominous, the tone of these novels is a little more high-strung than that of the first novel, and in his subsequent novels— *Tell Me How Long the Train's Been Gone* (1968), *If Beale Street Could Talk* (1974), and *Just Above My Head* (1979)—the pitch is harsh and loud, developments reflected in the essays. In one of those ironies that permeate African American literary history, Baldwin also wrote the same kind of protest novels, articles, and essays for which he criticized Wright and others. How did this happen? To answer this question, it is necessary to examine the effects that the developing Civil Rights movement, the black power spin-offs, the antiwar protests, and the Black Arts movement had on Baldwin's growth as an artist. That is, it is necessary to examine the cultural, social, and political upheavals of the 1960's and 1970's through the lenses of the African American writers who would emerge as distinctive literary voices.

THE 1960'S, 1970'S, AND 1980'S

The counterculture movements of the 1960's and 1970's affected all American artists, and African American novelists were no exception. Though his first two novels and various essays had gained him some notoriety, Baldwin had written himself into an aesthetic corner not unlike that inhabited by Ellison. Just as Ellison's essays after *Invisible Man* would put distance between his nineteenth century genteel aesthetics and the politicized aesthetics of the new African American writers, so, too, would Baldwin's criticism of Wright's *Native Son* as mere "protest" fiction alienate Baldwin from a new generation of African Americans anxious to relate literature to social concerns. For writers attempting to forge a black aesthetic based on the values of working-class African Americans, Baldwin was aesthetically and politically irrelevant. Worse, Baldwin's homosexuality only confirmed the suspicions of the largely homophobic Black Arts movement.

In 1967, one of the few novelists of the Black Arts movement, John A. Williams, penned *The Man Who Cried I Am*, a kind of roman à clef of African American literary history featuring Langston Hughes, Wright, and Baldwin under pseudonyms. Williams's novel, about a somewhat famous African American male writer who struggles with illness, the envy of his peers, and rampant racism, is composed with the crude urban realism of Himes and Wright, but its value is primarily archival.

It was during the same year, 1967, that John Edgar Wideman's first novel, *A Glance Away*, first appeared, presenting Wideman as a transitional figure between Ellison and Baldwin on one hand and the Black Arts movement on the other. Perhaps influenced by Baldwin's interest in the contingencies of sexuality and race, *A Glance Away* is a concentrated study—the narrative covers a single day—of the lives of an African American drug addict and a gay white professor. *Hurry Home* (1970), Wideman's second novel, focuses on the attempt of an African American to unite his European and African cultural heritages. Both novels are less concerned with racial issues per se than with philosophical ones. However, by the publication of his third novel, *The Lynchers* (1973), Wideman was under the influence of the Black Arts movement, though aesthetically the book remains outside its camp, a stance evident in Wideman's subsequent work such as *Damballah* (1981) and *Sent for You Yesterday* (1983).

Finally, 1967 saw yet a third auspicious debut. The most important male African American novelist to follow Ellison was Ishmael Reed. Eschewing the simplistic posturing of much of the Black Arts movement, *The Free-Lance Pallbearers* (1967) was a remarkable first novel, as Reed laid claim to being the best African American satirist since Schuyler. The form of his avant-garde novel was inspired as much by experimental jazz and film as James Joyce and Ellison. *Yellow Back Radio Broke-Down* (1969), his second novel, was an even greater triumph, a full-blown parody of the American Western as portrayed in dime-store novels and black-and-white films. Subsequent novels during the 1970's— such as *Mumbo Jumbo* (1972), *The Last Days of Louisi-*

ana Red (1974), and *Flight to Canada* (1976)—reinforced Reed's reputation as one of the most innovative comic spirits of his generation.

Ernest J. Gaines inaugurated the 1970's as the first major African American regional novelist since Jean Toomer, though he was soon followed by the equally talented Leon Forrest. Like Toomer, Gaines situates his novels in the complicated racial, sexual, and class mixtures of Cajun culture in Louisiana, Gaines's birthplace. His early novel, *The Autobiography of Miss Jane Pittman* (1971), was a major literary (and, later, television) event, as its 108-year-old narrator interweaves her personal history with that of the United States, allowing her to witness and comment on American history from nineteenth century slavery to the Civil Rights movement. Other significant novels would follow, including *In My Father's House* (1978); *A Gathering of Old Men* (1983), which was also made into a television movie; and *A Lesson Before Dying* (1993).

Forrest has staked a claim as the most important regional novelist of the North, as his four historical novels are all set in Forrest's native home, "Forest County"— that is, Cook County, Illinois. Focusing on the life and development of one central character, Nathaniel Turner Witherspoon, *There Is a Tree More Ancient than Eden* (1973), *The Bloodworth Orphans* (1977), *Two Wings to Veil My Face* (1983), and *Divine Days* (1992) trace the interrelated histories of two families by way of collage as Forrest draws on traditional oral storytelling, dream sequences, and mythological allusions to dramatize the intrinsic uncertainties of knowledge.

Forrest's redeployment of the serial novel—interrelated novels that follow a central theme, character, or family (for example, the Snopeses and Compsons in William Faulkner's fiction)—was mimicked by a number of other novelists, including Albert Murray. Unlike Faulkner, who used the serial novel to trace the disintegration of southern gentility, African American novelists such as Forrest and Murray used its epic possibilities to depict male heroism. Thus, Murray's trilogy of novels—*Train Whistle Guitar* (1974), *The Spyglass Tree* (1991), and *The Seven League Boots* (1995)—celebrate the spirit of adventure by linking the travels of an African American musician to those of the Greek hero Odysseus.

The serial novel has even been used by avant-garde writers such as the poet and novelist Nathaniel Mackey. His ongoing series of novels, From a Broken Bottle Traces of Perfume Still Emanate, has manifested itself in two epistolary novels: *Bedouin Hornbook* (1986) and *Djbot Baghostus's Run* (1993). Focusing on an ensemble of experimental jazz musicians, Mackey plays with polar oppositions usually taken for granted, especially those that supposedly define cultural borders, gender differences, racial and class biases, and natural and supernatural events.

The traditional novel, however, has not lost its viability among African American male writers. Yoking together the sophistication of northern urbanity and the penetrating eccentricity of southern folklore, David Bradley published *The Chaneysville Incident* (1981), a tour de force of historical guilt, murder, and atonement very much in the tradition of Dante's *La divina commedia* (c. 1320; *The Divine Comedy*, 1802).

Myth plays a fundamental role in the fiction of Charles Johnson. Like the early Wideman, Johnson was and remains essentially a philosophical writer. Johnson's first novel, *Faith and the Good Thing* (1974), is a good but unremarkable effort, though it already intimates the philosophical and theological concerns that would become more central to his next novel. *Oxherding Tale* (1982) could not be more different from the first book. Written under the influence of Zen Buddhism, *Oxherding Tale* revisits the slave narrative from an Asian philosophical perspective. Though not as pronounced in subsequent works such as the short-story collection *The Sorcerer's Apprentice* (1986) and the award-winning novel *Middle Passage* (1990), Johnson's Buddhist perspective tempers all his writings, both fiction and nonfiction. Oddly enough, Johnson's use of myth and philosophy has more in common with the experimental work of Mackey than it does with the mainstream novels of Toni Morrison, whose unique blend of myth, philosophy, folklore, and political outrage is unique, not only among African American women writers but also among all African American novelists.

AFRICAN AMERICAN WOMEN

Paule Marshall, the literary predecessor of the better known Morrison and Alice Walker, has labored in relative obscurity, perhaps, in part, because of her ethnicity. Born in New York City to Caribbean parents, Marshall draws on myriad cultural influences. Independent girls and women dominate her fiction, and when they are not strong, Marshall's narratives lead them back to healing sources, which are invariably African (as opposed to American) or pan-African in nature. Her novels—including *Brown Girl, Brownstones* (1959), *The Chosen Place, the Timeless People* (1969), *Praisesong for the Widow* (1983), and *Daughters* (1991)—counterpose, to varying degrees, American materialism and individualism to African American, Caribbean, and African spiritual ideals; these themes are also present in the writing of Marshall's literary descendant, Jamaica Kincaid.

Still, Morrison, who was awarded the Nobel Prize in Literature in 1993, was the most important African American novelist between the 1970's and 1990's. She has plumbed the depths of African American history with much insight, eloquence, and passion. Along with Walker, she takes seriously the feminist aphorism that the personal is political and redefines the relationship between African American women and their culture.

Like Walker, Gloria Naylor, Gayl Jones, and Toni Cade Bambara, Morrison focuses on the relationships between African American women and white women, African American women and African American men, and African American women and white America in general from a gendered and politically engaged perspective. Her novels—including *The Bluest Eye* (1970), *Sula* (1973), *Song of Solomon* (1977), *Tar Baby* (1981), *Beloved* (1987), *Jazz* (1992), *Paradise* (1998), *Love* (2003), and *A Mercy* (2008)—range across the landscape of African American culture. For example, while most of her novels—*Song of Solomon* is an important exception—feature women as central protagonists, none of the novels is determinedly feminist.

Morrison's work is primarily concerned with class and caste distinctions and divisions within African American culture; while slavery and racism, along with sexism, frame all the novels, Morrison's work cannot be deemed protest fiction because it is not addressed primarily to either male or white readers. Nevertheless, it certainly can be said that the novels have become increasingly political insofar as slavery, sexism, and racism loom larger in each succeeding novel. Although this process has been gradual, many critics, both detractors and proponents, cite *Beloved*, Morrison's best-known work and most controversial novel, as her representative work. The novel won a Pulitzer Prize in fiction in 1988.

Beloved, like *Jazz*, is based on a true story. It centers on Sethe, a former slave and a mother who attempts to escape from the South but pays a tremendous personal price. Trapped by slave hunters, she tries to kill both of her baby daughters rather than see them sold to slavery, succeeding only with the youngest, unnamed daughter. Years later, free in Ohio but ostracized from the African American community because of the murder, Sethe and Denver, her surviving daughter, are visited by the ghost of Sethe's dead daughter, Beloved, as well as Paul D., Sethe's lover, who wants to start a new life with her. Thus, the novel centers on the tug-of-war Sethe endures as she is alternately pulled back by the past (Beloved's claim of birthright) and toward the future (Paul D.'s claim on her as his wife).

The controversy over the novel centered on the question of the murder of Beloved. Was it indeed better to kill oneself or one's children than submit to the horrors of slavery? Or was it better to live, knowing that those who survived the ordeal would pass their indomitable genes and traditions on to a hoped-for, but unforeseeable, future of freedom? Morrison herself never directly addressed the issue, and readers are not helped by the ambivalence of the novel's last pages, which assert that the "story" was one "to pass on" and "not pass on." This ambivalence, a feature of all Morrison's novels, tempers the heightened political profiles of the stories. None of Morrison's contemporaries has achieved this precarious balance between political outrage and human complexity.

Walker's first novel, *The Third Life of Grange Copeland* (1970), appeared in the same year as Morrison's *The Bluest Eye*. *The Third Life of Grange Copeland* is a well-written, harrowing account of women who are not only physically and psychologically abused but also driven to madness by men. To this extent, Walker's writing is much more explicitly feminist than that of Morrison. However, *The Third Life of Grange Copeland* is also concerned with racism and class bias, as well as their relationship to violence against women.

Walker is best known, however, for her second novel, the controversial *The Color Purple* (1982), which won a Pulitzer Prize in fiction (1983) and the National Book Award (1983). An epistolary novel also made into a successful, award-winning film, *The Color Purple* explores the gradual sexual and feminist awakening of a young teenager, Celie, who has been abused by both her family and her husband, whom she calls Mister. Although she writes letters addressed to God, Celie is actually saved by Mister's mistress, Shug. The narrative of the novel implies that Shug's lesbian relationship with Celie is sparked, in part, by the oppression both undergo from Mister. This implication understandably angered feminist critics, who argued that Celie and Shug's relationship appeared to be simply a counter to Mister's misogyny and sexism instead of a willing relationship of attraction and desire. At the same time, the portrait of a misogynist and abusive Mister angered writers such as Ishmael Reed and Amiri Baraka, who believed that Walker and other African American feminists were unwittingly perpetuating the traditional demonization of African American men's sexuality. Largely unheard in the debate, however, was Walker's attempt to remind her critics that Celie is complicit in her own abuse and oppression and that Mister is transformed by the novel's end into a humane father and friend to Celie.

Walker sold the screen rights of the novel to director Steven Spielberg, whose 1985 film essentially deleted the sexual politics and romanticized the South, dismaying supporters and critics of the book. Although Walker continued to produce readable and successful novels, such as *The Temple of My Familiar* (1989) and *Possessing the Secret of Joy* (1992), she was made a marginal literary and cultural figure for focusing much of her work on black women's lesbian sexuality, a fate not unlike that suffered by James Baldwin (who was gay) for writing about gay men, and by lesbian poet and writer Audre Lorde, among many others.

Other black women writers, including Toni Cade Bambara, followed the lead of Morrison and Walker. Bambara, who died in 1995, was a brilliant short-story writer and a promising novelist. Her 1980 novel *The Salt Eaters* showcased complex narrative textures and jazz influences similar to those in Reed's early novels.

Gloria Naylor's first novel, *The Women of Brewster Place: A Novel in Seven Stories* (1982), was a major success that was made into an even more successful film for television. However, it was published in the same year as *The Color Purple* and, similarly, it suffered critically because of its depiction of black lesbian sexuality and black men's misogyny. Naylor rewrote and updated Baraka's *The System of Dante's Hell* (1965) with her second novel, *Linden Hills* (1985), revived the novel of manners in the vein of Jessie Redmon Fauset in *Mama Day* (1988), and, in *Bailey's Café* (1992), echoed the improvisational experiments of Morrison's *Jazz*.

Gayl Jones, author of *Corregidora* (1975) and *Eva's Man* (1976), among other novels, is, in many ways, the most interesting of the "new" African American writers. Her interest in the abnormalities of psychological profiles and their link to linguistic modes suggests an intelligence only partially realized in her first two novels. Jones, however, suffered a series of personal and professional traumas, and it was more than two decades before she published her next novel, *The Healing* (1998). This novel, along with her fourth, *Mosquito* (1999), suggests a return to creative and psychological health for Jones, and to the continuing development of African American fiction.

Tyrone Williams
Updated by David Peck

BIBLIOGRAPHY

Beaulieu, Elizabeth Ann. *Black Women Writers and the American Neo-Slave Narrative: Femininity Unfettered*. Westport, Conn.: Greenwood Press, 1999. Beaulieu discusses the efforts of African American women writers to redefine the slave narrative in the twentieth century. Among the novels discussed is Toni Morrison's *Beloved*.

Bell, Bernard W. *The Contemporary African American Novel: Its Folk Roots and Modern Literary Branches*. Amherst: University of Massachusetts Press, 2004. Broad, expansive history of African American literature. Focuses on distinctive elements and outlines the role of political and social influences in changing the focus of African American novels over time.

Braxton, Joanne M., and Andree Nicola McLaughlin. *Wild Women in the Whirlwind: Afra-American Culture and the Contemporary Literary Renaissance*. New Brunswick, N.J.: Rutgers University Press, 1990. Excellent anthology of critical writings on African

American women writers of several generations. The range of writers covered is impressive, and the language is free of jargon.

Butler, Robert. *Contemporary African American Fiction: The Open Journey*. Madison, Wis.: Fairleigh Dickinson University Press, 1998. Butler's book, as the subtitle suggests, covers a wide range of subject matter, from a study of the picaresque in the fiction of Zora Neale Hurston and Richard Wright to a discussion of Octavia E. Butler's vision of the twenty-first century.

Callahan, John F. *In the African-American Grain: Call-and-Response in Twentieth-Century Black Fiction*. Middletown, Conn.: Wesleyan University Press, 1988. Callahan examines the way novelists and short-story writers from Charles Waddell Chesnutt to Alice Walker have insisted on the importance of call-and-response in the creation of a personal identity that remains bound to larger ideals of African American culture.

Dickson-Carr, Darryl. *The Columbia Guide to Contemporary African American Fiction*. New York: Columbia University Press, 2005. Valuable reference work on the growth of the African American novel since 1970.

Gates, Henry Louis, Jr. *The Signifying Monkey: A Theory of African-American Literary Criticism*. New York: Oxford University Press, 1988. Ambitious, concise text that argues for the importance of the trickster figure in African American literature and its link to the problem of literacy and identity. For advanced readers.

Graham, Maryemma, ed. *Cambridge Companion to the African American Novel*. New York: Cambridge University Press, 2004. Scholarly essays examining "The Long Journey: The African American Novel and History," "Search for a Form: The New American Novel," and "African American Voices: From Margin to Center." Covers topics such as the Harlem Renaissance and the blues novel, as well as writers Richard Wright, Toni Morrison, John Edgar Wideman, and many others.

Joyce, Ann. *Warriors, Conjurers, and Priests: Defining African-Centered Literary Criticism*. Chicago: Third World Press, 1994. Joyce examines the work of neglected African American writers such as Ann Petry and Sonia Sanchez while taking on antifeminist critics such as Ishmael Reed. Joyce also provides the first tentative assessments of emerging writers such as Terry McMillan and E. Ethelbert Miller.

Kostelanetz, Richard. *Politics in the African-American Novel: James Weldon Johnson, W. E. B. Du Bois, Richard Wright, and Ralph Ellison*. New York: Greenwood Press, 1991. This investigation of the development of the African American novel charts the movement from the protest fiction of Johnson and Du Bois to the more complex and thus "better" work of Wright and Ellison.

Schwarz, A. B. Christa. *Gay Voices of the Harlem Renaissance*. Bloomington: Indiana University Press, 2003. Schwarz examines the work of four leading writers from the Harlem Renaissance—Countée Cullen, Langston Hughes, Claude McKay, and Richard Bruce Nugent—and their sexually nonconformist, or gay, literary voices.

The American Novel

America became a subject for literature after the Revolutionary War, when writers began the exploration of themes and motifs distinctly American. Continuing the Puritan belief in America as the New Eden, writers stressed the millennial nature of settlement and progress. Each milestone in improvement and enlargement marked a national movement toward spiritually sanctioned political dominion. Geographic, industrial, and social changes found justification in America's mythic vision of itself independent of England and free of European hierarchy.

A complex and often contradictory ethos emerged based on tensions in American dualities: Calvinistic sin and predestination opposed to romantic optimism; determinism opposed to free will; idealism versus materialism; European aristocracy opposed to democracy; capitalistic prosperity versus economic struggles. As the United States expanded, such dichotomies were complicated by tensions between long-settled areas in New England, the genteel South, the expansive plains states, and the wide open West. These contrary and interlocking forces created variety and crosscurrents in American fiction.

Puritan influence

The original Puritan experiment lasted less than one hundred years but indelibly marked American thought and expression. Emphasis on a godly life and personal motives shapes the journals of colonial governors William Bradford (1590-1649) and John Winthrop (1588-1694). Their documents reveal harsh dealings with merchandisers who invaded the colonies only to reap the wealth of the New World. The diaries of Judge Samuel Sewall (1652-1730) and Puritan cleric Jonathan Edwards (1703-1758) endorse the same catalog of virtues Benjamin Franklin lists in his *Autobiography* (1791). Puritan temperance, order, frugality, industry, and justice also suited the rational, moral sensibility of Franklin's Enlightenment God, the deistic Watchmaker-Creator who let the world tick on unhindered.

Though Edwards's harsh God had been replaced by a nearly indifferent craftsman, America's habit of thought was focused on the quest for personal identity and spiritual journeys central to Puritan self-examination. The search for identity and meaning articulated in Puritan journals appears in many guises in America's long-fiction tradition. Herman Melville's (1819-1891) Ishmael (*Moby Dick*, 1851), Kate Chopin's (1851-1904) Edna Pontillier (*The Awakening*, 1899), F. Scott Fitzgerald's (1896-1940) Amory Blaine (*This Side of Paradise*, 1920), and Toni Morrison's (born 1931) Milkman (*Song of Solomon*, 1977) all struggle with the context and significance of their lives.

Puritan practice shaped American novels metaphorically long after the Spartan spiritual regimen weakened. Puritan preachers reveled in comparisons between the biblical world and their own. Pairing events across time created a deeper sense of significance for American life. Moses's prophetic leadership made him a model for Puritan patriarchs. As men of God, their calling and authority mimicked that of Moses. Puritans were encouraged to see life's events as spiritual lessons designed to increase piety and faith or express God's nurturing. Persistent comparison made the nature of life metaphoric. Events in real time were seen as images of biblical experiences and were symbolically interpreted.

Overt transference of symbolism to fiction is clear in Nathaniel Hawthorne's (1804-1864) *The Scarlet Letter* (1850), in which protagonist Hester Prynne's scarlet letter A marks her as a symbol of fallen womanhood. The whale in *Moby Dick*, a massive symbol of evil, exhibits a subtle turn by making the evil force white rather than black. Modernists, following in the wake of late nineteenth century realists and naturalists, capitalized on this penchant for symbols, but their main figures were literary, not biblical. Ernest Hemingway's (1899-1961) code heroes rely on knowledge of traditional heroes to be effective. Jake Barnes's depressed wandering in Hemingway's *The Sun Also Rises* (1926) makes a hollow warrior's quest. He is an Odysseus without honorable men to lead or a homeland to reclaim.

Moving beyond storytelling to the theory of narrative, Gertrude Stein's (1874-1946) experiments with repetition of words and phrases invite skepticism about language and its reliability as an interpretive tool. In

"Melanctha" (*Three Lives*, 1909), her use of the word "love" causes readers to constantly redefine it. Stein moved beyond the Puritan equation, comparing two objects or people to question the process and means of comparison. Contemporary use of metaphoric construction influenced E. Annie Proulx's (born 1935) *The Shipping News* (1993), in which chapters are headed by the names of particular nautical knots, and the sea around Nova Scotia is ever-present as a force and locus of possibility in the character Quoyle's life. The ties for Proulx are elliptical and suggestive; readers must decide for themselves the significance and the connections.

Unlike the Puritans, contemporary American novelists draw no absolute lines between symbols and moral values or truths. The reader, not a minister, defines the significance of events. The novel itself, rather than Puritan beliefs or biblical passages, provides codes for translation. Still, the search for meaning requires cross-references between text and life—a Puritan strategy of interpretation.

Material prosperity fueled by the Industrial Revolution increased after the American Civil War, and the effect of money on American moral fiber became a dominant theme in fiction. Mark Twain (1835-1910) satirized the greed and hypocrisy in *The Gilded Age* (1873). William Dean Howells (1837-1920), one of the creators and promoters of American realism, reflected on acquisition and class structure in *The Rise of Silas Lapham* (1885), about a man who inherits and exploits a paint factory in New England. The Laphams attempt to enter Boston society, but, being nouveau riche, they know none of the behavior codes that signal breeding; they are never accepted by the upper class. Silas's moral compass is corrupted by market forces, as he wins material rewards through speculation and investment, not by his own labor. Only renunciation of wealth restores his moral stature.

THE TWENTIETH CENTURY NOVEL IN AMERICA

The effects of speculation and class aspirations on American moral character persisted into early twentieth century novels. Edith Wharton (1862-1937) portrayed the painful significance of class and wealth in a woman's life in *The House of Mirth* (1905). Her work explores the dislocation and struggle of people caught in social forces beyond their control. The post-Civil War transition to industrial strength and expansion left New England's shipping industry and economy weakened, signaling the end of America's cycle of origination and settlement. Writers Mary E. Wilkins Freeman (1852-1930) and Sarah Orne Jewett (1849-1909) recorded the details of village life and change in *Pembroke* (1894) and *The Country of the Pointed Firs* (1896), respectively, examining the lives of those who remained when those such as Howells's Silas Lapham migrated to the city. Unlike Silas, Jewett's Mrs. Todd Maine is not liable to be corrupted. Freeman's characters do not fare as well.

Although Freeman's novel's central dilemma seems romantic, the sources of tension and tragedy for the inhabitants of Pembroke are the versions of Puritan theology and moral strategies that control village households. Unlike later critics who marginalized the women as quaint, regional authors, Howells lauded their veracity in depicting American life, publishing them as his peers when he was editor of *The Atlantic Monthly*. Their frank look at economic and social changes makes them authoritative American voices.

The focus on capitalism's effect on American life was not always negative, however. Horatio Alger exploited the "rags-to-riches" myth in more than one hundred novels in which material success was, paradoxically, both the cause of and reward for moral virtue. Edwards's and Franklin's programs, now expunged entirely of sectarian doctrine, became a new "way to wealth." Alger's vastly popular novel *Ragged Dick* (1867), modeled in part on the life of American industrialist Andrew Carnegie, offered hope to thousands of trapped stock boys, shop girls, and factory workers. Many of them were part of the waves of immigration that began in the late nineteenth century. Their stories came into view when early twentieth century America's authors mined their own lives for writing material. In *The Bread Givers* (1925), Polish Russian Anzia Yezierska's (1885-1970) narrator, Sara, relates the poverty and need for education that urban Jewish immigrants felt so keenly in New York ghettos. Yezierska used a phonetic facsimile of Yiddish dialect to heighten the pathos of the immigrant struggle.

Willa Cather's (1873-1947) stories of frontier life recorded the American Dream unfolding in the West.

Alexandra of *O Pioneers!* (1913) and the immigrants cast in *My Ántonia* (1918) foreground the frontier's freedom for women and the opportunity Europeans experienced in America's western territories. Other immigrant groups found voices. O. E. Rölvaag's (1876-1931) *Giants in the Earth: A Saga of the Prairie* (1927; translated from *I de dage*, 1924, and *Riket grundlægges*, 1925) tells an eloquent saga of isolation, backbreaking labor, and temporary madness set in the Dakotas. Dutch truck farmers pursue their chance to rise socially through hard work on their farms south of Chicago in Edna Ferber's (1887-1968) Pulitzer Prize-winning novel *So Big* (1924).

THE HARLEM RENAISSANCE

The flowering of culture and identity known as the Harlem Renaissance was in full bloom during the 1920's, at the same time the novels of immigrant experience were appearing. Langston Hughes's (1902-1967) stories, poetry, and plays, along with Claude McKay's (1889-1948) *Home to Harlem* (1928), presented all aspects of African American life. McKay's work introduced the urban experience of working-class blacks that many black intellectuals chose to downplay. Later, Ann Petry's (1908-1997) *The Street* (1946) took another hard look at black urban life, portraying the pressures on a single mother trying to raise her son in Harlem, their lives beset by poverty and the temptations of the street.

Immigrant and African American experiences narrated in novels of the 1920's showed aspects of the American Dream that Alger overlooked in his optimistic portrayal of opportunity for most whites. However, McKay's cynical Ray and Cather's optimistic Alexandra still strove to enter the mainstream. They aspired to knowledge or property as a measure of success, adopting a version of the Puritan work ethic, even with backgrounds far from New England. Insistence on personal independence and the ability to affect one's destiny is a primary theme in early twentieth century novels.

MORALITY IN AMERICAN FICTION

The theme of testing moral formulas for material success was present in the stories of mainstream white America as well. *The Great Gatsby* (1925), by F. Scott Fitzgerald, illustrates the ironic coexistence of great wealth and moral carelessness. Like Silas Lapham, Jay Gatsby cannot rise in old-money society. The two characters replace the unifying moral framework of Ben Franklin's schema with faith in a tangible world of goods. For Fitzgerald, relational morality and context changes are emblems of modern society.

Sherwood Anderson (1876-1941) deals overtly with appearance and reality in *Winesburg, Ohio* (1919). Sinclair Lewis's (1885-1951) *Elmer Gantry* (1927) combines several American strains in the adventure of a rogue evangelist whose commodity is religion. E. L. Doctorow's (born 1931) *Ragtime* (1975) explores the interplay of public events and private lives as characters grapple with restless shifts in the American way of life after 1900. John Updike's (1932-2009) Rabbit series (1960-1990) chronicles striving in the span of one man's life and milieu. *That Night* (1987), by Alice McDermott (born 1953), measures love, loss, and success in post-World War II suburban neighborhood life. Finally, Wallace Stegner's (1909-1993) *The Spectator Bird* (1976) offers a retrospective on how one man's professional and private lives coincide in contemporary times. American characters ceaselessly question who they are and how they have arrived at their particular dilemmas and epiphanies.

The conflict between free will and determinism that informs American fiction can also be traced to the Puritan era. Ralph Waldo Emerson's (1803-1882) early defection from Puritanism's angry God to transcendental self-reliance (in *Essays: First Series*, 1841) set the stage for America's doctrine of manifest destiny. Emerson's themes fed a harmonic vision of America's purpose, as Americans set out to dominate a new continent and succeeded in a remarkably short time. In the latter half of the nineteenth century, personal, political, and religious activity devoted to progress and westward expansion had a redemptive purpose. All effort and experience took on spiritual significance for white Americans, which encouraged expansion as it provided the philosophic rationale for abuses of power leveled against the environment and American Indian cultures.

By the close of the nineteenth century America's central paradoxes also included the increasing duality of urban and rural lifestyles and the impact of Darwinism on the moral philosophies at the basis of human society.

William James's (1842-1910) *The Principles of Psychology* (1890) and Henry Adams's (1838-1918) *The Education of Henry Adams* (1907, 1918) explore the spiritual, educational, and behavioral bases on which modern life was founded. Adams in particular worried about how moral sensibility would keep pace with technological advances.

NATURALISM

In fiction, Stephen Crane's (1871-1900) *Maggie: A Girl of the Streets* (1893), Theodore Dreiser's (1871-1945) *Sister Carrie* (1900), and Frank Norris's (1870-1902) *The Octopus* (1901) exemplify the naturalist movement. Their novels, like those of the Frenchman Émile Zola (1840-1902), stress that the forces at work in nature work in humans as well. Transcendence was a myth.

The relentless effect of portraying life as a process controlled by indifferent natural forces put an end to the sentimental romantic tradition that had begun with Washington Irving (1783-1859). The fantastic quality of Irving's "The Legend of Sleepy Hollow" and his folk figure in "Rip Van Winkle" (both from *The Sketch Book of Geoffrey Crayon, Gent.*, 1819-1820) feature American landscapes and the phenomenal effects of the Hudson River Valley light but have no relationship to real events. James Fenimore Cooper's (1789-1851) work is an amalgam of American democratic ideas, Rousseauian philosophy, and Cooper's fascination with aristocratic England. His Leatherstocking Tales, produced between 1823 and 1841, romanticize Natty Bumppo as a knight-like figure who rights wrongs and is aided by the noble savage Chingachgook. Despite his aristocratic tendencies and the foolishness of some of his scenarios, Cooper's work remains popular because it promotes the mythic belief Americans have in individual determination, as well as their earlier romantic vision of the American wilderness as a place that could engender the highest ideals in people.

LOCAL COLORISTS

The pervasive optimism of American devotion to personal success accounts for other bridging novels of the late nineteenth and early twentieth centuries. Novels of local color or of regionalism capture the essence of different geographic areas of American life, which were beginning to erode as the United States was bound together by transportation and communication.

Critics tend to group all local-color writers in a quaint or nostalgic subgenre. In fact, there are distinct differences among the local colorists. The stories of Bret Harte (1836-1902) in the West, George Washington Cable (1844-1925) in Creole Louisiana, Joel Chandler Harris (1848-1908) in the South, and Mark Twain in the Midwest capture the rambunctious character of life in these regions with dialect and flamboyance. New England's local-color female writers, discussed previously, pay serious attention to social structure and the business of daily life. Their use of parochial dialect and event portrays one area's character without claiming superiority. Their work also tends to avoid the irony and satire that pervade most literature produced by men in this school.

Willa Cather's fiction embodies the serious attention to local detail these women engendered in their view of New England's rapidly shifting economic landscape. Although written later, her novels *O Pioneers!*, *The Song of the Lark* (1915), and *My Ántonia* chronicle events of an earlier time that all depend on the character of frontier life. Even later, Eudora Welty (1909-2001) and William Faulkner (1897-1962) molded their southern heritage into stories and novels that captured the gothic quality of southern life, which had seeped into the twentieth century. Faulkner created his mythic Yoknapatawpha County as an archetypal southern context. Contemporary African American writers Alice Walker (born 1944), in *The Color Purple* (1982), and Morrison, in *Beloved* (1987), focus on African American southern life with clarity and compassion, bringing local color's emphasis on region and cultural diversity into later twentieth century fiction.

MUCKRAKERS

Muckrakers are known for their crusading vision, as typified by Upton Sinclair's (1878-1968) *The Jungle* (1906), an exposé of the Chicago meatpacking industry that prompted enactment of the first pure food and drug laws. Such effort is a version of the Puritan quest for a new Eden.

Although not preoccupied with social change per se, other American novelists called attention to America's problems and their costs. Ellen Glasgow (1873-1945) wrote *Vein of Iron* (1935), the story of an Appalachian woman's struggle during the Great Depression. Character Ada Fincastle's Scotch-Irish immigrant history and gritty determination enable her to survive as she molds a new working identity for herself. John Steinbeck's (1902-1968) Pulitzer Prize-winning *The Grapes of Wrath* (1939) laid bare the vulnerability of the Joad family, caught, like a sea of other Americans, in the grip of big money and farmers who exploit migrant workers. Tillie Olsen's (1913-2007) heart-wrenching *Yonnondio: From the Thirties* (1974) was begun in the 1930's and tells the story of illiterate Anna and Jim Holbrook, who barely survive with their children. Hanging on to hope by the merest thread, they finally settle in a shack near slaughterhouses, where the stench and heat overwhelm them. These two books examine the desperate plight of workers denied the basic requirements of food and decent living conditions, as well as education for their children.

UTOPIAN NOVELS

Utopian novels offered another alternative to naturalism's grim paradigms between 1889 and 1900. The most famous, *Looking Backward: 2000-1887* (1888) by Edward Bellamy (1850-1898), influenced social philosophers such as John Dewey. Charlotte Perkins Gilman (1860-1935), an author and lecturer for social reform, wrote three utopian novels. *Herland* (1915 serial, 1979 book) posits a society free of men that functions perfectly, even on the reproductive level. Her use of humor and the plight of three men stranded in the strange land show just how gender-driven life is in Western society. All the utopian novels explore the interaction of context and culture. Far from the rigid Puritan dogmas, they investigate how to fashion a better world for oneself and society, a dilemma that has plagued Americans since their appearance on the continent.

From the earliest days of derivative sentimental and gothic novels, the creators of American literature sought an indigenous art and culture. They sought to establish aesthetic standards of their own on a par with the standards set by English and other European masters. This often led to consideration of the European preoccupation with hereditary class distinction and how Americans fit into such society, a theme raised to its highest form by Henry James (1843-1916). In *The American* (1876-1877), *Daisy Miller* (1878), and *The Ambassadors* (1903), he showed the dangers inherent in New World sensibilities braving European society, where moral superiority cannot measure up to European style and cultural sophistication. James's narrative style gave rise to an introspective novel that paved the way for later interior monologues.

THE LOST GENERATION

In the 1920's, European and American values collided in the works of the lost generation, a group of expatriate artists, including Ernest Hemingway, F. Scott Fitzgerald, Henry Miller (1891-1980), and Gertrude Stein. These writers fled the United States for the openness and sophistication of the Old World, though the Spanish Civil War (1936-1939) corrupted their idealistic beliefs.

Hemingway produced novels that explore individual male quests for masculinity and identity via the odd amalgam of free love, decadent travel, self-indulgence, and foreign civil wars. He filled the epic novel form with American expatriates looking for ultimate reality and self-expression among societies their immigrant forebears and settlers had abandoned. The character Barnes, in *The Sun Also Rises*, finds no way to exert himself for his own or anyone else's happiness. In 1925, while F. Scott Fitzgerald and Zelda Fitzgerald lived in Europe, *The Great Gatsby* was published, detailing, again, the sad hero's tragic search for meaning in the material world. In exile, these writers expressed a hopelessness and a cynicism that replaced the faith and vision that had propelled earlier Americans across the Atlantic. Ironically, their works ask more questions about individual worth and possibilities than they answer. The chief values of a European sojourn were cheaper living costs and proximity to new aesthetic trends.

The effect of European forms on American experience can also be seen in the development of the gothic genre in American literature. Edgar Allan Poe's (1809-1849) legacy lived on in the southern traditions fed by genteel aristocratic customs that exploited slaves, where graceful manners coexisted with the violence of lynchings and the Ku Klux Klan. Faulkner's broken perspective in *The Sound and the Fury* (1929) creates dislocation in reader and narrative progression. Carson

McCullers's (1917-1967) novels furnish a cast of unconventional characters who long for safety. Flannery O'Connor's (1925-1964) tortured Catholics clutch at a faith that offers only torment. Harper Lee's (born 1926) protagonist, Atticus, in *To Kill a Mockingbird* (1960), as well as plain-spoken characters from Welty's southern novels, counteract the gothic mutations. Their compassionate portrayals offer a South tolerant of eccentricity, a region trying to comprehend the effect of changing times on tradition and decorum.

AMERICAN MODERNISM

American modernism, launched by the 1913 Armory Show in New York, prefigured the collapse of spirit after World War I that led to the cynicism and materialism of the Jazz Age. Modernism's emphasis on the unpredictability of narrative time and voice echoed uncertainties about the permanence of values and life's possibilities. Doubt altered the form and emphasis of modern American novels. The search for identity became acutely personal in J. D. Salinger's (born 1919) *The Catcher in the Rye* (1951), as well as in Jack Kerouac's (1922-1969) Beat classic, *On the Road* (1957). The protagonists of Saul Bellow's (1915-2005) *Herzog* (1964) and John Irving's (born 1942) *The World According to Garp* (1978) search endlessly for meaning in a jumbled context. No underlying dogma but the certainty of change supports contemporary American expectations and the vision of society set in motion by pre-World War I modernist writers.

John Barth's (born 1930) experiments in discontinuity and narrative games that began in *The Sot-Weed Factor* (1960) are examples of contemporary fiction's exploration of its own form. Barth strips away conventional plot lines and chronology. Readers are forced to accept his books on terms dictated by form, not expectation. More and more, novel form began to echo the fragmented perspectives of contemporary life, with chapters or sections offering competing views of the same events and people.

A vibrant mix of ethnicity and place dominates contemporary fiction. Leslie Marmon Silko's (born 1948) *Ceremony* (1977) is set after World War II, when disillusioned American Indian war veterans return to their reservations and encounter even more discrimination from white America. Toni Morrison's *Song of Solomon* considers the conflict between races during the 1960's, as well as the conflicting annals of two black families. Her cautionary tale warns of the dangers of forgetting one's past and the risk of worshiping commercial success. Alice McDermott's (born 1953) Irish American Brooklyn family seen through the eyes of a child in *At Weddings and Wakes* (1992) evokes the urban neighborhood of the 1940's and 1950's, along with the suffocating closeness that is the legacy of immigrant communities.

Characters in all these novels search for meaning and identity within their cultural traditions, similar to Puritan introspection. However, they have no homogenous social or religious codes like those that unified early Americans. Cormac McCarthy's (born 1933) John Grady Cole in *All the Pretty Horses* (1992) may head for unknown lands, but he returns unsatisfied. Partial and very personal answers are merely implied. Ultimately, the vision of American identities is shaped by landscapes—literal, political, and social—but the contemporary sense of the field is more fluid and strives to be more inclusive than in times past. American novels continue to reveal people as they are.

David Sadkin; Karen L. Arnold
Updated by David Peck

BIBLIOGRAPHY

Adamson, Lynda G. *Thematic Guide to the American Novel*. Westport, Conn.: Greenwood Press, 2002. Discusses recurring themes in the American novel, including alienation, death, family, immigrant life, race, nature, and the search for identity. Features excerpts from novels of all literary periods that exemplify these themes.

Bradbury, Malcolm. *The Modern American Novel*. New ed. New York: Penguin Books, 1994. Provides insight into and critical commentary on the modern novel in the United States. A much-used resource.

Crane, Gregg. *The Cambridge Introduction to the Nineteenth-Century American Novel*. New York: Cambridge University Press, 2007. Comprehensive history of this century of literary romance and realism. Includes analyses of novelists Harriet Beecher Stowe, Nathaniel Hawthorne, Herman Melville, and Mark Twain.

Deneen, Patrick J., and Joseph Romance, eds. *Democracy's Literature: Politics and Fiction in America.* Lanham, Md.: Rowman & Littlefield, 2005. Essays on important novels of the nineteenth and twentieth centuries outlining the political nature of American literature and its profound philosophical underpinnings.

Elliott, Emory, et al., eds. *The Columbia History of the American Novel.* New York: Columbia University Press, 1991. Comprehensive collection of essays that explore the rise and development of American fiction, its recurrent themes, and the aesthetic principles on which it is based. Includes essays on race, gender, and regional novels.

Kazin, Alfred. *An American Procession: The Major American Writers from 1830 to 1930, the Crucial Century.* New York: Alfred A. Knopf, 1984. Weaves connections between the writers and their works and times. Kazin's broad knowledge of literary history makes this an excellent source for understanding a wide range of literature. Examines Ralph Waldo Emerson, Henry Thoreau, Edgar Allan Poe, Mark Twain, Henry James, Theodore Dreiser, Stephen Crane, Henry Adams, William Faulkner, and Ernest Hemingway.

Lauret, Maria. *Liberating Literature: Feminist Fiction in America.* New York: Routledge, 1994. Lauret explores the writing of American feminist writers of long fiction, including Marge Piercy, Marilyn French, Tillie Olsen, Alice Walker, Kate Millett, Agnes Smedley, Zora Neale Hurston, Toni Morrison, and Maya Angelou.

Minter, David L. *A Cultural History of the American Novel: Henry James to William Faulkner.* New ed. New York: Cambridge University Press, 1994. The history of this crucial period of the American novel—which includes analyses of individual works—is set against a larger American canvas, beginning with Henry James and continuing to the Armory Show of 1913, World War I, the Jazz Age, and the Great Depression.

Wagner-Martin, Linda. *The Mid-Century American Novel, 1935-1965.* New York: Twayne, 1997. Another volume in Twayne's Critical History of the Novel series, this book covers long fiction from the Depression era to the era of Vietnam and protest movements. Examines works by writers of color as well as popular literature and post-World War II novels.

ASIAN AMERICAN LONG FICTION

In the study of Asian American literature, the issue of authenticity is as problematic as the definition of "Asian American." While the racial boundary of the Asian American community is historically and geographically delineated by the origins of its immigrants and ontologically dictated by a common struggle for dignity and social justice, Asian American literature's cultural configuration is a subject of controversy. For example, *The Big Aiiieeeee! An Anthology of Chinese and Japanese American Literature*, edited by Chinese American writer and critic Frank Chin and others, was published in 1991, and the selections chosen for the anthology are as controversial as Chin's introductory article, "Come All Ye Asian American Writers of the Real and the Fake," in which he divides Chinese American and Japanese American writers into two groups: Asian American authors and Americanized Asian authors.

Chin posits that only those Asian American writers who are not susceptible to Christian conversion and who uphold traditional Chinese and Japanese values such as Confucianism, the Japanese sense of honor, and the samurai sense of nobility can be considered the "real" voice in Asian American literature. This group includes Chinese American writer Louis Chu (*Eat a Bowl of Tea*, 1961) and Japanese American writers Toshio Mori (*Yokohama, California*, 1949) and John Okada (*No-No Boy*, 1957). The "fake," according to Chin, include Chinese American writers such as Pardee Lowe (*Father and Glorious Descendant*, 1943), Jade Snow Wong (*Fifth Chinese Daughter*, 1950), Maxine Hong Kingston (*The Woman Warrior*, 1976; *China Men*, 1980; *Tripmaster Monkey: His Fake Book*, 1989; and the memoir *The Fifth Book of Peace*, 2003), and Amy Tan (*The Joy Luck Club*, 1989; *The Kitchen God's Wife*, 1991; *The Hundred Secret Senses*, 1995; and *The Bonesetter's Daughter*, 2001); Japanese American writers Mike Masaru Masaoka and Bill Hosokawa (*Nisei: The Quiet Americans*, 1969); and any Asian American writers who use the exclusively Christian form of autobiography and revise Asian history, culture, and childhood literature and myth. In their depictions of dual personality and identity crises, these writers, according to Chin, not only misrepresent their own cultural heritage but also betray its values.

In the foreword to *Reading the Literatures of Asian America* (1992), Korean American scholar Elaine H. Kim acknowledges that the pioneering work of the members of the Combined Asian-American Resources Project (CARP)—Chin, Chan, Lawson Fusao Inada, Nathan Lee, Benjamin R. Tong, and Shawn Hsu Wong—played an important role in helping to define the identity of the Asian American community and to establish Asian American literary voices. However, Kim points out that the terms of Asian Americans' cultural negotiations have changed, and are changing, over time because of differences in historical circumstances and needs. As the body of Asian American literature grows, it reflects desires to traverse the boundaries of unity and diversity, to enable the individual to take flight, and to claim infinite layers of self and community.

Chinese American Amy Ling agrees with Kim. In her article "Creating One's Self: The Eaton Sisters," Ling reiterates what has become almost a truism—that the self is not a fixed entity but a fluid, changing construct or creation determined by context or historical conditions and particularly by power relationships. By using the example of the Eaton sisters, who were Amerasians but, in their creative writing, had adopted identities of their choice—one Chinese and one Japanese—Ling convincingly reveals the dialectical relationship between creation and re-creation and between the permeability of the boundaries of the self and the influence of historical conditions.

In *Articulate Silence* (1993), Chinese American scholar King-Kok Cheung suggests that it is a distrust of inherited language and of traditional myth with a patriarchal ethos that brings Asian American writers, especially Asian American female writers, to the conclusion that they must cross cultural borders. They seek ways not only to revise history but also to transfigure ethnicity; the point is not to return to the original but to tell it with a difference. The "two-toned language" thus concretely objectifies the attempt of a large group of Asian American writers to negotiate a ground on which they can establish their own identity.

Many Asian American writers are trying to identify a voice that can describe the Asian American experience; they are not in search of a mouthpiece that can only echo what has already been expressed and described in Asian literatures. Given the fact that a person cannot achieve self-actualization without first identifying his or her relationship with her or his own cultural heritage, to be a hyphenated American means that a person is blessed with two cultures and can have the freedom and luxury to be selective. As Brave Orchid, the dynamic mother in Kingston's *The Woman Warrior*, puts it, "When you come to America, it's a chance to forget some of the bad Chinese habits."

ORIGINS

The development of Asian American literature can be divided into two periods. The first period lasted for almost a century. It started with journals, diaries, and poems written by new Asian immigrants in their native languages and culminated with semiautobiographical novels in the early 1980's. This period was marked by Asian American writers' interest in using the autobiographical approach to describe their experience and to define their relationship with mainstream American culture. Chinese American writers Pardee Lowe, in *Father and Glorious Descendant*, and Jade Snow Wong, in *Fifth Chinese Daughter*; Japanese American writers Daniel Inouye, in *Journey to Washington* (1967), and Monica Sone, in *Nisei Daughter* (1953); and Filipino American writer Carlos Bulosan, in *America Is in the Heart* (1943), use autobiography to describe the authors' struggles with both intercultural and intracultural conflict.

Asian American long fiction was born in the autobiographical tradition and Asian American writers' sharpened sensitivities built on an increased awareness of their own cultural heritage. From the mid-1960's to the early 1980's, Asian American literature was rich with fictionalized memoirs that can be read as semiautobiographies. Virginia Lee's *The House That Tai Ming Built* (1963), Chuang Hua's *Crossings* (1968), Kingston's *The Woman Warrior* and *China Men*, Shawn Wong's *Homebase* (1979), and Kazuo Miyamoto's *Hawaii: End of the Rainbow* (1964) could be (and often are) categorized as creative nonfiction rather than fiction. The au-

thors follow the autobiographical tradition in portraying the Asian American experience, in celebrating their cultural heritage, and in reclaiming their sense of history and identity.

The late 1980's through the early 1990's was a busy period in the development of Asian American literature. Established Asian American creative writers were able to continue their successful writing careers, while new Asian American novelists launched theirs. During this period, Asian American long fiction came of age. In 1989, Japanese American writer Cynthia Kadohata and Chinese American writer Amy Tan published their critically acclaimed novels *The Floating World* and *The Joy Luck Club*, respectively. Both heralded the Asian American renaissance of the early and mid-1990's. In 1991 alone, notable novels by four Chinese American writers appeared: Tan published her second novel, *The Kitchen God's Wife*; Gish Jen's first novel, *Typical American*, received positive reviews; Frank Chin published his first long work, *Donald Duk*; and Gus Lee, a lawyer, released an autobiographical novel, *China Boy*.

During the same period, Asian American novelists of Filipino, Korean, and South and Southeast Asian descent were ready to meet the challenge of diversifying the portrayal of the Asian American experience. Filipino American writers Cecilia Manguerra Brainard's *When the Rainbow Goddess Wept* (1994) and Jessica Hagedorn's *The Gangster of Love* (1996), Korean American writers Kim Ronyoung's *Clay Walls* (1987) and Chang-Rae Lee's *Native Speaker* (1995), Asian Indian American writer Bharati Mukherjee's *Jasmine* (1989), and Vietnamese American writer Jade Ngoc Quang Huynh's *South Wind Changing* (1994) enriched the voice and spectrum of Asian American long fiction and brought readers' attention to the diverse nature of the Asian American community.

CHINESE AMERICAN LONG FICTION

Maxine Hong Kingston's *The Woman Warrior* and *China Men* and Tan's *The Joy Luck Club* represent two distinctive periods in the development of Asian American literature to the end of the twentieth century. *The Woman Warrior* and *China Men* are representative of the early development and achievement of Asian American literature. Both use the autobiographical approach to describe their characters' struggles with their identities and their search for voice. Both use memories, oral stories, and traditional Chinese legends, and both interweave the past and the present, fact and fiction, reality and imagination, and traditional Chinese and modern American culture. As Chin observes, in *The Woman Warrior* Kingston mixes two famous Chinese legendary characters, Fa Mulan and Yue Fei, from two different stories. The attempt, contrary to what Chin argues, is not to rewrite Fa Mulan according to "the specs of the stereotype of the Chinese woman as a pathological white supremacist victimized and trapped in a hideous Chinese civilization" but to reveal the richness of the Asian American experience in general and of Asian American literature in particular. Kingston attempts to destroy both the traditional Chinese gender line, which places women at the bottom of the social totem, and the line that separates imagination and reality. The latter approach explains why both *The Woman Warrior* and *China Men* are often categorized as nonfiction.

Tan's *The Joy Luck Club* intermingles the thematic treatment of intercultural conflict with that of intergenerational conflict. The mothers who immigrated to the United States from China still have strong cultural ties to their old home, and they want to rear their children in the traditional way. Their Chinese American daughters, however, believe that they are trapped in the conflict between traditional Chinese culture and mainstream American society, between their aspirations for individual freedom and their sense of familial and social obligations, and between their false and their true identities. The conflict is both frustrating and constructive. The daughters are eventually led to conclude that they must embrace what they cannot culturally reject and to realize that they are as American as they are Chinese. Other Chinese American women writers include Jen (*Typical American*, 1991; *Mona in the Promised Land*, 1996; and *The Love Wife*, 2004), and Fae Myenne Ng (*Bone*, 1993, and *Steer Toward Rock*, 2008).

FILIPINO AMERICAN LONG FICTION

Filipino Americans occupy a unique place in the history of the United States. From the end of the Spanish-American War (1898) to the independence of the Philippines (1946), Filipinos were considered subjects of the United States, and there was no restriction on their immigration. For many years, therefore, Filipino Americans were the largest ethnic group in the Asian American community. This unique historical phenomenon created ambivalent feelings among Filipino Americans toward the United States. Whereas many appreciate the economic opportunities, Filipino American writers such as Joaquin Legaspi, José Garcia Villa, Alfred A. Robles, Bayani L. Mariano, N. V. M. Gonzalez, Samuel Tagatac, J. C. Dionisio, and Bienvenido N. Santos also aspire to reconnect with the native Filipino culture, literature, and art. Filipino American long fiction is largely built on this aspiration; it grows out of the fear of losing what Mariano, in his poem "What We Know," calls the "best of ourselves."

Cecilia Manguerra Brainard and Jessica Hagedorn are two leading Filipino American novelists. The main event of Brainard's *When the Rainbow Goddess Wept* occurs in Asia during World War II. The novel is narrated from a nine-year-old's perspective. With her family, Yvonne Macaraig flees the Japanese invasion of the Philippines to join the resistance effort. In the jungle she is nourished by the legends of Bongkatolan, the Woman Warrior, and the merciful rainbow goddess. Jessica Hagedorn is a novelist, critic, and anthologist whose novel *Dogeaters* (1990) was nominated for a National Book Award. In her 1996 novel *The Gangster of Love*, she portrays a new immigrant from the Philippines who, while excited about his new life in the United States, is haunted by the memory of the homeland he left behind. Both Brainard's *When the Rainbow Goddess Wept* and Hagedorn's *The Gangster of Love* represent Filipino Americans' effort to reclaim their sense of history and identity by making connections with their homeland and with the Filipino culture.

JAPANESE AMERICAN LONG FICTION

Japanese American literature started with logs, diaries, journals, and chronicles written in Japanese. Many Issei (first-generation Japanese immigrants to the United States) did not feel the need to learn English. They were not allowed to become U.S. citizens, and many had come to the United States with the intention of returning to Japan when they had saved enough money. Japanese American literature began to take shape with the emergence of Nisei (second-generation) writers. Some of these writers spoke fluent Japanese as well as English. Besides serving as a bridge between their parents' Japanese culture and American culture, many Nisei writers assumed the responsibility of making the Japanese American voice heard in what Japanese American poet and critic Lawson Fusao Inada calls "the Occidental world of mainstream American literature."

Japanese American novelist John Okada was one of the first Nisei writers to bring readers' attention to the traumatic experience suffered by many Japanese Americans during and after World War II. During the war, 120,000 Japanese Americans living on the West Coast of the United States were forced into relocation camps. The experience left an indelible impact on the Japanese American community and its literature. Okada's *No-No Boy* (1957) depicts a second-generation Japanese American's struggle to balance his loyalty to the Japanese culture, to his parents, and to his country, the United States. The protagonist, Ichiro Yamada, interned during World War II, is put in jail for refusing to forswear allegiance to Japan and join the U.S. Army. After he is released from prison, Ichiro moves back to Seattle and is caught between two seemingly irreconcilable worlds. On one side are his parents, very proud of being Japanese. On the other side is the United States, a country to which he still feels he belongs. During his search for his identity, Ichiro meets several people who help shape his perspective of himself and of his relationship with the United States. After witnessing the tragic deaths of several of his friends, Ichiro starts to think about his own future. He begins to chase the faint insinuation of promise that takes shape in his mind and heart.

In the second period of Japanese American literature, Sansei (third-generation) female writers made significant literary contributions. Cynthia Kadohata and Holly Uyemoto are two leading voices in the development of Japanese American long fiction. The narrator of Kadohata's *The Floating World* (1989), Olivia Ann, is a Sansei. As Olivia is growing up in the 1950's, her family is always on the move from job to job. Having to live in *ukiyo*, the floating world—"the gas station attendants, restaurants, and jobs," "the motel towns floating in the middle of fields and mountains"—the narrator learns early in her life that she and her family must rely on what

is stable while traveling through an unstable world. What is stable is the secret of the family's history, the strong role models in Olivia's mother and her grandmother (*obasan*), and the closeness of the family.

Uyemoto's *Go* (1996) also describes a Sansei's search for connectedness, for her identity, and for her spiritual home. Wil is a burned-out college student. After having an abortion and separating from her politically correct boyfriend, she returns to her family in search of support. Through the disentanglement of her family history, Wil learns about her grandparents' past, the experiences of Issei and Nisei in World War II internment camps, and a cultural heritage deeply embedded in her emotional and spiritual being. If *The Floating World* is exquisitely elegant, picaresque, and observant, *Go* is amusing, zany, and engaging. Both works celebrate Japanese American culture, both portray strong Japanese American female characters, and both suggest strong ties in characters' relationships with their family history and with that of the community.

KOREAN AMERICAN LONG FICTION

Korean American long fiction came into its own in the 1980's and 1990's. Because of the Korean War, Korean immigration to the United States had dramatically increased in the 1950's and 1960's. Children of first-generation Korean immigrants graduated from college in the late 1970's and early 1980's and began to contribute to the flourishing of Asian American literature. Kim Ronyoung was one of the pioneers in Korean American long fiction. Her novel *Clay Walls* (1987) chronicles the journey of a newly married Korean couple, Haesu and Chun, to the United States and their struggle to take root in the new land. The novel experiments with narrative points of view. Events are seen through the eyes of three characters: Haesu, Chun, and Faye, the couple's American-born daughter.

Like the literary works produced by writers from other ethnic groups in the United States, Asian American long fiction includes an important component that is frequently neglected in the study of Asian American literature. Asian American popular novels occupy a special place in Asian American literature and often introduce the culture to the reading public. Amerasian writer Ruthanne Lum McCunn's *Thousand Pieces of Gold*

(1981), Chinese American writer Bette Bao Lord's *Spring Moon* (1981) and *The Middle Heart* (1996), Evelina Chao's *Gates of Grace* (1985), and Gus Lee's *China Boy* (1991) and *Tiger's Tail* (1996) all fit into this category. In Korean American literature, Chang-rae Lee's *Native Speaker*, a detective story, also belongs in this company. The narrator of the novel, Henry Park, is a spy for a private business. His ethnicity provides him with an expedient cover for his work. This amusing and intriguing novel vividly and accurately introduces the customs and traditions of the Korean American community to the reader. Lee's later novels *A Gesture Life* (1999) and *Aloft* (2004) confirm his place as one of the most accomplished contemporary American writers.

SOUTH AND SOUTHEAST ASIAN
AMERICAN LONG FICTION

In the late 1980's and the 1990's, the spectrum of contemporary Asian American long fiction witnessed two major changes from its earlier period. First, autobiographical novels and fictional memoirs were replaced as the predominant voice in the description of the Asian American experience. Asian American writers became more interested in experimenting with different literary genres and in searching for literary forms that can accurately depict the Asian American experience. Second, Asian American writers other than Chinese, Japanese, Filipino, and Korean Americans began to attract attention. Jhumpa Lahiri's first collection of short stories, *Interpreter of Maladies* (1999), won the Pulitzer Prize in fiction in 2000 for tales set both in India and in the United States, and her novel *The Namesake* (2003), about the difficulties of moving from one culture to another, was made into a popular film.

One pioneering South and Southeast Asian American novelist is Asian Indian American writer Bharati Mukherjee. Mukherjee is a first-generation immigrant from India whose novel *Jasmine* depicts a new immigrant's journey from her native country to the United States. The narrator, Jasmine Vijh, was born in Hasnapur, India, and given the name Jyoti. She is her parents' fifth daughter and the seventh of nine children; as such, she was somewhat unwanted. An astrologer predicted that she was doomed to widowhood and exile.

Determined to chart the course of her own life, Jasmine married Prakash Vijh at the age of fourteen, and he renamed her Jasmine as a means of breaking her from her past.

After her husband is murdered by a Muslim fanatic, Jasmine fulfills Prakash's wish and goes to the United States. She first works as a caregiver for Taylor Hayes, a college professor in New York City. She then flees from Sukhwinder, the man who killed her husband, and moves to Baden, Iowa, where she falls in love with Bud Ripplemeyer and becomes his common-law wife, living as Jane Ripplemeyer. Taylor eventually finds Jasmine, and the two decide to move to California. In the novel, Jasmine has several identities; she is a different person to different people. To Prakash, she is Jasmine; to Half-Face, a man who rapes her, she is the goddess Kali; to Lilian Gordon, who helps her find a job in New York City, she is Jazzy; to Taylor, she is Jase; to Bud, she is Jane. Her various identities finally make Jasmine realize that she can be whoever she wants to make herself. At the end of the book, she is ready to take control of her own destiny.

Vietnamese American writer Jade Ngoc Quang Huynh is also a first-generation immigrant. Huynh was a college student in Vietnam, but he was sent to labor camps for "education in communist ideology, psychological and physical retraining, and lessons on how to become a happy and productive member in their new society." Huynh escaped Vietnam in 1977, a few years after the end of the Vietnam War, and went to the United States. His *South Wind Changing* (1994) follows the traditions established by Vietnamese American writers such as Le Ly Hayslip, whose two powerful autobiographies, *When Heaven and Earth Changed Places* (1990) and *Child of War, Woman of Peace* (1993), touched readers' hearts and were later made into a film (*Heaven and Earth*, 1993) directed by Oliver Stone. *South Wind Changing* is about family, traditions, and the stark contrast between the beauty of nature and the cruelty of war and ideological battles. The novel traces the narrator's footsteps from Vietnam to the United States. Its first-person narrative is believable, patient, and moving.

Qun Wang
Updated by David Peck

BIBLIOGRAPHY

Adams, Bella. *Asian American Literature*. Edinburgh, Scotland: Edinburgh University Press, 2008. Introductory guide to Asian American literature that includes historical and thematic perspectives. Focuses on works published after 1969, but earlier works are examined as well.

Chan, Jeffery Paul, Frank Chin, Lawson Fusao Inada, and Shawn Wong, eds. *The Big Aiiieeeee! An Anthology of Chinese American and Japanese American Literature*. New York: Meridian, 1991. Includes Frank Chin's article "Come All Ye Asian American Writers of the Real and the Fake," which discusses literary histories of Chinese American and Japanese American literature and criticizes the development of contemporary Asian American literature from a cultural-nationalist point of view.

Cheung, King-Kok. *Articulate Silences*. Ithaca, N.Y.: Cornell University Press, 1993. Examines the influential works of Japanese American writer Hisaye Yamamoto, Japanese Canadian writer Joy Kogawa, and Chinese American writer Maxine Hong Kingston in a discussion of women's contributions to the development of Asian American and Asian Canadian literature.

_____, ed. *An Interethnic Companion to Asian American Literature*. New York: Cambridge University Press, 1997. Collection of essays that survey North American writers of Asian descent in terms of both national origins (Chinese, Filipino, Japanese, Korean, South Asian, Vietnamese) and shared concerns.

Huang, Guiyou. *The Columbia Guide to Asian American Literature Since 1945*. New York: Columbia University Press, 2006. Excellent reference work with citations to a wide range of Asian American writers and literature published after World War II.

_____, ed. *Asian American Literary Studies*. Edinburgh, Scotland: Edinburgh University Press, 2005. Examines themes such as war and Asian American literary works, self-agency in Asian American autobiography, the "confines of binary oppositions of gender," and "pan-ethnicity."

_____, ed. *The Greenwood Encyclopedia of Asian American Literature*. Westport, Conn.: Greenwood Press, 2008. This comprehensive three-volume work contains more than 270 entries on writers, works, genres, events, and special topics in Asian American literature.

Kim, Elaine H. *Asian American Literature: An Introduction to the Writings and Their Social Context*. Philadelphia: Temple University Press, 1982. One of the pioneer works in the study of Asian American literature. Examines first- and second-generation Asian American writers and their portraits of Chinatown, the Japanese American community, the search for a new self-image, and other topics. An invaluable resource.

Lim, Shirley Geok-lin, and Amy Ling, eds. *Reading the Literatures of Asian America*. Philadelphia: Temple University Press, 1992. Collection of essays by leading scholars in the study of Asian American literatures and cultures. Essays include "The Ambivalent American: Asian American Literature on the Cusp" and "The Death of Asia on the American Field of Representation."

Canadian Long Fiction

Given the geographical and historical proximity of Canada and the United States, it stands to reason that their national literatures would reflect similar concerns. Early Canadian settlers traveled from Europe, with the majority emigrating from Great Britain and France. They were faced with a wilderness that seemed almost infinite—and would not be completely settled even into the twentieth century—inhabited by people whose appearance, beliefs, and customs were different from their own. Their national economy was closely linked to natural resources, dominated by such industries as farming, fishing, mining, logging, and milling. Little in their previous experience had prepared them for such an encounter, and few of the artistic models they had brought from Europe allowed them to completely express the reality of their relation to this "new" world. Like their cousins to the south, Canadians were continually renegotiating their identity relative to the surrounding landscape, and early Canadian writers sought to raise this daily phenomenon of encounter and compromise to an expression of national selfhood.

As such, it is strange to note how differently Canada and the United States developed, in both literary and historical senses. Where Americans were driven by their "manifest" directive to settle the continent, Canadian settlement was less rapid and headlong. Official groups such as the Royal Canadian Mounted Police often preceded settlers into the wilderness, carving out a habitable and "known" space for pioneers who followed. The emphasis was usually on order, which prevented the frenzied land rushes and cultural clashes occurring to the south. Where American settlement was often violent, punctuated by slavery and wars with American Indians, Canadian movements across the landscape were deliberate and, at some level, introspective. Relations with Indians, though not perfect, were enhanced by the Canadian government's simple willingness to adhere to its treaties. Other interchanges between cultures, despite friction, infrequently rose to the level of martial conflict that punctuated U.S. history. Indeed, the high premium that Canadians have historically placed on cultural dialogue continues to be exemplified by the coexistence of anglophone and francophone cultures.

Early Canadian novels, 1769-1852

The complexities of cultural interchange and of comprehending the landscape beyond simple conquest have epitomized Canadian long fiction from its inception. Chief among such works is Frances Brooke's *The History of Emily Montague* (1769), arguably the first North American novel. Written by an Englishwoman who had lived for five years in Canada and adhering closely to a standard romance plot, *The History of Emily Montague* nevertheless invokes the sense of dichotomy that would characterize later Canadian novels. The matrices that form the novel's thematic base—civilization versus savagery, urban versus rural, feminine versus masculine, and domestic order versus natural law—challenge the assumption that European society could be instantly transplanted to North America. While the lead characters, Emily Montague and Colonel Rivers, marry at the novel's end—per the genre's conventions—the negotiations that occur during their courtship in Canada suggest how Brooke's writing subtly undermines the moral, sexual, and political expectations of her English audience. Though no great upheaval occurs within the book's social order, the mere suggestion of necessary compromise (between characters of various backgrounds and between humans and the wilderness) creates a sense of cultural dialogue uncommon in works of the time.

Such dialogues are stressed in John Richardson's *Wacousta: Or, The Prophecy, a Tale of the Canadas* (1832), the next seminal novel in Canadian literary history. Similar to James Fenimore Cooper's Leatherstocking Tales in its depiction of a white army facing an Indian foe, *Wacousta* eschews the easy valorization of "civilization" over "savagery" implicit in Cooper's works. From the novel's start, Richardson refuses to uphold any character type as absolutely worthy or moral, and even the notion of identity itself—who people are, what qualifies them as good or evil, how rapidly they change—is negotiated at a frenetic pace. The title character is not even an Indian but a British man whose unrequited love for Clara Beverly has caused him to masquerade as a Scottish renegade, a French officer under Montcalm, and finally a lieutenant to Pontiac among the Ottawa. In this last capacity, he helps lead the Indians against Fort Detroit, home to Colonel De Haldimar (the widower of Clara Beverly) and his three children. The relationships formed by Haldimar's family with military personnel, Indians, and finally Wacousta himself weave an intricate cultural tableau in which Richardson presents his readers with a seemingly fixed version of the world only to invert the relationships in ensuing chapters.

The novel is finally presided over by the schizophrenic figure of Wacousta, whose negotiation of cultural borders suggests an ironic ability to alter his identity even as his ongoing psychological torment over Clara suggests his inability to elude the singular essence of what he is as a man. This metaphor could serve for most of the novel's characters, whose mores cannot keep pace with their rapidly changing situations in the novel, forcing them and their audience to reconsider the values they believe to be "permanent."

Wacousta is the most complex novel of early Canadian literature, outlining the thematic and cultural core of many works to follow, especially novels about the Canadian wilderness and cross-cultural contact. If Richardson is concerned with the way human identity both shapes and is shaped by the natural landscape, Susanna Moodie's *Roughing It in the Bush: Or, Life in Canada* (1852) offers an interesting thematic supplement, a chronicle of settlers attempting to deal with their environment after the wilderness has been largely "tamed." Of particular importance is the way that the novel serves both as a precursor to the "farm" or prairie novels of the early twentieth century and as a blueprint, with its vocal female protagonist, for the strong tradition of women's writing in Canadian letters.

The book is narrated by a woman named Susanna Moodie (not to be completely taken for the author herself) who recounts her failure, along with her husband, Dunbar, at farming in southern Ontario. Members of the gentry, the Moodies find themselves physically unprepared for the rigors of farm life and overly romantic about the promise of the land (unlike their poor neighbors, who are more accustomed to the labor that farming

requires). Offering a series of realistic sketches depicting the frontier in early Canada, the novel, like its predecessors, pits various opposites against one another: European versus North American, wealthy versus poor, urban versus rural. Again, it refuses to completely valorize any set of cultural mores; readers are disappointed by the literal failure of the optimistic Moodies yet skeptical of the unadorned, often menial physicality implicit in the lives of the more successful farmers. This ambivalence breaks down the absolute nature of the binaries that the author originally constructs, suggesting the inadequacy of using the Moodies, their neighbors, or any individuals as templates for a representative national identity.

THE INTERIM PERIOD, 1852-1920

Despite the impressive novels of the early nineteenth century, Canadians did not produce many long literary works from 1852 to 1920, and those that were produced did not rival the complexity of their predecessors; the best-known work from this period is a children's book, L. M. Montgomery's 1908 *Anne of Green Gables*. Indeed, a quick look at the number of Canadian titles produced throughout the nineteenth century would be enough to demonstrate that Canada was not developing the sizable literary tradition of the United States at the time. In part, this situation was the result of demographics: A small Canadian population spread over a broad area did not have the resources to support an indigenous publishing industry.

The disparity also was the result of U.S. history. Obsessed with becoming a world power, the United States engaged in not only a quick march across the continent but also a furious drive to place before the world a literature that could be considered emblematically American. Success against Britain in gaining independence, as well as the attention of European philosophers and a growing industrial economy, had made Americans keenly aware of their need for an intellectual apparatus to match their imperial aspirations. The novels they produced out of this sensibility were largely future oriented, singular in their belief in the eventual greatness of the United States, and philosophically rooted in a tradition that generally—if ironically—raised individual liberties, the spirit of revolution, and a proclivity for violence to the level of national-cultural persona.

Canadians, by contrast, often viewed the "chaos" of U.S. imperial designs with skepticism and dismay; many British loyalists had, in fact, fled north during the America Revolution. Canada, more than the United States, was forced to deal with crises of identity at an early stage of nationhood. Despite strong ties to the British crown, Canada was made up of a variety of cultural groups: loyalist English in Ontario, Maritime Scots sympathetic to the United States, French-speaking Catholics in Quebec, and numerous Indian tribes. Lacking the central (if dubious) myth of a unified predestined empire, Canada operated under a sometimes fragile sense of shared geography and cultural balance-of-power until confederation in 1867. Even after confederation, various groups continued to agitate for greater recognition, such as the Québécois independence movements that continued to occur throughout the twentieth century. Moreover, Canadian history and literature suffered from a kind of neocolonial complex, a sense of "inadequacy" in the face of both British tradition and the United States' burgeoning—if self-proclaimed—historic and artistic greatness.

Responding to this situation, Canadian writers in the early twentieth century worked to embrace their nation's "median" status, exploring the cultural borders on which Canadians found themselves and adopting analogues from British and American culture that represented their experience even as they rejected the idea of Canada as a mirror image of either foreign culture. Their job, as always, was to find in their multifarious history what was distinct about them as a people, a more introspective process than either British or American models probably allowed. This focus on "discovering" the past rather than pushing toward the future evolved into a quintessential feature of the Canadian novel, a direct outgrowth of the cultural exploration and self-analysis implicit in the earliest works of Brooke, Richardson, and Moodie.

What became important to Canadian intellectuals late in this period—and remained important through the twentieth century—was the idea of "process" by which a person or a nation comes to articulate an identity. Without a central cultural myth to which all others must refer, Canadian authors found themselves in the unique position of being able to write their own history well after it had unfolded—that is, to probe the past in an attempt not only to recount events but also to investigate how and why such events are told, to recognize the many viewpoints inherent in "making history," and to acknowledge the past not as a single set of incidents but as a more fluid series of interpretations constantly subject to review.

THE PRAIRIE AND THE WEST

During the 1920's and 1930's, a common metaphor for this process of discovering history recurred in novels about the Great Plains and the Western interior. Unlike the American frontier novel—where white pioneer-cowboys contend against American Indians, villains, and the forces of industry to settle the continent—Canadian Western novels deal with settlers coming to terms with the "vast absence" around them. If violent contests did occur in the Canadian West, they more often took the shape of humans versus the landscape or versus their own demons than a contest against those external forces struggling to prevent the advance of "civilization." Thus, while most American Westerns resolve themselves quite neatly—the defeat of the "savage" cleared the way for the nation's progress—Canadian Westerns were troubled both by the absolute moral oppositions of the American system and by the way that system failed to address Canada's own historical experience.

Implicitly aware of the multiple viewpoints shaping their past, Canadians struggled with the concept of how to build "history" out of many voices—or, more to the point, how to articulate Canadian identity when no one cultural voice told the nation's full story and history became a kind of "surrounding silence" incapable of revealing itself. Canadian experiences with both the prairie and the Western interior served as apt metaphors for this struggle, though for different reasons. The prairie—flat, empty, even desolate—offered a vacant site where the task of self-creation seemed simultaneously imminent and impossible, a blank slate on which to inscribe both personal and national identity that contained no external signposts to suggest exactly what that identity should be. The Western interior, by contrast, offered a mountainous landscape filled with spectacular topography and various cultures, a place full of external stimuli yet also filled with different people who encountered those stimuli through vastly divergent historical, economic, and personal contexts.

Of the prairie novels, the most notable are Frederick

Philip Grove's *Settlers of the Marsh* (1925), Martha Ostenso's *Wild Geese* (1925), Robert J. C. Stead's *Grain* (1926), and Sinclair Ross's *As for Me and My House* (1941). While all have been called works of realism, depicting the harsh nature of prairie life, later critics recognized them as psychological quests for self-understanding. *Grain* follows the attempts of a slow-witted man, Gander Stake, to come to terms with his own social and sexual identity even as the farm life to which he is accustomed slowly gives way to a post-World War I industrial economy. *Settlers of the Marsh* and *Wild Geese* explore the worlds of egomaniacal patriarchs trying to found personal dynasties on the plains, as well as the oppressed characters (often female) attempting to break free from their single-minded imperatives. *As for Me and My House* analyzes the process by which characters construct their identities away from civilization, isolated in a small prairie town.

Of these works, *As for Me and My House* is the most interesting because of the way it explores identity construction as more than a reaction to another's demagoguery; Ross's work excludes dominant, if detestable, central figures (such as Grove's Neils Lindstedt or Ostenso's Caleb Gare) in order to avoid amoral touchstones through which the actions of others can be measured and understood. Instead, he offers only the town of Horizon—a mere spot on the Saskatchewan map—during the Great Depression, where characters come to understand themselves through interactions with the community. The novel is rendered in journal format by the wife of Philip Bentley, Horizon's minister. Mrs. Bentley is a proud and stand-offish woman, a former musician who claims to detest everything about the small, isolated place to which her husband has been sent. Philip Bentley is an agnostic and a failed artist who has assumed his religious post more out of his sense of duty than out of belief or desire.

Together the Bentleys struggle to understand themselves against the backdrop of the desolate prairie, Philip's extramarital affair, an illegitimate child, and constant rancor. Despite her desperate need to be loved, Mrs. Bentley refuses to turn to Philip because of the many betrayals which she believes he has heaped upon her. Despite his desperate need for artistic stimulation and his overwhelming self-doubt, Philip refuses to leave

Horizon, motivated by the same pride that motivates his wife. In both cases, the prairie becomes a symbol of the isolation and emptiness that both characters feel. Even the one person who seems capable of escaping the oppressive psychological weight of Horizon—Philip's lover Judith—dies by the novel's end, and the Bentleys subsequently move back east.

Amid the despair, though, Ross's novel offers an ironic glimmer of hope in the figure of the prairie itself. Unending and oppressive, the prairie is ultimately the psychological catalyst that erases the characters' faulty self-conceptions and lets them see themselves for what they truly are. Mrs. Bentley regularly walks down the train tracks away from Horizon and into the prairie, an act that suggests her figurative desire to embrace the landscape's blankness and create a psychological space in which she can discover her true nature or even reinvent herself according to her deepest desires. Their insistence that the prairie stifles self-expression notwithstanding, both Bentleys explore various sides of their personalities while in Horizon and, while making critical mistakes, seem more self-satisfied by the novel's end. Their final move east can thus be read either negatively (as a retreat from that version of themselves that Horizon has revealed) or positively (as a redemptive shift toward grace following the Purgatory in which their souls have been laid bare). In either event, it is the process of identity discovery and even construction central to Canadian fiction that leads one Bentley family into Horizon and another away from it one year later.

Published almost concurrently with *As for Me and My House*, Howard O'Hagan's *Tay John* (1939) was the first work set in the Western interior to raise the prairie novel's quest for personal identity to the overt level of cultural politics and national myth. The protagonist of *Tay John* is a mixed-race Shuswap Indian navigating the margins of both Indian and white society. A failed messiah to his people and an enigmatic hunter-tracker among white people, Tay John is labeled time and again by the novel's other characters, only to disregard their expectations. Even his name, which changes several times, is evidence of the way that words fail to tell his story. He goes from being Kumkan Kleseem to Kumkleseem, to Tête Jaune, to Tay John—all very different names but each offering no more than a rudimentary assessment of his uncommonly yellow hair. Identity after identity is subverted until it becomes clear that no one—neither the Shuswap into whose tribe he was born nor the white people in whose camps he works—can begin to define him. His demise is equally enigmatic: Pulling a sled bearing his dead white wife, he appears merely to descend into a snow drift, dying but not dying, defying explanation again.

If one point of *As for Me and My House* is to demonstrate how difficult it can be to tell one's own story, then the point of *Tay John* is to demonstrate how impossible it must be to tell someone else's. In this sense, the ubiquitous Tay John—despite his mythic aspect—is one of the least compelling characters in the work. Rather, the book asks its audience to identify with those people who try, yet fail, to tell the protagonist's story: the Shuswap, who want Tay John to lead them to their promised land; Alf Dobble, the failed land developer who sees Tay John as a fixture in his mountain empire; and even Blackie, who tries to narrate Tay John's death as simply as possible, yet relegates him to myth again. These characters, O'Hagan suggests, are emblematic of the book's readers—people for whom names order the world, yet for whom names completely misidentify that world. As Jack Denham, the narrator of most of the book, observes, "naming is unnaming," tacitly admitting the way that a name ascribed by one person or culture necessarily undoes the name assigned by another. Interpersonal misunderstandings are raised to the level of cross-class, cross-race, and cross-gender miscommunication, underscoring the nearly complete futility of the notion of productive interchange among different people and cultures. Yet Tay John, both the man and the idea, remains indelibly fixed at the core of the tale—a story that cannot necessarily be told but one that undeniably exists.

These seemingly dichotomous elements—the need to tell the story despite skepticism that any one story can account for all the necessary viewpoints—has remained a feature of the Canadian Western since *Tay John*'s publication. Latter-day practitioners of the form have focused more specifically on the problems of cross-cultural interchange, keenly aware of historical frictions between Caucasians and Indians. For example, Peter Such's *Riverrun* (1973) inverts the "conventional" version of history by exploring the extinction of the Beothuck Indians of Newfoundland from the Indians' point of view. Rudy Wiebe's *The Temptations of Big Bear* (1973) challenges the idea of history proper by noting that any recorded version of the past marginalizes the Indian culture in whose language that history is not written. The story revolves around the Cree chief Big Bear—who refuses to select a reservation site for his people—and the numerous failed attempts of surrounding characters, Caucasians and non-Cree Indians alike, to understand him.

Other novels offer an occasionally humorous, if no less poignant, angle on this subject. Robert Kroetsch's *Gone Indian* (1973) tracks the attempts of an American graduate student to discover his "real" life as a mock Canadian Indian; George Bowering's *Caprice* (1987) comically inverts the normal order of the American Western by having two dry-witted, semi-omniscient Indians narrate the story of a whip-wielding cowgirl-heroine; and Philip Kreiner's *Contact Prints* (1987) follows the misadventures of a white teacher at an Indian school who makes a living covertly selling her art as "authentically" native.

Such an environment has also helped to foster a vibrant native literature in Canada. Despite hard-edged fiction that explores the brutal reality of some Indian lives—such as Beatrice Culleton's *In Search of April Raintree* (1983)—most Native Canadian novelists have echoed their white counterparts in adopting a sympathetic, even humorous, tone relative to Indian characters. As in the United States, the Native Canadian novel does not have a long tradition in itself, but many of its themes and devices derive from oral narratives that have existed since before first contact. In addition, Indian writers have been strongly influenced by the expansive tradition of the Canadian novel, especially the experimental styles of writers such as Kroetsch and Bowering. The Indians in Thomas King's *Medicine River* (1990) more closely resemble *Caprice*'s sardonic Indian narrators than more polemical protagonists, while his *Green Grass, Running Water* (1993) offers a multilayered postmodern tale in which members of one Indian family, several spirits, and an "omniscient" trickster figure are set on a course that brings them (and their immediate surroundings) to a farcical apocalyptic end.

As scholars have noted, later Indian novels focused

as much on the similarities between white and Native lives as on the differences. King's work—along with books by Maurice Kenny, Ruby Slipperjack, and Jeanette Armstrong—provides a version of everyday Indian life that seems quite similar to everyday white life even as it partakes of a lyricism and mysticism echoing its specific past. This duality, which acknowledges cultural similarities while being able to embrace differences, continues the careful balancing act of personal and cultural identity so precious to Canadian novelists. Nowhere is that process of national identity construction more evident than in Western Canadian fiction, from Richardson and Moodie through Ross and O'Hagan to Wiebe and King.

CANADIAN NOVELS AFTER 1960

While Native Canadians constitute the most prominent minority group writing in Canada, peoples of other races and ethnicities have found room within the nation's pluralistic literary tradition. Mordecai Richler has charted the Canadian Jewish experience in books such as *The Apprenticeship of Duddy Kravitz* (1959), *St. Urbain's Horsemen* (1971), and *Joshua Then and Now* (1980). Sky Lee's *Disappearing Moon Café* (1990) and Joy Kogawa's *Obasan* (1981) recount the sometimes tragic histories of Chinese and Japanese immigrants, respectively. Beginning around 1980, novelists of Middle Eastern, Asian Indian, and Sri Lankan descent also assumed a prominent place in Canadian letters. Before *The English Patient* (1992) won the Booker Prize, Michael Ondaatje was quite famous within Canada for experimental fiction such as *The Collected Works of Billy the Kid* (1970) and *Coming Through Slaughter* (1976). His continuing success, with, for example, *Divisadero* (2007), has been echoed by such writers as Rohinton Mistry, who won the 1991 Governor-General's Award for *Such a Long Journey* (1991) and has been short-listed for the Booker Prize for both *A Fine Balance* (1995) and *Family Matters* (2002). Lebanese-born writer Rawi Hage's *De Niro's Game* won a number of prizes following its publication in 2006. Even Caribbean writers have found their way to a northern home: Neil Bissoondath's *A Casual Brutality* (1988) recounts the moral devolution of a Caribbean island and one ordinary man's inability to cope with such changes.

Such inclusions do not mean that latter-day Canadian novels have completely lost a sense of their British "origins." The works of Robertson Davies, Canada's best-known writer, demonstrate a stylistic and thematic affinity for the Old World. Davies, who died in 1995, is best known for his trilogies—the Salterton trilogy, the Cornish trilogy, and the Deptford trilogy. His erudite language, fascination with psychology, and use of European mysticism and arcane lore make his sweeping sagas of Canadian families closely akin to John Galsworthy or Henry James.

Of Davies's work, the Deptford trilogy is probably the most famous. Following the lives of three men from the small town of Deptford, Ontario, the trilogy addresses the Jungian issues of how closely all human lives are interrelated, how issues of the spirit impact issues of the flesh, and how even the smallest actions can have profound effects on the future. The narrative begins when Percy "Boy" Staunton throws a stone-filled snowball at Dunstable Ramsay, who dodges, allowing the snowball to strike Mary Dempster instead. Mary gives birth prematurely to a son, Paul, before going insane. The rest of the trilogy follows the lives of Staunton, Ramsay, and Paul, never letting its audience forget the profound impact of a single snowball on all three characters and the people around them. On the surface, such connections seem only marginally related to the issues of historical investigation, revision, and self-creation typical of contemporaneous Canadian novels. At the same time, however, each novel in the trilogy is imbued with deep senses of guilt and responsibility.

In particular, *Fifth Business* (1970), the opening work in the series, emphasizes the Canadian impulse to understand the past, revolving around an autobiographical letter in which Dunstable Ramsay attempts to make sense of his place in the chain of events that led to Paul's birth and Mary Dempster's dementia. Such uncertainty—Ramsay's quest for the original definitive moment in his life—is what ultimately reinscribes Davies as a prototypical Canadian writer. The search for identity that many of his characters undergo echoes the larger quest of Canadians defining themselves both within and against Anglo-American ideas. Accused sometimes of being too urbanely English himself, Davies writes with the polish of British predecessors but always about characters whose lives undermine the historical sense of certainty often associated with the Anglo-American culture.

Beyond culture, Canadian novels have accommodated other differences. Most important is the strong tradition of women's writing present from the genre's inception by Brooke and sustained by writers such as Julia Catherine Hart, Moodie, Rosanna Leprohon, Nellie L. McClung, Laura Goodman Salverson, and Ostenso through the early 1920's. The second half of the twentieth century produced women novelists writing on every theme and in every style imaginable. Margaret Laurence's five Manawaka novels, especially *The Stone Angel* (1964) and *The Diviners* (1974), bear the distinct imprint of Ostenso and even Willa Cather in their epic record of women protagonists struggling to assert their identity after small-town beginnings. Aritha Van Herk's *The Tent Peg* (1981) and Anne Cameron's *The Journey* (1982) revise conventional Western plots, placing women in men's roles and even having women dress as men in an attempt to undermine the rigid gender inscription of the American West.

Sheila Watson's *The Double Hook* (1959), an experimental novel relying on modified stream of consciousness to navigate between characters' thoughts, anticipates the postmodern style of Alice Munro's *Who Do You Think You Are?* (1978; also known as *The Beggar Maid: Stories of Flo and Rose*, 1979), in which parallel episodes, flashbacks, seemingly random images, and nonlinear events piece together to delineate the complex relationship between a mother and daughter. Carol Shields's *The Stone Diaries* (1993) offers readers a graceful and straightforward depiction of a middle-class female protagonist, Daisy Stone Goodwill, whose Everywoman qualities resonate one of Laurence's realist portraits or even narratives from one century earlier.

Deserving special consideration is Margaret Atwood—a novelist, poet, and literary critic who has had such a profound effect on world literature since the late 1960's that it is impossible to discuss Canadian long fiction without mentioning her. More than her contemporaries, Atwood exploits ideas of duality and multiplicity, bringing together cultural binaries in ways that not only articulate the complexity of individual oppositions but also illustrate their relation to each other. From

early novels such as *Surfacing* (1972), in which a character's exploration of sexual identity leads her to question the meaning of her life generally, to later novels such as *The Robber Bride* (1993), which inverts the sexual mechanics of a Grimm's fairy tale to illustrate the influence of gender on larger cultural issues, Atwood demonstrates an uncanny ability to find the links among various kinds of identity and to balance those within single narratives.

Atwood's *The Handmaid's Tale* (1985)—an apocalyptic future narrative about an American theological revolution in which women become slaves—epitomizes this ability, demonstrating the links between gender and other identities but never allowing any one of these identities to predominate. For Atwood, identity is a matter of worldly forces in constant flux, with relationships changing daily. As such, she might be viewed as the consummate Canadian writer, a woman fundamentally concerned with how people define themselves but recognizing such definitions as a matter of ongoing process, never to be articulated finitely. Her later novels include *Alias Grace* (1996), *The Blind Assassin* (2000), and *Oryx and Crake* (2003), another dystopian narrative. All three were short-listed for the Booker Prize, and *The Blind Assassin* won the prestigious award.

MULTIPLICITY AND THE CANADIAN SELF

At its most basic level, Atwood's writing reminds readers of Canada's "differences." With its diverse geography and cultural history, the country frequently produces writers who seem more influenced by localized forces than national ones. Certainly this is true in the case of Quebec, where early novels such as *Les Anciens Canadiens* (1863; *The Canadians of Old*, 1864) by Philippe-Joseph Aubert de Gaspe and *Jean Rivard* (1874; English translation, 1977) by Antoine Gerin-Lajoie emphasize Québécois individuality and differences from anglophone Canada. English-language writers also have their regional traditions; one has only to consider Alistair MacLeod's Nova Scotia (*The Lost Salt Gift of Blood*, 1988; revised 1991), Matt Cohen's southern Ontario (*The Disinherited*, 1974), or Jack Hodgins's British Columbia (*The Invention of the World*, 1977) to recognize the indelible mark that such small places have left on Canadian literature.

However, such differences, always a part of Canada, have never quite overwhelmed the similarities. If one trend within the Canadian novel has been to emphasize separation, it has not been without some recognition of a larger geographical, social, and historical shared experience. Thus, a francophone farm novel such as Ringuet's *Trente arpents* (1938; *Thirty Acres*, 1940) or a work of psychological naturalism such as Gabrielle Roy's *Bonheur d'occasion* (1945; *The Tin Flute*, 1947), can address many of the same issues as works by Grove or Ostenso. Atwood's *Bodily Harm* (1981), a novel about a white Canadian woman witnessing a Caribbean revolt, can anticipate by several years the postcolonial fictions of Neil Bissoondath. Hodgins and King can use Irish and American Indian myth respectively to arrive at similarly satiric versions of the rise and fall of "civilization" in western Canada.

These incidental similarities, however, are less important than the process Canadian novelists have developed to discuss Canadian identity—a process ironically begun with the admission that pinpointing such an identity is impossible. Arnold E. Davidson has written that "the Canadian novel is especially Canadian in the very way in which it persistently unwrites and rewrites that problematic adjective, *Canadian*." In other words, it is their common belief in the absence of a single national identity that draws together Canadian novelists from all eras and backgrounds. Such a belief could be produced only by a country precariously united at times by the sheer fact of its common nationality. Then again, such a national literature thrives on ironies, oppositions, borders, and continual negotiations of selfhood. In refusing to stake out its exact parameters, the Canadian novel affirms its identity. Its pluralistic sensibility, its skill at balancing many cultural voices, and its belief in identity formation as an ongoing process continue to make it a progressive and intriguing literary tradition.

J. David Stevens
Updated by David Peck

BIBLIOGRAPHY

Atwood, Margaret. *Survival: A Thematic Guide to Canadian Literature*. Toronto, Ont.: McClelland & Stewart, 1996. Analysis of the chief issues in Canadian literature, in prose that is clear, witty, and accessible to a broad audience. A classic work of Canadian criticism by a renowned novelist.

Benson, Eugene, and William Toye, eds. *The Oxford Companion to Canadian Literature*. 2d ed. New York: Oxford University Press, 1997. Like Oxford's other companion volumes, this work offers insightful introductions to a broad range of Canadian writers and literary issues. Entries are as uniformly well written as they are diverse in subject matter. A thorough set of cross-references accompanies most entries.

Davidson, Arnold E., ed. *Studies on Canadian Literature: Introductory and Critical Essays*. New York: Modern Language Association of America, 1990. Collection of essays on both anglophone and francophone writers that explores Canadian literature from numerous critical perspectives. A fine overview of Canadian cultural issues, and a must-read for beginning students of Canadian literature.

Hammill, Faye. *Canadian Literature*. Edinburgh, Scotland: Edinburgh University Press, 2007. Combines historical and thematic approaches (for example, race and geography) into detailed analyses of the works of Alice Munro, Margaret Atwood, Michael Ondaatje, Leonard Cohen, Thomas King, and Carol Shields.

Harrison, Dick. *Unnamed Country: The Struggle for a Canadian Prairie Fiction*. Edmonton: University of Alberta Press, 1977. Preeminent work on the historical circumstances and cultural imperatives that precipitated the strong, if complex, tradition of Canadian Western writing.

Howells, Coral Ann. *Contemporary Canadian Women's Fiction: Refiguring Identities*. New York: Palgrave Macmillan, 2003. Analyzes the shift in Canada's literary perception of its identity through the writings of Canadian women.

Hutcheon, Linda. *The Canadian Postmodern: A Study of Contemporary English-Canadian Fiction*. New York: Oxford University Press, 1988. Analysis of late twentieth century Canadian literature from one of North America's foremost postmodern critics. Hutcheon makes the convincing case that Canadian literature—in its historic negotiation of borders and balancing of different cultural voices—has been "postmodern" for much of its history.

Kanaganayakam, Chelva, ed. *Moveable Margins: The Shifting Spaces of Canadian Literature*. Toronto, Ont.: TSAR, 2005. Literary critics address the issue of multiplicity in Canadian literature, and examine "how ideas of space and landscape complement and intersect with the constantly changing facets of Canadian society." Includes Asian Canadian, African Canadian, and indigenous perspectives.

Kröller, Eva-Maria, ed. *The Cambridge Companion to Canadian Literature*. Reprint. New York: Cambridge University Press, 2005. Comprehensive survey of major writers, genres, and topics in Canadian literature in one dozen essays by leading scholars in the field.

Moses, Daniel David, and Terry Goldie, eds. *An Anthology of Canadian Native Literature in English*. 3d ed. New York: Oxford University Press, 2005. Comprehensive selection of Native Canadian writing. Entries are representative, if not always extensive, and offer readers a solid sense of both the differences and similarities between the concerns of American Indians and Canadian Indians.

New, W. H. *A History of Canadian Literature*. 2d ed. Ithaca, N.Y.: McGill-Queen's University Press, 2003. Critical reading of Canadian literature from its indigenous origins in oral history to the writings of the twenty-first century. Astute and succinct work that also features a sixty-page chronology and an added final chapter covering works after 1987.

Vautier, Marie. *New World Myth: Postmodernism and Postcolonialism in Canadian Fiction*. Montreal: McGill-Queen's University Press, 1998. Explores how late twentieth century Canadian novels undermine the kind of New World myths that were central to settling the continent. Extends the discussion (prominent in Canadian letters) of the multiple meanings of "postcolonial" in Canadian cultural history.

The Caribbean Novel

Literary critic Roberto González Echevarría asserts that Latin American literature originated in the Caribbean. "It is in fifteenth century explorer Christopher Columbus's diary," he writes, "that we [readers] first encounter what will become the most persistent theme of Latin American literature." That theme, Echevarría argues, is "how to write in a European language about realities never seen in Europe before."

Caribbean writers find before them the tools of four European languages, imported by the imperial aspirations of the Dutch, English, French, and Spanish. Writers from Dutch Caribbean regions, such as Frank Martinus Arion and Astrid H. Roemer, have been translated into other languages, making their work available to non-Dutch-speaking readers, but the Dutch Caribbean tradition stands largely unexplored.

Caribbean literature unites literary works that have been studied not only in terms of national traditions (Haitian, Cuban, and so on) but also under a wide range of classifications, such as West Indian (meaning from the English-speaking Caribbean), francophone (French outside of France), and Latin American literatures, as well as African diaspora and postcolonial literature. Caribbean literature designates literature not only from the island nations but also from Central and South American continental territories such as Belize, Guyana, Suriname, and French Guiana, which share a common experience of slavery and sugar-plantation economies with the island territories. Because the indigenous populations of Arawaks, Tainos, and Caribs of the Caribbean basin were almost wholly exterminated through violence and disease, Caribbean peoples primarily descend from settlers exogenous to the region, most notably the large number of African slaves brought to toil on the plantations and the indentured Asian laborers brought to replace African labor after emancipation. Consequently, Caribbean writers must negotiate a relationship with both a colonial metropolitan culture and the memory of the other African and Asian cultures from elsewhere.

Early flourishings

If Caribbean literature began with Columbus's diary, the Caribbean novel, by contrast, was largely a product of the twentieth century. Nineteenth century Cuban antislavery novels, such as Anselmo Suárez y Romero's *Francisco* (1880), Cirilo Villaverde's *Cecilia Valdés* (first part 1839, completed 1882; *Cecilia Valdés: A Novel of Cuban Customs*, 1962), and Gertrudis Gómez de Avellaneda's *Sab* (1841; English translation, 1993), offered early intimations that nationalist, anticolonial thought in the Caribbean was inextricably bound to the legacies of slavery. For the most part, however, novelistic interrogations of Caribbean identities waited until the first decade of the twentieth century, when Haitian writers began their realist experiments and thus provided the seeds for the later, great genre of Haitian literature, the peasant novel.

In this early period, the novels of a writer claimed by the Harlem Renaissance proved paradigmatic. The Jamaican Claude McKay (1889-1948) was the first black anglophone Caribbean novelist. His first novel, *Home to Harlem* (1928), depicts Jake, an African American returned from World War I to the streets and nightlife of Harlem, and Ray, an exiled Haitian intellectual and aspiring writer, who instructs Jake in pan-Africanism and awareness of a global proletariat. Notably, Ray finds himself in the United States working alongside Jake as a Pullman Car porter because he has fled the U.S. occupation of his island. McKay's second novel, *Banjo* (1929), revisits Ray, this time as he pronounces on culture, world politics, and racial roots with an international assembly of drifters living on the Marseilles waterfront. Through Ray's debates with Banjo, McKay comments on colonialism and its racial manifestations while honing his portrait of the alienated intellectual. His final novel, *Banana Bottom* (1933), signals precisely the kind of nativist sentiment that his Haitian contemporary Jean Price-Mars advocated in his seminal study of Haitian folk culture, *Ainsi parla l'oncle* (1928; *So Spoke the Uncle*, 1983). McKay's novel depicts the return of Bita

Plant to the Jamaican rural community of Banana Bottom after her education in England (arranged by her white missionary guardians) and charts her rejection of both the stilted middle-class pruderies that her guardians expect from her and the mate they would choose for her. In returning to the "folk," Bita negotiates a more natural, integrated identity that takes what it can from the European intellectual tradition but is still most comfortable happily ensconced in the lush setting and rituals of rural black culture.

McKay's figure of the alienated, Western-educated intellectual returns countless times in Caribbean novels of the twentieth century, as does his appreciation of the folk culture. The effects of a colonial education—African Guadeloupians taught about "their ancestors the Gauls," Jamaican children taught to recite poems about daffodils and snow they have never seen—are a common touchstone in the Caribbean novel's depiction of childhood, particularly the popular bildungsroman genre, as epitomized by Michael Anthony's *The Year in San Fernando* (1965), Merle Hodge's *Crick, Crack, Monkey* (1970), Zee Edgell's *Beka Lamb* (1982), Jamaica Kincaid's *Annie John* (1985), Michelle Cliff's *Abeng* (1984), and Myriam Warner Vieyra's *As the Sorcerer Said* (1982). The perils of colonial education are treated with particular emphasis in Austin Clarke's pointedly titled *Growing Up Stupid Under the Union Jack: A Memoir* (1980). McKay's pan-Africanism predated the negritude movement spearheaded by the Martiniquan poet Aimé Césaire, and his privileging of rural folk culture resonated with the emphases of the peasant novel in Haiti, most notably Jacques Roumain's *Gouverneurs de la rosée* (1944; *Masters of the Dew*, 1946).

By contrast, the Trinidadians Alfred Mendes and C. L. R. James added an early urban spin to the Caribbean novel. James is primarily known for his studies of Caribbean history and culture—for instance, his study of the Haitian Revolution, *The Black Jacobins: Toussaint Louverture and the San Domingo Revolution* (1938), and his meditation on cricket, *Beyond a Boundary* (1963)—but he also authored one novel, *Minty Alley* (1936). *Minty Alley* joined Mendes's *Pitch Lake* (1934) and *Black Fauns* (1935) in inaugurating a tradition of social realism and protest that focused on the oppression of "yard," or slum, life. Later, Roger Mais's *The Hills Were*

Joyful Together (1953) and Orlando Patterson's *The Children of Sisyphus* (1964) revisited this theme.

ALEJO CARPENTIER

The Cuban writer Alejo Carpentier (1904-1980) shares the baroque style of the Cuban novel with José Lezama Lima, Severo Sarduy, Reinaldo Arenas, and Guillermo Cabrera Infante. Carpentier began his novelistic career under the influence of the *Afro-Cubanismo* of the 1920's and 1930's. His first novel, *¡Ecué-Yamba-O! Historia Afro-Cubana* (1933; Lord praised be thou), reflected the anthropological bent of the period by drawing on Carpentier's observations of the syncretic African Cuban Santería ritual. Influenced by the avant-garde, particularly the Surrealists, Carpentier's idea of the "marvelous real" of Caribbean life was transformed into the literary style of Magical Realism synonymous with the Colombian writer Gabriel García Márquez. A 1943 trip to Haiti, during which Carpentier came face-to-face with the magical presence of vodun (or Voodoo) in everyday life, led him to theorize that this commonplace "marvelous" quality was far superior to the contrived attempts by the European Surrealists to achieve similar effects.

In his prologue to *El reino de este mundo* (1949; *The Kingdom of This World*, 1957), Carpentier introduced his idea of *lo real maravilloso* produced by the hybrid nature of New World culture. Set in Haiti, the novel traces an arc from a slave insurrection to the establishment of a postcolonial state, from 1751 to 1831, depicting real historical figures and drawing on the mythical traditions associated with the revolt. Haitian Voodoo figures prominently as a factor in the quest for independence, and religion and music appear as two mediums for New World cultural mixture. The Haitian novelist Jacques Stephen Alexis would later elaborate his own theories on Haiti's marvelous realism, reflected in his novels *Compère Général Soleil* (1955; *General Sun, My Brother* (1999) and *Les arbres musiciens* (*The Musician Trees*, 1957). The late eighteenth century setting of *The Kingdom of This World* proved fertile ground for Carpentier's exploration of emerging New World identities; he returned to it in his novels *El siglo de las luces* (1962; *Explosion in a Cathedral*, 1963) and *Concierto barroco* (1974; *Concert Baroque*, 1976).

Carpentier is notable for his recognition of the centrality of African culture to New World cultural forms, as well as for an emphasis not on pure origins but on examples of cultural mixture, such as syncretic religious practice and Caribbean music forms. He also stands at the forefront of thought that began to envision a pan-Caribbean or inter-Antillian commonality, which began to take stronger hold at the end of the twentieth century.

Finally, Carpentier's preoccupation with elaborating a Caribbean history not fully accounted for by European intellectual traditions, an emphasis that offers a window on contemporary Caribbean life, is a common strategy of the Caribbean novel. For example, V. S. Reid's *New Day* (1949) links the granting of the 1944 Jamaican constitution to the 1865 Morant Bay Rebellion; Jean Rhys's *Wide Sargasso Sea* (1966) offers a perspective on 1830's postemancipation life in the British territories of Jamaica and Dominica; Pedro Mir's *Cuando amaban las tierras communeras* (1978) spans the years 1916 to 1965 and chronicles the dismantling of communal land ownership in the aftermath of the U.S. occupation of the Dominican Republic; and Caryl Phillips's *Cambridge* (1991) and *Crossing the River* (1993) return to Caribbean life of the eighteenth and nineteenth centuries. Michelle Cliff's *Abeng* and Maryse Condé's *La vie scélérate* (1987; *The Tree of Life*, 1992) also demonstrate a historiographic impulse by linking a young protagonist's investigations of her familial history to obscured features of Caribbean history.

WILSON HARRIS

In its emphasis on history and mythology, the work of Guyanese writer Wilson Harris (born 1921) has much in common with that of Carpentier. Harris's novels, however, leave all trappings of realism behind. His nonlinear, hallucinatory style is by far the most challenging of contemporary Caribbean novelists, although his experimental approach is shared by the fragmented and polyphonic novels *Jane and Louisa Will Soon Come Home* (1980), *Myal* (1988), and *Louisiana* (1994), by the Jamaican Edna Brodber. While Carpentier, too, plays with time, particularly in his best-known novel, *Los pasos perdidos* (1953; *The Lost Steps*, 1956), in Wilson's hands, it becomes even more fluid, looping in and out of itself in ways that defy any straightforward chronology. In an excellent metaphor for what it means to live with the history of the Caribbean, Harris's explorers in *Palace of the Peacock* (1960) encounter their dead selves and then die again. *Palace of the Peacock* is the first of the four novels known as *The Guyana Quartet* (1985), Harris's best-known work; the other three are *The Far Journey of Oudin* (1961), *The Whole Armour* (1962), and *The Secret Ladder* (1963).

Harris's novels are distinctive in their emphasis on the American Indian presence in the New World and for their evocation and symbolic use of the rivers and jungles of the Guyanese territory. His *The Eye of the Scarecrow* (1965), *The Waiting Room* (1967), *Tumatumari* (1968), and *Ascent to Omai* (1970) deploy a symbolic Guyanese landscape, and they "remember" perspectives of endangered communities, stretching back to before Columbus. Harris identifies a flute made by Carib Indians from the bone of an enemy as a symbol for what occurs in his work.

> Flesh was plucked and consumed and in the process secrets were digested. Spectres arose from, or reposed in, the flute . . . the flute became the home or curiously *mutual* fortress of spirit between enemy and other, an organ of self-knowledge suffused with enemy bias so close to native greed for victory.

In Harris's fiction, natives and European, African, East Indian, and Chinese settlers do commune, but with an unblushing acknowledgment of the violence of their mutual history. In this way, Harris's work both consumes what he terms "dilemmas of history" and becomes an "organ of self-knowledge," the bone flute that harmonizes the multihued peoples of Guyana with their historical struggles and conflicts.

GEORGE LAMMING AND V. S. NAIPAUL

Unlike Harris, Barbadian George Lamming (born 1927) and Trinidadian V. S. Naipaul (born 1932) embrace realism. These authors stood at the forefront of the anglophone literary boom in the 1950's. This decade was marked by an exodus of British West Indians to England to seek work and the burgeoning of independence movements that would come to fruition in the 1960's and 1970's, when British Caribbean territories began to gain their independence. Whereas Carpentier praises the "marvelous," in the sense of magical realities of Caribbean hybridity, Lamming and Naipaul focus rather unflinchingly on grim Caribbean realities. Both take a critical view of colonial status and its legacies in the West Indies and explore themes of alienation and exile in their depiction of West Indian life. Beyond this, however, their intentions and conclusions wholly differ.

In his collection of essays *The Pleasures of Exile* (1960), Lamming represents the voyage to London as initiating a mutual recognition between people of the various West Indian islands, related to but distinct from the homogenizing imperial gaze of the mother country. At home, these voyagers are Trinidadian, Jamaican, and Barbadian, but in England (on the way there, even), they become West Indian. Migration enables pan-Caribbean identification and community, a possibility also proposed in Samuel Selvon's trilogy *The Lonely Londoners* (1956), *Moses Ascending* (1975), and *Moses Migrating* (1983). In refusing to read "exile" as tantamount to a flight from identity, but rather as constitutive of it, in refusing to see migration as deracination, Lamming predates later studies of African diaspora culture, such as Paul Gilroy's *The Black Atlantic* (1993) and Carol Boyce Davies's *Black Women, Writing, and Identity: Migrations of the Subject* (1994), which see international flows as producing, rather than diluting, culture. As Gilroy suggests, "routes" are as important as "roots."

For Lamming, the voyage to England is also a voyage of enlightenment, a journey into the heart of colonialism that permits one to emerge from its darkness. London is one symbolic stop along the journey to independence. Lamming's *The Emigrants* (1954) brings black workers to London, and *Of Age and Innocence* (1958) returns them to the Caribbean and its growing independence movements. Approaching the themes of voyage and colonialism from another angle, his *Natives of My Person* (1972) charts the travels of a white crew of would-be settlers as they sail from the Guinea coast to the island of San Cristobal during the sixteenth century. The crew's shipboard interactions, particularly the male-female relationships, reveal ingrained patterns of conquest and domination and serve as an allegory for the society they will find in the New World. Lamming's voyagers were

succeeded by other novelistic travelers: Condé's Veronica in *Hérémakhonon: On doit attendre le bonheur* (1976; *Hérémakhonon*, 1982) and Cliff's Clare Savage in *No Telephone to Heaven* (1987) also undergo migrations that help them reflect on their personal identities and Caribbean heritage.

Lamming's later novel *Water with Berries* (1972) takes its title from a speech in William Shakespeare's *The Tempest* (1611) and presents guilt-ridden West Indian artists, the sons of Caliban, in London. This journey to London also involves an appropriation of the national bard. Both *Water with Berries* and *The Pleasures of Exile* develop the idea of Caliban as the colonial writer who has been taught the master Prospero's language and has learned to curse in it, a recurrent figure in the literature of the Caribbean, most notably in Aimé Césaire's play *Une Tempête, d'après "La Tempête" de Shakespeare: Adaptation pour un théâtre nègre* (1969; *The Tempest*, 1974). This figure also epitomizes Caribbean writers' ongoing dialogue with Western literary tradition, as demonstrated by Jean Rhys's appropriation of Charlotte Brontë's *Jane Eyre* (1847) in her *Wide Sargasso Sea* and Derek Walcott's Odyssean transformations in his Caribbean epic *Omeros* (1990).

Nobel Prize winner Naipaul became particularly invested in this Western tradition. Naipaul, who was awarded the Nobel in 2001, is largely regarded as the leading novelist in the anglophone tradition and among the region's most widely acclaimed writers. Ironically, however, he repeatedly demonstrates disgust with his Caribbean homeland, as evidenced in his nonfiction work *The Middle Passage: Impressions of Five Societies—British, French, and Dutch—in the West Indies and South America* (1962). Drawing on an education in nineteenth century realism, Naipaul gives his readers modern, alienated, West Indian protagonists who are trapped in claustrophobic, inauthentic, and ineffectual lives. In his deft hands, apparently trivial elements—a yellowed, filthy pillowcase; cooking odors; the ugly sound of an in-law's chewing—convey the hopelessness and degradation of his characters. Unlike Lamming, who critiques colonial Caribbean social organizations as a spur toward envisioning true political and ideological independence, Naipaul regards the faults of incompetent and corrupt government, poverty, poor educational opportunities, and general cultural provincialism as impediments to the full expression of individual Caribbean selves. Particularly adept at conveying the cultural conflicts within the East Indian communities of Trinidad, as well as their place within the mosaic of Trinidadian society, Naipaul's art is one of supreme vividness, humor, and despair.

Naipaul's first three novels are both comic tributes to and ironic commentaries on the place of his childhood. *Miguel Street* (1959) depicts the residents of the eponymous Port of Spain street, a slum to outsiders, through the wide eyes of a young artist who departs for England at the book's conclusion, never to return. The other two novels—*The Mystic Masseur* (1957) and *The Suffrage of Elvira* (1958)—establish Naipaul's distinctive critique of island politics. The first details the career of a lowly masseur who exploits his status as a mystic in order to rise in island politics, sacrificing his personal integrity along the way; the second depicts islanders who are ill prepared for universal suffrage and whose petty feuds and superstitions are exploited by self-interested politicians. Naipaul's two best-known Caribbean novels are *A House for Mr. Biswas* (1961) and *The Mimic Men* (1967). The former book richly but pessimistically depicts the struggles for autonomy of its sensitive, ineffectual title character. *The Mimic Men* represents Naipaul's most pointed exposure of the fraudulence of Caribbean political rhetoric, the pomposity and mimicry of the Caribbean's would-be leaders. Naipaul's ousted Caribbean politician, the self-loathing cynic Ralph Singh, flees his native Isabella and embraces the possibilities of exile, later recalling his participation in island politics as a "period in parenthesis." Ultimately, for Naipaul, exile is a strategy of survival, a preservation from the derivative mediocrity of Caribbean culture, a cultural "mimicry" that is the enduring legacy of colonialism.

ÉDOUARD GLISSANT

One response to this sense of Caribbean derivativeness has been a search for roots—not European ones, as in Naipaul's case, but African ones. The appreciation of "blackness" and the connection to Africa were epitomized by the highly influential negritude movement associated with Aimé Césaire and his seminal *Cahier d'un retour au pays natal* (1939, 1947, 1956; *Memorandum on My Martinique*, 1947; better known as *Return to My Native Land*, 1968), but the movement's positing of a historical black identity that serves as a prelapsarian preserve against the "fall" of the Middle Passage and enslavement came under fire for its essentialism and romanticized view of Africa. The Martiniquan poet, essayist, and novelist Édouard Glissant (born 1928) critiques this craving for pure, stable origins.

Glissant's theoretical work *Discours antillais* (1981; *Caribbean Discourse*, 1989) poses models of *métissage* (mixture and miscegenation) and *créolité* (creoleness) that destabilize notions of a fixed or permanent identity. These concepts are modeled on Creole, the mixed language that was born in the Americas. For Glissant, Creole is not a degraded cultural form, but the epitome of Caribbean cultural formations. From this perspective, other sites of hybridity, such as Caribbean music and the carnival ritual, prove valuable forms of Caribbean expression.

Glissant's theories inspired novelists, among them Raphaël Confiant and Patrick Chamoiseau, who choose to write in Creole. Chamoiseau's writing is increasingly available in English translation, particularly his Prix Goncourt-winning novel *Texaco* (1992; English translation, 1997). Puerto Rican writers Ana Lydia Vega and Luis Rafael Sánchez similarly embrace investigations of inter-Antillian traffic and commonalities, such as those posed in Glissant's *Poétique de la relation* (1990; *Poetics of Relation*, 1997). Sánchez's *La guaracha del Macho Camacho* (1976; *Macho Camacho's Beat*, 1980) and Guillermo Cabrera Infante's *Tres tristes tigres* (1967, 1990; *Three Trapped Tigers*, 1971) employ a regional Spanish strongly evocative of the French Creoles of Haiti, Martinique, and Guadeloupe. These writers also exhibit a preoccupation with popular culture and an ironic postmodern style that link them to other postmodern Caribbean novelists such as Marie Chauvet, Dany LaFerrière, and Willie Scott.

Glissant's novel *La Lézarde* (1958; *The Ripening*, 1985) recounts a series of voyages down the Lézarde River, using the Martinique landscape to meditate on the island's history. The titles of his later novels, including *Tout-Monde* (1993), particularly reflect his theoretical interests.

MARYSE CONDÉ

Like Glissant, the Guadeloupean writer Maryse Condé (born 1937) also strains against the return to African origins embraced by negritude thinkers, and her work displays a healthy postmodern irreverence. She leaves no sacred cows standing. Her first novel, *Hérémakhonon* ("welcome house" in Mandingo), records the internal monologue of the cynical, Sorbonne-educated Veronica, who travels to Africa to teach at a university. Confronted with a postcolonial Africa torn by internecine violence, an Africa that has moved on since her ancestors' removal from it to Guadeloupe, Veronica concludes her visit by reflecting, "My ancestors led me on. What more can I say? I looked for myself in the wrong place." The role of intellectuals and women's sexuality likewise emerge as legitimate means for exploring larger social and political issues. Her own critical study of French Caribbean women novelists, *La parole des femmes* (1979), reflects her insistence on the importance of women's perspectives in understanding Caribbean art and societies.

Condé stands among the most prolific and well-established writers of the Caribbean, with many of her novels available in English translation. She played a major role in debating the theoretical merits of creolization as a construct for understanding Caribbean culture. Her novels after *Hérémakhonon*, such as *Une Saison à Rihata* (1981; *A Season in Rihata*, 1988), deal with contemporary life in modern Africa as well as the epic sweep of its history, as in *Ségou: Les murailles de terre* (1984; *Segu*, 1987) and *Ségou II: La Terre en miettes* (1985; *The Children of Segu*, 1989). Her novella *Pays mêlé* (1985), translated as *Land of Many Colors* (1999), marks a return to Guadeloupe. Her subsequent novels, *Moi, Tituba, sorcière noire de Salem* (1985; *I, Tituba, Black Witch of Salem*, 1992), *La Vie scélérate* (1987, *Tree of Life*, 1992), *Traversée de la mangrove* (1989; *Crossing the Mangrove*, 1995), *Les Derniers Rois Mages* (1992; *The Last of the African Kings*, 1997), and *La migration des coeurs* (1995; *Windward Heights*, 1998), all deal with Caribbean and, more broadly, American settings.

Along with Merle Hodge, Marie Chauvet, Paule Marshall, and Simone Schwarz-Bart, Condé began her novelistic career before the explosion of writing by Caribbean women that began in the 1980's. The Antiguan Jamaica Kincaid is perhaps the best-known anglophone writer to emerge during this boom. Condé's later work nonetheless reflects the trends and attitudes in both the literature and scholarship of the Caribbean at the end of the twentieth century.

Throughout their century-long meditations on Caribbean identity, history, and culture, Caribbean novels have often explored connections to Europe, Africa, and Asia. Beginning in the 1980's, increasing attention was paid to both regional Caribbean and inter-American relationships, in particular with the United States. This focus was especially evident in the work of women novelists, presaged by Marshall's *The Chosen Place, the Timeless People* (1969). In the 1990's, Michelle Cliff's *Free Enterprise* (1993), Edna Brodber's *Louisiana*, and Evangeline Blanco's *Caribe: A Novel of Puerto Rico* (1998) paralleled Condé's *The Last of the African Kings*, *The Tree of Life*, and *I, Tituba, Black Witch of Salem* in representing intersections between U.S. and Caribbean history and culture. These works joined novels of Caribbean nationals' migrations to the United States, such as Kincaid's *Lucy* (1990), Julia Alvarez's *How the García Girls Lost Their Accents* (1991), Judith Ortiz Cofer's *The Line of the Sun* (1989), and Edwidge Danticat's *Breath, Eyes, Memory* (1994) in reorienting the transcontinental perspectives of Caribbean writing (Europe, Africa) to treat inter-American routes as well.

A similar type of hemispheric intercalation appears in the Puerto Rican writer Rosario Ferré's choice to compose her novels of Puerto Rico, *The House on the Lagoon* (1995) and *Eccentric Neighborhoods* (1998), in English. Caribbean writing at the end of the twentieth century reflects not only new patterns of migration and the Caribbean diaspora but also the century-long presence of the United States in the Caribbean region. Later Caribbean writers include Cuban-born Cristina García (*Dreaming in Cuban*, 1992) and Cuban American Oscar Hijuelos, whose *The Mambo Kings Play Songs of Love* won the Pulitzer Prize in fiction in 1990. Dominican American writer Junot Díaz's first novel, *The Brief Wondrous Life of Oscar Wao* (2007), was awarded the Pulitzer and the National Book Critics Circle Award in 2008.

CARIBBEAN TRANSIT

The idea of migration features prominently in the literature of the Caribbean region. Interestingly, other novelists not from the Caribbean region have also seen fit to "migrate" there for fictive purposes: Ernest Hemingway's much-acclaimed novella *The Old Man and the Sea* (1952) pits humanity against nature in the ocean off Cuban shores; war correspondent Martha Gellhorn's novelistic skills matured in *Liana* (1944), her tale of a powerless mulatto, or person of mixed race, living on a Caribbean island. Graham Greene chose Cuba on the eve of revolution as the backdrop for his satirical reflection on Cold War paranoia in his *Our Man in Havana: An Entertainment* (1958), and Toni Morrison created a fictional Caribbean island as the primary setting for *Tar Baby* (1981), a meditation on racial identity and race relations. As in the work of its more "native" authors, these novels mark the Caribbean as a vital hub in the traffic of global literature, a place of import and export and migration and exile, and the origin, endpoint, and transit zone of many cultural passages.

Nancy E. Castro
Updated by David Peck

BIBLIOGRAPHY

Arnold, A. James, ed. *A History of Literature in the Caribbean*. 3 vols. Philadelphia: J. Benjamins, 1994-2001. Excellent overview of all genres of Caribbean literature. Volume 1 surveys works of the Spanish- and French-speaking Caribbean, volume 2 examines the English- and Dutch-speaking Caribbean countries, and volume 3 provides a cross-cultural study of the Caribbean region as a whole.

Balutanksy, Kathleen M., and Marie-Agnès Sourieau, eds. *Caribbean Creolization: Reflections on the Cultural Dynamics of Language, Literature, and Identity*. Gainesville: University Press of Florida, 1998. Critics and writers, among them Maryse Condé, Edna Brodber, and Wilson Harris, provide an introduction to theories of Caribbean creolization.

Cudjoe, Selwyn R., ed. *Caribbean Women Writers: Essays from the First International Conference*. Wellesley, Mass.: Calaloux, 1990. Many anthologies on Caribbean women's writing have been published since this collection was produced, but with its depth of critical essays, author interviews, and pan-Caribbean bibliographic overviews, this work remains an excellent survey of the Caribbean women's literature.

Dance, Daryl C. *Fifty Caribbean Writers: A Bio-Bibliographical Critical Sourcebook*. Westport, Conn.: Greenwood Press, 1986. Quick and informative guide to the works and careers of writers from the anglophone, or English-speaking, Caribbean.

Dash, J. Michael. *The Other America: Caribbean Literature in a New World Context*. Charlottesville: University Press of Virginia, 1998. Arguing that broad critical categories, such as postcolonial and postmodern, elide the particularities of Caribbean literature, Dash provides a thematic and formal overview of Caribbean literature as a New World expression.

Figueredo, Danilo H., ed. *Encyclopedia of Caribbean Literature*. 2 vols. Westport, Conn.: Greenwood Press, 2006. Alphabetical listing of more than seven hundred entries covering writers, works, genres, themes, and national literatures, as well as political, cultural, and artistic events and movements.

Heady, Margaret. *Marvelous Journeys: Routes of Identity in the Caribbean Novel*. New York: Peter Lang, 2008. Uses the works of Jacques-Stephen Alexis, Alejo Carpentier, and Simone Schwartz-Bart to examine the transition from modernist to postmodernist consciousness in twentieth century Caribbean writings on identity.

James, Cynthia. *The Maroon Narrative: Caribbean Literature in English Across Boundaries, Ethnicities, and Centuries*. Portsmouth, N.H.: Heinemann, 2002. Traces the development of representations of the Caribbean in English fictional works from the seventeenth century through the twentieth century. Analyzes three works for each century and considers the theme of colonization, literary conventions, and women's contributions to the literature.

Kristal, Efraín, ed. *The Cambridge Companion to the Latin American Novel*. New York: Cambridge University Press, 2005. Comprehensive history of Latin American long fiction that includes analyses of Puerto Rican, Cuban, and Dominican novels, part of the literature of the Caribbean.

Ormerod, Beverley. *An Introduction to the French Ca-

ribbean Novel. Portsmouth, N.H.: Heinemann, 1985. Interprets novels by Jacques Roumain, Édouard Glissant, Jacques Stéphen Alexis, Simone Schwarz-Bart, and others. Still regarded as the best introduction to the French Caribbean novel.

Torres-Saillant, Silvio. *Caribbean Poetics: Toward an Aesthetic of West Indian Literature*. New York: Cambridge University Press, 1997. Comprehensive overview of the literature of the Caribbean region that also argues for the existence and integrity of a regional literary tradition. Joins J. Michael Dash in elaborating a pan-Caribbean approach.

THE EURO-AMERICAN IMMIGRANT EXPERIENCE IN LONG FICTION

Before the middle of the twentieth century, most immigrants to the United States were Europeans or enslaved Africans. The first U.S. census, in 1790, reveals that most free Americans were of English or other Northern European ancestry. That first census reported that 60 percent of white Americans described themselves as English, 14 percent as Scottish or Scotch-Irish, 9 percent as German, 4 percent as Catholic Irish, and 13 percent as other. Because of the English predominance, the earliest American fiction tended to follow English models. The Pennsylvanian Hugh Henry Brackenridge published *Modern Chivalry*, a satirical novel about American frontier life, in installments from 1792 to 1815. Although *Modern Chivalry* deals with American subjects, it was heavily influenced by English satirical writers such as Jonathan Swift and Henry Fielding. Even James Fenimore Cooper, often celebrated as the first great American writer of long fiction, showed the influence of the English author Sir Walter Scott.

Although early American novelists such as Nathaniel Hawthorne and Herman Melville distanced themselves from English models, American literature throughout the nineteenth century continued to develop out of the English tradition and to be written by people of English ancestry. For this reason, "immigrant literature" or "ethnic literature" in the United States has generally referred to writing that reflects the experiences of the non-English groups that arrived over the course of the nation's history.

THE "OLD IMMIGRANTS"

After 1820, European immigration to the United States began to increase greatly. Those who arrived between 1820 and the Civil War (1861-1865) are often referred to as the "old immigrants," in contrast to the "new immigrants," who began to arrive in the decades between the Civil War and World War I. Many of these immigrants came either from Germany, already the main country of origin for Americans who spoke a language other than English, or from Ireland. Germany, in particular, continued to supply the greatest number of immigrants to the United States, so that nearly one-fourth of

Americans of European origin in 1990 reported that they were primarily of German ancestry. German was widely spoken in the United States until World War I, and many German American communities had their own newspapers and schools. Some of the earliest literary expressions of the Euro-American immigrant experience, therefore, were produced by Germans.

One of the most important early immigrant writers from the German-speaking area of Europe was the Austrian Karl Postl, who changed his name to Charles Sealsfield after his arrival in New Orleans in 1823. Among his other writings, Sealsfield published a widely read historical novel, *Tokeah: Or, The White Rose* (1828), set in the Neches River area of Texas. Later in the nineteenth century, another major German American writer, August Siemering, also wrote about the experiences of Texas Germans during the Civil War in *Ein Verfeihtes Leben* (1876; the failure).

By the twentieth century, authors of German descent were frequently regarded as native-born American writers rather than as immigrant writers. Nevertheless, some continued to deal with the ethnic German or immigrant German experience. Theodore Dreiser's *Jennie Gerhardt* (1911) is notable as a work of long fiction about the German experience by a major American author. Other twentieth century works concerned with the German immigrant experience include George Hummel's *Heritage* (1935), Conrad Richter's *The Free Man* (1943), and George Freitag's *Lost Land* (1947).

The United States saw one of its greatest waves of immigration during the late nineteenth and early twentieth centuries. While most of the older immigrants had come from northern and western Europe, many of these new immigrants came from southern and eastern European nations, such as Italy, Greece, Poland, and parts of the Russian Empire. Although some of the immigrants during this time became farmers, many settled in cities, so that much of the new immigrant literature was urban. The immigrants who arrived after the Civil War also frequently met with prejudice from Americans of older stock. The great wave of immigration around the beginning of the twentieth century gave rise to a literature that was often self-consciously ethnic and was concerned with the problems of fitting into a new society; it took immigration and the consequences of immigration as a central subject.

SCANDINAVIAN IMMIGRANTS

Although Swedes and Finns settled in North America as early as 1638, when colonists established New Sweden at the mouth of the Delaware River, people from the countries of Sweden, Norway, Denmark, and Finland did not begin to arrive in the United States in large numbers until after the Civil War. Driven by political troubles and crop failures in their homelands, Scandinavian immigrants were exceptions to the general trends in immigration in two respects. First, they came from northern Europe, while most other immigrants at the time came from southern and eastern Europe; second, many of the Scandinavians settled in rural areas of the Midwest and became farmers, while immigrants from elsewhere generally settled in cities.

Establishing their own ethnic communities in isolated regions, Scandinavians were often able to resist Americanization and cling to their languages and traditions. They often wrote in languages other than English. The best-known Scandinavian American novelist, O. E. Rölvaag (1876-1931), wrote the two volumes of his masterpiece, *I de Dage* (1924) and *Riket Grundlægges* (1925), entirely in Norwegian. These two volumes became best sellers in Norway. They were combined in a single book for the English translation called *Giants in the Earth: A Saga of the Prairie* (1927). The English version became a Book-of-the-Month Club selection and also a best seller in the United States, making the author a celebrity in both Norway and America. Rölvaag's novel and its two sequels deal with the struggle to wrest a living from the American wilderness, and they exhibit nostalgia for the old country. These themes are embodied in the first book's main characters, Per Hansa, possessed by the urge to conquer the wilderness, and Beret Holm, a woman homesick for the land and traditions of Norway.

The best-known Scandinavian writer who worked in English was the Danish American Sophus Keith Winther, who arrived in the United States as a small child and grew up on a Nebraska farm. Winther, like Rölvaag, wrote about the difficult lives of immigrant farmers in novels that include *Take All to Nebraska* (1936), *Mortgage Your Heart* (1937), and *This Passion Never Dies* (1938). It is interesting to note that while Rölvaag is still considered a classic American author and is widely read in courses on American literature, Winther's work has been almost forgotten.

THE "NEW IMMIGRANTS"

Most of the "new immigrants," those who arrived after the Civil War, settled in cities. The United States industrialized rapidly at the end of the nineteenth century, creating jobs in urban areas. New York City, in particular, became a center for Italians and Jews from Eastern Europe. Unfamiliar with American ways and frequently impoverished, immigrants settled in some of the poorest neighborhoods of American cities. The term "ghetto," an Italian word that referred to Jewish areas in Italian cities, came to mean an urban concentration of minority-group members of any ethnicity. The earliest novels about immigrants, then, concern life in the ghetto.

Abraham Cahan spent his childhood in a Lithuanian Jewish village and arrived in the United States without a cent in 1882. Cahan worked in New York sweatshops, became active in labor unions, educated himself, and became known as a cultural leader in the ghetto of the Lower East Side. He published his first novel, *Yekl: A Tale of the New York Ghetto*, in 1896. Published just three years after Stephen Crane's *Maggie: A Girl of the Streets*, Cahan's novel is frequently compared to Crane's, because both writers were dedicated to realism in the portrayal of the hard facts of urban life. Among other novels in the "tenement fiction" genre—writing concerned with the social problems of the urban immigrant ghetto—are James Sullivan's *Tenement Tales of New York* (1895), about the Irish of New York's West Side; Julian Ralph's *People We Pass* (1896), about German and Irish youth in a New York tenement; and Isaac Kahn Friedman's *The Lucky Number* (1896), about an immigrant community in Chicago.

One of the recurrent themes of immigrant fiction in the years before World War I is the struggle of immigrant laborers for social justice. David M. Fine, author of *The City, the Immigrant, and American Fiction, 1880-1920* (1977), argues that the proletarian novel of the 1930's grew out of the immigrant labor novel. One of the greatest immigrant labor novels, *The Jungle* (1906), about immigrant workers in the meatpacking industry, was written by a nonimmigrant, Upton Sinclair (1878-1968). Isaac Kahn Friedman produced another notable novel about immigrant labor in *By Bread Alone* (1901), a dramatic story of strikes in a steel mill.

The predominant theme among urban immigrant writers of the early twentieth century was the struggle to fit into American society. The Jewish Russian immigrant Elias Tobenkin treats this subject in *Witte Arrives* (1916), which tells the story of Emile Witte. Tobenkin's hero had left Russia for America as a boy and managed to enroll at a university and then become a journalist. Although Witte is successfully Americanized, his adaptation to the new country involves conflict with his father, who clings to the traditions of the old country. Tobenkin's second novel, *The House of Conrad* (1918), deals with the same topics of assimilation into American society and intergenerational conflict. These topics became common in immigrant novels, many of which were heavily autobiographical.

The best-known and most highly praised novel of immigrant assimilation and upward mobility in the early twentieth century is Cahan's *The Rise of David Levinsky* (1917). Many other early immigrant novels, such as those of Tobenkin, wholeheartedly embrace the idea of assimilation into American society. Cahan, however, presents the immigrant success story as one of loss as well as gain. David Levinsky, Cahan's protagonist, arrives in America in 1885, a penniless young Jewish refugee from persecution in czarist Russia. He becomes a peddler, selling goods on the street, and also becomes familiar with crime, political corruption, and prostitution. He dreams of attending New York's City College, but poverty forces him to become a manufacturer. Through hard work, ruthlessness, and the willingness to take advantage of his own workers, Levinsky achieves material success. Although he manages to overcome his accent and his Russian Jewish ways, in the end the millionaire Levinsky feels that he has lost his own identity, and all his achievements seem empty to him.

By the 1930's, many of those writing about the European immigrant experience had either arrived in the United States as young children during the great wave of immigration before World War I or were born in the United States to immigrant parents. Growing up in an ethnic ghetto and youthful conflicts with the foreign ways of parents became recurrent topics in the writings of these authors. Mike Gold's *Jews Without Money* (1930) looks back at a boyhood in the ghetto. Henry Roth's *Call It Sleep* (1934) may have been the best young immigrant novel of the 1930's.

Roth (1906-1995) was born in an area of the Austro-Hungarian Empire that later became part of Ukraine and arrived in New York City with his parents as a small child. He was educated in New York public schools and graduated from New York's City College in 1928. Like so many other immigrant works of fiction, *Call It Sleep* is fictionalized autobiography. It tells the story of a young Jewish immigrant boy growing up in the lower East Side of New York in the years prior to World War I. The novel was highly praised by critics, who compared Roth to Irish writer James Joyce. However, sales of new books were slow during the Depression years, and Roth's first novel quickly went out of print. Roth was rediscovered by literary critics in the early 1960's, and *Call It Sleep* acquired a large, if belated, readership.

Roth did not publish another work of long fiction for many years, until the multivolume autobiographical work *Mercy of a Rude Stream*, which included *A Star Shines over Mt. Morris Park* (1994), *A Diving Rock on the Hudson* (1995), *From Bondage* (1996), and *Requiem for Harlem* (1998). Even though these books were published long after other works by authors of Roth's generation, they tell the story of Roth's younger years and provide a literary portrait of early twentieth century immigrant life.

Pietro di Donato, born in 1911 to an Italian immigrant family in New Jersey, presents the Italian immigrant experience in his work. His autobiographical novel *Christ in Concrete* (1938) tells the story of Italian immigrant workers in the United States. The book's protagonist, Paulino, is the son of an Italian bricklayer. After his father dies when a building collapses, the twelve-year-old Pietro must take up the responsibility of supporting his mother and seven younger brothers and sisters. *Christ in Concrete* achieved wide popular recognition, and it was a Book-of-the-Month Club selection in 1939. Di Donato's second novel, *Three Circles of Light* (1960), is the story of Paulino's family before the father's death.

This second novel did not achieve the critical or popular success of the first, and it was criticized as a loose assembly of impressionistic stories, rather than a coherent narrative.

LATER EUROPEAN IMMIGRANTS

The U.S. Congress passed legislation limiting immigration to the United States in 1924. As a result, immigration dropped drastically in the following years. In 1965, Congress changed the law to allow more people to enter the country, but the largest numbers of immigrants after 1965 came from Latin America and Asia, rather than from Europe. This meant that the immigrant experience in America largely ceased to be a European one. With the exception of older writers such as Henry Roth, most American authors of European Jewish, Italian, Scandinavian, or German ancestry in the 1960's and after had grown up in English-speaking families who had planted roots in the New World.

Some native-born American writers did look back at the immigration experiences of their families. For example, in his memoir-history *Unto the Sons* (1992), the Italian American Gay Talese looks at his own family's immigrant background. Among Jewish Americans, the mass murder of European Jews by the Nazis led to an intensified awareness of European Jewish heritage. American writers such as Philip Roth (born 1933), Bernard Malamud (1914-1986), and Saul Bellow (born 1915) present portraits of Jewish immigrants in the United States. Isaac Bashevis Singer (1904-1991) was one of the few Jewish American writers working in the second half of the twentieth century who was himself an immigrant. Born in Poland, Singer fled Europe for the United States in 1935, when he was thirty-one years old. He was a prolific author, and he composed many of his works in Yiddish, despite his fluency in English. Most of Singer's novels are set in Jewish villages before World War II, but he did sometimes write about immigrant life in the United States. In *Meshugah* (1994; crazy), Singer describes the encounters of Polish immigrant Aaron Greidinger with Holocaust survivors in New York during the 1950's.

Carl L. Bankston III
Updated by David Peck

BIBLIOGRAPHY

Bilik, Dorothy S. *Immigrant-Survivors: Post-Holocaust Consciousness in Recent Jewish American Fiction.* Middletown, Conn.: Wesleyan University Press, 1981. Bilik examines the new-immigrant novel, specifically Jewish immigrant novels after the 1950's. Argues that the Jewish immigrant, largely missing from American fiction after the 1930's, began to reappear around 1957. Whereas older works about immigrants are concerned with the efforts of Jews to fit into American society, the new writing is haunted by memories of the Holocaust.

Di Pietro, Robert J., and Edward Ifkovic, eds. *Ethnic Perspectives in American Literature: Selected Essays on the European Contribution—A Sourcebook.* New York: Modern Language Association of America, 1983. Collection of scholarly essays, each devoted to the literature of one European immigrant group in the United States. The essays examine literature both in English and in other languages.

Fine, David M. *The City, the Immigrant, and American Fiction: 1880-1920.* Metuchen, N.J.: Scarecrow Press, 1977. Still one of the best studies of American immigrant fiction of the late nineteenth and early twentieth centuries. Sets this writing in the context of U.S. immigration history and offers a particularly useful chapter on the writing of Abraham Cahan.

Howe, Irving. *World of Our Fathers: The Journey of the East European Jews to America and the Life They Found and Made.* New ed. New York: New York University Press, 2005. In this classic book, Howe tells the history of the immigration of more than two million Jews from East Europe from the 1880's to the 1920's. Discusses their efforts to maintain a Yiddish culture while establishing themselves in the United States.

Prchal, Tim, and Tony Trigilio, eds. *Visions and Divisions: American Immigration Literature, 1870-1930.* New Brunswick, N.J.: Rutgers University Press, 2008. Anthology of selections from key writers of the Progressive Era, when immigration from Europe increased and debates about it likewise rose.

JEWISH AMERICAN LONG FICTION

Approximately five hundred Jews lived in the United States in 1700. The majority lived in the Newport, Rhode Island, area, while the rest settled primarily in New York City; Savannah, Georgia; Charleston, South Carolina; and Philadelphia. Newport was particularly attractive because of the relatively liberal political administration of Roger Williams, who vied for a strict separation of church and state. There is little evidence to indicate a concentrated persecution of the Jews in any of the original American colonies. Many of the cultural values with which Jews were identified, such as thrift, industry, and a devout adherence to the word of God, were also values of a Puritan America; by the time of the First Continental Congress in 1774, when the chafe of British oversight had become intolerable, the colonists may well have felt an immediate kinship with the Jews in their midst. After all, Jews personified the Protestant work ethic, and many colonists believed that they, like the Jews, were God's chosen people, badly abused by a powerful nation.

EARLY JEWISH AMERICAN LITERATURE

The earliest Jewish American writers to produce widely recognized fictional narratives were journalists who also wrote for the popular stage, such as the early nineteenth century melodramatists Mordecai Manuel Noah and Samuel B. H. Judah. An editor of the *National Advocate* and the founder of the *New York Inquirer*, Noah avoided including Jews in his most popular melodrama, *Siege of Tripoli* (1820), as did Judah in his most popular work, *A Tale of Lexington: A National Comedy, Founded on the Opening of the Revolution in Three Acts* (1823). As such, there is nothing identifiably Jewish American about their writing.

The first Jewish American writers to speak from a decidedly Jewish perspective were women poets. Taking the ancient Jew as its subject matter, *Fancy's Sketch Book*, published in 1833 by Penina Moise, was one of the few such collections to reach a large audience in its day. However, Emma Lazarus's *The New Colossus* (1883) is by far the more familiar now, if for no other reason than

that one of its passages, "Give me your tired, your poor/ Your huddled masses," became the Statue of Liberty's invitation—and by extension, America's as well—to the disenfranchised of the world.

Lazarus's enthusiasm for America as a "melting pot" was shared by a number of early Jewish American novelists, Israel Zangwill to name but one. In *The Melting-Pot*, the 1908 drama that coined the phrase, Zangwill envisions a land where Jew and Gentile can live and labor in harmony, if only they are willing to become, first and foremost, "Americans."

There she lies, the great Melting Pot—Listen! Can't you hear the roaring and the bubbling? . . . There gapes her mouth—the harbor where a thousand mammoth feeders come from the ends of the world to pour in their human freight . . . Celt and Latin, Slav and Teuton, Greek and Syrian—black and yellow—Yes, East and West, North and South, the palm and the pine, the pole and the equator, the crescent and the cross—how the great alchemist melts and fuses them with his purging flame! . . . Ah, Vera, what is the glory of Rome and Jerusalem and all nations and races that come to worship and look back, compared with the glory of America, where all races and nations come to labor and look forward!

The possibility for inclusion must have been appealing to Jewish immigrants in particular. The history of Jews was one of persecution and homelessness; it is no wonder then that the possibility that the United States could provide a place where the Wandering Jew could finally put down roots became perhaps the single most persistent concern of the Jewish American novel. However, a second overriding theme surfaced more or less concurrently with this one.

Henry Harland's *Mrs. Peixada* (1886) and *The Yoke of the Thorah* (1887) deal with Jewish Americans who, while coming of age in the ghetto, are willing to marry outside their faith against the wishes of their elders. Such story lines anticipate the generational concerns of much later novels, such as Henry Roth's *Call It Sleep* (1934) and Albert Halper's *Sons of the Fathers* (1940), and later still the novels of Philip Roth and Saul Bellow, in which children come to feel estranged from their parents' way of life, yet have no meaningful alternative of their own. Hebrew, both literally and metaphorically, becomes the language of the father, a distant, often foreign tongue that speaks of restraint, denial, and suffering in a world of possibility and plenty. As Halper describes the relationship between the generations cited in the title of *Sons of the Fathers*,

> From his naturalized American lips issued Hebrew, an old world language, somberizing the room with its rich and mournful cadences. And though none of the children understood a word their father had said, they had the feeling they were in the synagogue. Every year their father sat upon a pillow during this service and every year, though enticing food lay within hands' reach, they forgot for a moment the prospect of eating as a feeling of solemnity stole into the room.

A related concern of early Jewish American novels is perhaps more daunting—namely, the fear that Jews may be able to find a proper place in mainstream, mercantile, American culture only by sacrificing what is most sacred to the Jew's human experience: being a Jew. This dilemma is first addressed seriously in Abraham Cahan's *The Rise of David Levinsky* (1917). Like Noah and Judah before him, Cahan was primarily a journalist, making his mark as an editor of the *Jewish Daily Forward*, a Jewish socialist newspaper. Unlike Noah and Judah, however, Cahan was more an artist than a popular entertainer. His novel deals with a young Russian Talmudic student who travels to the United States, enters the garment industry, educates himself, and begins his rise to the top of American society. If the American Dream is a dream of success, he achieves it. He becomes rich and powerful. He discovers, however, that the American Dream is most of all a secular dream; paradoxically, having found his place in America, he feels spiritually lost and without a home.

THE EARLY TWENTIETH CENTURY

Novels published shortly after World War I, such as Samuel B. Ornitz's *Haunch, Paunch, and Jowl* (1923), voiced some of the same concerns as Cahan, but only in passing. Most of these books were issued amid a great burst of postwar prosperity and therefore seem naïvely optimistic. Generally, these novels chronicled the ascent of their protagonists from the ghettos of New York City's lower East Side to the heights of American prosperity, for the sky, apparently, was the limit for any Jew who appreciated the value of personal initiative paired with formal education; however, such a vision of upward mobility was as short-lived as it was trusting in the promise of the United States, and these works were soon replaced by the proletarian novels written in response to the Great Depression.

Although novels such as John Steinbeck's account of Oklahoma sharecroppers, *The Grapes of Wrath* (1939), are classified as "proletarian" writing, the proletarian novel was an urban, Jewish American phenomenon. It signaled a new generation of Jewish American novelists, the American-born children of Jewish immigrants who were coming of age during a period when American capitalism was being challenged more seriously than ever before in the twentieth century. It also signaled the first time that Jewish American novelists as a group defined a place for themselves in American literature.

Their work reflects the left-of-center politics that became attractive to so many out-of-work Americans during the depths of the Depression. Michael Gold was surely the most doctrinaire of the group. Gold was the editor of *The New Masses*, the American Communist Party's influential literary magazine; in his *Jews Without Money* (1930), it is communism that promises a better future. So great was Gold's impact that a hard-line Marxist-Leninist agenda is often attributed to the other proletarian novelists as well, though Nelson Algren (*Somebody in Boots*, 1935), Roth (*Call It Sleep*), Meyer Levin (*The Old Bunch*, 1937), Halper (*The Foundry*, 1934), Isidor Schneider, and Daniel Fuchs demonstrated more faith in collective bargaining and trade unionism than in communist doctrine. Even at their most dogmatic they seemed to be utopian writers as much as anything else. They envisioned a way to bring the compassion and values of Jewish orthodoxy to the factory and the mill, a compromise between the sacred and the profane. To paraphrase Algren, theirs was a utopian socialism, a vision of "the New Jerusalem being built on the ashes of failure of American capitalism." The writing often has an almost religious fervor about it. In Schneider's *From the Kingdom of Necessity* (1935), for instance, readers are told that the protagonist

> had set out from the kingdom of necessity; he had found a way out, the escape from his class, only to find that, outside, he was homeless. He was to learn that no one enters the kingdom of freedom alone. He would return to his class. With it, he would march, taking his place in the advancing lines, in the irresistible movement of the masses of mankind from the kingdom of necessity to the Kingdom of Freedom.

The work of Fuchs should be of particular interest to anyone studying the development of the Jewish American novel. Fuchs is better remembered for his Hollywood screenplays (*The Human Jungle*, 1954; *Interlude*, 1957; *Jeanne Eagels*, 1957) than for his novels, yet his Williamsburg trilogy (*Summer in Williamsburg*, 1934; *Homage to Blenholt*, 1936; and *Low Company*, 1937; published in one volume as *Three Novels*, 1961; also as *Williamsburg Trilogy*, 1972) remains an important literary achievement. The trilogy takes its name from the Williamsburg section of Brooklyn in New York City. At the height of Jewish immigration to the United States, the lower East Side of Manhattan in New York City was more densely populated than Calcutta, India, and Jews gradually had to make their way across the Williamsburg Bridge to the outskirts of Brooklyn to find space in which to live. Fuchs's characters, who live in Williamsburg, begin to cast their eyes back toward Manhattan's Madison Avenue. In this regard their longings are reminiscent of those Ornitz characters who wished to leave their ghetto tenements and better themselves. However, there is a difference in how Fuchs treats such material: Unlike his predecessors, Fuchs infuses humor into his work. He is as much a satirist of human nature as he is a chronicler of upward mobility, and much that will be attributed to later Jewish American novelists such as Philip Roth—caricaturing the Jewish mother for comic effect, for instance—was pioneered by Fuchs.

The Holocaust and postwar fiction

World War novelsWar II and the Holocaust had a tremendous impact on Jewish literature, particularly in Europe. Holocaust survivors such as the Italian novelist Primo Levi and the Romanian Aharon Appelfeld offer unique perspectives on what it meant to be a Jew in the twentieth century by virtue of the ordeals they suffered. Levi addresses his experiences during the Holocaust in two autobiographies, *Se questo è un uomo* (1947; *If This Is a Man*, 1959; revised as *Survival in Auschwitz: The Nazi Assault on Humanity*, 1961) and *La tregua* (1963; *The Reawakening*, 1965), then drew from them obliquely in his novel *Se non ora, quando?* (1982; *If Not Now, When?*, 1985).

Appelfeld directed his attentions to the writing of fiction. His first novel was *Badenheim, 'ir nofesh* (1975; *Badenheim 1939*, 1980), and though he continued to publish after its translation, *Badenheim 1939* remains his best-known work. None of these chronicle the realities of his own internment and eventual escape, but the death camps are seldom far removed from the hearts and minds of his characters. They are often unwary Jews, well respected in their communities, whose lives are overtaken by the Nazis in the early years of the war, as in *Badenheim 1939*, *Tor-ha-pela'ot* (1978; *The Age of Wonders*, 1981), *Kutonet veha-pasim* (1983; *Tzili: The Story of a Life*, 1983), *To the Land of Cattails* (1986; also known as *To the Land of the Reeds*), *Be-'et uve'onah ahat* (1985; *The Healer*, 1990), and *Unto the Soul* (1994). Other novels depict Jews who are struggling after the war to reclaim their place in the world, as is the case in *Bartfus ben ha-almavet* (1988; *The Immortal Bartfuss*, 1988) and *Al kol hapesha'im* (n.d.; *For Every Sin*, 1989).

Jewish American fiction flourished after 1945. To offer even the slightest list of Jewish American authors who rose to prominence after World War II is to list some of the most influential writers in the canon of contemporary American literature: E. L. Doctorow, Joseph Heller, Bernard Malamud, Stanley Elkin, Bruce Jay Friedman, Cynthia Ozick, Isaac Bashevis Singer, Tillie Olsen, Grace Paley, Norman Mailer, Philip Roth, Saul Bellow, and Chaim Potok. Mailer's *The Naked and the Dead* (1948) was a debut that had a great impact following the war, earning its twenty-five-year-old author a berth at the forefront of American letters.

The novel recounts a long and lethal patrol by a U.S. Army platoon on an isolated island in the Pacific Ocean. Two of these soldiers, Herman Roth and Joey Goldstein, are Jewish. Roth, the better assimilated of the two, is more quickly accepted by the other men, but he is without the moral compass necessary to internalize what he is going through. Goldstein, by contrast, is devout. His worldview is that of an ancient Hebrew, and he is one of the few characters in the novel for whom the patrol has any meaning. Goldstein is paired in the novel's final chapters with Ossie Ridges, a Southern fundamentalist Christian, as they carry a wounded soldier on a litter through the jungle. Theirs is a Sisyphean chore that ends in failure, but it serves to unite them. Both Goldstein and Ridges have what the other men lack, a sense of a well-ordered universe in which humankind is in the hands of a punishing God, and such understanding stirs in each a compassion for the suffering of the other.

Philip Roth's first novel-length work, *Goodbye, Columbus* (1959), takes its title from the dream of its protagonist, Neil Klugman. Klugman's dream puts him aboard a masted sailing ship moored in the harbor of a paradisal island. An undertow begins to draw the ship out to sea. Powerless to stop the ship's departure, Klugman watches as beautiful native goddesses on the shore bid him farewell, chanting "Goodbye, Columbus, Goodbye," while the paradise before him grows more distant by the minute. The book's title and dream images befit much that Roth has written and certainly represent an experience shared by Roth protagonists as otherwise diverse as Alexander Portnoy, David Kepesh, Peter Tarnopol, and Roth's recurring alter ego, Nathan Zuckerman: The nearer one comes to the America of one's dreams, the more certain one can be that it will never be discovered.

Roth's work has at its core several additional consistencies. His novels often deal with Jewish American writers who are at or near the top of their public lives, rich and famous novelists with no shortage of creature comforts or sensuous and willing women in their lives; yet they live in the depths of personal despair, at odds with their current wives or former wives and haunted by their parents. Sooner or later this estrangement manifests itself in psychic and physical pain. The greater the suffering they experience, the more self-obsessed they become; the more self-obsessed they become, the more estranged they become from others and the greater their pains. It is a vicious cycle, but a comic one as well.

Roth gets much comic mileage out of psychosomatic—or at least undiagnosable—afflictions, including

Alexander Portnoy's trips to his analyst in *Portnoy's Complaint* (1969) and Nathan Zuckerman's wrenching back pains in *The Anatomy Lesson* (1983). His protagonists lack the spiritual wherewithal required to negotiate the problems they face; their complaints have more to do with their souls than with their minds and bodies. This harkens back to matters Roth deals with first in his depiction of Klugman, who is from a working-class Newark, New Jersey, Jewish household. Shortly after his discharge from the Army, Klugman falls in love with Brenda Patimkin, a Smith College student who is home for the summer and whose family lives in a fashionable and religiously mixed Newark suburb called Short Hills. Klugman resents Patimkin for the countless ways in which her life has been made easier than his own because of her parents' money, but he is envious as well. Is it Patimkin he loves, or is it Short Hills and all the material pleasures it represents? Late in the novel, Klugman uncharacteristically tries his hand at a prayer. "If we meet You at all, God, it's that we're carnal, and acquisitive, and thereby partake of You. . . . Where do we meet? Which prize is You?" Within moments, Neil thinks he has his answer: "Which prize do you think, *schmuck*? Gold dinnerware, sporting-goods trees, nectarines, garbage disposals, bumpless noses. . . ."

Klugman suspects that happiness is to be found not in physical pleasures or material possessions but rather in what in European shtetl tales of the nineteenth century would have been called being a "good and virtuous man." Still, virtue is a slippery concept. A ritzy department store and the goods available within it are not.

Roth's characters come to a situation with a much better grasp of secular matters than they have of their spirits, and something of the same thing is true of Saul Bellow's protagonists as well. Like those of Roth, Bellow's protagonists are second- and third-generation American Jews who are several times removed from their deepest spiritual roots and who have much clearer knowledge of themselves as consumers and Americans than they have of themselves as Jews. Therein rests their dilemma. They are often seasoned literary men, or at least highly successful in their chosen careers, and, like Bellow himself—who won the Nobel Prize in Literature, a Pulitzer Prize, and two National Book Awards—have been handsomely rewarded by the world at large.

In the course of the novel Bellow's protagonists go through a spiritual crisis. The dimensions of the crisis change from book to book, yet it is fundamentally the same in each work. Something is awakened in their souls that will not let them rest. Something, they sense, is amiss in how they have lived their lives, and the comedy begins as their attempts to set things right only make matters worse. Having accompanied his astrophysicist wife Minna to Eastern Europe, for instance, Albert Corde, the university administrator of *The Dean's December* (1982), senses that the court case in which he has been involved back in Chicago speaks of an evil that neither his wife's capacity for science nor his own capacity for logic and reason can comprehend. It is an amazing moment of recognition for a high intellectual such as Corde, yet it serves only to paralyze him rather than move him to act.

Bereft by personal and financial problems, Charlie Citrine, the artist protagonist of *Humboldt's Gift* (1975), turns to meditation and Rudolph Steiner's quasi-mystical Theosophy. The title character of *Herzog* (1964) tries to restore order to his life by writing letters and reconstructing his personal history for any and all who are willing to listen. The novel ends with Herzog in the Berkshire Hills of western Massachusetts, having left the big city behind. He lies on his couch in the novel's final pages and speaks aloud with no one there to hear him; though he thinks this will help him resolve his problems, he only succeeds in talking himself into further confusion. It is surely more than an autobiographical impulse that leads Bellow to make so many of his protagonists famous writers and fervent talkers, for the task he is putting before them is nothing short of articulating the unspeakable, and they fare no better than one might expect. Each protagonist has had a fleeting glimpse of some ultimate cosmic order in the universe. Each has experienced some longing of the spirit that defies translation into words.

Chaim Potok is the American novelist whose temperament and interests seem to be nearest to what readers expect of European authors. His earliest novels are his most formidable and perhaps still his most frequently read. Potok is at once a religious scholar and a creative artist, and his *The Chosen* (1967) and *The Promise* (1969) deal with the Jews' search for meaning, not only

through prayer and study but also through the protagonists' encounters with the diversity to be found in modern Judaism itself, such as Hasidism, Orthodox Judaism, and Conservative Judaism. Subsequent novels, such as *In the Beginning* (1975) and *The Book of Lights* (1981), cast a wider net in an attempt to locate the place of Jews in twentieth century history. His protagonists discover that the defining moments of the twentieth century were horrors of staggering dimension, such as the nuclear bombing of Hiroshima, but they avoid the alienation and despair to be found in so much of contemporary writing. They discover in these horrors the fruits of a spiritual quest that affirms rather than denies their most deeply felt religious beliefs.

LATE TWENTIETH CENTURY

The 1990's witnessed the emergence of several talented Jewish American writers, particularly Lev Raphael, Melvin Bukiet, Steve Stern, and Allegra Goodman. Crime novelist Raphael (*Winter Eyes: A Novel About Secrets*, 1992; *Let's Get Criminal: An Academic Mystery*, 1996; *The Death of a Constant Lover: A Nick Hoffman Mystery*, 1999) offers Nick Hoffman as his protagonist, an English professor at the State University of Michigan who finds himself solving murder mysteries between teaching classes and grading papers. These crimes inevitably shake him free of the ivory tower of academia in which he is trying to live his life, but they do more than that. In the process of investigating crimes, he is apt to be reminded that he is twice removed from the mainstream American experience he has sought in becoming a professor, first because he is a Jew, second because he is gay.

Bukiet, the child of Holocaust survivors, writes with the charming spirit of a fabulist in his short-story collection *While the Messiah Tarries* (1995). This dose of charm is somewhat deceptive, however, as he proves in *After* (1996) and *Signs and Wonders* (1999), both of which are laced with comic acid. *Signs and Wonders*, set at the end of the twentieth century, follows Snakes Hammurabi, a burlesque version of Christ-like savior, as it explores a modern world that is well beyond any chance of salvation. *After*, written in the picaresque tradition, is set in the final days of World War II as the Nazi concentration camps are being liberated by the Allies. Bukiet's picaro protagonist is nineteen-year-old Isaac Kaufman, a concentration camp survivor who emerges from his experience a rogue, a nihilist, and a victim who has learned to savor the pleasures of the victimizer. The novel follows Kaufman and two comrades across Europe in a scheme to liberate a fortune in Nazi gold and virtually anything else that might strike their fancy.

Steve Stern has published short stories (*Lazar Malkin Enters Heaven*, 1986), novellas (*A Plague of Dreamers*, 1994), and novels (*Harry Kaplan's Adventures Underground*, 1991), but perhaps his greatest achievement is his creation of Pinch, a backwater Jewish immigrant community in Memphis, Tennessee, in which much of his fiction is set. Ignored by upwardly mobile Memphis, Pinch is an enclave where magic is still possible, and, in Stern's quite competent hands, even probable. Stern has all the skills of shtetl storytelling at his disposal, but he has a distinctly modern sensibility that prevents his fiction from becoming an imitative homage to a literature that no longer seems to speak of contemporary times.

Many critics believe that Goodman has established herself as the Jewish American writer who is most clearly the heir of Grace Paley, Cynthia Ozick, Bellow, and Roth. In 1989, she published a novel titled *Total Immersion*, followed by two short-story collections—*The Family Markovitz* (1996) and *Kaaterskill Falls* (1998). A number of the stories in the collections first appeared in *The New Yorker*, and they benefit from collecting, if only because seeing them together makes one conscious of the consistency of her authorial concerns. The former novel deals with three generations of one Jewish American family; Rose, the grandmother, tries to make sense of two grown sons and a world that defy her understanding. The irony is that Rose is closer to her granddaughter Miriam than she is to either of her own children, not only because Rose and Miriam share a generational enemy in common but also because Miriam is willing to embrace a Judaic tradition that neither of Rose's sons can fathom. *Kaaterskill Falls* takes its name from an upstate New York town in which Jews are a minority. The stories follow several Orthodox Jews of the baby-boomer generation who have traveled to Kaaterskill for the summer. At the center of this community are the Shulmans, who have opened a general store in the area. The Shulman elders are much less able to embrace Judaism wholeheart-

edly than are their grown children, who are ultimately more comfortable being Jews than are their parents.

Jewish American literature continues to ponder whether assimilation into the fabric of American life is tonic or toxic to the Jewish experience. Is it possible to be a Jew in a meaningful sense and also take one's place within American culture? Whether written by Jews or Gentiles, American novels are no more sure today than they have ever been. Jay McInerney's *Bright Lights, Big City* (1984) is narrated by a yuppie whose ventures into the fashionable night life of New York City have resulted in a powerful cocaine addiction. This has cost him an enviable job, the woman he loves, his family, and his future. In one scene, he gets on the subway and sits beside a Hasidic Jew who is studying the Talmud. Says the narrator,

> This man has a God and a History, a Community. He has a perfect economy of belief in which pain and loss are explained in terms of a transcendental balance sheet, in which everything works out in the end and death is not really death. Wearing black wool all summer must seem a small price to pay. He believes he is one of God's chosen, whereas you feel like an integer in a random series of numbers.

Jewish American writers who continue to wrestle with the same issues as their predecessors include Michael Chabon (*The Amazing Adventures of Kavalier and Clay*, 2000, and *The Yiddish Policemen's Union*, 2007), Jonathan Rosen (*The Talmud and the Internet: A Journey Between Worlds*, 2000, and *Joy Comes in the Morning*, 2004), Nathan Englander (*The Ministry of Special Cases*, 2007) and Amy Bloom (*Away: A Novel*, 2007). Many, too, are pushing the limits of the novel form. These writers include Jonathan Safran Foer (*Everything Is Illuminated*, 2002, and *Extremely Loud and Incredibly Close*, 2005) and Art Spiegelman (*In the Shadow of No Towers*, 2004), whose widely popular, two-volume graphic novel *Maus: My Father Bleeds History* (1986) and *Maus: And Here My Troubles Began* (1991; also known as *Maus II: From Mauschwitz to the Catskills*) continues to be read and studied as a classic of Holocaust literature.

Jay Boyer
Updated by David Peck

BIBLIOGRAPHY

Chametzky, Jules, John Felstiner, Hilene Flanzbaum, and Kathryn Hellerstein, eds. *Jewish American Literature: A Norton Anthology*. New York: W. W. Norton, 2000. Comprehensive collection of works from colonial times to the present, including selections from Cynthia Ozick, Woody Allen, Allegra Goodman, Art Spiegelman, Philip Roth, and more than one hundred other writers.

Codde, Philippe. *The Jewish American Novel*. West Lafayette, Ind.: Purdue University Press, 2007. Theoretical study that contains sections on the cultural context (politics, religion, philosophy) of the Jewish American novel, and on "The French Existentialist Repertoire" in Saul Bellow, Bernard Malamud, Daniel Stern, and other postwar novelists.

Davidman, Lynn, and Shelly Tenenbaum, eds. *Feminist Perspectives on Jewish Studies*. New Haven, Conn.: Yale University Press, 1994. The title is misleading insofar as it suggests one political agenda or theoretical focus. The central focus of this collection of polished essays is gender and Judaism. Particularly useful is Joyce Antler's "Sleeping with the Other: The Problem of Gender in American-Jewish Literature."

Furman, Andrew. *Israel Through the Jewish American Imagination*. Purchase: State University of New York Press, 1997. Part of the State University of New York's Modern Jewish Literature series, this study examines fiction published between 1928 and 1995, specifically focusing on the place Israel occupies in twentieth century American letters as setting, myth, and metaphor.

Shapiro, Ann R., ed. *Jewish American Women Writers: A Bio-Bibliographical and Critical Sourcebook*. Westport, Conn.: Greenwood Press, 1994. Lists biographical, bibliographical, critical, and reference material on a wide range of Jewish American women writers, from the relatively obscure (Rhoda Lerman-Sniderman, Nessa Rapoport, Ilona Karmel) to those with a high popular readership, among them Erica Jong, Francine Prose, and Lynne Sharon Schwartz.

Shapiro, Gerald, ed. *American-Jewish Fiction: A Century of Stories*. Lincoln: University of Nebraska Press, 1998. This excellent collection of Jewish American fiction spans the twentieth century, beginning with pioneers such as Abraham Cahan and concluding with such writers as Francine Prose, Robin Hemley, and Allegra Goodman.

Shatsky, Joel, and Michael Taub, eds. *Contemporary Jewish American Novelists: A Bio-Critical Sourcebook*. Westport, Conn.: Greenwood Press, 1997. Collection of essays alphabetically arranged by novelist, from Walter Abish through Leon Uris, offering brief biographies and discussion of major works, themes, and critical reception for each writer.

Wade, Stephen. *Jewish-American Literature Since 1945*. Edinburgh, Scotland: Edinburgh University Press, 2001. Wide-ranging introduction to postwar Jewish American writers, including analyses of Cynthia Ozick, Philip Roth, and Chaim Potok.

Wirth-Nesher, Hana, and Michael P. Kramer, eds. *The Cambridge Companion to Jewish American Literature*. New York: Cambridge University Press, 2003. Essays in this collection cover material such as Hebrew literature in America, Jewish literary theory and poetics, the Jewish American renaissance, and the literary perspective of Jewish Americans on the Holocaust.

LATINO LONG FICTION

Latino fiction presents the experience and multiplicity of perspectives unique to Latinos—residents of the United States whose cultural, ethnic, and linguistic ties to Latin America connect them as members of a distinct yet multiethnic community. The principal Latino ethnic or cultural groups include Chicanos, or Mexican Americans; Puerto Rican Americans; Cuban Americans; and residents or citizens of the United States who trace their origins to Central and South America. Each of these constituent groups is distinct in its own right, with its own history, folklore, and traditions. However, they all share commonalities of language, culture, religion, experience, and values; these attributes distinguish Latino culture both from the dominant Anglo culture of the United States and from those of other immigrant populations. Much Latino long fiction is characterized by a sense of ethnicity and by the portrayal of ethnic experience.

MEXICAN AMERICAN/CHICANO LONG FICTION

In 1848, the Treaty of Guadalupe Hidalgo ceded all Mexican territories north of the Rio Grande to the United States. One year later, all former citizens of Mexico who still resided in the area automatically became U.S. citizens. These new citizens were a diverse group engendered principally from a mixture of European, Aztec, and indigenous North Americans; from each ethnocultural wellspring the group derived myths, values, religious and cultural traditions, laws, and literary models. In the ensuing years the overlay of Anglo influence enriched the mixture. The resulting culture came to call itself Chicano, a term used to designate the distinct history, culture, and literature of the American Southwest.

Chicano long fiction, like Chicano language and culture generally, derives from three distinct sociohistorical sources: Mexican Indian, predominant prior to 1519; Spanish Mexican, predominant from 1519 to 1848; and Anglo, emergent after the signing of the Treaty of Guadalupe Hidalgo in 1848. These sources provide a richness of myth, legend, history, and literary models and techniques, both oral and written, from which Chicano writers have drawn inspiration and material, the reactions to which have constituted the conflicts and tensions that drive all forms of Chicano literary expression.

Chicano long fiction is multilingual, employing Spanish, English, and Pocho, a hybrid blend of linguistic elements. Used together, these language options allow the Chicano novelist to express the full range of his or her experience, encompassing the dominant Anglo culture, the culture of origin, and the culture of the home and the *barrio*. Chicano novelists are conscious of their linguistic and ethnic heritage and depict a people proud of their history and culture, aware of their uniqueness, and committed to preserving their familial, social, and literary traditions. Their novels portray men and women who accept themselves as they are and resist pressures to become more closely aligned with the mainstream Anglo culture that threatens to Americanize them. Proximity to Mexico and movement both north and south across the border continually reinforce the Hispanic and mestizo ways, creating a cultural dynamic, unique to Chicano literature, which continues to influence the Chicano novel's vital, energetic, and creative momentum.

The first significant Chicano novelist was José Antonio Villarreal. His *Pocho* (1959) was the first Latino novel issued by a major publishing firm, and it is frequently regarded as the first work of real literary or historical value to reflect the Chicano experience. The protagonist is a boy who seeks self-discovery, but as a Chicano he also must decide which of the ideals, traditions, and attitudes of his parents to reject in favor of Anglo ones he likes. Though sometimes criticized for not placing appropriate emphasis on racial and cultural issues, *Pocho* remains an important work in Latino fiction. Richard Vásquez's *Chicano* (1970), like *Pocho*, has been criticized for its failure to depict the Chicano experience realistically, but in its portrayal of Chicano themes, the novel constitutes a seminal work. Raymond Barrio's *The Plum Plum Pickers* (1969) exposes the harshness of social and economic life for migrant Mexican and Chicano farmworkers in Southern California. Its literary excellence, the richness of its narrative technique, and its realistic depiction of the difficulties faced by Chicano laborers have earned it an important place in the evolution of Chicano fiction.

The novelists who represent the emergence into maturity and international acknowledgment of the Chicano novel include Rudolfo Anaya, Rolando Hinojosa, Ron Arias, and Sandra Cisneros. The critical acclaim accorded these novelists has established them as major twentieth century artists and has drawn attention to the genre of Latino fiction.

Anaya's *Bless Me, Última* (1972) uses dream sequences, Magical Realism, and mythological echoes to approach the fantastic. The novel's protagonist, through the agency of a folk healer named Última, achieves a level of spiritual and perceptual experience that awakens his awareness of the mythological figures of his Chicano heritage, teaching him respect for folk wisdom and custom and leading him to an alternate reality which, by extension, becomes available to the reader as well. The novel, widely read and critically acclaimed, established Anaya as a major force in American letters.

Hinojosa was the first Chicano writer to win an important international literary award. He was also the first U.S. citizen to be honored by the Casa de las Américas panel. His novel *Klail City y sus alrededores* (1976; *Klail City: A Novel*, 1987) was the second book in a trilogy that re-creates the reality, beliefs, and vision shared by generations of members of the Spanish-speaking community in south Texas, where Hinojosa was born. The other two volumes of the trilogy are *Estampas del valle, y otras obras = Sketches of the Valley* (1973; English revision, *The Valley*, 1983) and *Claros varones de Belken* (1981; *Fair Gentlemen of Belken County*, 1986). Hinojosa creates a collage of points of view, personalities, landscape snapshots, spots of time, and events both trivial and sublime that establish a palpable, vital fictional world through which a powerful sense of identity and continuity surges. Hinojosa suggested that he wrote the trilogy to help himself keep alive a past that grew in importance as it became more remote; in doing so, he has also made the Latino experience immediate and accessible to a broad spectrum of readers.

Arias's *The Road to Tamazunchale* (1975) reveals the influence of contemporary international literary currents. The emphasis on the subjective, internal reality of his protagonist, rather than on the exterior world of ob-

jects, is consistent with the emphases of many other modern novelists. The effect of this emphasis on alternative reality is to diminish the narrative distance between writer and reader by smearing the distinctions within the novel between illusion and reality. Arias's mastery of contemporary literary technique and his emphasis in the novel on the barrio experience, the problems of illegal Mexican immigrants in the United States, and the rejection of victimhood in favor of empowerment make *The Road to Tamazunchale* unique in the body of Latino fiction, perhaps setting a new standard for the Chicano novel.

Cisneros is one of an emerging group of Chicano writers who have graduated from a creative writing program; another is Helena María Viramontes, who has published the novels *Under the Feet of Jesus* (1995) and *Their Dogs Came with Them* (2007). Cisneros's first novel, *The House on Mango Street* (1984), was completed during her tenure as a National Foundation of the Arts Fellow, and it received the Before Columbus American Book Award in 1985. Employing fragmentation and montage, she depicts not only the Chicano experience from the unusual perspective of growing up in the Midwest among predominantly Puerto Rican Americans but also the emergence of her self-awareness as a writer and creator. Like Hinojosa, Cisneros admits a need to recapture the past in order to fulfill the needs of the present.

PUERTO RICAN LONG FICTION

The population of Puerto Rico is a blend of the cultures and races of Europe, Africa, and the Americas. From 1493 until 1898, Puerto Rico was a Spanish colony. Puerto Rican fiction assumed a mestizo identity, in opposition to Spanish pressures to assimilate; this emphasis evolved to reflect a more Latin American character in the twentieth century, when Puerto Rico became a U.S. territory. After World War II, almost one-third of the island's population immigrated to the United States, dispersing to points as far apart as Hawaii and New York. This distribution complicated the process whereby Puerto Ricans sought to define and protect their cultural and literary identity. Furthermore, by physically separating family and community members, the immigration reduced the efficacy of the oral tradition as a means of propagating values and traditions, making long fiction the culture's principal mechanism for articulating its vision of its own reality.

The language of the Puerto Rican American novel reflects the diversity of Puerto Rican ethnic and linguistic origins, a product of the melding of European (Spanish, French), African, and Native American cultures overlaid with an American patina. Puerto Rican American fiction has retained diverse elements of myth, culture, and value structures. Most Puerto Rican American fiction is bilingual, and it employs grammatical elements and vocabulary of the Caribbean patois and the Native American elements of its linguistic heritage.

The development of Puerto Rican literature has been constituted in part by a series of reactions. The reaction of nineteenth century Puerto Rican artists to Spanish dominance was to create a sense of identity that emphasized the values and linguistic elements of the indigenous, African, and mestizo aspects of its cultural heritage. From 1898 to about 1940, Americanizing pressures prompted Puerto Rican writers to emphasize the Spanish language itself and to use Latin American models in their efforts to define and protect their identity as a separate culture. Finally, since the end of World War II and in reaction to the new assimilating forces following the surge in emigration of the 1940's and 1950's, the efforts to preserve their cultural autonomy have increasingly led Puerto Ricans away from idealized depictions of the island and toward settings in New York, Chicago, and other enclaves of Puerto Rican American cultural influence.

The long fiction of the late twentieth century, written by the children of first-generation working-class immigrants, criticizes the complacency of an Americanized middle class as well as the oppressive dominance of Anglo culture. Typical of this class is Pedro Juan Soto's novel *Spiks* (1956; English translation, 1973), which emphasizes the anguish of the impoverished immigrants and looks wistfully back to an idyllic past. Another novelist who focused on the oppression and alienation of the Puerto Rican American in New York was José Luis González, with *En Nueva York, y otras desgracias* (1973; in New York, and other disgraces). Critics have come to regard these novels as reactionary, creating a distorted, idealized view of the reality that existed before American involvement in Puerto Rico and reflecting a skewed, one-dimensional image of Puerto Rican American life, focusing only on the tragedy, alienation, and exploitation of immigrants at the mercy of a cold and greedy America.

New York Puerto Rican writers of the late twentieth century were writing mostly in English and had inherited a popular tradition heavily influenced by Hispanic folklore and the multifaceted culture of one of the world's largest cities. Thematically and structurally, their work has much in common with the writings of African Americans, writers from the developing world, and other Latinos seeking identity through recognition of their multiethnicity rather than through acquiescence to pressures to assimilate. Nicholasa Mohr, one of the most productive and critically acclaimed Puerto Rican American novelists, moves away from the theme of alienation, creating characters who are not overly conscious of cultural conflict or crises of identity. *Felita* (1981) and *Rituals of Survival: A Woman's Portfolio* (1985) are examples of this fiction of self-determination.

CUBAN AMERICAN LONG FICTION

Cuban literary influence in the United States can be traced to the early 1800's, when José Martí and other patriots worked from the United States for Cuban independence. After Fidel Castro's 1959 victory in the Cuban Revolution and the large-scale emigration that followed, however, Cuban Americans emerged as a major contributing force to Latino culture and literature. Unlike Puerto Ricans, Cubans came as refugees rather than immigrants. Furthermore, although Cuba had been a U.S. protectorate since 1898, it was never a political colony of the United States in the same sense as Puerto Rico. At the time of the Cuban Revolution, then, Cuban writers, having felt no assimilationist pressure, had developed no literary expressions of defiance or protection against the imposition of mainstream American culture onto Cuban American identity. In fact, because it was sparked by a political and social revolution, the emigration involved a cross-section of Cuban society: workers, middle-class service personnel, professionals, intellectuals, and the wealthy. Many subsequently adapted to and became a part of U.S. and Hispanic mainstream culture.

The fiction of Cuban Americans in the 1960's was

primarily written in Spanish. One reason may be that the audience targeted by these first-generation exiles was primarily Spanish-speaking, either Cuban or Latin American. Another reason may be found in the essentially political, often propagandistic nature of the material. The themes were less concerned with discovery and preservation of an ethnic, cultural, or literary identity than with criticizing Cuba's communist economic and political system. Therefore, the Cuban American novel of the 1960's was almost devoid of the kinds of ethnic and linguistic self-consciousness that marked Chicano, Puerto Rican, and other minority ethnic fiction.

Fiction written by Cuban American novelists of the 1970's was less preoccupied with exile and looking back to the island past than with meeting the demands of the Cuban American communities then flourishing in the United States. Their novels were dominated by English, although code-switching (changing languages when expression in one seems richer or clearer than in the other) became more frequent, as did representation of a Cuban dialect heavily influenced by American idioms. Cuban American novelists of the late twentieth century have more in common with other Latino writers than did their forerunners of the 1950's and 1960's, having sought solidarity with the Latino community of writers and thinkers rather than returning to another, or remaining distinct as exiles. Immigration from Cuba continues to reinforce the dynamic nature of this evolution, however, and to provide an impetus resisting assimilation.

The first Cuban American novels, which began to be published in 1960, almost exclusively attacked Marxist doctrine in general and the political manifestation of it in the Cuban Revolution in particular. The first such novel, *Enterrado vivo* (1960; buried alive), written by Andrés Rivera Collado, was published in Mexico; the ensuing decade saw similar novels, published in the United States and abroad. At worst, these works were openly propagandistic and inflammatory, while at best they were unrealistically and ineffectively nostalgic in their idealization of prerevolutionary Cuba.

A change in direction for Cuban American fiction was initiated by Celedonio González, whose focus in *Los primos* (1971) was on Cuban life and culture in the United States. The thematic emphasis in González's subsequent novels, *Los cuatro embajadores* (1973; the four ambassadors) and *El espesor del pellejo de un gato ya cadáver* (1978; the thickness of the skin of a cat that's already a cadaver), is on the cultural and social conflicts experienced by Cuban Americans in a predatory economic system that keeps immigrants disadvantaged and alienated in order to exploit them. Like other Latino fiction, these novels depict a people not fully Americanized but clearly unable to return to or participate fully in their land or culture of origin.

Cristina García's work seeks resolution of the tensions between the first and subsequent generations of Cuban Americans; born in 1958 in Havana, she grew up in New York City and was educated at Barnard College and the Johns Hopkins School of Advanced International Studies. Her first novel, *Dreaming in Cuban* (1992), earned favorable critical reception and became widely popular. Neither harsh nor nostalgic, the novel avoids romantic excess, depicting a search for cultural and personal identity.

In the novels of Oscar Hijuelos, the evolution of Cuban American fiction moved even closer to integration in the American mainstream. Hijuelos was born in New York in 1951, and his parents were not exiles. Their experience, and his, is more consistent with that of Chicano and Puerto Rican American writers who lack the political agenda of writers in exile and whose thematic emphasis is on discovery and preservation of the integrity of their cultural and linguistic legacy. His first novel, *Our House in the Last World* (1983), is autobiographical, though often classified as a novel. He won the 1990 Pulitzer Prize in fiction. Further evidence of his acceptance by mainstream America was the film adaptation of his second novel, *The Mambo Kings Play Songs of Love* (1989).

Andrew B. Preslar
Updated by David Peck

BIBLIOGRAPHY

Allatson, Paul. *Key Terms in Latino/a Cultural and Literary Studies*. Malden, Mass.: Blackwell, 2007. Indispensable encyclopedia of hundreds of key concepts in Latino literary and cultural studies. Good starting place for students new to the literature.

Brady, Mary Pat. *Extinct Lands, Temporal Geographies: Chicano Literature and the Urgency of Space.*

Durham, N.C.: Duke University Press, 2002. Thorough and insightful discussion of the role of space and memory in Mexican American writing. Includes extensive footnotes and a bibliography.

Carlito, Delores M. *Cuban American Fiction in English: An Annotated Bibliography of Primary and Secondary Sources.* Lanham, Md.: Scarecrow Press, 2005. Comprehensive listings and annotations of Cuban American fiction (novels, anthologies, and short-story collections) from 1963 into the first decade of the twenty-first century.

Caulfield, Carlota, and Darién J. Davis, eds. *A Companion to U.S. Latino Literatures.* Woodbridge, England: Tamesis, 2007. Guide to Latino writers in the United States and the Caribbean, notably Puerto Rico and the Dominican Republic. Includes commentary on native-born Latino writers and Latin American immigrants to the United States.

Christie, John S. *Latino Fiction and the Modernist Imagination: Literature of the Borderlands.* New York: Garland, 1998. Examines the works of Cuban Americans, Mexican Americans, and Puerto Rican Americans, among other Latino groups. Includes thirteen pages of bibliographical references and an index.

Christie, John S., and José B. Gonzalez, comps. *Latino Boom: An Anthology of U.S. Latino Literature.* New York: Pearson/Longman, 2006. A 567-page collection that includes a historical overview of Latino literature in the United States and selections from the writings of Sandra Cisneros, Gary Soto, Junot Díaz, and dozens of other Latino writers. Also includes a bibliography and an index.

Day, Frances Ann. *Latina and Latino Voices in Literature: Lives and Works.* Westport, Conn.: Greenwood Press, 2003. Award-winning reference work covering Latino and Latina fiction writers Julia Alvarez, Rudolfo Anaya, Sandra Cisneros, and many others.

Gish, Robert Franklin. *Beyond Bounds: Cross-Cultural Essays on Anglo, American Indian, and Chicano Literature.* Albuquerque: University of New Mexico Press, 1996. Insightful exploration of the myths, languages, and literary traditions of the overlapping cultures of the American Southwest.

Horno-Delgado, Anunción, et al., eds. *Breaking Boundaries: Latina Writings and Critical Readings.* Amherst: University of Massachusetts Press, 1989. Focusing on the experience of female writers from all ethnic and cultural backgrounds, this collection of critical, scholarly essays on fiction, poetry, and linguistics offers introductory and analytical studies of issues relating to all aspects of Latina literary production.

Shirley, Carl R., and Paula W. Shirley. *Understanding Chicano Literature.* Columbia: University of South Carolina Press, 1988. Introductory work on Chicano long fiction, poetry, theater, and short fiction. Includes a list of suggested readings. Dense with information; appropriate for advanced high school and college-level students.

Torres-Padilla, Jose L., and Carmen Haydee Rivera, eds. *Writing Off the Hyphen: New Critical Perspectives on the Literature of the Puerto Rican Diaspora.* Seattle: University of Washington Press, 2008. Sixteen essays on both prominent and lesser-known Puerto Rican writers, written from a variety of contemporary theoretical perspectives.

NATIVE AMERICAN LONG FICTION

Although Native Americans, or American Indians, are an ancient people, most of their written literature is fairly recent. It was only in the twentieth century that Native American authors began to produce long fiction and that Native American ethnicity became a central theme in novels and other forms of writing. Nevertheless, the literature of America's oldest ethnic group does have deep cultural roots.

Long before the arrival of Europeans in the Americas, indigenous tribes and nations passed stories from generation to generation. These stories were intended to educate the young and to perpetuate cultural traditions, as well as to entertain. They told of the origins of the earth and of the human race, of the order of the universe and of the human place in it, and of bawdy tricksters who are mischievous but creative. Modern Native American fiction writers have frequently woven traditional narratives into their works.

Many of the earliest works of Native American written literature were autobiographies, intended for communication with the written culture of the invading Euro-Americans. In 1829, William Apes of the Pequot tribe published *A Son of the Forest: The Experience of William Apes, A Native of the Forest* to tell the story of the defeated and beleaguered Pequot people. Black Hawk, a Sauk, published *Black Hawk: An Autobiography* in 1833, after being defeated by Euro-American forces. The most famous of all Native American autobiographies is *Black Elk Speaks* (1932), the memoirs of the Oglala Sioux medicine man Black Elk, as told to poet John G. Neihardt. Although these autobiographies were generally intended for Euro-American audiences, they also influenced Native American writers. Much of contemporary Native American literature is heavily autobiographical.

The oral narratives and even the early autobiographies were works of people who saw themselves as parts of small communities, such as Pequot, Sauk, or Oglala. Over the course of the late nineteenth and early twentieth centuries, as anthropologist Peter Nabokov pointed out, Native Americans developed a sense of belonging to a wider group. By the mid-twentieth century, when Native American written fiction began to flourish, writers such as N. Scott Momaday and James Welch were writing self-consciously as people with an ethnic or racial identity and as members of specific tribes or nations. The sense of belonging to a single group, the autobiographical written tradition, and oral narratives may be identified as the primary cultural roots of modern Native American fiction.

EARLY NATIVE AMERICAN FICTION

The early twentieth century saw the first written works of fiction by Native American authors. In 1927, Mourning Dove published the romance *Cogewea, the Half-Blood*. During the same decade, the Oklahoma Cherokee John Milton Oskison became widely known as a short-story writer and novelist. His novels, which deal with life in and around the Indian Territory—which became Oklahoma—include *Wild Harvest* (1925), *Black Jack Davey* (1926), and *Brothers Three* (1935). Both Mourning Dove and Oskison are frequently criticized for their stock characters and their adherence to the conventions of popular fiction.

Literary critics generally regard the mixed-race Osage Indian John Joseph Matthews as a more sophisticated author than Mourning Dove or Oskison. Matthews wrote mainly history and autobiography, but he did publish one highly regarded novel, *Sundown* (1934). He set the story in the Osage country of Oklahoma, where the Osage are divided into the "full-bloods" and the "mixed-bloods" and into those who have money from oil leases and those who do not. The novel's hero goes away to college and then returns to struggle with his emotions about tribal life. Many of the themes, such as the tensions between tribal life and the modern economy and the struggle between assimilation and cultural traditionalism, became dominant in later Native American fiction.

D'Arcy McNickle (1904-1977), a member of the Confederation of Salish and Kutenai tribes of Montana, is often regarded as one of the best of the early Native American authors. Educated at the University of Montana and Oxford University, McNickle went to work for the U.S. Bureau of Indian Affairs in 1936, where he served as assistant to commissioner John Collier. McNickle dedicated himself to Collier's attempts to reverse the efforts of the U.S. government to force Native Americans to give up their cultural and political identities. McNickle gives passionate expression to the struggles of Native Americans in his novel *The Surrounded* (1936), which tells the story of a young man who returns from a government Indian school to his reservation.

THE NATIVE AMERICAN RENAISSANCE

By the 1960's and 1970's, a new generation of university-educated Native Americans, many of whom were influenced by the Civil Rights movement, began to produce novels that met with wide popular acceptance. N. Scott Momaday (born 1934) was one of the first of this generation to be recognized as a major American author. A professor of literature, Momaday has explored his Kiowa heritage in both poetry and prose. In 1968, he published the novel *House Made of Dawn*, which won the Pulitzer Prize in fiction in 1969. The protagonist of Momaday's novel, Abel, returns to his reservation after serving in the military in World War II. He kills an albino, whom he believes to have been an evil sorcerer, and serves a prison term. After his release, Abel settles in Los Angeles, where he meets with hardship and brutality from white society and the corruption of traditional ways by other Native Americans. At the end, he returns to the reservation and runs a ritual race against death and evil at dawn.

Gerald Vizenor (born 1934), whose father was Ojibwa, also became both a professor and a writer. A prolific author, Vizenor has written poetry, history, ethnography, and literary criticism, in addition to novels. His first novel, *Darkness in Saint Louis Bearheart* (1978; revised as *Bearheart: The Heirship Chronicles*, 1990), is an autobiographical work that examines his own experience as a Native American. Another of Vizenor's novels, *Dead Voices: Natural Agonies in the New World* (1992), draws on Native American traditions of oral narrative. This difficult, experimental novel looks at the trickster figure of Native American myth in the context of contemporary society.

Poet and novelist James Welch, part Blackfoot and part Gros Ventre Indian, looked at the Native American experience in works set in both contemporary and historical settings. Welch's first novel, *Winter in the Blood* (1974), is a story with some autobiographical basis, about a young Indian on a Montana reservation. The reservation and its social problems are also at the center of Welch's second work of long fiction, *The Death of Jim Loney* (1979), which deals with alcoholism and the confusion of a man of mixed race. *Fools Crow* (1986) tells of a band of Blackfoot Indians in Montana in the 1870's. A fourth novel, *The Indian Lawyer* (1990), returns to the modern reservation in a tale of a successful Native American's struggles with the temptations of political corruption. *The Heartsong of Charging Elk* (2000) follows its Native American protagonist from the Little Big Horn to France with Buffalo Bill's Wild West Show. He is abandoned in France and must struggle with late nineteenth century French culture on his own.

Leslie Marmon Silko (born 1948) achieved critical acclaim with her first novel, *Ceremony* (1977), which deals with a mixed-race Navajo veteran's struggles against insanity after returning from World War II. Under the guidance of a wise, elderly, mixed-race man, the protagonist finds peace and cosmic order through participation in traditional ceremony. Marmon's second novel, *Almanac of the Dead* (1991), is an epic that took the author ten years to complete. It covers five hundred years of the struggle between Native Americans and settlers from Europe.

THE NEW GENERATION

By the 1980's, the Native American novel was well established, and works of fiction on Native American themes were popular with a large readership. Louise Erdrich (born 1954), daughter of a Chippewa mother and a German American father, was one of the most successful Native American authors of the decade. In 1984, after having published a volume of poetry, Erdrich published her first novel, *Love Medicine* (revised and expanded, 1993). She followed this with a series of related novels: *The Beet Queen* (1986), *Tracks* (1988), *The Bingo Palace* (1994), and *Tales of Burning Love* (1996). The novels in this series tell the stories of three related Native American families living in North Dakota from 1912 through the 1980's. Sometimes compared to William Faulkner, Erdrich is concerned with universal patterns of family life, as well as with contemporary Native American issues. She collaborated with her late husband, Michael Dorris, on both fiction and nonfiction works. Her later novels mine the same areas and themes, at the same time as they explore new territory. *The Antelope Wife* (1998) is set in Minnesota, *The Last Report on the Miracles at Little No Horse* (2001) returns to North Dakota, *The Master Butchers Singing Club* (2003) explores Erdrich's German American family legacy, and *The Painted Drum* (2005) starts out in New Hampshire before returning with the sacred drum of the title to North Dakota.

New Native American novelists emerged during the last decade of the twentieth century. Ray A. Young Bear's *Black Eagle Child: The Facepaint Narratives* (1992) is an autobiographical novel in the form of a long blank-verse poem. It tells the story of Edgar Bearchild, a member of the Black Eagle Child settlement of the Mesquakie tribe. A dominant theme of the novel, one found in many Native American works, is the perplexing relationship between an individual who is part of modern American culture and the individual's ancient tribal heritage.

Sherman Alexie (born 1966) was the most widely praised new Native American author of the 1990's. A Spokane/Coeur d'Alene Indian, Alexie grew up on the Wellpinit Indian reservation and continued to live on the reservation after achieving literary renown. Most of Alexie's poetry and fiction focuses on contemporary reservation life, mixing portrayals of alcoholism and poverty with bitter but sympathetic humor and flashes of fantasy. *Reservation Blues* (1995) is set on a Spokane reservation. Its main characters are young Native Americans who have been out of high school for several years and face despair and a bleak future. After legendary blues guitarist Robert Johnson shows up, looking for a way to undo his deal with the devil, the young friends form a rock-and-roll band and reach fame after making their own deal with the devil, who happens to be a white man. Written after Alexie himself had achieved success, the story treats the problem of the threat to American Indian identity posed by succeeding in the white world, as well as with the frustrations and dangers of Native

American life. Alexie's 1996 novel *Indian Killer* is one of his few works not set on the reservation. The novel features a serial killer in Seattle who scalps his white victims, and it deals with issues of racial violence and loss of culture.

Carl L. Bankston III
Updated by David Peck

BIBLIOGRAPHY

Cox, James H. *The Muting White Noise: Native American and European American Novel Traditions*. Norman: University of Oklahoma Press, 2006. Comparative study that includes analyses of John Rollin Ridge, D'Arcy McNickle, Gerald Vizenor, Sherman Alexie, and other Native American novelists.

Hernández-Avila, Inés, ed. *Reading Native American Women: Critical/Creative Representations*. Lanham, Md.: Altamira Press, 2005. Examines Native American women's writings as "creative, cultural, and political expressions." Essays include "Relocations upon Relocations: Home, Language, and Native American Women's Writings," by Hernández-Avila, and "The Trick Is Going Home: Secular Spiritualism in Native American Women's Literature," by Carolyn Dunn.

Lincoln, Kenneth. *Native American Renaissance*. New ed. Berkeley: University of California Press, 1992. Still the most influential critical work on the Native American renaissance. Traces the writings of modern authors back to their roots in oral narrative and autobiography. Contains chapters devoted to N. Scott Momaday, James Welch, and Leslie Marmon Silko.

Lundquist, Suzanne Evertsen. *Native American Literatures: An Introduction*. New York: Continuum, 2004. Essential research tool for study of Native American literature. Includes both a broad overview of the history and scope of Native American literature as well as studies of individual authors and works. Includes excellent resources for further research.

Nabokov, Peter, ed. *Native American Testimony: A Chronicle of Indian-White Relations from Prophecy to the Present, 1492-2000*. Rev ed. New York: Penguin, 1999. In one of the best introductions to Native American history from the Indian perspective, anthropologist Peter Nabokov presents the recorded responses of Native Americans to the European and Euro-American incursion over a five-hundred-year period. Also introduces each historical period with a summary and commentary.

Parker, Robert Dale. *The Invention of Native American Literature*. Ithaca, N.Y.: Cornell University Press, 2003. Examines tradition and aesthetics in Native American literature. Includes essays examining the works of D'Arcy McNickle, Ray A. Young Bear, Leslie Marmon Silko, and others.

Porter, Joy, and Kenneth M. Roesmer, eds. *The Cambridge Companion to Native American Literature*. New York: Cambridge University Press, 2005. Dozens of essays on historical and cultural contexts and genres, as well as studies of N. Scott Momaday, James Welch, Leslie Marmon Silko, Gerald Vizenor, Louise Erdrich, and others.

Velie, Alan R., ed. *American Indian Literature: An Anthology*. Rev. ed. Norman: University of Oklahoma Press, 1991. Anthology containing a wide range of literature, including traditional tales and modern poetry and fiction, by Native Americans on Native American subjects. Useful commentaries on the different forms of literature.

Vizenor, Gerald, ed. *Native American Literature: A Brief Introduction and Anthology*. New York: HarperCollins, 1995. Collection of Native American writings assembled by an acclaimed Native American author. Part of the HarperCollins Literary Mosaic series.

Wiget, Andrew. *Native American Literature*. Boston: Twayne, 1985. Overview of Native American writing, from the earliest oral narratives to the writers of the Native American renaissance. Contains a chronology of Native American literary history from the development of agricultural myths to the publication of Leslie Marmon Silko's *Ceremony* in 1977.

THE SOUTHERN NOVEL

The American South can be defined historically, as an area consisting of the states south of the Mason-Dixon line or of the states that made up the Confederacy. It can also be defined topographically, as a region with three sections, one coastal, another hilly, and a third mountainous. However, from a cultural perspective, neither of these classifications is accurate. Coastal Savannah, Georgia, is unlike coastal Panama City, Florida, and there are few similarities among Birmingham, Alabama; New Orleans, Louisiana; and Dallas, Texas, except that they are all large cities. It might seem that the South is not a cohesive entity or that, if it once was, it vanished after the American Civil War or perhaps with desegregation.

The elements that make up the common heritage of the South are courtesy and honor; dedication to family, home, and home cooking; a love of slow talk and storytelling; a sense of humor, deeply rooted in rural life; a tendency toward nostalgia; a distrust of outsiders, especially those who are rude and arrogant; a willingness to tolerate eccentrics, at least those of known origins; and the conviction that good and evil forces are constantly at war, both in the outside world and in the soul of every human being. These elements are basic in southern literature. Where southern writers differ is not in how they define the South, but in how they define life, whether they look at it from the perspective of a romanticist or that of a realist, whether they see it as a tragedy, a comedy, or a farce.

NINETEENTH CENTURY FICTION

The romantic perspective pervaded nineteenth century southern fiction, whether in the form of historical romances or in ostensibly realistic works that presented an idyllic picture of plantation life, such as John Pendleton Kennedy's *Swallow Barn* (1832). Though "serious" fiction was considered the province of upper-class white men, sentimental, domestic novels by women such as Caroline Lee Hentz and Augusta Jane Evans Wilson, who, like Kennedy, romanticized the South, were immensely popular not only in the South but

also in the North, even during the Civil War. One of the novels in which Wilson defended the Confederate cause, *Macaria, or Altars of Sacrifice* (1864), was adjudged so dangerous that a Yankee commander in Tennessee banned his men from reading it.

However, these romantic novels did not have a lasting impact on southern fiction. By contrast, the realistic, earthy sketches classified as "southwestern" humor because they were set in the frontier states—Alabama, Georgia, Arkansas, Mississippi, Tennessee, and Kentucky—directly influenced later writers, including Mark Twain (1835-1910). Like those earlier sketches, Twain's *Adventures of Huckleberry Finn* (1884) was funny, farcical, and irreverent. It even satirized some of the most cherished beliefs of white southerners, including their assumptions about class and race. Other nineteenth century southern writers also attacked the prevailing romantic vision. In *Margret Howth* (1862), Rebecca Harding Davis wrote about the exploitation of workers in the iron mills, while in *The Awakening* (1899), Kate Chopin described the subjugation of women in a patriarchal society.

THE RICHMOND REVIVAL

At the beginning of the twentieth century, Richmond, Virginia, became the center of rebellion against the literary and social conventions of the Victorian South. Richmond had long been a center of journalistic activity and book publishing, but until the works of Amélie Rives (Princess Troubetzkoy; 1863-1945), Mary Johnston (1870-1936), Ellen Glasgow (1873-1945), and James Branch Cabell (1879-1958) began to appear, the one-time capital of the Confederacy was associated with a romanticized version of the past. None of the writers of the Richmond revival could be accused of having a nineteenth century sensibility. For example, although earlier writers would have been overly sentimental about a woman's obsession with her dead husband, in *The Quick or the Dead?* (1888), Rives approached her heroine with the detachment of a twentieth century psychologist. Rives's conclusion, that it is both unhealthy and impractical to be in love with loss, was not an idea that would have been advanced in a Victorian novel, much less in a Richmond drawing room. It has been suggested that the gothic ending of *The Quick or the Dead?* owes something to another Richmond writer, Edgar Allan Poe, but Rives's gothicism really anticipates that of William Faulkner and Flannery O'Connor.

Like Rives, Mary Johnston insisted on thinking for herself. Although she was sympathetic to the Confederacy, as is evident in her early novels, Johnston defied convention with *Hagar* (1913), a demand for women's suffrage; *The Witch* (1914), an attack on intolerance; and *Croatan* (1923), her version of what happened to the Lost Colony, which shows the settlers and the Native Americans retreating into the interior of the country, intermarrying, and establishing a utopian society.

Ellen Glasgow was also a feminist. Her southern heroines routinely rejected the protection of chivalric southern males and fled to New York City and freedom. Though, like Johnston, she was loyal to her own people, in her Civil War novel *The Battle-Ground* (1902) Glasgow opted for a realistic version of history. Instead of portraying all southern men as heroes and all Yankees as villains, as southern tradition dictated, Glasgow placed good and bad characters on each side. Similarly, her most famous novel, *Barren Ground* (1925), set in Virginia, works against many of the conventions of the Southern romance.

Glasgow's friend, James Branch Cabell, shared her passion for honesty. *The Cords of Vanity* (1909) was a satirical novel intended to expose the hypocritical nature of Richmond society. In his later fiction, Cabell continued to attack pretense, which he saw as the basis of southern life. The title character in *Jurgen* (1919) was a typical Cabell protagonist, an unashamedly hypocritical southerner. Cabell himself was finally rewarded for his uncompromising honesty; after *Jurgen* was banned in New York because of its sexual content, the author became a popular success and an international celebrity.

THE SOUTHERN RENAISSANCE

Shortly after World War I, a group of faculty members and students at Vanderbilt University in Nashville, Tennessee, began publishing a magazine called *The Fugitive*, a literary and critical journal that focused on the South and on its traditions. Most of these "Fugitives," including Andrew Lytle (1902-1995), Allen Tate (1899-1979), and Robert Penn Warren (1905-1989), later became Agrarians, opposing the inroads of industrialism into the South and urging a return to an agricultural economy. Some Fugitives and Agrarians, among them Tate, Warren, and Cleanth Brooks (1906-1994), also spearheaded the movement known as New Criticism. They taught their students to examine texts closely, rather than merely looking at them from a biographical standpoint or assigning them a place in literary history.

While the Nashvilleans were all important figures in the Southern Renaissance (1920-1950), that movement had no single geographical center; rather, it encompassed the entire South. Lytle's connection with Tennessee went back for generations, but Warren was born in Kentucky, and his best-known novel, *All the King's Men* (1946), evolved out of his stay in Louisiana during Huey Long's governorship. Other natives of Kentucky were the poet Tate, who wrote a Civil War novel, *The Fathers* (1938), and the fiction writer Caroline Gordon (1895-1981).

Among the fiction writers of the Southern Renaissance were William Faulkner (1897-1962) and Eudora Welty (1909-2001) of Mississippi; Thomas Wolfe (1900-1938) of North Carolina; Flannery O'Connor (1925-1964), Carson McCullers (1917-1967), and Erskine Caldwell (1903-1987) of Georgia; Peter Taylor (1917-1994) of Tennessee; and Katherine Anne Porter (1890-1980) of Texas. Probably the most famous African American writer of the period is Mississippi's Richard Wright (1908-1960), but James Weldon Johnson (1871-1938) and Zora Neale Hurston (1891-1960), both of whom were Floridians, are also significant.

The writers of the Southern Renaissance resembled each other only in that they recognized a common heritage. In emphasis and outlook, they could be as different as Caldwell, who in *Tobacco Road* (1932) and *God's Little Acre* (1933) blamed society for the misery and moral degradation of sharecroppers, and O'Connor, whose novels, like her short stories, revealed her commitment to the Christian faith. Each writer had a distinctive style as well. Wolfe's poetic prose was markedly different from the colloquial narratives and dialogues of Welty and Hurston.

WILLIAM FAULKNER AND
SOUTHERN LITERATURE

William Faulkner's continuing preeminence among southern writers is due in part to his amazing scope. His novels recapitulate southern history, and the characters in his fictional Yoknatapawpha County are drawn from every social class and represent various ethnic and racial groups. Moreover, the moral dilemmas and spiritual uncertainties that trouble all of his characters, except for the ones who are incapable of reflection or are resolutely amoral, are those that must be faced not just by southerners but by every human being.

Faulkner's stature in the international community was recognized formally in 1950, when he was awarded a Nobel Prize. Though his fiction has a universal appeal, however, it is profoundly southern. Faulkner was fascinated with families of all sorts: the Sutpens, the Compsons, the despicable Snopeses, and the poor, ignorant Bundrens, who in *As I Lay Dying* (1930) make a valiant effort to have a dead wife and mother properly buried. Faulkner liked to tell a good story, and he enjoyed comic exaggeration. Many of his accounts of the Snopeses' doings and his last novel, *The Reivers* (1962), are reminiscent of southwestern humor.

If Faulkner was sometimes nostalgic about the past, it was because, like Quentin Compson in *The Sound and the Fury* (1929), he saw such spiritual emptiness in the present. The contrast between the old world and the new is made explicit in the Civil War novel *The Unvanquished* (1938), in which the southerners try to live by a code of honor, while the Yankee invaders are merely rapacious. Faulkner knew that the southern distrust of outsiders and change was not just a long-lasting reaction to the Civil War and Reconstruction. As Isaac McCaslin pointed out in *Go Down, Moses* (1942), though the Old South was cursed by slavery and torn apart by racial prejudice, many southerners felt that the industrial, technological New South, with its gospel of greed, denied moral and spiritual values and might well end by destroying the natural world.

A CONTINUING RENAISSANCE

Although the Southern Renaissance is customarily described as lasting from 1920 to 1950, the continuing vitality of southern literature may prompt future literary historians to extend that second date at least to the end of the twentieth century. In the 1990's, at least seventy southern fiction writers appeared in almost every bibliographical listing, and new names were being added almost constantly.

Another sign of vitality is that instead of imitating Faulkner in theme and content, as many critics had expected, later southern writers proved to be highly original. Madison Smartt Bell's dark historical novel *All Souls' Rising* (1995) could hardly be more different from Robert Morgan's gentle Appalachian love story *The Truest Pleasure* (1995), nor could the poor white people in the fiction of James Dickey, Bobbie Ann Mason, and Lewis Nordan have less in common with the upper-class Atlantans in Anne Rivers Siddons's *Peachtree Road* (1988). Moreover, instead of imitating Faulkner's convoluted style, southern writers invented or developed their own. William Styron's prose, for example, is complex but less elaborate than that of Faulkner, while Reynolds Price and Fred Chappell are known for classical simplicity, and Mason is considered minimalistic.

Though the common heritage is the basis of all southern literature, evident even in the works of writers who have left the South or abandoned southern settings, one cannot generalize as to how life is defined in southern fiction. A southern novel can be comic or tragic, Romantic or realistic, gothic or satirical. It can exhibit stark pessimism, alienation and uncertainty, or profound religious faith. Cormac McCarthy emphasizes human depravity, Walker Percy believes love can provide relief from the modern malaise, and Reynolds Price holds to his belief in divine grace and ultimate salvation.

The final decades of the twentieth century brought one very important change to southern literature: The southern experience was no longer the province of white men alone. New voices began to be heard—voices of African Americans, such as Margaret Walker, Ernest J. Gaines, Alice Walker, Bebe Moore Campbell, and Dori Sanders; voices of white women, including Kaye Gibbons, Anne Tyler, Josephine Humphreys, Jill McCorkle, Jayne Anne Phillips, Lee Smith, and Mary Hood; and voices of gays and lesbians, such as Allan Gurganus and

Rita Mae Brown. In the fiction of these authors, the essential elements of the southern heritage are still apparent; however, because they had experienced alienation in ways that their white, male, or heterosexual contemporaries had not, these writers saw the South quite differently and thus added new dimensions to an already rich literary tradition.

Rosemary M. Canfield Reisman

BIBLIOGRAPHY

Abernathy, Jeff. *To Hell and Back: Race and Betrayal in the Southern Novel*. Athens: University of Georgia Press. 2003. Study of race in the southern novel. Includes analyses of the work of William Faulkner, Carson McCullers, Richard Wright, Alice Walker, and other twentieth century southern novelists.

Bassett, John E., ed. *Defining Southern Literature: Perspectives and Assessments, 1831-1952*. Madison, Wis.: Fairleigh Dickinson University Press, 1997. Selections arranged in chronological order reflect diverse views of the South and its literature, which the essays attempt to define.

Booker-Canfield, Suzanne. Introduction to *Contemporary Southern Men Fiction Writers: An Annotated Bibliography*, edited by Rosemary M. Canfield Reisman and Suzanne Booker-Canfield. Lanham, Md.: Scarecrow Press, 1998. In an introductory essay, Booker-Canfield points out the salient characteristics of southern literature in the final decades of the twentieth century. Excellent starting point for the study of contemporary writers.

Ciuba, Gary M. *Desire, Violence, and Divinity in Modern Southern Fiction: Katherine Anne Porter, Flannery O'Connor, Cormac McCarthy, Walker Percy*. Baton Rouge: Louisiana State University Press, 2007. Intensive study of four of the South's most important twentieth century writers and the themes and issues that unite them.

Crow, Charles L., ed. *A Companion to the Regional Literatures of America*. Malden, Mass.: Blackwell, 2003. Appraises regional literature in the United States from New England to the Pacific Northwest. Surveys the accomplishments and careers of regionalist geniuses such as Willa Cather, Bret Harte, and Mark Twain.

Flora, Joseph M., Lucinda Hardwick, and Todd W. Taylor, eds. *The Companion to Southern Literature: Themes, Genres, Places, People, Movements, and Motifs*. Baton Rouge: Louisiana State University Press, 2001. Massive (1,144 pages) encyclopedia on southern literature, with more than five hundred entries (alphabetical table of contents with a contents list featuring twenty-two subject headings).

Folks, Jeffrey J., and James A. Perkins, eds. *Southern Writers at Century's End*. Lexington: University Press of Kentucky, 1997. Attempt to survey southern writing during the final quarter of the twentieth century. The section "New Faces" examines the popular but critically neglected James Lee Burke and John Grisham, as well as some relatively unknown novelists.

Francisco, Edward, Robert Vaughan, and Linda Francisco, comps. *The South in Perspective: An Anthology of Southern Literature*. Upper Saddle River, N.J.: Prentice Hall, 2001. Selections are organized historically, from the colonial period, through the confederacy and Reconstruction, to the twentieth century. Nearly fourteen hundred pages conclude with a bibliography and an index.

Gray, Richard, and Owen Robinson, eds. *A Companion to the Literature and Culture of the American South*. Malden, Mass.: Blackwell, 2004. Essays by dozens of scholars on literary figures and movements, including Edgar Allan Poe, William Faulkner, and plantation fiction, and on southern society and culture, including music, sports, and politics. Indispensable to understanding the mind and literature of the American South.

Ketchin, Susan. *The Christ-Haunted Landscape: Faith and Doubt in Southern Fiction*. Reprint. Jackson: University Press of Mississippi, 2000. Examines whether religion plays as important a role in the lives of southern writers as in the society at large. Each of twelve sections consists of an interview with a writer, a selection from his or her works, and comments by the study's author.

Perry, Carolyn, and Mary Louise Weaks, eds. *The History of Southern Women's Literature*. Baton Rouge: Louisiana State University Press, 2002. Essays examine fictional interpretations of race, urbanization, feminism, gender, the myth of southern womanhood, the "southern belle" and the "mammy," poverty, and critical responses to novels such as *Uncle Tom's Cabin* and *Gone with the Wind*.

Rubin, Louis D., Jr., ed. *The History of Southern Literature*. Baton Rouge: Louisiana State University Press, 1985. Good comprehensive study of southern literature. Contains critical analysis and valuable back-ground information, a bibliographical essay, and an index.

Simpson, Lewis P. *The Fable of the Southern Writer*. Reprint. Baton Rouge: Louisiana State University Press, 2003. One of many volumes by a major literary historian. Simpson believes that since the Civil War, the literary imagination has been a vehicle for self-examination.

THE WESTERN NOVEL

The Western genre is rooted in the fertile soil of nineteenth century popular American literature. Among its antecedents are the Leatherstocking Tales of James Fenimore Cooper, a series of five novels of the American frontier featuring a self-sufficient and morally incorruptible backwoods character named Natty Bumppo, who is considered America's first literary hero. Though Cooper was ultimately ambiguous about the meaning of the frontier in American life, he clearly demonstrated that frontier materials could sustain serious literary consideration and that the frontier's pristine beauty, the savagery of its conflicts, and its colorful inhabitants could have immense popular appeal.

After Cooper came the House of Beadle and other dime-novel publishers, all ignoring the serious cultural questions that Cooper could at least identify, if not resolve. For the most part, the dime novels were cynically commercial in intention, with scant regard for all but the most lurid themes, episodes, and personalities in frontier history.

In addition, the Western was indebted to the local-color movement of the late nineteenth century, of which the works of Bret Harte are among the most familiar examples. Although the local colorists, by definition, failed to find in their materials matters of general cultural importance, they demonstrated the popular appeal and the literary validity of close attention to local and regional folkways, the distinctive personalities, dialect, and daily experience of common people, at times developing into the American tall tale.

OWEN WISTER AND ZANE GREY

Owen Wister (1860-1938), creator of the first genuine Western, *The Virginian: A Horseman of the Plains* (1902), is not the kind of person one would ordinarily think of as the author of cowboy novels. Born into a wealthy Philadelphia family, Wister received the best education his day could offer, culminating in a degree from Harvard. Culturally sophisticated, Wister enjoyed close friendships with Henry James, William Dean Howells, and Theodore Roosevelt, and his abilities as a pianist impressed even Franz Liszt, for whom he played at Bayreuth. Talent and family connections did not bring happiness: Unable to find a satisfying career in either the arts or the tawdry business world recommended by his father, Wister suffered a nervous breakdown in 1885, for which his doctor prescribed a recuperative trip to Wyoming. During this vacation on the cattle ranch of a family friend, he became impressed with the fictional potential of the American cowboy and began the literary experimentation that would lead to creation of the Western novel.

The Virginian was not the first appearance of the cowboy in American literature. The local colorist Alfred Henry Lewis, several dime novelists, Wister himself as early as 1891, and others had featured cowboy heroes in novels and stories. However, it was Wister's nameless Virginian who first provided just the right combination of colorful dress and speech, violent environment, and romantic potential to set the pattern for a new literary genre's success.

The critical novelist James expressed admiration for *The Virginian*, and many readers with more simplistic preconceptions regarding Westerns are surprised at the sophistication of the novel. Although the novel is somewhat episodic because it grew in part from short stories, *The Virginian*'s two main plots—the corruption of Trampas from an honest cowhand to a rustler, which results in the lynching of the Virginian's friend, Steve, and Trampas's death at the Virginian's hands in the famous walkdown; and the Virginian's courtship of the eastern schoolmarm, Molly Wood—are complex and skillfully narrated. Critics have observed that, although a cowboy novel, *The Virginian* contains not a single scene in which cowboys actually work with "cows," but such facile judgments do scant justice to the social and historical realism of the novel. The cowboy's dress, language, customs, ethics, and humor, and the environmental imperatives within which he operates, are carefully depicted and assessed.

Wister's literary output was not great, for he was not a prolific writer, and the West was only one of his concerns. Moreover, *The Virginian* is marred by much of the same confusion over the meaning of the West that had haunted Cooper: How can one relate the morally innocent—yet savage and violent—tenor of Western life to the culturally sophisticated, yet corrupt, East? The marriage of the Virginian and Molly indicates some sort of cultural accommodation, but in his final collection of Western stories, *When West Was West* (1928), Wister concludes that no such accommodation is possible.

As important as *The Virginian* was in the creation of the Western, no single work can create a genre, and it remained for Wister's innumerable successors and imitators to develop, out of the materials provided by *The Virginian*, the Western formula. By far the most prominent of Wister's early successors was Zane Grey (1872-1939). Grey's family had figured with some significance in the history of the Ohio River frontier, and he was reared on tales of ancestral exploits to compensate for the painful reality of the family's more recent decline from wealth and influence. Like Wister, Grey was unable to adjust idealistic youthful dreams and aspirations to the realistic necessities of earning a living. After undistinguished completion of a dental course at the University of Pennsylvania, Grey attempted to open a dental practice in New York City. He soon abandoned dentistry in favor of writing, but his early efforts, a trilogy recounting the exploits of his pioneer ancestors, sold poorly.

After a summer in Arizona and Utah in 1906, Grey discovered characters, settings, and themes that he was confident he could turn into literature, and his first Western, *The Heritage of the Desert* (1910), a story of Mormons, rustlers, and the redemptive qualities of the West, sold well enough to encourage him. Grey's phenomenal literary success began in 1912 with the publication of *Riders of the Purple Sage*, surely the most famous Western ever written. In that novel, Grey introduces a black-clad gunfighter hero, Lassiter, whose bloody encounters with the Mormons in the dramatic canyons of southern Utah established important literary precedents. Grey exhibited, in that and in many later novels, a much greater debt to the dime novels than did Wister: There is much less subtlety in Grey's violent scenes, much less complexity in his characters' emotions and motives, and much less restraint in his descriptions of setting.

Nevertheless, Grey shared with Wister an unfeigned love for the West and its history and culture, and he tried to portray it realistically. Grey chose a wide variety of western settings for his novels and an even wider variety of character types, including ethnic minorities who had interested few other authors. Furthermore, he invested his books with a philosophical burden often missing in popular writing: The West alone, in his view, offered free scope for development of complete human beings, including those primitive virtues and self-reliant skills that the overcivilization of the East had submerged.

Most of Grey's best work appeared during the years between *Riders of the Purple Sage* and *Under the Tonto Rim* (1926). Thereafter (and occasionally during that period as well), the urgency of his message, the originality of his characters, and the carefulness of his descriptions are much less poignant. Much of Grey's unevenness probably results from the sheer quantity of his work. During a career of some thirty years, Grey wrote nearly one hundred novels and stories and dozens of magazine articles.

Even at that, Grey's output is dwarfed by the production of perhaps the most prolific creator of Western literature since the dime novelists, a would-be epic poet named Frederick Schiller Faust (1892-1944), who supported both his literary aspirations and his sybaritic life in an Italian villa by producing more than six hundred Western novels and stories under some twenty pseudonyms, the best known of which was Max Brand. Though Faust, who was reared in California, knew the West well, there is little of the actual West in his books; he preferred instead to borrow his plots from the Greek and Roman classics, garbing Oedipus and Agamemnon in chaps and six-guns but cynically dismissing his Western works as "cowboy junk."

It is tempting to take Faust's cynicism at face value and disdain to consider seriously his Western works. However, in spite of his scornful attitude and rapid composition (during one thirteen-week period in 1920, he turned out 190,000 publishable words), Faust wrote some fine novels. *The Untamed* (1919), his first Western novel, features a memorable hero, Dan Barry, who lives an isolated, wild life in the desert, tames a wild horse and a wolf, and holds out against making an accommodation with civilization. *Destry Rides Again* (1930), later made into a popular motion picture, is a revenge story recounting the way a framed man gets even with the jury members. Unlike Grey's Lassiter, Harry Destry prevails more through guile and cleverness than through violence.

Faust's work, then, represents a considerable retreat from the realism of Wister and Grey, demonstrating that good novels need only be believable, not necessarily authentic. The career of Clarence Edward Mulford (1883-1956) followed Faust's in that respect and also called to mind the dime-novel tradition in his love of violence. Reared in Illinois, Mulford was working in a minor civil service position in Brooklyn when he began to write Westerns, but he did not visit the West until eighteen years after beginning to write about it. He was unimpressed and discovered that Western reality interfered with his imaginary conception of the West, so he never again left his eastern home. His first Western, *Bar-20* (1907), and many thereafter featured an actual working cowboy named Hopalong Cassidy, whose proletarian speech and bloodthirsty love for fighting made him a far cry from the character of the same name played on film by William Boyd.

Bertha M. Bower (1871-1940), by contrast, was as deeply rooted as a cottonwood tree in the real West. One of her four husbands, Clayton Bower, was a Montana cattleman, and she spent her entire life in the region about which she wrote. In *Chip, of the Flying U* (1906), which was illustrated by her friend, the cowboy artist Charles M. Russell, Bower established her trademark, the unglamorous cowboy character. Though Chip himself is extraordinary—he occasionally quotes William Shakespeare, and he is a gifted, untutored artist—Bower chose to make literature out of the smaller human dramas that occurred in the cowboy's daily work routine, forgoing any great universal truth.

ERNEST HAYCOX AND LOUIS L'AMOUR

Ernest Haycox (1899-1950), whom many critics consider the finest literary craftsman to emerge from the popular Western tradition, was one of a younger generation of writers who became popular during the heyday of Western fiction, 1930 to 1950. Like many of the older writers, he completed his apprenticeship in the pulp magazines, writing fast-moving Western romances with shallow characters and plenty of action. Like Faust, Haycox had serious literary aspirations, but unlike Faust, he wished to realize those aspirations through the use of

Western materials. In several mature novels toward the end of his career, beginning with *Bugles in the Afternoon* (1944) and culminating in his posthumously published masterpiece *The Earthbreakers* (1952), Haycox demonstrated the resilience of the Western formula.

Bugles in the Afternoon, a fictional account of General George Custer's Seventh Cavalry and the events leading up to its annihilation at the Battle of the Little Big Horn, is marred for many contemporary readers by its unabashed love for the military life. In spite of that, its main theme, how much the individual owes to the group, is extensively explored, and the depth of its realism, as seen in Haycox's poignant descriptions of bleak North Dakota towns and of the Seventh Cavalry soldiers and their equipment, is memorable.

Haycox was born, reared, and educated in Oregon, and it was of Oregon, with its moldy, misty forests, succulent soils, and salty, windy estuary towns that he wrote most effectively. The three great novels of Haycox's maturity, *Long Storm* (1946), *The Adventurers* (1954), and *The Earthbreakers*, are all set in Oregon's lower Willamette Valley. The main theme of each of the novels is the endurance and gradual victory of idealism over forces of savagery and cynicism. The great peril of such a theme is sentimentalism, and one must acknowledge that Haycox is occasionally ensnared by it, particularly in the two earlier novels. Haycox, like Grey, never learned to make sin attractive enough to make victories over it appear genuine; his villains, such as the Southern sympathizer Floyd Ringrose in *Long Storm*, who clumsily tries to subvert Oregon's strong Union commitment during the Civil War, are too often melodramatic caricatures. Ringrose abuses women and children, drinks too much, brags ridiculously, conspires ineptly, and fights poorly.

At his best, though, Haycox escapes the perils of sentimentalism. In *The Earthbreakers*, he places his hero, a former mountain man named Rice Burnett who has chosen to guide a wagon train to the Willamette Valley where he will stay and settle, in the midst of several characters representing various degrees of commitment to civilization and forces him to make genuine, often painful, choices concerning with whom and to what degree he will ally himself. Burnett has a yearning for civilization, though his love for the wild, free life of a trapper will not die easily or completely; still, defining what that civilization is, among the various choices available, is no easy matter. Burnett is an appealing hero, but he is a far cry from the superhuman gunslingers of much popular Western fiction and even from the overly idealistic characters of Haycox's earlier books.

Haycox's craftsmanship had a profound influence on popular Western literature. In 1952, a group of novelists, many of them Haycox disciples, founded the Western Writers of America (WWA). The WWA, which has grown steadily in size and sophistication, began publishing *The Roundup*, a monthly magazine with news, reviews, and articles on writing and the publishing business. The association also began making awards at each annual meeting for the best writing of the previous year in several categories of Western writing. The effect of the organization has been to establish higher literary standards and assist aspiring writers in meeting those standards.

Although Haycox's influence on younger writers was undeniable, none of his direct disciples or imitators climbed to the master's level. One of his leading competitors in sales, if not in literary quality, was Frederick Dilley Glidden (1908-1975), who wrote under the name of the Kansas gunfighter Luke Short. If many journalists are frustrated novelists, Glidden the novelist was a frustrated journalist. Born in Illinois, he graduated with a journalism degree from the University of Missouri. Though Glidden worked in various locations for brief periods on newspapers, the onset of the Great Depression cost him one job after another. Finally, in 1935, he began writing Westerns to support himself.

Like many writers of Westerns, Glidden was capable of massive production: During the 1940's alone, he wrote fourteen novels. His success enabled him to move to Aspen, Colorado, where he spent most of the rest of his life. At about that time, he began to lose interest in Western writing; during the 1950's, he wrote only six novels and began trying, with little success, to break into other genres.

Glidden admired Haycox and successfully competed with him for a time in the high-paying "slick" magazines such as *Collier's*; in literary quality, however, he was no match for Haycox. In fact, most of his novels could be regarded as throwbacks to the pre-Haycox days when

characterization and setting were not as important as action. Unlike most literary chroniclers of the masculine world of the frontier, Glidden knew how to develop convincing heroines. Both *Hard Money* (1940) and *Paper Sheriff* (1966), perhaps his best novel, feature at least one believably complex female character.

Undoubtedly the best-known modern Western writer is Louis L'Amour (1908-1988). From the age of fifteen, when he left his North Dakota home to ease the financial burden on his family, L'Amour lived a colorful life not unworthy of some of his characters. His travels throughout the United States working at a multitude of occupations inspired him with a clear vision of the diversity of American culture and the sturdy virtues required to settle the American continent. L'Amour began writing for magazines during the 1930's. Soon he conceived a plan for a massive fictional saga of the westward movement based on the stories of three families: the Sacketts, the Talons, and the Chantrys. Even with 101 books at the time of his death, not all of which were part of the saga, the project remained incomplete.

On the covers of his books and in his frequent television appearances, L'Amour was much more interested in discussing Western history than writing techniques and literary theory. He was convinced that his strongest suit as a writer was the authenticity of his novels, some of which even contain historical footnotes. Critics have argued that L'Amour confused authenticity with believability and that, like the works of Zane Grey, his novels often suffer from their heavy burden of undigested historical data.

L'Amour's *Hondo* (1953) expresses the opinion, well in advance of the current ecological movement, that humans are responsible for the use they make of their natural environment. Perhaps even more prevalent in L'Amour's fiction is the disillusioned, hard-bitten hero for whom survival is the only goal: *Shalako* (1962) is a notable example. Such novels were only the beginning of vast changes in values in the Western literature of the 1960's and 1970's, which paralleled changes in American culture as a whole.

Several publishers widened the chink opened by Doubleday's Double-D Western series, which featured, to the astonishment of readers of traditional Westerns, graphic descriptions of sex and violence and other formerly taboo material. Perhaps it is appropriate that the lead in establishing the subgenre of the "sex Western" was taken by Playboy Press. With its series written by staff writers under the collective name of Jake Logan, Playboy introduced graphic and lengthy sex scenes alongside more traditional Western elements. The trend caught on; as the Jake Logan series grew, other series appeared, such as the Longarm series published by Jove Publications. One can choose among several such series, each boasting several dozen titles. The assembly-line nature of those series, incidentally, is revealed in their packaging by number as much as by title. During its burgeoning years, the sex Western was a controversial issue: Much of *The Roundup* during 1982 was taken up by a heated debate regarding the validity of the sex Western, many writers haughtily disdaining its economic temptations. In response to the unprecedented openness of sexual discussion and expression in American life, often to the point of unabashed hedonism, the sex Western seems to have attained a solid place in the Western literary canon.

Equally noteworthy is the rise of the "violence Western," the leading proponent of which is an Englishman named Terry Harknett, creator of the Edge series under the name George Gilman. The depiction of extreme violence in Westerns clearly parallels larger cultural developments, yet the Edge series and the novels of another Englishman, J. T. Edson, are often revolting by any standard. Gilman's *The Living, the Dying, and the Dead* (1978), for example, after an assortment of shootings, stabbings, dismemberments, and disfigurements, culminates with a scene in which the rotting corpse of a dead prostitute is dissected.

Not all trends in popular Western literature, though, pandered to the most ignoble human instincts. Stephen D. Overholser's Molly series, for example, attempts to reach those calling for greater freedom and equality for women. The series contains sex, which the author says he tries to make a plausible and integral part of the story, but it also recounts the activities of an independent, resourceful woman on the frontier.

LARRY McMURTRY AND CORMAC McCARTHY

To some extent the Western novel has come into its own with its acceptance in the realm of real litera-

ture. Perhaps no contemporary writer of importance is more directly associated with the Western novel than Larry McMurtry. Born in 1936 in Wichita Falls, Texas, McMurtry earned degrees from North Texas State University and Rice University and did graduate work at Stanford as a Wallace Stegner Fellow. He entered the teaching profession as a creative-writing teacher at Rice but eventually turned to writing full-time, residing in Virginia, California, and Arizona before returning to his native Texas and settling in rural Archer City in 1986.

Although his earlier works, including *Horseman, Pass By* (1961; better known to many by the title of its film adaptation, *Hud*), *The Last Picture Show* (1966), and *Terms of Endearment* (1975), brought consistent, favorable attention to McMurtry and his work, it was not until *Lonesome Dove* (1985), which won the 1986 Pulitzer Prize, that McMurtry's fame moved into many diverse areas. The film versions of these works brought even more attention and acclaim to McMurtry.

Thematically, one can pigeonhole each of McMurtry's works into any one of four major concepts: initiation of the young man, the negative effect of modern civilization, a strong need to belong to a particular place, and the durability of America's Western myth. For instance, in *Horseman, Pass By*, the first novel in his Thalia trilogy, McMurtry places two value systems into conflict, much like James Fenimore Cooper does in his Leatherstocking novels. Homer Bannon represents the old values based upon belonging to the land and hard work, while his stepson Hud represents the change to a get-all-you-can-as-soon-as-you-can attitude that had engulfed much of the younger population of the West as it had the remainder of the country.

Leaving Cheyenne (1963) and *The Last Picture Show*, the concluding two parts of the Thalia trilogy, continue to portray the deteriorating life in the small-town West. In each, the reader is constantly told that the modern West must come to terms with changing times that often do not permit values long a part of Western lore to go unchallenged, most often shown in these three novels by the life-changing decisions that young characters must make.

Although McMurtry's earlier works deal almost entirely with the modern American West, he turned a new artistic corner in 1985 with the publication of *Lonesome*

Dove, the first installment of the adventures of aging Texas Rangers Woodrow Call and Augustus McCrae. These two Western archetype characters continue McMurtry's depiction of diametric opposites: Call fails to express any degree of emotion, and McCrae lives with his emotions just below the surface. After the work earned the Pulitzer Prize and spawned a successful television miniseries, McMurtry published such books as *Texasville* (1987), *Buffalo Girls* (1990), *The Evening Star* (1992), *Streets of Laredo* (1993), *Dead Man's Walk* (1995), and *Comanche Moon* (1997), among others. From the beginning of his career, McMurtry has fulfilled his reading audience's need for further installments of the continuing saga of America's mythical West. Although the names may change and situations may undergo major alterations, the story of the West looms large in the American imagination. The changes that McMurtry's characters undergo mirror the changes that America, itself, has undergone. With Diana Ossana, McMurtry wrote the award-winning screenplay for the film version of E. Annie Proulx's daring short story "Brokeback Mountain" (1998). The film of the same name, released in 2005 to critical acclaim and also controversy, tells the story of two young Wyoming ranch hands who fall in love while working together one summer. They remain lovers in the ensuing decades, although they meet infrequently (both are married to women) and must keep their intimate relationship secret.

Another writer of the West's story is Cormac McCarthy (born 1933). Like Owen Wister, McCarthy was not born in the West, and his writing career did not begin with novels about the western United States. McCarthy was born in Rhode Island but moved with his family to Knoxville, Tennessee, in 1947. McCarthy attended Knoxville's Catholic High School, graduating in 1951. He then entered the University of Tennessee but left in 1952. McCarthy joined the U.S. Air Force, after which he returned to Knoxville to pick up on the writing career of which he had dreamed.

McCarthy's early fiction (like the 1985 *Blood Meridian*) was replete with the violence and the grotesque that ensconced him in the world of modern gothic writers. However, in 1992, McCarthy moved to another realm of fiction when he produced the first installment of his Border trilogy. Although the locale changed from the Amer-

ican South to the American West, McCarthy continued to incorporate the violent and the strange into his fiction. The works of which McCarthy's Border trilogy consists, *All the Pretty Horses* (1992), *The Crossing* (1994), and *Cities of the Plain* (1998), continue the saga of the modern American West but with a McCarthy slant.

These three novels allow the reader to witness the initiation of two young cowboys, John Grady Cole in *All the Pretty Horses*, Billy Parham in *The Crossing*, and both in *Cities of the Plain*. As happened in many earlier Western novels, McCarthy's protagonists are thrown into situations that challenge all that they have been taught. The lesson that each learns is that the evil against which people must fight is most often found within themselves, echoing the quintessential American tragic hero, Captain Ahab of Herman Melville's *Moby Dick* (1851). They find that under the right circumstances they are able to kill other human beings with only minimal remorse, a lesson reminiscent of Natty Bumppo in Cooper's Leatherstocking novels. Cole and Parham are often forced to realize that they cannot meet their quests and that they must salvage whatever remains of their lives when their attempts are thwarted. In this manner, McCarthy contributes to moving Western novels further into the realm of realism and, to some extent, experimentalism through his less-than-positive endings and his use of the gothic techniques that characterized his earlier fiction about Knoxville and eastern Tennessee.

One of the most significant developments in popular Western literature during the 1970's, 1980's, and 1990's was the increasing acceptance of the Western among literary critics and intellectual historians. Some of this is certainly a result of the general democratization of American life after the 1960's and the rise of New Left historiography, with its emphasis on the life of common people. One may view this trend most graphically, perhaps, by comparing the two editions, ten years apart, of Richard W. Etulain's bibliography of Western literary studies. In *Western American Literature: A Bibliography of Interpretive Books and Articles* (1972), the entries on even popular writers such as Zane Grey often include some flawed and fugitive articles and reviews, and even those appear in limited numbers. By the time his *Bibliographical Guide to the Study of Western American Literature* appeared in 1982, Etulain could choose from a fertile field of books and articles from major presses and journals, and in much greater quantities than the previous decade. (A second edition of this guide was published in 1995 and edited by Etulain and N. Jill Howard.) Fred Erisman's *Fifty Western Writers: A Bio-Bibliographical Sourcebook* (1982) features essays on Grey, Glidden, and L'Amour alongside Frank Waters, John Steinbeck, and Jack London. The massive *Literary History of the American West* (1987), a volume sponsored by the Western Literature Association, gives ample space to the development of the popular Western.

Finally, the Western Writers of America began to take a more searching look at their craft through substantive articles in their revamped journal, *The Roundup*. Before 1988, *The Roundup* was little more than a trade journal that appeared ten times each year. Beginning in September of 1988, it changed to a much larger and intellectually substantial quarterly format. Similarly, *Western American Literature*, the journal of the Western Literature Association, based in Logan, Utah, has published serious and scholarly analyses of Western literature for some years.

The popular Western, then, gives every sign of remaining a living part of American literary legacy. Far from becoming ossified in outworn romantic horse opera clichés, the Western remains largely abreast with ongoing developments in the culture at large, while keeping in touch with important elements in American history and traditional values.

Gary Topping; Tom Frazier
Updated by David Peck

BIBLIOGRAPHY

Brown, Bill. *Reading the West: An Anthology of Dime Novels*. New York: Bedford, 1997. This anthology's extensive introduction to the dime novel is most important to any student. The works themselves put everything into perspective.

Etulain, Richard W. *Telling Western Stories: From Buffalo Bill to Larry McMurtry*. Albuquerque: University of New Mexico Press, 1999. Cultural historian addresses how fiction has influenced the public's images of the American West. Places Larry McMur-

try's work, for example, within a period of fiction about the West that exhibits increasing complexity and ambiguity.

Lape, Noreen Groover. *West of the Border: The Multicultural Literature of the Western American Frontiers*. Athens: Ohio University Press, 2000. Important corrective to the view of the West as exclusively white and male. Uses critical theory to examine the West as a borderland where writers initiate intercultural dialogue.

Lyon, Thomas J., ed. *The Literary West: An Anthology of Western American Literature*. New York: Oxford University Press, 1999. More than forty selections include pieces by Zane Grey, John Steinbeck, Wallace Stegner, and Amy Tan. Coverage from the sixteenth century to the late twentieth century.

Mitchell, Lee Clark. "What's Authentic About Western Literature? And, More to the Point, What's Literary?" In *Postwestern Cultures: Literature, Theory, Space*, edited by Susan Kollin. Lincoln: University of Nebraska Press, 2007. Mitchell questions the traditional definition of "Western" literature. Argues against the mandate for authenticity that haunts Western literature and for the idea of a literature built on seeing the West anew: As writers of the West, Mitchell argues, "Becoming more authentic is not the trick; we need simply to become more ingenious and creative."

Simonson, Harold P. *Beyond the Frontier: Writers, Western Regionalism, and a Sense of Place*. Fort Worth: Texas Christian University Press, 1989. Examines the myth of the West as a particular "place" and how the West is presented in the literature of the region.

Williamson, Alan. *Westernness: A Meditation*. Charlottesville: University of Virginia Press, 2006. Engaging, well-written look at how the American West has formed its own literary (and artistic) culture from the point of view of writers and artists who have been both westerners and easterners. Also addresses "the fear, anxiety, and sense of cultural vacancy that western artists have had to overcome in confronting their new landscape."

GENRE OVERVIEWS

The Academic Novel

A problem that every novelist confronts is the question of structure, of how to organize fictional materials—plot, character, setting—into a coherent and compelling whole. Some novels come with a built-in structure, such as stories about journeys (often called picaresque novels), in which a hero or heroes encounter various adventures. Another common fictional form is the bildungsroman, or the coming-of-age story, which follows a character from birth into adulthood. Finally, there is the form known as the ship of fools, in which characters, confined together (in, for example, a ship, plane, or prison), resort to sharing stories to pass the time. The academic novel follows this last structural format, as it is usually set in a single college or university community and tells about the lives and relationships of a group of faculty and staff. Related to the academic novel is the college or campus novel, as in F. Scott Fitzgerald's *This Side of Paradise* (1920) or Evelyn Waugh's *Brideshead Revisited* (1945, 1959). The college novel is an older form with similar settings, but it usually focuses on students and student life and is often a variant of the bildungsroman.

The academic novel emerged as a separate subgenre of the modern Anglo-American novel following World War II. Early examples include C. P. Snow's *The Masters* (1951), Kingsley Amis's *Lucky Jim* (1954), Mary McCarthy's *The Groves of Academe* (1952), and Randall Jarrell's *Pictures from an Institution* (1954). The reasons for the sudden emergence of the academic novel as a separate form at this time are fairly clear. First, there was a boom in college and university attendance after the end of World War II, as U.S. soldiers and other servicemembers returned from war seeking an education funded by the new G.I. Bill. State universities in particular began to enroll higher numbers of veterans—and then baby boomers and graduating high school students—in what came to be known as open admissions programs, after the 1960's.

Second, writers began to take jobs in academia. Before World War II, novelists rarely ventured onto college campuses; neither Ernest Hemingway nor James Joyce, for example, had any kind of academic background, although college dropout William Faulkner did become a writer-in-residence at the University of Virginia at the end of his career. After World War II, however, modern literature became a popular subject of study and creative-writing programs sprang up across the United States. Writers found that they were welcome at colleges and universities, encouraged to talk about their work and about the writing process itself. Their teaching schedules usually left them large chunks of time in which to write.

Out of this fortunate convergence of writer and setting came the academic novel. It made sense that the university, as it reflected larger and more diverse populations after World War II, became a closed but representative backdrop for fictional works. Writers began to use their new work surroundings as the dramatic settings of their fiction, leading to the new, distinctive genre.

The academic novel also appeared at a time when literature was challenging many social and cultural institutions. British writers after World War II, some of whom formed a group known as the Angry Young Men (for example, John Wain, Alan Sillitoe, and John Osborne), were deeply critical of society. Across the Atlantic were the Beat poets, who were equally critical of social convention. From Sloan Wilson's *The Man in the Gray Flannel Suit* (1955), to Jack Kerouac's *On the Road* (1957), to Joseph Heller's *Catch-22* (1961), and to Ken Kesey's *One Flew over the Cuckoo's Nest* (1962), American novelists after World War II began to attack particular American institutions (such as business and the legal system) for their cruel and impersonal treatment of humans. Heller's satire of war is a microcosm for an irrational society, as Kesey's mental hospital is a symbol of the craziness of the larger world. In the academic novel, similarly, the university community provided a microcosm for the larger society, and faculty foibles—personal, sexual, and political—became representative of larger societal failures.

The earliest academic novels were satirical. The exception is Snow's *The Masters*, considered the first academic novel, which centers on the election of a new don (tutor or professor) at an unnamed college in Cambridge, England—the setting for bitter political struggles—and is a work that seems closer as a historical novel to Anthony Trollope's *Barchester Towers* (1857) than to the contemporary academic novel. Amis's *Lucky Jim* is at the opposite extreme and is still perhaps the funniest academic satire in the history of this subgenre. Set in a red-brick university at a far remove from Cambridge, *Lucky Jim* satirizes academic politics, pretension, and scholarship, and its hero Jim Dixon is one of the funniest protagonists in twentieth century fiction.

One of the best American academic novels of the 1950's was McCarthy's *The Groves of Academe*. Set at a small Pennsylvania college named Jocelyn, *The Groves of Academe* focuses on a fight for faculty retention, and its satirical and cynical story identifies political correctness decades before that term became a fashionable catch phrase. Jarrell's *Pictures from an Institution*, dedicated to McCarthy and to philosopher Hannah Arendt (author of *The Origins of Totalitarianism*, 1951), follows an academic couple at Benton, a progressive college for women, which in Jarrell's portrait resembles a miniature totalitarian society. Bernard Malamud's *A New Life* (1961) focuses on academic conformity, complacency, and anti-intellectualism at a rural technical college in the northwest called Cascadia. Sy Levin, a displaced New York Jew, struggles to find meaning for himself and enact educational reform for his colleagues and students against entrenched traditions.

THE ACADEMIC NOVEL AT ITS PEAK

The high point for the academic novel came in the 1970's and 1980's and in the work of British writers Malcolm Bradbury and David Lodge. In contrast to the first wave of novelists in the 1950's, Bradbury and Lodge were full-fledged academics who continued their multiple careers as teachers, scholars, and creative writers (Lodge at the University of Birmingham and Bradbury at the University of East Anglia). Bradbury's first novel, *Eating People Is Wrong* (1959), focused on Professor Stuart Treece, head of the English Department at a university in the Midlands. That novel was followed by *Stepping Westward* (1965), set at a midwestern university in the United States (Bradbury had studied at Indiana University) and satirizing the new fad of hiring creative writers at universities. A British writer brought to Benedict Arnold University turns out not to be the Angry

Young Man the university thought they were getting but quite the stodgy reverse.

Bradbury's best work is *The History Man* (1975), a novel set at the University of Watermouth, England, and an attack on academic fads and trends of the late 1960's and 1970's, many of them sexual. Bradbury's protagonists, Howard and Barbara Kirk, lead the revolution, but Bradbury skewers them mercilessly. *Rates of Exchange* (1983) follows the linguist Dr. Petworth to the fictional East European country of Slaka for two weeks of misadventures in language and travel during the Cold War. The book is a dark comedy that was short-listed for the Booker Prize.

Lodge has been equally prolific and has produced a trilogy of academic novels. *Changing Places: A Tale of Two Campuses* (1975) centers on two professors of English literature, one British and one American, who swap jobs for six months. Philip Swallow takes the position at the State University of Euphoria, while Morris Zapp, from Euphoria, spends a year at Swallow's University of Rummidge. This exchange creates all kinds of comic cultural juxtapositions that Lodge fully exploits. Zapp—who is another memorable literary character, in the tradition of Amis's Jim Dixon—and Swallow return in *Small World* (1984), a novel that pillories the academic conference. Swallow and Zapp zip from one country to another to attend literary conferences. New characters also appear: Persse McGarrigle attends the conferences in search of the elusive Angelica Pabst and Fulvia Morgana, a feminist theorist, somehow ends up in bed with Zapp.

Lodge continues to play with academic politics and sexual exploits in the third volume of his trilogy *Nice Work* (1988). Zapp and Swallow appear once more in *Nice Work*, but the central figures here are Robyn Penrose, a professor of English, and Vic Wilcox, the managing director of an engineering company, who are asked to participate in a program to link the University of Rummidge more closely to industry. Their shadow careers help to highlight a number of moral, ethical, and ideological contrasts, and both characters learn and gain from each other.

Zapp is based on the famous American literary critic and academic Stanley Fish and also bears striking resemblances to the heroes of Philip Roth. If Lodge and Bradbury specialized in the academic novel in Britain, their American counterparts Roth and Don DeLillo are critically regarded novelists who occasionally used the genre, with powerful results. Roth published two academic novels in the 1970's, *The Professor of Desire* (1977) and *The Ghost Writer* (1979), using the campus setting and faculty figures to explore questions of Jewish identity, a continuing theme in Roth's novels. While there is the sexual obsession here that links *The Professor of Desire*'s David Kepesh to Zapp, Roth is less a satirist than a tragedian wrestling with ontological questions of life, death, and identity. Likewise in *The Ghost Writer*, where Nathan Zuckerman at Athene College tracks the reclusive writer E. I. Zonoff. Again, the setting is less important than the themes readers will find in other nonacademic novels by Roth: questions of human behavior, truth, and decency as well as the relationships between life and literature.

DeLillo's *White Noise* (1985), like Roth's novels, is set in a college campus and features satirical elements, including the extremes of academic specialization and the scholarly focus on trivia. Jack Gladney is chair of the Department of Hitler Studies. His colleagues lecture on the fast food, supermarkets, television, and films that make up popular culture. With its mordant humor, including its attacks on consumerism and the American fascination with death, *White Noise* has become a postmodern classic. It also won a National Book Award.

Roth returned to the campus setting with *The Human Stain* (2000) and to the fictional Athena College in the Berkshires. Zuckerman tells the story of Coleman Silk, a classics professor who loses his job over a supposed racial slur. Again, however, Roth has larger questions to pose, like those of racial and sexual identity, in what can be called a tragedy of self-discovery.

THE LATER ACADEMIC NOVEL

Increasingly, the academic novel after the 1980's began to reflect the influences of feminist and literary theories that were becoming staples of academic scholarship. A. S. Byatt's *Possession* (1990) won the Booker Prize in 1990 for its story of two British scholars of Victorian poetry, whose relationship shadows the secret affair of the two nineteenth century poets they are studying. The novel is steeped in contemporary feminist and literary theory and reflects its roots in metafiction (as in John Fowles's *The French Lieutenant's Woman*, 1969) as it jumps between centuries.

The academic novel of this time touches upon both the humorous and the serious, beyond the topic of scholarship. Jane Smiley's *Moo* (1995) is more satirical in its approach as it digs into the political machinations and consumerism both of faculty and administration at a large midwestern college named Moo U., well known for its agriculture department. (A giant hog called Earl Butz resides there.) While Richard Russo's *Straight Man* (1997), too, is a hilarious take on academic politics, J. M. Coetzee's *Disgrace* (1999), which won the Booker Prize in 2000, is a tragic novel about David Lurie, a professor at a South African university who resigns his position in the face of charges of sexual harassment and then faces the rape of his daughter.

The academic novel of the twenty-first century confirms the trends of the first decades of the form's existence. American author Jonathan Franzen's *The Corrections* (2001), which won the National Book Award, has academe as one of its subjects. British author Zadie Smith's *On Beauty* (2005) confirms the staying power of the academic novel. Beneath *On Beauty*'s satire of the idiosyncrasies at a suburban Boston college called Wellington lie issues of sexual and intellectual identity and struggles about the meaning of life. The novel even reveals the cross-cultural roots explored by Lodge's trilogy: *On Beauty* is the story of British academic Howard Belsey, married to an African American woman named Kiki, and his right-wing Trinidadian colleague and rival Monty Kipps and his wife, Carlene.

As writers continue to work in these campus settings and the colleges themselves remain stages for political, sexual, and ethical dramas, the academic novel will continue as a popular form. Writers as diverse as Vladimir Nabokov (*Pnin*, 1957), Alison Lurie (*Love and Friendship*, 1962, and *Foreign Affairs*, 1984), Gail Godwin (*The Odd Woman*, 1974), Carolyn Gold Heilbrun (*Death in a Tenured Position*, 1981; as Amanda Cross), Joyce Carol Oates (*Marya: A Life*, 1986), Francine Prose (*Blue Angel*, 2000), and Saul Bellow (*Ravelstein*, 2000) have all explored issues raised in academic novels, issues such as tenure and academic freedom, which have become representative of larger social issues.

David Peck

BIBLIOGRAPHY

Carter, Ian. *Ancient Cultures of Conceit: British University Fiction in the Post-war Years*. New York: Routledge, 1990. What Carter calls the "first study to connect literary, historical, and sociological aspects of modern British universities" finds a connection between the academic novel and the decline of British universities under Prime Minister Margaret Thatcher.

Connor, Steven. *The English Novel in History, 1950-1995*. New York: Routledge, 1995. Study of the academic or campus novel, as Connor calls the British version. Examines its themes and other distinguishing features in chapter two, "Conditions in England."

Moseley, Merritt, ed. *The Academic Novel: New and Classic Essays*. Chester, England: Chester Academic Press, 2007. Unusual collection of essays both critical and historical that examine the academic novel as a literary subgenre as well as a point of contention for its often unflattering depictions of academic life.

Rossen, Janice. *The University in Modern Fiction*. New York: St. Martin's Press, 1993. Examines the Anglo-American academic novel in terms of the power structures Rossen considers to be critical to campus life and the fate of faculty.

Showalter, Elaine. *Faculty Towers: The Academic Novel and Its Discontents*. Philadelphia: University of Pennsylvania Press, 2005. After a theoretical introduction, Showalter surveys the academic novel decade by decade, from the 1950's into the twenty-first century. Appends a "Bibliography of Academic Novels" that lists more than sixty examples of the form.

Womack, Kenneth. *Postwar Academic Fiction: Satire, Ethics, Community*. New York: Palgrave, 2002. Literary critique focusing on the writers who have the academy and its foibles as subject matter for their novels. Examines Kingsley Amis, David Lodge, Joyce Carol Oates, Vladimir Nabokov, Jane Smiley, and others.

THE BILDUNGSROMAN

Who has not been told that one learns more about oneself from failures than from successes? Is there a more reliable theme to draw readers than success following chronic failure? Literature's undying storyline is the determined progress of an unlikely hero against the odds.

Traditional fiction has no more crucial mandate than that by the end the protagonist exhibit major change: Proud Oedipus the king becomes blind Oedipus the exile. Although audiences in the golden age of Greek drama may have undergone catharsis in witnessing Sophocles' play concerning the tragic hero Oedipus's recognition of the losing hand that fate has dealt him, the audience may sometimes wish that even tragic destiny might just once be foiled. Readers are more receptive to a hero like Joseph Conrad's Lord Jim, who seizes the main chance and is redeemed, than to Thomas Hardy's Jude, who gives in to an indifferent universe.

Everyone begins in the infantlike state portrayed by James Joyce in the opening lines of *A Portrait of the Artist as a Young Man* (1914-1915 serial, 1916 book), proceeds as uncertainly as Ernest Hemingway's returning soldier in "Big Two-Hearted River," faces life-changing decisions like the heroines in Kate Chopin's stories, and ends as knowing as Theodore Dreiser's Carrie or as defeated as James T. Farrell's Studs Lonigan. The universal story is what happens when innocence confronts forces, human or cosmic, that are not innocent. For the playing out of that progress, literature has found an eighteenth century German word, bildungsroman, that has transcended the use of italics and become international.

ORIGIN OF THE BILDUNGSROMAN

It is far more difficult to locate the source of the bildungsroman—a term combining the German words *Bildung*, personal growth, with *roman*, novel—than it is to credit the book that is its exemplar. The *Encyclopedia of German Literary History* claims that the philosopher and literary historian Wilhelm Dilthey famously defined the term in an analysis in 1870 of Johann Wolfgang von Goethe's *Wilhelm Meisters Lehrjahre* (1795-1796, 4 vols.; *Wilhelm Meister's Apprenticeship*, 1824), almost eighty years after the publication of Goethe's masterpiece. In the bildungsroman, Dilthey wrote,

> [a] regulated development within the life of the individual is observed, each of its stages has its own intrinsic value and is at the same time the basis for a higher stage. The dissonances and conflicts of life appear as the necessary growth points through which the individual must pass on his way to maturity and harmony.

In 1942, in his comprehensive *English Novel in Transition, 1885-1940*, William C. Frierson applied the terms "life-novel" and "spiritual autobiography" to many of the novels that can be categorized as bildungsromans. As if unwilling to get bogged down by the Germanic bildungsroman and its cognates, Frierson never mentions the word or the novel by Goethe that exemplifies it. Other scholars prefer "education novel" or "apprentice novel." Thousands of novels—from Samuel Richardson's *Pamela: Or, Virtue Rewarded* (1740-1741) to J. D. Salinger's *The Catcher in the Rye* (1951), from Henry Fielding's *The History of Tom Jones, a Foundling* (1749) to F. Scott Fitzgerald's *The Great Gatsby* (1925)—could lay claim, if barely, to being chronicles of passage.

This survey discusses only a select few novels that both follow Dilthey's lead and meet the main criterion for any classic—endurance—concentrating on landmark works, most of them originally written in English. American literature is notable for writers whose oeuvres—career-long or in a sequence—have moved from innocence to experience but whose heroes, especially in contemporary novels (notably those of John Updike), are unchanging.

In the closing third of the twentieth century and the beginning of the twenty-first, the bildungsroman was given new vitality by novels dramatizing alternative patterns, especially women striving toward commensurate status with men. The feminist bildungsroman, given scant attention earlier, has become a major force in the revival of the form.

WILHELM MEISTER'S APPRENTICESHIP

The paragon for the nineteenth century novel of education was Goethe's *Wilhelm Meister's Apprenticeship*, translated by Thomas Carlyle. The earlier work introduces a hero whose object is to seek self-realization in the service of art: As actor and later manager of a stage company, he will make the German theater a primary agent of cultural change. In *Wilhelm Meister's Apprenticeship*, this aim must compete with many other intentions and values.

Scattered throughout the novel are many details and impressions adapted from Goethe's own experience: a childhood delight in puppets, the tension between visionary son and hardheaded practical father, efforts at amateur acting and firsthand observations of the vagaries of fellow-players, responses to the esoteric rituals of freemasonry, even Wilhelm's lovesick wandering of the streets. In most scenes, Wilhelm appears, sometimes as protagonist but more often as spectator or auditor, a young man whom Goethe viewed with marked ambivalence. Wilhelm's involvement with the theater makes possible an exploration and broadening of his personality. It offers him an adventurous life, a chance to broaden the self by accepting various roles, but it is life without direction. Following "Confessions," which closes the first half, Wilhelm gradually quits the theater for new rites, literal and figurative: those of passage and those of the secret Society of the Tower. Characteristically for the bildungsroman, entry is achieved only after many missteps.

THE NINETEENTH CENTURY ENGLISH
BILDUNGSROMAN

William Makepeace Thackeray's *The History of Pendennis: His Fortunes and Misfortunes, His Friends, and His Greatest Enemy* (1848-1850, serial; 1849-1850, book) is called by Thackeray's biographer Gordon N. Ray "the first true *Bildungsroman* in English fiction." Jerome Buckley rejects it as too conventional, perhaps because its hero comes to maturity more by accident than by design.

George Meredith's major bildungsromans derive from Charles Dickens, whom he dismissed as "a caricaturist who aped the moralist." Still, as Buckley argues, the later Victorian was indebted to the earlier, especially in *The Adventures of Harry Richmond* (1871) and in *The Ordeal of Richard Feverel* (1859). The method of narration and even the plotting of *The Adventures of Harry Richmond* recall Dickens's character David Copperfield, and the theme, the shattering of false illusions, resembles that of *Great Expectations* (1860-1861, serial; 1861, book). The frequent caricatures in *The Ordeal of Richard Feverel* are suggestive, according to Buckley, of "Dickensian shorthand."

Dorothea Brooke's two marriages in George Eliot's *Middlemarch* (1871-1872) symbolize a journey from naïve impressionability to practical wisdom and humane sympathy. Samuel Butler's *The Way of All Flesh* (1903) is the most directly autobiographical bildungsroman in English before D. H. Lawrence's *Sons and Lovers* (1913) and Joyce's *A Portrait of the Artist as a Young Man*. *The Way of All Flesh* remains, in Buckley's view, a "scientific" bildungsroman. Overloaded by digressions, *The Way of All Flesh* has gone virtually unread since World War II. Its author's hatred of the middle-class evangelism in which he had been brought up and his disavowal of Charles Darwin's evolutionary theories, which were rampant during the 1870's, when he wrote the novel, have affected the novel's later reception. The theme of Ernest Pontifex's childhood (the book's main link to the bildungsroman) is not developed with any dramatic immediacy.

In Thomas Hardy's *Jude the Obscure* (1895), Jude Fawley's life appears to have been doomed from the day of his birth. As the protagonist of a novel of education, Jude pays much attention to the hero's private study and none to formal schooling. A university education, however, is his great objective. The lure of learning fights an unequal battle with the appeals of sex as embodied in Arabella, the swine girl, who throws a piece of pig's flesh at Jude when they meet—an obvious symbol of the dismantling of Jude's illusions. Sue Bridehead, a truly interesting woman, becomes his mistress and mentor, but he buckles under her teaching.

Because it affirms the classic bildungsroman, Dickens's *Great Expectations* bears a closer look than any of the novels previously mentioned. The story of Pip falls into three phases that clearly display a progression. The reader first sees the boy in his natural condition in the country, responding and being instinctively virtuous.

The second stage involves a negation of childlike simplicity; Pip acquires his "expectations," renounces his origins, and moves to the city. He rises in society, but because he acts through calculation rather than instinctive charity, his moral values deteriorate as his social graces improve. This middle phase culminates in a sudden fall, the beginning of a redemptive suffering that is dramatically concluded by an attack of brain fever leading to a long coma. Pip rises from it regenerate. In the final stage of growth he returns to his birthplace, abandons his false expectations, and achieves a partial synthesis of the virtue of his innocent youth. Critic G. Robert Strange views *Great Expectations* as a moral fable in the tradition of stories of education. Like Stendhal's Julien Sorel and Honoré de Balzac's Eugène de Rastignac, Pip belongs in the nineteenth century gallery of children of the century.

THE LATER ENGLISH BILDUNGSROMAN

In 1948, literary critic and historian Mark Schorer wrote a famous essay, "Technique as Discovery," in which he declared that literary technique is nearly everything. It is

> the means by which the writer's experience, which is his subject matter, compels him to attend to it; technique is the only means he has of discovering, exploring, developing his subject, of conveying its meaning, and, finally, of evaluating it.

Without explicitly citing it as the high point in English of the bildungsroman, Schorer extols Joyce's *A Portrait of the Artist as a Young Man* as the crowning fictional study of passage in an especially rich period, the first quarter of the twentieth century. There is another reason to apply Schorer's strictures in the present context: He not only sets up Joyce's work as a classic in the bildungsroman tradition but also creates a literary rogues' gallery from other famous bildungsromans, including H. G. Wells's *Tono-Bungay* (1908), Lawrence's *Sons and Lovers*, Thomas Wolfe's *Of Time and the River* (1935), and Farrell's Studs Lonigan trilogy (1935).

As the bildungsroman's poet, Joyce, with *A Portrait of the Artist as a Young Man*, made the intuited destiny of Stephen Dedalus an attainment nonpareil. He utilized the subliminal so convincingly that it rendered the intrusive author in the long biographical novels of Goethe, Dickens, and Stendhal unnecessary. No writers of bildungsromans until Joyce had succeeded in making narrative serve theme contrapuntally. As a famous essay by poet and critic Hugh Kenner puts it,

> Each of the [five] chapters begins with a multitude of warring impressions, and each develops toward an emotionally apprehended unity; each succeeding chapter liquidates the previous synthesis and subjects its elements to more adult scrutiny in a constantly enlarging field of perception, and develops toward its own synthesis and affirmation.

Joyce presents a variety of styles, each appropriate to the movement of Stephen from childhood through boyhood into maturity. Flow of consciousness delineates the mind of the child not yet amenable to selection or judgment. Evocation of the world of sensual and bodily detail is rendered by internal and external emotional bursts—moments rescued from flux that Joyce called epiphanies—that mark Stephen's rejection of domestic and religious values. Gradually, Joyce conveys the intellectually assured Dedalus by dialectic as he asserts to himself his soul's call to be a poet.

OTHER ENGLISH BILDUNGSROMANS

Working from opposite directions, fiction's two principal figures in modernism between the two world wars were Joyce and Lawrence. Joyce, as noted, internalized fiction by evoking consciousness. Lawrence, who pioneered few technical innovations, broke down any notion that ego was stable. Books such as Lawrence's *Sons and Lovers*, *The Rainbow* (1915), and *Women in Love* (1920) blurred the usual partitions between and within genders and installed the primitive and savage emotions of "blood" over civilization's crippling decrees of "mind."

Neither the voluntarily exiled, hard-drinking Dubliner nor the Midlands coal miner's son who in his brief span would roam the world in a vain search for transcendence had anything good to say about the other. When Lawrence's *Lady Chatterley's Lover* (1928) began to vie with *Ulysses* (1922) as a book for tourists in Paris, the nearly blind Joyce asked a friend to read it to him. He listened carefully, then pronounced only one word: "Lush!" To Lawrence's puritan mind, *Ulysses* was a "dirty" book, a reduction of Sex (uppercase)—to him an icon in the merging of consciousnesses—to sex (lowercase)—a mechanical act for prurient readers.

A more fruitful pairing links Lawrence's *Sons and Lovers* with W. Somerset Maugham's *Of Human Bondage* (1915). In their sexual bildungsromans, the introspective hero that the reader met in Joyce's *Künstlerroman*, the artist-protagonist, gives way to lovers under siege. Paul Morel and Philip Carey spoke with candor to beleaguered young men everywhere. Lawrence's bildungsromans provided what Patricia Alden calls "the basis for a new, classless elite of the initiate [in which] sexual relationships recapitulate the fundamental conflict between bourgeois individualism and working-class communalism." More simply, Lawrence's novels always turn on crucial "splits." In *Sons and Lovers*, the conflict between Paul and his mother, Gertrude, vies with the conflict between kinds of love, physical and spiritual, which draw the son away and are represented by two young women, Miriam and Clara.

Critic V. S. Pritchett, whose short stories and autobiography celebrate his own emergence from late-Victorian squalor, demonstrates in a memorable essay how *Sons and Lovers* bears the defects of its virtues. Galvanic as he is in revealing Paul's drift into spiritual quandary, Lawrence "cheats" too: He almost entirely omits the story of Paul's education, his early teaching, and his gradual separation from the mining village of his birth. Alden agrees with Pritchett. For her, Lawrence isolates Paul's drive to become an individual from any social context. The story of how Lawrence left the Midlands becomes the story of how Paul leaves his mother; he is seen as the passive victim of three women who embody unmet social ambitions they seek to realize through him.

Joyce and Lawrence represent contrasting traditions with regard to the relationship in literary art between the creator and the created. Joyce, like Henry James and Gustave Flaubert, held that the artist must remain detached from life, producing narratives of experience somehow finished, exhausted, controllable, and manipulable. Lawrence confessed "one sheds one's sicknesses in books, repeats and repeats again one's emotions—to be master of them." Lawrence lives his experiences in the process of writing about them. Both Joycean and Lawrencean traditions have served bildungsromans well.

As a study of a youth's search for meaning and truth in a world of cruelty and deceit, *Of Human Bondage* stands apart from the remainder of Maugham's works. No one is spared, least of all its hero, Philip Carey. In a variation on Lawrence's confession that the writer "sheds" his or her "sicknesses in books," Maugham said he wrote *Of Human Bondage* to rid himself of his obsessions. Although written in characteristically spare prose, in contrast to the tropes of Joyce, *Of Human Bondage* joins *A Portrait of the Artist as a Young Man* in conveying the hero's life in stages. However, unlike the decisive Stephen, Philip matures in agonizing waltz-time, his steps advancing and retreating methodically. His ambivalence mirrors the way of troubled innocence.

Maugham titled the 1915 published version of his novel after the name of the fourth book of seventeenth century philosopher Baruch Spinoza's *Ethica* (1677; *Ethics*, 1870): "Of Human Bondage: Or, Of the Strengths of the Affects"—whose preface glosses perfectly the novel's theme.

> The impotence of man to govern or restrain the affects I call Bondage, for a man who is under their control is not his own master, but is mastered by fortune . . . so that he is forced to follow the worst, although he sees the better before him.

Philip's *Bildung*, or apprenticeship, can best be told as a series of releases whose permanency depends on his being able to understand a riddle. Critic Forrest Burt notes that the author's placement of the puzzle at the heart of the novel reflects the aging Maugham's "greatest drive," namely, to reshape his life into a pattern that would enable him to overcome a lifelong stammer, a desperate childhood, and rejection by an actor named Sue Jones, daughter of the playwright Henry Arthur Jones. Philip, following the lead of his creator, must free himself from a clubfoot, social restrictions, religious and moral hypocrisy, delusions, unrequited passion, and fear.

Of Human Bondage opens with the death of Philip's mother. Like the young Willie Maugham, the orphaned Philip is forced to move from his French home to England. There he lives with his uncle, the vicar of Blackstable, and kindly Aunt Louisa. They are childless and live a life quite unsuitable for their nine-year-old nephew, who speaks French more fluently than English. These early pages comprise a Victorian deprived-child paradigm. Unhappy school days with bullying masters and cruel classmates are reversed by an extraordinary year studying in Heidelberg, Germany, where Philip comes intuitively to the same conclusion he reached emotionally when his prayers to be delivered of his club-foot went unanswered: There is no God. The intuition of a kind of nihilism brings Philip not despair but joy. He will fail in a journeyman bid to study art in Paris but finds himself as a medical intern in London delivering babies. Philip will have his first sexual experience—brief and unsatisfying—before encountering a London waitress, Mildred Rogers, who, although ordinary in every way, holds him in near-fatal thrall.

Philip deludes himself about Mildred, suffers her brutal insults, rejects her and repeatedly takes her back, hates and adores her, and increasingly curses "the fate which [has] chained him to such a woman." It can be noted that Maugham, whose works are frequently adapted for film, lived to see three film versions of the novel, between 1933 and 1964—none of which reached beyond the theme of bondage to Mildred to explore the book as bildungsroman. As critic Buckley notes, "The novel is ultimately concerned with Philip's development and not just with his obsession."

It is easy for Philip to assume that he is fated to suffer and fail—that regret or blame is useless. He is also, however, eager to discover a pattern in his destiny. A drunken minor poet named Cronshaw tells him that he will find the answer to his questions in the pattern of a Persian carpet. One day, depressed by word of his close friend Hayward's useless death in the Boer War, he contemplates Greek funerary sculptures in the British Museum. Something reminiscent of Stephen Dedalus's vision of a maiden on the strand—an epiphany—comes to Philip: Life has no objective meaning; the design is in the mind of the individual.

THE BILDUNGSROMAN AND TIME

Shortly before beginning *Sons and Lovers*, the novel that launched his career, Lawrence revealed to his lover, Jessie Chambers, his despair upon reading Wells's *Tono-Bungay*: "Most authors write out of their own personality," Lawrence, then twenty-three, averred. "Wells

does, of course. But I'm not sure that I've got a big enough personality to write out of."

Thus, Lawrence is awed by the same quality in *Tono-Bungay* that critic Schorer deplores: a richness of vision, both retrospectively and futuristically, able to embrace at once the death of Victorianism and the emergence of the new spirit of advertising. For Schorer, in his manifesto favoring Henry James and formalism, Wells's best book proves to be not a novel but a hypothesis. Nearly a century later the issues between fiction and journalism still seethe.

What cannot be denied is that *Tono-Bungay*'s George Ponderevo—like Stephen Dedalus, Paul Morel, and Philip Carey—is the personification of a consciousness that seeks a secure handhold on life. Again and again this kind of hero proves a human test-site for every level and phase of society, with life always crowding in. As a boy living belowstairs in an estate called Bladesover, George becomes secularized early, inclined to follow the liberating force of scientific discovery late, and a survivor of the charlatanry of a bogus patent medicine called "tono-bungay" in between. The novel pursues a vertical—a futuristic—course. It presents a rocketlike macrocosm that allows Ponderevo to survive the wreckage of a marriage and a love affair, to withstand the "woosh" and sputter of tono-bungay, and, at last, to be the embodiment of a life force whose ambiguous symbol is a battleship forging ahead into the limitless sea. The purveyor of tono-bungay quackery—the catalyst for George's fall and rise—is a bubbling sprite of an uncle, Teddy Ponderevo. He, like the early Wells having escaped from pill dispensing, storms the bastions of society. Yet for this arriviste, to the manor born too late, the wages are corruption, defeat, and death.

It is curious that John Fowles has never mentioned Wells. In *The French Lieutenant's Woman* (1969), Charles Smithson, marooned in the midst of the Victorian era a generation before George Ponderevo, is also viewed as the man between. Each has lifted one leg out of one time frame and is about to put it down in another of whose substance he is uncertain. Like *Tono-Bungay*, Fowles's novel ends in a dramatizing of "postcultural man" through imagery of the sea. In Fowles's case, it is borrowed from Matthew Arnold's poem "To Marguerite."

[L]ife . . . is not a symbol . . . not one riddle and one failure to guess it, is not to inhabit one face alone or to be given up after one losing throw of the dice; but is to be, however inadequately, emptily, hopelessly into the city's iron heart, endured. And out again, upon the unplumb'd, salt, estranging sea.

Written three quarters of a century apart, these novels apply the bildungsroman strategies of passage to time itself. They instruct their audience imaginatively in the ways nineteenth century humans became twentieth century humans.

THE AMERICAN BILDUNGSROMAN

Writing his doctoral dissertation in 1948, Philip Young mounted a convincing wound-and-bow theory on Ernest Hemingway. The so-called Hemingway hero, as Young defined him, was Hemingway himself. For any real understanding of either the heroes of the novels or their creator, a Hemingway aficionado must take into account the young Ernest's severe injuries in the Italian campaign of World War I, which, according to Young, left permanent scars, visible and invisible. Over Hemingway's initial protests—he told Young that to try to psychoanalyze a writer is tantamount to destroying that writer—Young published the first literary study of Hemingway in 1952, and in 1965, four years after Hemingway's suicide, applied his "wound" thesis to all of Hemingway's books.

Young's ideas gave rise to the term "code hero," whose notion is that in a world dominated by violence and evil a decent young man, placed in testing situations, will maintain his "purity of Line" (a phrase applied to the matador Romero in Hemingway's 1926 novel *The Sun Also Rises*). Grace under pressure requires an earned style of conduct, a code that is a variation on the bildungsroman's conventional rites of passage. In his first book, *In Our Time* (1924, 1925), Hemingway combined stories and sketches that introduced Nick Adams, the young man who would grow up to be Jake Barnes, Lieutenant Frederic Henry, and all Hemingway's other warborn heroes. Young Nick is the outdoor man whose bliss is hunting and fishing. Even as an adolescent he reveals, always understatedly, a quality contemporary detractors call "macho" but which forces on Nick a "reckoning with his nerves" that leads to the ritual shutoff of mind

necessary to ward off the demons. Young aligns Nick Adams and Huckleberry Finn as exemplars of "a great American story because [theirs] is based not only on the experience of every man as he grows up but also on the particular and peculiar experience of this nation." The Huck-Nick stories tell what happens when a spontaneous virtue meets something alien.

After the appearance of J. D. Salinger's *The Catcher in the Rye*, critics throughout the 1950's extended Young's Huck-to-Nick line to Holden Caulfield. Huck and Holden speak in the first person and in boyish vernacular. Both heroes, in established bildungsroman custom, long to escape corrupting adult forces for a state of natural innocence. The unfunny Nick Adams lacks Huck and Holden's comedy, but his pattern is the same as theirs: improvisation.

A 1990's version of the bildungsroman is Frank Conroy's *Body and Soul* (1993). When this novel appeared, it was taken as either an anachronism or a refreshing return to the classic bildungsroman. *Body and Soul*, Conroy's only novel (he also wrote a distinguished autobiography, *Stop-Time*, published in 1967, and published a short-story collection, *Midair*, in 1985), records the romantic history of a musical prodigy's development from humble beginnings to concert fame as a piano virtuoso. The novel offers a chance for young readers to experience a genuinely happy novel, in which virtue and fidelity are rewarded and joy is made as plausible as divorce or nuclear meltdown. This is Dickens, updated and undistorted.

AMERICAN CHRONICLES AS BILDUNGSROMANS

Harry "Rabbit" Angstrom is a decent, unintelligent man who finds that the momentum that sustained him as a high school basketball star has slowed to a crawl in a dingy apartment where the dinner is always late and his wife has stopped being pretty. John Updike takes this common domestic tableau and turns it into a subtle expose of the frailty of the American Dream.

Written entirely in the present tense—in 1960, a virtually unheard-of technique in American fiction—to stress the immediacy of Rabbit's crisis, *Rabbit, Run* (1960) details the sterility of a society that offers television sets and cars but ignores spiritual loss and belief. As critic Donald J. Greiner puts it,

All [Harry's wife Janice] wants is for him to be like other husbands, to give in to the nine-to-five routine of selling Magi-peelers in the local dimestore, but Rabbit senses that loss of life's momentum means loss of life itself. So he runs.

Updike's quester is suggestive of Huck, Nick, and Holden, but Rabbit is neither as improvisatory as they nor as articulate—inside or outside. When asked to explain what he wants, all the uncomprehending Rabbit can do is hit a perfect tee shot, point to the grace of the soaring ball, and shout, "That's It!"

A decade later, in 1971, Updike reintroduced Harry, age thirty-six, in *Rabbit Redux* (Rabbit led back). The junk of ashtrays and closets from which Harry has run earlier is replaced by national events that promise to overwhelm him: Vietnam, the Civil Rights movement, the drug culture. For Rabbit, these "disasters" are redeemed by the first Moon shot but, try as he might to turn the spaceflight into a metaphor for his own need to soar gracefully and far, he can see in it only depersonalized technology making contact with a dead rock. In *Rabbit Redux*, any "lighting out for the territory" (Huck's solution) is negated by Rabbit's futility. He returns to his dingy house in the plastic suburb. The last words of the novel—"Sleeps. O.K.?"—are a long way from "Runs."

Rabbit Is Rich (1981) is about the 1970's. Now forty-six years old, Rabbit does not blame anyone for shopping malls or overflowing garbage cans beside failing restaurants. When he thinks of himself as "the star and spear point of the flourishing car dealership his family owns," readers know that he remains unreconstructed, his value system still defined in terms of athletic prowess. His youthful running has been slowed to gliding in golf carts. He acknowledges neither his son's drug addiction nor his own failing heart.

For *Rabbit at Rest* (1990), Updike combines reprise with sputtering evidence that passage for an unresponsive oldster like Harry merely repeats unalterable patterns. Rabbit runs one final time. He returns to the basketball court despite his weight, his age, and his heart. In short, he tries. His fear, however, presages the final stillness. Finally, in the novella *Rabbit Remembered* (2000), the family of the deceased Harry Angstrom continues life without him, after his wife, Janice, has remarried, his illegitimate daughter Annabelle has turned up, and his son, Nelson, has separated from his wife. Rabbit Angstrom has forged entry into the terrain of the modern bildungsroman's losers. Yet, as Greiner sums up the Rabbit books, "Harry has [also] joined the pantheon of American literary heroes like Natty Bumppo, Ahab, Huck Finn, Gatsby, Ike McCaslin, Holden Caulfield [in having learned] that no matter how far he runs in space, he cannot outrace time."

THE FEMINIST BILDUNGSROMAN

Ellen Morgan, in "Humanbecoming: Form and Focus in the Neo-Feminist Novel" (1972), identifies the bildungsroman as "the most salient form for literature influenced by" the feminist movement of the 1960's and 1970's. The feminist bildungsroman is a "recasting" of the old genre by modern women authors to meet their particular needs. The traditional bildungsroman is often an autobiographical novel depicting adolescent self-development and the educative experiences of youth. Endings to novels such as *Wilhelm Meister's Apprenticeship*, *Sons and Lovers*, *Of Human Bondage*, and *Tono-Bungay* become the beginnings for the protagonists, who either merge into their societies, like Philip Carey, or escape into the promise of a new world, like George Ponderevo.

The modern feminist bildungsroman concentrates on crises in which the female protagonist finds herself facing problematical dilemmas with no assurance, if they persist, of safe passage. A woman awakens in her late twenties or early thirties to what Bonnie Hoover Braedlin calls "the stultification and fragmentation of a personality devoted not to self-fulfillment and awareness, but to a culturally determined, self-sacrificing, self-effacing existence." These crises and concomitant struggles for oneness in cultures that fragment women into accepted roles provide the central themes of the feminist bildungsroman. Scholars have divided feminist bildungsromans into those that convey a "social quest" and those that focus on a "spiritual quest." The distinguishing factors are, with the former, a search for identity in the socioeconomic sphere and, with the latter, a journey involving a "transcendent deity."

Some structural features of female bildungsromans often stem from their confessional nature. The prevalence of first-person narration follows cause and effect. The recollection and reconstruction of memories and the utilizing of flashback are central strategies. Vivid recollections dominate—of girlhoods haunted by images of deadly mothers and absent fathers, demanding friends, first loves. Later, these heroines find themselves torn apart by the conflicting demands of marriage and motherhood on one hand and the longing for personal freedom and self-actualization on the other. Though the women in bildungsromans arrive at self-awareness through recalling, retelling, and analyzing their lives, they finally achieve the wholeness of selfhood by exploring their inner natures to unite the conscious elements of personality with the unconscious.

Included in an expanding list of authors of feminist bildungsromans cited frequently by scholars are Lisa Alther (*Kinflicks*, 1975), Margaret Atwood (*Surfacing*, 1972, and *Lady Oracle*, 1976), Sheila Ballantyne (*Norma Jean, the Termite Queen*, 1975), Francine du Plessix Gray (*Lovers and Tyrants*, 1976), Marge Piercy (*Small Changes*, 1973), and Doris Lessing (*The Golden Notebook*, 1962, and the five novels of the Children of Violence series, 1952-1969).

CONTEMPORARY BILDUNGSROMANS

The nineteenth and twentieth centuries saw no shortage of novels concerned with an adolescent's battle for an adequate extension of personality, a quest that brings the initiate into conflict with the constraining factors of parental wishes, first love, and economic and social sanctions. Many landmarks of world literature belong to this distinguished subgenre. In its classic form, the bildungsroman reached its peak in the nineteenth century. The twentieth century added more direct autobiography, an increasingly depersonalized society, and battles between the genders.

One of the first modern lesbian bildungsromans was Rita Mae Brown's first novel, *Rubyfruit Jungle* (1973). Writer Edmund White, author of an honored biography of French writer and iconoclast Jean Genet, published the coming-out novel *A Boy's Own Story* (1982) and *The Beautiful Room Is Empty* (1988), bildungsromans of alternative patterns of living as compelling as D. H. Lawrence's works of nearly a century ago. A coming-out novel such as *A Boy's Own Story*, besides depicting rites

of initiation as the bildungsroman has always done, reveals the harm psychotherapy can do to gays and lesbians and the self-hatred forced on a young man by society when it conceives of homosexuality only as a sickness, sin, or crime. E. Lynn Harris's *Invisible Life* (1991, self-published; 1994) is a bildungsroman about a gay African American man who comes out in law school.

There also has been a blossoming of novels that conflate the bildungsroman with the quest for ethnic and cultural identity by postcolonial, disfranchised, oppressed, immigrant, and other marginalized peoples. Readers have proven receptive to these works, which include Chicana author Sandra Cisneros's *The House on Mango Street* (1984); *The Buddha of Suburbia* (1990), by Hanif Kureishi, a British writer whose father was Pakistani; Irish novelist Roddy Doyle's *Paddy Clarke, Ha-Ha-Ha* (1993); *Breath, Eyes, Memory* (1994) by Edwidge Danticat, a Haitian-born American writer; and *The Kite Runner* (2003) and *A Thousand Splendid Suns* (2007), by Afghani American Khaled Hosseini.

The bildungsroman continues as an important form into the twenty-first century, accompanied by a new, intense interest in the memoir. Readers cannot get enough of stories—whether fictional or true—about the struggle for adulthood and selfhood. Many of these novels have also been made into feature films, including *White Oleander* (1999), by Janet Fitch; *The Secret Life of Bees* (2002), by Sue Monk Kidd; and *Brick Lane* (2003), by Monica Ali. Another twenty-first century bildungsroman, *Middlesex* (2002), by Jeffrey Eugenides, won the Pulitzer Prize in fiction.

Richard Hauer Costa

BIBLIOGRAPHY

Alden, Patricia. *Social Mobility in the English Bildungsroman: Gissing, Hardy, Bennett, and Lawrence.* Lewiston, N.Y.: Edwin Mellen Press, 1992. Confirms the difficulty of economically vulnerable youths, uncertain about aspiration and talent, and under no illusions that the provincial world of their childhood offers an alternative to their effort to escape.

Buckley, Jerome H. *Season of Youth: The Bildungsroman from Dickens to Golding.* 1974. Reprint. Bridgewater, N.J.: Replica Books, 2000. Engagingly written scholarly survey of more than a century of the English bildungsroman. Buckley demonstrates that gradual imaginative enlightenment has been vital to the hero's initiation and endurance. An indispensable book.

Castle, Gregory. *Reading the Modernist Bildungsroman*. Gainesville: University Press of Florida, 2006. Argues that the "vitality" of the bildungsroman comes from, primarily, "its ability to represent, in a self-consciously critical fashion, the complex and contradictory modes of self-development that have arisen in late modernity."

Feng, Pin-chia. *The Female Bildungsroman by Toni Morrison and Maxine Hong Kingston: A Postmodern Reading*. New York: Peter Lang, 1998. Analyzes repressed memory in African American writer Toni Morrison's bildungsromans *The Bluest Eye* and *Sula*, and Asian American writer Maxine Hong Kingston's bildungsromans *The Woman Warrior* and *China Men*.

Frierson, William C. *The English Novel in Transition, 1885-1940*. 1942. Reprint. New York: Cooper Square, 1965. Decades after it was originally published, this classic remains fresh and relevant. Displays Frierson's deep commitment to what he calls "life" novels. Especially sensitive to the relative darkness of "passage" novels of the 1930's, compared with those of the 1920's.

Gohlman, Susan Ashley. *Starting Over: The Task of the Protagonist in the Contemporary Bildungsroman*. New York: Garland, 1990. Protagonists are considered in this study in terms of their specific roles in the bildungsroman. Includes bibliographical references.

Japtok, Martin. *Growing Up Ethnic: Nationalism and the Bildungsroman in African American and Jewish American Fiction*. Iowa City: University of Iowa Press, 2005. Comparative study of the literary similarities between African Americans and Jews in interpreting "ethnicity"—in the early decades of the twentieth century—through their writing of bildungsromans, or coming-of-age novels.

Minden, Michael. *The German Bildungsroman*. New York: Cambridge University Press, 1997. Traces the development of the German bildungsroman during the nineteenth century, culminating in a discussion of early twentieth century examples of the form.

Moretti, Franco. *The Way of the World: The Bildungsroman in European Culture*. New ed. Translated by Albert Sbragia. New York: Verso, 2000. Using a unique combination of narrative and social and cultural histories, this study examines the profound effects of the bildungsroman on European literary culture. Argues the form ended in Europe with the advent of modernist experimentation around the time of World War I. Includes an informative new preface.

THE DETECTIVE NOVEL

The detective story is a special branch of crime fiction that focuses attention on the examination of evidence that will lead to the solution of the mystery. *The Oxford English Dictionary* records the first printed use of the noun "detective" in the year 1843. The term had become established in the language because of the formation of the first detective bureaus, the original of which was the Bow Street Runners, a group of detective-policemen organized by Henry Fielding and John Fielding in their capacities as magistrates in London. The Runners operated out of the Fielding residence on Bow Street and were the precursors of the detective branch of Scotland Yard. Some time later, early in the nineteenth century, the Sûreté Générale, the first modern police force, was formed in Paris with a detective bureau. With the establishment of such bureaus, the way was open for the detective story to be developed out of existing literary sources.

EIGHTEENTH AND NINETEENTH CENTURIES

In the eighteenth century, the chaplain of Newgate Prison in London was authorized to publish the stories of notorious criminals in *The Newgate Calendar*. From this practice sprang the often wholly fictional Newgate novels, accounts of sensational crimes. In France, François Vidocq, a criminal himself, became head of the Sûreté and later published his memoirs recounting his exploits in capturing criminals. It is also likely that some of the ambience of the early detective story was derived from the gothic novel. William Godwin's *Things as They Are: Or, The Adventures of Caleb Williams* (1794; also known as *The Adventures of Caleb Williams: Or, Things as They Are*; best known as *Caleb Williams*), for example, although not a detective novel, is a story of a crime solved in order to free an innocent man.

From these beginnings, it remained for Edgar Allan Poe to devise the detective story in its now familiar form. Poe wrote three short works that are certainly detective stories, as well as others that are sometimes included in the genre. The first of these was "The Murders in the Rue Morgue" (1841), which was followed by "The Mystery of Marie Rogêt" (1842) and "The Purloined Letter"

(1845). Poe initiated the device of establishing the character of the detective and then using him for several stories. Poe's detective, M. Dupin, is a recluse, an eccentric, aristocratic young man with a keen analytical mind. He has an unnamed but admiring friend who marvels at Dupin's mental prowess and is willing to be his chronicler. Dupin examines the evidence in a given case and solves the crime after the regular police have exhausted their methods—a circumstance that was to become one of the commonplaces of detective fiction.

Apparently impressed by *Mémoires de Vidocq, chef de la police de Sûreté jusqu'en 1827* (1828-1829; *Memoirs of Vidocq, Principal Agent of the French Police Until 1827*, 1828-1829; revised as *Histoire de Vodocq, chef de la police de Sûreté: Écrite d'après lui-même*, 1829), by François Vidocq, Poe set his stories in Paris and borrowed his policemen from the Sûreté. Meanwhile, in France itself, Émile Gaboriau began to produce detective stories that also owed much to Vidocq. His detective, M. Lecoq, a representative of the official police, became the chief figure in a number of tales of detection. The detective short story was thus established and enjoyed great popularity in the century to follow.

Probably the first full-length novel of detection was *The Notting Hill Mystery* (1865), by Charles Felix, but it was quickly followed by Wilkie Collins's *The Moonstone* (1868), which critics consider to be the first important detective novel. Collins introduced Sergeant Cuff of Scotland Yard, who, with the help of amateurs, was able to solve the mystery. The first detective in English fiction, however, antedated Sergeant Cuff by fifteen years: Inspector Bucket of Charles Dickens's *Bleak House* (1852-1853, serial; 1853, book). Detective novels were published at a slow, sporadic pace until the advent of Sherlock Holmes, the most famous of all fictional detectives, in Arthur Conan Doyle's *A Study in Scarlet* (1887, serial; 1888, book).

Holmes starred in four novels and fifty-six short stories and eventually came to have a life independent of his creator, Doyle, who even killed him off in one tale only to bring him back for further adventures. A house on Baker Street in London has been identified as the place where Holmes occupied a flat and is now a tourist attraction. Clubs honor his memory with birthday parties, and a biography has been written based on incidental remarks and inferences about his "life" in the works in which he appeared. The Sherlock Holmes stories follow the pattern established by Poe's Dupin: Holmes is a bachelor given to esoteric studies, an eccentric who plays the violin and occasionally takes cocaine. A keen observer with amazing talents for analysis and deduction, an amateur boxer who performs astonishing feats of physical strength, Holmes is a virtual superman, while the commonsensical Dr. John Watson, the narrator of his exploits, provides a perfect foil.

The success of the Sherlock Holmes stories resulted in an outpouring of detective fiction; many authors adopted the basic technique of establishing the character of the detective and then recounting a series of his "cases." R. Austin Freeman introduced Dr. John Thorndyke, who based his solutions on more strictly scientific evidence rather than the deductions favored by Holmes. An American writer, Jacques Futrelle, introduced Professor S. F. X. Van Dusen, who was called "the thinking machine" and who became one of the early omniscient detectives in the tradition of Sherlock Holmes.

DETECTIVE FICTION'S GOLDEN AGE

With *Trent's Last Case* (1913, revised 1929; also as *The Woman in Black*), by E. C. Bentley, the modern era of the detective story began. Mary Roberts Rinehart modified the pattern of the detective novel by providing a female amateur as a first-person narrator who worked with the official police and who provided the key to the solution almost by accident. Another prolific writer was Carolyn Wells, who wrote seventy-four mystery novels, most of which starred Fleming Stone as the detective. She also made an important contribution to the theory of the detective story with *The Technique of the Mystery Story* (1913).

As the detective story moved closer to its "classical" stage, it became more realistic and was written with more literary skill. The detectives became less bizarre and less inclined to become involved in physical danger or in personally grappling with the criminal in the manner of the great Holmes. The adventure-mystery involving a sleuth who was proficient both physically and mentally was given over to thrillers such as the Nick Carter stories, while the strict detective tale became purely analytical. In this form, the detective story featured the detective as its chief character and the solution to an interesting mystery as its chief interest. There was generally a narrator in the Watson tradition and an absence of any love interest, and neither characterization nor the tangential demands of the plot interfered with the central business of unraveling the puzzle. With these characteristics established, the detective story moved into its golden age.

The period of 1920 to 1940 represented the golden age of the novel of detection. It included the work of Dorothy L. Sayers, Agatha Christie, Earl Derr Biggers, and S. S. Van Dine (Willard Huntington Wright). Hundreds of novels were written during this period and were enjoyed by people at all levels of literary sophistication. The expectation of the reader was that a clever detective would be faced with a puzzling crime, almost always a murder or a series of murders, that had not been committed by a professional criminal; the solution of this mystery would come about by the examination of clues presented in the novel.

Dorothy L. Sayers was perhaps the most literary writer of the practitioners of the detective novel; she attempted a combination of the detective story and the "legitimate" novel. *The Nine Tailors* (1934) is a good example of the work of her detective, Lord Peter Wimsey, and of her careful research into background material. She is considered to be one of the finest of the mystery writers of this period. Lord Peter Wimsey is a snobbish man given to airy commentary and a languid manner, but he has the analytical skills necessary to solve the mysteries.

Although she may not have had the skill in characterization or the literary quality of Sayers, Agatha Christie surpassed her rivals in the sheer ingenuity of her plots and her manipulation of the evidence that her detective, Hercule Poirot, had to evaluate. Christie used such traditional ploys as the somewhat dense associate (in this instance, Captain Hastings), the least likely person as the murderer, the unexpected turn of the plot, and an exotic manner of committing the crime. Poirot, who became the most popular fictional detective since Sherlock Holmes, appears in thirty-three of Christie's novels.

Christie invented yet another fictional detective who became almost as beloved as Poirot: Miss Jane Marple is a quiet Victorian lady who figures in eleven novels and a collection of short stories. Her solutions come about from a shrewd knowledge of human behavior, keen observation, a remarkable memory, and the ability to make startling deductions from the evidence. Despite the popularity of Hercule Poirot and Miss Marple, neither stars in the book that is widely considered to be Christie's best: *Ten Little Niggers* (1939; published in the United States as *And Then There Were None*, 1940; also known as *Ten Little Indians*).

Rivaling M. Poirot and Miss Marple for the affections of detective novel fans was the Chinese Hawaiian American detective Charlie Chan, created by Earl Derr Biggers. Charlie Chan's widespread popularity was especially enhanced by the fact that his stories were turned into some forty-five motion pictures. Chan's characterization includes the frequent use of Chinese aphorisms, an extremely polite manner, and generally humane qualities. Chan is especially interesting in that come critics consider him to be the first example, in this kind of fiction, of an Asian who is a sympathetic character rather than a villain, while others consider him to be an offensive stereotype.

S. S. Van Dine is the author of twelve novels starring the detective Philo Vance, who, like Lord Peter Wimsey, is an English aristocrat, although all of his cases have an American urban setting. An extremely erudite man with a world-weary air, Vance was the best-educated and most refined detective of this era. Van Dine, under his real name of Wright, was a literary critic who made the detective story an object of research and study. The result was the publication of the "twenty rules for detective stories," only one of several efforts to define the exact characteristics of the form. Both readers and writers of this period had definite expectations and resented efforts in the field that did not follow certain specifications. The idea of fair play with the reader was essential; that is, the game must be played with all the evidence needed to solve the crime. There must be no love interest to detract from the business of solving the mystery, the detective could not be the criminal, and the solution could not come about as a result of accident or wild coincidence. During the detective novel's golden age, these rules were taken quite seriously by those who believed that a permanent form of popular fiction had been established.

While the classic detective story was being established in England and the United States, an American development turned the detective novel in a new direction. Manfred B. Lee and Frederic Dannay collaborated to create a detective who would achieve worldwide fame. Ellery Queen, ostensibly the author of the novels that describe his cases, is an amateur detective and professional writer who works with his father, Inspector Richard Queen of the New York Police Department. Inspector Queen provides the clues and investigative techniques while his son, Ellery, puts the evidence together. They are not supermen, after Sherlock Holmes, nor are they all-knowing in the manner of Philo Vance, but professionals dealing with a more realistic crime scene than that of their predecessors. Ellery Queen was thus a crossover figure leading to the police procedural story and to the kind of detective fiction that came to reflect the actual criminal class, as well as the working of the criminal justice system, in the United States.

HARD-BOILED DETECTIVE FICTION

In the 1930's, while the classic detective story was thriving, another kind of mystery story came into being—the hard-boiled detective novel. The preeminent writers of this school were Dashiell Hammett, Raymond Chandler, and—in the next generation—Ross Macdonald. Some of these writers began writing for *Black Mask*, a pulp magazine, in the 1920's. Hammett's Sam Spade, who appeared in *The Maltese Falcon* (serial 1929-1930, book 1930), is characteristic of the new detective: a private eye in a not-very-successful office who solves crimes by following people around in unsavory neighborhoods, having fights in alleys, and dealing with informers. He is cynical regarding the political dealings that go on behind the scenes and is aware of the connections between criminals and the outwardly respectable. He trusts no one, while he himself follows the dictates of a personal code. Hammett's *The Thin Man* (1934), which became the basis for a series of motion pictures, was a return to the more traditional form of detective fiction.

Another member of the hard-boiled school was Raymond Chandler, who wrote seven novels featuring his sleuth Philip Marlowe. Chandler, describing the ideal detective hero, said, "Down these mean streets a man must go who is not himself mean, who is neither tarnished nor afraid." Such a man is aware of the corruption he will find, but he is governed by a code that includes faithfulness to the client and an abhorrence of crime without an avenging or sadistic bent. Chandler specialized in complex plots, realistic settings, and snappy dialogue in novels such as *The Big Sleep* (1939), *Farewell, My Lovely* (1940), and *The Lady in the Lake* (1943). He was also a theoretician of the detective story, and his essay "The Simple Art of Murder" (1944) is an important document in the annals of crime literature.

After the introduction of the hard-boiled detective and the many stories involving the routine investigations of official law-enforcement agencies, the tradition of the superman detective declined. Fictional detectives lost their aristocratic manners and eccentricities, while the crimes being investigated gained interest not because they involved yet another bizarre or ingenious way to commit murder, but because of the influence of the psychological makeup or the social status of the criminal. The criminal was also less likely to be an amateur than a habitual malefactor. Limiting the suspects by setting the story in confined quarters—such as a country house or an ocean liner—gave way to a story that took the reader into the mean streets referred to by Chandler. These stories often involved the brutality of the police, more violence on the part of the detective, frankness in matters of sex, and the use of formerly taboo language. Mickey Spillane's Mike Hammer typified a new breed of private detectives, one who is given to acts of sadistic violence.

This often brutal social realism is also reflected in the work of Erle Stanley Gardner, best known for his creation of the lawyer-detective Perry Mason. The hero of more than eighty novels, Mason was first characterized in the hard-boiled tradition; early novels such as *The Case of the Velvet Claws* (1933) and *The Case of the Curious Bride* (1934) emphasize the fast-paced action and involuted plots that superseded the literary quality typical of Sayers's work. While retaining his early penchant for extralegal tactics, Mason gradually developed into a courtroom hero, allowing his assistant detective Paul Drake to do the research while Mason excelled in the

spectacular oral combat of the cross-examination. Many of Gardner's plots were drawn from his own legal experiences as an attorney; having founded the Court of Last Resort, Gardner demonstrated a concern for the helpless. In keeping with this concern, he modified the detective genre by introducing the state as the villain and attacking the urban evils of capitalistic greed for wealth and power.

In championing the defenseless, Gardner was the voice of a modern Everyman during the decades between 1930 and 1960. Viewing themselves as vulnerable to the dictates of the state (such as the establishment of Prohibition and income tax), readers achieved vicarious satisfaction in seeing the problems of average people solved. The mass popularity of Mason's cases was the result not only of their victories over the "system" but also of the medium they employed. Gardner was, by his own admission, a "product of the paperback revolution," and he further lowered the literary standards of classical detective fiction by dictating his novels. He was also the script supervisor for the television series *Perry Mason* (starring Raymond Burr and running from 1957 to 1966), which furthered the personal appeal and accessibility of the detective. Unlike the superhuman Lord Peter Wimsey and Philo Vance, whose intellectual and aristocratic qualities are extraordinary and intimidating, Perry Mason is a successful but common professional, combining the wit of the golden-age sleuth with the cynical pertinacity of the hard-boiled detective.

POLICE PROCEDURAL NOVEL

While the hard-boiled mystery developed one element of the classic detective novel—the appeal of a recurring hero with yet another case to solve—in a strikingly new direction, the sheer fascination of deduction that characterized the golden age of the detective novel was developed in a new subgenre: the police procedural, a kind of fictional documentary often purporting to be taken from actual police files. These stories detail the routines of investigative agencies, taking the reader into forensic laboratories and describing complex chemical testing of the evidence. Hardworking police officers interview suspects, conduct stakeouts, shadow people, and investigate bank accounts. Even if there is a major figure who is in charge of the case, the investigation clearly is a matter of teamwork, with standard areas of expertise and responsibility: in short, a realistic depiction of actual police methods.

These stories date from World War II and are typified by the television series *Dragnet* and Sidney Kingsley's Broadway play *Detective Story* (1949). One of the major writers of the police procedural is Ed McBain, who wrote more than thirty novels about the "87th precinct" in a fictional urban setting that closely resembles New York City. The police procedural has proved to be a versatile form that can be used as the basis for a symbolic story with intentions far beyond that of crime solving, as in Lawrence Sanders's *The First Deadly Sin* (1973). Similarly, Tom Sharpe's *Riotous Assembly* (1971) is a police procedural set in South Africa that uses the form to ridicule apartheid, hypocrisy, and racial stereotyping.

Ostensibly, the psychological crime novels of Georges Simenon should also belong in the police procedural category; however, Inspector Jules Maigret of the Paris Police Department uses neither scientific nor rational methods to identify murderers. Similar to Perry Mason in his bourgeois appeal (Maigret is heavyset, smokes a pipe, and is fond of domesticity) and in his delegation of research responsibilities to subordinates, Maigret solves crimes by absorbing the ambience of the place in which they were committed. By familiarizing himself with social customs, geography, and personalities, Maigret "becomes" the suspect and uses psychology and intuition to discern the criminal's identity. Patience rather than flamboyance characterizes Maigret; he relies on the hunches of his sympathetic imagination instead of on factual clues. While Maigret inhabits the sordid world of the hard-boiled detective, he sees himself as a "repairer of destinies" and acts more like a humble priest eliciting confessions than a vindictive policeman triumphing over evil.

In addition to departing from convention in Maigret's unique style of detection, Simenon also defies genre restrictions in the style of his work. *Pietr-le-Letton* (1931; *The Strange Case of Peter the Lett*, 1933; also known as *Maigret and the Enigmatic Lett*, 1963) was written in 1929, but it has little in common with the analytical works of the golden age. Accused of being too literary in his early psychological novels, Simenon probes the ambiguity of human behavior, acknowledging the capacity

of people to sin while maintaining a sympathetic understanding of their actions. Readers of the Maigret novels are unable to see evil in terms of black and white, as readers of Gardner's works do, and come away with as much compassion for the murderer as for the victim. Simenon denies both the mental action of the classical period of detective fiction and the physical action of the hard-boiled period, promoting instead the action of the heart. In so doing, he demonstrates the versatility of the detective fiction genre.

NEW SUBGENRES

While retaining many of its traditional core characteristics, detective fiction in the last decades of the twentieth century became increasingly varied, with many new subgenres emerging. Among the most popular and highly regarded writers that became prominent during this time were P. D. James and Dick Francis of England and Elmore Leonard of the United States. James writes in the so-called golden-age tradition of such authors as Agatha Christie and Ngaio Marsh (both of whom are still widely read). Her novels, longer and denser than most in the genre, have series detectives (Scotland Yard inspector Adam Dalgliesh and private eye Cordelia Gray) who are neither stereotypical nor two-dimensional but rather singular people whose private lives directly affect their professional activities. Dalgliesh, for example, is a poet whose wife died giving birth to their first child, a double tragedy that continues to haunt him. The cases he pursues are multifaceted; James develops complex milieus and characters, and there is always a thematic element (sometimes religious). Close to her in method is Ruth Rendell, whose Inspector Wexford novels also feature psychological probing and have equally complex puzzles but lack a thematic dimension. Both women's novels generally fall into the police procedural subgenre, as do Colin Dexter's Inspector Morse novels, which have an introspective, intellectual protagonist who is quite similar in temperament and method to Dalgliesh. Set in and around Oxford University in England, a Dexter novel usually has a religious element and a dollop of social criticism. Younger than James, Rendell, and Dexter but also a writer of procedurals is Peter Robinson, a Yorkshire native turned Canadian whose increasingly popular mysteries are set in his native northern England.

His detective is the gruff but sensitive Inspector Banks (closer to Wexford than to Dalgliesh or Morse), and each novel concurrently tracks several separate crimes at once, much as Ed McBain and J. J. Marric do in their police procedurals.

The many novels of former British steeplechase jockey Dick Francis have been best sellers on both sides of the Atlantic. Each is a fast-paced thriller, but at its heart is a narrative in the golden-age manner, a standard whodunit in which the nonprofessional sleuth exposes industrial corruption, a racing scandal, or some other crime. The admirable, even exemplary, hero inevitably finds himself in an unfamiliar situation, and in a predictable Francis set piece has a life-threatening encounter with an adversary at some late point in the book. Having overcome a variety of physical, intellectual, and emotional challenges, he restores a measure of normality to the society and returns to his normal pursuits. In a departure from the norm, the hero is not an outsider dealing with a case that just came his way but rather part of a group into which criminality has intruded. Holmes, Wolfe, Archer, Maigret, and Dalgliesh may never again come into contact with the principals in their cases; Francis's detectives, however, continue to live with their erstwhile clients, seeing them regularly at the Jockey Club and other familiar spots. The novels are formulaic, but Francis has maintained a freshness over the years by eschewing the series detective, although his heroes are basically alike. Another Francis standard is the first-person narrative, through which he gains immediacy as well as increased reader empathy with the hero.

Anything but formulaic are Elmore Leonard's best sellers, which are written in the hard-boiled tradition of Chandler, Hammett, and Macdonald. Like Francis, Leonard shies away from a series detective, but he revisits characters (law enforcers and law breakers), and though his milieus range far and wide, he also returns to such places as Detroit and south Florida. While he fills his varied novels with social misfits and assorted grotesques, many of his characters are ordinary people who find themselves in extraordinary situations. Readers can also expect a spare style in the Ernest Hemingway manner, dialogue that rings true to life, and a fast-paced narrative with a chase as a central element. Leonard began his career as a writer of Westerns, and this background is evident in his plotting and style. Another hallmark is his shifting point of view. His characters, good and bad, tell their own stories; Elmore thus avoids omniscient narrators. Further, he changes the narrative point of view several times within a book, carrying the practice to an extreme in *Maximum Bob* (1991), in which part of an episode is told from an alligator's point of view. Shifts in time between the past and present are another Leonard commonplace, and this characteristic and the others may reflect his experience as a writer of screenplays. Leonard is less predictable than most of his peers, for his subjects, settings, and plots run the gamut of possibilities. *The Hot Kid* (2005), for example, is set during the Great Depression, *Pagan Babies* (2000) is set in Rwanda and Detroit, and *Get Shorty* (1990), one of several of his books that have been adapted into feature films, takes its protagonist from Miami to Las Vegas to Los Angeles. Leonard's books are full of surprising protagonists, from a midwestern couple confined in the federal witness protection program to a loan shark turned music producer to an Arizona cowboy caught up in the Spanish-American War. Before he writes, Leonard or a surrogate visits potential milieus and does on-the-spot research to ensure verisimilitude. This process, coupled with his imagination, narrative skills, and incredible ear for dialogue, has led to critical and popular acclaim for Leonard.

Another popular crime novelist who engages in extensive prewriting research is Patricia Cornwell, who, before becoming an author, worked as a police reporter and for the Richmond, Virginia, chief medical examiner as a keeper of forensic records. She also studied forensic science and rode with homicide detectives as a first responder to crime scenes. This background and the preparation she does for each project have allowed Cornwell to produce graphically realistic novels that are almost case studies in such areas as forensic anthropology (*All That Remains*, 1992) and deoxyribonucleic acid (DNA) testing (*Postmortem*, 1990). Her series detective is Kay Scarpetta, a physician who is Richmond's chief medical examiner. Talented scientist though she is, Scarpetta is a woman with a personal life that occasionally intrudes upon her professional activities. Scarpetta's niece, like Cornwell herself, is lesbian, and the novels have always treated sexual identity matter-of-factly. Despite the characters' romantic problems and their confrontations with grisly inhumanity and irrationality, Scarpetta remains a decent person who copes and ultimately triumphs, sometimes over a local, state, or federal bureaucracy, but always over criminals.

Because the boundaries separating crime writing categories are often indistinct, Cornwell sometimes is placed with the hard-boiled group of writers and at other times is placed in the police procedural genre. The police procedural flourished during the 1980's and 1990's, not only because of new Ed McBain books but also because of such varied series as Tony Hillerman's New Mexico Navajo Indian mysteries, featuring Jim Chee and Joe Leghorn; James Lee Burke's Dave Robicheaux novels set in Louisiana; Archer Mayor's Joe Gunther books, which take place primarily in Brattleboro, Vermont; Reginald Hill's Dalziel and Pascoe Yorkshire whodunits; and Stuart Kaminsky's and Martin Cruz Smith's Soviet Union books.

The traditional mystery, increasingly called the "cozy," experienced a renaissance at the end of the twentieth century. Originally pejorative, the term "cozy" refers to novels in which the setting is noncriminal and in which the detective (usually not a full-time sleuth, but rather a college professor, bookstore proprietor, or English nobleman) engages in an intellectual chess match with the reader and faces a variety of suspects. The seriousness may be tempered with some humor, and the stories shy away from graphic violence, overt sex, and crude, lowlife characters. The cozy is often associated with British writers, with whom the form originated, but Americans such as Amanda Cross, Martha Grimes, Carolyn G. Hart, and Joyce Porter are popular practitioners of the form.

The private-eye subgenre also experienced a renaissance toward the end of the century, with a major change being that the stories were set in places other than New York, San Francisco, Chicago, or Los Angeles: Cedar Rapids (Ed Gorman's Jack Dwyer), Cincinnati (Jonathan Valin's Harry Stoner), Detroit (Loren D. Estleman's Amos Walker), North Carolina (Margaret Maron's Judge Deborah Knott), and a series of national parks (Nevada Barr's Anna Pidgeon). Female private eyes, perhaps influenced by the successes of P. D. James's Cordelia Gray, also started to come to the fore. Liza Cody's London agency operative Anna Lee first appeared in *Dupe* (1980). Two years later came two important American debuts: Sue Grafton's Kinsey Milhone in *A Is for Alibi* (1982) and Sara Paretsky's V. I. Warshawski in *Indemnity Only* (1982). Noteworthy, too, is Linda Barnes's Boston private eye Carlotta Carlyle, whose first appearance in a novel is in *A Trouble of Fools* (1987). Marcia Muller's Sharon McCone is sometimes considered the first of the hard-boiled female detectives. McCone has appeared in more than twenty-five novels, including *Edwin of the Iron Shoes* (1977) and *Burn Out* (2008), and Muller was awarded the Mystery Writers of America's Grand Master award in 2005.

Several detective novel subgenres either emerged or gained in popularity during the 1980's and 1990's. Series with religious themes and clerics as detectives include William X. Kienzle's Father Robert Koesler books, Joseph Telushkin's Rabbi Daniel Winter mysteries, and Ellis Peters's medieval Brother Cadfael novels. The Amanda Cross mysteries starring Professor Kate Fansler, M. D. Lake's campus cop Peggy O'Neill novels, and Edith Skom's literature lecturer Beth Austin books are academic whodunits, mysteries set on college or university campuses. New authors began featuring African American detectives (Walter Mosely, P. J. Parrish), Native American detectives (Thomas Perry, Aimée Thurlo), and gay or lesbian detectives (Lev Raphael, Katherine V. Forrest). Historical detective fiction, in which the action is set in the past, was a rarity until the 1970's, when it became a major subgenre, as practiced not only by Ellis Peters but also by such authors as Peter Lovesey, whose Victorian mysteries feature Sergeant Cribb; Jacqueline Winspear, whose sleuth Maisie Dobbs was a nurse on the front lines in World War I; and Edward Marston (pseudonym of Keith Miles), who has authored both medieval and Elizabethan novels. Marston's eleventh century Domesday Book series is developed around the device of William the Conqueror's men traveling the countryside to review problems stemming from the ruler's census and property survey. Spurred by sibling rivalry, the desire for material gain, and the determination to purge suppressed grievances, people murder and cause havoc in a society that remains insecure two decades after the upheavals of the Norman Conquest. By the time they leave an area, the king's men have adjudicated land claims and have exorcised real and imagined evils. Another Marston series, set in England at the end of the sixteenth century, centers on a London theater group whose stage manager turns to detection when deaths occur offstage.

The several plots that Marston typically orchestrates in each of his medieval and Elizabethan mysteries exemplify such subjects as unrequited love, political and social ambition, sibling rivalry, the intrusion of the past upon the present, and questions of personal identity. They are very much like the subjects of most other detective novels, whatever their category or subgenre. In other words, however much detective fiction changes, it retains fundamentals of early and golden-age crime stories, which traditionally used murder as a dramatic means of focusing on a wide variety of human issues.

At the beginning of the twenty-first century, the publishing industry began to decline in the wake of economic downturns and the availability of online media. In 2006, retail sales of mystery fiction had accounted for about $400 million in the United States, behind only romance novels, science fiction and fantasy, and classic literary fiction. Partially in response to marketing demands, a new wave of "cozy" detective series appeared. Apparently aimed at middle-age women, these new series had hobbies and careers as their "hooks." The detectives were women (often single mothers) who solved crimes while engaged in such activities as running coffeehouses, scrapbooking, blowing glass, repairing old houses, catering, selling candies or herbs, knitting, crocheting, or working in a library. Many of these books were short and less psychologically developed than the works of authors such as P. D. James and Patricia Cornwell—meant to be consumed quickly and in quantity, like the pulp fiction of the past. With the continued publication of books by authors including Elizabeth George, Michael Connelly, Michael Chabon, and Walter Dean Myers, however, the literary detective novel continued to thrive.

F. William Nelson
Updated by Gerald H. Strauss

BIBLIOGRAPHY

Barzun, Jacques, and Wendell Hertig Taylor. *A Catalogue of Crime*. New York: Harper & Row, 1989. Highly personal compilation by two voracious read-

ers of crime fiction contains more than five thousand brief descriptions and judgments of works in most categories of the genre as well as a variety of critical studies.

DeAndrea, William L., ed. *Encyclopedia Mysteriosa*. New York: Prentice Hall, 1994. Comprises alphabetically arranged entries about mystery authors, books, and characters as well as films and television and radio programs in the mystery genre. Includes ample cross-references and occasional longer entries (covering topics such as dime novels and the hard-boiled detective) by experts. Edited by a mystery novel writer and critic.

Frank, Lawrence. *Victorian Detective Fiction and the Nature of Evidence: The Scientific Investigations of Poe, Dickens, and Doyle*. New York: Palgrave Macmillan, 2003. Provides the framework for the development of the genre of detective fiction.

Gorman, Ed, Martin H. Greenberg, Larry Segriff, and John Breen, eds. *The Fine Art of Murder*. New York: Carroll & Graf, 1993. Collection of articles by crime fiction writers and critics is not intended as a definitive study of the genre but serves as a good introduction. Useful and entertaining, although some important writers are ignored.

Hadley, Mary. *British Women Mystery Writers: Authors of Detective Fiction with Female Sleuths*. Jefferson, N.C.: McFarland, 2002. Analyzes the works of women writers from the 1960's to the beginning of the twenty-first century, including P. D. James, Jennie Melville, Liza Cody, Val McDermid, Joan Smith, Susan Moody, Judith Cutler, and Lynda La Plante.

Kelleghan, Fiona, ed. *One Hundred Masters of Mystery and Detective Fiction*. Pasadena, Calif.: Salem Press, 2001. Collection of biographical and critical essays presents discussion of the most important figures in the genre before 1988.

Markowitz, Judith A. *The Gay Detective Novel: Lesbian and Gay Main Characters and Themes in Mystery Fiction*. Jefferson, N.C.: McFarland, 2004. Survey of series and stand-alone novels published since 1964 provides analysis of main characters, themes, and plot elements. Includes an extensive list of authors and their works.

Panek, LeRoy. *The Origins of the American Detective Story.* Jefferson, N.C.: McFarland, 2006. Covers the formative years of American detective fiction, from the late nineteenth century to the early twentieth century.

Rzepka, Charles J. *Detective Fiction.* Hoboken, N.J.: Polity Press, 2005. Presents the history of the genre from its modern beginnings in the early eighteenth century to its present state, focusing on urbanization, the rise of the professions, brain science, legal and social reform, war and economic dislocation, class-consciousness, and changing concepts of race and gender.

Symons, Julian. *Bloody Murder: From the Detective Story to the Crime Novel.* 3d rev. ed. New York: Mysterious Press, 1993. Update of a classic study by a major writer of crime novels and stories offers sound critical and historical analysis. Naturally reflects Symons's biases, but presents a balanced overview of the genre.

Thomas, Ronald R. *Detective Fiction and the Rise of Forensic Science.* New York: Cambridge University Press, 2004. Examines how the development of forensic science, from the invention of the lie detector to the uses of DNA, has influenced detective fiction in Great Britain and the United States.

THE EPISTOLARY NOVEL

The epistolary novel, a prominent form among modern fictions, is defined as a novel presented wholly, or nearly so, in familiar letter form. Its history reaches back to classical literature, taking special inspiration from the separate traditions of the Roman letter writers Cicero and Pliny, and of Ovid's *Heroides* (before 8 C.E.; English translation, 1567), a series of verse letters celebrating famous heroines of myth. Familiar letters, as such, developed slowly in a world where literacy was rare; but the epistle, a classic rhetorical form, defined by the rules of oratory, was a favorite means of expression for many scholars of the European Middle Ages and Renaissance, yielding learned letters in both prose and verse, most common at first in Latin, then in the vernacular.

The sixteenth century saw the first dated translation of Ovid's *Heroides* into French, in 1500. The mid-century welcomed with great enthusiasm the first "pure" epistolary novels: Juan de Segura's *Processo de cartas* (1548) and Alvise Pasqualigo's *Delle Lettere amorose* (1563). Letters were used as tools in the earliest modern novels and romances, for they answered the frequent problem of communication between separated lovers, as well as giving the opportunity to multiply complications and mischances by having letters discovered by enemies, lost and intercepted, misinterpreted, or received out of time and season. For example, within the five-volume bulk of Honoré d'Urfé's pastoral novel *L'Astrée* (1607-1628; *Astrea*, 1657-1658), there are 129 letters that are hidden in hats, stolen, found floating down rivers, or recited from memory.

The seventeenth century in France saw the development of a climate in which letters were one of the most popular forms of written material. The first printed edition of the letters of Abélard and Héloïse came in 1616, and the verse translation published in 1678 by Bussy-Rabutin (himself a celebrated social épistolier) was greeted with great enthusiasm. The collected epistles of Guez de Balzac, first published in 1624, had a great vogue, with many reprintings and new collections. His popular successor, Victor Voiture, was praised still more highly for the light tone and grace of his letters. Within the aristocratic salons of the day, the reading of letters within a circle of friends was a frequent social pastime, and many famous people of the day wrote their letters in the certainty of their being read to a group rather than kept private. Madame de Sévigné wrote to such correspondents as her cousin Bussy-Rabutin in the expectation that they would circulate and increase her reputation as a graceful wit.

Within the salons, expertise in letter writing grew through mutual compliment and criticism, but the appearance of popular letter manuals offered models to a wider circle of literate people. Jean Puget de la Serre published his enormously successful *Secrétaire de la Cour* in 1623 and followed it in 1641 with the *Secrétaire à la Mode*. These manuals were translated and reissued through countless numbers of printings, became very popular in England, inspired a great number of imitations, and had an untold effect on developing popular epistolary style and thematics. The letter writers, as they offered epistolary models on varied subjects and occasions, often offered responses as well and built up a series of letters that told the germ of a story. Samuel Richardson wrote a letter handbook, *The Complete Letter-Writer* (1741), in which can be found the prototype for his epistolary novel *Pamela: Or, Virtue Rewarded* (1740-1741).

Familiar letters were regarded as direct transcriptions of events seen or experienced by their writers, and although the epistles of writers such as Balzac were acknowledged to be polished productions, letters in general carried the cachet of truth and spontaneity. Thus, arising out of the ferment of epistolary literature, the early epistolary novelists claimed for their works, as a matter of course, the privilege of historical truth. The most frequent *topos* of epistolary novels is the statement that they are a collection of real letters, not literary fabrications, and that the author is only an editor of material from other hands. The first great French epistolary novel, *Les lettres portugaises* (1669; *Five Love-Letters from a Nun to a Cavalier*, 1678; better known as *The Letters of a Portuguese Nun*, 1893), now recognized as the work of

Gabriel-Joseph de La Vergne, was long believed to be a translation from the Portuguese of genuine letters written by a nun to her French lover. Letters offered a freedom of style, being rhetorically defined as written transcriptions of oral communication. Letters could deal with a variety of subjects, using a light touch, and were not forced to follow any subject through all its logical ramifications. Charles de Montesquieu, the author of *Lettres Persanes* (1721; *Persian Letters*, 1722), refers to these advantages of epistolary form in his "Réflections," which were added to the 1754 edition. Letters carried the atmosphere of lived experience, which gave credence and popularity to the memoir but had the added fillip of retelling stories whose ends were unknown. A memorialist has safely arrived at a point from which he or she can reflect on the past. Letters are written within the flow of present experience, looking back to the last letter written, forward to the next.

THE SEVENTEENTH AND EIGHTEENTH CENTURIES

Love themes are given a special privilege in the epistolary fiction derived from the tradition of Ovid, Abélard, and Héloïse, while the tradition descending from Cicero and Pliny to Guez de Balzac encourages the use of letters to treat a variety of topics of more general interest with the familiar touch of friends in social conversation. The seventeenth and eighteenth centuries saw the rise of the epistolary novel to a dominant prose form throughout Europe, first in France and England, then in Germany and Eastern Europe. Three of the most influential novels of the eighteenth century, Richardson's *Pamela*, Jean-Jacques Rousseau's *Julie: Ou, La Nouvelle Héloïse* (1761; *Eloise: Or, A Series of Original Letters*, 1761; also as *Julie: Or, The New Eloise*, 1968; better known as *The New Héloïse*), and Johann Wolfgang von Goethe's *Die Leiden des jungen Werthers* (1774, *The Sorrows of Young Werther*, 1779), were all in letter form. It was certainly the exploitation by the writers of the epistolary form itself that gave their novels their immense impact.

In *The Letters of a Portuguese Nun*, the epistolary novel is given an emotionally concentrated model, inspiring numerous translations, "completions," and imitations. The French edition of 1669, for example, was translated into English several times between 1678 and

1716. With its five letters, La Vergne's work is extremely brief, especially considered in the context of novels such as the five-volume *L'Astrée*. Presented by the author, in his guise as editor, as "a correct copy of the translation of five Portuguese Letters which were written to a noble gentleman who served in Portugal," the letters are univocal; that is, the reader hears only the voice of one correspondent. Every attempt is made to establish the credibility of the letters, which are said to have been circulating in private hands. Publication is resorted to only to ensure that a "correct copy" rather than a spurious compilation is in public circulation. The nun's voice cries in genuine pain, expressed through a correspondence whose failure destroys the romantic ties with her French lover. The expectation of a response is inherent in the nun's use of the letter and in the I-you couple that defines the alternate composers of a correspondence. Direct address calls for direct response. The nun's letters begin in answer to a letter from the absent lover, and a two-sided exchange is expected. In fact, while requesting frequent letters, the nun also tries to set the tone and admonishes her lover not to talk of useless things, nor ask her to remember him. The correspondence, and the romance, have run their course by the fifth and final letter, because the Frenchman does not respond within the expectations of the nun. At first he does not write at all; then his letters are inadequate to feed her passion.

Sentimental analysis, so important in this novel, is doubled by the analysis of the specific written form involved, by the problem of maintaining a satisfactory exchange of letters between parted lovers. The wounded heart of the nun is expressed in complaints of the lack of proper response in the letter chain, as well as of the lack of love. The author exploits the value of the letter as a tool for immediate access to his heroine's emotions, setting the tone for many later epistolary novels in the impassioned style of the nun's effusions. Even Madame de Sévigné joked that if she responded in like tone to a tender note from a gentleman friend, she would have to write a "portugaise."

In 1721, *Persian Letters* was published anonymously by Montesquieu. The introduction once again insists that the letters are a collection chosen from a great number written and received by Persians lodging with the author, letters copied and kept sometimes without the knowledge of the foreign travelers. The editor has "translated" the letters and adjusted them to European tastes, leaving out the flowery language, "sublime expressions," and long complimentary formulas of the originals. In choosing Persians for the chief characters of his novel, Montesquieu gave his novel an exotic background; in professing to adapt this exoticism to European tastes, he could add just as much as he liked for seasoning, without worrying about authentic Asian style. The choice of Persians also greatly emphasizes the theme of absence inherent in epistolary form; it is the chief difficulty facing Usbek in the administration of his distant harem and the reason for his ultimate downfall as a domestic tyrant. This exotic flavor also allows for comic exploitation in the naïve reactions of the Persians as their letters recount the manners and morals of Montesquieu's world.

Persian Letters includes letters attributed to numerous pens, although the chief correspondents are Usbek and his younger companion Rica. Usbek's exchange with the members of his harem and their keepers provides the story without which this would be no true novel, but this story is only one of the two major strains in the novel. There are a great many letters that serve as discussions of current events in France or deal with moral and philosophical questions. In all the letters, the name of the writer is given, in many of them a definite correspondent. All are dated according to the Persian calendar, covering a span of eight years. There are several complete letter circuits, letters given with their direct response, and subsequent letters to and from that same correspondent. There are also letter exchanges between secondary characters, such as that between the chief eunuch of Usbek's harem and a young protégé destined to replace him. The lapse of time indicated in the complete circuit of response is given great weight, especially at the denouement of the harem intrigue, when Usbek helplessly rages at the distances which make his own responses inadequate.

In letter 155, Usbek announces his return to Ispahan. His letters have often been received as much as six months late, and it is abundantly clear that he will not return to his harem until well after the horrible events chronicled in subsequent letters. Letter 148, Usbek's reply to letter 147, giving the chief eunuch universal power over the harem, arrives after the death of the addressee

and is kept by his elderly successor as a sealed relic (noted in letter 149). Letter 150, from Usbek, seeking to "reactivate" the sealed letter, is either intercepted by harem rebels (version given in letter 151) or lost during a robbery (letter 152). The last letter of the novel, 161, written by Usbek's favorite, Roxane, is composed after a self-administered dose of poison, noted in the text, and the process of death defines the compass of the letter. In this letter, the writer details the end of the harem world in her own death and ends the novel's text and her life when the pen falls from her hand and she dies.

The varied stylistic possibilities of letters are explored in the harem series; different writers are given different tones in which to express their characters, and the tones of the correspondents change as they address different people. Usbek does not write in the same manner to two different wives, and his tone and subject matter change again in addressing the chief eunuch or his own friend Nessir. The means of transmission of letters across the great distances is noted; letter 150 is to be delivered by some Armenian merchants traveling to Ispahan, but since the harem has moved to Usbek's country house, a servant is sent to fetch it; it disappears during a robbery on the servant's return trip. Letters are objects subject to many strange fates.

Letters serve a different function in the parallel series devoted to the exploration of various themes of French society and thought through the eyes of the Persian visitors. Here the epistolary form is used much as Voltaire later used it in his *Lettres philosophiques* (1734; originally published in English as *Letters Concerning the English Nation*, 1733; also as *Philosophical Letters*, 1961), where no story line is imposed within the letter framework to produce a true epistolary novel. In this use of the letter form, the epistolary license to touch on any subject with a light and familiar tone is the desired feature. The necessary epistolary use of the first person and direct address to the fictional correspondent gives the opportunity for the epistolary writer to build an automatic bridge of sympathy with the reader. In general, the formal fiction of the letter is given less weight as more is given to thematic development of the individual argument. In the Troglodyte series of letters (10 through 14), Usbek writes to his young friend Mirza, with the correspondence acting as a simple frame, an excuse for thematic development. Within the series, there are only the most perfunctory references to the correspondence, none to the letters themselves. Several texts succeed one another with no transition or attempt to explain differing circumstances of composition for different dates. Although written as a "response" to Mirza's letter, this series is a finished whole and requires no answer to complete it.

Persian Letters was followed by many epistolary novels set in exotic locales or using foreign characters for added interest and a pretext for letters. Laurent Versini, in his *Roman épistolaire* (1979), notes that half of the French epistolary novels between Montesquieu's success and 1750 were exotics. The great novels of the eighteenth century, however, concentrate on domestic situations, set within the countries of origin of their authors: *Pamela* in England, *The New Héloïse* in French Switzerland, and *The Sorrows of Young Werther* in Germany. These three works had enormous influence on the European reading public. All were translated into many tongues and inspired many imitators, both in literary terms and within the realm of everyday life. *The Sorrows of Young Werther*, said to have taken inspiration from *The New Héloïse*, in its turn supposed a direct descendant of Richardson's *Pamela* and *Clarissa: Or, The History of a Young Lady* (1747-1748), was not only one of the great propulsive works of German Romanticism but was said to have inspired a rash of suicides on its publication as well.

Pamela appeared in print one year before *The Complete Letter-Writer*, begun earlier, in which Richardson had set down the novel's premise: a series of letters telling a true story of a virtuous servant girl who defends herself from her employer's advances and eventually is rewarded by his hand in marriage. What is a skeleton in the letter manual is fleshed out to great length in the highly detailed development of the novel. Translated by no less a light than the Abbé Prévost, and succeeded by Richardson's own *Clarissa* and *Sir Charles Grandison* (1753-1754), *Pamela* was parodied by Henry Fielding in *An Apology for the Life of Mrs. Shamela Andrews* (1741), and by his *The History of the Adventures of Joseph Andrews, and of His Friend Mr. Abraham Adams* (1742). *Pamela* continues to arouse debate. Critics have often seen prurience in Richardson's theme and hypocrisy in his happy ending. Pamela's letters chronicle successive scenes of attempted seduction and rape in panting detail, while steadfastly defending the strictest principles of female chastity. Were Pamela's sufferings in some way a calculated "come-on" to a dupe due to be seduced into marriage? Although psychological credibility may be strained by the union of so much innocence and vulnerability with such a ferocious determination to resist and to recount every evidence of Mr. B.'s passion, the use of the letter form argues for Richardson's insistence on Pamela's candor. Richardson's first great epistolary novel is predicated on the assumption that the familiar letter is a direct window on the soul. Pamela may be taken at face value, and every letter carries what is supposed to be the free expression of the state of her soul.

Pamela is presented by the author as a collection of genuine letters, and he intrudes in his guise as editor to explain and provide transitions as well as to point out the moral at the end. In the opening pages, one finds complete letter circuits between Pamela Andrews and her aged, impoverished parents. These early letters introduce several of the major characters and establish the family's virtuous character, as well as a critical facet of Pamela's behavior. The favorable notice she had received from the lady whose death occasions the first letter had led her to take an inordinate interest in reading and writing, though yet very young (letter 4 gives her age as fifteen), and in general had raised her above her station in education and behavior. The first letter speaks explicitly of itself, drawing attention to rather than leaving in the background the epistolary pretext of the fiction: Pamela's tears are blotting her paper. The means by which the letter is to be sent are discussed, and a postscript opens the theme of letters hidden from and discovered by Mr. B.

As the novel progresses and Pamela passes through a series of harrowing experiences, including lengthy captivity by Mr. B., the letter exchange with her parents cannot continue, and Pamela writes to them in the hope that one day they will read her words and understand the trials through which she has come. Even her early letters are written in the anticipation of preservation and rereading by her entire family. The letters become a sort of journal, although an outward-turning one, in which the destined readers are often mentioned, and their reactions to a particular scene or reflection are imagined. The entries in this letter-journal are dated according to the day of the week, at times even with the time of day. All circumstances of composition are referred to, including the supply source of the paper, pen, and ink, as well as their places of concealment. Some letters from Mr. B. are included in the form of copies, and any communication received by Pamela is closely analyzed in her subsequent writing. First-person narration and direct address are used throughout. Pamela comments constantly on her style, the effect of her circumstances on her composition, and her intention to set down each event as it happens.

The status of the growing body of manuscript is very important indeed and is given a large place in the consideration of the epistolary text. Pamela's early letters are often intercepted and read by Mr. B. Her later journal is kept hidden from him by various expedients, sewn in Pamela's petticoats or, on threat of physical search, buried in the garden. In an attempt to have letters carried to her parents by the parson Mr. Williams, Pamela compromises that gentleman and brings him into disgrace with his patron. As a consequence, she has the piquant experience of reading a misdirected letter meant for Mrs. Jewkes, her keeper, and may contrast the style with the letter meant for herself and sent mistakenly to Jewkes. The recopying of Jewkes's letter serves a double purpose: to illustrate the severity of Mr. B. and to enter the text into the secret letter-journal. At last, when Pamela is dismissed from Mr. B.'s sight and is en route to her parents in disgrace, it is the story told by her letters, surrendered to him, which persuades him to change his resolution and marry her. The marriage restores epistolary commerce between Pamela and the elder Andrewses, and they learn the course of their daughter's acceptance into noble society, ending in their reunion on Mr. B.'s estates. The collection of Pamela's letters is left circulating among the family and friends of Mr. B. at the close of the novel, reconciling all to his choice of a wife.

While *Pamela* includes occasional letters from Mr. B. and other characters, the text is essentially univocal. *Clarissa*, Richardson's next novel, employs correspondence of several different characters in presenting and maintaining a multivocal epistolary narration. In Jean-Jacques Rousseau's *The New Héloïse*, it is the love duet of Julie and her Saint-Preux that holds the central posi-

tion. The letters are presented by the author as a collection of genuine letters, as the title of the 1761 translation announces: *Eloise: Or, A Series of Original Letters*. Letters are exchanged between inhabitants of a small town at the foot of the Alps and are collected and published by Rousseau. By linking his novel with the long-standing epistolary tradition of Abélard and Héloïse, Rousseau stresses the importance of letters as letters, as well as their aura of historic truth (since the first Héloïse was real, so is Julie), and the importance of the love intrigue, with its implication of suffering and sacrifice.

Letter form is given special weight in the first half of the novel, where, as the letters introduce the characters and lay the foundations for later narration, individual texts respond point-by-point to their predecessors. It is in answering Saint-Preux's letters, written while the lovers are in close daily contact, that Julie enters into a romantic relationship with him. It is in a letter that she first receives his expression of affection and through the letters that they are bound together, even over long absences. The letters are written in the first person, directed to a very definite correspondent, and the mode of communication between the lovers is discussed at length. Themes treated within the letters vary widely and include philosophical discussions, in which cases Rousseau uses the prerogative of the epistolary form to digress from his plot much as Montesquieu did. Within the line of the main narration, letters are important as physical testimony of the loved "other," substitutes for the loved one in absence, and as such they are kissed, caressed, preserved, and reread. Saint-Preux's handling of Julie's letters forces him to recopy them, since the originals are wearing out. This recopying in a certain sense establishes a prototext of the final letter collection represented in the novel. The time lapse between the letters is important, as is their method of transmission.

Letter 21 presents a highly dramatic scene in which Saint-Preux awaits and receives one of Julie's letters from the hand of the mail carrier. This passage highlights all the details of transmission: the necessity of naming oneself in claiming the letter, the opening of the outer packet in which the letter has traveled with the correspondence of others, the confirmation that there is indeed a letter for the narrator, and finally the confirmation of the letter itself as a physical object carrying the imprint of the loved one's hand in the superscription. Saint-Preux continues to recount in his own letter, in response to this one received with so much ceremony, the emotion he felt when he held the paper in his trembling hand and the conditions under which he finally opened and read it. The emphasis lies not only on the single letter so dramatized but also on the entire correspondence. In a text such as Voltaire's *Philosophical Letters*, no attention is given to building or embroidering the fiction of the epistolary text as a physical reality. In *The New Héloïse*, the highly charged, emotional intimacy between Julie and her Saint-Preux is served by the attention lavished on the mechanics of a letter exchange through which the narration may proceed and by which it is colored. The identification of the reader is sought through the attempt to engage belief in the reality of the characters involved. Again, as in *Pamela*, letters serve as a "hot" medium, transparent to the emotions of the individual writers and immediate to the events which affect them.

The Sorrows of Young Werther, the first major work of Goethe, is brief and concentrated in its impact, in contrast to the voluminous works of Rousseau and Richardson. Again, the book is presented by the editor as a collection of "all I could find" of Werther's letters. Almost all are addressed to Werther's intimate friend, Wilhelm, with a small number written for the beloved Lotte and her husband, Albert. The personality of the correspondent is seldom given much weight within the individual texts, although there are very few letters in which Werther does not use direct address or in which the intended reader is not clearly designated. Wilhelm is almost always the intimate *du* (the intimate, informal form of the pronoun "you"), infrequently *ihr* (plural form of "you") when in the company of Werther's mother. Lotte alone is *Sie* (formal "you"), until the last letter, while Lotte and Albert together are *ihr*, combining formal address for Lotte with familiar form for her husband. Significantly, as in *Persian Letters*, each epistolary text is dated, and the rhythm of the narration speeds or slows with the ebb and flow of the fictional correspondence. When Werther is overcome by the flux of his emotions during time spent with Lotte, the letters to Wilhelm are dated every two or three days, sometimes daily. When bored and depressed by exterior circumstances, such as his position on an ambassador's staff, the letters come

only once a week or so. The infrequent letters may be seen as an attempt at verisimilitude, since, although there is no break in the narration during these periods, the editor notes that certain letters of this period have been withheld as indiscreet.

Unlike Rousseau and Richardson, Goethe devotes little attention to the technical aspects of the epistolary commerce. One knows exactly where and how Pamela gets her pen and paper, and how Saint-Preux receives and treats Julie's letters, but there is no indication of how Werther's letters are written or exchanged with Wilhelm. The references to epistolary style are few, but there are some direct responses to Wilhelm's letters, with passages cited as they are answered. Beyond the faithful use of dates, which serves a dramatic purpose in emphasizing the speed with which Werther's passion enfolds and destroys him, there are very few uses of set letter forms. The letters vary greatly in length, some quite long and others reduced to the briefest of paragraphs. No opening formulas are used, and the formal closings are sparse, with at most a simple *Leb wohl* (farewell) inserted at the end. This manner of closing, however, can be effectively dramatized, as in Werther's closing to his suicide letter: "*Lotte! Lotte leb wohl! Leb wohl!*"

Goethe uses the letter form as a painfully intimate reflection of the state of mind of his suffering hero. The fragmentary sentences (which would be out of place in another narrative form), the stringing together of dated paragraphs that gain weight from their status as letters addressed to an outer eye, the license to speak in the first person about all the secret movements of the soul—these are all possibilities inherent in the epistolary form. That Werther makes what amounts to an aberrant use of the form in his emphasis on one pole of the correspondence, his own, is in a way a facet of the characterization of the tragic hero, so locked in on his own suffering that suicide becomes his only escape. The letter form is also open to the many descriptions of Werther's impressions of the people and things around him, yet even his sweeping pictures of the natural beauty he meets are transmuted into personal reflections. This is not the same use that Montesquieu, or even Rousseau, makes of the possibility of including material exterior to the story line within the narrative of a letter. The emotional impact of *The*

Sorrows of Young Werther is concentrated and focused through this use of univocal, inward-turning letter form.

The last days of Werther's life are chronicled by the anonymous editor's voice in a curious text formed by the third-person reminiscences of Lotte, Albert, Werther's servant, and other people who met or talked with Werther in that time. These bits of testimony are woven through by fragments of a last, undated letter addressed to Lotte and shorter bits directed to Wilhelm. This last attempt at writing anticipates the reactions of Werther's loved ones after his death, and frequent reference is made to their reading the text after the writer's burial. In it, Lotte changes from the formal *Sie* to *du* and is addressed in the most intimate and intense tones. The last words, addressed to her, are written immediately before the fatal shot. The impersonal editorial voice informs the reader that "From the blood on the back of the seat, one can determine, that he did the deed sitting before the writing desk." The contrast between Werther's own heated voice and the cold style of the editor is devastating, producing an impression of the "truth" of the fatal events and the finality of Werther's death.

The Sorrows of Young Werther, *The New Héloïse*, and *Pamela* all depend heavily on the convention that personal letters are the vehicles of personal truth, open and immediate to the individuals who write them. This understanding plays a part in the characterization of the fictional protagonists and in the emotional effects elicited by their letters. In contrast to these novels, *Les Liaisons dangereuses* (1782, *Dangerous Acquaintances*, 1784; also known as *Dangerous Liaisons*) of Pierre Choderlos de Laclos takes much of its impact from the use made by the libertine protagonists, the Marquise de Merteuil and the Vicomte de Valmont, of this same convention to conceal their emotions and intentions and to seduce and destroy their correspondents. The author plays with several correspondences exchanged within a small social circle, changing styles with each writer and according to each addressee. The totality of the letters is revealed, through various stratagems, to Madame de Merteuil and her sometime ally Valmont, and each letter becomes the object of discussion and analysis between them. If the progress of the seductions by Merteuil and Valmont is one interest of the narrative, the change in their relationship through the course of the novel is an-

other, a chance brought about in part through Valmont's own surrender to love for his victim Madame de Tourvel. The terms of his letters to Merteuil are held as a contract, forcing him to the destruction of the loved object and himself.

Dangerous Liaisons is preceded by a double preface, the first by the "editor," the second by the "writer." Together they form an ironic gem. The editor writes a bit of social commentary, saying that in spite of the author's attempts to make his work seem genuine, it must be a novel because the contemporary age is too moral for such events to take place. The writer produces the image of a pedantic hired hack who has pieced together the letters of the novel, chosen from a great body of possible correspondence, as the smallest number of texts necessary to tell the story. The writer complains that the third party, who commissioned him, did not allow him to change the grammar or style of the letters or to cut the chosen texts, "of which several deal separately, and almost without transition, with subjects altogether unconnected with one another." His employers maintain that a variety of styles, even errors, and a diversity of themes are expected of personal letters. Such features, the writer thinks, may both attract and repel the public, and since all the sentiments, or nearly so, are pretended, the identification of the public with the characters will be impaired. The reader of both the prefaces will find himself in a position of ironic suspension, where neither introductory voice can be believed or wholly rejected, and thus he must approach the novel with suspended judgment.

The complexity of *Dangerous Liaisons* and the literary virtuosity with which it was composed have attracted a great deal of critical attention. One of the most interesting of such studies, both in regard to this individual work and in its general overview of the epistolary genre, is Jean Rousset's "Le Roman par lettres," included in his collected essays, *Forme et Signification* (1962). Rousset discusses the important factors that enlist the reader's identification with the characters of the epistolary novel: the atmosphere of intimacy provided by the familiar letter form, the fact that the action of the novel is contemporary with the life and voice of the characters, and the seductiveness of the bipolar I-you structure that almost forces a reader to identify with the voices of the letters.

Rousset further points out that, in the case of *Dangerous Liaisons*, the reader is, like Merteuil and Valmont, in possession of an entire epistolary text, thus knowing the stratagems employed by the libertines in the composition of their letters. In Rousset's view, this knowledge renders the reader an accomplice of the libertines in their work of seduction.

What are the techniques used by Laclos to write these compromising letters that catch the reader in a dangerous liaison? Great importance is given to the individual letter and its ties with other letters. The names of writer and addressee are given, the dates of composition, and often the place. Frequent reference is made to letters received from the correspondent and other letters written or received by the writers. When Cécile de Volanges runs out of writing materials, Valmont smuggles some to her (letter 123). The mode of transmission of letters and where and how they are kept is a major motif, since so many of the exchanges are clandestine, and the various ruses of delivery and concealment are continuously under discussion.

In addition to the primary series of letters between pairs of correspondents, there is a secondary exchange within the letters of Madame de Merteuil and Valmont, of copies of letters to and from third parties, with detailed commentary and analysis of motivation and circumstances of character and composition. This commentary often completely changes the interpretation that must be given to individual passages or entire letters. One particularly titillating example is letter 48, written by Valmont to Madame de Tourvel. A naïve reader, such as Madame de Tourvel, sees in it nothing but Valmont's agitated state of mind, owing to his professed passion for his correspondent. In letter 47, however, Valmont sends the letter to Madame de Merteuil, who will post it for him from Paris, to preserve a pretense of his remaining in that city. Merteuil and the outside reader are informed that the letter was written on the back of a prostitute, the composition interrupted for intercourse, and that it gives an exact accounting of Valmont's situation and conduct in ambiguous terms. Thus when Valmont says, "The very table on which I write to you, consecrated for the first time to this use, becomes for me the sacred altar of love," the meaning is changed beyond recognition by the added information.

The reading and answering of letters are stressed as acts of self-engagement in the relations of the characters. Valmont sees the future success of his seduction in Madame de Tourvel's first reply to one of his letters; he sees its near accomplishment in the discovery that all his letters have been saved, even while the lady virtuously denies him any other sign of weakening. Several letters are dictated by one character to another, and the final letter with which Valmont must break Madame de Tourvel's heart, in order to fulfill his agreements with Merteuil, is copied verbatim from a model supplied in Merteuil's letter 141.

The chain of events by which all the letters are united in the hands of Madame de Rosemonde, thereby creating the novel text, is a chain of catastrophe. The production of the novel is the destruction of its chief characters. Of the victims, Cécile de Volanges enters a convent, the Chevalier Danceny goes into exile, and Madame de Tourvel dies of humiliation and a broken heart. Valmont is fatally wounded in a duel with Danceny, but as his last act he confides to the young man the packet of letters detailing his own relations with Madame de Merteuil, thus revealing the character of his beautiful and outwardly virtuous confederate. Danceny, after circulating some of these letters, passes the entire packet on to Valmont's elderly aunt, Madame de Rosemonde, the close friend of Madame de Volanges (Cécile's mother) and Madame de Tourvel. Madame de Merteuil herself is cast out of polite society, loses a court case that robs her of her entire fortune, suffers a severe case of smallpox that leaves her horribly disfigured, and finally flees the country, ill and utterly alone but carrying her diamonds with her. Laclos leaves no thread untied, as his bundle of letters is bound into a book.

Dangerous Liaisons opens with a quotation drawn from *The New Héloïse*. In its cynical use of letters as instruments of seduction and betrayal, it destroys the premise of emotional immediacy used to such advantage by Rousseau in his novel. For Saint-Preux, letters are a self-generating system by whose intervention he may always be in the presence of his beloved: "I can no longer separate myself from you, the least absence is unbearable to me, and it is necessary that I either see you or write to you in order to occupy myself with you without ceasing" (letter 11). For Madame de Merteuil, the letter is a tool to be used for definite ends: "What good would it do you to soften hearts with Letters, since you would not be there to profit from it?" (letter 33). Yet in the final analysis, it is through the letters united in the novel that Laclos paints compelling portraits of his characters, not in direct revelations but through the reflections and combinations of the continuing chain of correspondence. Valmont's inner truth finally does correspond with the appearance of love in his first letters to Madame de Tourvel, and it is Madame de Merteuil's letters that convince society of the evil character she had always before been able to conceal.

THE TWENTIETH CENTURY AND LATER

Epistolary novels passed into comparative disuse in the nineteenth and early twentieth centuries. Late in the twentieth century, however, writers of experimental and avant-garde fiction and criticism found the letter form, with its constant self-reflection and accepted freedom from certain formal structures, a tempting medium. Certain writers still used the letter as a form suited for naïve confidences, but, in general, its innocence was lost. In fact, even French deconstructionist critic and philosopher Jacques Derrida toyed with epistolary form in *La Carte postale: De Socrate à Freud et au-delà* (1980; *The Post Card: From Socrates to Freud and Beyond*, 1987), a series of letter texts with dates, direct address, and personal tone—sometimes fiction, sometimes criticism, but never a simple story.

John Barth's monumental work, *Letters* (1979), uses seven epistolary voices, one of them "John Barth," to simultaneously explore personal letters—letters in the sense of literature and letters of the alphabet. *Letters* opens with a formal invitation to "John Barth" to accept the honorary degree of doctor of letters from Marshyhope State University. This formal text from the provost is accompanied by a rambling personal postscript; the provost is also Germaine Pitt, the only female voice of the novel. "Barth" declines the honor but nonetheless launches into a dizzying interweaving of texts, stories, and word plays. The first six letters introduce the separate narrative voices; the seventh (from "John Barth" to "the Reader") belatedly announces the beginning of the novel.

The interrelations of the characters are complex, and this complication is mirrored by the complexity of their letter exchanges. Twice-married Germaine Pitt has been the mistress of a wealthy patron of Marshyhope. Her first husband, André de Castine, may be the alter ego of A. B. Cook VI or may simply be his cousin. A. B. Cook VI may be an extreme political conservative and the poet laureate of Maryland, or he may be André, the father of Germaine's missing son, born to a family of underground revolutionaries. He presents a series of letters that may have been written in the early nineteenth century by his ancestor A. B. Cook IV, a similarly enigmatic character, who may have died in the War of 1812. Germaine is caught up in a passionate affair with Ambrose Mensch, professor at Marshyhope, friend of "John Barth" and adapter of "Barth's" works for a motion picture. The film offers a stage for the novel's actions and reactions, as well as a frame for a debate on the viability of the written word in contrast to cinema.

Letters are written from "John Barth" to all his characters and vice versa, from one character to himself, from Ambrose to an unknown correspondent reached by placing letters in bottles and setting them adrift, from A. B. Cook IV to his unborn children and, after his supposed death, to his "widow," from a son to his dead father, and from "John Barth" to the reader. Letter conventions are scrupulously preserved in the date, salutation, direct address, and frequent reference to composition, means of transmission, and the physical particulars of each letter. One long, revealing letter from Germaine to "John Barth" tells about her affair with Ambrose. Later Germaine writes that a carbon copy of this letter has fallen into the hands of her college president. A digest is made from this carbon copy, and multiple copies are distributed to the trustees of Marshyhope. This doctored document is the pretext on which Germaine and Ambrose are fired from the university; Germaine is displaced for using the techniques of a professional writer on an all-too-personal letter.

In many cases readers are explicitly warned to distrust the identity of the letter writer. In no case are they encouraged to take anything at face value, not even the dates heading the letters or the names at their end. "John Barth" announces that he is writing a novel in which each of the characters is invited to participate; by this ambiguous invitation, he announces that those varied voices are all simultaneously imaginary constructs and separate "real" people. All the letter writers except Germaine are drawn from other works by the actual Barth, a theme that recurs explicitly in their letters. Each of the seven correspondents has a recognizable style and set of issues, and most events are told and retold through more than one narrator. The reader is never allowed to fully identify with the characters, for there is no consistent attempt to foster the illusion that these are "real" people. Few of the letters that form this novel are ever answered by other characters; in a work designed to test whether the epistolary novel can survive in the late twentieth century, the chain of direct response is lost.

The letters in *Letters* are built within an elaborate alphabetical and mathematical framework; value in advancing plot or revealing character is countered by arbitrary number and letter value. This relationship is emphasized by the comments of several characters about recurring events, number structures, and the "anniversary theory of history." Ambrose writes program texts, letters that offer plans for romance to Germaine. His propositions are based on esoteric number and letter puzzles. The film in which the characters are participating, based on the writings of "John Barth," in which they may or may not also have already appeared, repeats and distorts their lives. Letters from Germaine, for example, recount events in her affair with Ambrose that are reenacted for inclusion in the film. Their wedding day and costumes are planned to accommodate the filming of scenes in the motion picture, but Ambrose also enforces a strict schedule of copulation based on the number seven.

As the film spins out of control, the lives of the characters accelerate toward individual crises. In the traditional epistolary novel, the plot is knit together by the final letters; the collection of texts to and from the characters is enough to outline their fate. In *Letters*, the text ends while the most crucial questions remain unanswered. If the pregnant Germaine serves in some ways as a personification of *Letters*, her pregnancy and its outcome are important. However, the reader never learns the outcome of the pregnancy or even if Germaine is really pregnant or if the father is Ambrose or an ambiguous possible rapist. The only part of *Letters* that is satisfactorily brought to completion is the anagram of the title and subtitle built from the alphabetical letters that identify the individual letter texts. In the end, Barth's *Letters* refuses to give an authoritative answer to its own question: Is the epistolary novel still a viable literary form? However, the exuberant complexity of the text, the extravagant experimentation with letter form, and its ambiguities make Barth's work a convincing argument that there is still a long future for the novel of letters.

Indeed, several epistolary novels of note have appeared since *Letters* was published in 1979. Alice Walker's Pulitzer Prize-winning *The Color Purple* (1982) is perhaps the best-known example, told through the diary and letters of the protagonist, Celie, who grows from an abused teenager to a confident and empowered woman. As the novel progresses and Celie matures, the writing also becomes more mature, reflecting her growth. Canadian author Richard B. Wright used the form in *Clara Callan* (2001), about a woman in Ontario, Canada, in the 1930's. Testing the boundaries of the form, Mark Dunn's *Ella Minnow Pea: A Progressively Lipogrammatic Epistolary Fable* (2001) comprises letters and notes sent among the inhabitants of a fictional island, where the government forbids the use of one letter of the alphabet at a time until communication becomes impossible. In 2000, Matt Beaumont published what is considered to be the first "e-mail novel," *E: The Novel of Liars, Lunch, and Lost Knickers*, made up of e-mail correspondence among workers in an advertising office. *Love, Rosie* (2005), by Cecilia Ahern, depicts the friendship between two women through their letters, notes, e-mails, and instant messages.

The epistolary form has also become popular among writers for young adults, adopted by writers including Avi (*Nothing but the Truth*, 1991), John Marsden (*Letters from the Inside*, 1991), Steve Kluger (*Last Days of Summer*, 1998), Stephen Chbosky (*The Perks of Being a Wallflower*, 1999), and Daniel Handler (*Lemony Snicket: The Unauthorized Autobiography*, 2002, and *The Beatrice Letters*, 2006), Lenora Adams (*Baby Girl*, 2007). Beverly Cleary won the 1984 Newbery Medal for her 1963 novel *Dear Mr. Henshaw* (reprinted in 1983), which begins and ends with letters from the main character, Leigh Botts.

Anne W. Sienkewicz
Updated by Cynthia A. Bily

BIBLIOGRAPHY

Altman, Janet Gurkin. *Epistolarity: Approaches to a Form.* Columbus: Ohio State University Press, 1982. Focuses on the nature of the letter text and how it is exploited in epistolary fiction. Examples drawn from the English and French traditions. Many key citations are in French only. Bibliography includes both epistolary works and critical studies.

Beebee, Thomas O. *Epistolary Fiction in Europe, 1500-1850.* New York: Cambridge University Press, 1999. Covers the history of the epistolary novel from the Renaissance to the mid-nineteenth century, with a bibliography on major European epistolary fiction to 1850.

Bower, Anne. *Epistolary Responses: The Letter in Twentieth Century American Fiction and Criticism.* Tuscaloosa: University of Alabama Press, 1997. Innovative study of the letter form in novels and criticism of the twentieth century that explores the paradoxical quality of letters. Texts are analyzed through a feminist lens and include Alice Walker's *The Color Purple*, John Barth's *Letters*, and Jacques Derrida's *The Post Card*.

Bray, Joe. *The Epistolary Novel: Representations of Consciousness.* New York: Routledge, 2003. Argues that the eighteenth century epistolary novel represents consciousness in a way that influenced the later novel. Examines the works of Aphra Behn, Eliza Haywood, Samuel Richardson, Fanny Burney, Charlotte Smith, Jane Austen, and others.

Derrida, Jacques. *The Post Card: From Socrates to Freud and Beyond.* Translated by Alan Bass. Chicago: University of Chicago Press, 1987. Multifaceted deconstructionist meditation on the letter form. Both a novel and a critical genre study, with texts using date, salutation, and signature in letter style. For advanced readers.

Gilroy, Amanda, and W. M. Verhoeven, eds. *Epistolary Histories: Letters, Fiction, Culture.* Charlottesville: University Press of Virginia, 2000. Argues for a reexamination of the "association between the letter and the private sphere." Covering works from the seventeenth century to the late twentieth century, explores the intersection of the epistolary form with discourses on gender, class, politics, and commodification.

Goldsmith, Elizabeth C., ed. *Writing the Female Voice: Essays on Epistolary Literature.* Boston: Northeastern University Press, 1989. Critical look at women's use of the epistolary form, especially as a means to give voice to often-silenced concerns and perspectives.

How, James. *Epistolary Spaces: English Letter Writing from the Foundation of the Post Office to Richardson's "Clarissa."* Burlington, Vt.: Ashgate, 2003. Argues that the development in 1650 of a British post office led to the habit of letter-writing and then to the genre of the epistolary novel.

Kauffman, Linda S. *Special Delivery: Epistolary Modes in Modern Fiction.* Chicago: University of Chicago Press, 1992. Postmodernist and feminist perspective on seven writers, including Vladimir Nabokov, Roland Barthes, Jacques Derrida, Doris Lessing, Alice Walker, and Margaret Atwood, who chronicle the study and dismantling of the epistolary form at the hands of powerful scholars and novelists.

Simon, Sunka. *Mail-orders: The Fiction of Letters in Postmodern Culture.* Albany: State University of New York Press, 2002. Analyzes the work of Peter Handke, Ingeborg Bachmann, John Barth, Friedrich Schlegel, and Jacques Derrida, with a special nod to Edgar Allan Poe's "The Purloined Letter."

Singer, Godfrey Frank. *The Epistolary Novel: Its Origin, Development, Decline, and Residuary Influence.* New York: Russell & Russell, 1963. Dated but remains an excellent source for beginners. Explains the development of the epistolary novel, its wane, and its continuing influence on Western literature.

The Espionage Novel

Espionage—spying on enemies to obtain strategic information—is an age-old practice, but its treatment in fiction did not begin in earnest until the late nineteenth century. With this new theme, writers could begin to explore questions of courage, loyalty, and patriotism against a background of international conflict and intrigue. This combination of factors has proven attractive to readers, who have made many espionage novels best sellers. In time, a few espionage novels—those that explore not only the craft of spying but also what celebrated novelist Graham Greene called the human factor—have gained classic status. Even less successful efforts provide crucial insights into the social, political, and psychological makeup of their troubled times.

Espionage novels traditionally mirror world events. War, impending war, international crises, shifting perceptions of world power and influence, real-life episodes of espionage—all have inspired the durable and popular genre of espionage fiction.

EARLY CLASSICS

The first two decades of the twentieth century saw the appearance of half a dozen significant espionage novels of varying literary worth. The first is Rudyard Kipling's *Kim* (1901), set on the frontier of British India. The novel deals in part with the Great Game, the struggle between the British and Russian empires for control of Central Asia. The novel's engaging Anglo-Indian protagonist Kimball "Kim" O'Hara is an orphan who becomes involved in several aspects of the Great Game. Kim's growth to adulthood allows Kipling, who was born on the subcontinent, to explore a colorful and engaging cross-section of contemporary Indian society.

In the latter part of the nineteenth century, the prospect of war involving two or more of the great European powers fueled a popular genre known as the future war novel. Most examples of the genre have long since been forgotten. However, one—*The Riddle of the Sands: A Record of Secret Service* (1903)—is regarded as a classic of both espionage and sailing fiction. Written by Erskine Childers, the novel is set in the shallow waters off the North Sea coast of Germany and concerns the discovery by two Englishmen, Davies and Carruthers, that the Germans are preparing for a seaborne invasion of Great Britain.

Although Childers intended a serious warning about Britain's vulnerability, he wrote the novel as if it were an adventure, stressing action over character. Polish-born English novelist Joseph Conrad produced an entirely different work a short time later in *The Secret Agent* (1907). Set in London and based on real events, the novel centers on the activities of a slothful and conscienceless anarchist, Adolf Verloc, actually in the pay of the Russian embassy. Ordered to set off an explosion that will be blamed on his fellow revolutionaries, Verloc tricks his slow-witted stepson into planting the bomb—with fatal results. Although many readers were put off by the novel's somber tone and convoluted plot, later writers such as Graham Greene and John le Carré would find its linking of personal and political treachery instructive.

Working largely in the mold of Childers, Scottish writer and public servant John Buchan played a key role in the development of the espionage novel as a popular genre, writing a number of thrilling narratives of escape and pursuit. In *The Thirty-nine Steps* (1915), published during the second year of World War I, his resourceful protagonist Richard Hannay thwarts a plot to steal Britain's naval secrets. In *Greenmantle* (1916), Hannay uncovers the details of a German plot to incite a Muslim uprising in the Middle East that would threaten British India. Buchan subsequently produced several more sequels.

E. Phillips Oppenheim had written prolifically in the future war genre before publishing his masterpiece, *The Great Impersonation* (1920). Most of Oppenheim's works are forgotten, yet *The Great Impersonation* survives because of a strikingly original plot hinging on a double deception.

REALISM AND FANTASY

Later espionage writers emulated Buchan's fast pacing and suspenseful plotting, but most writers rejected his romantic outlook, conservative political attitudes, and unquestioning patriotism. Fellow British writers Greene and Eric Ambler completed the break with the romantic espionage novel, although they retained an interest in international intrigue that had been a hallmark of the future war novelists. The two also shared a more liberal political outlook than their predecessors, as well as deep suspicions of the machinations of powerful governments and what would later be commonly referred to as multinational corporations.

Greene portrayed a Europe sliding toward disaster in his first successful novel, *Stamboul Train: An Entertainment* (1932; also known as *Orient Express: An Entertainment*, 1933). He would continue to set most of his novels abroad, focusing on the world's trouble spots and dealing with geopolitical crises with remarkable prescience. Greene first dealt directly with espionage in *The Ministry of Fear: An Entertainment* (1943), which describes the dilemma of an innocent man who inadvertently involves himself in a spy ring. He returned to the theme of espionage with *Our Man in Havana: An Entertainment* (1958), a farcical take on spying in Cuba before the dictatorship of Fidel Castro, but reserved his fullest treatment for *The Human Factor* (1978), his last major novel. *The Human Factor* describes the fate of a British intelligence agent, Maurice Castle, who supplies classified information to the Soviet Union out of a sense of gratitude to a communist who saved Castle's South African wife and son. (Greene had worked for British intelligence during World War II.) By the time he died in 1991, he was acknowledged as one of the foremost writers of the twentieth century.

Few of Ambler's novels deal directly with spying, and those that do treat it somewhat tangentially. Nevertheless, his practice of examining serious geopolitical issues through exciting narratives helped shape the modern espionage genre. *Epitaph for a Spy* (1938), like Greene's *The Ministry of Fear*, describes the dilemma of an innocent bystander caught up in spying. Ambler's best work came the following year in *A Coffin for Dimitrios* (1939; also published as *The Mask of Dimitrios*), in which another innocent figure, writer Charles Latimer, pieces together the life and career of a sinister Turkish criminal. Latimer's investigations reveal the connections between the seamy criminal underside of contemporary Europe and the supposedly re-

spectable world of high finance. Years later, Ambler produced a sequel with *The Intercom Conspiracy* (1969; also known as *A Quiet Conspiracy*). Here, the dangerously naïve Latimer investigates the publishers of a tiny newsletter beginning to carry classified intelligence—a ruse, it turns out, to blackmail the governments of the countries involved.

Greene and Ambler were both popular writers, but neither achieved the kind of fame enjoyed by Ian Fleming and his most famous creation, James Bond. Bond's first outing was in *Casino Royale* (1953; also known as *You Asked for It: Casino Royale*, 1955), and the spy, code-named Operative 007, would appear in a number of sequels and a seemingly endless series of films. Despite Fleming's popular success, however, he did little to advance the espionage genre, relying instead on a titillating mixture of sex, violence, and upscale gadgetry to sell his books.

THE GOLDEN AGE AND AFTER

In the 1950's and 1960's, a series of sensational disclosures rocked the British espionage establishment and fueled public cynicism about the country's upper-class civil servants. The disclosures involved diplomats Guy Burgess and Donald Maclean and highly placed intelligence officer Harold "Kim" Philby, all of whom were exposed as agents working for the Soviet Union. Apparently tipped off by Philby that they were about to be interrogated, Burgess and Maclean defected to the Soviet Union in 1951; Philby himself followed in 1963. Nicknamed Kim for the title character of Rudyard Kipling's novel, Philby had been Graham Greene's superior in British intelligence. His duplicitous actions and those of his fellow spies inspired a number of novelists and gave rise to a two-decade-long golden age of espionage fiction.

John le Carré's first novel, *Call for the Dead* (1960; also known as *The Deadly Affair*), introduced a resolutely unromantic but highly competent protagonist, George Smiley. The novel attracted little attention, but with *The Spy Who Came in from the Cold* (1963), in which Smiley plays a minor role, le Carré produced a best seller that was also a critical success. The novel dramatizes the agonizing situation of British agent Alec Leamas, who has been tricked into protecting a ruthless

East German intelligence officer (and British mole) while sending the mole's upright colleague to his death.

Although many critics rate *The Spy Who Came in from the Cold* as the best espionage novel, others rate *Tinker, Tailor, Soldier, Spy* (1974) more highly. Here, Smiley returns to a central role, investigating four of his colleagues to determine which one has been leaking classified intelligence to the Soviets. Smiley's relationship with his beloved but adulterous wife, Ann, mirrors the professional challenges he faces. Two more novels, *The Honourable Schoolboy* (1977) and *Smiley's People* (1980), complete a trilogy that le Carré called the Quest for Karla, referring to the cunning (but ultimately human) Soviet spymaster who Smiley defeats in the final novel.

Le Carré took up the Palestinian-Israeli conflict in *The Little Drummer Girl* (1983) but returned to the world of Cold War politics in *A Perfect Spy* (1986). After the end of the Cold War, he wrote about a wider range of geopolitical subjects but did not neglect the complex and often tortured psychology of his characters.

Len Deighton's first novel, *The Ipcress File* (1962), introduced a hard-boiled British agent working for the imaginary intelligence agency WOOC(P). Whatever its ostensible purpose, WOOC(P) operates like many other bureaucracies; its leaders are intent on protecting their domains and infighting is rife. The bafflingly complex plot of *The Ipcress File* hinges on the cynical machinations of a double agent, yet the gritty realism of its details harks back to the work of W. Somerset Maugham. Deighton followed with *Horse Under Water* (1963) and *Funeral in Berlin* (1964). The latter is generally acknowledged as his best early novel and signals his first use of the divided German city of Berlin as a setting and metaphor for the ambiguities and vexed loyalties of the Cold War. Deighton wrote five more books for the series.

In the 1980's, Deighton began a series of nine novels featuring agent Bernard Samson and written in a more realistic vein. *Berlin Game* (1983), *Mexico Set* (1984), and *London Match* (1985) breathed new life into what had become by then an overly familiar theme—the penetration of the British intelligence services by a mole. However, the remaining two trilogies in the series failed to live up to the promise of the opening novels.

Most espionage novelists have been British. One American writer, Alan Furst, produced the first in a line of acclaimed espionage novels with *Night Soldiers* in 1988. Furst set his novels before and during World War II, writing about the difficult choices of those caught up in that dark conflict. Historical novels about espionage existed before Furst set out to write his own, but Furst's success suggested a new direction for the genre.

Grove Koger

BIBLIOGRAPHY

Ambrosetti, Ronald J. *Eric Ambler*. New York: Twayne, 1994. Comprehensive and sympathetic treatment of Ambler's writings. Includes a chronology and primary and secondary bibliographies.

Aronoff, Myron J. *The Spy Novels of John le Carré: Balancing Ethics and Politics*. New York: St. Martin's Press, 1999. Exhaustive analysis arguing that le Carré treats espionage as a metaphor for politics. Includes thumbnail biographies of le Carré's characters, detailed notes, and excellent primary and secondary bibliographies.

Bergonzi, Bernard. *A Study in Greene: Graham Greene and the Art of the Novel*. New York: Oxford University Press, 2006. Analysis by a major critic arguing that Greene's later novels, including *The Human Factor*, are examples of good storytelling but inferior to his earlier works. Rejects efforts by recent biographers to interpret Greene's writings through the details of his life.

Hepburn, Allan. *Intrigue: Espionage and Culture*. New Haven, Conn.: Yale University Press, 2005. Consideration of the spy novel as developed by genre writers and adapted by such noted mainstream novelists as Elizabeth Bowen and John Banville. Includes an extensive bibliography.

Hitz, Frederick Porter. *The Great Game: The Myths and Reality of Espionage*. New York: Alfred A. Knopf, 2004. A former Central Intelligence Agency officer compares espionage in fact and fiction, finding that the former is indeed stranger. Includes extensive endnotes.

Milward-Oliver, Edward. *The Len Deighton Companion*. London: Grafton, 1987. Alphabetical compendium of entries summarizing plots and identifying characters, settings, organizations, and miscellaneous references in Deighton's novels. Includes a long interview with Deighton and a detailed primary bibliography.

Panek, LeRoy L. *The Special Branch: The British Spy Novel, 1890-1980.* Bowling Green, Ohio: Bowling Green State University Popular Press, 1981. A history of the British espionage novel, through the earlier novels of John le Carré. Dated but essential to understanding the evolution of the genre.

Strout, Cushing. "John Buchan and the Great Game." *Sewanee Review* 114, no. 1 (Winter, 2006): 139-143. Analyzes Buchan's use of the espionage theme as a metaphor and discusses his influence on a wide range of later writers.

Winder, Simon. *The Man Who Saved Britain: A Personal Journey into the Disturbing World of James Bond.* New York: Farrar, Straus and Giroux, 2006. Argues that the popularity of Ian Fleming's James Bond character came at a time when Britain saw a war-weary and dispirited population.

Woods, Brett F. *Neutral Ground: A Political History of Espionage Fiction.* New York: Algora, 2008. Examines the manner in which contemporary international events have shaped the writings of such novelists as Kipling, Maugham, Greene, and le Carré. Includes a bibliography.

Experimental Long Fiction

Literature is forever transforming. A new literary age is new precisely because its important writers do things differently from their predecessors. Thus, it could be said that almost all significant literature is in some sense innovative or experimental at its inception but inevitably becomes, over time, conventional. Regarding long fiction, however, the situation is a bit more complex.

It is apparent that, four centuries after Miguel de Cervantes wrote what is generally recognized the first important novel, *Don Quixote de la Mancha* (1605, 1615), readers have come to accept a certain type of long fiction as most conventional and to regard significant departures from this type as experimental. This most conventional variety is the novel of realism as practiced by nineteenth century giants such as Gustave Flaubert, Leo Tolstoy, Charles Dickens, and George Eliot.

The first task in surveying contemporary experiments in long fiction, therefore, is to determine what "conventional" means in reference to the novel of realism. Most nineteenth century novelists considered fiction to be an imitative form; that is, it presents in words a representation of reality. The underlying assumption of these writers and their readers was that there is a shared single reality, perceived by all—unless they are mad, ill, or hallucinatory—in a similar way. This reality is largely external and objectively verifiable. Time is orderly and moves forward. The novel that reflects this view of reality is equally orderly and accountable. The point of view is frequently, though not always, omniscient (all-knowing): The narrators understand all and tell their readers all they need to know to understand a given situation. The virtues of this variety of fiction are clarity of description and comprehensiveness of analysis.

After reading Flaubert's *Madame Bovary* (1857; English translation, 1886), one can be confident that he or she knows something about Emma Bovary's home, village, and manner of dress; knows her history, her motivations, and the way she thought; and knows what others thought of her. Not knowing would be a gap in the record; not knowing would mean, according to standards against which readers have judged "conventional" novels, a failure of the author.

Modernism and its followers

Early in the twentieth century, a disparate group of novelists now generally referred to as modernists—James Joyce, Virginia Woolf, William Faulkner, Franz Kafka, Marcel Proust, and others—experimented with or even abandoned many of the most hallowed conventions of the novel of realism. These experiments were motivated by an altered perception of reality. Whereas the nineteenth century assumption was that reality is external, objective, and measurable, the modernists believed reality to be also internal, subjective, and dependent upon context. Reflecting these changing assumptions about reality, point of view in the modernist novel becomes more often limited, shifting, and even unreliable rather than omniscient.

This subjectivity reached its apogee in one of the great innovations of modernism, the point-of-view technique dubbed "stream of consciousness," which plunges the reader into a chaos of thoughts arrayed on the most tenuous of organizing principles—or so it must have seemed to the early twentieth century audience accustomed to the orderly fictional worlds presented by the nineteenth century masters.

Once reality is acknowledged to be inner and subjective, all rules about structure in the novel are abandoned. The most consistent structuring principle of premodernist novelists—the orderly progression of time—was rejected by many modernists. Modern novels do not "progress" through time in the conventional sense; instead, they follow the inner, subjective, shifting logic of a character's thoughts. Indeed, the two great innovations of modernist fiction—stream of consciousness and nonchronological structure—are inseparable in the modern novel.

Among the most famous and earliest practitioners of these techniques were Joyce (especially *Ulysses*, 1922, and *Finnegans Wake*, 1939), Woolf (especially *Jacob's Room*, 1922; *Mrs. Dalloway*, 1925; and *To the Lighthouse*, 1927), and Faulkner (especially *The Sound and the Fury*, 1929; *As I Lay Dying*, 1930). Many of the experimental works of post-World War II long fiction extended these techniques, offering intensely subjective narrative voices and often extreme forms of stream of consciousness, including disruptions of orderly time sequences.

In *La traición de Rita Hayworth* (1968; *Betrayed by Rita Hayworth*, 1971), Manuel Puig employs (among other techniques) the words of several sets of characters in different rooms of a house without identifying the speakers or providing transitions to indicate a change in speaker. The effect may be experienced by the reader as a strange solipsistic cacophony, or something like a disjointed choral voice; in fact, the technique is a variation on stream of consciousness and not so very different from the tangle of interior monologues in Faulkner's novels.

Tim O'Brien's novel of the Vietnam War, *Going After Cacciato* (1978, revised 1989), is another example of a work that makes fresh use of a modernist strategy. Here, reality at first seems more external and hence clearer than in *Betrayed by Rita Hayworth*. The bulk of the action concerns a rifle squad that follows a deserter, Cacciato, out of Vietnam and across Asia and Europe until he is finally surrounded in Paris, where he once again escapes. The chapters that make up this plot, however, are interspersed with generally shorter chapters recounting the experiences of the point-of-view character, Paul Berlin, at home and in Vietnam. In another set of short chapters, Berlin waits out a six-hour guard shift in an observation post by the sea. The most orderly part of the novel is the pursuit of Cacciato, which moves logically through time and place. The perceptive reader eventually realizes, however, that the pursuit of Cacciato is a fantasy conjured up by Berlin, whose "real" reality is the six hours in the observation post, where his thoughts skip randomly from the present to the past (in memories) to a fantasy world. As in the best modernist tradition, then, the structure of *Going After Cacciato* reflects an inner, subjective reality.

The post-World War II writer who most famously and provocatively continued the modernist agenda in long fiction was Samuel Beckett, especially in his trilogy: *Molloy* (1951; English translation, 1955), *Malone meurt* (1951; *Malone Dies*, 1956), and *L'Innommable* (1953; *The Unnamable*, 1958). In each successive novel, external reality recedes as the narrative voice becomes more inward-looking. In *Molloy*, for example, the title character searches for his mother, but he is lost from the

beginning. He can find neither her (if she truly exists) nor his way back home, wherever that is—nor can he be sure even of the objective reality of recent experience. In one passage Molloy notes that he stayed in several rooms with several windows, but then he immediately conjectures that perhaps the several windows were really only one, or perhaps they were all in his head. The novel is filled with "perhapses" and "I don't knows," undermining the reader's confidence in Beckett's words.

The subjectivity and uncertainty are intensified in *Malone Dies*. At least in *Molloy*, the protagonist was out in the world, lost in a countryside that appears to be realistic, even if it is more a mindscape than a convincing geographic location. In *Malone Dies*, the protagonist spends most of his days immobile in what he thinks is a hospital, but beyond this nothing—certainly not space or time—is clear. As uncertain of their surroundings as Molloy and Malone are, they are fairly certain of their own reality; the unnamed protagonist of the final volume of the trilogy, *The Unnamable*, does not know his reality. His entire labyrinthine interior monologue is an attempt to find an identity for himself and a definition of his world, the one depending upon the other. In those attempts, however, he fails, and at no time does the reader have a confident sense of time and place in reference to the protagonist and his world.

THE NEW NOVEL

With *The Unnamable*, long fiction may seem to have come a great distance from the modernist novel, but in fact Beckett was continuing the modernist practice of locating reality inside a limited and increasingly unreliable consciousness. Eventually, voices cried out against the entire modernist enterprise. Among the earliest and most vocal of those calling for a new fiction—for *le nouveau roman*, or a new novel—was a group of French avant-garde writers who became known as the New Novelists. However, as startlingly innovative as their fiction may at first appear, they often were following in the footsteps of the very modernists they rejected.

Among the New Novelists (sometimes to their dismay) were Michel Butor, Nathalie Sarraute, and Claude Simon. Even though Simon won the Nobel Prize in Literature, probably the most famous (or infamous) of the New Novelists was Alain Robbe-Grillet.

Robbe-Grillet decried what he regarded as outmoded realism and set forth the program for a new fiction in his *Pour un nouveau roman* (1963; *For a New Novel: Essays on Fiction*, 1965). His own career might offer the best demonstration of the movement from old to new. His first published novel, *Les Gommes* (1953; *The Erasers*, 1964), while hardly Dickensian, was not radically innovative. With *Le Voyeur* (1955; *The Voyeur*, 1958), however, his work took a marked turn toward the experimental, and with *La Jalousie* (1957; *Jealousy*, 1959) and *Dans le labyrinthe* (1959; *In the Labyrinth*, 1960), the New Novel came to full flower.

The most famous technical innovation of the New Novelists was the protracted and obsessive descriptions of objects—a tomato slice or box on a table or a picture on a wall—often apparently unrelated to theme or plot. The use of this device led some critics to speak of the "objective" nature of the New Novel, as if the technique offered the reader a sort of photographic clarity. On the contrary, in the New Novel, little is clear in a conventional sense. Robbe-Grillet fills his descriptions with "perhapses" and "apparentlys" along with other qualifiers, and the objects become altered or metamorphosed over time. After Robbe-Grillet's early novels, time is rarely of the conventional earlier-to-later variety but instead jumps and loops and returns.

One example of the transforming nature of objects occurs in *The Voyeur*, when a man on a boat peers obsessively at the figure-eight scar left by an iron ring flapping against a seawall. Over the course of the novel the figure-eight pattern becomes a cord in a salesman's suitcase, two knotholes side by side on a door, a bicycle, a highway sign, two stacks of plates, and so on—in more than a dozen incarnations. Moreover, Robbe-Grillet's objects are not always as "solid." A painting on a wall (*In the Labyrinth*) or a photograph in a newspaper lying in the gutter (*La Maison de rendez-vous*, 1965; English translation, 1966) may become "animated" as the narrative eye enters it, and the action will transpire in what was, a paragraph before, only ink on paper or paint on canvas.

Such techniques indeed seemed radically new, far afield of the novels of Joyce and Faulkner. However, it is generally the case with the New Novelists, especially with Robbe-Grillet, that this obsessive looking, these

distortions and uncertainties and transformations imposed on what might otherwise be real surfaces, have their origins in a narrative consciousness that warps reality according to its idiosyncratic way of seeing. The point-of-view character of *In the Labyrinth* is a soldier who is likely feverish and dying; in *The Voyeur*, a psychotic murderer; in *Jealousy*, a jealous husband who quite possibly has committed an act of violence or contemplates doing so. In all cases the reader has even more trouble arriving at definitive conclusions than is the case with the presumably very difficult novels of Joyce and Faulkner.

Ultimately, the New Novelists' program differs in degree more than in kind from the modernist assumption that reality is subjective and that fictional structures should reflect that subjectivity. As famous and frequently discussed as the New Novelists have been, their fiction has had relatively little influence beyond France, and when literary theorists define "postmodernism" (that is, the literary expression that has emerged after, and is truly different from, modernism), they rarely claim the New Novel as postmodern.

METAFICTION

A far more significant departure from modernism occurred when writers began to reject the notion that had been dominant among novelists since Miguel de Cervantes: that it is the chief duty of the novelist to be realistic, and the more realistic the fiction the worthier it is. This breakthrough realization—that realism of whatever variety is no more than a preference for a certain set of conventions—manifests itself in different ways in fiction. In metafiction, also known as self-mimesis or self-referential fiction, the author (or his or her persona), deliberately reminds the reader that the book is a written entity; in the traditional novel, however, the reader is asked to suspend his or her disbelief.

Often the metafictive impulse appears as little more than an intensification of the first-person-omniscient narrator, the "intrusive author" disparaged by Henry James but favored by many nineteenth century writers. Rather than employing an "I" without an identity, as in William Makepeace Thackeray's *Vanity Fair: A Novel Without a Hero* (1847-1848), metafiction makes clear that the "I" is the novel's author. Examples of this technique include the novels of José Donoso in *Casa de campo* (1978; *A House in the Country*, 1984) and of Luisa Valenzuela in *Cola de lagartija* (1983; *The Lizard's Tail*, 1983).

In other novels, the metafictive impulse is more radical and transforming. When Donald Barthelme stops the action halfway through *Snow White* (1967), for example, and requires the reader to answer a fifteen-question quiz on the foregoing, the readers' ability to "lose themselves" in the novel's virtual world is hopelessly and hilariously destroyed. Another witty but vastly different metafictive novel is Italo Calvino's *Se una notte d'inverno un viaggiatore* (1979; *If on a Winter's Night a Traveler*, 1981), in which the central character, Cavedagna, purchases a novel called *If on a Winter's Night a Traveler* by an author named "Italo Calvino." Cavedagna finds that his copy is defective: The first thirty-two pages are repeated again and again, and the text is not even that of Calvino; it is instead the opening of a Polish spy novel. The remainder of the book concerns Cavedagna's attempts to find the rest of the spy novel, his blossoming romance with a woman on the same mission, and a rambling intrigue Calvino would surely love to parody had he not invented it. Furthermore, the novel is constructed around a number of openings of other novels that never, for a variety of reasons, progress past the first few pages.

Metafiction is used to represent the impossibility of understanding the global world, particularly the complexity of politics and economics. Critically acclaimed metafictive novels include Australian Peter Carey's *Illywhacker* (1985), American Mark Z. Danielewski's *House of Leaves* (2000), Canadian Yann Martel's *Life of Pi* (2001), and South-African Nobel laureate J. M. Coetzee's *Slow Man* (2005). Junot Díaz won the Pulitzer Prize and the National Book Critics Circle Award for his first novel, *The Brief Wondrous Life of Oscar Wao* (2007). The novel is ostensibly a love story about a Dominican American man in New Jersey, but through a series of extended footnotes and asides the narrator relates and comments on the history of the brutal dictatorship of Rafael Trujillo in the Dominican Republic. The novel has different narrators and settings, as well as occasional messages from the author, and is filled with wordplay and lively slang in English and Spanish.

FICTION-AS-ARTIFICE

One might well ask if metafiction is not too narrow an endeavor to define an age (for example, postmodernism). The answer would be yes, even *If on a Winter's Night a Traveler*, for example, might more properly be described as a novel whose subject is reading a novel rather than writing one. Metafiction is best considered one variation of a broader, more pervasive impulse in post-World War II long fiction: fiction-as-artifice. Rather than narrowly focusing on the process of writing fiction (metafiction), in fiction-as-artifice the author directly attacks the conventions of realism or acknowledges that all writing is a verbal construct bearing the most tenuous relationship to actuality.

One of the earliest examples of fiction-as-artifice in the post-World War II canon is Raymond Queneau's *Exercices de style* (1947; *Exercises in Style*, 1958). The title states where Queneau's interests lie: in technique and in the manipulation of language, rather than in creating an illusion of reality. The book comprises ninety-nine variations on a brief scene between two strangers on a Parisian bus. In each retelling of the incident, Queneau uses a different dialect or style ("Notation" and "Litotes"). The almost endless replication of the single scene forces the reader to see that scene as a verbal construct rather than an approximation of reality. Such "pure" manifestations of fiction-as-artifice as *Exercises in Style* are relatively rare. More often, fiction-as-artifice is a gesture employed intermittently, side by side with realist techniques. The interplay of the two opposing strategies create a delightful aesthetic friction.

One of the most famous and provocative examples of fiction-as-artifice is Vladimir Nabokov's *Pale Fire* (1962). The structure of the work belies all traditional conventions of the novel. *Pale Fire* opens with an "editor's" introduction, followed by a long poem, hundreds of pages of annotations, and an index. The reader discovers, however, that this apparatus tells a hilarious and moving story of political intrigue, murder, and madness. Does *Pale Fire*, ultimately, underscore the artifices of fiction or, instead, demonstrate how resilient is the writer's need to tell a story and the reader's need to read one? Either way, *Pale Fire* is one of the most inventive and fascinating novels of any genre.

The same questions could be asked of Julio Cortázar's *Rayuela* (1963; *Hopscotch*, 1966), a long novel comprising scores of brief, numbered sections, which, the reader is advised in the introductory "Instructions," can be read in a number of ways: in the order presented, in a different numbered sequence suggested by the author, or perhaps, if the reader prefers, by "hopscotching" through the novel.

A similar strategy is employed in Milorad Pavić's *Hazarski rečnik: Roman leksikon u 100,000 reči* (1984; *Dictionary of the Khazars: A Lexicon Novel in 100,000 Words*, 1988). The work is constructed as a dictionary with many brief sections, alphabetized by heading and richly cross-referenced. The reader may read the work from beginning to end, alphabetically, or may follow the cross-references. An added inventive complication is the *Dictionary of the Khazars*'s two volumes, one "male" and the other "female." The volumes are identical except for one brief passage, which likely alters the reader's interpretation of the whole.

Although fiction-as-artifice is European in origin—indeed, it can be traced back to Laurence Sterne's *Tristram Shandy* (1759-1767)—its most inventive and varied practitioner is the American writer John Barth. In work after work, Barth employs, parodies, and lays bare for the reader's contemplation the artifices of fiction.

In his unified collection *Lost in the Funhouse* (1968), for example, Barth narrates the history—from conception through maturity and decline—of a man, of humankind, and of fiction itself. The story's telling, however, highlights the artificiality of writing. The first selection (it cannot be called a "story") of the novel, "Frame Tale," is a single, incomplete sentence—"Once upon a time there was a story that began"—which is designed to be cut out and pasted together to form a Möbius strip. When assembled, the strip leads to the complete yet infinite and never-ending sentence "Once upon a time there was a story that began Once upon a time. . . ." The novel's title story, "Lost in the Funhouse," contains graphs illustrating the story's structure. "Glossolalia" is formed from six brief sections all written in the rhythms of the Lord's Prayer. In "Menelaid," the dialogue is presented in a dizzying succession of quotation marks within quotation marks within quotation marks. Barth's experiments in *Lost in the Funhouse* are continued and intensified in later novels, especially *Chimera* (1972) and *Letters* (1979).

In *The Broom of the System* (1987) by David Foster Wallace, the protagonist, Lenore Stonecipher Beadsman, feels sometimes that she is just a character in a novel. Wallace's *Infinite Jest* (1996) is a massive work about a future North America where people become so engrossed in watching a film called *Infinite Jest* that they lose all interest in other activities. Wallace's fiction moves back and forth in time without warning and combines wordplay, long sentences, footnotes and endnotes, transcripts, and acronyms to create a disjointed postmodern language.

Mark Dunn's *Ella Minnow Pea: A Progressively Lipogrammatic Epistolary Fable* (2001) is an epistolary novel about a fictional island off the coast of South Carolina, where the government forbids the use of one letter of the alphabet, at a given time; in effect, the government is parsing the alphabet. The novel is a collection of letters and notes from inhabitants, often less than a page in length, written with a diminishing set of alphabet letters.

FICTION OR NONFICTION?

Even at his most experimental, however, Barth never abandons his delight in storytelling. Indeed, virtually all the long fiction addressed thus far show innovations in certain technical strategies but do not substantially challenge the reader's concept of what is "fictional." A number of other writers, however, while not always seeming so boldly experimental in technique, have blurred the distinctions between fiction and nonfiction and thus perhaps represent a more fundamental departure from the conventional novel.

The new journalists—such as Truman Capote (*In Cold Blood*, 1966), Norman Mailer (*The Armies of the Night: History as a Novel, the Novel as History*, 1968), Tom Wolfe (*The Electric Kool-Aid Acid Test*, 1968), and Hunter S. Thompson with his Fear and Loathing series (beginning in 1972)—blur the lines between fiction and nonfiction by using novelistic techniques to report facts. However, the subtitle of Mailer's work notwithstanding, the reader rarely is uncertain what side of the fiction-nonfiction line these authors occupy. The same cannot be said for Don DeLillo (*Libra*, 1988). For his interpretation of the Kennedy assassination, DeLillo spent countless hours researching the voluminous reports of the

Warren Commission and other historical documents. With this factual material as the basis for the novel and with assassin Lee Harvey Oswald as the central character, the degree to which *Libra* can be considered fictional as opposed to nonfictional remains a challenging question.

The question is even more problematic in reference to Maxine Hong Kingston's *The Woman Warrior: Memoirs of a Girlhood Among Ghosts* (1976). Kingston conducted her research for her memoir not in library stacks but by plumbing her own memory, especially of stories told her by her mother. At times, Kingston not only is imaginatively enhancing reconstructed scenes but also is inventing details. Is this a work of autobiography or a kind of fiction?

Publishers had trouble classifying Nicholson Baker's *The Mezzanine* (1988) and W. G. Sebald's *Die Ausgewanderten* (1992; *The Emigrants*, 1996). The reader is fairly certain that the point-of-view character in *The Mezzanine* is fictional, but in what sense is his experience fictional? The work, made up of essaylike contemplations of whatever the persona's eye falls on as he goes about his business on a mezzanine, recalls in some ways the intensely detailed descriptions of the New Novelists but with even less of an apparent conflict or movement toward climax one expects in fiction.

Sebald's work is in some ways even odder. His short biographies of a selection of dislocated Europeans have a documentary feel—complete with photographs. The photographs, however, have a vagueness about them that makes them seem almost irrelevant to their subjects, and the reader has the uneasy impression that the book may well be a fabrication.

The distinction between fiction and nonfiction was brought into new relief in 2003, when James Frey published *A Million Little Pieces*, his memoir of escaping drug addiction. The memoir was aggressively gritty in its detail of the author's struggles, and Frey was widely praised for his courage and honesty in revealing his own mistakes and weaknesses. In 2005 the book was named to Oprah's Book Club, and soon after topped nonfiction best-seller lists. In 2006, however, much of the material in the "memoir" was found to have been fabricated. The resulting clamor from talk-show host Oprah Winfrey, Frey's publishers, and readers led to a lively and interesting public debate over art and truth. Frey claimed that the work presented the "essential truth" of his life. Many readers continued to value the book as an honest accounting of what life is like for some addicts, but readers who felt that they had been defrauded were offered a refund. The Brooklyn Public Library, for example, moved the book to its fiction section.

Just as Baker and Sebald call into question what earlier generations would have thought too obvious to debate—the difference between fiction and nonfiction—one consistent impulse among experimenters in long fiction has been the question, What is necessary in fiction and what is merely conventional? Their efforts to test this question have brought readers some of the most provocative and entertaining works of fiction in the late twentieth and early twenty-first centuries.

Dennis Vannatta
Updated by Cynthia A. Bily

BIBLIOGRAPHY

Currie, Mark, ed. *Metafiction*. London: Longman, 1995. Collection of articles on experimental themes and techniques.

Friedman, Ellen G., and Miriam Fuchs, eds. *Breaking the Sequence: Women's Experimental Fiction*. Princeton, N.J.: Princeton University Press, 1989. Comprehensive study of women's English-language experimental fiction of the twentieth century. Includes an introductory chapter, followed by essays on various authors.

Levitt, Morton. *The Rhetoric of Modernist Fiction from a New Point of View*. Hanover, N.H.: University Press of New England, 2006. Accessible response to Wayne C. Booth's classic *The Rhetoric of Fiction* (1983) that considers point of view in modernist and postmodernist fiction, including novels by James Joyce, Virginia Woolf, Philip Roth, Don DeLillo, and Jose Saramago.

McHale, Brian. *Postmodernist Fiction*. 1987. New ed. New York: Routledge, 2004. Examines the theory and practice of writers such as Samuel Beckett, Alain Robbe-Grillet, and Vladimir Nabokov. Considered necessary reading for any study of postmodernist fiction.

Robbe-Grillet, Alain. *For a New Novel: Essays on Fic-*

tion. 1965. New ed. Translated by Richard Howard. Evanston, Ill.: Northwestern University Press, 1996. Single best statement, now a classic, on the aesthetic and philosophical assumptions underlying the New Novel, by the movement's highly influential writer and critic.

Seltzer, Alvin J. *Chaos in the Novel: The Novel in Chaos*. New York: Schocken Books, 1974. Addresses the chaos that seems to lie at the end of so many experimental novelists' search for truth. Traces the roots of contemporary experimentation to not only modernists but also nineteenth and eighteenth century writers.

Shiach, Morag, ed. *The Cambridge Companion to the Modernist Novel*. New York: Cambridge University Press, 2007. Essays explaining the concept of modernism and its influence on the novel. Detailed examination of works by writers from various countries, all influenced by the modernist movement. Includes a detailed chronology (1890-1945).

Waugh, Patricia. *Metafiction: The Theory and Practice of Self-Conscious Fiction*. New York: Routledge, 2005. Focuses on contemporary metafiction in Great Britain and the United States. Examines the factors that determine how certain works are judged to be metafiction.

THE FANTASY NOVEL

The term "fantasy" refers to all works of fiction that attempt neither the realism of the realistic novel nor the "conditional realism" of science fiction. Among modern critics, the primacy of the realistic novel is taken for granted. Realistic novels not only describe normality but also constitute the normal kind of fiction; fantasy, in dealing with the supernatural, seems to be almost perverse. Prior to the rise of the novel in the eighteenth century, however, this was far from being the case. Prose forms such as the imaginary voyage, the dialogue, and satire blurred even the basic distinction between fiction and nonfiction, let alone that between "realistic" and "fantastic" subject matter. The separation of realistic and fantastic began not with the casting out of fantastic genres from the literary mainstream, but rather with the withdrawal of a realistic genre—the novel—from a mainstream that had easily accommodated fantastic motifs.

EIGHTEENTH AND NINETEENTH CENTURIES

To speak of the "fantasy novel" in the context of the eighteenth century comes close to committing a contradiction in terms: Novels were about life as it was lived and had left behind the conventions of allegory and fable along with the decorations of the marvelous and the magical. It is arguable, though, that the withdrawal left behind a connecting spectrum of ambiguous works, and—more important—that it soon led to some important reconnections. Jonathan Swift's use of the techniques of narrative realism in his chronicling of the imaginary voyages of Lemuel Gulliver gave to his work a crucial modernity that is responsible for its still being widely read and enjoyed today.

The rise of the gothic novel in the last decades of the eighteenth century, in connection with the emergence of the Romantic movement that spread from Germany to France, England, and the United States, represents a definite reaction against the advancement of literary realism. The gothic novel, indeed, is almost an "antinovel" of its day, substituting a fascination with the ancient for a preoccupation with the modern, an interest in the bizarre for an obsession with the everyday, an exaltation of the mysterious for a concern with the intelligible, a celebration of the barbaric for a smug appreciation of the civilized. From the standpoint of today, the gothic can be seen to have been subversive in several different ways. It was subversive in a literary context because it opposed the dominant trend toward the development of the modern realistic novel. It was subversive in a sociological context because it reflected the fact that the values of the ancien régime were under stress and that the decadence of that regime was symptomatic of its imminent dissolution. It was subversive in a psychological context because it provided a parable of the impotence of the conscious mind to complete its oppressive victory over the forces of the unconscious, whose imprisonment could never be total.

Gothic novels dealt with strange events in strange environments, organized around the passions of the protagonists. The passions were frequently illicit in a perfectly straightforward sense, often involving incest and the breaking of sacred vows, but the more careful and controlled gothics—the archetypal example is *The Mysteries of Udolpho* (1794), by Ann Radcliffe—emphasized the extent to which the trend toward a less permissive morality would eventually rule, especially in England.

With the exception of the gothic novels, few of the products of the Romantic rebellion were cast in the form of long prose narratives. Short stories were produced in much greater quantity, and the evolution of the short story in Europe and America is closely intertwined with the Romantic reaction against realism and classicism. Poetry, too, was affected dramatically. Even the gothic novel underwent a rapid decline—not into nonexistence but into inconsequential crudeness. After the appearance, in 1824, of James Hogg's *The Private Memoirs and Confessions of a Justified Sinner*—a masterpiece of psychological terror involving paranoid delusions—there followed a long period in which gothic romance was primarily associated with the lowest stratum of the literary marketplace: with the partworks and "penny dreadfuls" marketed for the newly literate inhabitants of the industrial towns. Such interminable narratives as

Varney the Vampyre (1847), by James Malcolm Rymer, and *Wagner the Wehr-Wolf* (1846-1847), by G. M. W. Reynolds, achieved considerable success in their own time but have little to offer modern readers.

Although the gothic novel was primarily a species of horror story, its supernatural trappings did overflow into moralistic fantasies that might be comic extravaganzas, such as James Dalton's *The Gentleman in Black* (1831) and *The Invisible Gentleman* (1833), or earnest parables, such as John Sterling's *The Onyx Ring* (1839). The themes of these novels—tricky deals with the devil, invisibility, wish-granting rings, and personality exchange—were to become the staples of what Nathan Drake had called "sportive gothic," while curses, ghosts, vampires, and madness remained the characteristic motifs of "gloomy gothic."

The writers who produced the most notable works of fantasy in the middle of the nineteenth century—including Edgar Allan Poe and Nathaniel Hawthorne in the United States, George MacDonald and William Gilbert in England, and Théophile Gautier and Charles Nodier in France—primarily worked in the short-story medium. The novels written by these authors often have fantastic embellishments, but for the most part they pay far more heed to the restraints of conventional realism than do these authors' short stories.

VICTORIAN ERA

The revival of the fantasy novel in the last two decades of the nineteenth century was associated with several trends that can be traced through the fiction of the twentieth century. The partial eclipse of substantial work in fantastic fiction in the mid-nineteenth century is clearly related to the repressive morality of that period—it is notable that in France, where the repression was less effective than in Great Britain, the United States, and Germany, the Romantic heritage was more effectively conserved. It is possible, in consequence, to see the various threads of the revival in terms of reactions against and attempts to escape from that repression.

During this repressive period, indulgence in fantasy came to be seen as a kind of laxity: It was in the Victorian era that the notion of escapism was born. An exception was made in the case of children's literature (though even here there was a period when fantasy was frowned

upon), and there eventually arose in Britain a curious convention whereby fantasies were considered suitable reading for Christmas, when a little token indulgence might be overlooked, an idea that led to the emphasis on fantasy in the Christmas annuals to which Charles Dickens and William Makepeace Thackeray contributed. Such writers as Thackeray, MacDonald, and Lewis Carroll brought to the writing of books nominally aimed at children an artistry and seriousness that commended them to the attention of adults and helped to open a space for the production of fantastic novels within the British literary marketplace.

Another form of fantastic fiction that became to some extent associated with the British Christmas annuals was the ghost story, which became extremely popular in the 1880's and remained so for half a century, during which virtually all the classic British work in that genre was done. There is, however, something intrinsically anecdotal about ghost stories that keeps them more or less confined to short fiction. Though there have been some excellent novellas, there have never been more than half a dozen outstanding ghost novels. Joseph Sheridan Le Fanu, who stands at the head of the line of British ghost-story writers, produced several neogothic novels, but almost all of them are so ponderous as to be nearly unreadable. M. R. James wrote only short stories, and Algernon Blackwood's novels have not worn nearly as well as his shorter pieces.

The Victorian interest in ghosts, however, went far beyond the traffic in thrilling anecdotes. The influence of such contemporary fads as spiritualism and Theosophy sparked a new interest in the occult that began to be reflected quite prolifically in literary production. The great majority of the spiritualist fantasies of communication with the dead and accounts of the afterlife supposedly dictated by the dead through mediums are wholly inconsequential in literary terms, despite the eventual involvement in such movements of writers of ability, such as Arthur Conan Doyle. They did, however, lay important groundwork for those authors who followed. The fevered Rosicrucian romances of Edward Bulwer-Lytton, Marie Corelli's exercises in unorthodox theology, and commercially successful accounts of life "on the other side" by such writers as Coulson Kernahan and Elizabeth Stuart Phelps paved the way for much more substantial posthumous fantasies by Wyndham Lewis (*The Childermass*, 1928) and C. S. Lewis (*The Great Divorce*, 1945) and for the theological romances of Charles Williams and David Lindsay. Williams's *All Hallows' Eve* (1945) is possibly the best of the ghost novels, while Lindsay's *A Voyage to Arcturus* (1920) is a masterpiece of creative metaphysics.

The 1880's also saw a renaissance of comic fantasy, exemplified in Britain by the novels of F. Anstey and in the United States by Mark Twain's *A Connecticut Yankee in King Arthur's Court* (1889). The calculated irreverence of these stories reflects a self-confident rationalism that stands in opposition to the mystical movements inspiring most posthumous fantasy. The primary target held up for ridicule in these stories, however, is not the vocabulary of fantastic ideas itself but rather the moral pretensions of the contemporary middle classes. Anstey's stories use fantastic premises to expose the limitations of the attitudes that were rigidified within closed Victorian minds.

In the twentieth century, this tradition of humorous fantasy thrived more in the United States than in Britain—the leading American exponent of the species has been Thorne Smith—and this reflects, in part, the fact that as Britain has become somewhat less obsessed with the protocols of middle-class culture, the United States has become gradually more so. It was in the United States also that the absurd logical consequences of fantastic premises began to be exploited for pure amusement, largely in connection with the short-lived magazine *Unknown*, whose leading contributors were L. Sprague de Camp and Fletcher Pratt, who produced, in collaboration, a series of excellent comic fantasies.

A third species of fantastic fiction that first became clearly delineated in the last decades of the nineteenth century is the kind of story that translocates contemporary persons into fabulous imaginary worlds. Stories of this kind are among the oldest that are told. The mundane world has always had its fantastic parallels: its earthly paradises, the land of Cokaygne, and the land of Faerie. In the mid-nineteenth century these alternate worlds were retired into juvenile fiction, except for a few desert islands populated in a relatively mundane fashion. Victorian romances of exploration, however, celebrating the journeys of white men into the heart of the dark continent

of Africa, reopened imaginative spaces for more exotic traveler's tales.

Numerous "lost race" stories and a few "hollow earth" romances were published before 1880, but the writer who first made a considerable popular impact with exotic romances of exploration was H. Rider Haggard, first in *King Solomon's Mines* (1885), and later in *She* (1887) and *The Ghost Kings* (1908). The example that he set was rapidly taken up by others, and the fantasization of the lands where adventurers went exploring proceeded rapidly. Because this was also the period when interplanetary stories were beginning to appear among early scientific romances, it was perhaps inevitable that writers began to displace their more exotic imaginary worlds to the surfaces of other planets. The example set by Edwin Lester Arnold in *Lieut. Gullivar Jones: His Vacation* (1905) was rapidly followed by Edgar Rice Burroughs and many others. In *The Lost World* (1912), Arthur Conan Doyle revitalized remote earthly locations with survivals from prehistory, and this too was an example enthusiastically followed. A new vocabulary borrowed from scientific romance allowed later writers to send heroes through "dimensional gateways" of one kind or another into magical fantasy worlds as exotic as could be imagined: The most determined of all writers of this kind of escapist fantasy was the American Abraham Merritt, author of *The Moon Pool* (1919) and *The Face in the Abyss* (1932).

Though the lost-land story set on the earth's surface was gradually destroyed by news of real explorations—the last classic example was James Hilton's *Lost Horizon* (1933)—the borrowing of conventions from science fiction has allowed the basic story framework to be retained to the present day. Contemporary humans can still be precipitated into magical imaginary worlds with the aid of a little fake technology or even a light sprinkling of jargon. The removal of imaginary worlds from darkest Africa to other planets and other dimensions, however, coincided with another and possibly more important innovation in the use of the theme, which was to dispense with the protagonist from the familiar world.

FAIRY TALES AND HEROIC FANTASY

Although traditional fairy tales had, at the time of their origin, been set in the believed-in world, their remote printed descendants could not help but seem to their consumers to be set in an entirely imaginary milieu. The magicalized medieval milieu of such stories became a stereotype useful to modern writers, who began to repopulate it with complex characters whose adventures were filled with allegorical significance. The pioneers of this kind of enterprise were the German Romantic Friedrich de la Motte Fouqué, in his novel *The Magic Ring* (1813), and George MacDonald, in *Phantastes* (1958), but their example was followed in far more prolific fashion by William Morris, whose several romances of this kind include *The Wood Beyond the World* (1894) and *The Water of the Wondrous Isles* (1897). The form gathered further momentum in the work of Lord Dunsany, most notably in *The King of Elfland's Daughter* (1924) and *The Charwoman's Shadow* (1926); other contemporary examples include Margaret Irwin in *These Mortals* (1925) and Hope Mirrlees in *Lud-in-the-Mist* (1926). These sophisticated but slightly effete fairy tales then began to give way to a more active brand of heroic fantasy, first featured to extravagant extent in E. R. Eddison's *The Worm Ouroboros* (1922).

Modified fairy-tale fantasy reached new heights of popularity in the fantastic volumes included in James Branch Cabell's "Biography of Manuel," set in the imaginary magical European kingdom of Poictesme. It was also developed in a much more extravagant way by several of the contributors to the magazine *Weird Tales*, who used imaginary lands set in remote eras of prehistory in order to develop the subgenre commonly known as "sword-and-sorcery" fiction. Because it was initially restricted to the pages of a pulp magazine, this subgenre was developed primarily in the short-story form, although it is actually better adapted to novel length. Its most famous progenitor, Robert E. Howard, wrote only one novel featuring his archetypal hero Conan: *Conan the Conqueror* (1950; originally "Hour of the Dragon," 1935-1936). The first important novel of this kind to be published initially in book form was *The Well of the Unicorn* (1948) by George U. Fletcher (Fletcher Pratt), but since the advent of the paperback book the species has become established as a successful brand of pulp fiction.

The most notable modern novels set entirely in imaginary worlds tend to give the appearance of being hybrids of sophisticated fairy romance and a variety of heroic fantasy not too far removed from American sword-and-sorcery fiction. The masterpieces of the genre are *The Once and Future King* by T. H. White—published in its entirety in 1958 but absorbing three earlier novels—and *The Lord of the Rings* by J. R. R. Tolkien, published in three volumes between 1954 and 1955.

One of the most striking side effects of the development of fantasy novels of this kind for adults was the revitalization of work done primarily for the juvenile market, which is often remarkably sophisticated in both technical and ideative terms. Tolkien's juvenile novel, *The Hobbit* (1937), is an old example; later ones include Ursula K. Le Guin's six novels set in the world of Earthsea and various works by Alan Garner, Susan Cooper, and Lloyd Alexander.

The paperback publication of Tolkien's *Lord of the Rings* in the 1960's and the feature films released to great acclaim in 2001-2003 sparked countless exercises in imitation that proved popular enough to make the trilogy the basic form of modern fantasy fiction. The reborn genre went from strength to strength in commercial terms, making best sellers out of dozens of writers, many of them direly mediocre in terms of the quality of their prose. Nor is it simply oral fairytales that were rehabilitated within modern commercial fiction; following the success of Richard Adams's *Watership Down* (1972), animal fables—which were also popular in medieval times—were similarly produced in some quantity. The leading examples of this form are the twenty-one novels in the Redwall series by Brian Jacques, in which generations of woodland creatures inhabit a vaguely medieval world.

This exploitation of imaginary worlds is the most striking aspect of the evolution of fantasy novels during the twentieth and twenty-first centuries, and it is not entirely surprising that the "fantasy" label is now retained for such novels by publishers. There has, however, been a parallel evolution of occult and horrific fantasy. The Decadent movements at the end of the nineteenth century saw the emergence of a kind of fiction that reveled in the unnatural, and though most of the fantastic fiction of this kind was cast in short-story form, there were a few notable novels, including Oscar Wilde's *The Picture of Dorian Gray* (serial 1890, expanded 1891) and Hanns Heinz Ewers's *The Sorcerer's Apprentice* (1907) and its sequels.

TWENTIETH CENTURY GOTHIC FANTASY

In parallel with these works appeared a new wave of stories that developed the gothic images of fear into new archetypes, treating them with a determined quasi-scientific seriousness. The great success in this line was Bram Stoker's *Dracula* (1897), which has remained in print and which surely stands as the most heavily plundered fantasy of all time, being the sourcebook for literally hundreds of vampire stories and films.

This resurgence of fiction that deals with the supernatural in a deadly earnest fashion may seem rather paradoxical. It was possible for nineteenth century rationalists to imagine that their victory over superstitious belief was almost won and to look forward to a day when the irrational might be banished from human affairs. If anything, the reverse is true: Superstition, mysticism, and irrationality now thrive to a greater extent than ever before, and modern fiction reflects that fact.

Fantasy novels intended to evoke horror and unease are more prolifically produced and consumed today than they were in the heyday of the gothic, and one of the world's best-selling novelists, Stephen King, is primarily a horror writer. In addition, the role played by occult forces within the neogothic novel is crucially different; in gothic novels, normality was usually restored, and when the forces of the supernatural did break free, they usually did so in order to punish the guilty and liberate the innocent. In later neogothic fantasies, however—whether one looks at the respectable middlebrow tradition that extends from Mervyn Peake's Gormenghast trilogy to the works of Angela Carter or the lowbrow tradition that extends from Dennis Wheatley to James Herbert and Clive Barker—the gothic elements were superimposed in a wholesale manner upon the mundane world, subjecting it to a surrealization from which there could be no possibility of redemption.

This situation has been complicated by a marked tendency among writers of dark fantasy to subject the traditional monsters of gothic fiction to moral reappraisal. In modern vampire fiction, particularly the lush historical romances of Anne Rice, Chelsea Quinn Yarbro, S. P. Somtow, and Elizabeth Kostovo, the male vampire is more hero than villain, and his unusual existential plight is subject to a sympathetically fascinated scrutiny. Modern awareness of the extent to which such figures as the vampire and the werewolf embodied and exaggerated the sexual anxieties of the nineteenth century has enabled writers to redeploy them in fictions that champion the cause of liberalism, although the question of whether understanding automatically paves the way to forgiveness remains interestingly and sometimes achingly open. The psychoanalytical sophistication of much modern horror fiction has moved so far beyond traditional considerations of good and evil that it seems to some critics to have turned from stigmatization to glamorization—an argument supported by the strangely reverent tone adopted toward their all-too-human monsters by such writers as Poppy Z. Brite and Thomas Harris.

The concerted attempt made by many modern writers of supernatural fiction to redeem the Byronic literary vampire from the negative image foisted on him by John Polidori and Stoker extends beyond the limits of literary fantasy into lifestyle fantasy. Similarly intricate relationships between literary and lifestyle fantasies, aided and abetted by extravagant scholarly fantasies—a process that began with the modern reformulation of the idea of witchcraft—have developed across the entire spectrum of New Age philosophies, pretenses, and practices. The relationship between fiction and action has been further complicated by virtue of the spectacular success of fantasy role-playing games, pioneered by Dungeons and Dragons, and fantasy-based computer games. Although play has always been a significant medium of fantasy, it has never been the case before that so much play (involving adults as well as adolescents) has drawn so extensively upon a vocabulary of ideas established and embodied by literary and cinematic fantasies.

POSTMODERNISM

While the contents of popular fantasy fiction have overspilled in this remarkable fashion, fantastic motifs and literary methods have been imported again into the literary mainstream on a considerable scale. The mid-1960's and early 1970's saw the beginnings of a significant break with the American realist tradition in novels by such fabulists as John Barth, Thomas Berger, Richard Brautigan, Thomas Pynchon, and Robert Coover, which eventually expanded in the 1980's into an entire field of postmodern fiction closely connected—at least in the eyes of critics—with a series of formal challenges to the very ideas of realism and reality. British writers of a broadly similar stripe whose work spanned the same period include Angela Carter, Peter Ackroyd, Alasdair Gray, Robert Irwin, and Russell Hoban, although the notion of postmodern British fiction never took hold to the extent that their work began to be aggregated into a symptom of some crucial cultural transition.

Although postmodern fiction borrowed a good deal of imagery from science fiction—and postmodern critics happily conscripted such science-fiction writers as Philip K. Dick, William Gibson, and Bruce Sterling into the field—its mainstream practitioners usually deploy such imagery as a set of metaphors commenting surreally and satirically on contemporary society, in the manner of Kurt Vonnegut and Don DeLillo. The typical materials of commercial fiction bearing the "fantasy" label are far less diverse, but their potential in this regard has been demonstrated by such works as Samuel R. Delany's Nevèrÿon series and Steven Millhauser's *Martin Dressler: The Tale of an American Dreamer* (1996).

The translation into English during this postmodern period of several highly esteemed Latin American novels that productively and provocatively mingle mundane and supernatural materials, including key examples by Gabriel García Márquez and Jorge Amado, introduced the concept of Magical Realism to contemporary literary criticism. The style is widely, and perhaps rather promiscuously, applied to works that owe some allegiance to alternative cultural traditions, whether or not it requires translation. Key examples can be found among the works of Ben Okri, Milorad Pavić, and Salman Rushdie. The increasing interest of African Americans and Native Americans in their traditional cultures—previously obscured by the dominant Euro-American culture—and increasing curiosity about the folkways of Asiatic and African cultures, have led to a steady flow of new works into the American book market, much of which is advertised as Magical Realism for want of any other convenient label.

The relaxation of the realist norm allowed several varieties of fantasy that had long been dormant to resurface in the 1970's and 1980's. Although the classical models of the *conte philosophique* established by Voltaire were mostly novellas, their modern equivalents frequently take the form of novels. Significant examples include

Umberto Eco's *Il pendolo di Foucault* (1988; *Foucault's Pendulum*, 1989) and *L'isola del giorno prima* (1994; *The Island of the Day Before*, 1995) and the series of theological fantasies by James Morrow begun with *Towing Jehovah* (1994). The classical *Kunstmärchen* (art fairy tale) also was confined to shorter lengths, but its modern variants are similarly making increasing use of the novel form; key examples include John Crowley's *Little, Big* (1981) and Coover's *Briar Rose* (1996). Comic fantasy has been resuscitated with great success by such writers as Terry Pratchett—who was the best-selling novelist of the 1990's in Britain and whose work has been translated into dozens of languages—and by Pseudonymous Bosch, author of *The Name of This Book Is Secret* (2007) and *If You're Reading This, It's Too Late* (2008).

Although the bulk of the commercial fiction published under the fantasy label has become extraordinarily stereotyped and repetitive, with heavily promoted best sellers religiously following dumbed-down formulas derived from Tolkien, the fringes of the marketing category continue to play host to a number of highly imaginative and accomplished writers. These include Peter S. Beagle, Tim Powers, and James Blaylock. It is now commonplace for writers who produce excellent fantasy for children to extend their endeavors into adult fantasy; writers working with great facility on both sides of this increasingly ill-defined boundary include Jane Yolen, Patricia McKillip, and Nancy Willard. The Harry Potter series by J. K. Rowling, which has sold 400 million copies in dozens of languages, was marketed (if not written) for young adults but read by adults as well. In Britain, Rowling's publisher printed the books with alternate covers for adult readers who did not wish to be seen reading children's literature. Adults are also drawn to the witty absurdist *Artemis Fowl* series by Eoin Colfer and to Philip Pullman's *His Dark Materials* series. Pullman's books are marketed for young adults, yet their handling of complex religious—or antireligious—themes has made them a topic for serious scholarly debate.

The simultaneous extension of all these trends gives contemporary fantastic fiction such an extraordinary variety that it is becoming difficult to attach much meaning to the overarching notion of the fantasy novel—a difficulty clearly reflected in the comprehensive yearly summations of novel production offered by Terri Windling in her introductions to the annual *Year's Best Fantasy and Horror* anthologies that she coedits with Ellen Datlow. Windling routinely employs such fantasy categories as imaginary world, contemporary or urban, Arthurian, dark, religious, humorous, mysteries, historical, and literary fairytales but still requires such residual headings as "fantasy in the mainstream," "young adult fantasies," and "oddities" for the remainder. The priority traditionally awarded by critics to realistic fiction seems to be in the process of breaking down, and it may well be that a more elaborate literary taxonomy will have to be developed for the new millennium.

Brian Stableford

BIBLIOGRAPHY

Anatol, Giselle Liza, ed. *Reading Harry Potter: Critical Essays.* Westport, Conn.: Praeger, 2003. Fourteen scholarly essays examine the Harry Potter series, the biggest-selling fantasy series of all time. Topics include theories of adolescent development, book banning, literary influences, and morality and social values.

Attebery, Brian. *The Fantasy Tradition in American Literature: From Irving to Le Guin.* Bloomington: Indiana University Press, 1980. Comprehensive and intelligent study of the development of American fantasy, from Washington Irving to Ursula K. Le Guin.

Barron, Neil. *Fantasy Literature: A Readers's Guide.* New York: Garland, 1990. Guide with extensively annotated bibliographies of key texts. Includes a chapter on modern fantasy for young adults and sections on general reference works, history and criticism, author studies, and other sources for further study.

Bleiler, Everett F. *The Guide to Supernatural Fiction.* Kent, Ohio: Kent State University Press, 1983. Large collection of plot synopses and critical judgments of 1,775 books published between 1750 and 1960. A useful and near-comprehensive guide to the development and key themes of modern fantastic fiction.

Bleiler, Richard, ed. *Supernatural Fiction Writers: Contemporary Fantasy and Horror.* 2 vols. 2d ed. New York: Charles Scribner's Sons, 2003. Extensive collection of critical and biographical essays. The first volume deals with continental European and early British writers, the second with American and modern British writers.

Clute, John, and John Grant, eds. *The Encyclopedia of Fantasy.* New ed. New York: St. Martin's Griffin, 1998. Although less comprehensive and less well organized than its science-fiction companion, this remains one of the best general reference books on the fantasy genre that excludes horror and occult fiction.

Dickerson, Matthew T., and David O'Hara. *From Homer to Harry Potter: A Handbook on Myth and Fantasy.* Grand Rapids, Mich.: Brazos, 2006. Discusses Homeric and Biblical myth, Arthurian legend, nineteenth century fairytales, and contemporary writers including Ursula K. Le Guin, Philip Pullman, and J. K. Rowling.

Gray, William. *Fantasy, Myth, and the Measure of Truth: Tales of Pullman, Lewis, Tolkien, MacDonald, and Hoffmann.* New York: Palgrave Macmillan, 2009. Critical interpretations of the novelists' handling of reality, myth, and truth in their fantasy literature.

Hume, Kathryn. *Fantasy and Mimesis: Responses to Reality in Western Literature.* New York: Methuen, 1984. One of the best theoretical studies of the aesthetics of fantasy and its significance in postmodern fiction.

Lobdell, Jared. *The Rise of Tolkienian Fantasy.* Chicago: Open Court, 2005. One of dozens of scholarly books about Tolkien and the *Lord of the Rings* series, this book looks also to Tolkien's influences, and to his imitators.

Pringle, David, ed. *The St. James Guide to Fantasy Writers.* Detroit, Mich.: St. James Press, 1996.

_____. *The St. James Guide to Horror, Ghost, and Gothic Writers.* Detroit, Mich.: St. James Press, 1998. Matched pair of reference works on individual authors, with supportive bibliographies of their relevant books and biographical notes. These volumes cover more authors than Bleiler's *Supernatural Fiction Writers* and cover works untouched by Clute and Grant's *The Encyclopedia of Fantasy.*

Sandner, David. *Fantastic Literature: A Critical Reader.* Westport, Conn.: Praeger, 2004. Theoretical descriptions of fantasy literature, beginning with writings by Plato and Aristotle, through essays by Sigmund Freud and later twentieth century writers.

Feminist Long Fiction

Feminist long fiction features female characters whose quest for self-agency leads to conflict with a traditionally masculinist and patriarchal society. These novels have been harshly criticized and dismissed—and even ridiculed—for their nontraditional female characters.

Feminist ideology in the Western world traces its roots to the late eighteenth century. One particular work considered foundational to feminism is *A Vindication of the Rights of Woman, with Strictures on Political and Moral Subjects* (1792), by English writer Mary Wollstonecraft (1759-1797). Not until the twentieth century, more than one hundred years later, would women begin to reap some of the benefits of a long campaign for basic human rights. Feminism led to radical changes for women in politics, the public sphere, the workplace, the home, and the cultural realm, including the arts and literature. Popular literature, especially, began to reflect women's previously silenced voices.

As early as the end of the seventeenth century, however, women were publishing works of literature. Aphra Behn (1640-1689), likely the first Englishwoman to support herself through writing, published the highly popular *Oroonoko: Or, The History of the Royal Slave* (1688), a prose romance. This novel was the first in English to express sympathy for the plight of slaves.

The eighteenth century

Fiction, a genre that did not fully develop until the eighteenth century, provided a perfect vehicle for women who sought a voice through writing. The first long fiction in England consisted of what may generally be termed "romances." Men traditionally received credit for developing long fiction and, eventually, the novel form. Touted examples include Samuel Richardson's epistolary novel, *Pamela: Or, Virtue Rewarded* (1740-1741), and Henry Fielding's *The History of Tom Jones, a Foundling* (1749). However, earlier novels were written by women, a fact not widely acknowledged until the twentieth century. Mary de la Rivière Manley (c. 1670-1724) published *The Secret History of Queen Zarah and the Zarazians* in the early eighteenth century (1705). The novel is a version of the roman à clef. This type of fiction featured real-life personalities thinly disguised as its characters. Eliza Haywood (c. 1693-1756), a highly political figure, also wrote romances, including *The History of Jemmy and Jenny Jessamy* (1753). She is now frequently mentioned as an important figure in the development of the novel.

The nineteenth century

The nineteenth century became a golden age of writing for women. Jane Austen (1775-1817) wrote seven novels, often called novels of manners, that parody the ludicrous activities of genteel society and criticize inequitable social rules. *Sense and Sensibility* (1811), *Pride and Prejudice* (1813), *Mansfield Park* (1814), *Emma* (1816), *Persuasion* (1818), and *Sanditon* (1925) uncover the oppressive lives of women, including confining environments, a shameful lack of education, and pitiful dependence upon male relatives for survival. Austen's *Northanger Abby* (1818) satirizes as sentimental its heroine's love for the gothic genre, fiction that offers readers mysterious castles or mansions with secret passages, dark shadowy beings, a damsel threatened by death, a hero with an obscure past, and visions and ghosts.

Mary Wollstonecraft Shelley (1797-1851) would rejuvenate the public's appreciation for the gothic in her 1818 novel *Frankenstein*. Rather than emphasize the traditional elements of the gothic, Shelley produced a complex psychological study of her characters, imbuing her horror and science-fiction story with disturbing imagery of aborted creations and multiple deaths. Feminist critics link these elements to Shelley's real-life experiences.

By midcentury, Charlotte Brontë (1816-1855) and Emily Brontë (1818-1848) were producing novels featuring a new hero based on the Romantic ideals of the English poet Lord Byron (1788-1824). Named for the poet and the heroes of his poetry, the Byronic hero most generally had a brooding, dark, independent, and sometimes abusive personality. Charlotte Brontë's *Jane Eyre* (1847) includes a Byronic hero in the form of Edward Rochester. More important, however, the novel introduces a never-before-seen heroine in the shape of a plain, small governess, whose values for truth and justice lead to her rejection of the romantic attentions of Rochester, her master. The character of Jane undercuts the popular female stereotypes of fiction: the angel of the house, the "invalid," or the whore.

Although Charlotte Brontë's novel was well received by her contemporaries, Emily Brontë's masterpiece, *Wuthering Heights*, also published in 1847, was not. With its metaphysical suggestions that bordered on the gruesome and with an abusive, vengeful Byronic hero, its messages proved too strong for its time (especially so because they came from a woman). By the next century, however, this novel took its rightful place in the canon not only of feminist long fiction but also long fiction in general.

THE TWENTIETH CENTURY

Feminist fiction writer Kate Chopin (1851-1904) published *The Awakening* in 1899, a novel that many libraries refused to shelve, despite Chopin's earlier popularity as a writer of "traditional" fiction. Her book shocked readers with its heroine who took pleasure in sexual relations and its suggestion of the connections between the imagination, the artist, and sex. The hostile criticism it received centered on its heroine's rejection of the traditional oppressive role of wife and mother, causing even Chopin's hometown library in St. Louis, Missouri, to ban the book.

In 1920, the year women won the vote in the United States, Edith Wharton (1862-1937) published *The Age of Innocence*. She became the first woman to win a Pulitzer Prize in fiction for the novel in 1921, even though the work focuses on society's inequitable treatment of women.

As Wharton's career flourished in the United States, the English feminist Virginia Woolf (1882-1941), who was also an essayist and editor, also enjoyed popularity. She began her publishing career in 1915 with the novel *The Voyage Out*, which required seven years of work. In early adulthood, Woolf studied Greek, an unusual subject for a young woman of her time; taught at a college for working women; performed menial chores for the suffrage movement; and wrote for the *Times Literary Supplement*, a prestigious publication. All these experiences influenced her feminism.

In *Night and Day* (1919), Woolf shaped a heroine not unlike herself, who had experienced the trials of a young female writer. After *Jacob's Room* (1922), Woolf produced a highly influential novel, *Mrs. Dalloway* (1925). Departing from traditional novel structure, Woolf designed an analysis of post-World War I London society by moving, over a twenty-four-hour period, from her heroine's point of view to that of Septimus Warren Smith, a kind of insane alter ego for Mrs. Dalloway. Woolf's *To the Lighthouse* (1927), often studied by feminist critics, critiques the Victorian social mores that create an environment at once suffocating and stimulating for young women.

Woolf's intimate relationship with writer Vita Sackville-West likely inspired her 1928 novel *Orlando: A Biography*. *Orlando* is written as a biography of a character who lives more than four hundred years, during which time her gender evolves from that of a man to that of a woman. The novel represents the history of the aristocratic Sackville-West family and also the development of English literature. In 1929, Woolf produced a long essay published as *A Room of One's Own*, which focuses on the writing life of women; historians agree it represents the first major work of feminist criticism in English. Her most experimental novel, *The Waves* (1931), was labeled by Woolf herself a "poem-play." Made up of a number of monologues, the novel presents six characters, all lamenting the death of a young man named Percival, supposedly fashioned on Woolf's own brother, Thoby, who died many years before.

Additional works by Woolf include the nonfiction *Three Guineas* (1938), considered the most radical of her feminist writings in its examination of social oppression. Her final novel, *Between the Acts*, appeared in 1941, following Woolf's suicide in the same year.

Woolf's contemporary, English writer Rebecca West (1892-1983), was an actor, journalist, and suffragist. Born Cicily Isabel Fairfield, West adopted as her name that of a radical feminist character from Henrik Ibsen's play *Rosmersholm* (pb. 1886; English translation, 1889). Although much of West's work is in journalism and nonfiction, she published several important fictional works, despite some negative reactions to her writings and to her as an individual. Accounting for a portion of the hostility was her love affair with English novelist H. G.

Wells, an affair that led to an illegitimate son. The two writers' relationship challenged the conservative values of their society. After West gave birth to her son in 1914, she took a great interest in the situation of unwed mothers, leading her to write *The Judge* (1922). This novel featured the suffragist struggle with additional consideration of issues such as rape, illegitimacy, and motherhood.

In 1930, West produced more novels, expressing an enthusiasm for writings by Woolf. West's *The Harsh Voice* (1935), a collection of novellas, concerned economic and financial matters and focused on the 1929 global economic crisis. Many reviewers of the book declared its subject too harsh and its tone too pessimistic for a female writer. Others, however, noted with interest that West shaped female characters who differed from those in her earlier works. These heroines were strong, taking an active part in the determination of their own fate, something women were not encouraged to do in real life. This same strength of character informed West's most popular novel, *The Thinking Reed* (1936). Although some found the novel's heroine, Isabelle, ruthless, the book garnered much critical acclaim. In the novel, West criticized French, English, and American societies in a manner that some found offensive but most declared accurate.

By the 1950's, West departed from her feminist-socialist view to take up a conservative anticommunist stance. Her political reversal earned her the title of Dame Commander of the British Empire, a somewhat ironic circumstance for a writer who earlier had deeply criticized imperialism in print.

A FEMALE AESTHETIC

With the exodus of men fighting the two world wars in the first half of the twentieth century, American and English women entered the workforce in record numbers to occupy positions other than that of the traditional nurse, teacher, or secretary. As women's roles in the world changed, so did the characterizations of women in novels. Female writers began to connect their work and their lives. They discovered a number of disparities between their own ambitions, ingenuity, and creativity on one hand and the limited, often secondary, roles assumed by the majority of traditional female fictional

characters on the other hand. This reality was easily explained, as the majority of novelists were white men. By the mid-twentieth century, a plethora of long fiction by women began to appear, with realistic female characters. Women's fiction transformed from products of imitation of a male aesthetic to protests against that aesthetic, eventually becoming self-defining works of literature.

The success of these new novelists was propelled by the work of feminist literary critics, especially scholars in academia. In the 1960's, critics began questioning the characterizations of women as either angels or monsters. They also questioned the representation of women in popular literature written by men and, most important, refused to accept the exclusion of women from literary history. Their diligence in rediscovering female novelists from previous centuries and decades helped propel authors such as Woolf, George Sand (1804-1876), George Eliot (1819-1880), and West to their rightful place in the literary canon.

Feminist critics also traced the historical connections of recurring images, themes, and plots in women's writing that reflected their social and psychological experience in a culture dominated by men. One recurring image, for example, is that of the caged bird, which represents the suppression of female creativity or the physical and emotional imprisonment of women in general. Slowly, writings by women began to be accepted not only in the classroom but also the marketplace. Virago Press, which publishes the writings of women, reprinted, for instance, West's novels in affordable editions. While her work in its own day was deemed "too intellectual," feminist critics helped define a new study and a new appreciation of these works. In addition, the critical analyses of the aesthetic values that appeared in many of the novels that had long been considered classics led to a newly defined feminist novel.

Closely related to the formation of a feminist aesthetic was the development of a black women's aesthetic. Novels by African American women from the first half of the twentieth century, such as *Their Eyes Were Watching God* (1937) by anthropologist and writer Zora Neale Hurston (1891-1960), were reissued after decades of neglect. Hurston's novel—which tells the story of a young black woman involved in three abusive marriages who eventually finds redemption through her own strength and beliefs and through the support of her female friend—gained an important place in the feminist canon. Hurston's work prefigured that of Toni Morrison (born 1931), the first black woman to receive the Nobel Prize in Literature (1993). One of America's foremost novelists, Morrison is celebrated for her acute analyses of the dynamics of race and gender. Often framing her fiction in the fantastic and the mystical, Morrison is known for *The Bluest Eye* (1970), *Sula* (1973), *Song of Solomon* (1977), *Tar Baby* (1981), the Pulitzer Prize-winning *Beloved* (1987), *Jazz* (1992), *Paradise* (1998), *Love* (2003), and *A Mercy* (2008).

Like Morrison, Alice Walker (born 1944) explores the cultural inheritance of African Americans by examining universal moral issues and by celebrating supportive communities of women. In her critically acclaimed Pulitzer Prize-winning novel *The Color Purple* (1982), Walker presents her story in epistolary form, emphasizing her characters' struggles with articulating their feelings of identity from the perspective of African American experience. In her 1983 work of nonfiction, *In Search of Our Mothers' Gardens: Womanist Prose*, Walker coined the term "womanist" to describe the particular perspectives of feminist women of color.

By the 1950's, writers such as Iranian-born Doris Lessing (born 1919) were publishing works that feminists claimed as supportive of their cause. In Lessing's *The Golden Notebook* (1962), heroine Anna Wulf struggles with being a creative woman who fights solitude, has self-destructive impulses, and who practices self-censorship to conform to society. These are themes repeated in many of Lessing's novels. Lessing also is known for her vision of the writer as a morally responsible person, who criticizes capitalist inequities through a socialist philosophy.

Lessing was awarded the Nobel Prize in Literature in 2007. The Nobel Academy described her as "that epicist [writer of epics] of the female experience, who with scepticism, fire and visionary power has subjected a divided civilization to scrutiny."

Erica Jong (born 1942) wrote the widely popular *Fear of Flying* (1973). Even with its frank treatment of female sexuality, the novel sold more than five million copies by 1977 and prompted an avalanche of letters to Jong from women responding to the work as a revelation

of emotions they had never encountered in fiction. The book caused a flurry of mixed critical response as well, partly in reaction to its provocative cover images and to its content, which some labeled pornographic. Expressing in no uncertain terms the anger and energy of the women's rights movement, the novel also garnered praise for its frankness but also received criticism for what some called a banal tone and weak writing style.

The second half of the twentieth century saw feminist novels addressing race and ethnicity. This focus developed out of the work of feminists of color, who argued that race, gender, and class were inextricably linked. Maxine Hong Kingston (born 1940), born to Chinese immigrants, published *The Woman Warrior: Memoirs of a Girlhood Among Ghosts* (1976), which combines autobiography and fiction in a tale of "a girl-hood among ghosts." These ghosts emerge from Chinese myth to show how the definition of "feminine" is shaped in that culture. Frankly oppressive for women, ancient Chinese culture allows Kingston to investigate challenges to female physical and emotional survival. Louise Erdrich (born 1954), who is part American Indian, interrogates the social, economic, and emotional pressures suffered by dislocated women in her novel *Love Medicine* (1984). The book won the National Book Critics Circle Award. Novelist Julia Alvarez (born 1950), in her novel *In the Time of the Butterflies* (1994), tells the story of the historic Mirabal sisters and their resistance to Dominican dictator Rafael Trujillo.

Other feminist novelists who write from a multiethnic and multicultural perspective include Yvonne Vera (1964-2005). Her novel *Butterfly Burning* (2000) examines gender inequality in Zimbabwe. Monica Ali (born 1967), a British writer of Bangladeshi descent, tells the story of a woman in an arranged married in *Brick Lane* (2003). Chinese novelist Wang Anyi (born 1954) has had several of her short novels translated into English, including those examining women's lives in contemporary China (*Xiao cheng zhi lian*, 1988; *Love in a Small Town*, 1988). Lebanese novelist Ḥanān al-Shaykh (born 1945) is the author of *Misk al-ghazāl* (1988; *Women of Sand and Myrrh*, 1989), a novel that was banned in several countries in the Middle East for its harsh criticism of patriarchy; it was well-received in English translation.

By the beginning of the twenty-first century, it was no longer remarkable that stories about women's lives were indeed serious literature. However, much of the "seriousness" also has translated into increased sales and profits for publishers, especially because women surpassed men in terms of buying and reading novels. Books by women about women still are considered attractive primarily for female readers, whereas books by men about men are considered to have universal appeal.

Virginia Brackett

BIBLIOGRAPHY

Acampora, Christa Davis, and Angela L. Cotten, eds. *Unmaking Race, Remaking Soul: Transformative Aesthetics and the Practice of Freedom*. Albany: State University of New York Press, 2007. Collection of essays on the power of creativity—including writing—to transform the lives of women of color. Argues for the importance of "aesthetic agency" to literature and other forms of creative experience.

Gilbert, Sandra M., and Susan Gubar. *The Madwoman in the Attic: The Woman Writer and the Nineteenth-Century Literary Imagination*. New Haven, Conn.: Yale University Press, 1979. Classic text that considers nineteenth century stereotypes of female fictional characters and of the writers who created them, framing its discussion with ideas governing restrictive social mores. Essential reading for understanding feminist literature and writers.

_____, eds. *The Norton Anthology of Literature by Women: The Traditions in English*. 3d ed. New York: W. W. Norton, 2007. Comprehensive anthology of women's writing, featuring works from medieval times through the early twenty-first century. Biographies, works, and excerpts are presented chronologically, with each era preceded by introductions that examine the culture in which each woman wrote.

Lauret, Maria. *Liberating Literature: Feminist Fiction in America*. New York: Routledge, 1994. Lauret explores the writing of American feminist writers of long fiction, including Marge Piercy, Marilyn French, Tillie Olsen, Alice Walker, Kate Millett, Agnes Smedley, Zora Neale Hurston, Toni Morrison, and Maya Angelou.

Makinen, Merja. *Feminist Popular Fiction*. New York: Palgrave, 2001. Analysis of the move into popular fiction—detective fiction, science fiction, romances, and fairy tales—by feminist writers beginning in the 1980's. Includes a history of each genre and women's contributions to their formation. Also includes an introductory chapter, "Feminism and Genre Fiction: The Preliminaries."

Moers, Ellen. *Literary Women: The Great Writers*. 1976. Reprint. London: Women's Press, 1986. Moers, in part, makes visible a "subtext" in the writings of women. Argues that some works contain messages unrecognized in their own time because of assumptions and presumptions about gender. Includes a new introduction.

Robbins, Ruth. *Literary Feminisms*. New York: Palgrave, 2003. An introduction to feminist literary and critical theories in the United States and Great Britain. Examines the "pluralist" composition of feminist literary theory, which uses Marxist, postmodern, and other theories but remains centered on women. Includes readings of commonly taught feminist texts.

Whelehan, Imelda. *The Feminist Bestseller: From "Sex and the Single Girl" to "Sex and the City."* New York: Palgrave Macmillan, 2005. Overview of popular feminist fiction from the late 1960's to the end of the 1990's, examining the influence of Erica Jong, Marilyn French, and others on late twentieth century writers. Explains how these works are in dialogue with contemporary feminism.

GAY AND LESBIAN LONG FICTION

Homosexuality, traditionally regarded as a disease or perversion by church, state, and society, was rigorously denounced and condemned by those same institutions. In the case of the arts and literature, works featuring homoeroticism or gays and lesbians as characters were often censored, if they were recognized at all. English-language writers, for example, wrote "gay novels" under pseudonyms and published them either privately or in foreign countries.

Gay characters and sensibilities were introduced into literature only by arch subterfuge, with writers following society's unwritten decree that homoerotic fiction must end with the death, destruction, or extraordinary "conversion" of the questionable characters. In Bayard Taylor's *Joseph and His Friend* (1870), a disastrous marriage causes Joseph to drift toward Philip, a young, golden-haired man; the novel ends, however, with Joseph's sudden, almost inexplicable interest in Philip's look-alike sister. This plot shift presumably was made to "save" Joseph from a fate worse than death. Henry James's *Roderick Hudson* (1876) sketches wealthy Rowland Mallet's infatuation with a young sculptor, but after a rift between them, the eponymous character sinks into a decadent languor from which he is rescued only by Christina Light, a beautiful, bored girl. Like other novels of the time, homoerotic love is forced to yield to the heterosexual imperative.

Europe saw many clandestine homoerotic novels—such as the lurid *Gamiani* (1833; *Gamiani: Or, Two Nights of Excess*, 1923), attributed to Alfred de Musset and featuring lesbian sexuality—but none of these was a major work. Honoré de Balzac masked homosexuality by artifice. In his vast sequence of interrelated novels about French society, *La Comédie humaine* (1829-1848; *The Comedy of Human Life*, 1885-1893, 1896; also as *The Human Comedy*, 1895-1896, 1911), the exuberantly masculine Vautrin is imprisoned after taking the blame for a crime committed by Lucien, the gentle, handsome young man he loves. Vautrin dreams of owning a plantation in the American South, where he can have absolute power over his slaves, especially their bodies. Only by living outside hypocritical French society can Vautrin have insight into its excesses and his own nature.

Irish writer and poet Oscar Wilde defied Victorian hypocrisy, but he paid a mortal price. *The Picture of Dorian Gray* (serial 1890; expanded 1891) represents a Faustian pact between young Dorian and the forces of evil. Wilde defiantly embraces and gilds what his society deems evil. Society enjoyed the ultimate revenge by destroying Wilde's reputation and life: He was jailed for homosexual "offences" and went bankrupt while in prison.

If gay fiction wished to vividly portray homosexuality, it had to balance sensuality with social determinism—as in the case of Adolpho Caminha's Brazilian novel *Bom crioulo* (1895; *Bom-Crioula: The Black Man and the Cabin Boy*, 1982), the first explicitly gay work in Latin American fiction. The violent Amaro, often described with animal imagery, escapes from slavery and sexual strictures, but his "animal" nature drives him to kill his male lover in a jealous fit. Caminha uses laws of heredity to justify slavery and exploitation, and his novel is flawed by contradictions: Homosexuality is unnatural, yet heroic; it is against nature, yet it is natural for Bom Crioulo. Nevertheless, his novel is an example of the manner in which homosexuality haunts the "normal" world.

EARLY TWENTIETH CENTURY OBLIQUENESS

Lesbian sexuality was a major theme in Colette's novels about teenagers who were infatuated with older women. Male love figured in Robert Musil's *Die Verwirrungen des Zöglings Törless* (1906; *Young Törless*, 1955), set in a military school, and Thomas Mann's *Der Tod in Venedig* (1912; *Death in Venice*, 1925), the story of Gustav von Aschenbach's fatal infatuation with Tadzio, a fourteen-year-old Polish boy of Apollonian beauty and stillness.

Gay novelists in England and the United States resorted to setting love stories in faraway lands or using other techniques of evasion. Charles Warren Stoddard's *For the Pleasure of His Company: An Affair of the Misty City, Thrice Told* (1903), the story of Paul Clitheroe's love affair with two darkly handsome men, runs sour until Paul ends up in the company of three South Sea islanders. Edward Prime-Stevenson's *Imre: A Memorandum* (1906), privately published abroad in a small run of 125 copies, ends with a young Englishman, Oswald, in the arms of Imre, a twenty-five-year-old Hungarian army officer; but this "openness" is undercut by the novelist's pretense to be no more than the editor of a manuscript sent to him by a British friend. The guardedness of gay novelists continued for decades, even when the theme was a "coming out" of sorts. Henry Blake Fuller's *Bertram Cope's Year* (1919), set near Chicago, is about the ruined love affair between Randolph and Bertram Cope, but Fuller pretends that the rupture is based on age rather than on rival love.

The 1920's, an age of reckless, fast living, did not end gay fiction's camouflage. Sophisticates knew of Sigmund Freud's radical sex theories and D. H. Lawrence's carnal characters, but there was no progress in attitudes about homosexuality. Camouflage through euphuism became the mode, as in Ronald Firbank's high-camp affectation in his novellas or Carl Van Vechten's frothy tone in *The Blind Bow-Boy* (1923), where the notorious Duke of Middlebottom dresses as a sailor and has stationery printed with the motto "A thing of beauty is a boy forever." The spirit of the times did not welcome serious novels of social protest or self-disclosure, as Radclyffe Hall discovered when she published her semiautobiographical lesbian novel, *The Well of Loneliness* (1928). Virginia Woolf masked her love affair with Vita Sackville-West with the fantastical, androgynous world of *Orlando: A Biography* (1928).

Through the 1930's and 1940's, the "tough guy" novels of Ernest Hemingway and Raymond Chandler, as well as the war novels of Norman Mailer and James Jones, depicted gay characters with contempt, as if they were weak "pansies" and the antitheses of masculine heroes. In contrast, novels featuring African Americans and Jews, for example, often were proletarian novels of social protest. Consequently, gay fiction was left to hacks, with a few outstanding exceptions, including Parker Tyler and Frederick Rolfe. Tyler's *The Young and Evil* (1933; with Charles Henri Ford) is a slice-of-life story about life in Greenwich Village, New York, and Rolfe's *The Desire and Pursuit of the Whole* (1934) features a male protagonist who can entertain desire only when his beloved adopts male attire and behavior.

Other novelists, such as Frederic Prokosch, used numerous filters to conceal gayness in his works. His novels, including *The Asiatics* (1935) and *The Seven Who Fled* (1937), were lyrical tales of handsome bachelors in extreme circumstances and exotic places (such as Aden, Turkey, Iraq, or Tibet). Prokosch allowed his heroes, ostensibly heterosexual males, to be placed in sexually charged situations, but his filtrations and dilutions of homosexuality were concessionary. Djuna Barnes's *Nightwood* (1936) expressed the intensity of lesbian love, but its Parisian world was broodingly gothic. Researcher Alfred Kinsey's studies *Sexual Behavior in the Human Male* (1948) and *Sexual Behavior in the Human Female* (1953) rebuked assumptions about sexuality, including homosexuality, while the horrors of World War II prompted Americans to question traditionally accepted morals and values. Nevertheless, although the "open" homosexual in long fiction became increasingly frequent, literary camouflage and subterfuge remained necessary.

Novelist Carson McCullers, who was lesbian, did not concern herself principally with the subject of sexuality. Although each of her novels includes a man with a crush on another man, these works actually concern abnormality and yearning. In her *The Heart Is a Lonely Hunter* (1940), homosexuality is one of the few things not attributed to protagonist Singer by other characters, despite the fact that Singer's homoerotic love is his only joy and his only reason for living. Truman Capote writes of a young man's love for a handsome prizefighter in *Other Voices, Other Rooms* (1948), but Capote, too, skirted the issue of homosexuality by simply affirming that any love could be beautiful as long as it belonged to a person's intrinsic nature.

William Maxwell Jr.'s *The Folded Leaf* (1945) camouflages Lymie Peters's homosexual interest as an aesthetic one; worse, the athletic Spud Latham is never allowed to realize his friend's sexual desire for him. Novelist John Horne Burns, who thought it necessary to be gay to be a good writer, created a gay bar and a vivid set of rapacious, spontaneous, erotic characters in *The Gallery* (1947). However, his story is not about sex or love per se, but rather human nature. In *Lucifer with a Book* (1949), Burns acts almost apologetic about his erotic male characters by designing for them last-minute conversions to heterosexuality.

BREAKING THE PATTERN

The protagonist in Fritz Peters's *The World Next Door* (1949) admits that he loves a man while denying that he is gay. Helped by new trends in Europe, Patricia Highsmith and Gore Vidal dared to break the pattern of gay and lesbian invisibility and shame. Highsmith's *The Price of Salt* (1952, as Claire Morgan; also published as *Carol*) has a clear lesbian theme, while Vidal's *The City and the Pillar* (1948; revised 1965) depicts men undressing and kissing. Vidal's Jim Willard is presented as a reproach to society's censors: After Willard is vilely denounced by the man with whom he tries to rekindle their boyhood homoeroticism, he strangles the object of his affection

Vidal's all-male Eden was shocking to American literary critics. Vidal, however, was not in the league of Jean Genet, whose dark, decadent fiction—*Notre-Dame des Fleurs* (1944, 1951; *Our Lady of the Flowers*, 1949), *Miracle de la rose* (1946, 1951; *Miracle of the Rose* 1966), *Querelle de Brest* (1947, 1953; *Querelle of Brest*, 1966), and the semiautobiographical *Journal du voleur* (1948, 1949; *The Thief's Journal*, 1954)—never flinches from portraying the emotional and psychological depths of gay relations. Sex and violence are mixed with lurid and salacious density, and Genet often creates an extremely perverse but original perspective on theft, rape, and even murder.

Genet's deliberate idealization of outlawed desire is reflected in Yukio Mishima's Japanese fiction. A martial artist and sexual outlaw, Mishima resorts to metaphor for deception. The narrator of *Kamen no kokuhaku* (1949; *Confessions of a Mask*, 1958) enters into anonymous relationships with women, for whom he harbors secret distaste, simply to "fit" into conventional society.

THE 1950'S AND EARLY 1960'S

The 1950's was a time of anticommunist—and antigay—hysteria in the United States. Fearing the critics, gay male writers often became grotesque, parasitic, clownish, or campy characters in their own lives. Capote embraced Manhattan whimsy and capriciousness; Burns wrote a weak, straight novel shortly before he died; and Vidal put his energy into nonfiction and politics. Many versions of the "apprenticeship" gay novel appeared as well, with themes of a problematic childhood.

Gay fiction divided itself into two main categories: traditional realism (James Baldwin and J. R. Ackerley) and counterculture writing (William S. Burroughs), though there were fascinating exceptions to the rule—as in James Purdy's *Malcolm* (1959), an allegorical story about a teenager befriended by a possible pedophile; Peters's *Finistère* (1951) is set in a France more apt to accept the adolescent protagonist's burgeoning gayness than are his parents; James Barr's *Quatrefoil* (1950), a male love story told in a lofty, intellectual manner; and William Talsman's playfully witty and stylish *The Gaudy Image* (1958). Most of these novels, however, ended in wistfulness or death for the protagonist. Young Matt in *Finistère* drowns himself; Baldwin's *Giovanni's Room* (1956) ends on a bridge, where David tries to discard his lover's letter, only to have the wind blow the fragments back to him; and in *Quatrefoil*, Phillip, after his lover is killed in an aircrash, contemplates suicide, only to decide that love has made him strong.

Lesbian pulp novels, intended for a heterosexual readership, were sold at places such as drugstores and newsstands in the 1950's and most often featured a male-fantasy version of lesbian sex. The novels also cast women who have sex with women as shamed and isolated. Many of the later pulps, however, began to depict these young women as fully embracing their sexuality. The novels of Ann Bannon, for example, sent a crucial message to readers: that a condemning society, and not homosexuality, is morally wrong. For lesbians growing up around this time, the new pulp novels were, in many ways, lifesavers. Bannon's novels include her first, *Odd Girl Out* (1957), featuring college students Beth and Laura, and *Beebo Brinker* (1962), which introduces Bannon's favorite protagonist, the soft butch Beebo Brinker, to the lesbian world of Greenwich Village.

Gay writers in the early 1960's became increasingly open about homosexuality, having been inspired by the creative courage of the Belgian-born Marguerite Yourcenar, whose books defy classification because they mix modes as they tackle different kinds of love. She wrote of homosexuality, however, through her gay characters, and avoided, for the most part, the topic of lesbian sexuality. Her novels include the early work *Alexis: Ou, Le Traité du vain combat* (1929; *Alexis*, 1984) and the influential *Mémoires d'Hadrien* (1951;

Memoirs of Hadrian, 1954; also known as *Hadrian's Memoirs*).

The newly open writers include Baldwin, who, in *Another Country* (1962), depicts a sleazy New York hell where individuals are caught up in the general malaise of American society. However, Baldwin's gay characters have a greater awareness of their misery than does society at large, which remains ignorant. Christopher Isherwood's *A Single Man* (1964) affirms the value of an aging gay man who, in a departure from custom, is not a doomed homosexual with neurotic self-loathing or sexual guilt but a bachelor who entertains a fantasy of killing or torturing bigots unless they agree to end homophobic practices.

Isherwood's quiet prose contrasts with the louder brutality of Charles Wright's *The Messenger* (1963), where New York is a hell filled with junkies (and gays), or Hubert Selby's *Last Exit to Brooklyn* (1964), replete with pimps, whores, and thugs (and queers). The most controversial novels were John Rechy's *City of Night* (1963) and *Numbers* (1967). In *City of Night*, Rechy takes a hard look at the joyless and dangerous side of male prostitution, based on his own experiences, but his writing is not primarily confessional. It has a gritty realism that exposes its central character's refusal to express emotion for fear of revealing his sexual identity. *Numbers* is also a horror story with dark imagery, as its protagonist sets off on a journey of self-discovery, literally counting sexual experiences as if numbers could themselves ward off age and death.

NEW TAXONOMY

Homoeroticism became iconic after the Stonewall Inn bar uprising in New York City in 1969, a small revolt of bar patrons and others that ultimately strengthened an emerging modern gay and lesbian rights movement in the United States. Gay and lesbian writers began to produce works of full self-disclosure. By the end of the 1960's, gay and lesbian fiction expanded to include various subgenres: In other words, gay and lesbian literature was no longer simply about homosexuality as a "problem." In Europe, Pier Paolo Pasolini and Genet reveled in picaresque novels. Marie-Claire Blais brought stories of French Canadian lesbians to readers outside Canada, and Ursula K. Le Guin wrote science fiction in which fantasy worlds included gender equality.

The 1970's was rich in gay inventiveness. Anne Rice and Marion Zimmer Bradley also wrote in the science fantasy genre, with Bradley becoming one of the first science-fiction writers to use independent female characters to explore gender roles. Guy Hocquenghem explored the connections between the body and technology. Mary Renault used classical history to show how bisexuality was once a cultural norm.

During the 1970's and 1980's, the new taxonomy of gay and lesbian writing was consolidated. The rise of small presses specializing in gay and lesbian (and lesbian feminist) writing ensured the publication of diverse writers and genres. The "coming-out" and semiautobiographical novels of Andrew Holleran, David Leavitt, Rita Mae Brown, and Jeanette Winterson explore a wide range of experiences, including parental disgust and rejection, dispossession of home, the death of innocence, and various discourses on love. Also remaining popular was the "colonialist" tradition of upper-class men seeking erotic adventure with foreigners or working-class people—already encountered in nineteenth century and early twentieth century novels. Alan Hollinghurst is most notable in this tradition.

The 1970's also included Ann Allen Shockley's *Loving Her* (1974), the first black lesbian novel published in the United States. In 1977, Barbara Smith, in "Toward a Black Feminist Criticism," decried the overt dismissal of literature by black women and black lesbians. Her essay led to a radical rethinking of the place of African American literature in the literary canon. Novels such as Alice Walker's *The Color Purple* (1982), which feature lesbian sexuality as central themes, soon followed. Also in the 1970's, black gay men, working to promote literature by men of color, especially through small presses, were influenced by black lesbians and feminists of all races and ethnicities.

The confluence of the gay and lesbian rights movement and the rise of third-wave feminism ensured that lesbian writers could tell their stories from a lesbian-feminist perspective. June Arnold envisions women taking control of their own destinies and Dutch writer Anna Blaman uses language to upend social stereotypes. Feminist literary theorists helped to shape lesbian writing as well, even outside the academy. Canadian theorist and novelist Nicole Brossard associates the lesbian body with an "intelligent body," thereby envisioning utopia. In France, theorist and writer Monique Wittig suggests that women can liberate themselves only by using language in radical ways. Novelist-critic Hélène Cixous developed a theory and style called "writing from the body." Her bold celebration of lesbian sexuality as a lever to dismantle oppressive social structures helped clear a path for writers such as Dorothy Allison and Blanche McCrary Boyd.

While Allison won acclaim with *Bastard Out of Carolina* (1992) and *Cavedweller* (1998), which explores domestic, personal, and psychic violence from the perspective of a working-class lesbian, Boyd has ensured that each of her own novels is female centered. Each features a young woman who comes out as lesbian and learns to overcome obstacles to existential and sexual autonomy, as in the case of Ellen Larraine Burns, the protagonist of the Lambda Award-winning *The Revolution of Little Girls* (1991) and *Terminal Velocity* (1997).

The new consciousness enhanced gay and lesbian writers' gambits into social and political themes, even to the point of criticizing their own subculture—as with Larry Kramer's *Faggots* (1978), whose antipromiscuity theme aroused a backlash. Lisa Alther incorporates cultural satire into such works as *Kinflicks* (1975), *Original Sins* (1981), and *Five Minutes in Heaven* (1995). The preeminent writer of the era, however, is Sarah Schulman, who examines inherent tensions between the nature of art and the reality of politics in her novels, plays, and journalistic essays. Beginning with *The Sophie Horowitz Story* (1984), which reads like a detective story but is really a meditation on lesbian politics and sexuality, and continuing with *Girls, Visions and Everything* (1986), *People in Trouble* (1990), *Empathy* (1992), *Rat Bohemia* (1995), *Shimmer* (1998) and *The Child* (2007), Schulman examines, among other topics, individual responsibility and with the horrors of the AIDS crisis. *Rat Bohemia* is a favorite and ranks as one of the best novels of lesbian and gay fiction. Schulman's involvement with various gay activist groups deeply influences her writing. She was a cofounder of the New York Lesbian and Gay Experimental Film Festival and of the direct-action activist group Lesbian Avengers.

Gay and lesbian literature, however, does not limit itself to political themes. British novelist Sarah Waters's first novel, *Tipping the Velvet* (1998), is a lighthearted picaresque story of lesbian love featuring protagonist Kitty Butler, a stage performer and male impersonator in Victorian England. The novel was an immediate success, and it has been translated into more than twenty languages. Waters also set her next two novels, *Affinity* (1999) and *Fingersmith* (2002), in the Victorian period, but moved to the 1940's for *The Night Watch* (2006) and *The Little Stranger* (2009). Her first three novels were adapted for film and television. Katherine V. Forrest, a Canadian-born American writer, established the American lesbian detective novel with the first book in her Kate Delafield series, *Amateur City* (1984). Three of the eight novels in the series won the Lambda Literary Award, including *Hancock Park* (2004). Mark Richard Zubro is the author of two best-selling detective series, the Tom and Scott mysteries and the Paul Turner mysteries. *A Simple Suburban Murder* (1990), the first in the series about Chicago high school teacher Tom Mason and his pro-baseball-player husband Scott Carpenter, won a Lambda Literary Award as well. In the twelfth book in the series, *Schooled in Murder* (2008), a meeting at Tom's high school ends with a murder.

Schulman's playful experimentation with the detective genre, especially in *After Delores* (1988), a hard-boiled detective story in the style of James M. Cain and Dashiell Hammett, displays the modern gay and lesbian writer's literary freedom. English-language writers are no longer forced to envy foreign-language gay writers—such as Manuel Puig (*El beso de la mujer araña*, 1976; *Kiss of the Spider Woman*, 1979), Mutsuo Takahashi (*Zen no henreki*, 1974; partial translation, 1999 and 2000; Zen's pilgrimage of virtue), or Michel Tournier (*Gilles et Jeanne*, 1983; *Gilles and Jeanne*, 1987)—for their ability to take risks. Notable, too, are the achievements of Paul Monette, Armistead Maupin, and Kitty Tsui, as are the more experimental and ambitious works of Dale Peck, Edmund White, and Samuel M. Steward.

Reacting to the subtle and pervasive censorship inherent even in political correctness, Peck, White, and Steward began experimenting with mixed styles and modes. Steward's detective and modernist parodies examine the position of the artist in modern society, while promoting erotica as pure entertainment. Peck's *Martin and John* (1993) is an absorbing patchwork of conflicting stories, all with characters named Martin and John, but death is its driving force. His *Body Surfing* (2009) is a wild and funny story about the Mogran, a race of demons known primarily for their sexual appetites. However, neither writer matches White's mainstream success, especially with the semiautobiographical trilogy *A Boy's Own Story* (1982), *The Beautiful Room Is Empty* (1988), and *The Farewell Symphony* (1997), a mature example of the elegant sensitivity of modern gay fiction.

Keith Garebian
Updated by Cynthia A. Bily

BIBLIOGRAPHY

Austen, Roger. *Playing the Game: The Homosexual Novel in America*. Indianapolis, Ind.: Bobbs-Merrill, 1977. Dated but literate and still relevant history of the "gay novel" from its beginnings into the 1960's. Covers two hundred novels and includes a bibliography and an index.

Cart, Michael, and Christine Jenkins. *The Heart Has Its Reasons: Young Adult Literature with Gay/Lesbian/Queer Content, 1969-2004*. Lanham, Md.: Scarecrow Press, 2006. Examines the historical development of gay and lesbian young adult fiction. Comprehensive resource on an undervalued genre. Appendixes include "Young Adult Novels with GLBTQ Content, 1969-2004: Author/Title Bibliography with GLBTQ Portrayal, Inclusion, and Narrative Role," and "Young Adult Fiction with GLBTQ Content, 1969-2004: A Chronological Bibliography."

Castle, Terry, ed. *The Literature of Lesbianism: A Historical Anthology from Ariosto to Stonewall*. New York: Columbia University Press, 2003. Collection of hundreds of literary works about lesbian sexuality. Authors include William Shakespeare, John Donne, Aphra Behn, Alexander Pope, the Marquis de Sade, Samuel Taylor Coleridge, Emily Dickinson, Guy de Maupassant, Willa Cather, Virginia Woolf, Ernest Hemingway, Nella Larsen, and Graham Greene.

Lilly, Mark. *Gay Men's Literature in the Twentieth Century*. New York: New York University Press, 1993. Reintroduction to famous texts and an entry into less known work from the standpoint of gay men's experiences, sensibilities, and sexual desires.

Malinowski, Sharon, ed. *Gay and Lesbian Literature*. 2 vols. Detroit, Mich.: St. James Press, 1994, 1998. Extensive compilation of more than two hundred writers of the twentieth century. Inclusion in this work is based on thematic content, not sexual identity, forcing readers to rethink what makes a work "gay" or "lesbian." Each volume has a separate introduction to lesbian literature and gay literature, respectively.

Markowitz, Judith A. *The Gay Detective Novel: Lesbian and Gay Main Characters and Themes in Mystery Fiction*. Jefferson, N.C.: McFarland, 2004. Survey of series and stand-alone detective and mystery novels published since 1964, analyzing main characters, themes, and plot elements. Includes an extensive bibliography.

Pollack, Sandra, and Denise D. Knight, eds. *Contemporary Lesbian Writers of the United States: A Bio-bibliographical Critical Sourcebook*. Westport, Conn.: Greenwood Press, 1993. Biographical essays that include writers' personal history, an analysis of major works and themes, an overview of critical reception, and bibliographies. Introduction to this collection places lesbian literature in its historical and political contexts. Contains one hundred articles, a general bibliography, and appendixes of selected periodicals and journals.

Schwarz, A. B. Christa. *Gay Voices of the Harlem Renaissance*. Bloomington: Indiana University Press, 2003. Examines the work of four leading gay writers of the Harlem Renaissance—Countée Cullen, Langston Hughes, Claude McKay, and Richard Bruce Nugent—and their sexually nonconformist writings.

Slide, Anthony. *Lost Gay Novels: A Reference Guide to Fifty Works from the First Half of the Twentieth Century*. New York: Harrington Park Press, 2003. Detailed plot summary, character analysis, discussion of critical reception, and author biography for each of fifty "forgotten" works of lesbian and gay literature.

Summers, Claude J., ed. *The Gay and Lesbian Literary Heritage*: *A Reader's Companion to the Writers and Their Works, from Antiquity to the Present*. Rev. ed. New York: Routledge, 2002. This expanded edition features more than four hundred biographical essays on writers of all sexualities. Essays include overviews of ethnic literatures and literary themes, such as aesthetics, and cover genres such as modernism, science fiction, and young adult literature.

THE GOTHIC NOVEL

The gothic novel is a living tradition, a form that enjoys great popular appeal while provoking harsh critical judgments. It began with Horace Walpole's *The Castle of Otranto* (1765), then traveled through Ann Radcliffe, Matthew Gregory Lewis, Charles Robert Maturin, Mary Wollstonecraft Shelley, Edgar Allan Poe, Charlotte Brontë and Emily Brontë, Nathaniel Hawthorne, Charles Brockden Brown, Bram Stoker, Charles Dickens, Thomas Hardy, Henry James, and many others into the twentieth century, where it surfaced, much altered and yet spiritually continuous, in the work of writers such as William Faulkner, D. H. Lawrence, Iris Murdoch, John Gardner (1933-1982), Joyce Carol Oates, and Doris Lessing and in the popular genres of horror fiction and some women's romances.

The externals of the gothic, especially early in its history, are characterized by sublime but terrifying mountain scenery; bandits and outlaws; ruined, ancient seats of power; morbid death imagery; and virgins and charismatic villains, as well as hyperbolic physical states of agitation and lurid images of physical degradation. Its spirit is characterized by a tone of high agitation and unresolved or almost-impossible-to-resolve anxiety, fear, unnatural elation, and desperation.

The first gothic novel is identifiable with a precision unusual in genre study. Walpole (1717-1797), the earl of Orford, began writing *The Castle of Otranto* in June, 1764,; he finished it in August and published it in an edition of five hundred copies in early 1765. Walpole was a historian and essayist whose vivid and massive personal correspondence remains essential reading for the eighteenth century background. Before writing *The Castle of Otranto*, his only connection with the gothic was his estate in Twickenham, which he called Strawberry Hill. It was built in the gothic style and set an architectural trend, as his novel would later set a literary trend.

Walpole did not dream of what he was about to initiate with *The Castle of Otranto*; he published his first edition anonymously, revealing his identity, only after the novel's great success, in his second edition of April, 1765. At that point, he no longer feared mockery of his tale of a statue with a bleeding nose and mammoth, peregrinating armor, and an ancient castle complete with ancient family curse. With his second edition, he was obliged to add a preface explaining why he had hidden behind the guise of a preface proclaiming the book to be a "found manuscript," printed originally "in Naples in the black letter in 1529." The reader of the first edition was told that *The Castle of Otranto* was the long-lost history of an ancient Catholic family in the north of England. The greater reading public loved it, and it was reprinted in many editions. By 1796, it had been translated into French and Spanish and had been repeatedly rendered into dramatic form. In 1848, the novel was still active as the basis for successful theatrical presentations, although the original gothic vogue had passed.

Close upon Walpole's heels followed Radcliffe, Lewis, and Maturin. These three authors, of course, were not the only imitators ready to take advantage of the contemporary trend (there were literally hundreds of those), but they are among the few who are still read, for they made their own distinctive contributions to the genre's evolution. Radcliffe (1764-1823) was born just as Walpole's *The Castle of Otranto* was being published. She was reared in a middle-class milieu, acquainted with merchants and professionals; her husband was the editor of *The English Chronicle* and a fellow of the Society of Antiquaries. She lived a quiet life, was likely asthmatic, and seems to have stayed close to her hearth. Although she never became a habitué of literary circles and in her lifetime only published a handful of works, she is considered the grande dame of the gothic novelists and enjoyed a stunning commercial success in her day; she is the only female novelist of the period whose work is still read.

Radcliffe's works include *The Castles of Athlin and Dunbayne* (1789), *A Sicilian Romance* (1790), *The Romance of the Forest* (1791), *The Mysteries of Udolpho* (1794), *The Italian: Or, The Confessional of the Black Penitents* (1797), and *Gaston de Blondeville* (1826). She also wrote an account of a trip through parts of northern Europe, *A Journey Made in the Summer of 1794 Through*

Holland and the Western Frontier of Germany (1795). Her remarkably sedate life contrasts strikingly with the melodramatic flamboyance of her works. Her experiences also fail to account for her dazzling, fictional accounts of the scenery of Southern Europe, which she had never seen.

Lewis, called Monk Lewis in honor of his major work, conformed in his life more closely to the stereotype of the gothic masters. Lewis (1775-1818) was a child of the upper classes, the spoiled son of a frivolous beauty, whom he adored. His parents' unhappy marriage ended when he was at Westminster Preparatory School. There was a continual struggle between his parents to manage his life—his father stern and aloof, his mother extravagant and possessive.

Lewis spent his childhood treading the halls of large, old manses belonging both to family and to friends. He paced long, gloomy corridors—a staple of the gothic—and peered up at ancient portraits in dark galleries, another permanent fixture in gothic convention. Deeply involved with the literati of his day, Lewis (also homosexual) found an equivocal public reception, but his novel *The Monk: A Romance* (1796; also known as *Ambrosio: Or, The Monk*), an international sensation, had an enormous effect on the gothic productions of his day. Lewis died on board ship, a casualty of a yellow-fever epidemic, in the arms of his valet, Baptista, and was buried at sea.

Lewis's bibliography is as frenetic as his biography. Although his only gothic novel is the infamous *The Monk*, he spent most of his career writing plays heavily influenced by gothic conventions; he also translated many gothic works into English and wrote scandalous poetry. Among his plays are *Village Virtues* (pb. 1796), *The Castle Spectre* (pr. 1797), *The East Indian* (pr. 1799), *Adelmorn the Outlaw* (pr., pb. 1801), and *The Captive* (pr. 1803). He translated Friedrich Schiller's *The Minister* (1797) and August von Kotzebue's *Rolla: Or, The Peruvian Hero* (1799). He became notorious for his poetic work *The Love of Gain: A Poem Initiated from Juvenal* (1799), an imitation of Juvenal's thirteenth satire.

Maturin (1780-1824) is the final major gothic artist of the period. He was a Protestant clergyman from Dublin and a spiritual brother of the Marquis de Sade. He also was a protégé of Sir Walter Scott and an admirer of Lord Byron. His major gothic novel is *Melmoth the Wanderer* (1820), as shocking to its public as was Lewis's *The Monk*. An earlier Maturin gothic was *Fatal Revenge: Or, The Family of Montorio* (1807). His other works include the novel *The Milesian Chief* (1812); a theological novel, *Women: Or, Pour et Contre* (1818); a tragedy, *Bertram: Or, The Castle of St. Aldobrand* (pr., pb. 1816), produced by Edmund Kean; and the novel *The Albigenses* (1824).

Among the legions of other gothic novelists, a few writers (especially the following women, who are no longer generally read) have made a place for themselves in literary history. These writers include Harriet Lee, known for *The Canterbury Tales* (1797-1805), written with her sister, Sophia Lee, author also of *The Recess: Or, A Tale of Other Times* (1783); Clara Reeve (*The Champion of Virtue: A Gothic Story*, 1777; also known as *The Old English Baron: A Gothic Story*); Regina Maria Roche (*The Children of the Abbey*, 1796); Charlotte Smith (*Emmeline: Or, The Orphan of the Castle—A Novel*, 1788); Charlotte Dacre (*Zofloya: Or, The Moor—A Romance of the Fifteenth Century*, 1806); and Mary Anne Radcliffe (*Manfroné: Or, The One Handed Monk—A Romance*, 1809).

Critics generally agree that the period gothics, while having much in common, divide into relatively clear subclassifications: the historical gothic, the school of terror, and the *Schauer-Romantik* school of horror. All gothics of the period return to the past, are flushed with suggestions of the supernatural, and tend to be set amid ruined architecture, particularly a great estate house gone to ruin or a decaying abbey. All make use of stock characters. These will generally include one or more young and innocent virgins of both sexes; monks and nuns, particularly of sinister aspect; and towering male and female characters of overpowering will whose charismatic egotism knows no bounds.

Frequently the novels are set in the rugged mountains of Italy and contain an evil Italian character. Tumultuous weather often accompanies tumultuous passions. The gothic genre specializes in making external conditions metaphors of human emotions, a convention thought to have been derived in part from the works of William Shakespeare. Brigands are frequently employed in the plot, and most gothics of the period employ morbid, lurid imagery, such as a body riddled with worms behind a moldy black veil.

The various subdivisions of the gothic may feature any or all of these conventions, being distinguished by relative emphasis. The historical gothic, for example, reveals the supernatural against a genuinely historical background, best exemplified by the works of the Lee sisters, who, although their own novels are infrequently read today, played a part in the evolution of the historical novel through their influence on Sir Walter Scott. The school of terror provided safe emotional titillation—safe, because the morbidity such novels portray takes place not in a genuine, historical setting, but in some fantasy of the past, and because the fearful effects tend to be explained away rationally at the end of the respective work. Radcliffe is the major paradigm of this subgroup. The *Schauer-Romantik* school of horror, best represented by Lewis and Maturin, did not offer the reassurance of a moral, rational order. These works tend to evoke history but stir anxiety without resolving or relieving it. They are perverse and sadistic, marked by the amoral use of thrill.

There are very few traditional gothic plots and conventions; a discrete set of such paradigms was recycled and refurbished many times. Walpole's *The Castle of Otranto*, Radcliffe's *The Mysteries of Udolpho*, Lewis's *The Monk*, and Maturin's *Melmoth the Wanderer* represent the basic models of the genre.

THE CASTLE OF OTRANTO

The Castle of Otranto, emphatically not historical gothic, takes place in a fantasy past. It is not of the school of terror either; although it resolves its dilemmas in a human fashion, it does not rationally explain the supernatural events it recounts. This earliest of the gothics trembles between horror and terror.

The story opens with Manfred, Prince of Otranto, ready to marry his sickly son, Conrad, to the beautiful Isabella. Manfred, the pattern for future gothic villains of towering egotism and pride, is startled when his son is killed in a bizarre fashion. The gigantic statuary helmet of a marble figure of Alphonse the Good has been mysteriously transported to Manfred's castle, where it has fallen on and crushed Conrad.

Manfred precipitously reveals that he is tired of his virtuous wife, Hippolita, and, disdaining both her and their virtuous daughter, Mathilda, attempts to force himself on the exquisite, virginal Isabella, his erstwhile daughter-in-law elect. At the same time, he attempts to blame his son's death on an individual named Theodore, who appears to be a virtuous peasant lad and bears an uncanny resemblance to the now helmetless statue of Alfonso the Good. Theodore is incarcerated in the palace but manages to escape. Theodore and Isabella, both traversing the mazelike halls of Otranto to escape Manfred, find each other, and Theodore manages to set Isabella free. She finds asylum in the Church of St. Nicholas, site of the statue of Alfonso the Good, under the protection of Father Jerome, a virtuous friar. In the process of persuading Jerome to bring Isabella to him, Manfred discovers that Theodore is actually Jerome's long-lost son. Manfred threatens Theodore in order to maneuver Jerome into delivering Isabella. The long-lost relative later became a popular feature of the gothic.

Both Isabella and Theodore are temporarily saved by the appearance of a mysterious Black Knight, who turns out to be Isabella's father and joins the forces against Manfred. A round of comings and goings through tunnels, hallways, and churches ensues. This flight through dark corridors also became almost mandatory in gothic fiction. In the course of his flight, Theodore falls in love with Mathilda. As the two lovers meet in a church, Manfred, "flushed with love and wine," mistakes Mathilda for Isabella. Wishing to prevent Theodore from possessing the woman he thinks is his own beloved, Manfred mistakenly stabs his daughter. Her dying words prevent Theodore from revenging her: "Stop thy impious hand . . . it is my father!"

Manfred must now forfeit his kingdom for his bloody deed. The final revelation is that Theodore is actually the true Prince of Otranto, the direct descendant of Alfonso the Good. The statuary helmet flies back to the statue; Isabella is given to Theodore in marriage, but only after he completes a period of mourning for Mathilda; and order is restored. The flight of the helmet remains beyond the pale of reason, as does the extraordinary, rigid virtue of the sympathetic characters, but Manfred's threat to the kingdom is ended. Here is the master plot for the gothic of the Kingdom.

THE MYSTERIES OF UDOLPHO

Radcliffe's *The Mysteries of Udolpho* presents apparently unnatural behavior and events but ultimately explains them all. Not only will the sins of the past be nullified, but also human understanding will penetrate all the mysteries. In *The Mysteries of Udolpho*, the obligatory gothic virgin is Emily St. Aubert; she is complemented by a virginal male named Valancourt, whom Emily meets while still in the bosom of her family. When her parents die, she is left at the mercy of her uncle, the villainous Montoni, dark, compelling, and savage in pursuit of his own interests. Montoni whisks Emily away to Udolpho, his great house in the Apennines, where, desperate for money, he exerts himself on Emily in hopes of taking her patrimony while his more lustful, equally brutal friends scheme against her virtue. Emily resists, fainting and palpitating frequently. Emily's propensity to swoon is very much entrenched in the character of the gothic heroine.

Emily soon escapes and, sequestered in a convent, makes the acquaintance of a dying nun, whose past is revealed to contain a murder inspired by lust and greed. Her past also contains Montoni, who acquired Udolpho through her evil deeds. Now repenting, the nun (née Laurentini de Udolpho) reveals all. The innocent victim of Laurentini's stratagems was Emily's long-lost, virtuous aunt, and Udolpho should have been hers. Ultimately, it will belong to Emily and Valancourt.

This novel contains the obligatory gothic flights up and down dimly lit staircases and halls and into dark turrets; there are also fabulous vistas of soul-elevating charm in the Apennines, which became a hallmark of gothic, and blood-chilling vistas of banditti by torch and moonlight. There is also mysterious music that seems to issue from some supernatural source and a mysterious disappearance of Emily's bracelet, both later revealed to be the work of Valancourt. A miniature picture of the first marchioness of Udolpho, who looks unaccountably like Emily, threatens to reveal some irregularity about pure Emily's birth but in the end reveals only that the poor, victimized marchioness was Emily's aunt. In Udolpho, in a distant turret, Emily finds a body being devoured by worms. Emily is thrown into a frenzy, fearing that this is the corpse of her deluded aunt, Montoni's wife, but it is revealed to be merely a wax effigy placed

there long ago for the contemplation of some sinning cleric, as a penance. The dark night of the soul lifts, and terror yields to the paradise that Emily and Valancourt will engender. This is the master plot for personal gothic: the gothic of the family.

Radcliffe was known to distinguish between horror and terror and would have none of the former. Terror was a blood-tingling experience of which she approved because it would ultimately yield to better things. Horror she identified with decadence, a distemper in the blood that could not be discharged but rendered men and women inactive with fright. Lewis's *The Monk* demonstrates Radcliffe's distinction.

THE MONK

Lewis's *The Monk* concerns a Capuchin friar named Ambrosio, famed throughout Madrid for his beauty and virtue. He is fervent in his devotion to his calling and is wholly enchanted by a picture of the Virgin, to which he prays. A young novice of the order named Rosario becomes Ambrosio's favorite. Rosario is a beautiful, virtuous youth, as Ambrosio thinks, but one night Ambrosio perceives that Rosario has a female breast, and that "he" is in fact "she": Mathilda, a daughter of a noble house, so enthralled by Ambrosio that she has disguised herself to be near him.

Mathilda is the very image of the picture of the Virgin to which Ambrosio is so devoted, and, through her virginal beauty, seduces Ambrosio into a degrading sexual entanglement that is fully described. As Mathilda grows more obsessed with Ambrosio, his ardor cools. To secure him to her, she offers help in seducing Antonia, another virginal beauty, Ambrosio's newest passion. Mathilda, the madonna-faced enchantress, now reveals that she is actually a female demon. She puts her supernatural powers at Ambrosio's disposal, and together they successfully abduct Antonia, although only after killing Antonia's mother. Ambrosio then rapes Antonia in the foul, suffocating stench of a charnel house in the cathedral catacombs. In this scene of heavy breathing and sadism, the monk is incited to his deed by the virginal Antonia's softness and her pleas for her virtue. Each tear excites him further into a frenzy, which he climaxes by strangling the girl.

Ambrosio's deeds are discovered, and he is tried by

an inquisitorial panel. Mathilda reveals his union with Satan through her. The novel ends with Satan's liberation of Ambrosio from the dungeon into which the inquisitors have thrown him. Satan mangles Ambrosio's body by throwing him into an abyss but does not let him die for seven days (the de-creation of the world?). During this time, Ambrosio must suffer the physical and psychological torments of his situation, and the reader along with him. The devil triumphs at the end of this novel. All means of redressing virtue are abandoned, and the reader is left in the abyss with Ambrosio.

MELMOTH THE WANDERER

The same may be said of Maturin's *Melmoth the Wanderer*, a tale of agony and the failure of redemption. The book may be called a novel only if one employs the concept of the picaresque in its broadest sense. It is a collection of short stories, each centering on Melmoth, a damned, Faust-like character. Each tale concerns Melmoth's attempt to find someone to change places with him, a trade he would gladly make, as he has sold his soul to the devil and now wishes to be released.

The book rubs the reader's nerves raw with obsessive suffering, detailing scenes from the Spanish Inquisition that include the popping of bones and the melting of eyeballs. The book also minutely details the degradation of a beautiful, virginal island maiden named Immalee, who is utterly destroyed by the idolatrous love of Melmoth. The last scene of the book ticks the seconds of the clock as Melmoth, unable to find a surrogate, awaits his fall into Satan's clutches. The denouement is an almost unbearable agony that the reader is forced to endure with the protagonist. Again the horror is eternal. There will never be any quietus for either Ambrosio or Melmoth, or for the reader haunted by them. These are the molds for the gothic of damnation.

THE MODERNIZATION OF THE GOTHIC

The reading public of the late eighteenth and early nineteenth centuries was avid for both horror and terror, as well as for supernatural history. Such works were gobbled greedily as they rolled off the presses. Indeed, the readers of the gothic may have begun the mass marketing of literature by ensuring the fortunes of the private lending libraries that opened in response to the gothic

binge. Although the libraries continued after the gothic wave had crested, it was this craze that gave the libraries their impetus. Such private lending libraries purchased numerous copies of long lists of gothic works and furnished subscribers with a list from which they might choose. Like contemporary book clubs, the libraries vied for the most appetizing authors. Unlike the modern clubs, books circulated back and forth, not to be kept by subscribers.

William Lane's Minerva Public Library was the most famous and most successful of all these libraries. Lane went after the works of independent gothic authors but formed the basis of his list by maintaining his own stable of hacks. The names of most of the "stable authors" are gone, and so are their books, but the titles linger on in the library records, echoing one another and the titles of the more prominent authors: *The Romance Castle* (1791), *The Black Forest: Or, The Cavern of Horrors* (1802), *The Mysterious Omen: Or, Awful Retribution* (1812).

By the time *Melmoth the Wanderer* had appeared, this trend had run its course. Only hacks continued to mine the old pits for monks, nuns, fainting innocents, Apennine banditti, and Satanic quests, but critics agree that if the conventions of the gothic period from Walpole to Maturin have dried out and fossilized, the spirit is very much alive. Many modern novels set miles from an abbey and containing not one shrieking, orphaned virgin or worm-ridden corpse may be considered gothic. If the sophisticated cannot repress a snicker at the obvious and well-worn gothic conventions, they cannot dismiss the power and attraction of its spirit, which lives today in serious literature.

Modern thinking about gothic literature has gravitated toward the psychological aspects of the gothic. The castle or ruined abbey has become the interior of the mind, racked with anxiety and unbridled surges of emotion, melodramatically governed by polarities. The traditional gothic is now identified as the beginning of neurotic literature. In a perceptive study of the genre, *Love, Misery, and Mystery: Feeling in Gothic Fiction* (1978), Coral Ann Howells points out that the gothic literature of the eighteenth century was willing to deal with the syntax of hysteria, which the more prestigious literature, controlled by classical influences, simply denied or avoided. Hysteria is no stranger to all kinds of literature, but thinking today seeks to discriminate between the literary presentation of hysteria or neuroticism as an aberration from a rational norm and the gothic presentation of neuroticism as equally normative with rational control, or even as the dominant mode.

The evolution of the modern gothic began close to the original seedbed, in the works of Edgar Allan Poe. In "The Fall of the House of Usher," for example, the traditional sins of the gothic past cavort in a mansion of ancient and noble lineage. A young virgin is subjected to the tortures of the charnel house; the tomb and the catacombs descend directly from Lewis. So, too, do the hyperbolic physical states of pallor and sensory excitement. This tale is also marked, however, by the new relationship it seeks to demonstrate between reason and hysterical anxiety.

Roderick Usher's boyhood friend, the story's narrator, is a representative of the normative rational world. He is forced to encounter a reality in which anxiety and dread are the norm and in which the passions know no rational bounds. Reason is forced to confront the reality of hysteria, its horror, terror, and power. This new psychological development of the gothic is stripped of the traditional gothic appurtenances in Poe's "The Tell-Tale Heart," where there are neither swooning virgins nor charnel houses, nor ruined, once-great edifices, save the ruin of the narrator's mind. The narrator's uncontrollable obsessions both to murder and to confess are presented to stun the reader with the overwhelming force of anxiety unconditioned by rational analysis.

Thus, a more modern gothic focuses on the overturning of rational limits as the source of horror and dread, without necessarily using the conventional apparatus. More examples of what may be considered modern gothic can be found in the works of Nathaniel Hawthorne (1804-1864). Although Hawthorne was perfectly capable of using the conventional machinery of the gothic, as in *The House of the Seven Gables* (1851), he was one of the architects of the modern gothic. In Hawthorne's forward-looking tales, certain combinations of personalities bond, as if they were chemical compounds, to form anxiety systems that cannot be resolved except by the destruction of all or part of the human configuration. In *The Scarlet Letter* (1850), for example, the configuration of Hester, Chillingsworth, and Dimmesdale forms an interlocking system of emotional destruction that is its own Otranto. The needs and social positions of each character in this trio impinge on one another in ways that disintegrate "normal" considerations of loyalty, courage, sympathy, consideration, and judgment. Hester's vivacity is answered in Dimmesdale, whose violently clashing aloofness and responsiveness create for her a vicious cycle of fulfillment and rejection. Chillingsworth introduces further complications through another vicious cycle of confidence and betrayal. These are the catacombs of the modern gothic.

Another strand of the modern gothic can be traced to *Frankenstein* (1818), by Mary Wollstonecraft Shelley (1979-1851). The novel was published just as the gothic genre was on the wane. Shelley's story represents an important alternative for the gothic imagination. The setting in this work shifts from the castle to the laboratory, forming the gothic tributary of science fiction. Frankenstein reverses the anxiety system of the gothic from the past to the future. Instead of the sins of the fathers—old actions, old human instincts rising to blight the present—human creativity is called into question as the blight of the future. Frankenstein's mind and laboratory are the gothic locus of "future fear," a horror of the dark side of originality and birth, which may, as the story shows, be locked into a vicious cycle with death and sterility. A dread of the whole future of human endeavor pursues the reader in and out of the dark corridors of *Frankenstein*.

Bram Stoker's *Dracula* (1897) may be considered an example of a further evolution of the gothic. Here one finds a strong resurgence of the traditional gothic: the ruined castle, bandits ranging over craggy hills, the sins of the past attacking the life of the present, and swooning, morbidly detailed accounts of deaths. The attendant supernatural horror and the bloodletting of the vampires, their repulsive stench, and the unearthly attractiveness of Dracula's vampire brides come right out of the original school of *Schauer-Romantik* horror. The utterly debilitating effect of the vampire on human will is, however, strong evidence for those critics who see the gothic tradition as an exploration of neurosis.

Stoker synthesizes two major gothic subclassifications in his work, thereby producing an interesting affirmation. Unlike the works of Radcliffe and her terror school, *Dracula* does not ultimately affirm the power of human reason, for it never explains away the supernatural. On the other hand, Stoker does not invoke his vampires as totally overwhelming forces, as in the horror school. *Dracula* does not present a fatalistic course of events through which the truth will not win out. Humankind is the agency of its salvation, but only through its affirmation of the power of faith. Reason is indeed powerless before Dracula, but Dr. Van Helsing's enormous faith and the faith he inspires in others are ultimately sufficient to resolve gothic anxiety, without denying its terrifying power and reality.

THE GOTHIC IN THE TWENTIETH CENTURY
AND LATER

Significantly, in the contemporary gothic, reason never achieves the triumph it briefly found through the terror school. Twentieth and twenty-first century gothic tends toward the *Schauer-Romantik* school of horror. Either it pessimistically portrays an inescapable, mind-forged squirrel cage, or it optimistically envisions an apocalyptic release through faith, instinct, or imagination, the nonrational human faculties. For examples of both twentieth century gothic trends, it may be instructive to consider briefly William Faulkner (1897-1962), whose works are frequently listed at the head of what is called the southern gothic tradition, and Doris Lessing (born 1919), whose later works took a turn that brought them into the fold of the science-fiction branch of gothic. If there remains any doubt about the respectability of the genre and its writers, it may be noted here that both Faulkner and Lessing are winners of the Nobel Prize in Literature.

Faulkner's fictions have all the characteristic elements of the southern gothic: the traditional iconography; decaying mansions and graveyards; morbid, death-oriented actions and images; sins of the past; and virgins. *The Sound and the Fury* (1929) is concerned with the decaying Compson house and family, the implications of past actions, and Quentin's morbid preoccupation with death and virginity; it features Benjy's graveyard and important scenes in a cemetery. *As I Lay Dying* (1930) is structured around a long march to the cemetery with a stinking corpse. *Absalom, Absalom!* (1936) is full of decaying houses and lurid death scenes and features promi-

nently three strange virgins—Rosa Coldfield, Judith Sutpen, and Clytie—or five if Quentin and Shreve are to be counted. In this work, the past eats the present up alive and the central figure, Thomas Sutpen, is much in the tradition of the charismatic, but boundlessly appropriating, gothic villain.

These cold gothic externals are only superficial images that betray the presence of the steaming psychological modern gothic centers of these works. Like Hawthorne, Faulkner creates interfacing human systems of neurosis whose inextricable coils lock each character into endless anxiety, producing hysteria, obsession, and utter loss of will and freedom. The violence and physical hyperbole in Faulkner reveal the truly gothic dilemmas of the characters, inaccessible to the mediations of active reason. As in Hawthorne, the combinations of characters form the catacombs of an inescapable though invisible castle or charnel house. Through these catacombs Faulkner's characters run, but they cannot extricate themselves and thus simply revolve in a maze of involuted thought. The Compsons bind one another to tragedy, as do the Sutpens and their spiritual and psychological descendants.

There is, however, an alternative in the modern gothic impulse. In her insightful, imaginative study of the modern evolution of the gothic, *Ghosts of the Gothic: Austen, Eliot, and Lawrence* (1980), Judith Wilt assigns Lessing a place as the ultimate inheritor of the tradition. Lessing does portray exotic states of anxiety, variously descending into the netherworld (*Briefing for a Descent into Hell*, 1971) and plunging into outer space (the Canopus in Argos series), but Wilt focuses on *The Four-Gated City* (1969). This novel has both the trappings and the spirit of the gothic. The book centers on a doomed old house and an old, traditional family succumbing to the sins of the past. These Lessing portrays as no less than the debilitating sins of Western culture, racist, sexist, and exploitive in character. Lessing does indeed bring down this house. Several of the major characters are released from doom, however, by an apocalyptic World War III that wipes away the old sins, freeing some characters for a new, fruitful, life without anxiety. Significantly, this new world will be structured not on the principles of reason and logic, which Lessing excoriates as the heart of the old sins, but on the basis of something innately nonrational and hard to identify. It is not instinct and not faith, but seems closest to imagination. Lessing's ultimately hopeful vision, it must be conceded, is not shared by most contemporary practitioners of the genre.

The gothic enjoyed a resurgence in the 1980's that critics identified as a significant literary trend. Typical of the diversity of writers mentioned under this rubric are those represented in a collection edited by Patrick McGrath (born 1950): *The New Gothic: A Collection of Contemporary Gothic Fiction* (1991; with Bradford Morrow). McGrath, himself a writer of much-praised gothic fictions, assembled work by veteran novelists such as Robert Coover and John Hawkes as well as younger (now established) writers such as Jamaica Kincaid and William T. Vollmann; the group includes both the best-selling novelist Peter Straub and the assaultive experimental novelist Kathy Acker. These works were first collected by McGrath in the journal *Conjunctions* (1989), in which he contributed an essay outlining some of the characteristics of the new gothic. While resisting any attempt at rigid definition (the gothic, he says, is "an air, a tone, a tendency"; it is "not a monolith"), he acknowledges that all the writers whom he places in this group "concern themselves variously with extremes of sexual experience, with disease and social power, with murder and terror and death." That much might be said about most gothic novelists from the beginnings of the genre.

What perhaps differentiates many of the writers whom McGrath discusses from their predecessors—what makes the new gothic new—is a more self-consciously transgressive stance, evident in McGrath's summation of the vision that he and his fellow writers share.

> Common to all is an idea of evil, transgression of natural and social law, and the gothic, in all its suppleness, is the literature that permits that mad dream to be dreamt in a thousand forms.

Among popular-fiction writers, the gothic split into two main genres, one based on supernatural or psychological horror and the other based on women's fiction, featuring romance and, often, historical settings. Moreover, combinations of the two traditions most approach the hyperreal intensity and blend of fear and passion seen in the original gothic: for example, the saga of the Dol-

langanger family by V. C. Andrews (1923-1986) or the Blood Opera series—*Dark Dance* (1992), *Personal Darkness* (1993), and *Darkness, I* (1994)—by Tanith Lee (born 1947).

While horror writers often substitute the suburbs or small town for the isolated castle—and sometimes psychic abilities, deranged computers, or psychotic killers for ghostly nuns and predatory villain-heroes—they continue to explore the intense feeling, perilous world, tense social situations, and alluring but corrupt sexuality of the original gothic. Unlike the romantic gothic, which has seen periods of quiescence and revival, an unbroken line of the horror gothic persisted from *The Castle of Otranto* through *Dracula* and into the twentieth century with books such as *Ghost Stories of an Antiquary* (1904), by M. R. James (1862-1936), and the works of Walter de la Mare (1873-1956) and H. P. Lovecraft (1890-1937).

These stories continue the trend—seen in Poe, Hawthorne, Faulkner, and others—of maintaining morbid and sensational gothic elements while rooting the terror in psychology and even epistemology. Often, hauntings reveal, or are even replaced by, obsession and paranoia. Before the burgeoning of the modern commercial horror novel, Shirley Jackson (1916-1965), in two eerie and lyrical novels, *The Haunting of Hill House* (1959) and *We Have Always Lived in the Castle* (1962), uses the traditional gothic form and many of its motifs, with both psychological sophistication and true terror. Robert Bloch (1917-1994), with his novel *Psycho* (1959), also updates and psychologizes gothic conventions, substituting an out-of-the-way motel for a castle and explicitly invoking Sigmund Freud.

The horror genre grew with the (arguably) gothic novel *The Exorcist* (1971), by William Peter Blatty (born 1928), and with *Rosemary's Baby* (1967), by Ira Levin (1929-2007). The novel transplants to a New York City apartment building the hidden secret, supernatural menace, and conspiracies against the heroine of early gothics. Although the horror market withered in the 1990's, four best-selling authors continued in the gothic-horror vein: Dean R. Koontz (born 1945), Straub, Stephen King (born 1947), and Anne Rice (born 1941).

While much of Koontz's horror is better classified as horror-adventure, lacking the brooding neuroses and doubts about rationality prevalent in gothic fiction, gothic aspects do dominate his novels *Whispers* (1980), *Shadowfires* (1987), *Dean Koontz's Frankenstein: Prodigal Son* (2005; with Kevin J. Anderson), *Dean Koontz's Frankenstein: City of Night* (2005; with Edward Gorman), and *Dean Koontz's Frankenstein: Dead or Alive* (2007; with Gorman). Koontz's *Demon Seed* (1973) exemplifies the techno-gothic: A threatening setting and pursuing lover combine in a robot intelligence, which runs the house and wants to impregnate the heroine. Rice explores the gothic's lush, dangerous sexuality and burden of the past in the novels of the Vampire Chronicles, including *Interview with the Vampire* (1976), *The Vampire Lestat* (1985), *The Tale of the Body Thief* (1992), *Memnoch the Devil* (1995), *Blood and Gold: Or, The Story of Marius* (2001), and *Blood Canticle* (2003).

Straub's *Julia* (1975; also known as *Full Circle*), is a drawing-room gothic novel, focusing on the haunting—supernatural, mentally pathological, or both—of a woman dominated by her husband and his disturbing, enmeshed family. In *Ghost Story* (1979), *Shadowland* (1980), and others, Straub widens the focus, exploring and critiquing the small town, boys' school, or suburban setting while developing gothic themes, including dangerous secrets, guilt, ambivalent eroticism, and a threat from the past. In *Lost Boy, Lost Girl* (2003), the threats include a pedophile serial killer, a haunted house, and a missing man's obsession with his dead mother. Straub explores other genres as well, especially the mystery, but maintains a gothic tone and intensity.

Similarly, King's early work is more strictly gothic, such as *'Salem's Lot* (1975), in which vampires spread through a small town in Maine, and *The Shining* (1977), a story of madness and terror in an isolated, empty hotel. However, many later works, even mimetic ones such as *Gerald's Game* (1992), *Dolores Claiborne* (1993), *Bag of Bones* (1998), *From a Buick Eight* (2002), and *Cell* (2006), continue gothic themes and often a gothic tone. King is the undisputed best-selling author of the genre, having sold more than 330 million copies of his novels. Straub and King, admirers of one another's work, have collaborated on two fantasy novels, *The Talisman* (1984), and a sequel, *Black House* (2001).

The prolific Joyce Carol Oates (born 1938), author of more than fifty novels, has created several memorable gothic works, including a Gothic Saga series comprising *Bellefleur* (1980) and its sequels. Another memorable work is *Zombie* (1995), an exploration of the mind of a serial killer, based on the life of Jeffrey Dahmer. New voices on the gothic-novel scene include Donna Tartt (born c. 1964), author of *The Secret History* (1992) and *The Little Friend* (2002), and Elizabeth Kostova (born 1964), whose first novel, *The Historian* (2005), became a best seller and was translated into close to thirty languages.

Along with terror and horror, sentimental and romantic elements were established in the original gothic in the works of Ann Radcliffe, Clara Reeve, Susanna Rowson (1762-1824), and the Brontë sisters. In 1938, *Rebecca*, by Daphne du Maurier (1907-1989), the story of a young woman's marriage to a wealthy English widower with a secret, conveyed many gothic conventions to a new audience, paving the way for the genre of gothic romance. Combining mystery, danger, and romantic fantasy, such books tend to feature innocent but admirable heroines, a powerful male love interest and his isolated estate, ominous secrets (often linked to a woman from the love interest's past, as in *Rebecca*), and exotic settings that are remote in place and time.

In the early 1960's, editor Gerald Gross of Ace Books used the term "gothic" for a line of paperbacks aimed at women, featuring primarily British authors such as Victoria Holt (pseudonym for Eleanor Alice Burford Hibbert, 1906-1993), Phyllis A. Whitney (1903-2008), and Dorothy Eden (1912-1982). The mystery and love plots are inextricable, and the novels feature many gothic elements, including besieged heroines; strong, enigmatic men; settings that evoke an atmosphere of tension and justified paranoia; heightened emotional states; doubled characters (including impersonation); and lurid, sometimes cruel, sexuality. In the 1970's and later, erotic elements flourished and became more explicit, resulting in the new category of the erotic gothic.

Martha Nochimson
Updated by Bernadette Lynn Bosky

BIBLIOGRAPHY

Brown, Marshall. *The Gothic Text*. Stanford, Calif.: Stanford University Press, 2005. Scholarly examination of what it means to designate a literary work as "gothic." Brown explicates the antecedents of and ideologies that were contemporary to the birth of gothic literature. Brown also examines definitive gothic authors and works.

Ellis, Markman. *The History of Gothic Fiction*. New York: Columbia University Press, 2000. Historical survey of the gothic novel, with analyses of the female gothic, revolution and libertinism, science and conspiracy, vampires and credulity, and zombies and the occultation of slavery.

Frank, Frederick S. *Guide to the Gothic*. Lanham, Md.: Scarecrow Press, 1984.

_____. *Guide to the Gothic II*. Lanham, Md.: Scarecrow Press, 1995. Annotated bibliographies on gothic fiction and literary analyses of gothic works. With Frank's updated 1995 guide, impressively complete and helpful.

Geary, Robert F. *The Supernatural in Gothic Fiction: Horror, Belief, and Literary Change*. Lewiston, N.Y.: Edwin Mellen Press, 1992. Gothic fiction often contains elements of the supernatural. Geary discusses the most common works using use the supernatural as a theme.

Haggerty, George E. *Queer Gothic*. Urbana: University of Illinois Press, 2006. Considers the subtext of homoeroticism in gothic fiction. Examines topics such as gothic fiction and the history of sexuality, the gothic and the "erotics of loss," and the influence of gothic novelist Anne Rice on the "queering of culture."

Jackson, Anna, Karen Coats, and Roderick McGillis, eds. *The Gothic in Children's Literature: Haunting the Borders*. New York: Routledge, 2007. Argues that the gothic has always been a part of children's literature, contrary to assumptions about the gothic as a forbidden realm for adults only. Examines "the early intersection of the gothic and children's literature and the contemporary manifestations of the gothic impulse."

Kilgour, Maggie. *The Rise of the Gothic Novel*. Reprint. New York: Routledge, 1997. Explores the gothic novel's beginnings and its growth in popularity among writers, readers, and publishers. Includes bibliographical references and an index.

Mussell, Kay. *Women's Gothic and Romantic Fiction: A Reference Guide*. Westport, Conn.: Greenwood Press, 1981. Concise and insightful overviews and lengthy bibliographies concerning the female gothic, from Ann Radcliffe to commercial gothic romances of the late twentieth century.

Norton, Rictor, ed. *Gothic Readings: The First Wave, 1764-1840*. Reprint. New York: Leicester University Press, 2006. Study of the first novels of gothic literature. Edited collection of intelligent, readable essays.

Punter, David, and Glennis Byron. *The Gothic*. Malden, Mass.: Blackwell, 2004. Discusses backgrounds, contexts, themes, and motifs, and provides detailed introductions to dozens of individual authors. Includes a chronology and a bibliography.

Punter, David, ed. *A Companion to the Gothic*. Malden, Mass.: Blackwell, 2000. Twenty-four critical essays by leading scholars in the field, exploring the gothic's progression in Western literary history.

Varma, Devendra P. *The Gothic Flame: Being a History of the Gothic Novel in England—Its Origins, Efflorescence, Disintegration, and Residuary Influences*. Metuchen, N.J.: Scarecrow Press, 1987. Originally published in 1957, this groundbreaking study of the early gothic (1764-1826) provides descriptions, analyses, classifications, and a detailed history.

Wright, Angela. *Gothic Fiction*. New York: Palgrave Macmillan, 2007. From the perspective of aesthetic, political, psychoanalytic, and gender criticism, Wright explores "the moral and political panic" that accompanied the earliest rise of gothic fiction. Follows with a study of how the gothic survived the panic and then thrived as a serious form of literature.

THE HISTORICAL NOVEL

Popular legend records that the historical novel was born out of frustration—specifically out of Sir Walter Scott's frustration at having been displaced by Lord Byron as the most popular poetic romancer of his day. Scott's early narrative poems, such as *Marmion: A Tale of Flodden Field* (1808) and *The Lady of the Lake* (1810), had established him as the premier storyteller in verse in the first decade of the nineteenth century, but when Byron began publishing his Eastern tales (*The Giaour*, 1813; *The Bride of Abydos*, 1813; and so on), Scott saw his public turning away. Not one to acquiesce easily, Scott resurrected the manuscript of a prose work he had begun almost ten years earlier. In it Scott told of the climactic struggles of the Scottish barons to restore the House of Stuart to the throne, culminating in their final defeat in 1745, some fifty years before Scott had originally written the tale. Since an additional decade had now passed, Scott altered his subtitle and sent off to his publishers the manuscript of *Waverley: Or, 'Tis Sixty Years Since* (1814), thus creating what was to become one of the most popular forms of fiction.

The first edition of *Waverley* was published anonymously, presumably so that Scott would not suffer embarrassment if this experiment in prose were a failure. It was not; the reading public made *Waverley* a best seller, and a similar reception awaited the novels that followed its prolific author. Before he died in 1832, the father of the historical novel had brought to life the stories of Scotland, England, and, to a lesser extent, France during the Middle Ages, the Renaissance, and the eighteenth century. Historians may well claim that Scott's history is faulty, or that it is told from a slanted point of view; and literary critics may fault him for letting his penchant for adventure override concerns for character development, coherence of plot, and thematic exposition. Whatever faults scholars may find, though, none can deny the immediate success these novels had nor belittle the impact of this new literary venture on the development of fiction. The popularity of the historical novel has never abated, and it has consistently ranked with the detective story and the thriller as one of the forms of literature with the widest audience appeal.

The educated reader may well wonder, however, why certain novels have been singled out under the appellation "historical." The fact that all novels are set in some period links them to history; even novels set in the future share that link, however tenuously. What makes a particular novel "historical"? This problem of definition plagues critics, and virtually everyone who has written of the historical novel has evolved a standard that allows some novels to be included in this category while others are excluded. Most critics agree, however, that certain characteristics identify the historical novel. Writers of historical fiction have certain aims and limitations that mark their works as distinct from other forms of prose narratives and that form a general set of criteria by which their works may be judged.

Since the time of Aristotle, critics have generally contrasted the writings of the historian and the poet (or writer of imaginative literature), seeing their approaches to recording human events as essentially dichotomous. Aristotle believed that the historian dealt with the particular, the imaginative writer with the universal; the former wrote of what actually happened, the latter of what was probable in consonance with the verities of human character (*De poetica*, c. 334-323 B.C.E.; *Poetics*, 1705). While modern students of classical and medieval history have come to recognize that not all history is as factual as Aristotle would have liked to believe, the distinction is still useful. The historian is responsible for representing as accurately as possible past events as they really happened. Because the facts of the past do not of themselves speak to people in the present, historians must discern the significance of the data they collect. For most historians, however, any interpretation of the significance of those facts is clearly distinguished from the account of the facts themselves.

The notion of interpretation provides the key to understanding the relationship between historians and historical novelists. Like historians, historical novelists examine the facts of history, but rather than interpreting them analytically, they attempt to bring the past to life and interpret the significance of historical events through the conventions of literature: characterization, plot, and thematic development. They use the tools of their trade—image, symbol, juxtaposition, parallelism, and a host of other rhetorical devices—to provide their interpretation. Their aim is to transport the reader imaginatively to a period removed from the present. The best historical novelists accomplish their aims without violating the spirit of the historical process; they invent only when the chronicles are silent, and they rearrange only sparsely, or more often not at all. Thus, a main characteristic that sets apart the historical novel from other forms of fiction is the novelist's ability to present events of the past without remaining rigidly tied to historical documents (which themselves may be inaccurate). Coupled with the skill to delineate the interaction of human characters in the context of the historical period, their interest in recapturing the past distinguishes truly successful historical novelists from proponents of mere costume romance.

A large number of novels set in the past are indeed no more than costume romances, attempts to disguise modern situations or fantasies (usually involving sex or violence) in the garb of former times. Often, too, the use of history becomes a means of providing an apologia for present conditions or of producing a lament for times past without a serious attempt to examine the actualities of those times. Fiction of the American South (which includes some of the best historical novels) contains numerous examples of this kind of writing, the most notable being Margaret Mitchell's *Gone with the Wind* (1936). A best seller in the year of its publication and for years afterward, Mitchell's novel remains the most popular novel ever written by a southerner. The characters in the novel are stereotypes of the Old South: the gallant plantation youth (Ashley Wilkes), the demure southern belle (Melanie), the rebellious vixen (Scarlett O'Hara), the hardened and aristocratic outcast (Rhett Butler), the stern female house slave with a heart of gold (Mammy)—the list could be extended considerably. For all its popular success, the novel presents only a superficial view of the real conflicts that engulfed the South as it moved through this traumatic period of transition. For the majority of the American public, though, the portrait of the South that Mitchell creates has become the accepted one, largely because the work achieved wide readership among the general public and almost simultaneously provided the script for one of Hollywood's most successful motion pictures.

THE APPROACH TO THE HISTORICAL NOVEL

Generally, regardless of their intent, writers of historical novels have followed one of two approaches toward historical events and characters. By far the larger group has written works in which their major characters are fictional personages who live during periods in which great events occur: the glorious years of the Roman Empire; the age of the Crusades; the time of the English, American, French, or Russian revolutions; the Hundred Years' War; the Napoleonic wars; the American Civil War; or the two world wars. More often than not, the historical novel is set in a time of crisis. The fictional characters often, though not always, interact with real personages in some way. This technique of placing fictional characters on the fringe of great events, used by Scott in his novels and adopted by many others, can provide an effective sense of the period without violating (except, perhaps, for the purist) the sense of history that the reader brings to the work.

In novels that attempt to retain a high degree of verisimilitude, the contact between real and fictional characters generally remains slight; in works better termed "historical romances," such contact is often magnified, sometimes to the point of suggesting that the fictional character has had an impact on real-life events. Examples of this approach can be found in the World War II novels of Herman Wouk, *The Winds of War* (1971) and *War and Remembrance* (1978). Wouk's fictional hero, Victor "Pug" Henry, a U.S. Navy captain, becomes the confidant of President Franklin D. Roosevelt and his emissary to various foreign capitals, where he meets with world leaders Winston Churchill, Adolf Hitler, Benito Mussolini, and Joseph Stalin. Henry's influence in shaping Roosevelt's opinion about the war and his other exploits with foreign leaders is purely fictional and accounts in part for Wouk's own admission in the preface to *War and Remembrance* that he is writing a "historical romance."

Linking history to the narrative tradition of the romance has been a common practice for many writers who have chosen to focus on fictional characters living during a period of crisis. Among the more famous practitioners of this method is the French novelist Alexandre Dumas, *père*, who, through his loose weaving of historical fact and fancy, provided the worldwide reading public with figures and stories now part of the cultural heritage of the West: Porthos, Athos, and Aramis, the Three Musketeers, and idealistic young D'Artagnan, the real hero of several of Dumas's novels of the reign of Louis XIV. *Les Trois Mousquetaires* (1844; *The Three Musketeers*, 1846) is only one of many, however, that Dumas wrote about that period and about other episodes in French history, including explorations of the age of Henry IV, the Franco-Spanish War of the sixteenth century, the reign of Louis XV, and the French Revolution.

The methodology employed by artists who focus on fictional characters in real-life times of crisis can be seen most vividly in Charles Dickens's *A Tale of Two Cities* (1859). This chilling look at the impact of the French Revolution has given many generations of readers a feeling for that event that even Thomas Carlyle's history of the revolution fails to evoke. In this novel, Dickens recreates the horrors of the revolution by detailing the effects of the Reign of Terror on the lives of fictional characters whose destinies take them between Paris and London. Few major figures of history appear in Dickens's book, and those who do are given subordinate roles. The historicity of the novel lies in Dickens's graphic portrayal of the masses and of the individuals affected by the actions of the "citizens" of the revolution. The fictional Madame DeFarge, whose insatiable appetite for the blood of aristocrats is motivated as much by a desire for personal vengeance as by any desire for liberty and equality, reinforces the notion that the exploits of the real-life Robespierre and his henchmen were neither anomalous nor necessarily high-minded.

Similarly, the frustrations of the Manette family, as well as the heroism of both Sidney Carton and Charles Darnay, become representative of thousands whose stories are unnoted by the historian, whose personal tragedies and triumphs have been reduced to mere statistics. Thus, history is not violated but rather is vivified by the presentation of characters and incidents that, though unrecorded in chronicles of the period, might have easily occurred. In the best historical novels, the reader senses that, had these events occurred, they would have done so with the same consequences that the novelist has presented.

A second, less common approach to historical fiction is that of choosing as a main character a person who really did live and whose history is recorded in some form.

Such an approach is in many ways more difficult; those who choose this method are limited to a great degree by the facts of history in structuring plot, delineating character, providing motivation, and even in developing themes. Usually, the greater the figure chosen, the more restricted the novelist is in exploring the subject through the medium of fiction. Some have done so and been fairly successful. Howard Fast achieved popular acclaim for his portraits of George Washington (*The Unvanquished*, 1942) and Thomas Paine (*Citizen Tom Paine*, 1943). Robert Graves's *I, Claudius* (1934) is a daring attempt to present the decadent life of the emperor's court in post-Augustan Rome through the eyes of one of the major figures of that period.

Another highly successful examination of historical forces seen through the eyes of a major historical figure is found in Russian novelist Aleksandr Solzhenitsyn's *Avgust chetyrnadtsatogo* (1971; *August 1914*, 1972). In the novel, Solzhenitsyn is actually following the example set for him by his predecessor, Leo Tolstoy, whose *Voyna i mir* (1865-1869; *War and Peace*, 1886) has been called by some critics the greatest historical novel ever written. Chronicling events in Russia during the Napoleonic era, Tolstoy concentrates on the lives of fictional characters to reveal the nature of personal relationships as they are influenced by the forces of history. Looming large over the novel is the figure of General Kutozov, the commander of the Russian army who defeated Napoleon at Moscow. Also worthy of note is Gore Vidal's fictional chronicle of American history. In *Washington, D.C.* (1967), *Burr* (1973), *1876* (1976), *Lincoln* (1984), *Empire* (1987), and *Hollywood: A Novel of America in the 1920's* (1990), Vidal skillfully interweaves his fictional characters into the lives of Presidents Martin Van Buren, Abraham Lincoln, and Theodore Roosevelt, as well as luminaries such as John Hay, Henry Adams, and others easily recognizable by students of American history.

An even greater cast of historical personages comes to life in *Freedom* (1987), a novel by American journalist and critic William Safire. This long book (nearly one thousand pages of text and more than two hundred pages of notes and commentary that Safire calls his "Underbook") details life in Washington, D.C., and northern Virginia following the announcement of secession by the Confederate states and the momentous decision by

Lincoln to issue the Emancipation Proclamation. The daily lives—both public and private—of more than two dozen key figures involved on both sides of the Civil War are chronicled in Safire's lively and insightful account. Relying heavily on the historical record, Safire represents his figures with exceptional psychological sensitivity. His decision to steer clear of lengthy analyses of battles and concentrate instead on the political arena—in which decisions were often affected by personality clashes among men and women with oversized egos—makes this study of the causes and consequences of war particularly distinctive. For the student of historical fiction, Safire offers a perceptive observation about his process of composition: "The reader of any historical novel asks, 'How much of this is true?'" Safire's answer is to provide an "Underbook" citing the many sources from which he has drawn his portraits. This historical dimension "is close to the way it happened," reconstructed from "firsthand sources" such as letters and diaries. The rest, he reminds his readers, "is fiction, a device that overrides the facts to keep the reader awake or—when it works best—to get at the truth." Safire's novel gives the reader a sense of peering over the shoulder of real people whose lives seem a bit more dramatic than one might have imagined they could ever have been.

The same can be said of another fine historical novel about the American Civil War, Michael Shaara's *The Killer Angels* (1974). Focusing on the Battle of Gettysburg, Shaara mines the historical record for data about the principal generals and their chief lieutenants, bringing them to life as individuals and revealing some of the complexities of personality that shaped their decisions and, hence, the course of the war. In *Gods and Generals* (1996), the prequel to his father's novel *The Killer Angels*, Jeff Shaara follows his father's approach to research and focuses on two central figures. He has also published two novels about World War II: *The Rising Tide* (2006) and *The Steel Wave* (2008).

Writing about real people, however, is not without its dangers. One need only review the controversy surrounding the publication of William Styron's *The Confessions of Nat Turner* (1967). This Pulitzer Prize-winning novel is a fictional account of the leader of a slave revolt in the Tidewater region of Virginia in 1831. Historical records detailing Turner's revolt are sparse; the primary documentary evidence is contained in a twenty-page pamphlet written by the prosecuting attorney at Turner's trial and ostensibly dictated by Turner himself shortly before he was executed. Contemporary newspaper accounts offer some corroboration, but they are biased. From these slim historical sources, Styron creates what he calls "a meditation on history," a musing, first-person, reflective account of the motivation for Nat's actions.

In addition to taking the daring step of telling his hero's story in the first person, Styron also modifies the available facts to make his character more interesting psychologically. Omitting Nat's wife and father from the story, Styron attributes his hero's education to the efforts of good white masters and emphasizes the thin line between religious fanaticism and repressed sexual desire. Styron's Nat, believing that he is being driven by an Old Testament God who has made him the instrument of vengeance on the white community for their treatment of blacks, puts to use the education he received from whites to incite other slaves to revolt.

Effusive praise from white critics has been far overshadowed by the condemnations issued by African Americans. *William Styron's Nat Turner: Ten Black Writers Respond* (1968; reprinted, 1987), a collection of essays by noted black intellectuals, systematically attacks the novel on grounds both literary and historical. These critics assert that Styron's hero's meditations are the thoughts of white men, that his hero's aspirations are those that white men think black men have, and that his hero's rationale for acting is actually a reflection of the rationalization for slavery. Social historians have criticized the novel for not presenting a portrait of the real Nat Turner; they charge Styron with avoiding the real issues that led to Turner's revolt. In their view, the book simply does not fulfill one of the main criteria for good historical fiction: It is not sufficiently true to the historical record.

There is clear evidence, however, that the best historical novels can rank with the finest novels of any kind. One need only look to the works of one of America's foremost novelists of the twentieth century: William Faulkner. In many ways, the entire corpus of Faulkner's work is an extended study of the history of his region, the American South. Faulkner tries to make sense of what happened there in a society that contained, side by side, aspects of feudal or baronial European culture and the individualizing tenets of the American Dream. As one might expect, Faulkner focuses on the great crime of slavery; that dehumanizing institution on which southern society was based bred racial hatred that continued long after slavery was officially abolished as a result of the Civil War. That catastrophe plays a central role in Faulkner's fiction, either as a subject itself or as an event that looms in the consciousness of those who populate Faulkner's mythical Yoknapatawpha County.

Among his novels, *Absalom, Absalom!* (1936) is possibly the best example of a novel intensely concerned with the way people come to understand the past and the way they try to make sense of it so that the present becomes explicable. In the novel, a young southerner, Quentin Compson, and his Canadian roommate at college, Shreve McCannon, attempt to piece together the family history of Thomas Sutpen, a self-styled southern aristocrat whose grand design for establishing a dynasty in the wilds of northern Mississippi is ruined when his son kills the fiancé of Sutpen's only daughter, then flees the country. Quentin must piece together Sutpen's story from oral narratives and meager written accounts, none of which reveals the whole truth about the past. *Absalom, Absalom!* has been described as a kind of detective story, in which Quentin and Shreve make a "persistent attempt to understand the past from partially perceived fragments surviving about it" (Hugh Holman, *The Immoderate Past*, 1977). Because he is a son of the South, Quentin sees in the story of Sutpen the tragedy of his heritage. The novel reveals to the reader the impossibility of ever knowing the past completely; it is to humankind's credit, however, that it tries to do so, because in the past, one may find an explanation for the present, and thereby develop some hope for the future.

Absalom, Absalom! is, in the final analysis, a novel about the historical process itself, a story of the way one comes to understand one's own past. Ironically, these discoveries about the tenuousness and fragility of the historical method appear in a novel that contains almost no references to real personages; yet the reader senses that what is being read is as real as any historical account of the South. The saga of life in Faulkner's fictional Jefferson, Mississippi, and surrounding countryside may be far removed from places where great events have occurred, but the impact of history on the lives of men and women in this rural southern community is transformed by Faulkner into a statement of the way events mold the human race. In Yoknapatawpha County, one finds the engagement with the living past that continues to inspire the best historical novelists.

THE EVOLUTION OF THE HISTORICAL NOVEL

The appetite of the reading public for historical sagas has given several British and American novelists opportunities to write extensively about life in previous centuries. Among the more popular sagas is Patrick O'Brian's series of novels about the career of Jack Aubrey, a naval officer whose exploits at sea occur during the late eighteenth and early nineteenth centuries. Beginning in *Master and Commander* (1969) and extending through twenty volumes to *Blue at the Mizzen* (1999), O'Brian uses Aubrey's rise from midshipman to admiral as a fictional platform from which he is able to launch detailed accounts of naval life from the rebellion of the American colonists through the Napoleonic wars. Aubrey's constant companion at sea, Dr. Stephen Maturin, is not only a physician but also an employee of the state sent abroad to collect intelligence about foreign countries. Through him O'Brian is able to describe the political intrigues among nations and rogue groups whose actions influence international conflicts.

By carefully crafting plots that include significant naval engagements and a series of adventures on land, O'Brian creates for readers a sense of what life was like for both sailors and the land-bound populace during these turbulent decades. For example, in *The Hundred Days* (1998), Aubrey is assigned to intercept a shipment of gold intended to support Napoleon's efforts to recapture the French throne after he returns to the European continent from exile. Although few historical figures play a major role in the novel, readers nevertheless gain a sense of the impending European crisis by following Aubrey and Maturin across the Mediterranean as they negotiate with various leaders in the Arab world to block the transfer of gold that would allow Napoleon to equip a fighting force.

The same kind of historical ambience is created with exceptional skill by Charles Frazier in *Cold Mountain* (1997). In this Civil War tale, Frazier uses the conflagration between North and South as a backdrop to tell a story of love, courage, and endurance. His principal characters, the disillusioned soldier Inman and the southern belle Ada, find their lives disrupted and forever altered by the war. Inman is forced to behave brutally in his effort to return to Cold Mountain, where he hopes to rebuild his life with Ada. She, in the meantime, learns to fend for herself in a land where the social skills required for young women in antebellum North Carolina are of little value once the very necessities of life can no longer be obtained without succumbing to hard labor. Frazier's study in the adaptability of human nature and the power of strong emotions is made more poignant by the historical setting, a time of brutality and disdain for the norms of civil behavior.

Although many of their efforts have been dismissed as subliterary, perhaps because of their subject matter, women have used the historical novel to bring to light the contributions and the powers of women of the past. Historian-journalist Karen Essex examines the shrewdness of Cleopatra in two novels, *Kleopatra* (2001) and *Pharaoh* (2002), and she re-creates the little-known story of the powerful but forgotten Este sisters, Isabella and Beatrice, patrons and muses of Leonardo da Vinci, in *Leonardo's Swans* (2006). In *Stealing Athena* (2008), Essex tells a tale about the parallel lives of Mary Nisbet, the countess of Elgin, and Aspasia, Athenian philosopher and courtesan two millennia earlier—two powerful women deeply involved in the story of the long-contested Elgin marbles.

Philippa Gregory has written several well-researched novels, including her Tudor series, which recounts the behind-the-scenes life of Elizabeth I and the women in her circle. *The Other Boleyn Girl* (2002), about Mary Boleyn, the sister of Anne Boleyn, Henry VIII's second wife, became a best seller and was adapted as a British television series and a feature film. Jacqueline Winspear's character Maisie Dobbs, the protagonist of a series of award-winning mystery novels, was a front-line nurse at the Battle of the Somme in 1916. The novels, set in the years right after World War I, highlight the strength of the women and men who survived that battle.

Similarly, African Americans have used the historical novel to reclaim, rediscover, and reinterpret history, and to remind readers of a past that should not be lost.

Important novels in this vein include David Bradley's *The Chaneysville Incident* (1981); the Pulitzer Prize-winning *Beloved* (1987) by Toni Morrison, who won the Nobel Prize in Literature in 1993; Charles Johnson's *Middle Passage* (1990), which won the National Book Award; and Edward P. Jones's *The Known World* (2003), which won the Pulitzer Prize.

Traditional historical novels that follow the techniques used by Sir Walter Scott also found a large audience throughout the final decades of the twentieth century and the beginning of the twenty-first. Typical among the hundreds of historical fictions that populated best-seller lists is Steven Pressfield's *Gates of Fire: An Epic Tale of the Battle of Thermopylae* (1998). The novel recounts the heroism of the three hundred Spartans who stopped the advance of the Persian army at Thermopylae in the fifth century B.C.E. Through the story of Xeones, a fictional character who fights with the Spartans as squire to one of the nobles engaged in the battle, Pressfield not only relates a detailed account of the battle but also offers readers a glimpse into the lives of the Spartans and an analysis of their national character. Much as Scott employs historical personages to interact with his fictional heroes and heroines, in *Gates of Fire* figures such as the Spartan king Leonidas and the Persian emperor Xerxes are given prominence in the novel. Accounts of daily life in Sparta and of the battle itself are based on meticulous research. Characterization, imagery, and the use of literary devices such as similes bear strong resemblance to techniques used by the Greek epic poet Homer in *The Iliad* (c. 800 B.C.E.). Pressfield's novel offers modern readers a lesson in courage and sacrifice drawn from history.

There is a certain irony present in *Gates of Fire*, however, that highlights one of the basic tensions of the historical novel as a genre. Modern historians came to realize that "histories" by classical writers such as Herodotus and Thucydides must be read not as literal records but as creative attempts to paint one country or city-state in a favorable light, often at the expense of other societies—and even at the expense of historical accuracy. For decades, historiographers have demonstrated that the writer of history is more often than not a partisan chronicler. Hence, the line between fact and fiction is blurred not only in historical novels but also in the historical accounts on which they are based. Nevertheless, novels such as *Gates of Fire* and Pressfield's novel about Alexander the Great's invasion of Afghanistan, *The Afghan Campaign* (2006), attest to the continuing vitality of the genre, as readers find the blend of fact and fiction a particularly enjoyable way to learn about the past through the lives of characters who actually experience historical events. The historical novel continues to live up to Samuel Johnson's dictum that literature should teach by delighting.

Laurence W. Mazzeno

BIBLIOGRAPHY

Brown, Joanne, and Nancy St. Clair. *The Distant Mirror: Reflections on Young Adult Historical Fiction.* Lanham, Md.: Scarecrow Press, 2006. Thorough historical survey of this important genre, focusing on issues of faith, class, and realism. Includes suggestions for further reading and a bibliography.

Byerman, Keith Eldon. *Remembering the Past in Contemporary African American Fiction.* Chapel Hill: University of North Carolina Press, 2005. Focuses on the historical fiction of Toni Morrison, Ernest Gaines, Gloria Naylor, Raymond Andrews, Charles Johnson, and John Edgar Wideman.

Hughes, Helen. *The Historical Romance.* New York: Routledge, 1993. Study of more than forty romances. Explains how the writer's choice to ground a narrative in the historical past affords opportunities to create plausible fantasies. Looks at formal qualities of historical romances and the characteristics of readers who appreciate them.

Lukács, Georg. *The Historical Novel.* Translated by Hamma Mitchell and Stanley Mitchell. London: Merlin Press, 1989. Pioneering study of the genre, originally published in 1962. A Marxist analysis that praises writers who value the historical process.

Orel, Harold. *The Historical Novel from Scott to Sabatini: Changing Attitudes Toward a Literary Genre, 1814-1920.* New York: Macmillan, 1995. Explores changes in the concept of historical fiction between Scott's novels and those published just after the end of World War I. Concentrates on nine novels by British and Continental writers, and shows the divergent paths taken by writers of historical fiction and historical romance.

Sanders, Andrew. *The Victorian Historical Novel, 1840-1880.* New York: St. Martin's Press, 1978. Discusses more than one dozen novels by major and minor Victorian figures. Traces trends in historical fiction in the fifty years after Scott's death.

Shaw, Harry E. *The Forms of Historical Fiction: Sir Walter Scott and His Successors.* Ithaca, N.Y.: Cornell University Press, 1983. Defines the historical novel and explains how the genre was created. Provides criteria for evaluating historical fiction on its own terms and as part of the tradition of fiction in the nineteenth and twentieth centuries.

Ungurianu, Dan. *Plotting History: The Russian Historical Novel in the Imperial Age.* Madison: University of Wisconsin Press, 2007. Theoretically based analysis of a genre popular during the nineteenth century. Explains how novelists used history as the basis of their fiction, and why Russian readers were attracted to this form. Includes a chronology of historical novels published in Russia between 1829 and 1917.

Wallace, Diana. *The Woman's Historical Novel: British Women Writers, 1900-2000.* New York: Palgrave Macmillan, 2005. The first major study of this group of writers. Includes a wide survey, as well as focused attention on Naomi Mitchison, Georgette Heyer, Sylvia Townsend Warner, Margaret Irwin, Jean Plaidy, Mary Renault, Philippa Gregory, and Pat Barker.

Wesseling, Elisabeth. *Writing History as a Prophet: Postmodernist Innovations of the Historical Novel.* Philadelphia: J. Benjamins, 1991. Highly specialized study describing ways twentieth century novelists transform the traditional historical novel to explore the past and simultaneously explain how it can be apprehended. Traces relationships between historical fiction and fantasy literature, detective fiction, and science fiction.

Zimmerman, Everett. *The Boundaries of Fiction: History and the Eighteenth Century British Novel.* Ithaca, N.Y.: Cornell University Press, 1996. Examines eighteenth century notions of history that influenced major precursors of Sir Walter Scott. Explains how the necessity these novelists felt to ground their work in the historical record led to the development of the historical novel.

THE HORROR NOVEL

By the end of the nineteenth century, writers interested in exploring supernatural themes had abandoned the mode of gothic fiction pioneered by eighteenth century English novelist Horace Walpole. Walpole and his imitators had exploited such props as medieval ruins and gloomy manor houses riddled with secret passages, while later gothic novelists had accentuated madness and excessive violence. Newer writers emphasized character, practiced a more sophisticated narrative technique, and displayed an intuitive grasp of the workings of the human psyche.

Horror fiction continued to do what gothic fiction had done before it. In an era of growing emphasis upon science and reason, it explored humankind's darker and more irrational impulses. Increasingly, however, the boundaries between horror and gothic became more slippery, and individual authors or works are being categorized and analyzed in either genre.

HORROR'S GOLDEN AGE: 1872-1912

The four decades from 1872 to 1912 represent one of the two richest periods of horror fiction in the English language. Because such moods as dread and anxiety are easier to maintain in shorter forms, many of the most successful works from this period are stories and novellas.

The year 1872 saw the publication of *In a Glass Darkly*, by Irish writer Joseph Sheridan Le Fanu. Le Fanu also wrote novels in which the supernatural played some part, but he is remembered for his shorter works, among which is the novella "Carmilla" from this collection. Although not the first work in English to deal with vampires, "Carmilla" is one of the most sophisticated. It is not clear whether Carmilla is "really" a vampire or her feelings for the novella's young narrator are sexual. Nor is it clear what ultimate spiritual fate awaits the narrator herself, who is dead when the story begins. "Carmilla" is reprinted in countless anthologies of horror stories and has inspired numerous film versions, the most famous being Carl Theodore Dreyer's *Vampyr* (1932).

The same air of ambiguity hangs over *The Turn of the Screw* (1898), by Henry James. In this famous novella a governess charged with protecting two young children either battles malignant ghosts or projects onto imaginary ghosts her own destructive feelings toward the children—it is not clear which. Another writer who found the novella especially useful for exploring ambiguous psychological states was the Englishman Oliver Onions. In *The Beckoning Fair One* (1911), Onions described the disintegration of a writer whose sanity is sapped by his own ghostly creation.

Equally astute psychological analysis characterizes short novels produced by two writers famous for works in a variety of forms. Robert Louis Stevenson wrote the classic fictional treatment of the split personality in *The Strange Case of Dr. Jekyll and Mr. Hyde* (1886). Dr. Jekyll is a paragon of virtue, but the alter ego he releases by chemical means is a monster of murderous desire. In *The Picture of Dorian Gray* (serial 1890; expanded 1891), Oscar Wilde described a bon vivant whose portrait registers the ravages of sin while he himself retains his youthful appearance.

During this same period several British writers produced what American writer H. P. Lovecraft was to describe as "cosmic horror." These writers included Arthur Machen and William Hope Hodgson. Rather than embodying evil in stock figures such as ghosts, these writers located malignity in the universe itself. Machen's *The Great God Pan* (1894) is an early example. This novella describes a union between a young woman and Pan, ostensibly a minor classical deity but in this case a figure emblematic of a greater and far more frightening "reality" lurking beyond the everyday world. The experience drives the woman mad, and the daughter she subsequently bears instigates a cycle of destruction years later.

Unlike many talented supernatural writers of his time, Hodgson wrote effectively in longer forms, and his novels constitute a high-water mark of horror fiction. In *The Boats of the "Glen Carrig"* (1907), Hodgson drew upon his years at sea to describe the fate of a ship imprisoned in the weeds of a phantasmagoric Sargasso Sea. The tightly constructed short novel *The Ghost Pi-*

rates (1909) utilized another sea setting to describe a ship taken over by sailors from another dimension. In his masterpiece, *The House on the Borderland* (1908), Hodgson resuscitated the familiar gothic prop of the ruined manor—in this case a deserted stone house in the west of Ireland. Travelers recover from this ruin a manuscript describing an eruption of swinelike creatures from a nearby pit as well as an existentially chilling vision of the fate of the universe. Hodgson's enormous two-volume final novel, *The Night Land: A Live Tale* and *The Night Land: Volume Two* (1912), is written in a trying eighteenth century style but describes a world millions of years in the future. The remnants of humankind have gathered in a great pyramid known as the Last Redoubt, outside of which waits a horrifying assembly of malignant deities.

The best literary works often transcend apparent trends or categories. This is true of Bram Stoker's *Dracula* (1897), a melodramatic adventure novel that eschews the sophistication characteristic of much supernatural fiction of the period. Irishman Stoker mixed eastern European myths of the nosferatu (or vampire) with legends of Vlad the Impaler, a bewilderingly bloodthirsty tyrant of the fifteenth century. Told in the form of letters and journal entries, the novel carries its now-famous central character, Count Dracula, from Transylvania to England and back again. *Dracula* is a compelling and irresistibly readable account of the struggle between good and evil, and it has proven inestimably influential.

BETWEEN THE WARS

The major development in horror fiction in the United States occurred between World War I and World War II. American writers such as Nathaniel Hawthorne and Edgar Allan Poe had written prolifically in the gothic tradition, and drawing upon them and such British figures as Machen and Hodgson, Lovecraft created a highly influential body of work.

Lovecraft's major achievement was the creation of the Cthulhu mythos. The stories written within this framework suggest that Earth was once the realm of a host of malignant entities, or Old Ones—among them the dreadful Cthulhu—forever striving to regain their foothold. In addition to his many stories, Lovecraft

wrote two novels. The more important of them is *At the Mountains of Madness, and Other Novels* (1964), a thoughtful adventure novel concerning a scientific expedition to Antarctica that uncovers a dwelling place of the Old Ones. Lovecraft was a conscientious writer, but his work is often vitiated by a labored, mock-archaic style. For this reason and because of their bizarre subject matter, his stories appeared exclusively in amateur publications and garishly illustrated pulp magazines. Lovecraft's many followers and imitators published in the same markets, and as a result horror fiction in the United States was cut off from the mainstream of literary development for decades.

AMERICAN BOOM

After World War II, several American horror writers challenged the sometimes stultifying complacency of a society intent upon preserving the status quo. In *I Am Legend* (1954), Richard Matheson imagines a world in which almost everyone has become a vampire. In *The Body Snatchers* (1955), Jack Finney taps a similar vein of paranoia by imagining aliens who have taken over a small town's seemingly normal residents. Ray Bradbury describes another small town visited by a sinister carnival in *Something Wicked This Way Comes* (1962).

Most strikingly, writer Shirley Jackson challenges the era's normality with *The Haunting of Hill House* (1959), a coolly understated short novel in which the evil personality of a haunted house undermines the sanity of one of the group that comes to investigate its alleged supernatural nature.

In the late 1960's and early 1970's, several horror novels became best sellers, propelling the genre into public awareness. In *Rosemary's Baby* (1967) Ira Levin transferred the central situation of Machen's *The Great God Pan* to contemporary New York City, while in *The Exorcist* (1971), William Peter Blatty describes a case of demoniac possession. Both novels were rapidly paced and appealed to audiences unfamiliar with horror fiction. More poetic was Thomas Tryon's *The Other* (1971), an atmospheric tale of twins and their dark secret. Tryon's next novel, *Harvest Home* (1973), describes a New England fertility cult. Robert Marasco's *Burnt Offerings* (1973) posits a haunted house even more malignant than Jackson's Hill House.

These works set the stage for a writer who would transform horror fiction into a staple of contemporary culture. Stephen King's stories and novels have earned for him not only an enormous readership but also grudging literary respect. King's many works range from treatments of traditional themes to more original creations. *'Salem's Lot* (1975) is a straightforward but vividly realized vampire novel, while *The Shining* (1977) is an equally vivid haunted house novel, the "house" in this case being a snowbound hotel in the Rocky Mountains.

King's lengthy novels, *The Stand* (1978, unabridged 1990), *It* (1986), and *Lisey's Story* (2006), show his considerable talents stretched to their limits. In *The Stand*, a plague has wiped out most of humanity, setting the stage for the ultimate confrontation between good and evil. In *It*, a handful of characters—both innocent children and less-than-innocent adults—battle an unimaginably malevolent being buried far beneath Earth's surface. In *Lisey's Story,* a widow struggles to recapture memories of her dead husband, and faces a threat to her life.

King has been so prolific that he has written under more than one name. In one case, he simultaneously published *Desperation* (1996), as King, and another novel, *The Regulators* (1996), under the pseudonym Richard Bachman. These two books deal, appropriately enough, with a shift in the nature of reality and, like all King's best works, exhibit a grasp of realistic detail and an imaginative reach seldom equaled in the genre.

King's contemporaries have profited from his popularity, and some, such as Dean R. Koontz, have equaled him in production. Other writers include David Morrell, who provides a natural (if harrowing) explanation for supposedly supernatural phenomena in *The Totem* (1979), and Anne Rice, who initiated a ten-volume series of richly imagined if ultimately repetitive novels with *Interview with the Vampire* (1976). Others in the Vampire Chronicles series include *The Vampire Lestat* (1985), *The Tale of the Body Thief* (1992), *Memnoch the Devil* (1995), *Blood and Gold: Or, The Story of Marius* (2001), and *Blood Canticle* (2003). Suzy McKee Charnas has written works that are more restrained. Her novels include *The Vampire Tapestry* (1980) and *Stagestruck Vampires, and Other Phantasms* (2004).

King's most talented contemporaries include Peter Straub, T. E. D. Klein, and Jonathan Carroll. Straub's *Ghost Story* (1979) and Klein's *The Ceremonies* (1984) both recapitulate the history of the horror genre, and Straub, in *Shadowland* (1980), investigates the realm of a modern magician. Carroll's *The Land of Laughs* (1980) looks back to Matheson, Finney, and Bradbury as it exposes the dismaying reality behind a seemingly idyllic midwestern town. Elizabeth Kostova's first novel, *The Historian* (2005), became a best seller and was translated into twenty-eight languages. It tells the story of a young woman and her father who uncover the true history of Vlad the Impaler, or Dracula.

CONTINUING BRITISH TRADITION

The most enduring British horror fiction of the post-World War II period has been produced by writers working in the mainstream. Sarban (John William Wall) produced a haunting dark fantasy in *The Sound of His Horn* (1952), a short novel that combines time travel with a sadomasochistic fantasy positing Nazi triumph in World War II. In *The Feasting Dead* (1954) and *The Vampire of Mons* (1976), John Metcalfe and Desmond Stewart, respectively, each spin a psychologically compelling variation on the vampire theme. Richard Adams wrote a leisurely but grim ghost story, *The Girl in a Swing* (1980).

Noted biographer Peter Ackroyd has written a series of erudite horror novels, of which the best are *Hawksmoor* (1985) and *The House of Doctor Dee* (1993). *Hawksmoor* deals with an eighteenth century Satanist and architect of churches, while *The House of Doctor Dee* concerns a young man who discovers that he is living in the former abode of a famous alchemist.

The most accomplished postwar horror novel in Britain came from an unlikely source: famous comic novelist Kingsley Amis. His novel *The Green Man* (1969) features a libidinous and alcoholic innkeeper whose establishment is haunted by the ghost of a seventeenth century magician and terrorized by the magician's murderous creation.

Two other British novelists, Ramsey Campbell and Clive Barker, have written specifically within the horror and fantasy genres, and while they have gone on to explore a variety of themes and forms, their first novels remain their best. Campbell's short novel, *The Doll Who Ate His Mother* (1976), is as ghoulishly unsettling as its title suggests. Barker's lengthy and ambitious *The Dam-*

nation Game (1985) retells in contemporary terms the story of Faust, the sixteenth century figure said to have sold his soul to the devil.

Grove Koger

BIBLIOGRAPHY

Barron, Neil, ed. *Horror Literature: A Reader's Guide.* New York: Garland, 1990. Arranged alphabetically by author within broad chronological periods, this survey discusses most of the major works of the horror genre as well as many other, more obscure, authors and their works.

Bleiler, E. F., ed. *Supernatural Fiction Writers: Fantasy and Horror.* 2d ed. New York: Charles Scribner's Sons, 2003. Two-volume collection of accessible essays on the genres of fantasy and horror that examine every major figure in the field.

Bloom, Harold, ed. *Classic Horror Writers.* New York: Chelsea House, 1994. Collection of criticism of the works of major gothic and early horror writers.

_____. *Modern Horror Writers.* New York: Chelsea House, 1995. Continuation of *Classic Horror Writers*, covering late nineteenth century and twentieth century figures.

Burgess, Michael, and Lisa R. Bartle. *Reference Guide to Science Fiction, Fantasy, and Horror.* 2d ed. Westport, Conn.: Libraries Unlimited, 2002. Comprehensive guide to source materials on the genres of horror, fantasy, and science fiction. Lists relevant dictionaries, encyclopedias, and awards and provides bibliographies, fan guides, and price guides.

Docherty, Brian, ed. *American Horror Fiction: From Brockden Brown to Stephen King.* New York: Macmillan, 1990. Intriguing look at horror fiction from the eighteenth through the twentieth centuries, starting with Charles Brockden Brown to the vastly popular Stephen King.

Jones, Darryl. *Horror: A Thematic History in Fiction and Film.* London: Arnold, 2002. Thoughtful analysis of horror fiction and its critical reception. Examines how the form has been used to covertly explore national and cultural hatred. Includes a bibliography.

Jones, Stephen, and Kim Newman, eds. *Horror: One Hundred Best Books.* New York: Carroll & Graf, 1988. One hundred horror writers each choose and analyze an important work from the genre, including novels by Stephen King, Ray Bradbury, Edgar Allan Poe, Nathaniel Hawthorne, and Christopher Marlowe.

_____. *Horror: Another One Hundred Best Books.* New York: Carroll & Graf, 2005. Update of the editors' 1988 work, with a new set of writers analyzing their favorite examples of the horror genre. Excellent, intriguing, provocative volume.

Sullivan, Jack, ed. *The Penguin Encyclopedia of Horror and the Supernatural.* New York: Viking Press, 1986. Essays examine horror and the supernatural in literature, art, music, and film.

Wiater, Stan, Christopher Golden, and Hank Wagner. *The Complete Stephen King Universe: A Guide to the Worlds of the King of Horror.* Rev. ed. New York: Macmillan, 2006. Examines King's novels, short stories, motion pictures, miniseries, and teleplays, and includes story analyses, character breakdowns, and discussion of how the plots, themes, characters, and conflicts intertwine.

The Legal Novel

The roots of the legal novel can be traced to a variety of sources, including the heroic romance, the gothic novel, and even cowboy fiction, all of which provided models for characterization and plotting. From the mid-eighteenth century, novels have incorporated images and incidents from the law and many have turned on the discovery of a will or lost deed or a disputed claim over property. Important ancestors of the legal novel are the police memoir and true-life tale, popular during the nineteenth century, genres that gave rise to a number of highly popular forms such as the thriller, mystery, detective story, and police procedural. Generally, however, the legal novel is distinguished from these other genres by focusing on the law, making use of the courtroom in some way and having one or more lawyers featured prominently in the story.

DEVELOPMENT OF THE GENRE

One work often cited as a precursor to the modern legal novel is Charles Dickens's *Bleak House* (1852-1853, serial; 1853, book), which centers on a civil trial that lasts years in the Court of Chancery and eventually eats up the profits of the estate over which the legal dispute is centered. The work is populated with lawyers; however, the court proceedings are only one part of this lengthy critique of Victorian society, in which Dickens exposes some of the injustices of the legal system. Other British novelists of the nineteenth century, notably Wilkie Collins, also wrote fiction in which the law figures prominently. Among the first American writers to pay special attention to the law and lawyers was Melville Davisson Post. Post, an attorney who turned to writing fiction for diversion, in the 1890's began publishing stories featuring Randolph Mason, an unscrupulous lawyer who makes use of trickery and legal loopholes for his clients' benefit. A decade later, Post created a new persona, Uncle Abner, whose knowledge of the law matched Randolph's but whose moral character and sense of justice fostered a more idealized image of the legal profession. The popularity of Post's work suggests that the public was interested in stories about the law if these featured sharply drawn protagonists and intricate plots.

In the early decades of the twentieth century a number of writers tried their hand at legal fiction, borrowing many conventions of plotting and characterization from the detective novel. In 1926, Frances Noyes Hart published what is generally considered the first courtroom drama, *The Bellamy Trial*. Authors such as H. C. Bailey, initially a successful British mystery writer in the style of Dorothy Sayers, moved into the realm of the legal novel. Works by writers such as Englishmen Edgar Lustgarten, R. Austin Freeman, and Henry Cecil and American Harold Q. Masur were among hundreds that reached a modest but devoted audience.

One of the most important contributions to the development of legal fiction was made by Erle Stanley Gardner. His 1933 novel *The Case of the Velvet Claws* introduced readers to Perry Mason, a Los Angeles lawyer who specializes in defending murder suspects who appear guilty of the crime with which they have been charged. Trained as a lawyer, Gardner combined elements of the detective novel and the classic mystery tale with his own legal expertise. Many of the nearly one hundred Perry Mason novels and stories focus on the sleuthing talents of Mason, his secretary Della Street, and his private investigator Paul Drake. Occasionally, Mason or one of his associates is forced to face physical danger in the pursuit of key information, and they must frequently work at odds with the police. Each novel ends with a courtroom scene in which Mason is pitted against District Attorney Hamilton Burger, who often ends up exasperated and amazed by Mason's abilities, which include bending the law and engaging in courtroom theatrics to establish his clients' innocence and simultaneously reveal the real killer. Gardner's rather formulaic novels became favorites with millions of readers, and Perry Mason was later to achieve even greater notoriety in the long-running television series and made-for-television movies featuring Gardner's characters.

Legal fiction was not, however, always bound by strict conventions and aimed simply at arousing excitement and suspense in readers. Occasionally, the framework of the genre was used to explore serious social issues. Two acclaimed southern writers penned novels featuring dramatic courtroom scenes and lawyers as protagonists. In William Faulkner's *Intruder in the Dust* (1948), set in rural Mississippi, Gavin Stevens, a disillusioned and often out-of-work attorney, is called on to defend a black man accused of killing a white man. In addition to risking his life to save his client from a lynch mob, Stevens ends up investigating the murder and identifying the true killer. Faulkner's complex style limited the work's appeal to his first audience. By contrast, Harper Lee's *To Kill a Mockingbird* (1960) won the Pulitzer Prize and became a national best seller. Lee, the daughter of an attorney who had herself attended law school but not completed a degree, was able to use her considerable knowledge of the legal system to give the novel an air of realism about the justice system and courtroom proceedings. The story of lawyer Atticus Finch's attempts to defend a black man against a charge of rape, like the story told in *Intruder in the Dust*, exposed much about racism and concurrently dramatized the ways legal proceedings could be manipulated (or ignored) by those motivated by prejudices and interested in revenge.

The legal novel for most of the twentieth century, however, remained largely in the realm of popular literature, appealing to a readership that appreciated the intellectual puzzles created by writers who understood the law and its close relationship with all aspects of democratic life. Occasionally, legal fiction proved an attractive alternative for mainstream writers such as Louis Auchincloss, whose *A World of Profit* (1968) and *The Partners* (1974) both feature lawyers and legal proceedings at the center of the action. While most legal novels sold well, only a few became best sellers during this period. Notable among these is *Anatomy of a Murder* (1959), by Robert Traver (pseudonym of John Donaldson Voelker), a novel featuring a lengthy courtroom scene that authentically portrays the exchange between prosecution and defense. As with a number of more popular legal novels, *Anatomy of a Murder* was adapted for the screen, where its leading characters were portrayed by Hollywood legends James Stewart and George C. Scott.

THE MODERN LEGAL THRILLER

Although practicing attorneys had been writing novels about the law for decades, Scott Turow raised the profile of the legal novel with the publication of *Presumed Innocent* in 1987. Set in fictional Kindle County, Illinois, Turow's intricate plot revolves around the efforts of assistant district attorney Rusty Sabich to help identify the killer of fellow prosecutor Carolyn Polhemus. Because Sabich had secretly been having an affair with Polhemus, he ends up being the prime suspect, and much of the business of the novel is taken up with legal maneuverings by Sabich and his defense attorney to demonstrate his innocence. The plot is further complicated when the judge selected for the trial is found to have had an affair with the deceased as well. Readers are never certain whether Sabich is being framed or is really the killer, and even in the final scene, when there are strong hints as to who really committed the murder, there is only a presumption of Sabich's innocence.

Turow employed his considerable experience as a prosecutor to give the novel an exceptional aura of authenticity; his intricate descriptions of the legal process are reminiscent of police procedural novels that lay out the steps law-enforcement officials take to bring criminals to justice. Further, within the conventions of the thriller, Turow proves capable of depicting characters with exceptional subtlety, giving readers a sense that these men and women are not simply cardboard heroes and villains but are people one might meet in real life.

Turow followed *Presumed Innocent* with a series of best-selling legal thrillers and remained a favorite among devotees of the genre, but he almost immediately lost to John Grisham his place as the most celebrated writer of legal fiction. A Mississippi attorney who had a brief career in that state's senate, Grisham began writing during the mid-1980's and published his first novel, *A Time to Kill*, in 1989. Taking his cue from the work of Faulkner and Lee, Grisham develops his plot around the killing of two white racists by Carl Lee Hailey, a black man whose daughter had been raped by the pair. Jake Brigance, Grisham's protagonist, is determined to save Lee's life even though the residents of fictional Ford County, filled with the prejudices one normally associates with people in small southern communities, want revenge.

Although *A Time To Kill* did not achieve immediate success, Grisham followed with two novels that became almost instant best sellers, *The Firm* (1991) and *The Pelican Brief* (1992). The first features a young lawyer whose idealism is quickly shattered when he is hired at a firm that makes millions of dollars by handling legal affairs for the Mafia. The second focuses on efforts of a young law student to expose environmental pollution, corruption, and bribery involving powerful corporate interests and complicit politicians.

Two factors contributed significantly to the surge in popularity of legal fiction. First, both Grisham and Turow owe part of their success as novelists to having their books adapted into films with recognizable stars such as Harrison Ford in *Presumed Innocent*, Tom Cruise in *The Firm*, and Julia Roberts and Denzel Washington in *The Pelican Brief*. The popularity of these films drove many viewers to bookstores to purchase these novels and others by the same authors. The same would prove true for other writers in the decade that followed. Second, some critics have suggested that legal thrillers became popular as a replacement for spy novels, which were in vogue during the Cold War, from the late 1940's until the end of the 1980's.

Turow and Grisham were not the only attorneys-turned-novelists to benefit from the public's heightened interest in legal fiction. Among lawyers whose novels reached wide audiences were Lisa Scottoline, Richard North Patterson, Steve Martini, and David Baldacci. Some have combined conventions of the legal thriller with other popular genres, as James Patterson does in his Women's Murder Club series, where an assistant district attorney, police detective, and medical examiner work in tandem to solve crimes and bring criminals to justice. Among the more unusual adaptations of the genre are Randy D. Singer's Christian-themed legal novels. These writers make use of their own knowledge of the legal system to create stories that give readers a sense that they are seeing the inner workings of the justice system, both its good and bad sides. Further, each has managed to invent complicated plots and characters that meet readers' demands for stories that provide both a sense of escape from the real world and a feeling that they are somehow immersed in real-life situations that promise dire consequences for characters with whom they quickly come to identify.

RECURRING ELEMENTS AND THEMES

As the legal novel developed during the twentieth century, certain characteristics emerged to distinguish this type of fiction from the broader categories from which it emerged, such as crime or detective fiction and conventional thrillers. Although both prosecutors and defense attorneys have served as featured characters, it is more common to find protagonists operating outside large organizations such as district attorneys' offices or large law firms. Having them operate essentially as loners or parts of small teams such as Perry Mason's group of associates allows writers to focus on their personal struggles to get at the truth. When main characters are part of a larger organization, such as Rusty Sabich in *Presumed Innocent* or Mitch McDeere in *The Firm*, they are often placed at odds with superiors and coworkers to heighten the sense of conflict. Frequently, they are forced to break through the bureaucracy that surrounds the practice of law or expose corruption within the profession. In many instances they take an active role in solving crimes, often incurring great personal risk.

Two major forms of plot development dominate the genre. The first type is similar to the mystery novel: The lawyer-protagonist is cast in a role similar to the detective, forced to discover facts and expose criminals. In the second scenario, both the criminal and the crime are revealed early in the novel, and readers' interest lies in discovering how protagonists will win their cases.

Unlike police officers and private detectives, however, the heroes and heroines of legal novels are interested principally in using the law as a means of achieving justice. Most but not all legal novels feature courtroom scenes in which the protagonists are given the chance to bring about favorable resolutions for their clients or themselves. While a few novelists (notably Gardner) rely on courtroom theatrics and sudden confessions to achieve satisfactory resolutions, most create realistic give-and-take scenarios in which prosecution and defense marshal evidence and cite precedents to convince judges and juries that their side should ultimately prevail.

If there is one overriding theme in legal fiction, it is the exploration of the concept of justice. The best legal novels not only provide interesting and diverting reading; they expose for readers the fragility of the justice system, the potential for corruption, and the need for vigilance and determination by those who believe in this important cornerstone of democracy. Until the late twentieth century, most novelists worked from the premise that, if facts were presented to impartial judges and juries, justice would prevail. Hence, when a character such as Perry Mason exposes a killer in a dramatic courtroom scene, there is an unwritten assumption that District Attorney Burger will gain a conviction at that person's trial.

In time, however, novelists began writing about the foibles of the justice system, as readers became more aware of real-life examples of justice being trumped by legal chicanery or trampled by powerful figures able to influence courts and juries. At the turn of the twenty-first century it was not uncommon to find protagonists simultaneously risking their reputations and sometimes their own lives for their clients outside the courtroom while struggling to overcome obstacles within the justice system.

Laurence W. Mazzeno

BIBLIOGRAPHY

Bounds, J. Dennis. *Perry Mason: The Authorship and Reproduction of a Popular Hero.* Westport, Conn.: Greenwood Press, 1996. Scholarly analysis of the most famous fictional lawyer created during the twentieth century. Examines Mason as a cultural phenomenon, discusses key elements in the novels, and explores television and movie adaptations to explain the enduring appeal of this type of literary and visual entertainment.

Breen, Jon L. *Novel Verdicts: A Guide to Courtroom Fiction.* 2d ed. Lanham, Md.: Scarecrow Press, 1999. Extensive survey of legal fiction published in the United States and Great Britain. Annotated entries for nearly eight hundred novels provide brief plot summaries and evaluations. Introduction outlines elements of courtroom fiction and suggests criteria for critical analysis.

Klinkenborg, Verlyn. "Law's Labors Lost: The Lawyer as Hero and Anti-Hero." *New Republic*, March 14, 1994. Outlines the elements of legal fiction and explains the sociological and psychological reasons for the rise of the genre in the late 1980's. Supports general arguments with examples from several popular legal thrillers.

Macdonald, Andrew F., and Gina Macdonald. *Scott Turow: A Critical Companion.* Westport, Conn.: Greenwood Press, 2005. Analysis of Turow's fiction and his role in popularizing the legal novel. Includes a chapter on work that influenced Turow, including many key texts in the development of legal fiction in the nineteenth and twentieth centuries.

Pringle, Mary Beth. *John Grisham: A Critical Companion.* Westport, Conn.: Greenwood Press, 1997. Assessment of Grisham's career as one of the most popular authors of legal thrillers. Includes a chapter on the development of the genre in the United States. Analyzes a number of Grisham's novels.

_____. *Revisiting John Grisham: A Critical Companion.* Westport, Conn.: Greenwood Press, 2007. Continues Pringle's analyses of Grisham's works with an examination of the novels published from 1997.

White, Terry, ed. *Justice Denoted: The Legal Thriller in American, British, and Continental Courtroom Literature.* Westport, Conn.: Praeger, 2003. Compendium on the genre that includes an essay outlining components of the legal thriller, synopses of nearly two thousand novels and stories, a brief bibliography of secondary sources, a glossary of legal terms frequently used in this form of fiction, an index of characters that recur in popular series of legal novels, and brief responses by legal novelists to questions about their craft.

THE MODERN NOVEL

One way to understand the modern novel is to show its development in the work of writers such as Joseph Conrad, Marcel Proust, James Joyce, Virginia Woolf, Franz Kafka, and William Faulkner. This list is by no means exclusive, but it represents those authors who are essential figures of the modernist literary canon.

Along with their modernist contemporaries, Conrad, Proust, Joyce, Woolf, Kafka, and Faulkner are "modern" because they share certain literary preoccupations with an unstable modern world, have a diminishing belief in the idea of progress, are concerned with the radical subjectivity of the self, and, consequently, are preoccupied with the novelist's need to present "reality" from multiple perspectives. Of paramount concern to modernists is the question of how the world is perceived—or, rather, their concern is the difficulty of perceiving the world as an agreed upon or objective reality. Thus, the modern novel relies on stream-of-consciousness narrators and even unreliable witnesses to the present and the past, underscoring the strenuous effort by novelist and reader alike to arrive at a semblance of the truth. The modern novel, in other words, has an epistemological thrust, a dynamic questioning of what its characters know and how they think they know it.

JOSEPH CONRAD (1857-1924)

Many commentators on the modern novel date its inception to World War I—and its aftermath—because its horrors led to skepticism about moral values, religious principles, and political convictions that nineteenth century writers and readers believed were universal and enduring. The basic elements of modernism, however, evolved earlier; they appeared in Joseph Conrad's early work, completed before World War I.

Conrad experienced the sort of displacement and disorientation that are the hallmarks of high modernism, that is, of novels that inquire into the foundations of civilization, the core beliefs and modes of perception that nineteenth century novelists took for granted or only fitfully questioned. This was a time when Charles Darwin, Karl Marx, and Sigmund Freud first began to undermine the Victorian confidence in a coherent universe.

Conrad grew up in Russian-occupied Poland, the son of an impoverished Polish nobleman who wrote political plays and was persecuted by the Russians. Early on, Conrad absorbed the devastating history of Poland, an enlightened country that had been partitioned by Russia, Prussia, and the Austro-Hungarian Empire and had risen against its oppressors in several futile rebellions. Conrad left his native land and went to sea, deciding several years later to reestablish himself in England and pursue writing as a career.

Conrad doubted the Victorian notion of progress. His novels, such as *Heart of Darkness* (1899 serial, 1902 book), reminded the British that their island nation had once been a part of the Roman Empire and that the British "moment" in history—its pride in the achievements of imperialism—might be just that: a moment. Conrad ridiculed the European notion that its economy and political structures would prevail in history. He exposed the futile blindness of such pretensions in *Nostromo* (1904), a novel that prophetically described the repetitive round of revolution and counterrevolution and reaction that would pervade much of twentieth century South and Central America, even as Europeans and Americans invested in undeveloped countries and deluded themselves into believing their presence would result in a socially, economically, and politically improved world.

Charlie Marlow, Conrad's narrator in *Heart of Darkness*, *Victory* (1915), and other works, is a quintessential modernist because he cannot complacently accept civilization like his contemporaries. His views are antiheroic and anti-Romantic; he questions nineteenth century hero worship, which led Romantic and Victorian writers such as Thomas Carlyle and Ralph Waldo Emerson to argue that history is made by "great men" and that history itself is just the sum of innumerable biographies of great men. Kurtz in *Heart of Darkness* sets out to become one of these great men, and it is Marlow's task to discover why Kurtz fails—not merely as a person but as a representative of a Western civilization attempting to bring its values to the so-called savages in Africa.

Marlow meditates on Kurtz's intentions. Is Kurtz's

corruption, his assumption of absolute power over the indigenous peoples, the logical if unforeseen result of his arrogant quest to save them? Marlow questions and doubts his ability to understand not only Kurtz's story but also history itself. Does history, in fact, have a meaning? Even more troubling is Marlow's inability to tell the truth about Kurtz to Kurtz's fiancé, a proper Victorian woman who cannot begin to understand how Kurtz succumbed to evil, the heart of darkness that humans, the novel implies, are all too inclined to perpetuate.

Conrad's contribution to the modern novel is enormous. He brought a brooding, musing sensibility to narrative and an awareness of the way human consciousness feeds on itself and elaborates whole worlds rather than just describing them. The great tradition of nineteenth century was realism: The novelist attempted to accurately convey the world and render its complexity. The focal point, in other words, was the world, not human consciousness, although certain late nineteenth century writers such as Henry James began to demonstrate that it was the narrator—as much as or more than the story he or she had to tell—who was the cynosure of fiction. Thus, James's narrators, such as Lambert Strether in *The Ambassadors* (1903), anticipate the next major development in the modern novel, which occurs in the work of Marcel Proust.

MARCEL PROUST (1871-1922)

Like Conrad, Marcel Proust grew up in an atmosphere of societal upheaval. The Commune of Paris, a popular uprising for a more democratic government, had failed in the year of the novelist's birth, and France had been defeated in war by Prussia. In this demoralized and uncertain environment, with a declining aristocracy and dynamic middle class, the sensitive Proust was exposed to an era of rapid change. Like Conrad, Proust relied on the supple and subtle perception of his narrator to convey a conception of society and history as a construct, an extension of the human ego filtered through the sensibility of the artist. Proust could describe a town, a group of people, a country setting in the manner of a realist, yet it was his attention to language that made the descriptions stand out. Unlike the realist, in other words, Proust was not merely imitating nature to render an accurate picture of it; rather, he heightened sense through an exquisite attention to style (diction, imagery, and the rhythm of his prose).

Proust's masterpiece, *À la recherche du temps perdu* (1913-1927; *Remembrance of Things Past*, 1922-1931, 1981), is a standard modernist work, focusing on time and history as subjects in themselves. Proust's narrator is concerned not solely with his memories but with the way he remembers and with how others formulate their sense of the past and present. In Proust, human identity itself becomes a product of language, and thus the artist becomes not merely a reporter (as in the realist tradition) but also a symbolist; that is, the writer fastens on those objects, scenes, and anecdotes that are shaped to define the way his or her characters live and think of their lives.

JAMES JOYCE (1882-1941)

In *A Portrait of the Artist as a Young Man* (1914-1915, serial; 1916, book), James Joyce extended the Proustian effort to render reality as it appeared to human consciousness by resorting to different linguistic registers with their own vocabulary and grammar. Thus, the child Stephen Dedalus emerges with his own language in the opening passage about a "moocow." Joyce is not merely describing a child's world, or picturing that world from the child's point of view—as Charles Dickens does in *Great Expectations* (1860-1861, serial; 1861, book), for example. On the contrary, Joyce inhabits a child's world using the child's words and phrases to create a sense of immediacy, of what critics have called a stream of consciousness. Reality is not there to be observed but rather to be created in the child's mind. Stephen is the artist already making up stories in his unusual style. The modern novelist captures the fluid nature of perception as it is enacted in the mind.

Perhaps the most conspicuous example of Joycean stream of consciousness is Molly Bloom's famous soliloquy at the end of *Ulysses* (1922). Joyce daringly delves into Molly's private thoughts and feelings as she lies in bed dwelling on her lover's and her husband's behavior as well as on her own cravings for sex. Her constant repetition of the word "yes" to convey her obsessive desire shocked many of Joyce's contemporaries. He was breaking new ground in fiction, announcing, in effect, that what made the novel modern was the novelist's willingness to deal explicitly with subjects that heretofore had been deemed illicit and the province of pornographers. Joyce, however, believed that the novelist should not shy away from any feeling or desire expressed by his or her characters, even if this meant—as it did—that his or her work would be censored. *Ulysses* could not be legally published in the United States until 1933, when a court lifted the ban on the novel.

Joyce's modernism is defined then, not only by his method of narration but also his subject matter: women as fully active and demanding sexual creatures and who tell stories from their own point of view and with their own words. Similarly, the hero of *Ulysses*, Leopold Bloom, a Dublin Jew, is hardly a conventional male protagonist. He is, rather, what some critics have called an antihero because he engages in no daring actions and is not a leader of society or a military figure. He is, outwardly, unremarkable. What makes him noteworthy is the attention Joyce devotes to Bloom, including to his lively inner life, which is, in its own way, adventurous and absorbing. In other words, the modern hero or antihero acquires his or her status through the energy and imagination the novelist invests in him or her and not as the result of a record of accomplishment (namely in men) that society admires. Bloom is the common man as hero, making up the story of his own life as he lives it.

Like Proust, Joyce exercised a sort of sovereignty over his material, a superiority over the requirements of both classical literature—in the form of epics such as Homer's *Odyssey* (c. 800 B.C.E.)—and nineteenth century realism, which took society as a given, a template on which to place characters. Joyce's characters are alluring not because of what they do but because of the way Joyce invents them, endowing them with an interior language rather than just with certain mannerisms and tics, the externals of the characters that Dickens, for instance, was so adept at creating.

Joyce focused his novels on contemporary society and, it could be argued, from a male point of view, notwithstanding his sensitive creation of characters like Molly Bloom and Gerty MacDowell in *Ulysses*. One of Joyce's contemporaries, Virginia Woolf, wished to remake the modern novel so that it more fully reflected women's creativity in narratives that questioned the conventional ordering of history and traditional gender relationships.

Virginia Woolf (1882-1941)

Virginia Woolf sought to bring the full weight of women's concerns and talents to the development of the modern novel. She rejected the rigid hierarchies of a male-dominated society and sought in her own fiction to portray women as proactive, as makers of the world. She admired women writers and artists such as her contemporaries Rebecca West and Vanessa Bell (her sister) and based her eponymous heroine, Orlando, on Bell. *Orlando: A Biography* (1928) is a quintessential modernist novel that violates the standards of realistic fiction even as it mimics and burlesques biography, one of the most conventional literary genres that depends on linear development and chronological storytelling. Orlando, born in the Elizabethan period and still alive at the time of the novel, exemplified the development of civilization and gender. West was especially intrigued by the passages in which Orlando undergoes gender reassignment from a man to a woman. West maintained in her 1928 essay on Woolf, "High Fountain of Genius," that these passages made up the heart of the novel because Woolf was

> debating . . . how far one's sex is like a pair of faulty glasses on one's nose; where one looks at the universe, how true it is that to be a woman is to have a blind spot on the North Northwest, to be a man is to see light as darkness East by South.

In other words, Woolf was incorporating in her exploration of gender a typically modern concern with perception—that is, with the vantage point from which individuals view their world. That Orlando's gender itself transcended time was Woolf's way of exploring human identity in a context far larger than was available in the nineteenth century novel.

West, too, had been writing a novel—*Harriet Hume: London Fantasy* (1929)—exploring the differences between genders. She examined what would happen to a woman who could enter a man's mind and think his thoughts. Like Woolf, West employed the radical experimentation of the modern novel to challenge the social and political conventions of a patriarchal society. Woolf, West, and others, including Djuna Barnes (in *Nightwood*, 1936), added a vital element to modern fiction, developing the Joycean notion of how human identity develops from the creation of language and the artist's unique point of view.

FRANZ KAFKA (1883-1924)

The phantasmagorical aspects of modernism take on even greater political dimensions in Franz Kafka's novels, especially *Der Prozess* (1925; *The Trial*, 1937). One of the most influential modernists (his fiction gave rise to the term "Kafkaesque"), Kafka explored the terror of twentieth century society, in which an individual could be accused of a nameless crime (as in *The Trial*) and succumb to the bureaucratic maze of figures and institutions that prosecute him (or her). To many critics, the arbitrary nature of the trial, the arcane procedures used to determine the victim's guilt, and the constant pressing of a case against the individual until he begins to believe himself guilty of the charges, presaged the regime of the totalitarian state later dramatized in the novels of Arthur Koestler and George Orwell.

The very idea of a rational world is under attack in *The Trial*, and society seems like a modernist hell because there can be no standard of judgment, no principle of justice, no ethical code by which everyone is measured openly and fairly. Only the interests of the state are important, and the sole criterion for the individual's existence is whether he or she is deemed to have acted in conformity with the current line the authorities avow. In such an absurd world, the definition of reality keeps changing. Thus, Kafka elaborated the modernist attack on universal truths and obliterated the basis on which society had been organized since the Enlightenment.

Kafka's novels verge on nihilism, the conviction that there is no meaning in the universe. While he was certainly not the first writer to broach this notion of meaninglessness—after all, William Shakespeare's Macbeth decries a world that is full of sound and fury, signifying nothing—Kafka was an original because his work reflects this nihilistic tendency in alogical and nonlinear structures. In other words K, the protagonist of *The Trial*, lives in a world that does not make sense to him and that cannot be explained in terms of his own failings or ignorance.

WILLIAM FAULKNER (1897-1962)

William Faulkner's classic modernist novel *The Sound and the Fury* (1929) would seem to be a gloss on Kafka's nihilism. The novel is narrated both by an idiot named Benjy and by his highly intelligent brother, Quentin, a Harvard student who commits suicide after being tormented by a world that will not conform to his heroic expectations. The third part of the novel is narrated by Jason, the crass and cynical brother who survives on sarcasm.

The language of the novel is brilliant not only because Faulkner finds such distinctive voices for his narrators but also because each narrator represents a different way of looking at the world: Benjy focuses on images and the sense experience of the moment while Quentin intellectualizes and broods on his conflicted attitudes toward his family and society. Jason, the realist, simply accepts the status quo and looks for ways to profit from the weakness of others.

Set against these three troubling witnesses to a world gone awry is Dilsey, the faithful family servant who has brought up the brothers. While the novel does not endorse her simple Christian faith, it suggests that the reserves of strength in her character are an abiding aspect of civilization, an enduring sensibility that counters—even if it does not triumph over—the anarchic forces that envelop the brothers.

In Faulkner's novels, the search for meaning is heroic, and failure—while it is frequent—nevertheless conveys a certainly nobility in human efforts to comprehend the world. This is especially true in another of his masterpieces, *Absalom, Absalom!* (1936), an intense, multilayered historical work involving several generations of one family. The narrators piece together and argue over the story of Thomas Sutpen and his sons, a story that ultimately deals with the history of the South and the efforts of the narrators to construct a coherent interpretation of a man and his progeny.

THE POSTMODERN

After Faulkner, a new generation of writers emerging from World War II sought to define themselves in what came to be called a postmodern world, one that would have to find new ways of dealing with the radical subjectivity, nihilism, and the search for meaning that are the hallmarks of modernism. For this new postwar generation, Gertrude Stein became an inspiration. She was an uncompromising writer and poet who crafted several untraditional narratives that refused to rely on novelistic conventions such as plot and well-developed characters.

Stein's self-reflexive language, which suggests the writer creates his or her own reality rather than mirrors the reality outside that creation, elevated the notion of the novel's language as self-sustaining, that is, language did not have to refer to an outside world. Language itself, in other words, became the subject matter of novels. Attention to the power of words themselves, which was a key focus of Stein's work, was a defining feature of the modern and postmodern novelist. In this sense, modernism was not rejected but took a new shape in the postmodern novel.

Carl Rollyson

BIBLIOGRAPHY

Armstrong, Tim. *Modernism: A Cultural History.* Cambridge, Mass.: Polity Press, 2005. Well-regarded introduction to modernism that includes discussion of modernist authors Virginia Woolf, T. S. Eliot, and writers associated with the Harlem Renaissance.

Ayers, David. *Modernism: A Short Introduction.* Malden, Mass.: Blackwell, 2004. Primarily a literary study, with chapters on Ezra Pound, T. S. Eliot, Virginia Woolf, and James Joyce. Good for readers new to the subject.

Boland, Roy C., and Sally Harvey, eds. *Magical Realism and Beyond: The Contemporary Spanish and Latin American Novel.* Madrid, Spain: Vox/AHS, 1991. Magical Realism has been considered an aspect of modernism. Writers such as Jorge Luis Borges and Gabriel García Márquez employed invented histories and the supernatural, and dislocated and disrupted the conventions of realist fiction. Excellent introduction to the connections between Latin American and European modernism.

Childs, Peter. *Modernism.* 2d ed. New York: Routledge, 2008. A comprehensive introduction to modernism, including chapters on major thinkers (Karl Marx, Charles Darwin, Sigmund Freud, Friedrich Nietzsche, Ferdinand Saussure, and Albert Einstein) and genres (novel, short story, poetry, drama, art movements, and film). Includes a glossary and bibliography.

Dowling, David. *Mrs. Dalloway: Mapping Streams of Consciousness.* Boston: Twayne, 1991. Although Dowling focuses on a single text, Woolf's *Mrs. Dalloway* (1925), his work is indispensable for a discussion of the events affecting Woolf and her generation of modernists. Discusses World War I, theories of fiction, novelistic techniques, stream of consciousness, and other elements of modernism.

Kaplan, Carola M., Peter Mallios, and Andrea White, eds. *Conrad in the Twenty-first Century: Contemporary Approaches and Perspectives.* New York: Routledge, 2005. Collection of essays examines Conrad's depictions of postcolonialism, empire, imperialism, and modernism. Four essays discuss *Heart of Darkness.*

Karl, Frederick. *Franz Kafka: Representative Man—Prague, Germans, Jews, and the Crisis of Modernism.* New York: Ticknor & Fields, 1991. This critical biography integrates Kafka's writing into a portrait of the writer's many selves. A comprehensive study of Kafka in the context of the development of modernism.

Lamos, Colleen. *Deviant Modernism: Sexual and Textual Errancy in T. S. Eliot, James Joyce, and Marcel Proust.* New York: Cambridge University Press, 1999. Explores the "sexual energies" of modernism, focusing on Eliot's *The Waste Land,* Joyce's *Ulysses,* and Proust's *Remembrance of Things Past.* Argues that questions about sexual orientation, especially definitions of male heterosexuality, are an integral part of the aesthetics of modernism.

McCormick, John. *Fiction as Knowledge: The Modern Post-romantic Novel.* New Brunswick, N.J.: Transaction Books, 1999. Emphasizes the epistemological nature of the modern novel, with critical attention to the development of the antihero and the stream-of-consciousness narrative.

Neuman, Shirley, and Ira B. Nadel, eds. *Gertrude Stein and the Making of Literature.* Boston: Northeastern University Press, 1988. Essential reading for understanding how Stein was at the heart of modernism, influencing many of the major writers of her generation as well as postmodern writers.

Towner, Theresa M. *The Cambridge Introduction to William Faulkner.* New York: Cambridge University Press, 2008. Accessible resource, aimed at students and general readers. Detailed analyses of Faulkner's nineteen novels (and other works) and the critical reception of his fiction.

NATURALISTIC LONG FICTION

Naturalism is the application of scientific principles to literature, the examination of human life under the influence of heredity and environment. Although the movement flourished in the latter part of the nineteenth century through the early decades of the twentieth century, the term "naturalism" has far-reaching roots. In ancient philosophy, naturalism was used to refer to materialistic philosophies. During the eighteenth century naturalism referred to both a materialistic and a mechanistic view of the universe devoid of metaphysical principles. Denis Diderot considered the naturalists as atheists who viewed the world only as material and not spiritual. Naturalism entered the aesthetic field to describe painting that avoided the prescribed historical, mythological, and allegorical subject matter in order to convey a true depiction of nature. Naturalism's aim was to reproduce nature in all its grandeur. The term was later imported into literature by French writer Émile Zola to describe a literary style.

Literary naturalism is often confused with realism, and sometimes the terms are used synonymously. Both are based on the idea that art is mimetic (representational, aiming to mimic reality); each term suggests that fiction should deal with the ordinary and the contemporary and should use an objective methodology. Naturalism, however, has a more specific meaning than realism: Naturalistic fiction deals with more shocking subjects, uses stronger vocabulary, and employs photographic detail. Naturalism also espouses a view of life, in contrast to realism's relative neutrality.

THE RISE OF THE NATURALIST MOVEMENT

The historical and philosophical influences on the movement include the Industrial Revolution, the rise of venture capitalism, and the scientific age. By the mid-nineteenth century, the effects of the Industrial Revolution were manifest. The agricultural workforce had migrated to the cities, and thousands of large, new factories had been built. New technologies began to bring more efficient power sources, such as gas and electricity, to homes and businesses in urban areas. The steam loco-motive, the telegraph, and underground cables increased the speed of travel and communication. The new technologies opened new opportunities for entrepreneurs, and those few with access to capital built vast industrial empires. Increased wealth came into the hands of these businesspeople, and, for them, the standard of living rose dramatically.

The new industrialization had significant side effects. Factory workers were poor and underpaid, and they worked long hours in unsafe conditions. They had flocked to the cities from the country to find industrial jobs, and they were jammed together in squalid and overcrowded conditions. They lived a mean and brutish existence. The Industrial Revolution replaced romantic idealism with a new and harsh reality that focused on the accumulation of external goods—a new materialism.

Not only were material conditions changing, but new ideas were attacking the complacent Victorian order. In 1859 and again in 1871, Charles Darwin published his theory of evolution: Species are in constant battle to maintain their existence. Those that survive are better adapted to the environment and thus stronger. Through a process he called natural selection, new species evolve; humans had evolved from lower forms of animal life. Darwin had struck a blow to the metaphysical order and to most people's religious beliefs. No longer were humans privileged creatures created by a benign God in his own image: They were connected to the animal kingdom. The naturalists were influenced by Darwin and in their fiction would depict humans in a bestial state caught in the struggle for survival.

Although Darwin disapproved of the application of his theories to human beings (the process of natural selection required thousands, even millions, of years, not a few generations), a philosopher named Herbert Spencer applied the process of evolution to the economic and social order with his social Darwinism. Because social beings are evolving toward a higher order, he reasoned, nothing should tamper with that competitive system. The fittest will survive, prosper, and evolve. Those who do not prosper and survive—the poor and the lower classes—should perish because they are not strong enough to survive. The suffering and hardships of the unsuccessful, Spencer thought, are merely incidental conditions in humanity's evolution toward a perfect state. Social Darwinism allowed people in power to rationalize the exploitation of the working class as part of a grand design of nature. The economic system was not to be tampered with, since attempts to ameliorate the circumstances of the poor, immigrants, and children would encourage the propagation of weakness and ultimately work against society. Social Darwinism's element of natural determinism was reflected by the naturalist writers, who often depicted the struggle for survival.

Determinism also plays a role in the philosophy of Karl Marx. For Marx, economic conditions determine the highest goals of civilization. Individuals are caught in class warfare between the working proletariat and the capitalist class. The proletariat can escape oppression under the wheels of determinism through revolution and the formation of a socialist state. Unlike social Darwinism, Marxism sees the workers, not the capitalists, as triumphant. Some naturalist writers moved toward a socialist solution to the constant struggle for survival.

Another thinker, Hippolyte Taine, also influenced the naturalists. Taine made the Darwinian argument that the human animal is a continuation of the primitive animal, but he looked at three influences on human behavior. First, he said, humans are controlled by their heredity, which is passed on in their genes. The second influence is the environment in which a person is immersed. To these biological factors Taine added a third: the precise moment or circumstances that control a human's action. The naturalists used Taine's ideas concerning the controlling factors of heredity and environment. As a result, much naturalistic literature may seem fatalistic—the outcomes of events are less influenced by the characters' free will than dictated by deterministic factors.

CHARACTERISTICS OF NATURALISTIC FICTION

In naturalistic fiction, humans are observed as though they are specimens in a laboratory; the naturalist records their lives much the way an anatomist performs a dissection. The purpose of the naturalistic novel is to expose the truth, not to create an entertaining or sentimental fiction based on an inventive story driven by the rules of plot. Instead, the naturalistic novel is the life story of a person or a group of people whose actions are faithfully depicted.

The novelist depends heavily on documentation of facts. Upton Sinclair wrote a series of journalistic exposés on the meatpacking industry before writing his novel, *The Jungle* (1906). Zola rode a railway engine, descended into a mine, and measured the dimensions of a prostitute's bedroom before incorporating these locales into his novels. Zola's method was to take copious notes, observe with a keen eye, and let the observations shape the story. Naturalistic novelists had to remain impersonal about their observations and not comment on the story. Zola, however, believed observations should be filtered through a temperament (the author's) so that there would be latitude for the imagination and the perceptions of the observer. In some of his writings Zola went further. He believed in the author's creation of the grandeur of nature, in which writers reshape their observations to make an imprint of genius. For Zola, naturalistic novels are more than journalistic records.

In the romantic and melodramatic novel, which preceded naturalism, emphasis was placed on abstract virtues. In the naturalistic novel, moral absolutes are of no more importance than chemical products. Taine noted that virtue and vice were treated the same as vitriol and vinegar. Thus, naturalistic fiction was condemned by many readers and critics for its immorality or its amorality. The romantic novel created idealistic women, models of purity, and lovers who were admirably loyal. Often they were pitted against a stock villain. The naturalistic novel depicts both rogues and honest people without taking sides. It goes down into the gutters and reveals the seamy side of life.

Another trait of naturalism is its focus on the lower classes and on class struggle. Although Zola held that all subjects were open to the novelist, many naturalists focused on the squalid life of the lower-class poor and their reduction to bestial conditions. The naturalist was less interested in human beings living under ordinary conditions than in how people behaved in crisis. The naturalistic novelist creates a world in which humans are caught in the clutches of heredity and environment. Terrible things generally happen to the characters. Such a world is deterministic and has been viewed as pessimistic. Many criticized naturalism, equating it with fatalism or deterministic pessimism. Although some naturalistic fiction is indeed pessimistic, not all is so. Zola himself believed that deterministic thinking is not necessarily fatalistic. If the novelist can expose the cause of a deterministic cycle, there is room for reformers to change conditions and break the cycle.

Therefore, many naturalistic novels reveal a need for societal reform. The naturalists, like the muckraking journalists of the day, often used their writing to report facts that they hoped would open the eyes of their readers and encourage justice for working people victimized by ruthless capitalists and large economic forces beyond their control. Especially in American naturalism, labor strife became a pointed issue with both naturalists and muckrakers. The naturalistic novel is often critical of social institutions such as church and government, viewing them as corrupt and in need of reform.

One consistent theme in most naturalistic novels is the struggle for survival. Whether on natural terrain or in the social sphere, the characters in naturalistic novels are struggling to survive in an often ruthless world. There are no larger-than-life heroes who come to the rescue of those undergoing life-or-death struggles. Those who are weak and flawed are often destitute or dead by the end of the novel. The prose style of a naturalistic novel, in keeping with the philosophy that engendered naturalism, is often flat, bare of imagery, and lacking in rich ambiguity, yet stuffed with details. If imagery is used, it is often animal imagery. There is little room for the poetical and lyrical in naturalism.

NATURALISM'S ROOTS: ÉMILE ZOLA

Although there were precursors, the naturalistic novel emanated primarily from the works of Émile Zola (1840-1902). He collected a group of French writers around him, but Zola did not see naturalism as a school. One model for the naturalistic novel is Zola's *Thérèse Raquin* (1867; English translation, 1881). The plot is far from original. Thérèse and Laurent are driven to adultery by their passions, and they murder Camille, her husband, disguising the murder as an accidental drowning. Driven by remorse, they both commit suicide. The two lovers are not presented as characters with intellects

and consciences but as creatures driven by blood and nerves.

Zola states in his preface to the novel that they are animals devoid of soul. They are products of instinctual drives that pull them together, then, after the murder, drive them apart. Their behavior is the result of their natural, inherited constitutions. Thérèse's background is one of sexual repression, which explains the outpouring of her drives. Temperamentally, Laurent is sanguine and Thérèse is nervous. Thérèse lives in a cramped apartment with an overpowering mother-in-law, which further explains the chemical attraction between the two lovers. Zola is not particularly successful in establishing that their guilt is part of a physiological condition in which the woman's nervous temperament has driven the man to hysterical action. The chemical and physical attraction of two human beings is easily understood, but the organic underpinnings of moral conscience are not.

Throughout his lifetime, Zola assumed the monumental task of writing *Les Rougon-Macquart* (1871-1893; *The Rougon-Macquarts*, 1896-1900), which includes some twenty novels. The novels are connected in the tracing of the branches of two families throughout five generations. Zola traces the role of heredity through a series of stories of mental and physical diseases. He also explores society from all angles and from a variety of occupations. Each of these fields is thoroughly documented, providing the reader with a vivid picture of French society during the Second Empire.

NATURALISM IN ENGLAND: THOMAS HARDY

In England, naturalism did not take root as firmly as it did in France, and it expressed itself somewhat differently. Thomas Hardy (1840-1928) is one English novelist who is usually grouped with the naturalists. *Jude the Obscure* (1895) was one of his last novels. Because of the controversy over the novel's view of sex and marriage, Hardy ended his career as a novelist.

The character Jude Fawley, who aspires to study divinity at Christminster, is trapped into marriage with a vulgar woman who deserts him. His marriage ties make it impossible for him to court Sue Bridehead, whom he meets later and with whom he falls in love. Jude is unsuccessful in attaining admission to the university, and Sue becomes engaged to Philotson, Jude's old tutor.

During the engagement, Jude and Sue are thrown together, which expedites Sue's marriage to Philotson. However, Sue is repulsed by Philotson physically and goes to live with Jude in a nonconjugal relationship. Arabella, Jude's wife, returns, leading to Sue's capitulation to a sexual relationship with Jude. Jude and Sue drift from town to town with Arabella's child and eventually have two more children. Arabella's child kills all the children and himself. Stricken with remorse, Sue returns to Philotson. Jude, in a drunken stupor, remarries Arabella.

Jude, who has been ill, finally dies of consumption. The pull of physical attraction is seen in Jude's relationship with Arabella. Physical repulsion is seen in Sue's rejection of Philotson. Fatalism is shown as Sue accuses external forces of preventing Jude and her from working and loving. Jude spouts Greek philosophy as he blames all their miseries on a foreordained destiny. However, Hardy differs from other naturalists in that he sees the universe governed by a malign metaphysical force that toys with human destiny.

AMERICAN NATURALISM: STEPHEN CRANE, FRANK NORRIS, THEODORE DREISER

Although naturalism did not flourish in England, it did take root in the United States. In *Maggie: A Girl of the Streets* (1893), Stephen Crane (1871-1900) explores life in the New York slums. Maggie is part of a poor family living in the tenements of the East Side of Manhattan. She is an attractive girl who "blossomed in a mud puddle," a life filled with drunken rows. Trying to avoid the demeaning circumstances of her family, she seeks work in a collar-and-cuff factory, but life there is a monotonous routine filled with corruption. She meets a bartender named Pete, who takes her to beer gardens and theaters, giving her a romantic escape from drudgery and brutality. Seduced and abandoned by her lover and rejected by her family on moral grounds, Maggie is forced into prostitution and eventually drowns herself in the East River.

With no other choices, Maggie's fall into prostitution is inevitable: Her crippling environment, her work, and her romantic temperament have all ordained the outcome. No one cares about her, and she is consumed by degradation. Her crude brother and drunken mother survive in the human jungle of vice and hypocrisy. The influential American critic and novelist William Dean Howells wrote that Maggie's story had the quality of a Greek tragedy.

Frank Norris (1870-1902) showed how an ordinary working man can turn into a brute. *McTeague* (1899) has the plot line of a typical naturalist novel: All the data are provided, and the action flows from these facts. The protagonist, McTeague, thinks that he has taken a step upward from his working-class background by learning dentistry from a traveling quack. McTeague establishes a practice in San Francisco; he falls in love with and marries Trina, one of his patients. However, he makes an enemy of a rival, Marcus Schouler, who reports him for practicing without a license. When he is shut down, McTeague declines into drunkenness and brutality. He tortures his wife to find out where she has hoarded five thousand dollars that she won in a lottery. Eventually he kills her and flees to mining country in the Sierra Nevada, from where he came.

The story was suggested by a brutal murder in the poor section of San Francisco. Norris paints working-class life as he recorded it on Polk Street. The story takes the reader through eateries, bars, and the living quarters of the poor and middle classes. The world is violent: Beatings, two murders, torture, and mayhem typify the action. The story ends in Death Valley, in the desert of Southern California, as two men fight to the death. Unlike Crane, Norris depicts the violence in vivid detail. Though they are controlled, there are also scenes of sexuality: In one scene, McTeague grossly kisses Trina's mouth when she is anesthetized in his dental chair; in another, Trina lies naked in a bed of money as the instincts of greed and lust are combined.

Norris also shows reverse evolution. He displays how the latent beast inside a person emerges under certain circumstances, as shown in McTeague's biting through Marcus's ear: "It was something no longer human; it was rather an echo from the jungle." McTeague is described as an animal with enormous hands and the mind of a dumb brute. Slowly the animal reveals itself and turns into a ruthless killer.

Theodore Dreiser (1871-1945), perhaps the most famous American naturalist, created a masterpiece of naturalist fiction in *Sister Carrie* (1900), the story of Carrie

Meeber, who finds life harsh in the city, where everything is a commodity for sale. She becomes the mistress first of a cad named Drouet (who has no trouble seducing the young woman, predisposed to being seduced), and then of Hurstwood, a restaurant manager and a married man. As his fortunes decline, she rises as an actor. Carrie takes on and drops men as her needs determine. She knows that she has something that is valuable, her physical attractiveness, and she is able to deaden what little conscience she has.

Hurstwood is a creature of circumstances. He has a shaky marriage to a dominant wife and is looking for the first woman who will help him recapture his youth. He robs his boss. He opens the safe and takes out some money to fondle it; then, just as his conscience is telling him not to take it, the safe closes. Chance therefore plays a part in the deterministic outcome of the story, but Dreiser has shown that his character is predisposed to steal. Hurstwood sinks into illness and finally commits suicide. Inevitability is a major part of the pattern of life in this as in other naturalistic novels—as Dreiser warns in the first chapter. Carrie, at novel's end, is a successful stage actor. There is no punishment for her sins; her success grows out of her ability to cope with the corrupt world of the big city. For that reason, the novel shocked audiences when it was published, all the more so because Dreiser implied that Carrie's story was simply one of many that resembled it.

WOMEN AND THE NATURALISTIC NOVEL

Deeply influenced by but also very different from French naturalism was the work of Spanish novelist Emilia Pardo Bazán (1851-1921). One of the most outspoken of Spain's early feminists, she shocked the literary world for embracing French naturalism, to some degree. She decried its negation of beauty in favor of rawness, pessimism, obscenity, positivism, and determinism. Still, she agreed with naturalism's objectivity, its observational techniques, and its detailed study of the problems of everyday life.

Other naturalistic writers include Kate Chopin (*The Awakening*, 1899), Edith Wharton (*The House of Mirth*, 1905, and *The Age of Innocence*, 1920), and Ellen Glasgow (1873-1945), whose novels are focused mainly on a radically changing American South. Glasgow shunned

sentimentalism for a truth that "must embrace the interior world as well as external appearances." Exploring the "interior world" as well as externality set her apart from the realist writers of the time. Also, her naturalism is tempered by a sense of decorum and propriety, without shocking detail. She made the following plea to other southern writers:

> All I ask him [the writer] to do is to deal as honestly with living tissues as he now deals with decay, to remind himself that the colors of putrescence have no greater validity for our age, or for any age, than . . . the cardinal virtues.

Although naturalism as a movement was fading by the 1920's, naturalistic techniques found their way into detective fiction, and into the novels of Ernest Hemingway, William Faulkner, Norman Mailer, Truman Capote, Joyce Carol Oates, William Kennedy, Don DeLillo, and many others. An excellent example of the form reaching postcolonial writers is Indian Canadian Rohinton Mistry (born 1952). His novel *A Fine Balance* (1995) is set in Mumbai (formerly Bombay), India, between 1975 and 1977. As the earlier naturalists used their work to criticize church and state, Mistry tells in brutal detail the suffering of the poor because of governmental policies. His characters, Ishvar and Omprakash the tailors, Dina the widow, and Maneck the student, work hard and behave honorably but are continually beaten down by social and economic pressures.

Paul Rosefeldt

BIBLIOGRAPHY

Baguley, David. *Naturalist Fiction: The Entropic Vision*. New ed. New York: Cambridge University Press, 2005. First major study of naturalistic fiction as a distinct genre. Covers mainly the French naturalists, providing background to and theories of naturalism, but also examines naturalists from outside France. For advanced readers.

Bloom, Harold, ed. *American Naturalism*. Philadelphia: Chelsea House, 2004. A collection of critical essays on the major authors and works in American naturalism. Includes a chronology of significant cultural, literary, and political events of the naturalistic period in American literature.

Campbell, Donna M. *Resisting Regionalism: Gender and Naturalism in American Fiction, 1885-1915.* Athens: Ohio State University Press, 1997. Asks the question, What effect did the cultural dominance of women's local-color fiction in the 1890's have on young male naturalistic writers?

Civello, Paul. *American Literary Naturalism and Its Twentieth Century Transformations.* Athens: University of Georgia Press, 1994. Examines the rise of naturalism in the United States and how it influenced later authors such as Ernest Hemingway and Don DeLillo.

Furst, Lilian R., and Peter N. Skrine. *Naturalism.* 1971. Reprint. London: Methuen, 1978. Dated but excellent introduction to literary naturalism in France, Germany, England, and the United States. Includes an updated bibliography.

Lehan, Richard Daniel. *Realism and Naturalism: The Novel in an Age of Transition.* Madison: University of Wisconsin Press, 2005. Survey of the major American and European novels of naturalism and realism from 1850 to 1950, including gothic, urban, detective, and Western novels.

Stone, Edward, ed. *What Was Naturalism? Materials for an Answer.* New York: Appleton-Century-Crofts, 1959. Dated but still a relevant collection of primary sources on the rise of naturalism, including excerpts from the works of Charles Darwin, Karl Marx, and Émile Zola.

THE NOVELLA

The word "novella" comes from the Latin word *novellus*, a diminutive of the word *novus*, which means "new." The term "novella" first became associated with the telling of stories in the thirteenth century with collections of newer versions of old saints' tales, exempla, chivalric tales, and ribald stories. Eventually, the term became associated with tales that were fresh, strange, and unusual—stories, in short, that were worth the telling.

The most decisive historical event to establish the term "novella" as a designation for a new kind of fiction was Giovanni Boccaccio's decision to give the name "novella" to the tales included in his *Decameron: O, Prencipe Galetto* (1349-1351; *The Decameron*, 1620). What made Boccaccio's stories new was their marking a shift from the sacred world of Dante's "divine" comedy to the profane world of Boccaccio's "human" comedy. The resulting realism of *The Decameron* should not be confused, however, with the realism developed by the eighteenth century novel. The focus in Boccaccio's tales is not on a character presented in a similitude of everyday life but on the traditional world of story, in which characters serve primarily as "functions" of the tale.

With Miguel de Cervantes in the sixteenth century, as with Boccaccio before him, something new also characterized the novella. First, Cervantes, in his *Novelas ejemplares* (1613; *Exemplary Novels*, 1846), did not present himself as a collector of traditional tales but as an inventor of original stories. As a result, he became an observer and recorder of concrete details in the external world and a student of the psychology of individual characters. Although plot was still important, character became more developed than it was in *The Decameron*, and thus psychological motivation rather than story motivation was emphasized. Characters existed not solely for the roles they played in the stories but also for their own sake, as if they were real.

In Germany, in the first quarter of the nineteenth century, the novella began to detach itself from the notion of the form inspired by Boccaccio and Cervantes and became supported by a theory of its own. Friedrich von Schlegel agreed with the Renaissance idea that a novella was an anecdote that must be capable of arousing interest, but he noted that the modern retelling of already known traditional stories necessarily focuses the reader's attention away from mythic authority and toward the authority of the subjective point of view of the narrator. Johann Wolfgang von Goethe added an important new element to the definition of the novella form by arguing that it depicted an unheard-of event that actually took place; thus, although the event can be accounted for by the laws of nature, it must be strange and unusual.

In addition to this theorizing about the novella, numerous examples of the form contributed to its development. The first such example is Goethe's *Novelle* (1826; *Novel*, 1837), an exemplary story that dramatically changed the nature of the genre by shifting the focus from simple events to events that took on a symbolic meaning and form. After Goethe, the novella developed as a self-conscious genre, a sophisticated literary narrative that deals with the most basic metaphysical and aesthetic issues.

Whereas the logic of Goethe's *Novel* is governed by the narrative demands of the story and by aesthetic artifice, the logic of the most famous novella of Ludwig Tieck, *Der blonde Eckbert* (in *Volksmärchen*, 1797, 3 volumes), follows the convention of the fairy tale as an externalization of unconscious processes. This act of grounding the supernatural in the psychological is taken to further extremes in the novellas of E. T. A. Hoffmann, whose stories are often self-conscious manipulations of the relationship between fantasy and the everyday that had previously been developed in the fairy-tale form. In Hoffmann's best-known novella, *Der Sandmann* (1817; *The Sandman*, 1844), the protagonist is caught between fantasy and reality, a dichotomy that Hoffmann makes more explicit than does Goethe or Tieck. The advance of Hoffmann's tale over those of his predecessors lies in its ironic tone, which parodies the romantic view of reality. Hoffmann has the ironic sensibility of Franz Kafka in perceiving that the supernatural world is serious and sardonic at the same time.

Although the term "novella" is used to refer to both

the short pieces of fourteenth century fiction best exemplified by *The Decameron* and the highly developed nineteenth century German form, it was more often used in the twentieth century to refer to a number of works of midrange length, somewhat longer than the short story and somewhat shorter than the novel. The modern novella derives from various preexisting types. It began in the nineteenth century with a quasi-realistic normalizing of the old romance and parable forms and has maintained these romance conventions in such gothic novellas as Horace Walpole's *The Castle of Otranto* (1765), Charlotte Perkins Gilman's "The Yellow Wallpaper" (1892), and Henry James's *The Turn of the Screw* (1898). These conventions remain as well in such parabolic novellas as Gustave Flaubert's *La Légende de Saint Julien l'Hospitalier*, published in *Trois Contes* (1877; "The Legend of St. Julian, Hospitaler," in *Three Tales*, 1903), and Flannery O'Connor's *Wise Blood* (1952).

ROMANCE, REALISM, AND THE NOVELLA

It is not simply the gothic trappings and decorations that constitute the gothic novel, but rather the placing of characters into traditional romance tales and the resulting transformation of those characters into archetypes of the mythic story. The transformation of "real" people into parabolic figures by the latent thrust of the traditional romance story is characteristic of the novella form and can be seen in an explicit way in *The Castle of Otranto*, in which, even as characters act out their desires on the surface of the plot, desire becomes objectified and totally embodied in the latent and underlying plot.

In *The Turn of the Screw*, this basic combination is focused in a particularly explicit way, becoming the crux and central theme of the story. The issue of whether the ghosts in the story are real or are projections of the governess's imagination is reflective of the basic problem of the novella form—that is, whether a given story features characters who are presented as if they are real or as embodiments of psychological archetypes. This ambiguity is so thorough in James's novella that every detail can be read as evidence for both interpretations of reality at once.

Just as Walpole returned to the medieval romance for a model for his gothic tale, Flaubert returned to the medieval saint's legend or folktale for the exemplar for "The

Legend of St. Julian, Hospitaler." Furthermore, just as Walpole's romance differs from the medieval form by combining traditional story with psychologically real characters, so does Flaubert's moral fable differ from its medieval source by self-consciously foregrounding the static and frozen nature of the medieval story itself. The subject matter of Flaubert's story, although it has a moral issue at its center, is more particularly the generic means by which the medieval tale is moral and representative. The movement from the parable of Flaubert to the modern parables of O'Connor is a movement from a relatively simple story to a more complex and ironic form. Just as the narrative and symbolic aim of Flaubert's story is the spiritual transformation of its central characters, so also is the central aim of O'Connor's *Wise Blood* to lead its central character to a vision of his own fragmentation so he can be reborn.

Perhaps the two best-known modern parable forms of the novella are William Faulkner's *The Bear* (1942) and Ernest Hemingway's *The Old Man and the Sea* (1952). These two stories differ from the parables of Flaubert and O'Connor in that they both seem to be less illustrations of moral issues than reenactments of primitive rituals that enforce the moral issue. Although they are quite different in their individual syntactical rhythms, both stories are characterized by a highly formal structure and style in which moral values evolve ritually from the hero's encounter with the natural world. Of the two stories, *The Old Man and the Sea* seems closer to the parable form than does *The Bear*, primarily because of the conventional expectation that the parable is a relatively clean structural form, functional and bare in style and point of view.

One of the most common narrative devices of the novella is the convention of the Doppelgänger, or double. There are both historical and aesthetic reasons for the predominance of this motif in the form. Because the novella is a combination of the old romance form, in which characters are projections of psychic states, and the new realistic novel form, in which characters are presented as if they were real people with their own psychological lives, novellas often present both types of characters, especially in such works as Herman Melville's "Bartleby the Scrivener" (1853) and Joseph Conrad's *Heart of Darkness* (serial 1899, book 1902), in which the narrators seem to be realistic characters with individual psyches, while the central characters Bartleby and Kurtz seem to be manifested as psychological archetypes.

Perceiving reality to be a function more of mind than of external reality, nineteenth century fiction writers could present inner life by means of dreamlike romance projections. If, however, they wished to reveal the inner life in a realistic manner, yet avoid getting lost in a quagmire of introspection, the only answer was to present that subjective and often-forbidden side of the self in terms of external projections—as characters who, although the reader could respond to them as if they were separate external figures, were really projections of the mind of the protagonist. The most obvious means by which such an inner state could be projected as if it were outer reality was to present the projection as a figure somehow very much like the protagonist, not an identical double, but rather an embodiment of some hidden or neglected aspect of the self that had to be confronted and dealt with.

Robert Louis Stevenson's *The Strange Case of Dr. Jekyll and Mr. Hyde* (1886) is perhaps the purest example of this use of the convention; that Dr. Jekyll represents the conventional and socially acceptable personality and Mr. Hyde the uninhibited and criminal self is the most obvious aspect of Stevenson's novella. A more accomplished and subtle treatment of the convention can be seen in Conrad's "The Secret Sharer" (1910), for here the double is not merely a manifested hidden self or a figure imagined to be outside the protagonist, but rather an actual self whose crime is at the core of the moral issue facing the protagonist. Although it can be said that the double in "The Secret Sharer" represents some aspect of the captain's personality that he must integrate, it is more probable that he is brought on board to make explicit and dramatically concrete the dual workings of the captain's mind: He is distracted and split between his external responsibilities and his concealed secret.

Because of its moderate length, its highly formalized structure, and its focus on the ultimate metaphysical limitations of humanity, the novella has often been compared to classical tragedy. The central character of the novella often seems to be caught in the inevitability of fate or the story, being doomed at the same time as a victim of some limitation within the self. The essential issue is that the "tragic novella" creates the illusion that the characters are responsible for their own defeat, even though readers realize that they are witnessing the fatality demanded by the fable itself. The two most emphatic examples of this tragic form are Stephen Crane's "The Blue Hotel" (1898) and Katherine Anne Porter's *Noon Wine* (1937).

The three basic devices in "The Blue Hotel" that give it a sense of classical tragedy are its formalized structure, which suggests a classical five-act tragedy; a central character neither eminently good nor evil, whose misfortune results not from vice or depravity but from some error, frailty, or limitation; and the creation through metaphor and allusion of the sense that the events and characters are not contemporary and real but archetypal and ritualistic. The most essential requirement is that the protagonist is made to seem responsible for his or her own downfall, even though that downfall is governed by the rules of the ritual or fable itself. Whereas the tragedy in "The Blue Hotel" is brought on by the protagonist's mistake about the nature of the world around him, in Porter's *Noon Wine* the downfall is brought on by a limitation in the protagonist's ability to perceive himself. The tragic figure is Royal Earl Thompson; the other two figures, Helton and Hatch, are projections of two aspects of Thompson's personality and situation. Helton makes it possible for him to live a lie about himself, and Hatch forces him to confront that lie.

One of the narrative forms that serves as an important antecedent to the modern novella is the fairy tale, for fairy-tale devices appear in the novella in various self-conscious ways: as a dreamlike state of being that is laid bare, as a structural device to develop a parabolic story, as the means to create the sense of metaphysical mystery in external reality, and as a way to suggest traditional character types and story situations. The fairy-tale conventions in the modern novella are never allowed to lapse into the marvelous and the supernatural; rather, they reflect the extraordinary nature of ordinary life, in which extreme situations seem to transform the world into a kind of reality akin to that found in fairy tales. Carson McCullers's *The Ballad of the Sad Café* (serial 1943, book 1951) and Franz Kafka's *Die Verwandlung* (1915; *The Metamorphosis*, 1936) are two typical examples.

McCullers's story seems to take place in the realm of dreams rather than in external reality, for it is a story turned inward on itself, narcissistic and grotesque just as the central figure Miss Amelia's eyes are crossed, peering inward—sealed off from the ordinary world by the obsessions of the story itself. The effect of the work depends primarily on the poetic voice of the storyteller, which lyrically transforms the grotesque external reality into the inner story of the lover; the details of the story are thus transmuted by the teller until they bear no connection to the external world.

Perhaps the most successful example of this combination of fantasy and reality in the modern novella is Kafka's *The Metamorphosis*. The extreme step Kafka takes is to make the transformation of the psychic into the physical the precipitating premise from which the rest of the story follows. The only suspension of disbelief required in the story is that the reader accept the premise that Gregor Samsa awakes one morning from uneasy dreams to find himself transformed into a giant insect. Once the reader accepts this event, the rest of the story is quite prosaic and detailed, fully externalized in a realistic fashion. *The Metamorphosis* is an exemplar of the typical novella effort to present an inner state of reality as a fantastic but real outer event.

METAFICTION

The most common theme and technique in the contemporary novella is metafictional self-reflexivity, embodied in stories that have to do with the nature of storytelling itself. Philip Roth's *The Ghost Writer* (1979), in which external reality and fictional reality become inextricably blurred as the central character tells a story about the almost mythical figure Anne Frank, is one example. Perhaps the most commercially successful attempt at this kind of self-reflexive fiction, however, is Kurt Vonnegut's *Slaughterhouse-Five: Or, The Children's Crusade, a Duty-Dance with Death* (1969), which uses the popular science-fiction genre as a vehicle to explore methods of storytelling.

More sophisticated than *Slaughterhouse-Five* are the metafictional works of John Barth, Robert Coover, and William H. Gass. Barth's "Dunyazadiad" (in *Chimera*, 1972) reflects his own fascination with the notion of characters in fiction becoming readers or authors of the very fiction they inhabit. "Dunyazadiad" takes its premise and its situation from the classic Scheherazade story,

as told by her younger sister, Dunyazade. Barth transports a modern storyteller (himself) back to "Sherry's" aid to supply her with the stories from the future that she has told in the fictional past.

Coover traces his debts back to Cervantes, who created a synthesis between poetic analogy and literal history and thus gave birth to the modern novel. Coover's most popular novella, "The Babysitter" (in *Pricksongs and Descants*, 1969), is his most forthright example of this mixture of fantasy and reality. The story is a confused combination of the two realms in which, as is usual in the novella, unreality predominates over external reality. The story presents the fantasy reality in the same mode as external reality, so that in trying to unravel the two, the reader gets hopelessly lost in the mix.

Gass carries the self-reflexive mode to even further extremes. The primary premise of his novella, *Willie Masters' Lonesome Wife* (1968), is that the book the reader holds in his or her hands is Willie Masters's wife herself. This trope is carried out by such devices as varying the typography and the texture of the book pages and by using graphics and other purely physical devices to give readers the sense that they are not simply seeing through the medium of the book but are dealing with the medium itself.

The novella was not a popular form during the renaissance of the American short story in the 1980's, stimulated by writers, including Raymond Carver and Anne Beattie, who practiced a cryptic and abbreviated narrative style notoriously known as minimalism or hyperrealism, the ultimate extreme of which was the short-short story, sometimes dubbed sudden fiction or flash fiction. So many writers tried to profit from the popularity of the trend that reviewers began to criticize the form for lacking any moral or social content. The backlash spawned a return to a more expansive, discursive writing style in the 1990's, closer to the classic realism of the novel form.

Typical of this reaction against minimalism by a younger generation is Christopher Tilghman, whose debut collection, *In a Father's Place* (1990), features stories that affirm such novelistic middle-class values as family, the land, and tradition. The novella-length title piece casually meanders through a story about a traditional patriarch who sends his son's girlfriend away when she tries to convince her boyfriend to write a novel that "deconstructs" the family. Ethan Canin, who was first introduced to the public with his short-story collection, *Emperor of the Air* (1988), turned to the novella form with *The Palace Thief* (1994). Canin centers his title story on a teacher of ancient history, who retires from a private school after many years of teaching and tries to expose one of his former students, a powerful businessperson and politician who has become successful through cheating.

John Updike, one of the best-known practitioners of the often highly stylized stories that appeared in *New Yorker* magazine, began, in his later years, to write longer, more leisurely stories. "A Sandstone Farmhouse" (1990), the longest story in his 1994 collection *The Afterlife, and Other Stories*, is an understated, elegiac tale about a fifty-four-year-old man who must deal with his dead mother's possessions. As he goes through her things, comparing his own transitory life in Manhattan to the solidity of the stone house where his mother lived, he discovers that although he moved to New York City to be where the action is, the real action has occurred in the farmhouse. Perhaps best known for his four Rabbit series novels, which were published between 1960 and 1990, Updike returned to the series in 2000 with a novella, *Rabbit Remembered*, in *Licks of Love: Short Stories and a Sequel, "Rabbit Remembered."* Like *The Afterlife, and Other Stories* it shows the aftereffects of a death, as Rabbit's family moves on without him.

The stories of Andre Dubus, a writer who refused to follow the minimalists, are based on the conviction that most human beings are seeking love rather than sex, relationships rather than one-night stands, and family rather than thrills. In the long title story of *Dancing After Hours: Stories* (1996), a forty-year-old female bartender who lives alone finds new hope when she meets a disabled man using a wheelchair, who lives life with gusto in spite of his disability. The novella-length title story of Andrea Barrett's 1996 collection, *Ship Fever, and Other Stories*, takes place in the 1840's when thousands of poor Irish fled the potato famine, only to land on the harsh shores of Nova Scotia plagued by typhus and other diseases. The protagonist is a young doctor from Quebec who volunteers to work at a quarantine station on Grosse Island. A powerful abbreviated historical novel, *Ship Fe-*

ver creates a fully realized world focused on a social disaster.

A number of writers who were part of the minimalist or hyperrealist trend of the 1980's also published novellas afterward. Richard Ford's *Women with Men: Three Stories* (1997) includes a novella told from the point of view of a seventeen-year-old Montana boy who travels with his aunt to visit his mother. In contrast to her earlier minimalist narratives, Ann Beattie's later short fictions made more use of novelistic techniques of expanded character exploration and realistic, nonmetaphoric detail. In the novella-length title story of her *Park City: New and Selected Stories* (1998), the central character spends a week at a Utah ski resort during the off-season looking after her half sister's daughter, trying to find new meaning in her life.

Alice Munro, a writer of short fiction who began publishing in the 1960's, also began to write novella-length stories. The long title story of her collection *The Love of a Good Woman: Stories* (1998) begins in Wally, Ontario, a familiar Munro location, with three boys finding the body of the town's optometrist in his car in the river. Although one might expect the plot to focus immediately on the mystery of the drowned man, Munro is in absolutely no hurry to satisfy the reader's curiosity. She follows the three boys into their individual homes and leisurely explores their ordinary secrets.

Other collections of stories that featured novellas after the 1980's include Cynthia Ozick's *The Puttermesser Papers* (1997), which contains three novellas about her character Ruth Puttermesser; Amy Hempel's *Tumble Home: A Novella and Short Stories* (1997); and Saul Bellow's *The Actual*, which was published separately as a novella in 1997. Story collections by Robert Stone (*Bear and His Daughter,* 1997) and Charles Baxter (*Believers,* 1997) both feature novellas as their title stories. Other novellas by established writers include A. S. Byatt's *Angels and Insects: Two Novellas* (1992), Stephen Dixon's *Gould: A Novel in Two Novels* (1997), Richard Bausch's *Rare and Endangered Species* (1994), Antonya Nelson's *Family Terrorists* (1994), E. Annie Proulx's "Brokeback Mountain" (1997; in *Close Range: Wyoming Stories,* 1999), Steve Martin's *Shopgirl* (2000), Neil Gaiman's *Coraline* (2002; children's novella), and Philip Roth's *Everyman* (2006).

David Leavitt, one of the best-known writers on the lives of young gays, published *Arkansas: Three Novellas*, in 1997. The most controversial tale of the three is "The Term Paper Artist," in which a character named "David Leavitt" writes a term paper for a young, heterosexual male student in return for sex, after which he is pursued by a number of other straight male students with similar offers. In a short article on the novella, Leavitt wrote that if a novel is a marriage and the short story an affair, the novella is a "prolonged infatuation."

Charles E. May

BIBLIOGRAPHY

Clements, Robert J., and Joseph Gibaldi. *Anatomy of the Novella: The European Tale Collection from Boccaccio and Chaucer to Cervantes*. New York: New York University Press, 1977. Relevant historical survey and analysis of the theory and practice of the Renaissance novella from Giovanni Boccaccio to Miguel de Cervantes. Argues that because the form was middle-class in orientation, most novellas are ironic, dealing with characters thought to be inferior in power or intelligence to the reader.

Good, Graham. "Notes on the Novella." In *The New Short Story Theories*, edited by Charles E. May. Athens: Ohio University Press, 1994. Concise historical survey of the debate about the novella's basic characteristics and its relation to the short story and the novel. Focuses on the implications of the form being an imitation of a live telling in which the end of the story is known by the teller at the beginning.

Lee, A. Robert, ed. *The Modern American Novella*. New York: St. Martin's Press, 1989. Collection of essays by various critics on American novellas from the nineteenth and twentieth centuries. Examines, for example, Stephen Crane's *The Red Badge of Courage*, Kate Chopin's *The Awakening*, Ernest Hemingway's *The Old Man and the Sea*, and the novellas of J. D. Salinger and Saul Bellow.

Leibowitz, Judith. *Narrative Purpose in the Novella*. The Hague, the Netherlands: Mouton, 1974. Focuses on the European and American novella from the mid-nineteenth century to the early 1970's. Argues that the generically distinct nature of the novella is its double effect of intensity and expansion. Contends that although the repetitive structure and theme complex of the novella may also be found in the short story and the novel, they do not operate in those forms as mutually dependent devices, as they do in the novella.

Plouffe, Bruce. *The Post-war Novella in German Language Literature: An Analysis*. New York: AMS Press, 1998. Discusses developments in the novella in Germany in the second half of the twentieth century. Examines the "shared themes of uncertain existence and ambiguity of language" in the novella, the short story, and the *Novelle*.

Remak, Henry H. H. *Structural Elements of the German Novella from Goethe to Thomas Mann*. New York: Peter Lang, 1996. Tests the three constituents of Goethe's famous definition of the novella against his own novellas. Discusses his seminal role in the development of the novella as the supreme literary achievement of Germany in the nineteenth century.

Springer, Mary Doyle. *Forms of the Modern Novella*. Chicago: University of Chicago Press, 1975. Using the rhetorical approach of the Chicago school of criticism, Springer discusses five types of novella plots: serious plot of character, degenerative tragedy, satire, apologue, and the example.

THE PICARESQUE NOVEL

The Spanish words *picaresque* and *picaro* achieved currency in Spain shortly after 1600. Today they are terms in literary criticism, sometimes misused because of the vague meaning attached to them. The revival of the genre in the twentieth century was accompanied by an increased critical interest in this type of novel, with the result that some critics try to stretch the definition of the picaresque while others attempt to restrict it. Still, some features are generally accepted as distinct characteristics of the picaresque, including a loose, episodic structure; a rogue-hero (the picaro) who is on the move and goes through a series of encounters with representatives of a hostile and corrupt world; a first-person narrative; and a satirical approach to the society in which the adventures occur.

The typical social background of the picaresque involves a disordered, disintegrating world in which traditional values are breaking down. The instability of the social structure permits the emergence of the picaro, a resilient rogue but not a criminal, a person of low birth or uncertain parentage, an outsider whose adventures take him or her from innocence to experience. In this sense, the picaresque novel has affinities with the bildungsroman, but unlike the protagonist of the latter, the picaro is a fixed character. While he (traditionally a "he") learns survival techniques from his adventures, he does not change inwardly; he remains faithful to his healthy instincts without questioning the larger order of things. Pressured by circumstances to choose between integrity and survival, the picaro makes the pragmatic choice and learns to adjust to the corrupt values of his environment.

SIXTEENTH CENTURY SPAIN

The picaresque genre emerged in sixteenth century Spain, an age of turmoil and upheaval when medieval homogeneity and social stability were giving way to Renaissance mobility and a greater emphasis on the importance of the individual. All Spanish picaresque novels present a low-life character passing from master to master in search of some financial stability, thus providing a splendid occasion for the author to give an overall picture of Spain in an age of disintegrating values. The differences between the two first examples of the genre, however, already indicate its protean nature.

Lazarillo de Tormes, published anonymously in 1554 (English translation, 1576), presents a picaro, a victim of tricksters who by necessity becomes a trickster himself. The novel's anonymous author was the first to employ a realistic first-person narrator, creating a countergenre to the fastidious courtly literature of the period. Some critics suggest that both the anonymous author of *Lazarillo de Tormes* and Mateo Alemán, the writer of the second Spanish picaresque, were Jews or converted Jews, outsiders to the mainstream of Spanish society; in any case, the picaresque view of life is an outsider's point of view as far as protagonist and author are concerned.

Fear of starvation and anger are Lazarillo's true masters. The lesson he draws from his experience of privation and exploitation is not one of resistance or revolt; on the contrary, it is one of conformity. His is a kind of success story because, at the end of the novel, he finds a secure job as a town crier, but this is qualified success, since he pays for it with his honor, marrying the archpriest's mistress. He accepts the archpriest's advice to concern himself only with his own advantage. The advice, of course, reflects the hypocritical standards of Spanish society. Lazarillo is more than ready to heed the counsel; his bitter adventures have taught him to be content with low expectations. The feeling of being defenseless and unprotected against the wickedness of the world lends a tragic note to the story of his childhood and adolescence. Though most of his adventures make the reader laugh, anguish and despair prevail throughout the novel. The comic and the serious exist side by side, adding a note of ambiguity. *Lazarillo de Tormes* is a mixture of childish immaturity, innocence, and bitter cynicism; it excels in a fusion of modes and attitudes. At the end, Lazarillo compares his rising fortunes to Spain's rising political power; consequently, the unknown author not only puts his picaro's story in an ambiguous light but also extends that ambiguity to the whole empire of Charles V.

A DIFFERENT PICARO

King Charles V was succeeded by Philip II and Philip III; disillusionment followed triumph in the history of the empire. The picaresque novel, from the beginning a protean genre, adjusted to the new demands. Despair and anguish are present already in Lazarillo's story, but the picaro protagonist in Mateo Alemán's *Guzmán de Alfarache* (1599, 1604) is first of all a tormented soul. As an investigator of the prison system, Alemán was well acquainted with prison life. In Guzmán he presents a repentant sinner. The confessions reveal a lower-class character whom a dehumanizing society has forced to adjust to its corrupt values; the emphasis is not on Guzmán's adventures, however, but rather on his tormented soul. He is a kind of psychological picaro, one very much concerned with his soul. Guzmán compares the human predicament to warfare: an existence without any certainty or truth, a life full of hypocrisy and instability.

In spite of the many hilarious tricks played by the rogues on their masters, the Spanish picaresque novels were not intended to be amusing. There is a subtle balance of comedy and seriousness in *Lazarillo de Tormes* and *Guzmán de Alfarache*; at the same time, however, through the encounters of the rogue-hero with various masters—all of them representing the hypocritical, materialistic standards of contemporary Spanish society—these picaresque novels give a fragmented but valid and realistic picture of a society in change.

FRANCE AND GERMANY

The protean nature of the picaresque novel made it easy for the genre to spread rapidly through Europe. Adaptations of *Lazarillo de Tormes* soon appeared in France and England. *Guzmán de Alfarache* soon appeared in Germany. The Spanish original blended in each country with the native tradition, and the Spanish picaro turned into the English rogue, later a foundling; into the German *Schelm*; and in France, into a *gentilhomme*. Despite differences in each of these countries, the picaresque consistently performed the function of a countergenre, making legitimate the serious attention given to low-life characters. With the advance of capitalism, the middle class grew in size and influence, and its members found pleasure in a genre that centered on the plight of a low-life character seeking upward mobility. At the same time, printing techniques improved, and booksellers, in order to boost their profits, encouraged more and more printings of picaresque fiction because of its appeal to the taste of the bourgeoisie. In the following centuries the genre came to be adopted to reflect a bourgeois world view rather than a truly picaresque outlook. With the optimistic attitudes of the Enlightenment, the picaresque novel lost its quality of despair; the former picaro, though in different degrees and in different ways, came to be integrated into the mainstream of society.

In Germany, the Spanish picaresque merged with the native tradition of tales about false beggars. The most significant German novel of the picaresque type is Hans Jakob Christoffel von Grimmelshausen's *Der abenteuerliche Simplicissimus* (1669; *The Adventurous Simplicissimus*, 1912). The background of the book fits the requirements of the picaresque atmosphere: The Thirty Years' War was certainly a period of disorder and disintegration in German history. Simplicius Simplicissimus, as his name implies, is a naïve, simple, ignorant boy; his peasant background emphasizes this feature. He is almost another Parzival, a "pure fool," but the war destroys his pastoral life. His picaresque wanderings eventually lead him to live the life of a hermit. Compared to what is considered normal and sane in the gambling, warring, drinking, whoring society of contemporary Germany, the seemingly foolish idealism of the hermit is perhaps the only truly sane attitude amid universal madness. While society may consider Simplicissimus mad, his madness makes more sense than the reality created by the so-called respectable people. The German picaro, by tearing off the masks, shows the real face of society behind the facade.

In France, the Spanish picaresque merged with the tradition of criminal biographies and books on vagabonds; in the seventeenth century the genre came to be exploited by writers such as Charles Sorel and Paul Scarron, whose comic, realistic novels functioned as a countergenre to the improbable romances that flooded the market. The French picaro, born into the middle class, uses his tricks to unmask the society to which he belongs by birth; in consequence, the social criticism always implicit in the genre becomes more obvious. By far the most famous French picaresque novel is Alain-René

Lesage's *Histoire de Gil Blas de Santillane* (1715-1735; 4 vols.; *The History of Gil Blas of Santillane*, 1716, 1735; better known as *Gil Blas*, 1749, 1962). Though the adventures of this son of humble parents take place in Spain, Gil Blas is different from the original Spanish picaro. Influenced by Molière and La Bruyère, satirists of morals and manners, Lesage turned his Gil Blas into an observer of rogues rather than a participant in roguery. Indeed, Gil Blas is a noble-hearted adventurer who, in view of his virtuous behavior, deserves the success he achieves in the end.

ENGLAND

In England, the first translation of *Lazarillo de Tormes* appeared in 1576, the work of David Rowland; the first English *Guzmán de Alfarache* appeared in 1622. Soon thereafter, the Spanish picaresque merged with the native tradition of anatomies of roguery. The best early English picaresque is Thomas Nashe's *The Unfortunate Traveller: Or, The Life of Jack Wilton* (1594). *Guzmán de Alfarache* was very popular with translators; Richard Head's and Frances Kirkman's *The English Rogue* (1665, 1668) is the best among English adaptations of the original *Guzmán de Alfarache*.

In the eighteenth century, a kind of picaresque enjoyed a boom in English literature. Most of Tobias Smollett's fiction is in the picaresque vein. In his outstanding novel *The Adventures of Roderick Random* (1748), the protagonist, an orphan, foreshadows the English picaro as a foundling. He is a decent young person, and his inherent virtues contrast sharply with the cruelty and viciousness of most of the other characters in the novel. They stand for the attitudes of a dehumanized society that subjects the young protagonist to all kinds of hardships and misfortunes on land and on sea. Resilient, in the true picaresque spirit, Roderick Random bounces back after each misadventure. Although his personal fortunes are straightened out in the end when he finds his father and is happily married, on the whole, Smollett presents a rather gloomy view of the human condition.

Daniel Defoe's *The Fortunes and Misfortunes of the Famous Moll Flanders, Written from Her Own Memorandums* (1722) is an episodic fictional autobiography of a picara, a female rogue. She is a true criminal whose crimes are rooted in capitalistic attitudes. Indeed, Moll is a bourgeois picara; inspired by the spirit of profit and investment, she acquires the fortune necessary for investment in the New World by the only means available to her: thievery and prostitution. Her behavior and standards reflect on the materialistic values of the society to which she wants to conform.

Henry Fielding's *The History of Tom Jones, a Foundling* (1749) illustrates better than any other novel of the eighteenth century the transformation of the picaro from a roguish outsider to a belonger. Tom Jones is a foundling and thus an outsider—as a true picaro is expected to be—and in the course of the novel he must take to the road, where he undergoes various adventures. There is no doubt, however, that by the end of his journey he will be integrated into society. As a matter of fact, Tom Jones is a kind of vanishing picaro on his way to becoming the traditional English fictional hero. This hero always ultimately conforms to accepted norms. Tom Jones's place in the world of Allworthy is only being questioned in order to provide adventures for the amusement of the reader. The element of economic necessity is entirely lacking; in consequence, ambiguity and despair vanish and the adventures provoke wholehearted, easy laughter.

The next step on the path of the vanishing English picaro falls in the nineteenth century. In Charles Dickens's *Pickwick Papers* (1836-1837, serial; 1837, book), the picaresque structure is nothing more than a form of convenience. The rogue is Jingle, yet the hero of the adventure-series is the most respectable Mr. Pickwick. He is the picaro turned respectable, in an age when respectability, exemplified by Queen Victoria and the Prince Consort, dominated British society. Mr. Pickwick goes through a series of hilariously comic adventures, gains experience, and even goes to prison, but in the end he returns to society. Integration, so important in British fiction, is achieved at the end of the adventures.

THE UNITED STATES

The American development of the picaresque followed a radically different course. American dark humor, born on the pioneer frontier, recalls in its mixture of laughter and terror the atmosphere of the early Spanish picaresque. The early American, a lonely figure on a vast, unknown, and possibly hostile continent, is a distant cousin of Lazarillo and Guzmán. It is not surprising, then, that the novel from which, according to Ernest Hemingway, all American literature derives, Mark Twain's *Adventures of Huckleberry Finn* (1884), is an American picaresque story not only in the obvious picaresque pattern of Huck's adventures but also in the elements of loneliness and terror that fill up the frame.

Huck is an outsider, belonging to the lowest rank of whites in his society; he recognizes that society pays only lip service to ideals and decides to stay true to his own conscience. While the adventures of his trip down the Mississippi match Lazarillo's experiences of near starvation, the haunting experience with his own conscience over the case of Jim, the runaway black slave, makes Huck a relative of Guzmán, tortured about his soul. Huck, the American picaro, is a rogue with a conscience who chooses to listen to his own heart rather than follow the sham values of society.

THE PICARO IN MODERN FICTION

Many features of the original Spanish picaresque pattern and of its picaro-rogue hero correspond to trends in modern fiction and to the concept of the modern limited hero or antihero. The episodic, open-ended plot is an appropriate device for the modern writer, who knows "only broken images" for presenting the fragmented reality of a disorderly, chaotic universe. The picaro is not unlike the modern alienated individual, born into a world turned upside down. Many critics, therefore, consider the picaresque mode to be one of the most characteristic in twentieth century fiction, while others speak of a picaresque renaissance.

Irish writer James Joyce's *Ulysses* (1922), the archetype of modern fiction, shows striking similarities with the picaresque. Joyce's "joco-serious" recalls the unbalanced Spanish picaresque atmosphere of half-comical and half-serious attitudes. Leopold Bloom, a Jew in Ireland, is an outsider in society; as a betrayed husband, he also is an outsider in his family. Both *Ulysses* and the Spanish picaresque present a series of experiences rather than a coherent narrative. They present a roguelike hero, who is no criminal but still less than an example of virtue and whose life is a hard-luck story.

Bloom experiences a despair and anxiety which was alien to the more respectable picaros of the eighteenth and nineteenth centuries but which recalls the mood of *Lazarillo de Tormes*.

The English writer Joyce Cary also used the picaresque genre for his first trilogy, which concerns the life of the artist Gulley Jimson, a rascally but appealing picaro. Interestingly, only the first and third volumes can qualify as picaresque novels, for the narrator of the second book, *To Be a Pilgrim* (1942), is Thomas Wilcher, who does not fit the definition of a picaro. Wilcher is a member of the establishment, a rich, respectable lawyer who believes himself to be on the way to the Heavenly City. However, the first novel in the trilogy, *Herself Surprised* (1941), is narrated by a picara worthy to be classed with Moll Flanders; she not only habitually disregards the moral laws but also has no difficulty justifying even the most flagrant betrayal of trust—for instance, systematically stealing from Mr. Wilcher while she pretends to be the perfect housekeeper. Like Moll, Sara is eventually caught; *Herself Surprised* is written from prison. Gulley, who was probably the most important man in Sara's life, also falls victim to the law. *The Horse's Mouth* (1944, 1957), which he narrates, begins with his release from prison, an old man, but still adept at lying, cheating, stealing, and justifying his sins as necessitated by his art. Nevertheless, Gulley's zest for life and his ability to laugh both at the world and at himself make him a particularly appealing picaro.

The picaresque pattern also emerged in the novels of Britain's Angry Young Men in the 1950's. The angry picaresque novel of postwar Great Britain resulted from serious discontent with the welfare state. The decade found England in unsettled conditions, with the empire falling to pieces and the class system only slowly weakening in its traditional rigidity. Just as the Spanish picaresque novel arose in part as an expression of the social resentment of the underdog against the privileged classes, so Kingsley Amis's *Lucky Jim* (1954), John Wain's *Hurry on Down* (1953), and Alan Sillitoe's *Saturday Night and Sunday Morning* (1958) reject the values of the phony middle class. Yet their protagonists share Lazarillo's dream of belonging; in consequence, the angry picaresque stays within the pattern of integration characteristic of British fiction.

The American picaresque novel of the twentieth and twenty-first centuries may describe a restless small-town youth, as in John Updike's *Rabbit, Run* (1960), or a wild drive across the continent, as in Jack Kerouac's *On the Road* (1957). The present-day American rogues display an old American attitude; they try to recapture the heroic spirit of the frontier and confront the nature of humanity, of the self. The modern American picaro is an outsider; he may be a sensitive adolescent shunning the phony world, like Holden Caulfield in J. D. Salinger's *The Catcher in the Rye* (1951), or a man fighting the military in order to survive, like Yossarian in Joseph Heller's *Catch-22* (1961); he may be a member of a minority group—African American, like Ralph Ellison's Invisible Man in his novel *Invisible Man* (1952); Irish, like Ken Kesey's McMurphy in *One Flew over the Cuckoo's Nest* (1962); or Jewish, like Saul Bellow's Augie March in *The Adventures of Augie March* (1953).

Augie March is the product of the Chicago ghetto, the son of Jewish immigrants forced by his dehumanizing environment into a picaro attitude. A servant to many masters, resilient and ready to adjust, Augie ultimately refuses any attempt to be adopted and preserves his outsider status. Practical and pragmatic, he is able to do almost anything. While he is open to any new experience, he remains faithful to his own self, considering all his adventures as means to find his true identity. The Invisible Man, who is black, learns to accept his invisibility in white America; his picaresque experiences take him through a series of rejections at the end of which he emerges as a truly protean individual and even a trickster.

A PICARESQUE RENAISSANCE

Despite the protests of purists, who felt that the term "picaresque" was being applied too loosely, in the last three decades of the twentieth century novels thus described appeared in ever-increasing numbers, as did scholarly articles about specific works and books in which the genre was discussed more generally. Not surprisingly, much of the scholarship focused on the literature of Spain and Latin America, where the tradition has always flourished, and to a lesser degree on fiction from England and America. Occurrences of the picaresque novel were also found in some unexpected places, such as Morocco and Japan.

If the latter part of the twentieth century did see not only the preservation of the genre but also a very real picaresque renaissance, it can be explained by the fact that the form is so adaptable. Danny Deck, the successful writer-protagonist in Larry McMurtry's *All My Friends Are Going to Be Strangers* (1972), has little in common with the drug-dependent drifter in Jay McInerney's *Bright Lights, Big City* (1984), which is one of the few picaresque novels written in the second person. In *All My Friends Are Going to Be Strangers*, Danny travels from Texas to California and back to Texas, sometimes stopping for a time but always moving on, until at the end of the book he comes to a halt in the borderland between Texas and Mexico, his future uncertain. By contrast, all the adventures of McInerney's picaro take place in Manhattan over the course of one week, with frequent flashbacks into the past, and his story ends with his realizing that he must reclaim the values he was taught in childhood.

The quest of the picaro-narrator in Paul Auster's *Moon Palace* (1989) is also successful, though it takes some time for the aptly named Marco Stanley Fogg to realize that his own lack of purpose is rooted in his knowing nothing about his father and little about his mother, who is now dead. The scope of the novel is broadened geographically, temporally, and thematically by an interpolated narrative, a story told by the elderly man for whom Fogg works, which with the customary picaresque dependence upon happy coincidence enables the hero to identify his father and propels the hero westward across the continent to his own rebirth. The American Western novel, long a genre that easily accommodated the picaresque, reached what may be considered its literary pinnacle with the work of Cormac McCarthy, whose teenage runaway protagonist known only as "the kid" animated *Blood Meridian: Or, the Evening Redness in the West* (1985). In McCarthy's Western trilogy—the National Book Award winner *All the Pretty Horses* (1992), *The Crossing* (1994), and *Cities of the Plain* (1998)—each novel is a picaresque story of a young man on the move, facing tests and facing challenges from other men.

THE HISTORICAL PICARESQUE

Interjected narratives, letters, and diaries have sometimes extended the time frame of picaresque novels a short distance into the past, but as long as one aim of the genre was to satirize a corrupt society, it did not occur to writers to set such works in the distant past. Late in the twentieth century, however, a new form appeared, in which a fictional picaro operates within a historical setting. In his introduction to *Flashman* (1969), British writer George MacDonald Fraser pretends to have discovered the papers of a minor character in Thomas Hughes's *Tom Brown's School Days* (1858). In *Flashman* and in the twelve that followed it, including *Flashman on the March* (2005), Harry Paget Flashman exposes himself as an unprincipled rogue, a lecher, and a coward who not only seduces every woman who catches his eye but also survives such episodes as the Indian Mutiny, the Charge of the Light Brigade, China's Taiping Rebellion, John Brown's raid on Harper's Ferry, and Little Big Horn, winning a reputation as a hero and eventually rising to the rank of brigadier general. Fraser's plots are exciting, but the secret of his popularity is the character of Flashman, perhaps because no matter how much he deceives others, he is always honest with himself.

In other picaresque novels, however, the picaro is very different from Lazarillo de Tormes or Flashman. A first-person narrator with a need to survive, the picaro candidly relates his adventures, while also serving as an observer. Having attached himself to a historical figure, the picaro talks with and observes him or her, thus presenting the author's interpretation of history. In E. L. Doctorow's *Billy Bathgate* (1989), for example, the title character is involved with the Depression-era gangster Dutch Schultz, and in Larry McMurtry's *Anything for Billy* (1988), the inept train robber Ben Sippy develops a real affection for Billy Bone, or Billy the Kid, the legendary outlaw of the Old West. The primary goal of both narrators is to survive, Billy by finding a way out of the slums, Ben by fleeing from a household of females and the stifling life of a Philadelphia gentleman. However, they also have a boundless curiosity, and they knowingly risk their lives in order to satisfy it. The protagonist in *Johnny One-Eye: A Tale of the American Revolution* (2008), by Jerome Charyn, is a double agent who encounters historical figures on both sides of the conflict: George Washington, Alexander Hamilton, Lord Admiral Richard Howe, and Benedict Arnold. Like the other picaresque heroes, he is a close observer of the world

around him, and he describes everything in detail as he moves through the war and through the island of Manhattan looking for the identity of his father.

THE FEMINIST PICARESQUE

Another new development in the late twentieth century picaresque renaissance was the novel with a feminist slant. Though picaras had appeared in earlier works, such as *Moll Flanders*, now picaresque novels written by women and about women began to proliferate. They varied widely in content and in tone. Rita Mae Brown's semiautobiographical *Rubyfruit Jungle* (1973) is both a moving description of what it is like to be rejected by society and a defiant celebration of lesbian sexuality, as is Sarah Waters's *Tipping the Velvet* (1998), a lighthearted picaresque of lesbian love. Margaret Atwood's *Lady Oracle* (1976) features another kind of rebel, one who would be seen more and more frequently in fiction during the years that followed: a mature woman who becomes a runaway. Atwood's heroine, Joan Foster, a writer, is so tired of her marriage, her ongoing affair, and her fans that she decides to fake her own death and run off to Italy. By the time she is found out and forced to return, this picaresque heroine has made some important decisions about the direction her life will take. Bella, the protagonist of Helen Zahavi's *Dirty Weekend* (1991), is on the run from a neighbor who has molested her, and in her flight she meets and kills seven abusive men.

Picaresque novels by women have taken many different shapes. There are dozens of fantasies by writers such as Marion Zimmer Bradley, Jo Clayton, Sharon Green, Tanith Lee, Anne Maxwell, Anne McCaffrey, and Janet Morris, all of which are feminist in philosophy and picaresque in form. The picaresque is also allied with Magical Realism, as in Isabel Allende's *Eva Luna* (1987; English translation, 1988), in which the title character survives one crisis after another with the aid of unseen powers and the force of her own imagination. Erica Jong's *Fanny: Being the True History of Fanny Hackabout-Jones* (1980) is much more like the picaresque novels of the eighteenth century, the period in which it is set. The author uses not only the language, capitalization, and punctuation of novels written in that era but also a huge cast of characters and a plot dependent on mistaken identities, chance meetings, and improbable coincidences. As in the historical novels already mentioned, the fictional Fanny meets and comments on real people; among her customers in a brothel are Dean Swift, William Hogarth, and John Cleland, whose *Fanny Hill: Or, Memoirs of a Woman of Pleasure* (1748-1749) Jong insists is an inaccurate account of Fanny Hill's life. *Fanny* could well have been written in the eighteenth century, as it appears to be, were it not for the fact that the author's twentieth century sensibility and, specifically, her feminism are evident in every one of Fanny's pronouncements.

A GENRE OF LASTING VALUE

One of the reasons for the widespread use of the picaresque form at the end of the twentieth century was obviously its flexibility. It has been utilized by writers from very different cultures, representing a wide range of literary traditions, from the historical novel to Magical Realism and fantasy. Picaresque works can be confessional, autobiographical, philosophical, or savagely satirical, and their protagonists can range from the unfortunate to thoroughgoing scoundrels. Some picaros and picaras even reform. What they all share with their Spanish originals is an exuberant love of life and a determination to survive in order to enjoy it.

The picaresque renaissance can also be attributed to the times themselves. The disorder, instability, and chaotic nature of the age may remind one of the transitional character of the sixteenth century. Modern men and women, dwarfed by an awareness of their lack of control over events in the outside world as well as over their own behavior, cannot hope for heroism; the best they can achieve is a kind of picaro status—an unwilling conformist, a rebel-victim, a picaresque saint. In the protean genre of the picaresque, sixteenth century Spanish writers created a fictional form appropriate for presenting the human predicament in an age of turmoil and instability.

Anna B. Katona
Updated by Rosemary M. Canfield Reisman

BIBLIOGRAPHY

Benito-Vessels, Carmen, and Michael Zappala, eds. *The Picaresque: A Symposium on the Rogue's Tale*. Newark, N.J.: University of Delaware Press, 1994. Specific picaresque works are discussed in most of these essays, while others deal with more general topics, such as translation. In their preface, the editors explain the ongoing disagreements about what constitutes picaresque literature.

Bjornson, Richard. *The Picaresque Hero in European Fiction*. Madison: University of Wisconsin Press, 1977. History of the picaresque through the eighteenth century, presented through the examination of major works such as *Moll Flanders* and *The Adventures of Roderick Random*. Includes illustrations.

Dunn, Peter N. *The Spanish Picaresque Novel*. Boston: Twayne, 1979. Traces the development of the picaresque novel in Spain, from the sixteenth century's *Lazarillo de Tormes* through seventeenth century tales written by Miguel de Cervantes and others. Explains distinctive qualities of the genre and demonstrates how these continued in novels during the development of realistic fiction.

Friedman, Edward H. *The Antiheroine's Voice: Narrative Discourse and Transformations of the Picaresque*. Columbia: University of Missouri Press, 1987. Feminist and deconstructionist analysis of the effect of an author's gender and outlook on a novel with a picara as first-person narrator. Highly theoretical but thought-provoking.

Gutiérrez, Helen Turner. *The Reception of the Picaresque in the French, English, and German Traditions*. New York: Peter Lang, 1995. Explores ways a common tradition is adapted in various countries in Europe to meet the needs of individual writers and the expectations of the reading public. Discusses the development of the picaresque in three countries, examining examples from the sixteenth through the twentieth centuries.

Kaler, Anne K. *The Picara: From Hera to Fantasy Heroine*. Bowling Green, Ohio: Bowling Green State University Popular Press, 1991. After outlining the relationship among the picara, the picaro, and picaresque literature, the author considers the six characteristics that differentiate a picara from a picaro. Kaler points to many picaras in contemporary literature, notably in fantasies.

Miller, Stuart. *The Picaresque Novel*. Cleveland, Ohio: Press of Case Western Reserve University, 1967.

Scrutinizes six works in order to arrive at a definition of the genre. Although dated, this book is still valuable for Miller's comments about technical matters and for its accessibility.

Monteser, Frederick. *The Picaresque Element in Western Literature*. Tuscaloosa: University of Alabama Press, 1975. Traces the picaresque novel from its Spanish beginnings into France, Germany, Britain, Latin America, and the United States, but concludes that American society is now constituted so as to make the existence of a picaro impossible. Includes a chronological list of works.

Sherrill, Rowland A. *Road-Book America: Contemporary Culture and the New Picaresque*. Urbana: University of Illinois Press, 2000. Explores American fiction and nonfiction about life on the road, arguing these particular forms define a "new" picaresque.

Novelists discussed include John Steinbeck and E. L. Doctorow.

Viviès, Jean. *English Travel Narratives in the Eighteenth Century: Exploring Genres*. Burlington, Vt.: Ashgate, 2002. Focuses on the travel journals of James Boswell, Laurence Sterne, and Tobias Smollett to demarcate the line between fiction and nonfiction. Chapter four examines "The Vagaries of the Picaresque."

Wicks, Ulrich. *Picaresque Narrative, Picaresque Fictions: A Theory and Research Guide*. New York: Greenwood Press, 1989. In the first part of this important volume, the author examines the picaresque from a theoretical standpoint and provides a comprehensive list of secondary sources. In the second section, Wicks analyzes more than sixty picaresque fictions, films as well as novels, in alphabetical order.

THE POLITICAL NOVEL

In the narrowest sense, the political novel is a work of fiction that deals with politicians and the political process. In this category, Robert Penn Warren's *All the King's Men* (1946) and Sinclair Lewis's *It Can't Happen Here* (1935), and the work of British novelists such as Benjamin Disraeli and Anthony Trollope, are paramount examples of fictional narratives that attempt to recreate the business of politics—the speech making, campaigning, lobbying, and governing (both in public and behind-the-scenes). Although such works may derive from historical figures and events (Huey Long is the model for Willie Stark in *All the King's Men*), these novels remain in the realm of the imaginary because they posit outcomes that are hypothetical.

Another form of the political novel is historical fiction. Gore Vidal's *Burr* (1973) and Russell Banks's *Cloudsplitter* (1998)—a novel about John Brown that is narrated by one of his sons—deal directly with the historical record, inventing a voice for their protagonists and portraying a part of history that eludes historians for lack of evidence. These rather traditional political and historical novels have been challenged by postmodern uses of history and politics in works such as Robert Coover's *The Public Burning* (1977), half of which is narrated by an eroticized Richard Nixon, and Ishmael Reed's *Flight to Canada* (1976), featuring nineteenth century figures, including Abraham Lincoln and Harriet Beecher Stowe, who inhabit an anachronistic world of inventions that coexist with slavery. E. L. Doctorow's *Ragtime* (1975) represents a similarly playful and unconventional use of history.

Still another kind of political novel is ideological. Ayn Rand's *Atlas Shrugged* (1957) is a full-scale attack on collectivist societies similar to those established in the Soviet Union and other communist states. An uncompromising individualist, Rand created the future as a dystopia, in which the incentive to produce creatively would be stifled by a centralized government taking over the means of production. The human spirit itself is crushed in Rand's work—as it is in George Orwell's *Nineteen Eighty-Four* (1949), which agrees with Rand on communism, although Orwell shared none of her fervor for capitalism. In Rand's view, current definitions of society—and perhaps society itself—would have to perish for the world to be rebuilt on individualist principles. Other European novelists, such as André Malraux and Ignacio Silone, have portrayed the positive and negative aspects of Marxist and communist revolutions in the twentieth century without resorting to Rand's absolutist rejection of socialist values.

An earlier generation of novelists—Henry James in the *Princess Casamassima* (1886) and Joseph Conrad in *The Secret Agent* (1907)—deal with revolutionaries, anarchist conspiracies, and other underground political activities, which remain staples of the political novel in writers as diverse as Rebecca West in *The Birds Fall Down* (1966) and Russell Banks in *The Darling* (2004).

Still other forms of the political novel focus on espionage and, especially, the Cold War. Novelists such as Graham Greene, John le Carré, and Charles McCarry explore in considerable depth the cost of the Cold War to those nations that sought to maintain and, in some cases, extend their powers. The nature of covert work in organizations such as the Central Intelligence Agency (CIA) and MI5 (Great Britain's intelligence service) is detailed in Norman Mailer's *Harlot's Ghost* (1991) and le Carré's George Smiley novels.

A separate category might also be applied to the novels of writers such as Arthur Koestler (*Darkness at Noon*, 1940) and Conrad (*Nostromo*, 1904), both of which probe the nature of historical processes and question the course of the modern world. Orwell's fable *Animal Farm* (1945) as well as *Nineteen Eighty-Four* could belong to this category as well. Later novels in this category—Aleksandr Solzhenitsyn's *Odin den' Ivana Denisovicha* (1962; *One Day in the Life of Ivan Denisovich*, 1963) and *V kruge pervom* (1968; *The First Circle*, 1968), for example—explore how Stalinism and Soviet collectivism have attempted to destroy individual consciousness and to command the interpretation of history according to state dogma.

To some extent, all political novels project an idea or philosophy of history, a reading of where humanity is headed. Voltaire's *Candide: Ou, L'Optimisme* (1759; *Candide: Or, All for the Best*, 1759) is perhaps the earliest example of using a fictional narrative to comment on different forms of political organization and the way they impinge on the individual's life. Candide is exposed to an astonishing array of political systems and philosophies of government as well as to the faultiness of his mentor's optimistic claim that this is the best of all possible worlds. Similarly, William Godwin in *Things as They Are: Or, The Adventures Caleb Williams* (1794; also known as *The Adventures of Caleb Williams: Or, Things as They Are*; best known as *Caleb Williams*) used the plight of his protagonist to excoriate a British government bent on punishing dissenters and upholding a class system that threatened individual rights. The political novel yields an impressive panoply of approaches to imagining and assessing the way societies have been organized during the last 250 years.

POLITICIANS AND THE POLITICAL PROCESS

Both Sinclair Lewis and Robert Penn Warren focused on American forms of fascism that threatened to undermine American political institutions and to bring into disrepute the very nature of democracy. Lewis's *It Can't Happen Here* forecasts a nation so disheartened by the Depression that the calls for the equal distribution of wealth result in a kind of centralized police state. Liberal politicians such as President Franklin D. Roosevelt are unable to effect rapid change so the public turns to more radical solutions—just as the Germans, Italians, and Spaniards had done in Europe. Lewis's protagonist, Doremus Jessup, the liberal owner-editor of a small-town newspaper, heroically tries to resist the new dictatorial regime, but he is also part of the problem. Liberals are slow to heed the onset of evil, Lewis suggests.

In the novel, the country has to suffer a curtailment of liberty before it begins to right itself. As Joseph Blotner observes in his comprehensive study of the political novel, Lewis concludes that it is not outside forces that will subdue American democracy but rather a failure of will from within, of the "conscientious, respectable, lazy-minded Doremus Jessups who have let the demagogue wriggle in, without fierce enough protest." Liberals did not believe a dictatorship could form in the United States—that fascism could prevail in America—and Lewis set out to show just how wrong they might be.

Warren analyzed another weakness of liberalism in his Pulitzer Prize-winning novel *All the King's Men*. While Warren's hero Willie Stark was inspired by the career of Louisiana governor and senator Huey Long, Stark is more complex and tragic than his model. Warren's character begins as a naïve idealist who gradually realizes that he can do good only by becoming a part of the political system. He uses bribery and other forms of corruption to improve the lives of his state's citizens. In other words, he concludes that the end will justify the means—that he must use the corrupt practices in place to build a better world. However, Stark becomes in the process a dictator who does not merely put the idea of democracy in abeyance. On the contrary, he rules by force of personality to such an extent that there is no political system—only his power. This power was called Longism in Louisiana. Like Long in real life, Stark is assassinated, a victim of the unruly political passions that his own drive for power have provoked.

In the novels of Benjamin Disraeli and Anthony Trollope, the focus is on reform, on plots and characters that reveal the corruption at the heart of the British political system and the efforts of their heroes to expose injustice and restore a measure of fairness and truly representative government. Both writers deal with political institutions in a much more concrete fashion than do Lewis or Warren. In *Phineas Finn, the Irish Member* (1867-1869, serial; 1869, book), Trollope explores the career of a Liberal member of Parliament. Disraeli used novels such as *Sybil: Or, The Two Nations* (1845) to show how his Conservative Party could renew itself by addressing the inequities of society. Trollope based his characters on actual politicians and on the parliamentary process in *Phineas Redux* (1873-1874, serial; 1874, book) and *The Prime Minister* (1875-1876, serial; 1876, book).

THE HISTORICAL NOVEL OF POLITICS

Perhaps no novelist has devoted more careful attention to the lives and politics of political figures than has Gore Vidal. In *Lincoln* (1984) and *Burr* he not only creates vivid portraits of historical figures, he also shows them in political combat, so to speak. Thus, Thomas Jefferson becomes, in Aaron's Burr's narrative, a shifty, untrustworthy ally—much more of an opportunist than most historians and biographers are willing to concede. Burr becomes a perceptive dissenter free of the cant that Jefferson and his followers use to cloak their crude desire for power. Vidal's other political novels include *Washington, D.C.* (1967), *1876* (1976), *Empire* (1987), and *Hollywood: A Novel of America in the 1920's* (1990).

Postmodern novels go beyond Vidal's approach of reinterpreting history by also offering alternative scenarios and clearly fictionalized plots that nevertheless attempt to strike at the heart of what certain historical periods signify. Thus, in Robert Coover's *The Public Burning*, convicted American spies Julius and Ethel Rosenberg are publicly burned rather than executed in the electric chair because Coover believes their trial and conviction are part of the paranoid atavistic mood of 1950's America. During this time, tales of communist subversives planning to take over the free world are the equivalent of seventeenth century tales of witchcraft that led to the burning of dissenters or "witches" at the stake. From Coover's perspective, Nixon's anticommunism becomes a projection onto the Rosenbergs of his own perverted desires that he cannot acknowledge but must somehow express. Nixon craves what he condemns.

THE IDEOLOGICAL POLITICAL NOVEL

The works of André Malraux and Ayn Rand represent two extremes of the ideological novel, the former seeking in Marxism and collectivism a more just, democratic world based on collective principles (what is best for humanity as a whole), and the latter arguing that human freedom depends on the unfettered energy and creativity of individuals. Unlike Malraux, who portrayed individuals as highly confused about their own natures and lacking in self-knowledge, Rand posited supremely confident individuals who not only knew their own minds but resisted the modern world's tendency to subject powerful minds and achievers to some kind of socially determined core of values. The individual in Rand's view could live only in and for him- or herself. Only by doing so did individuals contribute to the development of the world. So powerful was her notion that the

modern world was attempting to enslave its greatest minds that Rand created in *Atlas Shrugged* a colony of superachievers that divorces itself from the world and attempts to create a new one based solely on the desires of its members to work (as artists, businessmen, and industrialists) for their own benefit.

Malraux's most important novel is *La Condition humaine* (1933; *Man's Fate*, 1934; also known as *Storm in Shanghai* and *Man's Estate*). Set during the Shanghai revolution of 1927, the story features an impressive array of characters of different nationalities and ideologies in conflict with themselves. Rather then seeing an intellectual, objective way out of this confusion—as Rand does in her portrayal of heroic individuals—Malraux sees in Marxism a vision of human solidarity, a fraternity of selves that collectively hold out at least the possibility of fighting for a fairer, more egalitarian world. Individuals cannot prevail; indeed the state of individuality is equated with solitude in Malraux's novels, and hence the need for a commitment to a cause greater than oneself.

THE UNDERGROUND POLITICAL NOVEL

In *The Princess Casamassima* (1886), Henry James explores the coterie of revolutionaries residing in late nineteenth century London. Hyacinth Robinson's grandfather died on the barricades in the French Revolution, and Hyacinth has been educated by a man involved in the revolutionary French Commune of 1871. Feeling the pressures of radicalism—a fervent desire to fundamentally change the world—Robinson vows to continue the cause, but then he is smitten by Princess Casamassima and as a result begins to question his devotion to revolution. The idea of obliterating the world the princess represents appalls him and eventually—unable to reconcile his conflicting feelings—he kills himself. James points out the way revolutionary politics tends to obliterate individual rights, even though revolutionaries argue they are fighting for a better, more equal world.

Similarly, in *The Birds Fall Down*, Rebecca West focuses on Kamensky, a double agent who works for a czarist aristocrat but also for the revolutionaries. Based on the case of an actual double agent known as Azeff, West's novel explores the conflicting claims of status quo (tradition) and revolution (change). Individuals torn between the two sides reflect the novelist's own ambivalent attitude about how best to improve the world while also preserving those aspects of government and society that remain essential to securing individual liberty and freedom of conscience. Joseph Conrad heavily influenced West. Her decision to set *The Birds Fall Down* shortly before the Russian Revolution aligns her with her illustrious predecessors, whose novels about the conflicting emotions of revolutionaries seem, in retrospect, prophetic of the confused and ultimately self-defeating ideology that led to the rise and fall of communism and of the Soviet state.

THE COLD WAR ESPIONAGE NOVEL

Like John le Carré, Charles McCarry uses his characters' biographies to encompass much of twentieth century political history. McCarry, a former employee of the CIA, has published a series of novels about spy hero Paul Christopher, a handsome Yale graduate and a poet. His father also was a spy; he was killed in Berlin in a setup by the Soviets. Christopher's mother, a courageous German woman against Nazi ideology, who aided many Jews to escape the Third Reich, was sent to a concentration camp during the war and then vanished. Each novel is a revelation, delving into Christopher's background and the widening network of contacts that implicate him in the major events of the Cold War. To read the sequence of the Paul Christopher novels is to not only journey through the complexity of contemporary history but also to revise perceptions of Christopher himself, just as perceptions of le Carré's George Smiley evolve from one novel to the next. Thus, biography, history, and psychology are melded into the plots of spy novels that are also contributions to political history.

Although well-known as a critic of American political institutions, Norman Mailer's view of the CIA is curiously positive—even heroic—when compared to McCarry's and le Carré's handling of intelligence agencies. In Mailer's *Harlot's Ghost*, the novel's protagonist, Harry Hubbard, is a protégé of the legendary Hugh Tremont Montague (Harlot) and a key participant in CIA operations in Berlin, Miami, Cuba, Uruguay, and Washington, D.C. Mailer's novel derives from a close reading of nearly one hundred books about the organization; it is also a harping on his well-worn subjects: the murder of Marilyn Monroe, Ernest Hemingway's suicide, and

the nature of Fidel Castro's heroism. Mailer portrays the CIA operative as a deceiver, a person who is playing more than one role, an actor whose sense of reality is constantly shifting, making it difficult to maintain loyalties and friendships, never sure of his or her own ground.

Harry Hubbard, the son of a fabled CIA agent, is a typical Mailer hero worried that he is not "tough enough" and takes on risky ventures such as the Bay of Pigs fiasco. As a matter of survival within the agency, he finds himself acting as a double agent—at one point reporting to both his mentor, Harlot, and to his father, Cal. Through Harry's letters, diaries, and first-person narrative, Mailer manages to cover most of the dramatic events involving the CIA from 1955 to 1963.

THE POLITICAL NOVEL AND HISTORICAL PROCESS

In *Darkness at Noon*, Arthur Koestler set the pattern of the postwar political novel that examined the trajectory of twentieth century history. The novel is the story of Nicolas Rubashov, an old Bolshevik (a true believer in the Russian Revolution). He has been schooled to believe that the communists are on the right side of history. His Marxism preaches that there are laws of history that the Communist Party follows no matter how they contradict an individual's ideas and convictions. The party, not the individual conscience, rules. Rubashov struggles to maintain his faith even as he himself is incarcerated, a victim of the Stalinist purges, and awaits a public trial for crimes he did not commit. However, Rubashov has been an enforcer of communist dogma and thus realizes that his own blind fealty to an ideology has brought him to this evil end. By forsaking his own moral and ethical codes, he has made it possible for the state to dispose of individuals in accord with its own idea of revolutionary justice and history.

The revolution that is eating its own in *Darkness at Noon* becomes in Orwell's *Nineteen Eighty-Four* a totalitarian state that is constantly at war, rewriting history to suit whatever political line the state currently pursues and treating all individuals as merely tools in a collective enterprise watched over by Big Brother on television screens. The fate of the old Bolsheviks has now become everyday reality for the state's subjects.

From its inception in novels such as *Candide* and

Things as They Are, the political novel has examined the basis on which modern society is organized. Certain political novelists—such as Conrad and James—do not seek to impose a view of history or of political events, except when they are exploring the inherent ambiguity and cross-purposes of their characters. Other novelists, such as Rand and Malraux, have an agenda, an argument they wish to propose as a solution to political problems. Other novelists, such as Koestler, demonstrate the futility of relying on ideology. West implies that the human character is too complex for a single system of thought to prevail and prove capable of governing the world. Still other novelists, such as McCarry and le Carré, have main protagonists who struggle to make the best of their flawed ideologies. Whereas traditionalists such as Vidal write from a coherent, liberal point of view, postmodernists such as Coover question both liberal and conservative principles, seeking to show that politics is not based on an objective reality, which Rand believed in, but rather on the human power to imagine and fabricate multiple ideologies, a power that leads postmodernists to the point of radical skepticism.

Carl Rollyson

BIBLIOGRAPHY

Blotner, Joseph. *The Political Novel*. 1955. Reprint. Westport, Conn.: Greenwood Press, 1979. Dated but comprehensive and important study of the genre, with short sections on significant political novels published since the eighteenth century. Also focuses on the role of women and on moral problems and values, international communism, proletarian literature, and imperialism. Bibliography divided into sections on American, English, Italian, German, French, Russian, and South African novels.

Boyers, Robert. *Atrocity and Amnesia: The Political Novel Since 1945*. New York: Oxford University Press, 1985. Chapters on Graham Greene, V. S. Naipaul, Aleksandr Solzhenitsyn, Nadine Gordimer, Günter Grass, Milan Kundera, and Holocaust fiction. A wide-ranging interpretation of individual novelists but also of the genre, including its treatment of time and ethics.

Cawelti, John G., and Bruce A. Rosenberg. *The Spy Story*. Chicago: University of Chicago Press, 1987.

Examines spy fiction as a way of exploring the complex and bewildering nature of twentieth century political institutions and groups. Argues that the secret agent represents the divided feelings of society. Discusses the work of Graham Greene, John le Carré, and others. Includes several bibliographies of spy novels, films, writers, and themes.

Crossman, Richard, ed. *The God That Failed*. New York: Columbia University Press, 2001. Originally published in 1950, this collection of essays is now a classic. Several distinguished writers, including Arthur Koestler, Ignazio Silone, Richard Wright, and Stephen Spender, describe their attraction to communism and why they ultimately rejected Marxism. An indispensable guide to studying political novels that deal with the development and demise of communism.

Harris, Sharon M, ed. *Redefining the Political Novel: American Women Writers, 1797-1901*. Knoxville: University of Tennessee Press, 1995. Study of American women writers of political novels who crafted their works long before women were assumed to have written such books. Especially valuable for its examination of how women helped to shape the male-dominated genre, despite cultural assumptions that women wrote "social commentaries" rather than political critiques, fictional or otherwise.

Howe, Irving. *Politics and the Novel*. Chicago: Ivan R. Dee, 2002. A classic study of the genre, with chapters on Henry James, André Malraux, Ignazio Silone, Joseph Conrad, and Fyodor Dostoevsky, as well as comprehensive discussions of the genre and the political world its seeks to describe and interpret.

Lord, Ursula. *Solitude Versus Solidarity in the Novels of Joseph Conrad: Political and Epistemological Implications of Narrative Innovation*. Montreal: McGill-Queen's University Press, 1998. Although Lord focuses on Conrad, her introduction is a wide-ranging study of the impact of thinkers such as Karl Marx and Charles Darwin on nineteenth century British political fiction.

Suleiman, S. R. *Authoritarian Fictions: The Ideological Novel as a Literary Genre*. Princeton, N.J.: Princeton University Press, 1983. Focuses on French political novels by André Malraux, Jean-Paul Sartre, and

Louis Aragon while exploring the way these ideological narratives challenge the premises of realistic novels.

Woods, Brett F. *Neutral Ground: A Political History of Espionage Fiction.* New York: Algora, 2008. Examines the manner in which contemporary international events have shaped the themes of political novels. Includes a bibliography.

Zinsser, William, ed. *Paths of Resistance: The Art and Craft of the Political Novel.* Boston: Houghton Mifflin, 1989. Essays by Isabel Allende, Robert Stone, Charles McCarry and others explore the role of politics in literature. Although these pieces may be regarded as special pleading for each author's respective work, the volume nevertheless is insightful as the novelists regard such matters as fidelity to fact, to ideas, and to the moral and ethical implications of political writing.

THE POSTMODERN NOVEL

Iconoclastic and irreverent, the postmodern novel is by definition a radical experiment that emerges when a writer feels the customary tropes of fiction have been exhausted. For the postmodernist, the well-worn genre of the novel is insufficient and no longer capable of conveying the imagination of the writer or the magnitude of historical events.

Several critics agree that postmodern fiction is a product of the post-World War II period. At that time, many of the major modernist writers, such as Joseph Conrad, Marcel Proust, Franz Kafka, James Joyce, and Virginia Woolf, had died. Other writers, including William Faulkner and Ernest Hemingway, had ceased publishing innovative and experimental work. Critics also tend to concur that postmodernism is an extension of rather than a decisive break or deviation from modernism, the defining literary movement of the twentieth century.

Many different authors have been labeled postmodernist. These writers include Thomas Berger, Richard Brautigan, Don DeLillo, William Gaddis, Vladimir Nabokov, and Thomas Pynchon, Peter Ackroyd, Angela Carter, Salman Rushdie, and Umberto Eco. Most critical discussion, however, focuses on American writers publishing since the late 1950's.

Like the modern novel, the postmodern novel is subversive; that is, it counters traditional notions of plot, narrative, chronology, and character development. Postmodern novels are often described as self-reflexive—that is, they center on the nature of fiction itself and are written as though fiction is independent of society, reality, and any realm outside itself. The origins of the "autonomous" postmodern novel can be found in the essays of early modernist writers such as Oscar Wilde, who argued against Aristotle's premise that art imitates life. On the contrary, Wilde contended that life imitates art.

Novelists spent most of the twentieth century elaborating on Wilde's thesis of art for art's sake—the idea that for art to be art it had to be independent of society and of political or extraliterary considerations—because the novel had been so thoroughly grounded in realism. Realist novels originated in the eighteenth century and

featured, among other literary devices, narratives that imitated the structure and style of biographies and histories so that their characters seemed real. That this realism, however, was only a kind of pretense, or willing suspension of disbelief, as Samuel Taylor Coleridge called it, was recognized early on by other eighteenth century writers, such as Laurence Sterne. In his novel *Tristram Shandy* (1759-1767), Sterne commented on his own fiction-making. In other words, he shattered the realistic frame of his own story to call attention to himself as narrator. Sterne's example, in the short term, earned him few followers, and it was not until James Joyce's playful introduction of the artist as narrator and character in the figure of Stephen Dedalus that modern novelists and their postmodernist successors focused on fiction as a self-sustaining universe of its own.

THE POSTMODERN NOVEL AS PASTICHE

Because literature itself is often the subject of postmodern novels, it is not surprising that genres such as the historical novel are parodied and satirized and become the subjects of pastiche. Thus, E. L. Doctorow's *Ragtime* (1975) introduces historical figures such as anarchist Emma Goldman and high-society player Evelyn Nesbit and has them interact in ways that would seem improbable in conventional historical fiction, in which the novelist is usually quite careful to portray history accurately. Referring to one scene in the novel, an interviewer asked Doctorow if Goldman had actually given Nesbit a massage, in "real life." The interviewer wanted to know whether or not the two had even met in real life. Doctorow responded with "they have now."

Doctorow's point was that fiction creates its own reality, a kind of truth that is not historically documented yet is of inestimable value. In this case, Doctorow was commenting on the gap between a romantic figure such as Nesbit and a down-to-earth radical such as Goldman, who also was a feminist who would have found Nesbit's plight as a sexual object deplorable. Nesbit needed the kind of care Goldman offered. That the two women never met would be irrelevant to the postmodern novelist, and that the two women should occupy such different places in society and be perceived as having nothing in common was precisely what Doctorow found as a fault in the world outside his novel, thus his creation of a parallel universe. Rather than slavishly repeat the historical record, the postmodern novelist seeks to invent a story that critiques the "real world."

Certain critics found Doctorow's work disturbing precisely because he would not respect their rigid ideas of fact and fiction. However, to the postmodern novelist, such distinctions make no difference because written history and novels are both narratives, a species of story. The language both genres share means that a fictional character or scene can seem as real as the so-called factual account because both are the product of words.

THE POSTMODERN NOVEL AND
HISTORICAL FICTION

Doctorow's willingness to employ historical figures is part of the postmodern novelist's revisionism. Like the modernist, the postmodernist seeks to overturn or disrupt conventional ways of apprehending history to demonstrate that the past is, in large part, an invention of the present and a projection of the story the novelist wants to tell.

Perhaps no postmodernist writer has subverted the conventions of the historical novel more than Susan Sontag. In *The Volcano Lover* (1992) she transforms the story of Admiral Nelson and Sir William Hamilton and his wife, Emma—the stuff of romantic fiction—into an inquiry about the nature of heroism, art collecting, and imperialism, and about a narrator who speaks in a voice close to Sontag's own. This method of narration provokes an exploration of the way narrative itself subsumes the content (the history) on which the narrator meditates. Similarly, *In America* (2000), based on the actual story of a famous Polish actress who established a community in California, begins with a preface in which Sontag identifies the writer featured in the novel. In doing so, Sontag shares much of her own biography and invites the reader to see the actress's story as exemplifying the career of ambitious women, including Sontag.

Other postmodern novels include John Barth's *The Sot-Weed Factor* (1960) and Robert Coover's *The Public Burning* (1977). In *The Public Burning*, narrated in part by Richard M. Nixon, history itself is overturned so

that Nixon lusts over convicted spy Ethel Rosenberg. Nixon's politics become a tormented psychodrama revealing the suppressed sexual tensions and paranoia that get displaced by attributing a society's anxieties about itself onto an external threat: in this case, the communist menace.

In *The Sot-Weed Factor*, Barth spoofs many of America's foundation myths—especially the sentimental story of Pocahontas and John Smith. A secret history of Jamestown (fabricated by Barth) reveals Smith's pornographic behavior, including his ability to enlarge his penis, which becomes the source of his power over American Indians.

Kurt Vonnegut's celebrated novel *Slaughterhouse-Five: Or, The Children's Crusade, a Duty-Dance with Death* (1969), considered his postmodernist masterpiece, is in part an explicit autobiography (which already marks a departure from novelistic conventions). Vonnegut opens with an account of his experience in Dresden, when the German city was firebombed during World War II. This horrendous event that destroyed a civilian population for no strategic purpose was seared into Vonnegut's memory. For more than twenty years, he explains, he sought a way to tell the story of his outrage and shame. Trying to convey the significance of what he saw to an Army buddy's wife, and recoiling from her accusation that he will tell the story in a conventional way—another one of those tales of how Americans survived the war—Vonnegut invented a narrative and character that constitute a repudiation of the traditional war novel. Whereas most war novels provide a chronological and panoramic structure with a cross section of representative characters (a good example is Norman Mailer's *The Naked and the Dead*, 1948), Vonnegut focuses on a single protagonist, Billy Pilgrim, who is not merely a product of his place and time. Indeed, Pilgrim is introduced as a person who has "come unstuck in time."

What follows in *Slaughterhouse-Five* is part observation of Vonnegut's contemporary world and his World War II past and part projection into the world of aliens, with Billy as the abductee. Consequently, Billy bounces around in time but is never simply a product of that time. Somewhat like Burroughs, who uses the world of drugs to gain a perspective on the monolithic and uniform blandness of his age, Vonnegut uses aliens, the

Tralfamadorians, as a way to defamiliarize the contemporary world and make Billy see his surroundings in a fresh way. *Slaughterhouse-Five* is liberating, a break from the imprisoning perceptions of cant, the weight of history, and the rule of orthodoxy. Just as Vonnegut has liberated himself from the established genre of the novel, so he expects his reader to eschew the crutches of chronology and plot. Meaning is not sequential but cyclical, so that events in *Slaughterhouse-Five* are repeatable and time becomes a kind of canvas on which human consciousness imprints itself. Rather than the form of history or of the novel being fixed, this fluid nexus of character and event promulgates a postmodern freedom for writer and reader alike.

THE POSTMODERN NOVEL AS METAFICTION

Ishmael Reed's utter disregard for verisimilitude and the irreverent verve with which he subverts the historical record in *Flight to Canada* (1976) has led critics to label the novel metafiction; that is, *Flight to Canada* is a novel that does not merely counter the conventions of literary realism but also insists on the primacy of the novelist's fictional universe. Thus, Reed concocted a novel based on the conventions of slave narratives but also on anachronistic language and discussion of modern inventions such as the airplane. The novel exaggerates the way past and present are mixed and confused in contemporary consciousness. History is not a linear continuum from past to present but rather a chaotic mélange of different periods and sensibilities that coexist and contradict one another in the reader's mind.

This elevation of the novel as its own justification, so that it is unconnected to any reality outside its pages, links the postmodern novel to *le nouveau roman*, or the New Novel, developed in the 1950's in France by writers including Alain Robbe-Grillet and Nathalie Sarraute and dramatists Samuel Beckett and Eugene Ionesco. Their self-reflexive fiction served as the model for contemporary postmodernists.

Two more examples of the postmodern novel as metafiction—Sontag's *The Benefactor* (1963) and *Death Kit* (1967)—reject the American realist school of fiction. Sontag is not concerned so much with the manners and mores of contemporary society as she is with literature itself; that is, she pursues a form of narrative

turned back on itself in which the narrator makes the idea of reality problematic and fictional. Perhaps the best example of her technique is to be found in *Death Kit*, in which she leaves the reader wondering if her protagonist, Diddy, really did murder a railroad worker or if the entire action of the novel is taking place in his mind. This doubt questions everyday perception. Similarly, *The Benefactor* focuses on the consciousness of its narrator, Hippolyte. To a great extent, he makes his world by fictionalizing it, transforming his friends and family into projections of his sensibility.

Perhaps the quintessential postmodernist novel is William S. Burroughs's controversial *Naked Lunch* (1959). Like James Joyce's *Ulysses* (1922), one of the defining works of modernism, *Naked Lunch* was deemed obscene by many courts in the United States. Sexual perversion and drug addiction are central themes in the novel, representing a shocking refutation of traditional moral values and literary conventions. Indeed, *Naked Lunch* contains far more extreme pornographic elements than Joyce's own novels that experiment with the language of illicit literature.

Naked Lunch had its champions in the literary community when it first appeared, and it exercised considerable influence on writers as diverse as Mailer and Sontag. Many older, more traditional writers, such as Rebecca West, however, deplored Burroughs's themes and style because he seemed to be attacking the integrity of the novel as a genre. *Naked Lunch* has no plot, no chronology, no realistic setting, and no conventional grammar to guide confused readers. The postmodern orientation of the novel is clear: Burroughs is dramatizing and criticizing the raucous and profane commercialization of a contemporary world that is brutally exterminating individuality.

Burroughs's style and ideology would later reach its political apogee in Coover's novel *The Public Burning*, which took a historical event—the electrocution of Julius and Ethel Rosenberg for spying for the Soviet Union at the height of the Cold War—and made it into a surrealistic event, a public burning, to emphasize the hysteria over communism in the early 1950's. A frightened, conformist population consented to the scapegoating of the Rosenbergs—so Coover's argument goes—rather than speak its own mind.

Burroughs's own recovery from drug addiction led him to write a book in which he uses his own sickness as the root fact about a contemporary world that is conspiring to deprive human beings of their dignity. Drugs, to Burroughs, are just one more product in a consumer society that promises alleviation of suffering by chemical means. The antidote to this world is the energy of the novelist's postmodern style. The greatest minds have always broken the rules, Burroughs implies, and have resisted the technicians of society who try to enforce bland and complacent behavior.

Naked Lunch still shocks readers with its originality, brutality, and profanity, for Burroughs assaults readers with a postmodern style that can never be fully digested. Indeed, this is his fundamental point: All too much is digested in contemporary society. People have become accustomed to quick-fix products—from junk food to microwave ovens. Burroughs's narrator, William Lee, gets a "junk-cure," a naked lunch that provides, as poet Allen Ginsberg told the Supreme Court of Massachusetts, clarity. The lunch in question, Ginsberg argued, would be the naked and raw meal of reality that society works so hard to camouflage.

OTHER INFLUENCES

A strong element of fantasy, too, distinguishes postmodern novels also linked to science-fiction writers such as Philip K. Dick, William Gibson, and Samuel R. Delaney. Thomas Pynchon, while relying on many of the tropes of science fiction, writes massive novels taking on nothing less than the entire course of world history in the nineteenth and twentieth centuries, exploring how science and its technological implications have come to dominate society. Modern inventions such as hot-air ballooning in his *Mason and Dixon* (1997) or the bombing of London in the waning days of World War II (in *Gravity's Rainbow*, 1973) become metaphors of humankind's Faustian need to seek dominion over a world that is falling apart, subject to the laws of entropy regardless of the never-ending race to renew and invent. Magical Realists, such as the Colombian Gabriel García Márquez and the Brazilian Jorge Amado, conflate history and fantasy and bridge both the modernist and postmodernist eras in their novels.

There is no critical agreement on how postmodernism

diverges from modernism. The divergence is, perhaps, made of nuance and subtle distinctions. One influential argument has been advanced by critic Brian McHale. Whereas modernism has an epistemological focus (what one can know about the world), postmodernism questions the very status of reality and the world. In postmodern fiction, in other words, characters can literally inhabit more than one world—as Billy Pilgrim does by residing both on Earth and on the planet Tralfamadore. Ontology (how one exists) replaces epistemology in the shift from modernist to postmodernist fiction. In the specific terms of Vonnegut's *Slaughterhouse-Five*, humans are wrong to suppose that what can be known can be counted on because it represents only the known world and not others that are beyond human perception or knowledge. What is real and what is really going on are not so easy to separate in the postmodernist novel.

Coleridge's famous formulation that a reader suspend disbelief to engage with a work of imaginative literature has been replaced, argues McHale, in postmodern literature by a suspension of belief. In other words, the reader can no longer take for granted that there is a settled and solid world by which the novel can be measured. Thus, it is difficult to come to any sort of resolution in a postmodernist novel, in which, it seems, questions about reality are far more important than any knowledge the novelist might be able to convey.

More traditional novelists, including Gore Vidal, deplore postmodernism, arguing that it is merely a fashionable academic game that always leads to the same predictable conclusions about the unknowability of reality. For Vidal and other traditionalists, the novel remains a prime vehicle for making sense of history, regardless of the novelist's perspective. Postmodernism, for all its impressive achievements, has not displaced conventional fiction or the desire of most novelists to seek coherence, not chaos.

Carl Rollyson

BIBLIOGRAPHY

Aldridge, John W. *Talents and Technicians: Literary Chic and the New Assembly-Line Fiction.* New York: Maxwell Macmillan International, 1992. Aldridge, a critic of American fiction, examines the nexus between modernism and postmodernism in the novels of Jay McInerney, Ann Beattie, Frederick Barthelme, Brett Easton Ellis, and others of the post-1960's generation.

Docherty, Thomas, ed. *Postmodernism: A Reader.* 1993. New ed. New York: Pearson Education, 2003. Excellent anthology of postmodernist theorists and critics, including Fredric Jameson, Ahab Hassan, Jean Baudrillard, and Richard Rorty. Topics covered include the relationship between feminism and postmodernism, postcolonialism and modernism, and the impact of postmodernism on literature, music, the visual arts, and philosophy. Includes an introduction and a comprehensive bibliography.

Fox, Robert Elliot. *Conscientious Sorcerers: The Black Postmodernist Fiction of Leroi Jones/Amiri Baraka, Ishmael Reed, and Samuel R. Delaney.* New York: Greenwood Press, 1987. A helpful study that integrates these writers into the postmodernist canon, emphasizing the self-conscious and self-reflexive nature of their fiction.

Geyh, Paula, Fred Leebron, and Andrew Levyeds. *Postmodern American Fiction: A Norton Anthology.* New York: W. W. Norton, 1998. A wide-ranging sampling of postmodern authors with helpful critical discussions of their own work. A comprehensive collection at 672 pages.

McCaffery, Larry. *The Metafictional Muse: The Works of Robert Coover, Donald Barthelme, and William H. Gass.* Pittsburgh, Pa.: University of Pittsburgh Press, 1982. Explores the ways Robert Coover, Donald Barthelme, and William H. Gass address ideology, the set of ideas that motivates their characters in contradistinction to the reality that they seem only fitfully able to recognize.

McHale, Brian. *Postmodernist Fiction.* 1987. New ed. New York: Routledge, 2004. Examines the theory and practice of writers such as Samuel Beckett, Alain Robbe-Grillet, Vladimir Nabokov, and Robert Coover. Considered necessary reading for any study of postmodernist fiction.

Malpas, Simon. *The Postmodern.* Reprint. New York: Routledge, 2007. Chapters examine the different definitions of postmodernism, its relationship to modernism, the role of subjectivity in postmodernist writing, the history of the concept, and its relationship to politics. Includes a glossary, suggestions for further reading, and a bibliography.

Maltby, Paul. *Dissident Postmodernist: Barthelme, Coover, Pynchon.* Philadelphia: University of Pennsylvania Press, 1991. Focuses on the critiques of vernacular language by Robert Coover, Donald Barthelme, and Thomas Pynchon and on how language distorts reality.

Parini, Jay, ed. *The Selected Essays of Gore Vidal.* New York: Doubleday, 2008. Includes the essay "The Hacks of Academe" (1976), Vidal's controversial and influential literary attack on postmodernist novels and the works of Thomas Pynchon, William H. Gass, John Barth, and others.

Reed, Peter J., and Marc Leeds, eds. *The Vonnegut Chronicles: Interviews and Essays.* Westport, Conn.: Greenwood Press, 1996. Collection includes three interviews with Vonnegut and eleven essays on his work. Among the topics that Vonnegut addresses in the interviews are postmodernism and experimental fiction. Includes a chronology, bibliography, and an index.

Scholes, Robert. *Fabulation and Metafiction.* Urbana: University of Illinois Press, 1979. Distinguished critic explores the fantasy element in postmodern fiction, concentrating on writers such as John Barth and Kurt Vonnegut. Includes an index.

Scott, Steven D. *The Gamefulness of American Postmodernism: John Barth and Louise Erdrich.* New York: Peter Lang, 2000. Applies postmodernist theories to an analysis of Barth's work. Addresses the motifs of play and games in American postmodernist fiction generally and focuses on "gamefulness" in the writings of Barth and Louise Erdrich.

Sim, Stuart, ed. *The Routledge Companion to Postmodernism.* Rev. ed. New York: Routledge, 2006. Collection of essays dealing comprehensively with the development of postmodernism as well with individual authors and theorists. Includes bibliographical references and an index.

Psychological Long Fiction

From the ancient belief in humors to the twentieth and twenty-first centuries' psychoanalytic and pharmacological methodologies, diverse theories about the mind have affected the literary production of novelists. Categorization according to these theories is difficult, because authors tend to mix them and use more than they admit. Hermann Hesse's works, for example, began to overflow with the analytical psychology of Carl Jung after the latter treated him, yet Hesse tended to belittle that influence and spoke of being closer to Sigmund Freud. Consequently, psychological long fiction is most easily categorized not according to medical theories but according to four literary techniques: playful etiology, unrepentant confession, stream of consciousness, and Kafkaesque fantasy.

PLAYFUL ETIOLOGY

Charles Baudelaire's novella *La Fanfarlo* (1847; the flaunter) attributes the idiosyncrasies of the protagonist, Samuel Cramer, to his mixed parentage (German and Chilean), his French education, and his heaven-bestowed partial genius. Baudelaire is thus practicing etiology—diagnosing the causes of a condition—but not with the seriousness a physician would adopt. Instead, he explains a condition through a whimsical mixture of rationales based on nature, nurture, and God. Such jocular syncretism (or, indeed, any extensive etiology) is common in fiction only from the eighteenth century onward. In Ovid's *Metamorphoses* (c. 8 C.E.; English translation, 1567), Myrrha's incestuous passion for her father creates the kind of situation that later fascinated psychologists, but the narrator simply comments on that passion as criminal and disgusting without investigating why Myrrha had such an unusual craving. Presumably, fate or the gods are somehow responsible.

With the rise of the sciences in the eighteenth century, however, tacit reference to supernatural influence was not enough to explain personality differences. Before the Romanticism of the early nineteenth century, the characters to be diagnosed seldom deviated far from normality and thus were little in need of lavish elucidation. Thereafter, however, neurotics and psychotics began multiplying through a growing interest in extreme expressions of individuality.

To demonstrate this individuality, authors must at some point diagnose characters' deviance from the norm; paradoxically, since what can be thus cataloged is not uniquely individual, the authors must also show a distaste for diagnosis itself. In *Washington Square* (1880), Henry James's narrator details the characters' psychological quirks quite directly, yet the story turns against such insights. The shrewd Doctor Sloper, known for diagnosing in too much detail, ruins his daughter's life by exposing her fiancé's temperament. In later works, James continues to provide etiological information, but it is filtered through points of view that render it ambiguous, as in his novella *The Turn of the Screw* (1898), which never establishes whether its ghosts are real or symptoms of a governess's hysteria.

Even more complexly, the narrator of Thomas Mann's *Doktor Faustus: Das Leben des deutschen Tonsetzers Adrian Leverkühn, erzählt von einem Freunde* (1947; *Doctor Faustus: The Life of the German Composer Adrian Leverkühn as Told by a Friend*, 1948) tries to demonstrate that the genius and mental illness of the composer Adrian Leverkühn are symptoms of both Germany's brilliance and its degeneration. Moreover, the narrator's mannered prose undercuts faith in his judgments. As Mann's essays also demonstrate, he considered the complexity of life to transcend simple categories. On a somewhat less sophisticated level, his method (obsessive use of etiology, yet skepticism about its conclusions) also appears in many thrillers, including Thomas Harris's *Red Dragon* (1981) and *The Silence of the Lambs* (1988). In these works, both a psychoanalyst-turned-cannibal and the investigating detectives employ psychological profiling. To this guesswork (which is not always accurate), Harris counterpoints pervasive religious imagery, meant to give the evil an apocalyptic quality, but without reducing it to any single theory, either psychological or theological.

In *Against Interpretation, and Other Essays* (1966), Susan Sontag combats the psychological and particularly the biographical study of literature. Accordingly, she peoples her novels with misfits on whom she comments in a manner that is more a parody of psychology than a reliance on it. Comparably, Thomas Pynchon took imagery from Jung's psychological introduction to the Tibetan Book of the Dead and travestied it in his comic novel *The Crying of Lot 49* (1966). As do others of Pynchon's fictions, it treats all analysis as itself a form of paranoia. Causing controversy, the New Novelist Alain Robbe-Grillet placed obvious allusions to Oedipus (a basic pattern in the Freudian system) throughout *Les Gommes* (1953; *The Erasers*, 1964); he denied publicly that they were there. In her essays, Nathalie Sarraute, another New Novelist, has explained that her characterization describes tropisms (behaviors with which people try to control one another), but she believes that no depths lie beneath these. Citations of psychological diagnoses merely to deny or ridicule them occur on a popular level in such novels as Ken Kesey's *One Flew over the Cuckoo's Nest* (1962), in which the character Nurse Ratched embodies a health care system eager to label patients as a way of demeaning and bullying them.

UNREPENTANT CONFESSION

In classic psychoanalysis, discovering etiology is largely the doctor's role. The patient engages in a secular form of confession, as a result of which (unlike the religious version) no one is required to repent. Literature has followed a similar path. In Fyodor Dostoevski's *Zapiski iz podpolya* (1864; *Letters from the Underworld*, 1913; better known as *Notes from the Underground*), the narrator's almost gloating self-exposure, without purgation or salvation, broke with Christian contrition and set a model for twentieth century confessional fiction. According to literary theorist Mikhail Bakhtin, Dostoevski's later novels, at their best, consist of a dialogue of voices presented without a commenting narrator. This would make Dostoevski's works confessional throughout, but, as Bakhtin admits, Dostoevski sometimes resorts to diagnosis and etiology, as in the epilogue to *Prestupleniye i nakazaniye* (1866; *Crime and Punishment*, 1886), with an obtrusive psychology based on Christianity.

At the beginning of the twentieth century, André Gide's *L'Immoraliste* (1902; *The Immoralist*, 1930) took the confessional mode further toward the secular. Until near the book's conclusion, its protagonist, Michel, is unaware of his homosexuality, so he cannot divulge it, except by reporting behavior he understands less than do the readers. Furthermore, since homosexuality in the novel is not an action but a tendency, it is not, in Christian terms, a sin; despite the guilt it instills, it does not seem susceptible to purgation. By persuasively associating the human condition with embarrassing impulses, *The Immoralist* sets a despairing tone for French fiction.

This tone continued at least as late as Albert Camus's *La Chute* (1956; *The Fall*, 1957). Its protagonist, Jean-Baptiste Clamence, is unwilling to risk his life to save a drowning man. Disillusioned by his own cowardice, Clamence abandons conventional behavior and slips into cruelty, intent on convincing everyone that his imperfection springs from an ineradicable strain within humanity itself: a fall for which there is no savior. Like Michel's homosexuality, Clamence's sadism is one of the conditions that the first half of the twentieth century brought to psychological attention. That age, shocked by the repressed, appears again in Kazuo Ishiguro's nostalgic novels. They show how reluctant people were to discover their own destructiveness, as shown in the disguised sadomasochistic relationship between Sachiko and Mariko in *A Pale View of Hills* (1982), or in the self-delusions of character Christopher Banks in *When We Were Orphans* (2000). Although Freud argued that aggressive and sensual drives might be sublimated into cultural achievements, novelists, along with the public, tended to be dismayed at psychology's disclosure of an unconscious prone to irrationality.

With the exception of such nostalgic works as Ishiguro's, confessional fictions in the twentieth century's second half were not as easily dismayed by implacable instincts. In Anthony Burgess's *A Clockwork Orange* (1962; reprinted with final chapter, 1986), the narrator, Alex, is a rapist and murderer who is treated with aversion therapy so that he becomes nauseated at the thought of sex or violence. In other words, he has been coerced into being as repressed as a stereotypical Victorian. Readers are expected to condemn his psychological castration. In a victory of free will, however, he overthrows the conditioning and returns to committing mayhem.

Comparably, in Orson Scott Card and Kathryn H. Kidd's *Lovelock* (1994), the narrator is an artificially enhanced capuchin monkey, who, like Alex, must overcome his conditioning to be capable of sex and violence. Here, even more clearly than in *A Clockwork Orange*, evil is an animal side of the mind to be freed. Liberation of the bestial permeates many first-person works that were popular in the 1960's, such as Jack Kerouac's *The Dharma Bums* (1958) and John Barth's *Giles Goat-Boy: Or, The Rev. New Syllabus* (1966). Although more conscious of evil than Kerouac, Barth makes psychological liberation sound relatively innocent compared with Burgess, whose acute awareness of human destructiveness is more typical of British fiction, such as J. G. Ballard's *Crash* (1973), which is about taking sadomasochistic joy in automobile accidents.

Perhaps because the nature of drama predisposes it to public rituals, in such plays as Peter Shaffer's *Equus* (pr., pb. 1973) and in countless films, psychoanalysis itself forms a setting for confession. In first-person fiction, however, the closest analogy to it is the relationship between narrator and reader. When psychoanalyst-like figures are present in fiction, they are often disguised to emphasize either the negative or positive associations of psychiatry. Thus, fresh from a productive therapy with Jung, Hesse made the rebellious, precocious title character of *Demian* (1919; English translation, 1923) into its narrator's unofficial analyst. Similarly, in J. D. Salinger's Glass family saga (such as in *Seymour: An Introduction*, 1963), although family members sometimes find themselves on a psychiatrist's couch, the older brothers, one of whom commits suicide, combine the functions of guru and therapist. Whether the analyst is a cannibal or a friend who helps people live with their sins, the process has less to do with penitence and forgiveness than with providing the readers entertainingly shocking revelations about what Joseph Conrad, in his 1902 novel of the same name, termed humanity's "heart of darkness."

STREAM OF CONSCIOUSNESS

According to Keith M. May, stream of consciousness—an attempt to represent barely conscious thinking—belongs to a relatively brief period when the two world wars led people to once again recognize human irrationality. Significantly, May omits mention of Édouard Dujardin's stream-of-consciousness novel *Les Lauriers sont coupés* (1887, serial; 1888, book; *We'll to the Woods No More*, 1938; also known as *The Bays Are*

Sere, 1991), which was published generations before World War I. More perceptively, Dorrit Cohn contends that ungrammatical fragments in stream of consciousness approximate a deep stratum of the mind, since the psycholinguist Lev Vygotsky has demonstrated such incoherence to be its nature.

According to Shiv Kumar, psychologist-philosopher William James originated the phrase "stream of consciousness" in 1890, but it was introduced to literary criticism in a 1918 article by May Sinclair about the novels of Dorothy Richardson. In *Pilgrimage* (1938, 1967), Richardson confines herself to her protagonist's consciousness, without providing the customary information readers expect early in a book. Fifty pages into the novel, the reader learns the character is a teenager. As Katherine Mansfield did for the short story, Richardson brought to the English novel the technique of stream of consciousness, whose major practitioners were Virginia Woolf, James Joyce, and William Faulkner.

The first of Woolf's novels to employ the technique is *Jacob's Room* (1922), about the life of an Englishman who dies in World War I. It repeatedly marks characters' inattention to traditional religion even when church bells chime in the background. (Her generation associated stream of consciousness with a world that was replacing theology with psychology.) By focusing on a single day, her next novel, *Mrs. Dalloway* (1925), achieves greater intensity in the depiction of relatively plotless mental flux. A unifying element, though, is repeated reference to Septimus Smith, who consults a psychiatrist and kills himself to avoid another physician. On an extreme level, his suicide parallels the importance that internal events have for the other characters.

Although stream of consciousness means something slightly different in each novelist's works, Joyce shows the greatest range of techniques. In his *A Portrait of the Artist as a Young Man* (serial 1914-1915, book 1916), most sections are in third person, but they are so attuned to their protagonist's developing mind that they range from baby talk (in the earlier ones) to the erudition of an educated young man (in the concluding ones). Joyce's *Ulysses* (1922), however, unifies each section by parodying some genre or style, such as journalistic prose or expressionist drama. The last section, rendering the mind of Molly Bloom as she falls asleep, is a flow of words without punctuation that particularly suits the term "stream of consciousness." Her monologue should not be confused with works whose authors simply provide their own musings.

In the first draft of *On the Road* (1957), Kerouac, at maximum speed, wrote the whole work as a single, unedited sentence to achieve spontaneous self-revelation. In contrast, Joyce is distancing himself from Molly's irrationality and somnolence. If stream of consciousness means representation of one mind at a time, then Joyce's monumental last work, *Finnegans Wake* (1939), has moved beyond it to a very nonlucid dream that takes incoherence almost to unintelligibility. Its readers enter something like Jung's collective unconscious: the whole human race's heritage of symbols.

After treating Joyce's daughter, Jung misunderstood even *Ulysses*, which he considered the spontaneous outpourings of hereditary madness, exacerbated by alcohol. Although no proof of its authors' insanity, the incoherence of stream of consciousness can well portray characters' mental aberrations. The first section of Faulkner's *The Sound and the Fury* (1929) records the barely comprehended sensory impressions occurring to Benjy, an idiot. Readers then encounter the mental contents of other witnesses to the same story, including a young man who killed himself because of incestuous feelings for his sister. Similarly, in Faulkner's next novel, *As I Lay Dying* (1930), Darl, a clairvoyant headed toward madness, is the character whose mind is most often sampled. Although interest in stream of consciousness was fostered by the rise of psychology, the technique itself implies that a mind is being observed not clinically but telepathically; thus, Darl's clairvoyance has much in common with those who write or read stream of consciousness.

Stream of consciousness began attracting a new generation of writers at the end of the twentieth century. Two examples are Patrick McCabe, whose narrator in *The Butcher Boy* (1992) is a young boy who deals with a troubled family by retreating to a fantasy world, and Irvine Welsh, whose *Trainspotting* (1993) is narrated by several drug users from the same town. Novels that employ wordplay, nonlinear structure, and footnotes in addition to stream of consciousness include Mark Z. Danielewski's *House of Leaves* (2000), Jonathan Safran Foer's *Everything Is Illuminated* (2002), and Junot

Díaz's *The Brief Wondrous Life of Oscar Wao* (2007). The most celebrated example, however, is Toni Morrison's *Beloved* (1987), winner of the Pulitzer Prize and numerous other awards. Its protagonist is Sethe, an escaped slave traumatized by the brutality she endured and by the despair that led her to murder her daughter, Beloved. Sethe's narration is fragmented, like the woman herself, and Morrison's use of stream of consciousness helps readers understand Sethe's psychological state.

KAFKAESQUE FANTASY

Stream of consciousness views characters' minds as if the author were separate from them. In Kafkaesque literature, however, characters and their authors converge. Indeed, Kafkaesque writers tend to place images of themselves within their works. Franz Kafka names the protagonist of *Das Schloss* (1926; *The Castle*, 1930) with the initial K., while the main character of *Der Prozess* (1925; *The Trial*, 1937) is Joseph K. (Kafka was named Franz for the emperor Franz-Joseph). Kurt Vonnegut puts himself in his own novel, *Slaughterhouse-Five: Or, The Children's Crusade, a Duty-Dance with Death* (1969), as a minor character who describes the book's composition and thereby tells the readers that the action is imaginary. Billy Pilgrim slips back and forth through time because of an association of ideas in Vonnegut's mind.

Milan Kundera makes his part in composition even more explicit by interrupting action with essays explaining how he created one character or another. In his novel *L'Insoutenable Légèreté de l'être* (1984; *The Unbearable Lightness of Being*, 1984; in Czech as *Nesnesitelná lehkost bytí*, 1985), he shapes the protagonist through meditations on living in truth as this idea is expressed by Kafka and Václav Havel. Although Kafka himself was subtler, examination of his works demonstrates that he structured events in quite as artificial a way as Kundera, with almost no attempt at verisimilitude. Rather, Kafkaesque fiction is like a lucid dream or nightmare in which the action, however exciting, is never quite real.

In non-Kafkaesque fiction, the work is a buffer between author and reader, so that they lose sight of each other. The Kafkaesque creates at least the illusion of transparency, where author and reader may glimpse one another as if they were characters. In Italo Calvino's *Se una notte d'inverno un viaggiatore* (1979; *If on a Win-*

ter's Night a Traveler, 1981), readers take an active part in the plot; indeed, a male reader of Calvino's book is described as having a romance with a female reader. *If on a Winter's Night a Traveler* is one of the most elaborate attempts to make "you" a character, but other notable novels that do this include Michel Butor's *La Modification* (1957; *Second Thoughts*, 1958; better known as *A Change of Heart*) and Carlos Fuentes's novella *Aura* (1962; English translation, 1965).

In Kim Newman's second-person novel *Life's Lottery: A Choose-Your-Own Adventure Book* (1999), the reader is invited to become Keith, the protagonist, and to make decisions on Keith's behalf; choosing one path over another directs the reader to another section of the novel. Kafka's fragmentary *Beim Bau der Chinesischen Mauer: Ungedruckte Erzählungen und Prosa aus dem Nachlass* (1931; *The Great Wall of China, and Other Pieces*, 1933) has both a first-person narrator, related complexly to Kafka himself, and a "you" as protagonist.

Like characters in nightmares, Kafkaesque protagonists may sometimes lack individual depth. Nonetheless, in its detailed probing of the authorial mind's dreaming its fictions, the Kafkaesque mode is at least as introverted and self-reflexive as are the other forms of psychological narrative.

James Whitlark

BIBLIOGRAPHY

Cohn, Dorrit. *Transparent Minds: Narrative Modes for Presenting Consciousness in Fiction*. Rev. ed. Princeton, N.J.: Princeton University Press, 1988. Cohn divides the fictional rendering of consciousness into three modes: "psycho-narration," which is both diagnosis and summary of mental contents; quoted (interior) monologue; and narrated monologue, a third-person narration that adopts the style of the character described.

Crosthwaite, Paul. *Trauma, Postmodernism, and the Aftermath of World War II*. New York: Palgrave Macmillan, 2009. Argues that the postmodern novel is not, as many critics claim, ahistorical, but deeply attuned to the cultural and social significance of trauma. Postmodernism has "reformulated" history in terms of a trauma "that is traceable, time and again," to the psychological horrors of World War II.

Edel, Leon. *The Modern Psychological Novel*. Reprint. Gloucester, Mass.: Peter Smith, 1973. This revision of Edel's *The Psychological Novel, 1900-1950* (1955) concerns modes of subjectivity in early twentieth century fiction, particularly stream of consciousness.

Hume, Kathryn. *American Dream, American Nightmare: Fiction Since 1960*. Urbana: University of Illinois Press, 2000. Analyzes the psychological responses of both writers and their fictional characters to the false promises of the American Dream in nearly one hundred novels.

May, Keith M. *Out of the Maelstrom: Psychology and the Novel in the Twentieth Century*. New York: St. Martin's Press, 1977. Ranging from the beginning of the twentieth century to the fiction of Jean-Paul Sartre in the 1960's, this study suggests analogies between psychology in novels and in the writings of psychologists contemporary with them.

Rosenberg, John. *Dorothy Richardson, the Genius They Forgot: A Critical Biography*. New York: Alfred A. Knopf, 1973. Aptly parallels events in Richardson's *Pilgrimage* to the writer's life. Concludes with an analysis of Richardson's pioneering impact upon the development of the modernist novel in general and stream of consciousness in particular.

Schur, Owen. *The Regulation of Consciousness in the English Novel: Desire and Power*. Lewiston, N.Y.: Edwin Mellen Press, 2002. Examines desire, consciousness, and hierarchies of power in the social practices of protagonists in the English novel. Covered novelists include Jane Austen, Charles Dickens, and Virginia Woolf.

Weinstein, Arnold L. *Recovering Your Story: Proust, Joyce, Woolf, Faulkner, Morrison*. New York: Random House, 2006. Analysis of eight novels, including *Mrs. Dalloway* by Virginia Woolf, *The Sound and the Fury* by William Faulkner, and *Beloved* by Toni Morrison, to show how fiction can help readers understand their own perceptions and dreams.

Whitlark, James. *Behind the Great Wall: A Post-Jungian Approach to Kafkaesque Literature*. Rutherford, N.J.: Fairleigh Dickinson University Press, 1991. Whitlark analyzes the psychological implications of Franz Kafka's fictions and of works by thirty-six authors influenced by him.

THE SCIENCE-FICTION NOVEL

The emergence of the "modern" novel in the eighteenth century, with its emphasis on narrative realism and its intimate involvement with the affairs of everyday life, is correlated with a gradual separation between mundane and imaginative fiction, a crucial breaking of categories that was later to be represented by such distinctions as that between "realism" and "romance." There have always been problems in defining the boundary that marks this categorical break, as there have always been problems in defining exactly what is meant by the term "novel," but from the end of the eighteenth century onward writers and critics have been aware of some such fundamental distinction and convinced of its propriety.

ROOTS OF SCIENCE FICTION

Many individual works lie within the borderland between mundane and imaginative fiction, but there is one entire genre that occupies a curiously ambiguous position, a genre that depends on the use of the imagination to a considerable degree but that tries to make its imaginative products responsible in some way to a realistic outlook. The names given to this genre all have a somewhat oxymoronic flavor in common: "scientific romance," "realistic romance," and "science fiction."

There are, as might be expected, two conflicting traditions in science-fiction criticism. One of these traditions stresses the close alliance between science fiction and other kinds of fantasy, and values the genre for its venturesome qualities. The other tradition emphasizes the responsibilities of the conscientious science-fiction writer in maintaining a firm base within scientific possibility and in the avoidance of any traffic with the occult. Brian Aldiss, in *The Billion Year Spree* (1973; revised as *The Trillion Year Spree*, 1986), suggests that science fiction is "characteristically cast in the Gothic or post-Gothic mode" and traces its ancestry from Mary Wollstonecraft Shelley's *Frankenstein* (1818). Robert A. Heinlein, by contrast, contributes to the symposium *The Science Fiction Novel* (1959), introduced by Basil Davenport, a spirited defense of science fiction as a species of realistic fiction, likening the method of science-fiction writers to the scientific method itself.

Not unnaturally, adherents of these two views differ markedly on the issue of which texts should be labeled "science fiction" and which ought to be cast out as pretenders. Everyone agrees, however, that publishers and critics tend to use the label irresponsibly—on one hand, extending it promiscuously to cover stories that are "really" fantasy, and on the other hand, refraining from its use in respect of many prestigious works that, though "really" science fiction, might somehow be stigmatized or devalued if they were so named in open court.

Despite the fact that several different histories of science fiction have been compiled by adherents of different definitions, it is to the history and development of the genre that one is inclined to turn in the hope of discovering a reasonable analysis of the genre's characteristics and relationships with other literary traditions. There is, in fact, no evidence whatsoever of a coherent tradition of literary endeavor extending from *Frankenstein* to more recent science fiction. Although there were echoes of gothic freneticism in a few of the works produced in the last decades of the nineteenth century, when fiction recognizably akin to what today bears the label began to proliferate, most of it was very different in character.

One can recognize four main stimuli that encouraged writers in the late nineteenth century to produce more or less careful and conscientious works about imaginary inventions, future societies, and alien worlds. The first was the revolution in transportation, which brought the products of the Industrial Revolution into the everyday world of the middle classes in the shape of steam locomotives and steamships. This stimulated the growth of the novel of imaginary tourism, the greatest and most popular exponent of which was Jules Verne, author of *Voyage au centre de la terre* (1864; *A Journey to the Centre of the Earth*, 1872), *De la terre à la lune* (1865; *From the Earth to the Moon*, 1873), and *Vingt mille lieues sous les mers* (1869-1870; *Twenty Thousand Leagues Under the Sea*, 1873). Most of the early novels of space travel have a distinctively Vernian flavor and represent the more ambitious extreme of this particular subspecies. Examples include *Across the Zodiac* (1880), by Percy Greg, and *A Columbus of Space* (1909), by Garrett P. Serviss.

A second important stimulus was the discussion provoked by the publication of Charles Darwin's *On the Origin of Species by Means of Natural Selection* (1859) and *The Descent of Man, and Selection in Relation to Sex* (1871). Literary reconstructions of the prehistoric past became common, and so did speculations regarding the possible evolutionary future of humankind. The most famous examples are *The Time Machine: An Invention* (1895), by H. G. Wells, and *The Hampdenshire Wonder* (1911), by John D. Beresford.

The same period saw a revitalization of speculation about the possibilities of social and political reform by virtue of increasing awareness of the extent that technology might encourage—and perhaps even compel— dramatic changes in the social and political order. Edward Bellamy's *Looking Backward: 2000-1887* (1888) became a runaway best seller in the United States and provoked numerous replies in kind, including *News from Nowhere* (1890), by William Morris, and *Caesar's Column* (1890), by Ignatius Donnelly. Whereas Morris's novel was one of many offering an alternative manifesto for the future utopia, Donnelly's was the first in what was later to become a thriving tradition of dystopian works developing the hypothesis that the world was getting worse and not better and that technology would help to secure its damnation.

The last important stimulus that proved prolific in this period was the anticipation of war in Europe and the fascination of exploring the potential of new weapons. George Griffith, in *The Angel of the Revolution* (1893), presented a dramatic image of war fought with aircraft and submarines, and this too became a continual preoccupation in the work of H. G. Wells, the most eclectic imaginative writer of the period, reflected in such works as *The War in the Air, and Particularly How Mr. Bert Smallways Fared While It Lasted* (1908) and *The World Set Free: A Story of Mankind* (1914). The perception by readers and writers that these disparate literary subspecies had something fundamental in common sent critics and publishers in search of a category label. The one most widely used at the time was "scientific romance."

The supposedly realistic quality of these stories was prejudiced in several different ways. For one thing, the writers were primarily interested in the more melodramatic implications of the premises on which they worked, and this led them toward the production of highly colored thrillers rather than sober speculations about the role of science and technology in future human affairs. This was largely a matter of the markets for which the authors worked: The advent of scientific romance coincided with an expansion of literacy and a corollary expansion of the kinds of reading matter that were available. It became possible for the first time for a fairly large number of writers to make a living from their work, provided that they appealed to a wide audience, and most of the successful science-fiction writers belonged to this cadre of new professionals.

Second, and perhaps more important, a realistic approach had to be compromised by the use of literary devices. It was not possible for Jules Verne to describe the operation of a genuinely sophisticated submarine or for George Griffith to describe a workable airship. Both writers had to guess what kind of physical principles such craft would depend on. Both, not surprisingly, guessed incorrectly. Wells faced a more serious problem in *The Time Machine* when he wished to expose for contemplation the long-term future of the human race and the planet Earth. No matter how well based in evolutionary theory his images of the future might be, in order to embed them in a literary work he needed a means of transporting an observer to report back news of them, and that means could only be a pure invention. Spaceships, too, are used in much science fiction simply as a literary device for opening up the immense imaginative territories provided by an infinite range of alien worlds. Whereas Verne, in *From the Earth to the Moon*, was concerned with the spaceship as a vehicle, an artifact in its own right, Wells, in *The First Men in the Moon* (1901), simply wanted a way to get his characters to the Moon so that they could investigate the mysteries of Selenite society and provide an eyepiece for a serious exercise in speculative sociology.

Science fiction has no option but to rely on such literary devices; there is no other way to avoid the logical trap pointed out by Karl Popper in the introduction to *The Poverty of Historicism* (1957)—that it is by definition impossible to know today what new knowledge will materialize tomorrow. Writers attempt to conceal the arbitrariness of these devices by the use of scientific or pseudoscientific jargon, which creates an illusion of plausibility, but this is merely laying a carpet over a hole in the floor.

The imaginative realms to which the writers of scientific romance built literary highways were soon invaded by writers who were not in the least concerned with fidelity to scientific possibility, but who merely wanted new playgrounds to incorporate into their dreams. There grew up, especially in the United States, a tradition of exotic interplanetary romance founded in the works of Edgar Rice Burroughs, author of *A Princess of Mars* (1917). Burroughs was the first of many to exploit a rich new vocabulary of ideas in the service of a purely romantic fiction. He set his fantasies in an imaginary world inside the earth and in a variety of undiscovered islands on its surface, as well as on other planets. The closest British parallel is to be found in Arthur Conan Doyle's novel *The Lost World* (1912), though the tradition has many affinities with the work of H. Rider Haggard.

When, in the 1920's, Hugo Gernsback began publishing pulp magazines in the United States specializing in science fiction, he issued a prospectus that strongly emphasized fidelity to scientific fact and the careful exploration of technological possibility, but in his own and rival magazines exotic interplanetary romance quickly took over. The audience that supported the pulp magazines demanded thrillers, the more highly colored the better. Gernsback's pretensions could not be maintained if the label "science fiction" was to be viable as a brand name for pulp fiction, and they were soon abandoned, although editorial propaganda continued to maintain a hollow pretense.

In Great Britain the situation was rather different. The literary marketplace was organized differently, and following World War I, cheap books displaced popular magazines to a large extent. The category label "science fiction" was not imported until 1945, and even "scientific romance" was not used freely or consistently. World War I had a tremendous impact on the attitudes of the nation, and postwar works of futuristic speculation were often desperately embittered. Their seriousness was rarely in doubt—many are grim stories of alarmism that try hard to impress the reader with the realistic nature of their forebodings.

There appeared a series of future-war stories looking forward to the possible self-destruction of civilization, the best of which are *The People of the Ruins* (1920), by Edward Shanks; *Theodore Savage* (1922), by Cicely Hamilton; and *Tomorrow's Yesterday* (1932), by John Gloag. Anxiety about the fruits of progress also ran high, with many European writers producing bitter parables in which the lot of humankind is made worse by unwise meddling with the secrets of nature or by the appropriation by power groups of sophisticated technological means of maintaining their power. Key examples include *Továrna na absolutno* (1922; *The Absolute at Large*, 1927), by Karel Čapek, and *Brave New World* (1932), by Aldous Huxley.

GROWTH OF THE SCIENCE-FICTION NOVEL MARKET

There is a certain irony in the fact that throughout the 1920's and 1930's, the works produced in the United States labeled "science fiction" actually bear far less resemblance to commonly held notions of the nature of the genre than the unlabeled speculative fiction produced in Europe. This situation began to change, however, in the 1940's. The dominant trend in American pulp science fiction from 1938 on—closely associated with the magazine *Astounding Science Fiction* and its editor John W. Campbell, Jr.—was toward a more sensible and more scrupulous development of hypotheses, while from approximately the same date the British literary community became gradually more aware of American science fiction. By the end of the 1940's, the label was used widely in Britain by both publishers and commentators. One of the effects of World War II was that the United States and Britain were brought much more closely together in cultural as well as political terms. American science fiction began to be imported into Europe on a large scale, bringing with it a diffuse cultural context that affected the attitude of literary critics toward futuristic and speculative works.

Although virtually all the science fiction produced in Britain between the wars was in the novel form—cheap books being the main form of mass-produced fiction in Britain—this was not true of American science fiction of that period. American science fiction rarely achieved book publication before 1950, so longer works were produced mainly as magazine serials. Several pulp magazines boasted that they presented a full-length novel in every issue, but "full-length" in this context could mean anything between twenty thousand and fifty thousand words—almost never anything longer. For some thirty years after Gernsback's founding of the first science-fiction magazine in 1926, science fiction's specialist writers devoted themselves first and foremost to the production of short stories and novellas. The long science-fiction novel was virtually nonexistent in the United States until the 1960's, though British writers regularly turned out works well over 100,000 words in length, including such epics as Olaf Stapledon's *Last and First Men* (1930) and Wells's *The Shape of Things to Come: The Ultimate Resolution* (1933).

This situation changed dramatically in the 1960's, mainly because of the spectacular market success of the paperback book. Paperbacks surpassed magazines as the chief medium of popular fiction in the United States and achieved the same degree of success in Britain. Once this happened, it became inevitable that writers would switch their main effort into the writing of novels. The old pulp writers adapted—the most important among them being Campbell's star protégés, Isaac Asimov and Robert A. Heinlein. The postwar generation of magazine writers adapted too, prominent among them being Arthur C. Clarke, Frederik Pohl, Frank Herbert, John Brunner, Robert Silverberg, and Philip K. Dick. In addition, there emerged in the 1960's many new writers who made their first impact on the literary scene as writers of science-fiction novels, including J. G. Ballard, Samuel R. Delany, Ursula K. Le Guin, and Norman Spinrad.

Some novelists have tried to avoid the science-fiction label because they have considered it to carry a definite stigma by virtue of its longtime association with pulp fiction. These writers include Kurt Vonnegut in the United States and John Wyndham in Britain, both of whom wrote abundant work that would be covered by any conceivable definition of science fiction. The willingness of American mainstream writers to borrow from the imagery of science fiction and the increasing interest in the genre taken by American academics have helped to overcome this stigma. Science fiction is no longer written exclusively by specialist writers or read almost exclusively by specialist readers, and the situation of the genre within American culture is now much more similar to the situation that existed in British culture between the wars. It is likely, however, that the most serious science-fiction novels are not taken as seriously as they deserve because

of the sheer number of exotic romances of various kinds that are also labeled "science fiction." The category continues to shelter a great deal of rather crude blood-and-thunder dream fantasy, which is frequently more evident to onlookers than is so-called literary science fiction.

DYSTOPIA, CYBERPUNK, AND NEW GENRES

Arguably, the main achievement of the science-fiction novel has been in helping people become more aware of the dangers posed by new technological developments. Science fiction has always been most effective in its alarmist and pessimistic moods, and its literary quality has been at its highest when its anxieties have run similarly high. Two science-fiction novels—Huxley's *Brave New World* and George Orwell's *Nineteen Eighty-Four* (1949)—may arguably be said to have had a greater impact on the popular imagination than any other literary works of the twentieth century. In its anticipation of social and environmental catastrophe, science fiction has been at its strongest; examples include *A Canticle for Leibowitz* (1959), by Walter M. Miller, Jr.; *The Drowned World* (1962), by J. G. Ballard; *Cat's Cradle* (1963), by Kurt Vonnegut; *Stand on Zanzibar* (1968), by John Brunner; *Do Androids Dream of Electric Sheep?* (1968), by Philip K. Dick; *This Is the Way the World Ends* (1986), by James Morrow; and the work of ecofeminist Sheri S. Tepper, author of *The Gate to Women's Country* (1988), *The Margarets* (2007), and many other novels.

Science fiction has also succeeded in emphasizing and popularizing hopeful possibilities. It is impossible to measure the contribution made by the imaginative stimulus of science fiction to the realized dream of reaching the Moon, but there can be no doubt that the inspiration of many rocket scientists originated from their reading of science fiction.

The use of science-fiction ideas as metaphors representing facets of the human condition has increased in scope. These developments, first seen in such novels as Ursula K. Le Guin's *The Left Hand of Darkness* (1969) and Robert Silverberg's *Dying Inside* (1972), have helped open up new common ground between science fiction and the mainstream novel so that a profitable cross-fertilization of images and methods can take place. This influence can clearly be seen in such works as Margaret Atwood's *The Handmaid's Tale* (1985) and Fay

Weldon's *The Cloning of Joanna May* (1989), two of the many novels that use science-fiction methods to explore the politics of feminism. Nicola Griffith won the Lambda Literary Award, given to the best lesbian, gay, bisexual, or transgender novel of the year, for her first science-fiction work, *Ammonite* (1993), and again for her second, *Slow River* (2005). Both feature strong lesbian protagonists. One of the few African American women writing in the field of science fiction was Octavia E. Butler, who used the genre to explore race, sexuality, religion, and other social issues. Her best-selling novel *Kindred* (1979) features a women who travels through time to meet her enslaved ancestors.

Science fiction is a uniquely changeable kind of fiction because it continually absorbs the implications of contemporary advancements in technology with an alacrity that compensates for its lack of authentic powers of foresight. The rapid elaboration and microminiaturization of information technology, in parallel with the development for medical purposes of partially mechanized human cyborgs, inspired the "cyberpunk" movement in the 1980's, spearheaded by such writers as William Gibson, Bruce Sterling, and Michael Swanwick. This movement combined dystopian ideas of the disintegration of civilization with images of superhumanly enhanced individuals equipped with exotic weaponry and the ability to enter the hypothetical "cyberspace" in which computer programs operate. Cyberpunk proved controversial because more traditionally inclined writers of "hard" (or technophilic) science fiction such as Gregory Benford and David Brin were critical of the movement's apparent moral nihilism (more reasonably regarded as moral skepticism). The emerging technologies of genetic engineering and hypothetical nanotechnologies (involving machinery whose microminiaturization has advanced by a further order of magnitude) subsequently began to feed into this kind of high-tech picaresque science fiction and made dramatic changes to the conceptual horizons of hard science fiction, as imagined in such works as Greg Bear's *Eon* (1985) and Gregory Benford's *Tides of Light* (1989).

In the meantime, however, the increasing popularity of horror and heroic fantasy fiction encouraged many writers to straddle genre boundaries in search of wider audiences. The vocabulary of ideas built up over the years by science-fiction writers became a key resource of horror writers such as Stephen King and Dean R. Koontz, while an increasing number of modern science-fiction stories were set in hypothetical alternative pasts rather than foreseeable futures—examples include James Blaylock's *Homunculus* (1986), Brian Stableford's *The Empire of Fear* (1988), and many novels by Harry Turtledove, including *The Misplaced Legion* (1987), set in the time of Julius Caesar, and *Homeward Bound* (2004), set during World War II. Hybrid works skillfully mixing science fiction and fantasy motifs, such as Tim Powers's *The Anubis Gates* (1983) and *Three Days to Never* (2006), also became increasingly common.

Given that science fiction is also a label under which religious fantasies such as James Morrow's *Only Begotten Daughter* (1990) and his Godhead trilogy (*Towing Jehovah*, 1993; *Blameless in Abaddon*, 1996; and *The Eternal Footman*, 1999) are sometimes marketed, it has become more difficult than ever before to see where the boundaries of the genre lie or to dictate where they ought to lie. As long as contemporary scientific discoveries continue to transform the spectrum of possible futures at a rapid pace, it will be sensible to argue that the science-fiction novel can serve as an essential tool of psychological adaptation for those who find reasons for hope, as well as reasons for anxiety, in the advancement of science and technology.

After 1980, the "science fiction" label—often shortened to "sci-fi"—was applied primarily to films, television shows, and their spin-off merchandise, including long series of tie-in novels. Within the popular genre, text-based materials were increasingly marginalized, a process completed by the successful colonization of the major publishers' science-fiction and fantasy lists by fantasy novels. Although works of serious hard science fiction continued to appear, it became increasingly common for them to be marketed individually as idiosyncratic items rather than as genre products.

The miniaturization of information technology facilitated by microprocessors has demonstrated that the future of space exploration rests with tiny machines that do not require the elaborate ecological support necessary to sustain humans in space. The image of the future as a gradual conquest of space, which obtained a broad consensus among science-fiction novelists of the 1940's who survived the 1980's, has in consequence been banished to the realms of fantasy, although "planetary romances" set on remote worlds remain an effective crucible for thought experiments in social design.

Intellectually respectable science-fiction novels that deal with extraterrestrial futures have been forced to treat humankind's expansion into space in terms that are far more problematic, as in Kim Stanley Robinson's Mars trilogy (*Red Mars*, 1992; *Green Mars*,1993; *Blue Mars*, 1995) and in Stephen Baxter's NASA trilogy (*Voyage*, 1996; *Titan*, 1997; *Moonseed*, 1998), or more far-reaching, as in Greg Egan's *Diaspora* (1997). Those novelists who have accepted that the foreseeable future will be earthbound have become, by necessity, more preoccupied with the seemingly high probability that the twenty-first century will be beset by a complex, interlinked series of ecological and sociopolitical crises; notable attempts to plot hypothetical historical routes through these crises include David Brin's *Earth* (1990), Marge Piercy's *He, She, and It* (1991), Octavia E. Butler's *Parable of the Sower* (1993) and its sequel *Parable of the Talents* (1998), and Jack McDevitt's *Odyssey* (2006). As the intellectually ambitious elements of science fiction are reabsorbed into the literary mainstream, abandoning the "sci-fi" marketing category to films, television shows, computer games, and toys, this will presumably remain the core activity of literary futurists.

Brian Stableford

BIBLIOGRAPHY

Aldiss, Brian W., and David Wingrove. *The Trillion Year Spree: The History of Science Fiction*. London: Victor Gollancz, 1986. Updated version of a history first published in 1973 (as *The Billion Year Spree*) provides a good introduction to the genre.

Barron, Neil. *Anatomy of Wonder: A Critical Guide to Science Fiction*. 5th ed. Westport, Conn.: Libraries Unlimited, 2004. Library guide features critical essays as well as extensively annotated bibliographies of key texts. Includes a four-part history, a chapter on young adult science fiction, and a section on secondary literature and research aids.

Bleiler, Richard, ed. *Science Fiction Writers: Critical Studies of the Major Writers from the Early Nineteenth Century to the Present Day*. 2d ed. New York: Charles Scribner's Sons, 1999. Collection of critical and biographical essays presents information on historical and literary contexts of particular works as well as critical commentary. Includes photographs, bibliography, and index.

Brake, Mark, and Neil Hook. *Different Engines: How Science Drives Fiction and Fiction Drives Science*. New York: Macmillan, 2008. Considers connections between science and science fiction through a series of "ages": the age of discovery, the mechanical age, the astounding age, the atomic age, the new age, the computer age, and the age of biology.

James, Edward, and Farah Mendlesohn, eds. *The Cambridge Companion to Science Fiction*. New York: Cambridge University Press, 2003. Collection of critical essays addresses a wide variety of topics, including science fiction's magazine era; the New Wave, feminist theory, and postmodernism in science-fiction writing; science fiction's approaches to race, gender, and ethnicity; and the various subgenres of science fiction.

Lefanu, Sarah. *Feminism and Science Fiction*. London: Women's Press, 1988. Comprehensive history focuses on the roles of women in science fiction and the uses of utopian and dystopian images of the future as instruments of feminist social critique.

Mann, George, ed. *The Mammoth Encyclopedia of Science Fiction*. New York: Carroll & Graf, 2001. Wide-ranging volume covers major authors, novels, films, television shows, magazines, and awards. Illustrated.

Roberts, Adam. *The History of Science Fiction*. New York: Palgrave Macmillan, 2006. Begins with science fiction and the ancient novel, then addresses works of science fiction in every century from the seventeenth through the twentieth, with a look ahead through the twenty-first.

_____. *Science Fiction*. New York: Routledge, 2000. Discussion of the genre includes chapters devoted to definitions, the history of science fiction, feminist science fiction, science fiction and race, and technology and metaphor.

Stableford, Brian. *Scientific Romance in Britain, 1890-1950*. London: Fourth Estate, 1985. History of the distinctive British tradition of speculative fiction is considered the definitive volume on this topic.

SELF-REFLEXIVE LONG FICTION

After a few minutes of reading stories that are not self-reflexive, readers sometimes forget what they are doing and feel transported into the world of the book. Considering this experience naïve, authors of self-reflexive fictions thwart it by such devices as commenting on their own composition and focusing on storytellers as characters. To some extent, literary self-awareness has existed at least since *Gilgamesh* (c. 3000 B.C.E.), which mentions its being recorded on stone, but that single reference is not enough to make it very self-reflexive.

Truly self-reflexive fictions fall roughly into four levels of introspection: misguided self-consciousness, in which narrators examine their own words, seeking an elusive self-understanding; the *Künstlerroman* (artist's novel), a novel about the education of a writer or some other analogous artist; "self-begetting" fiction, about its own creation; and extended Midrash, which focuses on its position within literature by combining narrative with literary criticism.

Self-reflexive authors tend to use language that is surprisingly contrived or casual, or to deviate from convention in countless other ways; this deviation highlights the text itself, thus making its portrayal of the world seem less real. This effect, called metafiction, is common to all self-reflexive works, though it is usually more extreme in each successive level.

MISGUIDED SELF-CONSCIOUSNESS

The malice-devoured narrator of *Zapiski iz podpolya* (1864; *Letters from the Underworld*, 1913; better known as *Notes from the Underground*), by Fyodor Dostoevski, set a pattern for misguided self-consciousness in twentieth century fiction: A narrator analyzes his or her own text, indeed is often a would-be artist, but lacks sufficient insight. Irony thus divides author and narrator. For example, Humbert Humbert, the protagonist of *Lolita* (1955), by Vladimir Nabokov, wishes to immortalize statutory rape as serious literature; however, his account is classified in the preface as a psychological case, and the novel is ultimately darkly comic, ridiculing Humbert Humbert.

Comparably, *The Great American Novel* (1938), by Clyde Brion Davis, purports to be the diaries of a jour-

nalist who spends his whole obtuse life planning a never-written novel. The first-person voice in *Grendel* (1971), by John Gardner, becomes fascinated with a narrative poet but ultimately rejects art, morality, and any other order. In fictions primarily about misguided self-consciousness, the monstrous or moronic narrator is an artist manqué.

THE *KÜNSTLERROMAN*

Near the start of *Metamorphoses* (second century C.E.; *The Golden Ass*, 1566), the author, Lucius Apuleius, predicts that its protagonist will have adventures worthy of being in a book. Although Apuleius writes the book, he declares his belief that the adventures themselves take precedence over the authorship of the story. Only with the nineteenth century did writers reach such a status that a genre arose to extol them—the *Künstlerroman*. Some of these works include Johann Wolfgang von Goethe's *Wilhelm Meisters Lehrjahre* (1795-1796; *Wilhelm Meister's Apprenticeship*, 1824) and Novalis's *Heinrich von Ofterdingen* (1802; *Henry of Ofterdingen*, 1842).

Like many imitations of this type, Thomas Wolfe's *Look Homeward, Angel* (1929), *Of Time and the River* (1935), *The Web and the Rock* (1939), and *You Can't Go Home Again* (1940) are disguised autobiography, depicting an artist's disaffection from contemporary society. More original are books that try to refresh the formula, such as Hermann Hesse's *Der Steppenwolf* (1927; *Steppenwolf*, 1929). At first it seems to be a novel of misguided self-consciousness, the ravings of a mad diarist, but Hesse portrays outpourings of the unconscious as an artist's proper education. Another variant of the formula is to counterpoise the perspectives of many writer characters, as in Aldous Huxley's *Point Counter Point* (1928), André Gide's *Les Faux-monnayeurs* (1925; *The Counterfeiters*, 1927), or Lawrence Durrell's *The Alexandria Quartet* (1962).

In the United States, authors frequently labor to keep self-reflection from turning into preciosity. Consequently, a popular variant of the formula is to disguise it as masculine adventure, as in Orson Scott Card's Ender novels. The first, *Ender's Game* (1985), seems to be about a prepubescent military leader, although his siblings become famous writers. In the second volume, *Speaker for the Dead* (1986), his education is shown to have prepared him to write the scriptures for a new religion. By the later volumes in the series, including *Shadow of the Giant* (2005), his powers as author have reached a magical dimension such that he can make characters literally live merely by imagining them. In the *Künstlerroman*, being a writer is deemed the ultimate expression of a person's potential, whereas the following level, the self-begetting novel, celebrates the author's godlike creation of a whole world.

THE SELF-BEGETTING NOVEL

In an attempt to define all self-reflexive long fiction, Steven G. Kellman devised the term "self-begetting novel," by which he means a work that appears to have been written by a character within that work. Although he admits that this is actually not the focus of all self-reflexive works, his phrase does suit those fictions that suggest self-enclosure by, for example, ending with references to their beginning.

Kellman sees self-begetting fiction as predominantly French, stemming from Marcel Proust's *À la recherche du temps perdu* (1913-1927; *Remembrance of Things Past*, 1922-1931, 1981). Henry Miller, in *Tropic of Cancer* (1934) and *Tropic of Capricorn* (1939), models his writer-protagonist's resistance to devouring time on Proust's work. Comparably, Jean-Paul Sartre's *La Nausée* (1938; *Nausea*, 1949) concludes with its main character, Antoine Roquentin, wishing to write a novel so that people might one day revere him the way he does a singer on a repeatedly heard record. As Kellman observes, the waitress who plays the record is named Madeleine, an allusion to Proust's madeleine cake, whose taste triggered the protagonist's paranormal, vivid recollection of his past. Significantly, Michel Butor, famous for his *La Modification* (1957; *Second Thoughts*, 1958; better known as *A Change of Heart*), and Samuel Beckett, author of *Molloy* (1951; English translation, 1955), *Malone meurt* (1951; *Malone Dies*, 1956), and *L'Innommable* (1953; *The Unnamable*, 1958), have written not only self-begetting fictions but also major essays on Proust.

The aforementioned Proust-like narratives are increasingly constricted and dissatisfied with life. Miller's world is designedly more tawdry and sordid than that of Proust. Sartre ventures further still into squalor, inspiring the "nausea" of Roquentin. Two decades later, rather than being by class a writer-intellectual like Roquentin, the protagonist of *A Change of Heart* works for a typewriter company, and Beckett's fictions concern barely human authors in nightmarish worlds. Kellman argues that Beckett's parodies of the tradition bring it to a close.

Anne Rice's best-selling *The Tale of the Body Thief* (1992), however, combines elements of this French tradition (such as slow movement, world-weariness, and prestigious allusion) with American self-begetting narrative (adventure, youthful perspective, and uncouth diction, as in J. D. Salinger's 1951 novel *The Catcher in the Rye*). Rice's French American protagonist Lestat alternates between poetic monologues about his centuries-long self-disgust and slang-filled expressions of his immortal youth. As epigraph, Rice quotes William Butler Yeats's poem "Sailing to Byzantium," about the need to leave the transience of life for the eternity of art or of the supernatural. Lestat achieves both: He writes the book and chooses a vampiric identity, which seems the next step beyond Beckett's almost dead narrators. In *Sofies verden: Roman om filosofiens historie* (1991; *Sophie's World*, 1996), by Jostein Gaarder, the protagonist is a woman who fears that she might be only a character in a book, a worry shared by Lenore Stonecipher Beadsman in David Foster Wallace's *The Broom of the System* (1987).

More purely American is the deliberate vulgarity of Kurt Vonnegut's *Slaughterhouse-Five: Or, The Children's Crusade, a Duty-Dance with Death* (1969), a fictionalized autobiography prefaced and repeatedly interrupted by the author's discussion of its composition. To emphasize circularity, he begins the story by accurately predicting that the final word will be a bird's song endlessly reheard by Billy Pilgrim, the time-shifting protagonist.

A frequent metaphor in American self-begetting novels (including Rice's) compares the self-begetting to physically sterile but psychologically productive sexual adventures. Two groundbreaking works of this sort are Philip Roth's *Portnoy's Complaint* (1969) and Erica Jong's *Fear of Flying* (1973). These forays are fraught with shame and angst. Roth's persona ends by wondering if he has allowed the irrational to govern his writings, and Jong's protagonist at least once dreads being caught in her own book. Sexual explicitness brought *Fear of Flying* its notoriety; nonetheless, it has much in common with more restrained, feminist, self-begetting novels such as Doris Lessing's masterpiece *The Golden Notebook* (1962).

In *The Golden Notebook*, the protagonist writes a series of notebooks culminating in the novel itself. This shows the closeness of the notebook form and self-begetting fiction. For example, Rainer Maria Rilke's *Die Aufzeichnungen des Malte Laurids Brigge* (1910; *The Notebooks of Malte Laurids Brigge*, 1930; also known as *The Journal of My Other Self*), although not precisely circular, frequently doubles back on itself, as Brigge keeps referring to earlier sections. His final discussion of the Prodigal Son involves the idea of cyclic return.

Comparably, the diarylike structure of Kōbō Abe's *Hako otoko* (1973; *The Box Man*, 1974) is possibly solipsistic and pervaded by metaphoric use of the box as an emblem of self-containment. Despite the form's fascination with autonomy, throughout the world variants of self-begetting fiction take on local color, as N. Scott Momaday's *House Made of Dawn* (1968) does from the Native American chant that begins and ends it, making the whole into the eternally repeating song of its protagonist.

EXTENDED MIDRASH

Because of its use by such critics as Harold Bloom, the term "Midrash" has come to denote literary interpretation in narrative form. Before there was a critical term for it, extended Midrash became fashionable through James Joyce's *Ulysses* (1922), based on a massive analogy between itself and Homer's *Odyssey* (c. 800 B.C.E.), though it links itself to a vast number of other works as well. For example, its character Stephen Dedalus (protagonist of Joyce's serialized *Künstlerroman* of 1914-1915 [1916 book], *A Portrait of the Artist as a Young Man*) spends a long chapter discussing William Shakespeare's *Hamlet* in a manner applicable to *Ulysses* itself.

In the same year that Joyce published the even more metafictional *Finnegans Wake* (1939), Flann O'Brien issued the almost equally experimental *At Swim-Two-Birds*, a parody of Irish literary tradition. The appearance of these works did not mark the opening of floodgates, since *Ulysses*—like extended Midrash—requires read-

ers who are able to comprehend a vertiginous play of allusions. Consequently, works of this sort are hardly plentiful. Even the most erudite readers do not always esteem them. In *Remembrance of Things Past*, for example, Proust's narrator condemned theorizing about art within a novel, likening it to leaving a price tag on a purchase.

Midrash first developed as an ancient form of Jewish biblical criticism. Some modern fictions continue applying Midrash to scriptures. For example, biblical hermeneutics are repeatedly foregrounded in Thomas Mann's multivolume *Die Geschichten Jaakobs* (1933; *Joseph and His Brothers*, 1934; also known as *The Tales of Jacob*), thereby underlining the fact that his retelling of Genesis is a speculation or even a fantasy. Its protagonist is himself both storyteller and dream interpreter, analogous to Mann himself. Comparably, Salman Rushdie's *The Satanic Verses* (1988) contains a Midrash-like dream about a character named Salman who finds that the Koran is imperfect, destroying Salman's belief in everything. This sense of unreality spreads into the dreamer's life, eventually causing him to kill himself. He has been an actor in religious roles, a part of the public's collective dreams, which mingle with their interpretation of scriptures. Caught in their pious fantasies, for much of the book he is transformed into an angel with a halo, a stereotyping that contributes to his suicidal depression.

Although stories about scriptures, myths, and fairy tales are the most common varieties of extended Midrash, authors' involvement with academia has resulted in other uses. For example, to his college class, Vladimir Nabokov presented an analysis of an apartment's structure in Franz Kafka's story *Die Verwandlung* (1915; *The Metamorphosis*, 1936). This analysis found its way into a poem, on which a crazed exegete then expatiates, in Nabokov's novel *Pale Fire* (1962). From an even more abstract source—a structuralist conference—Italo Calvino gleaned the idea of arranging tarot cards at random. The narrators of his *Il castello dei destini incrociati* (1969, 1973; *The Castle of Crossed Destinies*, 1976) connect these arrangements simultaneously to characters in the novel and to ones from world literature. Calvino's *Se una notte d'inverno un viaggiatore* (1979; *If on a Winter's Night a Traveler,* 1981) takes the self-reflectivity one step further: It is a novel about a reader trying to read a novel named *If on a Winter's Night a*

Traveler. In Julian Barnes's *Flaubert's Parrot* (1984), the narrator's obsessions with love and with scholarship on Gustave Flaubert converge.

Samuel R. Delany's series of fantasies, beginning with *Tales of Nevèrÿon* (1979), wanders among his personal concerns as a gay African American, the Conan parody he is writing, and the literary theories (particularly deconstruction) that inspire the narrative. In extended Midrash, nonfiction (criticism, autobiography) and fiction converge ambiguously, creating a feeling of uncertainty that life often gives as well.

Because of its ambiguities, ironies, and complexities, extended Midrash cannot be treated as if it were a simple statement of an author's opinions. Milan Kundera, for example, objects vociferously when critics treat the essays within his fictions as if they were his own views. Rather, he insists that their function is to reveal how he invents his characters. For example, as he reveals in *L'Art du roman* (1986; *The Art of the Novel*, 1988), his ruminations on the Romantic tradition led to his devising an imaginary member of it, the character Jaromil of *La Vie est ailleurs* (1973; *Life Is Elsewhere*, 1974). In that novel, Kundera's remarks about Romanticism are meant to create this character from the outside rather than through the devices of psychological fiction. His practice has its roots in eighteenth century characterization through recognizable types. Nonetheless, Kundera's version is significantly different from this conventional stereotyping. He not only breaks the illusion of reality by spending much of his novels explaining how he devises characters, but also, through meditations on language and literature, constructs new types and narratives about them. Certain words and scenes thus repeat as motifs.

Some comparable repetition pervades all self-reflexive fiction. As *Ulysses* and *Finnegans Wake* prove, despite this iteration, self-reflexive fiction can have great length without being necessarily tedious. Nonetheless, as Robert Scholes observes, self-reflexive fiction more commonly presents its complexity within the limits of the short novel, novella, or even short story, as in the metaphysical fictions of Jorge Luis Borges. Consequently, it tends toward unconventional, multilayered, integrated condensation reminiscent of experimental poetry.

James Whitlark

BIBLIOGRAPHY

Currie, Mark, ed. *Metafiction.* New York: Longman, 1995. Articles on experimental themes and techniques in literature, with essays contributed by writers of metafiction and by literary scholars. Essays include "What Is Metafiction, and Why Are They Saying Such Awful Things About It?" and "The Art of Metafiction."

Doody, Margaret Anne. *The True Story of the Novel.* New Brunswick, N.J.: Rutgers University Press, 1996. Comprehensive work in which the author traces self-consciousness in modern fiction to its use in the literature of the ancient world, which was connected to the mystery religions of the time.

Hutcheon, Linda. *Narcissistic Narrative: The Metafictional Paradox.* New ed. New York: Methuen, 1984. Study of the "forms and implications of metafiction." Hutcheon distinguishes the overt narcissism of metafiction from the covert narcissism of mystery novels, fantasy, eroticism, game structures, and puns. For advanced readers.

Kawin, Bruce. *The Mind of the Novel: Reflexive Fiction and the Ineffable.* 1982. New ed. Normal, Ill.: Dalkey Archive Press, 2006. Explores the essence of self-reflexive, or self-conscious, fiction and compares its structure to human consciousness. Kawin writes, "the self is the mystery at the heart of the reflexive novel." For advanced readers.

Kellman, Steven G. *The Self-Begetting Novel.* New York: Columbia University Press, 1980. Although it tries to do more, this study does especially well in tracing the self-begetting strand of metafiction. Chapters on Proust, Sartre, Beckett, and the English and American self-begetting novels.

Scholes, Robert. *Fabulation and Metafiction.* Urbana: University of Illinois Press, 1979. Excellent resource on metafiction as a means of storytelling. Dated but relevant study.

Waugh, Patricia. *Metafiction: The Theory and Practice of Self-Conscious Fiction.* New York: Routledge, 2003. Examines "the political, social, and economic factors" that affect judgments of fiction, including the self-reflexive novel. First published in 1984.

Sports Long Fiction

Few would think of Leo Tolstoy's *Anna Karenina* (1875-1877; English translation, 1886) as a novel with sport scenes, yet the book includes significant coverage of sports such as skating, tennis, and horse racing. Indeed, many famous writers have included sports in their novels. James Fenimore Cooper's *The Pioneers* (1823) depicts a turkey shoot, pigeon shooting, and bass fishing. Charles Dickens offers a colorful cricket match in *Pickwick Papers* (1836-1837, serial; 1837, book). Ernest Hemingway's *The Sun Also Rises* (1926) is renowned for its bullfighting sequence, but the loving presentation of the joys of fishing is equally vivid. The hero of Hemingway's *The Old Man and the Sea* (1952) is not just a fisherman but an avid baseball fan obsessed by Joe DiMaggio's quest to extend his record hitting streak. Beyond such occurrences, however, lies a wealth of fiction devoted mainly to sports.

For many years the most famous sports novels were those of Gilbert Patten. Writing as Burt L. Standish, Patten described the exploits of Frank Merriwell, a star in baseball, basketball, football, track, and crew at Yale University. In more than two hundred dime novels written between 1896 and 1930, Patten presents Merriwell as the epitome of virtuous American youth, always playing according to the rules, never drinking or smoking. Patten was obviously influenced by *Tom Brown's School Days* (1857), in which Thomas Hughes demonstrates how cricket and football (soccer) are necessary components of a British gentleman's education. The Merriwell tales established the template for such writers of young adult sports fiction as Clair Bee, Donald Honig, Jackson Scholz, and John R. Tunis. While many writers have been concerned with athletics, the best-known sports novels have been by American writers.

Baseball

While John R. Tunis's *The Kid from Thomasville* (1940) is a masterpiece of young adult baseball fiction, Bernard Malamud's *The Natural* (1952) is widely considered the first great baseball novel, paving the way for more literary examinations of the sport. By equating its

hero with the Arthurian knights Lancelot and Parsifal, Malamud created the first mythic baseball tale. His stories also draw from baseball history, notably the legend of Babe Ruth and the career of Eddie Waitkus, the first baseman for the Philadelphia Phillies shot in the chest by an obsessed fan in 1949.

With *The Great American Novel* (1973), Philip Roth borrows from *The Epic of Gilgamesh*, a Mesopotamian poem written before 2000 B.C.E. about a hero-king. Roth uses his more mundane baseball hero to satirize what he sees as the destructive American obsession with competition. In Jerome Charyn's *The Seventh Babe* (1979), a left-handed third baseman for the 1924 Boston Red Sox is banned from the sport for reneging on his marriage vows to a Boston socialite and ends up playing for the Cincinnati Colored Giants. Charyn uses baseball myths to imagine the game as played outside its official history.

Beginning with *The Southpaw* (1953), Mark Harris wrote four realistic novels narrated in the vernacular by pitcher Henry Wiggen of the New York Mammoths. Wiggen matures from a cocky, naïve youth prone to mistakes on and off the field to a more mature, philosophical man. In the final novel, *It Looked Like For Ever* (1979), the thirty-nine-year-old pitcher acknowledges his declining skills and faces life after baseball.

Canadian writer W. P. Kinsella is unusual for having devoted much of his career to baseball. Kinsella is best known for *Shoeless Joe* (1982), the source of the popular film *Field of Dreams* (1989), in which the spirits of Shoeless Joe Jackson, the most famous member of the infamous 1919 Chicago White Sox, and other dead stars play on a baseball diamond created in his cornfield by an Iowa farmer. In addition to such baseball novels as *The Iowa Baseball Confederacy* (1986), Kinsella has published several collections of baseball stories. Eliot Asinof's *Eight Men Out* (1963) is a detailed treatment of the 1919 game-fixing scandal involving several White Sox teammates.

The promise and disappointment faced by African Americans in baseball is part of Barry Beckham's examination of racism in *Runner Mack* (1972). A naïve and young black athlete believes he will be treated fairly in his efforts to break into the sport but finds himself with nowhere to go after his tryout is sabotaged. The years during which African Americans were banned from the major leagues is the subject of William Brashler's *The Bingo Long Traveling All-Stars and Motor Kings* (1973), which follows a traveling team of black players during the 1930's.

The protagonist of Robert Coover's *The Universal Baseball Association, Inc., J. Henry Waugh, Prop.* (1968), regarded by many as the greatest baseball novel, creates an elaborate baseball board game, rolling dice to determine outcomes. When the dice say his favorite player must die, his world descends into chaos, as Coover uses baseball to explore philosophical issues.

One of the most notable writers of baseball mysteries is Troy Soos. Beginning with *Murder at Fenway Park* (1994), set in 1912, Soos's hero Mickey Rawlings, a journeyman infielder, solves a murder at a different stadium in each novel. Soos lovingly re-creates the world of major league baseball in its early days, and historical figures often appear in the tales—including Ty Cobb in *Hunting a Detroit Tiger* (1997). In the historian G. S. Rowe's *Best Bet in Beantown* (2003), set in 1897, Will Beaman tries to prove to the Boston Beaneaters that he is worthy of a front-office job by finding out who assaulted the team's star shortstop. Crabbe Evers's excellent contemporary mystery series features colorful sportswriter Duffy House. Beginning with the New York Yankees in *Murderer's Row* (1991), each Evers novel deals with a different major league team.

Basketball

The most famous basketball player in literature is Harry "Rabbit" Angstrom, the protagonist of John Updike's *Rabbit, Run* (1960). This novel is the first of four about Angstrom, whose glory days as a high school basketball star are central in the formation of his character. A one-on-one game with a friend in *Rabbit Redux* (1971) proves the game has left him behind. The protagonist of Don DeLillo's *Americana* (1971) makes an autobiographical film about his high school playing days. DeLillo's *Ratner's Star* (1976) looks at the career of a

basketball star from his Bronx high school to an obscure community college in Antarctica.

The most productive writer of basketball fiction is Charles Rosen, former coach of the Oklahoma City Cavalry of the Continental Basketball League and the women's team at the State University of New York, New Paltz. Rosen's *The Cockroach Basketball League* (1992) looks at the lives of players and coaches in minor league basketball, hanging on desperately for a shot at the National Basketball Association. Rosen sees basketball as a metaphor for life's promise and disappointments. In *The House of Moses All-Stars* (1996), Rosen uses a barnstorming Jewish team in 1936 to depict the status of society's outsiders. Rosen's interest in the social and historical side of the sport can also be seen in *Barney Polan's Game: A Novel of the 1951 College Basketball Scandals* (1998).

Passing Off (1996), by Tom LeClair, who once played professional basketball in Greece, chronicles a year in the fictional Greek Basketball Association. Like a hero of Greek mythology, the protagonist undergoes a trial of his character on his odyssey about the country. LeClair attempts to do for basketball what Charyn, Malamud, and Roth have done for baseball. In *Playing the Game* (1995), Alan Lelchuk presents an Ivy League team's advance to the National Collegiate Athletic Association's Final Four basketball championship series. Lelchuk finds variations on the usual underdog saga, such as having the coach try to pass on the wisdom of writer-philosophers such as Ralph Waldo Emerson. Lawrence Shainberg's *One on One* (1970) is a metaphysical look at the sport, presenting a day in the life of a college player as he makes his Madison Square Garden debut and tries to block out his personal demons as well as the opposition.

Just as the importance of basketball in African American culture has been explored in numerous nonfiction books, it has also been examined in fiction. The hero of Paul Beatty's satirical *The White Boy Shuffle* (1996) moves to a "tough" section of Los Angeles after his parents' divorce and learns to fit in by playing basketball.

Football

A football hero's retirement leaves him with little reason to live in Thomas Wolfe's *The Web and the Rock*

(1939), a theme also explored in *Joiner* (1971), by James Whitehead. At six feet seven inches tall and weighing three-hundred pounds, Sonny Joiner has larger-than-life appetites but finds life after football glory disappointing. Don DeLillo's highly regarded *End Zone* (1972) follows a college running back through one season and equates the violence of football with the annihilation brought on by nuclear war.

The best known of many sports novels by longtime *Sports Illustrated* writer Dan Jenkins is *Semi-Tough* (1972), in which Billy Clyde Puckett pours as much energy into his off-the-field exploits as he does as the star running back for the New York Giants. In this parody of autobiographies by athletes, Jenkins pokes fun at those who want to add glamour to their lives by hanging around with football players. Jenkins continues Puckett's story in *Life Its Ownself: The Semi-Tougher Adventures of Billy Clyde Puckett and Them* (1984). While most football novels focus on players and coaches, sportswriter Mike Lupica makes an owner the hero of his satirical *Bump and Run* (2000) and *Red Zone* (2003). A Las Vegas casino worker inherits the New York Hawks from his father and finds the inhabitants of National Football League boardrooms just as greedy as his former colleagues.

Peter Gent, a basketball star at Michigan State University who became a wide receiver for the Dallas Cowboys from 1964 to 1968, wrote the satirical *North Dallas Forty* (1973). Gent presents professional football as a win-at-any-cost enterprise conducted by businessmen who care nothing about their players as human beings. His hero is forced to take painkillers to continue playing. Gent also writes about professional football in *Texas Celebrity Turkey Trot* (1978) and *The Franchise* (1983) and the corruption of college basketball in *The Conquering Heroes* (1994).

The football-related novel with the highest critical reputation is *A Fan's Notes* (1968). In Frederick Exley's autobiographical tale, the writer describes his numerous failures, including a drinking problem, and contrasts his life with the success of his University of Southern California classmate Frank Gifford, a football star in college and later with the New York Giants. Exley lives vicariously through Gifford, eagerly awaiting each Sunday and his idol's exploits, usually watched on a barroom television. *A Fan's Notes* has been acclaimed for its powerful portrayal of success and failure in America.

GOLF

In *Dead Solid Perfect* (1974), by Dan Jenkins, the uncle of an aging golfer, after years of barely making the cut on the Professional Golfers' Association tour, finds himself among the leaders at the master's tournament. Uncle Kenny, a self-mocking, profane, politically incorrect hero, nevertheless considers golf a mental disorder such as politics, gambling, and chasing women. Jenkins also looks humorously at the sport in *The Money-Whipped Steer-Job Three-Jack Give-Up Artist* (2001) and *Slim and None* (2005).

The mythical side of golf is addressed in J. Michael Veron's *The Caddie* (2004), as the spirit of Bobby Jones, the great American golfer of the 1920's, tries to save a struggling young player from self-destruction. William Hallberg's *The Rub of the Green* (1988) contrasts its hero's prowess on the course to his messy personal life. The lessons learned from golf also are prominent in Troon McAllister's *The Green* (1999) and *The Foursome* (2000) focusing on hustler Eddie Caminetti, whose victims deserve what they get. Beginning with *A Wicked Slice* (1989), the wife-husband team of Charlotte and Aaron Elkins offers mysteries featuring Lee Ofsted, who stumbles into murders while playing on the Ladies Professional Golf Association tour.

TENNIS

The first of John R. Tunis's many sports novels is *American Girl* (1928), an unflattering fictional treatment of tennis star Helen Wills Moody, and in *Sudden Death* (1983), Rita Mae Brown examines America's intolerance of lesbian athletes in women's professional tennis. In *The Tennis Handsome* (1983), Barry Hannah centers his dark, violent humor on an unusually attractive tennis player and his manipulative mentor, and the philosophical limits of tennis are contemplated in *Infinite Jest* (1996), by David Foster Wallace. The charismatic hero of *The Huge Season* (1954), by Wright Morris, set at a California college in the 1920's, is a would-be famous tennis player considered ideal by several of his classmates until he proves self-destructive and commits suicide.

BOXING

Fat City (1969), by Leonard Gardner is an especially gritty look at mediocre boxers who refuse to acknowledge that they will never become champions. A young man takes up boxing to escape Chicago's Polish ghetto in Nelson Algren's *Never Come Morning* (1942), and the corruption of professional boxing is the focus of Budd Schulberg's *The Harder They Fall* (1947). A Korean War veteran comes to grip with his problems only after killing a boxer during a bout in Michael Shaara's *The Broken Place* (1968), and Peter Lovesey presents a colorful portrait of Victorian-era boxing, from training to gambling, in his Sergeant Cribb mystery *The Detective Wore Silk Drawers* (1971).

HORSE RACING

The most beloved horse racing novel is Enid Bagnold's *National Velvet* (1935), the story of a young girl's love for her horse and their unlikely victory in England's Grand National. Arna Bontemps's *God Sends Sunday* (1931) profiles the life of an African American jockey. The most popular horse racing novels have been Dick Francis's mysteries, beginning with *Dead Cert* (1962), about an English jockey who turns to writing after sustaining a serious injury.

TRACK

The Front Runner (1974), by Patricia Nell Warren, depicting the sexual relationship between a cross-country runner and his coach, is one of the first sports novels to address homosexuality. The way politics sometimes interferes with sports is the subject of Hugh Atkinson's Olympic marathon novel *The Games* (1968). In Alan Sillitoe's *The Loneliness of the Long-Distance Runner* (1959), an imprisoned young man discovers the freedom offered by running.

SOCCER AND RUGBY

In Peter Handke's *Die Angst des Tormanns beim Elfmeter* (1970; *The Goalie's Anxiety at the Penalty Kick*, 1972), the protagonist's isolation on the soccer field reflects his alienation from society at large. David Storey's *This Sporting Life* (1960) contrasts the athletic success of its hero in rugby league football with failure in his romantic life.

OTHER SPORTS

The hero of Caroline Gordon's *Aleck Maury, Sportsman* (1934) finds an order and peace in fishing and hunting that is missing from the rest of his mundane life. Thomas McGuane depicts the decline of a Michigan hunting club in *The Sporting Club* (1969) and the rivalry between two Key West fishing guides in *Ninety-two in the Shade* (1973).

The Hustler (1959), by Walter Tevis and *Billy Phelan's Greatest Game* (1978), by William Kennedy look at contemporary mores through the experience of pool hustlers. A young woman becomes the greatest American chess player in Tevis's *The Queen's Gambit* (1983), and in Vladimir Nabokov's *Zashchita Luzhina* (1930; *The Defense*, 1964), a chess genius goes insane. Sports as a measure of manhood is the concern of James Dickey's *Deliverance* (1970), in which Atlanta suburbanites fight for their survival on a disastrous canoeing trip down a river in Appalachia.

In *Amazons: An Intimate Memoir by the First Woman Ever to Play in the National Hockey League* (1980), Don DeLillo, writing as Cleo Birdwell, creates a memoir of the first woman to play professional hockey in the United States. *Netherland* (2008), by Irish writer Joseph O'Neill, focuses on the expatriate cricket community in New York City. The novel's Dutch-born narrator, adrift following September 11, 2001, becomes involved with a man from Trinidad who wants to build a cricket stadium in Brooklyn. Beginning with *Deal Breaker* (1995), Harlan Coben has written several mysteries featuring character Myron Bolitar, an attorney and sports agent who solves crimes involving his clients. Each novel involves a different sport.

Michael Adams

BIBLIOGRAPHY

Cocchiarale, Michael, and Scott Emmert. *Upon Further Review: Sports in American Literature*. Westport, Conn.: Praeger, 2004. Essays explore the vastness of sports, athletes, fandom, mass media, and more and examine its representation in and influence on American literature. A comprehensive, scholarly, and readable collection.

Crowe, Chris. *More than a Game: Sports Literature for*

Young Adults. Lanham, Md.: Scarecrow Press, 2004. Chapters in this study of sports fiction for youths include "From the School Room to the Playing Field: A History of Young Adult Sports Literature" and "Sports Literature for Young Women."

Hill, Jeffrey. *Sport and the Literary Imagination: Essays in History, Literature, and Sport*. New York: Peter Lang, 2006. Essays by American and British writers study the influence of sports and athletics in crafting literature.

Oriard, Michael. *Dreaming of Heroes: American Sports Fiction, 1868-1980*. Chicago: Nelson-Hall, 1982. Covers sports fiction in the United States, considering themes such as history, myth, and aging. Includes chapters on "country and city" and "men without women" in sports fiction.

_____. *Sporting with the Gods: The Rhetoric of Play and Game in American Culture*. New York: Cambridge University Press, 1991. Examines sports, gaming, and other modes of "play" in the context of American culture. Discusses how these three themes have influenced American literature since the late eighteenth century.

Westbrook, Deeanne. *Ground Rules: Baseball and Myth*. Urbana: University of Illinois Press, 1996. Study of the role of myth in baseball fiction, with discussion of the works of W. P. Kinsella, Bernard Malamud, William Kennedy, and others.

YOUNG ADULT LONG FICTION

A distinctive literature about childhood has existed since the Victorian era, but not so about adolescence as a stage of life with its own integrity, concerns, and distinct problems. Teachers, librarians, and parents argue that the classics of world literature are accessible to reading teenagers. These classics include the work of Edgar Allan Poe, who is a lasting favorite with young people, as with adults. The romances of the Brontë sisters, Rudyard Kipling's exotic adventure tales, and the picaresque novels of Mark Twain feature youthful characters appealing to a wide range of readers. Young readers also seek out the novels of Jack London, Zora Neale Hurston, George Orwell, Pearl Buck, Ernest Hemingway, Harper Lee, Kurt Vonnegut, Chaim Potok, and others. Even though many classics endure as a type of literature for youth, a distinct junior or juvenile literary category did not emerge until the 1930's.

Rose Wilder Lane's *Let the Hurricane Roar* (1933) is widely credited as the first serious novel written specifically for young adults. Its story of hardscrabble family life on the Dakota plains, in which harsh problems are surmounted, set an optimistic tone for youth reading that was to dominate the field for many years. Publishers loosely defined young adulthood as ages twelve through twenty.

Less than ten years after Lane's groundbreaking novel, Maureen Daly published her own work of young fiction, *Seventeenth Summer* (1942). Betty Cavanna's *Going on Sixteen* followed in 1946. The success of these books meant that high school proms, sporting events, hot-rod adventures, adolescent infatuations, and career choices were soon the subjects of numerous novels. *Seventeen* magazine, addressing teenage girls, held writing contests and published examples of good teenage fiction. Publishers were eager to satisfy young readers with fiction about characters their own age and with problems similar to their own. The literature was still timid, however, hesitant to tackle subjects only whispered about at slumber parties or in locker rooms. Publishers understood that many of these books were purchased by adults, so the writing had to satisfy social values and expectations.

Several developments encouraged the expansion of junior books as a separate category. Public libraries appeared in more and more small towns. Mail-order department stores, including Montgomery Ward and Sears Roebuck, marketed books of all kinds. Urbanization provided greater access to libraries and bookstores, and teenagers were earning more discretionary money. "Penny dreadfuls" and subliterary pulp fiction had been marketed for several years, but in the 1960's the paperback industry accelerated; soon almost any book could be purchased in paperback, including young adult novels. Though prices increased, the books remained popular because of ease of handling and ready availability. Chain bookstores spread, demanding an increasing supply of new books for all tastes.

Established writers would soon be encouraged to write for young adults. One of these writers, Robert Cormier, became a best-selling author of young adult fiction with his immensely popular novel *The Chocolate War* (1974). As teenage fiction became a genre of its own, some stories would reach beyond the genteel boundaries of middle-class propriety to tackle the realities of youthful existence. Ethnicity, the immigrant experience, family dysfunction, sexual exploitation, drugs, and violence became popular topics. *The Chocolate War* is infamous for its sexual references, violence, and harsh language.

CHARACTERISTICS OF YOUNG ADULT FICTION

Publishers identified several characteristics of successful young adult fiction. First, protagonists were almost always young, and often through first-person narratives, their point of view prevailed. Second, plots dealt with adolescent dilemmas, such as Should one accept family expectations or fulfill personal goals? Was it better to "fit in" with high school cliques or assert one's individuality? and, Should employment, further schooling, or marriage be the choice for one's future beyond high school? Disappointment in love and friendship was another common theme. Third, problems were usually optimistically resolved by the end of a book. Fourth, stylistic experimentation was rare, even though many fine literary craftspeople were beginning to write works of young adult fiction.

With compulsory education extending through high school, publishers came to recognize the existence of a vast audience of those euphemistically referred to as "reluctant readers." Even though teachers and librarians promoted quality literature, many gradually concluded that any reading was preferable to none at all. This opened library shelves to books previously regarded as subliterary, including many formula Westerns, romances, and the previously scorned series books.

FAMILY LIFE

Novels of family life have always been a staple of youth literature. In Louisa May Alcott's *Little Women* (1868, 1869), four sisters and their mother form a supporting family circle, despite wartime deprivations and an absent father. In Kate Douglas Wiggin's *Rebecca of Sunnybrook Farm* (1903) and L. M. Montgomery's *Anne of Green Gables* (1908), orphaned children make happy homes with adoptive parents. *Cress Delahanty* (1953), by Jessamyn West is a realistic narrative of high school years made tolerable by empathetic parents. Although *Cress Delahanty* was praised throughout the 1950's for its keen insight into adolescent psychology and was used as a text in numerous college classes, the short novel rarely was read after the 1960's, illustrating the ephemeral nature of many quality books about young adults.

Not all young adult novels depict harmonious home environments. With divorce rates soaring during the last half of the twentieth century and the recognition that many children live in troubled or single-parent households, books started reflecting this reality. One of the pioneers of the nontraditional family story, whose enormous popularity did not extend into the new millennium, was Norma Klein. In *Mom, the Wolf Man, and Me* (1972), Klein introduced a child reared by her unmarried mother. In Klein's *Taking Sides* (1974), the loyalties of children were divided between a lesbian mother and a divorced father who took them on assignations with his girlfriend. Though Klein's characters are upper middle class and her books always end optimistically, her inclusion of socially taboo subject matter earned both praise and condemnation.

Klein paved the way for even more daring writers. In *The Hanged Man* (1994), Francesca Lia Block's protagonist lives through incest and child abuse. In *Peter* (1993), by Kate Walker, a fifteen-year-old Australian strives for his authentic identity, acknowledging his sexual orientation while fighting family and social stereotypes. Jim Naughton's *My Brother Stealing Second* (1989) concerns a family coping with suicide, while a high school freshman in Paula Fox's 1995 novel *The Eagle Kite* learns that his father is dying of complications from acquired immunodeficiency syndrome, or AIDS.

ETHNIC LITERATURE

With American urbanization and increased regional standardization, fiction turned to ethnic diversity as a way of generating interest. The ethnic complexity of American society was explored in numerous young adult books that satisfied readers in two ways: as an expansion of experience and as a celebration of cherished ancestral traditions. Through these books middle-class white teenagers could vicariously experience life in San Francisco's Chinatown or the Watts neighborhood of Los Angeles, for example. Chinese American youth claimed ancestry in the world's oldest continuous civilization, while the Watts youth gained pride in African folk traditions and the achievements of African Americans.

Sulamith Ish-Kishor's *Our Eddie* (1969), a much-acclaimed novel, easily transcends age categories. It is a realistic narrative of two contending generations of impoverished immigrants. Eddie is a disabled boy oppressed by his scholarly father, a harsh Hebrew teacher who ignores the needs of his family. With a sick mother, Eddie has only his sister to champion him. Defying the ethics of his father, he steals from his employer to provide a gift for his sister. Though Eddie never makes his peace, he does come to acknowledge his father's gift for bringing the rich panorama of Jewish history—with its mystics, prophets, and dramatic events—alive for his students. Having always been sickly, Eddie dies, but his death is not sentimentalized. The remaining family members find the strength to endure, and even the father, as in classical tragedy, gains a measure of wisdom. The book ends not with trite resolution but with reverent questioning, as Eddie's sister is left to wonder about God's mercy and power.

RELIGION

Although spiritual questions concern thoughtful young people, religion is a remaining taboo in young adult fiction. Fraught with complications in the public arena, religious books are purchased with great care by schools and public libraries. World religion may be an exception. Accepted books include those on religious ceremonies and customs when they form a central part of group identity, as with Orthodox Jews, the Amish, or early Quakers. In most other cases, religious matters tend to be approached only indirectly. Judy Blume's *Are You There God? It's Me, Margaret* (1970) is chiefly a coming-of-age tale, though the heroine does address God in the most superficial fashion.

Books with strong and specific religious affirmations may still be found in specialized Christian bookstores, which stock numerous young adult novels, many of them born-again variants of best sellers in the general market. Robin Jones Gunn's *Sisterchicks on the Loose* (2003) is chick lit for evangelicals. Ray Blackston writes books designed for young, Christian single men; his best is *A Pagan's Nightmare* (2006). The Left Behind series of books by Tim LaHaye and Jerry Jenkins (1995-2004), with their fictionalized accounts of Earth's last days, have been runaway best sellers and read by all ages.

THE OCCULT

If established religions are neglected in young adult fiction, the same cannot be said for the supernatural and the occult. Young people have always enjoyed the weird stories of Edgar Allan Poe and Washington Irving. H. P. Lovecraft's eldritch (or eerie) fictions, long regarded in Europe as classics, remain popular, and Stephen King's macabre thrillers remain best sellers.

The first decade of the twenty-first century witnessed a veritable epidemic of vampirism in teen literature. L. J. Smith's three-volume *Vampire Diaries* (1991) are based, according to the author, on her own nightmares. Cara Lockwood's Bard Academy books, with their intriguing, familiar titles—*Wuthering High* (2006), *The Scarlet Letterman* (2007), and *Moby Clique* (2008)—combine

mystery and family conflicts with ghostly elements. Darren Shan's *Vampire Blood Trilogy* (2003) mingles dark humor with graphic detail. His Demonata series introduces creepy country mansions haunted by violent demons, while his Cirque Du Freak series has been described as "teen gross-out fiction." By far the most popular specters are the romantic teen vampires of Stephenie Meyer's Twilight Saga (2005-2008).

MYSTERY AND WESTERNS

Young adults, like other readers, enjoy a good mystery. Arthur Conan Doyle, Agatha Christie, Ian Fleming, Sue Grafton, and Ruth Rendell are young adult favorites. Other mysteries have been written specifically for teens, with teen characters caught up in intrigue. Lois Duncan, Rosemary Wells, Patricia Window, Jay Bennett, and Joan Lowery Nixon are among the favorite writers of teen mysteries.

The Western, often called the American morality drama, with its courageous cowboy venturing forth to battle the forces of disorder, never goes out of fashion. Zane Gray, Louis L'Amour, and Walter Van Tilburg are important authors. Westerns written specifically for teenage readers include *The Man Who Killed the Deer* (1942), by Frank Waters, in which an American Indian youth must come to terms with two cultures, and *Walking Up a Rainbow* (1986), by Theodore Taylor, with its fourteen-year-old orphan hero setting out on a major adventure, driving sheep from Iowa to California.

SCIENCE FICTION AND FANTASY

Science fiction is less distinct in its target audience, and there is much cross-over appeal among different age groups. The classic science fiction writers—Jules Verne, H. G. Wells, Ray Bradbury, Arthur C. Clarke, Isaac Asimov, Robert A. Heinlein, Theodore Sturgeon—are well known to young readers. For young readers willing to tackle more complex styles, the novels of Philip K. Dick or Ursula K. Le Guin are challenging. Orson Scott Card arrived on the scene with his Ender series (1985-   ). Scott Westerfield's Uglies series (2005-   ) describes a future world in which each person, upon becoming sixteen years old, is subjected to compulsory surgery that transforms him or her into society's ideal of physical beauty. The uglies themselves are subversives who refuse beautification and retreat to Smoke, a distant settlement of conscientious objectors. Though of more appeal to boys than to girls, this series, which plays upon adolescent anxieties about appearance, is enjoyed by both genders.

Fantasy is a closely related genre, but unlike science fiction it does not have to establish authenticity through scientific extrapolation. Its readers are unapologetically projected into magical realms. The immensely popular Harry Potter stories (1997-   ), by J. K. Rowling, inventive and witty, are read by all ages, as are the classic fantasies of J. R. R. Tolkein and C. S. Lewis. Other fantasy writers read often by youths include Ann McCaffrey, Marion Zimmer Bradley, and Lloyd Alexander.

HISTORICAL ROMANCE

Historical novels at their best provide information as well as entertainment. Because they deal with the long ago and far away, they tend to romanticize. Sir Walter Scott and Alexandre Dumas, *père*, are often considered the first writers of historical fiction but are rarely read by modern teenagers. Their stories, however, are kept alive in films. Late twentieth century historical novels take special account of the narrower attention spans of young readers.

Rosemary Sutcliff has reconstructed early Great Britain in *The Eagle of the Ninth* (1954) and *The Shining Company* (1990). Patrick Raymond's *Daniel and Esther* (1989) and Bette Greene's *Summer of My German Soldier* (1973) are love stories set against a World War II background. No World War II era topic has attracted more attention in literature, youth or adult, than the Holocaust. *The Journey* (1990), by Ida Fink is an autobiographical novel about Jewish women hiding from the Gestapo. It is one outstanding example of the numerous young adult books about the Holocaust. Miriam Bat-Ami's *Two Suns in the Sky* (1999) is a story of forbidden love between a Roman Catholic American girl and a Jewish Croatian who meet in a refugee camp—in New York—for European Jews during the time of the Holocaust. Hans Peter Richter wrote three young adult novels about Nazi Germany and the Holocaust from the point of view of a German. Those novels are *Friedrich* (1961), *I Was There* (1962), and *The Time of the Young Soldiers* (1967).

Possibly the most distinguished American author of historical fiction for young adults has been Scott O'Dell, the winner of every major award in his field. In *The King's Fifth* (1966), sixteenth century Spaniards search for gold, while *Sing Down the Moon* (1970) tells the story of nineteenth century American Indian women suffering the advancement of white settlers. O'Dell's best-loved book remains *Island of the Blue Dolphins* (1960), a Robinson Crusoe-type narrative about a twelve-year-old girl unintentionally left behind on a Pacific island after the rest of her group is evacuated. It is a tale of survival under difficult physical and psychological conditions, of animal-human companionship, and of a lushly beautiful island.

HOT RODS, SPORTS, AND ADVENTURE

While much young adult fiction seems designed for female readers, there are many books that appeal chiefly to young males. The hot-rod and sports books produced in abundance since the 1940's have been largely formula driven, but other books are more substantial. Nelson A. Hutto's *Breakaway Back* (1963) is a serious novel about illegal sports recruitment in high school. Paul Zindel's *The Pigman* (1968) is a thoughtful exploration of interactions between young and old, while the novels of Robert Lipsyte and Robert Cormier always have important themes. Lipsyte, a professional sports writer, crafts sports fiction with special authority. In *The Contender* (1967) he introduces a young African American boxer, while *The Chief* (1993) features an American Indian heavyweight boxer. Cormier's *The Chocolate War*, set in a corrupt parochial school, and *We All Fall Down* (1991), a love story with "attitude," are admired for their stylistic skill as well as their powerful narratives.

SERIES BOOKS

Although the bane of teachers and librarians for decades, series books have been almost an addiction for many young people. Familiar characters following formula adventures to neat conclusions can be reassuring to unsteady or unsure readers. Harmless escapism or wish fulfillment are the chief offerings of these series, though a few add humor and occasional satirical wit.

The Stratemeyer Syndicate, with its large staple of writers, has been the most prolific supplier of series books for young adults. Among the heroes of the series, beginning early in the twentieth century, have been Tom Swift, the Bobbsey Twins, the Rover Boys, and the Hardy Boys. However, no series character has been more enduring than Nancy Drew, a girl detective, now as famous as Huckleberry Finn. Nancy Drew was created by Carolyn Keene and first appeared in 1930 in *The Secret of the Old Clock*. Nancy endured into the twenty-first century, as great-grandmothers shared fond memories of her with a new generation.

Nancy remains a liberated teenager, traveling to interesting places and meeting unusual people. Initially, she drove a roadster, carried a revolver, and was free of adult supervision. Her mother was deceased and her father was a distracted defense attorney. Though the early books contained ethnic stereotypes—chiefly of African Americans, Jews, and Eastern Europeans—later editions reflect a changed perspective. The early books were revised near the end of the twentieth century, reformed to educate as well as entertain. The books reference American Indian handicrafts, ecology, and the geography of the "exotic" places visited by Nancy. Also added to the Drew canon is a cookbook—though Nancy was never domestic—a handbook of detection, and an inspirational guide.

Other series proliferated throughout the 1940's, though none ever attained the popularity of the Nancy Drew books. Some attempted to combine mystery adventure with solid information about careers considered suitable for women. Helen Wells wrote both the Cherry Ames series and the Vicki Barr series. Betty Cavanna, writing as Betsy Allen, authored the Connie Blair series.

The series concept moved into the twenty-first century. Superficially, the later books appear more sophisticated and witty, though their plots still are predictable. They mirror—or wistfully project—an affluent youth culture in which designer clothes, neglectful parents, casual sex, drugs, and alcohol are the norm. Typical of the Clique series, so popular with young adult females, is *Bratfest at Tiffany's* (2008), by Lisi Harrison, a former senior director of programming at MTV. The Gossip Girl series (2002-   ), by Cecily von Ziegesar, is set in New York City's upper East Side, while Zoey Dean's A-List series (2003-   ) unfolds in the golden ghetto of Beverly Hills, California. The Princess Diaries series (2002-   ), by Meg Cabot, would seem to offer the ultimate in wish fulfillment for many American girls.

CENSORSHIP

The early, widespread conviction that books for youth should be didactic, or educational, as well as entertaining led to attempts to control their content. Well-meaning adults, often with little sensitivity to the aesthetics of literature and forgetting that adolescents are exposed to the seamier side of life every day, took exception to novels that would have attracted little notice if marketed for general adult readers.

Some books were condemned as racist or sexist while others were scorned for being too violent or for depicting sex. Novels about people with physical or psychological disabilities, too, often caused offense. The intent of an author or overall theme of a book would be ignored if even a single word was deemed inappropriate. In one extreme example, a novel as seemingly harmless as Walter Dumaux Edmonds's *Drums Along the Mohawk* (1936) was condemned in a Tennessee county because a parent found that the book included an expletive.

Established classics and books usually had some immunity to censorship, but not always. The most frequently banned book in schools had been Mark Twain's *Adventures of Huckleberry Finn* (1884), which many regard as the great American novel. Objections stemmed from Twain's use of substandard dialect and a misunderstanding of his satire, leading to charges of racism. In the 1960's, Twain's book was superseded in controversy by J. D. Salinger's *The Catcher in the Rye* (1951) despite this later novel's high moral direction and popularity with young readers. Its offense was a single obscenity, employed in realistic rather than salacious contexts. An awareness and understanding of the legal principle of a work's redeeming literary and social value has been slow to reach the general public, leading to much of the continuing controversy.

With the proliferation of books for all abilities and tastes, it was clear by the end of the twentieth century that young adult fiction was well established. Twayne's Young Adult Authors series published its first book in the 1980's, while the three volumes of the influential work *Writers for Young Adults* were published in 1997. Although competent reviewing existed for some time before these series began, these books helped to bring serious but accessible literary criticism to the field. With this development, it might be said that young adult literature truly came of age.

Allene Phy-Olsen

BIBLIOGRAPHY

Adamson, Lynda G. *World Historical Fiction: An Annotated Guide to Novels for Adults and Young Adults.* Phoenix, Ariz.: Oryx Press, 1998. Voluminous compilation on historical novels, with special attention to young adult literature. Includes annotations that are descriptive rather than evaluative.

Carlsen, G. Robert. *Books and the Teen-Age Reader: A Guide for Teachers, Librarians, and Parents.* 2d rev. ed. New York: Bantam Books, 1980. Dated but still a basic source. Carlsen identifies major features of young adult literature, discusses its appeal, and provides judicious recommendations.

Cyclopedia of Young Adult Authors. 3 vols. Pasadena, Calif.: Salem Press, 2005. Collection features more than two hundred authors whose works were written for or otherwise appeal to teenage and young adult readers. Each entry includes a description of the writer's impact on young adult literature, a brief biography, and discussion of the themes in his or her novels.

Donnelson, Kenneth L., and Alleen Pace Nilsen. *Literature for Today's Young Adults.* 7th ed. Boston: Pearson/Allyn & Bacon, 2005. A comprehensive single volume, frequently revised, covering the entire field of young adult fiction. Includes a brief history of the genre, discussions of popular culture and its relevance to the literature, and original essays by popular young adult authors.

Kies, Cosette N. *Presenting Young Adult Horror Fiction.* New York: Twayne, 1992. Kies understands the appeal of horror literature and distinguishes the quality works from the "lesser" novels. Volume in the distinguished Twayne series of critiques of young adult fiction.

Kutzer, M. Daphne, ed. *Writers of Multicultural Fiction for Young Adults: A Bio-Critical Sourcebook.* Westport, Conn.: Greenwood Press, 1996. Reference book on multicultural and multiethnic writers of fiction for teens and young adults. Entries include a biography, literary criticism of the writer's works, and a bibliography.

Mason, Bobbie Ann. *The Girl Sleuth.* New ed. Athens: University of Georgia Press, 1997. Informative book by one of America's leading fiction writers. Mason not only recalls her early love for Nancy Drew and other series books but also sheds light on the appeal of these books for young people. Includes a new preface.

Reid, Suzanne Elizabeth. *Presenting Young Adult Science Fiction.* New York: Twayne, 1998. Reid identifies some of the best science fiction written for young people or those works readily accessible to them. Another important volume in the Twayne critical series.

RESOURCES

BIBLIOGRAPHY

ORGANIZATION

This bibliography is divided into five sections. The first section lists books that either cover broad topics from a variety of critical perspectives or trace the historical development of world literature in a variety of languages. The remaining four sections are broadly divided by geographic region and list readings that examine African, Asian, Latin American, and Middle-Eastern long fiction; European long fiction, including Russian; American long fiction; and British long fiction, including English, Irish, Scottish, Australian, and Canadian.

SELECTION

Every effort has been made to include studies published in 2000 and later. Most items in this bibliography contain a listing of secondary sources, making it easier to identify other critical commentary on novelists, movements, and themes.

THEORETICAL, THEMATIC, AND HISTORICAL STUDIES

Altman, Janet Gurkin. *Epistolarity: Approaches to a Form.* Columbus: Ohio State University Press, 1982. Examines the epistolary novel, explaining how novelists use the letter form to develop characterization, further their plots, and develop meaning.

Beaumont, Matthew, ed. *Adventures in Realism.* Malden, Mass.: Blackwell, 2007. Fifteen essays explore facets of realism, which was critical to the development of the novel. Provides a theoretical framework for understanding how novelists attempt to represent the real and the common in fiction.

Brink, André. *The Novel: Language and Narrative from Cervantes to Calvino.* New York: New York University Press, 1998. Uses contemporary theories of semiotics and narratology to establish a continuum between early novelists and those of the postmodern era in their conscious use of language to achieve certain effects. Ranges across national boundaries to illustrate the theory of the development of the novel since the seventeenth century.

Brownstein, Rachel. *Becoming a Heroine: Reading About Women in Novels.* New York: Viking Press, 1982. Feminist survey of novels from the eighteenth century through the latter half of the twentieth century. Examines how "becoming a heroine" defines for women a sense of value in their lives. Considers novels by both men and women, and discusses the importance of the traditional marriage plot.

Bruzelius, Margaret. *Romancing the Novel: Adventure from Scott to Sebald.* Lewisburg, Pa.: Bucknell University Press, 2007. Examines the development of the adventure novel, linking it with the medieval romance tradition and exploring readers' continuing fascination with the genre.

Cavallaro, Dani. *The Gothic Vision: Three Centuries of Horror, Terror, and Fear.* New York: Continuum, 2005. Study of the gothic novel from its earliest manifestations in the eighteenth century to the early twenty-first century. Through the lenses of contemporary cultural theories, examines readers' fascination with novels that invoke horror, terror, and fright.

Doody, Margaret Anne. *The True Story of the Novel.* New Brunswick, N.J.: Rutgers University Press, 1996. Traces the roots of the novel, traditionally thought to have been developed in the seventeenth century, to classical Greek and Latin texts that exhibit characteristics of modern fiction.

Hale, Dorothy J., ed. *The Novel: An Anthology of Criticism and Theory, 1900-2000.* Malden, Mass.: Blackwell, 2006. Collection of essays by theorists and novelists. Includes commentary on the novel form from the perspective of formalism, structuralism, post-structuralism, Marxism, and reader response theory. Essays also address the novel through the lenses of sociology, gender studies, and feminist theory.

_____. *Social Formalism: The Novel in Theory from Henry James to the Present*. Stanford, Calif.: Stanford University Press, 1998. Emphasizes the novel's special ability to define a social world for readers. Relies heavily on the works of contemporary literary and cultural theorists. Provides a summary of twentieth century efforts to identify a theory of fiction that encompasses novels of many kinds.

Hart, Stephen M., and Wen-chin Ouyang, eds. *A Companion to Magical Realism*. London: Tamesis, 2005. Essays outlining the development of Magical Realism, tracing its roots from Europe through Latin America to other regions of the world. Explores the political dimensions of the genre.

Hoffman, Michael J., and Patrick D. Murphy, eds. *Essentials of the Theory of Fiction*. 2d ed. Durham, N.C.: Duke University Press, 1996. Collection of essays by influential critics from the late nineteenth century through the twentieth century. Focuses on the essential elements of fiction and the novel's relationship to the world it depicts.

Lodge, David. *The Art of Fiction: Illustrated from Classic and Modern Texts*. New York: Viking Press, 1993. Short commentaries on the technical aspects of fiction. Examples from important and minor novelists illustrate literary principles and techniques such as point of view, suspense, character introduction, irony, motivation, and ending.

Lynch, Deirdre, and William B. Walker, eds. *Cultural Institutions of the Novel*. Durham, N.C.: Duke University Press, 1996. Fifteen essays examine aspects of long fiction produced around the world. Encourages a redefinition of the genre and argues for inclusion of texts not historically considered novels.

Moretti, Franco, ed. *The Novel*. 2 vols. Princeton, N.J.: Princeton University Press, 2006. Compendium exploring the novel from multiple perspectives, including as an anthropological, historical, and sociological document; a function of the national tradition from which it emerges; and a work of art subject to examination using various critical approaches.

Priestman, Martin, ed. *The Cambridge Companion to Crime Fiction*. New York: Cambridge University Press, 2003. Essays examine the nature and development of the genre, explore works by writers (including women and ethnic minorities) from several countries, and establish links between crime fiction and other literary genres. Includes a chronology.

Scaggs, John. *Crime Fiction*. New York: Routledge, 2005. Provides a history of crime fiction, explores key subgenres, and identifies recurring themes that suggest the wider social and historical context in which these works are written. Suggests critical approaches that open crime fiction to serious study.

Shiach, Morag, ed. *The Cambridge Companion to the Modernist Novel*. New York: Cambridge University Press, 2007. Essays explaining the concept of modernism and its influence on the novel. Detailed examination of works by writers from various countries, all influenced by the modernist movement. Includes a detailed chronology.

Vice, Sue. *Holocaust Fiction*. New York: Routledge, 2000. Examines controversies generated by novels about the Holocaust. Focuses on eight important works, but also offers observations on the polemics surrounding publication of books on this topic.

Zunshine, Lisa. *Why We Read Fiction: Theory of Mind and the Novel*. Columbus: Ohio State University Press, 2006. Applies theories of cognitive psychology to novel reading, explaining how experience and human nature lead readers to constrain their interpretations of a given text. Provides numerous examples from well-known novels to illustrate how and why readers find pleasure in fiction.

BRITISH FICTION (INCLUDING AUSTRALIAN, CANADIAN, SCOTTISH, AND IRISH FICTION)

Ahern, Stephen. *Affected Sensibilities: Romantic Excess and the Genealogy of the Novel, 1680-1810*. New York: AMS Press, 2007. Explores the rise and rapid demise of various forms of fiction that feature excessive sensibility. Considers amatory fiction, sentimental fiction, and gothic narratives produced during the eighteenth century.

Crowe, Marian E. *Aiming at Heaven, Getting the Earth: The English Catholic Novel Today*. Lanham, Md.: Rowman & Littlefield, 2007. Surveys works of four twentieth century Catholic novelists. Introductory chapters provide detailed examination of the theory of the English Catholic novel, its history, and practices current in the last half of the twentieth century.

Damrosch, Leopold, Jr., ed. *Modern Essays on Eighteenth-Century Literature*. New York: Oxford University Press, 1988. Overview of critical commentary on important eighteenth century figures and literary works. Selections represent critical approaches popular during the 1970's and 1980's.

David, Deirdre, ed. *The Cambridge Companion to the Victorian Novel*. New York: Cambridge University Press, 2001. Eleven essays offer thematic analyses of issues important for understanding Victorian fiction. Discusses Victorian publishing practices and examines issues of gender, sexuality, race, aesthetics, religion, and science.

Eagleton, Terry. *The English Novel: An Introduction*. Malden, Mass.: Blackwell, 2005. Surveys English fiction by concentrating on the work of major authors. Considers novels from various theoretical perspectives, giving primacy to Marxist readings that stress the historical and sociological aspects of fiction.

ECW's Biographical Guide to Canadian Novelists. Oakville, Ont.: ECW Press, 1993. Brief sketches of the careers of forty-nine Canadian novelists, providing information on major works and principal literary interests.

James, Louis. *The Victorian Novel*. Malden, Mass.: Blackwell, 2006. Overview of the historical and social context in which Victorian novels were written. Also examines this fiction in relationship to historical, religious, and biographical works produced contemporaneously. Includes a chronology.

Kenyon, Olga. *Women Novelists Today: A Survey of English Writing in the Seventies and Eighties*. New York: St. Martin's Press, 1988. Extensive critical commentary on six important English women novelists. Introductory chapter examines the effect of the feminist movement on women novelists and reviews the importance of techniques such as realism in English fiction.

Levine, George. *The Realistic Imagination: English Fiction from Frankenstein to Lady Chatterley*. Chicago: University of Chicago Press, 1981. Examines the concept of realism and its application in important nineteenth century novels. Provides an overview of the development of fiction during this period.

McKeon, Michael. *The Origins of the English Novel, 1600-1740*. New ed. Baltimore: Johns Hopkins University Press, 2001. Theoretically based assessment of the cultural, political, and philosophical conditions in England that gave rise to the novel in the eighteenth century. Considers a number of important precursors to novelists Samuel Richardson and Henry Fielding.

MacLulich, Thomas D. *Between Europe and America: The Canadian Tradition in Fiction*. Toronto, Ont.: ECW Press, 1988. Explores the sources of Canadian fiction to identify its unique characteristics. Traces the development of that lineage from the nineteenth century through the twentieth century.

Nolan, Emer. *Catholic Emancipations: Irish Fiction from Thomas Moore to James Joyce*. Syracuse, N.Y.: Syracuse University Press, 2007. Traces the development of the Irish novel from 1820 into the twentieth century, concentrating on the influence of Catholicism on the production of fiction.

Norton, Rictor, ed. *Gothic Readings: The First Wave, 1764-1840*. London: Leicester University Press, 2000. Sketches the careers of important Gothic novelists, provides samples from their works, and discusses the development of the genre. Includes commentary on Gothic fiction from eighteenth and nineteenth century critics and readers.

O'Gorman, Francis, ed. *The Victorian Novel*. Malden, Mass.: Blackwell, 2002. Excerpts from dozens of influential twentieth century studies of Victorian fiction. Organized thematically; includes materials on formalist approaches, feminist readings, issues involving realism, historical approaches to fiction, postcolonial readings, discussions focusing on language and form, the impact of science on the novel, and the importance of publication practices.

Parrinder, Patrick. *Nation and Novel: The English Novel from Its Origins to the Present Day*. New York: Oxford University Press, 2006. Historical account of English fiction as a representation of the concept of nationhood and character. Organized chronologically. Includes significant critical commentary on important novels and novelists. Heavily reliant on theoretical studies of fiction and culture.

Peters, Joan Douglas. *Feminist Metafiction and the Evolution of the British Novel*. Gainesville: University Press of Florida, 2002. Uses feminist theory to reexamine the development of English fiction, demonstrating the key role women writers played in shaping the genre. Also discusses novels written by men that feature female protagonists.

Powell, Kersi Tarien. *Irish Fiction: An Introduction*. New York: Continuum, 2004. Handbook designed to introduce readers to Irish fiction. Explores themes common among most Irish writers and examines key novels that have shaped the genre.

Pykett, Lyn, ed. *Reading Fin de Siècle Fictions*. London: Longman, 1996. Twelve essays on writers who flourished between 1880 and 1910, applying contemporary critical theories to analyze individual works. Attempts to explore changes that transformed the novel during this period in English literary history.

Reed, Walter L. *An Exemplary History of the Novel: The Quixotic Versus the Picaresque*. Chicago: University of Chicago Press, 1981. Systematic study of the novel that examines its unique qualities and contrasts it with older forms of discourse. Offers close readings of several texts, explaining how the English novel fits within the larger developments in European fiction.

Richetti, John, ed. *The Cambridge Companion to the Eighteenth Century Novel*. New York: Cambridge University Press, 1996. Focuses on the cultural and historical context in which the novel developed. Chapters explore the work of major figures, the role of women writers, and the rise of gothic fiction.

_____, et al., eds. *The Columbia History of the British Novel*. New York: Columbia University Press, 1994. Collection of essays tracing the development of English fiction from the seventeenth century through the twentieth century. Explores important recurring themes and also writers not normally identified as the most notable. Contains brief biographies of one hundred novelists.

Ter Horst, Robert. *The Fortunes of the Novel: A Study in the Transposition of a Genre*. New York: Peter Lang, 2003. Reviews the rise of the English novel from its roots in early Spanish prose fiction, especially the work of Miguel de Cervantes, through the novels of Daniel Defoe, Sir Walter Scott, and Charles Dickens.

Focuses on the preoccupation of novelists with economic issues, broadly defined.

Van Sant, Ann Jessie. *Eighteenth-Century Sensibility and the Novel*. New York: Cambridge University Press, 1993. Thematic analysis of eighteenth century fiction, focusing on the concept of sensibility and the use of the sensual (both visual and tactile) as a technique in novels.

Willmott, Glenn. *Unreal Country: Modernity in the Canadian Novel in English*. Montreal: McGill-Queen's University Press, 2002. Attempts to identify the critical and cultural dimensions of a specifically Canadian literature. Relies on theories of modernism for establishing the theoretical framework in which individual novels are examined.

AMERICAN FICTION

Abernathy, Jeff. *To Hell and Back: Race and Betrayal in the Southern Novel*. Athens: University of Georgia Press, 2003. Examines novels of Mark Twain and several twentieth century Southern writers to determine how the pattern of friendship and betrayal has helped illuminate one of the most important dichotomies of American culture: the proclamation of democracy and trends supporting racial hierarchies.

Adamson, Lynda G. *Thematic Guide to the American Novel*. Westport, Conn.: Greenwood Press, 2002. Discusses important themes that recur in the American novel. Covers alienation, death, family, immigrant life, nature, multiracial offspring, and the search for identity. Examples from novels of all literary periods reveal the literary concern with these themes.

Alsen, Eberhard, ed. *The New Romanticism: A Collection of Critical Essays*. New York: Garland, 2000. Essays by novelists and critics explain the rise, since 1950, in romanticism in fiction as a resurgence transformed by novelists of the twentieth century. Brief readings of several nineteenth century novels to illustrate the scope of this change.

Anderson, Patrick. *The Triumph of the Thriller*. New York: Random House, 2007. Briefly traces the history of the thriller, a genre of American fiction that has achieved significant status among readers at the end of the twentieth century. Analyzes thrillers to explain why they have captured such a large reading audience.

Bell, Bernard W. *The Contemporary African American Novel: Its Folk Roots and Modern Literary Branches.* Amherst: University of Massachusetts Press, 2004. Extensive historical examination of the development of African American fiction, focusing on distinctive elements and outlining the role of political and social influences in changing the focus of African American novels.

Bell, Michael Davitt. *The Problem of American Realism: Studies in the Cultural History of a Literary Idea.* Chicago: University of Chicago Press, 1996. Examines how the concept of realism affected the production of novels in the late nineteenth and early twentieth centuries. Explains how works by important figures normally considered realists exhibit literary qualities that make it difficult to establish a monolithic definition of "American realism."

Bertens, Hans, and Theo d'Haen. *Contemporary American Crime Fiction.* New York: Palgrave, 2001. Surveys the work of crime and detective writers of the 1990's. Discusses ethnic crime literature, police procedurals, private detectives, and American fiction exploring other countries and historical periods. Special focus on the writing of women and people of color.

Budick, Emily Miller. *Nineteenth-Century American Romance: Genre and the Construction of Democratic Culture.* New York: Twayne, 1996. Surveys the development of the romance in America during the nineteenth century in light of new theoretical perspectives on the nature of romance narratives. Includes a lengthy bibliographical essay outlining the history of criticism of the American romance tradition.

Caulfield, Carlota, and Darién J. Davis, eds. *A Companion to U.S. Latino Literatures.* Woodbridge, England: Tamesis, 2007. Describes the achievements of Latino writers in the United States and the Caribbean region, notably Puerto Rico and the Dominican Republic. Includes commentary on native-born Latino writers and on immigrants from Latin America to the United States.

Cheyfitz, Eric, ed. *The Columbia Guide to American Indian Literatures of the United States Since 1945.* New York: Columbia University Press, 2006. Explores the emergence of fiction of Native Americans struggling against U.S. government oppression and sociocultural discrimination. Concentrates on works expressing resistance to oppressive actions and attitudes.

Clontz, Ted L. *Wilderness City: The Post World War II American Urban Novel from Algren to Wideman.* New York: Routledge, 2005. Examines the literary aesthetics underlying the representation of the urban environment in America since the end of World War II. Special focus on the use of "space" to create both scene and atmosphere in these works.

Cornis-Pope, Marcel. *Narrative Innovation and Cultural Rewriting in the Cold War and After.* New York: Palgrave, 2001. Systematic study of novels from the latter half of the twentieth century, considering how writers respond to the polarized political atmosphere of the time. Concentrates on American novelists, considering their work in the context of postmodern theories regarding the practice of writing.

Dineen, Patrick J., and Joseph Romance, eds. *Democracy's Literature: Politics and Fiction in America.* Lanham, Md.: Rowman & Littlefield, 2005. Essays on significant novels of the nineteenth and twentieth centuries outlining the political nature of American writing and the profound philosophical underpinnings of the best American literature.

Elliot, Emory, et al., eds. *The Columbia History of the American Novel.* New York: Columbia University Press, 1991. Explores the rise and development of American fiction, its recurrent themes, and its aesthetic principles. Discusses book production and publishing's impact on society. Includes essays on race, gender, and regional novels.

Hume, Kathryn. *American Dream, American Nightmare: Fiction Since 1960.* Urbana: University of Illinois Press, 2000. Surveys one hundred novels written between 1960 and 2000 that critique the idea of the American Dream and the failure of the nation to provide opportunities for happiness and prosperity to all of its citizens.

Karl, Frederick R. *American Fictions, 1980-2000: Whose America Is It Anyway?* Philadelphia: Xlibris, 2001. Surveys three decades of American fiction, organized thematically. Explores a wide range of topics.

American fiction from the World War II era to 1980 is covered in Karl's *American Fictions, 1940-1980* (Harper & Row, 1983).

Nelson, Emmanuel S., ed. *Asian American Novelists: A Bio-Bibliographical Critical Sourcebook*. Westport, Conn.: Greenwood Press, 2000. Brief biographical sketches and critical commentary on seventy Asian American novelists, including brief discussions of major works. Organized alphabetically.

Shatsky, Joel, and Michael Taub, eds. *Contemporary Jewish-American Novelists: A Bio-Bibliographical Critical Sourcebook*. Westport, Conn.: Greenwood Press, 1997. Reference guide outlining the careers and accomplishments of more than sixty Jewish American writers, most of whom wrote during the decades following World War II.

Thrailkill, Jane F. *Affecting Fictions: Mind, Body, and Emotion in American Literary Realism*. Cambridge, Mass.: Harvard University Press, 2007. Applies contemporary critical theories to a new reading of American novels written in the late nineteenth and early twentieth centuries. Stresses the importance of emotion and perception in creating pleasure for readers.

Tracey, Karen. *Plots and Proposals: American Women's Fiction, 1850-90*. Urbana: University of Illinois Press, 2000. Analyzes American women's novels of the late nineteenth century, arguing that they employ the double-proposal plot as a means of social critique.

Walter, James Frank. *Reading Marriage in the American Romance: Remembering Love as Destiny*. Plymouth, England: Lexington Books, 2008. Examines American romance from the work of Nathaniel Hawthorne through the late twentieth century. Explains the importance of marriage in determining the actions of characters caught up in complex social situations.

Weyler, Karen A. *Intricate Relations: Sexual and Economic Desire in American Fiction, 1789-1814*. Iowa City: University of Iowa Press, 2004. Examines novels of the early years of the American republic by concentrating on two significant literary topics: sexual desire and material desire.

Whelehan, Imelda. *The Feminist Bestseller: From "Sex and the Single Girl" to "Sex and the City."* New York: Palgrave Macmillan, 2005. Analyzes popular women's literature of the second half of the twentieth century. Explains how these works are in dialogue with contemporary feminist ideas.

EUROPEAN FICTION (INCLUDING RUSSIAN)

Baranski, Zygmunt G., and Lino Pertile, eds. *The New Italian Novel*. Reprint. Toronto, Ont: University of Toronto Press, 1997. Study of the "new" Italian novel from the last half of the twentieth century. Includes a brief history of the development of the new Italian novel.

Bartram, Graham, ed. *The Cambridge Companion to the Modern German Novel*. New York: Cambridge University Press, 2004. Combines broad historical discussions of trends in the development of fiction in Germany since 1890 with close textual analyses of key novels. Explores the influence of realism and modernism on German fiction, and traces the German novel's roots to its nineteenth century forebears, especially the bildungsroman.

Bondanella, Peter, and Andrea Ciccarelli, eds. *The Cambridge Companion to the Italian Novel*. New York: Cambridge University Press, 2003. Describes the development of the Italian novel from the seventeenth century through the twentieth century. Explores major themes common among Italian novelists and discusses works by several important writers.

Brown, Deming. *The Last Years of Soviet Russian Literature: Prose Fiction, 1975-1991*. New York: Cambridge University Press, 1993. Explores trends in Soviet Russian fiction during the final years of the Soviet Union. Also examines changes in publication practices that allowed for the rehabilitation of some dissident writers. Considers work by established writers and those who emerged on the literary scene during this period.

Clark, Katerina. *The Soviet Novel: History as Ritual*. 3d ed. Bloomington: Indiana University Press, 2000. Critical analysis of Soviet fiction by writers who followed the dictates of Socialist Realism, the only approved form of literature in the Soviet Union. Examines elements of this form of fiction and explains how the genre was intended to support larger political aims.

Emmel, Hildegard. *History of the German Novel*. Translated by Ellen Summerfield. Detroit, Mich.: Wayne State University Press, 1989. Abridged English-language version of a three-volume study organized around a number of key works defining the development of German fiction. Includes discussion of the relationship of the German novel to novels in English, Russian, and French.

Freeborn, Richard. *The Russian Revolutionary Novel: Turgenev to Pasternak*. New York: Cambridge University Press, 1982. Describes the phenomenon of the revolutionary novel and examines elements of the genre in a number of representative works. Stresses the importance of these novels in documenting imperialist rule and the totalitarian Communist state.

Gasperetti, David. *The Rise of the Russian Novel: Carnival, Stylization, and Mockery of the West*. DeKalb: Northern Illinois University Press, 1998. Study of eighteenth century Russian novels often ignored by literary historians. Explains how issues addressed in these works, and techniques developed by their authors, were important in shaping the great Russian novels of the nineteenth century.

Gillespie, David. *The Twentieth-Century Russian Novel: An Introduction*. Washington, D.C.: Berg, 1996. Study of characteristics of selected novels that illustrate the political situation in the Soviet Union during the seven decades of Communist Party rule. Provides brief plot summaries and critical discussions of key texts; also focuses on the fate of writers during this period.

Kohl, Katrin, and Ritchie Robertson, eds. *A History of Austrian Literature, 1918-2000*. Rochester, N.Y.: Camden House, 2006. Separate chapters survey the development of Austrian fiction to 1945, and from the end of World War II to 2000. Includes essays on the publishing industry in Austria and on Austrian writers' responses to the Holocaust.

Landeira, Ricardo. *The Modern Spanish Novel, 1898-1936*. Boston: Twayne, 1985. Surveys works by authors writing between the Spanish American War and the Spanish Civil War. Analyzes themes and techniques that make these works modern.

Merry, Bruce. *Encyclopedia of Modern Greek Literature*. Westport, Conn.: Greenwood Press, 2004. Brief synopses detailing the lives of Greek writers, significant works of Greek literature, and common topics and themes. Organized alphabetically.

Midgley, David, ed. *The German Novel in the Twentieth Century: Beyond Realism*. Edinburgh, Scotland: Edinburgh University Press, 1993. Traces the development of German fiction in the twentieth century. Focuses on the influence of narrative techniques in shaping the structure and themes of novels. Explains how certain novels relate historically.

Minden, Michael. *The German Bildungsroman*. New York: Cambridge University Press, 1997. Examines the development of the German bildungsroman during the nineteenth century, culminating in a discussion of significant works from the early twentieth century.

Motte, Warren. *Fables of the Novel: French Fiction Since 1990*. Chicago: Dalkey Archive Press, 2003. Searches for common themes in French literature and elucidates techniques shared by late-twentieth-century novelists who are not necessarily part of mainstream French fiction.

Prince, Gerald. *Narrative as Theme: Studies in French Fiction*. Lincoln: University of Nebraska Press, 1992. Examines representative examples of French fiction of the eighteenth, nineteenth, and twentieth centuries, focusing on how writers use narrative to establish truths in their works.

Rossel, Sven H. *A History of Scandinavian Literature, 1870-1980*. Translated by Anne C. Ulmer. Minneapolis: University of Minnesota Press, 1982. Surveys the work of Swedish, Norwegian, Danish, Faroese, and Icelandic writers. Explores the impact of modernism on literature in Scandinavian countries.

Samuels, Maurice. *The Spectacular Past: Popular History and the Novel in Nineteenth-Century France*. Ithaca, N.Y.: Cornell University Press, 2004. Examines the relationship between history and literature during a period when realism dominated fiction writing. Considers work by major French novelists of the nineteenth century and the influence of Sir Walter Scott's historical novels on French fiction.

Segel, Harold B. *The Columbia Guide to the Literatures of Eastern Europe Since 1945*. New York: Columbia University Press, 2003. Provides brief biographical sketches and a list of works for hundreds of writers from Eastern Europe. Introductory essay outlines the influence of politics on postwar literary production.

Turner, Harriet, and Adelaida López de Martínez, eds. *The Cambridge Companion to the Spanish Novel from 1600 to the Present*. New York: Cambridge University Press, 2003. Explores the development of the Spanish novel since the early seventeenth century. Focus on the characteristics of the novel's evolving form. Includes discussion of the regional novel, women writers, and the relationship between film and literature.

Ungurianu, Dan. *Plotting History: The Russian Historical Novel in the Imperial Age*. Madison: University of Wisconsin Press, 2007. Theoretically based analysis of a genre popular during the nineteenth century. Explains how novelists use history as the basis of their fiction, and why Russian readers were attracted to this form. Includes a chronology of historical novels published in Russia between 1829 and 1917.

Unwin, Timothy. *The Cambridge Companion to the French Novel from 1800 to the Present*. New York: Cambridge University Press, 1997. Examines the evolution of the French novel from the early nineteenth century to the late twentieth century. Emphasizes major changes introduced by modernism, World Wars I and II, and the postcolonial period.

AFRICAN, ASIAN, LATIN AMERICAN, AND MIDDLE-EASTERN FICTION

Allen, Roger. *The Arabic Novel: An Historical and Critical Introduction*. 2d ed. Syracuse, N.Y.: Syracuse University Press, 1995. Traces the growth of the Arabic novel from its roots in the nineteenth century. Includes a chapter on principal themes treated by Arab novelists, and examines twelve representative texts.

Booker, M. Keith. *The African Novel in English: An Introduction*. Portsmouth, N.H.: Heinemann, 1998. Provides background for understanding the African novel and an essay on its development. Critiques eight significant twentieth century African novels published in English.

Caiani, Fabio. *Contemporary Arab Fiction: Innovation from Rama to Yalu*. New York: Routledge, 2007.

Traces developments in fiction in the Arab-speaking world since 1979. Offers close textual analyses of representative novels to demonstrate the literary quality of work from the Middle East.

Hart, Stephen M. *A Companion to Spanish-American Literature*. London: Tamesis, 1999. Surveys the development of the novel in Latin America over five centuries, concentrating on nineteenth and twentieth century literature.

Heywood, Christopher. *A History of South African Literature*. New York: Cambridge University Press, 2004. Chapters on fiction trace the development of the novel as a product of the international, intercultural, and interracial climates in South Africa.

Hsia, C. T. *A History of Modern Chinese Fiction*. 3d ed. Bloomington: Indiana University Press, 1999. Analysis of Chinese fiction from 1917 to the end of the twentieth century. Examines the Chinese Communist Party's influence on the production of literature after 1949 and on the careers of writers. Also discusses the role of literature as a vehicle for political dissent.

Joshi, Priya. *In Another Country: Colonialism, Culture, and the English Novel in India*. New York: Columbia University Press, 2002. Applies contemporary theories of postcolonialism and political economy to a study of novels from the nineteenth through twentieth centuries. Also examines the influence of novels on readers in India and abroad.

Julien, Eileen. *African Novels and the Question of Orality*. Bloomington: Indiana University Press, 1992. Examines the influence of oral traditions on the production of novels in Africa. Using contemporary critical theory, explains the development of the genre and analyzes the way aesthetic, cultural, and social needs influence writers.

Keene, Donald. *Dawn to the West: Japanese Literature of the Modern Era—Fiction*. New York: Columbia University Press, 1998. Detailed commentary by a well-known scholar on the growth of Japanese fiction since the middle of the nineteenth century. Individual chapters feature major writers, discuss important advances in technique, and highlight key thematic issues. Volume three in the History of Japanese Literature series.

Kristal, Efrain, ed. *The Cambridge Companion to the Latin American Novel*. New York: Cambridge University Press, 2005. Outlines the development of the novel in Latin America during the nineteenth and twentieth centuries. Surveys characteristics of fiction from key regions in Latin America, and examines gender and sexuality. Analyzes six representative novels.

Mehrotra, A. K., ed. *A History of Indian Literature in English*. New York: Columbia University Press, 2003. Includes several essays that trace the growth of the Indian novel from its beginnings through the late twentieth century.

Mintz, Alan, ed. *The Boom in Contemporary Israeli Fiction*. Hanover, N.H.: Brandeis University Press, 1997. Collection of essays exploring Israeli fiction since the mid-1970's. Contributors examine how trends in publishing have given rise to new forms of fiction and new readership. Also discusses gender politics, the literature of minorities, the place of Magical Realism in Israeli fiction, and fictional depictions of the Holocaust.

Owomoyela, Oyekan. *A History of Twentieth-Century African Literatures*. Lincoln: University of Nebraska Press, 1993. Collection of essays examining fiction written in both English and French in countries throughout Africa. Traces the roots of written fiction to the oral traditions that existed across Africa for centuries.

Richie, Donald. *Japanese Literature Reviewed*. New York: ICG Muse, 2003. Brief essays on dozens of Japanese writers, organized chronologically. Discussions of novelists usually include brief plot summary and commentary on themes and techniques.

Wang, David Der-Wei. *The Monster That Is History: History, Violence, and Fictional Writing in Twentieth-Century China*. Berkeley: University of California Press, 2004. Interdisciplinary study tracing attempts by writers in China to deal with violent historical events, both on a personal and national scale. Explains how history has helped shape the direction of Chinese fiction, especially during the years of Communist rule.

Williams, Raymond Leslie, ed. *The Novel in the Americas*. Niwot: University Press of Colorado, 1992. Collection of essays highlighting the work of Latin American novelists. Contributors concentrate on the role of the imagination and on the influence of modernism and postmodernism on the production of Latin American fiction.

Laurence W. Mazzeno

GUIDE TO ONLINE RESOURCES

WEB SITES

The following sites were visited by the editors of Salem Press in 2009. Because URLs frequently change, the accuracy of these addresses cannot be guaranteed; however, long-standing sites, such as those of colleges and universities, national organizations, and government agencies, generally maintain links when sites are moved or updated.

African Literature and Writers on the Internet
http://www-sul.stanford.edu/depts/ssrg/africa/lit.html

This page is included in the Africa South of the Sahara site created by Karen Fung of Stanford University. It provides an alphabetical list of links to numerous resources about such African writers as Wole Soyinka and Chinua Achebe, online journals and essays, association Web sites, and other materials. Another page offers links to South African literature, including information about J. M. Coetzee, Nadine Gordimer, and other writers.

American Literature on the Web
http://www.nagasaki-gaigo.ac.jp/ishikawa/amlit

Among this site's features are several pages providing links to Web sites about specific genres and literary movements, southern and southwestern American literature, minority literature, literary theory, and women writers, as well as an extensive index of links to electronic text collections and archives. Users also can access information for five specific time periods: 1620-1820, 1820-1865, 1865-1914, 1914-1945, and since 1945. A range of information is available for each period, including alphabetical lists of authors that link to more specific information about each writer, time lines of historical and literary events, and links to related additional Web sites.

Australian Literature
http://www.middlemiss.org/lit/lit.html

Perry Middlemiss, a Melbourne-based blogger, created this useful resource about Australian writers and their works. It features an alphabetical list of authors that links to biographies and lists of their works; for some of the listed works, links to synopses and excerpts are provided. Peter Carey, Richard Flanagan, and Christina Stead are among the writers listed. The site also contains information about Australian literary awards.

Books and Writers
http://www.kirjasto.sci.fi/indeksi.htm

This broad, comprehensive, and easy-to-use resource provides access to information about hundreds of authors throughout the world, extending from 70 B.C.E to the twenty-first century. Links take users from an alphabetical list of authors to pages featuring biographical material, lists of works, and recommendations for further reading about individual authors; each writer's page also includes links to related pages on the site. Although brief, the biographical essays provide solid overviews of the authors' careers, their contributions to literature, and their literary influences.

The Cambridge History of English and American Literature: An Encyclopedia in Eighteen Volumes
http://www.bartleby.com/cambridge/index.html

This site provides an exhaustive examination of the development of all forms of literature in Great Britain and the United States, including novels. Volume 10, *The Rise of the Novel: Johnson and His Circle*, features information on the English novels of Samuel Richardson, Henry Fielding, Laurence Sterne, and Tobias Smollett; English novels from the Georgian, Romantic, and Victorian eras are covered in volumes 11 through 14. Volumes 15 through 18 focus on American literature, discussing writing from the early colonial period through the late nineteenth century, including the work of Mark Twain, William Dean Howells, and Henry James.

The Canadian Literature Archive
http://www.umanitoba.ca/canlit

Created and maintained by the English Department at the University of Manitoba, this site is a comprehensive collection of materials for and about Canadian writers. It includes an alphabetical listing of authors with links to additional Web-based information. Users also can retrieve electronic texts, announcements of literary events, and videocasts of author interviews and readings.

A Celebration of Women Writers

http://digital.library.upenn.edu/women

This site presents an extensive compendium of information about the contributions of women writers throughout history. The "Local Editions by Authors" and "Local Editions by Category" pages include access to electronic texts of the works of numerous writers, including Louisa May Alcott, Djuna Barnes, Grazia Deledda, Edith Wharton, and Virginia Woolf. Users can also access biographical and bibliographical information by browsing lists arranged by writers' names, countries of origin, ethnicities, and the centuries in which they lived.

Contemporary Writers

http://www.contemporarywriters.com/authors

Created by the British Council, this site offers "up-to-date profiles of some of the U.K. and Commonwealth's most important living writers (plus writers from the Republic of Ireland that we've worked with)." The available information includes biographies, bibliographies, critical reviews, news about literary prizes, and photographs. Users can search the site by author, genre, nationality, gender, publisher, book title, date of publication, and prize name and date.

Internet Public Library: Native American Authors

http://www.ipl.org/div/natam

Internet Public Library, a Web-based collection of materials, includes this index to resources about writers of Native American heritage. An alphabetical list of authors enables users to link to biographies, lists of works, electronic texts, tribal Web sites, and other online resources. The majority of the writers covered are contemporary Indian authors, but some historical authors also are featured. Users also can retrieve information by browsing lists of titles and tribes. In addition, the site contains a bibliography of print and online materials about Native American literature.

The Literary Gothic

http://www.litgothic.com/index_html.html

This site describes itself as a guide to "all things concerned with literary Gothicism," with the majority of its resources related to literary works written and published from 1764 through 1820. The site defines "gothic literature" in broad terms and includes some authors usually not associated with the genre, such as Louisa May Alcott and Honoré de Balzac. An alphabetical list of authors provides links to biographies and other Web-based resources. The "Titles" page enables users to retrieve electronic versions of numerous works of gothic literature.

LiteraryHistory.com

http://www.literaryhistory.com

This site is an excellent source of academic, scholarly, and critical literature about eighteenth, nineteenth, and twentieth century American and English writers. It provides numerous pages about specific eras and genres, including individual pages for eighteenth, nineteenth, and twentieth century literature and for African American and postcolonial literature. These pages contain alphabetical lists of authors that link to articles, reviews, overviews, excerpts of works, teaching guides, podcast interviews, and other materials. The eighteenth century literature page also provides access to information about the eighteenth century novel.

Literary Resources on the Net

http://andromeda.rutgers.edu/~jlynch/Lit

Jack Lynch of Rutgers University maintains this extensive collection of links to Internet sites that are useful to academics, including numerous Web sites about American and English literature. This collection is a good place to begin online research about the novel, as it links to hundreds of other sites with broad ranges of literary topics. The site is organized chronically, with separate pages for information about the Middle Ages, the Renaissance, the eighteenth century, the Romantic and Victorian eras, and twentieth century British and Irish literature. It also has separate pages providing links to Web sites about American literature and to women's literature and feminism.

LitWeb

http://litweb.net

LitWeb provides biographies of more than five hundred world authors throughout history that can be accessed through an alphabetical listing. The pages about each writer contain a list of his or her works, suggestions for further reading, and illustrations. The site also offers information about past and present winners of major literary prizes.

Luminarium: Anthology of English Literature

http://www.luminarium.org/lumina.htm

Luminarium has been a reliable source for more than a decade, providing information about English literature from the Middle Ages through the eighteenth century. The "English Literature: Restoration and Eighteenth Century, 1660-1785" section links to pages about individual writers of the period, including novelists John Bunyan, Daniel Defoe, Jonathan Swift, Aphra Behn, and Samuel Johnson. Users can access a biography, list of quotable remarks, and bibliographies of books about each author as well as links to electronic versions of the writer's works, essays about the writer, and related Web sites.

The Modern Word: Authors of the Libyrinth

http://www.themodernword.com/authors.html

The Modern Word site, although somewhat haphazard in its organization, provides a great deal of critical information about writers. The "Authors of the Libyrinth" page is very useful, linking author names to essays about them and other resources. The section of the page headed "The Scriptorium" presents "an index of pages featuring writers who have pushed the edges of their medium, combining literary talent with a sense of experimentation to produce some remarkable works of modern literature." The site also includes sections devoted to Samuel Beckett, Umberto Eco, Gabriel García Márquez, James Joyce, Franz Kafka, and Thomas Pynchon.

Nineteenth Century British and Irish Authors

http://www.lang.nagoya-u.ac.jp/~matsuoka/19th-authors.html

This site, part of the Victorian Studies Literary Archive, is maintained by Nagoya University in Japan. It contains links to information about almost four hundred nineteenth century British and Irish novelists, poets, playwrights, and other writers. The authors are listed chronologically by birth date, from 1751 through 1865. The site also provides a link for information about additional authors not included in the list.

Novels

http://www.nvcc.edu/home/ataormina/novels/default.htm

This overview of American and English novels was prepared by Agatha Taormina, a professor at Northern Virginia Community College. It contains three sections: "History" provides a definition of the novel genre, a discussion of its origins in eighteenth century England, and separate pages with information about genres and authors of nineteenth century, twentieth century, and postmodern novels. "Approaches" suggests how to read a novel critically for greater appreciation, and "Resources" provides a list of books about the novel.

Outline of American Literature

http://www.america.gov/publications/books/outline-of-american-literature.html

This page of the America.gov site provides access to an electronic version of the ten-chapter volume *Outline of American Literature*, a historical overview of prose and poetry from colonial times to the present published by the U.S. Department of State. The work's author is Kathryn VanSpanckeren, professor of English at the University of Tampa. The site offers links to abbreviated versions of each chapter as well as access to the entire publication in PDF format.

An Outline of the English Novel: The Short List

http://www.accd.edu/sac/english/bailey/engnovel.htm

This is one of the pages of the San Antonio College Lit Web, a compendium of biographical and bibliographical information about English literature. The page provides a chronological list of major English novels published from 1597 through 1940, with links to pages about authors ranging from John Bunyan, Daniel Defoe, and Fanny Burney to twentieth century writers Virginia Woolf, D. H. Lawrence, and Graham Greene. The individual author pages provide information about major works and links to additional online resources.

The Victorian Web

http://www.victorianweb.org

One of the finest Web sites about the nineteenth century, The Victorian Web provides a wealth of information about Great Britain during the reign of Queen Victoria, including information about the era's literature. The home page links to a section titled "Authors" that offers an alphabetical listing of more than 115 nineteenth century writers; the list links to additional pages of information about the individual authors, including biographies, bibliographies, analyses of their work, and, in some cases, excerpts of their writings. "Authors" also links to lists of pre- and post-Victorian writers and to British and other European authors associated with the aesthetic and Decadent movements. The information about some of the writers, such as Charles Dickens, Thomas Hardy, George Eliot, Charlotte Brontë, Anthony Trollope, and William Makepeace Thackeray, is quite extensive, with discussions of themes, characterization, imagery, narration, and other aspects of their works as well as essays and other resources placing their writings in social, political, and economic context.

Voice of the Shuttle

http://vos.ucsb.edu

One of the most complete and authoritative places for online information about literature, Voice of the Shuttle is maintained by professors and students in the English Department at the University of California, Santa Barbara. The site provides thousands of links to electronic books, academic journals, association Web sites, sites created by university professors, and many, many other resources about the humanities. Its "Literature in English" page provides links to separate pages about the literature of the Anglo-Saxon era, the Middle Ages, the Renaissance and seventeenth century, the Restoration and eighteenth century, the Romantic age, the Victorian age, and modern and contemporary periods in Britain and the United States, as well as a page focused on minority literature. Another page on the site, "Literatures Other than English," offers a gateway to information about the literature of numerous countries and world regions.

Western European Studies Section

http://wess.lib.byu.edu/index.php/Main_Page

The Western European Studies Section of the Association of College and Research Libraries maintains this collection of resources useful to students of Western European history and culture, and it is a good place to find information about non-English-language literature. The site includes separate pages about the literatures and languages of the Netherlands, France, Germany, Iberia, Italy, and Scandinavia where users can find links to electronic texts, association Web sites, journals, and other materials, the majority of which are written in the languages of the respective countries.

ELECTRONIC DATABASES

Electronic databases usually do not have their own URLs. Instead, public, college, and university libraries subscribe to these databases, provide links to them on their Web sites, and make them available to library card holders or other specified patrons. Readers can visit library Web sites or ask reference librarians to check on availability.

Bloom's Literary Reference Online

Facts On File publishes this database of thousands of articles by renowned scholar Harold Bloom and other literary critics, examining the lives and works of great writers worldwide. The database also includes information on more than forty-two thousand literary characters, literary topics, themes, movements, and genres, plus video segments about literature. Users can retrieve information by browsing writers' names, titles of works, time periods, genres, or writers' nationalities.

Canadian Literary Centre

Produced by EBSCO, the Canadian Literary Centre database contains full-text content from ECW Press, a Toronto-based publisher, including the titles in the publisher's Canadian fiction studies, Canadian biography, and Canadian writers and their works series, *ECW's Biographical Guide to Canadian Novelists*, and *George Woodcock's Introduction to Canadian Fiction*. Author biographies, essays and literary criticism, and book reviews are among the database's offerings.

Literary Reference Center

EBSCO's Literary Reference Center (LRC) is a comprehensive full-text database designed primarily to help high school and undergraduate students in English and the humanities with homework and research assignments about literature. The database contains massive amounts of information from reference works, books, literary journals, and other materials, including more than 31,000 plot summaries, synopses, and overviews of literary works; almost 100,000 essays and articles of literary criticism; about 140,000 author biographies; more than 605,000 book reviews; and more than 5,200 author interviews. It also contains the entire contents of Salem Press's MagillOnLiterature Plus. Users can retrieve information by browsing a list of authors' names or titles of literary works; they can also use an advanced search engine to access information by numerous categories, including author name, gender, cultural identity, national identity, and the years in which he or she lived, or by literary title, character, locale, genre, and publication date. The Literary Reference Center also features a literary-historical time line, an encyclopedia of literature, and a glossary of literary terms.

Literary Resource Center

Published by Gale, this comprehensive literary database contains information on the lives and works of more than 130,000 authors in all genres, in all time periods, and throughout the world. In addition, the database offers more than 70,000 full-text critical essays and reviews from some of Gale's reference publications, including *Contemporary Literary Criticism, Literature Criticism from 1400-1800, Nineteenth-Century Literature Criticism*, and *Twentieth-Century Literary Criticism*; more than 7,000 overviews of frequently studied works; more than 650,000 full-text articles, critical es-

says, and reviews from about three hundred scholarly journals and literary magazines; more than 4,500 interviews; and about five hundred links to selected Web sites. Users can retrieve information by browsing author name, ethnicity, nationality, years of birth and death; titles of literary works; genres; selected literary movements or time periods; keywords; and themes of literary works. Literary Resource Center also features a literary-historical time line and an encyclopedia of literature.

MagillOnLiterature Plus

MagillOnLiterature Plus is a comprehensive, integrated literature database produced by Salem Press and available on the EBSCO*host* platform. The database contains the full text of essays in Salem's many literature-related reference works, including *Masterplots, Cyclopedia of World Authors, Cyclopedia of Literary Characters, Cyclopedia of Literary Places, Critical Survey of Long Fiction, Critical Survey of Short Fiction, World Philosophers and Their Works, Magill's Literary Annual*, and *Magill's Book Reviews*. Among its contents are articles on more than 35,000 literary works and more than 8,500 writers, poets, dramatists, essays, and philosophers, more than 1,000 images, and a glossary of more than 1,300 literary terms. The biographical essays include lists of authors' works and secondary bibliographies, and almost four hundred overview essays offer information about literary genres, time periods, and national literatures.

NoveList

NoveList is a readers' advisory service produced by EBSCO. The database provides access to 155,000 titles of both adult and juvenile fiction as well information about literary awards, book discussion guides, feature articles about a range of literary genres, and "recommended reads." Users can search by author name, book title, or series title or can describe the plot to retrieve the name of a book, information about the author, and book reviews; another search engine enables users to find titles similar to books they have enjoyed reading.

Rebecca Kuzins

Glossary of Literary Terms

absurdism: A philosophical attitude, pervading much of modern drama and fiction, that underlines the isolation and alienation that humans experience, having been thrown into what absurdists see as a godless universe devoid of religious, spiritual, or metaphysical meaning. Conspicuous in its lack of logic, consistency, coherence, intelligibility, and realism, the literature of the absurd depicts the anguish, forlornness, and despair inherent in the human condition. Counter to the rationalist assumptions of traditional humanism, absurdism denies the existence of universal truth or value.

allegory: A literary mode in which a second level of meaning, wherein characters, events, and settings represent abstractions, is encoded within the surface narrative. The allegorical mode may dominate an entire work, in which case the encoded message is the work's primary reason for being, or it may be an element in a work otherwise interesting and meaningful for its surface story alone. Elements of allegory may be found in Jonathan Swift's *Gulliver's Travels* (1726) and Thomas Mann's *Der Zauberberg* (1924; *The Magic Mountain*, 1927).

anatomy: Literally the term means the "cutting up" or "dissection" of a subject into its constituent parts for closer examination. Northrop Frye, in his *Anatomy of Criticism* (1957), uses the term to refer to a narrative that deals with mental attitudes rather than people. As opposed to the novel, the anatomy features stylized figures who are mouthpieces for the ideas they represent.

antagonist: The character in fiction who stands as a rival or opponent to the *protagonist.*

antihero: Defined by Seán O'Faoláin as a fictional figure who, deprived of social sanctions and definitions, is always trying to define himself and to establish his own codes. Ahab may be seen as the antihero of Herman Melville's *Moby Dick* (1851).

archetype: The term "archetype" entered literary criticism from the psychology of Carl Jung, who defined archetypes as "primordial images" from the "collective unconscious" of humankind. Jung believed that works of art derive much of their power from the unconscious appeal of these images to ancestral memories. In his extremely influential *Anatomy of Criticism* (1957), Northrop Frye gave another sense of the term wide currency, defining the archetype as "a symbol, usually an image, which recurs often enough in literature to be recognizable as an element of one's literary experience as a whole."

atmosphere: The general mood or tone of a work; atmosphere is often associated with setting but can also be established by action or dialogue. A classic example of atmosphere is the primitive, fatalistic tone created in the opening description of Egdon Heath in Thomas Hardy's *The Return of the Native* (1878).

bildungsroman: Sometimes called the "novel of education," the bildungsroman focuses on the growth of a young *protagonist* who is learning about the world and finding his or her place in life; typical examples are James Joyce's *A Portrait of the Artist as a Young Man* (1914-1915, serial; 1916, book) and Thomas Wolfe's *Look Homeward, Angel* (1929).

biographical criticism: Criticism that attempts to determine how the events and experiences of an author's life influence his or her work.

bourgeois novel: A novel in which the values, preoccupations, and accoutrements of middle-class or bourgeois life are given particular prominence. The heyday of the bourgeois novel was the nineteenth century, when novelists as varied as Jane Austen, Honoré de Balzac, and Anthony Trollope both criticized and unreflectingly transmitted the assumptions of the rising middle class.

canon: An authorized or accepted list of books. In modern parlance, the literary canon comprehends the privileged texts, classics, or great books that are thought to belong permanently on university reading lists. Recent theory—especially feminist, Marxist, and poststructuralist—critically examines the process of canon formation and questions the hegemony of white male writers. Such theory sees canon formation as the ideological act of a dominant institution and seeks to undermine the notion of canonicity itself, thereby preventing the exclusion of works by women, minorities, and oppressed peoples.

character: Characters in fiction can be presented as if they were real people or as stylized functions of the plot. Usually characters are a combination of both factors.

classicism: A literary stance or value system consciously based on the example of classical Greek and Roman literature. While the term is applied to an enormous diversity of artists in many different periods and in many different national literatures, "classicism" generally denotes a cluster of values including formal discipline, restrained expression, reverence for tradition, and an objective rather than a subjective orientation. As a literary tendency, classicism is often opposed to *Romanticism,* although many writers combine classical and romantic elements.

climax/crisis: The term "climax" refers to the moment of the reader's highest emotional response, whereas "crisis" refers to a structural element of plot, a turning point at which a resolution must take place.

complication: The point in a novel when the *conflict* is developed or when the already existing conflict is further intensified.

conflict: The struggle that develops as a result of the opposition between the *protagonist* and another person, the natural world, society, or some force within the self.

contextualist criticism: A further extension of *formalist criticism,* which assumes that the language of art is constitutive. Rather than referring to preexistent values, the artwork creates values only inchoately realized before. The most important advocates of this position are Eliseo Vivas (*The Artistic Transaction,* 1963) and Murray Krieger (*The Play and Place of Criticism,* 1967).

conventions: All those devices of stylization, compression, and selection that constitute the necessary differences between art and life. According to the Russian Formalists, these conventions constitute the "literariness" of literature and are the only proper concern of the literary critic.

deconstruction: An extremely influential contemporary school of criticism based on the works of the French philosopher Jacques Derrida. Deconstruction treats literary works as unconscious reflections of the reigning myths of Western culture. The primary myth is that there is a meaningful world that language signifies or represents. The deconstructionist critic is most often concerned with showing how a literary text tacitly subverts the very assumptions or myths on which it ostensibly rests.

defamiliarization: Coined by Viktor Shklovsky in 1917, this term denotes a basic principle of Russian Formalism. Poetic language (by which the Formalists meant artful language, in prose as well as in poetry) defamiliarizes or "makes strange" familiar experiences. The technique of art, says Shklovsky, is to "make objects unfamiliar, to make forms difficult, to increase the difficulty and length of perception. . . . Art is a way of experiencing the artfulness of an object; the object is not important."

detective story: The so-called classic detective story (or mystery) is a highly formalized and logically structured mode of fiction in which the focus is on a crime solved by a detective through interpretation of evidence and ratiocination; the most famous detective in this mode is Arthur Conan Doyle's Sherlock Holmes. Many modern practitioners of the genre, however, such as Dashiell Hammett, Raymond Chandler, and Ross Macdonald, have de-emphasized the puzzlelike qualities of the detective story, stressing instead characterization, theme, and other elements of mainstream fiction.

determinism: The belief that an individual's actions are essentially determined by biological and environmental factors, with free will playing a negligible role. (See *naturalism.*)

dialogue: The similitude of conversation in fiction, dialogue serves to characterize, to further the *plot,* to establish *conflict,* and to express thematic ideas.

displacement: Popularized in criticism by Northrop Frye, this term refers to the author's attempt to make his or her story psychologically motivated and realistic, even as the latent structure of the mythical motivation moves relentlessly forward.

dominant: A term coined by Roman Jakobson to refer to

that which "rules, determines, and transforms the re-maining components in the work of a single artist, in a poetic canon, or in the work of an epoch." The shift-ing of the dominant in a *genre* accounts for the cre-ation of new generic forms and new poetic epochs. For example, the rise of *realism* in the mid-nine-teenth century indicates realistic conventions becom-ing dominant and *romance* or fantasy conventions becoming secondary.

doppelgänger: A double or counterpart of a person, sometimes endowed with ghostly qualities. A fic-tional character's doppelgänger often reflects a sup-pressed side of his or her personality. One of the clas-sic examples of the doppelgänger motif is found in Fyodor Dostoevski's novella *Dvoynik* (1846; *The Double*, 1917); Isaac Bashevis Singer and Jorge Luis Borges, among others, offer striking modern treat-ments of the doppelgänger.

epic: Although this term usually refers to a long narra-tive poem that presents the exploits of a central figure of high position, the term is also used to designate a long novel that has the style or structure usually as-sociated with an epic. In this sense, for example, Herman Melville's *Moby Dick* (1851) and James Joyce's *Ulysses* (1922) may be called epics.

episodic narrative: A work that is held together primar-ily by a loose connection of self-sufficient episodes. *Picaresque novels* often have episodic structure.

epistolary novel: A novel made up of letters by one or more fictional characters. Samuel Richardson's *Pamela: Or, Virtue Rewarded* (1740-1741) is a well-known eighteenth century example. In the nineteenth century, Bram Stoker's *Dracula* (1897) is largely epistolary. The technique allows for several different points of view to be presented.

euphuism: A style of writing characterized by ornate lan-guage that is highly contrived, alliterative, and repeti-tious. Euphuism was developed by John Lyly in his *Euphues, the Anatomy of Wit* (1578) and was emu-lated frequently by writers of the Elizabethan Age.

existentialism: A philosophical, religious, and literary term, emerging from World War II, for a group of at-titudes surrounding the pivotal notion that existence precedes essence. According to Jean-Paul Sartre,

"Man is nothing else but what he makes himself." Forlornness arises from the death of God and the concomitant death of universal values, of any source of ultimate or a priori standards. Despair arises from the fact that an individual can reckon only with what depends on his or her will, and the sphere of that will is severely limited; the number of things on which he or she can have an impact is pathetically small. Existentialist literature is antideterministic in the ex-treme and rejects the idea that heredity and environ-ment shape and determine human motivation and behavior.

exposition: The part or parts of a fiction that provide nec-essary background information. Exposition not only provides the time and place of the action but also in-troduces readers to the fictive world of the story, ac-quainting them with the ground rules of the work.

fantastic: In his study *The Fantastic* (1970), Tzvetan Todorov defines the fantastic as a *genre* that lies be-tween the "uncanny" and the "marvelous." All three genres embody the familiar world but present an event that cannot be explained by the laws of the fa-miliar world. Todorov says that the fantastic occu-pies a twilight zone between the uncanny (when the reader knows that the peculiar event is merely the re-sult of an illusion) and the marvelous (when the reader understands that the event is supposed to take place in a realm controlled by laws unknown to hu-mankind). The fantastic is thus essentially unsettling, provocative, even subversive.

feminist criticism: A criticism advocating equal rights for women in political, economic, social, psycholog-ical, personal, and aesthetic senses. On the thematic level, the feminist reader should identify with female characters and their concerns. The object is to pro-vide a critique of phallocentric assumptions and an analysis of patriarchal ideologies inscribed in a litera-ture that is male-centered and male-dominated. On the ideological level, feminist critics see gender, as well as the stereotypes that go along with it, as a cultural construct. They strive to define a particu-larly feminine content and to extend the *canon* so that it might include works by lesbians, feminists, and women writers in general.

flashback: A scene in a fiction that depicts an earlier event; it may be presented as a reminiscence by a character in the story or may simply be inserted into the narrative.

foreshadowing: A device to create suspense or dramatic irony in fiction by indicating through suggestion what will take place in the future.

formalist criticism: Two particularly influential formalist schools of criticism arose in the twentieth century: the Russian Formalists and the American New Critics. The Russian Formalists were concerned with the conventional devices used in literature to defamiliarize that which habit has made familiar. The New Critics believed that literary criticism is a description and evaluation of its object and that the primary concern of the critic is with the work's unity. Both schools of criticism, at their most extreme, treated literary works as artifacts or constructs divorced from their biographical and social contexts.

genre: In its most general sense, this term refers to a group of literary works defined by a common form, style, or purpose. In practice, the term is used in a wide variety of overlapping and, to a degree, contradictory senses. Tragedy and comedy are thus described as distinct genres; the novel (a form that includes both tragic and comic works) is a genre; and various subspecies of the novel, such as the *gothic* and the *picaresque,* are themselves frequently treated as distinct genres. Finally, the term "genre fiction" refers to forms of popular fiction in which the writer is bound by more or less rigid conventions. Indeed, all these diverse usages have in common an emphasis on the manner in which individual literary works are shaped by particular expectations and conventions; this is the subject of genre criticism.

genre fiction: Categories of popular fiction in which the writers are bound by more or less rigid conventions, such as in the *detective story,* the *romance,* and the *Western.* Although the term can be used in a neutral sense, it is often used dismissively.

gothic novel: A form of fiction developed in the eighteenth century that focuses on horror and the supernatural. In his preface to *The Castle of Otranto* (1765), the first gothic novel in English, Horace Walpole claimed that he was trying to combine two kinds of fiction, with events and story typical of the medieval romance and character delineation typical of the realistic novel. Other examples of the form are Matthew Gregory Lewis's *The Monk: A Romance* (1796; also known as *Ambrosio: Or, The Monk*) and Mary Wollstonecraft Shelley's *Frankenstein: Or, The Modern Prometheus* (1818).

grotesque: According to Wolfgang Kayser (*The Grotesque in Art and Literature,* 1963), the grotesque is an embodiment in literature of the estranged world. Characterized by a breakup of the everyday world by mysterious forces, the form differs from fantasy in that the reader is not sure whether to react with humor or with horror and in that the exaggeration manifested exists in the familiar world rather than in a purely imaginative world.

Hebraic/Homeric styles: Terms coined by Erich Auerbach in *Mimesis: The Representation of Reality in Western Literature* (1953) to designate two basic fictional styles. The Hebraic style focuses only on the decisive points of narrative and leaves all else obscure, mysterious, and "fraught with background"; the Homeric style places the narrative in a definite time and place and externalizes everything in a perpetual foreground.

historical criticism: In contrast to *formalist criticism,* which treats literary works to a great extent as self-contained artifacts, historical criticism emphasizes the historical context of literature; the two approaches, however, need not be mutually exclusive. Ernst Robert Curtius's *European Literature and the Latin Middle Ages* (1940) is a prominent example of historical criticism.

historical novel: A novel that depicts past historical events, usually public in nature, and features real as well as fictional people. Sir Walter Scott's Waverley novels established the basic type, but the relationship between fiction and history in the form varies greatly depending on the practitioner.

implied author: According to Wayne Booth (*The Rhetoric of Fiction,* 1961), the novel often creates a kind of second self who tells the story—a self who is wiser, more sensitive, and more perceptive than any real person could be.

interior monologue: Defined by Édouard Dujardin as the speech of a character designed to introduce the reader directly to the character's internal life, the form differs from other kinds of monologue in that it attempts to reproduce thought before any logical organization is imposed on it. See, for example, Molly Bloom's long interior monologue at the conclusion of James Joyce's *Ulysses* (1922).

irrealism: A term often used to refer to modern or postmodern fiction that is presented self-consciously as a fiction or a fabulation rather than a mimesis of external reality. The best-known practitioners of irrealism are John Barth, Robert Coover, and Donald Barthelme.

local colorists: A loose movement of late nineteenth century American writers whose fiction emphasizes the distinctive folkways, landscapes, and dialects of various regions. Important local colorists include Bret Harte, Mark Twain, George Washington Cable, Kate Chopin, and Sarah Orne Jewett. (See *regional novel.*)

Marxist criticism: Based on the nineteenth century writings of Karl Marx and Friedrich Engels, Marxist criticism views literature as a product of ideological forces determined by the dominant class. However, many Marxists believe that literature operates according to its own autonomous standards of production and reception: It is both a product of ideology and able to determine ideology. As such, literature may overcome the dominant paradigms of its age and play a revolutionary role in society.

metafiction: This term refers to fiction that manifests a reflexive tendency, such as Vladimir Nabokov's *Pale Fire* (1962) and John Fowles's *The French Lieutenant's Woman* (1969). The emphasis is on the loosening of the work's illusion of reality to expose the reality of its illusion. Other terms used to refer to this type of fiction include "irrealism," "postmodernist fiction," "antifiction," and "surfiction."

modernism: An international movement in the arts that began in the early years of the twentieth century. Al-

though the term is used to describe artists of widely varying persuasions, modernism in general was characterized by its international idiom, by its interest in cultures distant in space or time, by its emphasis on formal experimentation, and by its sense of dislocation and radical change.

motif: A conventional incident or situation in a fiction that may serve as the basis for the structure of the narrative itself. The Russian Formalist critic Boris Tomashevsky uses the term to refer to the smallest particle of thematic material in a work.

motivation: Although this term is usually used in reference to the convention of justifying the action of a character from his or her psychological makeup, the Russian Formalists use the term to refer to the network of devices that justify the introduction of individual *motifs* or groups of motifs in a work. For example, "compositional motivation" refers to the principle that every single property in a work contributes to its overall effect; "realistic motivation" refers to the realistic devices used to make a work plausible and lifelike.

multiculturalism: The tendency to recognize the perspectives of those traditionally excluded from the canon of Western art and literature. In order to promote multiculturalism, publishers and educators have revised textbooks and school curricula to incorporate material by and about women, members of minority groups, persons from non-Western cultures, and homosexuals.

myth: Anonymous traditional stories dealing with basic human concepts and antinomies. According to Claude Lévi-Strauss, myth is that part of language where the "formula *tradutore, traditore* reaches its lowest truth value. . . . Its substance does not lie in its style, its original music, or its syntax, but in the story which it tells."

myth criticism: Northrop Frye says that in myth "we see the structural principles of literature isolated." Myth criticism is concerned with these basic principles of literature; it is not to be confused with mythological criticism, which is primarily concerned with finding mythological parallels in the surface action of the *narrative.*

narrative: Robert Scholes and Robert Kellogg, in *The Nature of Narrative* (1966), say that by "narrative" they mean literary works that include both a story and a storyteller. The term "narrative" usually implies a contrast to "enacted" fiction such as drama.

narratology: The study of the form and functioning of *narratives*; it attempts to examine what all narratives have in common and what makes individual narratives different from one another.

narrator: The *character* who recounts the *narrative*, or story. Wayne Booth describes various dramatized narrators in *The Rhetoric of Fiction* (1961): unacknowledged centers of consciousness, observers, narrator-agents, and self-conscious narrators. Booth suggests that the important elements to consider in narration are the relationships among the narrator, the author, the characters, and the reader.

naturalism: As developed by Émile Zola in the late nineteenth century, naturalism is the application of the principles of scientific *determinism* to fiction. Although it usually refers more to the choice of subject matter than to technical conventions, those conventions associated with the movement center on the author's attempt to be precise and scientifically objective in description and detail, regardless of whether the events described are sordid or shocking.

New Criticism: See *formalist criticism*.

novel: Perhaps the most difficult of all fictional forms to define because of its multiplicity of modes. Edouard, in André Gide's *Les Faux-monnayeurs* (1925; *The Counterfeiters*, 1927), says the novel is the freest and most lawless of all *genres*; he wonders if fear of that liberty is the reason the novel has so timidly clung to reality. Most critics seem to agree that the novel's primary area of concern is the social world. Ian Watt (*The Rise of the Novel*, 2001) says that the novel can be distinguished from other fictional forms by the attention it pays to individual characterization and detailed presentation of the environment. Moreover, says Watt, the novel, more than any other fictional form, is interested in the "development of its characters in the course of time."

novel of manners: The classic examples of this form might be the novels of Jane Austen, wherein the customs and conventions of a social group of a particular time and place are realistically, and often satirically, portrayed.

novella, novelle, nouvelle, novelette, novela: Although these terms often refer to the short European tale, especially the Renaissance form employed by Giovanni Boccaccio, the terms often refer to that form of fiction that is said to be longer than a short story and shorter than a novel. "Novelette" is the term usually preferred by the British, whereas "novella" is the term usually used to refer to American works in this *genre*. Henry James claimed that the main merit of the form is the "effort to do the complicated thing with a strong brevity and lucidity."

phenomenological criticism: Although best known as a European school of criticism practiced by Georges Poulet and others, this so-called criticism of consciousness is also propounded in the United States by such critics as J. Hillis Miller. The focus is less on individual works and *genres* than it is on literature as an act; the work is not seen as an object but rather as part of a strand of latent impulses in the work of a single author or an epoch.

picaresque novel: A form of fiction that centers on a central rogue figure, or picaro, who usually tells his or her own story. The plot structure is normally *episodic*, and the episodes usually focus on how the picaro lives by his or her wits. Classic examples of the mode are Henry Fielding's *The History of Tom Jones, a Foundling* (1749; commonly known as *Tom Jones*) and Mark Twain's *Adventures of Huckleberry Finn* (1884).

plot/story: "Story" refers to the full *narrative* of *character* and action, whereas "plot" generally refers to action with little reference to character. A more precise and helpful distinction is made by the Russian Formalists, who suggest that "plot" refers to the events of a narrative as they have been artfully arranged in the literary work, subject to chronological displacement, ellipses, and other devices, while "story" refers to the sum of the same events arranged in simple, causal-chronological order. Thus story is the raw material for plot. By comparing the two in a given work, the reader is encouraged to see the narrative as an artifact.

point of view: The means by which the story is presented to the reader, or, as Percy Lubbock says in *The Craft of Fiction* (1921), "the relation in which the narrator stands to the story"—a relation that Lubbock claims governs the craft of fiction. Some of the questions the critical reader should ask concerning point of view are the following: Who talks to the reader? From what position does the narrator tell the story? At what distance does he or she place the reader from the story? What kind of person is he or she? How fully is he or she characterized? How reliable is he or she? For further discussion, see Wayne Booth, *The Rhetoric of Fiction* (1961).

postcolonialism: Postcolonial literature emerged in the mid-twentieth century when colonies in Asia, Africa, and the Caribbean began gaining their independence from the European nations that had long controlled them. Postcolonial authors, such as Salman Rushdie and V. S. Naipaul, tend to focus on both the freedom and the conflict inherent in living in a postcolonial state.

postmodernism: A ubiquitous but elusive term in contemporary criticism, "postmodernism" is loosely applied to the various artistic movements that followed the era of so-called high modernism, represented by such giants as James Joyce and Pablo Picasso. In critical discussions of contemporary fiction, the term "postmodernism" is frequently applied to the works of writers such as Thomas Pynchon, John Barth, and Donald Barthelme, who exhibit a self-conscious awareness of their modernist predecessors as well as a reflexive treatment of fictional form.

protagonist: The central *character* in a fiction, the character whose fortunes most concern the reader.

psychological criticism: While much modern literary criticism reflects to some degree the impacts of Sigmund Freud, Carl Jung, Jacques Lacan, and other psychological theorists, the term "psychological criticism" suggests a strong emphasis on a causal relation between the writer's psychological state, variously interpreted, and his or her works. A notable example of psychological criticism is Norman Fruman's *Coleridge, the Damaged Archangel* (1971).

psychological novel: A form of fiction in which *character*, especially the inner lives of characters, is the pri-

mary focus. This form, which has been of primary importance at least since Henry James, characterizes much of the work of James Joyce, Virginia Woolf, and William Faulkner. For a detailed discussion, see *The Modern Psychological Novel* (1955) by Leon Edel.

realism: A literary technique in which the primary convention is to render an illusion of fidelity to external reality. Realism is often identified as the primary method of the novel form: It focuses on surface details, maintains a fidelity to the everyday experiences of middle-class society, and strives for a one-to-one relationship between the fiction and the action imitated. The realist movement in the late nineteenth century coincides with the full development of the novel form.

reception aesthetics: The best-known American practitioner of reception aesthetics is Stanley Fish. For the reception critic, meaning is an event or process; rather than being embedded in the work, it is created through particular acts of reading. The best-known European practitioner of this criticism, Wolfgang Iser, argues that indeterminacy is the basic characteristic of literary texts; the reader must "normalize" the text either by projecting his or her standards into it or by revising his or her standards to "fit" the text.

regional novel: Any novel in which the character of a given geographical region plays a decisive role. Although regional differences persist across the United States, a considerable leveling in speech and customs has taken place, so that the sharp regional distinctions evident in nineteenth century American fiction have all but disappeared. Only in the South has a strong regional tradition persisted to the present. (See *local colorists.*)

rhetorical criticism: The rhetorical critic is concerned with the literary work as a means of communicating ideas and the means by which the work affects or controls the reader. Such criticism seems best suited to didactic works such as satire.

roman à clef: A fiction wherein actual people, often celebrities of some sort, are thinly disguised.

romance: The romance usually differs from the novel form in that the focus is on symbolic events and representational characters rather than on "as-if-real" characters and events. Richard Chase says that in the romance, character is depicted as highly stylized, a function of the plot rather than as someone complexly related to society. The romancer is more likely to be concerned with dreamworlds than with the familiar world, believing that reality cannot be grasped by the traditional novel.

Romanticism: A widespread cultural movement in the late eighteenth and early nineteenth centuries, the influence of which is still felt. As a general literary tendency, Romanticism is frequently contrasted with *classicism*. Although many varieties of Romanticism are indigenous to various national literatures, the term generally suggests an assertion of the preeminence of the imagination. Other values associated with various schools of Romanticism include primitivism, an interest in folklore, a reverence for nature, and a fascination with the demoniac and the macabre.

scene: The central element of *narration*; specific actions are narrated or depicted that make the reader feel he or she is participating directly in the action.

science fiction: Fiction in which certain givens (physical laws, psychological principles, social conditions—any one or all of these) form the basis of an imaginative projection into the future or, less commonly, an extrapolation in the present or even into the past.

semiotics: The science of signs and sign systems in communication. According to Roman Jakobson, semiotics deals with the principles that underlie the structure of signs, their use in language of all kinds, and the specific nature of various sign systems.

sentimental novel: A form of fiction popular in the eighteenth century in which emotionalism and optimism are the primary characteristics. The best-known examples are Samuel Richardson's *Pamela: Or, Virtue Rewarded* (1740-1741) and Oliver Goldsmith's *The Vicar of Wakefield* (1766).

setting: The circumstances and environment, both temporal and spatial, of a *narrative*.

spatial form: An author's attempt to make the reader apprehend a work spatially in a moment of time rather than sequentially. To achieve this effect, the author breaks up the *narrative* into interspersed fragments.

Beginning with James Joyce, Marcel Proust, and Djuna Barnes, the movement toward spatial form is concomitant with the *modernist* effort to supplant historical time in fiction with mythic time. For the seminal discussion of this technique, see Joseph Frank, *The Widening Gyre* (1963).

stream of consciousness: The depiction of the thought processes of a *character*, insofar as this is possible, without any mediating structures. The metaphor of consciousness as a "stream" suggests a rush of thoughts and images governed by free association rather than by strictly rational development. The term "stream of consciousness" is often used loosely as a synonym for *interior monologue*. The most celebrated example of stream of consciousness in fiction is the monologue of Molly Bloom in James Joyce's *Ulysses* (1922); other notable practitioners of the stream-of-consciousness technique include Dorothy Richardson, Virginia Woolf, and William Faulkner.

structuralism: As a movement of thought, structuralism is based on the idea of intrinsic, self-sufficient structures that do not require reference to external elements. A structure is a system of transformations that involves the interplay of laws inherent in the system itself. The study of language is the primary model for contemporary structuralism. The structuralist literary critic attempts to define structural principles that operate intertextually throughout the whole of literature as well as principles that operate in *genres* and in individual works. One of the most accessible surveys of structuralism and literature available is Jonathan Culler's *Structuralist Poetics* (1975).

summary: Those parts of a fiction that do not need to be detailed. In *Tom Jones* (1749), Henry Fielding says, "If whole years should pass without producing anything worthy of . . . notice . . . we shall hasten on to matters of consequence."

thematics: According to Northrop Frye, when a work of fiction is written or interpreted thematically, it becomes an illustrative fable. Murray Krieger defines thematics as "the study of the experiential tensions which, dramatically entangled in the literary work, become an existential reflection of that work's aesthetic complexity."

tone: The dominant mood of a work of fiction. (See *atmosphere*.)

unreliable narrator: A narrator whose account of the events of the story cannot be trusted, obliging readers to reconstruct—if possible—the true state of affairs themselves. Once an innovative technique, the use of the unreliable narrator has become commonplace among contemporary writers who wish to suggest the impossibility of a truly "reliable" account of any event. Notable examples of the unreliable narrator can be found in Ford Madox Ford's *The Good Soldier* (1915) and Vladimir Nabokov's *Lolita* (1955).

Victorian novel: Although the Victorian period extended from 1837 to 1901, the term "Victorian novel" does not include the later decades of Queen Victoria's reign. The term loosely refers to the sprawling works of novelists such as Charles Dickens and William Makepeace Thackeray—works that frequently appeared first in serial form and are characterized by a broad social canvas.

vraisemblance/verisimilitude: Tzvetan Todorov defines vraisemblance as "the mask which conceals the text's own laws, but which we are supposed to take for a relation to reality." Verisimilitude refers to a work's attempts to make the reader believe that it conforms to reality rather than to its own laws.

Western novel: Like all varieties of *genre fiction*, the Western novel—generally known simply as the Western—is defined by a relatively predictable combination of *conventions*, *motifs*, and recurring themes. These predictable elements, familiar from many Western films and television series, differentiate the Western from *historical novels* and idiosyncratic works such as Thomas Berger's *Little Big Man* (1964) that are also set in the Old West. Conversely, some novels set in the contemporary West are regarded as Westerns because they deal with modern cowboys and with the land itself in the manner characteristic of the *genre*.

Charles E. May

MAJOR AWARDS

NOBEL PRIZE IN LITERATURE

The Nobel Prize in Literature, which has been awarded annually since 1901, is generally regarded as the highest honor that can be bestowed on an author for his or her total body of literary work.

1901	Sully Prudhomme	1935	No award
1902	Theodor Mommsen	1936	Eugene O'Neill
1903	Bjørnstjerne Bjørnson	1937	Roger Martin du Gard
1904	Frédéric Mistral	1938	Pearl S. Buck
	José Echegaray y Eizaguirre	1939	Frans Eemil Sillanpää
1905	Henryk Sienkiewicz	1940	No award
1906	Giosuè Carducci	1941	No award
1907	Rudyard Kipling	1942	No award
1908	Rudolf Christoph Eucken	1943	No award
1909	Selma Lagerlöf	1944	Johannes V. Jensen
1910	Paul Heyse	1945	Gabriela Mistral
1911	Maurice Maeterlinck	1946	Hermann Hesse
1912	Gerhart Hauptmann	1947	André Gide
1913	Rabindranath Tagore	1948	T. S. Eliot
1914	No award	1949	William Faulkner
1915	Romain Rolland	1950	Bertrand Russell
1916	Verner von Heidenstam	1951	Pär Lagerkvist
1917	Karl Gjellerup	1952	François Mauriac
	Henrik Pontoppidan	1953	Winston Churchill
1918	No award	1954	Ernest Hemingway
1919	Carl Spitteler	1955	Halldór Laxness
1920	Knut Hamsun	1956	Juan Ramón Jiménez
1921	Anatole France	1957	Albert Camus
1922	Jacinto Benavente y Martínez	1958	Boris Pasternak
1923	William Butler Yeats	1959	Salvatore Quasimodo
1924	Władysław Reymont	1960	Saint-John Perse
1925	George Bernard Shaw	1961	Ivo Andrić
1926	Grazia Deledda	1962	John Steinbeck
1927	Henri Bergson	1963	Giorgos Seferis
1928	Sigrid Undset	1964	Jean-Paul Sartre
1929	Thomas Mann	1965	Mikhail Sholokhov
1930	Sinclair Lewis	1966	Shmuel Yosef Agnon
1931	Erik Axel Karlfeldt		Nelly Sachs
1932	John Galsworthy	1967	Miguel Ángel Asturias
1933	Ivan Bunin	1968	Yasunari Kawabata
1934	Luigi Pirandello	1969	Samuel Beckett

1970	Aleksandr Solzhenitsyn		1989	Camilo José Cela
1971	Pablo Neruda		1990	Octavio Paz
1972	Heinrich Böll		1991	Nadine Gordimer
1973	Patrick White		1992	Derek Walcott
1974	Eyvind Johnson		1993	Toni Morrison
	Harry Martinson		1994	Kenzaburō Ōe
1975	Eugenio Montale		1995	Seamus Heaney
1976	Saul Bellow		1996	Wisława Szymborska
1977	Vicente Aleixandre		1997	Dario Fo
1978	Isaac Bashevis Singer		1998	José Saramago
1979	Odysseus Elytis		1999	Günter Grass
1980	Czesław Miłosz		2000	Gao Xingjian
1981	Elias Canetti		2001	V. S. Naipaul
1982	Gabriel García Márquez		2002	Imre Kertész
1983	William Golding		2003	J. M. Coetzee
1984	Jaroslav Seifert		2004	Elfriede Jelinek
1985	Claude Simon		2005	Harold Pinter
1986	Wole Soyinka		2006	Orhan Pamuk
1987	Joseph Brodsky		2007	Doris Lessing
1988	Naguib Mahfouz		2008	J. M. G. Le Clézio

PULITZER PRIZE IN FICTION

The Pulitzer Prize in fiction has been awarded annually to American writers since 1918. In its initial years only novels were eligible for the prize, but in 1948 eligibility was broadened to include works of both long and short fiction.

1918	*His Family* by Ernest Poole		1935	*Now in November* by Josephine Winslow Johnson
1919	*The Magnificent Ambersons* by Booth Tarkington		1936	*Honey in the Horn* by H. L. Davis
1920	No award		1937	*Gone with the Wind* by Margaret Mitchell
1921	*The Age of Innocence* by Edith Wharton		1938	*The Late George Apley* by John P. Marquand
1922	*Alice Adams* by Booth Tarkington		1939	*The Yearling* by Marjorie Kinnan Rawlings
1923	*One of Ours* by Willa Cather		1940	*The Grapes of Wrath* by John Steinbeck
1924	*The Able McLaughlins* by Margaret Wilson		1941	No award
1925	*So Big* by Edna Ferber		1942	*In This Our Life* by Ellen Glasgow
1926	*Arrowsmith* by Sinclair Lewis		1943	*Dragon's Teeth* by Upton Sinclair
1927	*Early Autumn* by Louis Bromfield		1944	*Journey in the Dark* by Martin Flavin
1928	*The Bridge of San Luis Rey* by Thornton Wilder		1945	*A Bell for Adano* by John Hersey
1929	*Scarlet Sister* by Julia Peterkin		1946	No award
1930	*Laughing Boy* by Oliver La Farge		1947	*All the King's Men* by Robert Penn Warren
1931	*Years of Grace* by Margaret Ayer Barnes		1948	*Tales of the South Pacific* by James A. Michener
1932	*The Good Earth* by Pearl S. Buck		1949	*Guard of Honor* by James Gould Cozzens
1933	*The Store* by T. S. Stribling		1950	*The Way West* by A. B. Guthrie, Jr.
1934	*Lamb in His Bosom* by Caroline Miller		1951	*The Town* by Conrad Richter
			1952	*The Caine Mutiny* by Herman Wouk

1953 *The Old Man and the Sea* by Ernest Hemingway

1954 No award

1955 *A Fable* by William Faulkner

1956 *Andersonville* by MacKinlay Kantor

1957 No award

1958 *A Death in the Family* by James Agee

1959 *The Travels of Jaimie McPheeters* by Robert Lewis Taylor

1960 *Advise and Consent* by Allen Drury

1961 *To Kill a Mockingbird* by Harper Lee

1962 *The Edge of Sadness* by Edwin O'Connor

1963 *The Reivers* by William Faulkner

1964 No award

1965 *The Keepers of the House* by Shirley Ann Grau

1966 *Collected Stories* by Katherine Anne Porter

1967 *The Fixer* by Bernard Malamud

1968 *The Confessions of Nat Turner* by William Styron

1969 *House Made of Dawn* by N. Scott Momaday

1970 *Collected Stories* by Jean Stafford

1971 No award

1972 *Angle of Repose* by Wallace Stegner

1973 *The Optimist's Daughter* by Eudora Welty

1974 No award

1975 *The Killer Angels* by Michael Shaara

1976 *Humboldt's Gift* by Saul Bellow

1977 No award

1978 *Elbow Room* by James Alan McPherson

1979 *The Stories of John Cheever* by John Cheever

1980 *The Executioner's Song* by Norman Mailer

1981 *A Confederacy of Dunces* by John Kennedy Toole

1982 *Rabbit Is Rich* by John Updike

1983 *The Color Purple* by Alice Walker

1984 *Ironweed* by William Kennedy

1985 *Foreign Affairs* by Alison Lurie

1986 *Lonesome Dove* by Larry McMurtry

1987 *A Summons to Memphis* by Peter Taylor

1988 *Beloved* by Toni Morrison

1989 *Breathing Lessons* by Anne Tyler

1990 *The Mambo Kings Play Songs of Love* by Oscar Hijuelos

1991 *Rabbit at Rest* by John Updike

1992 *A Thousand Acres* by Jane Smiley

1993 *A Good Scent from a Strange Mountain* by Robert Olen Butler

1994 *The Shipping News* by E. Annie Proulx

1995 *The Stone Diaries* by Carol Shields

1996 *Independence Day* by Richard Ford

1997 *Martin Dressler: The Tale of an American Dreamer* by Steven Millhauser

1998 *American Pastoral* by Philip Roth

1999 *The Hours* by Michael Cunningham

2000 *Interpreter of Maladies* by Jhumpa Lahiri

2001 *The Amazing Adventures of Kavalier and Clay* by Michael Chabon

2002 *Empire Falls* by Richard Russo

2003 *Middlesex* by Jeffrey Eugenides

2004 *The Known World* by Edward P. Jones

2005 *Gilead* by Marilynne Robinson

2006 *March* by Geraldine Brooks

2007 *The Road* by Cormac McCarthy

2008 *The Brief Wondrous Life of Oscar Wao* by Junot Díaz

NATIONAL BOOK AWARD FOR FICTION

The National Book Award for fiction, which honors books by American writers, has been presented annually since 1950.

1950 *The Man with the Golden Arm* by Nelson Algren

1951 *The Collected Stories of William Faulkner* by William Faulkner

1952 *From Here to Eternity* by James Jones

1953 *Invisible Man* by Ralph Ellison

1954 *The Adventures of Augie March* by Saul Bellow

1955 *A Fable* by William Faulkner

1956 *Ten North Frederick* by John O'Hara

1957 *The Field of Vision* by Wright Morris

1958 *The Wapshot Chronicle* by John Cheever

1959 *The Magic Barrel* by Bernard Malamud

1960 *Goodbye, Columbus* by Philip Roth

1961 *The Waters of Kronos* by Conrad Richter
1962 *The Moviegoer* by Walker Percy
1963 *Morte D'Urban* by J. F. Powers
1964 *The Centaur* by John Updike
1965 *Herzog* by Saul Bellow
1966 *The Collected Stories of Katherine Anne Porter* by Katherine Anne Porter
1967 *The Fixer* by Bernard Malamud
1968 *The Eighth Day* by Thornton Wilder
1969 *Steps* by Jerzy Kosinski
1970 *them* by Joyce Carol Oates
1971 *Mr. Sammler's Planet* by Saul Bellow
1972 *The Complete Stories* by Flannery O'Connor
1973 *Chimera* by John Barth
1974 *A Crown of Feathers, and Other Stories* by Isaac Bashevis Singer
      Gravity's Rainbow by Thomas Pynchon
1975 *Dog Soldiers* by Robert Stone
      The Hair of Harold Roux by Thomas Williams
1976 *J. R.* by William Gaddis
1977 *The Spectator Bird* by Wallace Stegner
1978 *Blood Ties* by Mary Lee Settle
1979 *Going After Cacciato* by Tim O'Brien
1980 *Sophie's Choice* by William Styron
      The World According to Garp by John Irving
1981 *Plains Song* by Wright Morris
      The Stories of John Cheever by John Cheever
1982 *Rabbit Is Rich* by John Updike
      So Long, See You Tomorrow by William Maxwell

1983 *The Color Purple* by Alice Walker
      Collected Stories of Eudora Welty by Eudora Welty
1984 *Victory over Japan: A Book of Stories* by Ellen Gilchrist
1985 *White Noise* by Don DeLillo
1986 *World's Fair* by E. L. Doctorow
1987 *Paco's Story* by Larry Heinemann
1988 *Paris Trout* by Pete Dexter
1989 *Spartina* by John Casey
1990 *Middle Passage* by Charles Johnson
1991 *Mating* by Norman Rush
1992 *All the Pretty Horses* by Cormac McCarthy
1993 *The Shipping News* by E. Annie Proulx
1994 *A Frolic of His Own* by William Gaddis
1995 *Sabbath's Theater* by Philip Roth
1996 *Ship Fever, and Other Stories* by Andrea Barrett
1997 *Cold Mountain* by Charles Frazier
1998 *Charming Billy* by Alice McDermott
1999 *Waiting* by Ha Jin
2000 *In America* by Susan Sontag
2001 *The Corrections* by Jonathan Franzen
2002 *Three Junes* by Julia Glass
2003 *The Great Fire* by Shirley Hazzard
2004 *The News from Paraguay* by Lily Tuck
2005 *Europe Central* by William T. Vollmann
2006 *The Echo Maker* by Richard Powers
2007 *Tree of Smoke* by Denis Johnson
2008 *Shadow Country: A New Rendering of the Watson Legend* by Peter Matthiessen

PEN/FAULKNER AWARD FOR FICTION

The PEN/Faulkner Award for Fiction honors the best published works of fiction by American writers. The award has been presented annually since 1981.

1981 *How German Is It?* by Walter Abish
1982 *The Chaneysville Incident* by David Bradley
1983 *Seaview* by Toby Olson
1984 *Sent for You Yesterday* by John Edgar Wideman
1985 *The Barracks Thief* by Tobias Wolff
1986 *The Old Forest* by Peter Taylor
1987 *Soldiers in Hiding* by Richard Wiley
1988 *World's End* by T. Coraghessan Boyle
1989 *Dusk* by James Salter

1990 *Billy Bathgate* by E. L. Doctorow
1991 *Philadelphia Fire* by John Edgar Wideman
1992 *Mao II* by Don DeLillo
1993 *Postcards* by E. Annie Proulx
1994 *Operation Shylock* by Philip Roth
1995 *Snow Falling on Cedars* by David Guterson
1996 *Independence Day* by Richard Ford
1997 *Women in Their Beds* by Gina Berriault
1998 *The Bear Comes Home* by Rafi Zabor

1999 *The Hours* by Michael Cunningham

2000 *Waiting* by Ha Jin

2001 *The Human Stain* by Philip Roth

2002 *Bel Canto* by Ann Patchett

2003 *The Caprices* by Sabina Murray

2004 *The Early Stories, 1953-1975* by John Updike

2005 *War Trash* by Ha Jin

2006 *The March* by E. L. Doctorow

2007 *Everyman* by Philip Roth

2008 *The Great Man* by Kate Christensen

NATIONAL BOOK CRITICS CIRCLE AWARD FOR FICTION

Since 1975, the National Book Critics Circle has presented an annual award for the finest fiction published in the English language.

1975 *Ragtime* by E. L. Doctorow

1976 *October Light* by John Gardner

1977 *Song of Solomon* by Toni Morrison

1978 *The Stories of John Cheever* by John Cheever

1979 *The Year of the French* by Thomas Flanagan

1980 *The Transit of Venus* by Shirley Hazzard

1981 *Rabbit Is Rich* by John Updike

1982 *George Mills* by Stanley Elkin

1983 *Ironweed* by William Kennedy

1984 *Love Medicine* by Louise Erdrich

1985 *The Accidental Tourist* by Anne Tyler

1986 *Kate Vaiden* by Reynolds Price

1987 *The Counterlife* by Philip Roth

1988 *The Middleman, and Other Stories* by Bharati Mukherjee

1989 *Billy Bathgate* by E. L. Doctorow

1990 *Rabbit at Rest* by John Updike

1991 *A Thousand Acres* by Jane Smiley

1992 *All the Pretty Horses* by Cormac McCarthy

1993 *A Lesson Before Dying* by Ernest J. Gaines

1994 *The Stone Diaries* by Carol Shields

1995 *Mrs. Ted Bliss* by Stanley Elkin

1996 *Women in Their Beds* by Gina Berriault

1997 *The Blue Flower* by Penelope Fitzgerald

1998 *The Love of a Good Woman* by Alice Munro

1999 *Motherless Brooklyn* by Jonathan Lethem

2000 *Being Dead* by Jim Crace

2001 *Austerlitz* by W. G. Sebald

2002 *Atonement* by Ian McEwan

2003 *The Known World* by Edward P. Jones

2004 *Gilead* by Marilynne Robinson

2005 *The March* by E. L. Doctorow

2006 *The Inheritance of Loss* by Kiran Desai

2007 *The Brief Wondrous Life of Oscar Wao* by Junot Díaz

2008 *2666* by Roberto Bolaño

GOVERNOR-GENERAL'S AWARD FOR FICTION

The Canada Council for the Arts and the governor-general of Canada present this award annually to honor the best works of English- and French-language fiction by Canadian authors. From 1936 through 1958, the awards were presented only to English-language books or to French-language books published in English translation; in 1959, the awards were expanded to include a category for French-language fiction.

1936 *Think of the Earth* by Bertram Brooker

1937 *The Dark Weaver* by Laura G. Salverson

1938 *Swiss Sonata* by Gwethalyn Graham

1939 *The Champlain Road* by Franklin D. McDowell

1940 *Thirty Acres* (translation) by Ringuet (pseudonym)

1941 *Three Came to Ville Marie* by Alan Sullivan

1942 *Little Man* by G. Herbert Sallans

1943 *The Pied Piper of Dipper Creek* by Thomas H. Raddall

1944 *Earth and High Heaven* by Gwethalyn Graham

1945 *Two Solitudes* by Hugh MacLennan

1946 *Continental Revue* by Winifred Bambrick

1947 *The Tin Flute* (translation) by Gabrielle Roy

1948 *The Precipice* by Hugh MacLennan

1949 *Mr. Ames Against Time* by Philip Child

1950   *The Outlander* (translation) by Germaine Guèvremont

1951   *The Loved and the Lost* by Morley Callaghan

1952   *The Pillar* by David Walker

1953   *Digby* by David Walker

1954   *The Fall of a Titan* by Igor Gouzenko

1955   *The Sixth of June* by Lionel Shapiro

1956   *The Sacrifice* by Adele Wiseman

1957   *Street of Riches* (translation) by Gabrielle Roy

1958   *Execution* by Colin McDougall

1959   *The Watch That Ends the Night* by Hugh MacLennan

      Malagré tout, la joie by André Giroux

1960   *The Luck of Ginger Coffey* by Brian Moore

1961   *Hear Us O Lord from Heaven Thy Dwelling Place* by Malcolm Lowry

      Ashini by Yves Thériault

1962   *Running to Paradise* by Kildare Dobbs

      Contes du pays incertain by Jacques Ferron

1963   *Hugh Garner's Best Stories* by Hugh Garner

1964   *The Deserter* by Douglas LePan

      Les Terres sèches by Jean-Paul Pinsonneault

1965   *L'Incubation* by Gérard Bessette

1966   *A Jest of God* by Margaret Laurence

      La Joue droite by Claire Martin

1967   *Salut Galarneau* by Jacques Godbout

1968   *Dance of the Happy Shades* by Alice Munro

      Cocksure by Mordecai Richler

      Trou de mémoire by Hubert Aquin

      Manuscrits de Pauline Archange by Marie-Claire Blais

1969   *The Studhorse Man* by Robert Kroetsch

      Une Forêt pour Zoé by Louise Maheux-Forcier

1970   *The New Ancestors* by Dave Godfrey

      La Femme de Loth by Monique Bosco

1971   *St. Urbain's Horseman* by Mordecai Richler

      Le Cycle by Gérard Bessette

1972   *The Manticore* by Robertson Davies

      Don l'Orignal by Antonine Maillet

1973   *The Temptations of Big Bear* by Rudy Wiebe

      L'Hiver de force by Réjean Ducharme

1974   *The Diviners* by Margaret Laurence

      Don Quichotte de la démanche by Victor-Levy Beaulieu

1975   *The Great Victorian Collection* by Brian Moore

      Les Enfants du sabbat by Anne Hébert

1976   *Bear* by Marian Engel

      Les Rescapés by André Major

1977   *The Wars* by Timothy Findley

      Ces enfants de ma vie by Gabrielle Roy

1978   *Who Do You Think You Are?* by Alice Munro

      Les Grandes Marées by Jacques Poulin

1979   *The Resurrection of Joseph Bourne* by Jack Hodgins

      Le Sourd dans la ville by Marie-Claire Blais

1980   *Burning Water* by George Bowering

      La Première Personne by Pierre Turgeon

1981   *Home Truths: Selected Canadian Stories* by Mavis Gallant

      La Province lunaire by Denys Chabot

1982   *Man Descending* by Guy Vanderhaeghe

      Le Cercle de arènas by Roger Fournier

1983   *Shakespeare's Dog* by Leon Rooke

      Laura Laur by Suzanne Jacob

1984   *The Engineer of Human Souls* by Joseph Skvorecky

      Agonie by Jacques Brault

1985   *The Handmaid's Tale* by Margaret Atwood

      Lucie: Ou, Un Midi en novembre by Fernand Ouellette

1986   *The Progress of Love* by Alice Munro

      Les Silences du corbeau by Yvon Rivard

1987   *A Dream Like Mine* by M. T. Kelly

      L'Obsédante obèse, et autres agressions by Gilles Archambault

1988   *Nights Below Station Street* by David Adams Richards

      Le Silence: Ou, Le Parfait Bonheur by Jacques Folch-Ribas

1989   *Whale Music* by Paul Quarrington

      La Rage by Louis Hamelin

1990   *Lives of the Saints* by Nino Ricci

      La Mauvaise foi by Gérald Tougas

1991   *Such a Long Journey* by Rohinton Mistry

      La Croix du Nord by André Brochu

1992   *The English Patient* by Michael Ondaatje

      L'Enfant chargé de songes byAnne Hébert

1993   *The Stone Diaries* by Carol Shields

      Cantique des plaines by Nancy Huston

1994 *A Discovery of Strangers* by Rudy Wiebe
      Le Petit Aigle à tête blanche by Robert Lalonde
1995 *The Roaring Girl* by Greg Hollingshead
      Les Oiseaux de Saint-John Perse by Nicole
          Houde
1996 *The Englishman's Boy* by Guy Vanderhaeghe
      Soifs by Marie-Claire Blais
1997 *The Underpainter* by Jane Urquhart
      Cet imperceptible mouvement by Aude
1998 *Forms of Devotion* by Diane Schoemperlen
      La Terre firma by Christine Frenette
1999 *Elizabeth and After* by Matt Cohen
      La Danse juive by Lise Tremblay
2000 *Anil's Ghost* by Michael Ondaatje
      Un Vent se lève qui éparpille by Jean Marc Dalpé
2001 *Richard B. Wright* by Clara Callan
      Le Ravissement by Andrée A. Michaud

2002 *A Song for Nettie Johnson* by Gloria Sawai
      La Glorie de Cassiodore by Monique LaRue
2003 *Elle* by Douglas Glover
      La Maison étrangère by Élise Turcotte
2004 *A Complicated Kindness* by Miriam Toews
      Le Cercle parfait by Pascale Quiviger
2005 *A Perfect Way to Go to China* by David
          Gilmour
      Hotaru by Aki Shimazaki
2006 *The Law of Dreams* by Peter Behrens
      La Rivière du loup by Andrée Laberge
2007 *Divisadero* by Michael Ondaatje
      La Mer de la Tranquillité by Sylvain Trudel
2008 *The Origin of Species* by Nino Ricci
      Naissance de Rebecca à l'ère des tourments by
          Marie-Claire Blais

MAN BOOKER PRIZE

The Man Booker Prize has been awarded annually since 1969 to the best novel of the year that is written by a citizen of the British Commonwealth or the Republic of Ireland.

1969 *Something to Answer For* by P. H. Newby
1970 *The Elected Member* by Bernice Rubens
1971 *In a Free State* by V. S. Naipaul
1972 *G* by John Berger
1973 *The Siege of Krishnapur* by J. G. Farrell
1974 *The Conservationist* by Nadine Gordimer
      Holiday by Stanley Middleton
1975 *Heat and Dust* by Ruth Prawer Jhabvala
1976 *Saville* by David Storey
1977 *Staying On* by Paul Scott
1978 *The Sea, the Sea* by Iris Murdoch
1979 *Offshore* by Penelope Fitzgerald
1980 *Rites of Passage* by William Golding
1981 *Midnight's Children* by Salman Rushdie
1982 *Schindler's Ark* by Thomas Keneally
1983 *Life and Times of Michael K* by J. M. Coetzee
1984 *Hotel du Lac* by Anita Brookner
1985 *The Bone People* by Keri Hulme
1986 *The Old Devils* by Kingsley Amis
1987 *Moon Tiger* by Penelope Lively
1988 *Oscar and Lucinda* by Peter Carey

1989 *The Remains of the Day* by Kazuo Ishiguro
1990 *Possession* by A. S. Byatt
1991 *The Famished Road* by Ben Okri
1992 *The English Patient* by Michael Ondaatje
1993 *Paddy Clarke Ha, Ha, Ha* by Roddy Doyle
1994 *How Late It Was, How Late* by James Kelman
1995 *The Ghost Road* by Pat Barker
1996 *Last Orders* by Graham Swift
1997 *The God of Small Things* by Arundhati Roy
1998 *Amsterdam* by Ian McEwan
1999 *Disgrace* by J. M. Coetzee
2000 *The Blind Assassin* by Margaret Atwood
2001 *True History of the Kelly Gang* by Peter Carey
2002 *Life of Pi* by Yann Martel
2003 *Vernon God Little* by D. B. C. Pierre
2004 *The Line of Beauty* by Alan Hollinghurst
2005 *The Sea* by John Banville
2006 *The Inheritance of Loss* by Kiran Desai
2007 *The Gathering* by Anne Enright
2008 *The White Tiger* by Aravind Adiga

COMMONWEALTH WRITERS' PRIZE

The Commonwealth Writers' Prize was established in 1987 to encourage and reward outstanding works of fiction by writers from throughout the British Commonwealth. It presents two fiction awards annually—one for the best book and another for the best first book.

BEST BOOK WINNERS

1987 *Summer Lightning* by Olive Senior
1988 *Heroes* by Festus Iyayi
1989 *The Carpathians* by Janet Frame
1990 *Solomon Gursky Was Here* by Mordecai Richler
1991 *The Great World* by David Malouf
1992 *Such a Long Journey* by Rohinton Mistry
1993 *The Ancestor Game* by Alex Miller
1994 *A Suitable Boy* by Vikram Seth
1995 *Captain Corelli's Mandolin* by Louis de Bernières
1996 *A Fine Balance* by Rohinton Mistry
1997 *Salt* by Earl Lovelace
1998 *Jack Maggs* by Peter Carey
1999 *Eucalyptus* by Murray Bail
2000 *Disgrace* by J. M. Coetzee
2001 *True History of the Kelly Gang* by Peter Carey
2002 *Gould's Book of Fish* by Richard Flanagan
2003 *The Polished Hoe* by Austin Clarke
2004 *A Distant Shore* by Caryl Phillips
2005 *Small Island* by Andrea Levy
2006 *The Secret River* by Kate Grenville
2007 *Mister Pip* by Lloyd Jones
2008 *The Book of Negroes* by Lawrence Hill

BEST FIRST BOOK WINNERS

1989 *Women of Influence* by Bonnie Burnard
1990 *Visitors* by John Cranna
1991 *Shape-Shifter* by Pauline Melville
1992 *Divina Trace* by Robert Antoni
1993 *The Thousand Faces of Night* by Gita Hariharan
1994 *The Case of Emily V* by Keith Oatley
1995 *Seasonal Adjustments* by Adib Khan
1996 *Red Earth, Pouring Rain* by Vikram Chandra
1997 *Fall on Your Knees* by Ann-Marie MacDonald
1998 *Angel Falls* by Tim Wynveen
1999 *The Electrical Field* by Kerri Sakamoto
2000 *Prisoner in a Red-Rose Chain* by Jeffrey Moore
2001 *White Teeth* by Zadie Smith
2002 *Ama, a Story of the Atlantic Slave Trade* by Manu Herbstein
2003 *Haweswater* by Sarah Hall
2004 *The Curious Incident of the Dog in the Night-Time* by Mark Haddon
2005 *Purple Hibiscus* by Chimamanda Ngozi Adichie
2006 *Suspended Sentences: Fictions of Atonement* by Mark McWatt
2007 *Vandal Love* by D. Y. Béchard
2008 *A Golden Age* by Tahmima Anam

TIME LINE

60 C.E.	Petronius writes *Satyricon* (*The Satyricon*, 1694), a satirical look at the excesses of ancient Rome that is often described as an early novel. Only a fragment of the original remains extant.
Second century	The Roman writer Lucius Apuleius writes *Metamorphoses* (*The Golden Ass*, 1566), another forerunner of the novel genre.
c. 1004	Murasaki Shikibu, a Japanese noblewoman, writes *Genji monogatari* (*The Tale of Genji*, 1925-1933), a diary about her life that some scholars consider to be the first novel.
1349-1351	Giovanni Boccaccio's *Decameron: O, Prencipe Galetto* (*The Decameron*, 1620), a group of stories presented as told by ten Florentines escaping the Black Death, is published. This collection of *novelle* (stories) is similar in form to a novel.
1387-1400	*The Canterbury Tales* by Geoffrey Chaucer, a collection of stories with a structure similar to that of Boccaccio's *Decameron*, appears.
1485	*Le Morte d'Arthur*, a compilation of Arthurian romances by Sir Thomas Malory, is published. Perhaps the best-known work of Arthurian literature in English, the book has been the source of many subsequent works based on the Arthurian legend.
1508	*Amadís de Gaul* (*Amadís of Gaul*, 1619) is published. This was the first novel of chivalry, one of several forms of long fiction that enjoyed popularity during the Spanish Golden Age of Literature in the fifteenth through seventeenth centuries.
1532	*Pantagruel* (English translation, 1653) by François Rabelais is published, the first book in the series *Gargantua et Pantagruel* (1532-1564; *Gargantua and Pantagruel*, 1653-1694, 1929).
1553	*Lazarillo de Tormes* (English translation, 1576) is published anonymously in Spain. This work is generally conceded to be the earliest and best of the picaresque novels.
1578	John Lyly's *Euphues, the Anatomy of Wit*, the first notable English novel, is published. The book established euphuism—an artificial, elegant, and alliterative style—as a standard for other writers.
1590	Thomas Lodge's *Rosalynde: Or, Euphues Golden Legacy*, an imitation of Lyly's novel *Eupheus, the Anatomy of Wit*, and Sir Philip Sidney's *Arcadia*, a work of long fiction combining elements of chivalric romance and pastoral literature, are published in England.
1605	The Spanish Golden Age novel reaches its apogee with the publication of the first volume of Miguel de Cervantes' *El ingenioso hidalgo don Quixote de la Mancha* (*The History of the Valorous and Wittie Knight-Errant, Don Quixote of the Mancha*, 1612-1620; better known as *Don Quixote de la Mancha*). The second volume is published in 1615.
1669	Hans Jakob Christoffel von Grimmelshausen's *Der abenteuerliche Simplicissimus* (*The Adventurous Simplicissimus*, 1912), the first major German novel, is published.
1678	The first part of John Bunyan's Christian allegory *The Pilgrim's Progress from This World to That Which Is to Come Delivered Under the Similitude of a Dream, Wherein Is Discovered the Manner of His Setting Out, His Dangerous Journey, and Safe Arrival at the Desired Country* (commonly known as *The Pilgrim's Progress*) is published; the second part appears in 1684.
	Madame de La Fayette's *La Princesse de Clèves* (*The Princess of Clèves*, 1679), one of the earliest psychological novels, is published.

1688	The development of the English novel advances with the publication of *Oroonoko: Or, The History of the Royal Slave*, by Aphra Behn, who may have been the first British woman to write for profit.
1719	Daniel Defoe's *The Life and Strange Surprizing Adventures of Robinson Crusoe, of York, Mariner, Written by Himself* (more commonly known as *Robinson Crusoe*) is published. Defoe has been called the first true English novelist.
1722	Defoe publishes *The Fortunes and Misfortunes of the Famous Moll Flanders, Written from Her Own Memorandums* (better known as *Moll Flanders*).
1726	*Gulliver's Travels*, Jonathan Swift's satirical and fanciful indictment of humankind's corruption, is published.
1740-1741	*Pamela: Or, Virtue Rewarded*, by Samuel Richardson, is published. This epistolary novel enjoys instant success, going through five editions in less than a year and inspiring numerous parodies, including Henry Fielding's *An Apology for the Life of Mrs. Shamela Andrews* (1741).
1742	Henry Fielding's *The History of the Adventures of Joseph Andrews, and of His Friend Mr. Abraham Adams* (commonly known as *Joseph Andrews*) is published. In his preface to the novel, Fielding describes the elements of comic realism, the style of both *Joseph Andrews* and his 1749 novel *The History of Tom Jones, a Foundling* (better known as *Tom Jones*).
1759	*Rasselas, Prince of Abyssinia: A Tale by S. Johnson*, Samuel Johnson's only novel, is published. The novel is a moral tale about the vanity of human wishes.
	Voltaire's *Candide: Ou, L'Optimisme Candide* (*Candide: Or, All for the Best*, 1759; also known as *Candide: Or, The Optimist*, 1762), a philosophical novel by the greatest writer of the French Enlightenment, is published.
1759-1767	Laurence Sterne's multivolume sentimental novel *The Life and Opinions of Tristram Shandy, Gent.* is published. The novel's initial volumes are the rage of London, but sales of subsequent volumes fall.
1761	*Julie: Ou, La Nouvelle Héloïse* (*Eloise: Or, A Series of Original Letters*, 1761; better known as *The New Héloïse*), Jean-Jacques Rousseau's only novel, is published.
1766	*The Vicar of Wakefield*, Oliver Goldsmith's portrayal of English country life, appears.
1774	*Die Leiden des jungen Werthers* (*The Sorrows of Young Werther*, 1779) Johann Wolfgang von Goethe's first novel, is published. This epistolary work marks a major advance in the development of German prose literature and becomes a model for other Romantic novels in many other countries.
1792	*Hung-lou meng* (also known as *Hung-lou meng*; *Dream of the Red Chamber*, 1958), considered the greatest Chinese classical novel, is published anonymously. It is later revealed that the author is Cao Xueqin.
1794	*The Mysteries of Udolpho*, Anne Radcliffe's best-known novel and a classic of the gothic romance genre, is published.
1795-1796	*Wilhelm Meisters Lehrjahre* (*Wilhelm Meister's Apprenticeship*, 1825), a bildungsroman by Johann Wolfgang von Goethe, is published.
1798	*Wieland: Or, The Transformation*, an Americanized version of the gothic romance, is published. The book's author, Charles Brockden Brown, is one of the first significant American writers.

1811-1818	Jane Austen perfects the novel of manners with the publication of her six complete novels: *Sense and Sensibility* (1811), *Pride and Prejudice* (1813), *Mansfield Park* (1814), *Emma* (1815), *Northanger Abbey* (1818), and *Persuasion* (1818).
1814	Sir Walter Scott's *Waverley: Or, 'Tis Sixty Years Since*, the first in his series of historical novels, is published.
1818	Mary Wollstonecroft Shelley's *Frankenstein: Or, The Modern Prometheus*, one of the most famous works of gothic literature, is published.
1821	James Fenimore Cooper creates the spy novel with the publication of *The Spy: A Tale of the Neutral Ground*. Cooper also is credited with creating the Western novel with his Leatherstocking Tales, a series of novels that includes *The Last of the Mohicans: A Narrative of 1757* (1826), and the sea adventure with *The Pilot: A Tale of the Sea* (1823).
1825-1832	*Evgeny Onegin* (*Eugene Onegin*, 1881), a novel in verse by Russia's greatest poet, Alexander Pushkin, is published.
1829-1848	In one of the major achievements in world literature, Honoré de Balzac creates the multivolume novel *La Comédie humaine* (*The Comedy of Human Life*, 1885-1893, 1896 [40 volumes]; also known as *The Human Comedy*, 1895-1896, 1911 [53 volumes]), a sweeping depiction of nineteenth century French society. The works in the series, published during a nineteen-year period beginning in 1829, include *Eugénie Grandet* (1833; English translation, 1859), *Le Père Goriot* (1834-1835; *Daddy Goriot*, 1860; also known as *Père Goriot*), and *La Cousine Bette* (1846; *Cousin Bette*, 1896).
1830	*Le Rouge et le noir* (*The Red and the Black*, 1898), Stendhal's novel featuring the egotistical Julien Sorel as protagonist, is published.
1836-1837	*Pickwick Papers*, the first of Charles Dickens's published novels, appears. The most important novelist of the Victorian era, Dickens created some of the best-known characters and most enduring works of world literature, including *Oliver Twist* (1837-1839), *Nicholas Nickleby* (1838-1839), *David Copperfield* (1849-1850), *A Tale of Two Cities* (1859), and *Great Expectations* (1860-1861).
1842	The first part of *Myortvye dushi* (*Dead Souls*, 1887), by Nikolai Gogol, is published, with the second part appearing in 1855. Gogol is often described as the first great Russian novelist.
1844	*Les Trois Mousquetaires* (*The Three Musketeers*, 1846), the enduring tale of seventeenth century France by Alexandre Dumas, *père*, is published.
1847	Charlotte Brontë's *Jane Eyre* is published, and *Wuthering Heights*, by her sister Emily Brontë, also appears.
1847-1848	William Makepeace Thackeray's *Vanity Fair: A Novel Without a Hero*, one of the greatest novels of the Victorian era, is published.
1850	Nathaniel Hawthorne's *The Scarlet Letter* is published and becomes a best seller.
1851	*The House of the Seven Gables*, Hawthorne's follow-up to his successful novel *The Scarlet Letter*, is published.
	Herman Melville's *Moby Dick: Or, The Whale* is published to mixed critical reviews. With the rise of modernist literature after World War I, however, the book is reassessed as a relevant novel and achieves recognition as a great work of American fiction.
1852	Harriet Beecher Stowe's *Uncle Tom's Cabin: Or, Life Among the Lowly*, originally serialized in the *National Era*, is published in book form. The book remains a controversial depiction of American slavery.

1857	The publication of *Madame Bovary* by Gustave Flaubert, a master of literary style and one of the creators of the modern novel, stirs controversy in France. Flaubert is prosecuted on charges of obscenity and blasphemy, but these charges eventually are ruled to be "not proven."
	Barchester Towers, the second title in Anthony Trollope's series of Barsetshire novels, is published. Trollope is one of the most prolific novelists of the Victorian era.
1859	*Adam Bede*, the first of George Eliot's seven novels, is published. Eliot's work occupies a pivotal role in the history of British fiction; it is both a culmination of the panoramic Victorian novel and the beginning of the later psychological novel.
1860	Wilkie Collins's *The Woman in White*, one of the earliest mystery novels, is published. Collins further contributes to the development of the mystery and detective genre with his novel *The Moonstone* (1868).
1862	*Les Misérables*, Victor Hugo's epic story of former convict Jean Valjean, is published.
	Ivan Turgenov's *Ottsy i deti* (*Fathers and Sons*, 1867), one of the great works of the Russian Golden Age of Literature, is published.
1865	Lewis Carroll creates a new form of children's literature with the publication of *Alice's Adventures in Wonderland*. This whimsical account of a young girl's adventures lacks the overtly moralistic or didactic nature of previous children's fiction.
1865-1869	Leo Tolstoy's *Voyna i mir* (*War and Peace*, 1886) is published. In this book and in his other works, including *Anna Karenina* (1875-1877; English translation, 1886), Tolstoy destroys the Romantic conventions of Russian fiction, bringing a new realism and sharpness to the novel that strongly influences the work of other writers.
1866	Fyodor Dostoevski's *Prestupleniye i nakazaniye* (*Crime and Punishment*, 1886) is published. Dostoevski brings a psychological depth and a unique narrative style to the novel, anticipating many of the elements of modern fiction.
1868	*Little Women*, Louisa May Alcott's enduring story of the March family, is published.
1869-1870	Jules Verne's *Vingt mille lieues sous les mers* (*Twenty Thousand Leagues Under the Sea*, 1873) is published, fascinating nineteenth century readers with its account of Captain Nemo's submarine voyage.
1871	*La Fortune des Rougon* (*The Rougon-Macquart Family*, 1879), the first title in Émile Zola's multivolume series *Les Rougon-Macquart* (*The Rougon-Macquarts*, 1896-1900), is published. The series presents a naturalistic depiction of a nineteenth century French family and includes *L'Assommoir* (1877; English translation, 1879), *Nana* (1880; English translation, 1880), and *Germinal* (1885: English translation, 1885).
1874	*Far from the Madding Crowd*, Thomas Hardy's first important novel, is published. Although he considers himself primarily a poet, Hardy's naturalistic prose establishes him as one of the most important novelists of the Victorian era, second only to Charles Dickens.
1875	Mark Twain's *The Adventures of Tom Sawyer* is published.
1878	*Daisy Miller*, the book that establishes Henry James as a leading novelist in the United States and England, is published and becomes the only book in James's lifetime to attain commercial success. James's novels attract a large readership in the twentieth century, however, when his work is universally credited with bringing a new refinement and sense of vocation to the English-language novel.

1881	*Memórias póstumas de Brás Cubas* (*The Posthumous Memoirs of Brás Cubas*, 1951; better known as *Epitaph of a Small Winner*, 1952), by Brazilian writer Joaquim Maria Machado de Assis, is published.
1881-1882	*Treasure Island*, one of the highly regarded Romantic novels of Robert Louis Stevenson, is published in serial form.
1884	Mark Twain's *Adventures of Huckleberry Finn* is published.
1885	William Dean Howells, a major proponent of literary realism, publishes his best-known novel, *The Rise of Silas Lapham*.
1888	*A Study in Scarlet*, the first of Arthur Conan Doyle's four novels featuring Sherlock Holmes, is published in its entirety after being serialized the previous year.
1891	*The Picture of Dorian Gray*, Oscar Wilde's only novel, is published in its entirety after being serialized the previous year. The novel is condemned by Wilde's contemporaries and most critics, who maintain that it is immoral, promotes decadent behavior, and can corrupt its readers.
1895	*The Time Machine: An Invention* is published, the first of H. G. Wells's many works of science fiction.
	The Red Badge of Courage: An Episode of the American Civil War, Stephen Crane's impressionist account of one of the war's battles, is published and becomes a classic in its time.
1899	Kate Chopin's *The Awakening*, one of the last great works of nineteenth century American realist fiction, is published.
1900	Theodore Dreiser's novel *Sister Carrie* helps create an Americanized version of literary naturalism.
1902	Joseph Conrad's *Heart of Darkness*, previously serialized, is published as a book. Conrad is a major architect of the modern psychological novel.
1903	Jack London's *The Call of the Wild* is published.
1905	Polish writer Henryk Sienkiewicz, author of *Quo vadis* (1895-1986, serial; 1896, book; *Quo Vadis: A Narrative of the Time of Nero*, 1896), is awarded the Nobel Prize in Literature.
1906	Upton Sinclair's *The Jungle* is published. The novel's depiction of the Chicago meatpacking industry leads to the reform of food inspection laws.
1907	English writer Rudyard Kipling is awarded the Nobel Prize in Literature.
1908	*A Room with a View*, the third of E. M. Forster's six novels, is published.
1909	Swedish writer Selma Lagerlöf , author of *Gösta Berlings saga* (1891; *The Story of Gösta Berling*, 1898), is awarded the Nobel Prize in Literature.
1913	*Du côté de chez Swann* (*Swann's Way*, 1922), the first volume in Marcel Proust's seven-volume novel *À la recherche du temps perdu* (1913-1927; *Remembrance of Things Past*, 1922-1931, 1981), is published. The novel is notable for its intense psychological realism.
	Sons and Lovers, D. H. Lawrence's third novel and one of his best, is published.
1915	*Of Human Bondage*, W. Somerset Maugham's first significant novel, is published.
	Ford Madox Ford's *The Good Soldier*, one of the masterpieces of modernism, is published.
1918	Willa Cather's *My Ántonia* is published.
1919	*The Magnificent Ambersons*, by Booth Tarkington, wins the Pulitzer Prize in fiction.
1920	Agatha Christie's *The Mysterious Affair at Styles: A Detective Story*, is published and introduces readers to master detective Hercule Poirot.

1921	Edith Wharton's *The Age of Innocence* is awarded the Pulitzer Prize in fiction.
1922	James Joyce's *Ulysses* is published. The novel is banned from the United States as obscene until 1933, when a court ruling lifts the ban.
1925	*The Great Gatsby*, F. Scott Fitzgerald's chronicle of the Jazz Age, is published.
	Edna Ferber's novel *So Big* receives the Pulitzer Prize in fiction.
	Virginia Woolf's *Mrs. Dalloway* is published. The modernist novel recounts one day in the life of fifty-two-year-old Clarissa Dalloway, an accomplished London hostess and wife of a member of Parliament.
	Der Prozess (*The Trial*, 1937), Franz Kafka's absurdist tale of Joseph K, is published.
1926	*The Sun Also Rises*, Ernest Hemingway's first significant novel, is published.
1928	Thornton Wilder's *The Bridge of San Luis Rey* receives the Pulitzer Prize in fiction.
1929	*Im Westen nichts Neues* (*All Quiet on the Western Front*, 1929), Erich Maria Remarque's account of the horrors of World War I, is published.
	Look Homeward, Angel, Thomas Wolfe's first and most significant novel, is published.
	German writer Thomas Mann is awarded the Nobel Prize in Literature for a body of work that includes the novels *Buddenbrooks: Verfall einer Familie* (1901; English translation, 1924) and *Der Zauberberg* (1924; *The Magic Mountain*, 1927).
1930	*The 42nd Parallel*, the first volume in John Dos Passos's *U.S.A.* trilogy, is published.
	Sinclair Lewis becomes the first American to be awarded the Nobel Prize in Literature. His novels include *Main Street: The Story of Carol Kennicott* (1920), *Babbitt* (1922), and *Arrowsmith* (1925).
1932	*Brave New World*, Aldous Huxley's dystopian tale of a future society, is published.
	Pearl S. Buck's *The Good Earth* receives the Pulitzer Prize in fiction.
1937	*Their Eyes Were Watching God*, by Zora Neale Hurston, is published. The best and most prolific African American woman writer of the 1930's, Hurston makes use of folklore in her fiction and also draws on her own experiences growing up in all-black Eatonville, Florida.
1938	*Dimple Hill*, the last of the twelve volumes in Dorothy Richardson's *Pilgrimage*, is published. Richardson was the first novelist in England to restrict point of view entirely to the protagonist's consciousness .
1939	Frans Eemil Sillanpää of Finland is awarded the Nobel Prize in Literature.
1942	Ellen Glasgow's *In This Our Life* receives the Pulitzer Prize in fiction.
1945	Evelyn Waugh's *Brideshead Revisited* is published.
	John Hersey's *A Bell for Adano* receives the Pulitzer Prize in fiction.
	Hugh MacLennan's *Two Solitudes* receives Canada's Governor-General's Award for fiction.
1946	German writer Hermann Hesse, whose novels include *Siddhartha* (1922; English translation, 1951) and *Der Steppenwolf* (1927; *Steppenwolf*, 1929), is awarded the Nobel Prize in Literature. Hesse's novels will become anthemic works of the 1960's counterculture.
1947	French writer André Gide, whose novels include *L'Immoraliste* (1902; *The Immoralist*, 1930) and *Les Faux-monnayeurs* (1925; *The Counterfeiters*, 1927), is awarded the Nobel Prize in Literature.
	Robert Penn Warren's *All the King's Men* wins the Pulitzer Prize in fiction.
	The Tin Flute, the translation of Gabrielle Roy's novel *Bonheur d'occasion* (1945), receives the Governor-General's Award for fiction.
1948	*Cry, the Beloved Country*, Alan Paton's denunciation of South African racism, is published.

1949   *Nineteen Eighty-Four*, George Orwell's political novel depicting a dystopian future, is
         published.
         William Faulkner is awarded the Nobel Prize in Literature for "his powerful and artistically
         unique contribution to the modern American novel."

1950   Nelson Algren receives the first National Book Award for fiction for his novel *The Man with
         the Golden Arm.*

1951   *The Catcher in the Rye*, J. D. Salinger's only novel and one of the most widely read and
         influential works of American postwar fiction, is published.
         Morley Callaghan's *The Loved and the Lost* receives the Governor-General's Award for
         fiction.

1953   *The Old Man and the Sea*, by Ernest Hemingway, receives the Pulitzer Prize in fiction.
         Ralph Ellison receives the National Book Award for fiction for *Invisible Man.*

1954   *The Fellowship of the Ring*, the first novel in J. R. R. Tolkien's *The Lord of the Rings* trilogy,
         is published. In the trilogy and other works, Tolkien creates a new form of fantasy literature
         with intense philosophical insight, spiritual meaning, and serious purpose.

1955   *Lolita*, Vladimir Nabokov's best-known and most controversial English-language novel, is
         published and becomes a best seller.

1957   Jack Kerouac's *On the Road*, which becomes a classic work of the Beat generation, is
         published.
         French writer Albert Camus, author of such existentialist novels as *L'Étranger* (1942; *The
         Stranger*, 1946) and *La Peste* (1947; *The Plague*, 1948), is awarded the Nobel Prize in
         Literature.

1958   Chinua Achebe's *Things Fall Apart*, one of the first and most significant works of African
         postcolonial literature, is published.
         A Death in the Family, John Agee's posthumously published novel, is awarded the Pulitzer
         Prize in fiction.
         John Cheever's first novel, *The Wapshot Chronicle*, wins the National Book Award for
         fiction.

1961   Joseph Heller's *Catch-22* is published. The satirical novel captures the period's growing
         antiwar sentiment and becomes one of the most widely read and discussed books of the
         1960's and early 1970's.
         Bosnian writer Ivo Andrić, whose novels include *Na Drini ćuprija* (1945; *The Bridge on the
         Drina*, 1959), is awarded the Nobel Prize in Literature.
         To Kill a Mockingbird, Harper Lee's only novel, wins the Pulitzer Prize in fiction.

1962   American writer John Steinbeck, whose fiction includes *Of Mice and Men* (1937) and the
         Pulitzer Prize-winning novel *The Grapes of Wrath* (1939), is awarded the Nobel Prize in
         Literature.
         Walker Percy receives the National Book Award for fiction for his novel *The Moviegoer.*
         The Man in the High Castle, by science-fiction writer Philip K. Dick, is published.

1963   Nathalie Sarraute's *Les Fruits d'or* (*The Golden Fruits*, 1964), one of the best examples of
         the French New Novel, is published.

1966   Truman Capote creates the nonfiction novel with the publication of *In Cold Blood.*
         Israeli writer Shmuel Yosef Agnon, who during his lifetime is dubbed the "dean of Hebrew
         letters," is jointly awarded the Nobel Prize in Literature with poet Nelly Sachs.
         Margaret Laurence's *A Jest of God* receives the Governor-General's Award for fiction.

1967	Bernard Malamud receives the Pulitzer Prize in fiction for his novel *The Fixer*.
1968	Arthur C. Clarke's influential science-fiction novel *2001: A Space Odyssey* is published. Japanese writer Yasunari Kawabata, whose novels include *Yukiguni* (1935-1937, serial; 1947, book; *Snow Country*, 1956), is awarded the Nobel Prize in Literature. William Styron receives the Pulitzer Prize in fiction for *The Confessions of Nat Turner*. The novel's depiction of African Americans arouses controversy.
1970	Soviet dissident Aleksandr Solzhenitsyn is awarded the Nobel Prize in Literature "for the ethical force with which he has pursued the indispensable traditions of Russian literature."
1971	Mordecai Richler's *St. Urbain's Horseman* receives the Governor-General's Award for fiction.
1972	Wallace Stegner's *Angle of Repose* is awarded the Pulitzer Prize in fiction.
1973	Australian writer Patrick White is honored with the Nobel Prize in Literature. White, whose novels include *Voss* (1957), transforms Australian history into an epic and tragic vision. Eudora Welty's *The Optimist's Daughter* receives the Pulitzer Prize in fiction.
1974	Thomas Pynchon's *Gravity's Rainbow* obtains a unanimous vote to win the Pulitzer Prize in fiction, but a Pulitzer committee overturns this decision, calling the book "obscene," and no award is given for this year.
1975	*Ragtime*, by E. L. Doctorow, wins the first National Book Critics Circle Award for fiction.
1976	American writer Saul Bellow is awarded the Nobel Prize in Literature. Bellow's novels include *The Adventures of Augie March* (1953), *Herzog* (1964), and *Humboldt's Gift* (1975). William Gaddis's novel *JR* (1975) wins the National Book Award for fiction. John Gardner receives the National Book Critics Circle Award for *October Light*.
1977	*La tía Julia y el escribidor* (*Aunt Julia and the Scriptwriter*, 1982), by Peruvian writer Mario Vargas Llosa, is published.
1978	Isaac Bashevis Singer, whose Yiddish-language works chronicle Jewish life in Eastern Europe and the United States, is awarded the Nobel Prize in Literature. Iris Murdoch receives the Man Booker Prize for her novel *The Sea, the Sea*.
1980	Umberto Eco's *Il nome della rosa* (*The Name of the Rose*, 1983), a murder mystery set in an Italian monastery in 1327, is published and becomes a best seller. *The Executioner's Song*, Norman Mailer's novel about the execution of convicted murderer Gary Gilmore, receives the Pulitzer Prize in fiction. William Styron's novel *Sophie's Choice* receives the National Book Award for fiction, and John Irving's *The World According to Garp* garners the award for a paperback.
1981	*Rabbit Is Rich*, by John Updike, is published and receives the National Book Critics Circle Award for fiction; the novel goes on to be awarded the 1982 Pulitzer Prize in fiction and 1982 National Book Award for fiction.
1982	Colombian writer Gabriel García Márquez is awarded the Nobel Prize in Literature. García Márquez's masterpiece is the novel *Cien años de soledad* (1967; *One Hundred Years of Solitude*, 1970), one of the most influential works of Magical Realism. Isabel Allende's first novel, *La casa de los espíritus* (*The House of the Spirits*, 1985), is published.

1983   British author William Golding, author of *Lord of the Flies* (1954), is awarded the Nobel Prize in Literature.

Alice Walker receives both the Pulitzer Prize in fiction and the National Book Award for fiction for *The Color Purple*.

William Kennedy's *Ironweed* is published and receives the National Book Critics Circle Award for fiction; in 1984, the novel is awarded the Pulitzer Prize in fiction.

1984   Milan Kundera's *L'Insoutenable légèreté de l'être* (*The Unbearable Lightness of Being*, 1984; in Czech as *Nesnesitelná lehkost bytí*, 1985) is published. The novel tells the story of four characters whose lives are changed by the Soviet invasion of Czechoslovakia in 1968.

Sandra Cisneros's *The House on Mango Street* is published.

Anita Brookner receives the Man Booker Prize for *Hotel du Lac*.

1985   Don DeLillo receives the National Book Award for fiction for *White Noise*.

Anne Tyler's *The Accidental Tourist* receives the National Book Critics Circle Award for fiction.

Margaret Atwood's *The Handmaid's Tale* is honored with the Governor-General's Award for fiction.

1986   Nigerian writer Wole Soyinka becomes the first African to be awarded the Nobel Prize in Literature.

Larry McMurtry's *Lonesome Dove* receives the Pulitzer Prize in fiction.

1988   Egyptian writer Naguib Mahfouz becomes the first Arab writer to be awarded the Nobel Prize in Literature.

Australian writer Peter Carey's novel *Oscar and Lucinda* earns the author his first of two Man Booker Prizes.

1989   *The Joy Luck Club*, Amy Tan's novel about four Chinese American mothers and their daughters, is published and becomes a best seller.

Iranian religious leader Ayatollah Khomeini announces a fatwa calling for the death of writer Salman Rushdie, claiming the writer blasphemes the Muslim religion in his novel *The Satanic Verses* (1988).

1990   *The Mambo Kings Play Songs of Love* wins the Pulitzer Prize in fiction, making its author, Oscar Hijuelos, the first Latino writer to receive the award.

1991   Jane Smiley's *A Thousand Acres* is published and wins the National Book Critics Circle Award for fiction; it goes on to be awarded the 1992 Pulitzer Prize in fiction.

Nadine Gordimer becomes the first South African writer to receive the Nobel Prize in Literature.

1992   *The English Patient*, by Michael Ondaatje, wins both the Man Booker Prize and Canada's Governor-General's Award for fiction.

1993   *The Shipping News*, by E. Annie Proulx, is published and receives the National Book Award for fiction; in 1994 the novel is honored with the Pulitzer Prize in fiction.

Toni Morrison, whose novels include *Sula* (1973), *Song of Solomon* (1977), and *Beloved* (1987), becomes the first African American woman to receive the Nobel Prize in Literature.

The Stone Diaries, by Carol Shields, is published. This work garners three Canadian and American awards: the Governor-General's Award for fiction (1993), the National Book Critics Circle Award for fiction (1994), and the Pulitzer Prize in fiction (1995).

1994   Indian writer Vikram Seth's novel *A Suitable Boy* receives the Commonwealth Writers' Prize for Best Book.

1996   Richard Ford's novel *Independence Day* receives both the Pulitzer Prize in fiction and the PEN/Faulkner Award for Fiction.

1997   J. K. Rowling's *Harry Potter and the Philosopher's Stone* is published in Britain. The novel, retitled *Harry Potter and the Sorcerer's Stone* (1998) for publication in the United States, is the first of seven phenomenally popular books about the adventures of a young wizard and his friends.

1998   José Saramago of Portugal is awarded the Nobel Prize in Literature.

        Philip Roth receives the Pulitzer Prize in fiction for *American Pastoral*.

1999   German writer Günter Grass, whose works include *Die Blechtrommel* (1959; *The Tin Drum*, 1961), is awarded the Nobel Prize in Literature.

        Ha Jin's novel *Waiting* is published and wins the National Book Award for fiction; in 2000, the novel is honored with the PEN/Faulkner Award for Fiction.

        Michael Cunningham's *The Hours* receives both the Pulitzer Prize in fiction and the PEN/Faulkner Award for Fiction.

2000   Gao Xingjian, a Chinese author who emigrated to France, is awarded the Nobel Prize in Literature. His novels include *Ling shan* (1990; *Soul Mountain*, 2000) and *Yige ren de shengjing* (1999; *One Man's Bible*, 2002).

        Susan Sontag's novel *In America* is published and receives the National Book Award for fiction.

2001   Michael Chabon receives the Pulitzer Prize in fiction for *The Amazing Adventures of Kavalier and Clay*.

        White Teeth, by Zadie Smith, receives the Commonwealth Writers' Prize for Best First Book.

        Jonathan Franzen's *The Corrections* is published and receives the National Book Award for fiction.

2002   *Empire Falls*, by Richard Russo, wins the Pulitzer Prize in fiction.

        Ann Patchett's novel *Bel Canto* wins the PEN/Faulkner Award for Fiction.

2003   South African writer J. M. Coetzee is awarded the Nobel Prize in Literature. Coetzee's works include two Man Booker Prize-winning novels: *Life and Times of Michael K* (1983) and *Disgrace* (1999).

2004   *Gilead*, Marilynne Robinson's second novel, is published and receives the National Book Critics Circle Award for fiction; it goes on to win the 2005 Pulitzer Prize in fiction.

2005   John Barnes's *The Sea* receives the Man Booker Prize.

2006   *The Echo Maker*, by Richard Powers, is published and receives the National Book Award for fiction.

2007   British writer Doris Lessing becomes the oldest person ever awarded the Nobel Prize in Literature.

        Nigerian writer Chinua Achebe, often credited as the founder of modern African literature, wins the Man Booker International Prize for his life's work.

        Cormac McCarthy's postapocalyptic novel *The Road* receives the Pulitzer Prize in fiction.

2008   Herman Wouk, author of the Pulitzer Prize-winning novel *The Caine Mutiny* (1951), is honored with the first ever lifetime achievement award for fiction writing from the Library of Congress.

        Shadow Country: A New Rendering of the Watson Legend, by Peter Matthiessen, is published and receives the National Book Award for fiction.

Rebecca Kuzins

Chronological List of Authors

This chronology of the authors covered in these volumes serves as a time line for students interested in the development of long fiction from ancient to modern times. The arrangement is chronological on the basis of birth years, and the proximity of writers provides students with some insights into potential influences and contemporaneous developments.

Born up to 1700

Murasaki Shikibu (c. 978)
Malory, Sir Thomas (early fifteenth century)
Rabelais, François (c. 1494)
Wu Chengen (c. 1500)
Cervantes, Miguel de (September 29, 1547)
d'Urfé, Honoré (February 11, 1568)
Cyrano de Bergerac (March 6, 1619)
Grimmelshausen, Hans Jakob Christoffel von (March 17, 1621[?])
Bunyan, John (November 30, 1628 [baptized])
La Fayette, Madame de (March 18, 1634)
Behn, Aphra (July [?], 1640)
Defoe, Daniel (1660)
Swift, Jonathan (November 30, 1667)
Lesage, Alain-René (May 8, 1668)
Marivaux (February 4, 1688)
Richardson, Samuel (August 19, 1689 [baptized])
Voltaire (November 21, 1694)
Prévost, Abbé (April 1, 1697)

Born 1701-1800

Wu Jingzi (1701)
Fielding, Henry (April 22, 1707)
Johnson, Samuel (September 18, 1709)
Rousseau, Jean-Jacques (June 28, 1712)
Diderot, Denis (October 5, 1713)
Sterne, Laurence (November 24, 1713)
Cao Xueqin (1715[?])
Smollett, Tobias (March 19, 1721)
Goldsmith, Oliver (November 10, 1728 *or* 1730)
Goethe, Johann Wolfgang von (August 28, 1749)
Burney, Fanny (June 13, 1752)
Rowson, Susanna (1762)
Jean Paul (March 21, 1763)
Radcliffe, Ann (July 9, 1764)
Edgeworth, Maria (January 1, 1768)

Chateaubriand, François-René de (September 4, 1768)
Brown, Charles Brockden (January 17, 1771)
Scott, Sir Walter (August 15, 1771)
Lewis, Matthew Gregory (July 9, 1775)
Austen, Jane (December 16, 1775)
Hoffmann, E. T. A. (January 24, 1776)
Kleist, Heinrich von (October 18, 1777)
Maturin, Charles Robert (September 25, 1780)
Stendhal (January 23, 1783)
Manzoni, Alessandro (March 7, 1785)
Peacock, Thomas Love (October 18, 1785)
Cooper, James Fenimore (September 15, 1789)
Shelley, Mary Wollstonecraft (August 30, 1797)
Balzac, Honoré de (May 20, 1799)
Pushkin, Alexander (June 6, 1799)

Born 1801-1820

Hugo, Victor (February 26, 1802)
Dumas, Alexandre, *père* (July 24, 1802)
Mérimée, Prosper (September 28, 1803)
Sand, George (July 1, 1804)
Hawthorne, Nathaniel (July 4, 1804)
Ainsworth, William Harrison (February 4, 1805)
Stifter, Adalbert (October 23, 1805)
Simms, William Gilmore (April 17, 1806)
Gogol, Nikolai (March 31, 1809)
Gaskell, Elizabeth (September 29, 1810)
Stowe, Harriet Beecher (June 14, 1811)
Thackeray, William Makepeace (July 18, 1811)
Dickens, Charles (February 7, 1812)
Goncharov, Ivan (June 6, 1812)
Le Fanu, Joseph Sheridan (August 28, 1814)
Lermontov, Mikhail (October 15, 1814)
Trollope, Anthony (April 24, 1815)
Brontë, Charlotte (April 21, 1816)
Storm, Theodor (September 14, 1817)
Brontë, Emily (July 30, 1818)

Turgenev, Ivan (November 9, 1818)
Keller, Gottfried (July 19, 1819)
Melville, Herman (August 1, 1819)
Eliot, George (November 22, 1819)
Fontane, Theodor (December 30, 1819)

BORN 1821-1840

Dostoevski, Fyodor (November 11, 1821)
Flaubert, Gustave (December 12, 1821)
Goncourt, Edmond de (May 26, 1822)
Collins, Wilkie (January 8, 1824)
Valera, Juan (October 18, 1824)
De Forest, John William (March 31, 1826)
Verne, Jules (February 8, 1828)
Meredith, George (February 12, 1828)
Tolstoy, Leo (September 9, 1828)
Raabe, Wilhelm (September 8, 1831)
Carroll, Lewis (January 27, 1832)
Alcott, Louisa May (November 29, 1832)
Twain, Mark (November 30, 1835)
Butler, Samuel (December 4, 1835)
Aldrich, Thomas Bailey (November 11, 1836)
Howells, William Dean (March 1, 1837)
Machado de Assis, Joaquim Maria (June 21, 1839)
Pater, Walter (August 4, 1839)
Zola, Émile (April 2, 1840)
Daudet, Alphonse (May 13, 1840)
Hardy, Thomas (June 2, 1840)
Verga, Giovanni (September 2, 1840)

BORN 1841-1860

Hudson, W. H. (August 4, 1841)
James, Henry (April 15, 1843)
Pérez Galdós, Benito (May 10, 1843)
France, Anatole (April 16, 1844)
Cable, George Washington (October 12, 1844)
Eça de Queirós, José Maria de (November 25, 1845)
Sienkiewicz, Henryk (May 5, 1846)
Huysmans, Joris-Karl (February 5, 1848)
Strindberg, August (January 22, 1849)
Jewett, Sarah Orne (September 3, 1849)
Stevenson, Robert Louis (November 13, 1850)
Chopin, Kate (February 8, 1851)
Pardo Bazán, Emilia (September 16, 1851)
Moore, George (February 24, 1852)

Alas, Leopoldo (April 25, 1852)
Wilde, Oscar (October 16, 1854)
Frederic, Harold (August 19, 1856)
Gissing, George (November 22, 1857)
Conrad, Joseph (December 3, 1857)
Chesnutt, Charles Waddell (June 20, 1858)
Lagerlöf, Selma (November 20, 1858)
Aleichem, Sholom (March 2, 1859)
Doyle, Arthur Conan (May 22, 1859)
Heidenstam, Verner von (July 6, 1859)
Hamsun, Knut (August 4, 1859)
Garland, Hamlin (September 14, 1860)

BORN 1861-1880

Svevo, Italo (December 19, 1861)
Wharton, Edith (January 24, 1862)
D'Annunzio, Gabriele (March 12, 1863)
Unamuno y Jugo, Miguel de (September 29, 1864)
Merezhkovsky, Dmitry (August 14, 1865)
Kipling, Rudyard (December 30, 1865)
Rolland, Romain (January 29, 1866)
Wells, H. G. (September 21, 1866)
Valle-Inclán, Ramón María del (October 28, 1866)
Blasco Ibáñez, Vicente (January 29, 1867)
Reymont, Władysław (May 7, 1867)
Bennett, Arnold (May 27, 1867)
Pirandello, Luigi (June 28, 1867)
Galsworthy, John (August 14, 1867)
Gorky, Maxim (March 28, 1868)
Tarkington, Booth (July 29, 1869)
Gide, André (November 22, 1869)
Norris, Frank (March 5, 1870)
Proust, Marcel (July 10, 1871)
Dreiser, Theodore (August 27, 1871)
Deledda, Grazia (September 27, 1871)
Crane, Stephen (November 1, 1871)
Baroja, Pío (December 28, 1872)
Azuela, Mariano (January 1, 1873)
Jensen, Johannes V. (January 20, 1873)
Colette (January 28, 1873)
Glasgow, Ellen (April 22, 1873)
De la Mare, Walter (April 25, 1873)
Richardson, Dorothy (May 17, 1873)
Cather, Willa (December 7, 1873)
Ford, Ford Madox (December 17, 1873)

Maugham, W. Somerset (January 25, 1874)
Stein, Gertrude (February 3, 1874)
Chesterton, G. K. (May 29, 1874)
Mann, Thomas (June 6, 1875)
Buchan, John (August 26, 1875)
London, Jack (January 12, 1876)
Anderson, Sherwood (September 13, 1876)
Hesse, Hermann (July 2, 1877)
Döblin, Alfred (August 10, 1878)
Sinclair, Upton (September 20, 1878)
Forster, E. M. (January 1, 1879)
Grove, Frederick Philip (February 14, 1879)
Cabell, James Branch (April 14, 1879)
Van Vechten, Carl (June 17, 1880)
Pérez de Ayala, Ramón (August 9, 1880)
Hall, Radclyffe (August 12, 1880)
Asch, Sholem (November 1, 1880)
Musil, Robert (November 6, 1880)

BORN 1881-1900
Martin du Gard, Roger (March 23, 1881)
Macaulay, Rose (August 1, 1881)
Wodehouse, P. G. (October 15, 1881)
Roberts, Elizabeth Madox (October 30, 1881)
Woolf, Virginia (January 25, 1882)
Joyce, James (February 2, 1882)
Fauset, Jessie Redmon (April 27, 1882)
Undset, Sigrid (May 20, 1882)
Lewis, Wyndham (November 18, 1882)
Kazantzakis, Nikos (February 18, 1883)
Ha{scaron}ek, Jaroslav (April 30, 1883)
Kafka, Franz (July 3, 1883)
Zamyatin, Yevgeny (January 20, 1884)
Compton-Burnett, Ivy (June 5, 1884)
Lewis, Sinclair (February 7, 1885)
Ferber, Edna (August 15, 1885)
Romains, Jules (August 26, 1885)
Lawrence, D. H. (September 11, 1885)
Mauriac, François (October 11, 1885)
Tanizaki, Jun'ichirō (July 24, 1886)
Alain-Fournier (October 3, 1886)
Broch, Hermann (November 1, 1886)
Cendrars, Blaise (September 1, 1887)
Wilson, Ethel (January 20, 1888)
Bernanos, Georges (February 20, 1888)

Agnon, Shmuel Yosef (July 17, 1888)
Chandler, Raymond (July 23, 1888)
Sillanpää, Frans Eemil (September 16, 1888)
Cary, Joyce (December 7, 1888)
Cocteau, Jean (July 5, 1889)
Aiken, Conrad (August 5, 1889)
McKay, Claude (September 15, 1889)
Čapek, Karel (January 9, 1890)
Pasternak, Boris (February 10, 1890)
Porter, Katherine Anne (May 15, 1890)
Werfel, Franz (September 10, 1890)
Christie, Agatha (September 15, 1890)
Richter, Conrad (October 13, 1890)
Hurston, Zora Neale (January 7, 1891)
Larsen, Nella (April 13, 1891)
Bulgakov, Mikhail (May 15, 1891)
Lagerkvist, Pär (May 23, 1891)
Miller, Henry (December 26, 1891)
Tolkien, J. R. R. (January 3, 1892)
Barnes, Djuna (June 12, 1892)
Buck, Pearl S. (June 26, 1892)
Cain, James M. (July 1, 1892)
Aldington, Richard (July 8, 1892)
Andrić, Ivo (October 10, 1892)
West, Rebecca (December 21, 1892)
Sayers, Dorothy L. (June 13, 1893)
Marquand, John P. (November 10, 1893)
Gadda, Carlo Emilio (November 14, 1893)
Céline, Louis-Ferdinand (May 27, 1894)
Hammett, Dashiell (May 27, 1894)
Huxley, Aldous (July 26, 1894)
Rhys, Jean (August 24, 1894)
Roth, Joseph (September 2, 1894)
Priestley, J. B. (September 13, 1894)
Davis, H. L. (October 18, 1894; possibly 1896)
Giono, Jean (March 30, 1895)
Graves, Robert (July 24, 1895)
Gordon, Caroline (October 6, 1895)
Hartley, L. P. (December 30, 1895)
Dos Passos, John (January 14, 1896)
Cronin, A. J. (July 19, 1896)
Rawlings, Marjorie Kinnan (August 8, 1896)
Doderer, Heimito von (September 5, 1896)
Fitzgerald, F. Scott (September 24, 1896)
Tomasi di Lampedusa, Giuseppe (December 23, 1896)

Wilder, Thornton (April 17, 1897)
Faulkner, William (September 25, 1897)
Powell, Dawn (November 28, 1897)
O'Brien, Kate (December 3, 1897)
Remarque, Erich Maria (June 22, 1898)
Lewis, C. S. (November 29, 1898)
Nabokov, Vladimir (April 23, 1899)
Bowen, Elizabeth (June 7, 1899)
Kawabata, Yasunari (June 11, 1899)
Hemingway, Ernest (July 21, 1899)
Asturias, Miguel Ángel (October 19, 1899)
Silone, Ignazio (May 1, 1900)
Saint-Exupéry, Antoine de (June 29, 1900)
Sarraute, Nathalie (July 18, 1900)
Green, Julien (September 6, 1900)
Wolfe, Thomas (October 3, 1900)
Seghers, Anna (November 19, 1900)
Pritchett, V. S. (December 16, 1900)

BORN 1901-1910

Lehmann, Rosamond (February 3, 1901)
Sender, Ramón José (February 3, 1901)
Kavan, Anna (April 10, 1901)
Wescott, Glenway (April 11, 1901)
Hanley, James (September 3, 1901)
Malraux, André (November 3, 1901)
Boyle, Kay (February 19, 1902)
Steinbeck, John (February 27, 1902)
Laxness, Halldór (April 23, 1902)
Stead, Christina (July 17, 1902)
Waters, Frank (July 25, 1902)
Bontemps, Arna (October 13, 1902)
Paton, Alan (January 11, 1903)
Simenon, Georges (February 13, 1903)
Nin, Anaïs (February 21, 1903)
Queneau, Raymond (February 21, 1903)
Callaghan, Morley (February 22, 1903)
Yourcenar, Marguerite (June 8, 1903)
Orwell, George (June 25, 1903)
Horgan, Paul (August 1, 1903)
Mallea, Eduardo (August 14, 1903)
Cozzens, James Gould (August 19, 1903)
West, Nathanael (October 17, 1903)
Waugh, Evelyn (October 28, 1903)
Caldwell, Erskine (December 17, 1903)

Farrell, James T. (February 27, 1904)
Singer, Isaac Bashevis (July 14 or November 21, 1904)
Gombrowicz, Witold (August 4, 1904)
Greene, Graham (October 2, 1904)
Carpentier, Alejo (December 26, 1904)
O'Hara, John (January 31, 1905)
Rand, Ayn (February 2, 1905)
Warren, Robert Penn (April 24, 1905)
Bates, H. E. (May 16, 1905)
Sholokhov, Mikhail (May 24, 1905)
Sartre, Jean-Paul (June 21, 1905)
Canetti, Elias (July 25, 1905)
Renault, Mary (September 4, 1905)
Koestler, Arthur (September 5, 1905)
Snow, C. P. (October 15, 1905)
Green, Henry (October 29, 1905)
Powell, Anthony (December 21, 1905)
Roth, Henry (February 8, 1906)
Beckett, Samuel (April 13, 1906)
White, T. H. (May 29, 1906)
Narayan, R. K. (October 10, 1906)
Buzzati, Dino (October 16, 1906)
Michener, James A. (February 3, 1907[?])
MacLennan, Hugh (March 20, 1907)
Du Maurier, Daphne (May 13, 1907)
Heinlein, Robert A. (July 7, 1907)
Stuart, Jesse (August 8, 1907)
Moravia, Alberto (November 28, 1907)
Godden, Rumer (December 10, 1907)
Beauvoir, Simone de (January 9, 1908)
Ross, Sinclair (January 22, 1908)
L'Amour, Louis (March 22, 1908)
Prokosch, Frederic (May 17, 1908)
Arnow, Harriette (July 7, 1908)
Vittorini, Elio (July 23, 1908)
Maxwell, William (August 16, 1908)
Saroyan, William (August 31, 1908)
Wright, Richard (September 4, 1908)
Pavese, Cesare (September 9, 1908)
Rao, Raja (November 8, 1908)
Stegner, Wallace (February 18, 1909)
Roy, Gabrielle (March 22, 1909)
Algren, Nelson (March 28, 1909)
Welty, Eudora (April 13, 1909)
Aguilera Malta, Demetrio (May 24, 1909)

Dazai, Osamu (June 19, 1909)
Onetti, Juan Carlos (July 1, 1909)
Lowry, Malcolm (July 28, 1909)
Himes, Chester (July 29, 1909)
Clark, Walter Van Tilburg (August 3, 1909)
Alegría, Ciro (November 4, 1909)
Agee, James (November 27, 1909)
Morris, Wright (January 6, 1910)
De Vries, Peter (February 27, 1910)
Doerr, Harriet (April 8, 1910)
Genet, Jean (December 19, 1910)
Bowles, Paul (December 30, 1910)

BORN 1911-1920

Frisch, Max (May 15, 1911)
Sábato, Ernesto (June 24, 1911)
Goodman, Paul (September 9, 1911)
Golding, William (September 19, 1911)
O'Brien, Flann (October 5, 1911)
Mahfouz, Naguib (December 11, 1911)
Durrell, Lawrence (February 27, 1912)
Sarton, May (May 3, 1912)
Cheever, John (May 27, 1912)
White, Patrick (May 28, 1912)
McCarthy, Mary (June 21, 1912)
Amado, Jorge (August 10, 1912)
Pym, Barbara (June 2, 1913)
Wilson, Angus (August 11, 1913)
Davies, Robertson (August 28, 1913)
Simon, Claude (October 10, 1913)
Camus, Albert (November 7, 1913)
Burroughs, William S. (February 5, 1914)
Ellison, Ralph (March 1, 1914)
Duras, Marguerite (April 4, 1914)
Malamud, Bernard (April 26, 1914)
Hersey, John (June 17, 1914)
Purdy, James (July 17, 1914)
Cortázar, Julio (August 26, 1914)
Wouk, Herman (May 27, 1915)
Bellow, Saul (June 10, 1915)
Gonzalez, N. V. M. (September 8, 1915)
Hauge, Alfred (October 17, 1915)
Macdonald, Ross (December 13, 1915)
Fielding, Gabriel (March 25, 1916)
Cela, Camilo José (May 11, 1916)

Percy, Walker (May 28, 1916)
Ginzburg, Natalia (July 14, 1916)
Hardwick, Elizabeth (July 27, 1916)
Hébert, Anne (August 1, 1916)
Yerby, Frank (September 5, 1916)
Foote, Shelby (November 17, 1916)
McCullers, Carson (February 19, 1917)
Burgess, Anthony (February 25, 1917)
Powers, J. F. (July 8, 1917)
Auchincloss, Louis (September 27, 1917)
Clarke, Arthur C. (December 16, 1917)
Böll, Heinrich (December 21, 1917)
Gironella, José María (December 31, 1917)
Spark, Muriel (February 1, 1918)
Sturgeon, Theodore (February 26, 1918)
Settle, Mary Lee (July 29, 1918)
Solzhenitsyn, Aleksandr (December 11, 1918)
Salinger, J. D. (January 1, 1919)
Murdoch, Iris (July 15, 1919)
Pinget, Robert (July 19, 1919)
Levi, Primo (July 31, 1919)
Lessing, Doris (October 22, 1919)
Yglesias, José (November 29, 1919)
Asimov, Isaac (January 2, 1920)
Adams, Richard (May 9, 1920)
Tutuola, Amos (June 20, 1920)
James, P. D. (August 3, 1920)
Bukowski, Charles (August 16, 1920)
Bradbury, Ray (August 22, 1920)
Herbert, Frank (October 8, 1920)
Delibes, Miguel (October 17, 1920)

BORN 1921-1930

Sciascia, Leonardo (January 8, 1921)
Highsmith, Patricia (January 19, 1921)
Harris, Wilson (March 24, 1921)
Douglas, Ellen (July 12, 1921)
Moore, Brian (August 25, 1921)
Lem, Stanisław (September 12, 1921)
Jones, James (November 6, 1921)
Ćosić, Dobrica (December 29, 1921)
Kerouac, Jack (March 12, 1922)
Braine, John (April 13, 1922)
Amis, Kingsley (April 16, 1922)
Gallant, Mavis (August 11, 1922)

Robbe-Grillet, Alain (August 18, 1922)
Vonnegut, Kurt (November 11, 1922)
Saramago, José (November 16, 1922)
Gaddis, William (December 29, 1922)
Kemal, Yashar (1923)
Sembène, Ousmane (January 1, 1923)
Mailer, Norman (January 31, 1923)
Dickey, James (February 2, 1923)
Endō, Shūsaku (March 27, 1923)
Heller, Joseph (May 1, 1923)
Jolley, Elizabeth (June 4, 1923)
Calvino, Italo (October 15, 1923)
Gordimer, Nadine (November 20, 1923)
Abe, Kōbō (March 7, 1924)
Berger, Thomas (July 20, 1924)
Gass, William H. (July 30, 1924)
Baldwin, James (August 2, 1924)
Uris, Leon (August 3, 1924)
Connell, Evan S. (August 17, 1924)
Frame, Janet (August 28, 1924)
Škvorecký, Josef (September 27, 1924)
Capote, Truman (September 30, 1924)
Donoso, José (October 5, 1924)
Tournier, Michel (December 19, 1924)
Mishima, Yukio (January 14, 1925)
Cormier, Robert (January 17, 1925)
Wain, John (March 14, 1925)
Jones, Madison (March 21, 1925)
O'Connor, Flannery (March 25, 1925)
Salter, James (June 10, 1925)
Styron, William (June 11, 1925)
Hawkes, John (August 17, 1925)
Vidal, Gore (October 3, 1925)
Sinyavsky, Andrei (October 8, 1925)
Leonard, Elmore (October 11, 1925)
Williams, John A. (December 5, 1925)
Lispector, Clarice (December 10, 1925)
Fowles, John (March 31, 1926)
Donleavy, J. P. (April 23, 1926)
Lee, Harper (April 28, 1926)
Laurence, Margaret (July 18, 1926)
Konwicki, Tadeusz (July 22, 1926)
Adams, Alice (August 14, 1926)
Lurie, Alison (September 3, 1926)
Butor, Michel (September 14, 1926)

Knowles, John (September 16, 1926)
Wallant, Edward Lewis (October 19, 1926)
García Márquez, Gabriel (March 6, 1927)
Jhabvala, Ruth Prawer (May 7, 1927)
Matthiessen, Peter (May 22, 1927)
Ludlum, Robert (May 25, 1927)
Benet, Juan (October 7, 1927)
Grass, Günter (October 16, 1927)
Kennedy, William (January 16, 1928)
Stern, Richard G. (February 25, 1928)
Sillitoe, Alan (March 4, 1928)
Ozick, Cynthia (April 17, 1928)
Trevor, William (May 24, 1928)
Brookner, Anita (July 16, 1928)
Wiesel, Elie (September 30, 1928)
Fuentes, Carlos (November 11, 1928)
Dick, Philip K. (December 16, 1928)
Hinojosa, Rolando (January 21, 1929)
Potok, Chaim (February 17, 1929)
Wolf, Christa (March 18, 1929)
Kundera, Milan (April 1, 1929)
Marshall, Paule (April 9, 1929)
Garrett, George (June 11, 1929)
Grau, Shirley Ann (July 8, 1929)
Le Guin, Ursula K. (October 21, 1929)
Highwater, Jamake (1930's?)
West, Paul (February 23, 1930)
Elkin, Stanley (May 11, 1930)
Barth, John (May 27, 1930)
Bradley, Marion Zimmer (June 3, 1930)
McElroy, Joseph (August 21, 1930)
Ballard, J. G. (November 15, 1930)
Achebe, Chinua (November 16, 1930)
O'Brien, Edna (December 15, 1930)

BORN 1931-1940

Doctorow, E. L. (January 6, 1931)
Richler, Mordecai (January 27, 1931)
Bernhard, Thomas (February 9 or 10, 1931)
Morrison, Toni (February 18, 1931)
Wolfe, Tom (March 2, 1931)
Barthelme, Donald (April 7, 1931)
Weldon, Fay (September 22, 1931)
Le Carré, John (October 19, 1931)
Eco, Umberto (January 5, 1932)

Critical Survey of Long Fiction

Coover, Robert (February 4, 1932)
Appelfeld, Aharon (February 16, 1932)
Updike, John (March 18, 1932)
Dunne, John Gregory (May 25, 1932)
Naipaul, V. S. (August 17, 1932)
Aksyonov, Vassily (August 20, 1932)
Bradbury, Malcolm (September 7, 1932)
Hoagland, Edward (December 21, 1932)
Puig, Manuel (December 28, 1932)
Gaines, Ernest J. (January 15, 1933)
Sontag, Susan (January 16, 1933)
Price, Reynolds (February 1, 1933)
Lively, Penelope (March 17, 1933)
Roth, Philip (March 19, 1933)
Kosinski, Jerzy (June 14, 1933)
Storey, David (July 13, 1933)
McCarthy, Cormac (July 20, 1933)
Gardner, John (July 21, 1933)
Madden, David (July 25, 1933)
Bainbridge, Beryl (November 21, 1933)
Malouf, David (March 20, 1934)
Johnson, Diane (April 28, 1934)
Soyinka, Wole (July 13, 1934)
Johnson, Uwe (July 20, 1934)
Berry, Wendell (August 5, 1934)
Didion, Joan (December 5, 1934)
Gray, Alasdair (December 28, 1934)
Farrell, J. G. (January 23, 1935)
Lodge, David (January 28, 1935)
Brautigan, Richard (January 30, 1935)
Ōe, Kenzaburō (January 31, 1935)
Kiš, Danilo (February 22, 1935)
Shields, Carol (June 2, 1935)
Sagan, Françoise (June 21, 1935)
Lovelace, Earl (July 13, 1935)
Proulx, E. Annie (August 22, 1935)
Kesey, Ken (September 17, 1935)
Keneally, Thomas (October 7, 1935)
Kadare, Ismail (January 28, 1936)
Vargas Llosa, Mario (March 28, 1936)
McMurtry, Larry (June 3, 1936)
Byatt, A. S. (August 24, 1936)
DeLillo, Don (November 20, 1936)
Yehoshua, A. B. (December 9, 1936)
Wambaugh, Joseph (January 22, 1937)

McGinley, Patrick (February 8, 1937)
Condé, Maryse (February 11, 1937)
Pynchon, Thomas (May 8, 1937)
Godwin, Gail (June 18, 1937)
Desai, Anita (June 24, 1937)
Head, Bessie (July 6, 1937)
Myers, Walter Dean (August 12, 1937)
Stone, Robert (August 21, 1937)
Anaya, Rudolfo (October 30, 1937)
Kelley, William Melvin (November 1, 1937)
Harrison, Jim (December 11, 1937)
Ngugi wa Thiong'o (January 5, 1938)
Reed, Ishmael (February 22, 1938)
Oates, Joyce Carol (June 16, 1938)
Forsyth, Frederick (August 25, 1938)
Armah, Ayi Kwei (1939)
Bambara, Toni Cade (March 25, 1939)
Oz, Amos (May 4, 1939)
Paulsen, Gary (May 17, 1939)
Young, Al (May 31, 1939)
Drabble, Margaret (June 5, 1939)
Chase-Riboud, Barbara (June 26, 1939)
Atwood, Margaret (November 18, 1939)
McGuane, Thomas (December 11, 1939)
Coetzee, J. M. (February 9, 1940)
Plante, David (March 4, 1940)
Banks, Russell (March 28, 1940)
Carter, Angela (May 7, 1940)
Chatwin, Bruce (May 13, 1940)
Mukherjee, Bharati (July 27, 1940)

BORN 1941-1950

Theroux, Paul (April 10, 1941)
Wideman, John Edgar (June 14, 1941)
Rice, Anne (October 4, 1941)
Tyler, Anne (October 25, 1941)
Woiwode, Larry (October 30, 1941)
Irving, John (March 2, 1942)
Delany, Samuel R. (April 1, 1942)
Hannah, Barry (April 23, 1942)
Dorfman, Ariel (May 6, 1942)
Allende, Isabel (August 2, 1942)
Keillor, Garrison (August 7, 1942)
Crichton, Michael (October 23, 1942)
Handke, Peter (December 6, 1942)

Carey, Peter (May 7, 1943)
Barker, Pat (May 8, 1943)
Arenas, Reinaldo (July 16, 1943)
Tremain, Rose (August 2, 1943)
Ondaatje, Michael (September 12, 1943)
Robinson, Marilynne (November 26, 1943)
Miller, Sue (November 29, 1943)
Walker, Alice (February 9, 1944)
Ford, Richard (February 16, 1944)
Sebald, W. G. (May 18, 1944)
Emecheta, Buchi (July 21, 1944)
Brown, Rita Mae (November 28, 1944)
Butler, Robert Olen (January 20, 1945)
Dillard, Annie (April 30, 1945)
Conroy, Pat (October 26, 1945)
Banville, John (December 8, 1945)
Barnes, Julian (January 19, 1946)
Hegi, Ursula (May 23, 1946)
O'Brien, Tim (October 1, 1946)
Cliff, Michelle (November 2, 1946)
Auster, Paul (February 3, 1947)
Law-Yone, Wendy (April 1, 1947)
Prose, Francine (April 1, 1947)
Clancy, Tom (April 12, 1947)
Rushdie, Salman (June 19, 1947)
Butler, Octavia E. (June 22, 1947)
Abrahams, Peter (June 28, 1947)
Helprin, Mark (June 28, 1947)
Beattie, Ann (September 8, 1947)
King, Stephen (September 21, 1947)
Wiggins, Marianne (November 8, 1947)
Silko, Leslie Marmon (March 5, 1948)
Gibson, William (March 17, 1948)
Johnson, Charles (April 23, 1948)
McEwan, Ian (June 21, 1948)
Hinton, S. E. (July 22, 1948)
Boyle, T. Coraghessan (December 2, 1948)
Hagedorn, Jessica (1949)
Murakami, Haruki (January 12, 1949)
Turow, Scott (April 12, 1949)
Swift, Graham (May 4, 1949)
Kincaid, Jamaica (May 25, 1949)
Follett, Ken (June 5, 1949)
Russo, Richard (July 15, 1949)
Amis, Martin (August 25, 1949)

Smiley, Jane (September 26, 1949)
Gordon, Mary (December 8, 1949)
Naylor, Gloria (January 25, 1950)
Campbell, Bebe Moore (February 18, 1950)
Alvarez, Julia (March 27, 1950)
Wilson, A. N. (October 27, 1950)

Born since 1951

Hijuelos, Oscar (August 24, 1951)
McMillan, Terry (October 18, 1951)
Mosley, Walter (January 12, 1952)
Tan, Amy (February 19, 1952)
Hoffman, Alice (March 16, 1952)
Mistry, Rohinton (July 3, 1952)
Phillips, Jayne Anne (July 19, 1952)
Cunningham, Michael (November 6, 1952)
Bolaño, Roberto (April 28, 1953)
McDermott, Alice (June 27, 1953)
Erdrich, Louise (June 7, 1954)
Ishiguro, Kazuo (November 8, 1954)
Cisneros, Sandra (December 20, 1954)
Grisham, John (February 8, 1955)
Kingsolver, Barbara (April 8, 1955)
Jen, Gish (August 12, 1955)
Kadohata, Cynthia (July 2, 1956)
Everett, Percival (December 22, 1956)
Min, Anchee (January 14, 1957)
Hornby, Nick (April 17, 1957)
Powers, Richard (June 18, 1957)
Hamilton, Jane (July 13, 1957)
Doyle, Roddy (May 8, 1958)
García, Cristina (July 4, 1958)
Franzen, Jonathan (August 17, 1959)
Winterson, Jeanette (August 27, 1959)
Gibbons, Kaye (May 5, 1960)
Flanagan, Richard (1961)
Wallace, David Foster (February 21, 1962)
Chabon, Michael (May 24, 1963)
Patchett, Ann (December 2, 1963)
Hosseini, Khaled (March 4, 1965)
Rowling, J. K. (July 31, 1965)
Alexie, Sherman (October 7, 1966)
Whitehead, Colson (1969)
Danticat, Edwidge (January 19, 1969)
Smith, Zadie (October 27, 1975)

INDEXES

Geographical Index of Authors and Essays

CATEGORIZED INDEX OF AUTHORS

BLACK HUMOR. *See* SATIRE AND BLACK HUMOR

CHRISTIANITY. *See also* RELIGIOUS NOVEL

CIVIL WAR, U.S.

COLD WAR

COLONIALISM

COMMUNISM

DETECTIVE AND MYSTERY NOVEL

HISTORICAL NOVEL

HORROR AND THE SUPERNATURAL

HUMOR. *See* WIT AND HUMOR

IMPRESSIONISM

ROMANCE

ROMANTIC NOVEL

SATIRE AND BLACK HUMOR

WORLD WAR I

Subject Index

All personages whose names appear in **boldface type** in this index are the subjects of articles in *Critical Survey of Long Fiction, Fourth Edition.*

Critical Survey of Long Fiction

Critical Survey of Long Fiction